A Test of Time

and

A Test of Time Revisited

*The Volcano of Thera and the chronology and history
of the Aegean and east Mediterranean
in the mid-second millennium BC*

STURT W. MANNING

Oxbow Books
Oxford & Philadelphia

Published in the United Kingdom in 2014 by
OXBOW BOOKS
10 Hythe Bridge Street, Oxford OX1 2EW

and in the United States by
OXBOW BOOKS
908 Darby Road, Havertown, PA 19083

Hardback Edition: ISBN 978-1-78297-219-8
Digital Edition: ISBN 978-1-78297-220-4

A CIP record for this book is available from the British Library

Printed in the United Kingdom by Berforts Information Press, Eynsham Oxfordshire

For a complete list of Oxbow titles, please contact:

UNITED KINGDOM
Oxbow Books
Telephone (01865) 241249, Fax (01865) 794449
Email: oxbow@oxbowbooks.com
www.oxbowbooks.com

UNITED STATES OF AMERICA
Oxbow Books
Telephone (800) 791-9354, Fax (610) 853-9146
Email: queries@casemateacademic.com
www.casemateacademic.com/oxbow

Oxbow Books is part of the Casemate Group

*Front cover photographs: Sturt W. Manning – from top left – Minoan eruption pumice deposits, Thera;
view Minoan pumice deposits, Megalochori Quarry, Thera; view from Fira on Thera across the volcanic
caldera towards Nea Kameni (currently active volcanic area); view south from Fira on Thera along the
caldera wall showing the Quaternary volcanic series.*

Back cover illustration: Callista Manning

Contents

PART 1: A Test of Time

Abbreviations...vii
List of Figures xix
List of Tables xxv
List of Plates xxvi

Preface.. xxvii

I.   Introduction 1

II.   A brief history of the Thera debate 7

III. Aims and Preliminary issues for this Study 46

IV.   Archaeological and Historical evidence 69
      1.   Relative date of the Thera eruption in the Aegean and beyond 69
      2.   Dating Middle Minoan III in archaeological terms.........................76
      3.   Tell el-Dabᶜa, its frescoes, and early LBA Aegean chronology? 80
      4.   Linkages between the Late Minoan IA period, the Late Cypriot I
           period, and Egypt and the Levant 107
      5.   More on White Slip I, and the start of the Late Cypriot I
           and Late Minoan IA periods...150
      6.   Tempest Stela of Ahmose 192
      7.   Archaeology and the chronology of the Late Minoan IB period 202
      8.   Archaeology and the chronology of the Late Minoan II period 208
      9.   Keftiu in Theban tomb paintings and Aegean chronology..........................209
      10. Amenhotep III and Aegean chronology...220

V.   Absolute dating evidence 231
      1.   Radiocarbon evidence...232
      2.   Northern hemisphere climate event in the later 17th century BC 263
      3.   The identification of volcanic glass in the GISP2 ice-core. Potential
           confirmation of a 17th century BC date for the Thera eruption?................288
      4.   Aegean dendrochronology, and further evidence for a 1628BC
           climate-event consistent with the eruption of Thera 307

VI. Summary and Conclusions...321
    1.a. Problem Issues: Archaeology...322
    1.b. Problem Issues: Tell el-Dabᶜa...325
    1.c. Problem Issues: Science-Based Dating 329
    2.   The limited scope for a 'post-eruption-LMIA phase' and the
         importance of recognising an earlier phase of what seem to be long
         overall LMIB/LHIIA periods...330
    3.   Proposed Conclusions..335

VII. Some implications, and the problem of dating Alalakh VII...............341

Appendix 1: Egyptian chronology 367
Appendix 2: Why the standard chronologies are approximately correct,
             and why radical re-datings are therefore incorrect 415

References..421

Plates 481

PART 2: A Test of Time Revisited

REVISIT ESSAY The Thera/Santorini Debate 13+ years on

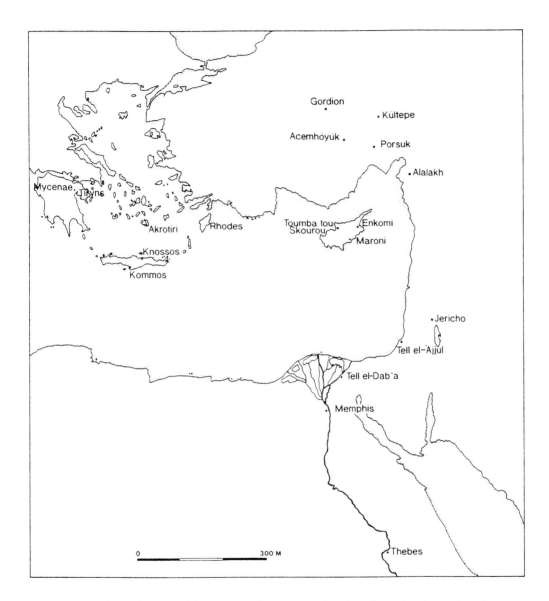

Fig. 1. Schematic map of the east Mediterranean showing the main sites referred to in the text.

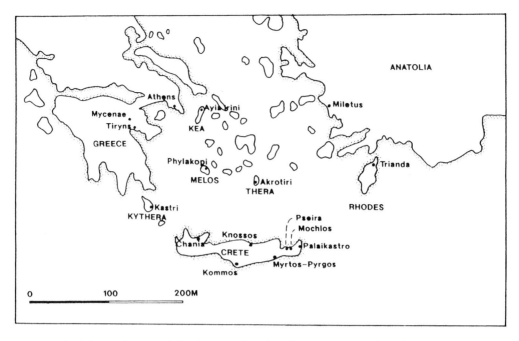

Fig. 2. Schematic map of the Aegean showing the main sites referred to in the text.

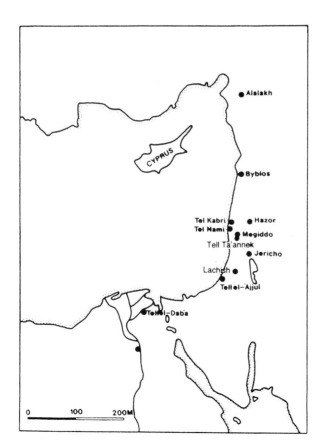

Fig. 3. Schematic map of the Levant showing the main sites referred to in the text.

Maps, main ceramic types, and abbreviations

For convenience, and because of general currency, several abbreviations are used in this book for the main stylistic phases and chronological periods in the archaeology of the Aegean and east Mediterranean during the second millennium BC (BCE). The general archaeological–chronological sequences of the Aegean and east Mediterranean

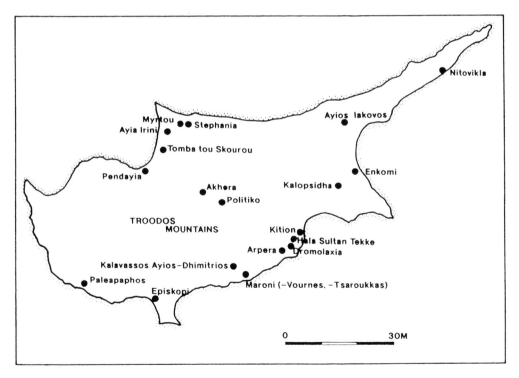

Fig. 4. Schematic map of Cyprus showing the main sites referred to in the text.

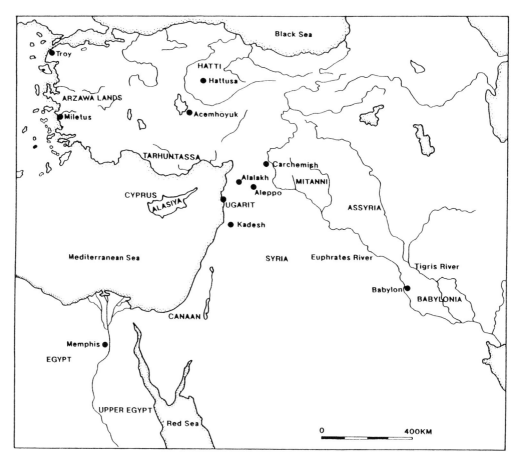

Fig. 5. Schematic map of Anatolia and the Near East showing the main sites and LBA entities referred to in the text.

follow a traditional tripartite system (Daniel 1943), with the Early Bronze Age roughly equalling the third millennium BC (Egyptian Old Kingdom), the Middle Bronze Age the first several centuries of the second millennium BC (Egyptian Middle Kingdom), and the Late Bronze Age the remainder of the second millennium BC (Egyptian New Kingdom). The exact dates are of course debated, and those for the middle of the second millennium BC are very much the subject of this book. In the Aegean, local regional names are then given which equate with the broad Early, Middle, and Late Bronze Age periods: thus Early, Middle, and Late Helladic in Greece, Early, Middle, and Late Cycladic in the Cycladic Islands, and Early, Middle, and Late Minoan on Crete. Each of these is then further subdivided into a number of detailed phases, e.g. Late Minoan IA, IB, II, IIIA1, IIIA2, IIIB, IIIC.

A major area of both popular and academic confusion in Aegean archaeology is that the same labels tend to be used both for stratigraphic time periods, and for stylistic

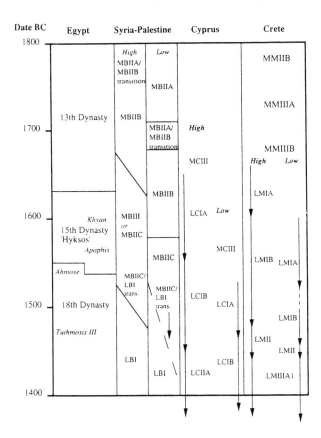

Fig. 6. Main existing chronological systems for Crete, Cyprus, Syria–Palestine, and Egypt in recent literature for the period c.1800–1400BC. Egyptian chronology after von Beckerath (1994a; 1997) or Kitchen (1996a 'high'); Syro-Palestinian 'high' chronology after Dever (1985; 1991; 1992) and 'low' chronology after Bietak (1991a; 1996a); Cypriot 'high' chronology after Merrillees (1992) and 'low' chronology after Eriksson (1992); Cretan 'high' chronology after Betancourt (1998b) and 'low' chronology after Warren (1998 as revising Warren and Hankey 1989).

phases. And both are defined through reference to the changing types and decoration of the pottery found. Thus pottery can be described as Late Minoan (LM) IA in style, but a stratigraphic context can also be said to be LMIA in date. In principle, the two are meant to go together, *but* in practice this is impossible and illogical. Styles and fashions do not start and end on appointed days. Nor do the building or architectural activities of people necessarily conveniently correlate with fashions in craft. Meanwhile, archaeologists can recognise various stratigraphic phases in their excavations. They can also recognise the main architectural phases and developments. These are then given a date according to the dominant and diagnostic features of the associated material culture (typically pottery in Aegean prehistory). The diagnostic feature looked for is the most recent stylistic phase represented. However, at the same time, there are always hangovers from past styles, or continuations. Thus if LMIB stylistic elements are clearly present (but no subsequent LMII), and despite the inevitable presence of many LMIA style examples, a stratigraphic context will be dated LMIB, and so on.

The inherent circularity of approach, when these two forms of dating and description are combined, has been noted by a number of scholars over the years. On Crete, an alternative stratigraphic-culture stage terminology is thus also used by many scholars. This is based around the key architectural cum civilisation stages of Minoan prehistory: prepalatial period (EM–MMIA), protopalatial or Old Palace or first palatial period (MMIB–MMIIB/MMIIIA), neopalatial or New Palace or second palatial period (MMIIIB–LMIB), monopalatial period (LMII–LMIIIA1), final palatial or third palatial period (LMIIIA2–LMIIIB), and postpalatial period (LMIIIC).[1] Various sets of material culture styles then may be associated with these main stages of the civilisation. In this book we are primarily concerned with New Palace, or neopalatial, Crete of the mid second millennium BC. This phase begins with the construction of a set of 'new' palaces and associated buildings (after the old palace group) at a time when MMIIIB–LMIA ceramics were in use, and represents the period of the use, modification, and development of these buildings until there was a major horizon of destruction, change, and re-orientation across Crete when mature LMIB style ceramics were in use.

The definition and recognition of the various Aegean ceramic style phases is not usually controversial. If Mycenaean pictorial vase-painting is left aside,[2] and it is not of relevance here, then some attempts have been made to recognise and to isolate specific vase-painters or workshops,[3] and some links between vase-painting styles and ideology advanced,[4] but the formal connoisseurship approach of Sir John Beazley, and the attendant problems in classical archaeology,[5] have had little relevance to the general classification and study of Aegean Bronze Age ceramics.[6] Small sherds may prove very difficult to relate to existing definitions, some styles are much easier to recognise than others, and there are of course various problems and debates in the specialist details (especially the 'transitions' or 'transition phases' between the major style phases), but, in general terms, the basic style phases are broadly accepted by all scholars.[7]

The Aegean ceramic styles of most concern to this book are the Cretan MMIIIB–early LMIA transition phase (variously also referred to by different scholars as MMIIIB or early LMIA), mature to final LMIA, and LMIB. Figures 7–10 show some examples

---

[1] See Rehak and Younger (1998a:92); Dickinson (1994:13 Fig.1.2); Hallager (1988:13 Table 1). Note, the one important point is that Rehak and Younger and Dickinson fail to note the important separate LMII–LMIIIA1 phase when there is effectively one dominant palatial site only on Crete (for central and west Crete in particular) at Knossos. This I term the monopalatial period after Hallager (see also Hallager 1978; Bennet 1985; 1987b; Rutter 1999: 148–149 n. 1).

[2] For this LHIII style (and so later than the period we are interested in), see Vermeule and Karageorghis (1982); for recent discussion concerning the recognition of individual artists within the style, see Morris (1993:47–51).

[3] E.g. Betancourt (1985:145 and refs.); Niemeier (1979b).

[4] E.g. Hiller (1995).

[5] See discussions of Neer (1997).

[6] In contrast to some other areas of Aegean art-history: see e.g. Cherry (1992); Broodbank (1992); cf. Morris (1993).

[7] Standard discussions for the periods/styles relevant to this book include: Furumark (1941a); Popham (1967); Niemeier (1980; 1985); Betancourt (1985; 1990b:41–46); Barber (1987); Warren and Hankey (1989); Warren (1991a); Mountjoy (1986; 1993); Dietz (1991); Dickinson (1994:110–130); Driessen and Macdonald (1997); Van de Moortel (1997). Further revisions are, however, always possible. For example, recent analysis of the Kommos material and sequence has led to the recognition of *three* phases of LMIA: early LMIA (= Warren's MMIIIB–LMIA transition), advanced LMIA, and final LMIA (= other scholars' late/final LMIA). This revises the two-stages recognised in previous work (Shaw *et al.* n.d.).

Fig. 7. Examples of MMIIIB–early LMIA transition, or early LMIA, ceramics. Drawings a. – d. (all at the same scale) from Akrotiri early Late Cycladic I seismic destruction horizon. Drawings after Marthari (1984). Drawings e. – m. from the MMIIIB–early LMIA transition assemblage from Knossos published by Warren (1991a).

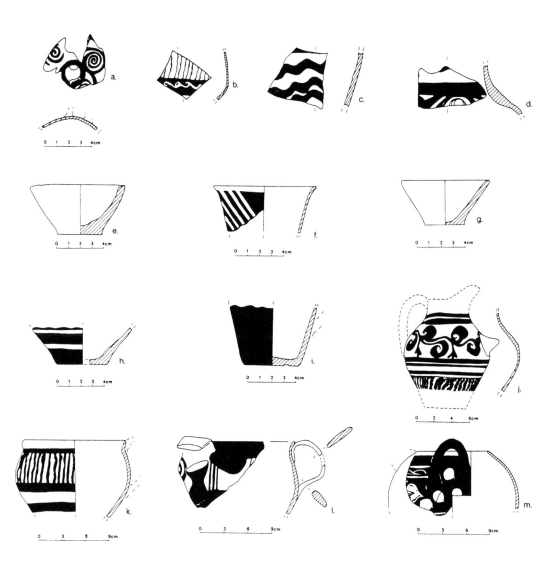

Fig. 8. Examples of MMIIIB–early LMIA transition, or early LMIA, ceramics from Kommos. Drawings (after Betancourt 1990b) are all to the same scale as a., unless otherwise indicated, and i. also has black paint on the interior surface.

Fig. 9. Examples of LMIA ceramics from mature to late/final LMIA contexts, including the volcanic destruction level at Akrotiri. Drawings after Betancourt (1985) and Marthari (1990).

Fig. 10. Examples of mature–late LMIB ceramics. Drawings after Betancourt (1985) and Popham (1967).

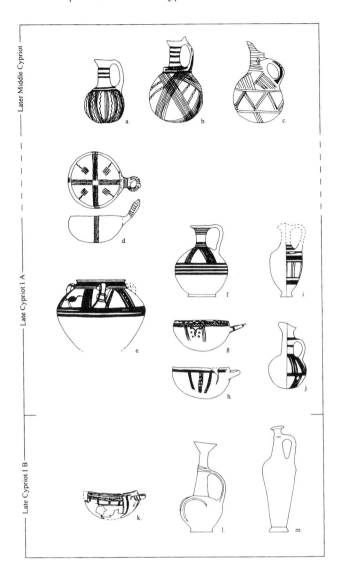

Fig. 11. Examples of the main decorated ceramic types from late MC, LCIA, and LCIB Cyprus found exported in the east Mediterranean. a. WP Pendent Line Style after Åström (1972b:Fig.9.4), b. WP Close Line Style after Åström (1972b:Fig.9.10), c. WP Fine Line Style after Maguire (1991:Fig.7.1 no.2), d. Red on Black after Åström (1972b:Fig.31.4) – note Red on Red is very similar, just different colour scheme, e. Bichrome Ware after Åström (1972d:Fig.44.3), f. Bichrome Ware after Åström (1972d:Fig.43.8), g. PWS after Popham (1972a:79.4), h. Early rope pattern lattice and ladder lozenge style WSI, as typified by the Theran WSI bowl, after Furtwaengler and Loeschcke (1886:pl.12.80), i. WPV after Åström (1972b:Fig.16.16), j. WPVI after Åström (1972d:Fig.41.2), k. Later LCIB WSI of the open, light, type, typified by the parallel line styles, as found in an example at Tell el-Dabʿa after Hein (1994b:258 no.352), l. LCIB BRI jug after Åström (1972d:Fig.49.4), m. Red Lustrous Wheelmade Ware spindle bottle after Åström (1972d:Fig.54.5).

of the varying types from within each of these phases as a guide during the discussions in the main text.

In addition, the discussions below find that Cypriot pottery types are crucial to the synchronisation of the history and chronology of the Aegean and east Mediterranean in the mid second millennium BC. Cypriot ceramic types from the late MC to LCIB chronological/stratigraphic periods on the island are thus frequently encountered in the following text. Figure 11 shows some examples of the main decorated types of Cypriot late MC to LCI types mentioned (found as exports).

BC   Before Christ (= BCE: Before Common Era). Note, all dates in this book which are not identified as BC or BP are to be interpreted as dates AD (Anno Domini).

BP   Before Present. Employed in this book with reference to radiocarbon dating. Here 'present' is arbitrarily deemed to be AD1950. Radiocarbon determinations are expressed in terms of radiocarbon years BP. These 'years' are relevant only to the radiocarbon timescale, and must be calibrated, via a radiocarbon calibration curve, in order to be expressed in calendar years BC and/or AD (see Chapter V.1).

BR   Base Ring, an LC ware. See Åström (1972d) and Vaughan (1991).

LBA   Late Bronze Age. The mid to later second millennium BC. The exact date for its beginning is the key debate discussed in this book. In the Levant the LBA phases are referred to as LBI, LBII, LBIII.

LB1   Term employed in this book to refer to the entire contemporary first phase of the Late Bronze Age in the Aegean region: i.e. LMI(A), LHI, and Late Cycladic I.

LC   Late Cypriot (phases LCI, LCII, LCIII; subdivisions LCIA – further sub-divided into LCIA1, LCIA2, LCIB, etc.). Name used to describe the Late Bronze Age of Cyprus. For basic definitions I have followed Åström (1972a) – this applies especially to the LCI subphases (see also Eriksson 1992:200–202), where Åström developed new definitions compared to earlier work.

LH   Late Helladic (phases LHI, LHII, LHIII; subdivisions LHIA, LHIB, LHIIA, LHIIB, LHIIIA1, LHIIIA2, LHIIIB, etc.). Name used to describe the Late Bronze Age of mainland Greece.

LM   Late Minoan (phases LMI, LMII, LMIII; subdivisions LMIA, LMIB, LMII, LMIIIA1, LMIIIA2, LMIIIB, etc.). Name used to describe the Late Bronze Age of Crete. The alternative reference scheme of MMIIIB–LMIB = New Palace or neopalatial Crete is also employed in the text.

MBA   Middle Bronze Age. The earlier second millennium BC.

late MBII, or late MBIIB, or MBIIC or MBIII

The MBA phases in Syria–Palestine are described as MBI, MBII, etc. Unfortunately, the terminology used is not consistent among various scholars and traditions. In this book we are concerned mainly with the late MBA, and the final MBA phase in particular. This is variously called late MBII with no later phase before the LBA, or (late) MBIIB with no later phase before the LBA (e.g. Kempinski 1983; 1992a:159), or MBIIC with no later phase before the LBA, and with previous MBII divided into an MBIIA and MBIIB (e.g. Dever 1992), or MBIII with no later phase before the LBA, and following an MBII phase (e.g. Oren 1997b; Marchetti *et al.* 1998). All four terms can, and roughly do, refer to the same archaeological phase. This final MB phase is conventionally dated c.1650–1550BC in current literature. Although an MBIIC or MBIII phase is widely referred to in scholarly literature (defined especially by Seger 1974; 1975), it remains the case that it is at best poorly defined in an area-wide sense (Kempinski 1983; 1992a; Bienkowski 1989). Kempinski (1992a:159), for example, concludes that 'it does not possess, in my opinion, sufficient characteristic features to merit a separate designation'. However, he is in effect rather redefining the usual periods to reach this view, since he chooses to regard the appearance of Bichrome Ware and LC ceramics as marking the end of the MBA/ start of the local LBI period (Kempinski 1992a:179), whereas it is these very features which demarcate the final MBA phase for most other scholars. In line with the majority of scholarship, I regard the second part of the final MBA phase, however designated, as characterised at major coastal sites by Bichrome Ware (and associated LCIA products) and also, and especially at inland sites, by Chocolate on White Ware (see Fischer 1999 – early Chocolate on White Ware may appear a little before Bichrome Ware, in the so-called pre-Bichrome Ware first phase of the MBIIC/MBIII period: see Fischer 1999:24). In this regard, the so-called MBIIC/MBIII phase is to an extent a regional (coastal) phenomenon.

MC Middle Cypriot (phases MCI, MCII, MCIII). Name used to describe the Middle Bronze Age of Cyprus.

MM Middle Minoan (phases MMI, MMI, MMIII; subdivisions MMIA, MMIB, MMIIA, MMIIB, MMIIIA, MMIIIB). Name used to describe the Middle Bronze Age of Crete. MMIB–MMIIB/MMIIIA is also often referred to as the Old Palace period.

PWS Proto White Slip, an initial LC ware. See Popham (1962).

SIP Second Intermediate Period. Period between the Middle and New Kingdoms of Egypt, and roughly occupying the later Middle Bronze Age to Late Bronze Age transition, when Dynasties of Canaanite origin controlled much of northern Egypt, conventionally c.1800–1550BC. The latter part of this period correlates with the so-called Hyksos, or 15th, Dynasty. For detailed studies of the political history of the period, see von Beckerath (1964) and recently Ryholt (1997); for the area of Hyksos control, see Redford (1997:21–22).

Tell el-Dabᶜa
Strictly speaking, this is one location within the greater 250ha ancient city of Avaris in the Nile Delta of Egypt (see e.g. Bietak 1996a:Fig.2). Other locations within the greater city of Avaris, such as ᶜEzbet Helmi and ᶜEzbet Rushdi, are distinct locations and sites. However, in general parlance, the initial main excavation site of Tell el-Dabᶜa has become synonymous with the whole site. Unless clearly qualified, the term Tell el-Dabᶜa is employed in this book in the general sense, meaning the whole Avaris site.

VDL Volcanic Destruction Level. Final mature to late LMIA cultural-occupation horizon on Thera, and especially at the site of Akrotiri on Thera, buried (destroyed) by the Minoan eruption of the Thera volcano.

WP White Painted pottery, an MC to LCI ware of Cyprus. See Åstrom (1972b; 1972d; also Frankel 1974; Maguire 1991).

WS   White Slip pottery, an LC ware. Types WSI (LCI) and WSII (LCII). See Popham
         (1972a).

I also use some abbreviations to refer to standard editions of ancient text material
and the standard *Cambridge Ancient History* volumes. Sources providing ancient texts
in translation are the primary reference in the text.

AT   Alalakh Tablets. See Wiseman (1953).
CAH   *The Cambridge Ancient History.*
CTH   Larouche, E. 1971. *Catalogue des textes hittites.* Paris: Klincksieck.
EA   The el-Amarna letters. See Moran (1992).
KBo   *Keilschrifttexte aus Boghazköi.*
KUB   *Keilschrifturkunden aus Boghazköi.*

Ancient Near Eastern names

I have chosen to spell Ancient Near Eastern names (that is Hittite personal and place
names, Babylonian and Assyrian personal and place names, etc.) in this book adopting
the simplest of the commonly used transliterations. In particular, I have avoided the
use of accents for ancient names. In general, I have followed the model of Bryce (1998).
For Bryce's justification of adopting the simplest of the commonly used transliterations,
see his p.4. To give some examples:

Burna-Burias – instead of Burnaburiaš
Hattusili – instead of Hattušili or Hattushili or Hattushilish
Kadasman-Enlil – instead of Kadašman-Enlil or Kadashman-Enlil
Mursili – instead of Muršili or Murshili or Murshilish
Samsi-Adad – instead of Šamši-Adad or Shamshi-Adad
Alasia – instead of Alašia or Alashiya

List of Figures

Most of the Figures were drawn by Jo Goffee, several by Sarah Monks, some by Elinor Ribeiro, and one was produced by David Sewell.

Fig. 1.   Schematic map of the east Mediterranean showing the main sites referred to in the text.
Fig. 2.   Schematic map of the Aegean showing the main sites referred to in the text.
Fig. 3.   Schematic map of the Levant showing the main sites referred to in the text.
Fig. 4.   Schematic map of Cyprus showing the main sites referred to in the text.
Fig. 5.   Schematic map of Anatolia and the Near East showing the main sites and LBA entities referred to in the text.
Fig. 6.   Main existing chronological systems for Crete, Cyprus, Syria–Palestine, and Egypt in recent literature for the period c.1800–1400BC. Egyptian chronology after von Beckerath (1994a; 1997) or Kitchen (1996a 'high'); Syro-Palestinian 'high' chronology after Dever (1985; 1991; 1992) and 'low' chronology after Bietak (1991a; 1996a); Cypriot 'high' chronology after Merrillees (1992) and 'low' chronology after Eriksson (1992); Cretan 'high' chronology after Betancourt (1998b) and 'low' chronology after Warren (1998 as revising Warren and Hankey 1989).
Fig. 7.   Examples of MMIIIB–early LMIA transition, or early LMIA, ceramics. Drawings a. – d. (all at the same scale) from Akrotiri early Late Cycladic I seismic destruction horizon. Drawings after Marthari (1984). Drawings e. – m. from the MMIIIB–early LMIA transition assemblage from Knossos published by Warren (1991a).
Fig. 8.   Examples of MMIIIB–early LMIA transition, or early LMIA, ceramics from Kommos. Drawings (after Betancourt 1990b) are all to the same scale as a., unless otherwise indicated, and i. also has black paint on the interior surface.
Fig. 9.   Examples of LMIA ceramics from mature to late/final LMIA contexts, including the volcanic destruction level at Akrotiri. Drawings after Betancourt (1985) and Marthari (1990).
Fig. 10.   Examples of mature–late LMIB ceramics. Drawings after Betancourt (1985) and Popham (1967).
Fig. 11.   Examples of the main decorated ceramic types from late MC, LCIA, and LCIB Cyprus found exported in the east Mediterranean. a. WP Pendent Line Style after Åström (1972b:Fig.9.4), b. WP Close Line Style after Åström (1972b:Fig.9.10), c. WP Fine Line Style after Maguire (1991:Fig.7.1 no.2), d. Red on Black after Åström (1972b:Fig.31.4) – note Red on Red is very similar, just different colour scheme, e. Bichrome Ware after Åström (1972d:Fig.44.3), f. Bichrome Ware after Åström (1972d:Fig.43.8), g. PWS after Popham (1972a:79.4), h. Early rope pattern lattice and ladder lozenge style WSI, as typified by the Theran WSI bowl, after Furtwaengler and Loeschcke (1886:pl.12.80), i. WPV after Åström (1972b:Fig.16.16), j. WPVI after Åström (1972d:Fig.41.2), k. Later LCIB WSI of the open, light, type, typified by the parallel line styles, as found in an example at Tell el-Dabᶜa after Hein (1994b:258 no.352), l. LCIB BRI jug after Åström (1972d:Fig.49.4), m. Red Lustrous Wheelmade Ware spindle bottle after Åström (1972d:Fig.54.5).

Fig. 12.   Schematic plan of the excavated part of the Bronze Age town at Akrotiri, Thera. After Doumas (1992).

Fig. 13.   Map of the eastern Mediterranean showing a number of the locations where airfall Theran tephra from the Minoan eruption has been identified either in geological coring or archaeological excavation (see text for details).

Fig. 14.   Approximate reconstruction of Late Bronze Age Thera/Santorini immediately prior to the Minoan eruption (after Druitt and Francaviglia 1992:Fig.10).

Fig. 15.   LHIIA?-style jug from the VDL at Akrotiri (no. 5115). Drawing after Marthari (1990:Fig.8).

Fig. 16.   Aegean relative chronology in schematic terms relevant to the Thera eruption period (MMIII–LMIB).

Fig. 17.   Comparison of the ice-core, dendrochronological, radiocarbon and archaeological dating relevant to the Thera eruption as in 1988 (after Manning 1988a:Figure). 1. Ice-core date of Hammer *et al.* (1987), 2. Tree-ring date of LaMarche and Hirschboeck (1984), add also Baillie and Munro (1988), 3. Most likely calibrated radiocarbon age range at 1σ confidence from Manning (1988a), 4. Revised archaeological age estimate of Betancourt (1987), and 5. Conventional archaeological age estimate of Warren (1984).

Fig. 18.   Comparison of some earrings depicted for élite females in the Akrotiri frescoes (a., d., e.) with others found in the Aegean (b. from Crete, f. from Shaft Grave 3, Mycenae) and examples found at late MBII (Hyksos) Tell el-ʿAjjul, Palestine (c. from hoard 1450, and g. from hoard 1313). Drawings after Doumas (1992:pls.108, 118, 130), Effinger (1996:pl.10 no.MaPM 1a), Higgins (1997:Fig.204), and Negbi (1970:pl.1 no.2, pl.3 no.10).

Fig. 19.   Comparison of earrings and arm bracelets/bangles depicted for élite females in the Akrotiri frescoes (a., b., d.) with examples of the same forms/motifs from Crete (e., g.) and western Asia (c., f.). No. b. is a detail of a. Drawings after Doumas (1992:pls.125, 126), Effinger (1996:39 no.KnS 5h, 27 no.PK 14l), Maxwell-Hyslop (1971: colour plate) and McGovern (1985:fig.17).

Fig. 20.   Comparison of similar crocus and papyrus motifs on an ikrea, necklace, and bracelet respectively a. Akrotiri, b. Tell el-ʿAjjul Grave 1073, and c. Akrotiri. Drawings after Doumas (1992:pls.37, 121) and Maxwell-Hyslop (1971:Fig.91).

Fig. 21.   Isopach map of Theran tephra falls from the Minoan eruption (primarily eastwards) after Pyle (1990a:Fig.1). Triangles mark locations where data on tephra deposit depth has been acquired. Tephra depth in cm. The data for the area of Crete are shown after Watkins *et al.* (1978).

Fig. 22.   Schematic plan of the citadel area of the late Hyksos period at ʿEzbet Helmi/Tell el-Dabʿa (after Bietak 1996a:fig.55).

Fig. 23.   Schematic stratigraphic sequence for the entire Avaris/Tell el-Dabʿa site after Bietak (1996a:Fig.3).

Fig. 24.   Schematic drawing of the published reconstruction of the bull-leaping tableau assembled from among the fresco fragments from the H/I and H/IV debris dumps after Bietak (1996a:pl.IV).

Fig. 25.   Comparison of a. the Tell el-Dabʿa ivy fresco fragment with b. an LMIB sherd with ivy motif from Kastri on Kythera and c. an LHIIA example from Ayia Irini, Keos. Drawings after Bietak and Marinatos (1995:fig.13); Coldstream and Huxley (1972:pl.57.287); and Cummer and Schofield (1984:pl.49 no.175).

Fig. 26.   Drawing of the Ahmose axe with Aegean-style griffin from the tomb of Ahhotep. After Morgan (1988:pl.63).

Fig. 27.   An example of an earlier Red Lustrous Wheelmade Ware spindle bottle from Stephania. Drawing after Eriksson (1993:frontspiece right).

Fig. 28.   The late MB Levantine brown burnished jug from LCIA Maroni *Kapsaloudhia* Tomb 1. Drawing after Herscher (1984:pl.7.3).

Fig. 29.   Distribution of the biconical type of Tell el-Yahudiyeh juglets after Bietak (1996a:Fig.48.B; 1991a:Fig.22); Kaplan (1980:Map 7). For site data, see Kaplan (1980:77–80).

Fig. 30.   An example of an exported SIP/Hyksos scarab: MT.140, a faience scarab, from Pit 18 at Maroni *Tsaroukkas* (see Manning and Monks 1998:340–341).

Fig. 31.   A drawing of the now lost early White Slip I bowl from pre-eruption Thera after Furtwaengler and Loeschcke (1886:pl.12.80). A wavy line below the rim, mentioned in one early description of the piece, is not evident in the Furtwaengler and Loeschcke plate. For the rest of the decorative scheme not visible in the view of the bowl shown in the Furtwaengler and Loeschcke plate, see Merrillees (n.d.).

Fig. 32. Examples of WSI bowls. a.–c. show the PWS-style ('rope pattern') lattice-band and pendent ladder/lattice motifs of earlier WSI. d.–f show the new open and airy elegance of classic WSI. a. and b. after Popham (1972a:Fig.80.6) – two views of same bowl from Enkomi Tomb 19; c. after Vermeule and Wolsky (1990:215 TI.137 P93); d. after Popham (1972a:Fig.59.1) from Saqqara in Egypt; e. after Popham (1972a:Fig.48.4); and f. after Popham (1972a:Fig.48.6).

Fig. 33. Drawing of a mature LCIB WSI vessel (Inv.-Nr.7949) from the ʿEzbet Helmi H/I citadel area at Tell el-Dabʿa after Hein (1994b:258 no.352).

Fig. 34. WSI sherds and one WP sherd from Cyprus and the Aegean. a., b., d. and e. from Phylakopi after Popham (1972a:Fig.58), c. from Knossos, Crete, after Popham (1963:Fig.1), f. from Trianda, Rhodes, after Furumark (1950:Fig.6), and g. from Zakros, Crete, after Popham (1963:Fig.1).

Fig. 35. Mature WSI bowl sherds, MT.710, from MT Tomb 15 at Maroni *Tsaroukkas*, southern Cyprus. The fabric of the bowl is made from a pure white clay/paste.

Fig. 36. Proposed chronology for later MC to LCIB Cyprus with the Aegean, Tell el-ʿAjjul and Tell el-Dabʿa. (Same as Fig. 62)

Fig. 37. a. Drawing of the LMIB? sherd (RAT 530.1301) from Kom Rabiʿa (Memphis), Egypt after Bourriau and Eriksson (1997: Fig. 9.1, pl. 1.a–c). b. and c. LMIB comparisons for the motif after Betancourt (1983:28 nos. 48 and 52).

Fig. 38. Depictions of two examples (3rd and 4th to right) of the Keftiu from the tomb of Senmut (TT71, Hatshepsut–early Tuthmosis III) wearing LMI loincloth (or breechcloth: Rehak 1996), and with the left figure carrying a massively over-size LM/LHI Keftiu cup. Drawing after photos kindly supplied by the Metropolitan Museum of Art (Metropolitan Museum of Art, Egyptian Expedition, Graphic Section, and the Metropolitan Museum of Art, Rogers Fund, 1930).

Fig. 39. Depictions of two examples (Figs. 15–16 of Register II) of the Keftiu from the tomb of Rekhmire (TT100, Tuthmosis III–Amenhotep II) with re-painted kilts. Drawing after photos kindly supplied by the Metropolitan Museum of Art (Metropolitan Museum of Art, Egyptian Expedition, Graphic Section, and the Metropolitan Museum of Art, Rogers Fund, 1930).

Fig. 40. Depiction of a member of the Keftiu (Fig. 4 of Register II) from the tomb of Rekhmire (TT100, Tuthmosis III–Amenhotep II) with re-painted kilt. Drawing after photos kindly supplied by the Metropolitan Museum of Art (Metropolitan Museum of Art, Egyptian Expedition, Graphic Section, and the Metropolitan Museum of Art, Rogers Fund, 1930).

Fig. 41. Depiction of a member of the Keftiu (Fig. 9 of Register I) from the tomb of Menkheperraseneb (TT86, Tuthmosis III) with kilt. Drawing after photos kindly supplied by the Metropolitan Museum of Art (Metropolitan Museum of Art, Egyptian Expedition, Graphic Section, and the Metropolitan Museum of Art, Rogers Fund, 1930).

Fig. 42. Examples of LMIIIA1 chevron and arc motifs found on pottery and very similar to the motifs repeated in registers on the kilts worn by the Keftiu in the Rekhmire and Menkheperraseneb tombs. Examples shown from Kommos; drawings after Watrous (1992:nos.682, 962, 1170, 963). See also Betancourt (1998b:Fig.29.2).

Fig. 43. Examples of LMIIIA1 infilled triangle motifs found on pottery and very similar to the motifs repeated in registers on the kilts worn by the Keftiu in the Rekhmire and Menkheperraseneb tombs. Examples shown from Knossos and Kommos; drawings after Popham (1967:pl.84a) and Watrous (1992:nos.774 and 988). See also Betancourt (1998b:Fig.29.2).

Fig. 44. The INTCAL98 radiocarbon calibration curve (Stuiver *et al.* 1998) for the period 1800–1400BC with 1σ (1SD) errors indicated. The Copenhagen weighted average radiocarbon age for the volcanic destruction level at Akrotiri on Thera, 3355±32BP, is also shown (see text for explanation). The main intersection, and likely calendar age range, is in the 17th century BC; the mid-16th century BC only just scrapes in within the respective 1σ errors. Note the steep slope (change in atmospheric radiocarbon levels) after 1535BC. The radiocarbon dating evidence relevant to the volcanic destruction level at Akrotiri cannot lie after about this point.

Fig. 45. The previous 1993 Seattle decadal radiocarbon calibration curve (Stuiver and Becker 1993), and 1986 Belfast bi-decadal radiocarbon calibration curve (Pearson *et al.* 1986), for the period 1800–1400BC, with the 1σ (1SD) errors on the constituent datapoints shown. The new INTCAL98 curve more or less lies in between these two previous curves (compare with Fig. 44). The calibration curves are essentially flat across the later 17th century BC and mid-16th century BC period, making it difficult or impossible to resolve calibrated calendar date ranges within this overall period. The 1993 decadal calibration curve of Stuiver and Becker (1993) offers a significant intersection for the Copenhagen weighted average date for the volcanic destruction level at Akrotiri, 3355±32BP, both in the 17th and mid-16th centuries BC. The relatively large errors on a couple of the mid-16th century BC datapoints exaggerates this region a little. In contrast, although also relatively flat across the period, the 1986 Belfast data strongly favours a 17th century BC intersection, and barely includes a mid-16th century BC intersection at 1550BC. The new INTCAL98 dataset includes a better later 17th century BC intersection (necessary to be potentially compatible with the 'early chronology' archaeological evidence, and *perhaps* the tree-ring and ice-core evidence), but, like the Belfast 1986 dataset, barely includes a mid-16th century BC intersection within 1σ confidence margins. All three curves record the steep slope (rapid change in atmospheric radiocarbon levels) after, variously, 1535BC, or 1530BC, and it seems impossible for the Thera radiocarbon age range to date much later than this. To quantify. Ruling out the aberrant and inconsistent Simon Fraser data with an inappropriate novel pretreatment (see Chapters II and V.1), and the aberrantly early Zürich data (see Manning 1995:208), the weighted average radiocarbon age range for the volcanic destruction level at Akrotiri from all the laboratories (Pennsylvania, Copenhagen, Oxford [Series I alone, Series I&II average, and Series I&II modified by 'residue' correction], and Heidelberg) which have run measurements on sets of appropriate short-lived samples are similar, respectively: c.3322±29BP, 3355±32BP, 3357±21BP or 3338±17BP or 3325±17BP, 3321±40BP (see Manning 1995:Table 2 and pp.208 and 211; Friedrich *et al.* 1990; Housley *et al.* 1990). Each has a 17th century BC and mid-16th century BC calibrated age range, with the respective 1σ and 2σ calibrated calendar age ranges *ending* at: 1528/1522BC, 1538/1527BC, 1617/1530BC, 1537/1528BC, 1530/1525BC, and 1527/1518BC (INTCAL98 calibration data and OxCal computer programme of Ramsey 1995 'round ranges off').

Fig. 46.   Calibrated calendar age range for the combined Copenhagen dataset for the Akrotiri VDL (see Tables 7 and 8) employing the INTCAL98 radiocarbon calibration dataset of Stuiver *et al.* (1998) and the OxCal computer calibration programme (Ramsey 1995, Round Ranges function 'off'). P = Probability (out of 1.0). The 1σ and 2σ calibrated age ranges are indicated by the upper and lower lines under the overall probability distribution.

Fig. 47.   Calibrated calendar age range for the combined Copenhagen dataset for the Akrotiri VDL (see Tables 7 and 8) employing the 1993 decadal radiocarbon calibration dataset of Stuiver and Becker (1993) from German wood and the OxCal computer calibration programme (Ramsey 1995, Round Ranges function 'off'). P = Probability (out of 1.0). The 1σ and 2σ calibrated age ranges are indicated by the upper and lower lines under the overall probability distribution.

Fig. 48.   The weighted average of the Chania and Myrtos-Pyrgos date sets reported in Housley *et al.* (1999:Table 1), each shown in relation to the INTCAL98 calibration curve (Stuiver *et al.* 1998). Compare to similar figure in Housley *et al.* (1999:Fig.2) where data are shown in relation to the 1993 decadal calibration curve of Stuiver and Becker (1993). The plausible calendar range where the two datasets may be placed relatively close to each other is indicated (c.1525BC to 1498BC). The possible earlier 15th century BC range for the Myrtos-Pyrgos dates can only come into play if a relatively long gap (40+ calendar years) is regarded as possible between the two respective later LMIB archaeological contexts.

Fig. 49.   a. Combined calibrated calendar probability distribution for the new Oxford Chania and Myrtos-Pyrgos data reported in Housley *et al.* (1999:Table 1) using the INTCAL98 radiocarbon calibration dataset of Stuiver *et al.* (1998). b. The same but adding also the two previous Pennsylvania data on identical samples from Myrtos-Pyrgos (Fishman and Lawn 1978:213) (compare to Housley *et al.* 1999:Figs. 7 and 8 based on the 1993 decadal radiocarbon calibration dataset of Stuiver and Becker 1993). Calibration data in each case from the OxCal computer calibration programme (Ramsey 1995, Round Ranges function 'off'). P = Probability (out of 1.0). The 1σ and 2σ calibrated age ranges are indicated by the upper and lower lines under each of the probability distributions.

Fig. 50.   Reduced growth/narrow ring event in dendrochronological data (ring-width plots) from Ireland, England, and Germany beginning in 1628BC. Drawing after Baillie (1990; 1995a).

Fig. 51.   Map showing the location of the main Greenland ice-core sites referred to in the text. Greenland ice-core sites: top left, Camp Century; centre left, GISP2; centre right, GRIP; bottom, Dye 3.

Fig. 52.   The Dye 3 ice-core acid profile showing the 1644BC spike suggested to represent the eruption of Thera (Hammer *et al.* 1987). Drawing after Hammer *et al.* (1987).

Fig. 53.   The SO_4^{2-} residual volcanic signals in the GISP2 ice-core for the period around the time of the Thera eruption after Zielinski and Germani (1998a). The scale of the AD1883 Krakatau signal in the GISP2 ice-core is shown at 46ppb (Zielinski *et al.* 1994a:Table 1). At the time of the maximum reduction in estimates of Thera's sulphur production, it was suggested that Thera's sulphur signal might have merely been similar to the rather smaller and more remote Krakatau eruption (Pyle 1990b:169 and 171, Tables 1b and 1c). The Krakatau signal might therefore be deemed to offer a likely minimum benchmark for a Thera signal, with anything lower being very unlikely to represent Thera.

Fig. 54.a   FeO (total iron) versus K_2O versus CaO+MgO ternary plot comparing the average value for the composition of the GISP2 volcanic glass with a range of published analyses of Theran volcanic glass. The approximate 2σ measurement error zones for both the average value of the GISP2 glass, and the Theran glass from Mochlos on Crete, are indicated (the latter measurement errors are considered as ±2% of stated figure after Vitaliano *et al.* 1990:58 = 1σ – it is not entirely clear how to apply the stated 0.05% precision error cited in Soles *et al.* 1995). The error region for the GISP2 glass is very large as there are very few constituent data (four shards).

Fig. 54.b   FeO (total iron) versus K_2O versus CaO+MgO ternary plot after Federman and Carey (1980:Fig.5) showing their defined Thera Minoan eruption field versus the Zielinski and Germani (1998a:Table 1) data for both Santorini (Thera Minoan eruption) and GISP2 1623 BC shards. The Zielinski and Germani GISP2 and Santorini data virtually plot on top of each other, and *neither* datum plots within the Minoan field as defined by Federman and Carey – although they are relatively close (and by definition the measurements on Theran glass in Zielinski and Germani 1998a *should* be within the Thera field). Hence Zielinski and Germani data offset versus true values? If measurement errors were indicated on either or both the Zielinski and Germani measurements, or the Minoan field data, then the Zielinski and Germani data and the Minoan field of Federman and Carey would overlap.

Fig. 55. Na_2O versus SiO_2 and TiO_2 versus SiO_2 covariation plots for the GISP2 glass sherds (solid circle and solid square) and a range of published analyses of Thera Minoan eruption volcanic glass with the 2σ measurement errors (where known) indicated. The Thera glass data come from: (a) Watkins *et al.* (1978:Table 1 tephra on land), (b) Watkins *et al.* (1978:Table 1 tephra in cores), (c) Zielinski and Germani (1998a:Table 1 Santorini), (d) Soles *et al.* (1995:Table 1 Mochlos and Thera 'Rose' pumice – 1σ measurement errors considered as ±2% of stated figure after Vitaliano *et al.* 1990:58), (e) Sullivan (1988:Table 1; 1990:Table 1) – Gölcük tephra, no measurement errors provided, (f) Guichard *et al.* (1993:Table 2 TRI172-22, GGC-79, and Minoan = east Mediterranean samples). Note, the 2σ errors cited by Guichard *et al.* for the 'Minoan' samples are the same as the 1σ errors cited for the identical sample series in Federman and Carey (1980:Table 2); thus it seems likely that Guichard *et al.* may be in error – hence the '2σ' errors I have employed after Guichard *et al.* may be considered as minima. The GISP2 glass data come from Zielinski and Germani (1998a:Table 1).

Fig. 56.   Comparison of the major oxide composition of the GISP2 volcanic glass from the c.1623±36BC layer and several published analyses of Theran Minoan eruption volcanic glass. a. without indication of measurement errors, b. indicating measurement errors at 2σ confidence where known. The Thera glass data come from: Zielinski and Germani (1998a:Table 1 Santorini), Soles *et al.* (1995:Table 1 Mochlos and Thera 'Rose' pumice – 1σ measurement errors considered as ±2% of stated figure after Vitaliano *et al.* 1990:58), Guichard *et al.* (1993:Table 2 TRI172-22, GGC-79, and Minoan = east Mediterranean samples). Note, the 2σ errors cited by Guichard *et al.* for the 'Minoan' samples are the same as the 1σ errors cited for the identical sample series in Federman and Carey (1980:Table 2); thus it seems likely that Guichard *et al.* may be in error – hence the '2σ' errors I have employed after Guichard *et al.* may be considered as minima.

The GISP2 glass data come from Zielinski and Germani (1998a:Table 1). Data described as <0.1 has been treated as 0.05.

Fig. 57.   The dendrochronological data from Porsuk, Turkey. The average behaviour in terms of percentage of normal growth by twenty-year moving average of the cedar, pine, juniper, and fir samples is shown both separately, and in terms of an overall Porsuk site combined average. The fit of the Porsuk data against the Aegean Dendrochronology Project Bronze–Iron Master Chronology is also shown (this is determined by a computer-calculated correlation). Note the growth patterns at extreme left and right are irrelevant due to very small (i.e. just one tree) sample numbers. Where there are good sample numbers note how all populations reflect the same major up or down trends, establishing the match of chronologies. Figure courtesy of Peter Ian Kuniholm.

Fig. 58.   The radiocarbon wiggle-match (best fit) of the 18 dendrochronologically-sequenced radiocarbon measurements on a section of wood from Gordion against the 1993 decadal calibration curve (Stuiver and Becker 1993). Figure after Kuniholm *et al.* (1996:Fig.1).

Fig. 59.   Figure showing, as of 1996, a population of juniper trees from Porsuk covering relative rings 800–900 of the Aegean Dendrochronology Project Master Chronology. In relative year 854 (shown by the vertical dashed line) the population exhibits a sudden growth event. Figure after Kuniholm *et al.* (1996:Fig.3).

Fig. 60.   Comparison of the 1993 decadal calibration curve data of Stuiver and Becker (1993) solely from German wood with the INTCAL98 dataset of Stuiver *et al.* (1998) and the Irish data of Pearson *et al.* (1986) for the period 1200–700BC. Errors on the calibration curve data are not shown.

Fig. 61.   Aegean Dendrochronology Project data for the 19th century AD. Note the effective *non*-impact of the Tambora and Krakatau eruptions. Small increases in growth do follow in each case, consistent with the model that cooler temperatures caused by volcanic aerosols promote tree growth in Anatolia, but the effect is very small and completely indistinguishable from normal growth variations. Data courtesy of Peter Ian Kunihom.

Fig. 62.   Proposed 'early' Aegean chronology for the mid-second millennium BC and its east Mediterranean context. (Same as Fig. 36)

Fig. 63.   Correlation of the Uluburun dendrochronological sequence, consisting of (for earlier part) one sample of cedar from shipframe and (for later part) one piece of cedar as cargo/dunnage aboard the ship, with the Aegean Dendrochronology Project Master Chronology. Correlation determined by computer calculation and checked by eye. The dramatic variation up and down in the Uluburun curve is solely because this consists of just one or two samples. This is in contrast to the relatively smooth overall average pattern of the master curve. The Uluburun sequence ends at relative ring 1177 or c.1305BC. The cargo/dunnage sample was not preserved to bark, thus an unknown number of additional rings are missing. A date c.1300BC for the wreck is a likely approximation. Figure courtesy of Peter Ian Kuniholm.

Fig. 64.   Schematic plan of Alalakh VII, the Yarim Lim palace, after Woolley (1955:Fig.35). Areas where LMIA-style frescoes found indicated (Rooms 4, 5, 11, 12 and 13: Woolley 1955:92, 94, 100, 102, 228–232). They were usually fallen from original locations on the floor above.

Fig. 65.   The ruling house of Alalakh VII and the chronology of relationships with the ruling houses of other Near Eastern cities (after Collon 1977; Charpin and Durand 1985; Astour 1989). Kings shown in CAPITALS. Names of females preceded by a superscript 'f'. It is possible that Hammurapi of Alalakh became king shortly before the sack of Alalakh VII, but this is not attested.

Fig. 66.   Stela now in the Louvre, Paris, with a relief scene at the top showing Hammurapi of Babylon standing before the throne of the sun-god. Hammurapi's legal code is inscribed below on the stela under this relief scene. See Frankfort (1970:119–122, Fig.134–135); Kuhrt (1995:Fig.11). Drawing after previous refs.

List of Tables

Table 1.   20th century AD evolution of the absolute chronology of the Aegean, Egypt, the Levant, and Cyprus around the middle of the second millennium BC.

Table 2.   Comparison of the pre-1987 conventional chronology of the earlier Aegean Late Bronze Age and the new 'early' chronology proposed in Betancourt (1987) and Manning (1988b).

Table 3.   The now current, mainstream, dates for the periods of Egyptian history relevant to this book, with accession dates listed for the pharaohs of the 18th and 19th Dynasties (data from von Beckerath 1994a; 1997; and Kitchen 1996a).

Table 4.   Kamose Stele. Translation of parts of the Stela of Kamose, last king of the 17th Dynasty of Thebes, describing the Hyksos city of Avaris (Tell el-Dabᶜa) after Redford (1997:13–15).

Table 5.   Tombs from Thebes in Egypt with paintings depicting Keftiu (Aegean people). Data from Wachsmann (1987).

Table 6.   List of Hittite Kings after Bryce (1998).

Table 7.   Radiocarbon determinations for samples from the VDL at Akrotiri from the Copenhagen Laboratory (from Friedrich *et al.* 1990:194 Table 3).

Table 8.   Calibrated calendar age range for the combined Copenhagen dataset for the Akrotiri VDL (see Table 7).

Table 9.   Radiocarbon determinations on samples from MMIII, early LMIA, and LMII contexts from the excavations directed by Prof. Joseph W. Shaw at Kommos, Crete, produced by the Oxford Radiocarbon Accelerator Unit as part of a project directed by Rupert A. Housley.

Table 10. Combined calibrated calendar age ranges BC for the radiocarbon data from LMII Knossos, LMII(?) Mochlos, and LMII Kommos. Data for Knossos and Mochlos from Hedges *et al.* (1990:227); and Soles (1997:426). Kommos determination from Table 9 above.

Table 11. Calibrated calendar age ranges for the radiocarbon data from later MBA Tell Es-Sultan (Jericho). Data from Bruins and van der Plicht (1995; 1996).

Table 12. Radiocarbon determinations relevant to the first Nuraghic phase on Sardinia. Data from Tykot (1994:125–126, 131).

Table 13. Major volcanic acid signals in the Dye 3, GRIP, and GISP2 ice-cores from southern (Dye 3), and central (GRIP, GISP2), Greenland for the period c.1700–1400BC. Data from Clausen *et al.* (1997:Table 3); and Zielinski *et al.* (1994a:Table 2); the 1688BC Dye 3 datum is from Hammer *et al.* (1987:519 and Fig.2).

Table 14. Highest attested year of reign for 18–20th Dynasty pharaohs after von Beckerath (1994a:117; 1997:201–202) compared to conjectured or interpolated years of reign in Kitchen (1996a), and, for late 20th Dynasty, Kitchen (1987).

List of Plates

Plate 1.   View of the Thera volcanic caldera looking south from Phira town. This overall caldera represents the outcome and evolution of a long series of volcanic eruptions.

Plate 2.   View of the massive Minoan eruption deposits in the Megalochori Quarry on Thera.

Plate 3.   View of part of the site of the Bronze Age settlement at Akrotiri buried by the eruption.

Plate 4.   View of part of the site of the Bronze Age settlement at Akrotiri buried by the eruption.

Plate 5.   View of a stream bed filled by the Minoan eruption deposits in the Phira Quarry on Thera.

Plate 6.   The Minoan land surface preserved directly beneath the pumice from the Minoan eruption (the straight dark line under the grey-white Minoan eruption pumice).

Plate 7.   Diver (Kate Mackay) recording one of the 45+ LBA-type stone anchors found on the seabed off the site of Maroni *Tsaroukkas*, southern Cyprus.

Plate 8.   White Painted pottery from an LCI deposit on the seabed off the site of Maroni *Tsaroukkas*, southern Cyprus.

Plate 9.   Proto White Slip sherd from an LCI deposit on the seabed off the site of Maroni *Tsaroukkas*, southern Cyprus.

Plate 10. Part of a Canaanite Jar from an LCI deposit on the seabed off the site of Maroni *Tsaroukkas*, southern Cyprus.

Plate 11. LMIA sherd from an early LCIA context at Maroni *Vournes* in southern Cyprus (P80 from trench M11 layer 12 #8814). Photograph courtesy of Gerald Cadogan.

Plate 12. A view of the Midas Mound tumulus at Gordion in Winter. Photograph courtesy of Peter Ian Kuniholm.

Plate 13. View of parts of the wooden structure inside the Midas Mound tumulus. Sections through some of the giant juniper logs preserved out to bark can be seen on the left. Photograph courtesy of Peter Ian Kuniholm.

Plate 14. Two examples of sections of logs taken as samples from the Midas Mound tumulus at Gordion. Photograph courtesy of Peter Ian Kuniholm.

Plate 15. Peter Ian Kuniholm collecting one of the wood samples at Porsuk, Turkey. Photograph courtesy of Peter Ian Kuniholm.

Preface

The modern archaeology of prehistoric Thera (Santorini) began as a result of a combination of two things: the construction of the Suez Canal (AD1859–1869), and a minor but violent eruption in the Thera caldera in late January AD1866. The first identified the island of Thera in the Aegean as offering a large and relatively proximate source for the quantities of volcanic pumice required in order to make the necessary cement, and so quarrying began on the island. The second led to a scientific mission to examine the geology of the island. It was soon discovered that the great pre-modern volcanic eruption which had blanketed the island in the tens of metres of valuable pumice had also buried a prehistoric (Bronze Age) civilisation.[8] Some have wondered if this eruption and the destruction of the island's civilisation might be behind the Greek legend of Atlantis. Marinatos further suggested in a famous article of 1939 that the eruption was responsible for the destruction of the palaces of Crete some 100km to the south. The extraordinary discoveries beneath the pumice on Thera, since modern archaeological excavations began in 1967 at the site of Akrotiri, have profoundly changed Aegean archaeology. An entire buried town, with houses preserved to two or more stories, has been revealed. The walls of many of the houses were decorated with remarkable frescoes, and these, in particular, have fascinated both tourists and scholars alike. But one question remains stubbornly unclear and vigorously debated: what was the date of this eruption? This question applies not only to a specific calendar date in years BC, but also to a relative date for the eruption in terms of the archaeological and historical sequences in Egypt, the Levant, Cyprus and the rest of the east Mediterranean. Yet the correct insertion of this great eruption into history requires a date.

In the last twenty years this has been perhaps the major controversy in Aegean archaeology. The conventional absolute calendar date offered through to the 1980s was c.1500BC; the eruption was also conventionally regarded in relative terms as occurring during the earlier 18th Dynasty of Egypt, shortly before the reign of Tuthmosis III, and during the LBI period of the Levant in general. However, over the

---

[8] Fouqué (1868; 1879; 1999); Mamet (1874); Sperling (1973); Forsyth (1998).

last two decades, a number of studies have proposed an absolute calendar date a little over a century earlier. Concurrently, several studies have argued that the eruption occurred in relative terms during the late MBA phase of the Levant, and the pre-18th Dynasty, Second Intermediate Period (SIP), of Egypt. The dates, both absolute and relative, for the eruption of Thera are central to many issues in Aegean and east Mediterranean archaeology and history, and their resolution is a key to a secure archaeology and history of the Aegean and east Mediterranean. In the Aegean, in particular, the potential significance is vast: did the New Palace civilisation of Crete, and the Shaft Grave culture of southern Greece, develop in communication with the MBA Levantine/Canaanite world, or instead the Egyptian 18th Dynasty led LBA world? This is no small difference, and the ramifications extend as far as the Classical world in consequence. The dating of the eruption is also important to several debates within volcanology and the environmental sciences. In addition, scholarly pride and raison d'être are transparently at stake. As Baillie (1995a:108) notes of the Thera eruption:

> Chronologically it is immensely important because, if the combined might of the archaeological and volcanological worlds cannot date an event of this magnitude, what chance is there of ever truly refining either archaeological or volcanological chronology....

The specific debate over high or low dates for the eruption of Thera is, moreover, symptomatic of a wider malaise in 20th century Aegean and Near Eastern archaeology and history. Giles (1997:5), at the beginning of a recent study on the history of western Asia in the second millennium BC, states:

> By far the most objectionable distortion of the historical record is that connected with schemes of chronology expressed in terms of western year dates. These theories have proliferated in recent times such that there is not only a High, Middle, and Low western chronology, but also some Ultra High and Ultra Low theories. Each one of these theories introduces its own distortions into history, and unfortunately there is no basis of agreement among these theorists, so that the discussion of these chronological theories in many cases displaces other perhaps more important historical research.

Time, as used by conventional archaeology and history, is a reference dimension;[9] in accordance with Darwinian logic, it does not explain.[10] Even modern theoretical approaches to the analysis of human culture – now prevalent in archaeology – which stress the reflexive and relative nature of all social life, still nonetheless employ chronology as a reference dimension in any archaeological applications.[11] Archaeological interpretation, and history, are impossible without some referential framework.

---

[9]   E.g. Bickerman (1980).
[10]   E.g. Cherry (1983). As Darwin (1886:82) writes: 'the mere lapse of time by itself does nothing, either for or against natural selection'.
[11]   E.g. Barratt (1994); Gosden (1994); Thomas (1996); Hodder (1992; 1996).

To the civilisations of ancient western Asia, through the Greco-Roman world, to the modern world, the standard reference system has been the earth's natural annual calendar made relevant to the lives of various (usually important) human individuals.[12] The result is that this solar timescale is central to history and archaeology. In archaeology, the aim is to correlate a relative chronology – a stratigraphically ordered sequence of phases found by excavation and study – with an absolute calendar timescale.

> To everything there is a season, and a time to every purpose under the heaven: a time to be born, and a time to die; a time to plant, and a time to pluck up that which is planted; a time to kill, and a time to heal; a time to break down, and a time to build up; a time to weep, and a time to laugh; a time to mourn, and a time to dance; a time to cast away stones, and a time to gather stones together; a time to embrace, and a time to refrain from embracing; a time to get, and a time to lose; a time to keep, and a time to cast away; a time to rend, and a time to sew; a time to keep silence, and a time to speak; a time to love, and a time to hate; a time of war, and a time of peace. (Ecclesiastes 3.1–8)

It is thus highly problematic for archaeology and history if this referential framework is totally mobile, ambiguous, and incapable of playing its necessary role as a frame of reference. And frustrating when reviews of recent standard works, such as *The Oxford Encyclopedia of Archaeology in the Near East*,[13] state that:

> The treatment of chronology is particularly inadequate. This is another key subject, especially for students, who might justifiably feel bewildered by the ample and inconsistently used terminology that they will encounter in the study of the ancient Near East.[14]

For although most aspects of human culture and history can be argued to be relative, and socially constructed, the western calendar system is in effect a cultural absolute. The writing and analysis of the archaeology and history of the second millennium BC in the eastern Mediterranean is usefully possible only with an agreed chronology. At present this is lacking, and, according to differing schemes, different rulers, peoples, fashions, and archaeological contexts are, or are not, contemporary and related. We urgently require the correct synchronisation of the Aegean and east Mediterranean civilisations.

The eruption of Thera is a key problem and opportunity in this regard. It offers a precise and dramatic event, and a clear horizon (time-line) across the entire Aegean region (and beyond); it should be datable (both archaeologically, and scientifically). This date should, moreover, be capable of being brought into precise correlation with the historical calendar chronologies in ancient western Asia (Egypt, Mesopotamia). It should be able to form the nexus of a new history. But controversy, argument,

---

[12] Cryer (1995).
[13] Meyers (1997).
[14] Baker (1998).

confusion, and debate are the order of the day. There was a conventional chronology; this was challenged; and a final resolution (new consensus) is still awaited. The result is that there are at present two different chronologies: the 'early' or 'high' chronology, and the 'conventional' or 'low' chronology. As Betancourt (1998b:291) notes, 'the two chronologies differ because of different interpretations of the Aegean imports in Egypt and Western Asia as well as eastern imports in the Aegean, and the fact that the "late chronology" rejects three types of scientific evidence'.

The present author has been writing about the eruption of Thera since an undergraduate essay, and has published a number of papers on the question of the date over the last decade. I will be considered partisan by some. But in fact I have always sought to review the totality of then available data (*both* archaeological and scientific), and to offer what *at that time* was the best working hypothesis. If new data or interpretations have emerged, or there have been improvements or revisions of scientific techniques, I have always accordingly re-assessed the debate. If new evidence showed that past positions I have supported were incorrect, then I would hope to be among the first to say so. This book is not a justification of past positions. This book is a sustained discussion of all the issues involved in the dating of the Thera eruption. Other studies may be criticised as narrowly based. Either they consider only the Aegean evidence and do not explore what this means in terms of the wider Mediterranean, or they concentrate on just one particular set of data, or approach, or technique. And there is a basic split between the archaeologists and the scientists. The exasperation of one famous Egyptologist is typical when he declares: 'If we were to adopt the more recent high chronology for the Santorini (Thera) explosion at about 1628BC, based on radiocarbon and dendrochronology, we would have to raise the dates of Egyptian chronology by some 130 years ... no Egyptologist would accept such a proposition'.[15] In fact, on examination, this is not the case, but the statement highlights the fact that a comprehensive study including all the relevant factors and their relationships with the wider archaeology and history of the Mediterranean is very necessary, and long overdue. The key absence to date of such holistic scholarship, of the non-integration of archaeology–history *and* science, is very evident if one reads another recent book by a famous scholar of ancient Egyptian chronology.[16] Just two pages (of over 200) concern science-dating techniques, the most recent reference cited on radiocarbon dating and calibration was published 31 years earlier in 1966, a few 'C14' dates with no explanation (just a reference to a paper of 1990) are given for no purpose, and a tone of (unjustified and inappropriate) scepticism is apparent. Meanwhile, some practicioners of archaeological science naively refer to Bietak's statement cited above about a supposed requirement for 'an additional 130 years of Egyptian history, something which no Egyptologist is likely to approve' as if this is *the* decisive data when they clearly have little or no clue about what they are referring to.[17] There is to date no useful integration of science and archaeology.

---

[15] Bietak (1996a:76).
[16] von Beckerath (1997).
[17] E.g. Buckland *et al.* (1997:587); Buckland *et al.* (1998:431).

One is reminded of the classic situation in many of the great debates and controversies in academic affairs. A convention reigns, and is then challenged. Some 'challenges' are quickly dismissed as wrong or unhelpful (and at best move into the twilight of alternative scholarship and conspiracy theories). Others are invariably at first denounced as radical and unproven and impossible. Then it is realised that they are not going away, and a general reassessment of the field begins. Sometimes this leads to the vindication of the challenge, sometimes to its ultimate rejection, and sometimes to a new position between original convention and challenge. Regardless, the health, rigour, and content of the field are enriched and strenghtened as a result of this cyclical process. Examples abound, but a good one in a Greek ancient history context is the work of H.B. Mattingly on ancient Athens – nicely summarised in his recently published collected papers.[18] Mattingly's radical redatings of key inscriptions, and so a new history of Athens, were at first rejected and criticised. But he was eventually vindicated, and the whole process of debate was constructive to scholarship. In Aegean prehistory we approach the beginning of the end of the Thera debate.

The present book reviews the history of the debate over the date of the Thera eruption, considers and analyses all the different types of evidence currently available from both archaeology and science, considers various problems and apparent contradictions, and finally proposes what seem on the balance of probabilities to be the most likely date or dates, both in relative and absolute terms. It then considers what these dates mean in terms of the archaeology and history of the Aegean and the east Mediterranean. It does not present all the data in detail, nor review and explore every related issue. This is beyond the scope of one book. Nonetheless, I hope to give a guide to where the debate is going in the next few years, and what we should now be working on. This book is cast as a discussion.

The original spur to write the present study came from a set of events in 1995–1996. Conferences in Tufts and Verona saw the topic of Aegean chronology thrashed out, and the existing debates gone over again and again (I thank especially Alessandro Guidi and Klavs Randsborg from the Verona meeting, and Miriam Balmuth and Robert Tykot from the Tufts meeting). But the debate seemed circular, and largely going nowhere. Scholars were wasting time attacking details published years ago, rather than concentrating on the state of play today. An attempt to write an up to date, relatively brief, but comprehensive, argument and synthesis dealing with the period under debate, c.1700–1400BC, seemed desirable. This could then provide a new focus; a point of reference, or attack. An invitation to lecture in Sweden at the universities of Lund, Uppsala, and Göteborg in early 1996 offered the prompt to start to bring together what became the initial draft of the following text (I thank Robin Hägg, Mary Blomberg, and Carole Gillis warmly for their wonderful hospitality – also Paul Åström for his friendly scepticism), and a seminar in Cambridge first brought several then recent developments together (I thank Sophia Voutsaki and Todd Whitelaw for the invitation).

---

[18]   Mattingly (1996). See pp.vii–xi by M. Chambers for a summary of the history of the debate.

Acknowledgements

This book represents closure on the last dozen years or so of my work on Thera and related matters. More directly, it is one outcome of research by the author as a member of the Aegean Dendrochronology Project over the last five years. I thank the US National Science Foundation and the Institute for Aegean Prehistory for research support, and I thank all the sponsors of the Malcolm and Carolyn Wiener Laboratory for Aegean and Near Eastern Dendrochronology for their indirect support of some of the work here. I have incurred many debts along the way. My key academic mentors have been forced to read Thera papers, though all expressly disliked chronology. I especially thank Bernard Knapp and John Cherry for not only publishing my first major study on the topic, but especially for many years of support, advice, and friendship. I similarly thank Anthony Snodgrass. I thank Martin Aitken, Mike Baillie, Philip Betancourt, Claus Hammer, and Valmore LaMarche, who were the scholars kind enough to reply when I sent letters or drafts off from Australia in 1985, and provided discussion, advice, and offprints then, and since. I thank Gerald Cadogan who has been a friend and source of support and advice over the last decade. I thank Colin Renfrew for an invitation to the Thera and the Aegean World III conference, and his interest since. I thank Peter Ian Kuniholm for his friendship and collaboration, likewise Bernd Kromer, and Bernhard Weninger. I also thank the rest of the Aegean Dendrochronology Project, and especially Mary Jaye Bruce, Jennifer Fine, Margaretha Kramer-Hajos, Maryanne Newton, Joan Ramage, Laura Steele, Isabel Tovar, and Carol Griggs. I have benefitted greatly from the friendship, knowledge, and advice of Malcolm H. Wiener, thankyou. His own forthcoming study, *The Chronology of the Late Bronze Age from Egypt to the Aegean: Science, Texts, Interconnections,* will be an important contribution, and is eagerly anticipated. Many other scholars have been kind enough to provide important comment, information, offprints, and advice, whether they agreed with me, or not. I cannot name everyone, but in particular I thank: Susan Allen, Dorothea and Dieter Arnold, Michal Artzy, Paul Åström, Celia Bergoffen, Manfred Bietak, Janine Bourriau, Eric Cline, Jack Davis, Oliver Dickinson, Christos Doumas, Jan Driessen, Kathryn Eriksson, Vronwy Hankey, Irmgard Hein, Ellen Herscher, Rupert Housley, Richard Jones, Vassos Karageorghis, Christine Lilyquist, Sandy MacGillivray, Louise Maguire, Nicoletta Martinelli, Floyd McCoy, Christopher Mee, Robert Merrillees, Wolf-Dietrich and Barbara Niemeier, Eliezer Oren, Jacke Phillips, David Pyle, Christopher Bronk Ramsey, Paul Rehak, Ian Rutherford, Jeremy Rutter, Hugh Sackett, Joseph and Maria Shaw, Tony Spalinger, Aleydis Van de Moortel, Alessandro Vanzetti, and Peter Warren.

In the preparation of this manuscript, I especially thank Jo Goffee and Sarah Monks for drawing work, research assistance, editorial assistance, and all their enthusiastic efforts and friendship. I also thank Elinor Ribeiro for several drawings, David Sewell for discussion, advice, several references, and the creation of some computer maps, and Thea Politis for research assistance and advice. I thank the Department of Archaeology, University of Reading, for providing facilities and a great place to work. I thank Peter Ian Kuniholm, Isabel Tovar, and Mary Jaye Bruce for printing and sending various figures and pictures, and for discovering and sending copies of several publications not accessible to me. I sincerely thank Oliver Dickinson, Kathryn Eriksson, Eliezer Oren, Celia Bergoffen, Jeremy Rutter, Maria Shaw, and another anonymous reader, for their critical and helpful comments on earlier drafts. I further thank Jo Goffee, Sarah Monks, and Peter Ian Kuniholm for reading through and criticising a subsequent draft. None of the above are responsible for remaining errors.

Final work was completed while I was Visiting Fellow at the Humanities Research Centre, Australian National University, Canberra. I thank the Director, Professor Iain McCalman, and Associate Director, Professor Graeme Clark, and the staff of the centre, for all their hospitality. I thank Sarah Monks, and Gerry Cox, for their critical support and assistance in bringing things to fruition. I thank Ruth Gwernan-Jones of Oxbow Books for her work seeing the manuscript to publication. I thank Georgia Nakou and Frank De Mita for work on the proofs and index.

Lastly, I wish to thank my wife, Leonie, who has always provided love, support, and belief, and put up with our home doubling as an office.

Chapter I: Introduction

This is a book about the chronology and dating of a key volcanic event – the great Minoan eruption of the Thera (or Santorini) volcano in the Aegean Sea – and the associated archaeological horizon, a little over 3,500 years ago. The date of this volcanic event and associated archaeological horizon, is central to, and has major implications for, the archaeology and history of the Minoan, Mycenaean, east Mediterranean, and even Egyptian worlds in the middle of the second millennium BC. This date has, however, been the subject of debate since 1939, and the focus of the major controversy in Aegean (and even general east Mediterranean) archaeology over the last decade. Different groups of archaeologists, historians, and scientists have proposed dates about a century apart. The correct history of the entire region in the middle of the second millennium BC hangs on the right answer, and so the resolution of the debate. This book seeks the best solution given the entire range of relevant archaeological and scientific data. It is thus concerned with the capabilities and limitations of current archaeological and scientific dating. It is also about the relevance of the dating of this volcanic eruption, and the associated archaeological horizon, to the archaeology and history of Aegean and east Mediterranean region from c.1700–1400BC.

Chronology, dating, is a fundamental both of archaeology, and the entire concept of socio-cultural evolution at the heart of all the social sciences over the last three centuries. The question of how old is this, or that, is about the first one asked of, and by, archaeologists. The ability to show a chronological succession through time formed the solid basis from the 19th century onwards to the concepts of evolution (biological and socio-cultural). The historiography of archaeology until very recently was in effect a history of chronology and dating. Most early scholarship in Egyptian and Near Eastern Studies was concerned with chronology and sequence. In later Mediterranean and European prehistory, after the initial Scandinavian-driven creation of relative and absolute chronology from natural stratigraphy and cultural typology (the 'Three Ages' terminology), the major phases were first a culture-historical framework centred on the historical dates offered by the civilisations of what Childe (1928) termed the 'most ancient East' (and the general 'diffusionist' model), and then, second, the radical re-think in many areas initiated by dendrochronology and the application of calibrated

2   *Introduction*

radiocarbon dating (and the general 'new', or processual, archaeology).[19] Even today, with the post-modern, post-processual, archaeology of the later 1980s and 1990s, and a host of new research interests and directions, the basic chronological frameworks developed over the course of the last century remain central to archaeological practice and theorising.

In the Aegean, the basic chronology was established towards the close of the 19th century AD. At the regional level, archaeological sequences, and interconnections (of exchanged objects and styles), allowed areas such as Crete, the Cycladic islands, and mainland Greece, to be tied together, and placed relative to each other through time. By the early 20th century, the general archaeological sequences on mainland Greece and Crete were established,[20] and an Aegean-wide synthesis became possible.[21] The potential for a calendar (or absolute) date arose because of the recognition that a couple of Old World civilisations (and in particular Egypt) had sophisticated calendar systems and long records of time in the forms of sequential king-lists (and other lists of various officials and priests) which can be recovered and reconstructed from a variety of written, or inscriptional, evidence to form a more or less continuous time-line back into the third millennium BC. Further, the analysis of a few astronomical observations recorded in these Egyptian and other records permits the approximate placement, or verification, of such dates.[22] Thus, for over a century, finds of 'datable' Near Eastern objects in the Aegean, or finds of imports from the Aegean in 'datable' contexts in the Near East (and especially Egypt), have enabled an approximate chronology to be constructed, and so the 'dating' of the relative archaeological sequences built up in the Aegean.

The absolute chronology of the second millennium BC Aegean region, in particular, began in the last decade of the 19th century AD, with the recognition by Sir Flinders Petrie (1891a) of Aegean ceramics from Twelfth Dynasty Kahun in Egypt, equated by Myres (1893–1895) with ceramic material found in the Kamares cave on Crete, and then the discovery of Mycenaean pottery, again by Petrie, at the capital of the Egyptian ruler Akhenaten (Amenhotep IV) at Tell el-Amarna which was inhabited for a short time in the mid-fourteenth century BC.[23] These initial Aegean–Egyptian linkages established the approximate absolute dating of the Aegean Bronze Age.[24] In the century since, many additional correlations have been found, and many refinements have been made to the relative sequences, and today we have a detailed relative Aegean ceramic sequence and a complex web of interrelations with Egypt, the Levant, and the Near East.[25] Despite various acknowledged shortcomings and areas of flexibility,[26]

---

[19] For discussions, see e.g. Gräslund (1987); Randsborg (1996a); Renfrew (1973); Trigger (1989). On the history of socio-cultural evolution, see Trigger (1998).
[20] Tsountas and Manatt (1897); Wace and Blegen (1916–1918); Evans (1906).
[21] Åberg (1933).
[22] See Meyer (1904; 1912); Gardiner (1961); Kitchen (1991; 1996a).
[23] Petrie (1894).
[24] See Newton (1878); Petrie (1890; 1891b). In general, see Cadogan (1978).
[25] E.g. Furumark (1941b); Popham (1970a); Hankey and Warren (1974); Hankey (1987; 1991/1992); Warren and Hankey (1989).
[26] Cadogan (1978); Manning (1996).

SOURCE	EGYPT Ahmose	EGYPT Amenhotep	EGYPT Tuthmosis III	LEVANT MBA/LBA Transition	CYPRUS LCIA	CYPRUS LCIB	AEGEAN LMIA	AEGEAN Thera eruption	AEGEAN LMIB
CAH¹ I (1923)	1580–1559	1559–1530	1501–1447				c.1580–1500		
Evans (1921–1935, vol.II.1)									1500–1450
Marinatos (1939)								1500	
Sjöqvist (1940)					1550–1450	1450–1400			
Furumark (1941b)							1550–1500		1500–1450
Tufnell *et al.* (1958)/Kantor (1965)				1600					
Amiran (1969)				1570					
CAH³ (1970–1973)	1570–1546	1546–1526	1504–1450	1570–1560			1570–1500	1500	1500–1450
Åström (1972a)					1600/1575–1525/00	1525/00–1425/15			
Avi-Yonah (1975)	1570–1546	1546–1526	1504–1450	1550					
Merrillees (1977)					1650/25–1575/50	1575/50–1475/50			
Cadogan (1978)							1550–1500		1500–1450
Kemp and Merrilees (1980)							*1675/50–1600/1575*		*1600/1575–1500/1475*
Baurain (1984)					1620–1520	1520–1420		1500	
Warren (1984)								1500	
Dever (1985)				1550 (to 1500)					
Betancourt (1987)							*1700–1610*	*1630/25*	*1610–1550*
Manning (1988b)							*1725/00–1630/20*	*1630/25*	*1630/20–1570/40*
Warren and Hankey (1989)							1600/1580–1480		1480–1425
Eriksson (1992)/Helck (1987)	1530–1504	1504–1483	1467–1413	1530	1530–1460	1460–1380	1530–1460	1460	1460–1430
Dever (1992)				1500					
Kempinski (1992a)				1600					
von Beckerath (1994a)	1550–1525	1525–1504	1479–1428						
Manning (1995)							*1675/50–1600/1550*	*1628*	*1600/1550–1490/70*
Kitchen (1996a)	1540–1515	1515–1494	1479–1427	1530 (to 1410)					
Bietak (1996a; 1997)								1515–1460	
Betancourt (1998b)							*?–1620/00*	*1627*	*1620/00–1490/70*
Warren (1998)							1580–1525/1490	1520	1525/1490–1450/25

Table 1. 20th century AD evolution of the absolute chronology of the Aegean, Egypt, the Levant, and Cyprus around the middle of the second millennium BC. The Aegean 'high', or 'early' chronology scholars are shown in the bold italics.

this ceramic and typologically based relative chronology – dated through the interpretation of links with Egypt and the Near East – has become the conventional chronology of the Aegean. It placed the eruption of Thera c.1500BC.

New science-based dating techniques relevant to Bronze Age prehistory became available to modern archaeologists after World War II; these primarily physics-driven techniques now form the core to chronometric dating in archaeology.[27] Here the Aegean was always going to be problematic. It sits at the junction between the historically dated east Mediterranean – and a century of archaeological tradition and assumptions – and genuinely pre-historic Europe. Not surprisingly, with the application of calibrated radiocarbon dating from the late 1960s onwards, the Aegean rapidly came to mark a chronological fault line between a new radiocarbon-dated Europe with rather earlier dates than previously thought from the old diffusionist logic, and a conventionally dated east Mediterranean.[28] Radiocarbon dating was applied (rather sparingly) in the Aegean itself from the 1960s.[29] It provided more or less the first solid evidence for the dating of the contexts earlier than the mid-third millennium BC, and, although not accepted by some traditionalists,[30] was held by most to offer useful evidence for these early periods.[31] The second millennium BC was thought to be different: archaeological correlations, and the general conventional chronology, were held to provide a sound and precise chronology to which radiocarbon dating could add little.[32]

However, by the 1970s, indications started to emerge that radiocarbon dating perhaps favoured a date for some Aegean archaeological phases in the middle of the second millennium BC rather earlier than the conventional chronology.[33] The dates in question came from archaeological sites on the islands of Thera (Santorini) and Crete: the former from the final volcanic destruction level phase at the site of Akrotiri buried by the great Minoan eruption of the Thera volcano, and the latter from the LMIB destruction at the site of Myrtos-Pyrgos. The dates from Akrotiri suggested a 17th century BC age, and not one c.1500BC, and those from Myrtos-Pyrgos indicated an age for the subsequent LMIB period in the 17th to 16th centuries BC, and not c.1500–1450BC. Here science-dating ran headlong into firm convention. For many archaeologists and historians, science-based dating had to agree with conventional dating in the Aegean and east Mediterranean, or be wrong.[34] And, indeed, across much of the second millennium BC radiocarbon dating offered dates consonant with the conventional chronology,[35] but, in the period around the start of the Aegean Late

---

[27] See progressively Aitken (1961; 1974; 1990); Taylor and Aitken (1997). For the dramatic changes in the immediate postwar decades compare Zeuner (1958) with Zeuner (1946).
[28] Renfrew (1970; 1973).
[29] Kohler and Ralph (1961).
[30] Milojčić (1967); Branigan (1973).
[31] Warren (1976a).
[32] Warren and Hankey (1974:142–143).
[33] Michael (1976); Betancourt and Weinstein (1976).
[34] E.g. Hood (1978a).
[35] Betancourt and Weinstein (1976); Weinstein and Betancourt (1978); Betancourt and Lawn (1984); Manning and Weninger (1992).

Bronze Age (LBA), or the middle of the second millennium BC, radiocarbon evidence clearly indicated an earlier chronology than the existing conventional one:[36]

> For some as yet unexplained reason, there are more problems with the LMIA and LMIB dates from Thera and Crete than there are for earlier and later periods in the Aegean.[37]

And so began a controversy that continues to this day. Some scholars simply declared radiocarbon dating to be incorrect in this case, and held to conventional interpretations (and all the entailed assumptions), some sought, or at least wondered about, a special problem with these particularly troublesome radiocarbon dates,[38] some plumped for science dating and even suggested that a plausible re-interpretation of the conventional archaeological chronology was possible, some searched for compromises, or best fits of both types of data, and many others regarded this as a horrible problem that would hopefully go away if ignored for long enough.[39]

Twenty years later the problem has not gone away. The date of the eruption of Thera, and hence the Late Minoan (LM) I period in the Aegean, remains fiercely disputed between those supporting the traditional archaeological chronology, those supporting a revised archaeological chronology, and those supporting science-dating evidence.[40] A major article published in 1998 reviewing the Aegean field simply states that 'for the last decade, Late Bronze Age Aegean chronology has been the subject of serious debate, centering around the dates for the earlier part of the period and particularly the date of the eruption of the Thera volcano'.[41] So, did the LMI period start in the 16th century BC as the conventional (or low) chronology holds, or did it instead begin earlier, in the 17th century BC (the 'early' or 'high' chronology)? Can we decide? Nor is this a small local affair. The problem has major ramifications for the chronologies of the rest of the east Mediterranean, the central Mediterranean, and also southeast Europe – all of which are archaeologically interlinked. Defenders of the conventional, lower, chronology are well aware of the significance of the debate. Driessen and Macdonald (1997:23) state that 'the responsibility of those who propose a 17th century date is great and what this might mean in broad Mediterranean terms has yet to be assessed'. The present book addresses the controversy, and this demand. It seeks both to establish what the date is, and to consider what this most likely date means in terms of Aegean and east Mediterranean archaeology and history. As often in research, we will discover that while the prime objective may remain problematic, a number of other issues become clear. At the heart of this whole subject is the question of the date of the Minoan eruption of the Thera volcano. The settlement of Akrotiri

---

[36] Weinstein and Michael (1978); Weinstein and Betancourt (1978); Betancourt *et al.* (1978); Michael (1978).

[37] Weinstein and Betancourt (1978:809).

[38] E.g. Weinstein and Betancourt (1978:806 and refs.); Biddle and Ralph (1980).

[39] Cf. Snodgrass (1985:36).

[40] E.g. Lohmann (1998:351–360); Schoch (1997); Forsyth (1998:106–113).

[41] Rehak and Younger (1998a:97–98).

on Thera buried by the eruption was the primary source of the original 'early' radiocarbon dates, and this volcanic event has remained the focus of the ensuing chronological debate over the last two decades.[42]

---

[42] Van Schoonwinkel (1990); Manning (1990b; 1992a; 1995:30–31, 200–216); Manning *et al.* (1994a:222–226); Warren (1990/1991; 1996; 1998); Rehak and Younger (1998a:98 and n.16); Forsyth (1998:106–113); Wiener (n.d.).

Chapter II:
A brief history of the Thera debate

The enormous eruption of the volcano of Thera (Santorini) in the Aegean a little over 3,500 years ago was a major event of global significance. The dramatic and eerie remains of the shattered volcano make this apparent to the millions of tourists who have visited the island: Plates 1 and 2.[43] It was a special eruption of a scale that occurs around the world only once in every 300 years; it was one of the larger volcanic eruptions of the last 10,000 years of the earth's history.[44] On current estimates, the eruption sent c.30–40km^3 of dense rock equivalent into the atmosphere.[45] The eruption buried and destroyed a prehistoric civilisation on the island of Thera under tens of metres of pumice, and in particular, a complete town at the site of Akrotiri:[46] Figure 12; two views in Plates 3 and 4. Akrotiri is the 'Pompeii' of the Aegean, a place where time stopped with the eruption. It provides a unique, and specific, window into a moment of time several thousand years ago. The eruption of Thera can be related to the surrounding contemporary cultures and areas: Crete, Greece, Cyprus, Anatolia, the Levant, and Egypt. There is thus an entire cultural horizon linked to the eruption of Thera in Old World archaeology and history. If the precise, and absolute, date of the eruption of Thera could be determined, then the moment time stopped on Thera would act as a chronological 'marker' across the Aegean and east Mediterranean. It would offer an independent test of existing chronologies, a refinement of current debates, and a pivotal event around which to build the chronology and history of the Aegean and east Mediterranean.

As stated, this study is about the quest to offer a precise and absolute date for the eruption of Thera, both in relative and absolute terms. En route, we will find that the long-standing conventional chronology of the subsequent LMIB to LMIIIA1

---

[43] For an excellent basic text on all aspects of the Thera volcano and island, with many pictures, see Friedrich (1994). I note that an English translation of this book, slightly revised and up-dated to 1997, will be published in the near future (W.L. Friedrich, pers. comm.; see Friedrich 2000).

[44] Decker (1990); Simkin and Siebert (1994).

[45] Pyle (1990a); Sigurdsson et al. (1990).

[46] Doumas (1983a; 1992).

West House

House of the Ladies

Xeste 5

House
of the Anchor

Xeste 2

Xeste 3

Xeste 4

South Building

0   40M

Fig. 12. Schematic plan of the excavated part of the Bronze Age town at Akrotiri, Thera. After Doumas (1992).

periods is definitely in need of (upwards) revision, and generally we will find that the Thera debate, and the challenge of the so-called 'early' or 'high' or 'long' Aegean chronology, has significantly changed the general status quo. A number of lazy assumptions have been highlighted. Thus the recent debate and period of controversy has been worthwhile and useful: a bright light has illuminated previously dark corners. Hence, even if the date of the eruption ends up in the 16th century BC, as the so-called low, or conventional, chronology maintains, it will not be the original c.1500BC date, nor will the evidence or arguments of the 1970s and 1980s be the reason for this decision. In the following investigation, the question of the date of the eruption itself is predictably found to be neither as simple nor clear-cut as proponents on either side of the debate initially thought. We can narrow down, and define, the parameters, but a definite answer remains the subject of agonised debate and some apparent contradictions. The following chapters explore the now possible dates, and consider what these mean in terms of the chronology and history of the wider Aegean and east Mediterranean. But first we must review the history of the Thera debate.

Systematic modern archaeological excavations began at Akrotiri, Thera, in 1967 under the direction of Spyridon Marinatos (1968–1976), and have been continued under Christos Doumas to the present day. The excavations, and the extraordinary discoveries, have revealed, and created, a dramatic, special, place which has become a focus of much research and interest. Allied with the discovery in the 1960s and early 1970s that the tephra (volcanic ash) fallout from the Thera eruption was widespread,[47] the subject of Thera, its eruption, and effects, have become a major joint archaeological and scientific project involving hundreds of archaeologists and scientists. Apart from many books and articles, four major international conferences have been held on the subjects of Thera, Akrotiri, and variously the geology, archaeology, and art-history, associated with the great volcanic eruption.[48]

As noted above, the sheer scale of the volcanic remains at Thera – a huge caldera – had attracted attention last century, especially once cultural remains were found in the later 1860s during quarrying on the island for pumice to be used in the construction of the Suez Canal.[49] The eruption buried a prehistoric (Minoan) land surface across the island: Plates 5 and 6. This early work (especially by Nomikos and Alafousos) revealed parts of several buildings at different locations, and, in the area of the modern excavations at Akrotiri, both Fouqué and subsequently Mamet and Gorceix found parts of buildings with Late Cycladic I fresco decoration. Work by Zahn from 1899 at Kamares (Potamos), only a 100m or so from the Akrotiri ravine, again found important Late Cycladic I material, and so, by the time Åberg (1933) wrote his comprehensive Aegean synthesis, there was a fairly detailed knowledge

---

[47] Ninkovich and Heezen (1965); Vitaliano and Vitaliano (1974); Cadogan *et al.* (1972).
[48] Marinatos and Ninkovich (1971); Doumas (1978a; 1980); Hardy *et al.* (1990a; 1990b); Hardy and Renfrew (1990); and a fourth conference, 'Wall Paintings of Thera', 30 August–4 September 1997, currently in press as I write.
[49] Fouqué (1868; 1879; 1999); Mamet (1874).

of prehistoric Thera.[50] In addition, whereas some scholarship tried to link Minoan Crete with the legendary Atlantis,[51] the question, the idea, of whether the cataclysm of Thera could hold the remains of the legendary civilisation of destroyed Atlantis was raised in the light of the early discoveries on Thera,[52] and has continued to be discussed ever since.[53] There is also literature which has proposed a possible link between the eruption of Thera and the legendary events of the Biblical Exodus.[54] Thera had entered the mainstream of both academic and popular interest.

As approximate Aegean relative archaeological chronologies were built and matured into their final general form in the early part of the 20th century AD, it became clear that the cultural remains on Thera buried by the eruption dated broadly to what Sir Arthur Evans had termed the LMI period on Crete, based on his excavations at Knossos and his study of Minoan finds across Crete. Evans had at one time thought that the Thera eruption deposits might correlate with the MMIII destruction at Knossos, but subsequently he observed the LMIA date of the Thera material,[55] opening a link with the mature LMIA seismic destruction at Knossos.[56] Renaudin (1922) likewise categorised the material from Thera buried by the eruption as LMIA.[57] But Thera was not yet a real focus of attention. This changed in 1939, when Marinatos published a now famous and controversial article in the journal *Antiquity* arguing that the eruption was responsible for the destruction of the Minoan palatial civilisation of Crete – and the editors of the journal insisted on adding a caveat at the end stating that the thesis required corroboration. Marinatos was not the first to suggest this hypothesis, but it was his article which caught the attention of the field.[58] Luce (1969) and Page (1970) then strongly re-iterated the case a generation later. Thera had become central to Aegean and Mediterranean prehistory.[59]

The finds of artefacts buried by the eruption, and there are literally millions from Akrotiri, provide a date for the eruption in terms of the material culture (the fashions, or styles) of the Cycladic region. In addition, finds of quantities of imported Minoan artefacts from Crete, and also Late Helladic (LH) artefacts from mainland (Mycenaean)

---

[50] See Åberg (1933:127–137). For a description of early work on Thera, see Fouqué (1879:94–131; 1999:94–131); Furtwaengler and Loeschcke (1886:18–19); Sperling (1973); for some of the finds, see Dumont and Chaplain (1888:19–42); Renaudin (1922). For a biographical note on Fouqué, see McBirney in Fouqué (1999:ix–xiii).

[51] E.g. Frost (1913); see discussions and review in Forsyth (1980:112–113, 159–168).

[52] Figuier (1872).

[53] Luce (1969); Galanopoulos and Bacon (1969); Ross (1977); Ramage (1978); Forsyth (1980:113, 115–158); Friedrich (1994:157–169); Castleden (1998). Some more recent examinations suggest looking elsewhere (and in particular in western Anatolia: James 1995; see also with less rigour Zangger 1992; 1993).

[54] E.g. Bernal (1991:291–293); Bruins and van der Plicht (1996); Baillie (1998:425 and refs.).

[55] Evans (1921–1935, vol.II:313 n.1).

[56] Evans (1921–1935, vol.II.320).

[57] Åberg (1933) considered the Thera assemblage on the whole a little more archaic, and linked it with the MMIIIB to earlier LMIA, and/or LMIA, Temple repositories at Knossos (cf. the initial dating of Evans). On the Temple Repository ceramics, see recently Panagiotaki (1998).

[58] Driessen and Macdonald (1997:107) note the article of Schoo (1937–1938), which was all but ignored.

[59] For a mid-1970s review of the subject, see Hiller (1975).

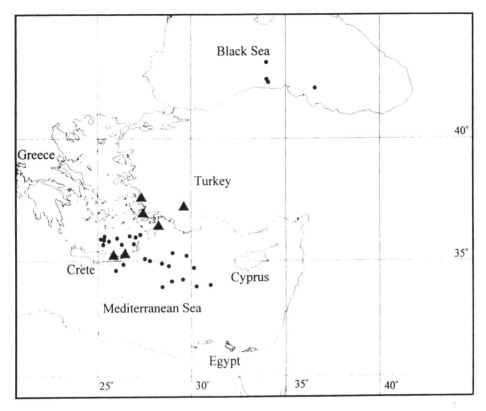

Fig. 13. Map of the eastern Mediterranean showing a number of the locations where airfall Theran tephra from the Minoan eruption has been identified either in geological coring or archaeological excavation (see text for details).

Greece, at Akrotiri synchronise the eruption precisely within the archaeological and cultural sequences of Crete and Greece.[60] Tephra from the eruption is also found stratified at sites in the Aegean (solid triangles), and in sediment cores from the Aegean, east Mediterranean, Anatolia, and the Black Sea (solid circles), delineating a widespread and important Thera eruption horizon: Figure 13.[61]

The eruption of Thera offers a pivotal event. Most of Aegean prehistory is at best the subject of approximate dating: via attempts to link finds of artefacts, and so the

---

[60] Doumas (1978b); Niemeier (1980); Marthari (1984; 1990); Warren (1990/1991); Driessen and Macdonald (1997:15–22).
[61] E.g. Davis and Cherry (1984); Cadogan and Harrison (1978); MacGillivray *et al.* (1992:134–137; 1998:241–242 and Fig.16); Soles *et al.* (1995); Doumas and Papazoglou (1980); Marketou (1988; 1990); Watkins *et al.* (1978); Stanley and Sheng (1986); Sullivan (1988; 1990); Guichard *et al.* (1993); Eastwood *et al.* (1998); Rehak and Younger (1998a:98 and n.21); W.-D. Niemeier, pers. comm. The tephra reported by Stanley and Sheng (1986) from the Nile delta in Egypt is highly problematic. Guichard *et al.* (1993); Liritzis *et al.* (1996) and Eastwood *et al.* (1998:679, referring to a forthcoming study by Eastwood *et al.*

timespan of some style, with the historical cultures of Egypt and the Near East; or via the irregular application of approximate scientific dating methods to samples which must then be interpreted in a cultural–archaeological context. Even in the best circumstances, a precise date from a technique like dendrochronology for some specific object does not date a wider archaeological assemblage, yet alone a site or culture. Archaeological interpretation and guesswork are necessary. Similarly, even sophisticated modern radiocarbon dating and analysis cannot resolve the typical open and non-bounded archaeological contexts found and excavated into more than an approximate framework.[62] In contrast, Akrotiri on Thera, like the cities of Pompeii and Herculaneum in Italy buried by the eruption of Vesuvius in AD79, offers a specific buried time-capsule: a complete town and associated widespread geological and archaeological horizon. If it could be dated, then the precise set of linkages would create a fixed point in time for the study of Aegean prehistory. Moreover, some east Mediterranean artefacts were found buried by the eruption on Thera, and the Minoan and Mycenaean cultures had trading relations with most of the cultures of the east and central Mediterranean. Thus the Thera eruption is specifically related to a whole nexus of relations across much of the Mediterranean (and thence into southern Europe), and even into Egypt and the Near East. It offers a potential point of reference for the prehistory of the entire region.

Relative date in the Aegean, and the initial historically derived date

The question, therefore, is whether the eruption can be dated. Fouqué, working in the 1860s–1870s, with little to go on, estimated the date of the Minoan eruption and the formation of the caldera as about 2000 years before the birth of Christ (and no later than c.1500BC).[63] He should be congratulated for his judgement. In the half century following Fouqué, Aegean archaeology developed as a discipline, and chronologies of the prehistoric cultures in the region were built on the basis of artefact linkages with Egypt, and these came to be used to date the eruption. As noted above, the pottery found buried by the eruption on Thera was studied and found to include, or be similar to, LMI types. Mature LMI was dated around 1500BC, through interpretation of, and interpolation between, finds of Minoan and Mycenaean artefacts in Egypt, and even wall paintings showing people (identified as Aegean) carrying Aegean style objects of LMI type in some 18th Dynasty tombs at Thebes in Egypt.[64] When Marinatos wrote

1999:24–26) all question the Theran attribution of this tephra. As evident in Guichard *et al.* (1993:Fig.2), and Figure 54.a below, the reported chemical composition of the glass shards found by Stanley and Sheng are significantly different from analyses of Theran (Minoan eruption) glass shards. On present evidence, it is impossible for the data reported by Stanley and Sheng to be Theran. It is thus best to discount the Stanley and Sheng data at this time.

[62] E.g. Bayliss *et al.* (1997).
[63] Fouqué (1868:28–29; 1879:130; 1999:130).
[64] E.g. Hall (1901–1902); Evans (1921–1935, vol.IV:265–266); Wace and Blegen (1939).

about the eruption in 1939, he could write that 'we can safely date the explosion to the last years of LMI, about 1500B.C.' (1939:431). This conclusion proved remarkably robust for half a century. Until the 1980s, LMI continued without serious question to be equated with the early New Kingdom of Egypt, and the eruption of Thera dated thereby c. 1500 BC (see next paragraph).

On Crete, Marinatos had noted that there were two styles of LMI artwork: LMIA, characterised by abstract or floral designs, and horizontally banded decorations often with spirals; and LMIB, characterised by marine style decorations, coherent single designs covering the whole vessel surface, or thematic representations. However, Marinatos did not think these two styles were necessarily chronologically distinct – he thought they were more or less contemporary (1939:428–429). Versions of this view persisted to the early 1970s, but the majority of scholarship accepted a chronological sequence from LMIA to LMIB (although clear stratigraphic evidence was absent until relatively recently). The classic typological, chronological, and historical studies of the Aegean material from the middle of the 20th century were by Arne Furumark.[65] He equated LMIA with the first part of the 18th Dynasty of Egypt before the reign of the pharaoh Tuthmosis III, and LMIB with the reign of Tuthmosis III. In view of the then current chronologies of Egypt, Furumark dated LMIA from 1550 to 1500BC, and LMIB from 1500 to 1450BC. The latest material from the early excavations on Thera, and associated with the volcanic eruption horizon, belonged to a mature stage of the LMIA period in stylistic terms. Scholes (1956:35) neatly and correctly summarised the pre-1967 evidence from Thera: no LMIB, but mature LMIA, and moreover some indications that LHIIA may have just about begun – hence late LMIA. The eruption therefore came to be placed as a matter of convention at the end of the LMIA period, and was dated, as noted above, c.1500BC. See also Table 1 in Chapter I.

The only potential challenges to this date in the period up to 1971 involved a downwards shift. Coldstream (1969:150), for example, noted one vessel *reportedly* found on Thera which could be placed in the LMIB period in stylistic terms, and this might have permitted the eruption to move down a little towards c.1450BC – if this vessel could ever be proved to have come from a secure pre-eruption context (whereas the opposite seems to be the case). He also noted another cup from Marinatos' excavations with a possible LMIB-style decoration, but Hood quickly responded, noting that the decoration in question is also found in LMIA contexts.[66] Page (1970), who wished to support Marinatos' (1939) theory that the Thera eruption caused the destruction of the palaces of Crete at the close of the LMIB period, hoped it was possible that Marinatos' view might prove correct whereby LMIB ran parallel to late LMIA, rather than being a subsequent stage. And, if this was not possible, he argued that perhaps there was a gap in the eruption sequence. Thus he proposed that the initial volcanic activity, and the abandonment of their homes by the population of Thera, could be dated to the end of LMIA, but the final decisive eruption activity occurred a generation or so later in LMIB. Page (1970:15) sought support in a much

---

[65] Furumark (1941a; 1941b; 1950).
[66] Hood (1970:104 n.10).

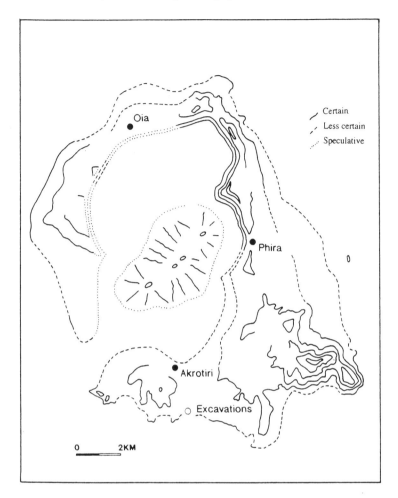

Fig. 14. Approximate reconstruction of Late Bronze Age Thera/Santorini immediately prior to the Minoan eruption (after Druitt and Francaviglia 1992:Fig.10).

earlier geological study published in 1936 by H. Reck, but, by the end of the first Thera conference,[67] this view seemed very unlikely. Pomerance meanwhile opted for a much more radical thesis.[68] He believed the eruption of Thera to have been on a cataclysmic scale, and argued that there was a lack of evidence for a comprehensive disaster around the Aegean and eastern Mediterranean anywhere close to 1500BC. Therefore, he suggested the eruption, or at least the decisive caldera collapse, did not occur until c.1200BC. This viewpoint attracted little support,[69] and has since been

---

[67] Marinatos and Ninkovich (1971).
[68] Pomerance (1970; 1971).
[69] Apart from van Effenterre (1974:193–209).

shown to be completely impossible.[70] Contrary to earlier reconstructions where pre-eruption Thera was thought to be one conical island which then blew apart and collapsed in the Minoan eruption,[71] subsequent work has demonstrated that prior to the Minoan eruption Thera was already a ring shaped island with a central bay-caldera,[72] and that, although dramatic, the scale of the Minoan eruption and likely tsunami would not have been of the supra-region-wide cataclysmic scale envisaged by Pomerance: see Figure 14. Finds of Thera eruption products, and waterborne pumice from the eruption, further confirm that the eruption processes occurred in the LMI period, and not centuries later.

The excavations by Marinatos at Akrotiri from 1967 confirmed that the last town at the site was Late Cycladic I and LMIA in date. There was a major earthquake during earlier Late Cycladic I/LMIA, followed by rebuilding. The site then ended subsequently in the mature to later LMIA period with the volcanic eruption. Since no human bodies were found, and portable precious items seemed to be missing, it appears that the population abandoned the town (or at least the area excavated) before its burial under meters of pumice. We do not yet know how many escaped the island, or whether much of the population will be found one day trapped, for example, unable to escape at the port. Despite enormous numbers of finds, there remained no indication of LMIB ceramics at Akrotiri. Thus, despite his 1939 theory, it seemed that the destruction of the Minoan palaces at the close of the LMIB ceramic period was a separate process a generation or more later.

In the early to mid 1970s debate centred on the details of this relative sequence at Akrotiri vis à vis the wider Aegean, and the possibility (or not) of somehow nonetheless arguing for an LMIB eruption. As noted above, a stylistic distinction had long been clear between what was defined as LMIA material and what was defined as LMIB material, but stratigraphic evidence for their temporal relationship was much less clear. Further, on Crete, material that looked like LMIA (i.e. was LMIA in style) appeared in contexts which also included material which was LMIB in style. Several scholars thus tried to place the eruption in the LMIB time period, and so link it with the LMIB destructions on Crete, either by simply conflating late LMIA with LMIB (with LMIB argued to be a special palatial style contemporary with later LMIA), or by proposing that there were extenuating circumstances to explain why LMIB stylistic material did not appear under the eruption pumice on Thera.[73] The ongoing excavations at Akrotiri largely put paid to these ideas once the material had been

---

[70] It is of course possible that *another* volcanic eruption or earthquake, and a resultant tsunami, was involved in some of the LMIIIB/LHIIIB destructions known from the later 13th to early 12th centuries BC, as suggested by Vallianou (1996:161–165).

[71] See e.g. Page (1970: Fig.10).

[72] I.e. largely the same shape found today. See Druitt and Francaviglia (1990; 1992); Heiken *et al.* (1990); Friedrich *et al.* (1988); Forsyth (1996).

[73] Proposals ranged from attempting to argue that there were one or two items (of many, many, thousands) from Akrotiri which might be considered LMIB in style, to arguments that Thera was more provincial or conservative in style than Crete itself and so late LMIA on Thera might equate with LMIB on Crete. For discussion of such ideas, see e.g. Höckmann (1974); Kleinmann (1974); Luce (1973; 1976); Bolton (1976); Platon (1984).

Fig. 15. LHIIA?-style jug from the VDL at Akrotiri (no. 5115). Drawing after Marthari (1990:Fig.8).

assessed. Despite many, many, thousands of ceramic finds, *nothing* was LMIB in style. This was clear in 1970 when Hood (1970:104) wrote that 'none of the pottery found ... has decoration characteristic of Late Minoan IB', and remains true nearly 30 years later. The latest Cretan, or Cretan-style, material was mature to late LMIA.[74] Geological evidence was also entering the debate. The Vitalianos searched for the presence of tephra from the Minoan eruption of Thera at archaeological sites on Crete, and argued that the pattern of its stratigraphic positions indicated an LMIA eruption date.[75] Although this initial study was criticised by some for its poor methodology,[76] it pointed the way to an eventual secure stratigraphic resolution a little over a decade later.

Excavation and study over the last two decades on Crete and elsewhere in the Aegean also clarified the stratigraphic situation. The LMIA period has now been clearly and stratigraphically distinguished from the LMIB period – the latter following the former.[77] LMIA styles do continue into the LMIB period (as Marinatos and many others observed), but the new styles which define the LMIB period do not occur in the LMIA period, and instead demarcate the second, LMIB, period of the overall LMI phase. The new palaces of Crete were destroyed during, or at the close of, the LMIB period.[78] Therefore, today, on the basis of the very large assemblage from the volcanic

---

[74] Marinatos (1968–1976); Doumas (1983a); Marthari (1984; 1990).

[75] Vitaliano and Vitaliano (1974; 1978).

[76] Pomerance (1975; 1976); Wilson (1976).

[77] Niemeier (1980); Betancourt (1985:115–148); Warren and Hankey (1989:72–81); Driessen and Macdonald (1997:15–22). The root cause of this problem was the fact that a clear LMIB horizon was not found by Evans at Knossos in his excavations at the beginning of the 20th century. Other sites thus had to provide the relevant stratigraphic relationships. Further work at Knossos in recent years has now found an LMIA to LMIB stratigraphic sequence (e.g. Warren and Hankey 1989:81 referring to the Royal Road excavations).

[78] Niemeier (1984; 1985:175–180); Driessen and Macdonald (1997).

destruction level (VDL) at Akrotiri on Thera, versus the sequence on Crete, the eruption of Thera may be placed during the mature to later LMIA period,[79] and, since one or two of the late LMIA vases from Akrotiri (see Figure 15) hint of features – e.g. the double axe motif – subsequently developed in LMIB/LHIIA,[80] a date relatively late in this mature–late LMIA phase seems likely.

The last vestiges of hope for those who wished to link the eruption, nonetheless, with the LMIB destructions on Crete was to hypothesise either some gap between the abandonment of Thera by humans, and the actual volcanic eruption, or a two stage eruption. The suggestion by Money (1973) that there was evidence of initial soil formation above some of the ruins at Akrotiri, but before the sealing volcanic pumice deposits, seemed to offer hope.[81] Money speculated that this could indicate quite a lengthy time interval. However, others were quick to dispute these findings and the possibility of a long gap before the eruption.[82] Although, as late as the second Thera conference in 1978, Page (1978) could still continue to argue that this sort of gap was not impossible, very few now regarded it as a likely scenario. While a period of volcanic activity over some years was geologically possible,[83] any lengthy gap or interval was considered improbable.[84] The accepted orthodoxy following the second Thera conference[85] held it as clear that the eruption of Thera occurred at the end of the LMIA period, and that this eruption was separate from, and had nothing *directly* to do with, the close of LMIB destructions on Crete.[86]

There were now very few dissident voices with regard to the relative chronology within the Aegean. As the debate entered the 1980s, only a couple of scholars went against the majority view, and argued that a possible LMIB date for the eruption had not been entirely excluded. Warren continued to allow it as a possibility, and Manning argued it was not an impossible view on the basis of the evidence available in the mid-1980s.[87] Indeed, a study of archaeomagnetic evidence from Thera and Crete by Downey and Tarling (1984) offered some new support. Downey and Tarling argued that their Aegean archaeomagnetic data revealed two patterns: (i) that the eruption of Thera occurred in two discrete phases, and (ii) that there were two chronologically discrete phases of LMIB destructions on Crete (central Crete, and then later eastern Crete). The first of these claims did not stand up to critical scrutiny.[88] But the second suggestion does remain supported.[89] The general correlations of archaeomagnetic date

[79] Niemeier (1980); Betancourt (1985:133); Hardy and Renfrew (1990); Warren (1990/1991); Shaw et al. (1997; n.d.).
[80] See Driessen and Macdonald (1997:73).
[81] E.g. Warren (1973:175).
[82] Doumas (1974:111–112; 1980:399); Davidson (1978:736–738); Luce (1976:10–11).
[83] Bond and Sparks (1976).
[84] E.g. Sparks (1976:289–290).
[85] Doumas (1978; 1980).
[86] E.g. Renfrew (1979); Popham (1979); Pomerance (1979); Doumas (1983a; 1983b); Pichler and Schiering (1980). For a recent review, and this same conclusion, see Lohmann (1998). For possible *indirect* role, however, see Driessen and Macdonald (1997).
[87] E.g. Warren (1984); Manning (1987:70–74; 1988b:21–24).
[88] Sparks (1985); Liritzis (1985); Evans and Mareschal (1988); Tarling and Downey (1990).
[89] Tarling and Downey (1989:352; 1990); Evans and Mareschal (1988).

proposed between the eruption of Thera and the Cretan destructions also remains – although there do seem serious questions over whether all the Cretan samples in the Downey and Tarling study in fact came from appropriate LMIB fired destruction levels.[90] It has been one of the odd situations of Aegean archaeology that this work has remained largely undiscussed by archaeologists.[91] Nor has the analysis been repeated on securely identified contexts.

Final resolution of the issue of whether the eruption was late LMIA and more or less immediately after the final human abandonment of Akrotiri, or perhaps in LMIB, came from further finds of Theran eruption products in secure archaeological strata in the Aegean: both airfall tephra and waterborne pumice. At the second Thera conference Renfrew reported microscopic traces of airfall Theran tephra from Late Cycladic I contexts at Phylakopi on Melos,[92] and, allied with the subsequent seriation analysis of the ceramics by Davis and Cherry (1984), these clearly indicated an LMIA date for the eruption. Moreover, the study of Davis and Cherry indicated a date before the end of LMIA. This study therefore raised the possibility that away from Thera (destroyed by the eruption) there was a post-Thera-eruption final phase of LMIA. Doumas and Papazoglou (1980) then reported a layer of Theran airfall tephra from Rhodes in what appeared to be a pre-LMIB (i.e. LMIA) context,[93] and definitive confirmation came in the later 1980s with the discovery of good, *in situ*, finds of undisputed Theran air-fall tephra stratified in LMIA, or pre-LMIB, contexts on Crete itself.[94] In agreement, finds were made of waterborne Minoan eruption pumice which had been used already in late LMIA or early LMIB building activity,[95] and perhaps even associated with a late LMIA destruction at Poros on the northcoast of Crete.[96] For all general purposes, these finds have settled the relative date of the eruption in Aegean terms as late LMIA. With regard to the Aegean relative sequence, the only debate which remains is whether the

---

[90]   As Tarling concludes in Tarling and Downey (1990:159).

[91]   Minoan archaeologists have been aware for some time that following the LMIB destructions the patterns evident in central and east Crete are rather different. For many years virtually no LMII material at all was recognised in east Crete (e.g. Popham 1980), and recently a distinct east Cretan LMII assemblage has been recognised (MacGillivray 1997b – fulfilling earlier suggestions that non-palatial or provincial LMII styles might exist in the east: Silverman 1978:84; Kanta 1980:318). Central Cretan LMII and LMIIIA1 are very strongly Knossian, and seem to reflect a central Crete oriented pattern (Haskell 1989:60). It is also widely agreed that no place names attested in the Linear B archive from Knossos can be securely located in east Crete. The known names may all be placed in central or west Crete (Killen 1977; Wilson 1977; McArthur 1981; Bennet 1985; 1986:78–81; 1987a:77–79). Thus, following Bennet (1987a), it is reasonable to conclude that when east Crete re-emerged in LMII–IIIA1, it was outside the Knossian sphere in central and western Crete (the only source so far of Linear B inscriptions – a fact in stark contrast to the island-wide finds of Linear A inscriptions: Bennet 1987b:fig.2). It is tempting to speculate that the indications from archaeomagnetic data of a different pattern of LMIB (or neopalatial) destructions in east Crete, versus central Crete, might have some relevance to this situation.

[92]   Renfrew (1978:412–416); Vitaliano and Vitaliano (1978:218–219).

[93]   Subsequently, see also Doumas (1988); Marketou (1988; 1990).

[94]   Soles and Davaras (1990); Soles *et al.* (1995); Betancourt *et al.* (1990); and several subsequent finds at these and other sites (e.g. Palaikastro: MacGillivray *et al.* 1991:134; 1998:241–242 and Fig.16).

[95]   Betancourt *et al.* (1990:96–97).

[96]   Tsunami? See e.g. Warren (1990/1991:32 and n.21); Driessen and Macdonald (1997:91).

eruption occurred merely during the mature–later LMIA phase, or instead at its very end. I will discuss this matter in a later chapter (IV.1).

Although the Minoan sequence is dominant in the southern Aegean at the beginning of the LBA, and the LMIA period is widely thought to represent the apogee of Minoan Crete, when it led and/or controlled/influenced an Aegean-wide region, even thalassocracy,[97] it is also important to note that the eruption of Thera is dated in terms of the local Cycladic sequence – it is defined as late in Late Cycladic I.[98] In addition, there are a number of mainland, LH, imports at Akrotiri.[99] Dietz (1991:310–311) characterises them as LHIB (i.e. later LHI as defined in his study). An element of debate, however, exists over the relative date of the final human occupation at Akrotiri in mainland terms. Dietz (1991:316) argues that the LHIB period continued after the eruption of Thera, perhaps for a whole generation. In agreement, Lolos noted the numerous imports at Akrotiri of the diagnostic mainland Vapheio cup, and, based on comparison with the chronological–developmental sequence of these cups in southern Greece, argued that the final LHI type was notably absent from the Theran assemblage, and so concluded that the eruption must have occurred before the end of the LHI period.[100] However, another vase from the excavations at Akrotiri (no. 5115) looks later, and indeed looks suspiciously like an LHIIA product:[101] Figure 15. If so, and despite the absence of the final type of Vapheio cup, the eruption might be placed in early LHIIA. Resolution of this debate is not yet possible. From a Cretan perspective, it has already been argued on other grounds that LHIIA began during late LMIA on Crete.[102] Hence, irrespective of the above small ambiguity with respect to the mainland correlation, we are still dealing with a mature–late LMIA date on Crete: see Figure 16. The intricacies of the mainland sequence need not detain us further here.

Absolute dating from AD1941 to 1988: science and the questioning of convention

While the relative chronology in the Aegean eventually became fairly clear, and is now more or less universally agreed in general terms, work was also being carried out aimed towards improving the absolute chronology of the Aegean sequences. Here there was little change in basic positions in half a century or more of scholarship. As noted earlier, finds of Aegean material in Egypt had led to a chronology by the 1940s which placed LMIA broadly contemporary with the early 18th Dynasty of Egypt, and LMIB contemporary with the major, and long reigning, pharaoh Tuthmosis III.[103] Scholarship from then to the 1980s essentially refined and supported the basic chronological scheme

---

[97] Doumas (1982); Hägg and Marinatos (1984); Wiener (1990); Dickinson (1994:244–248); Driessen and Macdonald (1997:esp.35–83); Rehak and Younger (1998a:100–149). Renfrew (1998) even proposes that the Versailles effects of the Minoan thalassocracy included a contribution to the linguistic development of the wider, early Greek (Mycenaean), Aegean.

[98] Marthari (1984; 1987; 1990); Doumas (1990).

[99] Marthari (1980); Dietz (1991:310–311).

[100] Lolos (1987; 1990).

[101] Marthari (1990:64 and Fig.8).

[102] Warren and Hankey (1989:97–98).

[103] Furumark (1941b).

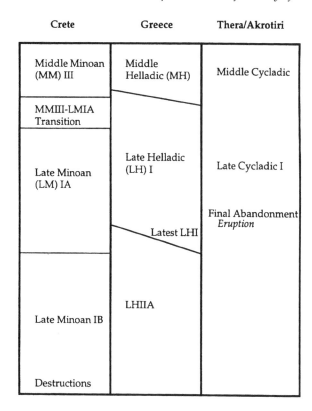

Crete	Greece	Thera/Akrotiri
Middle Minoan (MM) III	Middle Helladic (MH)	Middle Cycladic
MMIII-LMIA Transition		
Late Minoan (LM) IA	Late Helladic (LH) I	Late Cycladic I
		Final Abandonment *Eruption*
	Latest LHI	
Late Minoan IB	LHIIA	
Destructions		

Fig. 16. Aegean relative chronology in schematic terms relevant to the Thera eruption period(MMIII–LMIB).

of Furumark. LMIA was regarded as ending c.1500BC, and LMIB ran from then until c.1450BC; the only minor modifications came in the 1980s as a result of small changes in the datings of the Egyptian pharaohs by Egyptologists.[104] And so, the later LMIA eruption of the Thera volcano came to be conventionally dated c.1500BC.

However, the eruption of Thera is an independent event. Attempts to date it directly by various scientific means have been pursued for more than 30 years. For many years this led nowhere. The scientific techniques could not offer dates of a precision comparable to existing archaeological dating. And, even today, some techniques like thermoluminescence dating can only provide very broad approximate dates for Thera, e.g. 3600±200 years before present,[105] a 400 year span covering the entire range of modern debate, and much more. But a number of the techniques kept improving. As

---

[104] For the standard position up to the 1970s, see Popham (1970); Hankey and Warren (1974); Cadogan (1978). For the standard position in the 1980s, and the maintenance of the linkage of LMIB with Tuthmosis III, but the appreciation that the dates of this pharaoh had become lower in general Egyptological opinion (from c.1504–1450BC to c.1479–1425BC), see Warren (1985:151); Hankey (1987:53); Warren and Hankey (1989:138–144, 169 Table 3.1).

[105] Friedrich (1994:91). Some thermoluminescence dates on kilns on Crete believed to be of New Palace, LM, age (few precise details provided) were presented by Liritzis and Thomas (1980). The individual measurements have errors of the order of 5–6%, or c.160–210 years. The dates are given as years before

noted in Chapter I, by the 1970s radiocarbon dating was suggesting a worrying fact. Although the results varied, and had errors, they consistently pointed towards a date for the eruption about 100 years earlier than suggested by the archaeological chronology. Further samples from the 1980s onwards continued to indicate the same.[106] Archaeologists generally rejected these findings as aberrant. It was suggested that perhaps emissions of carbon dioxide from the volcano before the eruption had 'affected' (i.e. contaminated) the samples. Arguments pointing out that this phenomenon – which is known and observed – was very unlikely to be of relevance to the Thera samples were ignored.

As long as it was just radiocarbon dates, convention reigned; Aegean archaeologists wrote articles speculating on whether the radiocarbon method was accurate.[107] After all, a similar suggestion of an earlier (and long) chronology on the basis of radiocarbon had been made for Egypt and the Near East,[108] and this was quickly demonstrated to be in error[109] – a judgement subsequently confirmed by later appropriate radiocarbon-based work.[110] The climate of scholarly 'reception' was not promising for radiocarbon. Any evidence for problems and consequent refinements in radiocarbon dating practice were leapt upon as proof that the whole technique was somehow flawed. When a Danish team demonstrated that ice-cores from polar regions preserve a long-term record of past major volcanic eruptions,[111] and, upon noting that the only major evidence of a mid-second millennium BC volcanic eruption was at c.1390±50BC, went on to propose that this was Thera on the basis that it was about the only major volcanic eruption then known of the mid-second millennium BC, conventional Aegean archaeology was delighted, and regarded this as a further demonstration that the radiocarbon dates were incorrect. Indeed, a few even saw this 'late' dating as supporting a re-activation of the case for a time-lag between the destruction of Akrotiri and the eruption, and so the hypotheses of Marinatos and Page arguing that the eruption was temporally linked with the LMIB destructions on Crete.

Conventional archaeology was content, and was the agreed orthodoxy up to the start of the 1980s. Things then changed in several ways. In 1984 LaMarche and

---

present (presumably c.AD1980 since no other modern referent is stated). The neopalatial datum for Phaistos (kiln 1) provides a date of c.1486±208BC, and the average of three (rather varying) data on an LM kiln at Kato Zakros is 1407±97BC. Such data are not capable of resolving the current chronological disputes in the second millennium BC. Kuniholm (1990a:16) refers to work by R. Rowlett seeking to obtain a large number of thermoluminescence data on Theran ash with a view to a fairly tightly constrained average date, but no further details have emerged to date. It appears that the initial rather pessimistic assessment of Aitken and Fleming (1971) on the utility of thermoluminescence applications with regard to Thera will prove correct: 'It seems unlikely that useful dating information will ever be obtained from the pumice...' (p.300).

[106] The radiocarbon evidence is discussed below in Chapter V.1. In general, and with further references to the data, see Manning (1988a; 1988b; 1990a:33–35; 1990b; 1992; 1995:200–216; Manning *et al.* 1994a:222–226); papers in Hardy and Renfrew (1990).

[107] E.g. Hood (1978a).

[108] Mellaart (1979).

[109] Weinstein (1980); Kemp (1980); Munn-Rankin (1980); cf. Mellaart (1980).

[110] Hassan and Robinson (1987).

[111] Hammer (1977); Hammer *et al.* (1980). Based on finds of volcanic-derived acid products in the ice.

Hirschboeck published a study in the leading science journal *Nature* which showed that instances of frost damage in Bristlecone pines from the upper timber line in the White Mountains of California appeared to correlate in a number of cases with major volcanic eruptions. The hypothesis was that the stratospheric aerosol produced by a major volcanic eruption (principally the sulphur dioxide ejected high into the stratosphere, where it converts to H_2SO_4) lowered global surface temperatures because the aerosol back-scatters and reduces normal solar penetration of the atmosphere.[112] This in turn could cause low temperature related stress in trees growing in an environment particularly sensitive to any decrease in temperature. For example, it has been observed that the recent 1991 Mt. Pinatubo eruption lowered average global temperature in 1992 by about 0.4°C, a 0.7°C decrease from 1991,[113] and the AD1883 Krakatau and the AD1815 Tambora eruptions are estimated to have lowered global temperatures by c.0.3°C and c.0.4–0.7°C respectively.[114] LaMarche and Hirschboeck noted just one major incidence of frost damage in their second millennium BC tree-ring dataset at 1626BC (in fact 1627BC – LaMarche and Hirschboeck incorrectly had a year 0 in their computer programmes). Observing both that Thera was the major (then) known mid-second millennium BC northern hemisphere volcanic eruption, and also that the radiocarbon data from the archaeological contexts buried by this eruption offered dates typically in the 17th century BC, LaMarche and Hirschboeck went on to suggest a date of 1628–1626BC for the eruption of Thera.

LaMarche had suggested the link between frost damage and volcanoes as long ago as a paper of 1970, and, in fact, had already proposed the 17th century BC date for Thera on this basis in a quoted comment eight years previously in an article in the 'popular' journal *National Geographic Magazine*,[115] but the 1984 *Nature* publication could neither be overlooked, nor ignored, by Aegean archaeology. Peter Warren, a leading Aegean scholar, and an expert on the conventional archaeological chronology, published a reply.[116] He correctly noted that the tree-ring record was only an indirect record of past volcanism, and that it provided no direct linkage to any specific volcano. He further pointed out that not every major volcanic eruption showed up as frost damage, and vice versa. He thus maintained that no scientific date for past volcanic eruptions in general could provide a date for the specific case of Thera unless it agreed with the archaeological evidence from the Aegean and east Mediterranean, which he held to be both accurate and precise within quite small margins of error. In passing, Warren dismissed the relevance of radiocarbon evidence to the contrary, and cited the ice-core study of Hammer *et al.* to support a lower date, but also at the same time to reinforce the point that all these scientific techniques were offering dates that were less accurate or precise than the existing conventional archaeological chronology.

For many this was a classic paper. A brief and clear statement of the supremacy of

---

[112] See e.g. Sear *et al.* (1987); Hunt (1993); McCormick *et al.* (1995:esp. Fig.1).
[113] McCormick *et al.* (1995:402); Self *et al.* (1996).
[114] Pinto *et al.* (1989).
[115] Matthews (1976:610); noted also by Kuniholm (1990a:15).
[116] Warren (1984).

the conventional archaeological chronology over all challengers. Warren had even taken the care to note, and to argue against, a first suggestion from archaeology that the LMI period might have begun earlier than previously thought (see below). Many scholars thought things were now settled. Little did conventional archaeology know what was coming in a dramatic period from 1987 to 1988. In 1984 Hammer admitted that there were some major problems with the existing Camp Century ice-core used to supply the previously published 'Thera' date of 1390±50BC. He suggested that a much firmer chronology for the BC period would be available with analysis of the (then) new Dye 3 ice-core. In 1987, the Danish team publicly retracted the original 1390±50BC date, and published an article showing that the only major volcanic eruption recorded in the Dye 3 ice-core potentially compatible with Thera occurred at c.1644BC. Since this date correlated very well with the radiocarbon evidence from Thera, and Thera seemed (at this time) the only plausible candidate, Hammer *et al.* (1987) proposed a date of c.1645BC for the Thera eruption. They argued that the error on this date was about ±7 years, and at the outside ±20 years.

In a commentary on the paper, Gerald Cadogan (1987), an Aegean archaeologist and another expert on the conventional archaeological chronology, did his best to question the strength of the conclusions. His argument essentially consisted of noting that such a change in the conventional Aegean chronology would upset everything (i.e. surrounding periods and regions and all their carefully constructed framework of archaeological linkages and dates), and so was impossible given the strength of the overall conventional archaeological chronology. And, again, he could correctly note that there was no direct or positive evidence that this volcanic eruption was in fact Thera (and not some other volcanic eruption). There was a notable lack of the conviction of Warren (1984), but the conventional Aegean archaeological chronology was nonetheless held to be the best available. Importantly, though, Cadogan conceded that the traditional date of 1500BC for the Thera eruption 'is probably no longer tenable', and he concluded that 'taking everything into account, a date of the sixteenth century BC seems the most likely'. This was the beginning of the end of the conventional orthodoxy. Cadogan referred in particular to a study by Aitken (1988), published the next year. This reviewed the radiocarbon evidence from Thera. Aitken found that, taken together, and applying the then new high-precision radiocarbon calibration curves first available in the 1980s, the Theran radiocarbon dates could in fact date to either the 17th century BC (the now 'early' or 'high' chronology date), or in fact also to the mid-16th century BC, but definitely before about 1520BC (acceptable range at 95% confidence c.1670–1520BC). Cadogan not surprisingly saw hope here for what might be termed a 'modified' conventional chronology.

Next, a study of Irish tree-rings by Baillie and Munro (1988) found a pattern of occurrences of marked low growth which more or less correlated in general terms with the large volcanic events recorded in the Greenland ice-cores. As in the study of LaMarche and Hirschboeck (1984), it was again plausible that lowered temperatures caused by a volcanic aerosol would adversely affect tree-growth in the north of Ireland. The only significant low growth event of the mid-second millennium BC occurred from 1628BC. The correlation with the 1627BC date of LaMarche and Hirschboeck appeared perfect. Based on a review of the associated evidence, Baillie and Munro supported the identification of this tree-ring event with the Thera eruption. No positive proof or causal connection could be supplied, but there was a strong case from repeated coincidences and circumstances. Hughes (1988) subsequently argued that given the respective dating accuracies and precisions, tree-ring evidence offered absolute dates whereas the ice-core evidence was only approximately dated. Hence, given the close correlation of the tree-ring and ice-cores dates for major volcanic eruptions/climatic anomalies, Hughes argued that in the 17th century BC the various records were dating the same volcanic event which could be placed at exactly 1628BC.

A pattern was emerging. Ice-core evidence showed that a major volcanic eruption occurred in the second half of the 17th century BC, and tree-ring evidence showed that there was a significant climate anomaly affecting both the USA and Europe c.1628/1627BC. And these could well be the same event. Moreover, there was no evidence for a major volcanic eruption or climate anomaly in the century and a bit following (and thus no evidence consonant with the conventional archaeological date for the eruption of Thera). Although sceptics legitimately argued and demonstrated that the correlation between known eruptions and such records was not perfect[117] – which is hardly surprising – the overall correlation seemed quite strong, and, in particular, the later 17th century BC event kept showing up in all records from several areas of the northern hemisphere.[118] It is what Baillie has termed a 'marker' event – an event found in all records, and which may therefore be used to correlate records.[119]

The critical weak link, however, remained the absence of any direct or positive linkage between this recorded volcanic event and the specific eruption of Thera. As Buckland *et al.* (1997) argue, it is all too easy to be seduced by an apparently *possible* linkage,[120] and to begin to believe that it is real, despite the absence of tangible positive evidence. In the case of Thera, there was merely the approximate temporal correlation between these records and what at the time was about the only known large northern hemisphere volcanic eruption of the mid second millennium BC: Thera. Manning (1988a) published a response to the papers of Hammer *et al.* (1987) and Cadogan (1987) which showed that the directly relevant radiocarbon evidence then available from Thera did in fact clearly support a 17th century BC date range. But the thing resolutely at odds with the scientific evidence, as illustrated in the figure published in Manning (1988a), was the conventional archaeological chronology: see Figure 17.

As we have noted, for over half a century the date of the LMIA period was more or less fixed. It was correlated with the early 18th Dynasty before the reign of Tuthmosis III. Various debates in Egyptology and some new evidence had seen suggestions that Furumark's start date of 1550BC might be pushed back to 1570/1550±10BC,[121] but the link with the 18th Dynasty was regarded as established. This conclusion stemmed very

[117] Most thoroughly Buckland *et al.* (1997).
[118] Baillie (1990; 1995a:73–90, 108–121; 1996b:294–295); Kuniholm *et al.* (1996); Johnsen *et al.* (1992); Zielinski *et al.* (1994a); Clausen *et al.* (1997); etc. For a recent review of the science-dating evidence, see Schoch (1997).
[119] Baillie (1991a; 1995a).
[120] Something they themselves fell prey to with regard to AD1259: see Lowe and Higham (1998).
[121] Hankey and Warren (1974).

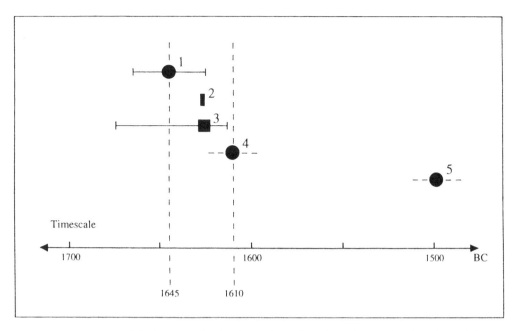

Fig. 17. Comparison of the ice-core, dendrochronological, radiocarbon and archaeological dating relevant to the Thera eruption as in 1988 (after Manning 1988a:Figure). 1. Ice-core date of Hammer et al. (1987), 2. Tree-ring date of LaMarche and Hirschboeck (1984), add also Baillie and Munro (1988), 3. Most likely calibrated radiocarbon age range at 1σ confidence from Manning (1988a), 4. Revised archaeological age estimate of Betancourt (1987), and 5. Conventional archaeological age estimate of Warren (1984).

much from Evans' original tripartite division of Minoan civilisation: Early Minoan went with the Old Kingdom of Egypt, Middle Minoan went with the Middle Kingdom of Egypt, and Late Minoan went with the New Kingdom of Egypt. There was, however, a total absence of any actual LMIA or LHI exports in Egypt, and no closely datable Egyptian or Near Eastern objects from initial LBA contexts found in the Aegean. The position was largely determined by assumption, and by an alabaster lid inscribed with the name of the Hyksos king Khyan found at the start of the 20th century AD by Evans at Knossos. Evans argued that this lid was found in an MMIIIA context;[122] hence the MMIII period correlated with the Hyksos-SIP era in Egypt, and the LMIA period plausibly went with the start of subsequent 18th Dynasty. Support was also sought from a jar found in a pre-18th Dynasty context at El-Lisht in Egypt which was argued to show MMIII style/derived dolphins.[123] Thus, since LMIB and contemporary LHIIA

---

[122] Evans (1921–1935, vol.I:418–421). In general, see Warren and Hankey (1989:136–137).
[123] Kantor (1965:23–24); Hankey and Warren (1974:145, 150). In general, see Warren and Hankey (1989:135–136).

items were found in contexts dated to the reign of Tuthmosis III (or later), it appeared obvious that LMIA must fit in between the MMIII–Hyksos, and LMIB–Tuthmosis III, synchronisms. A couple of Egyptian items from the start of the 18th Dynasty were argued to display influence from the Aegean LHI/LMIA styles,[124] and an assumption that this somehow dated the start of the LBA in the Aegean became a convention. The genuine scarcity of secure correlations or connections was noted, but somehow overlooked; similarly, few seriously considered the range of possible dates offered by the key Egyptian contexts, nor the vagaries of when and how particular objects came to be interred, nor the possible variations on when and how any influence was passed on.[125]

It was in fact not until the modern excavations at Akrotiri on Thera from 1967 onwards that scholarship was forced to begin to reconsider this assumption-convention. Finds there of MBII Levantine imports in a sealed LMIA context led Warren by 1979 to concede that there was evidence now for a significant pre-18th Dynasty, Hyksos/SIP, overlap for the LMIA period.[126] He thus suggested a start date for the LMIA period as early as 1600BC. But no one questioned the end date for the period. The c.1500BC close for the LMIA period had become one of those basic 'facts' of Aegean prehistory, despite an absence of any substantive positive evidence.

However, things were not all they seemed. A study of 1980 by Kemp and Merrillees started to sow the seeds of doubt concerning the rigour, foundations, and exact accuracy of the conventional Aegean archaeological chronology. Based on a consideration of Aegean pottery found in Egypt, these authors argued for a significantly earlier chronology for the Aegean LBA.[127] They dared to suggest that the LMIA period ended, rather than started, c.1600/1575BC. In particular, they highlighted how arbitrary some of the assumed correlations were, and how the actual *range* of the relevant Egyptian find contexts permitted a higher date for the Aegean ceramic periods in several instances. A short paper by Weinstein (1983) also raised some uncomfortable possibilities in this direction. Perhaps not surprisingly, neither of these works was by an 'Aegeanist'. It often takes an outsider to challenge a dominant paradigm. But, given Merrillees was already involved in a high versus low chronology debate over the dates for the Bronze Age periods on Cyprus,[128] some Aegean archaeologists undoubtedly thought that he was less than unbiased. In fact, surprisingly little serious, or prompt, attention was paid at first to the book of Kemp and Merrillees. The first review I am aware of was by none other than Weinstein (1982)! He agreed that much of the conventional evidence for MM chronology 'is based on synchronisms of dubious precision' (p.157), but for the LMI period he argues that the meagre evidence is not at all clear, and that Kemp and Merrillees

---

[124] Principally an axe with the name of Ahmose first king of the 18th Dynasty and a dagger and collar of his mother (?) Ahhotep, both found in the latter's tomb. For literature, see e.g. Niemeier (1985:185 and n.1435); Morgan (1995:36, 38, 47 ns.67 and 71). See further in footnote 505 below.

[125] A notable exception was the study of Merrillees (1972a).

[126] Warren (1979:88–90, 106–107 and n.2; 1985:149).

[127] Kemp and Merrillees (1980:250–267).

[128] Merrillees (1977).

overstate their case (pp.158–159). Although, his footnote 8 (p.160) refers to his paper on the Aniba alabastron,[129] and to Betancourt suggesting an LMII date for this vase, and Weinstein ends this note observing that 'such a date would have important implications' – a hint of what was to come a few years later. Two other, German language, reviews appeared in 1983–1984, and just two other reviews, period, up to 1987.[130] In retrospect, the lack of reviews in the major journals, like the *American Journal of Archaeology*, appears remarkable given the provocative issues raised. The work of Kemp and Merrillees thus really only came to wider attention in the mid-1980s when it was cited in Warren (1984), and was then the subject of a detailed and stern critical review by Warren (1985) in the following year. However, a stone *had* been cast, and as the ripples spread this study of Kemp and Merrillees prompted several scholars to reassess their positions, and in particular to question seriously the many long-standing assumptions in the field.[131]

And so we arrive at one of those critical turning points in any debate: an amazing change of mind, here by a leading Aegean archaeologist. In a study of 1976 Betancourt and Weinstein had discussed the 'early' evidence offered by the radiocarbon data from Akrotiri, but, in the light of a thorough review of the archaeological correlations with Egypt and the Near East, they concluded that the radiocarbon data appeared inconsistent with what they deemed to be a secure chronology derived from Egyptian linkages, and so should be rejected. Betancourt and Weinstein thus ended in firm support of the conventional chronology, and a date of c.1500BC for the end of the LMIA period. Primacy was given to the conventional interpretation of Aegean–Egyptian linkages. The study of Weinstein and Betancourt (1978:809) affirmed the view that:

> if an early radiocarbon chronology does exist for LMI, it cannot be explained by choosing alternative interpretations of the archaeological evidence. A small shift could be allowed by the Egyptian and Near Eastern correlations, but this would not be sufficient to explain the radiocarbon discrepancies (Betancourt and Weinstein, 1976).

Since they did not see any possibility of reinterpreting the conventional archaeological linkages, they continued to regard the conventional chronology as correct. There was thus a discrepancy in the radiocarbon data. And, in his standard textbook on Minoan pottery published in 1985, Betancourt again backed the conventional LM chronology (p.121).

But then, just two years later, Philip Betancourt (1987) stunned the Aegean archaeological community by recanting, and arguing that radiocarbon had been right all along, and, most critically, that all the key Aegean–Egyptian correlations could

---

[129] Weinstein (1983).

[130] See respectively: G. Walberg in *Gnonom* 55, 1983, 373–375; S. Hiller in *Archiv für Orientforschung* 29–30, 1983–1984, 162–165; and Warren (1985); V. Hankey in *Die Welt des Orients* 17, 1986, 152–154. The book was reviewed eight years after its publication date in *Journal of Near Eastern Studies* 47:304–307 by P. Lacovara, and no less than 10 years after its publication date in *Bulletin of the American Schools of Oriental Research* 274:87 by S. Getin.

[131] See also previously Merrillees (1972a).

plausibly, and best, be (re-)interpreted to support a consonant 'early' chronology. Meanwhile, working independently in Australia, Manning (1988b) presented a detailed study also arguing that a plausible re-interpretation of the (relatively few) archaeological synchronisms between the Aegean and Egypt was possible, and that a revised archaeological chronology was available consistent with the scientific evidence. The core radical proposal in each case was to break entirely with the supposed LMIA– early 18th Dynasty linkage, and instead to argue that the LMIA period was contemporary with the Hyksos–SIP era in Egypt, and consequently to revise upwards the subsequent Aegean period associations vis à vis Egypt. The outcome was a proposed chronology similar to, but even a little more radical than, the initial revisionist scheme suggested by Kemp and Merrillees (1980).

In retrospect, the key point from the studies of Kemp and Merrillees, Betancourt, and Manning was the conclusion that none of the *then* available archaeological data clearly or decisively required the conventional (now 'low') chronology, that some evidence actually favoured a high chronology, and that most data were ambiguous but could be consistent with either a high or a low chronology.[132] An 'early' or 'high' archaeological chronology for the beginning of the Aegean LBA consonant with the science data was born. The dates offered in these studies for the beginning of the LBA in the Aegean varied by over a century from the previous, conventional, chronology (see Table 2). They called for a chronological revolution.

The decade of controversy: AD1989–1998

And so began the Thera controversy in earnest. Following the article by Betancourt (1987) and a first reply by Warren (1987), a special section in the 1988 issue of the journal *Archaeometry* was devoted to the debate (vol. 30 no.1, pp.165–182), and positions were established. Proponents of the 'high' chronology pointed out that the available radiocarbon evidence from Akrotiri strongly favoured a later 17th century BC date for both the late LMIA period and the eruption,[133] that there were compatible indications from northern hemisphere ice-core and tree-ring evidence, and that the archaeological evidence then available could be plausibly interpreted to support such a 'high' Aegean chronology. Indeed, first reports of an important new archaeological find became available in 1989. A Minoan sherd had been found in an early (comfortably pre-Tuthmosis III) 18th Dynasty context at Kom Rabiᶜa, Memphis, and it seemed quite likely that it was LMIB in stylistic date.[134] Real evidence in favour of a 'higher' chronology potentially seemed to exist. Meanwhile, Peter Warren took up the role of defender of the challenged conventional chronology. He tried to argue that the radiocarbon evidence did not exclude the traditional 'low' date and generally to point to supposed problems with radiocarbon dating in the Aegean, he emphasised the

---

[132] E.g. Betancourt (1990a); Manning (1990a:31–33).

[133] Michael and Betancourt (1988:174) argued that the radiocarbon evidence favoured c.1639–1600BC, and that the conventional 'low' chronology had less than a 25% chance of being correct.

[134] Bourriau (1989); Warren and Hankey (1989:139). The sherd was initially considered Mycenaean, but subsequent study showed that it was LMI, and probably LMIB (Bourriau and Eriksson 1997).

	(i) Conventional Chronology until 1987 (e.g. Hankey and Warren 1974; Cadogan 1978; 1983)	(ii) New Chronology proposed by Betancourt (1987) and Manning (1988b)
Late Minoan IA	1575±25 to 1500 BC	1700 to 1630/1610 BC
Late Minoan IB	1500 to 1450 BC	1630/1610 to 1550± BC
Late Minoan II	1450 to 1425/1400 BC	1550± to 1490/1450 BC
Late Minoan IIIA1	1425/1400 to 1375± BC	1490/1450 to 1420/1400± BC

Table 2. Comparison of the pre-1987 conventional chronology of the earlier Aegean Late Bronze Age and the new 'early' chronology proposed in Betancourt (1987) and Manning (1988b). Dates given above slightly 'rounded' or approximated from minor variations in sources.

lack of a direct causal linkage between the ice-core and tree-ring evidence and the specific eruption of Thera, and he rejected the high chronology interpretations of all and any of the archaeological and art-historical evidence. Where an object might be argued to favour the 'high' chronology, Warren invariably demonstrated that it was possible (but not necessarily likely) that a lower date was correct.

In September 1989 matters adjourned to the island of Thera itself for the Thera and the Aegean World III conference. An entire session of papers was dedicated to the chronological debate.[135] Several radiocarbon laboratories presented new sets of measurements on samples from Akrotiri in an attempt to resolve the controversy. Most teams reported findings clearly in support of a 'high' 17th century BC date range: the Oxford team argued that their data showed a 70% probability for a 17th century BC date, and only a 30% chance for a 16th century BC date.[136] The complication was a divergent set of data from the Simon Fraser Laboratory.[137] They argued that if a novel pretreatment procedure was employed on the samples, then they could identify an older contaminant in the samples, and, by removing this, they could achieve lower ages more consistent with the conventional chronology. Sceptics such as Warren saw this as a good reason to dismiss all radiocarbon evidence from the debate. But the reality of this contaminant came under serious question. The Oxford laboratory tried to replicate the Simon Fraser results, and could not. The Copenhagen team simply stated that the Simon Fraser pretreatment was inappropriate. Thus the conclusion from the meeting was that radiocarbon evidence as of 1989 strongly supported the 17th century BC date for the Thera eruption.[138]

The other major new development relevant to the absolute date of the eruption announced at the conference was contained in the paper by Wolf-Dietrich Niemeier (1990). He had been excavating a major MBA site at Tel Kabri in Israel, and in particular

---

[135] Hardy and Renfrew (1990).

[136] Housley *et al.* (1990:213)

[137] Nelson *et al.* (1990).

[138] Thus, although one appreciates why he draws attention to this issue, it is inappropriate for Warren (1998:324) to refer to the Oxford 'Series II samples, from which the contaminants had been removed', because there is *no* evidence that *any* contaminant was removed. See further in Chapter V.1.

a later MBII destruction level dated around c.1600BC. He had just found LMIA-style fresco paintings in the Levant! He had also found Canaanite storage/transport jars very similar to an imported example found in the early 1970s by Marinatos at Akrotiri. The key Tel Kabri LMIA-style painted floor showed signs of wear, and had clearly been in use some time before the later MBII, c.1600BC, destruction at the site. Niemeier therefore argued that this evidence suggested that the LMIA style was clearly current sometime before c.1600BC, contemporary with the later MBII period of Syria–Palestine, and that imports of this time had gone to Akrotiri. The implication was clear: this evidence supported the 'high' chronology, and the later 17th century BC date for the late LMIA eruption of Thera. It showed LMIA was contemporary with the later MBII, pre-18th Dynasty, horizon in western Asia.

But the 'early' or 'high' chronology did not have everything its own way. The supposed tree-ring and ice-core evidence was again challenged strongly with regard to its relevance.[139] It was argued on the basis of then available data and techniques that the eruption of Thera had in fact not produced an enormous amount of sulphur dioxide, and so was unlikely to be responsible for the dramatic sulphur dioxide derived signal in the Greenland ice reported at 1645BC. This signal could therefore be another volcanic eruption altogether. And, in this regard, it was noted that there were in fact several other large northern hemisphere volcanic eruptions which could date to the 17th century BC.[140] Hence there was no necessary role for Thera. Similarly, no one disputed the existence of a marked tree-ring growth anomaly in several northern hemisphere locations at 1628/1627BC, but it was pointed out that it was not demonstrated that this reflected a volcanic eruption, yet alone the specific eruption of Thera. Neither the ice-core group present at the third Thera Conference, nor the tree-ring specialists, agreed, but this data was now seen by many to be of, at best, marginal relevance unless it could somehow be re-activated (and made relevant).

Nonetheless, by the end of the chronology session of the third Thera Conference, it is fair to say that things were not looking good for the supporters of the conventional chronology. In his closing address the session chairman, Colin Renfrew, despite his stated impartiality, concluded wondering whether the final determination of the date for the eruption would be 'within 20 years of 1620 BC'.[141] And, in 1991 to 1992, it got worse for the conventional chronology. One of Betancourt's startling claims in 1987 had been that the LMIIIA1 period had begun during the reign of Tuthmosis III in the mid-later 15th century BC, whereas it had previously been considered to belong a generation or more later. Betancourt had based this view on the stylistic analysis of one Aegeanising vase from a tomb at Aniba in Egypt which he dated to LMIIIA1. In opposition, Warren argued for LMI or LHIIA parallels, and thus claimed the vase was consistent with the conventional chronology.[142] But, although little observed for

---

[139] Pyle (1990b – see previously Pyle 1989); Sigurdsson *et al.* (1990).

[140] E.g. Nelson *et al.* (1990:204). See subsequently Vogel *et al.* (1990), where this case is developed.

[141] Renfrew in Hardy and Renfrew (1990:242).

[142] Betancourt (1987:46–47); Michael and Betancourt (1988); Warren (1987:207–208; 1988); Warren and Hankey (1989:144). For a summary, see Betancourt (1998b:293). He points out that Warren's counter arguments were based on 'incorrect parallels'. The shape simply was not invented until LMII/LHIIB.

another few years, a study by Barber (1991) suggested very important support for Betancourt's LMIIIA1–Tuthmosis III correlation based on the analysis of the designs illustrated on textiles worn by Aegeans (called Keftiu by the Egyptians) depicted in tomb paintings in Egypt dated quite precisely to the later part of the reign of Tuthmosis III. These appeared to be specifically LMIIIA1.[143] Today this initial observation has been widely accepted (see Chapter IV.9 below), and it means a significant raising of LMIB–LMIIIA1 chronology irrespective of the Thera question. Niemeier (1991) meanwhile developed his initial case from the Tel Kabri fresco finds, and linked in also existing Minoan-style fresco fragments from Woolley's excavations in 1937–1939 and 1946–1949 at Alalakh in the Turkish province of Hatay, to present a strong case in favour of the 'high' chronology, with LMIA correlated with later MBII in Syria–Palestine.

New scientific data seemed to point the same way. The first report of the GRIP ice-core from Greenland was published in 1992, and it again offered a single clear 17th century BC volcanic signal consistent within just a few years of the previous 1645BC signal, arguably linked with the 1628/1627BC tree-ring anomaly.[144] And a renewed relevance for these proxy records was possible in the aftermath of the great volcanic eruption of Mount Pinatubo in 1991.[145] One outcome of the study of Pinatubo was the observation that, as in the case of a couple of other 1980s eruptions, the standard petrologic method for estimating sulphur dioxide emissions had provided an estimate which was dramatically smaller than the actual amount of sulphur dioxide observed. It was thus possible that the existing petrologic estimates for the sulphur production of the Thera eruption also were much too small, and that the Thera eruption could have been responsible for the clear 17th century BC sulphur dioxide signal in the Greenland ice.[146] One of the main teams working on ice-core records of past volcanism quickly noted this issue, and stated that 'atmospheric loading estimates derived from the petrologic method may be unreliable'.[147] Looking back, AD1991–1992 was perhaps the first high water mark for the 'high' Aegean chronology. Radiocarbon, archaeology, and perhaps even the ice-core and dendrochronological evidence all seemed increasingly to indicate a later 17th century BC date for the late LMIA period and the eruption of Thera. Slowly, the general Aegean field took note, and the possible reality of the 'high' chronology started to appear in published works.

In the interim, advocates of the conventional chronology had not been inactive.[148] They did more than just follow the advice of Edmund Dantès, Count of Monte Cristo, always to 'wait and hope', but it was new information which offered them succour. Publications up to 1992 in favour of the low chronology were severely handicapped by their need in effect to dismiss or to ignore the radiocarbon evidence from Thera – yet this was directly relevant scientific data. Further, even the archaeological evidence

---

[143] See especially Barber (1991:348).
[144] Johnsen *et al.* (1992); Manning (1992b).
[145] Newhall and Punongbayan (1996).
[146] Manning (1992a).
[147] Zielinski *et al.* (1995:258).
[148] E.g. Warren (1990/1991); Muhly (1991); Hankey (1991/1992); Eriksson (1992).

seemed to be turning against them over the period from 1989–1991. Fresh hope came from two unexpected sources.

First, Manfred Bietak and an Austrian team had been excavating for many years (from 1966) at the site of Tell el-Dabᶜa in the Nile Delta. Today it is almost universally agreed that this site was Avaris, the great capital city of the Hyksos kings during the SIP when this Canaanite dynasty ruled part of northern Egypt.[149] Work now focussed on the area of the Hyksos citadel. In 1992 Bietak (1992b) announced dramatic findings of relevance to the Aegean. He too had found LMIA-style frescoes. These were said to be from a late Hyksos context (stratum D/2) at the site. This was in broad agreement with the Tel Kabri finds of Niemeier, and the old finds at Alalakh, and further supported a pre-18th Dynasty, Hyksos, date for the LMIA period. However, Bietak proposed a 16th century BC date for the Tell el-Dabᶜa context. His second announcement was the find of lumps of pumice at the site thought to be from the Minoan eruption of Thera (and subsequently positively identified as such in some cases) in what was said to be an early 18th Dynasty context. Since this was the only time such pumice was found at the site, Bietak argued that this indicated an early 18th Dynasty date for the eruption of Thera. The fact that this really only set an undefined and unquantified *terminus ante quem* (point before which) was ignored. All in all, this was a set of welcome news for the low chronology camp. The pumice at face value supported the conventional date for the Thera eruption, and, although it required the now admitted LMIA–Hyksos period overlap, the 16th century BC late Hyksos frescoes could be worked into a modified conventional chronology. In a subsequent review of the situation, a supporter of the low chronology was thus able to propose an LMIA period from c.1615–1525BC[150] – yes, starting even a bit earlier again than the 1980s position, but basically adhering to the principle of an early 18th Dynasty close for the period, even if 1500BC had had to be abandoned for c.1525BC.

The other succour came, ironically, from radiocarbon. In order to convert a radiocarbon determination on a sample in a laboratory into a date range expressed in calendar years, a radiocarbon calibration curve must be employed. This curve represents the currently best defined record of past natural radiocarbon levels in the atmosphere. Absolutely dated tree-rings are used to provide this record. Calibration curves have been around since the late 1960s, but the first internationally recommended high-precision calibration curves became available in 1986.[151] All the studies and statements about the radiocarbon dating of Thera published in 1987–1992 employed and relied on these 1986 calibration data. Given the set of radiocarbon determinations for samples from Akrotiri relevant to the volcanic destruction level and the eruption, these 1986 calibration data clearly favoured a 17th century BC date.

1993 saw the publication of a set of new, revised, high-precision radiocarbon calibration curves.[152] These were not internationally recommended, but they seemed

---

[149] Bietak (1979). See now in general Bietak (1996a).
[150] Negbi (1994:81–83).
[151] See the set of papers in *Radiocarbon* 28B (1986). For general statements, see Hassan (1986); Pearson (1987).
[152] See the set of papers in *Radiocarbon* 35(1) (1993).

on publication to offer the current state of the art. The slight changes and revisions in the constituent data of these new calibration curves were highly relevant to the Thera debate. They increased the likelihood of a mid-16th century BC calibrated date range for the Akrotiri determinations. The balance of probabilities still favoured the later 17th century BC, but it was now rather more ambiguous.[153] Indeed, one could legitimately argue that it was not now really possible in broad terms to decide between a later 17th century BC, and a mid-16th century BC, date range solely on the basis of radiocarbon evidence. The two calendar periods had almost the same radiocarbon ages. Thus, since the radiocarbon evidence was the one form of directly relevant scientific dating evidence then available, as of 1993 the possibility of a mid-16th century BC eruption became worthy of more serious scrutiny. The new radiocarbon evidence still ruled out a date after about c.1530–1520BC, and so the conventional date of c.1500BC, but one around c.1570–1530BC was entirely plausible. With analysis, the radiocarbon odds by themselves continued slightly to favour the 17th century BC, *but*, if other criteria could be said to require a 16th century BC date, then it had to be agreed that a mid-16th century BC date could be entirely compatible with the radiocarbon evidence. And, as we have noted, some argued that the finds at Tell el-Dabᶜa seemed to require just this. In his study of LBA trade between the Near East and the Aegean, Cline (1994:5–8), for example, adopted just such a compromise chronology, offering approximate dates for the early Aegean LBA phases in-between the 'early' or 'high' chronology, and the 'low' or 'conventional' chronology.

The academic tide was starting to ebb away from the 'early' or 'high' chronology. Nonetheless, other new reports were not, however, immediately encouraging for the low chronology camp. An American team reported finding major volcanic signals in a new ice-core at c.1623BC and c.1669BC, and proposed that either of these might represent the Thera eruption within the dating accuracy of the ice-core.[154] Moreover, critical consideration of the finds reported from Tell el-Dabᶜa[155] suggested that the picture was not as simple as first thought. The pumice finds in no way offered a date for the eruption, rather the time of their use in craft or other human activity. This could be much later. And the frescoes too needed further analysis. The stratigraphic associations known by 1994 were rather unclear, and, more critically, some of the Tell el-Dabᶜa examples might well post-date the LMIA-style examples known from Akrotiri. Indeed, opinions started to be expressed by experts that some of the frescoes from Tell el-Dabᶜa could in fact best be compared with subsequent LMIB art, and so these finds might in reality support the 'high' chronology contrary to first claims.[156] Finally, the excavator of Tell el-Dabᶜa, Manfed Bietak, supported a low MBA chronology in a separate dispute within Syro-Palestinian archaeology, and the dates offered for the D/2 stratum were the result of this and his arbitrary scheme allocating

---

[153] Manning (1995:200–216).

[154] Zielinski *et al.* (1994a:Table 2); Zielinski *et al.* (1995:Table 1).

[155] First properly reported in Bietak *et al.* (1994).

[156] Such views started to be articulated at conferences in 1994–1995, and various published statements appeared from 1994–1998. With regard to the pumice, see in summary Wiener and Allen (1998:25–27). With regard to the frescoes, see in summary Rehak (1997).

each of the MB phases at the site the same 30 year interval.[157] Thus a little flexibility was possible. Therefore, in overall terms, although the new finds at Tell el-Dab^ca, and the new radiocarbon calibration datasets, offered renewed hope to the low chronology, taken together with appropriate critical analysis, the full body of scientific and archaeological evidence available up to 1994–1995 undeniably continued still to favour the 'high' or 'early' chronology.[158] Davis (1995:733) went so far as to write that 'dendrochronology and reinterpretation of precision radiocarbon dates have now virtually resolved the dispute in favor of Betancourt and Manning'.[159] Work by the Aegean Dendrochronology Project completed in 1995, and announced at conferences that year (but published in 1996), seemed only to add to this picture. A remarkable tree-growth anomaly in the Aegean region could be dated to the later 17th century BC, plausibly to 1628BC, and might possibly be associated with the eruption of Thera.[160] There remained no direct causal connection,[161] but a conspiracy of data seemed to be leaning towards 1628BC. But, in reality, things were turning rapidly in scholarly opinion, and nearly all centred on Tell el-Dab^ca.[162]

In the 19th century AD French excavations on Thera in the area of Akrotiri one still unique find was made: an imported Cypriot White Slip (WS) I bowl was found in a volcanic destruction level context. This bowl had been lost by the time of an inventory and study of the French finds in 1920, but several drawings or photographs exist from the late 19th century. Thus WSI ceramics must have been in existence no later than the time of the eruption. When did WSI begin?[163] This was not clear from studies published in the 1970s to 1980s. One school supported a low chronology for Cyprus in which WSI began in the 16th century BC, but another had proposed dates from the mid-17th century BC.[164] In general, there was a debate similar to the one which came to surround LMIA: was the relevant Cypriot period (Late Cypriot IA2) contemporary with the Hyksos–SIP era, or instead the early 18th Dynasty. Existing data were less than clear-cut, compounded by the fact that almost no WSI had been found in Egypt (just two examples up to 1968).[165] When the 'high' Thera chronology was first proposed, this pre-existing Cypriot debate did not therefore appear to be a problem, and it even seemed that Thera might usefully resolve this debate in favour of the 'high' chronology for Cyprus. The ongoing excavations at Tell el-Dab^ca entered the fray at this time. In several publications before the mid-1990s Bietak stated that he had found WSI in pre-18th Dynasty, late

---

[157] See e.g. Bietak (1979; 1984; 1991a) versus Dever (1985; 1991; 1992).

[158] E.g. Manning *et al.* (1994a:222–226); Manning (1995:200–217); Baillie (1995a).

[159] See also the discussion of Bennet and Galaty (1997:83–84).

[160] Kuniholm *et al.* (1996).

[161] As pointed out by Renfrew (1996).

[162] See for example the study of Wiener (n.d.).

[163] This bowl, and the chronology of WSI, is discussed at length in Chapters IV.4 and IV.5. A new study by Merrillees (n.d.) now offers the best history of the bowl. Several illustrations showing just one side of this bowl are well known (esp. Furtwaengler and Loeschke 1886:pl.12.80); Merrillees importantly brings to light a key, but long-forgotten, illustration showing the other side of the bowl.

[164] Contrast e.g. Åström (1972a); Merrillees (1968; 1971; 1977); and Baurain (1984).

[165] See Merrillees (1968).

Hyksos, contexts.[166] Although he again insisted on his low mid-16th century BC date, the key point was the association of WSI with the late MBA horizon in western Asia. Like the news in 1992 of late Hyksos Aegean-style frescoes, this evidence appeared potentially consonant with the 'high' chronology.

But then Bietak changed his mind in a major volte-face. Publications appearing in 1995–1996 started to announce a major revision to the site chronology. Both the Aegean-style fresco fragments, and all finds of WSI, were now stated to be from early 18th Dynasty contexts, and *not* the late Hyksos period as first stated. No substantive explanation was provided for this major change, either then, or since; it was a simple diktat. Further, Bietak now started to state unequivocally that WSI did not occur *anywhere* before the start of the 18th Dynasty in Egypt. In consequence, he specifically argued that if the Egyptian historical chronology was even approximately correct, then this required a date no earlier than the mid to later 16th century BC for the eruption of Thera, given the WSI bowl found buried by the eruption.[167] The pumice, also from early 18th Dynasty contexts, was argued again perhaps to offer contemporary dating evidence.[168] Bietak saw the WSI issue in very simple, black and white, terms: initial WSI in Egypt equals initial WSI on Cyprus (whole island), and so WSI on Thera can be no earlier. He entirely failed even to consider the long-standing case of Merrillees (1971) that the LC wares developed as part of a specifically regional process on Cyprus, with the west/northwest of Cyprus the home of the LC styles, while the 'culturally retarded' (p.72) east of Cyprus continued in the MC WP tradition more or less until the beginning of the LCIB period when the already advanced WSI and BRI styles were adopted (from the west/northwest). And, of particular relevance to Bietak's argument, and own site, Bietak failed to consider Merrillees' (1971:74) case that eastern Cyprus supplied Egypt with most, if not all, its Cypriot ceramics. Thus the LC styles of WSI and BRI only arrived in Egypt from the time of LCIB when eastern Cyprus adopted these already developed styles from west/northwest Cyprus (where they began in LCIA). WSI had meanwhile already been in existence for some time in west/northwest Cyprus. Since the key site of Toumba tou Skourou in northwest Cyprus has demonstrable LCIA links with pre-eruption LMIA Thera (see Chapter IV.4), it is therefore entirely plausible that early northwestern LCIA WSI went to Thera *long before* eastern Cyprus-sourced LCIB exports of mature WSI and BRI went to Egypt. Bietak's entire WSI case is thus built on a false premise; he is, moreover, guilty of assuming that some (few) foreign finds can act as the arbiter of Cyprus' relative chronology without a thorough investigation of the archaeological evidence from Cyprus itself (again Bietak failed to note Merrillees' 1971:73 trenchant attack on Oren 1969 on just these grounds). This is a critical point for the current Thera debate. We will explore and return to the Cypriot MCIII–LCIB sequence a number of times in subsequent chapters.

Nonetheless, from 1996 the supporters of the conventional or low chronology claimed vindication. They pointed almost exclusively to Tell el-Dab^{c}a and the (revised)

[166] E.g. Bietak (1989a:79; 1995a:fig.1 and 27–28 n.47).
[167] See in particular Bietak (1996a:67–76; 1998); Bietak and Hein (n.d.); Wiener (n.d.).
[168] Bietak (1996a:76–78); Warren (1998:327).

dates and views of Manfred Bietak as clear proof of their position. Given the ambiguous radiocarbon position with the 1993 radiocarbon calibration datasets, and the lack of any direct connection between the ice-core and tree-ring evidence and Thera, they maintained that this scientific evidence was either potentially compatible (radiocarbon), or more likely irrelevant. The complete split of archaeology and art-history from science was if anything exacerbated.

Proponents of the 'early' or 'long' chronology were now all of a sudden under serious attack. Buckland *et al.* (1997) added to this siege, both with a trenchant critique showing that there was no necessary relevance for the ice-core and tree-ring data then available to the Thera debate, and with their general attack on the work of M.G.L. Baillie – who had sought to argue that the coincidences and correlations of different dates and environmental records offered a compelling (but unproven) case. In response, many of those who had supported the 'high' chronology could not understand how the largely unpublished and questionable stratigraphic sequence at one site in Egypt could be held to overturn a large body of scientific and other data. Some (unwisely) even refused to accept that the historical chronology of Egypt was necessarily such a certain fact (aided and abetted to some extent by a couple of popular books challenging Egyptian chronology which were published in the 1990s).[169] Others concentrated on the later MBII instances of LMIA-style frescoes at other sites (namely Tel Kabri and Alalakh), and previous claims of WSI ceramics from later MBII contexts at the site of Tell el-ᶜAjjul in Gaza,[170] whilst at the same time expressing scepticism over the security of the dates and correlations stated by Bietak from Tell el-Dabᶜa. There were also suggestions to re-evaluate the appropriate comparanda for the Tell el-Dabᶜa frescoes in Aegean terms.

General reviews of the evidence at about this time concentrated mainly on the almost total split between the scientific evidence and the conventional archaeological chronology. Without getting enmeshed in the complications of Tell el-Dabᶜa and Cyprus and White Slip, it was generally agreed that something more decisive was needed one way or the other to resolve this long-running controversy.[171] An objective observer held as of 1998 that 'in sum, the traditional archaeological chronology, based on alleged Egyptian/Minoan synchronisms, is not firm enough to rule out a seventeenth century date for the eruption of Thera'.[172] And, only science appeared to offer the prospect of the necessary truly precise and unambiguous evidence. The possible options appeared to be: (1) further refined radiocarbon dating, for example of the periods bracketing LMIA, in order to try to resolve the later 17th century BC *or* mid-16th century BC

---

[169] See Baillie (1995a:149–157; 1996b). For the popular books challenging conventional Egyptian chronology, see James *et al.* (1991a); Rohl (1995). For a brief discussion, see Appendix 2.

[170] For the frescoes, see e.g. Niemeier and Niemeier (1998); Rehak (1997). The WSI from Tell el-ᶜAjjul is from Palace I, and subsequently, at the site (Petrie 1931–1934, vol.II:pl.37; Merrillees 1974b; Bergoffen 1989; n.d.). These contexts, to the destruction of Palace II/City 2, are dated to the later MBA (Kempinski 1974; 1983:131–148; 1992a:189–192; Kempinski in Stern 1993:52–53; Oren 1997b; n.d.; Bergoffen n.d.). The site, its chronology, and its WS, are discussed below in Chapter IV.5. It is, needless to say, the subject of controversy.

[171] E.g. Schoch (1997); Forsyth (1998:106–113).

[172] Forsyth (1998:113).

ambiguity for the LMIA period if dated in isolation, or (2) finding a tree actually killed by the Thera eruption and obtaining a precise dendrochronological age for its final year of life, or (3) finding volcanic tephra from the Minoan eruption of Thera in a high-precision dated peat or sediment context, or (4) finding some way to fingerprint specific volcanic eruptions in the existing tree-ring records, or (5) finding some secure way of provenancing the volcanic acid signals in the Greenland ice and so identify (or not) the Thera eruption.

The first approach was tried by a team based at the Oxford Radiocarbon Laboratory, but sample availability led to useful data only for the LMIB to LMII periods. This data strongly supports a 'higher' LMIB–LMIIIA1 chronology consistent with the observations made concerning a link between the LMIIIA1 period and the later part of the reign of Tuthmosis III. However, it does not throw light on the date of the LMIA period; either a later 17th century BC date, or a mid-16th century BC date, for the close of LMIA could be compatible with the higher LMIB–LMIIIA1 chronology.[173] Only the conventional 'low' chronology end date of c.1500 BC may be excluded. Work with better MMIII through LMIB samples is necessary. The second approach has proved fruitless to date. No suitable dendrochronological samples exist at present. With luck, something will turn up one day. The third approach has worked elsewhere, for example the high-precision dating of the Hekla 4 volcanic eruption at 2310±20BC reported by Hall *et al.* (1994) and Pilcher *et al.* (1995), but finds of Theran tephra in a suitable peat or sediment context have not been reported to date. The fourth approach is the subject of ongoing work by the Aegean Dendrochronology Project. A volcanic signal may well be capable of detection; however, it is unlikely that a specific provenance for this signal will be able to be determined. Hence this approach will not provide a certain date for the eruption of Thera by itself.[174] The fifth approach is therefore about the last chance for the immediate future. Luckily, it is also the most realistic.

Tiny shards of volcanic glass (tephra) ejected by eruptions into the stratosphere can be carried as far as the Arctic or Antarctic, and can be deposited on the ice sheets there and so preserved in the annual ice laminations. Analysis of the chemical composition of such shards can enable the source volcano to be determined. So, the question was whether tephra particles could be found in any of the 17th century BC ice layers with notable concentrations of sulphur products which had been proposed as possibly relevant to the eruption of Thera? In the March 1998 issue of the *Journal of Archaeological Science* an article by Gregory Zielinski and Mark Germani (1998a) offered an apparent breakthrough. They reported the retrieval of tiny particles of volcanic glass from the c.1623±36BC layer of the American GISP2 ice-core in Greenland – this layer and its sulphur signal had been linked with Thera in earlier reports – but Zielinski and Germani claimed that the chemistry of these samples showed they did *not* come from Thera (Santorini). Hence they argued that this was important evidence against the 'early' or 'high' chronology date for the Thera eruption,[175] although they also stated that,

---

[173] Housley *et al.* (1999). This study is discussed in Chapter V.1 below.
[174] For a first preliminary mention of this work under John Chiment, see Kuniholm (1998a).
[175] News leapt upon by Warren (1998:328) in his most recent paper arguing for the low or conventional chronology.

notwithstanding their analysis, Thera could still have erupted in the 1620s BC since they had only analysed tephra found from one layer and another 72 years of ice *might* be relevant given their dating error.[176]

It is an understatement to say that this news was received with delight by the supporters of the conventional chronology. Of course, as just noted, Zielinski and Germani had merely claimed that one ice layer, dated by them to c.1623±36BC, was not linked to Thera. This left every other layer from the mid-17th century BC through the 16th century BC as possibly containing Theran tephra, and thus their data in no way supported the low chronology. In reality, Zielinski and Germani merely purported to rule out the c.1623±36BC acid signal. And there is perhaps no especial reason why this should represent the Thera eruption. Baillie (1996a) had already presented a plausible, neat, argument that what had been published as a c.1669BC volcanic acid signal in the GISP2 ice-core perhaps best correlated with the claimed Thera signal in the other ice-cores and the tree-ring evidence, while the team of Clausen *et al.* (1997:26,713), working on the European GRIP ice-core, publicly questioned the chronology of the American GISP2 ice-core in the second millennium BC interval. Further, if the Thera eruption did not produce a very large sulphur signal in the Greenland ice, as claimed by volcanologists in the 1980s, then there is no reason why its tephra will correlate with one of the major acid spikes; it may be happily lying in a less conspicuous section of core, whether in the later 17th century BC, or the mid-16th century BC. Nonetheless, the paper of Zielinski and Germani was billed as good evidence against the 'early' or 'high' date for the Thera eruption.

A further key point, therefore, is whether in fact Zielinki and Germani successfully demonstrated that the volcanic glass in the GISP2 ice-core could not have come from Thera. They published the major oxide chemistry of the samples. The problem is that the basic chemistry of many volcanic eruption products are, broadly, quite similar. Thus to discriminate a particular eruption from a number of possible fairly similar candidates it is often necessary to examine the very detailed composition of the samples. This means looking at the associated trace and rare earth elements. These alone tend to be specific (i.e. unique). This was not done by Zielinski and Germani. The analyses of Zielinski and Germani showed quite clearly that the tephra in the GISP2 ice layer did not come from some other volcanic eruptions which have been proposed as relevant, such as Avellino (Vesuvius) or Aniakchak, but, in broad terms, the composition of the GISP2 samples was not very different from analyses of Theran volcanic glass. In a response to their article, Manning (1998b) therefore suggested that some analyses of Theran volcanic glass were in fact potentially similar to the GISP2 samples, especially offering the rhyolitic (high silica content) characteristics sought. Zielinksi and Germani (1998b) countered on a narrow basis claiming to be able to discriminate the GISP2 samples from these and other Theran data (despite an incorrectly labelled ternary plot, and failing to allow for, yet alone include indication of, the measurement errors

---

[176] A caveat repeated in Zielinski and Germani (1998b:1,045). If the eruption shows up in tree-rings from 1628BC, then it may have occurred in 1629BC. Thus the possible dating window is 73 years against the GISP2 dating error. One year, 1623±36BC, only is claimed to be ruled out.

on their merely one standard deviation, 68.2%, confidence data), but, as I shall discuss in detail in Chapter V.3, the underlying point in fact remains if the data and analyses are examined more thoroughly. Some analyses of Theran glass (including those by Zielinski and Germani themselves) are similar to the GISP2 samples, and, within stated measurement errors, the composition of the GISP2 shards overlaps with several published analyses of Theran tephra. There also appears to be a case for a measurement offset. Hence the confident elimination of Thera as a possible source volcano by Zielinski and Germani is not necessarily valid. The final resolution of this issue will now only come either with news of secure tephra identifications (hopefully replicated) in the Danish-European Dye 3 and GRIP ice-cores (or subsequent cores), or after much more detailed analysis of the GISP2 ice-core in the 17th–16th centuries BC. Resolution via the former is in fact expected in the near future (see Chapter V.3 below; Claus Hammer, pers. comm.).

Late 1998 then brought one final important twist to the plot. There had been low-key criticism of some aspects of the production of the radiocarbon calibration curves published in 1993.[177] In particular, suggestions were made concerning unsupported data revisions, and there were claims that regional differences may exist which should be taken into account. As early as 1994, it was stated in print that the original 1986 data should be preferred 'for Hiberno-British archaeology, at least'.[178] And, as I noted above, the 1993 calibration datasets were not formally internationally approved by the wider radiocarbon community after collaboration and scrutiny. Thus their status was inherently problematic to many in the field. To resolve this situation, work was undertaken to produce a new internationally recommended radiocarbon calibration curve for general use. This became available in later 1998, and is named INTCAL98.[179] It will now be the standard reference for radiocarbon calibration for the next several years (and is employed as the primary referent in this book, along with comparisons with the 1993 decadal calibration curve on German wood). The relevant point here is that this new calibration curve slightly reduces the later 17th century BC versus mid-16th century BC ambiguity for the Akrotiri VDL in favour of the 17th century BC. To take the two main radiocarbon datasets from the 1989 Thera and the Aegean World III conference presentations, the Copenhagen and Oxford series, the calibrated calendar age range for the Copenhagen average date of 3355±32 radiocarbon years BP at 1σ (68.2%) confidence is 1690–1600BC (Probability, P=0.89), and 1560–1530BC (P=0.11), while the calibrated age range for the combined Series I and II Oxford data average of 3338±30 radiocarbon years BP at 1σ (68.2%) confidence is 1690–1600BC (P=0.71), and 1570–1530BC (P=0.29).[180] Thus, in radiocarbon terms, the odds now again more strongly favour (c.70% to 90% probability) the later 17th century BC for the date of late LMIA and the eruption of Thera. And, in reverse, a date after c.1530BC is

---

[177] See Bowman (1994:840–841); McCormac *et al.* (1995); Kromer *et al.*(1996).
[178] Bowman (1994:840–841).
[179] Stuiver *et al.* (1998).
[180] Copenhagen average age from Friedrich *et al.* (1990:195); Oxford combined Series I and II average age from Housley *et al.* (1990:213 Table 6 using the suggested ±30 year error). Calibrated age ranges from the OxCal computer calibration programme (Ramsey 1995) with round ranges function 'on' and employing the INTCAL98 dataset from Stuiver *et al.* (1998).

extremely unlikely to impossible. Supporters of the conventional, or low, chronology will of course ignore or overlook this: Warren (1998:328), for example, intransigently continues to support an eruption date around 1520BC. The current situation nicely exemplifies the almost total split between science and archaeology/art-history in this debate. Science is only cited when it agrees with the archaeological interpretation by supporters of the low chronology, whereas they accuse proponents of the 'early' or 'high' chronology of ignoring the archaeology.

Characterising the debate today

Since the Thera controversy erupted in 1987–1988, numerous published contributions have poured forth in a veritable frenzy of argument, attack, defence, and counter-attack. Once several scientific techniques were involved, and significant archaeological re-interpretation was suggested, a vigorous reaction was of course inevitable from the rest of the field. Scholars associated with the existing archaeological chronologies fought back with determination. As noted, the scholar most closely associated with the on-going defence of the traditional chronology is Peter Warren, who, in a substantial series of papers has attempted to reject and question all new proposals, and to defend the traditional chronology.[181] Other prominent scholars who wrote defending the conventional chronology included Vronwy Hankey, James Muhly, Kathryn Eriksson, Harmut Matthäus, Manfred Bietak, and most recently Malcolm Wiener.[182] The Aegean field thus split in the 1990s between those who decided to accept the new high chronology as likely (or at least possible), and those who steadfastly rejected it. But, even in the midst of this condemnation and point-scoring, one very interesting and important concession was quietly made by many: the cherished c.1500BC date for the Thera eruption was dropped, and instead a mid to later 16th century BC date was now conceded to be the minimum position by most scholars of the traditional position.[183]

Since the late 1980s, to the present day, a constant stream of publications have appeared presenting new data relevant to the Thera eruption, or discussing the date of the Thera eruption and the related chronology of the beginning of the LBA in the Aegean, whether in favour of the proposed new 'early' or 'high' chronology, against such an early chronology, in favour of the previous conventional chronology, or merely reviewing the subject. The standard 'textbook' in the field has a chronological table showing the split between the conventional chronology (supported by the work's author) and the rival 'early' chronology.[184]

---

[181] E.g. Warren (1984; 1985; 1987; 1988; 1990; 1990/1991; 1996; 1998); Warren and Hankey (1989:137–148).

[182] See Hankey (1987); Muhly (1991); Eriksson (1992); Matthäus (1995); Bietak (1996a:63–83; 1997:124–125; 1998); Wiener (n.d.).

[183] Cadogan (1987); Warren and Hankey (1989:215 postscript to p.142); Warren (1990/1991); Negbi (1994:82–83) – but cf. Bietak (1997:125) and Eriksson (1992) who continued to support the c.1500BC (or a later) date. Warren (1998:328) has now backtracked. He offers a date of c.1520BC for the eruption of Thera, and a date range of 1525–1490BC for the LMIA/LMIB transition. As noted above, this is almost impossible if any regard is paid to the scientific evidence.

[184] Dickinson (1994:19).

The debate has reached almost worryingly formalised proportions; each side is confident that they are right. Meetings at conferences have become a form of 'generalized feather-waving', where stress and conflict are managed and dissipated,[185] but progress is not made towards a new synthesis. The present battle lines were effectively drawn in the mid-later 1980s, and any new evidence has either been added to a list, or quickly rejected, depending on prior view point (a severe case of improper Bayesian thinking!). Of course, much progress has been made, but the central issue remains unresolved. I suggest that it is now time to stand back, and to reassess the whole situation; to identify the important data, and to see whether in fact we have the answer – or at least a clear working hypothesis which should now form the basis of an archaeological synthesis.

Is this important? Yes! The conventional chronology is the basis to the accepted history and art-history of the second millennium BC Mediterranean. It is indeed notable, and worrying, how MMIII–LMI Aegean and east Mediterranean art history, and thinking about its development, are now being constructed because of, and to fit with, both the conventional 'low' Aegean chronology, and the ultra-low Palestinian-SIP chronology of Bietak (1992a) – often by authors directly involved in the construction and defence of these same positions.[186] Thus, if the history, art-history, and material culture of the Old World is important – something I take as a given when writing for Old World, Mediterranean, and European archaeologists, historians, and readers – then the correct chronology is vital. And not just the chronology itself, but also the issue of how this chronology is constructed.

Moreover, the subject is urgent, since, as noted, the present situation is ridiculously circular; the 'conventional' history (i.e. that which developed largely before the advent of mature and sophisticated science-based dating, and which became the accepted orthodoxy in writings of the 1960s–1980s), and all the apparent certainties of many academic works based upon it, are now employed supposedly to reject independent arguments for a different 'earlier' chronology.[187] I wish to suggest that it is time to draw up a new convention; to consider a new paradigm.[188]

It is not an exaggeration to say that the Thera 'debate' is the most controversial and widely discussed issue in Aegean archaeology today. Further, due to the links between the Aegean and the east Mediterranean at the time – links especially accentuated since the recent discoveries of Aegean style frescoes and other Aegean material at Tell el-Dabᶜa in the Nile Delta region of Egypt, and at other Syro-Palestinian sites, and dramatic suggestions that a stela of the Pharaoh Ahmose

---

[185] G.A. Johnson (1982:405).

[186] E.g. Warren (1995:4–5); Bietak (1995a; 1996a); also see Morgan (1995), who completely adopts such a low chronology into her thinking; likewise Marinatos (1998).

[187] Eriksson (1992) is a classic of the genre. I wish to note in fairness to Eriksson that Bourriau and Eriksson (1997) withdraw from the polemically extreme, and low, chronology positions of Eriksson (1992). The paper of Eriksson (1992) also has many important observations relevant to the relative chronology of the Late Cypriot I period. I thank Kathryn Eriksson for interesting discussions, and advice, on these and related topics.

[188] I note that I am not going to discuss arguments by James *et al.* (1991a), Rohl (1995), and others for radically lower chronologies in the main text. For a brief treatment, see Appendix 2.

describing a great storm might perhaps be linked with the effects of the Thera eruption[189] – this controversy also keeps bubbling up in the fields of Egyptology, Near Eastern archaeology, and so on. Among other things, if the eruption of Thera could be precisely dated, then it offers a unique opportunity to test the chronology of ancient Egypt, and the traditional historical framework of the ancient Near East.

As quickly reviewed above, in the last couple of years a variety of new evidence has been published which both advances, and complicates, the quest for resolution. At present there remain serious cases in the scholarly literature for a Thera eruption date in:

1. the later 17th century BC (from radiocarbon, ice-core, and tree-ring evidence and a 'high' interpretation of the archaeological data),
2. the mid-16th century BC (from a revised but conventional consideration of the archaeological evidence and because c.1530BC is the about the latest date possible from the radiocarbon evidence), and
3. the range 'between 1515 and 1460 B.C., according to the present Egyptian chronology'[190] (from the finds of Theran pumice at Tell el-Dabᶜa, and Bietak's general 'low' chronological analysis).

As is evident from the difference of 100–150 years between positions 1. and 3. above, these positions, and the analyses behind them, are contradictory, and reflect respective decisions to reject or not to consider various data. In this regard, little improvement exists from the 1980s. For example, whereas Bietak (1997:125) dates the later LMIA Thera eruption 'into the period after Ahmose and before Tuthmosis III ... This seems to make a strong case for a date ... between 1515 and 1460 B.C.', Bourriau and Eriksson (1997) present compelling evidence from conventional archaeology that imported LMIB and later LHIIA material was in fact being deposited in Egyptian contexts dating somewhere between the reigns of Ahmose and Tuthmosis I. Since LMIB and later LHIIA are definitely subsequent to LMIA in relative stratigraphic terms, it is clear that these analyses cannot both be correct! Bietak simply does not discuss and consider the scientific evidence from radiocarbon, ice-core analysis, or dendrochronology (merely noting it sometimes and stating without proper discussion that it is impossible given conventional Egyptian chronology[191]). But, at the same time, Bietak is correct to highlight that the pattern of WSI finds in the east Mediterranean appears – as presently stated by himself (cf. above) – to be a major problem for the acceptance of a later 17th century BC date.[192] Needless to say, in general terms, the scientists behind the radiocarbon, ice-core, and tree-ring datings have not always mastered the intricacies of the archaeological evidence; many archaeologists have not mastered the scientific data; and many archaeologists of one region/specialism have not critically and rigorously examined

---

[189] For the frescoes, see Bietak (1995a; 1996a); Bietak and Marinatos (1995); Niemeier (1991; 1995a; 1995b); Niemeier and Niemeier (1998); Negbi (1994); Knapp (1998). See Chapter IV.3 below. For the 'Tempest' stela of Ahmose, see Davis (1990a); Foster and Ritner (1996). See Chapter IV.6 below.
[190] Bietak (1997:125).
[191] E.g. Bietak (1996a:76).
[192] See also Wiener (n.d.).

relevant archaeological evidence from other regions. Hence collective mutual incomprehension, and incompatibility, reigns. Position 2 is a compromise. For this reason alone it is unlikely to be correct – it just causes the least upset.

The new material, recent debates, and the resolution of various mutual incomprehensions form the core of the discussions in following chapters. It is argued that everything is in fact neither ambiguous, nor hopeless. There is clear evidence in favour of a revised earlier chronology for the LMIB to LMIIIA1 periods. However, the beginning of the LBA remains less certain, and there are at present good arguments in favour of *either* the full 'early', 'high', or 'long' chronology, *or* of a new shortened 'compromise' early chronology. Both of these are potentially compatible with much of the large variety of scientific *and* archaeological data. An answer which effectively ignores one or the other body of evidence is neither feasible nor realistic. Choice then between the early chronology and the compromise early chronology is not totally certain at present, and relies to an extent on rhetoric. Does the scientific evidence for a major volcanic eruption c.1628BC most *likely* relate to Thera, or not? Is there any perhaps decisive new scientific data which must overrule archaeological ambiguities? Does the absence of evidence for a major volcanic eruption in the mid-later 16th century BC rule out the compromise and low chronologies? Does a solitary Cypriot White Slip I bowl found last century on Thera, and now lost, and the pattern of exports of (relatively scarce) WSI elsewhere in the east Mediterranean, provide sufficient evidence to require the compromise chronology? Does the evidence provided by WSI in fact, on examination, support the case proposed by Bietak, *et al.*? And so on. We will explore these issues.

It is important to try to resolve the ongoing Thera debate, and to decide what is the appropriate date, or at least date range(s). Then the Thera eruption can act as the focus for a new chronology, a new history, of the Aegean and east Mediterranean in the mid-second millennium BC. This potential for certainty, for precision, is a rare situation in archaeology and prehistory: it must be grasped. And, this debate is not merely about Aegean LB1 chronology remote from other concerns. Among other things, the correct chronology will synchronise, and so permit valid analysis and explanation of, relations (cultural, trading, political, artistic) between the Aegean and Egypt, the Aegean and the Levant, and the Aegean and the Hittite world of Anatolia;[193] and it will offer the correct time frame for analysis of both the development and collapse of the new palace phase of civilisation on Crete, and the Shaft Grave phenomenon and the rise of the Mycenaean civilisation of Greece. Inherent also are several important methodological and theoretical issues, including: the relationship between archaeological timescales constructed from typological studies and evidence for exchange versus science-based dating information; and the relevance and potential for a precise linear timescale in pre- and proto-history.

Not surprisingly, it is the wider implications of any changes in Aegean chronology which have come to dominate recent discussions. For example, the ramifications of

---

[193] Cf. Gale (1991); Davies and Schofield (1995); Gillis (1995); Cline (1994); Negbi (1994); Giles (1997); Mee (1998); Bryce (1998); etc.

any 'early chronology' reach beyond the Aegean. A main counter-argument now follows the line that Aegean scholars cannot go raising their chronology because of the connections with other east Mediterranean chronologies and their supposed dates. But, in reverse, if the early Aegean chronology can be shown to be correct, then this conclusion must be incorporated into thinking not only in the Aegean, but also in Anatolia, Cyprus, the Levant, and Egypt, as well as the derived archaeologically-based chronologies of the central Mediterranean, and Europe. This wider argument is in fact the key issue today. The debate is not just about Thera, as if this is some isolated, discrete, problem; it is about the entire chronology, and so history and interrelations, of the Mediterranean in the mid second millennium BC. Indeed, the major arguments against the early chronology, and in favour of the compromise early chronology, come from the east Mediterranean.

At present, there are four issues in the way of a resolution of the Thera controversy.

(i) The controversy itself has almost come to obscure the evidence. Few now actually study and assess the corpus of relevant data; most scholars merely cite the 'debate', and leave the matter as controversial. Meanwhile, lost in the huge volume of publication, others are fighting battles ended several years ago, apparently unaware of subsequent work, and so on.

(ii) A need to stand back and neither privilege nor devalue any evidence at the outset of a proper, rigorous, analysis. No one site, nor set of *assumptions*, is inherently better than others, nor intrinsically correct. There are facts: the likely regnal dates of various Near Eastern rulers, radiocarbon determinations, dendrochronological data, ice-core data, and so on, but the relationship of many of these to Thera and/or to the Aegean relative archaeological chronology, needs interpretation, and none are correct just because tradition holds one view to be best.

(iii) Significant new data has started to emerge in the last few years which provides a route to all but ending the debate. But most scholarship seems as yet unaware of this data or potential, or happy to leave such developments aside, and instead merely refers to the controversy and what is regarded as a still unresolved debate. This is of course the path of least resistance. It does not require a careful, fair, and thorough review and analysis of what is now a very large body of relevant data.

(iv) The need to be critical of all data, both scientific *and* archaeological.

Much of the fault for this situation lies with the participants in the debate. In a welter of technical presentations, vigorous arguments with opponents, specialist summaries, and so on, a clear review of the current and relevant evidence has not been available for some time. In particular, there has not been a synthesis of both archaeological and scientific data. This book seeks to remedy the situation. It ends proposing the 'early' or 'high' chronology as perhaps the most likely from all the evidence, and on the balance of probabilities. However, the issue is not beyond reasonable doubt, and an alternative compromise chronology is also possible. The low chronology may be ruled out. The 'early' and 'compromise early' chronologies differ *only* in the dates of the LMIA period and the eruption of Thera – the dates for later LMIB to LMIIIA1 are the same in both. Hence I term them from here on as the 'early' chronology and the 'compromise early' chronology. I wish especially to focus the attention of Aegean archaeologists, Cypriot archaeologists, Syro-Palestinian archaeologists, Hittitologists, and Egyptologists on these new possible chronologies, and their wide-ranging, and solid foundations. I ask them to read the text below without prior prejudice, to reconsider convention, and to contemplate a paradigm shift. As they will find, with the exception of the early Aegean LBA, the implications are important and significant, but not really radical nor destructive. Of course, the new chronologies are not comprehensively proven, but the scholars in these fields cannot go on ignoring what are very likely facts. There are a few problems, but the overwhelming quantity and pattern of data supports the conclusions drawn in this work. This book provides both a future point of reference (since the weight of evidence as of the beginning of 1999 strongly suggests that future work will only confirm one or other of these chronologies), but also what should now be the point of attack for would-be critics (versus literature published some time ago). It is now time to make progress, despite the undeniable, if tautological, fact that everything in archaeology is 'always momentary, fluid and flexible'.[194]

---

[194] Hodder (1997). Hodder finds eerie resonance in 'the man' in Reza's (1998) *The unexpected man:* 'How can your complete works be anything more than a mishmash of approximations, of constantly shifting boundaries' (p.3). It is difficult not to empathise.

Chapter III:
Aims and Preliminary issues for this Study

'A feeling for chronology, gradually acquired, should help to dispel confusion'
(Braudel 1993:xxxii)

It is often said that chronology is the backbone of archaeology and history.[195] Indeed, the development of archaeological chronology very much formed the basis and background to the development of modern archaeology.[196] After all, 'an enquiry into the past which does not reckon with the dimension of time is obviously nonsense: the past *is* the past by virtue of the place it occupies in the time-scale'.[197] This conventional archaeological perspective follows the logic of the early chronographers of the Renaissance period, epitomised by Johnson (1962:136) when he refers to Jean Bodin's comment that 'without a knowledge of chronology "hardly an advantage is culled from history"'. Whereas the prevailing intellectual fashions in historical analyses moved away from a chronological approach last century,[198] most archaeology has necessarily remained concerned with chronology.

> Central to the process of doing archaeology is the necessity of understanding the chronological sequencing of archaeological entities and past events. Without a firm grasp of this sequencing, archaeologists would not be able to deal with issues of behavioural process and evolution. Archaeology as a discipline would be reduced to a dry cataloguing of artifacts and monuments with little hope of understanding the mechanisms and rates of change in past human cultures. For this reason, dating the past has been one of the most crucial methodological problems facing archaeologists.[199]

All field archaeology, from excavation to survey, is centred around chronological

---

[195] See for the central place of chronology and dating: e.g. Renfrew and Bahn (1996:111–162); Greene (1997:101–129); Trigger (1989:see index p.481 under 'chronology, continuing importance for archaeology').
[196] Gräslund (1987).
[197] Piggott (1966:63).
[198] See Johnson (1962).
[199] Fagan *et al.* (1996:168).

sequences; they provide the diachronic framework, and so the ability to discuss, interpret, and explain human development over time. Even R.G. Collingwood, the famous philosopher of history, and holder of a fairly relativist viewpoint, where 'an actually thought-out chronological scheme ... exists only as the organization of detail within an historical monograph', and for whom chronology may thus be compared to the time-beats of a musical symphony articulating the sequence into a simultaneous whole, nonetheless accepted the need for chronology,[200] and specifically notes the importance of the chronological studies of Bodin in disproving the 'four empires' scheme of history, and so setting the appropriate framework for historical study.[201] Similarly, although some post-modern, post-processual, archaeological theorising and writing largely avoids time, or takes an a-temporal rhetorical stance,[202] almost all archaeological practice finds time and chronology essential. Ian Hodder (1995:164), a leading post-processual archaeologist, himself specifically comments that 'the definition and dating of chronological phases or periods are fundamental to most, if not all, archaeological endeavour', and, as Gräslund (1987:2) notes, 'it is ... easy to forget that the chronological work of the scholars of earlier generations forms the platform without which archaeology could not have developed into a real social and humanistic science'.

Therefore, it does not matter whether the archaeological past, or time, is addressed from a traditional to processual perspective,[203] a theoretical perspective,[204] an *Annales* or historical perspective,[205] a political perspective,[206] or a post-modern perspective,[207] chronology, or chronologies, is/are the key to, and structure for, archaeological practice, analysis, and interpretation. In addition, the timescales upon which analyses and interpretations are undertaken are important to, and condition, archaeological inquiry,[208] and different conceptions, or types, of time and timescales, are relevant to different types of human activities and processes.[209] In all cases, time and chronology remain essential to analysis, from the near-instantaneous to the *longue durée*. With the advent of farming, in particular, diachronic progress also becomes central to the past societies themselves, and, from the development of state-level societies some 5000+ years ago, time and calendars have been at the heart of human civilisation.[210] Whatever and wherever one may subsequently make of, or take, the subject of archaeology, temporal existence and structure – that is chronology – lie at the heart of any higher analysis. Chronology is thus important to archaeology. Significant, justified, change

---

[200] Collingwood (1994:477–488) from his 'Outlines of philosophy of history' of 1928.

[201] Collingwood (1994:57).

[202] Hodder (1991; 1992; 1999). Hodder (1999:130) notes that time is central to archaeology, but argues that it has not been the subject of sufficient suitable theoretical discussion.

[203] E.g. Childe (1925); Renfrew (1972); Snodgrass (1985; 1987); Ehrich (1993).

[204] E.g. Bailey (1981; 1983; 1987).

[205] E.g. Knapp (1992); Last (1995); Bintliff (1991).

[206] I take as one example the project of Bernal (1987; 1991).

[207] E.g. Shanks (1992; 1996); Thomas (1996); Whitley (1998). For a classical archaeology review, see Dyson (1993).

[208] Gosden (1994).

[209] E.g. Meillassoux (1972); Gamble (1987); Whitrow (1989); Bradley (1991; 1998); Fletcher (1992).

[210] E.g. Whitrow (1989); Duncan (1998).

in an established, conventional, archaeological chronology is therefore even more important. It must not be undertaken lightly. It affects everything from totally conventional art-historical and archaeological taxonomy and synthesis, to post-modern, social theory, concerns with the situation and constitution of the diachronic practice theory of 'habitus',[211] structuration,[212] background,[213] being,[214] and related ideas in agency and the anthropology of art[215] – and critiques thereof.[216]

In following chapters we will examine, and rethink, mid-second millennium BC Aegean and east Mediterranean chronology, and see why this is necessary. The period of time concerned, and the cultural chronologies at issue, mean that both the prehistories of Crete, Greece, and Cyprus, and the proto-histories of Anatolia, Syria–Palestine, and Egypt, are all involved. Likewise the art-history of these societies. Existing ideas, frameworks, and models need review. The argument in the following pages may be about chronology, but the story is much larger: how we write the pre- and proto-history of the ancient Mediterranean over a period of some three centuries.

The format consists of an argument and synthesis on the basis of the most recent evidence. This seeks to follow up, integrate, revise, and reflect on the last two decades of work on the topic as of the beginning of AD 1999. The result is necessarily a detailed, multifaceted, investigation. The following text is meant to be provocative to convention, and to stimulate interest, reaction, and debate. It is not, however, intended to be a polemical, nor a one-sided, discussion. The aim is to suggest a new paradigm for the chronology and history of the Aegean and the eastern circum-Mediterranean area on the basis of *all* the available evidence (or at least the best resolution of all the sometimes contradictory data). I wish to end the situation where many scholars avoid the Thera controversy by way of a footnote, or by noting that it is only relevant to LMIA Thera and Crete. I also highlight that the possible chronological cases presented are not just based on any one type of scientific evidence. This is not just some 'radiocarbon' chronology at odds with everything else. Instead, the case is based on both a thorough reconsideration of the archaeological evidence, *and* a wide-ranging body of scientific evidence. All this data provides a consistent case in favour of the arguments presented in this book, and either the 'early' or 'compromise early' chronologies. In effect, I defy critics to make the same claim.

I wish to explain, and to emphasise, at the outset that the proposed 'early' or 'compromise early' chronologies affect directly *only* the earlier LBA of the Aegean. Here dates must go 'up' and moreover 'stretch out' (respectively either by a century, or about 50 years). This has major implications for Aegean history, and for the relations of the Aegean cultures with their neighbours. These must be explored, analysed, and tested. In particular, a revision of the traditional set of linkages between the Aegean and the historical civilisation of Egypt c.1700–1400BC is found to be both necessary,

---

[211] Bourdieu (1977; 1990).
[212] Giddens (1984).
[213] Searle (1995).
[214] Heidegger (1962); Karlsson (1997).
[215] Gell (1998).
[216] E.g. Turner (1994 – cf. Bohman 1997); see also Callinicos (1989).

and to be supported by the archaeological data. The effects of the new chronology beyond Thera and the Aegean, however, must be the subject of a careful consideration of the relevant linkages and archaeological contexts. For example, the 'early' chronology for Thera does *not* automatically transfer to other cultures unless directly associated with the eruption event: some of the very same data which support an 'early' Thera eruption date also support a 'low' Babylonian chronology. And, this is *not* contradictory – they are independent, and the resultant chronologies mesh well together.

I spend much of this book discussing the archaeological and scientific data and their analysis and interpretation; but I begin with a request to the reader to consider the situation objectively, to go beyond both first impressions, and pride and prejudice. There currently is *no* truth universally acknowledged in second millennium BC Aegean–east Mediterranean chronology. The summary is:

1. 'Early Chronology'

For: (a) that a wide variety of independent, high-quality, scientific data either strongly support, most likely support, or are consistent with, an 'early', or 'high', chronology for the Thera eruption (e.g. 1628BC), the early Aegean LBA, and directly related areas and cultures, (b) that analysis of the archaeological evidence clearly supports a compatible raised, or earlier, chronology for the later LMIB to LMIIIA1 periods, (c) that the archaeological evidence from the Aegean, Cyprus, the Levant and Egypt relevant to the MMIII–LMIB periods may almost all be interpreted as consistent with an early chronology and a later 17th century BC date for the eruption of Thera (including WSI), with the LMIA period in particular linked with the Hyksos (SIP) period in Egypt and the later MBII period in the Levant, and (d) that although there are of course a few discordant archaeological data, none of these is without problems, none may not be plausibly discounted, and, altogether, they represent a very few instances opposed to a vast majority, and a consistent pattern.

Against: (a) that a Cypriot WSI bowl was found on Thera in a pre-eruption context, and, since there is no good (or undisputed) evidence for exports of WSI in the east Mediterranean and especially Egypt before about the start of the 18th Dynasty in Egypt, some scholars, ignoring the evidence for important regionalism in ceramic production and trade in LCIA Cyprus, argue that this places the eruption no earlier than the start of the 18th Dynasty (a mid-16th century BC date), and (b) the revised current interpretation of the stratigraphy, architecture, and finds at the site of Tell el-Dabᶜa in the Nile Delta of Egypt.

2. 'Compromise Early Chronology'

For: (a) that the radiocarbon evidence also makes a mid-16th century BC date possible for the eruption of Thera, and this enables the WSI 'problem' as conceived by Bietak to be resolved, (b) that analysis of the archaeological and radiocarbon evidence which supports a raised, or earlier, chronology for the later LMIB to LMIIIA1 periods does not necessarily require a date for later LMIA (and the Thera eruption) earlier than about the start of the 18th Dynasty, and (c) that the archaeological evidence relevant to the MMIII–LMIB periods may almost all be interpreted as consistent with a mid-16th century BC date for the eruption of Thera with most of the LMIA period still contemporary with the (later) Hyksos (SIP) period in Egypt.

Against: (a) that a large body of evidence for a major mid-latitude northern hemisphere volcanic eruption in 1628BC, which seems remarkably consonant with the Thera eruption, must in fact be associated instead with another (as yet unknown) eruption, (b) that there is little or no evidence of a major mid-latitude northern hemisphere volcanic eruption in the mid-16th century BC, and (c) the radiocarbon evidence presently available seems to favour the 17th century BC option.

A further request to readers is to consider the quality of the data involved. For example, much of the data discussed below in Chapter V involves radiocarbon, and also other science-dating techniques.[217] Often, those who dispute the conclusions drawn from studies employing radiocarbon dating simply refer to 'errors', or 'problems'. They point to supposed discrepancies in dates run long ago and of non-modern quality, or fail to exclude dates known to be on samples unlikely to reflect the relevant cultural context at issue. The radiocarbon technique dates the moment a then living sample ceased to exchange carbon dioxide with the atmosphere (through breathing, photosynthesising) – i.e. died, or ceased growing (e.g. an annual tree-ring once laid down). How this date might be relevant to an archaeological context requires careful consideration of context: what was the origin of the sample? For example, a mass of charred seeds (of less than one year's growth) from a storage container should offer a near contemporary age for the moment that container was last used. In contrast, a sample of charcoal from wood might well derive from a building beam, and only the outside ring of the wood (last ring when the tree was felled) dates the time of this building activity. Inner rings offer irrelevant older dates. Further, building activity may in turn have occurred some years, to several decades or more, before the time of the final use of the building or its destruction – the circumstances that usually create archaeological deposits. Thus radiocarbon ages on wood/charcoal are often older than the cultural phase in which they are found (sequence: 1. building, 2. cultural use, 3. destruction/abandonment – with the radiocarbon determinations on wood/charcoal at latest dating 1. and only radiocarbon determinations on short-lived samples potentially dating 2. or 3.). Charcoal without specific architectural or use association may easily be residual (including sometimes firewood), and much older than the find context. These issues lead to the 'old wood' problem highlighted by Schiffer (1986). Most so-called problems in radiocarbon dating reflect either old inappropriate data, samples which were not appropriately pretreated to remove extraneous carbon compounds washed into samples while they were buried, use of inappropriate sample material, or a failure correctly to identify what the samples

---

[217] Generally, see Aitken (1990); Taylor and Aitken (1997).

obtained relate to and so a failure to consider whether the dated event is in fact the same as the target event for which a date was originally sought. The real laboratory and technique errors and problems in modern radiocarbon dating (and I am only discussing 1980s–1990s radiocarbon dating) are only both known, and quantified, because of the high accuracy and precision of the method. They are not mysterious 'problems', but defined numbers/parameters. Any 'mysterious' problems are invariably the fault of archaeologists: whether as noted above through a failure to employ relevant and secure samples,[218] or because of a failure to grasp the non-linear nature of the relationship between the radiocarbon and calendar timescales (see Chapter V.1).

A good modern radiocarbon laboratory has an offset versus other laboratories, or some agreed standard, which is known. The laboratory's counting/measurement accuracy is high, and precise, within stated errors. The radiocarbon calibration curve, which permits measurements of past natural radiocarbon levels as evidenced in organic samples to be converted into calendar dates, is established within relatively small margins of tolerance.[219] If one follows the technical literature, there are, of course, various current issues. The most interesting and problematic concerns location-dependent variations in atmospheric radiocarbon levels.[220] For the Mediterranean, where comparison is with calibration datasets from European or USA tree-ring series, the predicted modelled differences should be very small,[221] and, although recent data for USA versus Irish, and Irish versus European, wood suggest this model offers minimum values,[222] the observed differences are nonetheless so small as *usually* to be of little practical significance to the archaeologist.[223] Indeed, in other than very carefully controlled circumstances, such differences are barely distinguishable above normal

---

[218] Cf. Waterbolk (1971).

[219] See Stuiver *et al.* (1998) for the latest dataset. There is detailed discussion of the sources and errors involved in the construction of this dataset. On laboratory offsets among the calibration laboratories, see pp.1,044–1,045, and esp. Tables 1 and 2. Note the small offsets. Although this dataset is a revision to previous calibration curves, it is important to stress that in overall terms the high-precision radiocarbon calibration curve has remained more or less the same since high-precision data first became available in the 1970s (and these high-precision data themselves by in large narrowed and made much more precise – rather than changed – previous pre-high-precision calibration curves published by e.g. Damon *et al.* 1974; or Clark 1975). Changes have been quite small, and the various curves, *in toto*, look very similar. High-precision radiocarbon dating, and so high-precision calibration curves, started to be developed in the mid-1970s (e.g. Pearson *et al.* 1977; de Jong *et al.* 1979), and a first AD period true high-precision curve was published by Stuiver (1982). A long BC period curve relevant to prehistory was published a year later (Pearson *et al.* 1983). International, inter-laboratory, high-precision calibration datasets were then published in *Radiocarbon* 28B of 1986, *Radiocarbon* 35(1) of 1993, and *Radiocarbon* 40(3) of 1998.

[220] Damon *et al.* (1989); Jirikowic and Kalin (1993); McCormac *et al.* (1995; 1998); Damon (1995a; 1995b); Braziunas *et al.* (1995); Kromer *et al.* (1996:608–609); Stuiver and Braziunas (1998); Stuiver *et al.* (1998:1,045–1,046).

[221] Braziunas *et al.* (1995).

[222] E.g. McCormac *et al.* (1995).

[223] A current research project under the direction of the author in collaboration with Bernd Kromer, Peter Ian Kuniholm, Marco Spurk, and others, is investigating this very subject in order to establish the true situation for the Aegean–east Mediterranean region. Results available so far from this project indicate very good general correlation of the Aegean wood data with the international radiocarbon datasets for the northern hemisphere.

measurement error and inter-laboratory variance.[224] Where there are major latitude differences, altitude differences, oceanic input through coastal upwelling of deep waters, or hemisphere differences, the variations can mount up to a few decades. In these circumstances, or if trying to map overall global radiocarbon patterns, then the differences become important. But, important even then only in the case of true high-precision radiocarbon dating where measurement precision is so good ($\leq\pm10$–20 ^{14}C years) that the location differences assume significance. For archaeologists in the European-Mediterranean region, this is not a problem likely to be of concern in the great majority of situations.[225]

In contrast, what is of great importance to archaeology are developments in the quality of *routine* determinations,[226] and then the archaeologically relevant, or informed, application, analysis, and interpretation of these.[227] Current methodologies for the analysis and interpretation of radiocarbon data and their assessment in conjunction with archaeological (and other information) have of late reached a sophisticated level – especially through the implementation of Bayesian approaches – and bear no relation with the often inappropriate or crude work of past decades.[228] Today this is the minimum standard. Older work may well now be irrelevant, superseded, or in need of revision. Compare only like with like.

The other main forms of science-dating under consideration in the following discussions are dendrochronology and ice-core analysis. Dendrochronology has almost no error once a large replicated sample set has been analysed and checked.[229] Ice-core evidence is a little less precise, but also has impressive accuracy and precision through the last many thousands of years. The American GISP2 ice-core team claims a reproducible precision of better than 1% within sections of intact core,[230] and, even allowing for instances of visible stratigraphic data loss through episodes of non-intact core, estimates a precision level of just over 1%, or ±36 years, back to the mid-second millennium BC.[231] The Danish-European Dye 3 and GRIP cores have stated precisions within about a decade or so back to the same period.[232]

In marked opposition, much of the archaeological data often referred to in discussions on chronology result from trading and social practices of unknown, and different, types and durations. Most standard settlement, or non-single-burial, non-

---

[224] McCormac *et al.* (1998:1,321).

[225] The possible exceptions are likely to be times of rapid change in atmospheric radiocarbon levels, when regional or latitude-based differences may operate over the short-term. For an example, see Manning (1998a:Fig.30.4).

[226] International Study Group (1982); Scott *et al.* (1990); Rozanski *et al.* (1992) – see with Hogg *et al.* (1995); Gulliksen and Scott (1995); Scott *et al.* (1997; 1998); etc.

[227] See e.g. Bowman (1990; 1994); Bowman and Balaam (1990); Aitchison *et al.* (1991); Manning and Weninger (1992); Manning (1995); Day and Mellars (1994); Weninger (1997).

[228] See e.g. Bowman and Balaam (1990); Buck *et al.* (1991; 1992; 1994); Christen and Litton (1995); Ramsey (1995); Bayliss *et al.* (1997). On the general application of a Bayesian statistical approach to archaeological, and archaeological-science, data – including dating – see the book of Buck *et al.* (1996).

[229] Stokes and Smiley (1968); Schweingruber (1988); Baillie (1982; 1995a); Cook and Kairiukstis (1990); Dean (1997).

[230] Alley *et al.* (1997).

[231] Zielinski and Germani (1998a).

[232] Clausen *et al.* (1997).

foundation deposit, archaeological contexts are also, by the nature and processes of their formation, representative of a band of time (exact duration usually unknown), and not a specific instant.[233] Meaningful, or cherished, Aegean objects deposited in far off Egypt (or vice versa) in special contexts like tombs, and subsequently discovered by archaeologists, are either unique, or members of a very small sample – as far as modern archaeology is concerned – and so the data are incapable of control or replication. The definitions of the exact associations between the key exported/ imported artefacts at the heart of archaeological synchronisms, and specific persons and historical chronologies, are also usually difficult (if not impossible) to establish. Prior viewpoints, rather than solely the relevant data, tend inevitably to inform interpretations. A good example has been the long-held *assumption* of Egyptian agency in virtually all 'close of MBA' to early LBA destruction horizons at sites in Palestine, and so a conventional chronology and history which has been built around Egyptian pharaohs, whereas there is in fact remarkably little evidence to support this assumption in most cases:[234] see further below.

A core problem for archaeology in areas linked to the old world historical chronologies is the incompatibility of the historical chronologies comprised of lists of special or élite persons (e.g. king-lists), or lists of places conquered by such persons, and the material culture as found in archaeological excavations. Human beings tend to personalise their lives and the material correlates therefrom, and, as both individuals and groups, they personify their history such that an individual of importance or renown comes to have a life narrated which forms the reference for social history. But, once outside the relevant context (e.g. archaeologists examining millennia old strata), or when dealing with inanimate material culture in general, these past 'personal' linkages are not easily apparent. Thus, although a continuous list of kings may exist, and occasional lists of events, it is often impossible to relate closely particular styles in material culture, architectural phases, and events, let alone occasional or unique imports, with such lists. Different types of time, different entities, are being compared. Thus attempts to bring archaeological and historical evidence together (the event-historical model) are often almost inherently problematic because they represent fundamentally different facets of historical reality.[235] For example, even in the 'historical' Iron Age of the east Mediterranean (first millennium BC), the correlations of archaeology and supposed fixed points – records of Assyrian destructions – proves problematic on thorough examination.[236] The result is that, in any situation where there are no detailed records listing dates of buildings and the myriad ordinary events, there will be room for debate and interpretation. Hence, although Archaic Greece is bordering on the historical, the absence of such real detail

---

[233] See e.g. Schiffer (1987). On formation theory in archaeology, see the recent review of the subject by Shott (1998).

[234] Shea (1979); Redford (1979; 1992:138–139); Hoffmeier (1989; 1990; 1991); Na'aman (1994a).

[235] For a good review and critique, see Snodgrass (1983; 1987:36–66). Another example is offered by Finkelstein (1998a) in his critique highlighting the uneasy relationship between text history and archaeology, and the inappropriate power an historical paradigm has held over the relevant archaeological evidence, in the case of the discussion about the date and nature of the settlement of the Philistines in Canaan.

[236] Forsberg (1995).

has allowed heated debate even in recent years over the chronology of the main architectural and stylistic phases.[237] Another very recent scholarly fracas has broken out for the same reason in the area of the Iron Age chronology of Palestine.[238] In this case, historical dates and connections exist, and continuous king-lists are available from surrounding civilisations, and to an extent for Israel itself. But it is difficult securely to relate the archaeology to these dates and history. The situation stated by Finkelstein (1996a:180) is typical:

> The first important synchronism is the campaign of Pharaoh Shoshenq to Palestine in 926 BCE. But we need to admit that we do not have even one destruction layer which can safely be assigned to this campaign.

Once we move back to the Bronze Age Aegean, the whole process is even more distinctly approximate and indeterminate. Here we are attempting to compare true prehistoric archaeological assemblages built up on relative typological and/or stratigraphic criteria with lists of rulers of another distant country (e.g. Egypt). And, of course, the historical chronologies themselves are invariably less than perfect – the more so as they become further distant from their Iron Age anchors – and often have many errors and potential problems not all of which are precisely quantifiable.[239]

It is worth dwelling briefly also on the problems of transmission and deposition as regards archaeological chronology. First, there is a methodological issue rarely addressed. Classical and Aegean archaeology has rather tended both to equate people with pots, and ceramics with history, *and* to assume some special relevance or distinctiveness of Minoan, Mycenaean and (general) Greek civilisation.[240] But the Mediterranean of the middle of the second millennium BC was an international world – the product of a set of co-evolving, inter-linked, civilisations. Near Eastern traders made their mark in the MBA on Cyprus in order to secure metal supplies,[241] west Asian influence fused with Egypt during the SIP in a special, dynamic, phase, and the greater Near Eastern world system, based around the core Egyptian–Levantine–Mesopotamian area, expanded into the east Mediterranean in the MBII period.[242] But this does not necessarily mean direct political intervention, rather that there are various driving influences in fashion, symbolism, diplomacy, trade, and so on. For example, as discussed further in Chapter IV.4 , it may be observed that jewellery played an important role in Near Eastern religious practice, and status display, in the second millennium

---

[237] E.g. the challenge to convention by Francis and Vickers (1983; 1985 – see also Francis 1990; Vickers 1985; 1987); cf. Boardman (1984); Bowden (1991); Hannestad (1996). The early Iron Age is another area where there are rather more assumptions than facts, and some revision of traditional chronology may be in order (Morris 1998; Papadopoulos 1998).

[238] The challenge by Finkelstein (1996a; 1998b; 1999); cf. Mazar (1997); Ben-Tor and Ben-Ami (1998); Mullins (1999).

[239] Henige (1986); Gates (1988); Barnes (1991); Cryer (1995).

[240] The critical discussions making analagous points with regard to the Aegean early Iron Age, and especially the role of the Euboeans, by Papadopoulos (1996; 1998) are relevant.

[241] Courtois (1986).

[242] Generally, see Sherratt and Sherratt (1991; 1998). For the SIP in particular, and the expansionary contacts into the east Mediterranean by the major Hyksos kings, see Mellink (1995); Redford (1992:119–121); Ryholt (1997:138–142) – although cf. Ryholt (1997:143). For MM trade and contacts with the east Mediterranean, see Wiener (1987).

BC.[243] Earrings, in particular, seem very important, to both gods and humans. And it is thus significant that the élite women represented in the LMIA frescoes from Akrotiri on Thera wear earrings (and other items of jewellery) which have close and clear parallels not only with the contemporary Aegean but also the contemporary later MBII examples known from sites like later MBA Tell el-ᶜAjjul in Palestine (see Figures 18–20; see discussion in Chapter IV); and that the contemporary earliest LC jewellery from Cyprus is likewise similar and linked to the same later MBII Syrian–Palestinian world.[244]

Anachronistic concepts of nationality for aspects of material culture are often inappropriate in such circumstances.[245] This growing world system[246] became one inter-communicating zone (especially at élite, trading, level), with fluid boundaries with regard to trade, symbolic expression, art, and so on. Within the Aegean, we can note the merging of mainland and Cretan fineware ceramics in the LMIB/LHIIA periods, when it is often difficult to tell them apart; across the whole east Mediterranean, we might consider the horizon of so-called 'Aegean'-style wall paintings and just who was in fact influencing whom.[247] It is thus more useful to consider the whole picture – not to focus on any one type of material, or population group.

However, even if we adopt a more traditional approach and framework, we must nonetheless consider a number of issues which complicate any simple employment of dating via typology, and through archaeological correlations ('cross-dating').[248] For example, whereas in the cases of factory manufacture of known duration a quite precise archaeological chronology is possible, variation in time and space is likely when dealing with even relatively recent products which lack known manufacture timeframes and come from a variety of differing, non-standardised, local production processes.[249] Move to a prehistoric context, and the problems become acute. The complexities of style and its development must also be considered.[250] In the all-important cases of relatively rare long-distance imports/exports, which form our key synchronisms in mid-second millennium BC Aegean–east Mediterranean prehistory, we usually do not know (i) how much time elapsed between production in one culture and importation into another culture, and then (ii) how long the object was in use in its import context (and whether it was further exchanged), and finally (iii) how, after its period of deliberate use, the object actually came to enter the archaeological record.[251] All sorts of scenarios may be envisaged,[252] and these will vary according to the type of object and the exact mechanisms of trade.

---

[243] Maxwell-Hyslop (1971).

[244] Maxwell-Hyslop (1971:esp.127–131).

[245] Compare the discussion of Papadopoulos (1997) with regard to the Early Iron Age.

[246] Sherratt and Sherratt (1991).

[247] For the similarity without scientific analysis of some types of 'palatial' LMIB and LHIIA ceramics, see e.g. Mountjoy *et al.* (1978); Mountjoy (1993:41–52). For the issue of the direction of influence in the 'Aegean'-style frescoes, see Knapp (1998); Sherratt (1994).

[248] For the basic concepts involved in typological and assemblage dating, see Gräslund (1987:5–11); for further detailed discussion, see Adams (1988). For discussions of cross-dating as applied to the historical period, see South (1977).

[249] Dethlefsen and Deetz (1966); South (1977:207).

[250] Carr and Neitzel (1995); Hodder (1995).

[251] See Kristiansen (1985).

[252] E.g. Kemp and Merrillees (1980:160–161).

Fig. 18. Comparison of some earrings depicted for élite females in the Akrotiri frescoes (a., d., e.) with others found in the Aegean (b. from Crete, f. from Shaft Grave 3, Mycenae) and examples found at late MBII (Hyksos) Tell el-ʿAjjul, Palestine (c. from hoard 1450, and g. from hoard 1313). Drawings after Doumas (1992:pls.108, 118, 130), Effinger (1996:pl.10 no.MaPM 1a), Higgins (1997:Fig.204), and Negbi (1970:pl.1 no.2, pl.3 no.10).

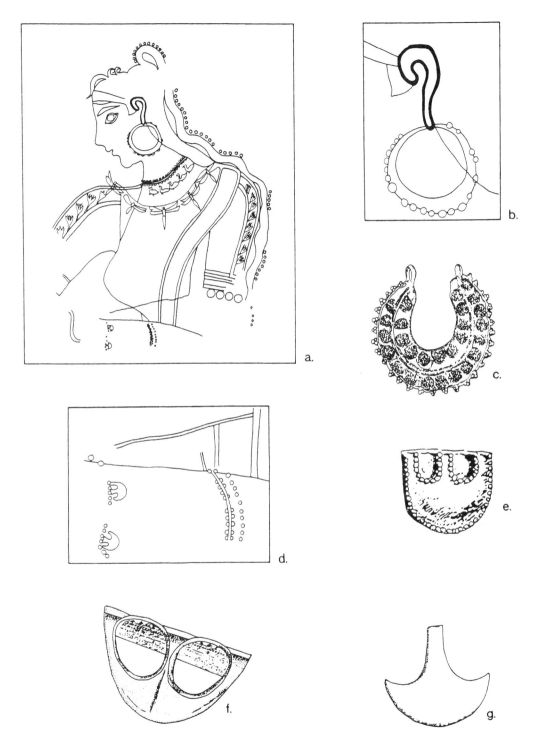

Fig. 19. Comparison of earrings and arm bracelets/bangles depicted for élite females in the Akrotiri frescoes (a., b., d.) with examples of the same forms/motifs from Crete (e., g.) and western Asia (c., f.). No. b. is a detail of a. Drawings after Doumas (1992:pls.125, 126), Effinger (1996:39 no.KnS 5h, 27 no.PK 14l), Maxwell-Hyslop (1971: colour plate) and McGovern (1985:fig.17).

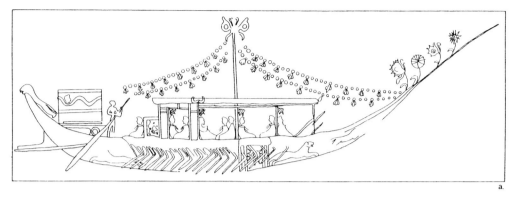

Fig. 20. Comparison of similar crocus and papyrus motifs on an ikrea, necklace, and bracelet from respectively a. Akrotiri, b. Tell el-ʿAjjul Grave 1073, and c. Akrotiri. Drawings after Doumas (1992:pls.37, 121) and Maxwell-Hyslop (1971:Fig.91).

In the cases of certain 'survival' technologies, archetypally weapons, rapid diffusion of new technologies may be expected.[253] But none of the key Aegean–Egyptian synchronisms – which form the basis of the Aegean LBA chronology – consist of such objects. Instead, they are either: various forms of small ceramic storage vessels, various forms of eating/drinking vessels, prestige art, or representations of Aegeans or Aegean iconographic features in élite Near Eastern art, or odd exotic imports of special or prestigious Near Eastern objects (seals, scarabs, figurines, etc.) into the Aegean. The simple fact that, until the later LBA period (LH/LMIIIA–B), we have only a very few synchronisms (from a couple of centuries of human time), suggests that until then Aegean–Egyptian exchanges were not part of a regular, commoditised, trade, but, instead, were very much in the realm of an infrequent, luxury, prestige-goods, token-currency/social storage, trade with the respective objects (and other goods – material, or otherwise) forming exotica, or biographies of value, in the recipient culture.[254] In

---

[253] E.g. Childe (1929:viii, 248); Wiener (1984:23 and n.61).
[254] See for discussion of non-commoditised, social, trade variously: Frankenstein and Rowlands (1978); Appadurai (1986); Kopytoff (1986); Helms (1988; 1992; 1993); Sherratt and Sherratt (1991); Voutsaki (1995); Halstead (1989; 1994); Wijngaarden (1999a – see also following comments by F.A. De Mita Jr., S. Voutsaki, and T. Whitelaw). For an extreme minimalist view of Aegean–Egyptian trade and contacts, see Merrillees (1998). This nonetheless nicely illustrates the general point about a lack of a regular, commoditised, trade in the early LBA.

such circumstances, there is no reason necessarily to assume either a linear, direct, trade, nor any rapidity in the process of transmission to final deposit (often the special context of a tomb) – indeed it is clear, for example, that 'Aegean ceramics in some cases could circulate for long periods of time, or were kept as heirlooms or antiques' as van Wijngaarden (1999b:38) observes citing Mycenaean finds from the Amman Airport site as a prime instance (see also Merrillees 1972a:281–283). Further, different mechanisms were probably operating simultaneously: some direct trade by merchants (but very possibly with one or more 'middle men', or subsequent 'down-the-line' exchanges involved, before goods reached final destinations), some 'gift' exchange between individuals (which may lead to a 'down-the-line' scenario again), some exchanges between respective rulers (which may then lead to subsequent disposal networks beneath the ruler), and so on.[255] We simply do not know the time-lag between production and deposition. Moreover, as Morris (1987:14–17) usefully emphasises, it is important to remember that ceramic (and other) populations and styles need to be considered in terms of being parts of active, living, material culture and social systems. There may thus be overlapping styles both in temporal and/or regional, and/or social status terms. Emulation, either between, or within, societies is an additional complicating issue. Chronologies built around style and rare imports/exports are therefore inherently fuzzy and flexible (and *non*-linear).

The lack of replication of the data in question often precludes any overall assessment, and clarification. All too often the synchronisms cited in Aegean Bronze Age chronological studies rely on just one object, or one context, or one site. There is no control on most of the data, and it is thus flexible within largely unknown limits. Only in the later LBA, post-1400BC, where we have many exchanges, and replicated patterns of finds of Mycenaean types across the eastern Mediterranean,[256] are we dealing with an active process of regular international trade, and secure linkages. Relative links between the Aegean and the east Mediterranean in the LHIIIA2–LHIIIB period are fixed within small margins of possible variation. This is not under dispute, nor is it the subject of the present book. The LMIA/LHI period, by total contrast, has very few linkages, and so, in such circumstances of transparent flexibility, appropriate interpretation becomes paramount.

A final issue is the dating of both find context, and exchanged object. In a large number of cases, the find contexts of key synchronisms are either not closely defined, ambiguous, or actively debated. This results from two causes. First, many of the well-known examples of exchanged objects were found in excavations from the later 19th or earlier 20th centuries AD; standards of excavation and recording do not necessarily match the demands placed on the evidence by today's scholarship. Second, although Egyptian archaeology has recourse to an historical chronology, and many monuments may be dated to particular rulers and officials, until relatively recently (1980s–1990s) the dating of Egyptian ceramic assemblages was not (almost correspondingly) a developed subject. The dating of archaeological assemblages instead tended to rely on the find of a scarab of a named ruler, and so on. However, convenient historical references are often not found, and scarabs may both stay in circulation a long time, and even be

---

[255] For evidence, and types, of trade, see e.g. Ericson and Earle (1982); Gale (1991); Knapp and Cherry (1994:123–155); Schortman and Urban (1992); Renfrew and Bahn (1996:335–368).
[256] E.g. Leonard (1994).

issued after the named individual is dead. Thus the precise dating of the find of Aegean and other exotic imports is often less than clear, and this is invariably the case for material excavated before the last couple of decades. Such imprecision and debate is an error range – it is not a reason simply to choose a date most convenient to an author. It is a mistake to think that these sorts of problems do not affect the LBA. Leonard (1988) has demonstrated the ridiculously circular logic, and unsubstantiated nature, of the dating of Levantine contexts by the Aegean exports supposedly themselves dated by the east Mediterranean contexts. And, even in the better cases, there are usually debates over details which create likely ranges in date of several decades at a minimum.

A number of scholars seek a route out of such inherent ambiguity by claiming only to employ the totally certain, good, evidence. Anything which may be in any way questioned is discarded. This is, however, a circular, and false logic in archaeology. It tends merely to replicate the status quo. It will also inevitably locate the main floruit of a period of exchange, rather than (for chronology) the all important beginning. The start of a new fashion and its exchange via trade will inevitably overlap with the concluding period of the previous fashion(s) and their trade. Requiring clean contexts and correlations will therefore usually lead to this beginning phase being discarded as 'questionable' or 'not secure', and instead only a date for the subsequent clear floruit period will be accepted. The result is completely predictable: it leads to a low or minimum chronology, at best defining *termini ante quos*.

Such a lack of genuinely firm foundations, and so the clash of differing scholars' interpretive constructs, appears to lie behind much of the existing archaeological debate, and the contradictory claims, with regard to the early Thera date and Aegean LB1 chronology. In essence, we may observe that the relevant cultural periods, LMI and Late Cypriot (LC) I, are transitional in terms of the key historical Egyptian and Syro-Palestinian sequences – they overlap the ending of the Middle Bronze Age (MBA) in Syria–Palestine and the start of the LBA and the 18th Dynasty in Egypt. This is a long-standing 'problem'; for years one group of scholars has tried to start LCI before the LBA/18th Dynasty,[257] and another has instead argued the contrary position that Middle Cypriot (MC) must equal Syro-Palestinian MBA and LC must equal Syro-Palestinian LBA (and the 18th Dynasty in Egypt).[258] But, as nicely summarised by Bourke,[259] the whole MB–LB transition debate is founded on false premises: first, proper, quantitative, stratigraphic studies of the MB–LB transition in Syria–Palestine based on settlement contexts are largely non-existent, and second, existing studies rely on one or more cherished 'facts' which are in essence deceiving assumptions ('factoids') incapable of withstanding rigorous scrutiny. Nor should we even expect

---

[257] E.g. Merrillees (1971:73–74; 1977; 1992); Warren and Hankey (1989:116).
[258] E.g. Oren (1969; n.d.); Gittlen (1981); Johnsen (1982); Eriksson (1992). However, only Gittlen and Eriksson really mean strictly MC=MBA and LC=LBA. Both Johnsen and Oren allow some initial LCI products in late MBA contexts in Palestine (esp. Monochrome and PWS), they merely argue that there are no indisputable claims of BRI and WSI from pre-LBIA contexts in Palestine and pre-18th Dynasty contexts in Egypt. Extremes aside, most scholars thus in effect almost agree, and the difference is one of emphasis. Did LCI just start during the Syro-Palestinian late MBA period (so maybe LCIA1=last MBA phase), or did rather more of LCI occur in the Syro-Palestinian later MBA period (so LCIA, even to start of LCIB=later MBA).
[259] Bourke (1993:esp.166).

great, pan-regional, correlation; Matthiae points out, for example, that what is termed the MBA ends in northern Syria some 50 years earlier than the end of what is called the MBA in Palestine.[260] And 'there was no Syro-Palestinian cultural unity during the Middle Bronze Age'.[261] Both these points are ignored by many writing about 'Syria–Palestine'. As already noted in Chapter II, similar temporal-regional issues dominate the archaeology of MCIII–LCI Cyprus, and must be taken into account in any analysis.

Bichrome Ware has been central to such debates, and, as nicely illustrated in the critique of Bimson (1981:137–171), the circular, and illusory, logic often employed in past analyses is all too evident. Bichrome Ware came to be regarded as a key indicator of the initial LBI period in the Levant. But at some sites, and especially Tell el-ʿAjjul, it was obviously in late MBA contexts. What to do? Some dismissed such early occurrences (a good example was a long-running dispute over whether Bichrome did, or did not, first appear in MBA level X at Megiddo, or only in LBA level IX), some re-dated Tell el-ʿAjjul, others re-defined what was LBI so as to include this earlier material, and others accepted that Bichrome did indeed first occur in the MBA. Once it was appreciated in the 1970s that the ware was Cypriot in origin, and not Syro-Palestinian as previously thought, the last position became a little easier to swallow, but confusion continued until recently (see further in Chapter VII). The central flaw was the reliance on any one ceramic type, rather than a comprehensive analysis of overall ceramic distributions by stratigraphic contexts. Today, as summarised by Gonen (1992:98–99), we know that Bichrome Ware did first appear in the last phase of the Levantine MBA (unless one re-defines what is the start of the LBA), but the prior history of confusion still permeates modern discussions.

Behind much of the logic, there was the old view (or assumption) that the end of the Palestinian MBA was the result of the campaigns of the first pharaoh of the New Kingdom in Egypt, Ahmose, and that the end of the MBA was therefore a defined, clear, horizon specifically linked with the start of the 18th Dynasty. Such a view is without any support.[262] Syro-Palestinian archaeologists increasingly appreciate the imprecision of defining the MB–LB transition in Egyptian terms. One school of thought nonetheless sticks with Egyptian agency, but now considers a series of campaigns by pharaohs from Ahmose to Tuthmosis III, and so an MB–LB transition phase of some half a century or so.[263] But the idea of starting with the old assumption of Egyptian 18th Dynasty agency, one way or another, remains falsely inscribed.[264] Many scholars

---

[260] Matthiae (1997:379–380); see also Kempinski (1997:327).

[261] Kempinski (1997:327).

[262] Weinstein (1981); Bimson (1981). The evidence for Ahmose's campaigning into the Levant primarily consists of an inscription from a tomb mentioning his seige of Sharuhen, another inscription from a second soldier's tomb mentioning a campaign in Zahi (see Breasted 1962, vol.II:§13 and §20), a reference to captured cattle from the Fenkhu (Breasted 1962, vol.II:§27), and a eulogistic mention of how Asiatics and people of the Fenkhu-lands are in terror of Ahmose in an inscription by Ahmose on a stela at Karnak (Breasted 1962, vol.II:§30). These comprise less than clear or comprehensive data.

[263] E.g. Dever (1992:14–17; 1991:74); Bietak (1991a); Weinstein (1991). There is good documentary evidence for Levantine campaigns by Tuthmosis I and Tuthmosis II (e.g. Breasted 1962, vol.II:§73, 81, 85, 125).

[264] And leads to the problems noted briefly by Kempinski (1997:326), which Kempinski pointedly observes 'Dever will have to tackle in the near future'.

argue that it is difficult even to associate the Egyptians with most of the relevant destructions.[265] The 'end' of the MBA at various sites might thus either pre-date or post-date Ahmose; and other agents (Mitanni or Hurrians) have been proposed for at least some of these destructions.[266] Indeed, as Kempinski (1997:329) stresses, much scholarship seems to be missing the big picture: there is an area-wide set of changes across the greater region including the destruction, or end of settlement, at several of the major MB sites, and a significant drop in total sites. The collapse of the Hyksos in Egypt, and the conquest of Avaris/Tell el-Dabᶜa by Ahmose, is merely part of this overall process, and quite possibly towards its end. The Theban kings Kamose and Ahmose took advantage in this case, but, elsewhere in Syria–Palestine, other factors were involved. In the specific case of the Hyksos, and despite his well-attested and long reign, the accession to, or seizure of, power at Avaris by Apophis some 40+ years before the fall of Avaris seems in fact to mark the beginning of the collapse of the overall 15th Dynasty state.[267]

Greater flexibility in interpretation and interpretative frameworks is required. The respective relative sequences which scholars have defined at regional, and inter-regional, level will often not have been parallel nor uniform. The 'logic' behind views that, for example, Tell el-Yahudiyeh ware and associated types are MBA in Syria–Palestine, therefore imports to Cyprus must be MC and anything from LCI contexts must be a *subsequent* local imitation of a now-defunct style in its place of origin, is inherently false because it is based on an arbitrary insistence that LCIA be parallel with the LBI/18th Dynasty of the Levant and Egypt, and a rejection of arguments that LCIA was instead contemporary with the close of the MBA.[268] However, work existing when Negbi wrote, and subsequent work and finds, clearly demonstrate that objects from what is defined as the LCIA period of Cyprus were deposited in the Levant in what is defined as the local late MBA (MBIIC or MBIII) period (see Chapter IV.IV and V below). If pan-regional alignment is nonetheless sought, then one or other (or both) of the respective periods must be redefined. Several scholars have noted this, proposing for example that the beginning of the LBA in material culture terms (i.e. the appearance of things like the LCIA imports of Bichrome Ware, PWS, Monochrome, and WPV–VI) should define the start of the Syro-Palestinian LBA, rather than the traditional association with the the 18th Dynasty of Egypt. The result is a higher date for the commencement of the LBA in the Levant, c.1600BC, or a little before.[269] Further, in the rigid application of terminological labels by Negbi, the regional patterns on Cyprus are overlooked. Negbi

[265] This observation had been made in the past on both archaeological and textual grounds: e.g. Shea (1979); Redford (1979; reiterated in Redford 1992:138–139); Weinstein (1981). However, it was brought prominently to the attention of the field by the papers of Hoffmeier (1989; 1990; 1991) and Na'aman (1994a), and the inadequate attempt at rebuttal by Dever (1990).

[266] Redford (1992:139–140); Na'aman (1994a). On the Hurrians (and so also the kingdom of Mitanni), see Wilhelm (1989).

[267] The latter case argued by Ryholt (1997:307).

[268] Negbi (1978). See p.147 for explicit rejection of Merrillees' arguments for LCIA being coeval with the late MBA of the Levant/SIP of Egypt.

[269] Examples of such views are provided by Kantor (1965); Tufnell *et al.* (1958:64–68); and Kempinski (1992a). The start of the Syro-Palestinian LBA is placed c.1600BC by these scholars as a result.

highlights that the (to her troublesome) LCIA occurrences of Cypriot imitations of Levantine MBA types occur especially in the area of Morphou Bay (northwest Cyprus); in the east the same vessels are more usually from MCIII or MCIII to LCIA contexts. She entirely fails to appreciate that these different areas of Cyprus had relatively distinct ceramic traditions over the same MCIII–LCIA period, and that all may in fact belong to more or less the same chronological horizon.[270] The cultural, economic, and political rationale behind exchange must also be considered. Dever (1992:16) refers to the 'easily recognizable Cypriot wares whose sudden and brief appearance [in Palestine] may be said to characterise "MBIII/LBIA"'. Why do they suddenly appear, and why only briefly? This relates to contemporary politics and economics – and *not* necessarily (or only) to the length, or dating, of the relevant Cypriot fashion phase. The 'absence' of Cypriot wares up until their 'appearance' in Syria–Palestine need not mean that they did not already exist (in Cyprus, or even elsewhere, as trade goods), just that there was little trade between Cyprus (or rather, the various and differing regions of Cyprus) and Palestine until late in the Syro-Palestinian MBA. Then, for some reason, there was a brief period of reasonably visible contact. And, in fact, this contact was strongly limited to the coastal area of the Levant. On analysis, only a very few sites have any real numbers of MCIII–LCIA imports: notably Tell el-ᶜAjjul, and to a lesser extent Tell el-Dabᶜa. For example, when Gittlen made a study in the 1970s of all the (then) known instances of Cypriot WS exports to the Levant, three-quarters of all the Cypriot Proto White Slip (PWS) exports from Palestine came from just one special site: Tell el-ᶜAjjul.[271]

Relevant factors will be the polity-formation processes and developments on Cyprus at exactly this time: both the general processes evident across the island in MCIII–LCI,[272] and specifically the polity formation processes in LCIA as visible at and around what became the major site of Enkomi,[273] and the three other coastal or near coastal centres which emerge at this time at Morphou *Toumba tou Skourou*, Hala Sultan Tekke *Vyzakia*, and Kourion *Bamboula*.[274] Two of the elements evident at this time seem particularly pertinent for our present discussion: first, that interregional trade is an important component of these changes, both in terms of exports from Cyprus including copper, and in terms of the acquisition of prestige goods for use within Cyprus by an emerging élite, and, second, that there is a clear change to the previous EBA–MBA settlement pattern on Cyprus, and a shift to, or founding of, a number of new coastal settlements in Cyprus,[275] with evidence from these of maritime trade with the Levant. The east/southeast of Cyprus is the area that Catling thought best typified the new LC settlement pattern, with a mixture of important new sites (e.g. Enkomi, Hala Sultan

---

[270] See Merrillees (1971). MCIII–LCIA regionalism, and the chronology of Tell el-Yahudiyeh ware, are both discussed in Chapter IV.

[271] Gittlen (1975; 1977). For an up-date, see Bergoffen (1989; 1991; n.d.); Oren (n.d.).

[272] See Knapp (1979; 1985:247–250; 1986a); Baurain (1984:27–103). Elements include regionalism, social instability/militarism, the growth of urban centres, the rise of literacy, the development of intensive copper production, and participation in interregional exchange. Mortuary data shows the rise of new élite groupings from the LCI period (Keswani 1989a:512–522; 1989b).

[273] Peltenburg (1996:27–35); Keswani (1989a:139–143).

[274] Negbi (1986).

[275] Knapp (1997:46–48); Catling (1962).

Tekke), and new coastal centres in long-established river valleys (e.g. the Maroni Valley, Kourion area). The evidence from the Maroni Valley is typical. A major new settlement appears on the coast at the very beginning of the LCI period, there is evidence of contemporary imports or influences from the Levant including direct evidence of LCI maritime trade from the seabed off the site (see Plates 7–10), and an LCI–II cemetery formed on a low coastal bluff overlooking the sea. This cemetery was not only rich in imported items, but excavations last century found two terracotta models of boats in the LC tombs; such finds highlight the link with the sea, and the role of maritime trade, in the development of local socio-political status and funerary display.[276]

The almost infamous regionalism, or territorial separation, of Bronze Age Cyprus is another highly relevant issue,[277] as argued especially by Merrillees (1971), when he proposed a split between the west of the island and the east of the island in LCIA (Chapter II above, and discussed in detail in Chapter IV.5 below). In addition, contemporary economic and political developments in Syria–Palestine may have been important at this time in making late MC and early LC Cypriot imports both accessible, and of value: for example, one might wonder about the establishment and rapid growth of a Hyksos trading world in the southeast Mediterranean, and its need for metal supplies.[278] And some Syro-Palestinian sites may have established trading links before others, or acted as key gateways for local distribution – one thinks especially of the port site of Tell el-ʿAjjul. In this regard, it is interesting to note, as Popham (1962:286) observed, that the main distribution of PWS in Cyprus coincides with the mining areas of central Cyprus, and that the technology and fabrics of PWS and WSI

---

[276] The LC coastal site in the Maroni Valley consists of the combined 'sites' of Maroni *Tsaroukkas*, Maroni *Vournes*, Maroni *Aspres*, and Maroni *Kapsaloudhia*. For initial occupation in earliest LCI (or MCIII–LCIA), see Cadogan (1983b:160–161; 1996); Herscher (1984); Johnson (1980). The Maroni Valley Archaeological Survey Project has not found any pre-LCIA material in the lower coastal area of the valley (e.g. Manning *et al.* 1994c; Manning and De Mita 1997:126–128; unpublished data in preparation for publication). The main MC occupation is a couple of kilometres inland at Psematismenos *Trelloukkas*. For initial LCI imports from the Levant, see Herscher (1984) for Maroni *Kapsaloudhia*, Gerald Cadogan (pers. comm.; and Cadogan *et al.* n.d) for Maroni *Vournes*, and, for finds of a number of late MBII–LBI Canaanite jars with an LCI assemblage including late WP, and PWS, in a deposit on the seabed off the Maroni *Tsaroukkas* site, see Manning and De Mita (1997:128–129, Figs.28–30); and especially the final report by Manning, Sewell and Herscher forthcoming. For the LCI–II cemetery, see Johnson (1980); Manning and Monks (1998); and Manning (1998d). For the boat models, see Johnson (1980:pls.9.15, 16.60). For discussion of these boat models, see also Wachsmann (1998:63–66).

[277] E.g. Merrillees (1965; 1992:47–48); Knapp (1979:19–26 with further refs.); Baurain (1984:27–103). This regionalism is primarily defined in material culture terms (and mainly ceramics), but it appears also to co-ordinate with contemporary trading, and geo-political, groupings on the island. In particular, an eastern territory around Enkomi may be proposed (see Peltenburg 1996), and seen as separate from other western areas. Thus this is not an inappropriate scenario where ceramics are arbitrarily treated as history. This east–west division is of course not absolute. There are rather a series of overlapping regions (for an MC example of a more detailed analysis, see Frankel 1974). Maguire (1990) offers in several places some useful critique of both the standard Swedish Cyprus Expedition (SCE) system of classification of Cypriot ceramics, and the ceramic-based approaches of previous scholars of MC–LC Cyprus, including Merrillees. She considers regionalism in her chapter 4.

[278] Generally see Oren (1997a) on the Hyksos world. For the suggestion of a need for metal supplies, see also Bietak (1997:124 and n.83); Philip (1995).

further link them to the piedmont and mountainous mining regions of Troodos.[279]

I will return to this Cypriot case later in Chapter IV.5. At this stage, I merely wish to emphasise the need to consider context and explanation. The conclusion I wish to draw is that we should not pre-judge, or pre-privilege, any data. Instead, let us try to understand how it came about (rather than merely applying labels). Thus I ask the reader to please consider all the data, its quality, and its relevance; then decide. And, by definition, note that science-based dating is a valid, independent, body of data. It is not there to be accepted if it supports some particular archaeological hypothesis, and dismissed if not.

One notable area in this regard for Aegean archaeology, ahead even of the often willful ignorance of modern science-dating techniques, is Egyptian chronology. This is usually merely taken as a 'given'. Aegean scholars who are critical of many things, and who are wary or sceptical of science, suddenly take the latest statement by an Egyptologist as gospel. Many Aegean scholars are both ignorant of the details of Egyptology, and especially of Egyptian chronology, and yet at the same time accord Egyptian data a special, sacrosanct, status – often from publications now well out of date in the Egyptian field.[280] Examine the situation carefully. Reviews of Near Eastern dating by Near Eastern scholars tend to be rather more appropriately cautious.[281] Egyptian chronology is subject at all points to some minor errors and debates, but, more crucially, the quality of the Egyptian chronology varies significantly at different times.[282] There are a number of problems or debatable assumptions, as highlighted by critical literature ranging from the 'serious' to the less than academically rigorous or credible.[283]

The conventional chronology of the Aegean (and surrounding regions) in the second millennium BC is based almost exclusively on reference to the chronology of Egypt – that is to correlations with contexts related to Egyptian pharaohs.[284] Thus the nature, quality, and soundness of Egyptian chronology for the period under investigation is central to the Thera controversy. It is important to grasp how this chronology is constructed, and to appreciate all the details and problems involved but often glossed over.

I do not mean to suggest that there is anything wrong with Egyptian chronology. I dismiss as incorrect recent attempts radically to down-date Egyptian chronology – they are contradicted both by clear science-dating evidence, *and* appropriate analysis of the inscriptional, textual, archaeological and historical evidence from Egypt and the

---

[279] See Courtois (1970:83); Courtois and Velde (1989:73 and refs. to previous work); Jones (1986:526–528); Knapp and Cherry (1994:57–59); Williams and Oren (n.d.; pers. comms.).

[280] Among many others one might cite, I unfairly note Rehak (1996:38 Table 1) employing the Egyptian chronology of Hayes (1970) from the *Cambridge Ancient History* of a generation ago, rather than a current chronological discussion – although, to be fair, one recent 'expert' work, Redford (1992), happily employs the same 'high' *Cambridge Ancient History* chronology: see p.104 n.23.

[281] Cryer (1995).

[282] In general, see Ward (1992); Kitchen (1991; 1996a); von Beckerath (1997).

[283] For 'serious' to attempted serious examples, see: Read (1970); Long (1974); Hari (1980); Wells (1989); James *et al.* (1991a:esp.220–259); Ward (1992); Rose (1994; 1997); Depuydt (1995); Goldberg (1995); Hagens (1996). For recent examples of the less than academically rigorous or credible kind, see e.g. Rohl (1995); Read (1995).

[284] E.g. Warren and Hankey (1989:127–169); Cadogan (1978); Hankey (1987; 1991/1992); Åström (1972a:755–762); Merrillees (1977); Dever (1992); Bietak (1991a); Weinstein (1996); Warren (1998).

Near East. However, it is wrong to think that everything is as neat and tidy as we are often told, or as it appears in various summary tables. As Hagens (1996:153) opens a recent paper: 'in spite of recent advances in scholarship, absolute dating of the Late Bronze Age ... remains poorly defined. There also seems to be a problem of lacunae in the records'. Hagens' overtly sensible critical analysis of the Egyptian Third Intermediate Period evidence finds that he cannot support the reconstruction of Kitchen (1986), and he concludes with a date for the accession of Ramesses II a century later than conventional! Of course, he must be wrong, one immediately asserts, but the point is that the historical data available from Egypt is *not* that transparently clear-cut nor secure. The limited astronomical data from second millennium BC Egypt with regard to the star Sirius (Sothis) and the Moon are widely stated to be either of debatable relevance, or capable of differing solutions, and so do not neatly resolve matters. They confirm the basic range of Egyptian chronology, but not the precise dates (see Appendix 1). The data from Assyria are better, but there is also a gap in the sequence, and a range of potential variation in the second millennium BC dates. Another lesson is that the traditional range of debate is not always a fixed parameter: in another instance of an overtly serious, sensible, scholarly work Gasche *et al.* (1998) propose a new Old Babylonian chronology outside, and independent, of previous arguments and schemes. The outcome therefore of a critical examination is that the 'historical' chronology of Egypt and the Near East for the mid-second millennium BC is 'approximate', and not as fixed or defined as convention holds (and as would be convenient).

There are certainly one or two particular points where an appreciation of what are no more than fixed assumptions based on one interpretation leads to a slightly greater flexibility which might permit some minor, but potentially important, chronological adjustment, although the overall basic chronological range of the Egyptian New Kingdom is not open to dispute. Among other things, radiocarbon and tree-ring dating demonstrate its approximate accuracy.[285] However, the real issue for Aegean and east Mediterranean archaeology is the correlation, or rather interpretation, of the archaeological data with the Egyptian, Babylonian, and Assyrian king-lists – precisely the problematic area discussed above. The controversy examined in this book is almost solely based here. In other words, New Kingdom Egyptian chronology is essentially correct give or take various minor problems (amounting to a few decades at most), but the question of which Aegean stylistic phases link with which parts of this chronology is rather less straightforward.

Rather than burden the text here with a detailed discussion on Egyptian chronology, I refer the reader to Appendix 1 at the end of this work for a critical review of the foundations of Egyptian chronology, and especially of some issues in the dating of the New Kingdom period. Reference below will be made to this discussion. In the meantime, in order for readers to have a basic reference point, I set out in Table 3 the currently standard chronologies of Egypt from von Beckerath and Kitchen for the period relevant to our discussions in Chapter IV.[286] I list the accession dates for each

---

[285] E.g. Hassan and Robinson (1987); Weninger (1990:223–226; 1997:96–101, 168–169, 182); Manning and Weninger (1992); Kuniholm *et al.* (1996).
[286] Dates taken from von Beckerath (1994a; 1997); Kitchen (1996a).

von Beckerath (1994a:118; 1997:188–190)	**Kitchen (1996a:11–12)**
Accession Year	*Accession Year*

Middle Kingdom

Dynasty 11, 2119–1976BC	Dynasty 11, 2116–1795BC
Dynasty 12, 1976–1794/93BC	Dynasty 12, 1973–1795BC

(1987–1795BC for Dynasty 12 in the recent, and exhaustive analysis of Obsomer 1995)

Second Intermediate Period

Dynasty 13, 1794/93–1648/45BC	Dynasty 13, 1795–1638/1627BC

Dynasty 14, Canaanite kings based at Avaris, contemporary with 13th Dynasty. Dynasty ends with conquest of Avaris by 15th Dynasty (after Ryholt 1997). Redford has proposed an alternative model. He argues the 14th Dynasty were non-ruling ancestors of Dynasty 15 (Redford 1992:106–107). Final possibility is another regional delta dynasty parallel with 13th and 15th Dynasties. Very few details known. Debates as to status and role (see e.g. O'Connor 1997:48–52 and refs. for a summary pre-Ryholt study).

? – 1648/45BC	184 years? (Manetho) or unknown number of years: probably parallel to Dynasty 13

Dynasty 15, main Hyksos rulers. There are six known (or accepted) kings: Salitis, Beon, Apachnas, Khyan, Apophis, Khamudy (there is no verification of this number: Redford 1997:34 n.267). There are a few other known names, which might be designated eldest sons, or otherwise require another explanation (Redford 1997:25–26). Dynasty 15 lasts 108 years according to the Turin Canon (the conventional figure), but rather

Table 3. The now current, mainstream, dates for the periods of Egyptian history relevant to this book, with accession dates listed for the pharaohs of the 18th and 19th Dynasties (data from von Beckerath 1994a; 1997; and Kitchen 1996a). Continued overleaf.

pharaoh. In some cases there was a period of co-regency (a subject often under debate by scholars) with the preceding ruler.[287] Points of detail or debate will either be mentioned where relevant in the following chapters, or reference made to the discussion in Appendix 1. The cornerstones of current convention are the claimed 'fixed' dates of 1479BC for the accession of Tuthmosis III and 1279BC for the accession of Ramesses II. If these dates are accepted as 'fixed' (i.e. absolute), then the only real debate in literature published in the 1980s and 1990s is about a 10 year variation in the dates for some of the earlier rulers of the 18th Dynasty (compare von Beckerath versus Kitchen in Table 2) – hence accession of Ahmose either c.1550 or 1540BC. There are also a few minor debates of a 0–5 year range over various other rulers depending on possible co-regencies, missing records, etc.[288] Whether the 1479BC and 1279BC dates are in fact both 'absolute', and whether there are any grounds for possible movements in these dates, are questions discussed in Appendix 1.

---

[287] See esp. Murnane (1977).

[288] See the discussion in von Beckerath (1994a), and the limits of debate for each ruler as listed in his table on pages 118–119.

longer according to Manetho, ending somewhere after Ahmose year (7–)11, and by Ahmose years 18 to 22. Parallel with Dynasties 16–17, and possibly Dynasty 14 if a non-Ryholt or non-Redford model is adopted.

        1648/45–1539/36BC   max dates 1638–1540BC
                                             min dates 1631/27–1523/19BC

Dynasty 16, very unclear. In most studies this Dynasty is identified as comprising minor Hyksos rulers (from Manetho, Africanus version), parallel with Dynasties 13–15. But Ryholt (1997) argues Dynasty 16 was a Theban dynasty, following the 13th Dynasty (after conquest of Thebes by 15th Dynasty), and before the 17th Dynasty. Very few details known. For other views on the constructions of Dynasties 13–17, see e.g. O'Connor (1997:Fig.2.4). There was also an Abydos Dynasty at about this time (Ryholt 1997:163–166, 202–203).

        ? Parallel with 15th Dynasty   ? parallel with 13–15th Dynasties

Dynasty 17, Theban kings following Dynasty 13 or Dynasty 16, but controlling only upper Egypt. Last ruler is Kamose, brother (? or father?) of Ahmose, who re-unifies Egypt and establishes the new 18th Dynasty. In contrast to the nearly century long span allotted by Kitchen and von Beckerath, Ryholt (1997) argues that the 17th Dynasty occupied only c.31 years.

        c.1645–1550BC   1638 or 1631/27 to 1540BC

18th Dynasty

Ahmose,	1550BC	1540BC
Amenhotep I	1525BC	1515BC
Tuthmosis I	1504BC	1494BC
Tuthmosis II	1492BC	1482BC
Tuthmosis III	1479BC	1479BC
(includes Hatshepsut from 1479/77/73BC)		(includes Hatshepsut from 1479BC)
Amenhotep II	1428BC	1427BC
Tuthmosis IV	1402 or 1397BC*	1401BC
Amenhotep III	1392 or 1388BC*	1391BC
Akhenaten‡	1355 or 1351BC*	1353BC
Smenkhkare	1338 or 1337BC*	1338BC (also Nefernefruaten? or
	separate reign for a female? ruler of this name for a few years around	
	here? See Murnane 1995:10; Allen 1994b)	
Tutankhamun	1335 or 1333BC*	1336BC
Ay	1325 or 1323BC*	1327BC
Haremhab	1321 or 1319BC*	1323BC

        ‡ Note: Akhenaten = Amenhotep IV

19th Dynasty

Ramesses I	1294 or 1292BC*	1295BC
Sethos I	1292 or 1290BC*	1294BC
Ramesses II	1279BC	1279BC
Merenptah	1213BC	1213BC
Amenmesses	1203BC	1203BC
Sethos II	1200/1199BC	1200BC
Siptah	1194/1193BC	1194BC
Tewosret	? ends 1186/1185BC	1188BC (ends 1186BC)

* The first date reflects von Beckerath (1994a), the second date is the revised date in von Beckerath (1997).

Table 3. continued.

Chapter IV:
Archaeological and Historical evidence

'Cannon to the right of them, Cannon to the left of them, Cannon in front of them'
(Tennyson, 'The charge of the Light Brigade')

We turn now to the evidence, and in particular the key data, sites, themes, and controversies of recent years. This is of course the core of the present book, and, among other things, the debates of the 1980s–1990s briefly reviewed in Chapter II are examined in detail. I have laid out this discussion in two long chapters: the present one, and Chapter V. First, in this chapter, I wish to explore the archaeological and historical evidence relevant to the date of the Thera eruption, and the associated archaeological phases (the 'conventional' evidence). I begin with the details of the Aegean sequence, and then move to the evidence from especially Egyptian and Cypriot archaeology for datable Aegean linkages, and so chronology, via Egyptian history. Much of the evidence here is well known to the specialist reader, and long discussed; I thus concentrate on key issues, and especially on recent finds, debates, and important new developments. For example, the 'White Slip problem' is explored in some detail, as it is claimed in recent literature to be the strongest argument against the early chronology. In fact, an examination suggests that a contrary conclusion is possible, even likely. Second, in Chapter V, I turn to the various bodies of scientific evidence: radiocarbon, ice-core, and dendrochronology. I explore these data, and, in the case of the ice-core and tree-ring records, consider whether they may in fact be linked (positively) with the Thera eruption. Exciting recent ice-core and tree-ring data suggests that this may now be almost possible. Arguments to the contrary are critically examined. At the same time, I raise the improbability of, and more or less total lack of evidence for, a 16th century BC eruption of Thera (or any very large mid-latitude northern hemisphere volcanic eruption) on the basis of the corpus of available scientific data. This situation appears to run strongly against the low, or conventional, chronology position, and is perhaps the main argument against the otherwise plausible 'compromise early' chronology.

1. Relative date of the Thera eruption in the Aegean and beyond

As reviewed in Chapter II, we can regard the relative chronology of the Minoan eruption of the Thera volcano in Aegean terms as more or less established and agreed: it occurred during the mature–late LMIA period of Crete: see Figure 16 (above p. 20).

No sensible scholar disputes this. The only debate at present is whether the eruption was at the very end of LMIA, at least in eastern Crete,[289] or whether it was in fact a little earlier during 'mature' LMIA. This debate hinges on the finds of Theran tephra at several sites on Crete and elsewhere in the Aegean, and detailed comparisons of LMIA ceramic assemblages at several key sites. It is also partly a relative, and definitional, question: the deposition of Theran tephra in some places, especially where heavier falls led to a significant impact on agriculture, buildings, and people, for example, may more or less mark the close of the local LMIA phase, yet sites elsewhere, and particularly in central or west Crete, and the mainland and islands to the west and north of Thera, may have continued in their local LMIA (or equivalent) phase before the LMIB fashion appeared at a later time.

The refined chronology of the Thera eruption is tied to the recognition of what seem to be two phases of 'seismic' activity/destruction in the southern Aegean, and – an assumption only – the linking of these with the seismic history of pre-eruption Thera. First, a number of archaeologists now link the earthquake immediately before the eruption of Thera, or one associated with the eruption itself (and possible tephra fall impact, tsunamis, etc.), with an apparent horizon of later or late LMIA destructions on Crete.[290] A recently published LMIA kiln at Kommos seems to go out of use at precisely this same time,[291] and may also perhaps be associated with this horizon on Crete. Second, a set of what are variously termed as 'MMIII–LMIA transition', or MMIIIB, or early LMIA destruction deposits on Crete[292] broadly correlate with the early Late Cycladic I earthquake destruction at Akrotiri and similar deposits from Melos and Keos and elsewhere.[293] The upshot of these two episodes is a widespread and fairly precise framework, linking Thera, Crete, and the southern Aegean both in what is variously referred to as MMIIIB, or MMIII–LMIA transition, or early LMIA, and then again in later LMIA.

The question of the precise relative place of the eruption in a hypothetical generic (island wide) Cretan LMIA phase is where we hit a problem. Although today there is widespread agreement that the Thera eruption, and/or these Cretan destructions, are *within* the late LMIA period, and certainly before the start of LMIB, there is active dispute over whether or not the eruption marks the end of the overall island-wide LMIA sequence, or instead occurred earlier. The arguments for the latter position primarily consist of: (a) the absence of a final stage of LHI ceramics at Akrotiri which may be linked to late LMIA elsewhere;[294] (b) the recognition of a mature, but apparently

---

[289] Most recently Soles *et al.* (1995); Bernini (1995); MacGillivray *et al.* (1998:241–242; 260).

[290] E.g. Soles and Davaras (1990); Bernini (1995); Macdonald (1996); Driessen and Macdonald (1997:17, 88, 91 re-Poros).

[291] Shaw *et al.* (1997:326; n.d.).

[292] Warren and Hankey (1989:61–65); Betancourt (1990b:41–48); Warren (1991a); Hood (1996:10); Macdonald (1996:17); MacGillivray *et al.* (1996); Van de Moortel (1997). At Kommos the sequence of transitional MMIII/LMIA or early LMIA, and then late LMIA, employed in Betancourt (1990b) and Watrous (1992), has now been revised as a result of new work since 1991. There are now three phases. Instead of the cumbersome transitional MMIII/LMIA label, the term 'early LMIA' is preferred. There follows 'advanced LMIA' and then 'final LMIA'. See Van de Moortel (1997:25–28); Shaw *et al.* (n.d.).

[293] Marthari (1984); Warren and Hankey (1989:65–67); Dietz (1991:313, 314–315, 321 Fig.93).

[294] Lolos (1990).

not the latest, LMIA seismic destruction horizon on Crete – tentatively linked to the Thera earthquake – and now a new similar deposit from a kiln at Kommos which went out of use at about this very time;[295] (c) a seriation study of the ceramic material from Late Cycladic I Phylakopi on Melos which found that the Theran tephra from the eruption predates a final phase of Late Cycladic I/LMIA,[296] and (d) the very recent announcement of the find of a piece of pumice – presumably Theran – stratified in a non-final LMIA deposit at Knossos.[297]

Overall, this debate is fairly restricted, with a period of only one to several decades at issue. There are two major contributing problems to the lack of a precise date within late LMIA. First, there are the clear regional differences in ceramic sequences within Crete in later LMIA. For example, Knossos had more or less abandoned the MM to MMIIIB/LMIA transition light-on-dark tradition by later (or mature) LMIA, but, in contrast, it continues to occur into late LMIA at Akrotiri, and in 'provincial' Crete at a site like Kommos.[298] This is why a scholar such as Cadogan expressed the view that the ceramics at Akrotiri did not represent the end of the LMIA period.[299] Over twenty years ago Popham (1977:195) highlighted the need for a more rigorous study and definition of the LMIA period, both at Knossos, and across Crete, and, although several recent studies have sought to address the beginning of the period (see above), it remains to be hoped that forthcoming studies will at last start to fill the gap in detailed knowledge for the remainder of the LMIA period.[300]

Second, there is the unavoidable fact that the division between late LMIA and early LMIB at sites with continuity is not clearly defined in stylistic terms, since LMIA *style* materials do continue into LMIB,[301] and, in the absence of decorated vessels in the select Marine Style, Reed Painter, Palace Style, etc., the majority of LMIA and LMIB standard ceramic types are very similar; moreover, the classic LMIB styles known from the close of LMIB destructions on Crete did not appear immediately at the beginning of the phase. Hence determining whether one is late LMIA, or early LMIB, is often not easy. With the addition of the problem that, at present, no stratigraphic sequence on Crete can resolve sub-phases of final late LMIA, the result is an unknown period of time – later LMIA to initial LMIB – over which we have little control.

Further, as noted above, why and how the LMIA period ended at each individual site (or specific excavation context) is relevant. At Phylakopi on Melos, where just a very light tephra fall from the eruption of Thera occurred (see Figure 21), and thus little real effect (i.e. damage), LMIA seems to just carry on.[302] But sites in the eastern

---

[295] Shaw *et al.* (1997; n.d.).
[296] Davis and Cherry (1984; 1990:195).
[297] Blackman (1997–1998:115); Peter Warren (pers. comm.).
[298] Shaw *et al.* (1997; n.d.).
[299] Cadogan (1987; 1988:99).
[300] The PhD dissertation of Van de Moortel (1997) is a key step in filling this need. The recent (1990s) work at Kommos (of which Van de Moortel is part), when published, promises to become the new baseline for understanding LMI ceramic history (along with ongoing work at other sites). See Shaw *et al.* (1997:325 and n. 10; n.d.).
[301] Niemeier (1980); Betancourt (1985:124, 133); Driessen and Macdonald (1997:15–16, 17–22).
[302] Davis and Cherry (1984); Driessen and Macdonald (1997:252–254).

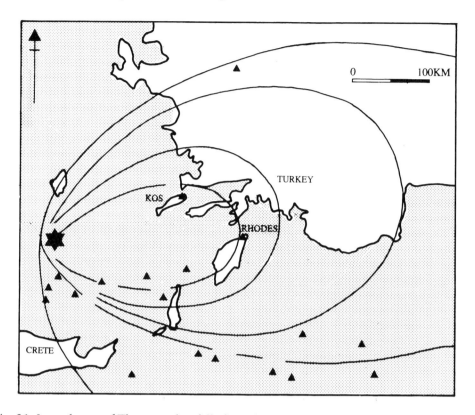

Fig. 21. Isopach map of Theran tephra falls from the Minoan eruption (primarily eastwards) after Pyle (1990a:Fig.1). Triangles mark locations where data on tephra deposit depth has been acquired. Tephra depth in cm. The data for the area of Crete are shown after Watkins et al. (1978).

Aegean, where heavy tephra falls occurred,[303] and perhaps also sites in north-east and eastern Crete, which were the only areas of Crete to receive potentially relevant tephra falls of 1–5cm (Figure 21),[304] and/or sites on the north coast of Crete, which may have felt the effects of a tsunami resulting from the eruption,[305] may have been seriously or noticeably affected by the eruption. A clear archaeological Thera eruption horizon is certainly evident in the east Aegean where significant tephra falls occurred.[306] At Tri016anda on Rhodes, for example, where there was a heavy tephra fall,

---

[303] E.g. 10–30+cm, the amount which will collapse roofs: see Blong (1980:221).

[304] Driessen and Macdonald (1997:93 and Fig.5.2).

[305] Kastens and Cita (1981); Cita and Rimoldi (1997); Bicknell (1996/1997; 1995); Johnstone (1997); Driessen and Macdonald (1997:89–90, 91 re-Poros); McCoy and Heiken (n.d.). The study of Dominey-Howes (1996), which considered the evidence for tsunami in the Aegean from the second millennium BC onwards, in fact found little good or clear evidence for a Minoan period tsunami linked with the eruption of Thera. However, a definitive and comprehensive study is yet to occur.

[306] E.g. Marketou (1990); Sullivan (1993).

there is a clear division of LMIA (before) and LMIB (after) a tephra horizon.[307] Real tephra-fall damage to buildings, and so on, probably occurred in this area. At the site of Mochlos on the north-east coast of Crete,[308] which, if anywhere in Crete, may have felt the effect of both a moderate tephra fall and perhaps a tsunami, the eruption of Thera may also effectively mark, and end, the main defined LMIA horizon. Consequent rebuilding and occupation occurred either in a combined (and irreducable) late LMIA–earlier LMIB phase, or even early LMIB phase after a brief interruption or hiatus (since finds of Theran ash to date at Mochlos are directly covered by LMIB deposits with no intervening LMIA occupation: see below). Again, at Palaikastro in east Crete, a reasonably significant tephra fall in effect seems to mark the end of the LMIA phase.[309] Although the picture at Palaikastro is complicated because the current evidence comes from an MMIIIB–earlier LMIA building (Building 6) which seems to have been abandoned (after a possible seismic destruction – possibly related to the mature LMIA Theran seismic destruction) and partly dismantled before the Theran tephra fall; hence this context inherently cannot offer good late LMIA resolution. Meanwhile, at Pseira in east Crete, the evidence is less clear.[310] Theran ash and water-borne pumice lumps are found in association with LMIA debris in a rubble/make-up level for a subsequent post-eruption floor (early LMIB, or late LMIA–early LMIB), and Theran ash is found elsewhere at the site, but no definite horizon is evident.[311]

However, in contrast to these examples, other sites in central, southern, and west Crete, and in the Aegean north and west of Thera, exhibit a far less clear picture, with little or no Theran tephra, and no general Thera eruption horizon. In these instances, we are considering traces, and not a distinct stratigraphic event. It would therefore appear appropriate to conclude that local site/context history, and especially the direct effects, or non-effects, of the Theran tephra fall (and other agents) are responsible for varying patterns in the late LMIA period across the southern Aegean region. Sites which experienced significant trauma, and where the tephra fall effectively ends the local LMIA phase, do not establish a wider chronological division applicable elsewhere.

I therefore believe that the cases of Soles *et al.* (1995) and Bernini (1995), and their claim that the eruption of Thera may be placed at the very end of the LMIA period (see below), is applicable at most to their own sites/contexts, and not to the pan-Cretan/southern Aegean region and phase. However, as this is an important matter, let us briefly consider the specific arguments of Soles *et al.* (1995) and Bernini (1995). Soles *et al.* (1995) argue that the eruption of Thera was right at the close of the LMIA period, and that there was no post-eruption-LMIA phase on Crete. Bernini argues that the evidence from Palaikastro is consonant with this hypothesis, and places the eruption of Thera 'near the end of the LMIA period'.[312] However, their respective arguments

---

[307] Doumas and Papazoglou (1980); Doumas (1988); Marketou (1988; 1990; 1996); Driessen and Macdonald (1997:248–251).

[308] See Driessen and Macdonald (1997:241–244) for a general review of the LMI site and for further refs.

[309] MacGillivray *et al.* (1998:241–242, 260).

[310] Driessen and Macdonald (1997:244–247).

[311] Betancourt and Davaras (1986:191–195; 1988:217–218); Betancourt *et al.* (1990).

[312] Bernini (1995:62–64, 67). Quote from p.67.

appear flawed (on current evidence). Soles *et al.* describe five deposits of Minoan tephra from Mochlos (A–E).[313] In the cases of deposits A–C, it is unclear why they do not in fact relate to use (as levelling, packing material) in an LMIB building (despite Soles *et al.* pp.390–391, where they attempt to rebut this possibility by referring to deposits D and E – which in fact seem to contradict their case: see below). And, of course, the ceramics from the last floor deposit do not necessarily date the construction of the platform and packing of the building (without much more evidence and details). However, the critical deposits are D, and especially E. Deposit E is cut into by an LMIB building (Building A). Therefore, Deposit E was already there for at least some time, and was stratified and part of the natural stratigraphy, by LMIB. The absence of pre-LMIB occupation is irrelevant; the tephra fell on the landscape, and became part of the stratigraphy. A subsequent (LMIB) building operation cut into it. From the descriptions provided regarding deposit E (and D seems to be fairly similar), the only chronology evident is that the tephra was already stratified before an LMIB building (and its foundations and walls) cut into it (the only other possibility seems to be that the tephra was put into the foundation trench). Thus the gap between tephra fall and LMIB building is completely unknown. The tephra fall could be mature LMIA (with subsequent latest LMIA following), or it could be later, but we cannot tell. Soles and Davaras describe another tephra deposit at Mochlos inside a yard near a wall to the rear of Building A.[314] It is an odd linear rectangle of a deposit, and Soles and Davaras note the artificial nature (taphonomy) of its preservation: '...it lay at ground level and is either another airbourne deposit, which was covered by earth and so preserved when the southern additions to the building were constructed and their lower floor levels excavated, or part of a deposit that was placed against the south wall of the building, shielded by the screen wall to the south, and saved to be put to some later use'. Soles (1997:427) subsequently speculates that this tephra may in fact have been stored for use as an abrasive – in which case it is irrelevant to the date of the initial tephra fall.

The study by Bernini (1995) argues that Theran tephra at Palaikastro occurs with LMIA material associated with an apparent earthquake (which she and others associate with the seismic destruction on Thera – it should of course be remembered that this is just an unproven hypothesis). The ceramics associated with the tephra are MMIIIB and LMIA, and, given the presence of the latter (and motifs such as the classic medallion spiral and foliate band), an LMIA date may be assigned (pp.62–63). She then attempts to date this earthquake-tephra episode within LMIA in relative terms by arguing that 'the pottery from the drain outside the east façade of building 3 ... is associated with the remodelling which followed this earthquake and contains some pieces whose shapes are nearing those characteristic of LMIB. Thus, the evidence at Palaikastro seems to support a late LMIA date for the Theran eruption and resulting earthquakes on Crete' (p.64). The problem in the logic is that we have no idea *when* after the earthquake the ceramics in the drain got there. The LMIA ceramics associated with the tephra are, at the latest, mature LMIA, and we still do not know what happened between this time and the start of the production of vessels nearing those characteristic of LMIB. We can

---

[313] See Soles *et al.* (1995:386–387).
[314] Soles and Davaras (1996:202–203, pl.58.c).

agree the eruption was late LMIA. The latest stylistic material from Akrotiri buried by the eruption informs us of this; as Betancourt (1985:133) concludes: 'the pottery must lie very late in LMIA, at the eve of the introduction of LMIB'. But neither Bernini, nor Soles *et al.*, throw light on whether or not there was a post-Thera-eruption final LMIA phase. And, as argued above, even if the tephra fall did in effect mark the end of local LMIA at these sites, such findings do not rule out post-Thera-eruption final LMIA phases at other sites. Since other studies suggest a mature (but not latest) LMIA tephra fall from more appropriate and specific evidence (see above), the correct working hypothesis at this time must be to regard the eruption as mature–late LMIA, and to allow for some possible (un-defined) post-eruption-LMIA phase. Nothing at present provides a clear case against the hypothesis of a post-eruption-LMIA phase, although, as Davis and Cherry (1990:193–195) highlight, the reverse also applies, and a clear post-eruption-LMIA phase has not been recognised at any Aegean site to date.[315] This very lack of clarity undoubtedly informs us that such a post-eruption-LMIA phase – if present – must have been relatively brief. It also suggests that this was a troubled time.[316] We might envisage a possible period of one to a few decades, but *not* a lengthy time interval.

To conclude. For the purposes of our discussion, I accept a relative date for the eruption of Thera in mature–late LMIA, and allow for the possibility of a short post-eruption phase of LMIA.[317]

One of the main reasons for exploring this subject is that mature LMIA and the eruption of Thera may be linked to a number of other cultures and regions. Beyond Thera and the Aegean, there is a veritable web of interrelations between the various cultures of the Aegean and the east Mediterranean – through artefact and stylistic transfers – which allows the mature LMIA period (and the contemporary LHI and Late Cycladic I periods) to be roughly placed in a number of other important regional sequences. Thus LMIA products and style, and contemporary LH products, may be clearly related to the LCI period in Cyprus, and also to the Hyksos and/or early 18th Dynasty period in Egypt.[318] Until now, this web of interrelations has been used to date the LMIA period; but, in reverse, if the eruption of Thera could be accurately and precisely dated, then this web of interrelations could be dated accordingly. Thera offers a chronological linch-pin.[319] Moreover, since Thera and LMIA, via LHI, also

---

[315] If the pumice reported from a non-final LMIA deposit, stratified beneath another small LMIA deposit, at Knossos (Blackman 1997–1998:115; Peter Warren pers. comm.) is verified as Thera Minoan eruption pumice, then this subsequent final LMIA deposit would offer an example from Crete of the very post-eruption-LMIA-phase in question. The Kommos evidence now seems to start to fill this absence also, with Akrotiri VDL equivalent material in the Advanced to initial Final LMIA phases, and the rest of the Final LMIA phase thereafter (Shaw *et al.* n.d.).

[316] As argued in considerable detail by Driessen and Macdonald (1997).

[317] That is a phase after the eruption, and before the development of the distinctive new stylistic elements which define the LMIB period.

[318] For the linkages, and references to literature, see Manning (1995:121–122, 198–199 end-note, 214 n.37; 1988b); Niemeier (1980:7–72; 1986; 1991; 1995a; 1995b); Bietak (1989a; 1995b; 1996a:70–78); Maguire (1995); Warren (1979: 88–90, 106–107 and n.2; 1998); Warren and Hankey (1989:116, 135–140); Catling (1991); Graziadio (1995); Cadogan *et al.* (n.d.); and Eriksson (1992 – who offers a detailed summary of the data, but from a starkly different viewpoint).

[319] Renfrew in his closing address to the Third Thera conference of 1989 (Hardy and Renfrew 1990:242)

have linkages to the west (Italy),[320] and to the north (Balkans/central Europe), the eruption of Thera offers in addition a date relevant for much of the Mediterranean and Europe.[321] Here is one area where scholars have quickly noted: that 'the updating of the Thera eruption to the 17th century ... would be welcome to those who would like to reconcile the C14 and traditional chronologies';[322] or, that the new early Aegean chronology 'corresponds well to the central and west European chronologies'.[323]

It is therefore important to explore in some detail the relative chronology, and relations, between the Aegean periods before, contemporary with, and following, the eruption of Thera, and the cultures and histories of the east Mediterranean and the Near East. The stratigraphic sequence on Crete runs: MMIII, LMIA (Thera eruption mature–late LMIA), LMIB, LMII, LMIIIA1. I therefore examine the evidence for linkages between these periods and the east Mediterranean and particularly Egypt, and the archaeological, art-historical, and textual evidence from Egypt argued to be relevant to the dating of parts or moments within this Aegean relative sequence. Where possible, I examine these various data in sequential terms, from MMIII times through to LMIIIA1. These various data offer both one approach to the dating of the eruption and earlier Aegean chronology, and also the framework by which an absolute date for the eruption of Thera may be applied to the chronologies of the east Mediterranean.

2. Dating Middle Minoan III in archaeological terms

The ceramic period before LMIA on Crete is MMIII. Thus the relative linkages of MMIII with the east Mediterranean should establish an upper limit (*terminus post quem*) for the subsequent LMIA period. Unfortunately, there is little, if any, useful evidence.

MM (Old Palace) Crete had relations with Egypt and the Levant during what is termed the MMII period (or MMIB–II depending on terminology). Some Egyptian scarabs are found in Crete, and MMII 'Kamares' pottery has been found at several Egyptian and Levantine sites, and, along with some other stylistic linkages, there is thus an approximate correspondence between the MMII period and the 12th–13th Dynasties of Egypt.[324] Unfortunately, none of the existing contexts in Egypt are particularly precise, and the dating of both the scarabs, and/or the find contexts, in Crete are equally problematic. In total, there are very few even approximately fixed (or closely defined) correlations for the MM period and a range of interpretations are

---

predicted (over-confidently) 'that by the fifth conference, it will no longer be a matter of using the Egyptian chronology to date the Thera eruption and to date the Aegean: it will be a case of using the Thera eruption, with its precise date, to give a sheet anchor ... for the Egyptian chronology'.

[320] Vagnetti (1993); Marazzi and Re (1986); Dietz (1991:301); Vanzetti (1998).

[321] Recent studies which highlight the relevance of the dating of the Thera eruption and the Aegean LB1 period to Europe include: Becker *et al.* (1989:441–442); Randsborg (1991); Bouzek (1994:217; 1996:178); Kristiansen (1998:31–34, Fig.13); Vanzetti (1998).

[322] Bouzek (1996:178).

[323] Kristiansen (1998:34).

[324] Warren (1980); Cadogan (1983a); Kemp and Merrillees (1980); Warren and Hankey (1989:131–135); Manning (1995:107–120); MacGillivray (1998:102–106); Betancourt (1998a).

accordingly possible.[325] Thus no precision is possible, merely the approximate correlation of some period within the 20th–18th centuries BC (dates for the 12th–13th Dynasties) with the span of MMII (or MMIB–II) on Crete. With regard to the eruption of Thera, our interest centres on the close of the MM period, and so the chronology of the MMIII period.

The MMIII period, which immediately precedes LMIA, has never been securely dated. It was a problem for Evans at the beginning of the century, and it remains as problematic – in terms of a clear MMIII–LMIA sequence in the Aegean – and ill-dated as it ever was. There are almost no solid correlations outside the Aegean, and indeed very few known exports at all.[326] A post-Kamares, MMIII, sherd has been recently found at Tell el-Dab^ca, but sadly it comes from a 19th Dynasty tree-pit and is thus unstratified and not relevant to its original 13th or 14th Dynasty importation and deposition.[327] MMIII evidence therefore offers no useful *terminus post quem* for the LMIA period. We may merely conjecture a 13th/14th Dynasty date.[328] The few potentially relevant later MM imports elsewhere in the Near East are invariably single items whose date of deposit need not be even closely contemporary with their respective date of production in the Aegean, and these 'dates' are themselves invariably debated constructs with significant possible variation. In the conventional chronology of Crete, the sequence ought to be MMIIIA, MMIIIB, LMIA. The distinction between MMIIIA and B is not however clear (or real) in many cases, and so the collective term MMIII is probably to be preferred.[329] Warren identified a subsequent late MMIII–early LMIA 'transition' horizon;[330] as noted earlier, this late MMIII–early LMIA 'transition' may be related to a similar horizon in the Cyclades, and especially the very early LBA (early Late Cycladic I, early LMIA) earthquake destruction at Akrotiri on Thera.[331]

As noted, no useful data exists at present for the dating of the close of the MMIII period in terms of Egypt and the Near East. However, some relatively new data exists of relevance to the opening (or earliest possible) date of MMIII, namely finds of preceding MMIIB vessels in Egypt. MacGillivray in particular provides an MMIIB (north-central Crete) Wavy-line Style attribution for a Kamares cup from Tell el-Dab^ca

---

[325] Regarding both how to characterise the material, and the dates to apply. For higher to lower or sceptical dates, see Warren (1980) versus Åström (1978; 1984), versus Walberg (1983:138–149; 1984; 1987). For different characterisation of the material, see Walberg (1976; 1983).

[326] Betancourt (1998a:6 and n.14) suggests that some sherds from MBA Hazor are probably MMIII (Yadin *et al.* 1960:91, pl.115 nos.12–13), but there are few other certain examples from the region.

[327] Bietak (1995:19; 1996a:29); Walberg (1992:159).

[328] The relationship between these dynasties in chronological terms is not entirely clear (see Appendix 1). For one recent view, see Ryholt (1997).

[329] E.g. Betancourt (1985:103–114).

[330] Warren (1991a); Hankey and Warren (1989:61–67). As noted above, this is in fact best regarded as early LMIA (Van de Moortel 1997; Shaw *et al.* n.d.). Hood (1996) discusses this same MMIIIB–early LMIA horizon, and argues that it is effectively what Evans termed MMIIIB – nonetheless, Hood agrees that, whether it be called MMIIIB, or early LMIA, or MMIIIB–LMIA transition as Warren and Hankey (1989), this horizon is contemporary with the penultimate, early Late Cycladic I, destruction at Akrotiri.

[331] For this horizon, see Marthari (1984); for the correlation of this with the late MMIII–early LMIA horizon, see Warren and Hankey (1989:67); Warren (1991a). This horizon is often referred to as the 'seismic' destruction at Thera.

stratum d/1=G/4.[332] Bietak (e.g. 1991a) correlates G/4 with the early 13th Dynasty of Egypt, and the early 18th century BC. Another MMIIB vessel comes from a likely mid–12th Dynasty context (to early 13th Dynasty),[333] and the Royal Road scarab from a debated MMIIB, or top of MMIIA, context at Knossos likewise is usually assigned a later 12th–earlier 13th Dynasty date.[334] Thus we might suggest that the MMIII period dates from after the earlier 13th Dynasty (after maybe c.1750BC, give or take a few decades, from the discussion in Appendix 1). A very recent find of a (MMIIB–) 'MMIIIA' pitcher in a Troy V period grave at Troy[335] provides another near contemporary export from the second half of the 18th century BC. The radiocarbon dating of the associated skeletal remains, and, in general, the comprehensive and refined science-dating programme of the entire Troy sequence under Korfmann,[336] may, in due course, offer useful absolute dating information for early MMIII.

The extent, and close, of the MM period is then left as most unsatisfactorily defined. A jug found at El-Lisht in Egypt has been the subject of a number of discussions over many years. The decoration includes some dolphins.[337] It has long been thought by some Aegean scholars that these dolphins reflected Minoan influence – a view rather ignoring the other motifs on the vessel.[338] The problem is that no precise stylistic date can be attached to the dolphins. They have been claimed as potential MMIIIA, or MMIIIB (–LMIA), imitations in recent years, and they remain debatable in every way.[339] The recent paper of Hankey and Leonard (1998:30–31) now dismisses any Minoan association at all,[340] and this appears the appropriate position. However, what they might have further noted is that this decision removes half the basis for the dating of the MMIII period in the basic conventional chronology study of Warren and Hankey (1989:135–137).

A study and publication specifically on the Lisht vase by Bourriau (1996) finds, in line with a Neutron Activation Analysis (NAA) study by McGovern *et al.* (1994), that the vessel is a Syrian/Palestinian product, and, although it is a unique piece, that it fits with a handful of comparanda into the ceramic traditions of Syria/Palestine.[341] The

---

[332] MacGillivray (1995; 1998:105). Walberg (1998) argues that MacGillivray is overly specific, and she regards the cup as datable merely to her Classical Kamares, or MMIIA–MMIIB (and some MMIIIA), category. Both agree it was a palatial product, from either Knossos or Phaistos.

[333] A bridge-spouted jar from Abydos: MacGillivray (1995:82; 1998:105); Warren and Hankey (1989:134); Kemp and Merrillees (1980:105–175, fig.38, pl.13).

[334] Manning (1995:119 and ns.169–172); Warren and Hankey (1989:134).

[335] Korfmann (1997:33–37 and 69–70 n.11, Abbs.29–32).

[336] E.g. Korfmann and Kromer (1993); see also Weninger (1995); Manning (1997).

[337] Kemp and Merrillees (1980:220–225, pls.29–30).

[338] As observed by Weinstein (1982). Near Eastern scholarship rather saw the vessel as related to Tell el-Yahudiyeh ware (Negbi 1978:145 n.23).

[339] Not least concerning whether the influence might not have been the other way around from a wider naturalistic Syrian–Palestinian–Hyksos tradition. For discussion and references with regard to this vase, see Manning (1995:25–26 postscript 9, 121–122, 217–219; 1988b:25–32); Warren and Hankey (1989:135–137); Warren (1995:3); Laffineur (1998:56); Åström (1998:257).

[340] Correcting Warren and Hankey (1989:135–136), and many previous publications by a number of authors.

[341] See also Bourriau (1997:165–166).

shaft tomb in which the vessel was found is not a closed context, but a deposition context during the early 13th Dynasty is likely (consistent with a potential MMIII stylistic link). The dolphin vase, from what is a rich high-status burial, thus belongs to the class of Syrian/Palestinian imports into Egypt which suddenly increase at this time.

The Khyan lid, an alabaster lid with the cartouche of the Hyksos king Seweserenre Khyan, was a further linch-pin of conventional chronology (and, with the El-Lisht jug, was the other half of the dataset employed by Warren and Hankey in their 1989 book[342]). The lid was found at the beginning of this century by Evans at Knossos, and the find context was dated by him to MMIII(A).[343] Thus it was held that LMIA must definitely post-date this Hyksos ruler, and so a ceiling of about 1600BC was stated.[344] But the find context was always unsatisfactory, as highlighted by Palmer,[345] and other scholars. It was found in an unstratified fill beneath an LMIII floor. This may not disprove Evans' dating,[346] but, in reverse, there is nothing concrete to support Evans' assertion. By the later 1980s several scholars thus stated that the Khyan lid should no longer be used to date MMIII,[347] and it seems finally to have passed away as a solid piece of evidence in most recent literature.[348] Contra Evans, the lid's entry into the stratigraphy at Knossos may probably at best be dated to LMI(A).[349] In consequence, the entire basis to the supposed dating of the MMIII period in the study of Warren and Hankey (1989) is revealed as non-existent.

There are a very few other extra-Aegean correlations, but none is particularly helpful. Perhaps the most important is a White Painted (WP) IV ware Cross Line style jug from (eastern–southern) Cyprus which was found with MMIII ceramics, and one transitional MMIII/LMIA piece, at Kommos.[350] This roughly allows us to correlate later MC with MMIII (even late MMIII). In turn, finds of similar Cypriot material in the Near East[351] offer links with the Syro-Palestinian later MBII (or MBIIB–MBIIC, or MBIIB–III) period. This is consistent with dates either in the 17th or earlier 16th centuries BC, but provides no precision. And, MC relative and absolute chronology is itself less than rigorous or secure.[352]

The conclusion is that archaeological synchronisms neither date the MMIII period, nor establish any clear upper ceiling date for the start of the LMIA period.

---

[342] See Warren and Hankey (1989:135–137).
[343] Evans (1900–1901:63–67, fig.20; 1921–1935, vol.I:418–421, fig.303).
[344] Warren (1984; 1985; 1987:206–207); Cadogan (1983a:517).
[345] Palmer (1964; 1981; 1984:74–80).
[346] Hood (1964); Warren (1990/1991:fig.5).
[347] E.g. Walberg (1987:71–72); Betancourt (1987:46).
[348] *Pace* Warren (1995:3); Warren and Hankey (1989:136).
[349] See Niemeier (1994:73 and n.21, 83–84; and 1995a:15 n.65), referring especially to Pomerance's (1984) dating of the associated stone ewers. For additional discussion and references, see Manning (1995:204 and n.17; 1988b:31); Phillips (1991:530–532); Betancourt (1987:46; 1997:429); Warren and Hankey (1989:136).
[350] Betancourt (1990b:192).
[351] Especially Tell el-Dabʿa strata E/1–D/3: Maguire (1995).
[352] Maguire (1992). Previously, contrast 'high' Merrillees (1977), 'middle' Saltz (1977), and 'low' Åström (1972b).

3. Tell el-Dab^ca, its frescoes, and early LBA Aegean chronology?

The first phase of what are termed palaces on Crete is termed the Old Palace period;
the floruit of Old Palace Crete corresponds with the MMII period. After seismic and
other events (and a rather murky MMIII period), a new set of palaces are constructed
at several sites in the MMIIIB–LMIA period. The era they demarcate is referred to as
the New Palace (or neopalatial) period. One of the notable features of the New Palace
period is the appearance of figural art in the form of wall paintings (frescoes) at most
major sites. Similar art forms occur elsewhere in the Aegean from this same MMIII–
LMIA transition phase (and onwards), with the incredible frescoes preserved beneath
the pumice at Akrotiri being the most complete and best known examples. These
New Palace wall paintings are one of the defining bodies of evidence of the early
LBA in the Aegean.[353] They have long been the subject of intense study, and
interrelations and distinguishing features between the paintings on Crete and the
various Cycladic islands (Phylakopi on Melos, Ayia Irini on Keos, and Akrotiri on
Thera), and the earliest paintings on the mainland (Mycenae), are well established.[354]
It had been suggested in the past that some links or parallels existed for these Aegean
paintings with paintings on plaster at Alalakh and Mari respectively in the Turkish
Hatay and Syria,[355] but general scholarship up to 1989 held that there was no useful
chronological linkage. Immerwahr (1990:35) is typical in writing of the Alalakh
examples that 'the paintings are very fragmentary and not really susceptible to stylistic
comparisons with the Minoan'. Thus, until the end of the 1980s, no clear stylistic links
existed between these Aegean wall paintings and any other closely dated art from
the Near East or Egypt.[356]

Then Niemeier (1990) announced the discovery at Tel Kabri in Israel of fresco
fragments with decorations which were very similar to those known from the LB1
Aegean.[357] The material includes both a couple of thousand fragments of wall
paintings, and parts of a painted plaster floor. Tel Kabri was a large (32ha) city on a
main coastal trade route. The paintings belong to the final major phase of the site – in
the later MBII period – before a destruction and general abandonment (and partial
short 'squatter' phase). The floor was *in situ*, but the wall painting fragments were
found as redeposited rubbish (deposited in the squatter phase, and thus the paintings
must be later MBII in original date). A link to the Syrian–Palestinian chronologies
thus became possible, and we draw tantalisingly close to Egypt and the heart of second
millennium BC historical chronology. And, just two years later, Bietak (1992b) stunned
the archaeological world with news of the finds of quantities of fresco fragments with
decorations very similar to Aegean examples from the site of Tell el-Dab^ca in Egypt.
Aegean scholars have reacted with barely concealed hysteria. These finds appear to

---

[353] E.g. Immerwahr (1990); Morgan (1988); Doumas (1992). For a brief summary of the palace period on
Crete, see Cadogan (1991).
[354] Cameron (1978); Davis (1990b); Morgan (1990); Shaw (1996); Chapin (1997:10–11).
[355] See Smith (1965:98–104).
[356] For a review of the earlier history of the topic, see Niemeier and Niemeier (1998:69–71).
[357] See further in Niemeier (1995a); Niemeier and Niemeier (1998:71–78).

offer the prospect of a good link between the start of the LBA in the Aegean and the historical world of ancient Egypt and the Near East. Let us examine this evidence, and consider what it tells us.

The enormous (250ha) site of Tell el-Dabᶜa, the Hyksos (15th Dynasty) capital of Avaris in the Nile Delta of Egypt, now plays a very prominent part in the archaeology of the Aegean and the east Mediterranean thanks to the extraordinary finds made during several decades of excavation campaigns directed by the Austrian Egyptologist, Professor Manfred Bietak.[358] The site was the centre and capital of the Canaanite 14th and 15th (Hyksos) Dynasties which controlled the Delta and northern Egypt during the SIP, c.1800–1550BC. The 15th, or Hyksos, Dynasty ended when the southern Theban king Ahmose invaded northern Egypt and conquered Avaris. Ahmose thus reunited Egypt and ruled a unified Egyptian state for the first time since the 12th Dynasty in the 19th century BC. In consequence, Ahmose became the founder both of what is referred to as the Egyptian New Kingdom, and also what is referred to as the 18th Dynasty.

Tell el-Dabᶜa, and finds made there, feature prominently in the discussions in this book. It has become one of the key sites for the archaeology and history of the entire eastern Mediterranean region in the second millennium BC, due in no small part to the numerous excellent and prompt publications produced by Bietak and his team. As noted above, one class of find deserves a separate initial discussion at this point: the spectacular discoveries of fragments of frescoes similar to Aegean New Palace (MMIIIB/LMIA–LMIB) frescoes in three areas at the ᶜEzbet Helmi area of the site (1. H/I and H/IV, 2. H/II, and 3. H/III): see Figure 22.[359] This material has become a major *cause célèbre* of Aegean, Levantine and Egyptian archaeology in recent years.[360] We must consider these Aegean-style frescoes, since they offer key evidence for linkages between the Aegean and Egyptian–Levantine worlds. I leave the detailed art-historical analysis, questions of reception and influence, and compositional reconstructions, to those now working on them, and others expert in these areas;[361] likewise, the question of how these 'Aegean'-style frescoes came to be painted at Tell el-Dabᶜa in Egypt. Apart from theories of Minoan princesses and dynastic marriages and/or other direct contact or supposed alliances,[362] one may note the general patterns of kingly rivalry and emulation in the field of élite ideology in the second millennium BC ancient Near East,[363] especially as constituted in palatial art and decoration,[364] which, along with

---

[358] In general, see Bietak (1996a).

[359] Bietak and Marinatos (1995); Jánosi (1995); Bietak (1995a; 1996a:72–79).

[360] E.g. Negbi (1994); Manning *et al.* (1994a); Sherratt (1994); Bietak (1995a; 1996a:72–79); Morgan (1995); Shaw (1995); Rehak (1997); Cline (1998a); Niemeier and Niemeier (1998); Knapp (1998); Laffineur (1998:56–60); Marinatos (1998). Cline (1998a:202) describes the scholarly output on the subject as 'positively astounding'.

[361] E.g. Bietak and Marinatos (1995); Shaw (1995); Bietak (1995a); Morgan (1995); Niemeier and Niemeier (1998); Hiller (1996); Marinatos (1998); etc.

[362] Originally Bietak (1992b:28; 1995a:26 and 28 n.51); for revised early 18th Dynasty 'scenario', see Bietak (1997:124; 1996b:esp.24) – cf. Niemeier and Niemeier (1998:87–88).

[363] Liverani (1990); Baines (1996).

[364] E.g. Kuhrt (1995:102).

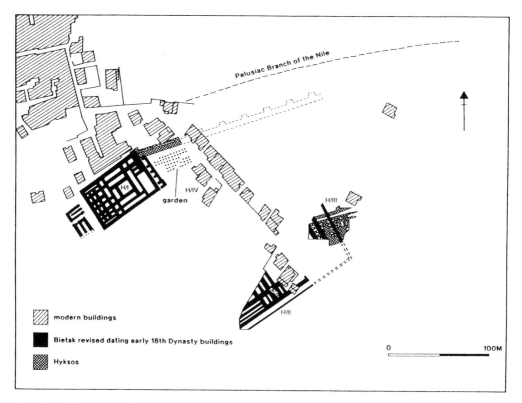

Fig. 22. Schematic plan of the citadel area of the late Hyksos period at ʿEzbet Helmi/Tell el-Dabʿa (after Bietak 1996a:fig.55).

travelling or exchanged craftsman/artists,[365] offer a suitable milieu for an explanation.[366] Instead, the main salient points for our purposes are the date of frescoes, both in terms of the sequence at Tell el-Dabʿa, and in terms of the Aegean comparisons.

STRATIGRAPHIC–CHRONOLOGICAL DATE OF
THE AEGEAN-STYLE FRESCOES AT TELL EL-DABʿA?

The discovery of these wall paintings was first announced in print in 1992,[367] and even in the short space of time between then and now the stratigraphic and historical date of these paintings at Tell el-Dabʿa has become a heated subject of debate thanks to a dramatic and somewhat confusing change of interpretation by the excavator,

---

[365] Zaccagnini (1983).
[366] Niemeier (1991; 1995a:10–11); Niemeier and Niemeier (1998:88–96); Laffineur (1998:60 and n.83); cf. Knapp (1998).
[367] Bietak (1992b).

Manfred Bietak, between publications appearing up to 1995, and those since. Not without reason, Cline (1998a) has written a study subtitled 'Tell el-Dabᶜa and the Aegean world – a guide for the perplexed'. Originally, the H/I and H/IV fragments found as rubbish in a garden area near a massive foundation platform (from the locus of the late Hyksos citadel) some 70.5m x 47m in size, were thought to be of Hyksos period origin, and were linked to the Hyksos palace.[368] The situation thus appeared to have some similarities of context and date with the Tel Kabri finds from a later MBII original context. In the initial publication Bietak specifically dated the platform to the late Hyksos period (1992b:26), and with regard to the fresco fragments concluded that:

> It is at present uncertain whether these painted plaster fragments originated from the structure on the foundation platform or from other buildings in the vicinity. They were scattered throughout the area of Ezbet Helmi, and many fragments were also transported by building activity into higher layers of the early Eighteenth Dynasty. *Nevertheless, it seems clear that their origin lay in the Late Hyksos period* [my italics].[369]

Complications were first really hinted at in a publication three years later.[370] Here some of the paintings were still attributed to the late Hyksos palace and period, but it was suggested both that some of the destruction (of earlier buildings) creating fragments was early 18th Dynasty, and that some of the buildings and paintings were in fact early 18th Dynasty. And now, from publications appearing in 1996 and since, Bietak argues that the H/I platform was built at the very beginning of the 18th Dynasty,[371] and that the H/I and H/IV fresco fragments belong with it.[372] He also dates the other Aegean-style fresco finds at H/II and H/III to this period. In the most recent site plan, Bietak (1996a:Fig.55) argues that he can isolate a set of early 18th Dynasty palatial structures on one orientation, above some previous Hyksos fortification walls and major structures on a different alignment (see Figure 22).

In order to be able to assess the validity of Bietak's dating of the frescoes, and in order to consider the relevant associations for the fresco fragments, it is necessary first to engage in a critical review of the stratigraphic sequence at the late Hyksos to early 18th Dynasty citadel compound at the ᶜEzbet Helmi area of Tell el-Dabᶜa.[373] I

---

[368] Bietak (1992b); Bietak *et al.* (1994); Jánosi (1995).

[369] Bietak (1992b:27).

[370] Bietak (1995a:20–23, 28n.47).

[371] Bietak (1996a:68–70; 1996b; 1997).

[372] Bietak (1996a:70, 73–76; 1996b).

[373] From Jánosi (1994; 1995); Bietak (1991b:289–315; 1996a; 1996b; 1997); Bietak *et al.* (1994); Hein (1998). Although lumped together, and although I use the generic term of Tell el-Dabᶜa to refer to the whole greater site as if one entity, I note that the two sequences of Tell el-Dabᶜa and ᶜEzbet Helmi are in fact quite separate (by about 1km). The correlation of stratum V at ᶜEzbet Helmi with stratum D/2 at Tell el-Dabᶜa, is only approximate. They are generally, but not necessarily exactly, synchronous. Quite a lot of Bietak's chronological case with regard to Cyprus and Thera rests on the assumption of approximate synchronicity.

review below the current sequence as published by Bietak and his team, and append some critical comments.[374] For the schematic stratigraphic sequence at the entire site, see Figure 23.

ᶜEZBET HELMI SEQUENCE

0. Hyksos phase

Late Hyksos citadel (of 5ha) enclosed within enormous fortifications. A huge Hyksos building at H/III seems to run under much of the central citadel; debris from the destruction of this structure might be expected all over the citadel area. This phase ends with widespread abandonment at the close of the D/2 phase. This is assumed to represent the siege/conquest of Ahmose, and, if Josephus's account from Manetho is followed, the exodus of the Hyksos – when Ahmose reached a treaty for their departure since he was unable to carry the siege.[375] However, exactly when the overall Hyksos period begins is unclear. As O'Connor (1997:53) writes: 'nine strata are *potentially* relevant to the Hyksos period, although only *some* of these are likely coeval with that period'. The first significant evidence of 'Canaanite' materials by no means should be regarded as indicating the Hyksos period; after all, the Canaanite 14th Dynasty preceded the Hyksos (15th) Dynasty at Avaris.[376] Bietak places three strata, E/1=later b/1 to a/2, D/3=later a/2, and D/2 as approximately contemporary with the Hyksos 15th Dynasty, or a period of c.108 years on the basis of the Turin Canon (see Appendix 1). Bietak in general places strata H=d/2 to D/2 as covering the period from the end of the 12th/start of the 13th Dynasty to the end of the SIP/conquest of Ahmose (linking H=d/2 with Amenemhat IV and the end of D/2 with Ahmose), a period of c.250–280 years, and, with just one or two very minor variations, Bietak allots roughly even

---

[374] For other reviews of the published evidence, and varying scepticism of the completely revised dating, see Niemeier and Niemeier (1998:79–80, 85–88); Cline (1998a). I note that this analysis and critique is based solely on the published data. In a response to Weinstein's critique of his chronology, Bietak (1997:126) notes that Weinstein has 'never visited Tell el-Dabᶜa to see or study the materials'. I admit to the same sin. My own archaeological fieldwork over the last decade has been in Cyprus and my travels in the Aegean and Anatolia, and I have not yet had the opportunity to visit Tell el-Dabᶜa at a time when the Austrian team is working at the site. But international scholarship in the humanities or sciences should be entitled to judge, analyse, interpret, and criticise on the basis of published materials (see also Cline 1998a). This is how academic scholarship works. Manfred Bietak is to be congratulated warmly for his prompt and detailed publication programme. Attention and examination therefore follow. Further, I stress that rigorous scholarship means that ideas, arguments, and conclusions *must* be both capable of scrutiny and capable of falsifiability. If there is a plausible alternative, or a plausible competing hypothesis, this requires full and thorough examination. No 'facts' are inherently sacred and right, unless *demonstrated* to be so. Opinion, convention, and tradition are irrelevant. While it may betray this author's intellectual approach as not trendily 'post-processual', I remind readers of the basic scientific (from the latin, *scire*, to know, with 'science' meaning knowledge) premise stated by Popper (1972:314): 'Varying and generalizing a well-known remark of Einstein's, one might therefore characterize the empirical sciences as follows: In so far as a scientific statement speaks about reality, it must be falsifiable: and in so far as it is not falsifiable, it does not speak about reality'.

[375] Josephus, *Contra Apionem* I.88–89.

[376] Ryholt (1997).

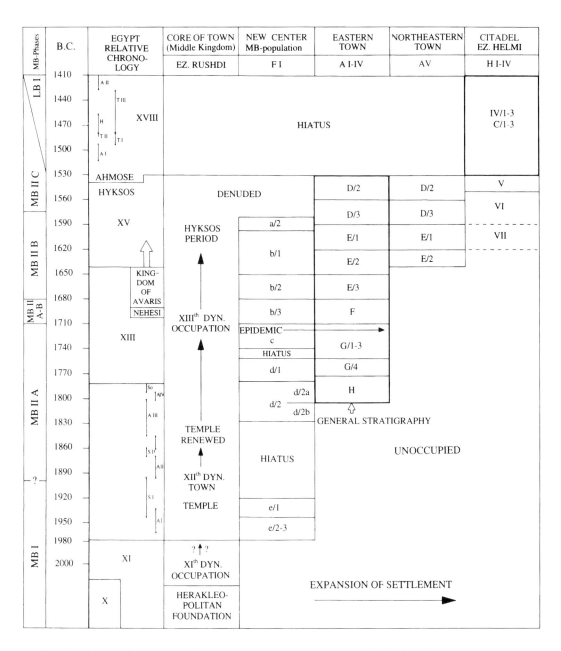

Fig. 23. Schematic stratigraphic sequence for the entire Avaris/Tell el-Dabᶜa site after Bietak (1996a:Fig.3).

30-year intervals to each of the nine strata.[377] This is clearly arbitrary, and so rather suspect and unlikely.

Comments
The period of especial concern in the present context is the final Hyksos period. Who built the new fortifications and new citadel of the final Hyksos period? One could propose Khamudy, final Hyksos ruler, on the basis that he was fortifying in the aftermath of the recorded attack of Kamose (final 17th Dynasty Theban-southern Egyptian-ruler, and immediate predeccesor of Ahmose), and in the face of subsequent renewed Theban advances under Ahmose. But the scale of the citadel fortifications seems to represent a real highpoint of power at Avaris. The walls are up to 6.2m wide, later enlarged to 8.5m, and there are impressive buttresses. They enclose some 5ha! It seems more likely to this author that the new palatial compound represents the building of either one of the greatest Hyksos rulers: Khyan, or Apophis,[378] or one or more of the three earlier kings of the dynasty (Manetho attributes to Salitis the rebuilding and fortification of Avaris with massive walls). Further, the Kamose stela informs us of the impressive fortifications at Avaris in the reign of Apophis, with the women of the palace looking out at the Egyptians from the citadel (see Table 4 below p. 99), and these therefore already exist in the mid to later reign of Apophis. Clearly they were both impressive and formidable. Bietak (1996a:64–65) also links the gardens inside the walls of the citadel near the H/I platform to those of Apophis described in the Kamose stela, and thus likewise assumes a construction date no later than Apophis, and quite possibly a preceding king. It is evident from the Kamose stela that Apophis refused combat outside the walls with Kamose, and Kamose could in consequence do nothing else against Avaris and Apophis, and so returned home to Thebes to celebrate his mission down the Nile.

Where does this leave the length of the final Hyksos D/2 stratum? The high point of Hyksos rule appears to be the reigns of Apophis, who is credited with 41 years, and his predecessor, Khyan, often credited with some 20+ years.[379] These two alone of the

---

[377] See also Bietak (1984) for discussion and origins of this chronology.

[378] As discussed in Appendix 1, the order of the 15th Dynasty kings is unclear. Only the final ruler, Khamudy, is placed by the Turin papyrus. Khyan is often thought to be the ruler before Apophis (e.g. von Beckerath 1997:137, 189; Ryholt 1997:119–120). But there seems a clear problem. Manetho has a king Iannas, whom von Beckerath for example equates with Khyan, but a stela of Ianassi from Tell el-Dabʿa names him as eldest king's son of king Khyan (Bietak in Hein 1994b:155–156). Thus as Bietak (in Hein 1994:155–156; Bietak 1997:114) argues, it is possible that Ianassi may have succeeded Khyan. But, as argued in Appendix 1, it seems likely this prince Ianassi never became king (the name Ianassi may however be linked with Manetho's Iannas: see also Görg 1993). Apart from the year 11 for an unknown king assumed to be either Khamudy or Apophis from the Rhind mathematical papyrus, and the fact Apophis has an attested year 33 on the same papyrus, and some reign lengths without names, or the name Khamudy but with no preserved reign length, on the Turin papyrus, we have no useful data from which to reconstruct the 15th Dynasty. The reign lengths in the list of six kings in Manetho adding up to some 260 years, or the whole of the period from the end of the 12th Dynasty to the start of the 18th Dynasty, seem completely unhelpful.

[379] I assume either his predecessor but one (with Ianassi in between), or his immediate predecessor. In the past it has been argued that this order based on the Turin Canon is incorrect, and that Khyan must

six known 15th Dynasty kings have monuments attested outside Tell el-Dabᶜa, and evidence of royal structures within the city. To this author, at least, the last minor ruler Khamudy appears unlikely to have done much major building; although various of the very late stratum D/2 modifications, and perhaps the readjustment of fortifications and military buildings inside the citadel, might well be linked to his 11+(?) years of reign (see Appendix 1). We might suggest that the distinct final D/2 phase is likely to reflect the building and expansion under either Khyan and/or Apophis, and then the prosperity of Apophis, before its decline and end under Khamudy. Thus the 30 years offered by Bietak might be considered a likely minimum, and the phase could last 40, 50, and even perhaps as much as 70 or more years. In support, as we shall discuss later, this stratum was contemporary with the *later* part of the LCIA phase on Cyprus (LCIA commenced late stratum E/1 or from stratum D/3: see Chapter IV.5 below). The overall LCIA period, and socio-political process, probably represents a significant amount of time. LCIA1, characterised by PWS, includes two or three phases following the recent analysis of Eriksson (n.d.), and so presumably represents a couple of 'generations', while LCIA2 covers the period from the advent of initial WSI, BRI, and Monochrome in the northwest of Cyprus to the subsequent adoption of the mature versions of these styles/wares across the whole island from the beginning of LCIB. Again, a couple of 'generations' may be supposed. All in all, a period of up to about a century may be involved.

The patterns of development in contemporary Palestine ought also to be considered – especially as this region was intimately linked with the Hyksos. Tell el-Dabᶜa strata later D/3 and all of D/2 are dated to the wider Palestinian MBIIC period (or MBIII period in other schemes) by Bietak.[380] How long was this phase in general? Unfortunately, there has been a set of rather unproductive disputes in the scholarly literature over the last decade around the historical interpretation of this period which have clouded the issue (see below). However, Dever (1997:291) is undeniably correct to point out that this late MB phase is distinct in the more coastal areas,[381] and that it seems to represent a reasonably significant interval of time. He correlates it with the entire 15th Dynasty (Hyksos) period in Egypt, and allocates c.120 years.[382] In accord, many scholars have given a general dating for this MBIIC or MBIII period of c.1650–1550BC.[383] Although it is difficult to judge from his diagram, Bietak (1996a:fig.3) appears to offer instead just c.50 years, or, in the text of this book, he refers to a period c.1600–1530BC which might also be considered as his MBIIC phase – i.e. up to c.70 years.[384] In

---

be an early (even the first) Hyksos king, because of a seriation analysis of Hyksos royal scarabs (W.A. Ward in Tufnell 1984:151–192, esp. at 161–168; Ward 1987:524 n.68). However, Krauss (1998a) demonstrates that this view from the scarab data is incorrect. It in fact transpires that the scarab data confirm that the reigns of Khyan and Apophis should be placed close to each other. Ryholt (1997:43) likewise found the conclusion of Ward impossible, and argued that Apophis was the direct successor of Khyan. Ryholt (1997:43–46) offers an alternative seriation consistent with this view.

[380] Bietak (1991:Figs.3 and 24; 1996a:fig.3; 1997:fig.4.3).
[381] See also Oren (1997b:271).
[382] Dever (1992; 1997:293).
[383] To take one recent example, see Marchetti *et al.* (1998:121 Table I).
[384] Bietak (1996a:63).

general sympathy with such a lower chronological position, Oren (1997b:271) starts his MBIII period c.1600BC, and this is a common date among the 'lower' chronological interpretations. Dever and Bietak have been engaged in a long-running squabble over MBA dates throughout the last decade,[385] but the 50–70 years between their two sets of dates is utterly crucial from an Aegean–Cypriot point of view. Moreover, the debate is not simple. For example, Dever's 'high' dates for the early MBA phases appear unlikely,[386] but the situation may be very different for the late MBA, and here other scholars express 'concern regarding the compression of the ... MBIIB and IIC strata that is demanded by the low chronology'.[387] If Tell el-Dabᶜa strata later D/3 and D/2 were in fact dated c.1650–1540/30BC – and also the general MBIIC or MBIII period – then many of the supposed *a priori* objections to the so-called Aegean 'early', or 'long', chronology could evaporate.

Bietak's (1997:115) choice of language shows that it is clear there is no good evidence for a specific date for the construction of the late Hyksos citadel. He writes that it was 'constructed during the late Hyksos period (after ca.1600 B.C.) ...'. The criterion for Bietak (1996a:64) is that there was no settlement in this area before the D/3–2 strata, but this clearly offers a flexible *terminus post quem* for the construction of the citadel. The stated c.1600BC *terminus post quem* is an arbitrary best guess given Bietak's existing (arbitrary) dates for the D/3 and D/2 strata. The logic is circular. There is in fact no evidence contrary to the somewhat longer final main late Hyksos phase proposed above.[388] A late 17th century BC construction date would be possible (or one in the early 16th century BC). Similarly, the c.1600BC date for the start of MBIIC, or MBIII, as stated by Oren (1997b:271), is merely an approximate guess – given the impressive developments Oren stresses in the MBIII period in Palestine a slightly longer period and earlier date is by no means impossible. His reference to Alalakh is not inconsistent (see discussion in Chapter VII below).

i. Start of stratum V
A massive Late Hyksos fortification wall encloses a palace area compound of over 5ha (0. above), and includes two phases of a garden with rows of trees or vines (traced as a regular series of pits east of the H/I platform at H/I–H/IV). Very little of the architecture remains other than a section of the enclosure wall at H/I, the exposure of part of a platform at H/III, and traces of another large structure at H/II.[389] Hein (1998:547–548) discusses the garden levels and the associated ceramics: 97% of the ceramics are SIP, but 3% are New Kingdom. Hein considers it possible that both garden levels are SIP and the New Kingdom material is intrusive, or that the lower garden level is SIP and the upper is New Kingdom, or that in fact both garden levels are New

---

[385] See Dever (1985; 1991; 1992; 1997:294 and fig.9.4 with further refs.); Weinstein (1996).
[386] Weinstein (1996); Beck and Zevulun (1996).
[387] Weinstein (1995:89).
[388] In the current stratigraphic diagram this means strata V and VI in the HI–IV area: Bietak (1996a:Fig.3; 1997:fig.4.3).
[389] For plan, see Bietak (1996b:Fig.5).

Kingdom and the SIP material is residual. In other words, dating is very difficult. Some Cypriot Bichrome Ware pottery was found;[390] this could be consistent with either a Hyksos or early 18th Dynasty date.

Comments
It is not clear what happened in the specific area of the H/I platform at this time on the revised sequence. Bietak (1997:115) writes that 'aside from the enclosure walls, the only monumental architecture of the Hyksos period found thus far is a platform construction of mudbrick in area H/III'. So, here is a Hyksos datum. Bietak then goes on to state that this H/III building has a 'good parallel' in the H/I platform. The only 'problem' is Bietak's new early 18th Dynasty date for H/I. Hein notes that evidence for the expansion of Hyksos settlement in this area of the site might make a Hyksos date most plausible for the garden and associated entities, but also points out that such circumstantial arguments cannot prove this.[391] All we really know for certain is that 'directly on top of the garden layers a settlement structure with poor house constructions was found'. This is dated on the basis of the associated black rim bowls to 'the early Eighteenth Dynasty'.[392] The gardens, and associated entities, are earlier. Thus Hyksos?

Another relevant fact should be noted. Very little MC, or MC-style LCIA, pottery (one sherd of WPV as of 1996), and very little other LCIA pottery, has been found in the ʿEzbet Helmi citadel area.[393] The Cypriot material there is arguably mainly LCIB and later (see Chapter IV.5). The latter represents the relatively small volume of LC ceramics known from the greater Tell el-Dabʿa site, in contrast to the relatively plentiful amounts of MC pottery (from the Tell el-Dabʿa site/mound). The LCIB material belongs with the earlier New Kingdom occupation at ʿEzbet Helmi. It correlates with the non-palatial, non-élite, use of the ʿEzbet Helmi area (and instead rather ordinary 18th Dynasty housing). The relatively plentiful MC material from the Tell el-Dabʿa site/mound likewise correlates with a settlement area, and not the contemporary ruling complex. The destroyed Hyksos palace at ʿEzbet Helmi thus might be argued to be likely to correspond chronologically with final MC and LCIA, only the ceramics of these periods are not represented in the palace debris (instead frescoes and other more 'high' art). The presence of a couple of MMIIIB–LMIA items (Chapter IV.4), contemporary with late MC–LCIA (see Chapter IV.4 and 5), provides compatible chronological evidence.

ii. Ahmose conquers Avaris
Many areas of the city appear simply to have been abandoned following the late Hyksos D/2 stratum. A transitional stratum may yet have to be inserted between strata D/2 and C/1, and this would post-date the Ahmose conquest as a block with either his name, or that of his mother, has recently been found.[394] There would thus

[390] Hein (1998:548).
[391] Hein (1998:548 and n.9).
[392] Hein (1998:548–549).
[393] Maguire (1990; pers. comm. 1996).
[394] Bietak (pers. comm. 1998).

be a very early 18th Dynasty stratum, followed by an early 18th Dynasty stratum running to about Tuthmosis III.

Comments

What happened in the citadel? Ahmose supposedly sacks the city. A soldier in his army recorded that 'Avaris was despoiled'.[395] Throughout Egypt the 18th Dynasty are said to have destroyed or erased all traces of the Asiatic-Hyksos dynasty,[396] and so it seems inevitable that Avaris – the great Asiatic-Hyksos capital – would have felt the force of this policy. However, the actual nature of this destruction is unclear in the excavations so far at Tell el-Dab'a. Bietak (1996a:67) writes that 'we have a little evidence for a conflagration in excavation area H/I but this may have been a very localised affair'. But, if anywhere was even symbolically 'despoiled', one might imagine that it was the Hyksos palace of the great enemy, Apophis, and his successor.[397] It seems likely this was in the H/I area. The existence of rubbish deposits with mainly late Hyksos material as a result of such a transfer of ownership, and in the area of H/I (e.g. in the garden area), is not unlikely? Are the rubbish deposits with the Aegean fresco fragments from the garden area not just this? Jánosi has argued that the fresco debris appears to represent material that was dismantled and then dumped.[398] Is there a better early 18th Dynasty story, or history, which explains such large-scale rubbish deposits of élite art (e.g. the frescoes)?

iiia. Very early in the 18th Dynasty

During the later part of the reign of Ahmose, conqueror of Avaris, an enormous platform is constructed at H/I overlaying/cutting at one corner part of the late Hyksos enclosure wall (and hence post-dates the later Hyksos fortification wall according to Bietak). This platform was originally dated to the late Hyksos period, but Bietak now proposes a redating. His case is: 'this redating may be explained in part by the fact that the platform [H/I] cuts into the late Hyksos ramparts, and also by its similarity in orientation to a second, larger palatial area to the south (area H/II), which can be dated to only the early Eighteenth Dynasty...'.[399] Bietak (1997:116) also suggests the comparison of the H/I platform with the southern palace at Deir el-Ballas. However, it is also evident that the case is hardly clearcut from the choice of language: '... the date of the platform now *appears* to be in the early Eighteenth Dynasty'.[400]

Comments

None of these arguments are particularly specific. Comparison to a fort (Deir el-Ballas)

---

[395] Kuhrt (1995:189); Redford (1997:15 no.70 line 14).

[396] Hayes (1990:11–39); Redford (1992:115–116); Bernal (1991:352–355).

[397] Cf. legendary literature such as the story of Apophis and Seqenenre: Redford (1997:17–18).

[398] Jánosi in Bietak *et al.* (1994:32).

[399] Bietak (1997:117); and (1996b:13) referring to imported Cypriot LCIB WSI, Bichrome Ware, BRI, and Red Lustrous Wheelmade Ware finds associated with H/II. See also Hein (1998:551–554).

[400] Bietak (1997:117, my italics). Note also again that Bietak (1997:115) considers the Hyksos H/III structure as having 'a good parallel' in the H/I structure. There is an alternative case if prior interpretation is excluded.

built in the later 17th Dynasty hardly proves an early 18th Dynasty date for the H/I platform. A building cutting into earlier Hyksos fortifications (i.e. re-modelling) again does not of itself require a post-Hyksos date. This defensive re-modelling and strengthening could make good sense as the work of either Apophis or Khamudy under threats from Kamose or Ahmose. The 'similarity in orientation' seems rather less than critical as dating evidence (the 13th Dynasty 'palace', or élite building, at the site has a roughly similar orientation as well, for that matter). It is unclear what (if anything) preceded this platform at H/I – the destruction of a later Hyksos structure is possible (and this too might be the source of the fresco fragments). Similarly, although later than the initial enclosure wall, the early 18th Dynasty building may have re-used a late Hyksos building. Finally, although subsequent to the fortification wall, there is no independent evidence that this is early 18th Dynasty, versus late Hyksos re-modelling – indeed, as suggested above, such military re-modelling and building seems very likely in the late Hyksos period under the direct threat of siege by the Theban kings. And, if the H/I platform was not Hyksos in date, then where was the palace of Apophis overlooking the Pelusiac branch of the Nile – right next to the H/I platform with it overlooking the curve of the river at this point – as described in the Kamose Stela? Coring has shown there is no other, older, building underneath the H/I platform.[401] And the (or a) previous Canaanite 14th Dynasty palace was perhaps what Bietak[402] has identitifed as a '13th' Dynasty palace in the F/I area about half a kilometer to the southeast.[403] Hence it seems likely that Apophis' palace must have been somewhere around the H/I area.

iiib. Very early in the 18th Dynasty
Other large structures at H/II and H/III on the same alignments are probably built at about the same time. The H/I platform covers some of the earlier garden. Bietak sees this as an Ahmose date structure covering late Hyksos gardens. In the remaining open area to the east of the H/I platform there is a second garden phase.

Comments
The latter seems very unlikely given the apparent use of the citadel area at this time: see v. below. The former is entirely feasible, but it could also be the latest Hyksos (i.e. Apophis-Khamudy) period re-modelling under military threat. Is this not post-dating the rubbish deposits, including the fresco fragments, found in the garden area?

iv. Also very early in the 18th Dynasty
After the initial construction of the H/I platform an extension is added subsequently at the east end.

---

[401] Bietak *et al.* (1994:27).
[402] Bietak (1996a:21–30; 1997:100–104).
[403] Ryholt (1997:104). In contrast, Wegner (1998:25) argues that the Tell el-Dabᶜa Area F building was not a palace (i.e. it was non-royal). He regards it instead as just a large élite building.

Comments
When? And is this, and all of the above – nos. iii, iv and v – to occur in the very first years of the 18th Dynasty? Or might the timespan, from a posited additional transitional very early 18th Dynasty stratum (see ii. above), and then the following existing main stratum C/1, in fact occupy the timespan from Ahmose to Tuthmosis III? The use of the site as a military base (see v. below) might then be seen as relevant *not* to Ahmose, but instead to one of the subsequent pharaohs who set off on campaigns into Palestine and Syria (esp. Amenhotep I, Tuthmosis I, or Tuthmosis III). The implications here are vast. The fresco fragments associated with the early 18th Dynasty buildings would then be dated to about this later time, and would have nothing necessarily to do with Ahmose. If this later period was somewhere from Amenhotep I to Tuthmosis III, then the similarity of some design elements in the frescoes to Aegean LMIB/LHIIA style art (see below) is not surprising.

v. Also very early in the 18th Dynasty
Immediately after the conquest, the citadel area is used as a military fort, and camp, as a base for further military activities (but cf. comment to iv. above).

> At the beginning of the Eighteenth Dynasty, most probably immediately after the fall of Avaris, the citadel was occupied by Upper Egyptian troops. Numerous postholes in the eastern part of the citadel give the impression that tents had been set up here. The presence of domestic pottery of the Kerma culture, as well as fine Kerma beakers, renders it likely that Nubian archers, brought by Ahmose from a Nubian campaign against the kingdom of Kush, had been stationed there. In addition, arrowheads of flint and whole bundles of bone arrowtips were found, as well as numerous slingshot projectiles. Remains of huge grain silos in area H/III also appear to have been intended for the temporary storage of provisions. Taken together, the evidence suggests that the former citadel of the Hyksos was used as a stronghold in the time of the early Eighteenth Dynasty, most probably intended for the concentration of troops needed for Ahmose's campaigns in southern Palestine.[404]

Comments
This is entirely plausible. Bietak specifically states that the large palatial area H/II 'can be dated to only the early Eighteenth Dynasty'. This area 'bears a resemblance to the Northern Palace at Deir el-Ballas'.[405] The Deir el-Ballas fortress was the military base of the later 17th Dynasty (Theban) kings. The finds date from the 17th Dynasty king Seqenenre (builder thereof) to Amenhotep I, and the ceramic finds also include Kerma pottery.[406] It is entirely likely that a building of this military sort constructed a generation later by Ahmose at Tell el-Dabᶜa would be very similar. And the need for a new forward military base for Ahmose makes sense. But, at the same time, it is

---

[404] Bietak (1997:115–116).
[405] Bietak (1997:117, see also pp.115–117).
[406] Lacovara (1990).

quite possible that some of this evidence for military encampment might also relate either to the Hyksos armed forces in the citadel in the last decades of Avaris when they were defending the besieged city against the Theban armies – Bietak has in fact offered no archaeological evidence related to this period and the sieges and eventual conquest – or to subsequent early 18th Dynasty kings who campaigned in Asia. Given apparent relations (even perhaps alliance) between the Hyksos and the kingdom of Kush,[407] even the presence of Nubian forces in late Hyksos Avaris is not impossible. The Kingdom of Kush = Kerma[408] received some SIP imports which may have come direct from the Hyksos delta region: Tell el-Yahudiyeh juglets, Syro-Palestinian juglets, and a Cypriot WPIV vessel.[409] It is not clear what to make of arrowheads said possibly to be of LH typology from the H/III area.[410] Depending on exact date, they could fit either scenario. Bietak (1997:117) refers to 'bags with arrowheads ... were found lying beside a large palace wall'. This sounds more like abandonment/hoarding, rather than casual loss. If so, the siege and then abandonment of final Hyksos Avaris might offer a more plausible scenario?

vi. Between stratum V and IV
A destruction or abandonment. The main product is debris east of the H/I platform over the garden area. This material includes the Aegean-style fresco fragments, and late Hyksos to early 18th Dynasty material.[411] In the garden area this debris is very mixed and does not form a discrete horizon.

Comment
Some of the material could well come from an earlier destruction or remodelling before, or as, the H/I platfrom in iii. was built, or extended. Thus between i, ii, or iiia above, and not later?

vii. Stratum IV
Early 18th Dynasty houses are built over the debris and garden area east of the H/I platform. The associated ceramics are early 18th Dynasty and include a Cypriot WSI bowl with a framed lozenge and two parallel line style (metope) decoration of the late phase of WSI belonging to the LCIB period.[412] A long scarab sequence is present, running more or less with the stratigraphy. The earliest scarab from right above the debris/garden belongs to Ahmose, and the latest ones to Tuthmosis III and Amenhotep II. As the houses encroach on the platform at H/I, it can only be assumed that it had gone out of use by this time. These houses are also of poor construction and seem

---

[407] Based on the comments of Kamose in his stela lines 20–22: Redford (1997:14–15); O'Connor (1997:45).
[408] Lacovara (1997:75). Bourrian and Eriksson (1997:108) argue that such Kerma pottery indicates a period before the campaign of Tuthmosis I which destroyed the capital of Kerma/Kush, and the subsequent 'Egyptian colonisation and the destruction of the Kerma culture in Nubia'.
[409] Lacovara (1997:78 and figs.3.5, 3.6, 3.7).
[410] Bietak (1997:117 and n.72; 1996b:12 and n.22).
[411] Hein (1994a; 1998).
[412] Hein (1998:548–549) for Egyptian ceramics. Hein (1998:549 and n.12); Bietak *et al.* (1994:Fig.12.d) for the WSI bowl. This bowl and the phases of WSI are discussed in detail in Chapter IV.5 below.

unlikely to be associated with the monumental platform structure. Given the very early 18th Dynasty scarabs from the houses, this leaves the platform, and its later east extension, as earliest 18th Dynasty at the latest.

Comment
A Hyksos date for the platform might work rather better.

PROBLEMS WITH THE ABOVE SEQUENCE

The presentation of the excavation evidence from the ʿEzbet Helmi area of Tell el-Dabʿa is still only preliminary, but some questions must be raised with regard to Bietak's current dating of the platform (as noted in the comments above), and especially his dating of the fresco fragments (issues which are probably, but not necessarily, linked). With regard to the fresco fragments from H/I, reference to the published section and description makes it very clear that there is _no_ secure stratigraphic association.[413] The fresco fragments are found in highly disturbed positions; the main group are worryingly close to the ploughsoil interface,[414] and the thin spread (lens) shown in the section looks suspiciously like a plough-action spread of material between the two walls. Other fragments are found rather deeper,[415] and the overall descriptions of all the fresco finds[416] indicates that they are in effect mixed from shallow to deeper locations, and in no sense associated with any architecture, or a clear stratigraphic horizon.[417] The surface of the H/I platform[418] meets the ploughsoil, thus anything from this building – whether dated Hyksos and stratum V (as in Jánosi 1995) or now later and stratum IV (as in Bietak 1996a and subsequent reports) – would be expected to be in hopelessly disturbed secondary contexts. The position of the fresco fragments in the section above the later 18th Dynasty buildings means nothing, since we must asume they have been transported horizontally from the west. Moreover, since some of the fresco fragments were found stratified in the foundations associated with the modifications of the H/I platform, they seem to be pre-18th Dynasty even on Bietak's revised dating.

Bietak (1995a:20) simply wrote that 'the find-circumstances are still partly obscure, because of agricultural levelling and extensive modern building in what is a growing rural village'. Describing this debris, Bietak (1996a:73) clearly states that it includes both late Hyksos _and_ early 18th Dynasty elements, and that while some finds are undoubtedly 18th Dynasty, 'some of the remains may have come originally from the Hyksos citadel'. The studies by Jánosi and Hein likewise report that this debris including the fresco fragments has both late Hyksos to early 18th Dynasty ceramics.[419]

---

[413] Jánosi (1995:passim, and Abb.2; 1994).
[414] Upper centre of Jánosi (1995:Abb.2).
[415] No.8 to far left of Jánosi (1995:Abb.2).
[416] Plan in Jánosi (1995:Abb.1).
[417] For a view of the shallow excavation area, see Bietak (1996a:pl.27B).
[418] No.1 in Jánosi (1995:Abb.2).
[419] Jánosi in Bietak _et al._ (1994:20–38); Hein (1994a; 1998).

Early 18th Dynasty buildings with scarabs from Ahmose through to Amenhotep II 'cover at least some of the wall-plaster fragments bearing Minoan frescoes',[420] and also 'run against the *eroded* northern ramp attached to [the platform]' (my italics),[421] suggesting they were later (and so the fresco fragments are earlier, and could easily be Hyksos period rubbish disturbed by 18th Dynasty building). Bietak suggests that these 18th Dynasty buildings must date after Ahmose, with the frescoes dating to the reign of Ahmose in his opinion, *but* given scarabs of Ahmose associated with the buildings, this seems special pleading. Nor is the then very short-lived life-span of the frescoes in the major building on the platform explained. Bietak (1996b:14 n.31) sums up his case: because he dates some frescoes as 18th Dynasty, he argues that they probably all are. He admits some fragments were found in late Hyksos contexts, but argues that it is impossible to show they are definitely of this date. But the reader can observe that the reverse also applies! The logic and evidence is less than compelling.

Further, we might note the east extension – the ramp heading northeast – to the original H/I platform (see Figure 22, p. 82 above). Of course, an extension may be added almost immediately after an original structure is built, but it could also be added some years, even decades, later. This extension is clearly not part of the original design concept for the neat, rectangular, H/I platform. Its addition, therefore, might suggest a change of purpose or use of the platform, or the building on it. Did such a process of original design, building, and then change of needs and additional building, all occur within the period of about a decade available in Ahmose's reign between his conquest of Avaris, after his year (7–)11 and by his years 18 to 22 (see Appendix 1), and his death in his year 25? A date for the extension after the reign of Ahmose is of course possible, *but* the scarab series (Ahmose to Amenhotep II) from the sequence of earlier 18th Dynasty houses built over the garden area east of the H/I platform, and the associated ceramics, suggest that they were constructed very early in the 18th Dynasty, and when they first built the ramp was already 'eroded'. Hence the east extension is likely to be very early in the 18th Dynasty *at the latest*. In turn, since the original H/I platform must date earlier again, this does make one wonder if Ahmose was not perhaps re-using a late Hyksos palace and/or foundation platform after he had set fire to it and perhaps stripped it of Hyksos features and decoration. This might be the origin of at least some of the debris[422] including the Aegean-style fresco fragments found to the east of the platform. Jánosi had previously argued just this, that the platform had been partly destroyed, or had become ruined, either because of the conquest of Ahmose, or in the period afterwards, before subsequent re-use of the area.[423] Indeed, since it is clear that fresco fragments were found in the foundations associated with such rebuilding and repair work, then, if this is (as Bietak argues) dated to the initial 18th Dynasty, it implies that the frescoes derive from a previous phase. Herein may lie some of the confusion in current literature.

---

[420] Bietak (1996a:72).
[421] Bietak (1996a:68); see also Jánosi (1995).
[422] Bietak (1996a:73).
[423] Jánosi in Bietak *et al.* (1994:38; 1995:68–70).

If, however, we accept the (revised 1996 onwards) Bietak sequence, and date the construction of the H/I platform to Ahmose, another interesting question arises. Why was it then destroyed almost immediately afterwards as Bietak (1996a:68–73) requires? Ahmose did not conquer Avaris until possibly reasonably late in his reign – and he was dead just 3 to 7 to 13(–18) years later. Bietak's best explanation is merely to write that 'the only solution to this conflicting evidence is to date the platform to the years immediately after the fall of Avaris and assume it was in official use for only a short time' (1996a:68). Why? Ahmose re-conquered and re-united Egypt, founded a new, successful, stable, dynasty, and is credited with carrying the war against the Hyksos into Palestine after the conquest of Avaris (before then turning his attention to the southern border).[424] Although he had already captured Sile (on the Egyptian-Sinai border) and the east Delta, it is entirely feasible to imagine Ahmose building a fort and new forward military stronghold at Tell el-Dab^c a (to replace the previous 17th Dynasty military base of Deir el-Ballas), and maybe there were other threats as Bietak suggests.[425] (However, as noted above, some of the evidence for military camps in the citadel might also be potentially linked either with the late Hyksos defence against the sieges of Kamose and/or Ahmose, or later earlier 18th Dynasty campaigns into western Asia – including perhaps especially Tuthmosis III.) But why, if so, would this new stronghold be destroyed – and not simply abandoned – only a few years later? Further, why would a relatively functional fortress have featured exotic fresco decoration/display (Niemeier and Niemeier 1998:95)? Something much more plausible at key structures of an established royal citadel in which visitors, who were to be impressed, were received. Bietak (1996a:81) proposes that it was a key strategic location, and became the base for Ahmose's subsequent campaigns in southern Palestine.[426] This is plausible, although there is no positive evidence. But why, to repeat the question above, if this was a military garrison and centre (like the southern palace at Deir el-Ballas to which Bietak compares it[427]), would it have been so decorated, and then destroyed so soon afterwards (and not just abandoned as no longer necessary, as occurred at Deir el-Ballas), and by whom was it destroyed? A Hyksos dating would allow a much better story and history.

Perhaps even more to the point, why would Minoan style frescoes be painted *here* in the early 18th Dynasty, and not at the main royal courts to the south, and, again, why would they be destroyed so soon afterwards? Further, why is there no trace of such art elsewhere in Egypt either before, and especially after, Ahmose? Bietak (1997:124) simply confesses that '... it is difficult to explain the presence of Minoan paintings in the Egyptian citadel of Avaris'. Such paintings make sense in a royal

---

[424] Summaries in Vandersleyen (1971:33–40); Kuhrt (1995:176, 188–190); Redford (1992:128–130); O'Connor (1997:45).

[425] Bietak (1997:124 and n.74).

[426] And the allied Minoan navy according to a suggestion of Bietak (1997:124; 1996b:24). This is merely fanciful, and supported by no actual evidence: also Niemeier and Niemeier (1998:87–88). The best one might point to is the reference to 'Amosis who excavated Lake Avaris...' cited by Clement of Alexandria I.101.3–4 from Apion's *Against the Jews*. Conceivably this could refer to Ahmose building a harbour, but is most likely irrelevant (or a garbled reference to Ahmose's seige activities when he might have sought to drain the Hyksos harbour or re-direct the Nile waterway).

[427] Bietak (1996a:68; 1997:116–117).

or élite building – in line with similar Aegean-style wall paintings from major port-trading sites in the eastern Mediterranean at Tel Kabri, Alalakh, Trianda on Rhodes, and Miletus[428] – but there is an embarrassing lack of evidence for Avaris fulfilling such a role *after* Ahmose's conquest. Even Bietak (1996a:82) admits that 'it is puzzling that we do not hear anything of Avaris during the 18th Dynasty in connection with military campaigns and trading expeditions to Asia', and has to argue that it had another name. Finally, some of the non-typical Aegean aspects of the paintings moreover hint at hybridisation, and the intervening cultural filter is likely to be the Levant, where such a tradition of painting clearly existed, rather than Egypt, where there is no other trace. The period of the later MBA Canaanite-Hyksos world offers a suitable milieu.[429] There is altogether a telling absence of evidence which directly associates Ahmose with this material. There is instead much conjecture, and few facts, with regard to the early 18th Dynasty scenario presented by Bietak. I suggest there is a better alternative, one involving the Hyksos period for any LMIA-style art at the site (e.g. the griffin which is closely paralleled at LMIA Thera[430]). The exclusive distribution of MMIIIB–LMIA objects and styles solely in the Delta at Avaris then makes sense as the link was with the Hyksos here, and *not* the world of 17th Dynasty Upper Egypt which was effectively cut off from the Mediterranean at this time. And, for other frescoes considered of early 18th Dynasty date, then the period of about Amenhotep I to Tuthmosis III offers a better home for examples of what might be considered to be LMIB/LHIIA to LMIIIA/LHIIIA-style art (see discussion in next section). There remains an absence of other known examples of Aegean wall-paintings from Egypt at this later date, but there is good evidence for knowledge of, and interest in, the Aegean including at royal level at this time (with the paintings of Keftiu in élite tombs at Thebes the best datum: see Chapter IV.9).

The rest of the city, and the wider story, are also revealing. Much of the great Hyksos city of Avaris of some 250ha – that is three times the size of the largest contemporary site in Palestine, several times the size of the 17th Dynasty capital of Thebes,[431] and almost four times the size of by far the largest site on Crete at Knossos – was abandoned at the end of the Hyksos period. Only the citadel area and one or two other areas show evidence of early 18th Dynasty occupation.[432] It is difficult to view this small

---

[428] Niemeier (1990; 1991; 1995a; 1995b); Niemeier and Niemeier (1997:238–240); Gates (1996:302 and fig.17); Marketou (1996:133); Negbi (1994). Bietak himself has remarked on what he sees as the royal nature of the Aegean-style fresco imagery in some cases (e.g. 1997:124). In this case the total absence of any compatible evidence from Middle or Upper Egypt runs against an 18th Dynasty date. The Delta and Levantine distribution instead matches an SIP date. In view of the remarkable finds made even on a random basis, it seems likely that a Bronze Age site under modern Beirut may well be added to this list in the future. See e.g. Saidah (1993–1994); and Ward (1993–1994). Other likely candidates might be suggested among the set of important late MBII or MBIII centres in Palestine – and perhaps especially Tell el-ʿAjjul, which was a key port site (Oren 1997b). I suspect we have much to learn about later MBII Levantine wall-paintings.

[429] I thank Professor Maria Shaw for her comments on this subject. See also Shaw (1995:110).

[430] Compare Bietak *et al.* (1994:52, pl.21) and Doumas (1992:pl.128). See also Bietak (1995a:pls.4.3 and 4.4). Bietak and Marinatos (1995:60) write that 'the similarity with the Theran griffin from Xeste 3 is indeed striking'.

[431] Thebes is estimated to have been 50–100ha(?) in size at this time (O'Connor 1997:58).

[432] Bietak (1996a:67–72 and 87 n.96).

and restricted early 18th Dynasty entity as a great mercantile centre. In stark contrast, the stela of Kamose,[433] rhetoric and bombast aside, describes the late Hyksos metropolis of Avaris with its fortifications and harbour, inside which were hundreds of ships of / from Retenu (the Levant) filled with foreign and exotic trading goods – all of which Kamose claims to have taken:[434] see Table 4. This sounds like the great and focal mercantile centre of the entire east Mediterranean and Levantine–Syrian–Palestinian region.[435] At least two other contemporary, major, later MBA trading/strategic centres in the east Mediterranean are notable for also having, in élite contexts, LMIA-style wall paintings similar to the ones from Tell el-Dabᶜa: Tel Kabri and Alalakh.[436] More importantly, in each case, these paintings are specifically late, but not latest, MBII (Hyksos period) in date.[437] To explain, they occur in the pre-Bichrome Ware stage of the later MBII period in Syria–Palestine – Bichrome Ware demarcates the final phase of the MBA, and is found in the last Hyksos stratum, stratum D/2, at Tell el-Dabᶜa (see further in Chapter VII). The Alalakh and Tel Kabri frescoes are thus not only before the conquest of Avaris by Ahmose, but at least one or two generations earlier again. The Alalakh and Tel Kabri contexts also show a correspondence of the later Syro-Palestinian MBII period with the LMIA period in the Aegean.[438] To return to Tell el-Dabᶜa, it seems plausible that if anywhere expressed such a koine of élite expression, it should be the great Hyksos capital and entrepôt of Avaris. Were its similar Aegean-style frescoes not broadly contemporary with the Alalakh and Tel Kabri examples? This appears a strong (if circumstantial) argument in favour of a late Hyksos date (strata D/3–D/2) for the original painting of at least some of the LMIA-style Aegean frescoes from Tell el-Dabᶜa.

Another issue is that, as noted above, the fresco fragments in the H/I area are only 'associated' with the platform by virtue of being found as secondary 'rubbish' in the same area. There is no reason necessarily to the link the two (except the 'logic' of large platform equals large building equals frescoes). It must not be forgotten that if the H/I platform is not part of the Hyksos palatial compound, then the main late Hyksos palace complex was also somewhere in the same area, and, on Bietak's revised model, destroyed by the new (now) start of 18th Dynasty palace structures.[439] Finally,

---

[433] Smith and Smith (1976); Redford (1997:13–15).

[434] Also Kuhrt (1995:180).

[435] See also Holladay (1997:201). Only Byblos may have been a rival (also Holladay 1997:209), and, at the high point of the Hyksos, Avaris probably surpassed it. Similar wall paintings and cultural features might be expected at Byblos in élite contexts.

[436] Generally, see Niemeier (1990; 1991; 1995a; 1995b); Niemeier and Niemeier (1998); Negbi (1994); Cline (1995a:266–270); Kempinski (1997:329–330).

[437] See in general Kempinski (1983). For Tel Kabri, see Niemeier (1995a:1 and 11–12 n.5 with further refs.); Niemeier and Niemeier (1998:71–78); for Alalakh, see Niemeier (1995a:14 n.49); Niemeier and Niemeier (1998:69–71, 82–85). See also the summary in Negbi (1994:77–80).

[438] Also Betancourt (1998a:7).

[439] Bietak (1996a:63–64). Against the Bietak model is the lack of evidence of previous palatial structures underneath the H/I platform (Bietak *et al.* 1994:27). Given the need for such impressive later Hyksos structures because of the description in the Kamose stela, this rather implies a likely Hyksos date for the H/I platform (also Niemeier and Niemeier 1998:86).

... I [Kamose] put in at *Per-djedken*, my heart happy, so that I might let Apopy [Hyksos ruler] experience a bad time... I made the mighty transport boat beach at the edge of cultivation, with the fleet behind it, as the sparrow-hawk uproots (plants) upon the flats of Avaris! I espied his women upon his roof, peering out of their windows towards the habour. Their bellies stirred not as they saw me, peeping from their loop-holes upon their walls like the young of *inh*-animal [rats, fledgings?] in their holes, saying: 'he is swift'! Behold! I am come, a successful man! What remains is in my possession, and my venture prospers! As mighty Amun endures, I shall not leave you, I shall not allow you to tread the fields even when I am not here with you! Does your heart fail, O you vile Asiatic? Look! I drink of the wine of your vineyards which the Asiatics whom I captured pressed out for me. I have smashed up your resthouse, I have cut down your trees, I have forced your women into ships' holds, I have seized [your? horses]; I haven't left a plank to the hundreds of ships of fresh cedar which were filled with gold, lapis, silver, turquoise, bronze axes without number, over and above the moringa-oil, incense, fat, honey, willow, box-wood, sticks and all their fine woods – all the fine products of Retenu – I have confiscated all of it! I haven't left a thing to Avaris to her (own) destitution(?): the Asiatic has perished! Does your heart fail, O you vile Asiatic, you who used to say: 'I am lord without equal from Hermopolis to *Pi-hathor* upon the *Rekhty* water. ...

Table 4. Selections from the inscriptions of Kamose describing the Hyksos capital of Avaris after Redford (1997:13–15). For originals, see Smith and Smith (1976); Helck (1975:no.119); Habachi (1972).

the existence of the late Hyksos garden inside the enormous citadel wall, close to the H/I platform, must be mentioned. Bietak (1996a:64–65) observes that it is quite plausible that this is in fact the famous royal garden of the Hyksos king Apophis referred to by Kamose in his stela. The finds of the fresco remains, spread as small rubbish fragments mainly in this garden, has to be suggestive of a possible link for some of these with a destroyed late Hyksos structure.

Further fragments of similar wall paintings were found in other locations at Tell el-Dab^ca. At H/II there is evidence again of major buildings, with three phases represented,[440] one late Hyksos, one from the start of the 18th Dynasty, and one from the end of the first half of the 18th Dynasty. It is not clear whether the fresco fragments belong to the late Hyksos or the start of the 18th Dynasty phases. Bietak and Marinatos (1995:49) write of these fragments that 'their stratigraphy is mixed'. Bietak implies that these fragments are also to be dated to the early 18th Dynasty,[441] but no location-specific explanation is provided. More fresco fragments were discovered at H/III. These are linked with a start of 18th Dynasty enclosure wall (associated with the new palace at H/II), and in particular a portal. Bietak and Marinatos (1995:49) write that 'on both sides of the wall and concentrating around a portal, more Minoan wall paintings were found. No doubt their primary function was the ornamentation of the gate'. They go on to refer to these paintings as *in situ*, but this is not at all clear from their description (just quoted). They sound rather more as if they were found associated with the wall and portal. Further, on p.57 of their article, Bietak and Marinatos (1995)

---

[440] Hein (1998:554).
[441] Bietak (1996a:70, 75, 76).

write: 'Plants can also be used as decorative motifs. A good example is a border composed of ivy which *probably* [my italics] decorated the previously mentioned portal of the early 18th Dynasty building (palace?) in area H/III'. The use of the word 'probably' does not indicate a fresco found actually attached to the portal/wall surface. But let us accept this association. Bietak (1997:117) states that the Aegean fresco fragments at H/III 'were found *in situ* in the context of the early Eighteenth Dynasty stratum'.

   Therefore, the evidence for a secure early 18th Dynasty date for any of the frescoes is at best debatable on strict criteria. The portal from H/III appears the most secure evidence so far, although even here the details (or semantics) are not completely rigorous. Perhaps the reasonable conclusion at present is to agree with Bietak and Marinatos (1995:49) that 'the Minoan wall paintings date to two periods: the late Hyksos period and the early 18th Dynasty'. I wish to stress that I do not seek to develop a case that Bietak is necessarily incorrect to propose an early 18th Dynasty date for these (or some of these) Aegean-style frescoes, merely to stress that his view rests on hypothesis, and not evidence, at this time. The final publication may well clarify the situation. The real point of the last several paragraphs has been to highlight the irretrievably mixed and non-secure associations of most of the fresco evidence, and especially the H/I and H/IV material. I accept that it might seem that I am failing to observe Popper's famous warning that 'the abandonment of real problems for the sake of verbal problems' 'is the surest path to intellectual perdition',[442] but, if Tell el-Dabᶜa is to form the centre-piece of Aegean chronology as argued by some leading scholars,[443] then it must be able to withstand scrutiny.

Stylistic date of the Tell el-Dabᶜa frescoes in Aegean terms?

Of rather greater significance than the preceding discussion is the date of the Tell el-Dabᶜa frescoes in Aegean stylistic terms, irrespective of whichever Egyptian association one accepts. This is inherently problematic. With the exception of the body of material from Akrotiri found conveniently sealed by the volcanic eruption, the majority of the comparanda from the key Minoan sites like Knossos are not securely dated.[444] Immerwahr (1990:63) writes that 'unfortunately the miniature paintings from Knossos had all fallen from the walls of the palace some time before its final destruction and are thus very fragmentary'. As a result, we are rather ignorant of LMIB frescoes, for example. The beginnings of the genre may, however, be established. In the Aegean, representational and naturalistic frescoes do not on present evidence begin before the New Palace, MMIIIB/LMIA, period.[445] Although possible Evans' 'MMIIIB' (= MMIIIB/LMIA transition) precedents may have existed at Knossos, figural scenes in

---

[442] Popper in Schilpp (1974:12, reversing the order of the two connected clauses in Popper's original sentence).

[443] E.g. Warren (1996:287–288).

[444] See e.g. Immerwahr (1990).

[445] And in specific terms at Knossos, not until the MMIIIB/LMIA second phase of construction: Niemeier (1994:84–85).

general are an LMIA (and later) phenomenon.[446] But this *minimum* LMIA stylistic date is by no means the only possible date for such art; it could well belong to the LMIB period. Although some of the Tell el-Dabᶜa fresco material, like the Alalakh and Tel Kabri examples, has good comparisons with (later) LMIA examples from Akrotiri,[447] some of the Tell el-Dabᶜa material may also, or better, be compared with later New Palace work from Crete,[448] or, like the male life-size face with beard,[449] have no good fresco comparisons of LMI date (on current data).[450] To date, rigour has been conspicuously absent in examinations of the Tell el-Dabᶜa fresco material. The fragments somehow all became LMIA in stylistic attribution when they were originally thought to be Hyksos in date,[451] and in general statements Bietak seems willing to continue to state this: '...they date to a period (Late Minoan IA) ...' (1997:117). But, in fact, several elements would as easily, even better, date to LMIB in terms of comparanda from Crete. Bietak and Marinatos (1995:60) expressly voice concern over this problem.

Recent assessments point clearly in this direction. Betancourt (1997:430) states that:

> The style of the paintings in Aegean terms is a developed, late phase of LMI, with the wealth of iconographic detail indicating that the painting tradition was already mature in the Aegean.

A 'late phase of LMI', with the painting tradition 'already mature in the Aegean', is code for an LMIB, rather than LMIA, date.[452] Laffineur (1998:60) likewise notes that the decorative border of half-rosettes at the bottom of the Tell el-Dabᶜa bull-leaping fresco is a late feature: see Figure 24. Even clearer guidance is offered from the examination of the 'bull-leaping ritual, which appears prominently among the recovered scenes at Tell el-Dabᶜa':[453] see Figure 24. Rehak (1997:400), referring to detailed studies on Minoan bull iconography[454] writes:

> According to the low (traditional) Aegean chronology, the early 18th Dynasty Dabᶜa paintings should be contemporary with LMIA. But as several recent studies have pointed out, the spread of bull iconography outside of Knossos is a feature of the end of the Neopalatial period. The Dabᶜa frescoes thus fit better into the revised high Aegean chronology, which makes them contemporary with LMIB.

---

[446] Warren (1995:4 and 14n.1); Morgan (1995); Immerwahr (1990:21–75); Walberg (1986:57–72); Blakolmer (1997).

[447] Negbi (1994); Bietak (1995a; 1996a:73–75; 1997:117); Morgan (1995); Warren (1995:4).

[448] For example, the comparanda cited by Bietak and Marinatos (1995).

[449] Bietak and Marinatos (1995:fig.7).

[450] Some larger-scale human figures are, however, known from Thera and Kea: Morgan (1995:38).

[451] E.g. Warren (1995); Morgan (1995).

[452] Betancourt (1998b:292) states that 'it is ... obvious that the paintings reflect a mature stage of the Aegean painting style, not its beginnings'. He further notes with regard to the Aegean-style wall paintings from the Levant and Tell el-Dabᶜa that the 'most often cited Aegean parallels are with ... LMIB for the Egyptian ones'.

[453] Quote from Bietak (1996a:79).

[454] By Hallager and Hallager (1995); Younger (1995); and Shaw (1995). See also Marinatos (1994).

Fig. 24. Schematic drawing of the published reconstruction of the bull-leaping tableau assembled from among the fresco fragments from the H/I and H/IV debris dumps after Bietak (1996a:pl.IV).

Thus we face the situation where careful consideration of Aegean stylistic date may both support Bietak's early 18th Dynasty date for (at least some of) the Tell el-Dabᶜa frescoes, but at the same time undermine the conventional low Aegean chronology which he takes for granted! 'Isn't it ironic … don't you think'.[455]

A little more might be said. Wall paintings and other media showing bull-games, and bull-leaping, appear on Crete from the beginning of the New Palace period[456] –

---

[455] Morissette (1995).

[456] The earliest representation of the genre appears to be on a clay sealing from the Temple Repositories at Knossos of MMIIIB–early LMIA date: Evans (1921–1935, vol.III:218, fig.149). For date of deposit, see Panagiotaki (1998). The MMIII? relief scenes from the East Hall in the palace at Knossos might also be relevant: Kaiser (1976:289–291); Immerwahr (1990:171 Kn No.8) – although an LMI date is likely. The date for the earliest wall painting evidence is less secure. One plaster relief fragment showing part of a bull's foot pre-dates the MMIII/LMIA transition (Niemeier 1994:84), but there is nothing else definitely (or even likely to be) so early (Niemeier 1994:84–85). Fragments of miniature frescoes from the cists of the 13th Magazine on the west side of the palace of Knossos (Evans 1921–1935, vol. I:442–445, 527–528 and Fig.385), including one showing a bull's head with the locks of the hair of a leaper/acrobat, were dated MMIIIB byEvans, but subsequent scholarship has favoured a later, LMII–IIIA, date (Immerwahr 1990:64, 173–174

although in no case for wall paintings is the chronology particularly secure[457] – and continue in LMI to LMII/IIIA.[458] The genre has long been considered a Cretan invention. The famous Toreador fresco from Knossos,[459] to which Bietak and others compare his bull-leaping scene, is in fact usually dated to the LMII–IIIA period,[460] up to a century later than the Dab‛a frescoes (even if painted in the late part of Ahmose's reign), although it should be noted that Evans did suggest a late LMI (i.e. LMIB) date: 'a date not later at least than the first Late Minoan phase' – and since he specifically mentions marine style pottery, we may interpret this as LMIB.[461] The appearance of bull-leaping scenes in Anatolia and Syria is placed from the 17th century BC.[462] A report of a dramatic new find of a bull-leaping scene depicted on a vase from Anatolia may now be added.[463] A date linked to the reign of the Hittite king Hattusili I is stated. The quoted numbers, 1650–1620BC, reflect the so-called Middle Chronology for the Babylonian Old Kingdom;[464] the Low Chronology would instead suggest dates either within the first half, or during the middle, of the 16th century BC;[465] and the reappraised Babylonian chronology of Gasche *et al.* (1998) would require dates even later again in the middle, to second half, of the 16th century BC. With the Aegean 'early' chronology, no chronological, and so artistic, precedence need be attached to the Anatolian examples, in accord with much perceived art-historical opinion which credits Crete and especially Knossos with the genre;[466] whereas, with the 'low' Aegean chronology, the situation is rather less satisfactory (also the case with other Aegean–Anatolian LBA linkages).[467]

Kn No.18; Morgan 1995:41 and 48 ns. 118 and 119). See generally Morgan (1998:18 and refs.).

[457] See references above; generally, see Immerwahr (1990:64–65, 90–92, 98–99, 161).

[458] For likely LMIB/II examples, see the stucco reliefs of charging bulls from the area of the West Loggia of the North Entrance at the palace of Knossos: Immerwahr (1990:174 Kn No.21 and refs.).

[459] See Shaw (1996:pl.C and D.1); Immerwahr (1990:175 with refs.).

[460] E.g. Hood (1978b:60–62).

[461] Evans (1921–1935, vol.3:210). Of course, if the Tell el-Dab‛a frescoes might in some cases date as late as Tuthmosis III (see previous section), then even LMIIIA comparanda could be relevant (see Chapter IV.9). In which case the chronological relevance of the corpus of paintings would become even more diffuse.

[462] Collon (1994).

[463] Lightfoot (1998).

[464] As in Bryce (1998:xiii).

[465] See Kuhrt (1995:229–231); Astour (1989:9–13, 77).

[466] E.g. Marinatos (1994), and her alternative view of the evidence compared to Collon (1994); see also Younger (1995); Hallager and Hallager (1995); Morgan (1995:40–44); Shaw (1996); Niemeier and Niemeier (1998:80 n.122); and Morgan (1998:18 and n.6). In an Aegean–east Mediterranean context the association of representations of bull-leaping (and bull-games) especially with Crete and Knossos is reasonable (despite Collon 1994). And, even if the Minoan exclusivity were challenged, the 17th–16th century BC 'appearance' of such representations might be regarded as a common koine of expression in the Aegean–east Mediterranean region, and might nonetheless be regarded as largely driven by the Minoan culture at its LMIA height. Of course, it is also worth remembering that Crete is not the only possible source of such images. The bull has long been a powerful symbol, and bull-leaping, and bull-games, occur widely across the prehistoric to early historic Indo-European world (Rice 1998). The specific nature (technical and stylistic) of the Tell el-Dab‛a wall paintings is what makes an Aegean influence likely (Niemeier 1998; cf. Knapp 1998).

[467] Mee (1998). See also Chapter VII below.

Shaw (1996) has recently published an interesting study of fresco fragments from Mycenae on the Greek mainland which show an early mainland Greek bull-leaping scene. She argues that it is close to the LMI originals of the genre, being in true miniature fresco technique. Like Younger (1995), Hallager and Hallager (1995), and Morgan (1995:40–44), she sees actual bull-leaping as a specifically Cretan, and probably Knossian, activity. Overall, the evidence is admittedly thin, but the art form very much begins in the 17th century BC, and in New Palace (MMIIIB–LMI) Crete. No secure wall-painted examples exist from MMIIIB–LMIA, but the evidence of LMIB and LMII–III examples, and the indications from other media, suggest that they did originally exist.[468] If the Tell el-Dabᶜa example is held to be rather similar in design and execution to Aegean wall-painted bull-leaping scenes, then these seem to centre at Knossos and only spread out from there in the LHII period (and onwards).[469] In Minoan terms, this is LMIB and later. Studies of representations in other media provide a consonant picture, and thus leave us with the position summarised by Rehak (above).

The fresco showing ivy from the area/context of the early 18th Dynasty portal (mentioned above) is of great interest in this regard. Whatever the semantics, in the article of Bietak and Marinatos (1995) this is the only fresco fragment specifically linked with the early 18th Dynasty. Bietak (1996a:75) is even more explicit: 'From area H/III – from around a doorway with a portico in an undisputed early 18th Dynasty context – we have decorative paintings with an ivy leaf and loop-pattern'.[470] The architectural elements are linked with an initial 18th Dynasty enclosure wall (associated with the new palace at H/II). A facsimile drawing of the fresco fragment is shown in an article by Bietak and Marinatos (1995:fig.13), with stylised, outline/hollow or x-ray detail, ivy with curling interior to leaf, in red on a yellow background. As in some other, later(?), examples from Tell el-Dabᶜa, the colours are not particularly Aegean.[471]

But much more interesting are the stylistic comparisons. Bietak[472] compares the loop to an Old Palace example from Phaistos,[473] but this is not an ivy leaf nor remotely similar in design (nor date, nor colours: note Aegean blue background at Phaistos). LMIA frescoes show ivy in a notably naturalistic style (if simplified) with

---

[468] As Morgan (1995:41) argues.

[469] With the Mycenae example perhaps the earliest in the Aegean: Shaw (1996). See p.190 for her best hypothesis on date.

[470] Bietak (1997:117) repeats this association. Although the fresco fragment shown in fig. 4.35, to which the reader is referred, is in fact a different fresco fragment.

[471] E.g. Theran ivy borders have blue leaves, greenish stems, a red stalk on a white background and reddish stems: Doumas (1992:pls.78–79, 83). The Monkey fresco from the House of the Frescoes at Knossos, of early New Palace date (MMIIIB–LMIA), has the same solid leaves alternatively blue or green (Immerwahr 1990:42–45, Fig.16, 170 Kn No.2; Hood 1978b:Fig.50A). The ivy in an LMIA fresco from Phaistos is similar (Hood 1978b:Fig.34; Immerwahr 1990:pl.17). In this regard one may compare the LMIA style spray behind the LMIA style griffin from among the Tell el-Dabᶜa H/I fragments where the colours *are* Aegean: Bietak (1997:120 Fig.4.31). The H/III ivy is quite different (and later).

[472] Bietak (1996a:75 and n.122).

[473] Immerwahr (1990:22, fig.6.b, 183 Phs No.1).

solid or part-solid leaves,[474] and most examples from ceramic decoration are similar.[475] Indeed, if one rules out a relief sculptural form of the motif from an MMIII columnar stone lamp[476] where the medium perhaps partly promotes this form of representation,[477] then the best comparisons for the less naturalistic, more stylised, representation of ivy, and especially with hollow, x-ray style, leaves with attention paid to curving/spiral interior decoration,[478] come from LMIB, and onwards into LMII and LMIIIA.[479] An example on an LMIB sherd from Kythera is very similar in type and is part of a running sequence off a stem as in the Dabʿa fresco.[480] The climbing motif in less naturalistic, more stylised, form occurs in LMII.[481] Indeed, it is notable that good comparisons of form and style may be found in Mycenaean LHIIA ceramic decoration.[482] In short, there seems no good reason for this ivy to be compared to LMIA examples (and MMIII comparisons are too early on any chronology); it is also in contrast both to the naturalistic, LMIA style, plants found in other (earlier) Tell el-Dabʿa fresco fragments,[483] and the relatively realistic pictorial design fashion seen in other earlier 13th Dynasty into Hyksos period art such as the pictorial representations on Tell el-Yahudiyeh and related ceramics from the Syrian–Palestinian–Egyptian region.[484] Thus it may be that the fresco associated with an early 18th Dynasty portal is best compared to LMIB/LHIIA styles. See Figure 25.

This offers an identical stylistic chronology to the bull-leaping case mentioned above. And there are other aspects of the material which can be similarly analysed. Thus we might correlate the early 18th Dynasty – and Bietak argues that this is earliest 18th Dynasty, and, in particular, Ahmose – with LMIB art on Crete. In fact, this is at present the only linkage definitely associated with the early 18th Dynasty on the basis of published literature. Where does this leave the rest of the fresco fragments? Some of these may also link with LMIB, but, if others do have best comparisons with LMIA style, this raises an interesting scenario. Might LMIA style fragments from other areas therefore be best dated to the late Hyksos palace? The alternative is to date them all 'neopalatial', and admit defeat on any closely refined chronology.

---

[474] Doumas (1992:pls.78–79, 83); Hood (1978b:Figs.34 and 50A); Immerwahr (1990:44–45, Fig.16; 180, pl.17); Niemeier (1985:66, figs.22.1–4). What looks like ivy on the MM Town Mosaic is similar: Immerwahr (1990:68 and Fig.21 upper left).

[475] Niemeier (1985:fig.22.9–14, 15); Popham (1967:pls.76.i, 77.d).

[476] Evans (1921–1935, vol.I:344–345, fig.249).

[477] The same applies to the later form on a metal cup: Hood (1978b:fig.165).

[478] What Furumark (1941a:268) refers to as the open and volute type of the motif.

[479] Niemeier (1985:67, fig.22.18, 22.23, 22.40); Popham (1967:pl.82.a, pl.83.b, pl.84.c); Cummer and Schofield (1984:56 no.175, pl.49.175, 62 no.274, pl.51.274).

[480] Coldstream and Huxley (1972:199 no.287, pl.57.287).

[481] Niemeier (1985:fig.22.45–46).

[482] Niemeier (1985:72, fig.23); Furumark (1941a:esp. fig.35 top, letters s, t, x, fig.35 nos. 2, 3, 8, fig.36 nos.9, 10, 30); Mountjoy (1993:fig.57, p.53 no.74, 168 Fig.393).

[483] Bietak and Marinatos (1995:figs.12, 14).

[484] E.g. Hein (1994b:231–233 nos. 282, 284, 285, 287 and 288); Vermeule and Wolsky (1990:pls.182–183); McGovern *et al.* (1994).

Fig. 25. Comparison of a. the Tell el-Dab^c a ivy fresco fragment with b. an LMIB sherd with ivy motif from Kastri on Kythera and c. an LHIIA example from Ayia Irini, Keos. Drawings after Bietak and Marinatos (1995:fig.13); Coldstream and Huxley (1972: pl. 57. 287); and Cummer and Schofield (1984:pl.49 no.175).

STYLISTIC DATE OF EGYPTIAN ELEMENTS IN THE TELL EL-DAB^C A FRESCOES?

This is a very short, but nonetheless important point. As Morgan (1998) observes and makes clear, it is noteworthy that the Egyptian comparanda for the themes evident in the Tell el-Dab^c a fresco fragments – such as the themes of man-lion, man-prey, and lion-prey hunts, acrobatics, combat sports, human fighting, and bull-fighting/tethering – are all Middle Kingdom, and *not* New Kingdom. The frescoes would therefore date best in Egyptian artistic terms to the late Middle Kingdom (or as derived from such), or, in other words, to the SIP. The developed themes, and the hybrid Egyptian–Aegean (or Levantine in view of the Tel Kabri, Alalakh and Tell el-Dab^c a examples) themes and representation modes would further make good sense especially during the special period of west Asian–Egyptian fusion during the SIP (see Chapter IV.4 below). These factors might provide further grounds for suspecting a Hyksos date for many of the Tell el-Dabᶜa fresco fragments, rather than an early 18th Dynasty one.

CONCLUSIONS

To conclude this discussion. It is quite possible that some (or more) of the Tell el-Dabᶜa frescoes belong to the early 18th Dynasty buildings at the site, but should be compared with LMIB (and later) art on Crete and in the Aegean. This supports aspects of Bietak's revision of the architectural sequence at the site, but undermines the conventional low Aegean chronology. Conversely, some (or more) of the Tell el-Dabᶜa frescoes may have been painted in the Hyksos period, and may be best compared with LMIA art in the Aegean, and Middle Kingdom traditions in Egypt. This is potentially consonant with either an 'early', or 'compromise early', Aegean chronology. And, in general, the fashion and display of LMIA-style frescoes in prominent large rooms of élite buildings in the east Mediterranean belongs to an apparent later MBA Canaanite (Retenu) world and ideology (later MBII Alalakh, later MBII Kabri, 14th–15th Dynasty Tell el-Dabᶜa).[485] In short, the Tell el-Dabᶜa frescoes do not as yet provide clear, yet alone decisive, chronological data. They may well provide evidence consonant with the Aegean 'early' chronology, and certainly do not provide strong evidence for the conventional low Aegean chronology. Any further conclusion is premature pending final publication of the material.

4. Linkages between the Late Minoan IA Period, the Late Cypriot IA period, and Egypt and the Levant

While exciting, the Tell el-Dabᶜa frescoes do not resolve the date of the start of the LMI period/Aegean LBA. Therefore, we now need to examine the other archaeological evidence of relevance to the dating of the initial Aegean LBA. This primarily consists of the evidence relevant to the LMIA period.

Until a few sentences by Bietak a couple of years ago, no certain LMIA ceramics had ever been found in Egypt.[486] The fact that the remarkable finds are at Tell el-Dabᶜa, and not anywhere else in Egypt, is itself highly significant (see the following paragraphs). In one of those exquisite ironies, all our attention with regard to the Thera controversy had been focused on the LMIA period, but there was no evidence from Egypt until the reports just a couple of years ago from Tell el-Dabᶜa of 'the first

---

[485] If the paintings were part of an early 18th Dynasty ideology, or even contemporary élite Egyptian values, it certainly seems strange that no other similar paintings, even themes and images, have been found in early 18th Dynasty art elsewhere in Egypt – in marked contrast to late MBII Canaan.

[486] Bietak (1996a:70–71; see also 1997:117). For the previous situation, see Kemp and Merrillees (1980); and Merrillees (1980). It is worth reminding ourselves that no MMIII ceramics either had been found in Egypt before the recent work at Tell el-Dabᶜa (e.g. Redford 1992:121 and n.125).

finds of imported pottery of MMIII and LMIA date within the citadel, unfortunately from secondary contexts so far'.[487] Thus the LMIA period has been somewhat problematic in terms of a date based on Egyptian chronology in scholarship up to the 1990s,[488] with, in effect, zero evidence. An initial hypothesis tied the start of the LMI period (i.e. LMIA) to the start of the New Kingdom in Egypt (just as MM, Old Palace, Crete went with the Middle Kingdom), but there was a lack of any precision in this best guess.[489] Popham (1970a:226) simply stated that 'Evans' date for the beginning of Late Minoan I is generally accepted but its basis is open to question'. Thus by 1979 Warren was happy to admit to SIP links for at least some of the LMIA period, and proposed starting the LMIA period during the SIP of Egypt (c.1600BC); Betancourt (1985:122) likewise observed that LMIA could start anytime from 1650–1550BC (i.e. SIP), and that 'there is no evidence for the more precise "traditional" view that it begins ca. 1580 B.C.' Hallager (1988:12) similarly admitted that 'it is important to stress that the renewed investigations of the traditional synchronisms of the MMIII/ LMIA material have shown the contexts – both the Egyptian/Near Eastern and Aegean – so dubious that a revised high chronology for the beginning of the LMIA is possible'.

In fact, it has become increasingly evident in recent years that much or all of the

---

[487] Bietak (1996a:70). No LMIA or contemporary Aegean ceramic material has yet been published or illustrated by Bietak and his team at the time this text is written. The Minoan in fact seems to be singular: 'It is a trickle decorated amphoriskos with an oval mouth (identified by Stephan Hiller and Peter Warren)' (Bietak 1997:130 n.71; see also Hankey and Leonard 1998:30). The other items referred to are: 'locally made Aegean ritual vessels, such as LMIA *rhyta* with red burnished surfaces', and 'Minoan and Aegean imports were also retrieved in the area of platform H/I, but unfortunately not in secure contexts' (Bietak 1997:117; Bietak 1996a:87 n.104 thanks Vronwy Hankey 'for consultation about the rhyta'). Bietak refers to Hein (1994b:245 no.314) as an example of one of these LMIA rhyta (Bietak 1997:130 n.70). This is the only available illustration to date. But the vessel illustrated in Hein (1994b:245 no.314) is not capable of being dated specifically as an imitation of an LMIA product (and personally I fail to see why it is necessarily an Aegean imitation at all). While conical rhyta are a classic LMIA type, they occur also in LMIB (and later), and, more to the point in this context, are well known in the reign of Tuthmosis III, as evident from their representation in the contemporary tomb paintings at Thebes (e.g. tomb of Rekhmire). In the footnote given following the mention of the other Minoan and Aegean imports (Bietak 1997:130 n.71), Bietak refers to Hein (1994b:261 no.359) as the only available illustration to date of such an item (Bietak 1996a:87 n.105 refers instead to 'Hein 1994b:261 no.358', but this is an error). This piece is stated to be 'sherds of a jug or amphoriskos with a painted representation of a leopard in flying gallop chasing an ungulate'. The illustrations in Hein (1994b:261) show a photograph of sherds with the head and fore legs of a leopard (which might be in flying gallop, but might also be crouched – the open mouth might favour the former) and a drawing showing sherds with two dark bands and above the legs of a running animal. A Cycladic association for the decorative motif is suggested. I discuss this vessel below, but suffice it to say here that while the decoration (or motif) might be linked to Cycladic examples (and even especially Theran ones), the vessel itself is probably not Aegean.

[488] Evans (1921–35, vol.IV:267 and fig.197) and Furumark (1950:209 and fig.18.A) originally identified an alabastron from Gurob as LMIA, but this vase is now considered to be a definite LHIIA product (Popham 1970a:226; Hankey and Warren 1974:146; Warren and Hankey 1989:144).

[489] The creation of the tripartite division of Minoan prehistory by Evans early in the 20th century in order more or less to correlate the Cretan sequence with the existing Old, Middle, and New Kingdom divisions in Egypt was a deliberate artificial construct. The problems of course are the problematic First and Second Intermediate Periods in Egypt, which lie respectively 'between' the EM and MM, and the MM and LM, periods on Crete. Herein lies the root cause of much of the modern Thera controversy.

LMIA period correlates with the late Syro-Palestinian MBA period, and the Hyksos/ SIP era in Egypt. There is no large body of clear-cut data (see above); but several lines of relevant argument lead this way.

A. MINOAN EXPORTS AND THE GENERAL HISTORICAL PATTERN

Consider a notable pattern. At the high-point of Middle Minoan, Old Palace, Crete, MMI–II products and influences are found over wide areas of the Aegean, east Mediterranean, Near East, and in particular at several sites in Egypt, including in Middle and Upper Egypt.[490] This corresponds with the unified Egyptian Middle Kingdom period. In the LMIB/LHIIA period Minoan, and especially Mainland equivalent, products and influences are again found from a variety of sites in the east Mediterranean and also in Egypt, including Middle and Upper Egypt and, in particular, via the paintings of the Keftiu, at Thebes in Upper Egypt.[491] This corresponds with the unified Egyptian New Kingdom (18th Dynasty). However, the LMIA period represents a stark contrast in Egypt outside the Delta. LMIA, and contemporary LHI and even rare Late Cycladic I,[492] products or influences are found all over the Aegean and in the east Mediterranean as far south as Palestine,[493] and this appears to be very much the high-point of Minoan civilisation.[494] Indeed, the holistic cultural corpus from pre-eruption, LMIA, Akrotiri on Thera – a major port – dramatically highlights the central importance of Aegean and east Mediterranean trade-exchange in the LMIA period[495] – and there is a good case for arguing that Minoan international trade declined noticeably in the wake of the Thera eruption and the destruction of Akrotiri.[496] But, despite this evident high-point and evidence of extensive foreign contacts, with the sole exception of the Hyksos capital of Avaris (Tell el-Dab'a) in the Nile Delta of Lower Egypt, *no*

---

[490] Warren and Hankey (1989:130–135); Kemp and Merrillees (1980); Cadogan (1983); Betancourt (1998a:6–7).

[491] Warren and Hankey (1989:138–144); Wachsmann (1987); Merrillees (1980); Leonard (1994); Hankey and Leonard (1998:32–33).

[492] Eastern exports of LHI and Late Cycladic I go at least as far as Cyprus: Dikaios (1969–1971:229–230); Cadogan (1990:95).

[493] For the latter, see Negbi (1989:61–62, pl.58.7). Confidently dated LMIA/LHI by Negbi, and compared to examples from Cyprus, but Leonard (1994:194 no.LM#6) suggests a more general 'LMI(?)' designation. Hankey and Leonard (1998:31) write 'LMIA/LHI (not certain?)'. A pithos from Tel Haror in Palestine with an incised Minoan sign might also be mentioned in this regard: Oren *et al.* (1996; Hankey and Leonard 1998:30). It is non-local, and may yet prove to be Cretan (postscript: *is* Cretan: P.M. Day *et al.* in *Aegaeum* 20, 1999). An 'LMI(?)' sherd from Tomb complex 104 at Palaepaphos *Skales* (Karageorghis *et al.* 1990:37 no.i, pl.4) is another possible early LM object in this region (whereas the sherd described by Karageorghis *et al.* 1990:50–51 no.vii, pl.4 mis-labelled as 'Tomb 105 Pit C (viii)', appears to be a likely LHIIA/LMIB find). A sherd described as LMIA was found closeby in one of the *Evreti* wells (Maier and Karageorghis 1984:71) (and, of course, other LMIA has been found elsewhere in Cyprus, especially at Toumba tou Skourou: see Chapter IV.5).

[494] Wiener (1990); Niemeier (1986); Driessen and Macdonald (1997:passim, and esp. pp.35–83); Rehak and Younger (1998:100–149); Renfrew (1998).

[495] Doumas (1991:44–48). Recent finds and announcements from Akrotiri add to this picture: in particular, there was a Linear A archive/administration on Thera (see Bennett and Owens 1999 and p.12 no.1 for other bibliography).

[496] Driessen and Macdonald (1997:80).

LMIA pottery or other product has ever been reported from Egypt: a long-standing position re-affirmed by Hankey and Leonard (1998:32). And, in particular, there is nothing in Middle or Upper Egypt.[497] The same applies to post-Kamares, MMIII, material – finds only in the Nile Delta at Tell el-Dabʿa.[498] Why? If LMIA was the overall high-point of Minoan Crete and its influence and trade, we may expect its products or influences at the major contemporary trading and élite centres of the period in the surrounding region. The total absence of LMIA finds in Egypt outside of the Canaanite-Hyksos capital in the Delta – in conspicuous contrast to previous MM, and subsequent LMIB/LHIIA and onwards, imports in Middle and Upper Egypt – *has* to suggest that it is likely that the MMIII–LMIA period correlated with the time of the Canaanite 14th and Hyksos-15th Dynasties in the Delta and their dominance in Egypt and the Levant and control of Egypt's access to the Mediterranean. This was a time when Upper Egypt (and the 16th and 17th Dynasties of Thebes) was in effect more or less cut off from the Mediterranean world.[499]

The stela of the late 17th Dynasty Theban king Kamose effectively confirms this situation until his reign when he states that: '... One chief is in Avaris, another in Kush, and I sit (here) associated with an Asiatic and a Nubian! Each man has his slice in this Egypt and so the land is partitioned with me! None can pass through it [surpass him – Apophis] as far as Memphis (although it is) Egyptian water! See he (even) has Hermopolis! No one can be at ease when they are milked by the taxes of the Asiatics...'.[500] The evidence suggests that 17th Dynasty Thebes looked further south for its exotic items in the main. Bourriau (1997:168) confirms this when she considers the ceramics from 17th Dynasty Thebes and area: 'The exotic element at Ballas [Deir el-Ballas, a major fort near Thebes] is not Middle Bronze Age Hyksos, but Kerma Nubian'. Even at Memphis, in Middle Egypt, in the Middle Kingdom, SIP, through early 18th Dynasty times, there are only a few fragments of imported Mediterranean ceramics (Cypriot, Aegean, Levantine), in marked contrast to the relative abundance at the Hyksos and Delta site of Tell el-Dabʿa.[501] And, in general, Bourriau (1997:160) observes that whereas the 17th Dynasty Theban kings enjoyed the resources (minerals) from the Eastern Desert, the Hyksos 'instead ... had the Levantine trade and, it now appears, trade with the Aegean'.

Even if we include the (only) two pieces of debatable evidence from Egypt and Nubia/Kush, the case remains: no potential LMIA or contemporary LHI object or clear stylistic influence has been found in a stratified context later than the *very beginning* of the 18th Dynasty (and both could well be SIP or late 17th Dynasty): (i) a small sherd from Kerma (Kingdom of Kush) apparently of LMI/LHI origin from either a late SIP

---

[497] This pattern is noted also by Niemeier (1995a:11 and 14–15 n.57 with refs.).

[498] Bietak (1996a:29, 70).

[499] For Hyksos control of much of Egypt, and the discomforture of the Theban dynasties, see Ryholt (1997); also the discussion of Redford (1992:112–115, 118–121). With further archaeological exploration in the Delta region, and of SIP sites in particular, additional finds of MMIII–LMIA ceramics might be anticipated in *this* region.

[500] Redford (1997:13).

[501] Bourriau (1997:165); Bourriau and Eriksson (1997).

or early 18th Dynasty context,[502] which, in view of the other main 'imports' of the period from Kerma being classic SIP types (Tell el-Yahudiyeh juglets, Levantine MBII piriform juglets, and a Cypriot WPIV vessel: Lacovara 1997:78), and the apparent end of international imports into Kerma with 'the beginning of hostilities between the Thebans, the Hyksos, and Kerma kingdoms', i.e. the reign of Kamose,[503] might very well also be a late SIP import (via the Hyksos delta region),[504] and (ii) the Aegean-influenced stylist features on items (some inscribed with the name of Ahmose) in the tomb of Queen Ahhotep, mother (?) of Ahmose founder of the 18th Dynasty: Ahmose axe shown in Figure 26.[505] The absence of any LMIA/LHI objects or clear stylistic

---

[502] Hankey and Warren (1989:138 with refs.); Smith (1965:39–40, fig.59); Lacovara (1997:78) – but cf. Hankey and Leonard (1998:31).

[503] Lacovara (1997:78–80).

[504] The sherd from Kerma from a late SIP=late 17th Dynasty or early 18th Dynasty context has in the past been described as 'LM/LHI' (Warren and Hankey 1989:138), although Dietz (1991:320 n.895) states that 'the fragment from Kerma cannot really be considered LMI/LHI'. Lacovara in his review of Kemp and Merrillees (1980) in the *Journal of Near Eastern Studies* 47 (1988) at p.305, referred to the sherd as identified as probably LHI by E. Vermeule, and he repeats this statement in a paper of 1997: '...there is one clearly identifiable Aegean sherd found at the site. This sherd ... has recently been examined by Mrs. Emily Vermeule, who attributed it to the Late Helladic I Period...' (Lacovara 1997:78). However, in the absence of an examination by a recognised specialist on early Mycenaean ceramics, this must be considered as less than satisfactory evidence.

[505] See Evans (1921–1935, vol.I:551 fig.402, 715 fig.537); Morgan (1988:51, 53, 186 n.80, 187 n.112, pl.63); Warren (1995:5); Bietak (1996a:80 and 89 n.139; 1997:124); also see below. Merrillees (1998:153) downplays the Aegean association, arguing that its presence may owe 'more to Levantine than Minoan workshops'. Mother of Ahmose is the usual view reported in Aegean literature. However, the exact genealogy of Ahmose's family is not certain, complicated by indications of some brother–sister marriages (for discussions, see Wente 1980a:123–127; Ryholt 1997:272–280). And with regard to Ahhotep, there is the long-standing problem that there seem to have been two high-status Ahhotep burials of about the same period (one found in the Deir el-Bahri cache, and one found at Dra Abu el-Naga). The burial of the Ahhotep from Dra Abu el-Naga contained the items inscribed with the names of Kamose and Ahmose (including those mentioned in the text above – for her coffin, see Tiradritti 1999:286–287). We know from several sources that Ahmose's mother was an Ahhotep. The question is which one, and to whom was she married? There are indications that kings Seqenenre Tao and Kamose were married to Ahhoteps. The name of Ahmose's father is not specifically attested. A statuette showing the eldest king's son Ahmose (not Ahmose who founds the 18th Dynasty, but perhaps an elder brother) now in the Louvre shows his name flanked by those of Seqenenre Tao and Ahhotep. If this is the later Ahmose's deceased elder brother, then this would suggest his parents were Seqenenre Tao married to Ahhotep (Ryholt 1997:275 n.1001, 277–278). But a problem occurs, because among the children of the king listed neither Kamose nor Ahmose appear. If Kamose was the elder brother of Ahmose this is a real problem, but he may more likely have been an uncle (younger brother of Seqenenre Tao). It is just possible to argue Ahmose had not been born (or was a baby) at the time of the statuette (and was thus a mere infant on accession). If we follow this line, one Queen Ahhotep (I) was the wife of King Seqenenre Tao and Ahmose's mother. The second Ahhotep (II) was a wife of Kamose. It is the latter whose burial contained the objects of interest. In this scenario she would be Ahmose's aunt (probably both paternal and maternal as the late 17th Dynasty seems to have practised brother–sister marriages and multiple use of the same names among children, and the two Ahhoteps are thus quite likely sisters). The other alternative is that Ahmose was the son of Kamose, and in this case the objects under discussion did belong to his mother (and this might best explain why objects with the names of both Kamose and Ahmose were found). Nothing is yet certain. An additional problem is how many kings had the nomen Tao? There seem to have been two (see Ryholt 1997:279), leading other scholars to propose slightly different family structures.

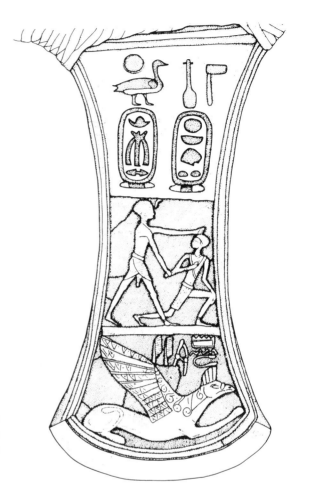

Fig. 26. Drawing of the Ahmose axe with Aegean-style griffin from the tomb of Ahhotep. After Morgan (1988:pl.63).

influence in the earlier 18th Dynasty anywhere in Middle or Upper Egypt would appear very odd if in fact LMIA was synchronous with the early 18th Dynasty (as the conventional chronology holds), given the pattern of just such imports and influences during the MM and then LMIB/LHIIA periods. Instead, this LMIA absence in early 18th Dynasty contexts (and in fact evidence for LMIB/LHIIA imports: see Chapter IV.7 below) strongly suggests that LMIA was contemporary with the Hyksos period, a time when Tell el-Dabᶜa was the major centre of Egypt, a major port, and a key part of a Hyksos-driven trading network in the east Mediterranean.[506] The recent news of the finds of LMIA ceramics and Aegean-style art at the Hyksos capital, Tell el-Dabᶜa / Avaris, and the general correlation observable in terms of space and time, between the LMIA period and its products, and the later MBA Canaanite-Hyksos world and its products, further supports this claim. And, it must also be noted that another pattern has long

---

[506] Bietak (1996a:59–63); Negbi (1994); Niemeier (1995a; 1995b).

been observed with reference to the early 18th Dynasty imports of LMIB/LHII material into Egypt: the majority are mainland (LHIIA) products.[507] This has only become more and more clear with further work. Thus, by the time of the early 18th Dynasty, it would seem that Cretan 'power' or trading 'influence' was on the wane. The early New Palace (MMIIIB–LMIA) acme of Minoan civilisation, power, and influence, on both a regional and interregional scale, had already passed, and must thus be placed in the SIP. Overall, New Palace period MMIIIB–LMIA–LMIB exports/links – in specific motifs, in ceramics, and in true *fresco* technique painting – 'was a rather short-lived phenomenon in the Levant and Egypt – in Egyptian terms, covering the Hyksos period and the very beginning of the early 18th Dynasty' (Niemeier and Niemeier 1998:96).

B. IMPORT PATTERNS IN THE AEGEAN

The datable imported Syrian–Palestinian or Egyptian material in the Aegean from LMIA (or contemporary) contexts is consistently of late MBA or Hyksos period (SIP) date[508] – the undatable imports, such as ivory and copper, are also entirely consistent with such a view.[509] The finds from the mature–later LMIA VDL on Thera are the clearest. The imports consist of several Syro-Palestinian MBII stone (gypsum) vessels, a Syro-Palestinian ('Canaanite') storage jar of likely later MBII (to LBI) date, and a Syro-Palestinian type tripod stone mortar from Marinatos' excavations at Akrotiri; in addition, there are also some Tell el-Yahudiyeh and related juglets (of later MBA/Hyksos period date) probably from pre-eruption Thera.[510] There are *no*

---

[507] Highlighted by e.g. Kantor (1947[1997]:48–50).

[508] A pattern observed and noted also by Niemeier (1995a:11); and Betancourt (1997:429).

[509] Rehak and Younger (1998b:235–242). Copper consistent with a Cypriot origin is found at LMIA pre-eruption Akrotiri on Thera (Stos-Gale and Gale 1990: 80 and Fig. 16). This is the earliest likely Cypriot copper found so far from the second millennium BC Aegean, and links nicely with evidence from Akrotiri for Late Cycladic I–LMIA–LCI contacts and trade.

[510] For the stone vessels, see Warren (1979:88–90, 106–107 and n.2). For the storage jar, see Marinatos (1968–1976, vol.VII:15, 30 and pls.19.b and 49.b). It is an example of a very long-lived type (Grace 1956; Parr 1973), and close dating is impossible. In general, it is of the MBII type, which continues into LBI, and pre-dates the bi-conical and 'knobbed' or pointed base types standard in the LBII period (see Amiran 1970:103, 140–142, pls.32 and 43). No consistent development is evident at every site in the Levantine region, making precise dating problematic. The Akrotiri vessel is unusual in detail (not helped by the photograph being taken looking slightly downwards: Marinatos 1968–1976:pl.49.b), and I have not found an exact parallel. It lacks the characteristic Palestinian MBII relatively slender ovoid shape which gracefully tapers to the base. The wide maximum diameter, and fairly straight, conical lower portion resembles some later MBII–LBI examples from Palestine (e.g. Amiran 1970:pl.32 no.6, pl.43 no.2). Marinatos (1968–1976, vol.VII:30) notes that the base is 'oval-shaped' (rather than flat or pointed). This again fits with MBII developments (which vary: Cole 1984:76). It is difficult to judge the exact form of the rim profile of the Akrotiri jar, but it seems quite everted and pronounced in Marinatos (1968–1976, vol.VII:pl.19.b esp. and also pl.49.b). The neck and rim appears plain, however (i.e. plain everted rim). There does not seem to be any ridge or other elaboration to the profile (cf. Cole 1984:Fig.22). Cole finds this to be a probable chronologically sensitive indicator in broad terms at Shechem of an earlier date: MBIIB, and not MBIIC (1984:73–74). In reverse, despite the plain profile, the relatively high neck, and especially the rim, which begins to flare outwards, are more typical of later MBIIB, and especially MBIIC(– LBI) (Seger 1974:123, 1965; Cole 1984:75). But the low position of the handles is more typically MBII

18th Dynasty, New Kingdom, imports from Thera.[511]

A further point is very important in this context. The single Aegean vessel described in any detail by Bietak among his finds of imported MMIII and LMIA ceramics at Tell el-Dabᶜa consists of 'sherds of a jug or amphoriskos with a painted representation of a leopard in flying gallop chasing an ungulate'.[512] Bietak notes that it is in fact not Minoan, but most likely Cycladic (the decoration, anyway – the vessel itself looks Levantine–Egyptian), in origin. I suggest we can be even a little more specific. This vessel's decoration seems to offer a link with pre-eruption Thera. The first reason is that pre-eruption Akrotiri was both the one and only large Cycladic centre of the later

---

than later (and more MBIIB than later, hence an older trait). Thus a date in later MBII is perhaps the most likely compromise. Although it is impossible to be precise. In Palestine (source of the evidence reviewed so far) the Akrotiri jar could fit in either a later MBII or LBI context. For example, the type would best fit in MBII Megiddo XIII/XII–X (Loud 1948:pls. 21.1, 27.3, 35.2, 43.1=129.1), rather than later, at Shechem an MBIIB–C date would appear acceptable (Cole 1984:73–76), at Jericho it fits generally with (later) MBII types of storage jar (Kenyon 1965:196–197, esp. Fig.122 no.3; Kenyon 1960:293), as also at Tel el-ᶜAjjul (Tufnell 1962:Fig.14 no.58). However, similar forms also occur among the early LBA material from Lachish, where it could belong with the range of storage jars of Class C (esp.) to B found in early LBI contexts – although it is noted that these 'jars of Class C survive from an earlier tradition' (Tufnell *et al.* 1958:221, 224); at the Fosse Temple the nearest examples belong with Temple I of early LBI date (Tufnell *et al.* 1940:pl.57.B nos.386, 387). And, then, just to render an ambiguous situation really complicated, a good parallel for the unusual body shape (but *not* everted rim, nor really the handles – too high and wrong shape) comes from Alalakh IV (Woolley 1955:pl.116 no.76, see p.335 for occurrence in Alalakh IV), of LBII date. But McClellan (1989:210) does note that many types of earlier levels occur into Alalakh IV. At Ugarit general comparanda may date from Ugarit Récent 1 (or 2: e.g. Schaeffer 1949:Fig.86). Other scholars have usually felt the Akrotiri vessel to be of an early type (e.g. Leonard 1996:243 characterises it as 'an early ovoid variant'), and have proposed either later MBII (Niemeier 1990:120–121; Niemeier and Niemeier 1998:87 n.207), or later MBII to LBI (Buchholz 1980:228), dates. These ubiquitous jars were probably mainly for wine trade along with other liquids (see McGovern and Harbottle 1997:152; Leonard 1996). For the tripod mortar, see Buchholz (1963; 1980:228–229) – Warren (1979:108) argues for local manufacture, but the type is well known in the east Mediterranean, and thus, even if he is correct, still offers a linkage between LMIA and later MBII in the east Mediterranean. For the Tell el-Yahudiyeh jugs, see Åström (1971); for the date for the biconical specimen, see the discussion of Bietak (1997:94). It must be admitted that there is no positive evidence that these jugs were found on Thera, but Åström (1971:415) makes a good case for their probably coming from the island and the LMIA volcanic destruction horizon. Further, their importation to Thera is plausible given other east Mediterranean finds at Akrotiri (and Akrotiri appears to have been a, or the, major international port of the LMIA period in the Aegean). The fact that a lump of pumice was found with one juglet may add to a Theran association.

[511] Cline (1994:201 no.598) is dated to either the Old/Middle Kingdom or 18th Dynasty, and hardly contradicts this statement. It is appropriate to note (again) that the MB stone vessels and the Canaanite jar from Akrotiri are not exactly clear diagnostic types. The late MBII dates are a best estimate. But it is fair to note in the case of the Canaanite jar, for example, that it is typically very difficult to distinguish between late MBII and early LBI contexts or products in Syria–Palestine (see previous footnote above). Thus sceptics might wish to argue that it is not necessarily impossible for these vessels to be early 18th Dynasty in chronological date. Yes, possible. But the useful contribution of this evidence is as part of a larger pattern. No evidence from LMIA contexts is certainly 18th Dynasty or Syro-Palestinian LBI in date, and all is either stated to be, or is consistent with, a SIP/MB (or earlier), date. Hence the position taken in the main text seems the most plausible and likely.

[512] Bietak (1996a:70–71 and 87 n.105). Illustration in Hein (1994b:261).

MBA–LB1 period, and the only Cycladic centre with regional and extra-Aegean connections.[513] Hence the export of any Cycladic product outside the Aegean, or evidence of a stylistic linkage (whether import or export) with an area outside the Aegean, is likely only via an active Akrotiri. In support, we may observe that the only other LCI Cycladic exports into the east Mediterranean are usually thought to be Theran.[514] We are by definition in the pre-eruption time period. The other reason is that the decorative motif shown on the vessel from Tell el-Dab^ca, on the basis of the description and available photograph, finds its only set of good parallels in the Aegean in the Late Cycladic I repertoire of pre-eruption Thera. A ceramic vessel found in the old French excavations on Thera offers a partial parallel for the ungulate running,[515] and another unprovenanced vessel undoubtedly from pre-eruption, Late Cycladic I, Thera,[516] shows likely cats or lions in flying gallop position (male pursuing female). Together, with cats/lions and ungulates, these two Theran vessels appear to offer good comparisons for the decorative scheme on the new Dab^ca vessel. It is unfortunate that the sherd is from a secondary context, but it nonetheless indicates a likely pre-Thera-eruption stylistic linkage with Tell el-Dab^ca.

Although scarce, the few other pieces of evidence from the Aegean yield a consistent pattern.[517] On the one hand, we may note that virtually all the (very few) other Syro-Palestinian-Egyptian imports specifically from the LHI–LMIA period are consistent with a SIP date. For example, a stone vessel either from Middle Kingdom or probably SIP Egypt, or perhaps instead better sourced to late MBA Syria/Palestine,[518] was found in either LHI, or later LHI (=LHIB) Shaft Grave V at Mycenae.[519] The Khyan lid may also be noted again; objects of this ruler are found over a wide area, and one from peak LMIA Knossos makes good sense.[520] The few other MMIIIB–LMIA (to 'LMI') Near Eastern imports are much less precise, but are consonant with a Syro-Palestinian MBA

---

[513] Wiener (1990); Davis and Cherry (1990); consider also the distributions of diagnostic artefacts in Niemeier (1986).

[514] Cadogan (1990:95); Vermeule and Wolsky (1990:382 and n.76, 394).

[515] Renaudin (1922:fig.29, pl.13).

[516] Demakopoulou and Crouwel (1993).

[517] I refer principally to the catalogue of orientalia in the Aegean assembled by Cline (1994).

[518] Lilyquist (1997:225).

[519] For vessel, see Phillips (1991:839 no.455); Hankey (1987:43); for later LHI/LHIB context, see Graziadio (1991:430–437); Dietz (1991:248–249, 250 fig.78). As I have noted before (e.g. Manning 1995:229 end-note 2), Cline's (1994:5–6 and 201 no.597) 18th Dynasty attribution is incorrect. Cline was following the original date offered by Warren in the 1960s, which Hankey and Phillips have since corrected/superseded. Warren (1997:211), in a paper not concerned with chronology, has subsequently persevered with his original date, but without any comment or discussion. The datings of Hankey and Phillips should be preferred in this regard. However, Lilyquist (1997:225 with refs.) has subsequently questioned the Egyptian attribution itself, and instead makes a strong case for a provenance in Syria–Palestine, and thus a likely date of manufacture in the later MBA: I thank C. Lilyquist for information and comment (see also in general Lilyquist 1996). In any case, the date of the vessel is pre-18th Dynasty.

[520] See Chapter IV.2 above for the lid, and for the probable LMIA date. For the foreign distribution of objects of this king, see Ryholt (1997:384 nos.7–10 File 15/4); Negbi (1994:85 and n.12); Mellink (1995:85–86).

association, for example: the Syrian seal from Poros,[521] the Syrian seal from Tylissos,[522] or the cylinder seal from Ayia Triadha.[523] Later material invariably either comes from imprecise contexts which include LMIB/LHIIA (or later), or the diagnosis of the 18th Dynasty/LBA date for the import is only part of a possible range including older dates (e.g. Middle Kingdom or SIP). Examples of such data drawn from the catalogue of orientalia found in the Aegean assembled by Eric Cline (1994) include: page 165 no.259 which is either 18th Dynasty or Middle Kingdom from an LMI (non-specific) context, 166 no.274 which is 18th Dynasty but from an LMI–II context (also 166–167 nos.275–277), 168 no.290 which is 18th Dynasty but from an LMIA–B context, 168 no.291 which is the same, 168 no.293 which is 18th Dynasty or Middle Kingdom from an LMI context (probably), 189 no.486 which is 18th Dynasty but comes from an MMIII–LMI (i.e. includes LMIB) context, 191 no.507 from a non-specific LMI context and which is 18th Dynasty or earlier, 202 no.609 which is 18th Dynasty but from an LMIA–B context, 204 no.626 which comes from an LHI context but is only possibly 18th Dynasty(?) or perhaps in fact of local manufacture(?), 204 no.630 which is early 18th Dynasty but from an MMIIIB–LMI (non-specific) context, 205 no.637 which is a LBA Syro-Palestinian import but from an LMIA–B context, 210 no.681 which comes from MMIII–LMIA but is only dated to anywhere from the Old Kingdom to the 18th Dynasty, 213 no.710 from a non-specific LMI context and assigned only to New Kingdom(?) or Minoan(?), and 221 no.785 which is 18th Dynasty but from an LMI–II context.[524]

There are in fact only three exceptions in the whole of the catalogue of Cline (1994). The first is some fragments of one or more Canaanite jars from an LMIA context at Kato Zakro on Crete.[525] These are given a Syro-Palestinian origin and an 'LB' date. However, this is simply of no value. Late MB and early LB (LB1) Canaanite jars can be, or are, indistinguishable from typical sherdage unless diagnostic parts are present (and even then it is difficult! – I speak from experience). The second is an 18th Dynasty(?) alabaster body fragment from LMIA Knossos which could as easily be from a SIP vessel instead.[526] The third is a faience vase from later LHI, LHIB, Shaft Grave II at Mycenae.[527] Cline gives this vase an 18th Dynasty date. If so, it is the only definite 18th Dynasty import of later LMIA or LHI date. This author in contrast does not find the vase distinctly diagnostic of the 18th Dynasty at all, and even Cline (1994:5–6) does not choose to mention this piece in his discussion on chronology.

On the other hand, we may note the probable total absence of definite 18th Dynasty objects in definite LMIA contexts (the one or two suggested items are highly questionable), but also the pattern of several later MBA, Hyksos-SIP, imports deposited in LMIB contexts *and*, during and by the end of the LMIB period, the appearance *then* of a horizon of the first Syro-Palestinian-Egyptian LBA/18th Dynasty material. Even

---

[521] Cline (1994:154 no.184 – cf. discussion in Manning 1995:218–220).
[522] Cline (1994:154 no.181).
[523] Cline (1994:160 no.223).
[524] I have ignored items in Cline's (1994) Catalogue III from disputed contexts, etc.
[525] Cline (1994:178 no.386).
[526] Cline (1994:166 no.269).
[527] Cline (1994:215 no.730).

allowing that the MBA-SIP imports were heirlooms by the time of their LMIB deposition, this does rather suggest that the preceding LMIA period was the likely time of import (if not earlier LMIB), and that LMIA, at least, was contemporary with the SIP-Hyksos period. It also suggests that the transition to the Syro-Palestinian-Egyptian LBA and 18th Dynasty occurred *during* the LMIB period. Examples of MBA-SIP material deposited in LMIB contexts include the good Hyksos period – 15th Dynasty(?) – scarab from an LMIB context at Knossos,[528] the stone sphinx from Malia,[529] and possibly the SIP or early 18th Dynasty faience vessels from LMIB Knossos.[530] The evidence from mainland Greece is compatible, with MBA-SIP material from LHI–II contexts,[531] with the earliest clear 18th Dynasty or Syro-Palestinian LBA material no earlier than LHIIA,[532] or from imprecise contexts where the available range includes LHII or later.

As noted, it is the mature LMIB period which witnesses the arrival of clear early 18th Dynasty imports, and Syro-Palestinian LB types likewise dated no earlier than the start of the 18th Dynasty. The examples of Egyptian imports from the catalogue of Cline (1994) include: 166 no.270 18th Dynasty alabaster fragments from an LMIB context at Knossos, 168 no.289 18th Dynasty alabaster alabastron from an LMIB context at Malia, 189 no.485 an 18th Dynasty faience bowl from an LMIB context at Knossos, 197 no.563 an 18th Dynasty ceramic fragment from an LMIB context at Kommos, 201 no.600 an 18th Dynasty alabaster fragment from an LMIB context at Knossos, and 221 no.783 an early 18th Dynasty frit vessel from an LMIB context at Knossos. Perhaps most significant of all are the appearance in LMIB contexts of the distinctive LBA/LCIB (from early 18th Dynasty onwards) Cypriot Red Lustrous Wheelmade Ware spindle bottles at LMIB Gournia and LMIB (or later) Kommos,[533] along with other LBA types:[534] see Figure 27 for a Cypriot example of the Red Lustrous Wheelmade Ware type.

Indeed, it is noticeable that, whereas the late MC to early LCI, and the first specifically early LCI, imports to the Aegean occur by mature LMIA, the Cypriot types which do not begin until during later LCI (i.e. are typical of 'LCIB' in the standard Swedish Cyprus Expedition terms of Åström 1972a) and which continue later, do not appear in the Aegean until the mature LMIB period. In the first category one may note, for example: the Red on Black ware later MC to LCI bowl fragment from an MMIII–LMIB context at Malia,[535] the WP Pendent Line Style sherd from a probable MMIIIB–LMIA context at Zakros (see Figure 34.g),[536] some LCI late handmade Red Slip from early

---

[528] Cline (1994:147 no.126).

[529] Michaelidis (1995).

[530] Cline (1994:211–212 nos. 696–698, 215 nos.731–733, 220–221 nos. 779–782); Cadogan (1976; 1983a:517 and n.183).

[531] E.g. Cline (1994:146 no.122, 213–214 no.716, and perhaps also 150 no.152).

[532] E.g. Cline (1994:150 no.152, 150 no.154, 163 no.244, 163 no.246, 165 no.257, 165 no.258, 179 no.396, 188 no.482, 204 no.631, 224 no.810); Rutter (1999: 142 and n.33).

[533] Cline (1994:214 nos. 717–718); Rutter (1999: Table 1 no.C2753); see in general Eriksson (1993; 1991).

[534] Cline (1994:173 no.330, 179 no.387, 194 no.532). See also the discussion of Rutter (1999:142 and ns. 33–34, and relevant data in his Table 1).

[535] Cline (1994:185 no.444).

[536] Popham (1963:89–91, Fig.1, pl.26.a).

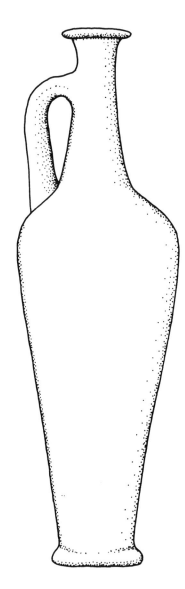

LMIA contexts at Kommos, a *possible* PWS? sherd from the middle phase of the three phases of LMIA at Kommos (LMIA Advanced), a group of Proto Base Ring and Monochrome vessels from either (and most importantly first) LMIA Final contexts (C10766, C10777, C10778, C10779) or early LMIB contexts (C10754, C10833, C11078) at Kommos, an occurrence of one (early? i.e. LCIA northwest/west Cypriot) BRI jug or tankard (C11215) from a LMIA Final context at Kommos (which, with the Thera WSI bowl, may reasonably be held to define the appearance of initial LCIA1/2 or LCIA2 northwest/west Cypriot WSI, BRI, etc., in the later LMIA period, and *prior* to the appearance of the full LCIB package of mature WSI, BRI, and especially additions like Red Lustrous Wheelmade Ware, during the subsequent LMIB period),[537] and, of course, the diagnostically earlier LCI WSI bowl from pre-eruption Late Cycladic I/ LMIA Thera.[538] The second category is typified by the Red Lustrous Wheelmade Ware spindle bottles from LMIB (or later) contexts, but also the find of classic later phase White Slip I (LCIB on Cyprus) in a definite LMIB context at Trianda on Rhodes,[539] along with other LCI imports from this time,[540] and LMIB period imports of LC coarse vessels.[541] Indeterminate, or in between these two groups, are some WSI bowls from several sites from 'LMIA–B' contexts.[542] Overall, we start to see a pattern to be examined in some detail in Chapter IV.5, where PWS and early WSI and the

---

[537] For news of the Red Slip and PWS? at Kommos, I thank Jeremy B. Rutter (pers. comm.). The *possible* PWS sherd is questionable at this stage, and may be late WP (V–VI)? For the Proto Base Ring, Monochrome and BRI at Kommos, see Rutter (1999: Table 1). Note, a Cypriot jug/amphora handle listed by Cline (1994:202 no. 608) from a MMIII–LMIA context at Kommos is left as find context date to be determined by Rutter (1999: Table 1 no. C11240/I53), and may or may not be relevant.

[538] Cline (1994:186 no.455); Manning (1995:31, 198–199 endnote); Merrillees (n.d.). See Chapter IV.V below for detailed discussion.

[539] Cline (1994:186 no.460).

[540] Cline (1994:219 nos. 765–768, 180 no. 404).

[541] Cline (1994:200 no. 594).

[542] Cline (1994:186 nos.454, 456, 458–460). Gjerstad (1926:324–325) discusses the find context information with regard to the Phylakopi sherds, and argues that the available evidence indicates a likely Late Cycladic I date.

Fig. 27. An example of an earlier Red Lustrous Wheelmade Ware spindle bottle from Stephania. Drawing after Eriksson (1993: frontspiece right).

LCIA period on Cyprus equate with LMIA, whereas classic WSI and the rest of the LCIB period on Cyprus equate with mature LMIB. This approximate division is confirmed from Cyprus.[543] The initial LMIA imports link with early LCI (LCIA) (see e.g. pp.126–127 below), whereas LMIB/LHIIA imports link with LCIB.

C. AEGEAN AND CYPRIOT EVIDENCE
AND THE LINKS TO SYRO-PALESTINIAN LATER MBII

The link of LMIA with early LCI (LCIA) is important (see also Chapter IV.5). Early LCI (LCIA) correlates with the late Syro-Palestinian MBA and Egyptian SIP periods, just as LMIA does. Both appear part of the horizon of culture and trade of late MBII Syria–Palestine (greater Canaan), of which Tell el-Dabᶜa was a, or the, focal centre.[544] This is not a new or radical suggestion. Warren and Hankey (1989:116) stated that it is clear that 'LMIA, like LCIA, was already in existence within the Second Intermediate Period'. However, although the doyen and doyenne of the conventional low chronology write this, it must be admitted that there has been a debate on this point for years (see Chapter III above). Some scholars have tried largely to align the beginning of the LCI period and the appearance of LCI products with the LBI period of Syria–Palestine and indeed the start of the 18th Dynasty in Egypt.[545] The studies of Gittlen are typical;[546] he argues against all previous claims of MBA Syro-Palestinian finds of LC products – except Monochrome ware where he admits defeat[547] – but, in consequence, finds himself confessing (1977:384) that perhaps early LCI WS production had almost ended in Cyprus (i.e. we are well into LCI) by the time imports first arrived in Syria–Palestine – i.e. LCI began in the late MBA of Syria–Palestine.[548] There is, of course, no *a priori* reason why the beginning of a new stylistic period on Cyprus (or on Crete) should correlate with those in Syria–Palestine. Indeed, the notable, and sudden, popularity of late MC to early LC types in late MBA to early LBA contexts in the Levant and Egypt rather indicates that these 'new' Cypriot styles and associated products caught the interest of the east Mediterranean at this time, and were *leading* rather than following general trends.

Despite expressions to the contrary in the past, the evidence available today clearly

---

[543] Vermeule and Wolsky (1978; 1990); Eriksson (1992); Warren and Hankey (1989:116–117); Cadogan *et al.* (n.d.).

[544] Just what is Canaan, greater or otherwise, is not especially clear in the second millennium BC. The term is used in a general, or ambiguous, or non-specific sense in ancient Near Eastern textual material of the second millennium BC. It can at best be described as the general Levantine region, or what archaeologists have tended to refer to as Syria–Palestine (despite obvious differences within this region). By greater Canaan I mean the Levantine region. See Lemeche (1991; 1996; 1998); cf. Na'aman (1994b; 1999); Rainey (1996).

[545] Oren (1969; n.d.); Gittlen (1977; 1981); Dever (1992:16–17); Eriksson (1992); Bietak (1996a).

[546] Gittlen (1975; 1977; 1981).

[547] For MBIIC Monochrome finds, see Oren (1969:140–142); Gittlen (1977:304–324, esp. 321 and n.47; 1981:49 n.6).

[548] Gittlen is mistaken in his views on the PWS from Megiddo, where the vessel from level X is a sound datum (see Chapter IV.5 below), and Tell el-ᶜAjjul, where PWS and probably WSI occur in late MBII contexts (see Chapter IV.5 below).

supports a date for the start of what is defined as the LCI period in the standard works of Åström (1972a, d) during the later MBA of Syria–Palestine, or the SIP in Egypt. The evidence from Tell el-Dabᶜa is exemplary. Initial LC products (PWS, WPV–VI) are found in the final MBA, D/2, stratum,[549] parallel with an instance of Cypriot Bichrome Ware.[550] Bietak (1996a:63) tries to restrict this overlap to just very initial LCI by stating that 'no imported Base Ring or Red Lustrous ware have yet been found in strata dating to the late Hyksos period'.[551] But Bietak is evading by means of a footnote the find of an LC BRI jug in a secure SIP context at Memphis.[552] BRI is a typical mature LCI ware; indeed, conventionally, BRI does not mark the beginning of LCIA, but appears with WSI (or just before) in LCIA2, and is typical of the mature later LCI (i.e. LCIB) period.[553] Indeed, in the east of Cyprus, the main BRI and WSI phase is almost exclusively LCIB (Merrillees 1971). Bietak has suggested that this Memphis deposit is perhaps not SIP, as there are a few New Kingdom types present in the deposit,[554] but this view fails to consider how ceramic fashions and trait dissemination work in practice. The 'New Kingdom' types began as the prevailing fashions of 17th Dynasty Thebes (and area).[555] These types then characterise deposits all over Egypt once the country is re-united under Ahmose. But, some of these 'New Kingdom' types start to be distributed before then into other areas of Egypt – at a time contemporary with the later 17th Dynasty (or SIP). The few 'New Kingdom' types in the relevant Memphis deposit are best seen in this light, as 17th Dynasty in date; the deposit as a whole is SIP, and pre-18th Dynasty – more specifically, the deposit pre-dates the sand deposits at the site which are dated to the time of the Hyksos-Theban wars, and thus the SIP deposit presumably pre-dates the campaign of Kamose.[556] This shows that typical LCIA1–2 (to early IB) objects were arriving in Egypt during the SIP, and that the LCI period began during the SIP (at an unknown point).[557] There are in addition the LC Monochrome bowls found in MBIIC contexts

---

[549] Bietak (1991b:313 no.4 [2100] and Abb. 288.4 [note mis-labelled as '2010b']; 1996a:63); Maguire (1992; 1995); Fuscaldo (1998:62).

[550] A sherd was found in the same grave, no.10, as the PWS sherd just referred to: Bietak (1991b:313 no.3 [2010b] and Abb. 288.3 [note mis-labelled as '2100']).

[551] Bietak is of course ignoring previous publications (Maguire 1992:117 Fig.2) where it has been stated that BR occurred in his own late Hyksos D/2 stratum. This is presumably because this BRI, along with the frescoes and the WSI, has now been re-assigned to the early 18th Dynasty.

[552] Bietak (1996a:86 and n.85). For the find, see Bourriau (1990; pers. comms.); Merrillees (1992:50–51); Eriksson (1992:169). Kathryn Eriksson (pers. comm.) confirms to me that the vessel is BRI, and *not* proto-BR. I thank her for her advice.

[553] For main LCIA2–IB range, see Åström (1972a:700–701 chart); Eriksson (1992:204–217). As typical of LCIB, see e.g. Åström (1972a:758). It should be noted, however, that the relative chronology of the BR typology (BRI–II) is unclear (Vaughan 1991).

[554] Bietak and Hein (n.d.); Bietak (pers. comm.). Bietak argues that all the Memphis deposits involved should be analysed and published before any conclusion is reached. One is tempted to make the same statement about another site.

[555] See generally Bourriau (1997).

[556] For a general review of the stratigraphy and the 'sand' layer, see Bourriau (1997:161–165).

[557] I thank Janine Bourriau and Kathryn Eriksson for discussion and advice. It is of course unfortunate that the context at Memphis is not more satisfactory. A decisive and clear stratigraphy is simply not

in Palestine,[558] and, as Bietak (1991a:58) himself notes, 'in the stratum XVIII destruction level at Gezer and at some other sites there is evidence of Base Ring ware within late MB IIC ceramic collections'.[559]

In conclusion, there appear good grounds for proposing that earlier LCI (LCIA) began in the Syro-Palestinian later MBA, or during the Egyptian SIP. The earliest Cypriot imports into these regions demonstrate this. LMIA correlates with LCIA. Thus a date for LMIA in the late MBA of Syria–Palestine, or the SIP of Egypt, makes sense.

Undoubtedly, the source of the 'problem' in some scholars' minds is that an overlap is involved. The correlation is *not* MC/MM with the Syro-Palestinian MBA (SIP), and

---

found in the area, and a certain scepticism will invariably exist. The find is also singular. Replication is required. It must be admitted that at present no other BRI finds in Egypt from clear and undisputed contexts are as early. Merrillees (1968; 1975) claimed some possible cases, but Oren (1969) showed that none of these contexts were certain. It remains the case, however, that some of these ambiguous cases *could be* SIP in date (as Merrillees suggested). In particular, out of the tomb deposits reviewed by Oren (1969:128–130), one may point to a few instances suggestive of just such a date (see also Oren 1969:143). The first is Tell el-ʿAjjul tomb 369, where BRI occurs with WPVI and the cylindrical juglet; the second is Megiddo tomb 3005, where BRI occurs with WPVI and the baggy dipper juglet. WPVI does occur into the LBI period, but it is also typical of the final MBII (MBIIC or MBIII) period, and the final Hyksos stratum at Tell el Dabʿa. Thus, apart from a *belief* that BRI does not pre-date the LBI period, these two finds could be late MBA. Tell el-ʿAjjul tomb 374, where BRI occurs with the Black Lustrous juglet and a bowl form, could also easily be late MBA. Several other possible instances of pre-LBI BRI from Palestine and Syria are all contested by Oren (1969:144–145), but some of these remain 'possible'. What Oren showed was that the pre-LBI date was not established or clear for any of this material, and that a lower chronological construction of this evidence is also possible. But, as Merrillees (1971) argued, the mainly 18th Dynasty/LBI date of initial export occurrences in Egypt of BRI does *not* date the appearance of this ware on Cyprus – rather its belated adoption in *eastern* Cyprus which in turn was the source of most of the Cypriot exports to Egypt. Merrillees builds a strong case that the LC package, including BR and WSI, developed in the west/northwest of Cyprus in LCIA, but was only adopted by the east of Cyprus in the LCIB period. Oren (n.d.) presents a case similar to his 1969 article when he disputes the existence of any absolutely certain and indisputable finds of WSI in pre-LBIA/18th Dynasty contexts. Again, he is right that one can question most such claims, and that in a number of cases proper and specific context data are not known; but this does not necessarily mean all such claims or possible 'early' finds are invalid. We are left with a situation in which it is apparent that LCIB products are found in early 18th Dynasty contexts, but it may be debated whether or not LCIA2 to initial LCIB products are found earlier, in SIP contexts. A couple of data say yes, but more, and more satisfactory, data are necessary. I argue that the Memphis BRI find is an exception which proves a rule. Nearly all BRI from Egypt is mature BRI of LCIB date. This material is found in earlier (onwards) 18th Dynasty contexts. It was exported from eastern/ southeastern Cyprus in the LCIB period. But BR was developed in the LCIA period in west/northwest Cyprus, and the odd product (whether directly, or via eastern/southeastern Cyprus, or via a Levantine intermediary) reached Egypt. This was SIP in Egyptian chronology terms. Most if not all Hyksos–Egyptian SIP trade with Cyprus was with east/southeast Cyprus. LCIA period = later SIP Cypriot ceramic imports were thus of the late WP types which persisted in this region in LCIA, along with new eastern LCIA inventions such as Bichrome Ware.

[558] E.g. Oren (1969:140–142). These are *not* successfully dismissed by Eriksson (1992:167 with refs.) in an otherwise tendentious section fudging on this issue by referring to the difficulties of defining a Syro-Palestinian LBI culture (an important, but separate, issue: see above, Chapter III). Note Monochrome appears to develop in northwest Cyprus (like PBR to BRI, and early style WSI): Pilides (1992:esp.296–297).

[559] And in view of the Memphis data, we must consider a modification of the view in Oren (1969:143–

LC/LMI with the Syro-Palestinian LBA (18th Dynasty), in some extraordinary pan-regional co-ordination of style and stratigraphy.[560] Instead, LCIA/LMIA starts during the late Syro-Palestinian MBA and SIP and then LCIB and LMIB continue into the early Syro-Palestinian LBA (or MBIIC/LBI transition period) and the early 18th Dynasty (to about the early part of the reign of Tuthmosis III). We see this 'overlap' played out on Cyprus where MBA Tell el-Yahudiyeh ware and fashion occurs mainly in later MC contexts, but overlaps into early LCI (see below), and on Thera where the VDL (mature LMIA) contains late Tell el-Yahudiyeh ware, a probable later Syro-Palestinian MB amphora, some Syro-Palestinian MB stone vessels, and an early WSI bowl.

Another part of the 'problem' often not appreciated sufficiently by those working outside of Cyprus is that the exact definition and recognition of the beginning of the LCI period on Cyprus is debated, or imprecisely defined[561] – transitions between stylistic phases are, of course, by definition problematic. Åström's (1972a) criteria were subjective, nor were they based on clear, stratified, settlement data. The comparison of material from tombs and settlements is fraught with difficulties, since 'burials ... are likely to contain material anything up to a generation later than its true horizon on settlement sites'.[562] On current data, different ceramic types first appear at different sites at differing times (and various site deposits reflect differing stages within the overall periods). For example, Cypriot Bichrome Ware is reported from Tell el-Dabᶜa strata D/3–D/2,[563] and D/2,[564] and elsewhere in the Levant it first occurs

---

145, 146–149) that BR did not appear until the time of Tuthmosis III. Bietak tries to explain this evidence away by linking it with the long so-called MBIIC–LBIA transition he posits from the mid-16th century BC through to the reign of Tuthmosis III (1991a:Fig.24), but, as discussed in Chapters III, IV.5 and V.1 (re-Jericho), this concept is both problematic and unnecessary. It effectively continues to assume Egyptian agency in the close of MBA destructions and changes in Syria–Palestine, whereas there is little evidence to support this view. The high-precision radiocarbon evidence from Jericho also runs directly contrary to the Bietak hypothesis. There is no positive reason to try to pull this MBIIC evidence into the 15th century BC; it clearly belongs in the mid-16th century BC as part of an area-wide horizon from Syria to Palestine and the Nile Delta region. In view especially of the Memphis find, it is not unreasonable to view BRI as occurring in the Levant from the late MBA/SIP through early 18th Dynasty. As discussed in the main text below, a key point is that early WSI, early BRI, and early Monochrome, all seem to be ceramic types which develop in, and are first exported from, the northwest of Cyprus (and contrast Bichrome Ware which is an eastern Cypriot type). This initial LCI-style northwestern phase in Cyprus is contemporary with the late MC-style, but LCI in date, contemporary phase in the east of Cyprus. Only Levantine sites in contact with northwest Cyprus received late MBII (MBIIC or MBIII) 'LCIA' exports. Tell el-ᶜAjjul appears to have been the prime such import site for the Canaanite region. Tell el-Dabᶜa, and Egypt in general, in contrast, received its Cypriot imports from eastern/southeastern Cyprus (and thus they *appear* to still be MCIII, but are in temporal terms LCIA).

[560] Given we now keep and use the designated regional styles – and do not re-name them, and re-coordinate them: cf. suggestions of Finkelstein (1996b). Kempinski (esp.1992a:179) is the only scholar who has approached this position. He re-defines the Syro-Palestinian LBI as beginning c.1600BC with the appearance of Bichrome Ware and other LCIA products (whereas conventional scholarship sees this as later MBIIC or MBIII).

[561] See e.g. Eriksson (1992:195–217); see also Merrillees (1971); Herscher (1976; 1984).

[562] Hennessy (1963:55).

[563] Maguire (1992:117 Fig.2).

[564] Maguire (1992:117 Fig.2; 1995); Bietak (1996a:63; 1989a:79). A Bichrome Ware sherd was found with the PWS vessel from a stratum D/2 grave (Bietak 1991b:313 no.3 [2010b] and Abb. 288.3 [note mis-labelled

in late MBA contexts. Åström regards Bichrome Ware as an indicator of earliest LCI in Cyprus.[565] Indeed, occurrences of Bichrome Ware in MCIII contexts are reported,[566] although its presence in late MCIII *style* assemblages in the east of Cyprus may be considered as contemporary with the LCIA period of the west and northwest of the island.[567] Among other sites, Maroni offers a good example: Bichrome Ware occurs with PWS, WPV–VI, and other late MC to earliest LC types in very early LCI.[568] However, not every site on Cyprus has an identical record in this regard. At the major site of Enkomi, Bichrome Ware does not appear until Level IB, supposedly the second phase of LCI at the site,[569] and similar situations were observed at the important sites of Myrtou-Pigadhes, Kalopsidha, and Toumba tou Skourou,[570] where Bichrome Ware appeared in each case in a post-initial LCIA1 horizon, with WSI, and BRI. Thus we find in the case of some sites that WSI, BRI, and Bichrome Ware mark the beginning of local mature LCI, whereas, at others, an 'early' LCI phase minus one or more of these types is recognised, and so on.[571] In the conventional chronological scheme, this situation was seen as primarily temporal, with LCIA1 characterised by an absence of BRI and WSI, and LCIA2 marked by the appearance of these wares. Whether Bichrome Ware fits in (let alone helps to define) the former, or the latter, varies across Cyprus.

In an observed reality, the data pattern available seems to be the result of a mixture of chronology and regional difference. Thus whereas Toumba tou Skourou in the west/northwest of Cyprus has an LCIA1 phase,[572] the first 'LC' deposit at Enkomi in the east may be characterised as LCIA2 (even LCIB),[573] which implies that its final 'MCIII' ran into LCIA1–2 elsewhere.[574] Further, specific local variations are possible. At Kalopsidha WSI was absent in the first LCI layer, but Åström acknowledges that this may merely be a local peculiarity.[575] And, in other instances, it should be noted that WSI is in fact not necessarily common in many LCIA2 layers (in fact it is quite

---

as '2100']). Bietak (1996a) refers to 'late' Cypriote Bichrome Ware which is regarded as either stratum C *or* D/2: pl.26C caption. Hein (1998:548) mentions finds of Cypriot Bichrome Ware in the garden levels in Areas H/I and H/IV, which could either be SIP (with 97% of the associated material) or New Kingdom (the other 3% of the associated material). New Kingdom finds of Bichrome Wheelmade Ware come from the H/II area (Hein 1998:551).

[565] Åström (1972a:758); also Merrillees (1971:65); Baurain (1984:64–66).

[566] Åström (1972b:171–172); Hennessy (1963:54–55); Epstein (1966:132–133); Artzy (1972:58); Baurain (1984:64–66); Gonen (1992:98–99).

[567] Following Merrillees (1971:65).

[568] Herscher (1984:25); Cadogan *et al.* (n.d.).

[569] Eriksson (1992:212).

[570] Eriksson (1992:205–206, 214).

[571] For further discussion of Bichrome Ware, see Chapter VII below.

[572] Eriksson (1992:213–217). Minus eastern Cypriot initial LC Bichrome Ware.

[573] Eriksson (1992:211–212). As Merrillees (1971) argues, the northwestern LC wares (WSI, BRI, Monochrome) basically only appear at Enkomi, and in the east generally, in LCIB. For the situation at Enkomi, see especially Merrillees (1971:67–70).

[574] Merrillees (1971:72–73). And there does not appear to be a clear PWS, pre-WSI, horizon. Dikaios (1969–1971, vol.I:225) writes that 'the global evidence collected in the present excavation, shows that it occurred in Level I together with White Slip I'. Popham (1962:287) had previously argued to the contrary from one isolated find at the site.

[575] Åström (1966:54, 57); Eriksson (1992:206).

rare in many cases outside northwest/west Cyprus), and it becomes a typical find only in LCIB. Thus, when one considers the Cypriot imports at Tell el-Dab^{c}a, Bietak is wrong to place too great an emphasis on the apparent absence of one ware in a small sample. Åström, for example, did not entirely exclude the possibility that all 20 LC sherds from Kalopsidha trench 9 layer 71 (the initial LCI layer) were intrusive.[576] We have the general pattern that the early LCI (LCIA) 'package' appears as a combined entity in Syria–Palestine–Egypt from the late MBA and SIP, but how to regard the LCIA1 and LCIA2 elements is less than straightforward. The later LCI (LCIB) package (including especially BRI and Red Lustrous Wheelmade Ware) appears with the early 18th Dynasty. The latter is not controversial. But, as Merrillees (1971:74) argues, the appearance of these mature LCI types in Egypt probably occurred only *after* these types became part of the eastern Cypriot assemblage in LCIB. The absence of early LCI northwestern Cypriot products in 18th Dynasty Egyptian contexts, and instead the near total dominance of eastern Cypriot products, offers support for this hypothesis. Thus the LCIA period is contemporary with the later MBA/SIP.

Further, the subtleties in the development of LCI Cyprus must be considered, and continually emphasised. As noted above (Chapter III), this was a time of major change, instability, and transformation on Cyprus.[577] The archaeology of the period is characterised by the appearance of what have been termed 'forts' and by weaponry, along with new settlement, stylistic, and trading patterns. Even in what his great rival and sparring-partner James Muhly (1985:23) described as 'a complex and persuasive interpretation of the regional issues involved in the beginning of the Late Bronze Age on Cyprus', Robert Merrillees argued for an apparent differentiation between development processes in east and west Cyprus across the MCIII–LCI period.[578] As already noted above, and as I will emphasise again, Merrillees argued that the 'new' LCI styles of WSI and BRI (and also Monochrome[579]), for example, developed in the 'west' of Cyprus (central, west and northwest areas, especially), whereas the White Painted and Red on Black painted traditions carried on for longer in the east and south of the island. By the time the LCI assemblage appeared in the east of Cyprus it was already a mature fashion and, chronologically, mature LCI (i.e. LCIB).[580]

---

[576] Åström (1966:52); Eriksson (1992:207).

[577] E.g. Merrillees (1971); Åström (1972c); Knapp (1979; 1985; 1986a; 1994:282–293); Baurain (1984); Peltenburg (1996:27–35); Keswani (1996:219).

[578] Merrillees (1971). See also Åström (1972c). The development of the dominant 'regional' model for the analysis of Cypriot society in the Bronze Age is summarised by Knapp (1979:19–26). The basic divisions are clear from the MC period onwards (into LCI): 'two distinct cultural areas can be distinguished in Cyprus, an Eastern and a Western one' (Åström 1972b:275). Merrillees (1965:140) writes that: '...it is becoming increasingly apparent that regionalism is the key-note to the cultural history of the Bronze Age, and that it is only in terms of this phenomenon that the island's civilisation in all its aspects can be properly understood'. See also comments of Merrillees (1992:47–48).

[579] See Pilides (1992:esp. 296–297).

[580] Eriksson (1992:217), without reference to Merrillees (1971), suggests that perhaps PWS and PBR were innovations of the northwest, whereas WSI and BRI were eastern creations. But this seems unlikely. The northwest has a clear developmental sequence of PWS into WSI and PBR into BRI (e.g. Toumba tou Skourou: Vermeule and Wolsky 1990; or Kazaphani: Nicolaou and Nicolaou 1989). At Enkomi a little PWS appears with WSI and BRI in the initial 'LC'; the likely view is that this represents LCIA2 when the

What is the timescale? Merrillees (1971) did not quantify, but merely argued that: 'it is evident ... that the cultural transmission from M.C.III to L.C.I was very gradual' (p.56), and commented further that 'when account is taken of the long time it took the L.C. fabrics fully to oust their M.C. predecessors...' (p.57). Vermeule and Wolsky (1990:395) admit to a considerable lack of precision and possible flexibility for this MC–LC transition period: 'it may occupy two, or three, generations': thus c.50–75 or more years? They correlate it with the Shaft Grave period in the Aegean (itself usually placed over several generations). Peltenburg (1996:27–37) adds to this picture, with his detailed discussion of the formation of a polity centred on the eastern centre of Enkomi in LCI.[581] This regional entity marks a geopolitical territory, potentially separate from the west and especially west/northwest (e.g. the area around Toumba tou Skourou), and the south coast. Merrillees (1971) argued that the new 'LC' western (and northwestern) grouping was in contact with Syria–Palestine, but not Egypt, whereas east (and southeast) Cyprus traded especially with Egypt but was also in contact with the Levant. Now of course no such generalisation holds completely true, and some Egyptian contacts for the west and northwest are evident, but this general picture of the regional, and geopolitical, development of the LCI period on Cyprus, and the power-polity structures of the hierarchical LC period (in contrast to the relative lack of such evidence in the MC period), remains useful. Peltenburg (1996:35), for example, specifically argues that eastern Cyprus, 'and that must mean Kalopsidha and Enkomi, had the closest links with the Levantine mainland at this time'. And, in confirmation of these approximate patterns, Louise Maguire observes that the comparanda within Cyprus for the Cypriot ceramic material from Tell el-Dab^ca and the Levant are primarily eastern/southeastern:[582]

> Of the White Painted tradition, Pendent Line Style, Cross Line Style and White Painted V Style, *predominantly southeastern styles,* form the largest component of exported pottery at over thirty sites in the Levant and at Tell el-Dab^ca, Egypt (Maguire 1986).[583]

---

two types were both current in the northwest, before the 'proto' wares decline. The east received the developed package.

[581] See also Pickles and Peltenburg (1998:87).

[582] Maguire (1991:64; 1992:118; 1995:54); Pickles and Peltenburg (1998:87). Further suggestions that such apparent associations may lead to historical hypotheses are premature. Baurain (1984), for example, argued that the developments of LCIA (e.g. the building of fortresses) could be attributed to the influence/infiltration of Syro-Palestinian peoples into Cyprus. Several scholars previously saw the building of the LCI forts as linked with SIP/Hyksos kings seeking to control access to Cyprus' copper. There is as yet little positive evidence. The proposal of Helck (1993) that the Hyksos themselves were derived from Cypriot or Anatolian pirates lacks any basis. There are MC–LC imports at the Hyksos capital Avaris (Tell el-Dab^ca) (Maguire 1986; 1990; 1995), but these comprise only a tiny fraction of the total finds. Bietak (e.g. 1996a:59) has suggested that a Cypriot community lived among the Canaanites at Tell el-Dab^ca from stratum G onwards, since there are local objects made with Cypriot techniques or imitations of Cypriot objects in local clays (see in Maguire 1990:chapter 2), but he clearly envisages only a small group as part of the much larger population of the overall great city. Such foreign communities are of course typical of the great mercantile centres.

[583] Maguire (1991:64, my italics).

Indeed, she notes at the time of writing her 1991 article, that there is just one example of the more typically northern or central Cypriot Fine Line WP workshop[584] – contrasted to the southern 'broad band' styles – in the whole of Egypt and the Levant.[585] Maguire (1991:64) concludes that:

> It is evident, in the first instance, that *separate* distributions of contemporary styles exist on the island[586] and, secondly, that a dichotomy is also noticeable in the distribution of their numbers abroad.

The time frame at issue[587] was MCIII–LCI, and particularly pre-LCIB.[588] Peltenburg sees Enkomi building a polity at this time.[589] But the ceramic assemblage of initial LC Enkomi is in effect 'MC'.

To anticipate the discussion in Chapter IV.5 below, it would therefore be very possible for an early WSI product (one with more than a trace of PWS style in the lattice band below the rim, for example – and one even once attributed to the PWS category by a leading scholar in print) to have been exported from the west/northwest of Cyprus, where, as Vermeule and Wolsky (1990:393) observe, WSI 'comes to us earlier', at a time when later 'MC'-style, but LCIA date, WP juglets from the east/southeast of Cyprus were still going to Egypt and the Levant (along with LCIA PWS from, or via, the southcoast). This would all be, in chronological terms, early LCI (e.g. LCIA). Some significant time period could be represented herein. The imported LMIA sherd from an early LCIA context at Maroni *Vournes* in southern Cyprus (Plate 11),[590] and another from what seems to be a very early LCI (LCIA1) context in the niche burial of Tomb III at Toumba tou Skourou,[591] certainly show that the LMIA period was underway (already) at the time of earliest LC, and that there was contact between

---

[584] Defined at Maguire (1991:61). This sherd is DAB 200.

[585] Maguire (1991:64). This is a rim fragment from Tell el-Dabʿa (and the presence of the exception at the great site of the eastern Mediterranean is of course most likely). See also P. Johnston (1982:68) who notes the conspicuous absence of northern 'geometric' styles of WP ware in Palestine. P. Johnson (1982:68–70) makes a tentative case against assuming that these two different stylistic groupings were necessarily contemporary (although the historical summation on p.70 reverts to the conventional view), but this suggestion fails as it leaves large vacant gaps in the material culture of northern Cyprus. The general regional model applies. And, in fact, on careful and detailed examination (Frankel 1974), it is not a simple broad east–west division at all, but a set of overlapping regions where links break down with distance from source zone (associated by Frankel with trade, marriage, and other social relations). Only on an overall scale does this mosaic merge together to create basic over-arching east and west groupings.

[586] See also Maguire (1992:118 and Figs. 5 and 6).

[587] The 'this time' of Peltenburg (1996:35) quoted above.

[588] Cf. Peltenburg (1996:33 n.20 and reference to Merrillees 1994).

[589] See also Keswani (1996:221–224).

[590] Cadogan *et al.* (n.d.). The sherd (P80 from trench M11 layer 12 #8814) comes from one of the earliest LCIA contexts at the site, dated within the initial Vournes Ia phase.

[591] Vermeule and Wolsky (1990:266–267, also 393, 394). Eriksson (n.d.) questions this correlation (and the general correlation of LMIA with PWS). She argues that although found in Tomb III, which has no WSI or BRI or other post-initial LCIA material, the LMIA was not actually in direct association with the PWS. The LMIA sherd came from Niche I, whereas the PWS was all found in the tomb's main Chamber. The early date still seems appropriate, however. Nothing from the Tomb (Chamber plus Niche) is post LCIA1. Further, the Niche did contain a juglet similar to Proto BR and/or later MBA Levantine shapes

the LMIA Aegean and initial LC Cyprus. The east and southeast of the island was probably still exporting late WP and Red on Black/Red on Red vessels (along with 'new' PWS) at this same time to Egypt, the Levant, and the Aegean.[592] But the LMIA period had already begun in the Aegean, and, probably, so too had early WSI production in the west/northwest of Cyprus.

However, we should also note that only a relatively few early 'LCI' Cypriot exports (PWS, early WSI, and contemporaries) of the period are known. With the exception of Tell el-ᶜAjjul, in particular, and a few coastal locations in Syria–Palestine in general, early LCI exports are best described as uncommon at most sites in the eastern Mediterranean:[593] a few items at a few sites, and just a handful at a couple of the major trading locations of the era. Several major contexts at even the great city of the eastern Mediterranean at this time, Avaris/Tell el-Dabᶜa, in fact have very little Cypriot material. Fuscaldo (1998:62) writes of late Hyksos contexts at ᶜEzbet Helmi (Tell el-Dabᶜa) that: 'a very few Cypriote pottery sherds ... were found in the settlement'.[594] This is not a reflection of continuous, very regular, trade in such items. Over the time-spans involved, exchanges could be described as sporadic in most cases. Thus these items do not offer a representative sample of some frequent process of exchange. They reflect maybe one or two, or a few, exchanges – out of a potentially significant, and long, period of style/fashion on Cyprus. If the evidence for imports and exports are not representatives of commodity trade – e.g. containers for commodities – then the precise quantitative and temporal data may be difficult to assess from material evidence alone.

For an example of a cautionary tale, we may note that there are in fact very few direct imports/exports of material objects between Crete and Cyprus during the MM–LMI period;[595] as Swiny (1997) recently entitled a paper comparing Bronze Age Crete and Cyprus: 'so near and yet so far...'. But, when a written script appears on Cyprus at the beginning of the LBA period (if not a little earlier), it is quite similar to Minoan Linear A,[596] and so was named the Cypro-Minoan script by Evans.[597] Evans proposed that the Cypriot script was a derivative from the Minoan script. This hypothesis that the genesis of the Cypro-Minoan script was somehow connected with the Aegean linear systems

(Vermeule and Wolsky 1990:267 TIII.3 P642), for which an LCIA1 date would be appropriate. And, to confirm PWS = LMIA, we may now refer to the Maroni *Vournes* sherd, and also the possible/probable PWS sherd from LMIA Kommos (see Chapter IV.4.B above).

[592] For example, the initial phase of LCIA at Maroni *Vournes* in southern Cyprus, Vournes Ia, contained, along with the LMIA import just mentioned, PWS, WPV, WPVI, Composite (Black Slip and WP) ware large bowls, Red on Black, Red on Red, Black Slip II and III, Bichrome Wheelmade Ware, and Proto Base Ring (Cadogan *et al.* n.d.). In other words, this is the Cypriot export assemblage associated with later MBII (MBIIC or MBIII) in Syria–Palestine, and strata D/3 and especially D/2 at Tell el-Dabᶜa. For the export of eastern WP to the Aegean at about the same time, see the WP PLS sherd from Zakros (Popham 1963:89–91, Fig.1, pl.26.a).

[593] See e.g. Gittlen (1977); Bergoffen (1991); Cadogan (1979); Portugali and Knapp (1985); Oren (n.d.).

[594] See also Fuscaldo (1998:Fig.3) where Cypriot pottery is too negligible a quantity to make the statistics shown.

[595] Cadogan (1972); Portugali and Knapp (1985); Catling (1991). Recent work at the major port at Kommos in south central Crete shows that this site was an exception with several Cypriot imports (Rutter 1999).

[596] Palaima (1989:136–140).

[597] Evans (1909:69, generally see 68–77)

of writing has been widely accepted,[598] and the development has been attributed to the influence of Crete and its trading world,[599] and the comparative ease of learning the Aegean script system compared to the complicated cuneiform ones of the contemporary ancient Near East.[600] Of course, it is also possible that the reverse occurred. The Cypro-Minoan script has some links with other Anatolian–Syrian–Palestinian scripts and languages, and it must be noted that a number of the Cypriot signs do not have Minoan parallels[601] – although Palaima (1989:137–139) suggests this is an over-statement. However, since recent finds indicate that scripts similar to 'Minoan' Linear A were in use before, during, and after its current attestation on Crete, both in the north Aegean and west Anatolia, and in the Levant,[602] it is now clear that a common home in one of these areas for Minoan Linear A and Cypro-Minoan is indeed possible. The case for some relationship (several words in common at least) with the Semitic language group is quite strong for both,[603] and arguments may also be advanced in favour of Anatolia.[604] Cyprus and its copper were drawn into the literate (clay tablet archive) Near Eastern trading world from about the 18th century BC.[605] Thus it may be that the Cypro-Minoan script of Cyprus derives from its neighbouring MBA Syrian–Palestinian–Anatolian literate milieu,[606] and that Minoan trading brought them into contact with such scripts (in Cyprus, and probably also Anatolia and Syria), and that this in turn led to developments in the Aegean. Either way – and I do not wish to make any 'issue' of the point since resolution is currently impossible – the bare handful of MM–LMI objects from Cyprus, and the reverse, perhaps hide a rather more significant relationship – presumably centred on the Minoan need for metal supplies.[607] The material evidence are thus odd exotica (or occasional meeting–drinking gifts, since nearly all the Aegean finds of WS vessels are examples of the hemispherical bowl), perhaps randomly spread over the temporal span of the relationship based on trade in metals or other things without ceramic containers.[608] They provide evidence of contacts and exchanges, but no data, or control, on the relationships of the respective stylistic and stratigraphic phases.

---

[598] E.g. Palaima (1989:140).

[599] E.g. Masson (1961–1962); Wiener (1990:147–148).

[600] Palaima (1989:161–162).

[601] Knapp and Marchant (1982:15–17); Knapp (1979:74–76, 80–82); Vládar and Bartonèk (1977).

[602] See Finkelberg (1998) summarising finds from Samothrace, Troy, Miletus, Tel Haror, and Lachish. The Tel Haror find only counts if the clay of the ceramic vessel with the Linear A graffito is demonstrated not to be from Crete. This is not yet certain. In a recent review of the evidence, Duhoux (1998) suggests that Minoan Linear A may derive from a non-Indo-European Anatolian language. A Semitic origin is the other main suggestion. It is possible that the Neolithic settlers to Crete and Cyprus came from the same general language area (either Anatolia or the Levant, with geography perhaps favouring the former).

[603] Gordon (1966); Betancourt (1998a:7).

[604] Whether to a non-Indo-European language, or instead to a proto-Indo-European language (see Renfrew 1998:257–260 for a review advocating the latter position with further refs.).

[605] Courtois (1986).

[606] E.g. the Hurrians: although cf. Knapp and Marchant (1982); or a Semitic grouping: Gordon (1966).

[607] See also Wiener (1987; 1991).

[608] And without Aegean/Cypriot ceramics becoming fashionable prestige goods in either foreign destination at this time – contrast the situation where the much later LHIIIA2 kraters become key prestige goods on Cyprus in the LCII period (Steel 1998).

We must bear such factors in mind when considering the Cypriot exports to the east at the beginning of the LBA. The study of Gittlen (1977) is illuminating in this regard when we consider the nature of these links. First, at the time of his study, only a very few pieces of the initial LC assemblage (and especially PWS – just 11 finds in total) were known from the Levant (and indeed the corpus from Cyprus is not large). The majority came from one site: Tell el-ᶜAjjul (64%).[609] This could literally reflect only a few shipments, and hardly offers a sample from a continuous and consistent trade in current Cypriot ceramic fashions. By the time they are interred in Palestine, they may not indeed reflect contemporary reality on Cyprus. Gittlen more or less reaches this conclusion in his study. He argues that these imports were early LBIA, but notes that: 'It would appear that this rare ceramic was at the end of its production-life when its importation to Palestine occurred' (1977:403). He offers a similar argument for (subsequent) WSI: 'The distribution of WSI pottery suggests that a limited and restricted variety was imported into Palestine during a relatively short period, probably because WSI was no longer being produced in any large quantity at a time when WSII pottery was becoming increasingly popular on Cyprus and available for export. The paucity of WSI finds, the concentration of these finds in southwestern Palestine and particularly at Tell el-Ajjul, and the location of the finds in domestic structures at these sites, all result from the waning production of WSI pottery on Cyprus'.[610]

The additional conclusion I therefore wish to draw in this discussion of the Cypriot evidence is that, until eastern Mediterranean trade and exchange patterns reached the frequent and commoditised levels of the 14th–13th centuries BC,[611] it is very difficult, even dangerous, to reach any specific and precise chronological conclusions, and especially *phasal* correlations, from finds of a few 'exotic' traded items. This is of course done all the time in earlier periods in Aegean prehistory, but, for the 17th–15th centuries BC, the required precision is not give or take 50 or even 100 years as is the case in the Aegean EBA, rather it is a couple of decades. Hence we must exercise considerable care, critique, and rigour.

D. Tell el-Yahudiyeh ware and related types

Another related evidential cluster permits us to reach a similar conclusion. Tell el-Yahudiyeh ware offers a clear linkage between Thera, Cyprus (both eastern Cyprus, and northwest Cyprus), and SIP Tell el-Dabᶜa, since it is found along with LMIA/Late Cycladic I imports at Thera and Toumba tou Skourou.[612] Tell el-Yahudiyeh ware has thus been a subject of debate between the 'high' and 'low' chronological interpretations. Eriksson (1992:158–162) argues that imported (Near Eastern) Tell el-Yahudiyeh ware on Cyprus pre-dates LCI, in accord with an earlier study by Negbi (1978).[613] Negbi's

[609] Gittlen (1977:379, 449).
[610] Gittlen (1977:384).
[611] See Sherratt and Sherratt (1991: esp. 370–373).
[612] Kaplan (1980); Åström (1971); Merrillees (1971; 1978); Negbi (1978); Bietak (1989b; 1997:91–96); Vermeule and Wolsky (1990).
[613] And before that Oren (1969:136–137 with previous refs.). Contrast Merrillees (1971:esp.73).

argument was based on the assumption that Tell el-Yahudiyeh ware is an MBA type in Syria–Palestine, and so is not contemporary with LCI (since she wanted MBA=MC, LBA=LC). Instead, Negbi argued that LCI examples are local Cypriot imitations of a no-longer available type. But, apart from its clear presence in LCIA2 at Enkomi, and other eastern LCIA contexts,[614] the logic is poor, since imitations are likely to begin with (even if they go on to continue after) the floruit of a fashion. Across the Levantine region, similar jug forms appear in the late MBA.[615] Further, we can note the contrary evidence from Tell el-Dabᶜa. Here, from stratum G onwards (G–E/3), Bietak reports Tell el-Yahudiyeh jugs developed from the Cypriot ceramic tradition,[616] and, in particular, notes the use of a Cypriot technique for attaching the handle.[617] Thus we might expect a roughly synchronous period of contact and exchange of products, fashions, and techniques.[618] In turn, simply on logical grounds, we should not assign an exclusively post-MBA date to all 'Cypriot' imitation Tell el-Yahudiyeh ware, and hence a beginning for LCI contemporary with latest MBII in Syria–Palestine is both plausible and likely. As we will review below, the extant data require just such a position.

Cypriot data referred to by Bietak in his various discussions in fact offer a rough sequence of Tell el-Yahudiyeh impact on Cyprus from first imports in MC through imports *and* imitations in LCIA. An assemblage found in Arpera *Mosphilos* Tomb 1[619] included Tell el-Yahudiyeh ware jugs of the piriform type. The tomb is usually dated to the later MCIII period.[620] Bietak has compared the Tell el-Yahudiyeh ware jugs with examples from stratum E/3–2 at Tell el-Dabᶜa, and so an earlier Syro-Palestinian MBIIB date. He also compared examples of Tell el-Yahudiyeh ware from stratum E/2–1, or later MBIIB, at Tell el-Dabᶜa with finds in Tomb V at Toumba tou Skourou.[621] Tomb V at Toumba tou Skourou is the earliest tomb at the site, datable to the close of the MC period.[622] In particular, it is earlier than Tomb I, which has LMIA imports.[623] This sequence leaves the subsequent LCIA examples, and the Cypriot imitations,[624] as synchronous with Tell el-Dabᶜa strata D/3–2, or MBIIC=MBIII.[625] In turn, LMIA is MBIIC=MBIII.

The distinction of MC from LC constructed by Negbi (1978), and used to support her argument with regard to Tell el-Yahudiyeh ware, has also been criticised by the excavators of the key site, Toumba tou Skourou. Vermeule and Wolsky (1990:386–387)

---

[614] For Enkomi find, see Eriksson (1992:212); Dikaios (1969–1971:546 no.2283/1). For other eastern LCIA examples, see Merrillees (1971).

[615] Nicely shown in Hein (1994b:133–137, 218–219).

[616] Bietak (1996a:59 and fig.49).

[617] Also Negbi's (1978) key criterion, see e.g. pp.139–140.

[618] Compare Maguire in Hein (1994b:216).

[619] Merrillees (1974a:43–77).

[620] Merrillees (1974a:75–77); Baurain (1984:68–70); cf. Åström (1987:57–58).

[621] Bietak (1979:235 and n.1).

[622] Vermeule and Wolsky (1990:287–307).

[623] Vermeule (1974); Vermeule and Wolsky (1990:159–243).

[624] Negbi (1978).

[625] When Negbi (1978) was written it was feasible for the author to argue that LCIA was not contemporary with the Syro-Palestinian MBA (and instead LBA/18th Dynasty). She said she rejected the chronology of Merrillees who had proposed such an LCIA–MBA link. However, the contemporaneity (or at least significant overlap) of LCIA with the Syro-Palestinian MBA is now almost universally accepted: see below.

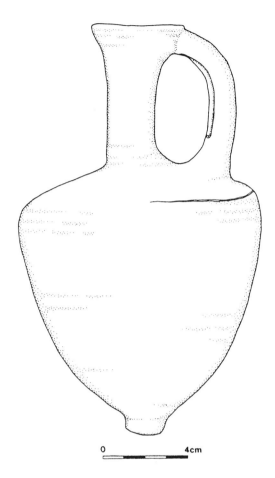

0   4cm

Fig. 28. The late MB Levantine brown burnished jug from LCIA Maroni Kapsaloudhia *Tomb 1. Drawing after Herscher (1984:pl.7.3).*

point out that there are close comparisons between the Tell el-Yahudiyeh examples in Tomb V (no LC in the tomb) and Tomb I (which has LCI materials, also an LMIA vessel with good parallels with one from Akrotiri on Thera[626]), and so raise the likelihood of an overlap of Tell el-Yahudiyeh fashion from late MC into early LC, and hence an overlap of later Syro-Palestinian MBA with the start of LCI.[627] Further confirmation comes in the form of a WP imitation of a Hyksos button-based juglet from an early LCI context from the foundations of an LCIA wall at Toumba tou Skourou,[628] and a late MB Levantine brown burnished jug from LCIA Maroni *Kapsaloudhia* Tomb 1: Figure 28.[629] Maroni *Kapsaloudhia* tomb 1 contained a PWS vessel, and may be dated to early LCIA.[630] The irregular piriform shape of the Maroni jug, truncated, almost conical body, very pronounced shoulder, long narrow neck, and handle attached from the rim to shoulder, are all typical of a comparison with Syro-Palestinian MBIIB or MBIIC examples,[631] although Cypriot manufacture, and comparison, is also possible.[632] The jug's shape, type, and button base might be compared with Syrian Red Burnished examples.[633] Examples of such vessels first appeared in MBIIB, and have been found in contexts of MBIIC or later SIP period date.[634] It is not a pretty vessel,

---

[626] Vermeule and Wolsky (1990:382 and n.76, 394); Cadogan (1990:95).

[627] Vermeule and Wolsky (1990:395).

[628] Vermeule and Wolsky (1990:84–85, 87, 88, 89, pl.47).

[629] Herscher (1984:25 and pl.7.3); Cadogan (1986:106). Although one might wonder whether the handle is perhaps a Cypriot feature (?) (cf. Negbi 1978:esp.139–140); I thank Gerald Cadogan and Ellen Herscher for allowing me to examine this jug.

[630] Herscher (1984:25); Cadogan *et al.* (n.d.).

[631] E.g. Amiran (1970:107, 112, 119).

[632] See footnote 629 above. Compare Negbi (1978:141 fig.6).

[633] Åström (1972b:132 types IIA1b and IIB1a); also Åström (1971:416 fig.3).

[634] Åström (1972b:240).

nor a fine ware type. It is unlikely to have been an heirloom when it was deposited. Instead, it probably shows the approximate correlation of later Syro-Palestinian MBII style with early LCI(A).

We have seen that early LCI (LCIA) correlates with LMIA, and it seems likely that some (MBA) Tell el-Yahudiyeh juglets (and other contemporary items) were in all probability found in a pre-eruption LMIA context on Thera itself (Chapter IV.4.B above). Therefore, again, the data highlights the likelihood of the LMIA period in the Aegean correlating with the later Syro-Palestinian MBA period, or the SIP of Egypt. The correlation of initial LCI(A) with the late Syro-Palestinian MBA is well established, with finds of WPV, WPVI, Monochrome, PWS, and Cypriot Bichrome in late MBA contexts in the Levant and Nile Delta.[635]

It is therefore time to reconsider the Negbi-Eriksson view of Tell el-Yahudiyeh ware and chronology with reference to Cyprus and Thera. The important elements are the regional chronology of MCIII–LCIA Cyprus, the chronology of the types of Tell el-Yahudiyeh juglets, and the Levantine date for the end of Tell el-Yahudiyeh use and its relationship to Cyprus. Negbi (1978) observed that LCIA occurrences of Cypriot imitations of Tell el-Yahudiyeh and related juglets (Black Punctured, Black Burnished, Red Burnished, Black Slip) occur especially in the area of Morphou Bay (that is northwest Cyprus). In the east of Cyprus, such juglets are dated MCIII–LCIA. Negbi sees the former as subsequent imitations, whereas, in fact, initial LCIA style assemblages from the northwest of Cyprus are broadly contemporary with MCIII–LCIA assemblages in eastern Cyprus. In chronological terms, both are LCIA. The presence of imitations especially in the northwest of Cyprus might rather be argued to indicate that this region was not in direct trading contact with Egypt, and was derivative in this regard from eastern Cyprus (i.e. the Merrillees 1971 model).

A more refined chronology is thus necessary, based around the different types of Tell el-Yahudiyeh ware.[636] An early phase may be characterised by the piriform juglets at Arpera *Mosphilos* Tomb 1. As noted above, these link with examples from Tell el-Dabᶜa strata E/3–2. This tomb is comprehensively MCIII, with WPIII, Red Polished III, Black Slip II and just one vessel in Red on Black as the latest element.[637] WPIII–IV from eastern Cyprus is found at Tell el-Dabᶜa from stratum G through D/3, and strata E/3–2 might be argued to offer a likely main linkage for this material.[638] Tomb V at Toumba tou Skourou perhaps identifies the next phase. This is final MC (in the northwest). The tomb included examples of piriform Tell el-Yahudiyeh and related juglets.[639] No biconical Tell el-Yahudiyeh is present. As noted above, Bietak has offered parallels from Tell el-Dabᶜa strata E/2–1.[640] Later finds at Toumba tou Skourou are

[635] Oren (1969; n.d.); Bietak (1991a:46; 1996a:63); Maguire (1986; 1990).
[636] For the chronology of the different types of Tell el-Yahudiyeh juglets, see e.g. Bietak (1989b; 1996a:Figs.46 and 47; 1997:94). See previously Kaplan (1980).
[637] Merrillees (1974a:47–59).
[638] With the finds primarily from tombs from stratum E/1 (though plentiful) marking the end (not floruit) of the period of linkage. Bietak and Hein (n.d.) view the odd find from stratum D/3 as probably residual.
[639] Vermeule and Wolsky (1990:296–297); Negbi (1978:nos.6, 8, 11, and 12).
[640] Negbi (1978:145 and n.18) linked the (now lost) juglet from Tomb V with an incised decoration of

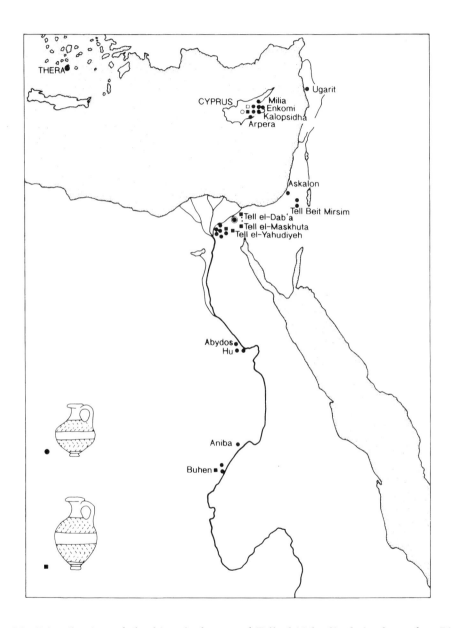

Fig. 29. Distribution of the biconical type of Tell el-Yahudiyeh juglets after Bietak (1996a:Fig.48.B; 1991a:Fig.22); Kaplan (1980:Map 7). For site data, see Kaplan (1980:77–80).

LCIA. Meanwhile, in the east of Cyprus, examples of the late biconical types of Tell el-Yahudiyeh juglets, used in Tell el-Dabᶜa strata E/1 to D/2, are found at several sites: see Figure 29.[641] This preferential eastern/southeastern distribution for the type offers a corollary on Cyprus for the evidence of nearly all the Cypriot imports to Tell el-Dabᶜa coming from eastern Cyprus (see Chapter IV.4.C above, and also Chapter IV.5). These finds date from the local MCIII period and into the MCIII–LCIA period. In east Cyprus initial LCIA remains MC-style, with WPV–VI, and so on, without, or with little, PWS/WSI, PBR/BRI. An LCIA date is indicated only by subtle indicators, such as flat bases on the WPV–VI jugs (several WPV examples found at Tell el-Dabᶜa[642]). The contemporary period at Toumba tou Skourou, and especially early Tomb I where a solitary biconical specimen of a Syro-Palestinian juglet of the Tell el-Yahudiyeh or related Levantine MBA type occurs,[643] is also LCIA, but has the new (northwest origin) LC styles of PWS and WSI and PBR and BRI. A southcoast site, like Maroni *Kapsaloudhia* Tomb 1, combined elements of both regions, with a late MBA Levantine juglet in an early LCI context including PWS.[644]

It is clear, however, that Tell el-Yahudiyeh ware and its associates only just overlap into LCIA. The main phase is MC (Tell el-Dabᶜa strata E/3–2 to E/1). Only the late biconical type seems broadly to correlate with LCIA. Importantly, this type is represented on Thera. This late type is not, however, well attested in the Levant.[645] In the Levant, Tell el-Yahudiyeh ware has basically vanished by the time Late Cypriot Bichrome Ware appears.[646] The absence of Tell el-Yahudiyeh ware in Tell el-ᶜAjjul City 3/Palace I is telling. Thus, as Oren (1969:136) concludes, the evidence 'strongly indicates that Tell el-Yahudiyeh ware and piriform juglets became almost extinct well before the end of [the] Middle Bronze Age'. The biconical type is different. It is a product of the Egyptian Delta,[647] and thus it seems that, whereas trade occurred employing these late biconical juglets between Egypt and Cyprus, and Egypt and Thera (indirect via Cyprus?), and a few sites in the Levant (rare class of local copies?[648]), the Tell el-ᶜAjjul trade group was outside of, or separate from, this late biconical Tell el-Yahudiyeh trade group contemporary with Tell el-Dabᶜa strata E/1 to D/2.[649] Tell el-ᶜAjjul received initial LCIA material from northwest Cyprus, along with Red on Black from northeast

---

flowers and water birds (Negbi 1978:ills.1–4; Vermeule and Wolsky 1990:pls.182–183) to examples from Tell el-Dabᶜa stratum E/2.

[641] After Bietak (1996a:Fig.48.B; 1991a:Fig.22); Kaplan (1980:Map 7). For site data, see Kaplan (1980:77–80).

[642] Maguire (1990).

[643] Vermeule and Wolsky (1990:218 TI.548 P440); Negbi (1978:no.2).

[644] The Maroni juglet may be compared with one from Toumba tou Skourou Tomb I (Vermeule and Wolsky 1990:218 TI.237 P193; Negbi 1978:no.1).

[645] Kaplan (1980:72).

[646] Oren (1969:136).

[647] Kaplan (1980:63).

[648] Kaplan (1980:63).

[649] Bietak (1991a:60) has also observed these differential patterns, noting that the 'ware seems to be a sensitive indicator for cultural provinces in Palestine'. He further notes that 'cultural patterns are often indicators of political differentiations'. Bietak cites Kempinski (1983:191–196) who previously identified several different ceramic groups, or 'provinces', in MBII Palestine.

Cyprus, and Bichrome, WP, and Red Slip wares from eastern Cyprus, but *not* Tell el-Yahudiyeh juglets from the Nile Delta.[650] The indications of the separateness of some aspects of the trade of Tell el-ʿAjjul versus Tell el-Dabʿa is highly important, and should be borne in mind when we return to discuss Tell el-ʿAjjul and WSI in Chapter V. That all these different products (northwest Cypriot, eastern Cypriot, and Nile Delta), and the trade involving these items, are, however, approximately contemporary, is shown by the find of one of the same biconical type Tell el-Yahudiyeh juglets on pre-eruption Thera. Here the jug is LMIA; and LMIA independently links both with LCIA in northwest Cyprus at Toumba tou Skourou (and so late MBA Tell el-ʿAjjul), *and* initial LCIA in southern Cyprus at Maroni *Vournes* (and so the eastern WPV–VI, Red on Black, Black Slip, PWS, horizon, and so in turn to Tell el-Dabʿa strata E/1 to D/2).

Therefore, the conclusion to be drawn is that the late biconical type of Tell el-Yahudiyeh juglet links pre-eruption LMIA Thera with LCIA Cyprus and late MBA Tell el-Dabʿa (strata E/1 to D/2).

E. FRESCOES

We should briefly note again the pattern of finds of similar frescoes from Tel Kabri, Alalakh, and Qatna of later Syro-Palestinian MBA date which show strong links with earlier New Palace (MMIIIB–LMIA) examples from Crete, the Cycladic Islands, or Miletus.[651] In view of the available data, the common association of all these sites best makes sense in the late Syro-Palestinian MBA when all appear to have been part of a unified east Mediterranean trading area typified in ceramic terms by the exchange of, and common fashions/imitations in, small, narrow-necked, containers (juglets especially).[652] Some examples of these were transported to LMIA Thera, along with contemporary MBII stone vessels and a Canaanite Jar (see above), and imports of ostrich eggs and other exotic but not dated items entirely consistent with Hyksos period trade and fashions.[653] Until the re-dating by Bietak, the initial reports of late Hyksos wall paintings from Tell el-Dabʿa seemed to add to a consistent picture,[654] where there is a notable koine of élite expression among a set of late MBA east Mediterranean *and* Aegean centres. This is the real point, rather than a debate over the 'ethnicity' of the art form. Ethnicity is a social construction, a decision and statement of belonging–association, versus exclusion (and is defined only in relative terms vis à vis others[655]). The so-called 'Aegeanising' wall paintings represent a

---

[650] Bietak (1991a:60 and Fig.23) further identifies another separate grouping in inland Palestine defined by the distinct Piriform 3 type of Tell el-Yahudiyeh juglet. Thus several distinct trading–cultural groupings exist.

[651] See Chapter IV.3. See: Niemeier (1991; 1995a; 1995b); Niemeier and Niemeier (1997:238–240; 1998; pers. comm.); Negbi (1994); Manning *et al.* (1994a:); Morgan (1995); Warren (1995:4); Cline (1995:266–270); Knapp (1998).

[652] See Chapter IV.4.D. above. Also see Maguire (1990:chapter 3); Karageorghis (1995).

[653] Negbi (1994:85–86).

[654] Bietak (1992b).

[655] '...ethnic groups are categories of ascription and identification by the actors themselves' (Barth 1969:10). See further in Barth (1969); Jones (1997); Hall (1997).

common mode and language of élite representation and symbolism across key centres in both the Aegean and the east Mediterranean – they specifically represent a common statement of association with a (self) perceived grouping. They thus represent a more or less contemporaneous, communicating, phenomenon.

The evidence from Tel Kabri and Alalakh, and the evidence from the Aegean, suggests that this is a later MBA, or Hyksos, horizon, linked to LMIA in the Aegean. Only Bietak's revised dating of the fresco fragments from secondary rubbish contexts at Tell el-Dabᶜa is contradictory (see Chapter IV.3 above). Some arguments and circumstances to the contrary have already been examined earlier in this chapter. A consideration of some other factors is also relevant, and the discussion of these in the remaining sections of this chapter may offer a likely resolution of the problem.

F. Exploring context: inter-élite communication, fashion, and the key late MBA-SIP cultural and artistic fusion

We have already noted the lack of LMIA exports to Egypt in any context *other than* secondary contexts at Tell el-Dabᶜa, and specifically their absence from any definite early 18th Dynasty context, and in reverse, the similar absence of early 18th Dynasty exports to the LMIA/LHI Aegean. And, in contrast, we have noted the positive evidence for LMIA-Hyksos associations (which could include the Tell el-Dabᶜa finds). We may now extend this pattern to the clear evidence for ruler to ruler, royal, contact. Mellink (1995) highlights the specifically royal, king-to-king, gifts sent by the Hyksos king Khyan to both Knossos (main centre on Crete) and Hattusa/Boghazköy (the Hittite capital in Anatolia). No such evidence exists of early 18th Dynasty date. It is a specific circumstance, and one is entitled to wonder whether the appearance of Minoan-style art and Minoan imports at Tell el-Dabᶜa (and not elsewhere in Egypt) is entirely unrelated. Mellink (1995:86) writes that:

> The coincidence that an Egyptian vessel with the name of Khyan, suitable as a present among royalty, was found in each of two foreign capitals, leads one to opt for the conclusion that Khyan indeed sent these objects (presumably among other gifts) as tokens of personal and dynastic interest in establishing friendly relations with each of two dynasties formerly not officially approached by Egyptian rulers.

She concludes (p.89) that these gifts intrinsically represent:

> signs of a new cultural and political perspective on the part of Khyan, and proof of a new initiative by a cosmopolitan ruler of great ambition.

As noted in Chapter IV.2, and in revision to the original date given by Evans, an LMIA date for the deposit of the inscribed lid at Knossos is possible, even likely (instead of an MMIIIA date). And the LMIA period represents a suitable historical context as a time when Crete was a major international power, and Knossos was the dominant site of Crete and its greater region. Other objects linked to Khyan (as king) complete a wide distribution map of apparent contacts or connections for this important ruler.[656] The Hyksos capital of Avaris is described even by their enemy, the 17th Dynasty Theban king Kamose from Upper Egypt, as a major, and especially international, port (see Table 4 above p. 99). Oren (1997a:xxiii) simply states that Hyksos Avaris (Tell el-Dabᶜa) was 'no doubt one of the largest towns in Egypt and probably the entire Levant during the Middle Bronze Age'. The Hyksos period (or contexts which might well be associated with it) appears to offer the best evidence for the communicating world system at issue above. It is a time of a clear and specific international prestige goods economy across the whole eastern Mediterranean driven from the Levant/Hyksos world,[657] seen for example in:

1. The koine of élite expression via the medium of similar frescoes – see Chapter IV.4.E above, and Chapter IV.3.
2. The koine of élite and ritual expression via the medium of similar jewellery – see below.[658]
3. The common/similar scarab forms found in both Egypt and Palestine, from those bearing the names of rulers, to exports and local productions of Egyptian scarabs with private names or the titles of officials, from Canaanite SIP Egypt to Palestine,[659] and, notably, the export of these also to the rest of the east Mediterranean and their deposition in final burial contexts from the earlier LBA,[660] and onwards through the LBA: Figure 30. The original Egyptian usage of these scarabs as funerary amulets appears to have been transferred to Palestine and the rest of the east Mediterranean.

---

[656] Redford (1992:118–122); Negbi (1994:98 n.12); Ryholt (1997:384 nos.7–10 File 15/4). On Crete, Knossos is clearly the largest site, and elements of cultural leadership may be noted. Several scholars argue LMI Crete was unified under Knossian rule. This may be debated, but in LMIA (in particular, and in contrast to LMIB) Knossos does seem to have been the centre of a wider territory (Schoep 1999: esp. 217–220; see her p. 202 and ns. 3 and 4 for previous scholarship).

[657] In general, see Negbi (1994); and for Syria–Palestine, see Kempinski (1983).

[658] Negbi (1970:22–29); Merrillees (1986); Matthiae (1997:407–409). It is important to note that Negbi's (1970) LBI date for the Tell el-ᶜAjjul City 2/Palace II hoards should be revised to late MBII=MBIII (see Kempinski 1974; 1983:131–148; 1992a:189–192; Kempinski in Stern 1993:52–53; Oren 1997b:271; pers. comm). In essence, this is a revision of the date horizon for Bichrome Ware. Negbi (1970:37, also 18–19) dates the famous hoards of goldwork from Tell el-ᶜAjjul – which includes the relevant earrings – 'precisely to the floruit of Bichrome Ware at Tell el-ᶜAjjul and other Syro-Palestinian sites'. Negbi, following Epstein (1966) and eventually Albright (1938), regarded this horizon as LBI. She sought support from the associated LC ceramics (WPVI, Monochrome, PWS, WSI: Negbi 1970:19). However, it is now clear that Bichrome Ware occurs from the late MBII period (what is called MBIIC or MBIII), and indeed that Bichrome Ware very much defines this late MBA phase (Kempinski 1983; Gonen 1992:98–99; Oren 1997b:271). Similarly, LCIA WPVI and PWS occur in late MBA Syria–Palestine. Hence much of the relevant jewellery from Tell el-ᶜAjjul can be regarded as late MBA (consistent with linkages to material from Ebla: Matthiae 1997:407–409). The few assemblages associated with BRI (Negbi 1970:20–21) may be a little later (i.e. LCIA2–LCIB, and into Syro-Palestinian LBI/early 18th Dynasty), although it is possible that BRI first appears during the SIP (LCIA2 presumably), especially as this site was in contact with northwest Cyprus where BR developed. See further in discussion of Tell el-ᶜAjjul in Chapter IV.5.

[659] E.g. Kempinski (1992a:179; 1983:68–78); Weinstein (1981:8–12, Fig.3); Ryholt (1997:105–111, 130); Ben-Tor (1994). For local productions, see Ben-Tor (1994:12 ns.12–13).

[660] In the Aegean in LHI–II or LMIB (e.g. Cline 1994:146 no.122, 147 no.126); in Cyprus from LCI, or I–IIA (e.g. Jacobsson 1994:52 no.275, 53–54 no.279, 54 no.280).

4.   The common Tell el-Yahudiyeh juglet, and
     Cypriot and other small juglet/container,
     phenomenon visible across the region.[661]

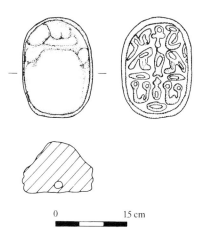

This period is also the high-point and culmination
of the Mediterranean trade network established
earlier in the MBII period, and, generally, the last
MBA phase represents the zenith of the urban
MBA civilisation in Palestine[662] – marked especially by the appearance specifically in this final
phase of several major new 'palatial' centres.[663]
As noted by Oren (1997b:271), in Palestine,
Bichrome Ware very much distinguishes this
particular late MBII phase (including Tell el-Dabᶜa
stratum D/2), along with the export appearance
of late MC to LCI *types* (i.e. all probably LCIA in
date). I suspect the Aegean also may probably be
associated with this specific Syro-Palestinian
stylistic horizon, for example through jewellery,
and also pottery.

*Fig. 30. An example of an exported
SIP/Hyksos scarab: MT.140, a
faience scarab, from Pit 18 at Maroni
Tsaroukkas (see Manning and
Monks 1998:340–341).*

The extraordinary LMIA frescoes found in the
Xeste 3 building at Akrotiri show a number of what must be considered high-status
women in impressive dress. But apart from the elaborate flounced skirts, jewellery is
also a conspicuous feature of these representations, and this jewellery offers good
links with the world of later MBII Syria–Palestine.[664] Let us consider just a few
examples here. The large and impressive gold hooped earrings worn by the female
figures, both human and divine ('mistress of the animals') in the Xeste 3 suite,[665]
including some with clear indications of granulation,[666] find good general parallels in
crescent, penannular, and annullar earrings not only elsewhere in the Aegean, but
especially in the impressive Tell el-ᶜAjjul assemblage of gold jewellery.[667] There are
also good linkages for some bracelets/bangles, and for the crocus and papyrus motif:
see Figures 18–20 above pp. 56–58. In past literature, the Tell el-ᶜAjjul examples have
been dated LBI, but the correct date for these City II/Palace II, or earlier, finds (and

[661] Kaplan (1980); Karageorghis (1995).

[662] Seger (1974; 1975); Dever (1987; 1997:291–292); Kempinski (1992a); Bourke (1997:107). This last MBA
phase is variously called the late MBII, MBIIC, or MBIII period. In the coastal areas a separate MBIIC or
MBIII phase may be recognised.

[663] E.g. in Palestine: Tell el-ᶜAjjul, Tel Haror, Tel Seraᶜ: Oren (1997b:257).

[664] I thank Thea Politis for discussion and advice.

[665] Doumas (1992: pls. 100–102, 105–109).

[666] Especially Doumas (1992: pls. 116, 118–121, 122–126, and 129–130).

[667] Petrie (1931–1934, vol.IV:pls.13–14 nos.26–31, pls.19–20 no.132); Petrie *et al.* (1952:pl.6 nos.4–5); Negbi
(1970:38 nos. 1–13, 39 nos. 26–38, 40 nos. 41–61, 40–41 nos. 62–80, and 41 nos. 81–91, pls.I.2, III.10 centre);
Maxwell-Hyslop (1971:116–117 'earrings with granular decoration', pls.78–81); Lilyquist (1993:47–50)
for a summary.

the general tradition to which they belong) is later MBII in Syro-Palestinian terms.[668]

Links in the ceramic evidence are less clear; direct imports to the Aegean are virtually non-existent, and only Akrotiri on Thera offers a glimpse of sea-trade bringing later MBII products (stone vessels, Canaanite jars, and so on). However, as Merrillees (1974a:5–6) and also Buchholz (1980:228) suggest, some 'Black-on-Red' to 'polychrome' vessels from late MH/earlier LHI contexts at Mycenae (and a few other contemporary contexts on the mainland and Crete), and late Middle Cycladic/early Late Cycladic I contexts at Phylakopi and other Cycladic sites including Akrotiri, appear in some way related to, influenced by, or derived from, the Cypriot-Palestinian Bichrome Ware style.[669] In particular, one may note both (i) the common accent on bird and fish representations (and disks and geometric decorations/filling) in 'Black-on-Red' (so-called 'Temple Repository style') and Bichrome Ware, and (ii) the general similarities in the representations of some quadrupeds in LCI Theran art, including in Black and Red, and Bichrome Ware.[670] Åström (1971:418) proposed the same tentative association, and, importantly, that the influence perhaps ran from the Aegean to the east Mediterranean; Artzy (n.d.) has now turned this into a strong argument. In terms of the relative chronologies this makes good sense, and it is perhaps an idea worthy of further consideration. Various stylistic elements in the Aegean during the early to mid 17th century BC thus influence the development of Bichrome Ware on Cyprus in the later 17th century BC, and so in turn the subsequent main Bichrome Ware phase in the Levant in the final MBII (MBIIC or MBIII) period from the end of 17th century BC through to the mid 16th century BC.

Stressing the Hyksos links is not to re-invent ideas of a Hyksos 'world empire' as previously suggested,[671] but to highlight, as in Chapter III, a contemporary 'world

---

[668] Kempinski (1974; 1983; 1992a:189–192); Kempinski in Stern (1993:52–53); Oren (1997b:271; pers. comm.). See also footnote 658 above.

[669] A manuscript by Michal Artzy (n.d.) explores and develops this case in some detail. I thank her for generously sending me a copy.

[670] For 'Black-on-Red' ware in the Aegean, see Davis (1977); Davis and Williams (1981:295–297); Andreou (1974) – with Davis (1977); Dietz (1991:298 and 299 Fig.88, 309–312); Cummer and Schofield (1984:47). One may also add for consideration the dramatic 'polychrome' vessels from LMIA Akrotiri on Thera (Marinatos 1968–1976, vol.V:colour pl.A; VI, colour pl.11), apart from fragments of Black-on-Red bird vases from the early LMIA seismic destruction (Marthari 1984:Fig.7.c). Davis (1977) outlines a two-stage development in the style, from late MBA to LMIA. For Bichrome Ware, see Epstein (1966). For birds in the Red-on-Black style at the Temple Repositories at Knossos, see Evans (1921–1935, vol.1:556–561). This deposit is difficult to date, but lies somewhere in either the MMIIIB–LMIA transition period, or the LMIA period (Panagiotaki 1998). Panagiotaki (1998:197) considers linking the destruction of the Temple Repositories with either the early LMIA seismic destruction at Thera, or the VDL at Thera, or some other local Knossos destruction 'close in date to the Theran destructions'. For birds in Bichrome Ware, see Epstein (1966:31–40). For quadrupeds in Black and Red from Thera, see e.g. Renaudin (1922:fig.29, pl.13; also Åberg 1933:128 Abb.237). For quadrupeds in Bichrome Ware, see Epstein (1966:40–51). In an early study of pictorial Bichrome Ware, Heurtley (1939:33–34) noted the suggestion of a link to the Mycenae vases, but discounted it (understandably as there was then a lack of other evidence to support such an association). He however admitted that the fish motif on one Bichrome vase from Tell el-ʿAjjul was like Cycladic or Minoan examples (p.34). Evans (1921–1935, vol.I) linked the Cycladic style birds to the flying gallop griffin motif (p.558), and also noted the link to west Asian styles (pp.559–560).

[671] von Bissing (1936–1937); cf. Redford (1992:120); Oren (1997a:xxii).

system' of which the Hyksos, and the general region of 'greater Canaan',[672] were both a part, and perhaps a core or driving centre, for a period of a century or so.[673] This area both generated, but also drew in, influences from the greater east Mediterranean trading world. The corresponding periods seem to be late MC style and early LCI style = LCIA in Cyprus, and LMIA, Late Cycladic I, and LHI in the Aegean.

In reverse, we may note the strong west Asian-Nilotic and/or African element and/ or 'royal' or 'eastern' element (lions, leopards, griffins, sphinxes), in a variety of specifically early Cretan New Palace (MMIIIB–LMIA), Late Cycladic I, and LHI art. This link has been noted often before, and much discussed.[674] Conventional scholarship has concentrated on the one approximately datable Egyptian synchronism, and the one instance where even the ever-critical Furumark (1950:220) agreed on 'an absolutely certain instance of Aegean influence': the discovery of an (agreed) Aegean style griffin on an axe (Figure 26 above p. 112), along with some (not completely agreed) possible 'Aegean'-style rockwork and animals in the supposedly 'Aegean'-style flying gallop on an inlaid dagger blade, from the tomb of Ahhotep.[675] As a result, a date contemporary with the accession of Ahmose somehow became the accepted date for the start of the LMIA/LHI periods. But this logic is incorrect, as Furumark argued. The Ahhotep link

---

[672] Syria–Palestine: see Niemeier (1995a:9 and 13 n.46). Cf. footnote 544 above.

[673] I am employing the loaded term of 'world system' very loosely. The term was developed with reference to modern capitalism (16th century AD and onwards) by Wallerstein (1974). Some scholars have suggested the utility of his concept when studying earlier history, and indeed prehistory back into the Bronze Age (see Frank and Gills 1993; Algaze 1993; Sherratt 1993; Chase-Dunn and Hall 1991; 1995). In particular, such scholars point to the core–periphery economic dynamic, and processes of capital accumulation, as common across the last 5,000 years in the Near East and eastern Mediterranean (especially). It is in this sense of variously inter-connected core–periphery economic systems that I use the term 'world system' for the Bronze Age (for an Aegean-oriented summary, see Sherratt and Sherratt 1991). I appreciate problematic definitional issues, and some problems with the evidence, but believe that the characterisation is useful and reasonable. I adopt the necessary view of Algaze that Wallerstein's concentration on political/military control in the capitalist era may be modified in antiquity, where 'in many cases the extent of ... economic hegemony far outreached the boundaries of political control' (Algaze 1993:8), and thus that – in antiquity anyway – economic dominance and political/military control are not mutually exclusive categories (Algaze 1993:9). Another major issue of definition is that Wallerstein regards trade primarily in luxury goods as defining a system of trade between separate systems (however defined), whereas trade primarily in bulk goods (which he regards as necessities) defines an integrated world system. This then leads on to the debate concerning whether the ancient Near East and related areas was a form of 'ancient world system', or instead another set of structures. This debate, and whether or not modern capitalism of the sort discussed by Wallerstein may be considered equivalent to forms of ancient capital accumulation, need not concern us here, since the system or systems of the ancient Near East and east Mediterranean – however defined – may nonetheless be characterised by their varying core–periphery relations, and because the interrelated nature of the élite prestige goods systems in the ancient world largely parallels the logic of the modern world system analysis (with preciosities here the 'necessities': from Schneider 1977), even if it should be regarded as different (for the case for the ancient world system, and for critique and debate, see Frank and Gills 1993; see also papers in Sanderson 1995).

[674] See e.g. the classic study of Furumark (1950:215–222); see also recent review in Laffineur (1998:64– 67). For a more general treatment, see Crowley (1989).

[675] See footnotes 124 and 505. For a list of scholarship on the griffin on the axe, and for the locations of illustrations, see especially Morgan (1995:47 n.71).

plausibly marks the *end* of this stylistic linkage, or fusion. Nor is the wider pattern being considered.

Furumark (1950:219) argued that 'the "flying gallop" is apparently one of the many new features that were created in the Near East during the Second Intermediate period, as a result of the conflux of impulses from various sources', and in general he saw the introduction of the griffin and a whole new range of art as linked to this dynamic period in the Near East (1950:218–221). Furumark specifically highlighted the prior (i.e. SIP) existence of the flying gallop in Hyksos art,[676] and its absence in general Aegean art before the beginning of the New Palace period (pp.218–219).[677] Syria appears to play a key role in the process of transmission.[678] In the Aegean, the appearance of the flying gallop motif is very much associated with a new prestige art-craft form, the inlaid bronze dagger[679] – and interestingly the dagger from Ahhotep's tomb is of the same type. In one of the few instances of potential agreement between Kantor and Furumark, Kantor pointed out that the inlaid ('niello') technique did not originate in the Aegean, but in MBA west Asia.[680]

These conclusions remain as true today as they did half a century ago. The initial LB1 phase in the Aegean (LHI, Late Cycladic I, LMIA) appears to be in stylistic communication with a key new art-craft phase in the Near East (an aspect of the late MBII, or MBIII/MBIIC, urban zenith) linked especially with the time of the SIP and a visible fusion of western Asian influences, and ending more or less with the start of the Egyptian New Kingdom. Let us consider some of the evidence.

(i)   The appearance of the exciting and new 'flying gallop' motif in general art, and especially its use for the representation of exotic animals such as lions, leopards/cats, and griffins, which have eastern associations, and are also the creatures of power and royalty in the Near East and Egypt. In the Aegean, this form appears all of a sudden on highly prestigious weapons (and notably inlaid-technique

---

[676] Smith (1965:155). Furumark even took Kantor to task for ignoring this point: Furumark (1950:219 n.6). Kantor was aware that there was potential evidence contrary to her view of an Aegean origin for the flying gallop representation (1947[1997]:63 discussing the work of Edgerton), but chose to dismiss this. I must disagree with Laffineur (1998:54), who follows Kantor, and regards the Ahhotep I dagger as the start of the representation.

[677] A few representations of animals in more or less 'flying gallop' pose do occur on MM seals (Crowley 1989:113–114; Immerwahr 1990:30 and Fig.10; Morgan 1995:36 and 47 n.64), but not elsewhere. Similarly, although the odd griffin and lion occurs from this time also (e.g. Immerwahr 1990:Fig.10.a [griffin] and perhaps d and e [lions? – or dogs?]), there is a clear group or horizon of representations using these motifs together in LM/LHI in a new range of media. The ultimate origin of the flying gallop pose has been much debated. Kantor (1947[1997]) supported an Aegean home, but one in Syria is equally likely (especially for the initial LBA group/horizon). Hood (1978b:235) points out its primitive and non-specific nature, and wider use in painted art from the Palaeolithic onwards.

[678] Aruz (1995:39–40).

[679] In the past often, but in fact inappropriately, referred to as niello technique, or damascene – discussed below.

[680] Kantor (1947[1997]:65). See e.g. Frankfort (1970:237, 244). Sites like later MB Byblos, and Ugarit (Ras Shamra), have some early examples, and were perhaps the source of such prestige technology, then imitated and developed in the Aegean, and at the Hyksos centres: see further below.

daggers) from the LHI Shaft Graves at Mycenae and elsewhere.[681] An inlaid technique dagger-sword was found also on pre-eruption LMIA Thera.[682] As noted above, the inlaid technique itself is widely accepted to be of West Asian later MB origin[683] – and Dickinson (1997) and Boss and Laffineur (1997:194–196) find little reason to involve Minoan Crete in the transmission process in any key way. Thus this fairly direct instance of Levantine–Aegean correspondence appears to offer further evidence for the linking of the LHI, LMIA, and Late Cycladic I periods to the late MBA of the Levant. In Egypt, similar examples of the inlaid technique begin during the Hyksos period, and end with Ahmose;[684] it is evident that the former period offers the main synchronism, with Ahmose marking the end of the relationship. In addition to the Shaft Grave examples, the flying gallop motif with lions and other ungulates appears also on a group of Late Cycladic I vases – notably from pre-eruption Thera which was a major international port at this time.[685]

(ii)   One of the extant mature LMIA wall paintings from Akrotiri on Thera is distinctly Nilotic: the river scene with exotic 'Nilotic' flora and fauna from Room 5 of the West House.[686] Other paintings include Nilotic elements, for example: the lions in chasing or 'flying gallop' pose in the miniature frieze from Room 5 of the West House along a river and emblazoned along the side of the most prominent ship in the flotilla;[687] the papyrus plant/flower both as a feature or compositional element in several scenes;[688] the 'African' from the area of Sector Alpha;[689] and the monkeys from Building Beta and Xeste 3.[690]

(iii) Some other likely LMIA wall-paintings from Crete include distinctly Nilotic elements, for example: the monkeys in two frescoes from Knossos;[691] the cat from Ayia Triadha;[692] perhaps the 'MMIII' (Evans) fragment of a lion's mane from Knossos;[693] and perhaps the LMI and MMIII–LMIB, and LMIB?, griffins and sphinxes from Knossos.[694]

---

[681] E.g. Hood (1978b:178–181); Negbi (1978:147 and n.30); Marinatos and Hirmer (1960:167, pls.35–38); on the technique and its correct characterisation, see Demakopoulou *et al.* (1995); Boss and Laffineur (1997).

[682] Vermeule (1964:pl.13.C); Hood (1978b:181 and n.57).

[683] Laffineur (1990–1991:269–276; 1996); Demakopoulou *et al.* (1995:137–138); Dickinson (1994:99–100); Xenaki-Sakellariou and Chatziliou (1989:18–24); Hood (1978b:181 and n.56); Betancourt (1998a:6); Cline (1998a:214 and n.148).

[684] The examples usually cited are the dagger of Apophis, and then the items from the tomb of Ahhotep: e.g. Cline (1998a:213–214). See above.

[685] Demakopoulou and Crouwel (1993).

[686] Doumas (1992:64–67, pls.30–34).

[687] Doumas (1992:68–77 pls.35–37).

[688] E.g. Doumas (1992: 36–37, pls. 2–5, 86 pl.50 left, 87 pl.51, etc.); see also Warren (1976b).

[689] Doumas (1992:187, pl.148).

[690] Doumas (1992:120–123, pls.85–89, 159, pl.122; etc.); in general, see: Morgan (1988:146–150, also 21–28, 41–54, 172).

[691] Immerwahr (1990:170, Kn Nos. 1 and 2).

[692] Immerwahr (1990:49, 179–180, pl.17).

[693] Immerwahr (1990:177, Kn no.34).

[694] Hood (1978b:62 and Fig.45); Immerwahr (1990:171, Kn no.8e, 177, Kn no.35).

(iv)   As noted, contemporary LHI art on prestige objects from the Shaft Graves at Mycenae and elsewhere with motifs such as lions, cats chasing waterfowls amongst papyrus, and cats and palms, links specifically with Asian-Nilotic art and origins.[695]

The scenario of 'a whole series of features of Egyptian origin' appearing at the beginning of the neopalatial period in Crete and the Aegean is a well accepted observation.[696] The question is the source of this new imagery, these techniques, and these associations? Some might wish to suggest Crete when discussing the Mainland, or even Thera. But overall it is an Aegean-wide adoption from elsewhere. Nor is Egypt the source (and certainly not the 18th Dynasty). As Furumark (1950:219) argued with specific reference to the 'flying gallop': 'it seems extremely probable that both the Aegean and the Egyptian representations of this kind are derived from a common outside source. And this source can have been situated nowhere else than in Asia'. When? The only plausible conclusion is the SIP when Asian influences fused with the Egyptian and a new Levantine–Egyptian culture dominated the east Mediterranean[697] – and in the case of the flying gallop, for example, a clear SIP example at least half-way towards the full motif exists in the dagger of the Hyksos king Apophis thought to have been made in Syria,[698] along with SIP scarab representations. In the Aegean, the marine motifs associated with these Nilotic images in some cases (the Miniature frieze from Akrotiri), or found on other similar inlaid bronze daggers from Greece,[699] or on the plaster offering table from Akrotiri,[700] perhaps accentuate the link with the international world and the exotic, far away, Asian–Nile region. Doumas (1992:180) even comments referring to the marine decorated table of offerings that '...the manner in which the dolphins are portrayed displays closer affinities with the Egyptian principle...'. The riverine symbolism itself, whilst generally 'Nilotic', is also perhaps more especially representative of a connection with the marshes–delta region of Egypt, and the core of the Hyksos world when Avaris/ Tell el-Dabᶜa was the great centre of the ancient world.

In overall terms, the exotic components in the Akrotiri frescoes appear linked to a prestige socio-political economy encapsulating and displaying esoteric knowledge,[701] and are part of a general model where the creation and display of these elaborate wall-paintings form a display of power and wealth by important individuals or groups.[702] Although actual visits or familiarity with the source of the images is therefore

---

[695] E.g. Marinatos and Hirmer (1960:167, pls.35–38); Morgan (1988:42–43); Hood (1978b:178–181); on the lion motif at Mycenae: Immerwahr (1990:137 and 218 n.12).

[696] Furumark (1950:221).

[697] As Furumark (1950:219 and n.6)

[698] Evans (1921–1935, vol.I:717 fig.540, 718–719); Warren (1995:5); Morgan (1995:47 n.66). Both the gazelle and lion shown each only have one pair of their legs up in the air in flying gallop pose (respectively back and front). The intent is there. It is generally assumed that this dagger is a product of Syrian workmanship (Frankfort 1970:245–246, fig.282 caption).

[699] Marinatos and Hirmer (1960: pl.38).

[700] Doumas (1992:181–183, pls.142–144).

[701] Doumas (1992:27); Manning *et al.* (1994a:219–222); Knapp (1998); Niemeier and Niemeier (1998:96).

[702] Boulotis (1992); Chapin (1997:23).

not necessary for most in the society, it nonetheless seems unlikely that these images were created and displayed with reference to a time or period when the Aegean seems to have had *no* contact with Egypt. As Barthes (1971:9) states, style is essentially a citational process. The total lack of other archaeological evidence for definite LMIA–early 18th Dynasty contacts (this Chapter) therefore cannot make the early 18th Dynasty the likely source of the Nilotic imagery in the Theran frescoes, or the other essentially Asiatic-source art from the Shaft Graves and Thera. Instead, the evidence for some LMIA contact and involvement with the late MBA trade system of the Hyksos world has to form a persuasive argument in favour of an LMIA-Hyksos correlation, and a Hyksos-Delta source for the Nilotic imagery. It is notable that this linkage is well represented at pre-eruption Thera, which was a major port and regional and inter-regional centre of this time. As Doumas (1992:27) writes, 'numerous objects imported from Eastern Mediterranean lands (Syria, Palestine, Egypt) have been found in the excavations at Akrotiri, attesting relations with the Oriental world'. This is something which conspicuously cannot be said of any other contemporary Aegean site. The axe and dagger from the tomb of Ahhotep mark more or less the *end* of this dynamic period of Asian-driven international artistic development involving much of the east Mediterranean in the SIP. And there is, in fact, no reason they do not represent later LMI (i.e. LMIB) influence (with much LMIB-use prestige art carried over from LMIA – see Driessen and Macdonald 1997:62–70) early in the reign of Ahmose.

G. CONCLUSIONS

In sum, there is a strong case and pattern in the data in favour of an Egyptian SIP-Hyksos date for the LMIA period (or at least much of the LMIA period). As noted above, this is not a particularly radical idea. Since 1979 Warren has proposed at least some overlap. And, as already quoted above, Warren and Hankey (1989:140) state that 'Late Minoan IA was in existence before the end of MBII, that is within the time of the Second Intermediate Period in Egypt'. The relevant synchronisms Warren had in mind came from mature to late LMIA on Thera, hence this overlap need not have been insignificant, even on these terms. I am merely arguing that the overlap is substantial. And, in reverse, that there is in fact almost no good evidence for the original, conventional, linkage with the early 18th Dynasty. Nothing supports a link later than the very beginning of the 18th Dynasty. Thus a primarily LMIA=Egyptian SIP equation may be offered. Furthermore, this overlap or period should not be regarded strictly as 'Hyksos'. The preceding 'Canaanite' 14th Dynasty seems if anything to have had more extensive links with the Levant,[703] and, if the 'early' Aegean chronology is correct, parts of the earlier LMIA, LHI, and Late Cycladic I periods before the eruption of Thera will have been contemporary with the later 14th Dynasty (extent depending on Egyptian chronology).

---

[703] Ryholt (1997:105–111).

H. COMPLICATIONS?

Is there any evidence which contradicts this conclusion? Two things have been discussed in recent years. First, Eriksson (1992:170–172) raises an Egyptian razor from chamber 1 of Tomb I at Toumba tou Skourou, Cyprus. She argues that this form does not pre-date Tuthmosis III (or perhaps it is better stated that it is a New Kingdom type from current evidence). I accept this, and have not investigated the point in Egyptian terms.[704] However, this has *no* bearing on the date of the LMIA period. Although imported LMIA ceramics were in the tomb chamber, there were more than 20 burials, and the range of the local Cypriot material extends from MCIII to LCIB. The razor can belong to LCIB comfortably, while the LMIA imports can go with the earlier (and hirsute) LCIA burials. Bourriau and Eriksson (1997:99–100) return to this object, and reach a similar conclusion: LCIB continues into the reign of Tuthmosis III (and hence this razor), but LCIA, which equals LMIA from finds elsewhere such as at Maroni *Vournes* (see above this Chapter), and Enkomi,[705] may lie earlier (not delimited). Bourriau and Eriksson (1997:100) write that the LCIB=LMIB overlap with Tuthmosis III 'does not mean that the transitions from LCyp IA to LCyp IB and from LMIA to LMIB could not have occurred well *before* the beginning of the reign of Tuthmosis III'. In support of a post-LMIA correlation for LCIB, one may note especially Tomb II at Toumba tou Skourou. Chambers 2 and 3 have mature LCI, i.e. LCIB, products, *and* LMIIIA1 ceramics.[706] Thus the LCIB period is running through to later Tuthmosis III (when LMIIIA1 begins: see Chapter IV.9), and it is therefore reasonable to correlate the earlier portion of the LCIB period with LMIB–LMII, and *not* LMIA. This is confirmed by the mature WSI, that is LCIB, sherd from Trianda on Rhodes found in an LMIB context (see Chapter IV.5 below).

Second, the last of several recent, exciting, if complicating, discoveries at Tell el-Dabᶜa which we must consider are the finds of pieces of pumice identified in some instances as Theran (Minoan eruption) in a workshop context, and elsewhere, dated to the earlier 18th Dynasty.[707] Similar pumice has also recently been identified at a couple of other related sites. Bietak, Warren, Driessen and Macdonald, and others, regard these finds as very strong – indeed decisive – evidence in favour of an early 18th Dynasty date for the eruption of Thera (i.e. that the eruption is deemed as being contemporary with the find contexts of this pumice).[708] Is this the case? I wish to explain why this evidence is far from decisive, and why it is not suitable for chronology.[709]

---

[704] Kathryn Eriksson (pers. comm.) suggests that the razor type is definitely not Middle Kingdom or SIP on current evidence, and is a New Kingdom type. She proposes that it is classically Tuthmosis III, but cannot rule out an earlier 18th Dynasty date.

[705] Eriksson (1992:173).

[706] Vermeule and Wolsky (1990:254–257).

[707] See Bietak *et al.* (1994:35, 53–54, fig.10.B); Bietak (1996a:78, pls.34A and B; 1997:124–125); Warren (1995:13).

[708] E.g. Bietak (1996a:77–78); Bietak and Hein (1998); Warren (1996:287–288; 1998:327); Driessen and Macdonald (1997:23).

[709] See also e.g. Wiener and Allen (1998:25–27).

In terms of the local stratigraphy and correlations, the pumice is dated by the excavator to the early 18th Dynasty and perhaps to the reign of Tuthmosis I,[710] with overall limits of between Ahmose and pre-Tuthmosis III. Now there are two sets of points and possibilities to consider. First, in the absence of (direct) airfall tephra from the eruption in a stratified context, it is not necessary to regard the pumice as at all contemporary with the eruption. It cannot have been transported direct to Egyptian or Levantine coasts by tsunami associated with the eruption. The study of McCoy and Heiken (n.d.) argues that within the time interval of the Theran eruption pumice could have been washed ashore only at distances of up to c.100km (i.e. within the Aegean region). To explain finds of Theran pumice beyond this range, they refer instead to other, *later*, tsunami, storms, or human activity. Such pumice may relate to use (whether novel, or just now attested or archaeologically recovered) of existing previous drift material, to later drifts of pumice from Thera, or, even more likely, to deliberate acquisition and trade in pumice (at any later, post-eruption, time) – whether for craft purposes, and/or ritual activity.[711] In the Aegean, Theran pumice (and tephra) has been found from many later contexts in craft-use and other (including ritual) circumstances.[712] And a similar pattern is probably evident at some other Palestinian sites. At Tel Nami on the coast of Palestine, pumice is found in the main courtyard and environs in LBII, along with conical cups.[713] This is likely to be Theran pumice, and, regardless, highlights the use of pumice as a resource in the LBA east Mediterranean.

Second, if the alternative case is made, and the appearance of pumice at this time at several sites is seen to be a remarkable coincidence,[714] then we must consider three possibilities: (i) the pumice was apparently used for craft activities, and in such use

---

[710] Bietak *et al.* (1994:35).

[711] See the discussion of Artzy (1995:22–25; 1991). For finds of pumice with conical cups in Crete in a 'ritual' context, see Hood (1978c:688; also see Wiener and Allen 1998:27 n.53 first paragraph); for other uses and contexts of pumice, see summary in Wiener and Allen (1998:26 with refs.). Artzy refers to the study of Hiller (1978) which proposes that a Cretan goddess known from Linear A, and adopted by the Mycenaeans and found in Linear B, whose name is read Qe-ra-si-ja, is the 'Theraean one'. As Hiller (1978:678) argues: 'Her revenge [the eruption and destruction of Akrotiri] was a most horrible one. It was never forgotten after that till the end of the Bronze Age'. Finds in Crete of pumice in association with conical cups – used among other things for ritual purposes – lend credence. Pumice is also found in contexts associated with metalworking, and was employed to smooth and burnish metal. Both elements probably coincide in the area of metal-work, where, as Artzy notes, sanctuaries and workshops often occur together in association. In a sense, the unprecedented and cataclysmic nature of the Theran eruption and the destruction (indeed disappearance) of LBA settlement on Thera might be supposed to have had a long-lasting effect on cultural memory, much as the great religious revolution of Akhenaten appears to be the basis in human memory of the figure of Moses in the Bible (Assmann 1997).

[712] Faure (1971); Renfrew (1971); Wiener and Allen (1998:25–27 with refs.); Manning (1995:31); Manning *et al.* (1994a:223 and refs.); Soles (1997:427); Driessen and Macdonald (1997:91). See also the discussions in Bietak (1995b:121–125).

[713] Artzy (1995:22–25).

[714] Bietak (1996a:78); Warren (1996:287). Although note that the stratigraphic record of sites in the area through late MBIIC is notoriously problematic and incomplete, and at Tell el-Dabʿa there is a lack of continuity in most areas after the late MBA and one find from a secondary context *might* belong to the Hyksos level (Bietak 1996a:78).

pumice by definition wears away; therefore, the finds of lumps are only made when/ where they are abandoned for some reason, and have no bearing on whether pumice also was used in earlier phases, hence the 'appearance' at Tell el-Dabᶜa is of no especial significance; (ii) Aegean exploitation of Theran pumice seems to be primarily LMIB/ LHIIA *onwards*,[715] and a similar pattern of *subsequent* use may have occurred in Egypt – and Theran pumice may even have been traded to Egypt by LMIB/LHIIA Aegeans; or (iii) the possibility that the pumice does suggest a link to the relatively immediate post-eruption period,[716] and that the Tell el-Dabᶜa find context is in fact dated to within a few years of the eruption of Thera.

The last is, of course, the position held by the scholars of the conventional (low) chronology who have reviewed the matter. Since they 'know' the dates of the early 18th Dynasty, they believe that this dates the eruption to the later 16th century BC. However, I suggest the reverse. If a range of other independent evidence suggests a possible date for the Thera eruption in the later 17th century BC, and archaeological evidence seems to indicate that the LMIA period of the eruption correlated with the pre-18th Dynasty, SIP, period, and so the eruption was mid-16th century BC at the latest, then there are only two logical possibilities: (a) adoption of one of the time-lag arguments offered above which distances the Thera eruption from the time the pumice was employed (or places its original context within the Hyksos period); or (b) the radical alternative, which is to date the Tell el-Dabᶜa context to the later 17th century BC. However, in view of the Egyptian historical data, the latter option is not possible. The 18th Dynasty is restricted to the 16th century BC. Therefore, we may conclude that the only viable explanation is that the later 17th century BC pumice is subsequently found in its secondary, final resting place, in the early 18th Dynasty. Why should we adopt this former explanation (apart from the reasons discussed above)?

I begin with an examination of the recent discussion of the Tell el-Dabᶜa finds in the (otherwise) excellent review of Aegean–Egyptian relations by Warren (1995). On page 4 of his paper Warren correctly identifies the many clear LMIA period associations evident in the Tell el-Dabᶜa fresco fragments. But then he realises that the Theran pumice found at the site is later than the frescoes in stratigraphic terms. And, in order to support and reconcile his pre-existing chronological views, Warren chooses to regard this craft-use pumice as contemporary with, and so dating, the eruption (see his page 13). However, this leaves the Tell el-Dabᶜa frescoes if anything *earlier* than the Theran

---

[715] Faure (1971); Rapp *et al.* (1973); Pichler and Schiering (1980:26–30); Evely (1984:290 ns.33 and 35); Warren and Puchelt (1990:80 where Theran examples [D–J: see p.79] derive from LMI, LMII–III, LMIIIC and Iron Age contexts); Bietak (1995b:121–125). With regard to the Nichoria evidence of Rapp *et al.* (1973), I note that Oliver Dickinson (pers. comm.) drew my attention to the fact that although the majority of finds were from LHII contexts as reported, one find was in his view from an undoubted LHI context. Thus we have one more or less contemporary occurrence (as on Crete at e.g. Pseira), but a pattern of mainly later use from the next period, and for then many many years and centuries afterwards elsewhere around the Aegean.

[716] When this 'new' resource floats up on Palestinian and Egyptian shores; evidence of drifts of Theran pumice – not necessarily at all contemporary with the eruption – in the Aegean and east Mediterranean exists: Francaviglia (1990).

ones! Warren rather fudges on this point as he realises his predicament, and, of course, suitable Aegean comparanda are conspicuously lacking. Warren finds himself noting that 'almost no naturalist or figural painting in Crete can be dated any earlier or even so early' (p.4). Warren has then to engage in special pleading, suggesting the existence of non-attested MMIII paintings (on the 'authority' of a postulation by Evans), and Warren admits this is all rather unsatisfactory. He thus develops the extraordinary argument that the Tell el-Dab^ca frescoes – *in Egypt* – were in fact 'the first such Minoan frescoes to be painted' (p.5)! It is surprising that Warren is comfortable with the obviously unlikely, rather turning-a-blind-eye, logic here (pre-supposing Minoan inspired/executed work in Egypt earlier than any examples from the Aegean).[717] But he is forced into this position because of a determination to give precedence to his belief in a low Aegean chronology, rather than to step back and to consider the evidence in a holistic manner. To try to square the circle, Warren has in the end to adopt the special explanation of a Minoan princess going to Avaris. But even this still does not explain how the 'first' New Palace period Minoan frescoes were painted in Egypt, and not Crete. This entire scenario seems most implausible.

Is there a better alternative? Yes. Instead of the elaborate hypothesis just reviewed, it seems much more likely, especially given other such similar artworks from Tel Kabri and Alalakh, that the Tell el-Dab^ca frescoes are more or less contemporary with the mature LMIA comparanda (irrespective of debates over who was influencing who). It is especially relevant to note again that naturalist and figural wall paintings do not, as far as we currently know, have a pre-LMIA tradition in the Aegean. As Warren observes, there were earlier frescoes at Akrotiri preceding the ones buried by the eruption, but there is so far no evidence for naturalist and figural scenes.[718] Instead, the last occupation phase at Akrotiri, and the contemporary mature LMIA phase elsewhere, date the genre. The link to Egypt in these mature LMIA paintings is clear from various Nilotic elements,[719] which then continue into LMIB ceramic decorations. Therefore, it seems likely that the earlier (and so Hyksos?) Tell el-Dab^ca frescoes are contemporary with the period around the eruption of Thera, and were not significantly earlier. The later ones, and for instance the ivy fresco found *in situ* in an early 18th Dynasty context (before or at latest contemporary with the context of the pumice), are best dated LMIB/LHIIA (in other words post-Thera-eruption: see Chapter IV.3 above). This later stage is the time of the Theran pumice at Tell el-Dab^ca. In support

---

[717] Laffineur (1998:57–58) also notes the problematic nature of Warren's case. Now it must be noted that the view that the 'Aegean-style' frescoes from the Levant and Nile Delta are derived from the Aegean is more a matter of faith than proof. Although it runs against all the mainstream Aegean scholarship on the topic in the last few years (except Knapp 1998), it is not impossible that the influence ran the other way, from east to west. But, even if this were ever to be shown to be the case, the strong similarities between the Tell el-Dab^ca frescoes and those from the Aegean (and for some features, such as the griffin wing: Bietak 1995a:pls.4.3 and 4.4, with the frescoes from Akrotiri in particular) must indicate that both east Mediterranean and Aegean examples are broadly contemporary. The same artistic conventions, the same artists and copybooks/mental templates, are involved, and a common expression of élite values.

[718] Warren (1995:4 and 14 n.1).

[719] E.g. cat and bird theme seen in paintings at Akrotiri, Knossos, and Ayia Triadha, and carried into other media: see Morgan (1988:146–150). See also Chapter IV.4.F above.

of this position, LMIB/LHIIA ceramics are found elsewhere in Egypt from very early 18th Dynasty contexts earlier than, or contemporary with, the context of the pumice at Tell el-Dab^{c}a (see below Chapter IV.7). This demonstrates that both the LMIA linkage with Tell el-Dab^{c}a, and the actual eruption of the Thera volcano, were earlier, and so probably Hyksos-SIP, since the eruption must have happened significantly before these LMIB/LHIIA ceramics were produced, yet alone exported and deposited in their Egyptian find contexts. The pumice found at Tell el-Dab^{c}a thus most probably derives from post-eruption exploitation of the resource. This is the only way to avoid the contortions of Warren above.

Indeed, the scientific examination of the now celebrated pumice from Tell el-Dab^{c}a offers some interesting support for this view. Bichler *et al.* (1997) report on the analysis of three pumice samples from Tell el-Dab^{c}a.[720] The find context of these samples is not stated in the publication, but it is understood that they are from the earlier 18th Dynasty finds discussed above.[721] Bichler *et al.* (1997) found that only two of the three pumice samples analysed from Tell el-Dab^{c}a came from the Minoan eruption of Thera. The third sample, in contrast, comes from another eruption. This third sample is very similar to pumice found at Antalya, Turkey, and on the Greek island of Chios.[722] This finding has two important and interesting ramifications. First, the finds of different pumices strongly suggests either use of drift material from the coastline of various types and ages, or distribution by trade of Aegean pumices for craft use, at an unknown time *subsequent* to the eruption of Thera. This finding thus challenges the *a priori* assumption of special, contemporaneous, and unique use of Thera pumice and the idea that its use at Tell el-Dab^{c}a can be seen as a chronological marker. Instead, volcanic pumice from several sources is relatively common on the coasts of the eastern Mediterranean.[723] Second, if one looks for another suitable, roughly contemporary, and chemically consistent, volcanic source, then one might speculate that a likely source of the pumice in the Tell el-Dab^{c}a3, Antalya, and Chios, samples in the study of Bichler *et al.* (1997) could well be the Yiali (Nissyros) volcano in the east Aegean.[724] There is a long history of volcanic activity in the Kos, Yiali, Nissyros area, but the Nissyros volcano in particular offers a relatively recent eruption which may in fact date in the mid-second millennium BC. Recently reported Thermoluminescence dates obtained for this eruption are only approximate (four widely ranging dates each with a large measurement error), and preclude any precision, but they do suggest a mid-second millennium BC date.[725] More obviously, they indicate a date *after* either the later 17th century BC or the mid-16th century BC, that is *after* the possible date range of the Thera eruption: the quoted average date is 1460BC. Hence, if the Tell el-Dab^{c}a3,

---

[720] I thank Max Bichler for an offprint.

[721] They were certainly stated to be the early 18th Dynasty pumice finds discussed above in a presentation by M. Bichler at the symposium 'The Synchronization of Civilizations in the Eastern Mediterranean during the Second Millennium B.C.', Schloß Haindorf, Langenlois, 15–17 November, 1996.

[722] Bichler *et al.* (1997:Fig.5).

[723] Francaviglia (1990).

[724] Keller *et al.* (1990); Galloway *et al.* (1990).

[725] Liritzis *et al.* (1996); this study is discussed in Chapter V.2 below.

Antalya, and Chios, samples in the study of Bichler *et al.* (1997) do derive from the second millennium BC Nissyros eruption, this pumice may offer the latest, near contemporary, pumice at Tell el-Dab^c^a, and so would only further highlight the irrelevant *terminus ante quem* nature of the older Theran pumice.[726]

5. More on White Slip I, and the start of the Late Cypriot I and Late Minoan IA periods

It has already become clear in previous sections that the WSI bowl from Thera, and the chronology of WS in the eastern Mediterranean in general, are now held to be critical to the entire Thera debate. For example, Manfred Bietak (1998) has entitled a recent paper 'The Late Cypriot White Slip I-Ware as an Obstacle of the High Aegean Chronology', and Malcolm Wiener (n.d.) has entitled another recent paper 'The White Slip I of Dab^c^a and Thera: Critical Challenge for the Aegean Long Chronology'. I wish in this section to argue that the nature and relevance of WS to the debate is rather more subtle and complex than hitherto appreciated by those involved. First, I wish to argue that the existing WS evidence is not at all in solid support of the position advocated by Bietak where he states that WSI is decisively in favour of a 'low', late 16th century BC, date for the Thera eruption,[727] and, second, I wish to explore the apparent subtlety and patterns in WS which might in fact offer a useful chronology, and one moreover potentially consistent with the 'early' chronology. The outcome of this investigation suggests that the WSI bowl from Thera is very early WSI in stylistic date, that is LCIA1–2 in temporal-period date, whereas the secure early 18th Dynasty WSI at Tell el-Dab^c^a is of a late phase of WSI, and dated to the LCIB period. In consequence, the pattern of WSI occurrences across the Aegean and east Mediterranean, and Cypriot pottery in general, are potentially compatible with the 'early' Aegean chronology. One group probably stems from LCIA trade from northwest Cyprus to the Aegean, the other group from LCIB trade from eastern Cyprus to Egypt. This does not, of course, mean that the 'early' Aegean chronology is necessarily correct, but it does mean that it remains possible, and is not ruled out by WSI. Let us now consider the details.

The WSI bowl from Thera

Earlier LCI, Late Cycladic I, LMIA, and the eruption of Thera are linked especially via the WSI bowl found below the eruption deposits on Thera in the 1870 excavations of Gorceix and Mamet in the area of Akrotiri:[728] Figure 31. There is a lack of clarity

---

[726] Despite the above arguments against the relevance of the pumice samples from Tell el-Dab^c^a to the dating of the Thera eruption, I agree, however, with Bietak (1996a:78) that further research looking for stratified Theran eruption products – and especially airfall tephra – at Tell el-Dab^c^a could offer an important means to correlate the eruption of Thera with Egyptian chronology.

[727] Bietak (1996a:76; 1996b:16 and n.35; 1997:117, 124–125; 1998).

[728] Fouqué (1879:v, pl.42.6; 1999:caption to pl.XLII between pages 272 and 273, pl.42.6). Fouqué does

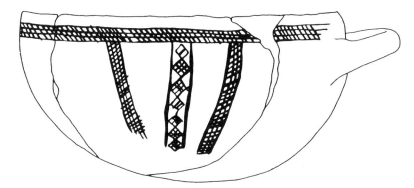

Fig. 31. A drawing of the now lost early White Slip I bowl from pre-eruption Thera after Furtwaengler and Loeschcke (1886:pl.12.80). A wavy line below the rim, mentioned in one early description of the piece, is not evident in the Furtwaengler and Loeschcke plate. For the rest of the decorative scheme not visible in the view of the bowl shown in the Furtwaengler and Loeschcke plate, see Merrillees (n.d.).

concerning the exact find circumstances of this particular vessel, but it was almost certainly found in the 1870 campaign – it was recorded and drawn in 1872, and illustrations were published in several works between 1879 and 1888.[729] The account of Fouqué is the fullest,[730] and leaves no doubt that the bowl comes from the work of Gorceix and Mamet in 1870 – but it is not stated whether this was their work on prehistoric buildings in the area of the Akrotiri ravine southeast of the modern village of Akrotiri (the area of the current excavations and most likely location), or the exploration of prehistoric remains located to the northwest of the modern village of Akrotiri close to Balos.[731] Furtwaengler and Loeschcke (1886:19) merely state of the group of objects from Thera including this bowl in their plate 12 that 'Die Objecte

---

not discuss the WS bowl; the closest is reference on p.127 to 'other jars identical to some of those at Akrotiri have been found on Cyprus'. For literature on the bowl, see: Gjerstad (1926:324); Cadogan (1972:5–6 no.4); Niemeier (1980:72–73, Abb.44); Buchholz (1987:164); Cline (1994:186 no.455); Merrillees (n.d.). The latter paper offers what will be the definitive modern discussion, and includes re-discovery of an early drawing showing the other side of the bowl which has until now been effectively unknown to scholarship.

[729] Burnouf (1879:end plate no.3); Fouqué (1879:pl.42.6; 1999:pl.42.6); Furtwaengler and Loeschcke (1886:pl.12.80); Dumont and Chaplain (1888:pl.2.23).

[730] Fouqué (1879:v and 107–125; 1999:caption to pl.XLII between pages 272 and 273, and pp.107–125). Note especially that Fouqué specifically discusses the identification of both buildings and finds as belonging to contexts covered by the pumice (that is the volcanic destruction level – or earlier).

[731] Sites B, C and D respectively in Mamet (1874:map, cf. pp.28–31). I have not found any further information in the earlier preliminary reports on the French work which I have been able to locate. As Merrillees (n.d.) observes, an important, but now missing, document may have been the 'mémoire' written by Gorceix and Mamet which was not published. This document was consulted by Dumont, Fouqué, and others, but since its return to Burnouf at the École française in Athens in 1873 its whereabouts are not attested.

stammen aus den Ausgrabungen von Thera'. The context is clearly the Late Cycladic I/LMIA VDL. The associated material illustrated is consistent with this conclusion.

In addition to this infamous WS bowl definitely originating from the VDL on Thera, there have also been suggestions of a second WS bowl which may have been found on Thera.[732] However, this bowl is of early WSII style, and so probably early LCIIA in date, and cannot have any connection with pre-eruption Thera. The provenance attributed to the vase may thus be seriously doubted.[733]

The exact nature of the WSI bowl from Thera has, until very recently, been less than clear. Several of the 19th century illustrations are poor in one way or another, and it is only with Merrillees' (n.d.) re-discovery of the Burnouf (1879) illustration that the entire decorative scheme on the bowl is now known. The three illustrations referred to in literature from AD1880–1998 all show just one aspect of the decoration of the bowl. The watercolour drawing published by Fouqué (1879:pl.42.6; 1999:pl.42.6), without any associated description, is very schematic and poor in detail. It shows a partly mended hemispherical WS bowl upside down, with only the bases of the wishbone handle preserved. It shows a horizontal lattice band with diagonal hatching (Popham's 'rope pattern') of PWS-style variety below the rim. There is no clear representation of a wavy line above it and below the rim; although it is possible that there is a thin wavy line shown on the right side (as published upside down, left side if right way up) which dips down above the edge (right as published, left if right way up) of the central pendent lozenge chain. There is a central decoration of a pendent lozenge chain inside parallel lines, and then two pendent lattices (rope pattern) on either side of this. The colour of the paint is not clearly represented, but could be blackish and reddish. The slip appears to be pinky-white.

The illustration of Furtwaengler and Loeschcke (1886:pl.12.80) shows the bowl standing right way up in a more formal (to scale) black and white lithograph drawing based on a photograph. By this time the vase has been comprehensively mended and an incorrect loop (versus wishbone) handle attached. The outer two pendent lattices (rope pattern) are not shown, just a central framed lozenge chain flanked on each side by a single pendent lattice. The diagonally hatched, PWS-style, lattice band below the rim is visible. There is no trace in the drawing of a wavy line below the rim – the way the light is shown and the nature of the reproduction render such detail invisible. This drawing is said to be at a scale of 1/3, suggesting the bowl was about 23cm in diameter, and 12 cm high, which is perfectly suitable for a WSI bowl.

Finally, Dumont and Chaplain (1888:pl.2.23) show just a WS sherd. This is clearly the main front part of the bowl from the Furtwaengler and Loeschcke drawing. Chaplain made his drawing in 1872,[734] so this undoubtedly reflects the sherdage before

---

[732] Merrillees (1974:6) referring to a WS bowl in the Cairo Museum: *Journal d'entré* 36792. The list in Portugali and Knapp (1985) lists an apparent additional WSI bowl from Thera; this is a mistake, the original bowl from Thera is referred to twice.

[733] See Merrillees (n.d.). Bietak (1998:321) recently refers to the investigations by Merrillees, but, in stating that 'Robert Merrillees was able to locate a second White Slip I-bowl from Thera in the Cairo Museum', Bietak completely misreports the conclusions of Merrillees (who says the bowl in question is early WSII).

[734] Dumont and Chaplain studied the material in the École française in Athens in 1872 (Dumont and Chaplain 1888:i).

mending. This sherd has a lattice band around the rim (and no wavy line, nor dotted rim, is shown – although cf. description in text), a pendent framed lozenge chain, and single pendent lattice on each side. It matches the decoration shown in the previous two illustrations. More importantly, however, the vessel is described in relative detail at p.24 no.37. The most important things noted are: the colour of the fabric (clay), which is said to be brown; the colour of the painted decoration, which is said to be a mixture of red and black; a wavy line is mentioned on the upper body (below the rim); and the decorative scheme is stated to be repeated four times around the vessel. And then there is the final observation: 'plusieurs traces semblent indiquer une réparation ancienne'. When was this? And what does this mean for the bowl's biography of travel from Cyprus to Thera (and when)?[735]

The drawing in Figure 31, after Furtwaengler and Loeschcke, shows the bowl as known from these three studies. The description of Dumont and Chaplain allows us to add a wavy line around/below the rim. The detective work of Merrillees (n.d.) permits us now to go further. The drawing, presumably by Burnouf, at the rear of his 1879 volume, and reproduced with discussion by Merrillees, shows the front of the body of the bowl as well as the side. As a result, Merrillees offers what is the best description of the bowl one can hope for without actually being able to see it. The decoration consists of:

> a wavy line round top of the body, below the rim; underneath a horizontal band consisting of four parallel straight lines with diagonal hatching, either side of a vertical row of cross-hatched lozenges framed on each side by a vertical straight line; descending down the front of the body, two parallel vertical rows of cross-hatched lozenges, each linked to the horizontal band by a short wavy line and framed on the outer sides by a vertical row of dots and enclosed by a vertical band of four parallel vertical lines with diagonal hatching; descending from the horizontal band on either side of the handle base, a vertical band of four parallel straight lines with diagonal hatching; between them and the next vertical band on the side of the body, a vertical row of dots and dashes.[736]

The key question is the relative date of this bowl within the Cypriot typological sequence. While, in overall terms, clearly attributable to the WSI class, the decoration, consisting of a horizontal lattice-band with slanted cross-lines, and pendent framed lozenge and lattice pattern, comes directly out of the preceding PWS style.[737] The latticed band around the rim, and especially the quite slanted vertical lines (rope pattern),[738] is in fact rather PWS in style. Later, or developed, WSI has 'ladder lattice'

---

[735] It might be argued that the reported signs of repairs in antiquity mean that the bowl must have been extant for some time before its burial by the eruption. Perhaps. But ceramic vessels can also have relatively short use-lives, or be easily damaged, and, given this bowl's rarity as the only WS import known from Thera, and one of just a handful of WSI imports from the Aegean, a repair when it was accidently broken is not implausible, and could have occurred at any time: literally from its first day on Thera, onwards. Of perhaps greater concern is whether this ancient repair was prehistoric?

[736] I quote the manuscript of Merrillees (n.d.).

[737] Popham (1972a:433, 442, Figs.46g.1, 47).

[738] Popham (1972a) uses the term 'rope' pattern.

pattern where the cross lines are at right angles.[739] The simple ornamentation is PWS to early WSI. The wavy line under the rim and above the latticed band is typical of early WSI. The brown fabric (clay) is typical of PWS to WSI, but not some special developed WSI nor subsequent WSII. The red and black paint mix is quite typical of either PWS or so-called Bichrome WSI (and can be traced to origins in WP pottery). Thus, overall, although the standard conclusion is that the bowl is early WSI,[740] it has clear hang-overs from the PWS style. It is not developed or late WSI. The Thera bowl compares well with early WSI examples from Toumba tou Skourou (see Figure 32.c),[741] or examples from Palaepaphos *Teratsoudhia*,[742] or an example from Enkomi Tomb 19 (see Figure 32.a).[743]

The Thera bowl belongs to the earliest stylistic phase recognisable in the WSI sequence: the horizontal rope pattern lattice with pendent ladder/lattice framed lozenge style.[744] It is unfortunately not easy to confirm this early date in stratigraphic terms from Cyprus, as few contexts offer the necessary tight chronology. At Toumba tou Skourou,[745] Tomb I has a substantial series of bowls in these styles and a number of bichrome examples, and Padgett (1990) argues for their early date as some retained PWS features, but, the overall contents of the tomb ran from MCIII to LCIB, so, in strict terms, the early date of the ladder lattice framed lozenge style is not demonstrated. Toumba tou Skourou Tombs IV and VI offer better evidence suggestive of an early date: several WSI bowls with rope pattern rim lattices and vertical ladder lattice framed lozenges in overall assemblages of mainly MCIII–LCIA date including PWS in Tomb IV.[746] The latest items apart from one example of mature WSI in Tomb IV are a few vessels described in the publication as BRI. Early BRI should be contemporary with early WSI (and may even appear first in some places);[747] further, as Bergoffen (n.d.) reports, Åström is of the view that all but one of these vessels are

---

[739] This is an important distinction. Early WSI like the Thera bowl has PWS-style lattices where the cross lines are diagonal (or at least not at right angles). This type may be distinguished from first, ladder lattice pattern, where usually four horizontal or vertical parallel lines are joined by vertical/horizontal cross lines, and second, ladder pattern, where two horizontal or vertical parallel lines are joined by vertical/horizontal cross lines (this latter style might also be usefully described as railway track style). See Padgett (1990:373 n.31).

[740] See especially Niemeier (1980:72–73; 1990:122); also Popham (1972a:461); Cadogan (1972:5–6); Åström (1971:417–418); Manning (1995:198–199 End-Note).

[741] E.g. Vermeule and Wolsky (1990:215 TI.137 P93, 280 T.IV.24 P700; the former is shown here in my Figure 32.c).

[742] Especially Karageorghis *et al.* (1990:pl.6 Tomb 104 Chamber E (ii) top left). Another bowl is similar on three sides (Karageorghis *et al.* 1990:pl.15 no.E.11) – except for a double lozenge on one face and the lack of two lines framing the lozenges (dots are used instead).

[743] Popham (1972a:Fig.80.6); Niemeier (1980:Abb.45).

[744] Popham (1972a:442); Padgett (1990:374).

[745] Vermeule and Wolsky (1990).

[746] Vermeule and Wolsky (1990:270–287, 307–320). For the earlier style WSI, see p.280 T IV.24 P700, T IV.32 P708, T IV.44 P720, p.286 T IV.79 P755 = T IV.91 P767, and p.317 T VI.25 P1069.

[747] BRI occurs earlier than WSI in some eastern and southern Cypriot contexts, in particular. In the northwestern heartland of the 'LCI' styles – Proto Base Ring to BRI, PWS to early WSI style, and early Monochrome – all seem to appear more or less together, and demarcate the new phase.

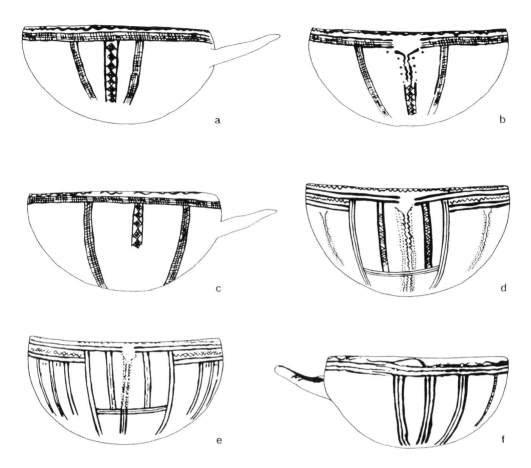

Fig. 32. Examples of WSI bowls. a.–c. show the PWS-style ('rope pattern') lattice-band and pendent ladder/lattice motifs of earlier WSI. d.–f show the new open and airy elegance of classic WSI. a. and b. after Popham (1972a:Fig.80.6) – two views of same bowl from Enkomi Tomb 19; c. after Vermeule and Wolsky (1990:215 TI.137 P93); d. after Popham (1972a:Fig.59.1) from Saqqara in Egypt; e. after Popham (1972a:48.4); and f. after Popham (1972a:Fig.48.6).

in fact Proto Base Ring. Hence the 'early', LCIA, nature of these two contexts seems likely,[748] and so in turn the ladder lattice framed lozenge style of WSI. A tomb published by Karageorghis (1965), Pendayia *Mandres* Tomb 2, seems to offer further evidence in support of the early date of the ladder lattice framed lozenge style of WSI, and an early phase of WSI centred in the west/northwest of Cyprus. Pendayia *Mandres* Tomb 2 had been robbed before excavation, but the remaining assemblage was solely MCIII–

---

[748] With the example of mature style WSI (Vermeule and Wolsky 1990:286 T IV.115 P780) deemed an early, LCIA2, instance of this more typically LCIB genre.

LCIA, and included PWS and a sherd of what looks like WSI with ladder lattice and pendent lozenge chain framed by solid dots.[749] The solid dots are critical. When the circles of the PWS style become dots, this is WSI; similarly the ladder lattice here is more WSI style than the PWS rope pattern.[750] Karageorghis regarded this tomb as exactly contemporary with the unrobbed Pendayia *Mandres* Tomb 1, which was also solely MCIII–LCIA in date. No such 'early' evidence exists for the other styles of WSI, nor can they be seen to have evolved straight from PWS. Thus, although the evidence is scarce and hardly overwhelming, it does seem likely that the ladder lattice framed lozenge style of WSI was the initial WSI style, and that the Thera bowl, of this style, may therefore have been a product of initial WSI production.

It is important, and notable, that this same ladder lattice framed lozenge style of WSI is, as Popham noted, 'particularly well represented' as exports: both in the Aegean (Thera), and in the Levant (especially Tell el-ᶜAjjul).[751] Further, at Tell el-ᶜAjjul, where there is the one reasonably substantial assemblage so far found of this type, Bergoffen notes that bichrome painting – as described by Dumont and Chaplain for the Thera bowl – is particularly associated with this style, and, generally, with the earlier styles of WSI.[752] The fact that the first, novel, version of a new style is found widely (not necessarily numerously) exported is quite plausible. Novelty is interesting, different, potentially valuable, and perhaps even useful. It may travel for reasons beyond the routine. Such circumstances may not necessarily apply to later derivatives. The fact that two dozen examples have been found at Tell el-ᶜAjjul, and on the basis of the available information a number came from late MBII contexts (Palace I), further indicates that this early WSI style spread contemporary with the late MBII (MBIIC or MBIII) floruit period in the Levant.[753] I have already noted earlier in this Chapter that other contemporary imports from the Levant have been found at LMIA Akrotiri, and observed the close parallels in some jewellery (especially earrings) painted in the frescoes at Thera and late MBII examples found at Tell el-ᶜAjjul. Both sites seem to have been major harbour towns. The early WSI bowl found on Thera fits perfectly into the wider pattern. It is perhaps possible that Levantine merchants were involved in bringing it to the Aegean. This is all part of a pre-18th Dynasty horizon in the eastern Mediterranean.

---

[749] Karageorghis (1965:pl.4:1, row 2 third from left).
[750] Compare Padgett (1990:373): 'The use of circles instead of solid dots, the very slanted lines of the latticed bands ... are some of the elements that distinguish Proto White Slip from White Slip I'.
[751] Popham (1972a:442). It is important to note that these exports are rare examples at all sites except for Tell el-ᶜAjjul, where there is, in relative terms, a remarkable number of early LC finds. For the two dozen examples at Tell el-ᶜAjjul, and for a similar analysis of the stylistic date, see Bergoffen (n.d.). It is very striking that the few export sites include some of the main trading/port centres of the time, sites already suggested to be connected on other grounds in the late MBA as part of a greater Canaanite/Levantine later MBA world system. This horizon ends with the close of MBA destructions across Syria and Palestine, and the subsequent wars and conquests by the kings of the 18th Dynasty. It is not LBI/early 18th Dynasty.
[752] Bergoffen (n.d.). Bergoffen adds the ladder framed lozenge style to the lattice framed lozenge style to make up her group of earlier WSI styles.
[753] See Bergoffen (n.d.). The WSI from Tell el-ᶜAjjul is discussed further below. Peter Fischer has now also found WSI in what seems likely to be a late MBA level at Tell Abu al-Kharaz in Jordan (1999:24; oral presentation at the White Slip Ware conference, Nicosia, 30 October 1998).

A reasonable view, therefore, is that the Theran WSI bowl belongs in an almost transitional period between PWS and WSI when 'there is obviously considerable overlap between the two styles' and when 'many of the bowls from Toumba tou Skourou are painted in a transitional style that makes hard and fast divisions almost meaningless'.[754] Not surprisingly, one leading Cypriot archaeologist has in fact once described it as PWS,[755] although the consensus (now, and then) is that it is in fact early WSI. On the basis of the typological seriation of Åström (1972a), earlier WSI means the LCIA period, rather than the subsequent LCIB period when developed or later WSI occurs (with the second, 'LCIA:2', stratum – to be considered today as LCIB following Åström (1972a) – at Kourion *Bamboula* nicely defining LCIB and the later WSI styles[756]). I have reviewed what evidence there is at present to support such an early LCI, or LCIA, date above. Merrillees (n.d.) offers a similar analysis, and agrees that the bowl stands early in the WSI sequence, but ends up suggesting a slightly later date around the transition from LCIA to LCIB for the Thera bowl because he draws a comparison to parallels in shape and decoration from Palaepaphos *Teratsoudhia* Tomb 104. Referring to the publication of Karageorghis *et al.* (1990:60), Merrillees says nothing found in this funerary complex requires a date earlier than transitional LCIA to LCIB. In general this is correct,[757] however, there is nothing to indicate that the 'Thera' style WSI in this tomb marks the appearance of the style on Cyprus; in fact, the co-appearance of some other types of WSI including the rare white fabric-paste type (see below), would indicate the opposite. The comparanda from Toumba tou Skourou and Pendayia – not mentioned by Merrillees – suggest an LCIA date for the beginning of the style. Overall, the point is not that the 'Theran' WSI style is necessarily solely of such an early date; rather, that it begins at this early date, is the only WSI style at this time, and an export horizon seems to correlate with this initial LCIA production.

Popham (1972a:442) suspected a central Cypriot origin for the framed lozenge and ladder pattern decoration (out of PWS), but we may note a further observation of Padgett (1990:374) with regard to Toumba tou Skourou: 'no other site has produced so many of these early White Slip I bowls with the latticed bands and lozenge chains'. Bergoffen (n.d.) concurs, and proposes that the early WSI from Tell el-ᶜAjjul came

---

[754] Padgett (1990:373).

[755] Merrillees (1974:6 and n.16).

[756] For the Kourion *Bamboula* WS sequence, see Benson (1961); for the site stratification, see Benson (1969; 1970), and esp. the summary at Benson (1970:40); for relevant dating review, see Eriksson (1992:207–209). What Benson describes as 'LCIA:1' would today be called LCIA2 (since WSI and BRI are present), what he describes as 'LCIA:2' is LCIB (since the phase is characterised by plentiful mature WSI, and there is also BRI and Red Lustrous Wheelmade Ware), and his 'LCIB' is LCII (since it marks the appearance of WSII and BRII).

[757] Chamber K includes a few potential LCIA/B finds (Karageorghis *et al.* 1990:29–31, 57–60), although these need not necessarily date before LCIB. It is also important to note that Tomb 104/105 includes a couple of notably PWS-WSI transitional ladder-lattice decorated WS pots (Karageorghis *et al.* 1990:pl.15 E.4, pl.18 K.41+T.105/B.12). The vertical dots on the latter are even more PWS-style circles than WSI dots. Thus *some* rather early WSI (and so LCIA2) items are present within the long period of use of this impressive tomb complex. The 'Thera'-style WSI may be placed at the early end of this range.

from Toumba tou Skourou (and region). The association with Toumba tou Skourou not only hints at a regional provenance,[758] but is of chronological value. As Padgett notes, other nearby LCI sites, such as Ayia Irini and Stephania, do not have this early transitional WSI style. The assemblage at Toumba tou Skourou, of which WSI bowls comparable to the Thera find are part, occupies an early phase of LCI not widely attested at other published sites. It seems a time of overlap with PWS (a transitional phase), and is before the time of mature or classic WSI and the new non-PWS-derived WSI decorative styles (see below). Therefore, the Thera WSI bowl may fairly be attributed to initial WSI, or even transitional PWS-WSI, and, temporally, may be contemporary with late PWS production (especially elsewhere in Cyprus – e.g. southern Cyprus – where the new WSI style was not yet present). Hence, it would not be impossible for the Thera bowl and contemporaries at Tell el-ᶜAjjul Palace I to be seen as close to contemporary with other PWS exports – quite possibly late PWS exports – which appear from the late MBII (MBIIC or MBIII) period in the Levant (see below); especially if the latter were being produced and exported from/via southeast/east Cyprus, while west/northwest Cyprus had commenced earlier WSI production. The export patterns may even support this view of marked regional differences in production and trade, with different sites maintaining different trading relations. For example, Tell el-Dabᶜa received eastern/southern Cypriot WP and so presumably had its trading links with this area. It has a handful of late MBA examples of PWS (from or via the south/east too?), and little early WSI (and so few to no links to LCIA west/northwest Cyprus). In contrast, Tell el-ᶜAjjul has late MBA early WSI and trading links with west/northwest Cyprus. The plentiful Red on Black/Red on Red at Tell el-ᶜAjjul, in contrast to Tell el-Dabᶜa, also indicates links especially with the northcoast-Karpass region of Cyprus.It is of course not possible on present evidence to prove that this scenario occurred; but the important point is that such a scenario is possible, and perhaps even likely, given the evidence available.

TELL EL-DABᶜA AND ITS WSI: A CRITIQUE

Bietak chooses to place great significance on the WSI bowl from Thera.[759] In an (other) important revision to previous publications on his excavations at Tell el-Dabᶜa, Bietak now states that he has no Cypriot WSI pottery until his 18th Dynasty levels.[760] He had

---

[758] Merrillees (n.d.) disagrees. His draft manuscript does not refer to Toumba tou Skourou. He instead cites the Enkomi parallel, the Palaepaphos *Teratsoudhia* tomb 4 examples, and another from Milea *Vikla Trachonas* T.10, and proposes a south coast provenance for the Thera bowl. Proof is impossible given the limited evidence, but, even if one grants his view as possible, one can state that it is by no means established or likely. Toumba tou Skourou (and area) is a definite candidate. Further, it can be said that such material is not common in the east/southeast of Cyprus on current evidence, and this region is therefore not a likely source (despite an example at Enkomi – possibly imported of course – and another at Milea).

[759] Now in fact lost, since before 1920: cf. Renaudin (1922:114); Niemeier (1980:72 n.299); Merrillees (n.d.). Merrillees speculates that it probably went missing during the period of the First World War.

[760] Bietak (1996a:70; 1996b:16 n.35).

in the past stated that WSI occurred in MBA stratum D/2,[761] and, indeed, his recent book (1996a) remains rather ambiguous at p.63 where he writes of MBA trade and Tell el-Dabᶜa that:

> In addition to southern Palestine, another major trading partner of that period [later MBA] was Cyprus... An enormous increase in Cypriot pottery...can be observed in strata D/3–2... At Tell el-Dabᶜa the whole spectrum of early types of LC pottery appears: White Painted V, White Painted VI, Proto White Slip, *probably White Slip I* and Bichrome ware... No imported Base Ring ware or Red Lustrous ware have yet been found in strata dating to the late Hyksos period [my italics].

Previously Maguire had stated of stratum D/2 that:

> In addition to the Middle Cypriot ... [wares seen in D/3], Late Cypriot pottery is present for the first time. There is White Painted ... V ware ... true Bichrome ... Proto White Slip ... and White Slip ... Ware, Black/Red Slip Ware, and Red-polished Ware.[762]

The problem (and revision) came about as there are (as of 1998) in total only some 20 WS sherds from Tell el-Dabᶜa, and only at ᶜEzbet Helmi is WS found in a stratified sequence.[763] Originally, two sherds respectively of probable or possible WSI were thought to belong with the MBA D/2 stratum, but subsequent work by Irmgard Hein showed that one (7057 C) probably came from a pit cut from the early 18th Dynasty levels (see below), while another (6461 Z) is perhaps best diagnosed as PWS and comes from a non-closed D/2 context which includes some later material[764] – hence the revised dating. Although, as Bietak and Hein (n.d.) specifically admit, it nonetheless remains possible that one probable WSI sherd, 7057 C,[765] *could* have come from a stratum D/2 (late Hyksos) context, and several other sherds, including all of those of *potentially* earlier styles of WSI (ladder lattice framed lozenge, and ladder framed lozenge, styles) come from secondary contexts and *could* be residual pre-New Kingdom in origin (also Bergoffen pers. comm.). Sherd 7057C was found in a D/2 tomb chamber; however, the vault of the tomb had collapsed and the tomb had been robbed in the New Kingdom, and it was then used as a rubbish pit during stratum C. Hence any material found could easily be New Kingdom. But, at the same time, the WS sherd quite likely originally came from a tomb context, and may be a relic of the primary tomb contents – hence a stratum D/2 date is possible. Thus a D/2 date cannot be excluded, nor proved. In fact, all that seems really definite is that the sole largely complete (and hence *in situ*?) WSI vessel found so far at Tell el-Dabᶜa (ᶜEzbet Helmi),

---

[761] E.g. Bietak (1989a:79; 1995a:fig.1 and 27–28 n.47); Maguire (1995:55 and fig.7) referring to the late Hyksos Area A/V.

[762] Maguire (1986, cited by Holladay 1997:187).

[763] Hein (1998:549); Irmgard Hein, pers. comm. The WS from the site will be published by M. Bietak and I. Hein (n.d.). I also thank Celia Bergoffen for information and comments on early WS in the Levant and at Tell el-Dabᶜa.

[764] Bietak (1998); Bietak and Hein (n.d.); I. Hein (pers. comms.).

[765] The sherd preserves the bottom of a three parallel line motif. This is a classic mature WSI decoration.

bowl 7949 (Figure 33), of later WSI style and LCIB date (see below), comes from an *early* 18th Dynasty context. To this one may add a small stray sherd (7946 F) possibly of the framed wavy line style, consistent also with a later WSI, LCIB, date, which derives from a similar context, and a sherd of ladder framed lozenge style (7944 U), of early to later WSI, LCIA–LCIB range date (see below), from a secondary context of the New Kingdom. Thus one might argue that the evidence shows that later WSI and the LCIB period correlate with the early New Kingdom, and, by definition, this in turn requires earlier WSI and the LCIA period to be SIP. *And*, all the potentially earlier style WSI of either LCIA or LCIB date at Tell el-Dab^ca, comes from secondary contexts such that they may derive from original SIP import and use. However, nowithstanding, and not considering the relative WSI sequence nor the regional-chronological sequence on MCIII–LCI Cyprus, the excavator of Tell el-Dab^ca, Manfred Bietak, holds no secure WSI has been found at Tell el-Dab^ca before the start of the 18th Dynasty. Even so, a member of his team notes that, in time, earlier finds may be made elsewhere at the site.[766] But, for the present anyway, Bietak states his view that there is clear evidence of WSI (treated as one entity) only from the start of the 18th Dynasty.

Therefore Bietak argues that all the LC WSI, and also BRI and Red Lustrous Wheelmade Ware, should be assigned to 18th Dynasty contexts. Further, since Bietak has a large corpus of later MC into earliest LCI pottery (PWS, WPV, WPVI, Bichrome Ware) in his pre-18th Dynasty levels, but (now) no WSI, he argues that this offers a significant pattern, and implies that WSI was not made – or at least exported to Egypt – until about the start of the 18th Dynasty, which he dates c.1540BC (totally ignoring Merrillees' 1971 case that such exports, from eastern/southern Cyprus to Egypt, may only be expected from the LCIB period). Because the WSI bowl was found on Thera beneath the Minoan pumice in a pre-eruption context, Bietak argues that this shows that the eruption cannot have occurred until the middle of the 16th century BC.[767] However, as already noted above, the data are not as secure as they might at first seem, and do not permit Bietak's logic as summarised above. Let us engage in a critique of the available evidence.

First
It must be stressed that none of the WSI finds at Tell el-Dab^ca are from precise nor secure, *in situ*, use, or sealed deliberate-deposit, contexts.[768] Only the finds from ^cEzbet Helmi even come from a good stratigraphic sequence.[769] In the types of deposit defined by Elizabeth French in an important, but sadly unpublished, paper presented to the 6th International Colloquium on Aegean Prehistory, Athens, 1987,[770] the Tell el-Dab^ca WSI sherds are *not* from the types of context directly useful for stratigraphic-chronology construction: principally 'primary' contexts, and sometimes 'cumulative' contexts.

---

[766] Hein (1998:549) is careful to note that the evidence for an early 18th Dynasty appearance of WSI in this case 'does not exclude an earlier production date, nor appearances of the ware elsewhere'.
[767] Bietak (1996a:76, see also 70–72; 1998); Bietak and Hein (n.d.).
[768] Maguire (1992; 1995).
[769] Hein (1998:549).
[770] See MacGillivray (1997a:194) for a summary.

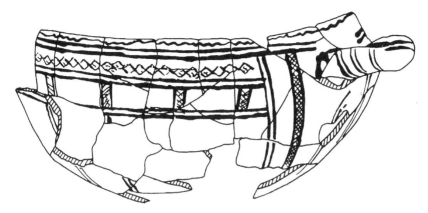

Fig. 33. Drawing of a mature LCIB WSI vessel (Inv.-Nr.7949) from the ᶜEzbet Helmi H/I citadel area at Tell el-Dabᶜa after Hein (1994b:258 no.352).

Instead, they are from 're-deposited' contexts. As MacGillivray (1997a:194) concludes: 'the primary context is the only one to which any confidence may be attached'. And, in addition, it is important to remember that there are in fact not that many finds of WSI, or PWS, at the whole of the very large Tell el-Dabᶜa/Avaris site from over 30 years of excavation by the present Austrian team! Bietak and Hein (n.d.) refer to 10 WSI occurrences, five with early 18th Dynasty stratigraphic contexts, and 10 PWS occurrences, six from MBA stratum D/2, in total.[771] Thus there is no large sample, and so no rigorous, or significant, pattern to the data. This is not an unusual situation in Egypt. Gittlen (1981:54) had previously noted that WS pottery was 'rare in Egypt' – so rare that no WS had been found in a scientifically controlled archaeological excavation when Merrillees compiled his exhaustive compendium of Cypriot material found in Egypt in the 1960s.[772] Instead, the relatively few finds at Tell el-Dabᶜa are currently unique, and are moreover all sherdage from generalised 'fills' taken out of 'strata' excavated. To quote Maguire (1995:55):

> ...we are dealing with sherdage within a Tell site and sherds reflect a date of deposition or even redeposition and not an accurate date of period of use or period of manufacture within either the country of origin or export.

Hence the processes of deposition and redeposition are difficult to reconstruct.

Second
The stylistic, and chronological, date of the key WSI sherds from early 18th Dynasty Tell el-Dabᶜa is not necessarily at all contemporary with the Theran WSI bowl. *I stress this point.* The best preserved WSI bowl found to date at the site comes from the citadel

---

[771] Bietak and Hein (n.d.). Previously, see Bietak (1998). Eight other sherds are diagnosed as WS Indeterminate (Robert Merrillees proposes that one of these, K5216–5, can be classified as WSI), and these may therefore hide additional PWS or WSI data. There are also four later WSII sherds.
[772] Merrillees (1968).

area at ᶜEzbet Helmi, and is the key stratified early 18th Dynasty occurrence of WSI: Figure 33.[773] Although with a slightly uncommon decorative scheme, this bowl with bichrome decoration is a slightly more complex (horizontal elements) variant of the mature or classic WSI framed lozenge and two parallel line metope school (see further below), with no trace of PWS origins. It may be contrasted with the 'early' ladder lattice framed lozenge style export group:[774] see Figures 32.a–c and contrast with Figure 32.d and e and Figure 33. This bowl is of the late phase of WSI. It is LCIB in date. Partial parallels abound at Kourion *Bamboula*, which may be dated LCIB,[775] Stephania, dated to LCIB,[776] Toumba tou Skourou, including one example securely dated to LCIB,[777] and elsewhere.[778] It is notable that such parallel line style is rare at Tell el-ᶜAjjul, and totally absent in the Palace I and likely MBA contexts. One late (post-MBA) find at Tell el-ᶜAjjul in this style offers a good parallel for the decoration on the Tell el-Dabᶜa bowl.[779] The sole 'mature' or late phase of WSI find in the Aegean with a secure and precise find context, and a closely related decorative scheme, is the sherd from Trianda on Rhodes: Figure 34.f (below p.175).[780] It was found in a clear LMIB context.[781] This is significantly later than the VDL context on Thera.

A similar conclusion appears to apply to most of the *few* other WSI sherds from earlier New Kingdom contexts at Tell el-Dabᶜa.[782] The material includes decorative schemes typical of the mature or later styles of WSI; and, in contrast, the simple early style of WSI with single lattice band with slanted cross lines under the rim, of the type seen on the Thera bowl, is absent. The New Kingdom Tell el-Dabᶜa WSI may be contrasted further with the large early WSI assemblage from Tell el-ᶜAjjul;[783] the New Kingdom Tell el-Dabᶜa assemblage is thus rather later (latest elements, anyway). Ruling out secondary sherds from mixed SIP-New Kingdom/Ramesside, or post–early New Kingdom stratum C, or very late Ramesside, find contexts (6462 E, 8205 M, 8441 H,

---

[773] Bietak *et al.* (1994:43 Abb.12.d, taf.13.B); Hein (1994b:258 no.352; Hein 1998:549); Bietak and Hein (n.d.:no.7949). This bowl came from ᶜEzbet Helmi H/I-k/25, Inv.-Nr.7949.

[774] Popham (1972a:442); Padgett (1990:374 and n.41).

[775] Benson (1961:passim, with pl.5 Fig.3 top left the closest specific parallel; Benson 1972:pl.40 'WSI'); for the correct modern dating of the site, see Eriksson (1992:207–209). The WSI bowl from tomb 13 at Kourion *Bamboula* (Benson 1972:pl.86 B86), with a design not unlike the ᶜEzbet Helmi bowl, comes from an LCIB–II tomb, and nicely illustrates the typically later nature of this mature WSI.

[776] Hennessy (1963:pl.37 tomb 7 no.5). For the date, see Hennessy (1963:52 and pl.64).

[777] Vermeule and Wolsky (1990:235, TI.300 P228, fig.46; 217 TI.101 P58A, pl.161). The latter is not bichrome, however. Parallels minus the horizontal elements connecting the pendent lines are common: e.g. p.216 TI.672 P878, TI.507 P399; p.217 TI.211 P167, TI.518 P410; p.257 TII.76 P594 Ch.3.13. Likewise there are several other related variations, e.g. p. 217 TI.121 P77 Ch.I.39A. The one good context which establishes the typically later date of this style is TI.121 from Tomb II Chamber 3, where the assemblage is all LCIB, and includes an LMIIIA1 sherd (p.257 TII.80 P598 Ch.3.17, pl.175). The rest come from contexts which include LCIB.

[778] Popham (1972a:438 fig.48 nos.3 and 4, 460 Type IA b').

[779] Petrie (1931–1934, vol.II:pl.37).

[780] Padgett (1990:376) concurs, regarding this sherd as belonging to the late phase of WSI.

[781] Marketou (1988:31); Furumark (1950:166 and Fig.6 no.97). See further below.

[782] I wish to thank Irmgard Hein for discussion, and for sending copies of figures from the forthcoming *Tell el-Daba IX.* I also thank Celia Bergoffen for information and comments.

[783] Bergoffen (n.d.). See further below.

8441 R, 8476 H), definite early New Kingdom finds – albeit from secondary contexts which may include earlier material – other than LCIB bowl 7949 (above) are very few and less than decisive: 7944 U, 7945 P, 7946 F, and 8894 F (data here and below from Bietak and Hein n.d.). 7944 U is a sherd of a ladder framed lozenge style of either LCIA or LCIB; for this author the harder fired grey fabric colour and the decoration which is mature, elegant, and of linear style, with neat ladders, would be most comfortable in LCIB (see also discussion of Phylakopi sherds below). The find context is early New Kingdom but into plough zone. 7946 F is a handle fragment perhaps of the framed wavy line style typical of later WSI and LCIB finds. This could fit with an early New Kingdom context. 8894 F is a body sherd with part of a vertical lattice with cross lines not at right angles and with a circle (PWS tradition, versus usual dots of WSI) beside it. This looks most likely to be earlier style WSI, and could easily fit in as LCIA at Toumba tou Skourou on Cyprus, for example. The find context is a secondary deposit in a well in the early New Kingdom. The sherd could very easily represent re-deposited SIP material. Of the sherds found in later New Kingdom to Ramesside, or mixed SIP to New Kingdom/Ramesside, contexts, some could potentially be earlier style WSI of LCIA date, although all but one (8205 M) look better to this author as LCIA–LCIB. 6462 E is of the parallel line framed lozenge style,[784] of likely LCIB date, and from a SIP-Ramesside context. 8205 M is a sherd of bichrome ladder lattice framed lozenge style, with slanting cross lines in the lattice. This is a design found from PWS through WSI,[785] and could be LCIA. The sherd came from a secondary, late (post–early New Kingdom, stratum C), context, and could be either a residual LCIA-SIP import, or a later LCIB-New Kingdom import. 8441 H is a tiny sherd from a secondary Ramesside context with two parallel lines. With a grey fabric one might speculate on a later LCIB parallel line style attribution, but nothing be certain. 8441 R is a rim fragment of the ladder lattice framed lozenge style. This could be earlier (LCIA), or LCIA–LCIB. The context is secondary Ramesside. Nothing can be said about earlier date of original import and use. Finally, 8476 H consists of parts of a bowl of the ladder framed lozenge style. This could be earlier, although the neater, railway-track, ladder is more LCIA–LCIB. However, the find context is Ramesside fill of a well/pit, and again nothing can be said about date of earlier import and use. As in several earlier cases, this could be an original LCIA-SIP import re-deposited in late New Kingdom/Ramesside activity. Overall, there is an absence of very early WSI of the 'Thera bowl' style (except perhaps 8894 E and maybe 8205 M), and the only really secure early New Kingdom find (bowl 7949) shows that the WSI deposited in early 18th times at Tell el-Dab^ca was later WSI style and of LCIB (=LMIB in the Aegean) date. Earlier WSI, and the LCIA period, are therefore contemporary with the SIP (and any such material at Tell el-Dab^ca comes from

---

[784] 6462 E is a totally ubiquitous type of the framed lozenge and two parallel lines style, and the sherd is like Popham (1972a:Fig.80.3 or Fig.46g.2 top row second in from the left); or Padgett (1990:Fig.46 TI.300 P228); etc.

[785] Compare for PWS Vermeule and Wolsky (1990:212 and Fig.46 TI.182 P138), and for WSI Vermeule and Wolsky (1990:215–216 TI.505 P397, TI.99 P56 TI.229 P185, TI.531 P423, TI.545 P437); Karageorghis *et al.* (1990:pl.8 Tomb 105 Chamber B (iii), pl.7 Tomb 105 Chamber B (v) bottom right).

secondary deposits where it may be considered to reflect re-deposition of original SIP imports).

This relative stylistic date is critically important when one considers the arguments of Bietak against the 'high' or 'early' Aegean chronology. He argues that if WSI began before the early 18th Dynasty, then there should be WSI at Tell el-Dabᶜa from stratum E/1 onwards.[786] But he is *entirely* missing the point. Unlike Tell el-ᶜAjjul, Tell el-Dabᶜa lacks clear evidence of contact with the initial LCI phase of northwest Cyprus, and, in particular, the initial phase of WSI (see above). The secure Tell el-Dabᶜa WSI dates from the LCIB period. That is to say that the WSI probably came from eastern Cyprus, as nearly all the Cypriot imports at late MBA–early 18th Dynasty Tell el-Dabᶜa, and so only *after* eastern Cyprus adopted the WS and BR tradition in the LCIB period. A sentence of Merrillees (1971:74) remains highly pertinent:

> in this respect the data from Egypt precisely reflect the ceramic history in *eastern* Cyprus, as L.C.IA was marked by the continuance of the W.P. pottery industry and L.C.IB saw the take-over by B.R. and W.S. at a similarly advanced stage of development [my italics].

The New Kingdom Tell el-Dabᶜa WSI (of LCIB date, from eastern and southeastern Cyprus) is therefore entirely at home in the mid–later 16th century BC according to the 'early' chronology. It is not odd that Tell el-Dabᶜa did not receive more than one or two instances at most of the early style WSI. Few sites overseas did, and, in the Levant, Tell el-ᶜAjjul seems to have been the main (known) recipient. Tell el-Dabᶜa was instead receiving mainly eastern/southeastern Cypriot, MC-style (but into LCIA date) imports; thus, although initial WSI may have existed in northwest Cyprus, and been exported to Tell el-ᶜAjjul and Thera, we need not expect much if any in later MBA Tell el-Dabᶜa. To repeat the key point above: only when all Cyprus adopted the classic WSI styles in the LCIB period, and so also the eastern and southeastern sites supplying Tell el-Dabᶜa, does WSI necessarily appear at Tell el-Dabᶜa. The 'chronology' of WSI at Tell el-Dabᶜa is therefore irrelevant to the early WSI from northwest Cyprus as found in 1870 on Thera.

Third

Taken as a whole, the striking feature of the Cypriot material from the greater Avaris site is that there is a long MC to very initial LCIA assemblage from Tell el-Dabᶜa – the main MBA site area – whereas there is a very different LCIB and onwards assemblage from the citadel area at ᶜEzbet Helmi.[787] The two assemblages do not link; there is a sharp break between them. Contrary to Bietak (1998:321), there is thus not a complete spectrum of MC to LC wares at Tell el-Dabᶜa. At present, the early phase of WSI (as found in numbers at late MBA Tell el-ᶜAjjul) is *not* (or barely – as residuals) represented at the greater Tell el-Dabᶜa (Avaris) site, and other types typical of early LCI assemblages, such as Red on Black, Red on Red, and early Monochrome, are also rare or absent at Tell

---

[786] See Hein and Bietak (n.d.) for this case in explicit terms.
[787] Maguire (1990; 1995); Eriksson (n.d.).

el-Dab^ca, whereas they are well represented at Tell el-^cAjjul. This gap is both chronological, *and* regional. The products of northwest Cyprus are absent; this is where the initial early WSI style seems to have developed. The missing phase might correlate with the uppermost plough disturbed layers on the MBA Tell el-Dab^ca, or as yet undiscovered later Hyksos levels elsewhere (presumably including in the ^cEzbet Helmi area). But it may very well simply not be represented at Avaris due to different trading relationships. Indeed, the fragmentary evidence available possibly points towards the latter explanation. A find of Cypriot Red on Black has been mentioned in the past from Tell el-Dab^ca stratum E/1 (a bowl handle), and, in the most recent accounts, Bietak adds also Red Slip from stratum E/1.[788] These types span the late MC to LCI transition on Cyprus, and are typical of LCIA contexts in the east.[789] At Maroni *Vournes*, for example, Red on Black and Red Slip are characteristic of LCIA, with, as typical of the eastern–southeastern Cypriot tradition, Black Slip, Bichrome Ware, WPV–VI, and PWS.[790] Red on Black also characterises the City 3/Palace I to City 2/Palace II period at Tell el-^cAjjul, with a higher proportion in City 3/Palace I.[791] An example of Red Slip at Tell el-^cAjjul is specifically noted as of eastern Cypriot fabric.[792] The presence in Tell el-Dab^ca stratum E/1 could well indicate that late MC, *or* even initial LCIA (eastern Cypriot – the region from which all the Cypriot imports to Tell el-Dab^ca came), was underway on Cyprus by this time,[793] and that the subsequent stratum D/3 is in fact definitely contemporary with LCIA (despite, to date, finds only of WPV – presumably from eastern Cyprus and so quite plausibly contemporary with initial LCIA in the northwest, and remembering that WPV is a typical LCIA ware).[794] Since Tell el-^cAjjul (later) City 2b/Palace II correlates

---

[788] Maguire (1992:Fig.2); Bietak and Hein (n.d.). Bietak and Hein (n.d.) state 'In Str. E/1 the occasional presence of Red on Black and of Red Slip Ware can … be observed'.

[789] Åström (1972a:700–701 chart, 718; 1972b:226–227); Maguire (1990). Merrillees (1971:70) argued that Red on Black was primarily produced in the northeast (Karpass region) in MCIII to LCI. When found abroad, Red on Black occurs primarily in MBA/Hyksos contexts. The accompanying Cypriot products range from later MC (WP PLS, PW CLS, WPV) to initial LCIA (the WPVI, early Monochrome, Red on Red, PWS horizon).

[790] Cadogan (1983b:160–161); Herscher (1984:25); Cadogan *et al.* (n.d.).

[791] Oren (1969:140; n.d.).

[792] Åström (1972b:225).

[793] It is important to note that the WP (Pendent Line Style and Cross Line Style) found in stratum E/1 is mainly from tombs. It first occurs from late stratum G (more than a century earlier). Thus, although the majority of finds at the site come from these tombs, it is quite possible that there is an element of an heirloom scenario at work for these final tomb deposits, as well as a false sense of the floruit (due to these tombs preserving material not available from strata G through E/1). The main WP PLS/CLS correlation might in fact be within the time range of strata F through E/2.

[794] In support, one might note an observation made by Bietak (1996a:63). He writes that 'an enormous increase in Cypriot pottery … can be observed in strata D/3–2 … on the other hand, a large quantity of biconical jugs of Tell el-Yahudiya ware was exported from Egypt to Cyprus'. This Cypriot pottery nearly all came from eastern Cyprus, and, as we noted earlier, the Tell el-Yahudiyeh exports from Egypt went also mainly to eastern Cyprus. This pattern, and the change and the enormous increase Bietak cites, plausibly may be explained especially in terms of a new regional politico-economic entity in eastern Cyprus. The major eastern site of Enkomi develops into a regional polity in LCIA (to LCIB) (Peltenburg 1996:27–35), and it is likely that the changes therefore broadly correlate with the emergence of LCIA Enkomi. LCIA1–2 Enkomi, and eastern Cyprus, is, more or less, late 'MC' in style, but contemporary

with Tell el-Dab^ca stratum D/2 (and the Tell el-^cAjjul phase probably ends with the seige of the city, Sharuhen, by Ahmose), the PWS and WSI from Palace I onwards at Tell el-^cAjjul would necessarily correlate with Tell el-Dab^ca strata E/1 and D/3, supporting the suggestions above.[795] In turn, a later 17th century BC date becomes entirely plausible.

Given the link between this absent early WSI style, and LMIA Thera and its frescoes, it is tempting to speculate whether this currently missing time horizon at the greater Tell el-Dab^ca (Avaris) site might be relevant to some of the LMIA-style fresco fragments found redeposited as rubbish at ^cEzbet Helmi? In other words, Bietak may be quite right to date the stratum C or IV architecture at ^cEzbet Helmi to the New Kingdom, but wrong to make an association with the redeposited Aegean MMIII–LMIA ceramics, or the redeposited LMIA-style fresco fragments (except for the former setting a *terminus ante quem* for the latter).

Fourth

As Maguire (1992) argues with regard to the MC correlations, it is important to remember that these finds in Egypt of Cypriot wares set only a *terminus ante quem* for the date of use at the site; there is then further time back to the date of export from Cyprus, and finally to the date of manufacture in Cyprus. The length of the *ante* is not known. Thus, even if later WSI is first deposited as sherdage in initial 18th Dynasty contexts, the date of import may have easily been some time earlier, and manufacture of the ware on Cyprus may have been occurring from an even earlier date. Early WSI was before this time again.

Fifth

Tell el-Dab^ca is an enormous site (some 250ha.), and only several relatively small, and discrete, areas have been excavated,[796] In addition, the late MBA has been denuded in several excavated areas, and importantly the central area is already lost by the final MBA stratum of D/2. Further, following Bietak's interpretation, the key Hyksos palace area was largely destroyed by early 18th Dynasty construction.[797] The citadel area is the only excavated area with an early 18th Dynasty sequence,[798] but the citadel area is perhaps *not* the most likely place to find – *in situ*, anyway – the best range of Cypriot imports at the site; the study of Gittlen (1977:382) found that 'WSI bowls were only infrequently found in the administrative and cultic buildings that were excavated at Tell el-Ajjul, Hazor and Lachish', and there is no reason to propose a different pattern for Tell el-Dab^ca. Bietak's work seems only to reaffirm this impression; the non-citadel areas of the Hyksos city have reasonable amounts of Cypriot pottery,[799] and Bietak (1997:109) notes especially that the late Hyksos houses at area A/V, some

---

with initial LC-style LCIA in the northwest. A common LC culture only exists across the island in LCIB. The consequence is that LCIA correlates with Tell el-Dab^ca strata D/3 to D/2 (and LCIB correlates with Tell el-Dab^ca stratum C or IV).

[795] See further below.

[796] Bietak (1991a:27; 1996a:7); for areas excavated, see Bietak (1996a:4 fig.2).

[797] Bietak (1991a:45–47, 32 Fig.3); Bietak (1996a:6 Fig.3, 63–67).

[798] Bietak (1996a:6 fig.3; 1997:fig.4.3); Hein (1998).

[799] Maguire (1995).

1km from the citadel, had a relatively high percentage of Cypriot imports. And, of course, relations between the different areas and strata of the greater site are by interpolation. Thus the value of 'negative' evidence – a lack of secure WSI from stratum D/2 – might be seriously questioned.

One may further note that the last Hyksos phase is particularly poorly represented for a couple of reasons. On the one hand, it was plundered by the conquering army of Ahmose.[800] In an inscription in the tomb of Ahmose, son of Ibani, a soldier in king Ahmose's army, Ahmose describes that after its conquest 'Avaris was despoiled and I brought spoil from there'.[801] Bietak (1979:268) writes of the end of the final Hyksos D/2 stratum that 'settlement was obviously abandoned abruptly, and this may be connected with the fall of the Hyksos rule in Egypt. All the graves were plundered, and this is unlikely to have happened while the buildings were inhabited'. On the other hand, Bietak explains the poor state of the stratigraphy and lack of *in situ* finds because 'modern plowing removed whatever evidence existed from the centre of the site'. Similarly, discussing what happened at the close of stratum D/2, Bietak states that 'the evidence for ... this stratum is largely destroyed by deep Ramesside (stratum B) and Late Period (stratum A/2–3) foundations and by *sebakh* digging'. Finally, I highlight again the statement that '...the tombs show signs of *thorough* plundering' [my italics]. Apparently, 'the large chambers were easily recognizable ... Occasionally, small single burials remained unnoticed'.[802] The larger or richer tombs might especially be the ones where imported objects would be expected to be found (and elsewhere in the region finds of imported LC and Aegean ceramics strongly correlate with tombs). The value of negative evidence becomes very questionable in these circumstances. The D/2 stratum is inherently not well defined.[803]

Sixth
As noted in Chapter IV.4 above, an LC BRI vessel is reported from a pre-18th Dynasty context at Memphis.[804] On Cyprus, BRI appears either no earlier than WSI, or just fractionally earlier than WSI in some instances, so this should suggest the possibility of pre-18th Dynasty finds of WSI (in the model of the occasional early LCI northwestern Cypriot product finding its way to the Nile Valley during the SIP[805]). This is all that is necessary. WPV appears by (or before) Tell el-Dabᶜa stratum D/3 (pre-D/2).[806] PWS will not have been far behind on Cyprus. Maguire (1995:55) notes

---

[800] Ryholt (1997:138).
[801] Kuhrt (1995:189). For Ahmose, son of Ibani, and the full inscription in his tomb, see Breasted (1962, vol.II:§1–16). The translation of Breasted is slightly different.
[802] Bietak (1991a:45 and 47).
[803] See also Hein (1998).
[804] As noted in Chapter IV.4, BR has previously been mentioned from pre-18th Dynasty stratum D/2 at Tell el-Dabᶜa also (Maguire 1992:117 Fig.2), but, presumably, this too has been re-dated based on Bietak's (1996a:63) statement that 'no imported Base Ring ware ...[has] yet been found in strata dating to the late Hyksos period'.
[805] Merrillees (1971:74).
[806] Maguire (1992:117 Fig.2).

that the classic MC WP styles (Pendent Line Style, and Cross Line Style) show a floruit in Tell el-Dab^ca stratum E/1; accordingly, the full WPV–VI and associated MCIII–LCIA assemblage may be expected from the subsequent stratum, D/3, onwards, and not just in D/2. The stratum D/2 PWS bowl from a grave need in no way set the beginning of the style on Cyprus;[807] rather, it is a *terminus ante quem*. The origin of this PWS is another relevant issue in this regard. If it is from eastern or southern Cyprus (whether made there, or traded from there), as nearly all the other Cypriot ceramic imports at the site, it need in no way date the very beginning of the PWS style in northwest, west, and central Cyprus.[808] Bietak (1998:321) in fact emphasises that all the few PWS finds at Tell el-Dab^ca have been made in pre-18th Dynasty, MBA stratum D/2 contexts (or in one case a New Kingdom fill solely with SIP material). If stratum D/2, or even D/3–D/2, were dated from the later 17th century BC to the mid-16th century BC, all the 'early' chronology evidence may be accommodated. We have noted already that there is a sharp break in the general nature of the Cypriot import assemblage between the MBA areas and strata, and the early New Kingdom ^cEzbet Helmi contexts.[809] This is because the assemblages do not appear to be sequential; instead, as noted above, the Cypriot material from the latter seems already to be LCIB (and/or later), and a clear LCIA horizon is not present.[810] This implies some time interval may have passed between the two assemblages, and clearly suggests a new 18th Dynasty trading pattern in operation in the latter area. However, what happened in-between the two assemblages represented at Tell el-Dab^ca is not clear. A reasonably significant time interval may be involved.

WSI in particular was a long-lived style on Cyprus (more than a century). Hector Catling (1991:2–3), even employing the low, short, Cypriot chronology of Paul Åström,

---

[807] See arguments of Maguire (1992) referred to above.

[808] If it is from the southeast coast, where there are also contemporary links to the Levant, then the PWS could be interpreted as from any point(s) within what seems, on the evidence from Maroni *Vournes*, to have been a long LCIA period in this area (see Cadogan *et al.* n.d.). Again, the few export occurrences need not date the beginning of PWS production.

[809] Maguire (1995:55, 63).

[810] The New Kingdom contexts at ^cEzbet Helmi include several LC types (Maguire 1995:Fig.4) most likely to date from the later LCI period (i.e. LCIB): Red Lustrous Wheelmade Ware (see Eriksson 1993), late phase WSI (see text above), BRI in reasonable quantity (see Oren 1969), White Lustrous ware (Hein 1998:549), and what looks like a 'monochrome' or 'WP' painted Bichrome Wheelmade Ware krater (Hein 1998:551; Hein 1994b:258 no.353, and colour plate). Together, these definitely require an LCIB date for this horizon (Åström 1972a; Eriksson 1992:204–217; n.d.). Some would even be at home in LCIIA (e.g. the Red Lustrous pilgrim flask sherd shown in Maguire 1995:pl.5.6 – Kathryn Eriksson, pers. comm.). An LCIA horizon appears missing in stratigraphic terms between the initial LC in the D/2 stratum and here. An initial LCIA1 assemblage is evident from stratum D/2 with its late WP ware, PWS and first Bichrome Ware. Missing, however, is Monochrome ware (found at Tell el-^cAjjul by contrast: see text below), Black Slip (a few sherds were found in Area A/IV and one sherd of either Black Slip or Red Slip was found at Area A/V in Maguire 1995:Figs.6 and 7) or Proto BR or Red on Black/Red. An LCIA1–2 horizon is totally absent. There is no (or at most one re-deposited) early WSI of the lattice-band (rope pattern) with simple pendent ladders and/or lozenges (as found at initial LCI Toumba tou Skourou and also Thera and Tell el-^cAjjul), and again no early Monochrome (again contrast Tell el-^cAjjul). All that can be noted is the mention in Maguire (1995:Fig.4) of one find of Red Slip from ^cEzbet Helmi. This is an LCI type (non-specific), and could well go with the LCIB types.

still concludes that WSI was in production for nearly 150 years.[811] Even the ultra-low and short Cypriot chronology of Eriksson (1992:218) would permit 130 years of WSI production.[812] As we will discuss below in detail, the evidence from Tell el-ʿAjjul nicely concurs: WSI appears in later MBA Palace I and then continues through to the early 18th Dynasty/LBI period, a period of about a century to a century and a half. Therefore, the presence of (mature) WSI in the new early 18th Dynasty assemblage hardly precludes its possible presence in the preceding stratum D/2, and on Cyprus, and in the Aegean, in the period from the later 17th century BC onwards. This is particularly the case when it is noted that the WSI from early 18th Dynasty Tell el-Dabʿa includes, or consists of, late phase WSI, and is of LCIB date (see above, also see further below). I would suggest that the early 18th Dynasty imports of LCIB mature WSI (and Red Lustrous Wheelmade Ware, etc.) are contemporary with the LMIB period in the Aegean; as noted above, what we are presently missing at Tell el-Dabʿa from stratified (non re-deposited, secondary) contexts are earlier LCIA WSI = LMIA imports – these might be hypothesised to belong chronologically to stratum D/3 to D/2 and into the denuded stratigraphy and/or disruption and/or hiatus and reorientation between D/2 and the early 18th Dynasty contexts (in fact they were probably/possibly not received at all, since the site does not appear to have been trading with northwest Cyprus at this time). Here the lack of good stratum D/2 contexts is also relevant. It is a shallow and compact horizon and usually disturbed by the subsequent New Kingdom levels. As a result, there is very little temporal control within the time period of this stratum. We effectively have only a few *in situ* finds, and instead mainly redeposited material which may belong to this stratum (perhaps including the LMIA-style fresco fragments and the MMIII–LMIA ceramic imports). Further, as noted several times, and I repeat again as it is a critical point, the Cypriot contacts at the site seem mainly to have been with the east and southeast region of Cyprus (for the WP, and also the Bichrome), and not the northwest, whether due to trade patterns or other factors.[813] PWS exports from or via the east and southeast region may well be

---

[811] For similar views, see also Popham (1972a); Åström (1972a:675–781); Gittlen (1975); Padgett (1990).

[812] Warren (1998:327) writes of 'the fact, emphasized to me by Vassos Karageorghis, that WSI had a short *floruit*, to be followed by the long period of WSII'. What is meant by short floruit is not stated, nor the evidence to support this statement. Most scholarship holds a rather different view. WSII undoubtedly had a very long period of currency, some two and a half to three centuries from the mid 15th century BC. But the issue is the century and a half of WSI before WSII.

[813] Bergoffen (n.d.) expresses disbelief that products enjoyed at Tell el-ʿAjjul would not have been available simultaneously at Tell el-Dabʿa. Of course, in temporal terms, contemporary products *could* have been available at both. However, she is not considering the very different nature of the Cypriot imports in the late MBA at the two sites (see Oren n.d.; and discussion in text above), nor the conspicuous absence of Nile Delta Tell el-Yahudiyeh ware at Tell el-ʿAjjul. Along with imported closed vessel types from Cyprus, Tell el-ʿAjjul conspicuously has a large number of Cypriot open bowl imports in Red on Red and Red on Black which are unparalleled in Canaan or Egypt (including Tell el-Dabʿa). This suggests the deliberate importing of tableware items, and the use of Cypriot imports by the élite in their social activities. In contrast, Tell el-Dabʿa mainly received just the closed vessel category. Thus it was importing merely desired contents, and not the eating/drinking paraphernalia and associated symbolism and practices. As Oren (n.d.) notes, in the LBA Egypt again avoided the open vessel types produced in LBA Cyprus, and there is a marked contrast with Levantine sites where such Cypriot items are widely spread.

contemporary with initial LCIA WSI in the west and northwest of Cyprus (e.g. at Toumba tou Skourou). The latter is therefore not necessarily represented at Tell el-Dab^ca. The relevant period of time was during the late MBA, prior to the early 18th Dynasty and its LCIB mature WSI.

Seventh

The types of vessels are relevant. Maguire (1995) shows that the MBA and LBA Cypriot imports were mainly small transport containers (of something precious). WS was not used for such vessels. It instead relates to drinking activities (using bowls, kraters, etc.), and so especially to élite, prestige, and ceremonial drinking and feasting,[814] and funerary display, and also interment as funeral goods. Not accidentally, one PWS bowl found at Tell el-Dab^ca came from a stratum D/2 grave,[815] likewise the imported MM Kamares cup.[816] Thus, in the absence of stratified élite settlement areas, or of graves, from the late Hyksos period at Tell el-Dab^ca, the supposed absence of WSI is a non-statistic. Moreover, as noted in footnote 813, Egypt in the Bronze Age seems to have had different customs or needs compared to other areas, and open vessels from Cyprus were never popular, in contrast to the Levant. Thus only a few examples may have ever existed.

RELATIVE CHRONOLOGY/SEQUENCE OF WSI

And so, at this point, I suggest that the type of evidence Bietak is relying on is far from solid or conclusive. However, I now also wish to explore briefly some further subtleties of WS. We return once again to the development of the LC styles in Cyprus, and the apparent regionalism involved in this process. As is well known, the changes from MCIII to LCI did not occur simultaneously across the island,[817] and we need to try to understand some of the processes involved.

It must be admitted at the outset that the 'evidence' with regard to the chronology of WS is problematic, as we have seen above; although a well-known, even ubiquitous, type on Cyprus, clear stratified sequences remain lacking in the published literature.

Thus something cultural may be at issue. Therefore, despite many links and similarities between Tell el-^cAjjul and Tell el-Dab^ca (Oren 1997b), some marked differences in aspects of the imported Cypriot ceramic assemblages are perfectly reasonable, and are observed. A further source of difference are the relevant traders, and their trading partners. Different traders at the various major maritime cities of the Levant and at Avaris were in competition with each other. They will have sought to establish different trading relation-ships, and if possible to secure exclusive arrangements in certain places or with certain people. Tell el-^cAjjul and Tell el-Dab^ca may have been closely linked sites, but the various traders will have been competing with vigour (both between, and within, each city). It is thus perfectly plausible that one site may have had a trader or traders associated particularly with one or more key sites in west/northwest Cyprus, whereas the other had a long-standing association with one or more key sites in east/southeast Cyprus.

[814] The importance of ceremonial drinking cannot be over-emphasised: see recently the discussion of Holladay (1997:199–201).

[815] See above. Bietak (1991b:313 no.4 [2100]); Hein (1994b:217 no.248; 1998:549).

[816] MacGillivray (1995); Walberg (1992).

[817] E.g. Merrillees (1971); Herscher (1976); Baurain (1984: 27–103).

Further, no stylistic divisions are in any way absolute. Nonetheless, some patterns and processes are apparent, and are of considerable importance for the relationship of Thera to Tell el-Dabʿa and vice versa. I have begun to advance a suggestion concerning earlier, versus later, WSI in the foregoing discussion. It is time to consider the matter in the wider context on Cyprus.

Previous scholars have noted a curious fact. PWS decoration seems to evolve or stem fairly clearly from some later WP decorative schemes, but WSI appears to owe little to PWS, whereas the later WSII decoration is again similar to PWS decoration and is little derived from WSI.[818] In the most general terms, and considering only the bowl form, since this is most relevant to our discussion here, the PWS style sees the development of the lattice-band below the rim of the bowl (e.g. Plate 9) with pendent lattices or lozenges. This decorative genre follows on from later WP decorations. Although this PWS-style continues in (earlier) WSI, in almost complete contrast, distinctive new style WSI specialises in elegant linear decoration with parallel lines, and new motifs and variations not seen before, with an altogether 'open' and 'light' syntax (an 'airy elegance'[819]) that is far removed from WP ware and not at all like most PWS. For example, contrast new-style, classic WSI in Figure 32 nos. d, e, and f, with old PWS-style lattice WSI in Figure 32 nos. a, b, and c above p. 155. WSII however returns to the PWS style lattice band and cross-hatching, and often a greater 'heaviness' of syntax. How is this evolution to be explained? Dikaios proposes that WSI was influenced or derived from contemporary Painted Wheel-made wares from Syria–Palestine, whereas PWS represents a local development from Cypriot WP. WSI also shows some influence of the Bichrome Ware geometric decorative schemes and effect,[820] and it is notable that several interesting 'bichrome' WSI examples were exported to the Levant.[821] WSII thus represents the merging of these divergent traditions and especially the triumph in the main of the local heritage.

An important element of regionalism seems apparent also. Although examples are of course found in the east, PWS is undeniably more common in the centre, west, south, and northwest of Cyprus,[822] and, in general, the development of the early 'proto' WS and BR wares, and the development of the LC styles, seems to lie reflected in the objects found at sites in the northwest and west, rather than anywhere in the east. There is additionally a clear link to the Troodos foothills and the copper belt of Cyprus (both as observed, and for technical reasons as the slip relies on the geology of these areas and an association with metal production), and to the close-by areas in the plains associated with these (or down a river valley). Popham's map demonstrates this for the centre and west/northwest of Cyprus, and for the west and southwest of Cyprus Maliszewski's review finds the main MCIII–LCI cluster in the Troodos foothills in the upper Dhiarizos river with a few other sites or tombs lower down this or nearby

---

[818] Popham (1962 and refs.; 1972a); Dikaios (1969–1971:226–227).
[819] Padgett (1990:374). See also comments of Benson (1961:63).
[820] E.g. Vermeule and Wolsky (1990:pl.160.A, B).
[821] E.g. to Tell el-ʿAjjul: Merrillees (1974b:92 nos.40, 44 and 45, 98 nos. 85, 87 and 88, etc.); Bergoffen (n.d.).
[822] E.g. Popham (1962:Fig.6). For south (e.g. Episkopi *Phaneromeni*, Maroni *Vournes*), see Swiny (1979:237–239); Carpenter (1981:64); Cadogan *et al.* (n.d.).

river valleys.[823] One might also link in PWS finds in southern Cyprus, for example from the Maroni and Vasilikos Valleys (in contrast to eastern Cyprus).

Another consideration is that, as noted above, PWS seems to evolve most logically, and almost visibly, from MC WP wares.[824] These are all but absent (occasional imports only) from the southcoast to southwest area of Cyprus,[825] and are instead found in the southeast/east and north to northwest regions.[826] The area of greatest contact or overlap is central to west/northwest Cyprus, and particularly the greater Morphou Bay area and inland regions south and southwest from there to the northern Troodos foothills. With, I admit, an undoubted worrying generality and circularity of argument, this area suggests itself as perhaps the most likely home for the development of PWS. Our archaeological knowledge is still incomplete, and, in particular, the western area around Paphos is not to be ignored as PWS is found there (although largely unpublished). But, from currently published data, it is the west/northwest sites like Toumba tou Skourou, and Pendayia *Mandres*, which offer clear examples of a 'proto' to full LCI assemblage, in contrast to sites in the east. The presence of odd exceptions elsewhere in Cyprus, and especially at the key focal, and coastal-trading, sites in eastern and southern Cyprus does not undermine this conclusion – Enkomi, in particular, always has at least a little bit of everything due to its special status in LCI–II, but the general character of its assemblage is distinctly different.

In a notable contrast to the above regionalism, mature WSI is found all over the island. Although some sub-styles of decoration appear to exhibit regional preferences,[827] and earlier LC fine wares (such as WSI and BRI, etc.) seem relatively rare in general in some areas of southwest Cyprus,[828] it is clear in overall terms, that the LCIB period marks a new homogeneous culture across the island. The west–east division of MC–LCIA ends. We need not enter the old debates over the building of fortresses, military symbolism, supposed mass graves, destructions, and the other significant changes in the archaeological record in the LCIA period,[829] but the point which needs to be grasped is the key element of regionalism, linked to trading and polity formation, in the development of early LC culture. It is clear that warfare, or social turmoil, was involved, and that the competing polity groupings were perhaps quite distinct from each other. This is why it is difficult to define what is MCIII and what is LCIA,[830] and why the answer is different in different regions.

---

[823] Maliszewski (1997:75, 79, Map 2).

[824] Gjerstad (1926:199); Popham (1962; 1972a:431–432, 436); Karageorghis (1965); Benson (1967:316); Eriksson (n.d.) discusses this subject at length.

[825] Catling (1962); Herscher (1981); Swiny (1981); Herscher and Fox (1993:74–75).

[826] Åström (1972b).

[827] See below; Popham (1972a:442).

[828] See e.g. Bilde (1993:7); Swiny (1981); Hadjisavvas (1977 – where only one site cluster, southwest of Souskiou, in the areas surveyed has LC, and it is not clear if this includes early LC: p.230 nos.5, 6, 7, 9, 10 and 11). However, across the region as a whole, some tombs and sites of MCIII–LCI, or LCI and later, date are known (Maliszewski 1997).

[829] Knapp (1979:17–150; 1985:247–250; 1986a; 1986b:73); Merrillees (1971); Åström (1972c); Baurain (1984:27–103); Keswani (1989a:133–147).

[830] Muhly (1985:26).

The key WP to PWS, and PWS to WSI transitions are best attested in the west/ northwest. The tombs at Pendayia *Mandres* mentioned earlier, near the southern end of Morphou Bay nicely encompass the first,[831] with late MC WP types together with earliest LCIA types including PWS, and a probable sherd of 'Thera-style' early lattice ladder and lozenge WSI, and no later WSI nor BRI. It is notable also in this regard that the PWS includes forms (jugs) in common with the preceding MC period, whereas such shapes are not found in later WSI.[832] WP wares in general seem to provide the origin of PWS. At Toumba tou Skourou, in particular, one can then witness the transition from PWS to earliest WSI (even a 'transitional' style) (see below), before the appearance of the classic WSI style.[833] This transition is not really evident in the material found to date at any other site on Cyprus, and, as Padgett (1990:374) speculates, it may be that WS developed in the region of Toumba tou Skourou (i.e. the greater Morphou area to the north of the Troodos foothills and the copper-associated area around Politiko). Some chronology is also evident. In the settlement (Area A) at Episkopi *Phaneromeni* on the south coast of Cyprus the material in general belongs to the south coast MC tradition, but the latest elements, taking the date to initial LC, consists of WPV and at least 151 PWS sherds.[834] There is nothing later. One may note similar situations among some other MC to early LC assemblages with PWS but no WSI from the southwest.[835] WSI then appears at other sites in the region as part of a subsequent LCIB horizon. Similar instances from intact tomb assemblages of late MC/earliest LC classification also exist, where PWS is the latest element.[836] Thus PWS is revealed as appearing earlier than WSI.[837]

The chronology of PWS to early WSI to mature WSI is shown at Toumba tou Skourou. Tomb VI with its early LCI assemblage has an early PWS-style WSI bowl with a lattice-band and lozenge chain,[838] and no classic WSI pieces. In contrast, Tomb II Chambers 1–3 has none of the PWS-style lattice-band decorated WSI bowls, and is instead full of classic open, airy, WSI decorated bowls or a classic WSI decorated krater.[839] This is more or less the difference between LCIA and LCIB.[840] Eriksson (n.d.) quibbles over a

---

[831] Karageorghis (1965:15–70).

[832] Popham (1962:279); Karageorghis (1965:50).

[833] Padgett (1990:373–374).

[834] Swiny (1979:237–239); Carpenter (1981:64).

[835] Bilde (1993:6 sites 86-K-2 and 86-D-47, and perhaps 83-E-23). The LC tombs at Kouklia might offer important data on the developmental sequence when published. They range from LCI–III in date (Catling 1979; Maier and Karageorghis 1984:51–52). There is PWS material from the vicinity (Popham 1962:39), but the subsequent later LCI (LCIB in the main with some hints of LCIA in cases) and onwards deposits, such as in the Palaepaphos *Teratsoudhia* tombs (Karageorghis *et al.* 1990), do not have any PWS. Hence we might guess at a chronological sequence in the material.

[836] E.g. Pendayia Tomb 1: see above; Maroni *Kapsaloudhia* Tomb 1: Herscher (1984:25); Akhera Tomb 1: Karageorghis (1965:74–76, 80–111). Note, to reach this view of the Akhera tomb 1 assemblage I note that, like Popham (1972b:699–700), I consider all the WS from Akhera Tomb 1 to be PWS. This is contra Karageorghis' (1965:106–107) original publication (and also Åström 1972a:678 who follows Karageorghis).

[837] As Popham proposed (1962:290–291; 1972b:699–700).

[838] Vermeule and Wolsky (1990:317, TVI.25 P1069).

[839] Vermeule and Wolsky (1990: pp. 250, 255, and 257).

[840] It is relevant to note that there has been some debate over whether there is an even, island-wide,

few of the details, and the not perfect differentiation, but the big picture is clear enough.

How does this relate to Thera and Tell el-Dab[c]a? Well, the presently known imports of PWS and WSI to the Aegean in fact form two quite distinct groups. There is an early group of at present just two examples, characterised by the PWS-style lattice band below the rim (with slanting vertical lines: Popham's 'rope' pattern), consisting of a PWS sherd from Miletus,[841] and the celebrated early WSI bowl from Thera (and perhaps also the possible PWS? sherd from Kommos, p. 118 above). Then there are some classic WSI imports without the distinctive lattice band, and instead with the 'new', and different, WSI decorative schemes: a sherd from Knossos on Crete[842] (Figure 34.c), the sherds from one bowl from Phylakopi on Melos[843] (Figure 34 nos. a, b, d, and e), and some sherds from Rhodes[844] (Trianda one shown in Figure 34.f). With this division, I must note that I am disagreeing slightly with the views expressed by Cadogan and Padgett among others, and the implication of Popham, all of whom see the Phylakopi sherds as belonging to the earlier group of WSI.[845] Padgett states that earlier WSI bowls with lozenge chains and ladders were exported to several Aegean sites, and specifically at p.374 links the Thera bowl with the sherds from Phylakopi. But it is entirely a mistake to compare the Thera bowl with the Phylakopi sherds. Taken as a whole, the decoration on the Phylakopi WSI sherds exhibit the taut, clean, and refined lines, and some of the new additional motifs (e.g. parallel lines with neat 'railway-track' cross-lines, see Figure 34.b and e, and neat pairs of vertical lozenge chains framed by dots, see Figure 34.e), of classic, i.e. later, WSI. There is a telling absence of the PWS lattice-band/rope pattern, or of any other early 'cumbersome' features.[846] There are comparisons for the fabric-paste (see further below), rim decoration (a ladder framed lozenge type) and the bowl shape from Palaepaphos *Teratsoudhia* Tomb 5,[847] but there is no reason to regard the relevant parallels as among the earliest WSI present at this site – and, indeed, the combined decoration (not just rim ornament), and especially

---

linear succession whereby 'Proto' Base Ring and 'Proto' White Slip necessarily pre-date BRI and WSI respectively. Some have suggested that Proto-BR and PWS are to an extent 'regional' styles of BR and WSI (see Eames 1994 on Proto Base Ring, and Eames 1994:140 n.67 referring to Bourke 1981 for Proto White Slip; cf. Eriksson 1992:216). However, although there is clear evidence for regionalism, and for differing developmental sequences (the whole point of the present discussion), this extreme alternative argument does not hold up for WS. There is increasingly good evidence for a chronological succession of PWS to WSI to WSII (see text). This is apparent in the sequence of deposits in the tombs at Toumba tou Skourou, and is stratigraphically attested in the excavations at Maroni *Vournes* (Cadogan *et al.* n.d.; Ellen Herscher, pers. comm.; Gerald Cadogan, pers. comm.; for an early report, see Cadogan 1983b:160–161).

[841] Niemeier and Niemeier (1997:235 and fig.66).

[842] Popham (1963:91–93, Fig.2, pl.26.b).

[843] Popham (1972a:Fig.58); Cadogan (1972:6); Cline (1994:186 no.454). Merrillees (n.d.) presents a thorough investigation of the Phylakopi finds.

[844] Furumark (1950:Fig.6 no.97); Catling (1991:2 Fig.1).

[845] Cadogan (1972:6 no.5); Padgett (1990:374); Popham (1972a:442).

[846] Cf. Padgett (1990:374).

[847] Adduced by both Merrillees (n.d.) and Eriksson (n.d.). See Karageorghis *et al.* (1990:57 n.28) for comparison of fabrics. For parallels in decoration for the Phylakopi sherds, see Karageorghis *et al.* (1990:pls. 5 Tomb 105 Pit C (ii) row 1 centre, pl.6 Tomb 104 Chamber E(iii) several sherds, pl.6 Well (v) row 2 far right, pl.7 Tomb 105 Chamber B (vii) row 1 far right, row 2 second in from left, pl.8 Tomb 105 Chamber B (ii) row 2 second in from left, pl.33 B13, B52).

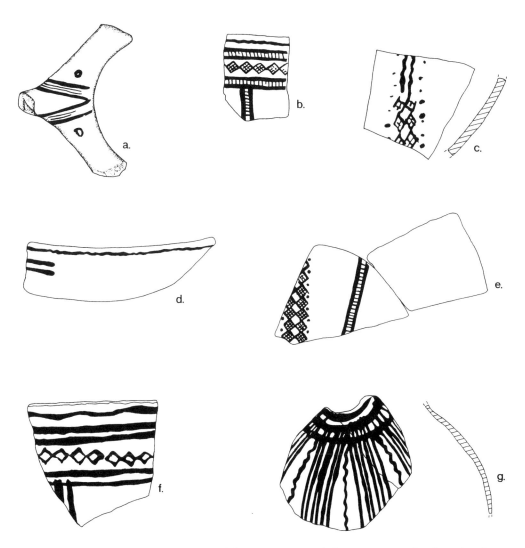

Fig. 34. WSI sherds and one WP sherd from Cyprus and the Aegean. a., b., d. and e. from Phylakopi after Popham (1972a:Fig.58), c. from Knossos, Crete, after Popham (1963:Fig.1), f. from Trianda, Rhodes, after Furumark (1950:Fig.6), and g. from Zakros, Crete, after Popham (1963:Fig.1).

the unusual fabric-paste (see below), support a later, LCIB, date. At present, therefore, with a questionmark against the Phylakopi sherds, in the Aegean only Thera received an early type WSI bowl; all the others are classic WSI and best dated in Cypriot terms to LCIB.[848]

---

[848] Padgett (1990:376) concurs with regard to the Knossos and Rhodes examples as belonging to a late phase of WSI.

Further, Popham (1963:92) notes that both the Knossos and Phylakopi WSI sherds are unusual in being made of a white clay fabric or paste (with very few inclusions/ grits) – stating that 'both are clearly high-quality products of a rare type'. Other exports of WSI made of this white paste have been found at Alalakh and Tell el-ᶜAjjul.[849] Popham noted that on Cyprus the examples he was aware of came from sites in the east or south.[850] The pattern he observed 30 years ago basically holds true today, with the addition of the southwest. For the south coast one can, for example, add the recently recovered sherds from a large white paste WSI bowl (MT.710) from MT Tomb 15 at Maroni *Tsaroukkas*: Figure 35. The decoration offers a parallel for the Knossos sherd. The accompanying material included WSI, BRI, and even a WSII Early bowl, and was generally LCIB–early IIA. A WSI bowl from a tomb at Enkomi (topographical point 1336) offers a further member of this group. Described as 'a masterpiece', it has fine white clay, and also offers a parallel for the decoration on the Knossos sherd. It features a very similar pair of vertical wavy lines bordered by dots splaying out at the top, and below this a pair of vertical lozenge chains also bordered by dots.[851] In the southwest, the WSI objects found in the impressive tombs at Palaepaphos *Teratsoudhia* include, among many other WSI examples of usual kinds, some vessels with white (to yellow) 'eggshell' fabric.[852] Karageorghis notes the link with the Aegean finds, and even proposes Palaepaphos as the source of the sherds from Phylakopi.[853] One (or more) special workshop(s) might almost be considered for these vessels; there are furthermore similarities in the decoration of these pots which might support a restricted number of production loci. Although some white clay fabric WSI sherds are known from elsewhere, including the centre of the island,[854] and despite the lack of any detailed, comprehensive, study (and one is sorely needed), it is tempting nonetheless to speculate about an eastern, southern, to southwestern source or preference for this type. But for our present purposes, the key point is that this group is late phase WSI, and LCIB in date.

The last point is critical. The evidence in general, and the secure evidence in particular, shows that examples of the distinctive (new, or late phase) WSI style appear to be chronologically later in those (few) cases where a chronology can be determined. For example, the classic WSI sherd from Trianda is in an LMIB context (see above). And, as noted above with reference to Toumba tou Skourou on Cyprus, distinctive 'new' airy and elegant style WSI tends to occur in LCIB contexts, and tends to occur with other typically LCIB types like developed BR (not Proto Base Ring) and Red Lustrous Wheelmade Ware. And, although the evidence is at best suggestive, a late LCI date seems most likely. The Enkomi tomb (1336) is typical: most of the material

---

[849] Popham (1963:92 n.14); Bergoffen (n.d.). The Tell el-ᶜAjjul example is described by Bergoffen as having pendent criss-cross lines bordered with dots and pendent parallel lines. It thus belongs like the others of this class to the later styles of WSI.

[850] Popham (1963:92 n.14; 1966:95). See also Åström (1972c:49).

[851] Johnstone (1971:91–92 no.216, Fig.21.1).

[852] Karageorghis *et al.* (1990:26 no.4, 28 nos.15 and 16, 53 nos. i–iv).

[853] Karageorghis *et·al.* (1990:57 n.28).

[854] E.g. one sherd recently found at by the Sydney Cyprus Survey Project: I thank A.B. Knapp for letting me see this ceramic material.

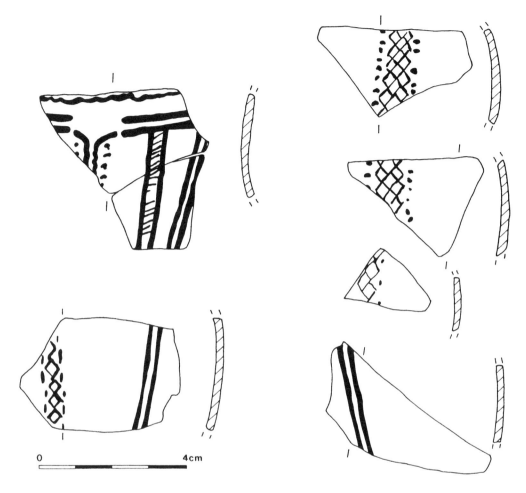

Fig. 35. Mature WSI bowl sherds, MT.710, from MT Tomb 15 at Maroni Tsaroukkas, southern Cyprus. The fabric of the bowl is made from a pure white clay/paste.

is in fact post-WSI,[855] and the deposit thus seems to start with late WSI (and LCIB) and continues into LCII. Sadly, the serpentine vase with the probable cartouche of Ahmose from Dromos L in Tomb 104 at Palaepaphos *Teratsoudhia* was not found in a precise or closed context (and of course many objects with cartouches of Egyptian rulers are not found in contemporary contexts on Cyprus).[856] Nonetheless, there is no

---

[855] The four MC sherds from the tomb chamber are described as 'intrusive': Johnstone (1971:110).

[856] Karageorghis *et al.* (1990:31–32 Dromos L no.1, pl.20); Clerc (1990). The identification is likely but not certain (Clerc 1990:95–96). See also the comments of Helck in Åström (1989:53). For finds of objects with cartouches in later contexts, see e.g. Åström (1979).

PWS nor a real indication of earlier LCIA in the tomb in general,[857] and, in particular, in Dromos L and the associated Niche M and Chambers N and O.[858] Hence an LCIB *terminus post quem* might be set.[859] Even though the true context may be rather later, this evidence does not contradict the pattern of LCIB mainly equating with the earlier 18th Dynasty (and so LCIA with the SIP).[860]

If one returns to the arguments of Merrillees (and others) discussed in Chapter IV.4 concerning the development of the LCI styles, what we seem to have is the development in LCIA of the PWS and then WSI styles predominantly in the west/ northwest and central region of the island, while the east and southeast predominantly continues with its WP tradition. As Padgett (1990) notes, Toumba tou Skourou seems to lead its region into the WSI style, thus early WSI here may be precocious vis à vis earlier LCI in general (although the western area around Paphos should not be discounted). In particular, no other site has produced anywhere near as much early (or transitional) WSI material with the lattice-bands and lozenge chains. It is of course notable that Toumba tou Skourou also produced several contemporary LMIA or Late Cycladic I imports – two with clear links to pre-eruption LMIA Thera,[861] along with Tell el-Yahudiyeh imports and imitations – another link with pre-eruption Thera (see Chapter IV.4 above). The PWS style lattice-band, and overall ladder lattice framed lozenge style, WSI bowl from Thera might be considered a likely export from this west/northwest region, and dated no later than LCIA2, and perhaps even LCIA1/2. The eastern/southeastern to southern region of Cyprus meanwhile is exporting later WP styles, Bichrome Ware, and PWS (and itself importing the odd early WSI vessel). Examples of these specific eastern/southeastern WP types (and *not* of the western/ northwestern WP Fine Line Style type) have been noted at Tell el-Dabᶜa,[862] and, interestingly, a likely similar eastern export of a WP Pendent Line Style sherd is known from a probable MMIIIB–LMIA context at Zakros on Crete (see Figure 34.g).[863]

No such divisions are absolute, of course. Although the southcoast has a distinctive MC to LCIA tradition, 'imported' PWS style material is known.[864] Exactly where the divisions between 'west/northwest/central' Cyprus, southcoast Cyprus, and 'east/ southeastern' Cyprus, should be drawn is inevitably a moot point, and the southcoast has some interrelations with the other two regions in LCIA. The Maroni valley roughly marks the western edge of the general eastern/southeastern WP grouping, whereas, much further west along the southcoast, one is into the distinct southcoast grouping. But the southcoast region, as far as the Maroni Valley, receives PWS (indeed has a long sequence) and exhibits several clear links with the west/northwest/centre region

---

[857] Just Chamber K includes a few potential LCIA/B finds (Karageorghis *et al.* 1990:29–31, 57–60), although these need not necessarily date before LCIB.

[858] 'Stage 2' in the history of the Tomb 104 complex: Karageorghis *et al.* (1990:24, 31–37, 60–66).

[859] Cf. Åström (1987:57).

[860] Karageorghis *et al.* (1990:37). Chamber O also had an LMI? import.

[861] Vermeule and Wolsky (1990:381–383); Cadogan (1990:95).

[862] Maguire (1991); see discussion above.

[863] Popham (1963:39–91, Fig.1, pl.26.a).

[864] Popham (1962:Fig.6); Herscher (1991).

in the LCIA period,[865] but, at the same, it recieves Bichrome Ware from the east. Only a little 'imported' PWS is found further to the east (usually only bowls). What is largely missing on the southcoast is the ladder lattice framed lozenge phase of early WSI; there is a good PWS phase, and then a subsequent mature WSI phase characterised by framed wavy lines and lattices. PWS thus occupies most if not all of LCIA here, with the (already mature) WSI then largely LCIB. Both PWS and early WSI are less common, to rare, further east.

However, if one takes the evidence as a whole, there is a clear separation of the basic groupings. At Toumba tou Skourou there are many transitional or 'proto' pieces between the late MC, the initial LC, and then LCI styles in several of the main types, and especially in the WS, where there is, as noted above, almost a transitional period when 'there is obviously considerable overlap between the two styles' and when 'many of the bowls from Toumba tou Skourou are painted in a transitional style that makes hard and fast divisions almost meaningless'.[866] In contrast, this process is not visible in the south and east. Further, whereas in the west/northwest continuous deposit sequences (e.g. tombs) can be found with an approximate sequence (or co-occurrence) of late MC, then PWS, proto BR, and then early WSI, before classic WSI and BRI,[867] deposits in the east and southeast tend either to be generally late MC in character with some of the new early LCIA types making them part of a recognisable MCIII/LCIA horizon in eastern Cyprus (chronologically = LCIA),[868] or instead they include clearly evolved LCI (especially LCIB) types such as the distinct open airy and elegant style WSI.

The earlier tombs at Enkomi are typical:[869] PWS is entirely absent. Tombs either contain MC/LCIA tradition materials only,[870] or they include mature LCI (e.g. WSI, BRI), and often also later types.[871] No transition assemblage is evident. If it did exist it ought to have been in Tombs 32, 3, or 134; Tomb 32 has a predominantly MCIII/ LCIA assemblage, but lacks any transition group, and instead also has finds of WSI, BRI and other mature LCI types, Tombs 3 and 134 meanwhile lack WSI, but include BRI, and are LCI in date with no trace of an early LCI transitional assemblage. A very similar situation is seen in the two tombs at Dromolaxia *Trypes* from near Larnaca in southeastern Cyprus reported by Admiraal (1982). Tomb 1 includes a range of late MC objects, especially several WP types, and then a range of LCI–II objects, but no PWS or transitional assemblage. WSI is in fact represented only by five vessels, three

---

[865] Cadogan (1983b:161); Herscher (1984:27).

[866] Padgett (1990:373).

[867] Especially the Toumba tou Skourou Tombs: Vermeule and Wolsky (1990).

[868] E.g. Herscher (1984:25 and n.13); Merrillees (1971:62–70).

[869] Taking as representative the relatively intact chamber groups in Courtois (1981); and Dikaios (1969–1971). Eriksson (n.d.) points to one possible exception to the pattern summarised below. She reports a PWS bowl shown with a selection of finds from a tomb at Enkomi in a publication of 1936 by Schaeffer. As she notes, there are no other details. I suggest that this bowl, if confirmed, may act as the exception which proves the rule. It is an example of an occasional LCIA import from elsewhere into the east.

[870] E.g. Tombs 240, 390, 365 from Courtois (1981); and Cypriot Tomb 3 from Dikaios (1969–1971). Åström (1972a:676) dates Cypriot Tomb 3 at Enkomi to LCIA1.

[871] E.g. Tombs 32, 126, 3, 134, 110 from Courtois (1981); and Tombs 2, 5, 10, 13, 14, 20, 22 from Dikaios (1969–1971).

preserved just as fragments (versus no less than 65 WSII examples), and the WSI seems 'mature'. Of the two WSI vessels which are described, no.106 is of the open and airy type with bands of horizontal lines,[872] while no.107 is classified as WSI but sounds to be almost like transitional WSI–II (to WSIIA) ware (like no.110) with 'on rim bands of ladder pattern and solid bands, on front of body a composition of two broad vertical ladder pattern bands with a similar horizontal band in between with four lozenges above and a simple ladder pattern below, at either side a vertical row of dots'.[873] The PWS to early WSI stage is thus entirely absent. Tomb 2 is predominantly MC, but has a few early LCI objects. However, there is no PWS or WSI, and the transitional assemblage of early LCI found elsewhere in the west/northwest of Cyprus is missing. The presence of one BRI juglet (no.8) in Tomb 2, and typologically the latest object interred, might support the view that BRI appeared in general shortly before WSI in eastern Cyprus.[874]

The same picture exists in the material from Cyprus available up to the writing of the seminal studies of Merrillees (1971), and Åström (1972a; 1972c), and respectively summarised therein, with most intact eastern MCIII–LCIA (and not later) tomb assemblages, or settlement deposits, lacking PWS and the other transitional signs evident in the west and northwest.[875] Or, if PWS does occur, it tends to be a rare 'import', and the rest of the initial LC 'proto' or transitional assemblage known from the west and northwest is absent. Different but contemporary Cypriot cultural, fashion, production, and trading systems appear to be in operation, one primarily western/northwestern (to northern/Karpass zone if one considers the Red on Black/Red in the Levant), and one primarily eastern/southeastern. This only ends when the new, distinctive, style of classic WSI becomes standard across the island in what may be best defined as LCIB (after some undoubted late LCIA overlaps: especially western/northwestern PWS to PWS-style early WSI to mature WSI – as evident in Tomb I at Toumba tou Skourou).

How does Tell el-Dabᶜa fit in? As noted several times, most of its MC-style imports are from the east/south-east region of Cyprus, and its WSI is mainly of the distinctive 'new' or late WSI style. Early western/northwestern style WSI is largely absent (certainly from secure New Kingdom contexts). And, if one observes the indications of regional fashions within classic WSI in Cyprus,[876] the general northwestern penchant for cross-hatched bands and filling ornaments is not evidenced at Tell el-Dabᶜa. An eastern or southern Cypriot origin would be quite possible (although not certain) for most of the Tell el-Dabᶜa WSI. The one other illustrated example of WSI from Egypt, reportedly from Saqqara (Figure 32.d),[877] in older publications, is likewise of the new

---

[872] Admiraal (1982:47, pl.6.13, 50 n.18).

[873] Admiraal (1982:47). The vessel is not illustrated.

[874] Åström (1972a:676 and n.6). BRI appears similarly as the solitary harbinger of LCI in Ayios Iakovos *Melia* Tomb 12, and Nitovikla Tomb 2: see below. This precedence appears also on the southern coast: in the stratigraphic sequence at Maroni *Vournes* BRI appears in Vournes Phase Ib, before WSI (Cadogan *et al.* n.d.).

[875] Tombs: e.g. Ayios Iakovos *Melia* Tomb 12: Gjerstad *et al.* (1934:341–345); or Nitovikla Tomb 2: Gjerstad *et al.* (1934:410–414); settlement: Kalopsidha: Åström (1966).

[876] E.g. Popham (1972a:442).

[877] Merrillees (1968:28 no.60); Popham (1972a:Fig.59.1).

WSI style and similar to examples from the south or east of Cyprus. Thus it is likely, if never capable of proof, that the WSI from New Kingdom Tell el-Dab^ca is not only LCIB in date/style, but from eastern/southeastern Cyprus (and follows the Merrillees 1971:74 model of LC exports to Egypt only in LCIB once these styles were adopted by eastern Cyprus). The Tell el-Dab^ca WSI, and the early 18th Dynasty stratum C horizon at the site, could therefore be significantly later than the PWS-style lattice-band, ladder lattice framed lozenge, early WSI bowl found on Thera (probably from the west/ northwest of Cyprus). How much later we do not know. What we can determine, however, is that PWS and early WSI in the west/northwest of Cyprus are linked to mature LMIA both at Toumba tou Skourou, and on Thera. Contemporary Proto Base Ring, early BR, early Monochrome and possible/probable PWS, likewise first appear and link with mature–late LMIA at Kommos (Chapter IV.4.B above). The new distinctive WSI style seems in the main to be diagnostic of LCIB, and links to a period running from LMIB, LHIIA, and the start of the 18th Dynasty, through to the reign of Tuthmosis III and the first appearance of LM/LHIIIA1. However, it is important at the same time to note that WSI is in fact very rare in Egypt. The finds from Tell el-Dab^ca significantly increase the total, very small, corpus. It would therefore be very unwise to attach too much chronological weight to these few rare finds in Egypt (not one of them to date found in a secure or primary context, moreover). But we might nonetheless speculate that a situation not dissimilar to the one for LMIA pottery imports appears to exist (see Chapter IV.4 above). The excavation of the key Canaanite-Hyksos centre of Tell el-Dab^ca is now producing rather more WSI than ever before found in Egypt. And it is of course well known that the important Canaanite centre of Tell el-^cAjjul produced significant finds of PWS and WSI.[878] The almost total absence of PWS or WSI elsewhere in Egypt might thus suggest that, like LMIA, this fashion period was partly, or even predominantly, contemporary with the SIP period when the rest of Egypt was cut off from Mediterranean trade. Certainly, any potential earlier LCIA WSI at Tell el-Dab^ca may be attributed to re-deposited original SIP material, and this view may even apply to some of the mature WSI. Like LMIB/LHIIA (see Chapter IV.7), LCIB *may* have begun before the end of the SIP.

The critical and poorly understood site of Tell el-^cAjjul very much forces itself into our consciousness at this point.[879] It has a so far unique collection of Cypriot pottery of early LC date. In particular, it has significant amounts of PWS and WSI,[880] including quantities of earlier WSI comparable to the Thera WSI bowl – as *not* found in early 18th Dynasty Tell el-Dab^ca – as well as a little, later, or 'classic' WSI material.[881] The

---

[878] See above; Gittlen (1977); Bergoffen (1989; n.d.); Eliezer Oren (n.d.; pers. comms.). See further in the following paragraphs.

[879] Petrie (1931–1934); Petrie *et al.* (1952); Stewart (1974); Kempinski (1974; 1983:131–148; 1992a:189–192); Bergoffen (1989; n.d.); Gonen (1992:118–123); Oren (1997b; n.d.).

[880] Bergoffen (1989:135–147; 1991:66 and Figs.10 and 11; n.d.); Merrillees (1974b); Gittlen (1977:379, 382); Oren (1969:144; n.d.).

[881] Bergoffen (n.d.; 1989; pers. comm.). I warmly thank Eliezer Oren for discussion, and in particular for spending time with me going through the collection of material from Petrie's excavations at Tell el-^cAjjul

later MB deposits at Tell el-ʿAjjul (City 2b/Palace II) thus appear to include the time of Tell el-Dabʿa stratum D/2 (both have PWS and Bichrome Ware),[882] *and* a little later (Palace II includes mature WSI and also BRI). But they are pre-stratum C (or IV at ʿEzbet Helmi) at Tell el-Dabʿa. However, the major initial problem is the much vexed chronology of the sequence at Tell el-ʿAjjul. Petrie's excavation and recording was clearly less than satisfactory, and the original reports are summary and opaque to the point of being useless.[883] The topography and taphonomy of the tell were not properly understood, nor recorded (only in the final report did more rigour occur, and by then it was too late[884]). The recorded information for many finds is also inadequate; some sherds which were kept have loci (rooms) written on them which may be related to specific excavation areas[885] and to recorded heights, but many only preserve the broad phase (e.g. City 2) to which Petrie and other project members assigned them (and we have little or no information concerning this process). There are accordingly many difficulties when it comes to interpreting the site. Much potentially crucial information has sadly been lost, or must be considered suspect.

Problems with Petrie's publications on Tell el-ʿAjjul were immediately apparent. Albright provided a swift critique of the whole venture, and denounced the dates offered by Petrie.[886] Albright substituted his own chronology for the various layers of the tell. Whereas Petrie dated Palace levels I–IV as pre-Egyptian 18th Dynasty (variously 6th–8th to 16th Dynasties), Albright allowed only Palace I to be pre-18th Dynasty (Hyksos), and dated the rest to the New Kingdom. Albright further associated the earliest of the three city levels recognised by Petrie (City 3) as contemporary with Palace I. This radical 'low' chronology for Tell el-ʿAjjul – much in keeping with Albright's general chronological synthesis – remained current for many years. Influential studies by Tufnell (1962), Epstein (1966), and Negbi (1970) all employed it without serious question.[887]

However, subsequent work has shown that Albright was overly enthusiastic in his down-dating. Further, there is no stratigraphic connection between Palace I and City

---

held in London. I note that he does not necessarily share my views on chronology, and should not be held responsible for my statements here concerning Tell el-ʿAjjul.

[882] The early WSI at Tell el-ʿAjjul, and not at Tell el-Dabʿa stratum D/2, may be inferred to be of northwest Cypriot origin, with eastern Cypriot late WP, and southcoast PWS (as at Tell el-Dabʿa), extending into the time range of initial northwestern WSI production. The later part of Tell el-ʿAjjul City 2b/Palace II and Tell el-Dabʿa stratum D/2 are thus contemporary, but the Cypriot imports at the respective sites include objects from different, but themselves contemporary, ceramic and cultural groupings on Cyprus at this time.

[883] Petrie (1931–1934).

[884] See Petrie *et al.* (1952).

[885] See Kempinski (1983:plans 5, 6, 7).

[886] Albright (1938); Albright's paper was reprinted in Stewart (1974:64–75). For further critical comments on the site recording, see also Stewart (1974:9–14).

[887] Other important studies to accept this Palace I = City 3 correlation, and the basic chronological placement of Albright, included Kenyon in the *Cambridge Ancient History* (1973:553–554); Stewart (1974:11–13); and Weinstein (1981:5). The City and Palace strata are both referred to in the existing literature with Roman numerals (e.g. Palace I/City III). I have chosen to use Arabic numerals for the City strata to avoid confusion.

3, and their destructions could have been unrelated. Aharon Kempinski has been the major scholar in this regard.[888] Through careful analysis of the finds from the site and re-evaluation of the stratigraphy, he has proposed various revised, and rather 'higher', chronologies for the site. Oren and Bergoffen have continued the re-analysis of the site and its finds.[889] In Kempinski's recent analyses he placed Palace I as running from the time of City 3 through to early in the time of City 2 (City 2b); and he places the end of Palace I contemporary with the reign of the Hyksos king Khyan. Kempinski regards the subsequent Palace II as contemporary with the main Bichrome Ware phase in Canaan, and he equates the end of this palace with the reign of Apophis. Some Bichrome Ware was found in City 3 contexts (Oren n.d.), but Palace II and City 2b mark the main late MBA 'Bichrome Phase' (Kempinski has argued that the Palace I finds from the courtyard could be debris from Palace II or III since this area remained in use). This main Bichrome Ware phase begins c.1600BC (during the reign of Khyan, with most of the phase linked to Apophis).[890] Hence the basic datum that City 3 and Palace I lie before this point. Palace II then ran from the earlier phase of City 2 (City 2b) through the remainder of the late MBII (MBIIC or MBIII) period and to the end of the MBA/ very beginning of the LBA, and the time period of the very early 18th Dynasty (City 2a). City 2b (and the areas of City 3 which were not destroyed) is wholly MBA. There are good links with Tell el-Dabᶜa stratum D/2. Burnt debris contained a scarab of Apophis, and this is the most recent datum. It is quite plausible that City 2b/Palace II was the city of Sharuhen destroyed by Ahmose in the mid to later part of his reign.[891] City 2a is early LBI and early 18th Dynasty. City 1 and Palace III are later again.

When did WSI appear at Tell el-ᶜAjjul? This has proved a controversial question, as the excavation records clearly run against the conventional low chronology synthesis. Petrie specifically claimed that some 40 sherds of WSI came from Palace I contexts.[892] There is also PWS from City 3/Palace I.[893] Despite this, some later scholars have simply ignored the evidence, and indicated that WSI did not appear until after Palace I; but even this view leaves City 2b/Palace II finds as late MBA.[894] The problem, of course, is that WSI has not been found elsewhere in an MBA context in Palestine.[895] However, no other site has produced *anywhere* near the quantity of early WS found at Tell el-ᶜAjjul,

---

[888] Kempinski (1974; 1983:131–148; 1992a:189–192); Kempinski in Stern (1993:52–53). See also Gonen (1992:118–120).

[889] Oren (1997b; n.d.); Bergoffen (1989; n.d.).

[890] The picture is further complicated by the fact that not all sections of City 3 were destroyed, and some parts continued to be used during the subsequent City 2b. The c.1600BC date is not entirely independently derived, and partly comes from one interpretation of the sequence at Alalakh, in what is undeniably a somewhat circular set of arguments overall (see e.g. Oren 1997b:271).

[891] The identification was proposed strongly by Kempinski (1974). However, it is not certain, as recently argued by Rainey (1993).

[892] Petrie (1931–1934, vol.II:pl.37); Bergoffen (1989; n.d.); Merrillees (1974:95); Gittlen (1975:113; 1977:404).

[893] Oren (n.d.); Bergoffen (1989; n.d.).

[894] Tufnell (in Stern 1993:52).

[895] Although one should now note that Peter Fischer has reported a find of WSI in what seems likely to be a late MBA level at Tell Abu al-Kharaz in Jordan (1999:24; oral presentation at the White Slip Ware conference, Nicosia, 30 October 1998). If confirmed, this would strongly support the Tell el-ᶜAjjul evidence.

and it may very well preserve special, even unique, evidence. Indeed, the scarcity of WSI at other major Palestinian sites such as Hazor, Lachish and Megiddo is conspicuous. Epstein (1966:176–177) adopted this line, arguing that Tell el-ᶜAjjul was an important trade town and so the unexpected appearance of WSI here may have been because it was the first site in the region to receive such Cypriot imports. I see no reason not to believe that WSI was found in Palace I contexts, and that these date from the time of Khyan and further back into the 17th century BC. The evidence in question is not one stray sherd, but a large group. Moreover, the WSI in question from the Palace I and related post-Palace I (but pre-Palace II) contexts is notably of the earlier WSI styles (and probably from the west/northwest area of Cyprus).[896] Tell el-ᶜAjjul also has early Monochrome ware from Palace II. This too is a northwestern Cypriot product.[897] Neither of these types are represented at other LBI contexts in the region, including early 18th Dynasty Tell el-Dabᶜa/ᶜEzbet Helmi. Thus they make sense in the preceding later MBII period, contemporary with 'MCIII'-style to LCIA exports from eastern Cyprus at other sites.[898]

Later City 2b and Palace II contexts and assemblages at Tell el-ᶜAjjul are broadly comparable with Tell el-Dabᶜa stratum D/2 (although the Tell el-ᶜAjjul context starts earlier = Tell el-Dabᶜa stratum D/3, and ends slightly later).[899] Apart from ceramic correlations, scarab evidence attests the contemporaneity of the close of the phase with

---

One might also consider the historiography of this debate. Kenyon (1970:553) considered the Tell el-ᶜAjjul evidence as problematic as she considered that neither Bichrome Ware nor WSI had been found anywhere else in MBA levels. However, Bichrome Ware is now considered to be the very hallmark of the last MBA (MBIIC or MBIII) phase. In time, early WSI from northwest Cyprus may be seen to be another later MBA element in the Levant.

[896] Bergoffen (n.d.; 1989). Stewart (1974:62–63) also recognised the early character of the assemblage. The low chronology sceptical viewpoint would argue that, considering only the totally secure data, all stratified WSI from City or Palace contexts at Tell el-ᶜAjjul are LBA/New Kingdom. However, it remains the case that many other less secure (but stated by Petrie), or unstratified, WSI sherds from the Palace area may very well have derived from earlier, that is MBA, contexts. Further, consideration of the unusual early character of the Tell el-ᶜAjjul LCIA assemblage points firmly in this direction.

[897] Pilides (1992:esp. 296–297).

[898] The scenario appears to be that whereas the polity that formed around Enkomi in east Cyprus in MCIII–LCI exported to Tell el-Dabᶜa, the northwestern polity around Toumba tou Skourou exported to Tell el-ᶜAjjul. These respective polity formations on Cyprus were very probably rivals and quite distinct on the island. Largely exclusive relations are plausible; since the two regions of Cyprus were at this time operating differing styles of ceramic production and decoration, quite different patterns in the evidence of Cypriot imports in late MBA Palestine and Hyksos Egypt are therefore likely. The basis to the trade was probably copper.

[899] The 14th Dynasty seals from Tell el-ᶜAjjul (Ryholt 1997:106 n.356) can be seen as dating from City 3 through to the construction of City 2 (Kempinski 1983:140–141). Kempinski in his 1983 book regarded king Sheshi of the 14th Dynasty as marking more or less the end of City 3 *and* Palace I (since a scarab of Sheshi was found in the construction fill of City 2). In his 1993 study (in Stern 1993:52–53) he allows Palace I to run on to the time of Khyan. Kempinski (1983:225) dates Sheshi and the close of City 3 c.1670/60BC, whereas Ryholt (1997:200) places Sheshi c.1745–1705BC. Either way, City 2 begins by, or in, the earlier 17th century BC. On the latest assessment, Place II would commence around 1600BC. The latest scarab evidence from the City 2 destruction belongs to Apophis (Kempinski 1983:138), hence City 2 may be considered as ending about the close of his reign, or slightly later (sack of Ahmose). The Tell el-ᶜAjjul City 2 and Palace II LCI finds thus co-ordinate nicely with the 'early' Aegean chronology.

the 15th (Hyksos) Dynasty king Apophis. Imported finds include late MC to early LC ceramic types (i.e. typical of an LCIA asssemblage), along with contemporaries emanating from the eastern Cyprus region such as Bichrome Ware. The important difference is that Tell el-ᶜAjjul City 2/Palace II seems to continue a little longer than the stratigraphic sample excavated to date at Tell el-Dabᶜa stratum D/2. Thus PWS (as in Tell el-Dabᶜa stratum D/2) and earlier style WSI (as in the Palace I and post-Palace I grouping) still occur, but we also see the appearance of the later styles of WSI along with BRI and Monochrome from Palace II and onwards.[900] The metope, framed wavy line, and two parallel line styles of WSI link the end of this phase with the time of early 18th Dynasty Tell el-Dabᶜa and ᶜEzbet Helmi stratum IV.[901] In the main, much of the City 2/Palace II assemblage 'fits' stylistically from, and then *in between*, the Cypriot assemblages represented at Tell el-Dabᶜa in strata D/2 and then C (and ᶜEzbet Helmi stratum IV).[902] Only the latest elements link to Tell el-Dabᶜa stratum C and ᶜEzbet Helmi stratum IV. A rare 'time window' is on view. As Bergoffen (1991:69) concludes, 'The phase of importation represented by Proto White Slip, White Slip I, Red on Black/Red on Red and Monochrome bowls of type I, is not represented in Egypt or in northern Sinai...'. This could reflect temporal difference and/or different or changing trade patterns. Without doubt, later MBA Tell el-ᶜAjjul appears a primary trading partner for initial LBA northwestern Cyprus, whereas later MBA Tell el-Dabᶜa was not (on current data), and instead had its links with eastern Cyprus. What happened in the period immediately after the conquest of Ahmose at Avaris is not clear; when evidence for trade with Cyprus resumes, it is with LCIB period (eastern/southeastern?) Cyprus.

Where does this leave a chronology of WS? Redford (1992:138–139) correctly

---

[900] Merrillees (1974b); Bergoffen (1989; n.d.). Hardly suprising given WSI in Palace I, even if deemed to be late Palace I. However, it should be noted again that this is a highly contentious issue. Based on the loci recorded on the sherds kept by the project, the statement in the text is correct, and Merrillees and Bergoffen state the same. The trouble is that many of the WSI sherds in question invariably do not have a specific excavation context (a room) recorded, but have merely been assigned to City 2 by the excavators. Thus some scepticism is justified – the issue is how much? And can both the 40 odd Palace I, *and* also all the City 2/Palace II, examples be dismissed? In summary, it is clear that the late MBII (MBIIC or MBIII) horizon definitely is coeval with the eastern Cypriot Bichrome Ware and PWS, and late WP wares grouping, and generally LCIA, since a variety of these sherds are found with specific good loci recorded on them. But the placement of the initial LCIA northwestern Cyprus grouping causes concern to some scholars, who would argue that it is only somewhere between probable to possible that WSI also occurs by the end of the same late MB phase. At the extreme, a case could be made by excluding everything not absolutely certain and with recorded specific locus (i.e. most of the assemblage!) that WSI and BRI do not necessarily occur until the start of the Palestinian LBIA phase. This is the absolute minimum position. But it fails to appreciate the marked stylistic differentiation of western/northwest Cyprus from eastern Cyprus at this key LCIA stage. The accepted eastern Cypriot LCIA material *should* be contemporary with the initial WSI and BRI production in northwestern Cyprus (and probably the region around Toumba tou Skourou). This author therefore believes that sufficient of the Palace I, City 2 and Palace II finds probably stand, and that the temporal correlation of the earlier WSI style to the later Syro-Palestinian MBII period (=MBIIC or MBIII periods, depending on how defined) can be accepted.

[901] With a metope, two parallel-line style, WSI vessel from Tell el-ᶜAjjul offering a very good comparison for the WSI bowl from Tell el-Dabᶜa (Petrie 1931–1934, vol.II:pl.37).

[902] One might note the presence of early Monochrome, along with other early LC types (Bergoffen 1989:153–210; 1991:66 and fig.12).

emphasises that we are as yet ignorant of much concerning the late MBII–LBIA transition in Syria–Palestine. Clear lines may not be drawn in the sand. Among many very unclear parameters is the length of time to be allotted to the very important overall late MBII (MBIIC or MBIII) phase. It has become apparent that what was originally an afterthought is in fact a key phase, the zenith of MBA development in the region.[903] Solid data are scarce, other than a broad parallelism – variously for the latter part of the phase, or for all of it, or for the earlier part of it – with the Hyksos 15th Dynasty who presumably derived from this dynamic later MBII urban 'Canaanite' world.[904] Dever, in broad terms, allows 150 years for this period; Bietak around half this time.[905] Both then allow c.50 years for a supposed 'MBIIC/LBIA' transition phase.[906] The former can be made compatible with the 'early' Aegean chronology, whereas the latter is incompatible. The one thing that is agreed between Dever and Bietak is that the situation is less than certain. If the Aegean and consequently Cypriot situation became clear, it does not appear that there is any overriding reason why the assigned chronological length of the late MBII period could not be modified accordingly. Nor are the data fixed; we must do our best with the palimpsest of data currently available.

At present, we therefore have evidence for PWS to early WSI from later MBII Tell el-ᶜAjjul: PWS (and proto BR) and WSI from MBII City 3 and/or Palace I contexts, and PWS and WSI (from earlier styles into mature and later styles) from late MBII (MBIIC or MBIII) City 2 and Palace II contexts.[907] Contemporary late MBII (MBIIC or MBIII) finds of PWS bowls have been made in Megiddo level X,[908] and elsewhere in

---

[903] See above; Kempinski (1983); Dever (1987; 1997:291–292); Oren (1997b:257; pers. comm.).

[904] Redford (1992:102, 105–106); Ryholt (1997:302–303).

[905] Dever (1987:149; 1992:Fig.1); Bietak (e.g. 1991a).

[906] This supposed 'MBIIC–LBIA' transition phase is a very problematic concept, and the use of this term in the literature is creating a false impression of what is in fact occurring in the archaeology. Its basis is that many scholars assume that the close of MBA destructions in Palestine were the work of the Egyptians. Since Ahmose did not conquer all of the region, other pharaoh's campaigns as late as Tuthmosis III are proposed (see esp. Weinstein 1981; 1991). Hence some scholars view the end of Palestinian MBA culture as occurring between Ahmose and Tuthmosis III. But this is seriously missing the point. There is a more or less contemporary set of destructions and changes in Palestine (and Syria) which mark the end of the late MBII (i.e. MBIIC or MBIII) period. The assemblages involved are very similar, and contemporary with LCIA. There is a macro-regional change in progress. The end of Avaris and the advance of Kamose, and then Ahmose, are merely parts of this wider phenomenon of the end of the late MBII 'world system'. The Egyptians may in fact be a late element in a process which began further north. The late MBII (MBIIC or MBIII) period ended in the 16th century BC. Whether earlier or later then depends on the chronological debates such as the date of the Thera eruption, etc., discussed in this book.

[907] Gittlen's (1977:499 n.108) view that the then recent proposal for the re-dating of Tell el-ᶜAjjul by Kempinski (1974) was not possible, must now be rejected. With this 'problem' out of the way, Gittlen's general insistence on artificially aligning the start of the LC period with the start of the Syro-Palestinian LBI period can be seen for what it is, and ignored.

[908] (Loud 1948:pl.45.21), as accepted by Popham (1962:286–287), Oren (1969:144), Åström (1972a:757 and n.12), and Kempinski (1983:190) – notwithstanding the strained efforts to argue against this piece claiming a less than secure context by Gittlen (1975:113; 1977:403 and ns.110, 112). The general character of the Megiddo X assemblage is appropriate for a PWS import; in particular, there is Bichrome Ware (Loud 1948:pl.42.1). Oren (pers. comm.) has further investigated the context of this find from the original field notes, and regards it as coming from a good, clear, level X context.

Canaan.[909] Tell el-ᶜAjjul City 2b/Palace II belongs to the later MBII period, from somewhere in the earlier 17th century BC (post Sheshi) onwards for the city, and from around a point during the reign of Khyan and later for the Palace, through to the (likely) attack of Ahmose in the mid-16th century BC. The Tell el-ᶜAjjul evidence suggests that the early WSI style of west/northwestern Cyprus was in existence from before and/or around the reign of Khyan. On the basis of the only useful evidence, the Turin Canon, and an assumed end of the Hyksos Dynasty c.1540/1537BC, von Beckerath (1997:137) suggests that the reign of Khyan dates c.1610/1607 to 1590/1587BC. The Tell el-ᶜAjjul evidence is thus entirely consistent with the find of, and dating of, a similar early WSI style bowl in a later 17th century BC context on Thera. Therefore, the available evidence for the development and chronology of early WS ceramics is not inconsistent with, and arguably even supports, an 'early' chronology for LCIA, and in turn the LMIA period and the eruption of Thera.

Although I can sense the tangible disbelief of a few readers with a vested interest in the low chronology, we may thus conclude that the presence of the early WSI style bowl on Thera does not in any way preclude an 'early' date for the eruption of Thera, and the LMIA period. The conclusion above does not, of course, rule out a later date; but it does mean that the 'early' chronology is entirely plausible. The WSI finds from 18th Dynasty or LBA Tell el-Dabᶜa are likely to be quite distinct, both regionally, and especially chronologically, from the early WSI of Thera, MBA Tell el-ᶜAjjul, and LCIA Toumba tou Skourou and related horizon in west/northwest Cyprus. It is unfortunate that there is at present a conspicuous lack of independent chronometric evidence relevant to the dates of either PWS or WSI from Cyprus which could confirm or deny the interpretation from the ceramic data. As outlined in Manning (1996:21 n.9), a solitary radiocarbon date relevant to the last phase at Episkopi *Phaneromeni* in southern Cyprus, which sees the appearance of WPV and PWS (see above), but not yet WSI, suggests a *terminus post quem* range for WSI from somewhere in *either* the 17th or 16th centuries BC (i.e. a radiocarbon age range broadly contemporary with the radiocarbon evidence from LMIA Akrotiri).[910] This could be consistent with either an early 17th century BC appearance of the ware, or a mid-16th century BC appearance as Bietak argues, and so offers no independent resolution (while in probability terms rather favouring the earlier, or longer, chronology). If securely linked to the context of the PWS, the radiocarbon dating of the short-lived seed samples recovered from the final phase at Episkopi *Phaneromeni* might offer crucial, directly relevant, chronological data on this point.[911]

---

[909] See the important review of early WS finds in Canaan in Oren (n.d.). This replaces Gittlen (1975) and relevant parts of Gittlen (1977).

[910] HD7071–6609, 3350±100BP. With the OxCal programme (Ramsey 1995) and the INTCAL98 radiocarbon calibration curve (Stuiver *et al.* 1998), the 1σ calibrated calendar age range is 1746–1517BC. With the 1993 decadal calibration curve on German wood measured at Seattle (Stuiver and Becker 1993), the 1σ calibrated calendar age range is 1736–1705BC (P=0.12), 1694–1498BC (P=0.88).

[911] The seeds are mentioned by Carpenter (1981:65). An AMS programme might prove fruitful.

CONCLUSION AND SUGGESTED OUTLINE SEQUENCE

A number of strands have been pursued in this and the preceding two sections (Chapter IV.3 and 4), and it is time to bring them together. First, evidence from Cyprus shows that LMIA imports link both with earliest LCIA in southern Cyprus (Maroni *Vournes*) and early LCIA in northwest Cyprus (Toumba tou Skourou). The early WSI bowl from Thera, and the LC late handmade Red Slip, possible/probable PWS, Proto Base Ring, Monochrome, and BRI finds in LMIA (progressively from the Early, Advanced, and Final phases) at Kommos, offer reciprocal evidence. The west/ northwest Cypriot LCIA and eastern 'MCIII'-style/LCIA Cypriot horizons link directly with the later MBA period of Palestine (and the MBIIC or MBIII period): this section. The later MBA period of Palestine is itself linked directly back to pre-eruption LMIA Thera via artefact finds at Akrotiri, the jewellery represented in the frescoes painted at Thera, and the Aegeanising frescoes found at Tel Kabri and Alalakh (Chapter IV.3 and 4). LMIA is thus largely parallel to the late MBII period (SIP) and world system driven out of greater Canaan (Chapter IV.4 above, and see also Chapter IV.7 below). The potential historical chronology comes via Palestine and the Canaanite Nile Delta. The broad horizon is the late MBII period, or what is referred to as the MBIIC or MBIII period. This is conventionally dated c.1650–1550BC. Further, the pre-Thera-eruption relationship specifically dates to, or at least begins, in the pre-Bichrome Ware stage, or from before, to around, the reign of Khyan. This requires the first half of the above span; such a date range is consistent with, and supportive of, the 'early' Aegean chronology which dates mature LMIA to the same later 17th century BC period.

Classic or later WSI style products of the LCIB period are then found in later export contexts. In the Aegean and on Cyprus this horizon generally corresponds to the time period of LMIB/LHIIA. These Aegean phases end *during* the reign of Tuthmosis III, and perhaps rather early (see Chapter IV.7 below). In the Levant, later WSI correlates with the time range from the close of the MBA period through the LBI period up to the time of Tuthmosis III.

WSI style and production, *in toto*, early to late, thus occupies a significant chronological period, from the later 17th century BC through to the early 15th century BC – some c.150–175 years.

To return now to where this section began (p. 150 above), and Bietak's view of WSI as an obstacle for the Aegean high chronology. I think we have to view Bietak's argument for a start of the 18th Dynasty *terminus post quem* as clearly not sound. His dating evidence is at best relevant only to the distinct 'open', 'light', style of classic or later, LCIB period, WSI, and not to the early WSI style of LCIA of which the Thera bowl is a conspicuous example. The presence of an early WSI bowl on pre-eruption Thera in no way precludes a SIP date for this context in Egyptian terms, and does not require a correlation with the first 'secondary context' finds of a few pieces of classic or later LCIB period WSI at Tell el-Dab^ca.

The approximate summary sequence I suggest is as follows (see also Figures 36 and 62):

(i)   later MM (and even start MMIIIB/LMIA transition) = late MC. See WPIV jug from Kommos. Tell el-Dab^ca stratum E/1. This marks the transition also from

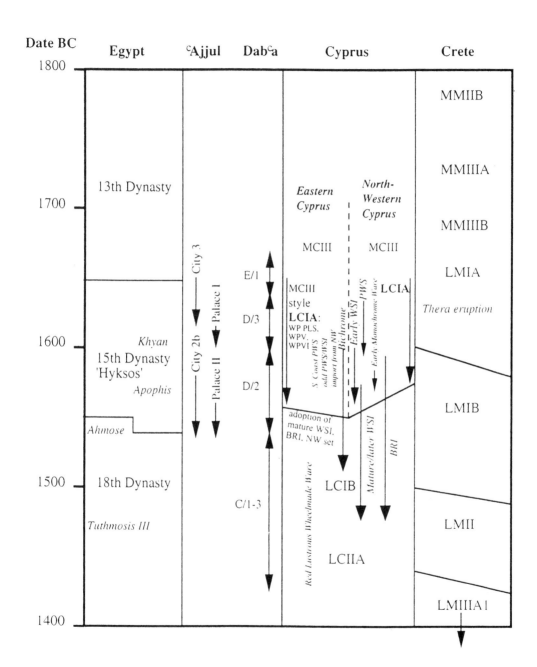

Fig. 36. Proposed chronology for later MC to LCIB Cyprus with the Aegean, Tell el-ᶜAjjul and Tell el-Dabᶜa. (Same as Fig. 62)

the later MC WP Cross Line Style and WP Pendent Line Style to the end MC and then LCIA 'WPV–VI' (begins in stratum E/2), 'WPV' (in reasonable quantity from stratum E/1), Red on Black (stratum E/1), and Red Slip (stratum E/1).[912] Further, it should be remembered that in eastern Cyprus, WP CLS is not solely late MC, but is also very typical of LCI contexts, with the transition to a predominance of WP PLS versus CLS perhaps a diagnostic feature that demarcates LCIA on the basis of Åström's (1966) sequence (layers 71, 70) at Kalopsidha.[913] In the proportional occurrence diagrams of Maguire (1995) for Cypriot pottery at Tell el-Dab^ca, only in Area II is WP PLS dominant (more MC), whereas in Areas A/IV and F/I CLS is clearly predominant (more LCIA). (Some influences from Aegean polychrome, and polychrome geometric design, styles start to reach the east Mediterranean from MMIIIB/early LMIA, early LHI, Middle Cycladic/early Late Cycladic I, and link in with WP tradition to form the origin of Cypriot Bichrome Ware in eastern Cyprus.)

(ii) Early to mature LMIA = earlier LCIA (LCIA1). Tell el-Dab^ca stratum E/1–D/3. WPV exports continue to Tell el-Dab^ca from eastern/southeastern Cyprus. Tell el-Yahudiyeh juglets travel in opposite direction. First inlaid dagger deposited in 'MHIIIB' = MMIIIB/LMIA transition to early LMIA grave N in circle B at Mycenae.[914] PWS sherd to Miletus from west/northwest Cyprus. LC late handmade Red Slip, and possible/probable PWS, exports to Kommos now, or, for the PWS, into (iii) below.

(iii) mature LMIA = LCIA. See LMIA sherds from initial LCIA at Maroni *Vournes* (or ii. above), and niche burial, Tomb III at Toumba tou Skourou. Enkomi and east/southeast still predominantly 'MC' in style with WP (Merrillees 1971 model revised), as are their exports to the Levant and Egypt, and we might also add the WP Pendent Line Style sherd from Zakros on Crete and late WP CLS and PLS from Tell el-Dab^ca strata D/3. PWS in west and south Cyprus. The eastern Cypriot WPVI exports, and imitations thereof, found in both early and late settlement strata at SIP Tell el-Maskhuta in the Delta, and other sites, occur.[915] Initial western/northwestern Cyprus Monochrome exports to the Levant in late MBII. Tell el-Dab^ca stratum D/3. Later Tell el-Yahudiyeh juglets to eastern Cyprus, and as far as Thera. PWS to Levant now and into (iv) below. LMIA-style frescoes painted at later, but not final, MBA Tel Kabri and Alalakh.

(iv) Mature to later LMIA. LCIA1/2 transition early WSI bowl exported to later LMIA Akrotiri on Thera, presumably from the west/northwest of Cyprus (and probably Toumba tou Skourou region, or perhaps Paphos region). Similar exports to Palace I Tell el-^cAjjul, and Proto Base Ring, early BRI, and early Monochrome exports to late LMIA Kommos from the same west/northwest region of Cyprus. Enkomi yet to adopt WSI (exports still 'MCIII' in style, but of LCIA date – the WPV–VI and associated material [cf. Maguire 1995:55 noting transition between 'Cypriot

[912] Maguire (1992:Fig.2); Bietak and Hein (n.d.) for the Red Slip.
[913] See also Merrillees (1971:65–66).
[914] Dietz (1991:298 with Figs.78 and 93).
[915] Redmount (1993:4; 1995:71).

MBA wares, such as the classic PLS and CLS styles, and what would appear to be later so-called WPV wares ... the late Hyksos settlement revealed in Area AV ... illustrates this succession']). Later phase of WPVI at Tell el-Maskhuta. PWS still produced and exported, perhaps especially from/via south and southwest, whereas northwest region has gone PWS–WSI transitional to early WSI (i.e. Thera bowl above). Bichrome Ware appears in eastern Cyprus in early, but perhaps not earliest, LCIA onwards; exports follow.[916] Tell el-Dabᶜa stratum D/3 mid to later. Bichrome Ware at Tell el-Dabᶜa from stratum D/2–D/3 and D/2 period.[917] Late Tell el-Yahudiyeh juglets exported to eastern Cyprus and as far as Thera. Hyksos LMIA-style frescoes painted? Eruption of Thera.

(v) late/final LMIA continues through LCIA2, and includes early in LCIA2, or at LCIA1/2 transition, the eruption of Thera (above). See Tomb I imports at Toumba tou Skourou. Tell el-ᶜAjjul continues to receive earlier to mature WSI. Overall LMIA period, including a post-LMIA-eruption phase, ends around or during the reign of Khyan. Enkomi and the east and south still have not adopted WSI, and continue to produce largely late 'MC'-style products, and the southcoast has PWS. Main clear Cypriot Bichrome Ware export phase. Tell el-Dabᶜa D/3 to D/2. Eastern Cypriot products arrive at Tell el-Dabᶜa (so far no, or no in context, northwestern products, but early WSI may very well be found in the future, and one or two SIP residual sherds are already possible candidates). BRI (from west/northwest Cyprus?) is available for deposit at Memphis by now or just before (and note BRI seems to appear slightly before WSI in several areas on Cyprus especially in the south and east). Late Hyksos period LMIA-style to hybrid frescoes painted at Tell el-Dabᶜa? Final Tell el-Yahudiyeh juglet production.

(vi) Early LMIB/LHIIA = LCIA/B transition to early LCIB (interpolated, rather than securely attested). Mature to later WSI appears at Tell el-ᶜAjjul before the close of the MBA. Final MBA phase in Levant. Tell el-Dabᶜa stratum D/2. Late Hyksos period early LMIB-style to hybrid frescoes painted at Tell el-Dabᶜa? This period is the least satisfactory in terms of correlations, but it must be remembered that, at the beginning of the period, the Aegean close of LMIA and early LMIB linkages may have been significantly affected by the consequences of the eruption of Thera, including the loss of the international port of Akrotiri on Thera, while, at the end of the period, late Tell el-Dabᶜa stratum D/2 trade relations may have been interrupted to some (even significant) extent by warfare (from seige of Kamose through reign of Khamudy, perhaps last c.15 or more years).

(vii) LCIB = mature LMIB/LHIIA phases to the close of the LMIB/LHIIA periods,

---

[916] It is striking that Toumba tou Skourou has only a small quantity of poor quality Bichrome Ware, despite its significant assemblage of MCIII–LCI ceramic material (I thank Kathryn Eriksson for highlighting this to me). In conformity with the archaeometric analyses showing Bichrome Ware's eastern Cypriot origin in the area around Enkomi (Artzy *et al.* 1973; 1978; 1981; Artzy 1973), this rather suggests that it was not a local product of north-western Cyprus (as stated by Vermeule and Wolsky 1990:385), and hence it might appear that Bichrome Ware is another aspect of the west–east split in MCIII–LCIA Cyprus.

[917] Maguire (1992:Fig.2) for D/2–D/3 beginning.

and the early 18th Dynasty to the early years of Tuthmosis III.[918] Classic late
phase WSI style exports, and other LCIB exports, such as Red Lustrous
Wheelmade Ware, go to LMIB Crete and Rhodes, and classic LCIB onwards BR
is exported around the east Mediterranean.[919] LHIIA/LMIB exports go to LCIB
contexts on Cyprus,[920] and contexts in the east Mediterranean with LCIB
products.[921] If correctly identified, and if a contemporary export, a serpentine
vessel with the cartouche of Ahmose arrives in Cyprus. LCIB period mature–
late WSI imports to Tell el-Dabᶜa H/I–IV area, early 18th Dynasty.

6. Tempest Stela of Ahmose

In a recent article Foster and Ritner (1996) argue that a record of a major storm during
the reign of Ahmose might be linked to the effects of the eruption of Thera, and so
provide a date for the eruption c.1530BC, and thus provide evidence in support of the
'low' Aegean chronology. This record is inscribed on a stela found at Karnak (Thebes)
in Egypt, and is referred to as the 'Tempest Stela of Ahmose'. It is not, however, a new
text; it had been included or discussed a number of times in Egyptological literature[922]
– although it had not entered into the literature and discussions of the Aegean field
before Davis (1990a). It is not appropriate or necessary here to engage in a long and
detailed discussion of everything relevant to the article of Foster and Ritner, since a
response by Wiener and Allen (1998) offers a full critique and commentary. However,
since the article of Foster and Ritner (1996) claims to provide a case exactly contrary
to the overall thesis found to be plausible in the present book, it is necessary to present
a brief review. The general summary is that the assumption of Foster and Ritner –
linking the events described to a major earthquake, and associating this with a volcanic
eruption (which they propose is Thera) – is completely unwarranted, and in fact likely
to be false from an analysis of the text itself.[923]

   The first major problem is the translation of the text offered by Foster and Ritner
(1996:11–12). It appears less than satisfactory in several regards, and the translations
of either Allen or Redford are to be preferred.[924] This more or less rules out reference
to, or agency by, an earthquake.[925] Since this was the only link to a specific volcano-
related hypothesis, the central proposal of Foster and Ritner (1996) is also rendered
most unlikely or unnecessary.[926] The text of the Tempest Stela after the translations of

---

[918] See below Chapter IV.7; Graziadio (1995); Eriksson (1992); Warren and Hankey (1989:116–117).
[919] See Catling (1991); Eriksson (1991; 1992:177–181; 1993); Merrillees (1968).
[920] See Graziadio (1995); Eriksson (1992:172–173, 181).
[921] E.g. Saqqara Tomb NE1: Warren and Hankey (1989:117, 144); Merrillees (1968:21–22); see Chapter IV.7.
[922] E.g. Vandersleyen (1967); Helck (1975:no.124); Goedicke (1992:60–61 and refs. in note 50); Porter
and Moss (1994a:73 and refs.); Baillie (1995a:154–156).
[923] Similar scepticism is expressed by Ryholt (1997:144–148).
[924] Allen in Wiener and Allen (1998:3–6); Redford (1997:16). See also comments of Ryholt (1997:144–
145).
[925] See especially Wiener and Allen (1998:19–20).
[926] See Wiener and Allen (1998).

first Allen in Wiener and Allen (1998:3–6), and then second Foster and Ritner (1996:11–12), follows (and, for the critical description of the 'storm', also the translation of Redford 1997:16). The text appears on both sides of the stela, although the layout differs, with just 18 lines of text on the front (F), but 21 on the back (B). The stela is damaged, with approximately a quarter of the original text lost. The first ten lines in particular are very fragmentary, and some lacunae remain despite the best efforts of proposed readings and textual restorations. This is critical for the 'storm'. As Davis (1990a:232) writes, the locations of the missing text means that there are 'many lacunae in the metrological description'. The other problems concern the meaning or interpretation of the text.

Lines 0–3
(i) Wiener and Allen
[Regnal Year 1 ... during the Incarnation of the Horus "Great of Developments", Two Ladies "Perfect of Birth", Gold Falcon "Who knots together the Two Lands", King of Upper and Lower Egypt NEB-PEHTI-RE, Son of Re AHMOSE, alive forever – at the coming of His Incarnation [to ...], the Sun himself having designated him king; for though His Incarnation had settled in the habour-town of "Provisioner of the Two Lands" [...] of the south of Dendera, A[mun-Re, lord of thrones of the Two Lands] was in Thebes.

(ii) Foster and Ritner
(1) [Long live the Horus "Great of Manifestations," He of the] Two Ladies "Pleasing of Birth," the golden Horus "Who Binds the Two Lands," King of Upper and Lower Egypt, Neb-pehty-ra, son of Ra, Ahmose, living forever. Now then, His Majesty came [...] (2) Ra himself had appointed him to be King of Upper Egypt. Then His Majesty dwelt at the town of Sedjefa-tawy (3) [in the district just to] the south of Dendera, while A[mon-Ra, Lord of the Thrones of the Two Lands was] in Thebes.

Lines 3–6 F, 3–8 B
(i) Wiener and Allen
Then His Incarnation sailed upstream to [give him a] pure [...]. Now, after this offer[ing-ceremony ... th]em, and they were put on the [... in/of] this [nome], while the processional image [...], his body united with this temple, his limbs in joy. [Then His Incarnation sailed downstream to the Palace, 1lp. But] this great [god] was desiring [that] His Incarnation [return to him, while] the gods were asking for [all] their cult services.

(ii) Foster and Ritner
It was His Majesty (4) who sailed south to offer [bread, beer, and everything good] and pure. Now after the offering [...] (5) then attention was given in [...] this [district (?)]. Now then, the cult image [of this god...] (6) as his body was installed in this temple while he was in joy. (7) Now then, this great god desired [...] His Majesty [...] while the gods declared their (8) discontent.

Lines 6–10 F, 8–12 B
(i) Wiener and Allen
[Then] the gods [made] the sky come in a storm of r[ain, with dark]ness in the western region and the sky beclouded without [stop, loud]er than [the sound of] the subjects, strong[er than ... howling(?)] on the hills more than the sound of the cavern in Elephantine. Then every house and every habitation they reached [perished and those in them died, their corpses] floating on the water like skiffs of papyrus, (even) in the doorway and the private apartments (of the palace), for a period of up to [...] days, while no torch could give light over the Two Lands.

(ii) Foster and Ritner
The gods [caused] the sky to come in a tempest of r[ain], with darkness in the western region and the sky being (9) unleashed without [cessation, louder than] the cries of the masses, more powerful than [...], [while the rain raged (?) on the mountains louder than the noise of the (10) cataract which is at Elephantine. Every house, every quarter that they reached ...] (11) floating on the water like skiffs of papyrus opposite the royal residence for a period of [...] days, (12) while a torch could not be lit in the Two Lands.

(iii) Redford
they were angry [...] of (?) the gods. They sky came on with a [rain]-storm, and [darkness] was in the western heavens; (9) it rained without [let-up...the cr]y of the people, powerful [...] [the thunder] upon the mountains, louder than the noise of (10) the 'Cavern' which is in Abydos. Then every house collapsed and hut [where] they had repaired [collapsed and the detritus was] (11) in the flood of water; like reed canoes, at the very gate by the palace; and for a period of [...] days (12) no lamp was ever lit in the Two Lands.

Lines 11–14 F, 12–16 B
(i) Wiener and Allen
Then His Incarnation said: "How much greater is this than the impressive manifestation of the great god, than the plans of the gods"! What His Incarnation did was to go down to his launch, with his council behind him and [his] army on the east and west (banks) providing cover, there being no covering on them after the occurrence of the god's impressive manifestation. What His Incarnation did was to arrive at the interior of Thebes, and gold encountered the gold of his processional image, so that he received what he had desired. Then His Incarnation was stabilising the Two Lands and guiding the flooded areas. He did not stop, feeding them with silver, with gold, with copper, with oils and clothing, with every need that could be desired.

(ii) Foster and Ritner
Then His Majesty said: "how much greater this is than the wrath of the great god, than the plans of the gods!" Then His Majesty descended (13) to his boat, with his council following him, while the crowds on the East and West had hidden faces, having no clothing on them (14) after the manifestation of the god's wrath.

Then His Majesty reached the interior of Thebes, with gold confronting (?) gold for this statue so that he (i.e., Amon-Ra) received that which he desired. (15) Then His Majesty began to reestablish the Two Lands, to drain the flooded territories without his [...], to provide them with silver, with (16) gold, with copper, with oil, and cloth of every bolt that could be desired.

Lines 14–18 F, 16–21 B
(i) Wiener and Allen
What His Incarnation did was to rest in the palace, 1ph. Then one was reminding His Incarnation of the entering of the sacred estates, the dismantling of tombs, the hacking up of mortuary enclosures, and the toppling of pyramids – how what had never been done (before) had been done. Then His Incarnation commanded to make firm the temples that had fallen to ruin in this entire land: to make functional the monuments of the gods, to erect their enclosure walls, to put the sacred things in the special room, to hide the secret places, to cause the processional images that were fallen to the ground to enter their shrine, to set up the braziers, to erect the altars and fix their offering-loaves, to double the income of office-holders – to put the land like its original situation. Then it was done like everything that His Incarnation commanded to do.

(ii) Foster and Ritner
Then his Majesty made himself comfortable inside the palace (life! prosperity! health!). (17) Then His Majesty was informed that the mortuary concessions had been entered (by water), with the tomb chambers collapsed, the funerary mansions undermined, and the pyramids fallen, (18) having been made into that which was never made. Then His Majesty commanded to restore the temples which had fallen into ruin in this entire land: to refurbish (19) the monuments of the gods, to erect their enclosure walls, to provide the sacred objects in the noble chamber, to mask the secret places, to introduce (20) into their shrines the cult statues which were cast to the ground, to set up the braziers, to erect the offering tables, to establish their bread offerings, (21) to double the income of the personnel, to put the land into its former state. Then it was done in accordance with everything that His Majesty had commanded.

Let us now review the main problems and issues with the case of Foster and Ritner (1996).

(i) Location, date and context
This is very specific and significant, and should inform interpretation of the entire document. Ahmose has clearly just become king. He appears to have been in the town 'Provisioner of the Two Lands' south of Dendera. This title belongs to Kamose according to Redford.[927] The location is, as Vandersleyen suggests, probably one of

---

[927] Redford (1997:31 n.175) referring to an oral communication from H. Goedicke.

the palaces at Ballas, perhaps the fortress of Deir el-Ballas built by Kamose as a base for his military campaign against the Hyksos. The point of the opening section is:

> The two clauses, together with the mention of the king's "designation" in l.2, suggest that Ahmose had been crowned outside Thebes [due to the death of Kamose], perhaps at his residence in Ballas. In that case, he would have had an obligation as one of his first official duties to visit Karnak, where his coronation could be confirmed by Amun-Re, "lord of thrones of the Two Lands"[928]

> ...the stela probably dates to Ahmose's first regnal year; this conclusion is supported by several orthographic features of the text.[929]

The text is thus evidently very much concerned with the divine legitimation of Ahmose, and with the restoration of Egypt (of the two lands) – the prime mission of the late 17th Dynasty kings. In a key sense, the text is thus *not* about the storm at all. This is a device to accentuate the overall purpose: the restoration of order after the disorder of the Hyksos (who are referred to metaphorically as a great destructive storm[930]). The year 1 date, nonetheless, rules out any link to the events referred to in the entry on the Rhind Mathematical Papyrus shortly before the fall of Avaris (a decade or more later): the sound of thunder and the rain from heaven.[931]

An example of the need for a more subtle interpretation – compared to the literal one offered by Foster and Ritner – is lines 8 F to 9 or 9 B to 10: 'loud]er than [the sound of] the subjects, strong[er than ... howling(?)] on the hills more than the sound of the cavern in Elephantine'. As Wiener and Allen (1998:19) note, this is the only place an earthquake could be mentioned (as argued by Foster and Ritner) in one or two missing clauses beginning with 'strong'. But the real point of this sentence is the 'sound of the cavern in Elephantine'. Foster and Ritner express this totally literally as the cataract on the Nile, but Redford (1997:31 n.178) is surely correct to note that the 'cavern' at Abydos is referred to, and so 'the wailing for Osiris in the pantomime of his passion, enacted yearly at Abydos'.

(ii) The tempest stela text itself

This is an interesting narrative, but dramatic accounts of major floods, storms, and similar events are a feature of several Egyptian records (and especially of important rulers or historical moments),[932] along with other ancient Near Eastern and derived texts, including of course the Bible, Manetho (e.g. frag.42)[933] where a 'blast of god smote us', and Artapanos who records 'But as the king still persisted in his folly, Moses

---

[928] Wiener and Allen (1998:7).
[929] Wiener and Allen (1998:17).
[930] Also Ryholt (1997:144).
[931] Redford (1997:16 no.71). This text is dated to year 11 of an unknown king. However, it seems very likely that the southern prince referred to is Ahmose, and hence the document probably dates to Khamudy year 11: see discussion in Appendix 1.
[932] Goedicke (1992:60–61) offers examples for Amenhotep I, Ahmose, and Hatshepsut.
[933] Preserved in Josephus, *Contra Apionem* I.75.

caused hail and earthquakes by night, so that those who fled from the earthquakes were killed by the hail, and those who sought shelter from the hail were destroyed by earthquakes. And at that time all the houses fell in and most of the temples'.[934] Note especially the ending; it alerts us to the generic construction of an Egyptian 'disaster'; it is the same *topos* as in the Ahmose stele. In all cases, there is a lack of clear evidence that these literary phrases, or devices, are to be directly connected with the historical, climatic, or geological record. Foster and Ritner acknowledge that similar accounts exist in many sources (p.5), but fail to explain why their single example is so special, merely suggesting that the destruction was more severe than any other such storm.[935] One especially wonders why they do not discuss the other various major storms and events of Hatshepsut year 7 and Ahmose's reign to which Goedicke has drawn attention, the former referring to nine days of raging storms and total darkness?[936] The conclusion must be that there are all too many such dramatic storms, and there is no clear evidence or reason to associate any particular one with the eruption of Thera on present evidence. Moreover, a volcanically induced storm is in fact unlikely to have wrecked Egypt in the way the Ahmose stela inscription describes (flooding in the upper Nile – around Thebes as described in the stela – typically relates to Monsoonal-belt storms and rainfall). A similar and analogous problem surrounds the account and date of the Exodus of the Israelites.[937] The darkness that could be felt, and the column of fire, tempt one to make an association with the Thera eruption,[938] but no firm data exists by which to date the Exodus, and to know with what exactly to associate it.[939]

(iii) Political-cultural context
One wonders whether Foster and Ritner might not be mistakenly treating as literal what is in fact an obviously metaphorical text dating to, and related to, the accession of a new ruler (Ahmose, succeeding Kamose)? We perhaps should return again to the

---

[934] The extant portions of Artapanos' original work on the Jews are to be found in Jacoby (1958:no.726). This particular passage is preserved in Eusebius' *Praeparatio Evangelica* 9.27.33. The passage is cited by Rohl (1995:284).

[935] It should be noted that any supposed analogies from non-Egyptian sources are irrelevant: there is no evidence that the Egyptians thought and conceived of events and descriptions in the same way that other cultures in western Asia did.

[936] Goedicke (1992:61; 1986:40–41); see also Eriksson (1992:194).

[937] E.g., see Vandersleyen (1995:232–237) who discusses the date and debate in relation to the present topic. Hoffmeier (1997:150–151) draws an analogy between the seventh plague (*Exodus* 9:22–24) and the Ahmose Tempest stela, and notes how in both the storms are as a result of divine activity.

[938] Recently Bruins and van der Plicht (1996); previously e.g. works cited in Redford (1992:421n.136).

[939] Although, as Redford concludes, out of a morass of useless data and debate (1992:258–269), a memory of the Hyksos move into Egypt and subsequent removal is perhaps one likely origin for the story: Redford (1992:408–422); Assmann (1997:esp.28–43). Others, however, support later dates and varying degrees of greater historicity for the exodus tradition. The main 'conventional' date range for a semi-historical exodus is somewhere towards the close of the LBA (13th century BC) or in the earlier 12th century BC, see e.g. Hoffmeier (1997); Malamat (1997); Yurco (1997); and, with little enthusiasm, Weinstein (1997). For recent scholarly discussions on the subject, see Hoffmeier (1997) and Frerichs and Lesko (1997).

issue of the point of the inscription: the great and special power of Amun is stressed. How was this related to Ahmose? Very closely! The family of Ahmose (the *Theban* 17th Dynasty) had an especial affinity with the local Theban god Amun. Let us consider Redford (1967:70):

> Since the rebellion against the Hyksos had begun right in Thebes, it was Amun himself who had rebelled against the Hyksos Baal. And if Thebes had won, had it not been Amun who had triumphed over Baal? *Ipso facto* Amun was destined to receive the booty, and the free-will gifts of king and people besides. Ahmose set about to embellish the small provincial shrine that had survived from Middle Kingdom times, and presented to the gods the spoils of his wars and all sorts of cultic paraphernalia. Overnight, as it were, Amun of the backwoods, so long impoverished during the years when Thebes was cut off from the products of Asia and Kush, found himself the possessor of vast riches undreamed of two generations earlier.

This is a text which concerns the founder of a new dynasty, the conqueror of the Hyksos, a ruler who is the bringer of order, and the restorer of the Egyptian state. Moreover, it is about the founder of a new dynasty which stressed its continuity from the previous 12th Dynasty.[940] Major events and changes in Egyptian history are often set in such dramatic, all-encompassing, terms; and the find of the stela at Karnak is not a coincidence. In both regards, one may compare especially the Restoration Stela of Tutankhamun.[941] The full text is not really about a specific flood, or earthquake, it is instead as much about the restoration of the Egyptian state: to the order and station of the Middle Kingdom and 12th Dynasty – after the dislocation (all-wrecking storm) of the Hyksos era, and the destruction of Middle Kingdom shrines and tombs under the 13th Dynasty and Hyksos.[942] Note especially the section:

> Then His Incarnation commanded to make firm the temples that had fallen to ruin in this entire land: to make functional the monuments of the gods, to erect their enclosure walls, to put the scared things in the special room, to hide the secret places, to cause the processional images that were fallen to the ground to enter their shrine, to set up the braziers, to erect the altars and fix their offering-loaves, to double the income of office-holders – *to put the land like its original situation* (my italics).

One might even argue that the whole Theban text is a symbolic encoding of Ahmose's defeat of the Hyksos, his fulfilling of Amun-Re's desires, and his creation of a new civilised order – e.g the victory of Theban Amun over Hyksos Baal. As Goedicke (1992:61) argues, the 'dramatic' date is Kamose's final (3rd) year or

---

[940] See Redford (1967:78). For literature on the great Amun temple complex at Thebes, see Porter and Moss (1994:21–110).
[941] Bennett (1939).
[942] Compare also the Speos Artemidos Text of Hatshepsut (Breasted 1962, vol.II:§296–§303), and the story of Apophis and Seqenenre, see Redford (1997:16–18).

Ahmose's first year. This would not have been an easy time. Kamose, in a very short time of just three years, had waged successful campaigns to the south and then to the north to Avaris itself.[943] But his death was clearly a major setback for the Thebans. If our current chronology is correct, Ahmose required over a decade to recover to this position, and to mount his own finally successful military campaign against Avaris. It is also often assumed that Ahmose was only young on accession. The need to stress his divine propriety, favour, and power, would have been critical. A key section is perhaps: 'What His Incarnation did was to go down to his launch, with his council behind him and [his] army on the east and west (banks) providing cover, there being no covering on them after the occurrence of the god's impressive manifestation'. It is difficult to know exactly how to read this.[944] Why is the army providing cover for the king's river journey? Wiener and Allen (1998:19) suggest that 'the extra measure of security may have been deemed necessary either because of the unrest attendant on Ahmose's ongoing struggle with the rival Hyksos regime or because the king feared being overwhelmed by a population demanding relief from the disaster, if not both'. In either case, and especially if Ahmose was just a young boy (?), it suggests a degree of crisis of a *political* nature, and the immediate need to highlight the divine-sanctioned station of the new king *in Thebes*. Pharaoh's special relationship with Amun-Re was his basis of power: 'What His Incarnation did was to arrive at the interior of Thebes, and gold encountered the gold of his processional image, so that he received what he had desired'. Ahmose then acts as the restorer of Egypt, both immediately and literally with the relief of the Tempest, and generally by restoring the sanctuaries of the other gods, and rebuilding (and linking to) the desired state as under the 12th Dynasty.

(iv) Some of the details do not match the hypothesis of Foster and Ritner
For example, the 'darkness' is actually mentioned as only in the western region. And the west is not exactly where you would expect a hypothesised Theran darkness to be. Thera is to the northwest, and given the easterly distribution of ash from the eruption, and the easterly direction of atmospheric circulation in the northern hemisphere at mid-latitude, a darkness in the 'north' would be expected – if anywhere. The torches are mentioned separately. The rains raged on the mountains, but what mountains are these – presumably those in Middle-Upper Egypt, and, like Thebes, a very long way from Thera? All sorts of things, hyperboles, are being dragged into a typical cataclysm account.

Moreover, a volcanically induced storm is in fact unlikely to have wrecked Egypt in the way the Ahmose stela inscription describes. It is actually a long way, more than 1300km, from Thera to Thebes and not in the direction of tephra fall and atmospheric transport.[945] The violent storms associated with major Plinian volcanic eruptions are

---

[943] It has long been assumed that Kamose campaigned in the south (Nubia), but Krauss (1993) argues that there is in fact no solid evidence for this assumption. Thus Kamose may only have fought the Hyksos.
[944] See Wiener and Allen (1998:13–14).
[945] It has been claimed that traces of Theran tephra fall were found in the Nile Delta – still a long way

confined to the region of the volcano. Some effect (i.e. cloud and even a storm) might have travelled further away, but south and east to Egypt is not the most likely direction for maximum impact – which would have been easterly and then gradually northerly given the general circulation patterns in the atmosphere. The text refers to a rainstorm and severe flooding. This is distinct from a Nile Flood (seasonal event), but nonetheless, a flood in the Nile will be caused by unusual rainfall in its relevant catchment areas. Since the flooding in the text appears most notable at Thebes in Upper Egypt, the rainfall must have been in (or included particularly) this area, and the region further south, in order to lead to floods here.[946] Rainfall leading to flooding in far south/ Upper Egypt relates to storms now well over 1,500km from Thera in the northern equatorial climate zone.[947] Storms here are unlikely to derive solely from the Thera eruption, but instead will have been related to Monsoonal-belt storms and rainfall – usually a late Autumn/early Winter threat, such as the devastating rainfall and floods in October–November 1994 which affected Upper Egypt[948] – even if some mid-latitude to equatorial latitude spill-over of Thera eruption effects might have contributed to unusual weather following the eruption.

The very dramatic and all-encompassing scale of effects apparently felt in Egypt due to the storm event are notable. Although, one might compare the Tutankhamun Restoration Stela, or the Speos Artemidos inscription of Hatshepsut.[949] The latter refers to the terrible disorder of the Hyksos period and the delivery of Egypt and its restoration under Hatshepsut. A non-literal genre appears evident.

Moreover, if, as Foster and Ritner suggest, this havoc is to be literally interpreted, and is the outcome of a massive volcanic eruption, and if this is dated as they argue c.1530BC (p.10), then it must be of some serious concern that none (of the several) northern hemisphere records of past major volcanism reveal *any* major volcanic event at all at this time (see Chapter V.2 below). The evidence from these records shows no major volcanic eruption within a generation or more of c.1530BC. The possible earlier 16th century BC events are well before Ahmose was born, unless a radical review of Egyptian chronology is considered. The later 17th century BC major volcanic event is

---

north of Thebes – in an article by Stanley and Sheng (1986). However, as noted earlier in Chapter II, it should be observed that it is fact most unlikely, if not impossible, that these glass shards are from the Minoan eruption of Thera: see Figure 54.a below. Their chemical compositions are very significantly different from those for the Thera eruption products. See Guichard *et al.* (1993:esp. Fig.2); Liritzis *et al.* (1996); and Eastwood *et al.* (1998:679, referring to a forthcoming study by Eastwood *et al.* 1999:24–26).

[946] Storms in Nubia or Punt are associated with Nile floods in ancient sources: Lloyd (1975:54–55); also Wiener and Allen (1998:18 n.17).

[947] Typically, floods in Middle–Upper Egypt are the result of monsoonal-derived storms and rainfall in equatorial Africa (see Lamb 1988:194–214), and in particular in the region around and feeding into Lake Victoria (near the equator) and the Nile river system. For example, when the level of Lake Victoria rose by almost 2m in 1961, the discharge into the Nile doubled from $20km^3$ to $41km^3$ a year (Lamb 1988:203). This caused disastrous floods. The alternative is unusual direct rainfall in Upper Egypt, or Nubia, or ancient Punt causing flooding (Wiener and Allen 1998:18 and n.17). Again, a link to Thera some 1,500km away is not clear.

[948] Referred to by Wiener and Allen (1998:18).

[949] Gardiner (1946); Fairman and Grdseloff (1947).

even earlier again. Thus a link between the Tempest Stela and a major volcanic eruption is doubtful.[950] There is also a conspicuous lack of archaeological evidence for such a devastating storm and flood – especially in the Delta (e.g. Tell el-Dabᶜa) where its effects might have been most severe.

(v) The references to darkness must also be explored in possible non-literal terms
The Egyptians were very concerned with the threat of being plunged into permanent darkness;[951] hence the central importance of the universal creator, Amun-Re, who was light, and who was reborn/resurrected during the darkness and brought the new sunrise (and so also the promise of life after death). Thus the great devotion to him, and the care put into being ready for the sunrise each morning. The failure of the torches might thus be the might/wrath of god. Moreover, the religious connection and the role of Pharaoh as intermediary is stressed. The pharaoh was after all the son of Re and responsible for Egypt's well-being. Note that the lack of clothing may even link in here in a metaphorical context (devotees/priests of Amun-Re of course had to be pure). Pharaoh goes to the divine statue, and light is reborn.

(vi) Relevance of human agency, and no link in text between storm and most of the damage
Foster and Ritner link together the storm and damage described after line 17 – problems Ahmose is 'reminded' about. They also suggest an associated earthquake. But Wiener and Allen (1998:20, 25) point out that the text specifies that this other damage was purposeful damage, caused therefore by human agency. The damage relates to things in the realm of the gods and a proper respect for the past. This damage Ahmose then properly sets to right. There is no actual connection made in the text between the tempest/storm of earlier in the text, and these actions once Ahmose is king, except that they offer a parallel: the first of dramatic contemporary damage by a storm which Ahmose relieves, and the second of a long-standing situation (SIP era) which Ahmose also sets to rights.

(vii) Conclusion: no Thera link
And so, contra Foster and Ritner (p.10), the Ahmose stela is not a 'straightforward description of storms, darkness, noise, and damage throughout Egypt'. The specific historical, yet alone chronological, relevance is not established. No link to a volcanic eruption or associated earthquakes is established. This 'text' should not be considered as relevant to the present discussion on the chronology of the Thera eruption and the Aegean LBA.

This is also the moment to mention that there are a number of other ancient literary texts which might possibly, or potentially, be associated with a large volcanic eruption

---

[950] Critics might cite the Theran pumice found at Tell el-Dabᶜa from contexts dating after the reign of Ahmose to before the reign of Tuthmosis III (see Chapter IV.4 above). Yet the text dates the storm to Ahmose year 1. His reign was at least 22 (and probably 25 years) long, and the two contexts are clearly separate. They cannot be used to support a joint hypothesis.

[951] It is in this context that the ninth plague in the story of the Exodus sees the darkening of the sun, and thus Yahweh showing his superiority over the Egyptian creator-god.

in the mid-second millennium BC (17th–16th centuries BC). These range from Joseph and the famine in *Genesis* 41, to the Exodus of the Israelites from Egypt and the associated pestilence, storms, pillar of cloud/fire and parting of the sea (*Exodus* 8–9, 13–14), to Chinese, Mesopotamian, and Irish texts which may contain evidence of climatic or atmospheric anomalies, to the Greek legend of Atlantis or the events described in Hesiod's *Theogony*, and so on.[952] These data are either not precisely dated, or cannot definitely be linked with a volcanic eruption. A specific link with the Minoan eruption of Thera is most certainly not established. Therefore, while they are interesting, and tantalising, I do not discuss such data further with regard to the dating of the eruption of Thera.

7. Archaeology and the chronology of the Late Minoan IB period

In contrast to the extreme paucity of LMIA period/style products in Egypt (Chapter IV.4), a few distinctive mature LMIB style artefacts, and also rather more of their mainland LHIIA equivalents, have long been known from Egypt and the Near East.[953] Many of these LMIB/LHIIA objects in fact do not have secure contexts,[954] but of those that do most were found in contexts which are dated/related to the early 18th Dynasty, usually including the long reign of Tuthmosis III.[955] In addition, wall paintings from some tombs at Thebes in Egypt dated to the reign of Tuthmosis III show figures named as Keftiu (Aegeans), who were dressed like LMI Minoans, and carried objects reflecting LMI types:[956] see Figure 38 below (p.210). For many years, the archaeologically and historically 'visible' reign of Tuthmosis III was therefore regarded as offering a date for more or less the entire LMIB period. Over time, an approximation became a convention. This was an error; the evidence always indicated that the early 18th Dynasty prior to Tuthmosis III was also relevant.[957] Further, as Betancourt (1998b:292) reminds us, 'one must remember that the LMIB pottery we have as intact vases in Crete is from the very end of the period, at its destruction'. Thus the earlier part of the LMIB phase was prior

---

[952] Among much literature on such subjects, see e.g. Luce (1969); Scranton (1976); Ramage (1978); Vitaliano (1973:218–271); Pang and Chou (1985); Pang *et al.* (1988; 1989); Stanley and Sheng (1986:735); Warner (1990); Bernal (1991:278–319); Baillie (1995a:149–158). Greene (1992:esp.46–63) makes the specific claim that Hesiod's *Theogony* contains an account of the Thera eruption. He writes (p.54): 'I am suggesting that a detailed record of the actual eruption survived to be written down by Hesiod. In other words, that the details of an event which took place in the middle of the second millennium were accurately preserved (whether in oral tradition in Greece or in written form as part of a Near Eastern theogony) for more than seven hundred years, and faithfully recorded as a part of the story of the origins of the world and the gods'.

[953] Evans (1921–1935, vol.IV:269–276); Furumark (1950:203–215); Hankey and Warren (1974:146, 149–150); Helck (1979:83–92); Warren (1985:150–151); Warren and Hankey (1989:138–144); Hankey and Leonard (1998:32–33). Rodziewicz (1988:45) mentioned the finds of Mycenaean ceramics at the Treasury of Tuthmosis I at Karnak, but I am not aware of any further details.

[954] Merrillees (1980).

[955] Or contexts which might be so attributed, e.g. Lilyquist (1994:208 no.01).

[956] Especially the Senmut and Useramun Tombs: Wachsmann (1987:27–28, 31–32, pls.23, 27–32).

[957] See Merrillees (1972a) for a study which critiqued convention.

to these early 18th Dynasty to Tuthmosis III correlations with exported mature to late LMIB/LHIIA examples.

Artefact evidence now shows without doubt that mature LMIB/LHIIA style products were current during the early 18th Dynasty, before the reign of Tuthmosis III. It is even possible that evidence suggests that mature LMIB products were current by about the end of the Hyksos period in Egypt. The most important recent find is undoubtedly the small Minoan rim to neck sherd from Kom Rabica, Memphis: see Figure 37.a.[958] This sherd comes from a stratified settlement context (530).[959] Earlier imported material from the same context includes a Cypriot WPV Tangent Line Style sherd.[960] In a detailed study, Bourriau and Eriksson (1997) argue that context 530 at Kom Rabica dates from somewhere between the period after Ahmosis' conquest of Avaris to the end of the reign of Tuthmosis I (and following the SIP sand layer at the site[961]). The sherd is undoubtedly Minoan as they suggest (and not Mycenaean), and it is most likely of LMIB stylistic date, and probably from an LMIB bridge-spouted jar[962] with a 'sub-LMIA' = LMIB degenerative, or carelessly painted, foliate band motif.[963] It is not a dot band;[964] the careless foliate band motif,

Fig. 37. a. Drawing of the LMIB? sherd (RAT 530.1301) from Kom Rabica (Memphis), Egypt after Bourriau and Eriksson (1997: Fig. 9.1, pl. 1.a–c). b. and c. LMIB comparisons for the motif after Betancourt (1983:28 nos. 48 and 52).

with either one or two (or no) central bands is common, but is not LMIA in date (and is absent at Akrotiri). Comparisons for the decoration are instead LMIB:[965] see Figures

---

[958] Warren and Hankey (1989:139, RAT 530.1301); Eriksson (1992:169–170); Hankey and Leonard (1998:31 and n.18); Bourriau and Eriksson (1997). The sherd and context were described by J. Bourriau in lectures in New York and Philadelphia in 1989, and a written text circulated (1989); a proper publication is now available (Bourriau and Eriksson 1997); I thank Bourriau for letting me examine the sherd. I thank both Bourriau and Eriksson for correspondence and discussion on the sherd and the context.

[959] For context 530: see Bourriau (1997:Fig.6.3); Bourriau and Eriksson (1997:101–108, Fig.1).

[960] Bourriau and Eriksson (1997:107, Fig.9.2, pl.1.d–e).

[961] For which, see Bourriau (1997:161–163).

[962] As suggested by Bourriau and Eriksson (1997:97–98).

[963] A view supported by Prof. Philip P. Betancourt, whom I thank warmly for discussion and references.

[964] Contra Warren (1998:326).

[965] E.g. Betancourt (1983:28 nos. 48 and 52).

37.b. and 37.c. Without more of the body decoration, further precision is impossible.[966] The use context for the vessel from which this sherd derives may be regarded as ending somewhere between late in the reign of Ahmose and the end of the reign of Tuthmosis I, but the date of production is clearly at least a little earlier: certainly early in, even the very beginning of, the 18th Dynasty.

An LMIB sherd from a tomb at Abydos (tomb 328.A.07) might permit us to go further, and to offer a Hyksos period correlation as argued by Kemp and Merrillees (1980). The counter argument for a Tuthmosis III date involves ignoring most of the evidence, and then taking the latest possible date for one vessel (whereas it could equally date earlier – and in general the vessel types involved are exceedingly difficult to date closely!).[967] But there is clearly a slight question mark over this evidence, given the debate in the literature. Perhaps more important, therefore, is the LHIIA alabastron and cup found in Tomb NE 1 near the Teti Pyramid at Saqqara.[968] Bourriau and Eriksson (1997:100) discuss the local Egyptian objects from the burial: the coffin, which is of the probable late 17th to very early 18th Dynasty non-banded *Rishi* type, and a jar of very early 18th Dynasty type. As a result, they suggest that a date very early in the 18th Dynasty – indeed during the reign of Ahmose – is likely.[969] Christine Lilyquist (pers. comm.) suggests that this diagnosis is overly prescriptive, and instead proposes a date from the 17th Dynasty through to Amenhotep I for the coffin type, and favours a date during the reign of Amenhotep I for the burial. In their discussion of the Egyptian painted jar Bourriau and Eriksson concur with a date *before* the reign of Tuthmosis I. Either way, this burial occurred in the first two to four decades of the 18th Dynasty. But the real interest arises because Warren and Hankey (1989:144) argue that the Mycenaean cup is of a type which only appears at the end of the LHIIA period and went out of use by the LHIIIA1 period; i.e., it is of a type usually dated to the LHIIB period.[970] Thus the conclusion is that late LHIIA, at a minimum, exists as an import for burial in a tomb within the first decades of the 18th Dynasty![971] This datum requires a significant, and important, upwards revision to the conventional chronology of Warren and Hankey (1989).[972]

---

[966] As stated by Hankey and Leonard (1998:31).

[967] For the sherd, and debate, see Kemp and Merrillees (1980:232–236, 252–253); Manning (1988b:32); Warren (1985:149–150); Warren and Hankey (1989:141); Hankey (1991/1992:16); Eriksson (1992:175–176); Bourriau and Eriksson (1997:99).

[968] Firth and Gunn (1926:69–70, pl.42.D); Merrillees (1968:21–22, 194–195); Warren and Hankey (1989:144).

[969] Contra the Tuthmosis III date suggested by Hankey and Warren (1989:144). This revises the view reported in Merrillees (1968:22), where, although he notes that the *Rishi* coffin type reached its fullest development in the 17th Dynasty, he nonetheless offers a Tuthmosis III date in this case based on a comparison with a coffin from Deir el Medina (cf. Bourriau and Eriksson 1997:100 and no.32).

[970] Mountjoy (1986:46); Warren and Hankey (1989:98).

[971] As noted in Chapter IV.5, this tomb also contained LCIB Cypriot products: a Red Lustrous Wheelmade Ware spindle bottle and two BRI jugs. Apart from demonstrating the co-occurrence of LCIB and LHIIA, this context therefore shows that LCIB dates from the early 18th Dynasty (and certainly from significantly before the reign of Tuthmosis III: contra the chronological scheme in Eriksson 1992). This evidence is part of the early New Kingdom LCIB horizon as represented also at the ʿEzbet Helmi area of Tell el-Dabʿa (see Chapter IV.5).

[972] Warren (1998:326) is rather disingenuous with regard to this datum. He admits the Egyptian context

What is the relationship between late LHIIA and LMIB? In the Aegean, it is clear, especially from the sequence at Ayia Irini, Keos, that the subsequent LH phase, LHIIB, began before the end of the Cretan LMIB phase.[973] Ayia Irini Period VIIa contains mature LMIA but also the new LMIB and LHIIA styles, and so may be regarded as earlier LMIB in date. Period VIIb contains later LMIB styles – Marine Style and Alternating Style – and has close comparisons to the close of LMIB destruction deposits both on Crete and at Kastri on Kythera, and so may be regarded as late LMIB in date.[974] But Ayia Irini Period VIIb also sees the first appearance (still rare) of the mainland LHIIB Ephyraean goblet;[975] hence we may determine that LHIIB began during the late LMIB period on Crete. Therefore, we may further place the preceding late LHIIA phase within mature–later LMIB.[976] In turn, if we refer back to the Saqqara tomb, we may conclude by dating, at a minimum, a point no earlier than mature–later LMIB somewhere in the first c.45 years of the 18th Dynasty.[977] The beginning of the LMIB/LHIIA periods is then earlier again. A date for the start of the LMIB/LHIIA periods during the (late) SIP/Hyksos period is almost inevitable, especially as it is becoming increasingly clear that the LMIB period represents a significant period of time (see Chapter VI below).

The broad correlation of the LMIB/LHIIA period with the LCIB period has already been noted. The later LCI (LCIA2–LCIB) BRI jug in a likely (later) SIP (Hyksos) context at Kom Rabiᶜa (Chapter IV.4), and late phase LCIB WSI and LCIB Red Lustrous Wheelmade Ware from early 18th Dynasty Tell el-Dabᶜa (Chapter IV.5), thus offer consonant evidence from Egypt for a late SIP *through* early 18th Dynasty date range for this period. These data disprove the interpretation of Eriksson (1992), who, apart from the evidence from Tell el-Dabᶜa, found that there was little evidence even to allow us to take the beginning of LCI(A) back to the start of the 18th Dynasty, and tried to argue that the Tell el-Dabᶜa stratum D/2 evidence perhaps was really all

---

may now be considered rather earlier, but chooses to say 'possibly the time of Tuthmosis I'; this is about the latest possible date given the revised views in favour of a date range from Ahmose to Amenhotep I. Further, he entirely ignores his own previously published views that the cup type only appears at the *end* of the LHIIA period, and thus this synchronism dates late LHIIA (and so mature to late LMIB). Instead, Warren suggests that this evidence 'would slightly raise and offer firmer evidence than hitherto for the date of the LMIA–B transition'! This is clearly turning a blind eye. For a more honest reaction from a leading Aegean archaeologist who has supported the conventional chronology in the past, I quote the concluding portion of an e-mail posting of 10 March 1998 by Oliver Dickinson to Aegeanet (see: http://www.umich.edu/~classics/archives/aegeanet/aegeanet.980310.03): 'Anyway, the dating of the Keftiu paintings relative to what's going on in the Aegean has now become a very complex issue. There seems good reason to believe that a grave context containing late LH IIA and (early) LH IIB types at Saqqara can date no later than Tuthmosis *I*. A nuisance, but there it is'.

[973] See Schofield (1984; 1985); Cummer and Schofield (1984). Note the caveats by Cummer and Schofield (1984:143–144).

[974] Warren and Hankey (1989:79–80).

[975] Schofield (1984:181); Cummer and Schofield (1984:143–144). For the very few actual occurrences, see the very short list at Cummer and Schofield (1984:143 n.12).

[976] Warren and Hankey (1989:71 Table 2.6, 79–81, 97–98).

[977] It is important to note that this conclusion proves to be in remarkably good agreement with the independent conclusion reached from the radiocarbon data from close of LMIB contexts on Crete: see Chapter V.1 below; Housley *et al.* (1999).

effectively contemporary with the early 18th Dynasty.[978] In all, the LCIB period must occupy some 75–100 years. The Kamose stela shows that until his reign the Theban 17th Dynasty did not have control north of Cusae,[979] and the arrival of the main, characteristic, early 18th Dynasty ceramic assemblage at Memphis may probably be dated during and following the reign of Ahmose.[980] The BR vessel and its pre-18th Dynasty context was therefore deposited at an unknown time before c.1550–1520BC (depending on choice of a high, middle, or low Egyptian chronology). A variety of other evidence from Alalakh to Egypt might offer consonant data.

The pattern of the few early finds of LMIB, LHIIA and LCIB indicates that the LMIA period not only correlates with the Hyksos period, but probably ended by no later than during the late Hyksos period. Mature LMIB and LHIIA correlate with the earliest 18th Dynasty, and very likely the late Hyksos period, onwards to the beginning of the reign of Tuthmosis III (see below). Evidence compatible with such a chronology exists in reverse from the Aegean in the form of Hyksos to early 18th Dynasty period objects which were deposited in LMIB contexts on Crete (see Chapter IV.4).

A variety of other LMIB/LHIIA material is found in contexts which date from the early 18th Dynasty to the reign of Tuthmosis III.[981] For no good, or explicit, reason, this material has usually been ascribed (solely) to the reign of Tuthmosis III, and the potential earlier 18th Dynasty aspect ignored. The case of the LHIIA vessel from Medinet el-Gurob is a case in point. Warren and Hankey (1989:144) admit 'the tomb had nothing specifically datable to that pharaoh [Tuthmosis III]' and note that 'Kemp and Merrillees (1980, 242) accept an early XVIIIth Dynasty context for the vase', but Warren and Hankey nonetheless begin their discussion of date by saying that the context was 'probably of the time of Tuthmosis III'! Merrillees (1972a), among others, has commented critically on this, and other circular or illogical arguments, but the practice has remained as a convention.

In fact, the 'body' of LMIB material from secure contexts in Egypt is remarkably small. As first pointed out by Wace and Blegen (1939), much of the material is actually LHIIA, and many other pieces often illustrated are unprovenanced.[982] Other 'evidence' is vanishing, or in need of significant re-interpretation. In particular, the three sherds from an LMIB(?)[983] spouted jar from Tell Ta'annek (a little south of Megiddo) have for many years been held to offer a fixed point *terminus ante quem* synchronism for LMIB. The argument was that the destruction deposit with these sherds could be associated with the Tuthmosis III year 23 conquest of nearby Megiddo.[984] But it has now become apparent that either: (i) there is in fact no correlation with Tuthmosis III, or, (ii) if the

---

[978] Eriksson (1992:163).

[979] Smith and Smith (1976); Redford (1997: 13–15 nos. 68–69).

[980] Bourriau (1997).

[981] Kemp and Merrillees (1980:226–245); Hankey and Warren (1974:146 and 149–150); Warren (1985:150–151); Warren and Hankey (1989:138–144, 172 n.22).

[982] Merrillees (1980).

[983] It would seem that it is in fact quite likely to be LHIIA: see Hankey and Leonard (1998:33 n.30).

[984] See e.g. Hankey and Warren (1974:146); Betancourt and Weinstein (1976:338); Cadogan (1978:210 Table 1). The revolt in Asia, and battle, siege, and sack of Megiddo and territory, is described in the Annals of Tuthmosis III (see Breasted 1962:§415–437).

link with Tuthmosis III's year 23 conquest of Megiddo and Tell Ta'annek is maintained,[985] that the LMIB sherds were in fact heirlooms, since the latest import in the cache is a WSII vessel from Cyprus.[986] Finds of WSII are relatively widespread in the Aegean, but are all LMIIIA1 (or later) in date where known.[987] Thus, if anything, this suggests the correlation of Tuthmosis III year 23 with a point in the LMIIIA1 period (see further below).[988]

Nonetheless, all scholars in the field can agree that a few LMIB and LHIIA vessels were put in tombs dating no later than the early 18th Dynasty and/or to the reign of Tuthmosis III: e.g. the Medinet el-Gurob alabastron discussed above; or the Abydos tomb 328.A.07 sherd discussed above. A few other finds *may* also belong to such a time-range: e.g. a baggy alabastron from Sidmant tomb 137, where Warren and Hankey (1989:142) note that this context '...may be datable to the time of Tuthmosis III. Petrie and Brunton list no dated object in the tomb...'. Bourriau and Eriksson (1997:100–101) refer in addition to the LHIIA kylix from near the altar in Structure I of the Fosse Temple at Lachish. This context is dated between the end of the reign of Tuthmosis III and the beginning of the reign of Amenhotep III.[989] Although this almost starts to sound like an heirloom from a special/religious context, since the LHIIB and probably even LMIIIA1 periods have begun during the later part of the reign of Tuthmosis III (see below), Bourriau and Eriksson (1997:101) conclude that we thus 'have confirmation of an LHIIA (and thus also LMIB) correlation with part of the reign of Tuthmosis III'. The important point is that anything definitely into the reign of Tuthmosis III offers us the *latest* datable LMIB/LHIIA correlations. This is the end of the period (as deposited in a foreign country). There is of course no reason that LMIB was even still current in the Aegean when these vessels were interred, given time-lags in transmission, *but*, even if one takes a positive view, there is no reason to extend the period beyond the first years of Tuthmosis III.[990] All of the LMIB period lies before this point. Work on Crete and in the Aegean in recent years has clearly shown that the *overall* LMIB period represents a significant (i.e. fairly lengthy) interval of time: see Chapter VI below. The ceiling pattern from the tomb of Amenemhet at Thebes perhaps offers about the latest good evidence. This ceiling pattern is quite similar to the decorative scheme on the dress of a female figure from an LMIB fresco at Ayia Triadha on Crete. The Egyptian context is early in the reign of Tuthmosis III; the use of pattern books need not mean entirely contemporary transfer of the image (even far

---

[985] As e.g. Warren and Hankey (1989:142); Warren (1987:209–210).

[986] See discussion and references in Manning (1995:224–225).

[987] Manning (1995:225); Watrous (1992:157–159); Rutter (1999: Table 1), where secure initial WSII is LMIIIA1 in date (C4249, C340, C2046, C4432, C4773) (C993 from a 'LMI mixed with some LMIIIA2' context may be discounted, and the WSII associated with the later material). Other examples, both at Kommos and elsewhere on Crete, are LMIII (Rutter 1999: 142 and n.27, Table 1).

[988] Warren (1998:328) simply ignores these facts. He continues to state that it is an LMIB bridge-spouted jar (although Hankey and Leonard now regard it as probably LHIIA), and fails to mention or consider the WSII. He takes cover in a spurious reference to a Syro-Palestinian 'transitional MBIIC/LBI phase'.

[989] Warren and Hankey (1989:144).

[990] The exact synchronism of late LMIB and LHIIA is debated: cf. differing dates offered by Warren and Hankey (1989:169 Table 3.1).

from it), but it seems quite plausible that a stylistic image current in LMIB was in use until early in the reign of Tuthmosis III.[991]

8. *Archaeology and the chronology of the Late Minoan II period*

The LMII period follows the island-wide destructions on Crete at the close of the LMIB period. Until recently, very few sites attested any LMII occupation, and in publications up to 1990 there were only about a dozen sites with definite LMII material.[992] Work in the last couple of years has identified a few more sites, and an east Cretan LMII–IIIA1 style has also been isolated,[993] but, even so, the total numbers and scale of LMII settlement represents a sharp decline from LMI.[994] Many LMI sites simply are not occupied at this time on the basis of ceramic data. LMII might thus be predicted to be problematic, and it is indeed one of those annoyingly hazy concepts and periods in Aegean chronology.[995] There are more than a few links with later LMIB[996] – as a new LMII deposit at Mochlos illustrates[997] – and an evolutionary process is evident,[998] whilst the dividing line in stylistic terms between LMII and the succeeding period, LMIIIA1, is difficult in many cases,[999] and requires care and argument.[1000] In the past, some have thus argued that LMII is either merely a limited tradition contemporary with late LMIB,[1001] or that it is effectively part of the LMIIIA1 period.[1002] Instances of a good stratigraphic distinction between LMIB and LMII remain difficult, but LMII has now been shown as later than LMIB at Knossos,[1003] and at Chania,[1004] and stylistically is defined as distinct from LMIB with new shapes appearing.[1005] Meanwhile, a clear stratigraphic relationship between LMII and

---

[991] For the comparison of the Amenemhet tomb ceiling and the decorative scheme on the Ayia Triadha female figure's dress, see Barber (1991:colour plate 2 and plate 3 top left). For the date of the Amenemhet tomb, see Barber (1991:339 Table 15.1). The Ayia Triadha fresco was part of the LMIB destruction, hence it was on the wall in LMIB. However, it may be argued to be LMIA in style, and so may have been extant for a considerable period. See Immerwahr (1990:49, 180 A.T. no.1 with refs.). Warren (1998:326) argues for the linking of LMIB to early Tuthmosis III on the basis of this evidence.

[992] Popham (1980); Haskell (1989:84); Driessen (1990:127 and n.444).

[993] See MacGillivray (1997b; 1997a).

[994] Driessen and Macdonald (1997:36–41).

[995] Betancourt (1985:149); for a review at Knossos, see Driessen (1990:117–122).

[996] Warren and Hankey (1989:82).

[997] Soles (1997:425–426); Soles in Tomlinson (1996:46).

[998] Furumark (1941a:166–169; 1950:256).

[999] Warren and Hankey (1989:83).

[1000] E.g. Andreadaki-Vlasaki and Papadopoulou (1997:137–144, 147).

[1001] E.g. Vermeule (1964:144–146).

[1002] Niemeier (1979a).

[1003] Warren and Hankey (1989:81).

[1004] Catling (1983:60). At Kommos there is also a good sequence in some areas (e.g. House X), and LMII can be shown to seal previous LMIB floor contexts (see Shaw and Shaw 1993:131–161; Jeremy B. Rutter, pers. comm.).

[1005] Popham (1967:343–344); Betancourt (1985:149–150).

LMIIIA1 is evident from a couple of sites,[1006] with a group of late LMII destructions (at Knossos, Kommos, and Malia) first recognised by Popham effectively marking the division.[1007] Thus it is now generally agreed that the LMII period is a separate chronological entity.

No LMII objects have been found in Egypt or the Near East, but based on a largely extrapolated synchronism between LMII and LHIIB,[1008] the LHIIB vessel from the Tomb of Maket at Kahun with a scarab of Tuthmosis III[1009] shows an approximate correlation with some (disputed) point in the reign of Tuthmosis III.[1010] Further, even if Eriksson (1992:185–186) is correct to suggest a late Tuthmosis III date for the deposit, it hardly means that the imported LHIIB alabastron was made at this time, rather, it comes from an unknown earlier time (reasonably the early to middle part of the reign of Tuthmosis III). Remember, the Saqqara cup offers an end of LHIIA, or LHIIB correlation, with a point no later than about the end of the reign of Amenhotep I (Chapter IV.7 above). This suggests the existence of the LMII style/period no later than early in the reign of Tuthmosis III (even allowing that LHIIB commences before LMII). It is also important to remember that the correlation of LHIIB to LMII in the Aegean is approximate and unclear at best;[1011] for example, we have no information at present from which to decide whether the end of LHIIB was during the course of LMII, or all too conveniently at the end of LMII, or in early LMIIIA1, in terms of the Minoan sequence. We do know that mainland LHIIIA2 seems to have begun before the end of LMIIIA1 on Crete.[1012]

9. Keftiu in Theban tomb paintings and Aegean chronology

Figures identified as 'Keftiu', from the 'Isles in the Midst of the Great Green [i.e. Sea]', are found in a group of élite tombs at Thebes in Upper Egypt dating from the reign of Tuthmosis III to shortly afterwards:[1013] see Table 5; Figures 38–41. These figures look like Minoans, and carry objects which in many cases look Aegean. Despite the critical minimalism of Furumark (1950:223–239), who accepted only the initial Senmut rep e-sentation as establishing an Aegean connection (p.239), it is widely agreed that these figures and the term 'Keftiu' represent people from the Aegean, and probably Crete, or

---

[1006] Watrous (1981); Popham (1984); Warren and Hankey (1989:83).

[1007] Popham (1975; 1988:223).

[1008] Since LMIB = later LHIIA, and early LHIIB begins in late LMIB, and then LMIIIA1 = LHIIIA1, it seems clear that most of the LHIIB period broadly correlates with LMII. It shares forms such as the Ephyraean goblet (which appears first on Crete in LMII: Hallager 1997:23 and n.29). Two instances of imported LHIIB goblets from solid LMII contexts are recently reported at Kommos (Rutter 1999: Table 6), further strengthening the conventional correlation/chronology. See Warren and Hankey (1989:80–81, 83–84, 97–98).

[1009] Hankey and Tufnell (1973).

[1010] Manning (1988b:35); Warren and Hankey (1989:145–146).

[1011] E.g. Warren and Hankey (1989:98).

[1012] Pålsson Hallager (1988; 1993:269 n.53).

[1013] Furumark (1950:223–239); Vercoutter (1956); Wachsmann (1987).

Tomb	Date
Senmut	Hatshepsut (probably prior to her year 16)
Puimre, Intef	Early Tuthmosis III
Useramun	Early Tuthmosis III (before his year 28 but after his co-regency with Hatshepsut had ended – i.e. after her year 16)
Menkheperraseneb	Late Tuthmosis III (tomb completed prior to the accession of Amenhotep II)
Rekhmire	Late Tuthmosis III–very early Amenhotep II (tomb completed soon after accession of Amenhotep II, but scene with Keftiu clearly associated with reign of Tuthmosis III, and so likely to be late Tuthmosis III in date [cf. Wachsmann 1987:36])

Table 5. Tombs from Thebes in Egypt with paintings depicting Keftiu (Aegean people). See Vercoutter (1956); Wachsmann (1987). Dates are those offered by Wachsmann (1987:103).

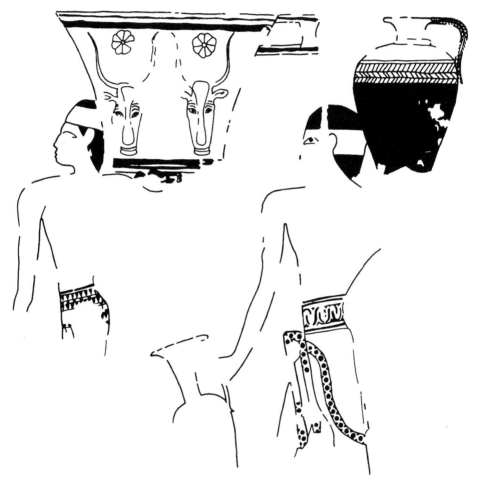

Fig. 38. Depictions of two examples (3rd and 4th to right) of the Keftiu from the tomb of Senmut (TT71, Hatshepsut–early Tuthmosis III) wearing LMI loincloth (or breechcloth: Rehak 1996), and with the left figure carrying a massively over-size LM/LHI Keftiu cup. Drawing after photos kindly supplied by the Metropolitan Museum of Art (Metropolitan Museum of Art, Egyptian Expedition, Graphic Section, and the Metropolitan Museum of Art, Rogers Fund, 1930).

Crete and other Aegean islands.[1014] A couple of scholars have tried instead to link the Keftiu with Cyprus,[1015] but these cases are much weaker, and ignore the specifically Minoan features of the costumes worn and objects carried. Such counter arguments are moreover essentially determined by another, separate, debate: unsuccessful attempts to overthrow the usual equation of Cyprus with the ancient name of Alasiya.[1016]

Two groups within the depictions of Keftiu have long been evident. An earlier group with figures wearing Minoan-style loin cloths, and a later group wearing kilts.[1017] The conventional view held the former to be LMI Minoans, whereas the latter perhaps reflected the new supposedly Mycenaean fashions of the LMII period – since kilts were worn by the male figures in the LMII Procession Fresco at Knossos.[1018] Thus it was often argued that the change to the kilts corresponded to the transition from LMIB to LMII on Crete, and, from the dates of the paintings in the Theban tombs,

Fig. 39. Depictions of two examples (Figs. 15–16 of Register II) of the Keftiu from the tomb of Rekhmire (TT100, Tuthmosis III–Amenhotep I) with re-painted kilts. Drawing after photos kindly supplied by the Metropolitan Museum of Art (Metropolitan Museum of Art, Egyptian Expedition, Graphic Section, and the Metropolitan Museum of Art, Rogers Fund, 1930).

this was said to be placed in the later years of Tuthmosis III.[1019] However, the Keftiu represented in these paintings have been receiving some welcome attention of late, and the previous conventional interpretation has to be significantly revised.

[1014] E.g. Vercoutter (1956); Wachsmann (1987); Haider (1990); Betancourt and Weinstein (1976:338); Sakellarakis and Sakellarakis (1984); Knapp (1985); Warren and Hankey (1989:145); Cline (1994:32); Matthäus (1995); Quack (1996).

[1015] Strange (1980); Merrillees (1972b; 1982).

[1016] I do not go into this matter here, see especially Knapp (1996:3–13; 1985:234–241; 1979); and Muhly (1972; 1982:258–261) for the positive case. Hellbing (1979) prevaricates. Merrillees (1972b; 1982; 1987) has pursued a campaign against the identification, a position also argued by Strange (1980). The case of Strange does not withstand critical scrutiny (Knapp 1985), while Merrillees, and a few other archaeologists who have doubted the Alasiya-Cyprus equation, are not familiar with the ancient Near Eastern textual data (Knapp 1985:236). The identification may be regarded as likely (Knapp 1996:3–13), but Merrillees (esp. 1987) is correct to argue that it is not proved on current data.

[1017] Recently, see Rehak (1996); Matthäus (1995).

[1018] Immerwahr (1990:88–90). The Procession Fresco, with its use of the horizontal register system, has widely been thought to reflect the influence of Egyptian conventions at this time (e.g. Hood 1978b:65 and 248 n.104), but as Immerwahr (1990:89–90) discusses, the processual theme appears to begin from at least LMIA in Aegean art.

[1019] E.g. Warren and Hankey (1989:145); Betancourt and Weinstein (1976:338).

The paintings in the Rekhmire and Menkheper-raseneb tombs are the latest of the group, and show the Keftiu in the new form of dress – the kilt – compared to the earlier paintings where the Keftiu wear a form of the Minoan loincloth and codpiece. For chronology, the figures in the Rekhmire tomb are the most crucial: figures actually named as Keftiu were originally painted in the Minoan loincloth with codpiece, but, after the completion of the painting, the garments were repainted as kilts. Both these tombs seem to record the same visit by new fashion Keftiu somewhere in the later years of Tuthmosis III: since although Rekhmire was vizier from late in the reign of Tuthmosis III and into the early years of Amenhotep II, the Menkheperraseneb paintings were done before the death of Tuthmosis III, and so the date of the 'new' image belongs to the later years of Tuthmosis III.

Wachsmann (1987) and Vercoutter (1956) provide detailed analyses of the chronology of the corpus of Keftiu paintings and their sources relative to the regnal years of Tuthmosis III. In brief, the 'loincloth and codpiece' paintings in the Useramun tomb pre-date Tuthmosis III years 20–28, and those in the Senmut tomb are probably pre-Hatshepsut year c.16 (or a few more years).[1020] The supposed 'fall' from power or favour of Senmut around Hatshepsut year 16 is not well understood,[1021] and his subsequent death is not exactly dated, and it is possible that he died either a few years before the death of Hatshepsut herself or a few years afterwards.[1022] Given the general similarities between the paintings in these two tombs, a common source behind the copy books used by the artists for both tombs may be conjectured, and Wachsmann suggests a 'source' visit

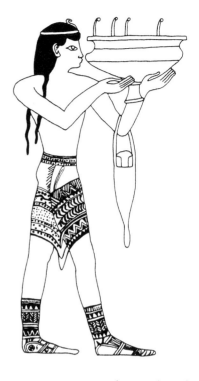

Fig. 40. Depiction of a member of the Keftiu (Fig. 4 of Register II) from the tomb of Rekhmire (TT 100, Tuthmosis III–Amenhotep I) with re-painted kilt. Drawing after photos kindly supplied by the Metropolitan Museum of Art (Metropolitan Museum of Art, Egyptian Expedition, Graphic Section, and the Metropolitan Museum of Art, Rogers Fund, 1930).

to Egypt of Keftiu earlier during the reign of Hatshepsut.[1023] Work on Senmut's tomb began in Hatshepsut year 7 = Tuthmosis III year 7,[1024] and activity is attested until

---

[1020] Wachsmann (1987:27).

[1021] Dorman (1988:141–164).

[1022] Dorman (1988:177–179).

[1023] Who was particularly associated with foreign trade/expeditions: Wachsmann (1987:121–123); Tyldesley (1996).

[1024] Dorman (1988:34–35, 95–97).

Fig. 41. Depiction of a member of the Keftiu (Fig. 9 of Register I) from the tomb of Menkheperraseneb (TT86, Tuthmosis III) with kilt. Drawing after photos kindly supplied by the Metropolitan Museum of Art (Metropolitan Museum of Art, Egyptian Expedition, Graphic Section, and the Metropolitan Museum of Art, Rogers Fund, 1930).

year 11 and perhaps continued until Senmut's death.[1025] Hence a date for the paintings around or before then is likely, and so the relevant visit of the LMI Keftiu was earlier again. Vercoutter (1956: 410–412) postulated a source visit as early as the reigns of Tuthmosis I or II. Thus LMI Keftiu need not post-date the first decade of the reign of Tuthmosis III, and could well be earlier. Furthermore, the stylistic 'date' of the prestige objects carried by the Keftiu may pre-date the context. Driessen and Macdonald (1997:62–70) make a strong case that many of the prestige objects found in LMIB contexts on Crete were in fact produced in the LMIA period, and thus finally deposited in LMIB after a significant period of continued use. And so, LMIB period Keftiu may well have presented LMIA production/style prestige gifts to the royal court in Egypt, which could explain any apparent anachronisms/archaicising. One might also further suspect that the Senmut (phase) representations of Keftiu in the tombs of a few of the Egyptian élite at Thebes has more to do with the Egyptian politics of foreign links and representations under Hatshepsut (who stressed these, e.g. in her mortuary temple at Deir el-Bahri), than with a specific chronological and historical reality. The bizarrely over-size representations of Aegean objects (the Vapheio cups) in the Senmut tomb may then be explained both by a lack of real familiarity, and a desire to impress with details of the relevant exotica: see Figure 38. Thus there is no reason to associate any particular part of the LMI period with this time, although a general link with the LMIB period seems likely.

We turn now to the 'revised' Keftiu image. Rekhmire became vizier in Tuthmosis III year 28. It is assumed he got to work on his tomb more or less at once, but the paintings probably do not pre-date his appointment, as he is always described as vizier. Thus the original 'loincloth and codpiece' painting of the Keftiu costume was quite possibly done in the first few years he was vizier (perhaps Tuthmosis III years 29–34, or so). This does not necessarily imply any sighting at this time of LMI Keftiu, merely that this was still the current copy book image, and a continuation of the tradition from the earlier Theban tombs. Something significant, an embassy of new-

---

[1025] Dorman (1988:95–97, 172 and n.47).

style Keftiu, then occurred subsequently, and the dress on the Keftiu figures was revised. As noted, the Menkheperraseneb tomb paintings offer the clearest evidence for dating: all relate to Tuthmosis III, and, unlike Rekhmire's tomb, there is no mention of Amenhotep II. Hence it seems likely that the paintings of new-style Keftiu in the Menkheperraseneb tomb were completed late in the reign of Tuthmosis III. The same date can be applied to the Rekhmire paintings since there appears a direct relationship between the Keftiu in both the Rekhmire and Menkheperraseneb paintings (a common source, or one copied from the other). In addition, in the relevant scene showing the Keftiu from Rekhmire's tomb, Rekhmire is shown receiving gifts/tribute meant for Tuthmosis III, and the scene thus presumably dates to this time, confirming the above observation. The Menkheperraseneb paintings identify the kings of the Keftiu, Hatti, and Tunip; as Wachsmann argues (1987:35), the Hittites first appear in the Egyptian historical record in Tuthmosis III year 33,[1026] therefore, a reference before that date in a private tomb seems unlikely. This may provide a *terminus post quem*. Wachsmann goes on to suggest that the key visit of new 'kilted' Keftiu was perhaps in Tuthmosis III year 42, although this is conjecture.

As noted above, for many years it had been recognised that the new dress was much more like the post-LMIB dress seen for example in the Procession Fresco at Knossos. Since Mycenaeans were widely held to have arrived in, or conquered, Crete at this time, and to have been responsible for the new developments on Crete in LMII–IIIA, it has long been held that the new-look Keftiu represented a change from a Minoan to a Mycenaean delegation, and, in effect, the Mycenaean take-over of Crete. Thus these paintings have been held to offer a date for the LMIB/LMII transition.

However, new studies change all this 'convention'. The brilliant and detailed study of Elizabeth Barber (1991:330–357) has led to two important revisions. First, she has highlighted the importance of textiles in prehistory, and the links between elaborate textiles as prestige goods, and status. For example, the Keftiu and others (Syrians) are shown as bringing bolts of cloth to the pharaoh in these same Theban paintings.[1027] Rehak has developed this point further, and with specific attention to the kilt.[1028] He finds that elaborately decorated kilts appear to reflect high status in Aegean (Cretan and Cycladic) representations from MMII–LMIIIA. They appear to be the male equivalent of the elaborate, high or special status, flounced skirts worn by women featured in ritual or important activities from Crete and Thera over the same period. Elaborate, highly-crafted, costumes may therefore be recognised as of considerable importance in the Aegean world. It is thus of significance when Keftiu are shown wearing elaborately decorated kilts.

The second observation by Barber concerns the careful examination of the decoration on the kilts. Since this is the main detailed aspect of the paintings of the Keftiu, these details may be regarded as our best evidence. Barber finds that the decorations on the Rekhmire and Menkheperraseneb textiles do not find their best

---

[1026] In the Annals of Tuthmosis III. The relevant section is in Breasted (1962, vol.II:§485).
[1027] Wachsmann (1987:75).
[1028] Rehak (1996; 1998).

parallels in the Knossos frescoes and LMII art; instead, the correct parallels are with the new styles of LMIIIA. Betancourt has pursued the subject, and finds that close parallels exist from LMIIIA1 ceramic decorations.[1029] Notable are repeated motifs usually in horizontal and/or vertical and/or curving registers/bands or fields consisting of in-filled triangles, chevrons, arcs, and other distinctively LMIIIA motifs.[1030] A few of these motifs do first appear in LMII,[1031] but the complete 'package' is LMIIIA1. See Figures 42–43 for some examples, and compare to the motifs on the kilts worn in Figures 38–41. This is an important correlation. Various past scholarship has regarded the decorations on the kilts as non-Aegean.[1032] In fact, what they identified was that they were not LMI in character. They are, however, very much LMIIIA1. The form of the kilts with tassels may be compared with those in the LMII–IIIA Procession Fresco from Knossos,[1033] but the form and type of single field of decoration depicted on the kilts in the Procession Fresco, consisting of elaborate inter-locking, 'metallising', designs with net-pattern, stylised ivy, etc.,[1034] is quite different from the Theban examples.[1035] Such elaborate, taut, stylised, inter-locking designs

Fig. 42. Examples of LMIIIA1 chevron and arc motifs found on pottery and very similar to the motifs repeated in registers on the kilts worn by the Keftiu in the Rekhmire and Menkheper-raseneb tombs. Examples shown from Kommos; drawings after Watrous (1992:nos.682, 962, 1170, 963). See also Betancourt (1998b:Fig.29.2).

are, moreover, more typical of the LMIB(–LMII) special 'palatial' tradition in ceramic decoration,[1036] and might be contrasted with the new styles of LMIIIA.

Mark Cameron (1967:341 n.27) observed that there was a close relationship between ceramic and fresco decoration in LMII–IIIA1. The link between painted designs on ceramics and the woven or printed motifs on kilts represented in frescoes may also be sustained in other periods; for example, two male figures – notably in procession as most other key examples – of LMIA/Late Cycladic I date from Akrotiri on Thera wear kilts decorated with LMIA/Late Cycladic I spiral decoration.[1037] And, as Rehak notes,

[1029] Betancourt (1998b:293); also Barber (1991:348; 1993; 1998:16); Rehak (1996:36–37).

[1030] E.g. Watrous (1992:nos. 527, 682, 774, 963, 988, 1170, 1431); Betancourt (1985:fig.119).

[1031] Popham (1984:pl.147.1, 156.1, pl.164.1–6, pl.166.64, etc.); Watrous (1992:nos.348, 352, 383, 500); Betancourt (1985:150 and fig.110).

[1032] See Wachsmann (1987:43).

[1033] Immerwahr (1990:174–175).

[1034] Evans (1921–1935, vol.II.2:fig.456).

[1035] Also Barber (1991:336–338); Rehak (1996:45).

[1036] Betancourt (1985:140–144).

[1037] Doumas (1992:176, pl. 138); Rehak (1996:47 and fig.10).

Fig. 43. Examples of LMIIIA1 infilled triangle motifs found on pottery and very similar to the motifs repeated in registers on the kilts worn by the Keftiu in the Rekhmire and Menkheperraseneb tombs. Examples shown from Knossos and Kommos; drawings after Popham (1967:pl.84a) and Watrous (1992:nos.774 and 988). See also Betancourt (1998b:Fig.29.2).

it is very interesting to observe a figurine with kilt of perhaps SIP date which is decorated with running spirals in strips[1038] – i.e. an LMIA-derived kilt, versus the LMIIIA1 examples seen in the Rekhmire and Menkheperraseneb tombs. One might also wonder about the typically LMIB saw-tooth (lines and/or dots) motif[1039] which occurs on the Knossos Chariot Fresco,[1040] on a yellow background.[1041] Although Immerwahr supports Cameron's (1967) preference for an LMII–IIIA1 dating for the composition (versus Alexiou's pre-LMII date), an earlier (LMIB) stylistic date might be suggested for this fragment.[1042] It would then fall into a pattern of LMIA, LMIB, LMII, and LMIIIA1 linkages between clothing decoration in frescoes and ceramic decoration, and confirm Cameron's observation.

The metal objects carried by the Keftiu in the Theban paintings have recently received careful analysis by Matthäus (1995). He finds that the metal objects depicted in the earlier paintings with LMI-clothed Aegeans (tombs of Senmut, Useramun) compare

---

[1038] Rehak (1996:37 n.12); (Riefstahl 1972).
[1039] For examples of the motif, see e.g. Betancourt (1985:pl.22.D, H).
[1040] Immerwahr (1990:92–94, Kn No.25).
[1041] Alexiou (1964: figs.2.II, 4.II).
[1042] As in Hood (1978b:58–60).

well with New Palace types (mainly LMIA/LHI, but range MMIII–LMII).[1043] In contrast, in the tomb of Menkheperraseneb, where the Keftiu are clothed in the later kilt costume with LMIIIA1 style motifs, Matthäus (1995:183) finds the metal objects to include LMII/LHIIB to LMIIIA/LHIIIA types. Matthäus (1995:184) reaches a similar conclusion from an examination of the pithoid jars and amphorae. Overall, the tombs of Senmut and Useramun have depictions of types manufactured in the Aegean until the end of LMIB/LHIIA, whilst the tomb of Menkheperraseneb has types which begin in LMII/LHIIB and continue into LMIIIA/LHIIIA in Aegean terms.[1044] The findings of Matthäus are thus entirely compatible with the observations made from the clothing. This is even more so if one considers the likely 'heirloom' effect with a number of valuable or prestige LM metal craft items.[1045] The later paintings reflect features datable to LMII at the earliest, and, considering all the features together, best date to LMIIIA1.[1046]

In conclusion, the examination of both textile decoration and metal types reveals good evidence that the LMIIIA1 period had begun by late in the reign of Tuthmosis III, and this evidence does not appear inconsistent with the wider cultural-historical

---

[1043] Matthäus (1995:182).

[1044] Matthäus (1995:184–186).

[1045] Rehak (1998:46 and refs.); Driessen and Macdonald (1997:62–70).

[1046] Matthäus is an acknowledged expert on east Mediterranean metal objects (e.g. Matthäus 1980; 1985) but the other comments made by, and conclusions drawn by, Matthäus (1995) about Aegean chronology are unfortunately naïve, incorrect, or ill-informed. This note summarises the main flaws in his arguments. (i) re-Matthäus (1995:177–179). The Betancourt-Manning 'high' chronology is not based on radiocarbon evidence. Instead, it is based on a plausible re-interpretation of all the archaeological data, and, we supported this re-interpretation in the studies cited because it was consistent with a wide range of independent scientific dating evidence (including particularly radiocarbon data). In contrast, the conventional, or 'low', position must reject all this science data. Warren and Hankey (1989) was not a 'reaction' to the 'high' proposals – rather a long awaited work which sought to avoid the issue as best as possible, and to defend its pre-conceived chronology. (ii) re-Matthäus (1995:180). There are no 'distortions' in the radiocarbon time scale! This implies some sort of odd occurrences, problems, etc. No! These 'wiggles' are simply the known history of natural radiocarbon variations. They are not an excuse – they are facts, and, moreover, offer distinct fingerprints in time which can be employed via wiggle-matching to obtain very precise dates. Matthäus cannot, on the basis of ignorance and incorrect knowledge, state he has 'no confidence in radiocarbon dating'. He is adopting 'flat-earth', or anti-Copernican, logic! Matthäus mentions ice-core and tree-ring evidence – all one can say is that he is wrong, and that there is a great deal of evidence and reason why the 1628BC climatic event could plausibly be linked with the very large, 1 in 300 years scale, eruption of Thera (see Chapter V.2, 3, and 4; also Baillie 1995a; 1996a; Kuniholm *et al.* 1996; Manning 1995:200–216; 1992a). (iii) re-Matthäus (1995:180–181). The interpretation of the Amenhotep III scarab from Sellopoulou Tomb 4 is not simple (see Manning 1995:226–227; and a further detailed discussion in Chapter IV.10 below); the correlation shows that the reign of Amenhotep III began before the last burial with the scarab in the tomb – it does not mean LMIIIA1 began only during Amenhotep III's reign. (iv) re-Matthäus (1995:180 n.9 last two lines). Matthäus says that Manning (1992a) apparently contradicts Manning (1990b), and Matthäus says he finds this 'incomprehensible'. What has not been comprehended is Manning (1992a – see also Baillie 1995a:121); new scientific evidence and analyses became available which showed that some petrologic estimates of sulphur emissions from volcanoes were serious underestimates and indeed useless (see further in Chapter V.2; Kuniholm *et al.* 1996). Thus, whereas the existing scientific view based on petrologic estimates at the time of the third

evidence.[1047] Once this is accepted, the alabaster vase with the Tuthmosis III cartouche from LMIIIA1 (and perhaps into IIIA2) Katsampas tomb B need not be explained away as an heirloom,[1048] likewise, the view that the Aniba alabastron imitates LMIIIA1 makes good sense.[1049] We have already noted a similar possible dating to be derived from Tell Ta'annek via its White Slip II vessel (Chapter IV.7). Finally, Watrous refers to an Egyptian vessel from LMIIIA1 Kommos and notes that it may have a Tuthmosis III period date (referring to views of D. Arnold and material from Karnak),[1050] and Manning (1988b:36) mentioned two other compatible linkages.[1051] I explain below why the Amenhotep III scarab from Sellopoulou Tomb 4 does *not* undermine the 'early' chronology. The end result, therefore, is that there is no reason why LMIIIA1 cannot have begun during the reign of Tuthmosis III. This position is just about accepted now even by the doyen of the conventional, low, chronology: Peter Warren.[1052] Indeed, there are several pieces of evidence clearly showing that it probably did commence by the middle–later years of his reign.

Further, before leaving this subject, it is tempting to reflect on those high-status kilts. From Aegean evidence, these go with important people,[1053] and, in the Rekhmire tomb we may further note that two of the Keftiu wear exotic 'leopard' skin kilts (nos. 5 and 14). Given the occurrences of lions and wild cats in prestige Aegean art (Akrotiri miniature frescoes, specialist-crafted inlaid dagger blades[1054]), they add to the idea that the costumes depicted represent high status. The inscriptions from the Rekhmire and Menkheperraseneb paintings specifically refer to the 'prince/chief of Keftiu', whereas

---

Thera Congress (in 1989) was that the output of sulphur from Thera was insufficient to account for the large acidity level recorded in the 17th century BC in Greenland ice-cores (a view reported in Manning 1990b; see also the review of this issue, and the change in geological evidence since 1990, by Baillie 1995a:113), it became clear from 1991 onwards that this view was incorrect. Manning (1992a) reported this change. (v) re-Matthäus (1995:181). The idea of employing Cyprus to sort out Aegean–Egyptian linkages and chronology will be received with mirth amongst Cypriot archaeologists! The ceramic and stratigraphic sequences on LCI–II Cyprus are relatively poorly dated in absolute terms at present, and rely on Aegean and Egyptian–Near Eastern links for their chronology. Further, many of the key Cypriot ceramic types/wares are long-lived and lack precise stratigraphic correlations (see e.g. Barlow *et al.* 1991; Knapp and Cherry 1994:41–92; Eames 1994), and, as stressed in the discussions in Chapter IV.4 and IV.5, regionalism is a major complicating factor. Typically the Aegean imports to Cyprus are used as key chronological diagnostics – thus Matthäus is recommending the circular logic correctly derided by Leonard (1988). Matthäus of course mentions Tell el-Dab^ca. One MMIIB Kamares vessel in an early 13th Dynasty context means nothing significant, and especially new; it merely confirms a well known *terminus ante quem* (Manning 1995:25–26 n.9; MacGillivray 1995). On the frescoes, see Chapter IV.3 above. For WSI, see Chapter IV.4 and IV.5 above.

[1047] E.g. Rehak (1998).

[1048] *Pace* Warren and Hankey (1989:137).

[1049] For this view, see Betancourt (1987:46–47; 1998b:293); Michael and Betancourt (1988:170); Manning (1988b:34–35); against, see Warren (1987:207–208; 1988:177); Warren and Hankey (1989:144); Eriksson (1992:182–184).

[1050] Watrous (1992:162 no.1960)

[1051] Cf. Hankey and Leonard (1998:31).

[1052] Warren (1998:326, 328; 1996:288).

[1053] Rehak (1996).

[1054] Morgan (1988:41–49).

the earlier paintings do not, or at best do not name the Keftiu, but show a Keftiu-like figure in a group of the princes/chiefs from the northern lands. The context is a set of paintings showing gifts-tribute from the various lands and their rulers.[1055] Is it possible that a specific high-status ('royal') embassy went from the Keftiu to Egypt during the later part of the reign of Tuthmosis III? Potentially high-level contacts are evident from the annals of Tuthmosis III year 34, which refer to his receiving supplies for his Syrian wars from Keftiu ships.[1056] The jar with the cartouche of Tuthmosis III from Knossos' harbour town from an LMIIIA context could be related to this, or reciprocal activity? The Syrian, versus Egyptian, provenance of a number of stone vessels from LMII–IIIA1 Crete previously thought to be Egyptian[1057] might well also link to this period, and to Egyptian royal activity and presence in Syria? With Knossos' take-over of central (and western) Crete in the LMII–IIIA1 period,[1058] it became the sole super-site of the island.[1059] The rulers of Knossos were of a new order of magnitude in power and status (and ambition) compared to LMI, when Knossos was just one of several major players on Crete – yet alone the Aegean, where Akrotiri on Thera, among others, was a significant 'player' in LMIA. Moreover, although Crete perhaps enjoyed 'royal' links with the Hyksos (Khyan lid, nexus of 'Aegean' frescoes), similar *close* relations may not have been established with the early 18th Dynasty rulers before Tuthmosis III (in late LMIB).

LMIIIA1 would be a suitable historical time for the rulers of the new 'super-site' Knossos to make their mark, and to be recognised, on the international stage. Tuthmosis III was a great, conquering, pharaoh with international ambitions,[1060] carrying out major wars from his year 23 to 42. 'Impressed and probably not a little disturbed by Tuthmosis III's conquests, most of the other nations of western Asia and the eastern

[1055] See Cline (1995b:146–147) for the argument that these are specifically gifts from the rulers of Crete to the pharaoh.

[1056] See Wachsmann (1987:119–121; 1998:51). The relevant text is in Breasted (1962, vol.II:§492).

[1057] See Lilyquist (1996; 1997).

[1058] Bennet (1985; 1987a; 1988:38–39 and n.65); Hallager (1978); Niemeier (1985:217–231); Doxey (1987); Haskell (1989); Rutter (1999: 139 and ns.1–3).

[1059] I ignore the controversial, and for present purposes irrelevant, issue of whether Knossos was now ruled by Mycenaeans: see previous references; also Niemeier (1983; 1985:195–216); Driessen (1990:124–125); Firth (1992–1993); Olivier (1992); various papers in Driessen and Farnoux (1997); Rehak and Younger (1998:148–150). The issue of whether or not LMII to early LMIIIA2 Knossos was ruled by Mycenaeans is of course central to the interpretations of scholars who have written on this period. The very relevance of the Linear B archive at Knossos is at stake. However, the complexities of this argument need not concern us here. On the one hand, if a Cretan, Knossian, regime ruled in LMII–IIIA1 (and Minoan Linear A is attested until LMII, even LMIIIA1, see Vandenabeele 1985; Dimopoulou *et al.* 1993:esp.505), and Mycenaeans arrived only in LMIIIA1/2, then this important Cretan (if Mycenaenising) regime had dealings with Egypt, and was a/the dominant power centre in the Aegean until the end of LMIIIA1 (or the 'fall' of Knossos and other perhaps related Aegean changes and realignments: Doxey 1987; Catling 1989; Shelmerdine 1992). On the other hand, if the Mycenaeans were already present and ruling as an élite at Knossos during LMII–LMIIIA1, then this Mycenaean Knossian state had dealings with Egypt late in the reign of Tuthmosis III, and again was a/the dominant Aegean centre until early LH/LMIIIA2. Who invented Linear B is yet another long-running and related debate.

[1060] E.g. Kuhrt (1995:193, 321–323); Hayes (1990:114–116); Drower (1973:444–459); Weinstein (1981); Hayes (1973); Gardiner (1961:181–193).

Mediterranean area hastened to make friendly overtures to the pharaoh'.[1061] The inscription referring to the Keftiu in the Rekhmire tomb makes this connection explicit: 'When they [the princes of Keftiu] hear of his victories over all the countries, they bring their gifts on their backs in order to obtain the breath of life in order to submit to his majesty [Tuthmosis III] in order that his power could protect them'.[1062] A nexus between LMIIIA1 and later Tuthmosis III thus appears reasonable and likely. LMIIIA1 is the period of conspicuous international trade at the port of Kommos, and, until the end of LMIIIA1, the majority of orientalia in the Aegean are from Crete, with, in particular, a number of stone vases from LMII–IIIA Knossos conspicuous amongst these.[1063] The Isopata 'royal tomb' stands out, especially.[1064] Even though looted – and precious metals and jewellery were undoubtedly taken based on 'dropped' beads, pendants, gold pin, and 'missed' silver bowls – the tomb contained the largest group of Near Eastern artefacts ever found on Crete in a single context. Crete, and especially Knossos, appears the dominant regional locus in the Aegean at this time (although, in a sign of things to come, a prince of Tanaja = mainland Greece, following Cline 1994:32; 1995:146; Chapter IV.10 below, sends a gift soon after in Tuthmosis III year 42 – we might link this best with the rise of the newly formed palaces/states of LHIIB–LHIIIA1 mainland Greece, see footnotes 1083 and 1091 below, and perhaps especially the centre at Mycenae).

10. Amenhotep III and Aegean chronology

For some years a great deal of importance has been attached to a scarab with the name of the Egyptian pharaoh Amenhotep III from Sellopoulou Tomb 4 at Knossos.[1065] Warren and Hankey (1989:148) write that it is 'one of the best Aegean–Egyptian synchronisms'. They regard a 'fresh' scarab of Amenhotep III as coming from 'an LMIIIA1 single period burial, including an LHIIIA1 imported vase for good measure'. Warren and Hankey consider this scarab as proving beyond doubt that LMIIIA1 must (at some point) correspond with the reign of Amenhotep III, and they regard it as the key evidence which disproves an 'early' date for the LMIIIA1 period (and the Tuthmosis III correlation). I wish to explain (again) why each of these assumptions or arguments is incorrect, and why the scarab does not pose any hindrance at all to the 'early' chronology.

[1061] Hayes (1990:115); see also Gardiner (1961:193); Drower (1973:456–457).

[1062] Vercoutter (1956:57; trans. Bernal 1991:426).

[1063] For foreign trade at Kommos, see Rutter (1999; previously Watrous 1992). For orientalia and stone vases, see Cline (1994); Warren (1991b); Lilyquist (1996). Stone vases formerly held to be Egyptian, but probably Syrian, or non-Egyptian in origin: Lilyquist (1996). As noted above, they may link to Tuthmosis III's activities in the Levant.

[1064] Evans (1903–1904:5–6; 1905:526–562; 1921–1935, vol.IV.2:771–776); Warren (1969:112–113); Phillips (1991:583–594).

[1065] Popham *et al.* (1974:216–217, 224 no.J14); Popham (1973; 1970a:228). For a recent study of the reign of Amenhotep III, see O'Connor and Cline (1998). For his relations with the Aegean, see pp.236–241.

Let us consider the burials themselves to begin with. There were three: two males, and a female. The two males were buried first, and had the majority of the grave goods (ceramics and metals of LMII–IIIA1 date),[1066] with the first burial associated with an imported LHIIIA1 vessel. Subsequently, the third and last burial of a female was installed. This was positioned differently. The gap of time between the first and last burials is unknown, but at least some time had transpired (hence the tomb is not a single burial context). However, a solitary stirrup jar of LMIIIA1 date was associated with her, and a necklace including the Amenhotep III scarab was near the lower jaw. What does one LMIIIA1 stirrup jar mean? It could place the last burial in the (now later) LMIIIA1 period, but the time period concerned could also be a little later. After all, the definition of the early LMIIIA2 period at Knossos is as 'a time when the majority of the vases in use were still LMIIIA 1 in style'.[1067] With just one vase we cannot know. Since some of the LMIIIA1 vessels with the earlier burials are quite comparable to material from early LMIIIA2 (or LMIIIA1/2) deposits at Knossos, it is by no means clear that these burials are earlier LMIIIA1, and, in general, we see the natural blurring of stylistic/fashion boundaries which inherently are not clear-cut (thus: LMII–IIIA1 merge, and LMIIIA1–IIIA2 early merge). There is, therefore, no necessary reason to date the last burial in the tomb to LMIIIA1 in strict logical terms, and it is quite possibly early LMIIIA2. Furthermore, some significant range of time is available between the first and last burials (e.g. earlier–mature LMIIIA1 to late LMIIIA1/early LMIIIA2), and, in particular, LHIIIA1 is *not* associated with the last burial and the necklace with the scarab.

What about the relationship between LMIIIA1 and LHIIIA1? More could be learnt, but on present evidence it is clear that LHIIIA2 began and was current during LMIIIA1 on Crete.[1068] Thus at a minimum later LMIIIA1 equates with earlier LHIIIA2. Although Warren and Hankey (1989:84) note this evidence and write that 'this indicates that LHIII A 2 had already begun within the time of LMIII A 1', they then fail to make any allowance for it in their final absolute chronology, where they entirely synchronise LMIIIA1 and LHIIIA1, and LMIIIA2 and LHIIIA2.[1069] When one considers the Sellopoulou tomb, there is no reason that the mainland LHIIIA2 period cannot have begun by the time of the last burial – whether seen as late LMIIIA1 = early LHIIIA2, or early LMIIIA2 = mature LHIIIA2. The transition to LHIIIA2 could be placed between the first burial and the last. Therefore, the scarab quite possibly offers a late LMIIIA1/early LMIIIA2 *and* earlier LHIIIA2/mature LHIIIA2 synchronism.[1070]

[1066] As Hallager (1997:25–27) states, the large plain goblet type (it was probably tin-covered originally) is diagnostically typical of an LMIIIA1 date, and the type does not continue into LMIIIA2. The goblets from Sellopoulou Tomb 4, associated with the first and second burials, are of this type (Hallager 1997:26–27 and n.54).

[1067] Popham (1970b:81), quoted by Warren and Hankey (1989:83).

[1068] Pålsson Hallager (1988; 1993:269 n.53).

[1069] Warren and Hankey (1989:169 table 3.1).

[1070] Warren (1998:328) suggests that 'everyone, except perhaps Sturt Manning, is in any case agreed that

Was the scarab 'fresh'? Warren and Hankey (and others) have quoted this description of the scarab as somehow implying that it was brand new when buried, and thus more or less contemporary with the pharaoh. However, there is no basis to this view. The scarab cannot have been 'fresh'. It had been made into part of a necklace and definitely 'used' in some way. This was a relatively common practice at Knossos; several scarabs are known from LMIIIA necklaces.[1071] Further, Phillips (1991:597) describes the condition of the scarab as with 'flaking glaze and worn stone (?) edges' – hardly fresh, just intact. Two further details are also important. First, the scarab in fact appears to be made of stone (perhaps quartz). This hard material may explain the scarab's good state of preservation (versus what might be expected if it had been made from one of the usual softer materials employed for scarab manufacture), rather than any particular newness. Second, the hieroglyphic inscription is unusual, and Popham *et al.* (1974:216–217) even quote the view of the distinguished Egyptologist I.E.S. Edwards that the scarab was possibly made by someone 'not familiar with the hieroglyphic script, perhaps a foreigner'.[1072] Thus it may well not be a product of the pharaoh's workshops.

It must be remembered that 'it is possible that this is a commemorative scarab made after his reign, as demonstrably later examples of his name are well known'.[1073] And, perhaps more to the point, that this scarab was probably the feature ornament of the necklace of which it was part. Since there seems a good case that there was some sort of special 'embassy' or linkage between Amenhotep III and the Aegean,[1074] based on a remarkable number of objects inscribed with his name (or that of his wife, Queen Tiyi) known from the Aegean, and the 'Aegean list' inscribed on Amenhotep III's funerary temple at Kom el-Hetan, the association of Amenhotep III with status, and prestige, is reasonable, and so the presence of the scarab in a rich tomb at Knossos is plausible.

When was this embassy or linkage? Cline goes to some effort to argue for an LMIIIA1/LHIIIA1 date on the basis of the Sellopoulou scarab, since it was supposedly the earliest, best-dated, correlation as far as he was then aware. However, we have

---

LM/LHIIIA1 is closely linked to Amenophis III ... through the Sellopoulo tomb 4 scarab'. Apart from noting that Wiener (1998:311) accepts some of the problems I highlight with regard to the conventional interpretation of this datum, I wish to point out that I do not dispute that the LMIIIA1 period may have lasted into the reign of Amenhotep III. I instead raise the logical possibility that the third burial with the scarab could have been early LMIIIA2, but I agree it may have been later LMIIIA1 (and used the formula LMIIIA1/early LMIIIA2 in the main text). I particularly wish to highlight that this point in time (whichever) could well be contemporary with earlier LHIIIA2 on the mainland. Overall, I wish to argue that it is both plausible, and from other evidence likely/required, that the LMIIIA1 period begins rather earlier (by late in the reign of Tuthmosis III). Contra Warren, the Sellopoulou tomb 4 scarab sets the end date for the LMIIIA1 period, and not its beginning or floruit.

[1071] Phillips (1991:160 and n.88), who lists three other examples apart from the Sellopoulou example, from tombs at Zaphor Papoura, Gypsades and Aghia Pelagia (LMIIIA–B); see pp.364–366 no.1, 596–598 no.217, 601–602 no.219, 614–615 no.229.

[1072] A view highlighted also by Lilyquist (1996:146 n.120), who questions the Egyptian provenance of this and several other supposedly 'Egyptian' products in the Aegean.

[1073] Phillips (1991:597 n.252).

[1074] Cline (1987; 1990; 1990–1991:22–27; 1994:38–39; 1998b). For a recent review of general Aegean–Egyptian linkages and history in the LBA, including the Amenhotep III–Aegean issue, see Haider (1996).

seen that it is no such thing; it was very possibly buried in earlier LHIIIA2 (late LMIIIA1/early LMIIIA2), and it seems in some way a derivative object, perhaps even locally produced,[1075] and certainly re-used. The other objects of Amenhotep III (or his wife) from the Aegean have been found in contexts which either include LHIIIA2, are LHIIIA2, or are later than LHIIIA2.[1076] LHIIIA2 pottery is first found in Egypt from contexts contemporary with his reign.[1077] And, before we reach a conclusion, consider one other circumstance brought out by the studies of Cline.[1078] Until the end of LMIIIA1, the vast majority of orientalia (Egyptian or Near Eastern objects) in the Aegean are found in Crete. However, from LHIIIA2 onwards, there is a major shift, with the vast majority now found on the mainland, and only a very few on Crete. The pharaohs following Tuthmosis III – Amenhotep II, Tuthmosis IV and Amenhotep III – mark the transition. Up to the end of the reign of Tuthmosis III, orientalia primarily offer links with Crete (LMIB to LMIIIA1); from Amenhotep II on they instead primarily offer links with mainland, Mycenaean, Greece (LHIIIA1 to LHIIIA2). In the case of Amenhotep III, it is very noticeable that while some objects inscribed with his name are found in Crete, a large group was found on the mainland, and especially at Mycenae. The Argolid region around Mycenae was the heart of the newly dominant Mycenaean world, and the production centre from which most known LHIIIA2 exports into the eastern Mediterranean derive.[1079] With the traditional view of the Sellopoulou correlation removed, there is every reason to suggest an LHIIIA2 = late LMIIIA1/early LMIIIA2 date for the Amenhotep III embassy/linkage. Indeed, the find of a scarab of his predecessor, Tuthmosis IV, in tomb 8144 at Hazor with a number of imported Mycenaean vases which are of LHIIIA2 date in all but one case (of LHIIIA1), might even raise the possibility of the LHIIIA2 period beginning shortly before, or at the latest very early in, the reign of Amenhotep III.[1080]

We may also integrate textual historical evidence to support the chronology suggested above, with LHIIB–LHIIIA1 occupying the later part of the reign of Tuthmosis III into the reigns of his successors Amenhotep II and Tuthmosis IV, and LHIIIA2 primarily correlating with Amenhotep III. As noted in Chapter IV.9, the Egyptian term 'Tanaja', which may probably be identified with the Greek mainland,[1081] first occurs late in the reign of Tuthmosis III.[1082] Keftiu (Crete) had been referred to in

---

[1075] One may note by way of analogy that Cline (1990:209–210) suggests that one of the Amenhotep III plaques from Mycenae was locally produced. C. Lilyquist (pers. comm. and forthcoming) goes further, and questions whether any of the plaques are Egyptian. She instead suggests production in Levantine workshops. This does not necessarily rule out a diplomatic linkage, however.

[1076] Another scarab of Amenhotep III has been found at Panaztepe in western Anatolia. The context is referred to as probably 'LHIIIA', without subdivision (see summary in Cline 1998b:246 n.107; Warren and Hankey 1989:148).

[1077] Warren and Hankey (1989:149–154); Hankey and Aston (1995:69).

[1078] Cline (1994; 1990–1991:21–22).

[1079] E.g. Jones (1986:542–571); Mommsen *et al.* (1992); Leonard *et al.* (1993:118–119).

[1080] Scarab: Yadin *et al.* (1960:153 no.15 and pl.137 no.15 on left page but no.14 on right page); Mycenaean vases: Yadin *et al.* (1960:150–151).

[1081] Faure (1968:145–147); Cline (1994:32).

[1082] 42nd year: Cline (1994:114 no.A.32, also 110 no.A.15).

Egyptian records for several centuries previously. A prince of the Tanaja sends among
other things a silver shawabti-vessel in Keftiuan workmanship. This would be the
LHIIB–LHIIIA1 period, as the mainland centres in Greece start to become fully-formed
states around palatial centres.[1083] It is perhaps significant that the prince is listed as
sending as his prime gift a vessel of Cretan workmanship. Knossos and the workshops
of Crete are still dominant in the Aegean as producers of prestige goods (e.g. weapons)
until the end of LMIIIA1.[1084] Two Egyptian monkey figurines with the cartouche of
the successor of Tuthmosis III, Amenhotep II, one from Mycenae and one from
Tiryns,[1085] could be argued to offer evidence of such new direct contacts between the
mainland and Egypt developing and continuing (and Amenhotep II and Tuthmosis
IV perhaps occupy the remainder of the time-span of the LHIIIA1 period in the
Aegean). The main group of mentions of, or references to, Tanaja occur then during
the reign of Amenhotep III,[1086] suggesting a specific link with the now established
and dominant early LHIIIA2 Mycenaean states. We might consider placing the
Amenhotep III embassy or linkage with the Aegean (discussed above) shortly before
the destruction at Knossos in early LHIIIA2.[1087]

Cline (1990–1991:26–27) makes the interesting suggestion that Amenhotep III may
have been establishing links with the states surrounding the Hittites as part of his
strategy of trying to contain the threat that the Hittites posed to Egypt and its empire
in Syria–Palestine.[1088] As noted in Section 9 above, the Hittites appear in Egyptian
history only from Tuthmosis III year 33.[1089] This is later in the LMII period, or almost
into the LMIIIA1 period, in Aegean terms. With Tuthmosis III's conquests and
ambitions in western Asia, Syria had become the strategic buffer area between the
main powers: Egypt, Mitanni, and Hatti. His successors Amenhotep II and Tuthmosis
IV were engaged especially in dealings with the Mitanni, and the issue of control of
Syria.[1090] Tuthmosis IV campaigned in Syria. From an Egyptian perspective, the aim
seems to have been by diplomatic means to contain both the Hittites and the
Mitannians. There is little evidence, however, of much direct contact between the
Egyptians and the Hittites through this period. It is not in fact until the reign of
Amenhotep III that the Hittites first seem to become genuinely important players in
Egyptian eyes (and concerns).

[1083] Earliest 'palaces' from LHIIB: Rutter (1993:796); cf. Barber (1992).

[1084] E.g. Driessen and Macdonald (1984); Niemeier (1983); Hiller (1984:30).

[1085] For the figurines, see Cline (1991). The Mycenae example probably came from an LHIIIB find context,
and was first published in Hall (1901–1902:188). The Tiryns example came from an LHIIIA find context.
We might hypothesise original (mature–later) LHIIIA1 import.

[1086] Cline (1994:32, 114–116).

[1087] I suggest this date since Crete and Knossos still feature as receivers of objects with the names of
Amenhotep III or Queen Tiyi, and Amnisos, Phaistos, Kydonia and Knossos are found on the Kom el-
Hetan list, but mainland sites, and especially Mycenae, are now their equals if not pre-eminent (from
'special' nature of collection of Amenhotep III objects at Mycenae). Thus we might call this point either
late LMIIIA1 or early LMIIIA2 on Crete, and earlier LHIIIA2 in mainland terms (with the mainland
LHIIIA2 period beginning during late LMIIIA1 on Crete).

[1088] See also Cline (1998b:248–249).

[1089] Breasted (1962, vol.II:§485); Bryce (1998:128–129); Wachsmann (1987:35).

[1090] Bryce (1998:156–158); Wilhelm (1989:28); Cline (1998b:241–250).

Let us turn back to the Aegean. How might all this fit into the world of international politics and diplomacy? The period concerned covers the rise of the Mycenaean states; the Minoans/Keftiu are no longer so important after the lifetime of Tuthmosis III. The development of the Mycenaean states, and Mycenaean expansion into the Aegean and western Anatolia, seems to occur during the LHIIB–LHIIIA1 phase;[1091] palaces and extensive trading links are established and evident from LHIIIA2. If Mycenaean Greece is to be associated with the place name 'Ahhiyawa' in various Hittite texts,[1092] then Ahhiyawa and related concerns first appear in Hittite documents relating to the reigns of the Hittite Great Kings Tudhaliya I and Arnuwanda I. Whilst it is fair to say that there is some uncertainty concerning the exact reconstruction of Hittite New Kingdom royal genealogy before Suppiluliuma I,[1093] these kings are dated somewhere in the late 15th century BC to early 14th century BC, at least one/two generations before Suppiluliuma I. The chronology comes from linkages evident in extant written correspondence, which show that the reign of Suppiluliuma I overlapped the later years/decades of the reign of Amenhotep III, and continued until shortly after the death of Tutankhamun.

An Ahhiyawan presence in Anatolia, and Hittite attention and concern about this, is specifically recorded from the reign of Tudhaliya I in the Indictment of Madduwatta[1094] composed in the reign of Arnuwanda I,[1095] where an Attarisiya of Ahhiya (an older form of the name Ahhiyawa) is engaged in warfare in western Anatolia until checked by the Hittite general Kisnapili. He subsequently also campaigns in Alasiya (Cyprus). The initial appearance of Ahhiyawa in western

---

[1091] Dabney and Wright (1990:47–52); Mountjoy (1993:11–15); Mee (1988; 1998); Rutter (1993:796); French (1993:155–157); Cline (1994:68–77); Gates (1995).

[1092] As now widely accepted – if not proven: e.g. Güterbock (1983; 1984); Bryce (1989b; 1998:59–61); see Mee (1998:142 n.71) for a collection of other recent discussions. For a good recent review and extensive bibliography on this issue, and also the related question of whether Millawanda = Miletos, see now also Niemeier (1998:20–25).

[1093] Among recent reviews, see Bryce (1998:132–133); Giles (1997:259–295). The Hittite New Kingdom starts after the assassination of the interloper Muwatalli. The first king is named Tudhaliya. But how many kings should be placed before Suppiluliuma I is debated. The time interval between the first Tudhaliya and Suppiluliuma I is three generations. The crux of the problem is that there are several kings named Tudhaliya, and it is not clear on present evidence whether there were two or three of them in this time period. Among scholars who assume there were three, there has also been a further debate in which the order of Arnuwanda I and Tudhaliya II is reversed in many accounts, with the former the son of the latter (e.g. Gurney 1990:181, rather than the reverse, as in Astour 1989:74 chart 1). The best evidence towards a resolution of these problems comes from a recent find at Hattusa which shows that Suppiluliuma I's father was named Tudhaliya (Neve 1993:57 Abb.147). Now, since another Tudhaliya (conventionally Tudhaliya III) was his short-reigned brother who Suppiluliuma I replaced in a coup d'état (Astour 1989:73; Bryce 1998:168), this must make it likely that his father was a Tudhaliya II (and not the original founder of the dynasty, Tudhaliya I), and in turn Arnuwanda I was the father of Tudhaliya II, and Tudhaliya I was in turn the father of Arnuwanda I. Hence we have a king-list running: Tudhaliya I, Arnuwanda I (who may have had an elusive Hattusili 'II' as a co-regent?: see summary in Bryce 1998:153–154), Tudhaliya II, Tudhaliya III (very short-lived reign of months before coup by his brother), and then Suppiluliuma I. For a slightly different reconstruction, see Giles (1997:294–295).

[1094] Beckman (1996:144–151 no.27); CTH 147; KUB 14.1 + KBo 19.38.

[1095] Otten (1969); Houwink Ten Cate (1970:63–65); Bryce (1986; 1998:140).

Old Kingdom	
Labarna	
Hattusili I	(grandson?)
Mursili I	(grandson, adopted son)
Hantili I	(brother-in-law)
Zidanta I	(son-in-law)
Ammuna	(son)
Huzziya I	(brother of Ammuna's daughter-in-law)
Telipinu	(brother-in-law)
Alluwamna	(son-in-law)
Tahurwaili	(interloper)
Hantili II	(son of Alluwamna?)
Zidanta II	(son?)
Huzziya II	(son?)
Muwatalli I	(interloper)
New Kingdom	
Tudhaliya I	(grandson of Hazziya II?)
Arnuwanda I	(son-in-law, adopted son)
Hattusili II?	(son? – emphemeral king/co-regent)
Tudhaliya II	(son?)
Tudhaliya III	(son)
Suppiluliuma I	(brother, son of Tudhaliya II)
Arnuwanda II	(son)
Mursili II	(brother)
Muwatalli (II)	(son)
Urhi-Tesub (=Mursili III)	(son)
Hattusili III	(uncle)
Tudhaliya IV, 1st period as king	(son)
Karunta	(cousin)
Tudhaliya IV, 2nd period as king	(cousin)
Arnuwanda III	(son)
Suppiluliuma II	(brother)

Table 6. List of Hittite Kings after Bryce (1998).

Anatolian affairs might therefore be placed from the later 15th century BC (and thus the later LHIIIA1 period into early LHIIIA2).[1096] As Mee (1998:142) argues, the campaigning Attarisiya of Ahhiya, and the irrepressible Madduwatta, were rather incompatible with the conventional Aegean chronology, where they were contemporary with LHIIB at the latest. This seems too early, as Mycenaean Greece was

---

[1096] For the Hittite texts, Ahhiyawa, and dating, see e.g. Güterbock (1983; 1984); Houwink ten Cate (1970); Bryce (1983; 1986; 1989a; 1989b; 1998); Astour (1989); Gurney (1990:20–22, 38–45); Cline (1994:69, 121); Kuhrt (1995:229–238, 250–252). The 'redating' of some of the Hittite texts – namely the association of some documents including the Madduwatta text mentioned above with the late 15th–earlier 14th century BC kings Tudhaliya and Arnuwanda and not like-named kings of the 13th century BC – as a result of work in the late 1960s and 1970s – is now widely accepted. A few scholars disagree and maintain the traditional dates (e.g. Heinhold-Krahmer *et al.* 1979; and most recently, and in detail, Giles 1997:123–

barely a power by then, and only emerged as a regional and inter-regional force in the next periods. As Mee notes, some scholars even cited this problem as a reason to reject the 'Ahhiya(wa) = Achaiwa' equation – alternatively one had to insist on the old, much later, dating of this text.[1097] However, with the 'high', or 'early', Aegean chronology, and the recognition of the correlation of LMIIIA1 (and thus LHIIIA1) with the last years of Tuthmosis III (Chapter IV.9), a good and suitable historical–archaeological context and correlation exists.

This might be called international phase 1 for Mycenaean Greece/Ahhiyawa: correlating a period in (later) LHIIIA1 with Tudhaliya I. Tudhaliya I's long reign seems to end a few years after the accession of Tuthmosis IV according to Astour (1989:52), or in the 1390s BC according to conventional Egyptian chronology. In other words, we are pre-Amenhotep III.

When did Amenhotep III become involved in Hittite history, and diplomacy with the surrounding powers? The key prompt seems to have been a set of intra-Anatolian wars at some point during the reign of Tudhaliya II (son of Arnuwanda I and Asmunikal, daughter of Tudhaliya I), about a generation later, which we learn about from the preamble in a decree of Hattusili III.[1098] Up to this point, the Egyptians had been interested solely in Syria, and the control of this region vis à vis the Mitanni and the Hittites. The Egyptians first made the so-called Kurustama treaty with the Hittites, simply agreeing upon basic territorial status.[1099] The Egyptians subsequently made a treaty, even alliance, with the Mitanni, and seem to have become increasingly concerned about Hittite power. Negotiations with the Mitanni began during the reign of Amenhotep II, and a treaty and marriage alliance was formalised in the reign of Tuthmosis IV.[1100] The Egyptians appear to have been keen to build up a series of strategic alliances in order both to consolidate their empire, and to constrain the Hittites – about whom, given the extraordinary conquests and successes of Suppiluluima I just a generation later, they had reason to be concerned.[1101]

However, the whole status quo seemed to change in a few years during the reign of Tudhaliya II,[1102] when a text informs us that a number of countries all around the Hittite homeland seceded from the Hittites and attacked them.[1103] Among these the Arzawans are named, and they occupied a significant area of west and southwest Anatolia. The Hittites' loss of territory was extremely serious from their own (even if

---

143), but, as the review of Gurney (1982), and a number of other papers of the early 1980s stress, this seems very unlikely. For a brief review with further references, see Bryce (1998:414–415). The arguments of Giles (1997:123–143) are flawed by their overly-literal, and simplistic, interpretation of history and archaeology.

[1097] As for example by Giles (1997:134–135).

[1098] Bryce (1998:158–159); KBo 6.28; CTH 88. Kuhrt (1995:251–252) incorrectly associates these events with Madduwatta, and the reign of Arnuwanda I.

[1099] Tudhaliya I with Amenhotep II?: see Astour (1989:65–67); CTH 134.

[1100] Bryce (1998:156–158); Astour (1989:66–67).

[1101] See Bryce (1998:168–205); Kuhrt (1995:252–254).

[1102] This Tudhaliya = Tudhaliya III of Bryce (1998).

[1103] Dated by the Suppiluliuma-Sattiwaza treaty to the time of the father of Suppiluliuma I, hence Tudhaliya II.

exaggerated) account. Most significantly of all, the capital, Hattusa, was burned down.[1104] This was an event of international significance, and changed the apparent power-balance and make-up of the wider region. It is in this context that we should consider one of the el-Amarna letters (EA31), sent by Amenhotep III to Tarhundaradu, king of Arzawa, in which Amenhotep III seeks to establish friendship and alliance, and proposes to marry a daughter of the king.[1105] We may also speculate that this was the first such royal contact between Egypt and the Arzawans, as the Arzawan scribe notes at the end of a reply (EA32) that correspondence should be in Hittite (the language of the two known letters in the Amarna archive);[1106] clearly, therefore, the Egyptians had no prior established protocol with this state. Amenhotep III specifically comments on the fact that: 'I have heard that everything is finished, and that the land of Hattusa too has gone to pieces'.[1107] It is difficult to construe this as anything other than an obvious reference to the dramatic troubles besetting Tudhaliya II, including the burning of his capital, and the letter as an attempt by Amenhotep III to react to, and even take advantage of, the apparent new geo-political situation by making relations with Arzawa, who had suddenly emerged in international terms as a major power and rival/enemy of the Hittites.[1108]

While it is unlikely that there will ever be any positive evidence, it is therefore

---

[1104] Bryce (1998:158–159); Astour (1989:70 and 125–126 n.487); CTH 88; KBo 6.28 + KUB 26.48.

[1105] Bryce (1998:160–161); translations of the letter in Moran (1992:101); Kuhrt (1995:251–252).

[1106] Moran (1992:103).

[1107] Translation of Güterbock (1967:145); Moran (1992:101) is very similar. Moran (1992:102–103 note 8) notes an alternative translation by Starke which renders the end as 'is at peace'. Starke argues that the word order is Egyptian-based and that the key verb 'igait' (is icy, is cool, is sluggish, is inactive) could from Egyptian idiom mean 'is at peace'. Moran says this is ingenious, but prefers the conventional reading due to the historical evidence. More pertinent perhaps is that Starke is failing to accommodate the active nature of the verb. A reading of 'is inactive' or 'is sluggish' does in fact seem applicable and relevant to a country that has stalled, is collapsing, or otherwise is in chaos and disruption. Thus the general meaning of the conventional translation may be regarded as safe. I thank Ian Rutherford for his advice.

[1108] For a general account of this period, see Bryce (1998:158–161). Cline (1996) discusses a sword recently found at the Hittite capital of Hattusa. It appears to be of, or imitating/developed from, an Aegean Type B sword of LHII–LHIIIA2 date (pp.138–139 with refs.). The inscription on the sword reads 'As Duthaliya the Great King shattered the Assuwa country, he dedicated these swords to the storm-god, his lord'. However, this find, while interesting, is of no specific chronological utility as it is in fact not clear which Great King named Tudhaliya is involved. Cline states Tudhaliya II throughout his article, but employs the mid–later 15th century BC dates of Tudhaliya I (even citing at p.141 n.28 pages specifically relevant to Tudhaliya I in Astour 1989). Cline (p.141 and n.27) links all the main Hittite documents referring to Assuwa to Tudhaliya II and the rebellion against him which he eventually crushed (see main text). But other scholars plausibly argue that some of these texts relate instead to Tudhaliya I (e.g. Astour 1989:52–53). As a result, both kings claimed military victories over Assuwa: one in the mid–later 15th century BC, one in the early 14th century BC. Either scenario could work well with the 'early' Aegean chronology, whereas, on the conventional Aegean low chronology (Warren and Hankey 1989:169 Table 3.1), Tudhaliya I corresponds either to late LHIIA or to LHIIB, and, as noted in the main text, this seems too early for significant Mycenaean=Ahhiyawan influence or involvement in west Anatolia. Thus the low chronology would prefer this sword to relate to Tudhaliya II. If the sword does relate to the rebellion under Tudhaliya II, and if Aegeans were involved in this conflict (Cline 1996:146–149 and refs.), then it is all the more apparent why Amenhotep III chose to initiate contact with the Aegean (and the king of Ahhiyawa) at this time. Ahhiyawa would very much have appeared part of the new anti-Hittite political geography.

tempting to associate the unusual evidence of some link between Amenhotep III and the Aegean, via the finds of a number of objects linked to this ruler's name, with this same period. As Cline (1998b:248–249) notes, Amenhotep III initiated contacts with almost all the countries surrounding the Hittites, and a pattern is evident in which he was seeking both new alliances and a means to take advantage of, and to constrain, the Hittites when they were (temporarily) weak. If Amenhotep III was seeking out friendship with previously unknown or minor states surrounding the Hittites, and perhaps especially those known to be hostile to them (such as the Arzawans), the king of Ahhiyawa would also seem a likely target of Egyptian interest. And this was a short window of interest and activity. As it turned out, Amenhotep III misjudged the situation, and Tudhaliya II mounted a campaign of reconquest, and returned the Hittites to their dominant regional position. Nonetheless, we can see that Amenhotep III was interested in the whole Aegean–Anatolian area for a period during his reign, and that Ahhiyawa had become important in the regional power struggles of the early rulers of the Hittite New Kingdom. In conclusion, the chronology of Hittite involvement with Ahhiyawa, and the context of Amenhotep's interest in western Anatolia, are consistent with a link between Amenhotep III and the Mycenaeans in the late LHIIIA1 period at the earliest, and, more probably, during the early LHIIIA2 period (see above). We might refer to this as international phase 2 for Mycenaean Greece/Ahhiyawa.

Hence the conclusion adopted here is that some point, plausibly early, in the reign of Amenhotep III correlates with the beginning of (or early part of) the LHIIIA2 period, and the beginning of the established (palatial) dominance of Mycenaean Greece. A ceiling of Amenhotep III's palace at Malkata is decorated in Aegean style,[1109] and LHIIIA2 pottery is found in Egypt from his reign.

[1109] Barber (1991:348–350 and fig.15.24).

Chapter V: Absolute dating evidence

Absolute dating refers to the ability to provide accurate and precise calendar dates in terms of our modern Julian-Gregorian Calendar.[1110] This 'western' chronology extends continuously back to the Classical Greek period. Dates to this point are absolute in historical terms. The earlier ancient civilisations of Egypt and Mesopotamia also had sophisticated calendar systems and historical records (see Appendix 1). It has proved possible to link these calendars and records to the Greco-Roman calendar because the worlds of Persia, Egypt, and Greece (and its history as known from Herodotos and other records) intersected from 525BC onwards when the Persian king Cambyses conquered Egypt.[1111] Further, these chronologies are confirmed through, or are consistent with, the analysis of some recorded astronomical observations.[1112] Thus Egyptian and Mesopotamian king-lists, and some similar lists of priests or other officials, may be dated, and form a chronology, back through the second millennium BC. These dates range from the near absolute, to the approximately absolute, give or take certain errors (on Egyptian chronology, see Appendix 1; for further discussion, including of Mesopotamian chronology, see Chapter VII).

The problem is that it is often very difficult, even problematic, to link archaeological strata and material culture styles with these calendar systems. One is comparing two completely different forms of reference, which are often unrelated (see Chapter III). And while the king-list may be near absolute (although invariably not completely so), any purported linkage often comes encumbered with a set of cultural filters and factors which could affect the appropriate date by unknown, or significant, amounts. The find of a piece of Aegean pottery in a tomb related to the time of the reign of a pharaoh does no more than establish an approximate association, or *terminus ante quem*. The nature and length of the 'ante' is usually unknown. Therefore, although I

[1110] For the story of the modern calendar, see Duncan (1998). For the history of time-keeping and the role of time in human life, see Whitrow (1989).

[1111] For discussion of this date, see Depuydt (1996a).

[1112] Although these are not without their own problems: see e.g. Bickerman (1980); Ward (1992); Cryer (1995); Kitchen (1996a:9; 1996b:xlv); von Beckerath (1997:42–51). See further in Appendix 1.

will scandalise traditionalists, I do not discuss Egyptian or Mesopotamian chronology under this heading of 'absolute chronology' for Aegean prehistory.

The quest for absolute dates in prehistoric archaeology has instead to turn to other means, and in particular to a set of physical sciences techniques which offer the potential to achieve absolute (precise calendar) dates independent of cultural filters.[1113] These science data are testable, replicable, and potential errors are capable of being specified and quantified. An added advantage of science-based dating techniques is that they are directly dating the context or object at issue, and so avoid the usual cumbersome and subjective step-wise transfers involved in archaeological cross-linkages.[1114] In this second part of the review of the evidence relevant to the dating of the Thera eruption, I wish to summarise a variety of relevant (or potentially relevant) evidence of an independent, scientific, nature, and to which the adjective 'absolute' may be attached.

1. Radiocarbon evidence

The radiocarbon technique provides a means of determining the time when an organic being/thing stopped exchanging carbon dioxide with the atmosphere (i.e. died, or stopped growing). Radiocarbon, or ^{14}C, is an unstable (radioactive) isotope of carbon produced in the atmosphere when cosmic rays interact with Nitrogen atoms. Once formed, radiocarbon then decays at a constant rate. A radioactive 'clock' is thus available, since the amount of radiocarbon found today in a sample represents what *was* the past atmospheric level *minus* the known process of decay since that time. A complication is that the rate of production of radiocarbon varies through time, but luckily the history of past levels of radiocarbon in the atmosphere can be determined from the study of tree-rings, since each annual ring incorporates and so records that year's average atmospheric radiocarbon content (across growing season). This record of past natural radiocarbon levels from tree-rings runs from the present backwards for many thousands of years. The observed measurement of the radiocarbon age of a sample (of unknown age) may therefore be compared with, or calibrated against, the known values for past time intervals in order to obtain a real calendar date (in practice a range since several years may be compatible, or more or less compatible, with the measurement).[1115]

[1113] Taylor and Aitken (1997).

[1114] Such direct dating of the relevant human cultural contexts is the only way to overcome the tyranny of the study of material culture (art-historical) typology and chronology for its own sake, and as our only option, in Aegean prehistory. It is the means to move beyond the sort of situation criticised by Shanks (1996:157) when he writes: 'so, for example, what stage in the pottery sequence was reached when Knossos was destroyed? Was it Late Minoan II or IIIA1 or IIIA2? ... These are typical questions which have concerned, sometimes obsessed, Aegean prehistorians...'.

[1115] For details, see e.g. Bowman (1990); Aitken (1990:56–119); Taylor (1997; 1987); Weninger (1997). For the basics of calibration, see Pearson (1987). For the original development of the radiocarbon dating method *before* recognition of the need for calibration, see Libby (1955). For the development of radiocarbon science from the 1950s to 1990s, see Taylor *et al.* (1992). There is an excellent introduction to radiocarbon dating and calibration, with extensive bibliography, by T. Higham available via: **http://c14.sci.waikato.ac.nz/webinfo/**

In practice, archaeological applications usually relate to the analysis or dating of charcoal, bones, and seeds found during excavations. The relevance of the resultant date depends on the sample and the find context. For example, if one wishes to date the end of a phase of human settlement (a so-called destruction horizon for instance), then one only wishes to date samples which were effectively dying or ceasing to grow just before this event. Thus a charcoal sample is relevant only if the outermost tree-rings are dated, and this tree was felled literally in the year of the destruction. This is unlikely in most circumstances. Wood is usually felled for construction (i.e. it relates to the building, and not destruction, of a house), or for fuel (although old wood lying around may also be collected for firewood if available – a further problem: Schiffer 1986); further, it is only rarely that one knows whether or not one is dating the outermost tree-rings. Radiocarbon determinations on charcoal are therefore often likely to produce dates rather older than their final deposition context. If the aim is to date a construction phase, then they may well offer the relevant information, otherwise they set merely a *terminus post quem*.

The attempt to date the eruption of Thera by radiocarbon means has centred on trying to date the final habitation at the site of Akrotiri, buried by the eruption. Seeds stored in pots at the time the settlement was abandoned, and so presumably harvested only a year or so beforehand at most, have been the focus of several dating campaigns by a variety of radiocarbon laboratories. These 'short-lived' samples ought to offer a date almost contemporary with the final habitation of the settlement. Since the eruption is thought to have occurred shortly thereafter, these seeds, give or take a couple of years, date the eruption.

Thus far it seems simple; unfortunately, practice has proved otherwise.[1116] Four central problems exist. First, radiocarbon levels vary constantly, thus although 10 and 20 year 'averages' may be precisely determined from dendrochronologically dated wood for given time periods, samples from short time intervals (e.g. seeds of annual, or sub-annual, growth) will have varying radiocarbon levels *around* the longer term trend. The seeds from Akrotiri thus exhibit quite a bit of variation in the dates produced. This has caused both confusion, especially to those not familiar with radiocarbon issues, and analytical difficulties. Second, a few of the sets of results appear simply wrong, whether due to an unresolved contaminant issue/inappropriate sample treatment/inappropriate sample materials, or a problem with the particular laboratory (something only evident when tight precision is necessary and comparisons with other laboratories are at issue, as in this case). Third, the relevant calendar period, somewhere between c.1700–1500BC, sees similar radiocarbon levels in both the later 17th century BC and the mid-16th century BC. This was particularly the case with the 1993 decadal radiocarbon calibration curve based on measurements of wood from Germany for the BC era, but is evident to a varying extent in all of the 1986–1998 radiocarbon calibration curves. There is an inherent dating ambiguity if the radiocarbon age one wishes to calibrate lies across such a plateau in the radiocarbon timescale:[1117] see Figures 44 and 45. With the 1993 decadal calibration data, this was certainly the case; and, considered

---

[1116] See Hardy and Renfrew (1990); Manning (1990b; 1995:200–216).
[1117] Baillie (1995a:109–111); Manning (1995:200–201, 206–213).

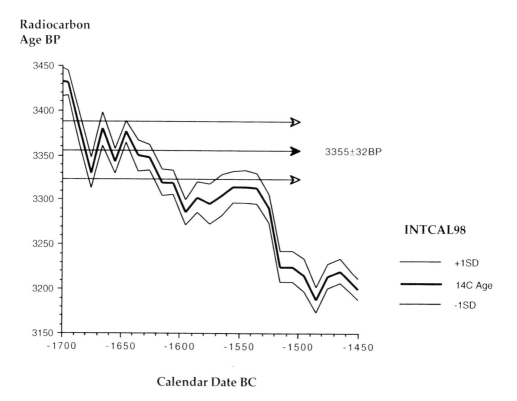

**Radiocarbon
Age BP**

Calendar Date BC

Fig. 44. The INTCAL98 radiocarbon calibration curve (Stuiver et al. 1998) for the period 1800–1400BC with 1σ (1SD) errors indicated. The Copenhagen weighted average radiocarbon age for the volcanic destruction level at Akrotiri on Thera, 3355±32BP, is also shown (see text for explanation). The main intersection, and likely calendar age range, is in the 17th century BC; the mid-16th century BC only just scrapes in within the respective 1σ errors. Note the steep slope (change in atmospheric radiocarbon levels) after 1535BC. The radiocarbon dating evidence relevant to the volcanic destruction level at Akrotiri cannot lie after about this point.

in isolation, no amount of normal statistical manipulation, nor use of techniques like 'boot-strapping',[1118] could overcome this limitation for the radiocarbon data from Thera at this time. Only the inclusion of additional parameters could have potentially resolved the ambiguity.[1119] However, the new, revised, and internationally recommended, 1998 INTCAL98 radiocarbon calibration curve means this problem is now of less concern (see below) – although the truth probably lies somewhere in between. Fourth, volcanoes emit carbon-dioxide and can affect normal radiocarbon levels in the atmosphere close

---

[1118] Aczel (1995:esp. p.847 re-Thera).
[1119] Manning (1992a:249–250).

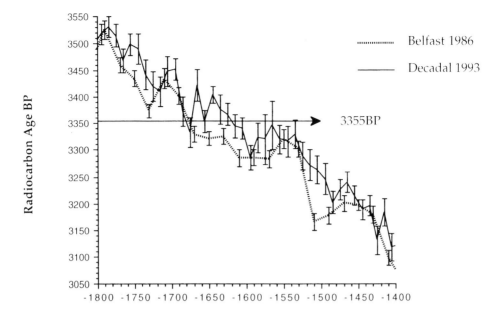

Fig. 45. The previous 1993 Seattle decadal radiocarbon calibration curve (Stuiver and Becker 1993), and 1986 Belfast bi-decadal radiocarbon calibration curve (Pearson et al. 1986), for the period 1800–1400BC, with the 1σ (1SD) errors on the constituent datapoints shown. The new INTCAL98 curve more or less lies in between these two previous curves (compare with Fig. 44). The calibration curves are essentially flat across the later 17th century BC and mid-16th century BC period, making it difficult or impossible to resolve calibrated calendar date ranges within this overall period. The 1993 decadal calibration curve of Stuiver and Becker (1993) offers a significant intersection for the Copenhagen weighted average date for the volcanic destruction level at Akrotiri, 3355±32BP, both in the 17th and mid-16th centuries BC. The relatively large errors on a couple of the mid-16th century BC datapoints exaggerates this region a little. In contrast, although also relatively flat across the period, the 1986 Belfast data strongly favours a 17th century BC intersection, and barely includes a mid-16th century BC intersection at 1550BC. The new INTCAL98 dataset includes a better later 17th century BC intersection (necessary to be potentially compatible with the 'early chronology' archaeological evidence, and perhaps the tree-ring and ice-core evidence), but, like the Belfast 1986 dataset, barely includes a mid-16th century BC intersection within 1σ confidence margins. All three curves record the steep slope (rapid change in atmospheric radiocarbon levels) after, variously, 1535BC, or 1530BC, and it seems impossible for the Thera radiocarbon age range to date much later than this. To quantify. Ruling out the aberrant and inconsistent Simon Fraser data with an inappropriate novel pretreatment (see Chapters II and V.1), and the aberrantly early Zürich data (see Manning 1995:208), the weighted average radiocarbon age range for the volcanic destruction level at Akrotiri from all the laboratories (Pennsylvania, Copenhagen, Oxford [Series I alone, Series I&II average, and Series I&II modified by 'residue' correction], and Heidelberg) which have run measurements on sets of appropriate short-lived samples are similar, respectively: c.3322±29BP, 3355±32BP, 3357±21BP or 3338±17BP or 3325±17BP, 3321±40BP (see Manning 1995:Table 2 and pp.208 and 211; Friedrich et al. 1990; Housley et al. 1990). Each has a 17th century BC and mid-16th century BC calibrated age range, with the respective 1σ and 2σ calibrated calendar age ranges ending at: 1528/1522BC, 1538/1527BC, 1617/1530BC, 1537/1528BC, 1530/1525BC, and 1527/1518BC (INTCAL98 calibration data and OxCal computer programme of Ramsey 1995 'round ranges off').

to vents. This effect has been observed.[1120] Thus it has been suggested that the radiocarbon determinations from Thera have been contaminated, and are not correct. In practice, such effects are strictly limited to plants growing very close to the volcanic source (a vent), and are virtually non-existent at >100m (unless the local environment traps air and does not permit rapid atmospheric mixing). It is unlikely that numerous different samples from both cereal and pulse crops would be consistently affected (the source of the samples dated from Thera); further, the relative consistency of the great many radiocarbon determinations from Thera from different plant species and different agricultural fields in the landscape,[1121] and the high-level of atmospheric mixing on this windy island, render a significant volcanic effect negligible. If such a volcanic effect were present, it should, moreover, be evident in anomalous $\delta^{13}C$ values; this does not appear to be the case for the Thera samples with known $\delta^{13}C$ values. Nonetheless, some 'doubt' remains in some minds.

The radiocarbon dating of the VDL on Thera has effectively consisted of two phases. First, work in the late 1960s to early 1980s principally carried out at the University of Pennsylvania (with a few other laboratories running a few other samples), and then, second, several sets of new data produced by several laboratories (Oxford, Copenhagen, Zürich, Heidelberg, and Simon Fraser) in the late 1980s and presented at the Third Thera and the Aegean World conference in 1989.[1122] In general terms, these data favour an 'early' chronology, and in particular a 17th century BC date for the eruption of Thera.[1123] However, this body of evidence has also created more than its share of confusion. Significantly differing individual age ranges are provided by the same laboratory for supposedly similar samples in several cases; there has been a dispute between the Simon Fraser and Oxford Laboratories over whether or not there was an older contaminant present in some samples;[1124] and there are different possible radiocarbon calibration curves which offer significantly different calendar age ranges. It is self-evident why many archaeologists simply despair, and abandon the method.

It is time to offer a critical review of this subject, and to ask whether radiocarbon has any useful role to play in the precise and accurate dating of the Thera eruption. The basic issues are remarkably simple: (i) we need to reconsider what exactly is being dated; (ii) we need to reconsider which samples are strictly relevant to the radiocarbon age of the Akrotiri VDL; and (iii) we need to understand why there have been different calibration curves, and the potential significance of these differences, and the current state-of-play. I wish to suggest that (i) and (ii) encapsulate the Simon Fraser v. Oxford dispute, and much of the apparently puzzling variation in radiocarbon dates from

---

[1120] See e.g. Hubberton *et al.* (1990); Bruns *et al.* (1980); Calderoni and Turi (1998).

[1121] See Sarpaki (1990).

[1122] For the various 'first' phase datasets, see Olson and Broecker (1959:20); Fishman *et al* (1977:191–193); Fishman and Lawn (1978:215–217); Friedrich *et al.* (1980); Meulengracht *et al.* (1981:229–230). For the 'second' phase datasets, see Housley *et al.* (1990); Nelson *et al.* (1990); Hubberten *et al.* (1990); Friedrich *et al.* (1990); Bonani *et al.* (1990); Wölfli (1992:40–41). For reviews of this evidence, see Manning (1988b:38–46; 1990a; 1990b; 1995:200–216).

[1123] E.g. Manning (1988a; 1990a; 1990b; 1995:200–216); Bruins and van der Plicht (1996).

[1124] See Nelson *et al.* (1990); Housley *et al.* (1990).

Akrotiri. Meanwhile, the new INTCAL98 internationally recommended radiocarbon calibration curve offers the current general purpose frame of reference, but the range of possible variation in Aegean calibration needs to be allowed for.

When one looks at the radiocarbon data from Akrotiri it is clear that something odd is going on. Too often apparently similar samples yield quite different radiocarbon ages. The Simon Fraser versus Oxford controversy highlighted this. Employing a novel sample preparation treatment, the Simon Fraser team claimed to detect and isolate an older contaminant in seeds from Akrotiri.[1125] The Oxford laboratory tried to replicate these results (obtaining a supposed 'contaminant' sample and a supposedly appropriate 'residue' sample), but they reported that they could not replicate the Simon Fraser data, and ended up seriously questioning the Simon Fraser claims.[1126] In the process, the Oxford laboratory produced some rather odd data. For example, in the Oxford data, it seems extraordinary that the date for normally processed OxA-1557 is 3240±60 BP, whereas the supposed 'residue' age (OxA-1692) for seeds from the same batch (2070) is 3325±60 BP, some 85 radiocarbon years older, despite the removal of the supposed older 'contaminant' (OxA-1693) aged 3420±60 BP which is a further 95 radiocarbon years older again! Such results simply do not make sense. And, generally, the variations between a century difference to just 20 radiocarbon years difference between the other normal versus 'residue' ages further suggest a lack of a consistent process. But the real point to note is this variation. Indeed, this almost characterises the data from Akrotiri: otherwise usually excellent laboratories note that they achieved markedly varying ages specifically on seeds from Akrotiri.[1127]

The problem is, of course, the nature of the samples, and their archaeological contexts. A number of the seeds dated by Oxford and Simon Fraser were *not* fully carbonised – and one may assume this applies to many of the other short-lived samples dated from Akrotiri.[1128] In usual archaeological circumstances this is not a major problem. However, the burial circumstances at Akrotiri are far from typical. The pumice which covers the site is extremely porous, and provides a buried context very different from usual archaeological circumstances, and one in which the samples could easily have exchanged carbon with permeating water.[1129] If samples are regularly exposed to groundwater, and in effect solutions of water and surrounding materials,

---

[1125] Nelson *et al.* (1990).

[1126] Housley *et al.* (1990).

[1127] E.g. Hubberten *et al.* (1990:184) reporting data from the Heidelberg laboratory. The Oxford data provide another good example (Housley *et al.* 1990). The range of quoted ages is 3465BP to 3240BP, but the average estimated error for the set at one standard deviation is ±64. The (unweighted) mean and standard variation of the set of 15 non-'contaminant' Oxford data is: 3344±74 BP. In other words, the standard variance within the set of radiocarbon determinations (±74) is of the same order as, and indeed greater than, the quoted measurement errors on the determinations (average for set: ±64).

[1128] Nelson *et al.* (1990:200) remark that this was certainly the case for the data measured at the Pennsylvania laboratory, referring to a personal communication from B. Lawn, who worked in the Pennsylvania laboratory. Friedrich *et al.* (1990:193) comment that 'part of the Akrotiri plant material has only been lightly charred without really being carbonized. This may be a question of the position of the seeds in the storage jars, and the temperature to which the jar has been heated'.

[1129] From surface to buried contexts, and regularly over the last three and a half thousand years.

we may expect some (not well understood) exchanges of carbon into and out of the samples. With fully carbonised samples this is not a problem. They may be properly pretreated with an alkaline solution to remove the contaminating humic acids. This is standard practice. However, non-fully carbonised samples dissolve in the pretreatment, and thus cannot be properly pretreated. Younger or older carbon in the form of humic matter may have become included in such samples, and cannot now be recognised nor removed. Non-carbonised samples are in effect themselves humic acids! Humic acids therefore do not offer an appropriate sample/date for the relevant archaeological context (especially in the circumstances on Thera).

This was the problem that the Simon Fraser laboratory discovered,[1130] and why they proposed a novel form of pretreatment. What this really means is that any radiocarbon determination from Akrotiri not on a *fully carbonised* sample should be discarded (and the problems just outlined probably account for much of the 'variation' in existing datasets through differing humic matter).

The further question is whether the solution to the problem proposed by the Simon Fraser team is appropriate, i.e., is their novel (and in effect untested) pretreatment system valid? The Copenhagen Laboratory team concluded fairly bluntly that it is not. Friedrich *et al.* (1990:193) write:

> If the sample is not really carbonized, the whole sample material will be dissolved when treated with alkaline solutions, with the result that an effective extraction of humic matter is excluded. Such samples therefore cannot be considered safe. Extraction with ultrasonication in acid solutions has been tried on not fully carbonized seeds (Nelson *et al.* 1990), but this can hardly be considered a safe extraction method for humic matter.

The appropriate conclusions are two. First, all not fully carbonised samples from Akrotiri must be regarded as effectively unsafe (i.e. discarded); it is impossible to be confident that the measured radiocarbon age correctly relates to the time the seeds were alive/growing. This eliminates most current data! (and unfortunately much time, money, and effort). Second, following Friedrich *et al.*, one must question the validity of the novel pretreatment of the Simon Fraser group. I repeat the conclusion in the study of Housley *et al.* (1990:210): the novel Simon Fraser technique 'was simply a mild way of dissolving the whole sample [not the objective!], rather than a procedure which was removing a specific contaminant [the objective, if possible, and if relevant]...'. There is no evidence that this novel procedure removed the post-burial humic acids, nor that it takes us anywhere nearer the correct radiocarbon age relevant to when the samples were alive/growing.[1131]

Where does this leave us? The only unquestionably sound data on suitable short-lived sample matter from the VDL at Akrotiri currently available are the set of data

---

[1130] Nelson *et al.* (1990:200); see also Housley *et al.* (1990:209) where they describe the problem of the samples 'solubilizing', and how about 30% of the sample weight was lost in the attempted pretreatment.

[1131] Confirmed by the confusing and contradictory results obtained by the Simon Fraser team (Nelson *et al.* 1990). See also discussion in Manning (1995:207–208).

Sample	Material	Context	δ¹³C PDP	Radiocarbon Age BP
K-5352	Pulses	West House, Room 3 Ground-floor, Pot 3	–22.5	3310±65
K-5353	Pulses	Bronos 1a, hearth	–20.5	3430±90
K-3228	Pulses	West House, Room 5 Delta 3	–20.6	3340±55
K-4255	*Tamarix*	House 3, Delta 1	–23.8	3380±60

Table 7. Radiocarbon determinations for samples from the VDL at Akrotiri from the Copenhagen Laboratory (from Friedrich et al. 1990:194 Table 3).

from the Copenhagen laboratory. The Copenhagen laboratory carefully and deliberately selected only fully carbonised seeds (three samples) and a twig of *Tamarix* with ten growth rings.[1132] Friedrich *et al.* deserve great credit for recognising the humic acid situation, and for adopting a deliberate strategy to avoid it. All other currently published samples are either known to be less than appropriate, or are not explicitly known to be fully carbonised – and so must be treated with suspicion.[1133] We thus have a set of data:[1134]

[1132] Friedrich *et al.* (1990:193–195, Table 3). To quote their rationale: 'In order to avoid such contaminants, it was ensured that the samples dated in this study consisted only of pure, single faba/*Lathyrus* seeds, all fully carbonized'. A similar review of the Akrotiri radiocarbon samples, and the conclusion that the Copenhagen data are the only currently available high-quality and totally reliable data, was offered in Manning *et al.* (1994a:226).

[1133] For example, the samples dated by the Oxford laboratory clearly fall in this category, since they note (Housley *et al.* 1990:209): 'that the 0.1 M NaOH treatment was reduced [from the normal laboratory pretreatment protocol] to a rinse of a few seconds because of its effect in solubilizing the seeds'. In other words, the samples were in effect humic acids. Even with this reduced procedure 'about 30% by weight of the sample was lost by dissolution'. This is not normal.

[1134] Some readers may suspect they are detecting a sleight of hand. They may feel I am in some way removing much data to the benefit of my own argument. This is *not* the case. The other main datasets on routinely, or normally, processed short-lived samples from the Akrotiri VDL which have been published with full details in fact offer very similar data to the Copenhagen dataset: e.g. Copenhagen weighted average – 3355±32BP, Oxford Series I weighted average – 3357±21BP (3351±23BP with just the final VDL stages 2/3 samples), Pennsylvania weighted average of all the 15 short-lived, or thought to be short-lived, samples from the Akrotiri VDL – 3373±16BP: see Friedrich *et al.* (1990:195) for their weighted average; Housley *et al.* (1990:213 and Table 6) for their weighted average; Manning (1995:209) for Pennsylvania weighted average. Furthermore, a generalised frequency histogram of all the radiocarbon determinations on short-lived samples relevant to the VDL at Akrotiri strongly centres on this same general interval (Baillie 1995a:110 Fig.7.1). Therefore, despite the correct decision above to exclude the other datasets because the samples were not fully carbonised, or are not known to have been so, it would nonetheless seem very likely that the Oxford and Pennsylvania data do more or less offer reasonable approximations for the real radiocarbon ages of the Akrotiri samples (albeit with 'noise'). This probably reflects the fact that although some (or more) of the samples were in effect humic acids (and water soluble, mobile, and easily open to contamination by other percolating carbon compounds), they probably also in the majority of cases reflect the actual burial age of the samples. Hence an average date is not far off the mark.

The other major issue raised earlier is the appropriate calibration curve for the conversion of the radiocarbon ages for samples from Akrotiri to calendar ages. Unfortunately, there has been a little controversy and confusion over calibration curves in the last few years, and this has not helped the resolution of the Thera debate. The first set of full-scale high-precision radiocarbon calibration curves for general employment were published in *Radiocarbon* 28(2B), 1986.[1135] The key players were the Belfast laboratory, which produced a bi-decadal calibration dataset from measurements of Irish oak,[1136] and the Seattle laboratory, which produced a decadal dataset from measurements for the BC period of German wood.[1137] These both seemed to agree with each other to a quite remarkable degree, and a precisely-placed, hemisphere-valid, high-precision radiocarbon calibration curve was heralded. In consequence, a general purpose calibration curve was provided for routine use which combined both the Belfast and Seattle data (an average in effect).[1138] These curves were recommended for general use at the 12th International Radiocarbon Conference in Trondheim. But then, in *Radiocarbon* 35(1), 1993, the Seattle laboratory published a revised decadal dataset, stating and explaining that there had been a radon contamination problem in the laboratory (which had affected the Stuiver and Becker 1986 dataset).[1139] The effect was that their calibration curve was slightly 'raised', and so the resultant calendar ages became slightly later (more recent). At the same time, and with no proper explanation – just reference to the re-calculation of the 'efficiency correction' due to a suggestion of a possible, but not detectable, scintillant leakage – Pearson and Qua (1993) published a revised Belfast dataset. Oddly enough, this revision just happened to keep the Belfast dataset in more or less near perfect agreement with the Seattle dataset (and a belief in such close agreement is apparent in a preliminary overview published the year before[1140]). The rest of the Belfast team chose not to be co-authors of this paper. A new combined general purpose curve was also provided.[1141]

These new calibration curves were not internationally recommended. And in the next couple of years serious questions were raised over the validity of the revision to the original 1986 Belfast data. Sadly, there are now no records, or easy means to resolve this matter. Pearson left the Belfast Laboratory. A number of papers, most including members of the Belfast Laboratory under its new director F.G. McCormac, subsequently made a case for discarding the 1993 Belfast dataset, and instead employing the original 1986 Belfast dataset of Pearson *et al.* (1986) pending systematic

---

[1135] Various high-precision calibration data and curves had previously been published for some time periods by individual teams (e.g. Pearson *et al.* 1977; 1983; de Jong *et al.* 1979; Stuiver 1982), but the 1986 publication represented the first coherent international statement on high-precision radiocarbon calibration for the whole field.

[1136] Pearson *et al.* (1986).

[1137] Stuiver and Becker (1986).

[1138] Stuiver and Pearson (1986); and Pearson and Stuiver (1986).

[1139] Stuiver and Becker (1993).

[1140] Stuiver and Pearson (1992).

[1141] Stuiver and Pearson (1993); Pearson and Stuiver (1993).

rechecking and new measurements.[1142] The result was a confusing situation for the radiocarbon user community: for example archaeologists. A new, internationally recommended, and properly vetted, calibration curve was urgently required for general use. This has now been supplied with the publication and distribution of the multi-laboratory, internationally recommended, INTCAL98 radiocarbon calibration dataset of Stuiver *et al.* (1998). The INTCAL98 dataset forms the current standard radiocarbon age calibration for the northern hemisphere, and is accordingly employed in this text as the main point of reference.

The INTCAL98 curve combines several sets of high-precision radiocarbon calibration data to offer the best general purpose approximation for standard radiocarbon levels in the northern hemisphere from the present backwards through the Holocene and into the late Pleistocene. This does not, of course, mean that all the contemporary constituent data are exactly the same – and nor should they be. It was a mistake to expect exact agreement. Some of the small differences may reflect inter-laboratory variations/offsets – and so are an inescapable feature of any laboratory's biography when compared to another, some element may reflect real minor regional, or temporal/regional, differences in atmospheric radiocarbon levels,[1143] and some of the variability may be just that: inherent measurement variability. No resolution is yet possible. With reference to the Aegean region, some arguments may be made to support the better relevance of the data on German versus Irish wood,[1144] but this is as yet a rather insubstantial case. Work is underway at the time of writing by the Aegean–East Mediterranean Radiocarbon Calibration Project to try to resolve this issue for the Aegean and east Mediterranean region, and results should be available within a couple of

---

[1142] E.g. Kalin *et al.* (1995); McCormac *et al.* (1995); van der Plicht and McCormac (1995); van der Plicht *et al.* (1995); Kromer *et al.* (1996:608). It is important to remember that these differences are small, and of 'academic', versus useful or significant, relevance in most non-high-precision archaeological situations.

[1143] See discussion above in Chapter III for a brief review of recent literature. The possibility of differential ^{14}C activity was mentioned as a possible factor in minor inter-laboratory differences by Stuiver and Pearson (1992:21; 1993:1). However, they regarded it as of at most of ≤20 ^{14}C years relevance, and so effectively discounted it. In many ways they were correct. New work has shown that regional differences do exist (McCormac *et al.* 1995; 1998; Stuiver and Braziunas 1998), but for the core mid-latitude northern hemisphere regions (excepting coastal areas next to major deep-water upwelling) the differences are of about ≤20 ^{14}C years relevance, and so of interest, but effectively of no concern to archaeologists in most situations. Except in near perfect, high-precision, laboratory conditions the differences are so small as to be difficult even to detect (and up to 1996 the evidence was still largely inconclusive because of inevitable 'noise' in the data: Kromer *et al.* 1996:608–609). Nonetheless, over systematic high-precision radiocarbon datasets (e.g. the calibration curves), such regional differences in source organic material, allied with systematic laboratory offsets, can (even should) create small differences in average trend between laboratories (i.e. slightly differing calibration curves). A more subtle possibility is a very minor regional/temporal difference. The argument here is that trees in different climate zones do the majority of their growing at slightly differing times during the year (e.g. spring in the Mediterranean, and summer in northern Europe), and, therefore, since natural radiocarbon levels do vary in a systematic way through the year (with highest levels in the late summer: see Levin *et al.* 1992, and a low in early spring: Stuiver and Braziunas 1998:331), some systematic minor variation in recorded radiocarbon content between trees from different climate zones might be expected (Stuiver and Braziunas 1998:331; McCormac *et al.* 1998:1321). I thank Bernd Kromer for discussion.

[1144] Kuniholm *et al.* (1996); Manning (1998a). See further in Chapter V.4.

years.[1145] Preliminary indications show excellent general correlation with the INTCAL98 dataset, but might nonetheless support both the existence of some very minor regional/ temporal variations at some past time intervals between contemporary tree-rings from Anatolia and Germany, but also, on average, the slightly greater relevance of German oak versus Irish oak data for the Aegean region. For the present, the INTCAL98 dataset offers the best approximation of general northern hemisphere radiocarbon levels, and is therefore employed as the primary reference in this text. However, I also give for comparison the data derived from the 1993 Seattle decadal calibration curve (determined from German wood for the BC period) as this may in the end prove relevant. I note that the latter works *against* the 'early' Aegean chronology; hence I am trying not only to be non-partisan, but to allow for the range of possible variation.

I pause for a moment to note that some readers may feel that the foregoing discussion only demonstrates that radiocarbon dating has many errors, and thus should not be taken too seriously. I wish to stress that this is not the case. First, the variations and errors at issue are remarkably small. The atmospheric radiocarbon level around one hemisphere at any one time is typically homogeneous within 0.1 to 0.2%.[1146] Proposed possible regional or temporal–regional differences are of interest, but are usually very small (with rare special exceptions involving major latitude or altitude shifts, or major ocean interaction with continental margins – none of which are relevant in the case of Thera). Appropriate pretreatment of wood samples, and correction using $\delta^{13}C$ measurements, can ensure that in effect all trees yield true reflections of past atmospheric radiocarbon content for where they were growing,[1147] and so, within the broadly similar continental-latitude grouping of the USA and Europe,[1148] an 'average' northern-hemisphere radiocarbon calibration curve should be of utility. The variation in measurement data between the high-precision radiocarbon laboratories is also remarkably small in real terms (less than 1–2%), and usually within quoted measurement errors (typically less than 1%). Finally, it must be highlighted that such issues are quantifiable in radiocarbon dating, and are capable of investigation and resolution. Thus, for example, Stuiver *et al.* (1998:1045) are able to report the offsets observed between the main high-precision calibration laboratories, and their dendro samples, involved in the INTCAL98 project, based in each case on a large number of comparisons. For example, the comparisons on similarly dendro-dated wood range from offsets of a mere –2±2 ^{14}C years (Pretoria/Groningen versus Belfast) to typically something like 12±1 ^{14}C years (Belfast versus Seattle) or 19±2 ^{14}C years (Heidelberg versus Seattle) to a maximum of 30±3 ^{14}C years (Heidelberg versus Belfast). In total contrast, conventional archaeological dating from correlations and art-historical linkages is not easily quantifiable, nor capable of such rigorous control. Nor are the errors anywhere near so small.

[1145] This project, allied with the Aegean Dendrochronology Project, is directed by the author with the collaboration of a number of scholars, including especially B. Kromer, P.I. Kuniholm, and M. Spurk.

[1146] Braziunas *et al.* (1995).

[1147] McCormac *et al.* (1998:1321).

[1148] Braziunas *et al.* (1995).

INTCAL98 calibrated age ranges (Stuiver *et al.* 1998):
    1σ (68.2%):   1687–1604BC (P=0.97), 1549–1548BC (P=0.01), 1541–1540BC (P=0.01)
    2σ (95.4%):   1735–1714BC (P=0.07), 1691–1599 (P=0.71), 1588–1527BC (P=0.21)

Seattle 1993 calibrated age ranges (Stuiver and Becker 1993):
    1σ (68.2%):   1686–1670BC (P=0.18), 1659–1650BC (P=0.10), 1638–1603BC (P=0.38), 1584–1557BC (P=0.28),
             and 1540–1534BC (P=0.06)
    2σ (95.4%):   1724–1712BC (P=0.03), 1690–1598BC (P=0.59), 1591–1526BC (P=0.37)

Belfast 1986 calibrated age ranges (Pearson *et al.* 1986):
    1σ (68.2%):   1738–1723BC (P=0.19), 1687–1626BC (P=0.66), and 1552–1537BC (P=0.15)
    2σ (95.4%):   1747–1713BC (P=0.20), 1702–1608BC (P=0.58), 1599–1583BC (P=0.02), and 1570–1526BC
             (P=0.20)

Table 8. Calibrated calendar age range for the combined Copenhagen dataset for the Akrotiri VDL (see Table 7) employing OxCal (Round Ranges function 'off'). P = Probability (out of 1.0 – although note that occasionally a rounding error means that total probability described only equals 0.99, as in the case of the 1σ INTCAL98 range above, or 1.01). The calibrated age ranges are given at 1σ and 2σ (1 or 2 standard deviation, 68.2% and 95.4%) confidence.

To return now to Thera. We have a relevant dataset from the Copenhagen laboratory (Table 7), and the 1998 internationally recommended radiocarbon calibration curve, and the 'alternative' 1993 Seattle decadal radiocarbon calibration curve derived from trees growing in Germany. All that remains is to select a computer programme to perform the calibration process. The current programme of choice is the OxCal programme by Ramsey (1995, and subsequent modifications).[1149] The combined calibrated calendar probability distributions for the four data in the Copenhagen VDL

[1149] The other main computer calibration programmes (Calib 4.0 and 4.1 by Stuiver and Reimer –see Stuiver and Reimer 1986; 1993 and Stuiver *et al.* 1998, and Cal25 by J. van der Plicht – see van der Plicht 1993) offer largely similar to identical date ranges. Some variations are of course evident, either because of slightly different approaches to extrapolating the calibration curve between/among calibration datapoints (linear extrapolation, versus tightly fitted splines, versus looser best fit splines), or computation differences and rounding. In general, the OxCal programme if anything favours slightly wider, and therefore includes lower, calibrated age ranges. For Thera, it gives a little more significance to the mid-16th century BC range, for instance. Thus use of OxCal as the standard calibration programme in this text by no means favours the author's argument. I compare as an example the OxCal and Calib 4.1 calibrated ranges for the Copenhagen and Oxford Thera average ages of 3355±32BP and 3338±30BP, both employing the INTCAL98 calibration dataset, for the interest of readers. 1. 3355±32BP. Calib 4.1 (intercept method): 1σ 1687–1615BC, 2σ 1738–1707BC, 1694–1524BC; (probability method): 1σ 1688–1606BC (P=1.000), 2σ 1736–1712BC (P=0.066), 1693–1527BC (P=0.934). OxCal (round ranges 'off'): 1σ 1687–1604BC (P=0.89), 1554–1538BC (P=0.11), 2σ 1736–1712BC (P=0.08), 1691–1599BC (P=0.67), 1589–1527BC (P=0.24). 2. 3338±30BP. Calib 4.1 (intercept method): 1σ 1683–1666BC, 1663–1647BC, 1643–1601BC, 1569–1531BC, 2σ 1731–1718BC, 1690–1522BC, (probability method): 1σ 1680–1665BC (P=0.114), 1664–1602BC (P=0.623), 1560–1534BC (P=0.263), 2σ 1686–1526 (P=1.000). OxCal (round ranges 'off'): 1σ 1682–1668 (P=0.16), 1661–1649BC (P=0.14), 1640–1603BC (P=0.41), 1564–1533BC (P=0.29), 2σ 1687–1524BC (P=1.00).

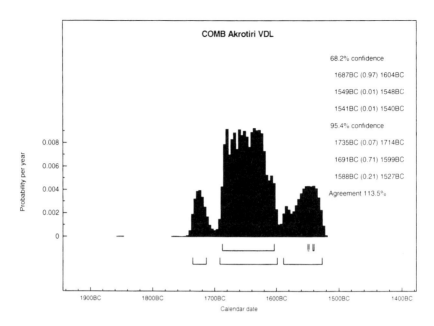

Fig. 46. Calibrated calendar age range for the combined Copenhagen dataset for the Akrotiri VDL (see Tables 7 and 8) employing the INTCAL98 radiocarbon calibration dataset of Stuiver et al. (1998) and the OxCal computer calibration programme (Ramsey 1995, Round Ranges function 'off'). P = Probability (out of 1.0). The 1σ and 2σ calibrated age ranges are indicated by the upper and lower lines under the overall probability distribution.

dataset (Table 7) are shown in Figures 46 and 47, and the date ranges for the combined calibrations are set out in Table 8.

The odds strongly favour a 17th century BC date range. With the current INTCAL98 calibration dataset, at 1σ (68.2%) confidence there is 97% probability for a 17th century BC date, and, even at 2σ (95.4%) confidence, there is only a 21% probablity for a date range after 1599BC. With the Seattle dataset, there is a greater than 60% probability of a date in the 17th century BC, but a mid-16th century BC date clearly cannot be ruled out. With the original Belfast 1986 bi-decadal dataset, there is only a 15–22% probability of a date in the 16th century BC, in contrast with a very good probability for the 17th century BC date range.[1150] A betting person would have little hesitation about where to place their money.

As noted above, previous studies have noted a problematic 17th century BC *or* mid-16th century BC ambiguity in the calibrated data from Thera. This was a result of the shape of the radiocarbon calibration curve (i.e. the past history of natural

---

[1150] This comparison stresses the small, but significant, difference between the data solely on Irish trees versus the data solely on German trees.

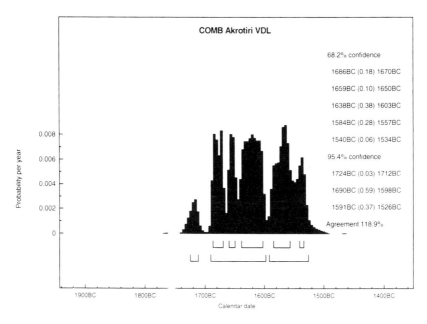

Fig. 47. Calibrated calendar age range for the combined Copenhagen dataset for the Akrotiri VDL (see Tables 7 and 8) employing the 1993 decadal radiocarbon calibration dataset of Stuiver and Becker (1993) from German wood and the OxCal computer calibration programme (Ramsey 1995, Round Ranges function 'off'). P = Probability (out of 1.0). The 1σ and 2σ calibrated age ranges are indicated by the upper and lower lines under the overall probability distribution.

variations of radiocarbon levels in the atmosphere), whereby radiocarbon ages from the later 17th century BC are effectively similar to, or the same as, those of the mid-16th century BC. This is especially the case with the Seattle 1993 decadal dataset of Stuiver and Becker (1993): see Figure 45 and compare with Figure 44. However, the above analysis largely avoids this problem. The late 17th century BC and mid-16th century BC plateau still exists (see Figure 44), but the combination of the Copenhagen dataset, and the slightly revised INTCAL98 calibration curve, mean that the previously 'ambiguous' period is now later than the preferred radiocarbon age for the appropriate, fully carbonised, short-lived samples available from Thera.

To consider the relevance of this change, it is necessary to examine the shape of the calibration curve in general from 1700–1450BC. The relevant radiocarbon age for the VDL at Akrotiri appears to be c.3355BP (the weighted average of the Copenhagen data[1151]), or thereabouts. This age does not intersect with any of the 16th century BC

[1151] The average of the Copenhagen data: Friedrich *et al.* (1990:195). I calculate 3356BP using the Ward and Wilson (1978) approach. The series I (no unusual procedures) data from the Oxford laboratory offers a remarkably similar average age of 3357±21BP (Housley *et al.* 1990:213 Table 6).

radiocarbon calibration data in the INTCAL98 dataset within the stated 1σ errors of the calibration curve (cf. Figure 44).[1152] Indeed, only a radiocarbon age of less than 3334BP now intersects with anywhere in the 16th century BC even allowing for the 1σ errors on the calibration curve. And, only if the radiocarbon age is less than 3315BP, does it actually intercept with the midpoint of the calibration data (i.e. the measurement without its error component) anywhere in the 16th century BC. The Copenhagen data offer a radiocarbon age a little, but clearly above, this divide. Indeed, analyses of the other major datasets relevant to the VDL at Akrotiri, the Oxford and older Pennsylvania suites, show that they too indicate a preferred radiocarbon age somewhere above this latter divide.[1153] It might therefore seem that the correct radiocarbon age for Thera is just slightly higher than, and so avoids, the late 17th century BC and mid-16th BC century radiocarbon plateau. If so, one of the main problems for the 'early' Aegean chronology is overcome, and a major new obstacle stands before advocates of the 'low' Aegean chronology.

We may therefore conclude that the good quality radiocarbon data presently available from Thera (the Copenhagen data from the VDL at Akrotiri) cover both the Aegean 'early' and 'compromise early' chronological alternatives, but very clearly favour the 17th century BC and so the 'early' chronology. A date after c.1530/1520BC is impossible.[1154] The steep slope in the radiocarbon calibration curve after 1535BC, and especially 1525BC (see Figure 44), reflecting rapidly changing radiocarbon levels in the atmosphere at this time, takes the radiocarbon calibration curve decisively away from the Thera age range. Thus the traditional date for the Thera eruption c.1500BC[1155] is ruled out – and the recently proposed date for the eruption 'between 1515 and 1460 B.C.'[1156] is simply not possible.

[1152] For comparison we can review the situation for the 1993 Seattle decadal curve, and the 1986 Belfast bi-decadal curve. 3355BP does not intersect with most of the 16th century BC 1993 decadal calibration data within 1σ errors (cf. Figure 45) – only the problematic 1575BC and especially the 1565BC data points with their unusually large errors – and, if one considers the 1986 Belfast bi-decadal calibration curve, there is in fact *no* intersection for any radiocarbon age greater than or equal to 3342BP in the 16th century BC: see Figure 45.

[1153] Housley *et al.* (1990:213) consider two possible outcomes from their data. The overall average of both their series I and II data is 3338±17BP (which they consider as 3338±30BP). However, they also allow for the possibility of the reality of an older contaminant factor in their series I, and thus also consider a revised overall average age of 3325±30BP. The average age of the consistent subset of the Pennsylvania data on short-lived samples relevant to the age of the VDL was calculated at 3321±18BP in Manning (1988a; 1988b:44; 1990a:34). Different subsets with either NaOH pretreatment, or δ13C normalisation, offered average ages of 3330±25BP or 3351±32BP (Manning 1990a:35).

[1154] The calibrated age range at 2σ (95.4%) confidence ends at 1527BC for the combined calibration of the Copenhagen data in Table 7. We might compare other radiocarbon ages suggested for the VDL at Akrotiri (using OxCal with round ranges 'on' and INTCAL98). The Oxford averages of 3338±30BP or 3325±30BP both end at 2σ (95.4%) confidence at 1520BC. The Pennsylvania average of 3321±18BP ends at 2σ (95.4%) confidence at 1520BC. See also Figure 45 caption.

[1155] E.g. Warren (1984).

[1156] Bietak (1997:125). Even lower proposed dates, such as c.1460BC in Eriksson (1992:219), are totally impossible, unless one chooses to ignore not only the radiocarbon evidence from Akrotiri, but also a variety of other recent radiocarbon evidence including the new late LMIB determinations presented by

We can go no further with the direct radiocarbon evidence from Thera itself. The probable situation is transparently clear with the new 1998 INTCAL98 calibration dataset, but a final choice between the likely date in the later 17th century BC, *or* the possible but much less likely date in the mid-16th century BC, must be made on other criteria (see below). Some degree of ambiguity remains, and this, and a variety of other problems, from the genuine to the spurious, will be noted by critics. For a purely radiocarbon-based resolution, what are required, in addition to the current body of evidence, are either: (i) samples from locations other than Thera, beyond suggestions of carbon dioxide emissions from the volcano, and moreover related to the several surrounding ceramic periods so that a number of parameters constrain and date the LMIA period, and the eruption, precisely;[1157] (ii) dendrochronological samples from Thera providing fixed sequence tree-ring or radiocarbon data directly related to the eruption (i.e. trees killed by the eruption) which could be matched, respectively, against either the Aegean dendrochronology (see Chapter V.4 below), or the radiocarbon calibration curve (so-called 'wiggle-matching'), in order to obtain a precise and specific date;[1158] or (iii) securely provenanced Minoan eruption Thera airfall tephra found in a peat or sediment context which can be radiocarbon dated via wiggle-matching with extreme high precision.[1159]

One project which sought to begin the process of resolving the Thera ambiguity by obtaining radiocarbon data from other related sites, and from the archaeological periods and phases around the eruption, was based at Oxford under Rupert Housley. Samples of short-lived materials (i.e. samples whose radiocarbon age should be approximately contemporary with their find context) relevant to the LMIB destructions at Myrtos-Pyrgos and Chania on Crete, and the LMII destruction of the Minoan Unexplored Mansion at Knossos on Crete, were, among others, collected for this project, and measurements performed at the Oxford Radiocarbon Accelerator Unit. The LMIB period results of this project appeared in a paper by Housley *et al.* (1999). The results suggest that the end of the LMIB period at these sites cannot be later than c.1525–1490BC. This conclusion was derived from the 1993 decadal calibration curve. Use of the INTCAL98 dataset offers a similar result.[1160] At 2σ (95.4%) confidence there is a 78% probability that the data calibrate *before* 1487BC (c.1482–1445BC has a 22% probability). The most likely calibrated age range is 1526–1494BC. This particular

---

Housley *et al.* (1999) – discussed below – along with clear archaeological evidence for a pre-Tuthmosis III beginning for the (subsequent) LMIB period (a situation subsequently recognised and accepted by Eriksson: see Bourriau and Eriksson 1997). The recently proposed date of about 1520BC by Warren (1998:328) is also practically impossible given the viable radiocarbon date range *within* which a specific date must be sought. Those who wish to support lower Aegean chronologies need to consider an eruption date in the range c.1550–1530BC.

[1157] Cf. Manning (1992a:249–250).

[1158] For an example of the latter approach from New Zealand, see Sparks *et al.* (1995).

[1159] A good example of what could be achieved is offered by the study of Hall *et al.* (1994) and Pilcher *et al.* (1995). This established a date (2310±20BC) with realistic total dating error of just ±20 calendar years for the deposition of Hekla 4 tephra. Radiocarbon dates exist from sediment/pollen cores from Turkey pre-, or post-, dating Theran airfall tephra; these confirm the mid-second millennium BC age, but do not so far offer useful chronological precision: e.g. Sullivan (1988). See now Eastwood *et al.* (1999:26–28).

[1160] Employing the OxCal calibration programme (Ramsey 1995).

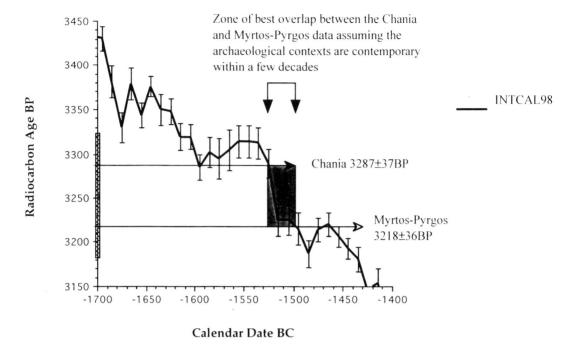

Fig. 48. The weighted average of the Chania and Myrtos-Pyrgos date sets reported in Housley et al. (1999:Table 1), each shown in relation to the INTCAL98 calibration curve (Stuiver et al. 1998). Compare to similar figure in Housley et al. (1999:Fig.2) where data are shown in relation to the 1993 decadal calibration curve of Stuiver and Becker (1993). The plausible calendar range where the two datasets may be placed relatively close to each other is indicated (c.1525BC to 1498BC). The possible earlier 15th century BC range for the Myrtos-Pyrgos dates can only come into play if a relatively long gap (40+ calendar years) is regarded as possible between the two respective later/late LMIB archaeological contexts.

date range is arrived at because of the shape of the radiocarbon calibration curve. The samples from the close of LMIB destructions at Chania (Houses I and IV and an associated context closeby) and Myrtos-Pyrgos (the 'country-house') ought, according to conventional archaeological analysis, to be closely similar (to almost con-temporaneous) in age. No one believes these contexts could be more than a couple of decades apart in age, and both exhibit similar classic mature LMIB types in the respective ceramic assemblages.[1161] But the radiocarbon data are quite different for the two sites: the Chania data are rather older than the Myrtos-Pyrgos data. The only way this information can be accommodated *with* the archaeological information, is for the two sets of data to fit in the period c.1526–1494/1487BC (see Figures 48 and 49), when there is a brief period with a sharp change in atmospheric radiocarbon

---

[1161] See the recent review of each site in Driessen and Macdonald (1997:121–124, 217–281).

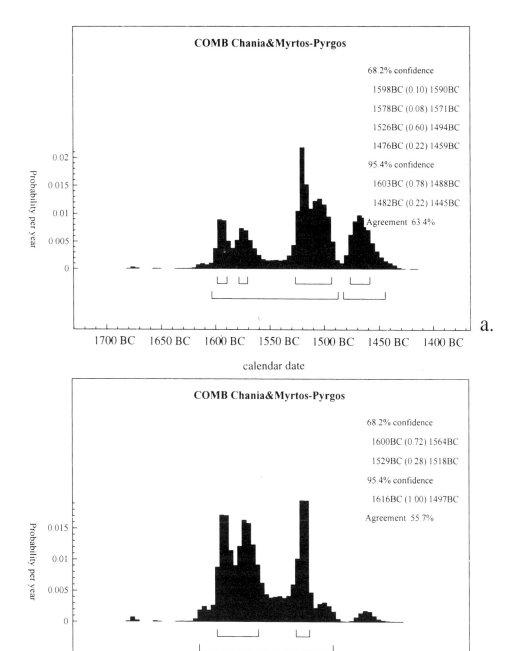

Fig. 49. a. Combined calibrated calendar probability distribution for the new Oxford Chania and Myrtos-Pyrgos data reported in Housley et al. (1999:Table 1) using the INTCAL98 radiocarbon calibration dataset of Stuiver et al. (1998). b. The same but adding also the two previous Pennsylvania data on identical samples from Myrtos-Pyrgos (Fishman and Lawn 1978:213) (compare to Housley et al. 1999:Figs. 7 and 8 based on the 1993 decadal radiocarbon calibration dataset of Stuiver and Becker 1993). Calibration data in each case from the OxCal computer calibration programme (Ramsey 1995, Round Ranges function 'off'). P = Probability (out of 1.0). The 1σ and 2σ calibrated age ranges are indicated by the upper and lower lines under each of the probability distributions

levels.[1162] Some previous radiocarbon dates on essentially identical short-lived samples from the LMIB destruction of Myrtos-Pyrgos (P-2113, 3320±60BP; P-2114, 3320 ±60BP)[1163] yielded ages similar to those from LMIA Akrotiri (and now those from LMIB destruction Chania).[1164] The combined calibrated calendar age range at 2σ (95.4%) confidence for the eight new Oxford close of LMIB determinations and these two Pennsylvania data is 1616–1497BC.

The only conclusion from all this evidence seems to be that the radiocarbon age of sample matter relevant to the mature–late LMIB period ranges from being very similar to, to somewhat later than, the radiocarbon age of the short-lived material from the VDL at Akrotiri. This is entirely to be expected given the shape of the radiocarbon calibration curve (i.e. the history of past natural variations in atmospheric radiocarbon levels): Figures 44 and 45. We have seen that the late 17th century BC and mid-16th century BC had similar radiocarbon ages, followed by a steep change (down) in radiocarbon age in the late 16th century BC. The individual close of LMIB short-lived determinations wish to date either between (i) the later 17th century BC or mid-16th century BC 'wiggle' in the calibration curve, or (ii) the 16th through 15th centuries BC. As a set, these determinations straddle the mid-16th century BC through late 16th century BC pattern of radiocarbon ages. The lower range resolves the initial ambiguity. The unique fit for the radiocarbon range exhibited by LMIB short-lived samples ties the close of the LMIB ceramic phase to the period from the mid-later 16th century BC to c.1490BC, it cannot move further up, it cannot move further down: see Figures 48 and 49. In consequence, the LMIA short-lived samples which *could* date either to the later 17th century BC or the mid-16th century BC are shown most likely to belong to the later 17th century BC option, since the mid-16th century BC is already occupied by the mature to late LMIB short-lived samples.[1165]

It must be emphasised that the LMIB samples at issue are dating the *end* of the LMIB period, thus the rest of the period must be 16th century BC. LMIA then lies before this, and (from the large body of data from Akrotiri) mature/late LMIA lies in the later 17th century BC. The Oxford project produced two other highly relevant age determinations in this regard from Kommos: see Table 9.[1166]

[1162] For detailed discussion, see Housley *et al.* (1999).

[1163] Fishman and Lawn (1978:213).

[1164] See Housley *et al.* (1999).

[1165] Manning (1992a:249–250); Housley *et al.* (1999). It is important to note the relevance and potential usefulness of the past natural variations in radiocarbon levels, and not merely to cite the overlap of some LMIA and LMIB date sets as grounds for 'inconsistencies', and thus abandon the method. Warren (1987:208–210; 1996:284–285; etc.; and Warren and Hankey 1989:127, 141) has repeatedly argued, because some LMIB date sets seem to have radiocarbon ages similar to LMIA date sets, and vice versa, that radiocarbon dating is of no utility for this period. But, as discussed in the main text, the relevant date sets are in fact correctly reflecting past radiocarbon patterns, and, when considered against these, a correct 'fit' of the data patterns is available which is both consistent with, and usefully dates, the known archaeological sequence.

[1166] LMIA period data were also acquired by the project from Trianda on Rhodes, and Palaikastro on Crete. The Trianda data have not yet been finalised, and will be published elsewhere. A small set of analyses on bone samples from Palaikastro proved problematic. The only samples available at the time were uncharred bone, and most on chemical analysis proved unsatisfactory, with at best one offering a possibly reliable age. The aim was to extract and date the ion-exchanged gelatin from the collagen, but

Lab. No.	Context	Material	δ¹³C	¹⁴C Age BP	Calibrated Calendar Age Ranges BC		
						Seattle 1993 data	INTCAL98 data
OxA-3673	MMIII Kommos Hillside 45A/12	charred bone	−20.5	3400±65	1σ:	1766–1763 (P=0.02) 1741–1603 (P=0.83) 1584–1557 (P=0.13) 1539–1535 (P=0.02)	1860–1844 (P=0.07) 1771–1606 (P=0.93)
					2σ:	1876–1842 (P=0.05) 1828–1791 (P=0.05) 1779–1512 (P=0.90)	1878–1840 (P=0.09) 1828–1793 (P=0.06) 1782–1525 (P=0.85)
OxA-3429	early LMIA Kommos Room 25B Building T Tr.66B	charcoal	−27.8	3350±70	1σ:	1721–1715 (P=0.03) 1689–1525 (P=0.97)	1731–1720 (P=0.06) 1689–1599 (P=0.59) 1588–1528 (P=0.35)
					2σ:	1771–1451 (P=1.00)	1873–1843 (P=0.03) 1775–1492 (P=0.95) 1477–1456 (P=0.02)
OxA-3674	LMII Kommos Hillside 41A1/26	charred bone	−20.2	3090±80	1σ:	1431–1418 (P=0.06) 1412–1243 (P=0.87) 1229–1216 (P=0.05) 1197–1194 (P=0.01)	1436–1259 (P=0.94) 1233–1218 (P=0.06)
					2σ:	1501–1105 (P=0.99) 1096–1079 (P=0.01)	1521–1125 (P=1.00)

Table 9. Radiocarbon determinations on samples provided by Joseph W. Shaw from MMIII, early LMIA, and LMII contexts at Kommos produced by the Oxford Radiocarbon Accelerator Unit as part of a project directed by Rupert Housley. I thank Joseph Shaw and Rupert Housley for permission to refer to these data here, and Jeremy Rutter for information and advice on the contexts at Kommos. Calibrated results from the OxCal programme (Ramsey 1995). Round Ranges function 'off'. Calibration datasets from Stuiver et al. (1998); and Stuiver and Becker (1993). P = Probability (out of 1.0 – although note that occasionally a rounding error means that total probability described only equals 0.99 or 1.01). The calibrated age ranges are given at 1σ and 2σ (1 or 2 standard deviation, 68.2% and 95.4%) confidence.

Both these (MMIII and early LMIA) samples should date before the VDL at Akrotiri, the MMIII sample by a reasonable amount, the early LMIA sample by at least a few decades. They thus nicely constrain the upwards limit of the dating of Thera, and provide the only recent, high-quality, radiocarbon evidence for these periods currently available. It is immediately interesting to note that the radiocarbon ages of the two

---

collagen can undergo degradation as part of the process of bone diagenesis – especially if the bone is not fully charred before burial – and it is impossible to remove exogenous contaminants like humic acids if the sample was not fully carbonised. The quality of any isotope measurement therefore depends on two factors, the degree of preservation of the endogenous collagenous material, and the success in removing exogenous contaminants (like humics). In order to assess the Palaikastro dates, the project undertook a chemical characterisation of the protein (van Klinken and Hedges 1992; van Klinken et al. 1994). This showed that at best only one of the samples had only relatively little collagen degradation and a high concentration of the tripeptide Glycine-Proline-Hydroxyproline. The conclusion was therefore to discount these data as unsatisfactory.

samples are just higher than, or more or less the same as, the radiocarbon age for the mature–late LMIA VDL at Akrotiri. We are looking therefore for a plateau in the radiocarbon calibration curve for early to late LMIA where a period of several decades had more or less the same radiocarbon age, and an upwards slope before this where a slightly older preceding MMIII sample might be accommodated. The theoretically possible 16th century BC calibrated date ranges for each sample may be discounted given the LMIB evidence (above), and the need also to accommodate the late LMIA evidence from Akrotiri between the LMIB data and these earlier data. These Kommos samples should hence date in the 18th–17th, and 17th, centuries BC (respectively) – appropriately the main calibrated age ranges for each sample (see Table 9). The early LMIA sample is likely to be from roof collapse; it was an c.8cm in diameter round charcoal/wood sample from room 25 of Building T.[1167] This sample ought to offer a *terminus post quem* for the LMIA period at Kommos. We may further note that radiocarbon determinations on long-lived samples relevant to the date of early LMIA run some time ago are broadly consistent with the new Kommos data.[1168] Excluding those data which are manifestly aberrant for whatever reason, MMIII data congregate around or just before 3400 radiocarbon years BP, and LMIA long-lived samples group just a couple of decades later. The most likely calibrated ages lie in the 18th–17th centuries BC for MMIII, and the 17th century BC for LMIA.

At the lower end of the LMI (i.e. LMIB) period of interest here, we might consider the radiocarbon evidence relevant to the LMII period, to see whether it is compatible. Two small sets of data on relevant short-lived sample matter from Crete have been published: one from Knossos and one from Mochlos; there is also a single new date from Kommos (see Table 10).

The set of three LMII destruction (i.e. end of the LMII period) determinations on samples of charred barley from the Unexplored Mansion at Knossos are less than clear-cut; two offer radiocarbon ages quite similar to each other (OxA-2098, 3220±65BP; OxA-2097, 3190±65BP), but one is much more recent (OxA-2096, 3070±70BP).[1169] The data, once calibrated, could be compatible with an end for the LMII period either in the earlier or later 15th century BC: see Table 10. As a set, these data are not very specific. If the inconsistent most recent sample is discounted, then a date range 1515–1436BC becomes most likely. Two radiocarbon determinations on olive pits from a workshop area at Mochlos, Crete, have recently been published: 3240±50BP, and 3180±40BP.[1170] This workshop dates somewhere from LMIB to LMII on the basis of the description of the associated ceramics.[1171] Soles describes a single occupation episode, with uniform stratigraphy and material throughout; this includes LMIB *and* LMII ceramics. In another preliminary statement, Soles writes that 'the most startling find of all was that much of the pottery which lay alongside LMIB material here should be classified as LMII. Pottery of these two styles appears to have been used

---

[1167] Shaw (1986:253, Figs. 6.a, 6.b, Pls. 53.a–c).
[1168] Manning (1988b:49–55).
[1169] Housley *et al.* (1990:214–215); Hedges *et al.* (1990:227).
[1170] Soles (1997:426, pl.CLXV).
[1171] Soles (1997:425–426).

Context	Combined Calibrated Calendar Age Ranges BC	
	Seattle 1993 data	INTCAL98 data
Minoan Unexplored Mansion at Knossos, LMII destruction (all three samples)	1σ: 1488–1480 (P=0.10) 1453–1392 (P=0.90) 2σ: 1502–1370 (P=0.90) 1359–1346 (P=0.03) 1336–1317 (P=0.07)	1495–1474 (P=0.24)* 1460–1405 (P=0.76) 1518–1386 (P=0.96) 1333–1321 (P=0.04) *OxA-2096 has a poor agreement statistic
MUMK with just two consistent 'older' samples (excluding OxA-2096)	1σ: 1499–1430 (P=0.89) 1420–1411 (P=0.11) 2σ: 1600–1586 (P=0.02) 1581–1570 (P=0.01) 1531–1374 (P=0.95) 1331–1321 (P=0.02)	1515–1436 (P=1.00) 1601–1560 (P=0.06) 1532–1394 (P=0.94)
Mochlos Workshop	1σ: 1493–1472 (P=0.40) 1460–1432 (P=0.53) 1417–1413 (P=0.08) 2σ: 1521–1407 (P=1.00)	1512–1510 (P=0.04) 1501–1440 (P=0.96) 1520–1414 (P=1.00)
Kommos, OxA-3674	1σ: 1431–1418 (P=0.06) 1412–1243 (P=0.87) 1229–1216 (P=0.05) 1197–1194 (P=0.01) 2σ: 1501–1105 (P=0.99) 1096–1079 (P=0.01)	1436–1259 (P=0.94) 1233–1218 (P=0.06) 1521–1125 (P=1.00)
Knossos-Mochlos-Kommos LMII Combined (note OxA-2096 has a poor agreement statistic)	1σ: 1486–1482 (P=0.09) 1451–1429 (P=0.54) 1422–1410 (P=0.37) 2σ: 1494–1470 (P=0.18) 1462–1405 (P=0.82)	1492–1478 (P=0.31) 1454–1426 (P=0.60) 1420–1415 (P=0.09) 1513–1509 (P=0.02) 1502–1410 (P=0.98)
Knossos-Mochlos-Kommos LMII combined excluding OxA-2096	1σ: 1488–1480 (P=0.23) 1453–1432 (P=0.60) 1418–1412 (P=0.18) 2σ: 1498–1409 (P=1.00)	1497–1473 (P=0.45) 1461–1432 (P=0.55) 1516–1428 (P=1.00)

Table 10. Combined calibrated calendar age ranges BC for the radiocarbon data from LMII Knossos, LMII(?) Mochlos, and LMII Kommos. Data for Knossos and Mochlos from Hedges et al. (1990:227); and Soles (1997:426). Kommos determination from Table 9 above. Calibrated results from the OxCal programme (Ramsey 1995). Round Ranges function 'off'. Calibration data after Stuiver et al. (1998); and Stuiver and Becker (1993). P = Probability (out of 1.0 – although note that occasionally a rounding error means that total probability described only equals 0.99 or 1.01). The calibrated age ranges are given at 1σ and 2σ (1 or 2 standard deviation, 68.2% and 95.4%) confidence.

simultaneously'.[1172] On strict grounds, this suggests an LMII date for the deposit (and a general contemporaneity and comparison with the Unexplored Mansion deposits at Knossos), but Soles notes complicating problems of regionalism and exact definition. The radiocarbon ages are very similar to those for the two consistent, older, LMII destruction samples at Knossos: OxA-2097 and OxA-2098 (see above). A solitary LMII radiocarbon determination from Kommos, OxA-3674, is a little more recent, consonant with the most recent determination from the Unexplored Mansion at Knossos. The combined Knossos–Mochlos–Kommos LMII calibrated calendar date range in Table 10 should offer a reasonable guide to the real calendar age of some part(s) of the LMII period. The likely age range is the first three-quarters of the 15th century BC.[1173] Moreover, the evidence from Knossos (and probably the other samples also) relates to a close/ late LMII destruction deposit. Much of the LMII period should be earlier than the age of the short-lived samples. A date for the LMII period somewhere in the earlier to mid 15th century BC, and *before* c.1430/25BC seems very likely from this evidence.

This independent evidence for the chronology of the LMII period is very important in three ways. First, it directly contradicts the conventional 'low' chronology dates for the LMII period. Warren and Hankey (1989:169) dated the LMII period 1425–1390BC. The radiocarbon evidence makes it fairly clear that the LMII period very probably ends by no later than c.1430/25BC. Second, this radiocarbon evidence from Knossos, Mochlos, and Kommos for LMII nicely supports the chronology derived above for the preceding LMIB period from the radiocarbon data from Chania and Myrtos-Pyrgos. This found the evidence to support a date for the respective close of LMIB destructions at these sites around or before c.1525–1490BC. Data from the succeeding LMII period provides evidence that it ends by c.1430/25BC, and suggests a date range for the overall period c.1490–1430BC (consonant with the LMIB data). Third, the radiocarbon evidence and chronology is entirely consistent with the archaeological evidence. As discussed above, recent archaeological and art-historical work has shown the need to raise previous dates for the LMIB period, due to finds such as the Minoan sherd at Memphis (see Chapter IV.7), and also the need to raise LMII to LMIIIA1 dates, since it is now widely agreed that the LMIIIA1 period must have begun late in the reign of Tuthmosis III because of an analysis of the designs represented on kilts of Aegeans in a couple of tombs from Thebes in Egypt (see Chapter IV.9). According to current consensus in Egyptian chronology, Tuthmosis III died in 1425BC.[1174] If the LMIIIA1 period had begun at least a few years prior to this point, we must conclude that the LMII period is very much dated in line with the radiocarbon evidence. Hence radiocarbon and archaeology are in near perfect agreement, and the previous conventional chronology is shown to be too low, and in need of revision. Further, the prejudice against, and criticism of, radiocarbon evidence

---

[1172] J.S. Soles in Tomlinson (1996:46).

[1173] The most recent determination from the Unexplored Mansion (OxA-2096) has a poor agreement statistic with the rest of the data (the similarly aged Kommos determination just survives due to its larger measurement error); if it is discounted on this ground, then the probability for a date somewhere in the 15th century BC *before* c.1432 BC increases: see Table 10.

[1174] Kitchen (1996); von Beckerath (1994; 1997).

by the advocates of this disproven low chronology is shown to have been misplaced.

In conclusion, the available modern, high quality, radiocarbon evidence from the Aegean is consistently supportive of an earlier chronology both for the date of the eruption of Thera, and for the MMIII to LMII archaeological periods. The independent radiocarbon evidence rules out the conventional low date for the Thera eruption c.1500BC, and clearly supports a 17th century BC date. The 'compromise early' chronology, which would place the eruption in the mid-16th century BC, is rather less likely with the new INTCAL98 calibration dataset than it was with the 1993 decadal dataset. But, even now, it is not entirely ruled out. If other evidence required a mid-16th century BC, or 18th Dynasty, date for the later LMIA period, then this 21% probability (at 2σ, 95.4%, confidence) would have to come into play. However, as reviewed in Chapter IV, the archaeological evidence is in fact entirely consonant with, and indeed supportive of, a date for the later LMIA period, and the LCIA period (and early WSI style and early BRI), in the late 17th century BC (around and/or before the reign of Khyan). It most certainly does not require a date after the beginning of the 18th Dynasty. Thus the 17th century BC radiocarbon age for the VDL at Akrotiri should stand as likely and plausible. The radiocarbon evidence from Crete shows that the LMIB period lies *no later* than in the 16th century BC through to c.1526–1494BC, and the LMII period from then to *before* c.1430/25BC. All this evidence fits together to form a coherent framework. It requires a new 'early' Aegean chronology.[1175]

Apart from the above directly relevant radiocarbon evidence from Thera and the Aegean, two other bodies of radiocarbon data might be briefly considered. One has already been argued in print to be relevant to the dating of the Thera eruption, and the other has the potential to be relevant.

I. RADIOCARBON EVIDENCE FROM JERICHO

New high-precision radiocarbon evidence reported by Bruins and van der Plicht for the close of MBA destruction at Tell Es-Sultan (Jericho) in Palestine has been discussed both in connection with the Thera debate, and the chronology of the important later Palestinian MBII period.[1176] Bruins and van der Plicht obtained determinations on both a set of charcoal samples, and a set of grain samples, from the last MBA stratum at the site. The latter should effectively date the final MBA destruction; the former might well offer dates for wood used either during the phase, or in the construction of the structures of the final MB phase. Bruins and van der Plicht (195:215) calculate the combined average radiocarbon age of the long-lived charcoal determinations (from 11 consistent determinations, minus one early outlier: GrN-18538) as 3370±6BP. This

---

[1175] Warren (1998) admits that the radiocarbon evidence favours the 'early' chronology (p.324), but then goes on to argue that the pattern of all the archaeological evidence favours the low chronology (pp.325–328); hence he rejects the radiocarbon probabilities. However, as discussed in detail in Chapter IV, a coherent alternative interpretation of all the archaeological evidence is available. Indeed, a number of pieces of archaeological evidence support, rather than just permit, the 'early' chronology. Therefore, the positive evidence from radiocarbon should be taken into account.

[1176] Bruins and van der Plicht (1995; 1996).

offers a calibrated, calendar, age range in the 17th century BC: see Table 11. The combined calibrated calendar probability distribution from all the samples excepting the one earlier outlier is similar, and offers a total dating range at 2σ (95.4%) confidence of 1687–1638BC. The combined average radiocarbon age for the six short-lived grain samples is appropriately a little more recent. Bruins and van der Plicht (1995:216) arrive at an average radiocarbon age of 3306±7BP. However, this in fact has an unsatisfactory chi-square agreement at the 95% confidence level.[1177] Bruins and van der Plicht (1996:213) suggest using the consistent central sub-set of four data yielding an average radiocarbon age of 3311±8BP, or 3311±13BP with an additional measurement error allowance. All of these average ages offer likely calibrated calendar age ranges in the first three-quarters of the 16th century BC: see Table 11. In particular, at 1σ, 68.2% confidence, the possible date range variously ends 1529–1528BC. Bruins and van der Plicht offer very similar calibrated data from a different computer calibration programme and a slightly modified (splined and thus smoothed) calibration dataset, and they demonstrate that very similar results are achieved whichever high-precision calibration dataset is used.[1178] If a combined calibrated calendar probability distribution from the short-lived grain samples is considered, then one with an acceptable agreement statistic can be achieved with the central four data. The 1σ, 68.2% confidence, range ends respectively at 1530BC: see Table 11. The most likely date range for the destruction of late MBA Jericho from this evidence is 1571–1530BC. This date is remarkably compatible with the conventional date for the end of the Palestinian MBA, and specifically Jericho, c.1550BC.[1179]

Although these samples do not come from a current excavation (rather the old excavations at Jericho by Kenyon), and some sceptics will inevitably challenge their relevance, these data are exciting for offering the first set of high-precision radiocarbon determinations applicable to the problematic time of the close of the MBA period in Palestine. They offer a date which is independent of the various circular assumptions in conventional Syro-Palestinian chronology. The date demonstrated for the end of the MBA at Jericho somewhere in the mid-16th century BC (and probably *before* c.1530BC) is broadly consistent with conventional dates, and certainly excludes radically lower alternatives.[1180] Bruins and van der Plicht (1996) go on to suggest a correlation with the Exodus and place the destruction of Jericho 40 years after this (which they tie to the eruption of Thera and the 'darkness that can be felt' of *Exodus* 10:21[1181]). But here they have (unfortunately) ventured into the realm of speculation.

The important point for our present purposes is that these radiocarbon data suggest that the later MBII occupation at Jericho covers a range from the earlier to mid-17th century BC through to some point in the first three-quarters of the 16th century BC.

[1177] Calculated statistic of 24.1 ≥ upper acceptable value of 11.1: see Ward and Wilson (1978).

[1178] Bruins and van der Plicht (1995:Fig.4; 1996:Figure).

[1179] As employed in the study of Marchetti *et al.* (1998). Two new radiocarbon determinations on short-lived samples relevant to the *end* of the succeeding LBIA period (preserved/from the violent conflagration which brought this phase to an end) from Period V at Tell Abu al-Kharaz nicely support the general Jericho chronology (see Fischer 1999:13, 17–19). These data provide a most likely (probability = 96%) 1σ combined calibrated calendar age range c.1525–1442 BC with the INTCAL98 dataset and OxCal (round ranges 'off'), and suggest a LBIA period from the mid/later 16th century BC through to the earlier/mid 15th century BC. This matches very well with the MBIIC/MBIII Jericho dates.

[1180] As Bruins and van der Plicht (1995) note.

[1181] Cf. Vandersleyen (1995:232–237).

	Calibrated Calendar Age Ranges BC	
	Seattle 1993 data	INTCAL98 data
1.a. Jericho final MBA phase long-lived (charcoal samples), average ^{14}C age 3370±6BP (minus GrN-18538)	1σ: 1688–1679 (P=0.13) 1674–1668 (P=0.09) 1661–1649 (P=0.18) 1640–1614 (P=0.40)	1σ: 1686–1680 (P=0.16) 1670–1658 (P=0.35) 1651–1632 (P=0.49) 1575–1560 (P=0.21)
	2σ: 1727–1711 (P=0.06) 1690–1603 (P=0.68) 1586–1554 (P=0.22) 1544–1532 (P=0.04)	2σ: 1732–1716 (P=0.07) 1690–1621 (P=0.93)
1.b. Jericho final MBA phase long-lived (charcoal samples), combined calendar probability distribution (minus GrN-18538)	1σ: 1690–1680 (P=0.23) 1640–1620 (P=0.64) 1570–1560 (P=0.13)	1σ: 1685–1683 (P=0.23) 1670–1661 (P=0.77)
	2σ: 1690–1610 (P=0.82) 1580–1560 (P=0.18)	2σ: 1687–1681 (P=0.21) 1671–1658 (P=0.52) 1650–1638 (P=0.27)
2.a (i). Jericho final MBA phase short-lived samples, average ^{14}C age 3306±7BP	1σ: 1601–1566 (P=0.50) 1561–1524 (P=0.50)	1σ: 1601–1600 (P=0.03) 1587–1528 (P=0.97)
	2σ: 1682–1672 (P=0.06) 1616–1499 (P=0.94)	2σ: 1618–1524 (P=1.00)
2.a (ii). Jericho final MBA phase short-lived samples, average ^{14}C age 3311±8BP	1σ: 1602–1598 (P=0.07) 1591–1526 (P=0.93)	1σ: 1616–1601 (P=0.22) 1585–1580 (P=0.09) 1572–1529 (P=0.70)
	2σ: 1683–1670 (P=0.08) 1619–1500 (P=0.92)	2σ: 1678–1672 (P=0.04) 1621–1525 (P=0.96)
2.a (iii). Jericho final MBA phase short-lived samples, average ^{14}C age 3311±13BP	1σ: 1677–1676 (P=0.02) 1602–1597 (P=0.08) 1592–1525 (P=0.90)	1σ: 1616–1600 (P=0.25) 1585–1580 (P=0.09) 1571–1529 (P=0.67)
	2σ: 1684–1671 (P=0.08) 1619–1500 (P=0.92)	2σ: 1679–1670 (P=0.05) 1623–1522 (P=0.95)
2.b (i). Jericho final MBA phase short-lived samples combined calendar probability distribution (5 samples, excluding GrN-19063 which yields a poor agreement statistic)	1σ: 1585–1554 (P=0.87) 1546–1539 (P=0.13) 2σ: 1690–1670 (P=0.06) 1610–1520 (P=0.94) OK agreement statistic	1583–1557 (P=1.00) 1588–1527 (P=1.00) Poor agreement statistic
2.b (ii). Jericho final MBA phase short-lived samples combined calendar probability distribution (4 central samples, excluding GrN-19063, and GrN-19064)	1σ: 1589–1570 (P=0.49) 1557–1541 (P=0.39) 1533–1528 (P=0.12)	1σ: 1613–1612 (P=0.03) 1605–1604 (P=0.03) 1584–1583 (P=0.03) 1571–1530 (P=0.90)
	2σ: 1679–1674 (P=0.04) 1603–1523 (P=0.96)	2σ: 1617–1599 (P=0.19) 1588–1527 (P=0.81)
	good agreement statistic	good agreement statistic

Table 11. Calibrated calendar age ranges for the radiocarbon data from later MBA Tell Es-Sultan (Jericho). Data from Bruins and van der Plicht (1995; 1996). Calibrated results from the OxCal programme (Ramsey 1995). Round Ranges function 'off'. Calibration data from Stuiver et al. (1998); and Stuiver and Becker (1993). P = Probability (out of 1.0 – although note that occasionally a rounding error means that total probability described only equals 0.99 or 1.01). The calibrated age ranges are given at 1σ and 2σ (1 or 2 standard deviation, 68.2% and 95.4%) confidence.

This is very much in accord with conventional scholarship which dates the later MBII (or MBIIC or MBIII) period to the same approximate range.[1182] In general terms, these data may be said to favour one of the 'higher' Palestinian chronologies. In contrast, they appear rather unlikely to be compatible with the ultra low and short chronology of Bietak,[1183] where the whole relevant phase is meant to be in the 16th century BC, and to last about 60 to 70 years (or extend into an MBIIC/LBI phase stretching into the late 15th century BC).[1184] Nor, given conventional Egyptian chronology (see Table 3; Appendix 1), can the destruction of Jericho be linked with the campaigns of any of the Egyptian rulers from Amenhotep I to Tuthmosis III which have, in recent scholarship, been proposed as accounting for the series of Syro-Palestinian destructions marking the close of the local MBA phase.[1185]

It is just possible that the first ruler of the 18th Dynasty, Ahmose, was involved, as was argued in older literature. Such an Egyptian campaign under Ahmose is unlikely to pre-date the time he entered northern Egypt and conquered Avaris. The conquest of Avaris is variously dated by different scholars from Ahmose years 7 or 11–18/22 (see Appendix 1). The accession date for Ahmose has been getting lower and lower in a number of recent studies by leading students of Egyptian chronology. It was formerly placed c.1580BC[1186] to c.1570BC;[1187] then became c.1552/1550BC[1188] in what is currently termed the 'conventional' chronology by Kuhrt (1995:186); then Krauss proposed an even lower date of c.1542–1539BC,[1189] and Kitchen (1996a) now offers c.1540BC based on 'dead-reckoning'; and finally Helck (1987) suggested the presently ultra-low date among 'serious' scholarship of c.1530BC. The low and ultra low dates rely on the absolute minimum attested reign lengths for some of the early 18th Dynasty pharaohs. However, this is a time notable for its lack of data, and so minima are inherently dubious. Further, if credence is given to the Sothic date in the Ebers Papyrus, and this is placed as relevant to Thebes (at least), then the 'conventional' chronology is necessary.[1190]

The lower chronologies are barely, if at all, compatible with Ahmose's involvement with the Jericho destruction. *If* he was involved – for example associated with his three year siege of Sharuhen, or his move into Djahi in central Syria – then the evidence would favour the need for either a high, or at least 'conventional', accession date.

[1182] Kempinski (1983); Dever (1997:293–294; 1992).

[1183] Bietak (1984; 1989a; 1991a; 1997).

[1184] As Bruins and van der Plicht (1995:218) point out, the radiocarbon data also comprehensively rule out the very low Palestinian chronology of Bimson (1981; Bimson and Livingston 1987), or the attempt of Wood (1990) to date the Jericho context to the LBA and c.1400BC (against the latter, see also Bienkowski 1990; Weinstein 1997:101–102 n.28). In general terms, these new data are again good evidence against the radically low chronologies proposed by James *et al.* (1991a) and Rohl (1995).

[1185] Weinstein (1981; 1991); Dever (1990; 1992:13–14); Bietak (1991:57–62); Kuhrt (1995:189–193, 320–323). Weinstein (1997:97) continues to support an Egyptian agency as more plausible than other suggestions, but, although he notes the radiocarbon evidence for a 16th century BC date for the Jericho destruction (1997:101–102 n.28 last paragraph), he fails to consider which if any 18th Dynasty pharaoh might be responsible at such a date.

[1186] Breasted (1962, vol.I:§66).

[1187] Hayes (1970); Wente and Van Siclen (1976).

[1188] Hornung (1964); Kitchen (1987 'high'); von Beckerath (1994a; 1997).

[1189] Krauss (1978; 1985); Kitchen (1987 'low').

[1190] As argued in detail by von Beckerath (1994a); cf. Krauss (1995).

However, as noted in the discussion in Chapter III, good evidence for Egyptian military involvement with most of the Palestinian destructions is lacking, and there is no necessary reason to associate Ahmose (or any other Egyptian ruler) with the destruction of Jericho. Thus the close of MBA destructions in Palestine might have occurred either a little before or a little after the start of the 18th Dynasty in Egypt.[1191]

No Bichrome Ware was found in the relevant MBA deposits at Jericho. This might suggest that the later MBII destruction at Jericho was during the earlier part of the horizon of late MBA change and collapse in Syria–Palestine, and that the destruction of Jericho might be linked with the destruction at Tel Kabri, for example, where there were also no finds of Bichrome Ware. In this case, the possible calibrated date range in the second quarter of the 16th century BC might apply. But, since Bichrome Ware is rare outside the coastal strip in Palestine, not too much emphasis should be placed on its non-appearance at inland Jericho. The destruction context may well have been contemporary with early Bichrome Ware on the coast. The Jericho context otherwise appears typically later MBII, i.e. MBIIB, or MBIIC or MBIII, according to the various terminological systems.[1192] If this view were correct, a date in either the second or third quarters of the 16th century BC might be relevant. Further, if two sealings from Jericho are attributed to Khamudy, the final Hyksos king, as Ryholt suggests,[1193] then this would indeed suggest a late MBII (MBIIC/MBIII) date for the Jericho context, and could permit a link for the destruction of Jericho with Ahmose. If accepted, the Khamudy association clearly favours either a high or middle (conventional) Egyptian chronology.

The radiocarbon evidence from Jericho is not of direct relevance to the chronology of Tell el-Dabᶜa unless either the possible Khamudy sealings (above) are considered, or the traditional model is accepted where Ahmose conquers Avaris, and then initiates further Egyptian conquests and destructions across Palestine (by himself and his successors). If either of these were the case, then, since the close of the MBA at Jericho is linked to the general close of the late MBA at other Syro-Palestinian sites, and so to the same situation seen at Tell el-Dabᶜa stratum D/2,[1194] the date chosen by Bietak for the fall of Avaris would be challenged by the data from Jericho. Bietak's date of around or after c.1530BC for the fall of Avaris,[1195] would then be barely within the possible range of dates for the destruction of Jericho, an event seen as subsequent in the traditional 'historical' scenario. The outcome of this logic is that it seems unlikely that either Ahmose, or any of the other 18th Dynasty rulers, was responsible for the destruction of Jericho. To argue to the contrary would require a higher

---

[1191] Niemeier (1995a:14 n.49) refers to 'the radiocarbon datings of a series of samples from the destruction level of the palace at Kabri, currently under AMS-analysis by the Institut für Mittelenergiephysik der Eidgenössischen Technischen Hochschule Zürich'. As far as I am aware, these data have not yet been published at the time I write. When available, they should offer good evidence for the date of the later MBII period, and for one example of Aegean-style wall paintings in Syria–Palestine, and should allow confirmation (or not), and refinement, of the chronology presently available from Jericho.

[1192] See Kempinski (1983:70–71, 123–125, 151–165, 222; 1992a; 1992b); Bienkowski (1990). Kempinski (1992a) links the end of MBA Jericho (V) with Megiddo level X, and places both c.1600BC, with neither as very latest MBA.

[1193] Ryholt (1997:52, 121, 387–388 File 15/6).

[1194] See e.g. Dever (1992:7 fig.2).

[1195] E.g. Bietak (1996:76).

Egyptian chronology. The so-called conventional chronology for Ahmose, c.1550–1525BC, is the minimum acceptable scenario if any involvement is to be sustained.

The conventional chronology of Egypt requires no special justification. A slightly higher chronology is not, of course, impossible, but runs against current scholarship. It would involve a Memphite solution for the Ebers Papyrus. Although most Egyptologists regard the conventional Egyptian chronology as closely fixed down, it must be noted that 'dead reckoning' of the available very partial palimpsest of Egyptian chronological data[1196] is not, and can never be, definitive.[1197] It cannot therefore be so accurate, and so precise, as to be able to discount a small amount of movement. And, whereas critics are always trying to shrink Egyptian chronology, and to offer hyper-critical, hyper-compressed, readings, it is in fact more likely that we are lacking various records, and missing various highest attested years of rulers. Nearly nine centuries exist between the last really fixed point in Egyptian chronology in the 7th century BC and the accession of Ahmose (and just over a millennium from the truly fixed point of Cambyses' conquest of Egypt). A little upwards movement is, if anything, more than possible/plausible in these circumstances (see Appendix 1). It is certainly not impossible that radiocarbon and/or dendrochronology may in the future find against the current lowest (minimalist) as possible Egyptian chronologies for the New Kingdom, and instead require something around, or even slightly earlier than, the so-called conventional chronology (i.e. accession of Ahmose *no later* than c.1550 BC).

II. BEYOND THE AEGEAN TO ITALY AND SARDINIA[1198]

Aegean chronology has always been very much a derivative of scholarship concerning Egypt, the Near East, and the eastern Mediterranean. It is one aspect of the old diffusionist paradigm which has never gone away. Aegean archaeologists have always tended to turn to the Near East to acquire, or test, or extrapolate, any chronological data. However, it is also possible to test Aegean chronology by looking elsewhere. It might even be argued to be an important step, since there are many circular problems of evidence,[1199] interpretation and chronology, and conflicts between approximate 'historical' chronologies, versus archaeological synchronisms, versus science-based dating, when one considers the chronologies of the Aegean, east Mediterranean, and Near East/Egypt.[1200]

Tykot (1994:128) argues that 'the presence of Mycenaean artefacts in the Western Mediterranean ... makes it particularly possible for Sardinia, with its many findspots of Mycenaean pottery and oxhide ingots ... to make a contribution to Aegean chronology...'. The reverse is therefore also true. Furthermore, in this case, the two correlated archaeological stratigraphic sequences can be compared in order to see whether the radiocarbon evidence from the west Mediterranean is consonant with

---

[1196] E.g. Kitchen (1996a; 1996b).
[1197] See e.g. Hagens (1996).
[1198] This section is a short version of some of Manning (1998a). For current reviews of the Sardinian archaeological evidence, see the other papers in the Balmuth and Tykot (1998) volume.
[1199] As highlighted by Leonard (1988).
[1200] Hence the appeal for an independent chronology of the Near East by Bruins and Mook (1989).

the artefact linkages between the Aegean and Sardinia, and whether it supports the 'early', or instead, the conventional, Aegean chronology.

The dates for imported Aegean objects in the west Mediterranean can either be contemporary with their Aegean context, or slightly later, depending on the time-lag in transport, use, and then deposition. The central Mediterranean data thus set *termini ante quos* for the Aegean production date of imports (as indeed do the Egyptian contexts with Aegean imports, although this logical fact is often rather overlooked). The evidence from the central Mediterranean in effect offers an independent test on existing ceramic and radiocarbon chronologies in the Aegean and east Mediterranean. Italy and Sardinia seem especially relevant in this regard, as LHI linkages have been long known, and are regarded as very much a cornerstone of traditional dating in Italian prehistory. I do not propose here to begin a comprehensive review of Italian and Sardinian archaeology and radiocarbon evidence,[1201] rather to give the example of one case: the phase in Sardinia relevant to the Late Bronze 1 period in the Aegean.

In Italy and Sardinia, we are conventionally referring to the EBA/MBA transition, with MBI (Protoappennine B) equated with LHI (or the Shaft Graves at Mycenae in broad terms). With older Aegean chronologies this led to a start date c.1600BC or later;[1202] with newer Aegean chronologies, and especially the proposals to date the eruption of Thera c.1628BC, a revised date of c.1700BC is now often given.[1203] However, let us reverse the logic, and consider the direct and independent radiocarbon evidence provided from Sardinia, and see how this fits with Aegean chronology. Does it support the 'early', or conventional low, Aegean chronology?

The initial problem is exactly what radiocarbon dates to employ, as Sardinian archaeologists have been busy redefining their periods. Whereas formerly it was standard to regard the first nuraghi ('corridor', protonuraghi, earliest tholos nuraghi) as MBI (and so Protoappennine B and LHI–II),[1204] Lilliu and Webster instead regard these as EBA to EBA–MBA (Bonnanaro B, or Nuragic I)[1205] – although in advocating 'early' dates for the first nuraghi Webster appears to place over-reliance on a couple of very unsatisfactory 'early' radiocarbon determinations with very large measurement errors. Nuragic II, which sees the appearance of the true, tholos, tower, nuraghi is now instead regarded as defining the start of the MBA,[1206] and Nuragic II is linked to Protoappennine B – although, of course, some overlap of the protonuraghi and tholos type is apparent.[1207] Dates for the earliest tholos nuraghi should therefore approximately correlate with LHI(–II) in Greece and the Aegean.[1208]

LHI–II ceramics are known from several Italian sites,[1209] and, as noted, they are corre-

---

[1201] See Skeates and Whitehouse (1994); Guidi and Whitehouse (1996). Vanzetti (1998) offers a detailed analysis of Italian data, and finds it to be consistent with, and to work well with, the early Aegean LB1 chronology and the early, later 17th century BC, date for the eruption of Thera.

[1202] E.g. Ugas (1992).

[1203] E.g. Cardarelli (1993:368); Guidi (1993:420–421).

[1204] Ugas (1992).

[1205] Lilliu (1982); Webster (1988; 1996:18–19, 87).

[1206] Ugas (1992) instead sees this as MBII.

[1207] Tykot (1994:126 and refs.).

[1208] Combining Ugas (1992); Contu (1992); Lilliu (1982); Tykot (1994:125–126).

[1209] E.g. Vagnetti (1993:145, fig.2); Dickinson (1994:249).

lated with the Italian Protoappennine B culture and thence to the MBI period on Sardinia.[1210] LHI, which is broadly comparable with LMIA in chronological terms,[1211] should thus be more or less contemporary with the first phase of tholos nuraghi on Sardinia.

Tykot (1994) collects a number of radiocarbon determinations relevant to the first phases of the Nuraghic period on Sardinia (Nuragic I–II), ranging from Bonnanaro B to pre-comb-decorated (*a pettine*) ceramic contexts (Q-3031, R-963a, Gif-?, K-151, Q-3070, I-14,774, Gif-243, Gif-242, Q-3169, and P-2788): see Table 12. The combined calibrated calendar age range of this set of 10 determinations at 2σ (95.4%) confidence using the OxCal computer programme (Ramsey 1995, with round ranges function 'off') and the INTCAL98 calibration dataset of Stuiver *et al.* (1998) is: 1739–1703BC (P=0.43), 1695–1678BC (P=0.20), and 1671–1624BC (P=0.37). However, the set has a poor agreement statistic, with I-14,774 in particular revealed as aberrant (*even with* its huge quoted measurement error), and it is thus not a consistent set of data. Webster (1988:467) employs I-14,774 to argue for an initial use of Tower A at Duos Nuraghes c.2000–1800BC; but reliance on this very poor quality measurement seems unwise, and its age may be clearly distinguished from the other 'initial' Nuragic I–II radiocarbon determinations available – making it unlikely to offer a valid Nuragic I–II date. Instead, it is most probably revealed as an irrelevant, aberrant, datum. The other serious concern involves the fact that a number of the determinations have (very) large measurement errors by modern standards, which render them seriously suspect (or, at best, of little utility); further, measurements carried out before the significant improvements in radiocarbon dating procedures and analysis in the early 1980s, and without proper pretreatment, must also be regarded as suspect. The set of data above looks decidedly unhealthy in these terms.

If one were rigorous, at least half the measurements should be deleted from analysis. However, whether by luck or good management, the various determinations are largely similar, even if of different quality. Thus, for example, if one ignores the date of laboratory measurement, and merely removes determinations with measurement errors ≥±200 radiocarbon years, then the remaining six determinations (Q-3031, R-963a, Gif-?, Q-3070, Q-3169, P-2788) offer a set with an almost acceptable agreement statistic, and a combined calibrated calendar age range at 2σ (95.4%) confidence of 1738–1708BC (P=0.33), 1694–1678BC (P=0.19), and 1671–1623BC (P=0.48). This is not significantly different from our previous conclusion.

These calibrated calendar age ranges from charcoal/wood samples, where known (Skeates 1994), should offer *termini post quos* for the Nuragic I–II period, and, in turn, the date of the Nuragic I–II period offers a *terminus ante quem* for the LHI period in the Aegean from the archaeological synchronisms. The results are notable for two reasons; first, they (again) confirm the general Aegean chronology derived from archaeology, history, and radiocarbon versus recent attempts radically to lower Mediterranean chronology;[1212] and second, the Sardinian dates offer approximate support for a chronology broadly consistent with the 'early' LBA chronology in the Aegean, with the LHI period underway by, or before, a date range from the mid–later 17th century

---

[1210] E.g. Ugas (1992).

[1211] Warren and Hankey (1989:96–97); Dietz (1991).

[1212] E.g. James *et al.* (1991a); Rohl (1995).

Lab. No.	Site	Context	Radiocarbon Age BP
Q-3031	Grotta Filiestru	Layer B(2)	3440±40
R-963a	Sa Turricula	Hut 1, Layer 2	3460±50
Gif-?	Nuraghe Pizzinnu	Tower	3350±50
K-151	Barumini	Beam, main chamber	3420±200
Q-3070	Nuraghe Noeddos	Gb(3)1	3360±50
I-14,774	Duos Nuraghes	Tower A floor	4180±320
Gif-243	Brunku Madugui	Layer e	3770±250
Gif-242	Nuraghe Albucciu	Lower layer 6	3170±250
Q-3169	Nuraghe Noeddos	Gb(12)	3330±70
P-2788	Ortu Còmidu	Pavement, tower S	3310±50

Table 12. Radiocarbon determinations relevant to the first Nuraghic phase on Sardinia. Data from Tykot (1994:125–126, 131).

BC. In particular, there is strong support for an earlier–later 17th century BC start for the LHI period (depending on the extent of the average 'old wood' offset relevant), and so the general case for a later 17th century BC date for the eruption of Thera.

2. Northern hemisphere climate event in the later 17th century BC

The Minoan eruption of Thera will undoubtedly have had some climatic impact, since it injected large amounts of volatiles and tephra high (c.36km) into the stratosphere. In a recent review of the issue, David Pyle (1997:60) states that:

> Analysis of the observed cooling patterns following major eruptions of the past 140 years (Robock and Mao 1995) suggests that the first two winters following the Minoan eruption would have been marked by a slight warming in high-latitude parts of North America and Eurasia, and an enhanced cooling of high-latitude continental areas for two or three summers. These conclusions would not be greatly changed even if the sulphur injection from the Minoan eruption were an order of magnitude larger than currently estimated.

The question for Aegean archaeologists is whether this injection of volcanic products, and consequent climatic impact, can be detected successfully in various environmental records, and thus accurately and precisely dated? Needless to say, the subject is complicated and controversial. Finding an apparent volcanic signal or effect is one thing, tying it to Thera is another.

As noted in Chapter II, it has been observed for 20 years from analyses of both long-term ice-core, and tree-ring, records from several locations in the northern hemisphere that there was some sort of major climatic anomaly in the later 17th century BC. Moreover, the ice-core evidence specifically records the effect of a large, climatically-effective, volcanic eruption because of the sulphur-dioxide signal preserved in the ice. It was immediately proposed that this event might be the eruption of Thera. The initial logic was pretty poor. Thera just happened to be about the only major volcanic eruption known from this approximate time-span. There was no positive correlation. Even today, the positive case remains relatively weak in much published literature. Buckland *et al.* (1997:581–587) recently highlighted this situation, arguing that there was no sound date for Thera on the basis of either ice-core or tree-ring evidence.

Much ink has already been spilt on this topic over the last decade or so, both in the archaeological and scientific literature. It might be felt that there is little new to say here. However, this is not the case. Several new data and analyses have recently become available which are very significant. Two of these are discussed in detail in Chapter V.3 and V.4 below. But first we need to summarise the history of the subject, and review the current situation. Progress may be made here also.

Precisely (i.e. absolutely) dated tree-ring records from three continents (North America, Europe, Asia Minor) reveal a major climate anomaly in 1628–1627BC (and nowhere else within a couple of hundred years): e.g. Figure 50. The anomalies are all consistent with, and best explained by, a lowering of the 'normal' temperature in the northern hemisphere. The effects *could* therefore be consistent with those of a large, climatically-effective, volcanic eruption whose aerosol backscatters solar radiation and lowers average summer surface temperatures. It has been regularly observed in long-term tree-ring chronologies covering the last several thousand years that 1628BC fits a pattern where such events do more or less match major volcanic eruptions.[1213] However, this by itself is not proof. In historical periods tree-ring records from climatically sensitive growth areas, or tree species, do show strong correlations between tree-growth anomalies and both unusual climate events and major volcanic eruptions,[1214] but again these types of records do not by themselves, or without further analysis, provide any direct evidence of either temperature lowering, or a volcanic cause. Therefore, in the late 1980s, all that could be said was that there was a coincidence, and a plausible causal model based around observations of surface cooling and short-term climate change resulting from large and/or sulphur-rich volcanic eruptions.[1215] Critics were thus justified to note that this evidence was not sufficient. Warren, Parker, and Pyle all correctly pointed out that there was a less than perfect correlation between every known eruption and every defined tree-ring anomaly, nor could any specific anomaly necessarily be tied to any particular eruption.[1216]

For the direct link to a volcanic eruption, one had to turn to evidence from cores drilled deep into the polar ice caps (and for Thera to cores drilled in Greenland). This field in effect began in 1977, when Claus Hammer announced the apparent correlation of the dates of acid traces in the Greenland ice with the dates of historic volcanic eruptions. The model was simple. Volcanic eruptions inject sulphur dioxide and other gases and particles into the atmosphere (and most importantly the stratosphere), and

---

[1213] LaMarche and Hirschboeck (1984); Baillie and Munro (1988); Baillie (1990; 1991a; 1995a; 1996b); Manning (1992a; 1995:202, 214–216 end-note 1); Stothers and Rampino (1983); Rampino *et al.* (1988).

[1214] E.g. LaMarche (1974); LaMarche and Hirschboeck (1984); Lough and Fritts (1987); Baillie and Munro (1988); Briffa *et al.* (1988; 1992); Scuderi (1990; 1992); Baillie (1995a); Vogel *et al.* (1996). I am not discussing here the possible effects of volcanoes on 'near-vent' forests (see Yamaguchi 1993:Table 1).

[1215] Rampino and Self (1982); Sear *et al.* (1987); Rampino *et al.* (1988); Chester (1988); Handler (1989).

[1216] Warren (1984; 1998:324); Parker (1985); Pyle (1989; 1990b; 1992); see also Yamaguchi (1993); and see now the critical review by Sadler and Grattan (1999:187–190).

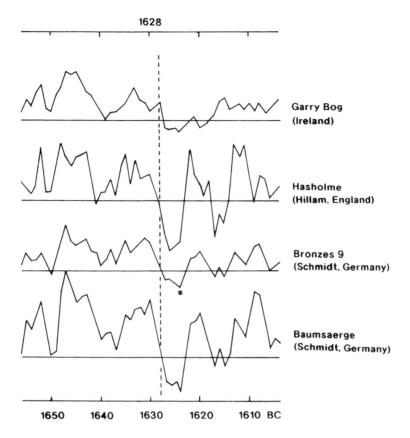

1628

Garry Bog
(Ireland)

Hasholme
(Hillam, England)

Bronzes 9
(Schmidt, Germany)

Baumsaerge
(Schmidt, Germany)

1650   1640   1630   1620   1610 BC

Fig. 50. Reduced growth/narrow ring event in dendrochronological data (ring-width plots) from Ireland, England, and Germany beginning in 1628BC. Drawing after Baillie (1990; 1995a).

these are subsequently deposited via precipitation on the polar ice sheets. Further, on the basis of analogy with studies of the fallout of radioactive substances from atmospheric nuclear bomb tests on the polar ice, the processes of stratospheric injection, transport, and fallout, could be modelled, and it is even possible to estimate the original quantities injected into the stratosphere.[1217] In suitable polar regions where summer melting is restricted, the ice-sheets build up with the precipitation (i.e. snow fall) in annual laminations, and preserve records of past precipitation and ice composition (and so also proxy climate and temperature data) for many thousands, to hundreds of thousands, of years.[1218] In particular, a specifically volcanic acid signal may thus be detected for various years in the ice, when large eruptions occurred,

---

[1217] Hammer *et al.* (1980); Clausen and Hammer (1988).
[1218] E.g. Alley *et al.* (1993); Dansgaard *et al.* (1984; 1985; 1993). A special issue of the *Journal of Geophysical Research*, volume 102 no. C12, 1997 (pp.26,315–26,886), contains 47 papers on the recent GISP2 and GRIP cores and associated research, and provides a useful summary of the current state of research.

backwards for many thousands of years.[1219] Ice-cores therefore offer evidence of past volcanism.

The dating of prehistoric ice-cores is, however, less accurate than the dating of tree-rings (from suitable temperate tree species). With multiple replication, tree-ring chronologies are absolute – that is ±0. The tree-ring chronologies from the USA and Ireland referred to above are of this quality for the relevant period: that is absolute, ±0.[1220] Ice-cores cannot claim such perfection. For example, an initial date of 1390±50BC for the major mid-second millennium BC volcanic signal[1221] – suggested to be Thera on the sole ground that, at the time, it was the main known second millennium BC volcanic eruption – was subsequently retracted after problems became evident with part of the core,[1222] and replaced with a date of c.1645BC.[1223] The dating error on this revised estimate was said to be probably ±7 years at one standard deviation (68.2% confidence), with an estimated error limit of ±20 years. Even today, ice-core layers of only a few hundred years age have errors of up to c.±2 years,[1224] and, in the period 3000–4000 years ago, current errors are variously stated to be from a probably unrealistic minimum of ±c.7 years[1225] to a more realistic estimate of ±36 years.[1226]

Nonetheless, several ice-cores from the late 1980s onwards showed that there was one (or more) major volcanic eruption(s) in the northern hemisphere somewhere around the mid to later 17th century BC.[1227] It was even possible to suggest that, since the ice-core dates were to a degree flexible, the tree-ring and ice-core records were very possibly reflecting the same, and therefore volcanic, climate event c.1628BC.[1228] But, again, direct proof of an association between the acid layer and any specific volcano was lacking. In the recent past the relationship between acid signal and known historic volcanism was close enough to permit fair confidence, but once back several hundred years or more this was not the case. Large volcanic eruptions are relatively common on a global scale over the last many thousands of years,[1229] so there should be no *a priori* assumption that the eruption of Thera is necessarily responsible for any given distinctive signal.

Thus the 1980s ended with arguments built on coincidences and likely associations, versus appropriate critical scepticism. But belief is not science. Luckily, developments in the 1990s have revolutionised both the tree-ring and ice-core fields.

An exciting technique built around density measurements of tree-rings now offers

---

[1219] E.g. Hammer *et al.* (1980); Hammer (1980); Zielinski *et al.* (1996).

[1220] For the history and methods of building these chronologies, see Baillie (1982); summary in Baillie (1995a:18–31). The long bristlecone pine chronology of western USA was the work of Ferguson (1969). The western European long chronologies became absolute with Pilcher *et al.* (1984).

[1221] Hammer *et al.* (1980).

[1222] Hammer (1984).

[1223] Hammer *et al.* (1987).

[1224] de Silva and Zielinski (1998:Fig.2 caption).

[1225] Clausen *et al.* (1997).

[1226] Zielinski and Germani (1998a).

[1227] Hammer *et al.* (1987); Johnsen *et al.* (1992); Zielinski *et al.* (1994a); Clausen *et al.* (1997).

[1228] Baillie (1996a); Manning (1992b; 1995:202 n.9); Hughes (1988).

[1229] Zielinski *et al.* (1994a; 1996); Simkin and Seibert (1994).

the ability approximately to reconstruct past temperatures.[1230] It is thus possible to state definitely that the tree-ring anomalies previously only tentatively linked with lowered temperatures are in fact positively associated with unusually cooler summers. A strong coincidence was observed in these regional dendroclimatic reconstructions between localised cold summers and known volcanic eruptions,[1231] and a paper published in 1995 identified some potential for recognising large volcanic signals in a combined set of North American and European tree-ring chronologies.[1232] Work published in 1998 announced the creation of a northern hemisphere-wide set of correlated dendrochronologies and derived proxy temperature data from c.AD1400 to the present day.[1233] For the first time it was possible to consider the coherent relationship between volcanic eruptions and temperature variability. From this work it is clear that a positive relationship exists, with several unusually climatically effective eruptions having a marked effect on hemisphere temperature both at an annual, and even decadal, timescale.

Over the last few years a similar revolution in precision and detail has also occurred in ice-core studies. In the 1980s volcanic acid traces could be identified, but the source volcano could only be surmised. Now fragments of volcanic glass from major eruptions are being identified in such ice-layers enabling the positive correlation of signal with specific volcanic source.[1234] The result is that it is increasingly possible to tie together precisely and unequivocally tree-ring and ice-core evidence with lowered temperatures and specific volcanic activity. For example, the major Huaynaputina eruption in AD1600 can be shown from a combination of ice-core and dendroclimatic data to have had a significant effect on northern hemisphere temperature and climate.[1235] In reverse, it is also possible to demonstrate that other specific eruptions, for example the Asama eruption in Japan in AD1783, had minor to minimal impact on climate.[1236]

Where does this leave the 17th century BC. As noted above, the suggestion has been repeatedly made that the volcanic eruption detected in the ice-cores and reflected in the tree-ring data is Thera. The Minoan eruption of Thera was an enormous volcanic eruption, sending some c.27–30km^3 to c.39km^3 of dense rock equivalent into the

---

[1230] E.g. Briffa *et al.* (1990); Luckman *et al.* (1997); Kalela-Brundin (1999).

[1231] Briffa *et al.* (1992); Briffa *et al.* (1994).

[1232] Jones *et al.* (1995).

[1233] Briffa *et al.* (1998).

[1234] See e.g. Palais *et al.* (1987; 1990; 1992); Fiacco *et al.* (1993; 1994); Zielinski *et al.* (1995; 1997). One important cautionary point should be noted. These studies have, to date, mainly relied on the comparison of major oxide (element) data. In many cases this is sufficient to distinguish among possible source eruptions (especially with rigorous statistical treatment: e.g. Stokes and Lowe 1988; Stokes *et al.* 1992). However, in other situations, where a number of volcanic eruptions might be involved, major oxide (element) data alone is not sufficient, as many volcanic eruption products have broadly similar compositions, and so, combined with variations in eruption product compositions, and in laboratory measurements, discrimination is not possible. Therefore, further analysis considering the overall distinctive profile of each relevant eruption is necessary in such circumstances, in particular, the investigation of the trace element chemistry, and of the rare earth elements (see, with reference to Thera: Vitaliano *et al.* 1990:61–70; Eastwood *et al.* 1998; 1999).

[1235] de Silva and Zielinksi (1998); Briffa *et al.* (1998); Pyle (1998).

[1236] Zielinski *et al.* (1994b).

atmosphere.[1237] The total volume of the tephra fall alone from the eruption preserved in deposits across the east Mediterranean (see Figures 13 and 21 above pp. 11 and 72) was some c.38–42km^3.[1238] This makes the Thera eruption more than twice the size of Krakatau in AD1883 (c.18 km^3 of total bulk volume products[1239]), and three–four times the size of Mt. Pinatubo in 1991 (8.4 to 10.4km^3 of total bulk volume products[1240]). And, as more and more tephra from the Thera eruption is found,[1241] these estimates only rise. Finds of Theran tephra deposits in recent archaeological excavations in east Crete increasingly suggest that the estimated data in Watkins *et al.* (1978:Fig. 1.b) for this area – fresh tephra falls of up to 4cm – are likely minima.[1242] The eruption clearly had a significant local-regional effect.[1243]

However, when it comes to tying volcanic eruptions to ice-core and tree-ring data, the issue is hemisphere-scale climatic effect. A volcanic eruption has a climatic effect if it injects quantities of sulphur dioxide into the stratosphere. The volcanic sulphur dioxide oxidises and spreads to create a sulphate aerosol layer (H_2SO_4) around the hemisphere (and beyond in some cases). This layer intercepts incoming solar radiation, and so disturbs and typically lowers surface temperatures.[1244] When it reaches northerly latitudes, precipitation deposits some of this acid on the polar ice, and, if this is in sufficient quantity, a volcanic signal can be found through analysis. Climatically effective eruptions can have a c.1–3 year climatic–atmospheric effect/presence.[1245] This

---

[1237] Pyle (1990a); Sigurdsson *et al.* (1990).

[1238] Pyle (1990a:116 Table 2a); Sigurdsson *et al.* (1990:102).

[1239] Simkin and Fiske (1983).

[1240] Scott *et al.* (1996). The largest 20th century AD eruption is Novarupta (Katmai) in Alaska in June 1912. This produced c.28±4km^3 of total tephra (from Scott *et al.* 1996:569), and had a marked and immediate effect on northern hemisphere climate, and is clearly evident in the tree-ring data.

[1241] E.g. Guichard *et al.* (1993); Eastwood *et al.* (1998; 1999).

[1242] Driessen and Macdonald (1997:93).

[1243] Driessen and Macdonald (1997). See also two projects in progress on the physical/environmental impacts of the eruption in the Aegean: an Australian-based project (Bicknell 1996/1997; 1995); and a UK PhD project (David Sewell, University of Reading, UK).

[1244] The role of suphur products in the atmosphere is complex. SO_2 in the lower atmosphere is in fact a warming, greenhouse, gas. However, once SO_2 converts into an H_2SO_4 aerosol in the upper atmosphere (i.e. the stratosphere), it then intercepts incoming solar radiation and so leads to surface cooling. For a summary of the key role of sulphur dioxide in creating climatic impact, see Rampino *et al.* (1988:75–79). But a caveat must be stressed to this general picture: the climatic effects of any particular eruption may vary for reasons other than volume of sulphur production according to a complex set of circumstances including time of year of the eruption, residence time and optical depth of the aerosol, location of the volcano, nature of the high altitude circulation systems, precursor conditions, etc. Further, the effects may vary regionally around the world (e.g. cooler in the USA but warmer in central Europe). See now Sadler and Grattan (1999).

[1245] E.g. Rampino and Self (1982); Rampino *et al.* (1988); Sear *et al.* (1987); Luhr (1991); Dutton and Christy (1992); Hunt (1993); McCormick *et al.* (1995); Robock and Mao (1995); Seol and Yamazaki (1998). Dutton and Christy (1992) however note favourably literature showing that such volcanic signals can exist for 3–5 years after a major eruption, considering especially ocean-heat storage, and point out that the effect from the El Chichón eruption lasted 2–5 years after the eruption. Chemical and physical feedback mechanisms in the stratosphere are argued to limit the temporal duration of an effective aerosol to no more than another few years. The type of 1–3 year, or <5 year, effect discussed here applies to the large volcanic eruptions of historical times. Past super-eruptions had much more devastating effects: potentially a so-called volcanic winter (see Rampino *et al.* 1988). The enormous Roza eruption, some 15 million

'effect' is usually relatively minor,[1246] however, and in general terms recent volcanic eruptions have had little significant effect beyond the scale of other variations in climate,[1247] and, over the long-term, the climatic impact of volcanic eruptions is currently the subject of debate.[1248] It has been suggested that occurrences of a cluster of volcanic eruptions may have a more significant, decadal, to multi-decadal, impact,[1249] and in recent times the period AD1815–1837 is intriguing in this respect (and also the 17th century BC as we shall see below), but, in general, there is little evidence for detectable volcanic forcing of climate beyond a 1–3 year period.[1250]

Nonetheless, even a minor volcanic effect may be sufficiently significant to affect trees growing in a sensitive environment. The average temperature drop in such cases is potentially larger, by a factor up to 3–4 times, in high-latitude, or high-altitude, circumstances.[1251] A number of studies (such as those cited earlier) provide examples of more or less systematic records via tree-rings of volcanic eruptions. A critical element in the specific climatic effect of any particular eruption is its latitude. The vertical distance to the stratosphere is less at high latitude (c.7–10km at the poles, versus c.14–16km at the equator), and this makes it easier for a high latitude volcano to inject sulphur into the stratosphere, but, due to poleward transport in the atmosphere, the aerosol is less likely to spread over the rest of the hemisphere and so have a widespread effect at middle and lower latitudes. In contrast, if a mid-latitude eruption successfully injects sulphur dioxide into the stratosphere, then the resultant aerosol spreads all over the hemisphere, and so has a more marked, widespread, and long-lasting impact on climate.[1252] The big question is thus what climatic effect did the mid-latitude eruption of Thera produce, and can we expect a signal from it in the Arctic ice and northern hemisphere tree-rings? The resolution of this issue is multi-faceted, and we need to work through several arguments.

Let us begin by considering the case *against* the eruption of Thera having any major impact, as this has been held to be the main stumbling block on scientific grounds for linking Thera with the 17th century BC climate signals. It has been argued that the sulphur production of the Thera eruption – estimated by petrologic analysis (see below) – was far too small to account for the volcanic sulphur products found in the later 17th

---

years ago, of the Columbia River Plateau, was 50 times the size of the Tambora eruption of AD1815. It would have blocked out over 99% of sunlight (Stothers *et al.* 1986; Rampino *et al.* 1988:92–93). More recently, the Toba super-eruption of about 75,000 years ago produced a Plinian ash fall alone some 20 times the size of Thera's, and may have been expected to have had a dramatic climatic impact (see Rampino and Self 1993; Rampino *et al.* 1988:90–92).

[1246] E.g., as noted in Chapter II, there was an average global temperature drop of just 0.4°C after the large, VEI 6, Pinatubo eruption in 1991 (McCormick *et al.* 1995; Self *et al.* 1996). Observed cooling of 0.5°C to 0.6°C occurred in the northern hemisphere. Dutton and Christy (1992) report a very slightly larger number for average cooling effect: 0.5°C. They too note that the effect in the northern hemisphere (0.7°C) was slightly greater than in the southern hemisphere. They attribute this to the 'the presence of greater land mass which cools more readily than ocean areas in the event of diminished solar heating' (p.2,316).

[1247] Mass and Portman (1989; 1990); see now Sadler and Grattan (1999).

[1248] Birks (1994); Buckland *et al.* (1997); see now Sadler and Grattan (1999).

[1249] Porter (1986); Scuderi (1990; 1992); Brunstein (1996:71–72); Schimmelmann *et al.* (1998; 1999).

[1250] Crowley *et al.* (1993); Crowley and Kim (1993); Stuiver *et al.* (1997:260–261).

[1251] Cf. Cuffey *et al.* (1995); Stuiver *et al.* (1997:262).

[1252] Bluth *et al.* (1997).

century BC acid spike recorded in the Greenland ice-cores.[1253] This was leapt upon by critics of the 17th century BC date,[1254] and was cited by other scholars as the principal reason to support the potential relevance of other possible volcanic eruptions.[1255]

However, this whole logic must now be dismissed. The sulphur production estimates employed by Sigurdsson _et al._ and Pyle (and others)[1256] were made on the basis of the petrologic technique. This involves analysing glass inclusions from phenocrysts – assumed to contain representative samples of pre-eruption magma composition – and glass from erupted tephra – assumed to represent the composition of the degassed magma – and then comparing these in order to reach an approximate estimate from the difference for the yield of volatile emissions to the atmosphere. The method was only ever claimed to give a minimum estimate of volcanic volatile yield. However, opinion in the volcanological field has significantly changed since the 1980s (when the work relevant to Thera was carried out). It has recently become clear that petrologic estimates can _seriously_ underestimate SO_2 emissions.[1257] New measurements of total sulphur emissions from volcanic eruptions are now possible through data from the Total Ozone Mapping Spectrometer (TOMS) satellite. Comparisons of these data to petrologic estimates show a huge discrepancy (e.g. petrologic estimate just 12% of remote sensing); and independent plume analysis measurements obtain similar results. Now, of course, the TOMS system itself has some errors, _but_ even at the minimum, the TOMS data still reveal total sulphur production much higher than the petrologic estimates.[1258] Even by 1991, it was becoming clear from published analyses of several recent eruptions that petrologic estimates were very significant underestimates.[1259] The eruption of El Chichón in Mexico in 1982 had an estimated SO_2 production of just 23 thousand tons from petrologic analysis, but TOMS satellite data estimated the yield as 2.7 _million_ tons.[1260] Likewise, the estimates for the eruption of Mt. Pinatubo in the Phillipines were 0.3–3.0 million tons of SO_2 from petrologic analysis, but 19, or 17±2, million tons from the TOMS satellite data.[1261] The petrologic estimates were 20 to 100 times too small![1262] This makes a mockery of the confident assertion by Sigurdsson _et al._ (1990:110) that the petrologic estimates had a maximum error factor of two. Gerlach _et al._ (1996:430) conclude that their study 'reinforces growing evidence, based on smaller eruptions (VEI ≤5), that petrologic emission estimates for SO_2 are many times lower than estimates based on remote sensing, and indicates that petrologic estimates may also seriously underestimate the SO_2 emissions of larger explosive eruptions'.

[1253] See Sigurdsson _et al._ (1985; 1990:105–110); Pyle (1990b).

[1254] E.g. Warren (1990/1991:33).

[1255] See e.g. Vogel _et al._ (1990:536); Sigurdsson _et al._ (1990:101, 110).

[1256] Following originally Devine _et al._ (1984).

[1257] Gerlach _et al._ (1994; 1996).

[1258] For TOMS errors, see Krueger _et al._ (1995).

[1259] See summary in Manning (1992a:246); Baillie (1995a:113–114).

[1260] Andres _et al._ (1991); Luhr _et al._ (1984).

[1261] Bernard _et al._ (1991); Gerlach _et al._ (1996). Gerlach _et al._ (1996:416) specifically note that the 17 million ton figure is the _minimum_ estimate of the total SO_2 emissions.

[1262] Gerlach _et al._ (1996:420) conclude that 'the petrologic method pedicts an SO_2 emission ... that is not significantly different from zero but is significantly different indeed from the 17-Mt remote sensing result'.

In the light of these problems, and the evidence that several recent eruptions produced significant excess sulphur in terms of previous models and data analysis, Kress (1997) has now proposed an exciting new magma-mixing model to explain such 'excess' sulphur production.[1263] The circumstances he describes as capable of producing much more sulphur than would formerly have been predicted are relatively common among volcanoes. In general terms, it is also evident that the overall geological setting of a volcano may be as crucial to determining volatile yield (including sulphur) for a major eruption as the composition and yield of the particular juvenile magma (as investigated by the petrologic technique), especially if there is dissociation of sulphur-rich sediments at depth (anhydrite). It is quite possible that Thera could be a candidate for an upwards revision of its total sulphur production on such grounds.[1264] At a minimum, it needs to be stressed that our understanding of the final dynamic processes in explosive volcanism remains poor,[1265] and rigid categorisation is thus inappropriate. Finally, where sea-water enters the eruption process, as at Thera, further excess volatiles may result beyond those determined by petrologic analysis.

In view of both the observed major discrepancies, and the new theoretical model of Kress (1997), we may conclude that the petrologic estimates of SO_2 production by the Thera eruption, and the supposed discrepancy between these and the recorded SO_2 fallout in Greenland in the ice-cores by a factor of 6–12, or 8–20, times,[1266] are therefore completely irrelevant (pending a major review and new work). This is a significant revision to the 'state of play' in 1990. And, even before the TOMS data, geologists should have been more cautious of petrologic estimates; proponents admitted an error factor of 2, but analysis of relevant data shows that in practice the real errors were in fact up to 4–8 times the estimate (e.g. the case of Krakatau – often compared to Thera), and the constituent logic and data were shaky.[1267] From the analogy of the recent high-quality TOMS satellite data, the existing petrologic estimates of Thera's SO_2 production probably imply that the real SO_2 production was in fact quite possibly up to some 10–20 (or more) times larger, and we might therefore speculate that Thera's SO_2 production potentially correlates very comfortably with the recorded acid spike in the Greenland ice-cores in the later 17th century BC. Indeed, as we shall see in Chapter V.3, there is now potential positive confirmation for this view.

Therefore, it is abundantly clear that the petrologic evidence previously cited as relevant to Thera may now be dismissed as completely irrelevant. This does not mean that all petrological estimates (of other) volcanic deposits are equally problematic (some data in Sigurdsson *et al.* 1985 correlate relatively well with independent measurements), nor that recent improvements to the petrological technique may not

---

[1263] See also Carroll (1997). For other discussion on the sources of the excess sulphur, see Gerlach *et al.* (1996:425–429); and the several other papers in Newhall and Punongbayan (1996:687–891).

[1264] Luhr and Melson (1996:748) suggest some criteria for the identification of ancient sulphur-rich eruptions, and these, and other relevant data acquired as a result of Mt. Pinatubo and El Chichón, should now be considered in relation to the Minoan eruption (Bo) Thera deposits.

[1265] Dingwell (1996); Mader *et al.* (1996); Papale (1999); Melnik (1999).

[1266] Sigurdsson *et al.* (1990:106–107); Pyle (1990b:171).

[1267] Baillie (1995a:113); Manning (1995:202–203, 215).

lead to better estimates.[1268] But, as Self and King (1996:280–282) conclude in a recent review, it is clear that petrologic estimates at best establish *minimum* estimates: in recent cases ranging from too small by a factor of about two, to far too small by one or more orders of magnitude. Petrologic estimates work best for relatively mafic-rich or sulphur-rich magmas, but tend to be serious underestimates for oxidising magmas, or in circumstances where there was magma-mixing (common in calc-alkaline systems), or magmatic volatile saturation at the time of inclusion entrapment.

Let us thus discount the 1989–1990 negative case from petrologic evidence, and instead now consider the positive case for the eruption of Thera linking with the later 17th century BC climatic event/anomaly in the tree-ring and ice-core evidence. The positive case consists of three strands: (1) a strong general circumstantial case (rest of this Section), (2) likely or potential positive confirmation of Theran eruption products linked to a 17th century BC volcanic signal in the Greenland ice (Chapter V.3 below), and (3) good evidence for a specific and significant climate event in the Aegean region in 1628BC which is most plausibly linked to the eruption of Thera (Chapter V.4 below). Before turning to the two sets of direct, positive, data, I wish to spend the remainder of this Section setting the parameters and constraints on the cause and source of the 17th century BC climate event. These alone make the eruption of Thera the most plausible and likely of the currently proposed candidates.

Rampino *et al.* (1988) state that 'probably any explosive eruption bigger than Krakatau's in 1883 can be detected in one or both of the polar ice-sheets, because so much magma is erupted that the sulphur release is bound to be fairly large in any case'.[1271] The Minoan eruption of Thera was significantly bigger than Krakatau,[1272] hence, as a mid-latitude northern hemisphere eruption, it can be expected on common-sense grounds to be represented in the northern hemisphere ice-core data. If we turn to the record of historical volcanism we find support for this view. The standard descriptive statistic for volcanic eruptions is the volcanic explosivity index (VEI).[1273] This scale is logarithmic, with each category representing a volume of erupted tephra an order of magnitude greater than the last. Thus an VEI 6 eruption is c.10 times the volume of an VEI 5 eruption, and 100 times that of an VEI 4 eruption, for example. The sulphur emissions produced do not, on average, increase on the same logarithmic scale;[1274] nonetheless, on the basis of recent eruptions for which there is satellite data, the total quantity of sulphur emissions do on average increase significantly with, and so correlate with, overall eruption size.[1275] Therefore, there is a broad approximate correlation between the scale-explosivity of the eruption and the total sulphur emissions. The Minoan eruption of Thera is estimated at VEI 6.9,[1276] significantly larger than any recent eruption. On an average, modelled, basis, its sulphur dioxide output should be at least

---

[1268] See Self and King (1996).

[1271] Cited also by Baillie (1995a:112).

[1272] See above; this applies even from the now discredited petrologic data (Sigurdsson *et al.* 1990:108–110).

[1273] Newhall and Self (1982).

[1274] Pyle *et al.* (1996); Schnetzler *et al.* (1997:20089–20090).

[1275] Schnetzler *et al.* (1997:20088–20089).

[1276] Decker (1990).

getting close to the *minimum* c.0.6 x 10^5 kt range estimated for a VEI 7 'arc' eruption.[1277] This is already some 6 to 7.5 times larger than the total sulphur yields estimated by Pyle (1990b), or 3.5 times larger than the estimate of total sulphur emissions by Sigurdsson *et al.* (1990) (and, if it fell above the minimum estimates, the estimated sulphur dioxide production range for a VEI 7 eruption goes up to 50 to 62.5 or 45.5 times larger). It would thus be very odd if the eruption of Thera were not represented in the Greenland ice-core record. We can therefore expect Thera to be represented somewhere within the possible dating window. The last twenty years of analysis and debate in the combined fields of archaeology and science have undoubtedly established the maximum potential dating window for the Thera eruption as c.1650–1500BC.[1278]

Several recent, high-quality, Greenland ice-cores from different parts of Greenland (see Figure 51) provide records of northern hemisphere volcanic activity for the period, in particular the Dye 3, GRIP, and GISP2 cores.[1279] The different latitudes of these cores (e.g. central versus southern Greenland for the GRIP versus Dye 3 cores), and the differences between the volcanic records as a result, in addition permit a degree of discrimination of the latitudinal band of some eruptions and the ability to identify and discount minor (local, high-latitude) eruptions of non-hemisphere-wide significance. Major volcanic acid signals in these cores for the period c.1700–1400BC are set out in Table 13. See also Figures 52 and 53.

We can immediately reach one highly relevant conclusion. There is a notable absence of any even vaguely significant volcanic activity for a century between c.1569/1566BC[1280] and 1463BC or 1459BC in all three ice-cores. It should be noted that the core sites in Greenland receive 'sufficient amounts of annual precipitation to rule out the possibility of missing annual snow deposits'[1281] thus, especially in view of the replication across three different ice-cores, it must be concluded that we are dealing with a complete record, and so a real absence of major volcanic activity during this period. It would seem very unlikely, bordering on impossible, for the massive eruption of Thera to have occurred in this period. The dating accuracy on each ice-core varies, and is not absolute. From a comparison of the Dye 3 and GRIP cores, Clausen *et al.* (1997) argue for an error range of only ±c.7 years for the GRIP/Dye 3 dates; the GISP2 dates in this time range are held to be accurate only to ±c.36 years.[1282] Nonetheless, the consistent absence of evidence from this period across three cores appears very strong evidence against a date for the eruption of Thera c.1560 to 1470BC. In agreement with the radiocarbon evidence (Chapter V.1), and the archaeological evidence (Chapter IV), this seems to provide further strength to the case against the 'low' or conventional

---

[1277] Schnetzler *et al.* (1997:Table 1).

[1278] E.g. combining and including each of: Warren (1984; 1990/1991; 1996; 1998); Warren and Hankey (1989:137–141, 214–215); Betancourt (1987; 1998b); Manning (1988a; 1988b; 1992a; 1995:200–216); Hammer *et al.* (1987); Baillie (1995a); Kuniholm *et al.* (1996); Clausen *et al.* (1997).

[1279] Hammer *et al.* (1987); Clausen *et al.* (1997); Zielinski *et al.* (1994); Zielinski and Germani (1998a).

[1280] Signals linked as the same by Clausen *et al.* (1997:Table 4).

[1281] Hammer *et al.* (1987:518).

[1282] Zielinski and Germani (1998a:282).

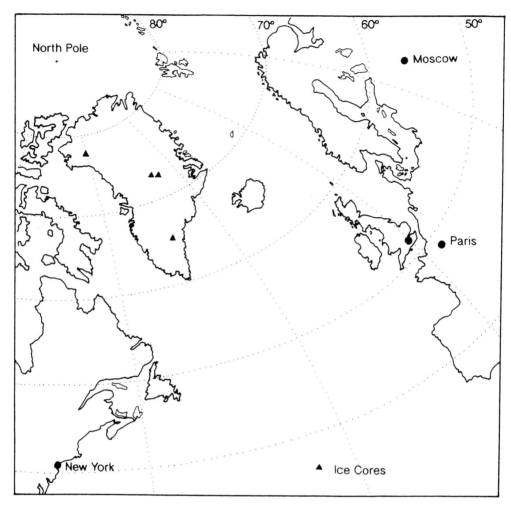

Fig. 51. Map showing the location of the main Greenland ice-core sites referred to in the text. Greenland ice-core sites: top left, Camp Century; centre left, GISP2; centre right, GRIP; bottom, Dye 3.

date for the eruption of Thera and the LMIA period. With less force, this evidence also runs against the 'compromise early' chronology, since the nearest signal is in the earlier 1560s BC, and none of the earlier 16th century BC signals appear to represent major volcanic eruptions.[1283]

Tree-ring data from the USA and Ireland likewise provide no evidence for any

---

[1283] However, given dating errors, and the fair possibility that Thera did not necessarily produce a high sulphur yield to the stratosphere, one of the signals in the c.1560s BC *could* be brought into play by advocates of a 'compromise early' chronology.

Dye 3 BC	Mton H$_2$SO$_4$	Group	GRIP BC	Mton H$_2$SO$_4$	Group	GISP2 BC	SO$_4^{2-}$ ppb
						1695	213
1688	not stated						
						1669	78
1644	186*	G4					
			1636	139*	G4		
						1623	145
1622	15	G1					
			1618	53	G3		
						1602	58
						1600	40
						1594	30
						1577	29
1569	62	G2					
			1566	39	G3		
1463	110	G3					
						1459	104
1457	98	G3				1457	67
						1454	164
						1442	57
1440	93	G3					
1428	41*	G2					
			1425	141*	G4		

Table 13. Major volcanic acid signals in the Dye 3, GRIP and GISP2 ice-cores from respectively southern, central, and central Greenland for the period c.1700–1400BC. Data from Clausen et al. (1997:Table 3); Zielinski et al. (1994a:Table 2); the 1688BC Dye 3 datum is from Hammer et al. (1987:519 and Fig.2). Note, there is no relationship between the two different units of scale of signal cited by the Danish-European (Dye 3, GRIP) and U.S.A. (GISP2) teams. The Group (G1–G4) refers to a scale dividing acid signals in the Dye 3 and GRIP cores according to signal strength in relation to background acid deposition at each site (see Clausen et al. 1997:26,713 and Table 2). 'The acid signals of group G4 are the most obvious candidates for major volcanic eruptions in the northern hemisphere'. Signals marked with the asterisk (*) are identified by Clausen et al. (1997:26713, Table 5) as the major volcanic signals in the combined Dye 3-GRIP record.

significant growth-climatic anomaly or event in the 16th century BC.[1284] Warren,[1285] and Sigurdsson *et al.* (1990:109), and others, object that this tree-ring evidence does not reflect every volcano, hence Thera could easily be missing in the tree-ring record. And, it is true that not every major volcanic eruption produces a clear signal in any one set of tree-ring data (*and* the effects of any specific eruption can vary around the world by region), but the data also needs appropriate contextualisation before any broad generalisations can be made.

[1284] LaMarche and Hirschboeck (1984); Baillie and Munro (1988); Baillie (1990; 1995a).
[1285] Warren (1984; 1990/1991:38 n.28; 1998:324).

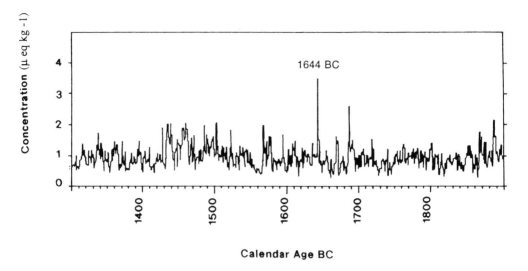

Fig. 52. The Dye 3 ice-core acid profile showing the 1644BC spike suggested to represent the eruption of Thera (Hammer et al. 1987). Drawing after Hammer et al. (1987).

   Trees in environmentally sensitive locations where unusual temperature decreases will have a significant impact on their growth do usually reflect climatically effective volcanic eruptions.[1286] Suitable tree data can thus provide part of a *positive* case for the recognition of a volcanic eruption climate signal – but, since trees do *not* record all eruptions, the reverse does not necessarily apply (i.e. no tree signal does not mean no eruption). For any particular volcanic eruption, it is necessary to consider how this might have impacted such trees. Trees in the White Mountains of California, for example (the source of the LaMarche and Hirschboeck dataset), may not have been overly affected by less than very large high-latitude eruptions since rapid polewards transport of eruption products may have rendered effects at mid-latitudes relatively minor. The time of the year of the eruption will also be important if the effect is only short-lived (if it misses the growing season, then it may leave no significant trace). For the upper-timber line Bristlecone pine the relevant time period is the end of June through mid-September;[1287] variations in temperature in May or October appear irrelevant (and of course November through April). Again the relatively short-lived effects of high-latitude or non-major eruptions may have no significant impact.
   Major mid-latitude eruptions thus come more into the picture. As noted above, if one of these successfully injects sulphur dioxide into the stratosphere, then the resultant aerosol spreads all over the hemisphere, and so has a more marked, widespread, and long-lasting impact on climate, and so things like tree-growth across

---

[1286] E.g. Briffa *et al.* (1998).
[1287] Brunstein (1996:69 and Fig.4).

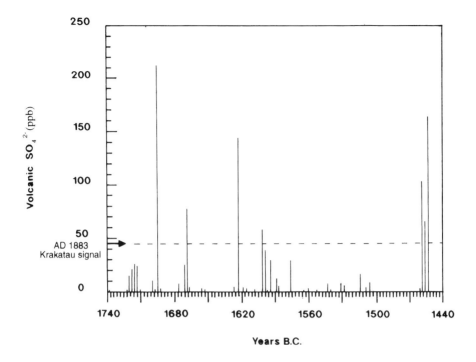

Fig. 53. The SO$_4^{2-}$ residual volcanic signals in the GISP2 ice-core for the period around the time of the Thera eruption after Zielinski and Germani (1998a). The scale of the AD1883 Krakatau signal in the GISP2 ice-core is shown at 46ppb (Zielinski et al. 1994a:Table 1). At the time of the maximum reduction in estimates of Thera's sulphur production, it was suggested that Thera's sulphur signal might have merely been similar to the rather smaller and more remote Krakatau eruption (Pyle 1990b:169 and 171, Tables 1b and 1c). The Krakatau signal might therefore be deemed to offer a likely minimum benchmark for a Thera signal, with anything lower being very unlikely to represent Thera.

the northern-hemisphere.[1288] Such an eruption can have a 1–3 year climatic impact, and so can affect tree-growth through the complete one or more years afterwards, and thus 'catch' the growing periods of different trees around the northern hemisphere. In contrast, equatorial eruptions (and those in the southern hemisphere) have much less marked and certainly less immediate effects on northern hemisphere climate. Hence the huge eruption of Novarupta (Katmai) in Alaska in June 1912 had a marked and immediate effect on northern hemisphere climate, and is clearly evident in the tree-ring data,[1289] whereas the similarly large eruption of Santa Maria in Guatemala in October 1902 is effectively invisible in the high northern latitude tree-ring data of Briffa *et al.* (1998). Some effect is registered in the mid-latitude Bristlecone pine frost-

---

[1288] Bluth *et al.* (1997).
[1289] LaMarche and Hirschboeck (1984); Brunstein (1996:Table 1); Briffa *et al.* (1998).

damage indices, however, where frost damage is noted in AD1902 by LaMarche and Hirschboeck (1984), and AD1903 by Brunstein (1996:Table 1), although this may also reflect the near contemporary and equatorial zone eruptions of Soufrière, St. Vincent, and Pelée, Martinique.

Sigurdsson *et al.* (1990:109) cite two supposedly telling instances of non-representation in tree-ring data: a Japanese and Icelandic eruption of AD1783 (respectively Asama, and Laki), and an unknown eruption of AD1259. It is worth exploring these cases as they nicely illustrate the need to consider the evidence carefully, and in context. The first does show up as a colder year in the dendroclimatological data of Briffa *et al.* from high-latitudes (1998:Fig.1), but more to the point both are high-latitude eruptions, and the Asama eruption in particular had little climatic impact,[1290] while the sulphur and volatiles cloud from the Laki eruption in Iceland was largely restricted to the troposphere (did not reach the stratosphere) and so the eruption had severe local to regional, but not hemisphere-wide, effects.[1291] The lack of frost damage in western USA is thus to be expected (and is not an anomaly at all). The AD1259 eruption is again an interesting case.[1292] It is a special and unusual event because a large volcanic acid signal is found in both Greenland and Antarctic ice cores at about this time (give or take one to two years), but there is a lack of northern hemisphere tree-ring evidence (and in general the climatic effect at this time is enigmatic in the northern hemisphere). The source eruption is unknown, but it is guessed to be equatorial – perhaps El Chichón in Mexico.[1293] Depending on time of year and the state of the stratospheric quasi-biennial oscillation,[1294] the sulphur aerosol from such an equatorial eruption might have been stored and dispersed in the tropical stratosphere for one or two years before being transported to higher northern latitudes,[1295] and so its effect on mid-latitude trees in the northern hemisphere may have been relatively minor.

What one finds, therefore, when one explores the evidence in detail, is that the climatic effects of volcanic eruptions can vary significantly, and likewise the tree-ring reflection thereof, depending on where, and when, an eruption occurred. It is also important to remember that other climatic forces, such as strong El Niño events, can also create similar tree-ring growth anomalies independent of volcanoes.

The choice of dendrochronological data is another relevant factor. The critiques of Warren (1984); Sigurdsson *et al.* (1990); and most recently Buckland *et al.* (1997), all referred solely to the frost damage record presented by LaMarche and Hirschboeck (1984). However, this one record is neither unique, nor privileged. It was very much a first, approximate, and rather simplistic, statement on the subject of the relationship between trees from one area and wider volcanic activity. But for LaMarche's untimely death, much more sophisticated further work might have been expected in the next decade. LaMarche and Hirschboeck did not present a huge, totally representative,

---

[1290] Zielinski *et al.* (1994b).
[1291] Sigurdsson (1982); Grattan and Charman (1994); Thordarson *et al.* (1996).
[1292] Lowe and Higham (1998).
[1293] Lowe and Higham (1998:428 with refs.); Palais *et al.* (1992).
[1294] Trepte and Hitchman (1992).
[1295] McCormick *et al.* (1995:400–401); Pyle (1998:415).

sample; even in the worst years not every tree necessarily suffers frost damage, because much depends on extremely local factors. Thus, for example, a number of latewood frost rings in the record from Almagre Mountain, Colorado,[1296] are additional to the record from the White Mountains, California, of LaMarche and Hirschboeck (1984). What *is* highly significant are years where many trees at several diverse sites all reflect an identical event. In the last 1000 years the 14 relevant years in common between the LaMarche and Hirschboeck (1984) and Brunstein (1996) data are: 1965, 1941, 1912, 1903–1902, 1837, 1828, 1817, 1805, 1761, 1680, 1660, 1453, 1171, and 1029. Of these, only four events do not clearly correlate with known major volcanic eruptions or large volcanic acid signals in ice-cores: 1965, 1941, 1828 and 1805. 1965 and 1941 do correlate, however, with two strong El Niño events,[1297] and 1805 was an unusually poor summer in the western USA with snowstorms from mid-August,[1298] and was in a decade where hemisphere temperatures went into temporary freefall on average.[1299] Only 1828 lacks clear cause or association.

The nature of the critique of Buckland *et al.* (1997) is thus mis-directed. They happily use recent mid-1990s ice-core data against the one solitary 1984 tree-ring dataset of LaMarche and Hirschboeck (see their Table 1). They conspicuously fail to refer to, yet alone employ, rather more sophisticated and comprehensive tree-ring data (contrast Briffa *et al.* 1998 as the current state of the art). The 'evidence' derived by Buckland *et al.* (1997) from their Table 1 is thus very much an unfair, or irrelevant, and anachronistic statistic (even by their own standards[1300]). They are, however, right to highlight the complex nature of the relationship between events such as volcanic eruptions and climate, and correct to note that the effects of volcanic eruptions are usually only relatively minor in overall climatic terms (see above).

To return therefore to the 16th century BC. The current tree-ring evidence indicates no major climate event potentially consistent with a major volcanic eruption in the whole of the 16th century BC.[1301] It was a volcanologically quiet time. The few volcanic

---

[1296] Brunstein (1996:Table 1).
[1297] Brunstein (1996:70).
[1298] Brunstein (1996:Table 2).
[1299] E.g. Briffa *et al.* (1998:Fig.1).
[1300] Baillie (1998:Table 1).
[1301] The steep slope in the radiocarbon calibration curve c.1530–1515BC (marking a rapid increase in $\delta^{14}C$) does not by itself indicate volcanic activity in the total absence of positive evidence from ice-core records. Such changes in radiocarbon levels are more likely linked to solar forcing. The recent suggestion by Schimmelmann *et al.* (1998; 1999) that a period of climate change at the beginning of the 17th century AD was primarily caused by a cluster of volcanic activity cannot, contra their initial paper, explain the sharp increase in $\delta^{14}C$ from about the same time. This radiocarbon episode lasts for most of the century, and thus may not be associated with the short-term effects of volcanic activity (sub-decadal). As van Geel *et al.* (1999) point out, a similar century-scale period of $\delta^{14}C$ increase occurs in the period c.850–760BC. No major volcanic eruption is correlative. The time-scale is also again too long to be accounted for by volcanic activity. Hence, as van Geel *et al.* (1999) conclude, solar forcing must be a more likely causal mechanism. This is not to say that the marked volcanic activity c.AD1600 did not lead to short-term climate effects, and, given its coincidence with the beginning of a century-scale period of solar-forced climate change, the effect may have seemed significant. However, the volcanic activity did not create the overall climate episode in the 17th century AD.

acid signals in the various ice-cores from the earlier 16th century BC are all relatively small and minor. The one apparently larger one, 1569BC in the Dye 3 core, may probably be discounted as it occurs against a high background acidity[1302] – hence only a G2 rating in Clausen *et al.* (1997:Table 3). This alone does not rule out one of these signals being Thera, but positive statements to this effect, e.g. by Pyle (1990b:171), were influenced by the very low petrologic estimates for Thera's sulphur production, which are now discredited. However, it is notable that mid-latitude eruptions have the most marked and direct effect on hemisphere climate, and that the mid-latitudes of the northern hemisphere are also particularly sensitive to the effects of large volcanic eruptions.[1303] Given the enormous scale of the Thera eruption, and the general correlation of eruption scale with bulk sulphur yield (see above), this would have to lend some *a priori* weight to the case against the likelihood of the relatively small earlier 16th century BC signals possibly representing Thera.

Thus the preliminary conclusions are: (i) that a Thera eruption date c.1560BC to 1470BC is extremely unlikely to impossible from the ice-core data (and consistent tree-ring data); and (ii) that while an eruption in the range 1602–1569BC is possible (minor ice-core acid signals, but no tree-ring support), and so could co-ordinate with the 'compromise early' chronology, it is not intrinsically likely. The latter possibility relies to an extent on the view that Thera had a low sulpur yield to the atmosphere, and so little significant climatic effect.

The main volcanic and climate signal within the potential Thera date window lies in the mid to later 17th century BC. In the three ice-core records in Table 13 there is a significant volcanic eruption variously dated 1644BC (Dye 3), 1636BC (GRIP), or 1623BC (GISP2 – it remains possible that the 1669±c.36BC signal in the GISP2 core may also be relevant). The 1644BC and 1636BC signals are equated as being the same volcanic signal,[1304] and it is quite possible (to likely) that the 1623BC signal in the GISP2 core is also the same event.[1305] The ages are consistent with the radiocarbon evidence for the eruption of Thera, and in each case a link with the eruption of Thera has been proposed at some stage by the ice-core teams.[1306] The only significant tree-ring growth anomaly among temperature sensitive trees in the USA and Ireland (and elsewhere in the UK and Germany) for the period c.1700–1450BC occurred more or less contemporaneously, at 1628/1627BC.[1307] These workers have suggested that this is also Thera – and a major

---

[1302] Cf. Hammer *et al.* (1987:Fig.2).

[1303] Robock and Mao (1995).

[1304] Clausen *et al.* (1997).

[1305] The dating error on the GISP2 core over this period would indicate that the 1669BC signal would have a dating error of about ±36 years (following Zielinski and Germani 1998a). Thus it could easily be contemporary with the respective Dye 3 and GRIP signals. It could also be contemporary with the radiocarbon data relevant to the Thera eruption. The stated date and error would just, by 5 years, appear to exclude contemporaneity with the dendrochronological event at 1628BC. However, whether the date is defined with such accuracy and precision is debatable (see Section 3 below; also see Baillie 1996a).

[1306] Hammer *et al.* (1987); Clausen *et al.* (1997:26,713, 26,721); Zielinski *et al.* (1994a:Table 2) – but cf. Zielinski and Germani (1998a; 1998b), which in turn should be read with Manning (1998b) and *especially* with Chapter V.3 below.

[1307] LaMarche and Hirschboeck (1984); Baillie and Munro (1988); Baillie (1990; 1995a).

volcanic eruption is certainly a plausible cause, or causal factor. Although there is at present no positive correlation, it seems quite likely in addition that the ice-core and tree-ring datasets are reflecting the same major volcanic climate signal, and that all this evidence may therefore be dated precisely to 1628BC.[1308]

Thus it seems likely that a large volcanic event occurred in the later 17th century BC which (via its SO_2 aerosol) caused low temperatures, increased rainfall, and almost no spring growth in oaks in the north of Ireland in 1628BC (hence probably a winter to spring eruption timing), and a sufficient lowering of the northern hemisphere temperature so that in 1627BC frost damage occurred at the upper timber-line in trees growing in the White Mountains of California.[1309] A provisional temperature reconstruction for Fennoscandia across the second millennium BC is not yet absolutely dated, but is constrained within narrow margins ($\leq\pm50$ years) by radiocarbon data.[1310] Interestingly, and importantly, it reveals that the two marked periods of temperature reduction in the whole of the second millennium BC occur at, or very close to, the known major tree-ring anomalies of 1628BC and 1159BC, and the contemporary major volcanic signals in the Greenland ice-cores.[1311] We thus perhaps have a situation where a major volcanic eruption (or cluster thereof) in the later 17th century BC (1628BC in particular) coincided with a cooler climate episode across the same period. The combined result may have been quite a clear climatic signal (unusual tree-ring evidence), and general effect. A similar set of circumstances seems to have occurred in the period around the eruption of Tambora in AD1815; a cooler climate episode, combined with this eruption, caused the year without a summer, and the last great subsistence crisis in human history.[1312] No such temperature drop or volcanic effect is found in the 16th or 15th centuries BC. The only question remaining, therefore, is which volcano, or perhaps it is volcanoes, was/were responsible for the 1628BC eruption and the volcanic part of the associated climate event?[1313]

[1308] Hughes (1988).

[1309] Baillie (1995b:34; 1996b:295) reports that frost damage has now also been identified in two new foxtail pine chronologies from the Sierra Nevada.

[1310] Briffa (1994).

[1311] Baillie (1995b:36 and fig.18).

[1312] See Rampino *et al.* (1988:83–85) for a summary. For a contrasting account, see now Sadler and Grattan (1999:184–187).

[1313] As noted, I am not suggesting that Thera by itself caused this marked temperature drop over several decades. This is contrary to all observations and models of the effects of major volcanic eruptions of Thera's scale. The Anatolian tree-ring evidence (Chapter V.4) further indicates a local marked effect for only a few years. But, we might consider either: (i) that several major volcanic eruptions occurred in this period and, combined, these forced a lower average temperature over a several decade period; or (ii) that for other reasons northern hemisphere temperatures were lowered and that when the Thera eruption occurred at this time it may therefore have had a greater than usual impact on marginal environments (i.e. relevant precursor conditions). The correlation of these two cooler episodes with the notable collapses and re-orientations of civilisation in the Old World in the SIP (with Egyptian and other testimony of famine) and then the collapse of the LBA in the 12th century BC (Ward and Joukowsky 1992; Drews 1993) may also be noted as an interesting coincidence. The sorts of disasters associated with the climate cooling and then great Tambora volcanic eruption in AD1815 may offer a hint of what a similar, but more serious, episode, might lead to, especially in the pre-modern world.

As noted, Thera has been proposed. But this was an admittedly unjustified assumption in the 1980s based on it being about the only 'then-known' very large volcanic eruption from the approximate period. In fact, volcanic eruptions are quite common, and even relatively large volcanic eruptions occur with a reasonable frequency.[1314] On the Volcanic Explosivity Index of Newhall and Self (1982), an eruption of VEI 4 or greater sends eruption products into the stratosphere, and is thus capable of creating a climatic effect. As Pyle summarises, about three eruptions of VEI 4 or greater scale occur on average each decade in the northern hemisphere.[1315] Significantly larger eruptions are much more rare. Over a 150 year period some five eruptions of VEI 5 or greater occur on average. On the basis of these numbers, Pyle argued that there should have been several (to many) other volcanic eruptions during the period of the Thera dating window which could have been responsible for the 17th century BC climate signal in the ice-core and tree-ring evidence. This is a fair conclusion taking the history of past volcanism as a whole. Another pattern of note is that the distribution of large eruptions across time is not always very even. Some centuries have much more volcanic activity than others, and indeed clusters of major volcanism exist, such as the period AD1815–1835. Other periods have a low level of volcanic activity. The 16th century BC is one such 'quiet' century. As noted above, it seems most unlikely that the massive eruption of Thera can be hiding here.

It is evident from the ice-core evidence (and especially the GISP2 data) that there were several large volcanic signals in the 17th century BC, consistent with the argument of Pyle from history that Thera should not be seen as some isolated event (see Table 13). Several other potential major northern hemisphere volcanic eruptions exist in about the same general time-frame (18th–17th centuries BC) in addition to Thera: Avellino in Italy, Aniakchak II in Alaska, the Mount St. Helens Yn tephra eruption in western USA, Avachinsky in Kamchatka, and the Nissyros volcano (Yiali) in the Aegean,[1316] and more may be found in the future. The question is therefore which of these several possible signals is most likely to have caused the one clear signal in the later 17th century BC found in both ice-core and tree-ring data? So far, the debate with regard to rivals to Thera's candidacy has not centered on rigorously establishing any of these other candidates as better claimants – merely the offering of a few

---

[1314] Simkin and Siebert (1994); Simkin (1994).

[1315] Pyle (1990b:169; 1998:Fig.2).

[1316] See e.g. Vogel *et al.* (1990); Begrét *et al.* (1992); Braitseva *et al.* (1993; 1997); Liritzis *et al.* (1996). Although there are many volcanoes in the Kuril-Kamchatka region, only the Avachinsky AV_1 eruption is potentially relevant on dating criteria (see Braitseva *et al.* 1995; Ponomareva *et al.* 1998). I have not seen the paper by Melekestsev and Miller (1997) – merely the reference. It apparently proposes that the c.1645BC volcanic acid signal in the Dye 3 ice-core in Greenland represents the eruption of Aniakchak. I assume this is on the basis of the potentially compatible dating of the eruption (something not in dispute), since the authors will not have been in a position to present new tephrachronological data from the ice-core. However, as discussed below, the compositional analyses of Zielinski and Germani (1998a) provide some grounds for ruling out Aniakchak as the source of the c.1623BC signal in the GISP2 ice-core (probably = 1636BC GRIP = 1644BC Dye 3), and a set of other factors indicate that a high northern latitude eruption (e.g. Aniakchak) is inherently unlikely to have been the cause of the later 17th century BC volcanic-climate signal at issue. I thank David Sewell for drawing this reference to my attention.

radiocarbon dates, and noting that they might, or could, match the 17th century BC date, as if this is sufficient. We need to explore the data in order to answer the question above on a rigorous basis.

The answer to the provenance question above is threefold. First, three of the eruptions (Avellino, Avachinsky, and Nissyros) may be dismissed on dating grounds as not compatible with a later 17th century BC date. The lack of precision in the dating of the Avellino eruption in the paper of Vogel *et al.* (1990) has already been discussed,[1317] and recent dendrochronological, radiocarbon, and archaeological analysis comprehensively demonstrates that this eruption occurred a little earlier than 1650BC, and in fact probably within the late 18th century BC to early 17th century BC.[1318] The Avellino eruption correlates quite closely with the transition between the EBA (Palma Campania facies) and the MBA (Protoapennine facies). The eruption buried advanced EBA sites like Palma Campania, whereas subsequent post-eruption site assemblages include early MBA Protoapennine pottery (e.g. at Ariano Irpino). Such material correlates well with the earliest level at Vivara island in the Bay of Naples. The subsequent level at Vivara saw true Protoappenine pottery, and the first imports of LHI material. It is thus evident that the preceding Avellino eruption occurred a little before the appearance of LHI ceramics in Italy, and in turn, broadly, a little (50–100 years) before the time frame of the eruption of Thera in later LHI in the Aegean. The AV_1 tephra layer and eruption of the Avachinsky volcano in Kamchatka is dated c.3512±18 ^{14}C years BP on the basis of ten radiocarbon determinations.[1319] This is some 150 ^{14}C years earlier than the radiocarbon evidence relevant to the eruption of Thera. The lower limit of the 2σ (95.4%) confidence calibrated calendar date range for the Avachinsky eruption is 1746BC or 1737BC.[1320] Even allowing for an off-set for long-lived sample matter, of up to 50 years or so, this evidence yields a calibrated age range significantly earlier than the later 17th century BC, and so is clearly earlier than the evidence from Thera. The proposed candidacy of the Nissyros volcano (Yiali)[1321] does not deserve serious consideration on current evidence. On the basis of just four extremely widely differing thermoluminescence (TL) dates with huge quoted measurement errors (apparently only 1σ, 68.2%, confidence even so) covering more than a thousand years (1018±400BC, 1014±430BC, 1714±714BC and 2088±750BC), Liritzis *et al.* propose that this volcano might be relevant to the Thera debate and the LMI period! This data is of such poor quality and consistency as to be useless. Their claim of the relevance of the 'mean' of this data set of 1460 BC is ridiculous (the differing weighted mean of 1260 BC is similarly irrelevant[1322]).

Second, to anticipate the discussion below in Chapter V.3, shards of volcanic glass have been recovered, and analysed, from the c.1623BC volcanic acidity signal in the

[1317] Manning (1992a; 1995:214–215).
[1318] Levi *et al.* (n.d.); Vanzetti (1998); Vanzetti, pers. comm.
[1319] Braitseva *et al.* (1997).
[1320] Stuiver *et al.* (1998); and Stuiver and Becker (1993) data respectively; employing Ramsey (1995).
[1321] Liritzis *et al.* (1996).
[1322] Liritzis *et al.* (1996:368–370).

GISP2 ice-core.[1323] The composition of these shards is quite different from, and completely incompatible with, products from the Avellino, Mount St. Helens, and Aniakchak eruptions.[1324] Thus, although on dating grounds Mount St. Helens or Aniakchak could well date to the 17th century BC,[1325] neither is responsible for the c.1623BC volcanic signal in the GISP2 core. Whether the Mount St. Helens eruption produced sufficient sulphur products to be relevant is also doubtful.[1326] Whereas, as will be discussed in detail in Chapter V.3 below, and contrary to the conclusions of Zielinski and Germani who employed inappropriate comparative analyses,[1327] the composition of the volcanic glass from the 1623 BC layer in the GISP2 core is potentially consistent with the volcanic glass produced by the eruption of Thera. Moreover, if the relevant radiocarbon dating evidence is examined in detail, the most likely dating for both the Aniakchak and Mount St. Helens eruptions is a little earlier than the radiocarbon date range for Thera (average radiocarbon ages respectively of 3435±40BP and 3420±50BP, versus c.3355±32BP for Thera). Even allowing for some off-set for long-lived sample matter,[1328] the calibrated calendar ranges favour a date range in the 18th–17th centuries BC, and slightly earlier on average than the radiocarbon evidence from Thera. The Aniakchak eruption could thus be proposed as a possible source for one of the other volcanic signals in the earlier 17th century BC.

Third, we can make some estimate of the likely latitude of the source eruption of the later 17th century BC volcanic signal/climate event. The pattern of occurrences of frost damage in the Bristlecone pine record from the western USA shows a stronger correlation with low to mid-latitude volcanic eruptions, versus high northern latitude volcanic eruptions. High northern latitude eruptions tend to have less, or indeed no clear, effect, and so representation as frost events. In support, as noted above, the study of Lough and Fritts (1987) showed that large lower-latitude eruptions were more likely to produce the cool conditions in the western USA likely to cause summer growing season frost damage. But, at the same time, we must include the ice-core evidence.[1329] The 1644BC Dye 3, 1636BC GRIP, and 1623BC GISP2 volcanic signals are large, but not enormous, and last as clear signals over nearly 2.5 years of deposition.

The raw signal is probably too large to be the result of an equatorial (or southern hemisphere) eruption on the basis of analogies.[1330] It is generally agreed that the eruption of Tambora in 1815 (VEI 7) was slightly larger than Thera, but, due to its equatorial location, the raw acid trace in Greenland is rather smaller than the 17th century BC signal at issue; similarly Krakatau in 1883 (VEI 6) left a relatively modest signal; and the very large Huaynaputina eruption of AD1600 in Peru is difficult to pick up as a

---

[1323] Zielinsky and Germani (1998a). Following here the view of Zielinski and Germani (1998a) that the 1623±36BC signal is the relevant one, and not the 1669±c.36BC one. Both were offered as possible Thera signals in the original publication: Zielinski *et al.* (1994a:Table 2).

[1324] Zielinski and Germani (1998a:284–285, Table 1, Fig. 3).

[1325] Vogel *et al.* (1990); Begét *et al.* (1992).

[1326] Vogel *et al.* (1990:536).

[1327] Zielinski and Germani (1998a; 1998b).

[1328] Vogel *et al.* (1990:535).

[1329] Zielinski *et al.* (1994a); Clausen *et al.* (1997); Hammer *et al.* (1987; 1980).

[1330] Clausen and Hammer (1988).

distinct major event in the Greenland ice.[1331] Alternatively, the 17th century BC acid signal is not likely to be a high-latitude northern eruption, because the signal is picked up as strongly (even more strongly) in southern Greenland (Dye 3 core) when compared to central Greenland (GRIP, GISP2). Several recent high-latitude northern eruptions, such as Novarupta (Katmai) in the Aleutian Islands in AD1912, left only minimal acid signals in the south Greenland Dye 3 core record versus clear signals in central and north Greenland cores,[1332] and it is clear that this is due to strong general poleward transport in the high-latitude stratosphere. The 1644BC, 1636BC, 1623BC signal is also not phenomenally large, and so is unlikely to be a local volcano close to Greenland, in contrast to the large acid spikes of AD1783, Laki, Iceland, AD1106, Hekla, Iceland, or c.AD934, Eldgjá, Iceland.[1333] And, in reverse, the clear mid-latitude climate signal in the proxy tree-ring records from the western USA, Ireland, and Europe[1334] differentiates the later 17th century BC signal from Icelandic (and other 'local' high latitude) eruptions, such as Eldgjá in c.AD934, which show up clearly in the ice-core data from Greenland, but left little clear trace in mid-latitude historical or proxy climate/temperature records.[1335] A final factor to consider in this regard is that Hammer *et al.* (1987:Fig.3 caption) specifically note that the acid peak for the later 17th century BC event (c.1644BC in the Dye 3 core) was primarily sulphuric acid, and that the Cl⁻ concentration was 'not enhanced during the event'. The HCl component of the eruption products is much more soluble than the sulphur dioxide component, and is thus thought not to travel as far from the eruption source.[1336] Significantly enhanced Cl⁻ concentrations in the ice-core data tend to correlate with relatively local, high northern latitude, eruptions.[1337] The lack of an enhanced Cl⁻ component thus further supports a more distant, low–mid latitude, eruption source for the later 17th century BC volcanic signal.

Thus the circumstantial and analogy-derived indications point strongly towards a low–mid latitude northern hemisphere volcanic eruption. This makes the Alaskan and Kamchatkan volcanoes unlikely sources of the combined volcanic–climatic signal/effect seen in the later 17th century BC. Avellino, Mount St. Helens, and Nissyros are already out of the running for one or two reasons each (see above). The eruption of Thera is the prime available and suitable candidate which meets the relevant criteria: a very large lower mid-latitude northern hemisphere volcanic eruption.

In conclusion, an examination of the current evidence quickly finds either that none of these other eruptions is convincingly dated to the later 17th century BC, and/or that none of these other eruptions is consistent with the chemical composition of the volcanic glass from the c.1623BC volcanic acid signal from the GISP2 ice-core, and/or that locational indications discount some of these other suggested eruptions. In contrast,

---

[1331] de Silva and Zielinski (1998:457); Clausen *et al.* (1997:26,716).

[1332] Clausen *et al.* (1997:26,715); Hammer *et al.* (1987:518).

[1333] Clausen *et al.* (1997:26,716, 26,721); Hammer (1984).

[1334] LaMarche and Hirschboeck (1984); Baillie and Munro (1988); Baillie (1990; 1995a).

[1335] Zielinski *et al.* (1995:136–139).

[1336] Tabazadeh and Turco (1993).

[1337] E.g Eldgjá in c.AD934: Zielinski *et al.* (1995); Clausen *et al.* (1997:26,721, pl.4.g); Novarupta (Katmai) in AD1912: Clausen *et al.* (1997:26,715, pl.4.a).

for reasons to be discussed in Chapter V.3 below, the c.1623BC ice-core volcanic signal *is* potentially consistent with the eruption of Thera, and the locational indications are likewise consistent with Thera as the source of the main later 17th century BC volcanic–climatic signal (the 1669BC signal in the GISP2 ice-core also requires investigation, however). As discussed below in Chapter V.3, this c.1623BC signal in the GISP2 ice-core appears possibly to equate with the c.1636BC signal in the GRIP ice-core, and the c.1644BC signal in the Dye 3 ice-core, and, all three of these quite probably equate with the 1628BC tree-ring event. The eruption of Thera is (and remains) by far the best dated candidate for the target date range. In addition, Thera was an exceptionally large eruption, matching the nature of the ice-core signal and the 1628BC climate event.[1338] (Note: the Dye 3 ice-core is considered the best dated ice-core back to 6000BC, and the c.'1636BC' date from the GRIP ice-core is regarded as really c.1644BC – and this really as a 1646/1645BC volcanic eruption: Claus Hammer, pers. comm. – Hammer n.d. has further argued that the c.1623BC GISP2 signal is not Thera, and does not equate with c.1636/1644BC in GRIP/Dye 3, but this further issue is not yet resolved – and this author considers it still possible/plausible that some or all of these ice-core signals equate with the 1628BC tree-ring event.)

On present estimates, Thera was an extraordinary, 1 in 300 years, estimated Volcanic Explosivity Index 6.9, volcanic event.[1339] Moreover, as more and more Theran tephra is found in the Black Sea, Anatolia, and the east Mediterranean, the scale of the eruption just gets bigger. It has to be the best working hypothesis candidate on current data for the major mid to late 17th century BC volcanic–climate signal. It is of course also possible that another large volcanic eruption happened around the same time (and there are several candidates as noted, apart from other unknowns). Indeed, it has been argued that the climate anomaly attested in Ireland – one to two decades of affected tree-ring growth in environmentally sensitive locations – following 1628BC is far too long-term to be the result of one single eruption, since the effects of observed recent eruptions have been both relatively minor, and of a shorter, 1–3 years, periodicity.[1340] This might lead to speculation of a multiple eruption scenario, or significant climate forcing during a century of heightened volcanic activity.

However, such speculation is perhaps premature for two reasons. First, the situation of a prolonged post-1628BC effect is especially notable only in wood from bogs in the north of Ireland. This is an unusual and environmentally sensitive location. The normal growing season is relatively short, and even a slight lowering of temperature and increased rainfall is a major threat/stress factor for trees in the area. The effect could thus be longer and more severe here than in many places. In addition, the input of volcanic volatiles, and especially acids, may have had an especially significant effect in such a location.[1341] The bog environment is inherently somewhat acidic, and so

---

[1338]In general, see the papers in Hardy *et al.* (1990b) – noting the major revision to the petrologic analyses as discussed above.

[1339] Decker (1990:451).

[1340]As noted in discussions above. In general, see Kelly and Sear (1984); Bradley (1988); Mass and Portman (1989; 1990); cf. Dutton (1990).

[1341] Grattan and Charman (1994); Grattan and Gilbertson (1994).

marginal for tree growth/survival, and further changes in the bog pH (measure of acidity/alkalinity) may have been critical.[1342]

Second, it must be remembered that the observations of 1–3 years only of significant effects are all based on modern eruptions. There have been no recent eruptions of the scale of Thera at mid-latitude, thus we really do not have comparable modern data. And, even more importantly, an obvious counter argument to the critique of Pyle,[1343] and others, in this regard is to point out that modern, post-Industrial Revolution, data are quite possibly seriously misleading with reference to pre-modern circumstances. The recent study of Bluth *et al.* (1993) reveals in the modern world that 'the total volcanic contribution of SO_2 to the Earth's atmosphere totals only approximately 5–10% of the annual anthropogenic flux' (p.329). This implies a relatively small role for volcanic eruptions in *modern* climate change. For, even though most sulphur compounds emitted into the atmosphere do not reach the stratosphere, and so have a very short residence time and are of little net effect by themselves, the continuous high modern anthropogenic flux in the atmosphere forms part of the now vast modern anthropogenic 'greenhouse' warming effect which strongly counteracts, even swamps, any injection of long-term (1–2+ years) cooling sulphates into the stratosphere by volcanoes. A large volcanic eruption like Mt. Pinatubo only just exceeded the opposite greenhouse-gas forcing pattern, and so made AD1992 one of the coolest years of the last 30.[1344]

But this situation will not have existed before the Industrial Revolution, because the modern enormous levels of anthropogenic emissions of both SO_2 and other greenhouse gases have occurred (and increased exponentially) only since then.[1345] Even so, and despite the modern opposite (warming) effects of 'greenhouse' gases, a few recent SO_2-rich volcanic eruptions have, as noted, had an observed impact on global climate for 1–3 years (e.g. El Chichón, Mt. Pinatubo). In pre-modern times there will have been a dramatically reduced anthropogenic input of all types. Among the regular natural sources of SO_2 emissions, major irregular explosive volcanic eruptions would then stand out as key contributors of dramatic short-term increases in the stratospheric/atmospheric flux. In a relatively 'clean' pre-modern atmosphere, with no counteracting greenhouse-gas forcing, such significant sudden inputs would have produced marked effects.[1346] Major prehistoric volcanic eruptions may be hypothesised to have had a greater climatic impact than any recent volcano.

[1342] Baillie (1989) proposed that a short, volcanically-forced, period of cooler temperatures and increased precipitation could have triggered raised water tables in the bog environment of the north of Ireland, and so long-term water-logging from which the system took some time to recover. Grattan and Charman (1994:104) criticise this suggestion, but the work of Caseldine *et al.* (1998) finds that in some cases this is not an impossible occurrence (pp.109, and 110). The study of Dwyer and Mitchell (1997) could also not be conclusive, but tephra impact did correlate with wetter conditions. They stress the need to consider the individual sensitivity of any specific environment to change.

[1343] Pyle (1989; 1990b).

[1344] McCormick *et al.* (1995:Fig.3).

[1345] Bluth *et al.* (1993); Charlson *et al.* (1992); on the increases in CO_2 and other greenhouse gases: e.g. Oeschger and Siegenthaler (1988); Watson *et al.* (1990); Lorius *et al.* (1992:231–232).

[1346] Cf. Hobbs (1993).

And so, we may conclude that Thera is the best candidate to be responsible for the later 17th century BC volcanic and climate events. Even if the later 17th century BC was a time when two or more major eruptions coincided within a very short time to cause a significant, relatively long-term, climate anomaly, then the list of best dated candidates for membership of the package begins with Thera.

3. The identification of volcanic glass in the GISP2 ice-core. Potential confirmation of a 17th century BC date for the Thera eruption?

We have noted how large volcanic eruptions send a sulphur aerosol into the stratosphere, and how, as this settles into the troposphere, snowfall/precipitation deposits traces of this on the polar ice. However, it is also possible for some of the tiny pieces of volcanic glass (tephra) produced by an eruption to be transported to the polar regions and to be deposited on the ice along with the sulphur aerosol component. In principle, recovery and analysis of these volcanic glass shards is the only way to establish the provenance of a volcanic acid signal with good confidence.[1347] Clearly, therefore, the best route to resolving the entire Thera-dating debate would seem to be to establish whether or not any of the 17–16th century BC volcanic acidity signals in the ice-cores are, or are not, compatible with Thera. This has been noted as the necessary and potentially definitive route to the resolution of the Thera dating debate by several scholars;[1348] the problem is the difficulty, time, and expense involved in obtaining, and then carrying out, the necessary detailed analysis of deep polar ice-cores. And even with the best will in the world, volcanic glass shards are not always found. Further, as evident from debates in the literature, rigorous establishment of provenance is not straightforward.[1349]

It was thus something of a sensation when Zielinski and Germani (1998a) announced the discovery of four tiny tephra shards in the c.1623±36BC layer of the GISP2 ice-core associated with the major c.1623BC volcanic acidity signal. Each shard has a long axis of only 2–4 thousandths of a millimetre. Were these compatible with Thera? Zielinski and Germani (1998a) said no. They argued that the shards did not match the composition of those from the Minoan eruption of Thera (Santorini), and that this therefore 'severely challenges the 1620s BC age for the Santorini eruption' (p.281). On the *assumption* that the c.1623BC layer in the GISP2 ice-core correlates with the 1628BC tree-ring event (suggested by Zielinski and Germani – but with no real supporting case[1350]), and that it also probably correlates with the 1644/1636BC volcanic signals in the Dye 3 and GRIP ice-cores (although Clausen *et al.* specifically comment on the lack of satisfactory correlation between the GISP2 and GRIP/Dye 3 ice-cores in the second millennium BC[1351]), then, if it were correct that the volcanic glass in the c.1623BC layer is not even potentially compatible with Theran eruption

---

[1347] E.g. Palais *et al.* (1990); Zielinski *et al.* (1995; 1997).

[1348] E.g. Schoch (1997:61); Kuniholm *et al.* (1996:782); Manning (1995:203); etc.

[1349] See the discussions of Hunt and Hill (1993; 1994); Bennett (1994).

[1350] Zielinski and Germani (1998b:1045) state that 'we believe that the large SO_4^{2-} peak ... in the GISP2 core at 1623BC is correlative to signals in other proxy records that suggest a volcanic eruption around 1627/1628BC'.

[1351] Clausen *et al.* (1997:26,713–26,714).

products, this would be a serious blow to the early chronology.[1352] Although some have argued that the dating of the GISP2 core is problematic enough that the 1669BC volcanic signal could in fact be Thera, and really dated 1628BC in absolute terms,[1353] and, of course, there are other smaller later 17th century BC and early 16th century BC volcanic signals which could become relevant, and, all up, Zielinski and Germani merely claim to rule out one of the 73 candidate years in the GISP2 core given the stated dating error, leaving 72 other possible years, it is undeniable that the 'strong' Thera case would like the c.1623±36BC signal in the GISP2 ice-core to be Thera.

It is therefore of great importance that the conclusion of Zielinski and Germani is demonstrably incorrect.[1354] The composition data they present for the GISP2 volcanic glass shards *cannot*, within the quoted measurement errors (totally ignored by Zielinski and Germani), legitimately be distinguished from data on Theran Minoan eruption volcanic glass. Let me explain the details.

CHARACTERISATION OF THE c.1623BC GISP2 GLASS SHARDS,
AND WHY THERA CANNOT BE RULED OUT AS THE SOURCE

Zielinski and Germani seek to characterise, and to discriminate, the GISP2 volcanic glass shards from Thera eruption glass products on the basis of three comparisons: (i) a ternary plot of Fe_2O_3 (total) versus K_2O versus CaO, (ii) a plot of SiO_2 versus Na_2O, and (iii) a plot of SiO_2 versus TiO_2.[1355] Two points should be noted. First, standard practice for establishing the provenance of Theran volcanic glass involves not a Fe_2O_3 (total) versus K_2O versus CaO ternary plot, but an FeO (total iron) versus K_2O versus CaO+MgO ternary plot.[1356] Why the change? For one very good reason: if the GISP2

[1352] For example, Warren (1998:328 Addendum) has quickly drawn attention to the news and cites it as supporting the low or conventional chronology. He concludes that 'thus liberated from any attachment to 1628BC we are now free to return to the case for the (long argued) late 16th century date for the late LMIA eruption'.

[1353] Baillie (1996a).

[1354] I wrote an initial response to the paper of Zielinski and Germani (1998a): Manning (1998b). I admit that this was a less than successful critique because it did not deal comprehensively with all aspects of the data and analyses of Zielinski and Germani. As a result, Zielinski and Germani (1998b) were able in their reply to seem to dismiss or avoid my criticisms, to create a red-herring by criticising my graph (a fault I accept), and to go off on a tangent about zoned magma chambers, and all without the basic issue of the overlap of the respective data *within measurement errors* being addressed. I attempt to make a more useful and comprehensive critique in the present text. Hammer (n.d.) has also argued against the conclusion of Zielinski and Germani (1998a). Hammer argues that Zielinski and Germani analysed the wrong signal due to a combination of bad luck and a section of missing core. Hammer believes that the 1644BC Dye 3=1636BC GRIP volcanic signal remains the best candidate for Thera. Hammer may be right; but for the present in the text below I consider it possible that the c.1623BC GISP2 volcanic signal may be re-considered as potentially Theran, and, in turn, potentially coeval with the 1644/1636BC Dye 3/GRIP volcanic signals.

[1355] Zielinski and Germani (1998a:Fig.2; 1998b:Fig.1).

[1356] See with reference to identifying Thera glass e.g. Watkins *et al.* (1978:Fig.2); Federman and Carey (1980:166, 170, Fig.5); Sullivan (1988:Fig.3); Guichard *et al.* (1993:Fig.2). Federman and Carey (1980:170) conclude that 'a ternary plot of Fe, Mg + Ca, and K for tephra glasses can be used to distinguish between the widespread layers and correlate them to their terrestrial sources'.

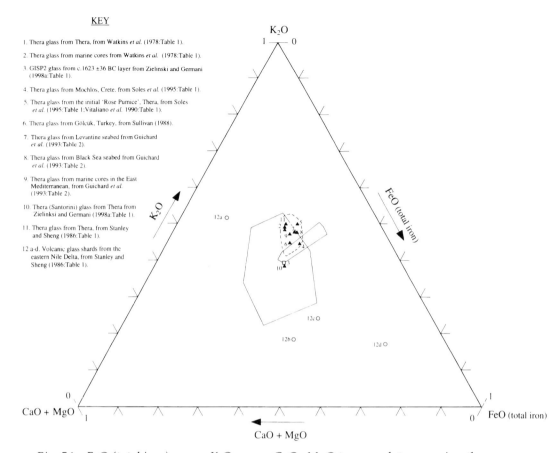

KEY

1. Thera glass from Thera, from Watkins *et al.* (1978:Table 1).

2. Thera glass from marine cores from Watkins *et al.* (1978:Table 1).

3. GISP2 glass from c.1623 ±36 BC layer from Zielinski and Germani (1998a:Table 1).

4. Thera glass from Mochlos, Crete, from Soles *et al.* (1995:Table 1).

5. Thera glass from the initial 'Rose Pumice', Thera, from Soles *et al.* (1995:Table 1;Vitaliano *et al.* 1990:Table 1).

6. Thera glass from Gölcük, Turkey, from Sullivan (1988).

7. Thera glass from Levantine seabed from Guichard *et al.* (1993:Table 2).

8. Thera glass from Black Sea seabed from Guichard *et al.* (1993:Table 2).

9. Thera glass from marine cores in the East Mediterranean, from Guichard *et al.* (1993:Table 2).

10. Thera (Santorini) glass from Thera from Zielinksi and Germani (1998a:Table 1).

11. Thera glass from Thera, from Stanley and Sheng (1986:Table 1).

12 a-d. Volcanic glass shards from the eastern Nile Delta, from Stanley and Sheng (1986:Table 1).

Fig. 54a. FeO (total iron) versus K_2O versus CaO+MgO ternary plot comparing the average value for the composition of the GISP2 volcanic glass with a range of published analyses of Theran volcanic glass. The approximate 2σ measurement error zones for both the average value of the GISP2 glass, and the Theran glass from Mochlos on Crete, are indicated (the latter measurement errors are considered as ±2% of stated figure after Vitaliano et al. 1990:58=1σ – it is not entirely clear how to apply the stated 0.05% precision error cited in Soles et al. 1995). The error region for the GISP2 glass is very large as there are very few constituent data (four shards).

and Santorini (Thera) major oxide composition data presented by Zielinski and Germani (1998a:Table 1) were plotted on an Fe_2O_3 (total) versus K_2O versus CaO+MgO ternary diagram, then they virtually lie on top of each other and are indistinguishable (see Figures 54.a and 54.b)! Moreover, *even if* one considers the selective Fe_2O_3 (total) versus K_2O versus CaO ternary plot of Zielinksi and Germani, the GISP2 and Thera data points are not that far apart at all (and certainly overlap within errors, see next point) and in fact about half the Thera data points are very near to being compatible

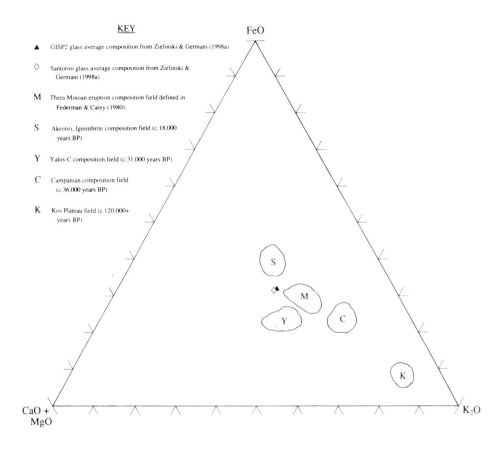

Fig. 54b. FeO (total iron) versus K₂O versus CaO+MgO ternary plot after Federman and Carey (1980:Fig.5) showing their defined Thera Minoan eruption field versus the Zielinski and Germani (1998a:Table 1) data for both Santorini (Thera Minoan eruption) and GISP2 1623 BC shards. The Zielinski and Germani GISP2 and Santorini data virtually plot on top of each other, and neither datum plots within the Minoan field as defined by Federman and Carey – although they are relatively close (and by definition the measurements on Theran glass in Zielinski and Germani 1998a should be within the Thera field). Hence Zielinski and Germani data offset versus true values? If measurement errors were indicated on either or both the Zielinski and Germani measurements, or the Minoan field data, then the Zielinski and Germani data and the Minoan field of Federman and Carey would overlap.

with the GISP2 field: this is particularly evident in Zielinski and Germani (1998a:Fig. 2 ternary plot). Second, individual microprobe measurements have measurement errors, and, among individual measurements of the major oxide compositions of volcanic glass and pumice, data differ for each sample from a suite of samples from the same eruption context (within a range – variously tight to loose depending on the volcano); there can also be further variation among the specific eruption products and stages of any particular eruption.[1357] In the presence of water (or ice), selective leaching of the glass is also a potential complication, altering the original geochemical fingerprint. Thus any single measurement, and any set average datum, has a stated error, and a particular set of eruption products offers a field of data (rather than a single precise point). Only with a significant number of datum points can relative homogeneity or heterogeneity be quantified, assuming careful analytical methodology and controls of the sort detailed by Westgate *et al.* (1998:108–109). Zielinski and Germani (1998a:Table 1) cite the 1 standard deviation (1σ, 68.2%, confidence) errors for their average data. These errors are not insignificant![1358] But they are not subsequently mentioned, nor allowed for, by Zielinski and Germani in their ternary plot of Fe_2O_3 (total) versus K_2O versus CaO, nor in their plot of SiO_2 versus Na_2O, nor in their plot of SiO_2 versus TiO_2. If these cited errors were allowed for, and especially a more appropriate 2σ (95.4% confidence) error margin, then it is manifestly apparent that the GISP2 data significantly overlap with published analyses of Minoan eruption Thera glass, and vice versa, in each of the three comparisons employed by Zielinski and Germani: see Figures 54.a and 55.

This overlap of composition ranges does not, of course, mean that the GISP2 shards necessarily come from Thera; but it does mean that they cannot rigorously be distinguished from Theran eruption products on the basis of the comparsion of major oxide data. The broad compositional similarity of a number of eruptions is a well known fact. In such cases, only detailed analysis and comparison of trace and rare earth elements can provide a rigorous discrimination and provenance analysis.[1359]

So, let us re-appraise the data and arguments of Zielinski and Germani with regard to the GISP2 c.1623BC volcanic shards. Their argument is that microprobe analyses of the c.1623BC GISP2 volcanic glass shards are significantly different from analyses of volcanic glass samples from the Minoan eruption deposits on Thera itself, and that they must therefore derive from another, different, volcanic eruption. Thus let us run through all the various comparisons drawn by Zielinski and Germani to see whether they stand up.

[1357] For examples of variation within sets of measurements on Theran Minoan eruption (Bo) samples, see Vitaliano *et al.* (1990:Figs.4, 5, 6, 19 upper). The detailed data on the compositions of matrix glass from the 1991 Pinatubo eruption nicely demonstrate limited but significant variation (within a tight overall range, or field): e.g. Pallister *et al.* (1996:710–713, esp. Fig.15B); Luhr and Melson (1996:741–743, esp. Fig.2). Similarly, a high-quality recent study on the characterisation of the great c.75,000 years ago Toba eruption products found a discrete, but reasonably large, field (Westgate *et al.* 1998:Fig.2).

[1358] Hunt and Hill (1993:276) note in general of such tephra geochemical diagrams that 'in these diagrams error bars or fields ... are particularly useful but seldom used...'.

[1359] Zielinski and Germani (1998b:Fig.2) nicely demonstrates this. They (fairly) seek to criticise this author's earlier graph (Manning 1998a:Fig.1), and so plot several other eruptions to show how they all look broadly the same. But, in so doing, they merely highlight the fact that comparison of major oxide data is a less than successful method of discriminating among similar eruption products. A detailed and rigorous discrimination and provenance analysis must instead use rare earth and trace elements: see, with reference to Thera, Eastwood *et al.* (1998; 1999); Vitaliano *et al.* (1990:61–70).

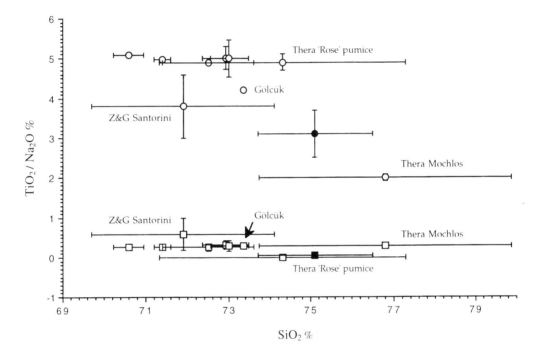

Fig. 55. *Na$_2$O versus SiO$_2$ and TiO$_2$ versus SiO$_2$ covariation plots for the GISP2 glass sherds (solid circle and solid square) and a range of published analyses of Thera Minoan eruption volcanic glass with the 2σ measurement errors (where known) indicated. The Thera glass data come from: (a) Watkins et al. (1978:Table 1 tephra on land), (b) Watkins et al. (1978:Table 1 tephra in cores), (c) Zielinski and Germani (1998a:Table 1 Santorini), (d) Soles et al. (1995:Table 1 Mochlos and Thera 'Rose' pumice – 1σ measurement errors considered as ±2% of stated figure after Vitaliano et al. 1990:58), (e) Sullivan (1988:Table 1; 1990:Table 1) – Gölcük tephra, no measurement errors provided, (f) Guichard et al. (1993:Table 2 TRI172-22, GGC-79, and Minoan = east Mediterranean samples). Note, the 2σ errors cited by Guichard et al. for the 'Minoan' samples are the same as the 1σ errors cited for the identical sample series in Federman and Carey (1980:Table 2); thus it seems likely that Guichard et al. may be in error – hence the '2σ' errors I have employed after Guichard et al. may be considered as minima. The GISP2 glass data come from Zielinski and Germani (1998a:Table 1).*

1. Zielinski and Germani state that 'the Santorini glass is less rhyolitic with a higher alkali composition (i.e., 72% SiO_2 and 7.5% Na_2O+K_2O) than the highly rhyolitic, moderately alkaline GISP2 glass (i.e. 75% SiO_2 and 5.1% Na_2O+K_2O)'.[1360] But, in fact, some of the glass produced by the eruption of Thera was indeed highly rhyolitic (e.g. 74.3% up to 76.8% SiO_2) and so potentially compatible with the GISP2 shards.[1361] The Na_2O data are only very slightly different between the GISP2 and Santorini shards reported by Zielinski and Germani: 3.1±0.3% versus 3.8±0.4%.[1362] Even at these quoted 1σ measurment errors, the data overlap, and they certainly overlap at 2σ, 95.4%, confidence. The only tangible difference is in fact the values of K_2O reported by Zielinski and Germani. Here the average of the just four measurements of K_2O for the GISP2 shards is admittedly lower than the data for Santorini glass (2.0±0.3% versus 3.7±0.2%).[1363] However, there is quite a degree of variation in K_2O content through the time period of the Minoan eruption of Thera. The initial Plinian glass found at Mochlos has relatively low K_2O content (3%), whereas the initial Plinian 'Rose' pumice from Thera has a higher value (3.4%), and the later pumice is lower again. There is in fact evidence 'for inversion of a zoned magma chamber during the eruption. This is best displayed by the positive correlation of MgO and inverse correlation of K_2O with stratigraphic height … so that the most fractionated material, with lowest MgO and highest K_2O, came out first'.[1364] Some of the initial phase, or later cataclysmic phase, Thera products would in fact overlap with the GISP2 data within 2σ measurement errors. Overall, other data show that the alkalic composition of Thera glass varied significantly from moderate (e.g. 5% Na_2O+K_2O)[1365] to higher (e.g. 8.3% Na_2O+K_2O).[1366] The former (a sample from Mochlos on Crete) is potentially compatible with the GISP2 shards.

2. As already noted, Zielinski and Germani compare the composition of the volcanic glass found in the c.1623BC layer of the GISP2 core with the composition of glass from Santorini using an Fe_2O_3 (total) versus K_2O versus CaO ternary plot.[1367] Their diagram is rather less than satisfactory. Not only are measurement errors ignored, but in Zielinski and Germani (both 1998a:Fig.2 and 1998b:Fig.1) the labels do not relate to the associated axes of the ternary plot. The more normal comparison is an FeO (total iron) versus K_2O versus CaO+MgO ternary plot. I show the GISP2 data published by Zielinski and Germani versus a range of published analyses of Thera glass on an FeO (total iron) versus K_2O versus CaO+MgO ternary plot in Figure 54.a. The GISP2 datum is admittedly a little below (in this figure) most of the Thera data points,

---

[1360] Zielinski and Germani (1998a:283).

[1361] Soles *et al.* (1995:Table 1 samples 3 and 4); Vitaliano *et al.* (1990:76 sample E).

[1362] Zielinski and Germani (1998a:Table 1).

[1363] Zielinski and Germani (1998a:Table 1).

[1364] Vitaliano *et al.* (1990:72). See also especially their Fig.19 top left. For data, see Table 5.

[1365] Soles *et al.* (1995:Table 1 sample 3).

[1366] Soles *et al.* (1995:Table 1 sample 4).

[1367] On ternary plots, see West (1981). I thank John Chiment, Peter Ian Kuniholm, and Mary Jaye Bruce for sending me literature on ternary plots and their employment.

but it virtually overlaps with Zielinski and Germani's own average datum for Thera glass – since these two sets of data were obtained on the same microprobe they should be comparable, and so this basic similarity is significant. And, more particularly, if the measurement errors on all the analyses are taken into account, then the data cannot be discriminated. I show the approximate 2σ error zone of the GISP2 average datum. This overlaps with several of the Thera data (and if the errors on the Thera data were all shown, then this overlap would be even more apparent). In reverse, I also show the approximate 2σ error zone for the Thera glass from Mochlos. This just about includes the GISP2 average datum, and certainly significantly overlaps with the GISP2 error zone. While I accept that the GISP2 data presented by Zielinksi and Germani tend to be very slightly different,[1368] they are not distinguishable within measurement errors. There tends to be a reasonable range of values (around a norm) among any set of microprobe analyses of volcanic glass from any one eruption, and even more so among different sets of analyses on the same samples. The GISP2 data and the Thera data are potentially compatible within such normal variation.[1369] Calculation of a relatively small confidence region on a ternary plot requires both many more datum points than the four available for the GISP2 glass, *and* the assumption of sample homogeneity (not established from just four samples).[1370]

We can also consider another complementary approach. Federman and Carey (1980:Fig.5) defined a Thera Minoan eruption field on an FeO (total iron) versus K_2O versus CaO+MgO ternary plot on the basis of a large set of measurements.[1371] We can then add to this plot the Zielinski and Germani data for their average Santorini glass composition and average GISP2 glass composition: see both Figure 54.a and Figure 54.b.[1372] What we find is that the Zielinski and Germani data for

---

[1368] See also Zielinski and Germani (1998a:Fig.2 top), where the basic similarities of the two sets of data are evident. And note in particular the apparent pattern in the Thera data. They almost divide into two groups: about half the values seem to lie to the below left of the average value, and about half to the upper right. The latter are very close to the GISP2 mean value, and some visibly overlap with GISP2 datapoints. Why are the Thera values reported by Zielinski and Germani so disparate in this diagram?
[1369] For another example of such minor variations, see the study of Bichler *et al.* (1997:Fig.4) considering rare earth elements in Theran Minoan eruption pumice samples. The range of Thera Bo pumice data, and further the error ranges, are significant, and the elemental data for the two Theran pumice samples from Tell el-Dabᶜa vary inside, and from just, to a little, *outside* the Thera range established from samples from Thera itself. Perfect matches cannot be expected. Only samples consistently well away from the Theran range can be satisfactorily distinguished (e.g. the Tell el-Dabᶜa3 sample).
[1370] Watson and Nguyen (1985). On the assumption of sample homogeneity, as numbers of samples increase, the 95% or 99% confidence space should decrease. Failure to do so would be a good indication of heterogeneity in sample compositions. It should be noted that an assumption of sample homogeneity in geochemical data may not always be appropriate, as recent detailed work on lead isotope fields has revealed (Baxter 1999). Apparent low dispersion of composition data on a ternary plot can never prove sample homogeneity – it is merely not inconsistent with the assumption.
[1371] See also Watkins *et al.* (1978:Fig.2).
[1372] Note: the ternary plots in Figures 54.a and 54.b are shown at differing orientations. The spatial relationships are the same whichever orientation is employed.

both Santorini and GISP2 virtually overlap, *and* that neither datum actually plots within the Minoan field defined by Federman and Carey (although relatively close, and certainly within measurement errors)! But, by definition, the analyses of Theran glass reported by Zielinski and Germani should do so. The reason is most likely not significantly differing glass compositions – indeed the relative homogeneity of the Thera Minoan eruption glass within measurement errors is widely noted[1373] – rather differing microprobe conditions for the different analyses.[1374] Thus the apparent *slight* difference between the Zielinski and Germani composition data for the GISP2 shards and the usual range of values for Thera Minoan eruption glass may be a minor difference among laboratories, microprobes, analytical circumstances, controls, or techniques, rather than any significant difference between the actual volcanic glass compositions. If the Zielinski and Germani Thera data were calibrated to the Theran field of Federman and Carey, then it would be very likely that the GISP2 shards would also overlap with the Theran field.

3. Zielinski and Germani present Na_2O versus SiO_2 and TiO_2 versus SiO_2 covariation plots. They argue that the GISP2 samples may be distinguished from the Thera samples. This at best applies only if no allowance is made for the quoted measurement errors (and, even on the most recent plot by Zielinski and Germani themselves, the distinction is less than apparent).[1375] I show Na_2O versus SiO_2 and TiO_2 versus SiO_2 covariation plots for the GISP2 sherds and a range of published analyses of Thera glass with the 2σ measurement errors (where known) indicated in Figure 55. The TiO_2 versus SiO_2 covariation plot reveals the GISP2 datum happily overlapping with two Thera data (the Mochlos and Rose Pumice analyses),[1376] and, generally, looking part of the Thera set (even if to one edge of the overall set range). Perhaps most importantly, within 2σ measurement errors, the Santorini glass data of Zielinski and Germani just about overlaps with their GISP2 data, and, if the measurement errors were known, the Thera Gölcük glass data would also have to overlap comfortably. The Na_2O versus SiO_2 plot is similar. The GISP2 datum is not an outlier within the overall range offered by the analyses on Thera glass; yes, it is to the bottom right edge of the overall set, but it comfortably overlaps with the Zielinski and Germani Santorini data within measurement errors, is not far away from the Thera Mochlos data, and would probably overlap with the Thera Gölcük glass data if the measurement errors were known.

[1373] Federman and Carey (1980:162) note the 'marked compositional homogeneity of the glass'; Vitaliano *et al.* (1990:72, 76) make the same observation. Zielinski and Germani (1998a; 1998b) also highlight this observation. See now also Eastwood *et al.* (1999:Tables 1–5).

[1374] Inter-laboratory/inter-microprobe/inter-microprobe runs variability is a major issue. With reference to an inter-comparison in progress when they wrote, Hunt and Hill (1993:275) note that 'whilst some results are still awaited, the initial findings are not encouraging, and may have wider geological implications'. Sodium migration is suggested to be a major likely problem. It must also be remembered that the relationships shown in linear space on a ternary plot, where three dimensions have been reduced to two via normalisation, distort the true radial differences within the data (Philip and Watson 1989).

[1375] Zieinski and Germani (1998b:Fig.1 lower).

[1376] Compare Zielinski and Germani (1998b:Fig.1 lower).

One may therefore conclude that the composition of the GISP2 glass shards is not clearly distinct from the range of Thera glass, and, indeed, could potentially be regarded as compatible. In this regard, it is important also to remember that there were only four GISP2 glass shards, and that the resultant analytical data clearly vary quite a bit.[1377] Thus the available information is well short of what might be termed a representative dataset, and a closely defined field of values. A Thera match cannot at present be excluded. For a final comparison, we can consider the overall major oxide profile of the GISP2 shards versus several published analyses of shards of Theran glass, first without, and then with, indication of error measurements: Figure 56.[1378] In all categories, except for MgO and K_2O, the GISP2 average value lies within the range of values for the Thera glass, and, when measurement errors are considered, the MgO overlaps with other Theran data, and the K_2O is only just short of overlapping with the Thera value range. When comparing the volcanic tephra from Mochlos with the Thera 'Rose Pumice', Soles *et al.* (1995:387) wrote: 'the composition of the major elements … are closely equivalent. The elements Si and Mg, which are the most critical indices of differentiation, are within 2%'. One could make exactly the same observation comparing the analyses of the GISP2 shards with the range of published data for Thera glass.

In general, one of the more suitable potential comparisons for the GISP2 glass samples is the Theran glass from Mochlos on Crete; this was a key point made by the present author in a brief response to the initial paper of Zielinski and Germani.[1379] This Mochlos glass offered some evidence contrary to the claims of Zielinski and Germani (1998a) that there was no Theran glass potentially compatible with the GISP2 glass. It further provided important evidence contrary to the statements of Zielinski and Germani that 'past studies on the composition of Santorini glass both from areas close to the source and in more distal marine cores all indicate that glass composition remained constant throughout the Minoan eruption' … and that 'the differences in the GISP2 glass and the Santorini glass … cannot be explained by fractionation of the Santorini glass with long-distance transport or by changes in the magma composition during the eruption'.[1380] Instead, these samples, and also the initial Plinian 'Rose' Pumice from Thera,[1381] showed that there is in fact variation in Thera products from particularly evolved glass as found at Mochlos to the evolved glass of the initial Plinian 'Rose' Pumice on Thera to more basic glass from other (later in the eruption sequence) deposits on Thera to the even more basic bulk tephra samples;[1382] and that, as Soles *et*

[1377] See the hollow squares in Zielinski and Germani (1998a:Fig.2).

[1378] To avoid the criticism of Zielinski and German (1998b:1,044) concerning a graph I used in Manning (1998b:Fig.1), where they (fairly) argued that 'by plotting all the oxides on the same scale and given the 70–75% SiO_2 content, one cannot reliably and consistently detect the 1–2% difference that can occur in many oxides and particularly those of TiO_2, MgO, CaO, Na_2O, and K_2O', I have employed a log scale. This stresses variation at the bottom of the scale, and largely compresses the SiO_2 peak.

[1379] Manning (1998b); the Mochlos samples are reported and discussed in Soles *et al.* (1995:387–390, Table 1). Zielinski and Germani were apparently not aware of this publication when they wrote their first paper (1998a).

[1380] Zielinski and Germani (1998a:283–284).

[1381] Vitaliano *et al.* (1990:Fig.3, Table 2).

[1382] Vitaliano *et al.* (1990:Table 2 Base Surge and Upper Unit, Table 5).

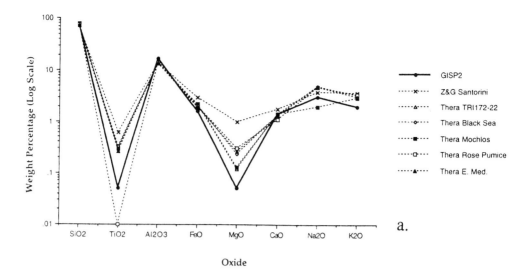

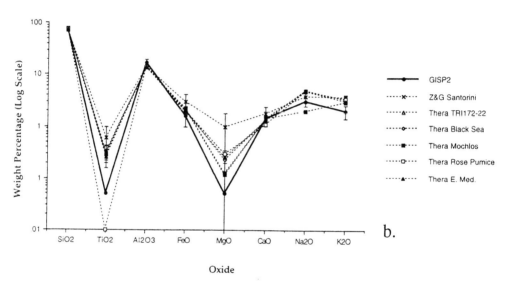

Fig. 56. Comparison of the major oxide composition of the GISP2 volcanic glass from the c.1623±36BC layer and several published analyses of Theran Minoan eruption volcanic glass. a. without indication of measurement errors, b. indicating measurement errors at 2σ confidence where known. The Thera glass data come from: Zielinski and Germani (1998a:Table 1 Santorini), Soles et al. (1995:Table 1 Mochlos and Thera 'Rose' pumice – 1σ measurement errors considered as ±2% of stated figure after Vitaliano et al. 1990:58), Guichard et al. (1993:Table 2 TRI172-22, GGC-79, and Minoan = east Mediterranean samples). Note, the 2σ errors cited by Guichard et al. for the 'Minoan' samples are the same as the 1σ errors cited for the identical sample series in Federman and Carey (1980:Table 2); thus it seems likely that Guichard et al. may be in error – hence the '2σ' errors I have employed after Guichard et al. may be considered as minima. The GISP2 glass data come from Zielinski and Germani (1998a:Table 1). Data described as <0.1 has been treated as 0.05.

al. (1995:390) go on to argue, the Theran evidence does show slightly different degrees of evolution in the glasses, and that the particularly evolved glass (as found at Mochlos) was probably from high in the magma chamber, and so the first to be erupted (in the initial Plinian phase).

In their reply to Manning (1998b), Zielinski and Germani (1998b:1,044–1,045) spend some time disputing the relevance of the Mochlos glass. They note the evidence for a zoned magma chamber, with more evolved glass in the higher portions of the chamber, but they go on to argue that the initial Plinian eruption phase is not as likely as the later, larger, ignimbrite-forming eruption phase to have sent volcanic products as far as Greenland. However, although there is no reason why the later phase of the eruption, when the main co-ignimbrite cloud forms, could not have produced tephra which was transported far away, as Zielinski and Germani argue, it remains the case that the Plinian phase produces the highest cloud of eruption products. Height is quite possibly critical; it is the exteme heights achieved by the Plinian phase that injects material well into the stratosphere, and there is every reason to suspect that these might be among the eruption products which subsequently found their way to Greenland. The fact that just such initial Plinian tephra was deposited on Crete means it clearly could have made it much further. Zielinski and Germani conclude by claiming that 'even if these [initial Plinian] phases of the eruption were able to get glass high enough to eventually reach Greenland, the composition of the Mochlos and Rose Pumice glass does not match that of the GISP2 glass', but, as discussed above, this simply is not the case. The GISP2 glass, and the Mochlos glass, in fact compare quite well within measurement errors. Further, as highlighted in 2. above, the specific microprobe measurements of Zielinski and Germani are arguably systematically slightly offset from others on Minoan Thera glass and require slight calibration. Therefore, Plinian products from Thera, where more variability in compositions might be expected,[1383] *could* have been the source of the GISP2 glass shards.

We may therefore conclude that highly evolved Thera glass, as initially erupted in the Plinian phase, and so quite possibly able to travel far/furthest, and so be found in places like a Greenland ice-core, and particularly as found at Mochlos on Crete, is both compatible with (highly rhyolitic), and indeed characteristic of (low MgO and TiO_2), the GISP2 tephra shards. In other words, the four shards in the c.1623BC layer of the GISP2 core *could* be from the eruption of Thera. I stress *could*. There is no positive proof, but I have demonstrated above that, on the evidence currently available, the arguments of Zielinski and Germani, which try to distinguish the GISP2 glass from Theran glass, are not sound.

The situation is thus ambiguous. The GISP2 glass is not Theran in an obvious and decisive fashion, but at the same time it could be compatible with Theran glass, especially if the measurement errors on the data are allowed for. If it is Theran, then it might best come from the initial Plinian phase of the eruption, and there is no reason why this is not possible. To move to a positive case other forms of data are necessary. Although Thera potentially fits the relevant profile, it is of course possible that there are other eruptions in addition to Thera which produced volcanic glass with a similar

---

[1383] See Vitaliano *et al.* (1990:72, 76 re sample E).

major oxide composition at around this time; definitive discrimination and provenance of eruption products to a specific volcanic eruption requires additional rare earth element and trace element comparison.[1384] Such analysis and data are now required for the GISP2 shards.

SOME OTHER ERUPTIONS CAN, HOWEVER, BE EXCLUDED

Nonetheless, despite the Theran ambiguity, the study of Zielinski and Germani (1998a) does, however, provide one very important and relevant finding. They examined the composition of volcanic products from four of the other volcanic eruptions which have been proposed in recent years as possible alternative sources of 17th century BC eruption signals or products (Aniakchak, Vesuvius-Avellino, and two eruptions of Mt. St. Helens). Although this was not a comprehensive comparison, and the Avellino and Aniakchak data are not from their own measurements on the same microprobe which produced the analyses of the GISP2 shards, the analyses clearly demonstrate that none of these four eruptions offers data even vaguely compatible with the c.1623BC GISP2 glass shards.[1385] This further strengthens the candidacy of Thera. The composition of its glass can at least offer approximately similar data within measurement errors. Of course, other eruptions may exist of the relevant time period, and one or more of these may also have a compatible chemical composition (and several Kamchatkan, Alaskan and Icelandic eruptions have produced relatively similar glass). But we can probably rule out suggestions of high northern latitude possibilities (see Chapter V.2 above), and so other Alaskan, Kamchatkan, or Icelandic eruptions.[1386] The glass shards in the c.1623±36BC layer of the GISP2 core support such a view. They are very small, and as Zielinski and Germani (1998a:285) argue, this supports a model of long distance transport, and thus a lower latitude to equatorial eruption source. Thera is suitable, and other would-be candidates probably have to come from a similar mid to lower latitude source.

Therefore, it is reasonable to suggest the possibility that the volcanic glass shards in the c.1623±36BC layer of the GISP2 core could come from the eruption of Thera. As noted above, further positive evidence to confirm or deny this identification is now required (if possible): e.g. trace-element and rare earth element analyses.[1387] Additional composition data are also required, both to build up a rigorous composition field for

---

[1384] For Thera, see Vitaliano *et al.* (1990); Eastwood *et al.* (1998; 1999).

[1385] Zielinski and Germani (1998a:284–285 and Table 1 and Fig.3).

[1386] Contrary to Zielinski and Germani (1998a:285).

[1387] See Vitaliano *et al.* (1990:61–70); Eastwood *et al.* (1998; 1999). The major problem with such further analytical techniques is that they are destructive forms of analysis; hence, if huge cost and much time is required to find just a couple of tiny volcanic glass shards, then one wants to be very confident of the measurement facility before destroying the evidence. In addition, traditional forms of further analysis required reasonably large amounts of sample, and these are simply not available from ice-core finds of tephra. Therefore, the ability to analyse very small samples, indeed on a single-shard basis, via laser ablation ICP-MS (Eastwood *et al.* 1998) is a major development, and should lead to much greater rigour in tephra-provenance, and tephrachronological studies.

the GISP2 shards,[1388] and to characterise all other potentially contemporary major, climatically-effective, northern hemisphere volcanic eruptions. This will permit a rigorous characterisation and provenance of later 17th century BC tephras.[1389]

DATING ACCURACY OF THE GISP2 CORE AND THE IMPLICATIONS FOR THE THERA DEBATE?

If these GISP2 volcanic glass shards are potentially of critical importance – whether in positive or negative terms – then the obvious next question concerns the exact accuracy and security of the c.1623BC date of the volcanic acid signal, and these associated shards, in the GISP2 core. Zielinski and Germani (1998a:282) claim an accuracy of 'just over 1%' – which they quantify as ±36 years – on the dating of the GISP2 ice-core in the 17th century BC (depth 766.8–766.9m). Previous publications stated a conservative error of the order of 2%,[1390] and the recent study of Meese *et al.* (1997:Table 2) again repeats this, stating an 'estimated error' of 2% for depth 719–1371m. Zielinski and Germani are at pains to point out that 'these errors are very conservative and should be considered as a maximum possible error', but they fail to address the one salient issue raised in the earlier publications of the GISP2 team: namely that the GISP2 core is not complete. Alley *et al.* (1993:528 Table 1) state that 'recovery of intact core exceeded 97%', but therefore specifically mean that recovery of intact core was also clearly less than 98% (i.e., 2% is non-intact). In particular, Baillie (1994:216) has highlighted that some 14m of core was unrecoverable between c.AD614±15 and AD545±15. In a response to such suggestions, Zielinski and Germani (1998b:1045) in fact rather avoid this issue; they state there is a dating error, but generally claim that the depth of any core which was not sampled is known, that ice accumulation rates did not vary by more than 10% during the entire Holocene, and that, overall, such errors add up only to 'tenths of 1%'.

The detailed analysis of Alley *et al.* (1997) provides further details and a more useful account. Across good (intact) sections of core the GISP2 team can achieve an excellent, ±1%, reproducibility of visual stratigraphic measurements, *but* some 87m of core was not suitable for analysis. Sometimes, although it was not usable, the length of core was still known, other times the intervals lost had to be estimated from typical ice accumulation rates. In the absence of multi-core replication, an unknown error may have been introduced with such estimates. Some 30 incidents of visible stratigraphic data loss occurred by depth 766m (17th century BC) in the GISP2 core.[1391] Therefore, as Alley *et al.* (1997:26,378) state: 'we thus must accept that single-core dates, and especially single-core/single-indicator dates, involve some uncertainty'.

The exact stated date of c.1623BC may thus prove a little more flexible than Zielinski and Germani suggest (or it may not – the point is that accuracy and precision are not replicated, and at present are only estimated). One appropriate test for the accuracy

---

[1388] Ten or more measurements would be an appropriate basis on which to describe the range of the GISP2 glass.

[1389] Compare the work in New Zealand by Stokes and Lowe (1988); Stokes *et al.* (1992).

[1390] E.g. Alley *et al.* (1993:528 Table 1); cf. Zielinski *et al.* (1994a:948).

[1391] Alley *et al.* (1997:Fig.2).

and precision of the GISP2 age scale is to compare it with the two other recent long ice-core sequences: the Dye 3 and GRIP cores. Replication provides certainty in the observational sciences. In this case there is an initial caveat. The nature of the ice-core record does not permit the total accuracy and precision of the annual tree-ring records. It is possible to achieve better than ±1% error in replicate analyses of the same intact core sections, but there is inherently some small variation.[1392] Reference to historical markers (e.g. precisely dated volcanic eruptions) permits further precision in the recent period, but, even less than 400 years ago, a small, ±2 year, error is nonetheless possible in the GISP2 core.[1393] For the GISP2 core the last claim of a securely dated event is the eruption of Vesuvius in AD79. But in fact no positive confirmation has been established, as no glass shards could be identified.[1394] The logic is merely that there is a large acid signal, and no other large volcanic eruption at this approximate time is known (a logic now widely criticised for the Thera debate!). Before Vesuvius, the oldest 'secure' eruption date cited by the GISP2 team is some nine centuries later: Eldgjá in Iceland. Analysis of the GISP2 core dates this signal (and positively identified tephra) c.AD938; the Danish-European team report a date of c.AD934 for the same signal.[1395] Despite no further totally secure volcanic signals, it is nonetheless clear for the most recent three millennia, back to 1084BC, that there is, in general, a very good agreement between the volcanic signal records and chronology for the GISP2 and GRIP ice-cores, with only a maximum ±10 year discrepancy at 1084BC.[1396] The GRIP core in turn is well replicated over the same period by the Dye 3 core with variations of only a couple of years maximum.[1397]

Unfortunately for present purposes, the accuracy and precision available for the period 1000–2000BC is less impressive. There are some rather more significant differences, or non-correlations, between the timescales reported for the GISP2 versus GRIP cores. Clausen *et al.* (1997:26,713) observe that 'between the ages 1000 B.C. and 2000 B.C. the uncertainty of the two timescales deviates too much to make a safe comparison'. In favour of the superiority of the GRIP timescale is the relatively good replication achieved with the Dye 3 core. The two agree to within ±7 years in the 15th and 17th centuries BC.[1398] Clausen *et al.* thus conclude that 'it is possible that the GISP2 timescale at these ages should be reconsidered'.[1399]

One approach to resolution appears to be to search for key 'marker' volcanic events which almost certainly have to be represented in both the GISP2 and GRIP ice-cores. The cores were taken just 30km apart, and it is unlikely that one or the other represents significantly different precipitation patterns. For example, in the period 1–2000BC, it has been noted before that just two major climate events compatible with the effects of

---

[1392] Alley *et al.* (1997).

[1393] This is a maximum error: de Silva and Zielinski (1998:fig.2 caption).

[1394] Meese *et al.* (1997:26,413).

[1395] Meese *et al.* (1997:26,413); Zielinski *et al.* (1995); Clausen *et al.* (1997:26,721).

[1396] Clausen *et al.* (1997:26,713).

[1397] Clausen *et al.* (1997).

[1398] Clausen *et al.* (1997:26,713).

[1399] Clausen *et al.* (1997:26,713–26,714). See also Hammer (n.d.).

large volcanic eruptions occur with clarity in *both* the absolutely dated Irish and USA tree-ring records *and* the Danish-European Greenland ice-core (GRIP and Dye 3) data:[1400]

Event 1:   42–44BC (tree-ring) = 49/50±5BC (ice-core);
Event 2:   1626–1628BC (tree-ring) = 1636±7BC or 1644±7 BC (ice-core)

The spacing between these two events is also important: 1584 (tree-ring) or 1595/94 or 1587/86 (ice-core) years.

Where are these two events in the GISP2 record, and this spacing? In the GISP2 core only one SO_4^{2-} (sulphur dioxide derived) signal in the two century period between c.AD50 and 150BC exists which could possibly represent a very large volcanic eruption which had a major effect on northern hemisphere climate: the enormous signal dated to c.54BC.[1401] On common sense, *a priori*, grounds this is likely to be the c.49/50BC signal in the GRIP/Dye 3 cores (pending positive identification). And the error is only ±4–5 years, GISP2 offering the 'older' dates. By the start of the second millennium BC this trend seems to have increased. There is a clear large volcanic signal in both the Dye 3 and GRIP ice-cores dated at 1074BC. The corresponding signal has to be the one dated ten years earlier at c.1084BC in the GISP2 core (there is no other significant signal within ±40 years, and no other 'major' signal within a century). The GISP2 chronology has thus stretched to 10 years older than the GRIP/Dye 3 timescale. But let us return to the 54BC signal, and the spacing to the 17th century BC signal. 1584 (tree-ring) or 1595/94 or 1587/86 (Danish-European ice-core) years earlier than 54BC is 1638BC, 1640/41BC or 1648/49BC. There is no volcanic signal at this time in the GISP2 core; instead, the major volcanic signals nearby are at c.1623 or c.1669 BC. This implies a real flexibility in the GISP2 timescale of at least 15–30 years by the 17th century BC, since, unless something very problematic has occurred, one of these two signals must match the GRIP and Dye 3 signals. And, to be fair, the GISP2 team claim only a ±36 year maximum error for this period, and so are proved accurate and precise within their stated confidence.

However, we need to know which signal. The solution requiring the least error is the c.1623BC signal, especially as the GRIP core provides a slightly lower chronology for this period than the Dye 3 core. In this case, the overall error is within ±15 years, and this roughly conforms to the scale of error/discrepancy found in the previous first and second millennium BC comparisons. And, it in fact would seem inherently likely that neither ice-core timescale is entirely correct, and that the real date is 1628BC, in line with the one clear climate-event signal found over a period of several centuries in the absolutely dated tree-ring evidence.[1402] (There is of course an element of circular logic involved here, but there is a strong circumstantial case from the notable pattern of a set of 'marker' volcanic/climate event-clusters found in both tree-ring and ice-core records over the last several millennia.[1403])

[1400] See Manning (1992b; 1995:202 n.9). For the primary data, see LaMarche and Hirschboeck (1984:Table 3); Baillie and Munro (1988); Clausen *et al.* (1997); Johnsen *et al.* (1992:Table 1).
[1401] Zielinski *et al.* (1994a:Table 2).
[1402] E.g. Hughes (1988); Zielinski and Germani (1998a:282; 1998b:1,045).
[1403] Stothers and Rampino (1983); Baillie (1991a; 1995a).

Baillie (1996a) has, however, made a case for the 1669BC volcanic signal in the GISP2 core being the equivalent of the 1636BC and 1644BC volcanic signals in the GRIP and Dye 3 cores (and all really being c.1628BC). In general support, one could note that the GISP2 core was offering older dates than the GRIP/Dye 3 cores at the start of the second millennium BC. The trend may have continued. It is difficult to disprove absolutely Baillie's suggestion in the absence of tephra identifications from each of the respective ice-core layers, but Zielinski and Germani (1998a:282) argue that this revised chronology is both unnecessary, and probably unlikely. Further, the inability of the GRIP team to correlate their second millennium BC data with the GISP2 data implies that something other than gradual stretching of the GISP2 timescale has occurred during the second millennium BC, and this runs against Baillie's linear scheme. We might suspect one of those instances of visible stratigraphic data loss. In such circumstances, the GISP2 core could, through incomplete data and less than perfect interpolation, become suddenly a bit over a decade younger at this point than the GRIP core.

Moreover, if the data is examined, it is plausible to offer a set of correlations among the various ice-cores in contrast to Baillie's scheme.[1404] To begin, there is a good match for the major volcanic acidity signals in the Dye 3, GRIP, and GISP2 cores at 1074BC, 1073BC, and 1084BC, and again at 1183BC, 1182BC, and 1192BC, with GISP2 offering dates about a decade older. This continues the first millennium BC pattern. But then there is no major GISP2 signal corresponding to the 1428BC and 1425BC signals in Dye 3 and GRIP. 1442BC is the closest relatively minor signal in the GISP2 record. If associated, this is then a c.14–17 year older date for GISP2 and suggests a little further upwards stretching of the timescale to this point. The 15th century BC then appears to be when things change around. One or more of the volcanic signals in 1463BC, 1457BC and 1440BC in the Dye 3 core might correlate with the large volcanic signals in the GISP2 cores in 1454BC, 1457BC and 1459BC. But here it seems something is going wrong with the GISP2 timescale. If these three signals in each core are the same, then the GISP2 core has suddenly become very compacted, and lost about 15–20 or so years, such that by 1459BC it is now 4 years younger than the Dye 3 and GRIP timescales. These signals are not clearly represented in the GRIP core (and the explanation for this is not apparent[1405]). Perhaps warmer temperatures or some other process created some variations in the core records in the mid-15th century BC? The next major signals in all three ice-cores are the 1644BC, 1636BC, and 1623BC signals. Since these are the first major signals after the apparent problems of the 15th century BC, there is no control on whether these data are in fact correlative. On face value there seems no reason not to correlate these three signals (rather than the 1669BC signal in the GISP2 core), but neither is there any positive case. If so, the less than enormous 1669BC signal in the GISP2 core might then correlate with the more minor 1688BC signal in the Dye 3 core (continuing the now 15–20 year younger timescale); this might well be one of the other possible 17th–18th century BC volcanic eruptions

---

[1404] For data, see Table 13; Clausen *et al.* (1997); Zielinski *et al.* (1994); Hammer *et al.* (1987).
[1405] Cf. Clausen *et al.* (1997:26,713–26,714).

proposed by Vogel *et al.* (1990) – see Chapter V.2 above. In general, the lack of major signals in the Dye 3 or GRIP cores to match the 1669BC and 1695BC signals in the GISP2 core seems to indicate that these were not huge marker events, but for some local reason were more prominent at the GISP2 site whereas they lie hidden in the minor signals in the Dye 3 and GRIP records.[1406] The alternative is that 'the GISP2 timescale at these ages should be reconsidered' (Clausen *et al.* 1997:26,713–26, 714); in turn, the analysis of Zielinski and Germani (1998a) would then have no necessary relevance to the 1620s BC, nor Thera (Hammer n.d.), and we may continue to consider a mid–later 17th century BC Thera date.

MIGHT THERA IN FACT BE REPRESENTED BY
ONE OF THE LESS DRAMATIC VOLCANIC ACID SIGNALS?

The initial assumption by those working in the ice-core field was that a large volcanic signal in the mid second millennium BC might well be Thera. Since Thera was a very large eruption, it was more or less just assumed that it would be obvious in the ice-core record. Sulphur production is the key; both in terms of climatic effect, and representation as an acid signal in the polar ice. Thus when petrologic estimates in the 1980s cast serious doubt on the scale of Thera's sulphur production, this assumption looked mistaken. Now, I have outlined in Chapter V.2 why these petrologic estimates for Thera may be inappropriate. Some recent volcanoes have produced much greater amounts of sulphur products than indicated by petrologic estimates. However, this does not mean that all petrologic estimates are in serious error, rather only for certain categories of volcano/eruption. It is therefore entirely possible that Thera's sulphur output was not enormous (even if a little higher than the minimum data of Pyle and Sigurdsson *et al.*).[1407] If so, and if the eruption does lie in the later 17th century BC (probably) or mid 16th century BC (possibly), as indicated by the directly relevant radiocarbon evidence from Akrotiri, then it *could* be represented by one of the smaller volcanic signals in the ice-core records, such as 1622BC in Dye 3, 1618BC in GRIP, or 1602BC or 1600BC in GISP2. We can in fact just about limit ourselves to this range, and exclude the 16th century BC. Why? Zielinski *et al.* (1994a:951 n.32) briefly considered this issue. They noted that 'Pyle [1990b] … suggested that the amount of sulfur produced by the Santorini eruption may have been similar to that produced by Krakatau (A.D. 1883); thus, there was a low sulfur/total volume erupted ratio. If that suggestion is true, one of the smaller SO_4^{2-} residuals in the 1600s B.C. may be from the Santorini eruption'. The point is that the eruption of Krakatau, and a minimum analogue for Thera, nonetheless left an SO_4^{2-} residual signal of 46ppb in the GISP2 ice-core, despite its equatorial location. Pyle

---

[1406] Clausen *et al.* (1997:pl.3).

[1407] One interesting aside is that the c.1623BC GISP2 glass is highly rhyolitic (silica-rich), and silica-rich eruptions often tend not to yield large volumes of sulphur dioxide. Thus one might question whether the eruption that produced these shards necessarily was capable of explaining all of the reasonably major c.1623BC volcanic acid signal in the GISP2 core. This might even lead to the possible issue of whether there may have been more than one volcano contributing to the annual flux in this year (cf. Manning 1995:216). Thera could well be a candidate in such a case.

calculated the *minimum* sulphuric acid yield of the Thera eruption at a little over c.3 megatonnes, and Krakatau produced only slightly less.[1408] Thus, if Krakatau, in a distant equatorial location, produced a residual signal of 46ppb, Thera should have left as large, or larger, a signal by definition, given its larger size, greater sulphuric acid yield (even on minimum petrologic estimates), and closer mid northern hemisphere latitude. Therefore, since there is *no* SO_4^{2-} residual signal greater than 30ppb in the whole 16th century BC in the GISP2 record,[1409] and given the likelihood that the minimum sulphur production estimates for Thera by Pyle (and Sigurdsson *et al.*) from the petrologic technique are in fact absolute minima (Chapter V.2), it appears unlikely, and perhaps impossible, that the eruption of Thera could be represented by one of the two small 16th century BC signals. An SO_4^{2-} residual signal of ≥c.50ppb would seem to be a realistic minimum candidate. In the 17th century BC, apart from c.1623BC at 145ppb, and c.1669BC at 78ppb, the GISP2 ice-core only has volcanic signals of any significance at c.1600BC (40ppb), c.1602BC (58ppb), and c.1695BC (213ppb). The last is clearly too old to be Thera (unless the core chronology is seriously in error), but it is conceivable that 1600BC or especially 1602BC, could represent Thera on a lower sulphur-production scenario. These are the realistic possible alternatives, and should be investigated. The stated ±36 year dating error for this section of the GISP2 ice-core applies to each of these dates. Whether or not these dates could correlate with the tree-ring evidence is another question.

At present, partial provenance data exists for the volcanic source of just one year in the potentially relevant range of the Thera eruption (or rather one of the typically bi-annually sampled ice horizons in the GISP2 core[1410]). Within the stated dating error of ±36 years, this leaves many other years also potentially relevant to a c.1628BC, or later 17th century BC, eruption of Thera which have not been explored. Thus, *even if* Zielinski and Germani are right that the c.1623BC volcanic glass is not Theran, then, as they themselves conclude: 'Santorini still could have erupted in the 1620s BC. We cannot disprove that possibility' (1998b:1,045). Until all the potentially relevant ice is examined, and a positive Theran match is identified (wherever this is), then the matter is unresolved. After all, it may turn out that no other tephra c.1700–1450BC offers a better match for Thera than the c.1623BC glass. And, as we have seen, within error margins, and in overall terms, the GISP2 glass could already be considered as consonant with Thera Minoan eruption volcanic glass.

Conclusion

In correction to the interpretations of Zielinski and Germani, the tephra shards from the c.1623BC layer of the GISP2 ice-core do not discount the possibility of a 1628BC date for the Minoan eruption of the Thera volcano. They may even be compatible

---

[1408] Pyle (1990b:169 and Table 1c for Thera, 171 and Table 1b for Krakatau).

[1409] Zielinski *et al.* (1994a:Table 2). The just two signals of any significance listed are: 1577BC at 29ppb, and 1594BC at 30ppb. Neither of these dates are particularly compatible with the available mid-16th century BC radiocarbon range for Thera, nor the 'low' archaeological chronology.

[1410] See Zielinski *et al.* (1994a:948). Some sections were evaluated at subannual resolution (Zielinski *et al.* 1994a:951 n.19).

within measurement errors. And, suitable analogues for extremely distal Theran tephra may not have been analysed before. Although the dating error should not be ignored, the c.1623±36BC date is entirely compatible with the previous suggestions of a 1628/ 27BC date for the Thera eruption from tree-ring data (Chapter V.2) or a c.1636±7BC or c.1644±7 (to a maximum of ±20) BC date for the Thera eruption from other ice-core evidence,[1411] or the most likely date range for the Thera eruption from the radiocarbon evidence relevant to the eruption (Chapter V.1 above[1412]). Further positive confirmation and replication must now be sought, both from the GISP2 core, but also the Dye 3 and GRIP cores.[1413] This will hopefully offer the final proof, high or low, for the date of the Thera eruption. Needless to say, the present author believes that such data and final resolution will support a mid–later 17th century BC date. Professor Claus Hammer very kindly informs me (pers. comm. 1999) that results of the relevant analyses of samples from the Dye 3 and GRIP ice-cores with regard to Thera are expected during AD2000. These should offer a final resolution based on well-dated ice-cores. As of 1999, Professor Hammer continues to consider a 17th century BC date as the most likely for Thera. If so, the general archaeological synthesis developed in the current work will be required, versus a likely possibility. However, *even if* the final resolution should favour the mid-16th century BC and so the 'compromise early' chronology (the low or conventional chronology is not a possibility following *both* the archaeological and scientific arguments in this book), then the general *relative* archaeological synthesis developed in the current work remains valid.

4. Aegean dendrochronology, and further evidence for a 1628BC climate-event consistent with the eruption of Thera

Professor Peter Ian Kuniholm and his team – the Aegean Dendrochronology Project – have over the last three decades built up many thousands of years of tree-ring chronologies for the east Mediterranean: at present some 6,500 years of chronologies across several tree species.[1414] One major constituent chronology begins with the wood found in the extraordinary Midas Mound Tumulus at Gordion, capital of the Phrygians, in central Anatolia: Plate 12. Here a man-made mound still 53m high and 300m in diameter contained a small wooden building with the rich burial of one male aged 60–65 years,[1415] plausibly King Midas himself – on the basis of the finds, scale of the tomb, and other circumstantial evidence.[1416] The logs forming the wooden tomb

---

[1411] Clausen *et al.* (1997); Hammer *et al.* (1987:519).

[1412] See also Manning (1995:200–216).

[1413] No finds of tephra shards from the GRIP or Dye 3 cores in the relevant period are yet reported at the time I write this, and it must be hoped that evidence will be forthcoming in the future (cf. Schoch 1997:61 and n.118; Lohmann 1998:Nachtrag): see below this paragraph.

[1414] Kuniholm and Striker (1982; 1987); Kuniholm (1993; 1996a; 1996b; 1998a; 1998b).

[1415] Young (1981:79–190).

[1416] Prag (1989); Prag and Neave (1997:85–104). These studies present a tentative reconstruction of the face of 'Midas' from the skull in the tomb.

were preserved out to the bark (i.e. cutting year), and had hundreds of preserved rings, with as many as 918 in one log: see Plates 13–14.[1417] Altogether, a 1028-year tree-ring chronology was constructed from Gordion. The date of the Midas tomb was considered to be late 8th century BC or early 7th century BC from the stylistic dating of the finds and historical evidence. A long tree-ring chronology reaching back into the Bronze Age was thus forming. Wood from three other key sites, Porsuk (a 321-year chronology) (Plate 15), Acemhöyük (a 164-year chronology), and Kültepe (a 435-year chronology) was able to be matched together, and to the Gordion chronology, to build an overall 1503-year Bronze-Iron Age chronology.[1418] Most important for present purposes is the section from Porsuk: see Figure 57. This chronology has since been extended and further replicated through new work and finds,[1419] and, with one still tentative join in the 23rd century BC, runs as of summer 1998 from c.627BC back to c.2687BC.[1420] But, for present purposes, I will refer to the published 1503-year chronology in this discussion.

Based on archaeological materials at the respective sites, this 1503-year chronology must cover the period from the late 3rd millennium BC through to the earlier 1st millennium BC. However, as the 1503-year chronology is not at present connected to a fixed dendrochronology from living trees backwards, it is a floating chronology within these approximate archaeological constraints. A series of high-precision radiocarbon measurements was therefore obtained on specific decades from this chronology in order to place the floating chronology in absolute terms through the wiggle-matching of the radiocarbon measurements to the decadal resolution high-precision radiocarbon calibration curve of Stuiver and Becker (1993). As of 1996, this enabled the chronology to be accurately dated at 95.4% confidence within small calendar errors (+76/−22 years): see Figure 58.[1421]

At the same time, in the several thousand years of the Aegean dendrochronology, it was observed that there is just one, unique, exceptional, and dramatic growth anomaly (sudden much increased growth, from over 200% to over 700% normal growth), starting in relative ring 854 of the 1503-year chronology: see Figure 59, see also Figure 57.[1422] It is important to note that this growth anomaly is not just in one, or a few, trees. Individual trees show all sorts of seemingly dramatic ups and downs in growth for all sorts of very individual, or site, or tree-specific reasons. This is instead a major growth anomaly in the average trend across an entire sizeable population of trees. The trees were also of widely differing ages at the time of the event (from 19 years of age through to greater than 244 years of age), and from several different species (cedar, pine, juniper and fir). There is no reason to assume all the trees were growing close to each other. The growth event is thus not a result of some unusual micro-environmental cause: such as young trees suddenly forcing their way through

[1417] Kuniholm (1977).
[1418] Kuniholm (1993); Kuniholm *et al.* (1992); Kuniholm and Newton (1989).
[1419] See in Kuniholm (1996b; 1998a; 1998b).
[1420] P.I. Kuniholm (pers. comm.); Wiener (1998:313–314).
[1421] See Kuniholm *et al.* (1996).
[1422] This growth spike was detected in wood from Porsuk (see Kuniholm *et al.* 1992).

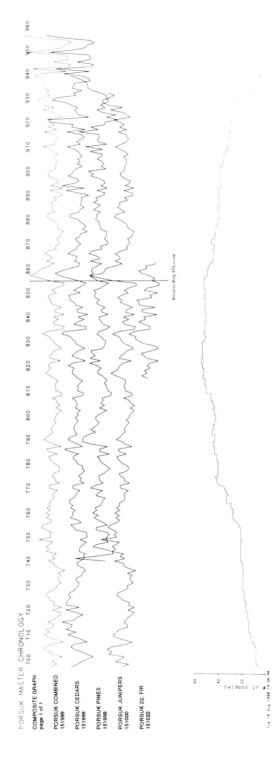

Fig. 57. The dendrochronological data from Porsuk, Turkey. The average behaviour in terms of percentage of normal growth by twenty-year moving average of the cedar, pine, juniper, and fir samples is shown both separately, and in terms of an overall Porsuk site combined average. The fit of the Porsuk data against the Aegean Dendrochronology Project Bronze–Iron Master Chronology is also shown (this is determined by a computer-calculated correlation). Note the growth patterns at extreme left and right are irrelevant due to very small (i.e. just one tree) sample numbers. Where there are good sample numbers note how all populations reflect the same major up or down trends, establishing the match of chronologies. Figure courtesy of Peter Ian Kuniholm.

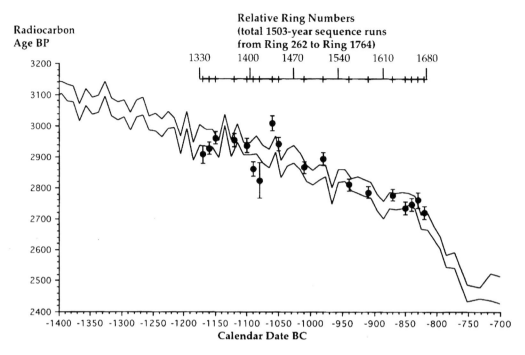

Fig. 58. The radiocarbon wiggle-match (best fit) of the 18 dendrochronologically-sequenced radiocarbon measurements on a section of wood from Gordion against the 1993 decadal calibration curve (Stuiver and Becker 1993). Figure after Kuniholm et al. (1996:Fig.1).

the forest canopy and growing without restraint, or a recovery from insect attack. The report of Kuniholm *et al.* (1996) was based on a population of 36 trees relevant to this growth anomaly; further work since that date meant that there were 54 trees involved as of 1998: see Figure 57. At the time of writing, that number has now risen to 62. The marked growth anomaly remains across this large population, and so has been further replicated, and made totally secure.

It is thus clear that at the time of relative ring 854 a remarkable thing happened; whereas normally in the dry Mediterranean environment growth largely slows in summer, at this time growth continued all year. In other words, the climate was unusually cooler and wetter. The growth surge in the tree populations from this time is hundreds of percent greater than usual. On the basis of the radiocarbon wiggle-match published in Kuniholm *et al.* (1996), the growth event was dated 1641 +76/−22 BC.[1423]

[1423] Since the writing and publication of the Kuniholm *et al.* (1996) paper, some further radiocarbon determinations have been run on the Gordion dendrochronological sequence as wiggle-matched (Bernd Kromer, pers. comm.). The aim was to replace one poor datum with a large error (versus the other data),

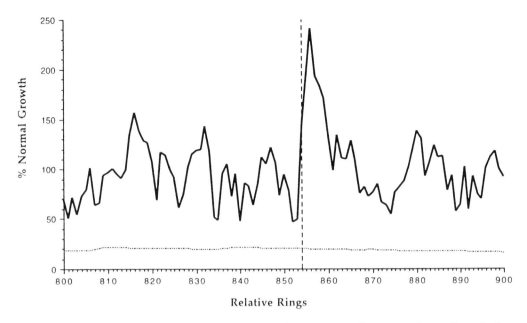

Fig. 59. Figure showing, as of 1996, a population of juniper trees from Porsuk covering relative rings 800–900 of the Aegean Dendrochronology Project Master Chronology. In relative year 854 (shown by the vertical dashed line) the population exhibits a sudden growth event. Figure after Kuniholm et al. (1996:Fig.3).

This match was against the radiocarbon calibration curve of Stuiver and Becker (1993) – a set of measurements carried out at the Seattle radiocarbon laboratory on German wood (for the relevant BC period). The new INTCAL98 radiocarbon calibration curve of Stuiver *et al.* (1998) has subsequently been produced, combining data from several laboratories. A match against this chronology, like a match against the Belfast 1986 or 1993 calibration data, or the 1993 combination of Belfast and Seattle data,[1424] offers a slightly older fit. But one which, comfortably within error margins, would still include the dendrochronological fit proposed in Kunihom *et al.* (1996). However, parallel high-precision measurements of contemporary radiocarbon levels in Anatolian versus German wood currently underway at Heidelberg for the Aegean–East Mediterranean Radiocarbon Calibration Project lead the members of this project

---

and to test others. Four new measurements are now available, three replacing previous data points. The wiggle-match is little affected as would be expected. The best fit point moves slightly upwards on the new data (by 9 years following a chi-square fit against the Stuiver and Becker 1993 data), *but* the margin of downwards error on the fit increases accordingly since the general possible range of fit at 95% confidence is almost identical to that reported in Kuniholm *et al.* (1996:Fig.2). Thus there is in effect no change to the general dating window and arguments in the paper of Kuniholm *et al.* (1996). I therefore refer to the published paper of Kuniholm *et al.* (1996) in the main text.

[1424] Manning (1998a:Table 30.2).

to believe that the more appropriate match for the radiocarbon age of Anatolian wood at this time (and generally) is against the radiocarbon age of German wood, rather than against the radiocarbon age of Irish oak.[1425] For many periods, there is excellent agreement between the German, Anatolian, and INTCAL98 data, and generally, there is hemisphere-wide stability in radiocarbon levels, but, at some other times, and especially when radiocarbon levels are changing rapidly and significantly, there are minor but potentially significant differences in contemporary radiocarbon levels between different areas, such as between Anatolia–Germany and then Ireland or the USA. At such times, a wiggle-match may vary by a few decades depending on which regional calibration dataset is employed. The period around 1100BC, and the 9th century BC, are such times of changing radiocarbon levels, and there is a several decade difference between the German–Anatolian versus Irish data (with the new INTCAL98 dataset more or less in-between): see Figure 60. Thus, for the present, I continue to use the wiggle-match published in Kuniholm *et al.* (1996) based on German wood; the errors quoted on this wiggle-match date more than cover the possible variation caused by employing other calibration curves. We continue to believe that this match is the best available on published data; it offers good agreement with historical dates for wood from the end of the sequence.[1426]

Two things are apparent with regard to the ring 854 anomaly. First, there is a remarkable near coincidence of this date and effect – evidence of significant cooling and increased rainfall/reduced evapotranspiration – in the Anatolian dendro-chronology with the only major tree-ring event plausibly representing significantly cooler surface temperatures and increased rainfall in the Irish dendrochronology from the middle of the second millennium BC, and absolutely dated at 1628BC.[1427] Further, this event correlates with the 1627BC frost damage event (again showing evidence of significant surface cooling) reported from the bristlecone pines of the White Mountains of California.[1428] There is also other consonant (if less decisively clear) evidence from 1628BC in UK and German chronologies.[1429] All in all, 1628BC represents a northern hemisphere-wide tree-ring event of some significance (a 'marker event'[1430]), and it is both not surprising, and indeed likely, that evidence for it should show up in the Anatolian dendrochronology. The same contemporary effect, a sudden reduction in northern hemisphere surface temperatures and increased precipitation/reduced evapotranspiration, led to different effects depending on local environment and

---

[1425] I thank my collaborators on this project: Bernd Kromer, Peter Ian Kuniholm, Marco Spurk, and others. I especially thank Bernd Kromer for discussion and analytical work on the comparison of contemporary radiocarbon levels in Anatolian and German wood.

[1426] The dates for final available tree-rings from a coffin at Gordion Tumulus B and for bark from wood linked with the later years of king Rusa II of Urartu offer dates within a very few years of historical estimates: Kuniholm (1997; 1996c; pers. comm.); Wiener (1998:313–314).

[1427] Baillie and Munro (1988).

[1428] LaMarche and Hirschboeck (1984), correcting their 1626BC date since they had a year 0 in their chronology. Baillie (1995b:34; 1996b:295) reports that frost damage has now also been identified in two new foxtail pine chronologies from the Sierra Nevada.

[1429] Baillie (1990; 1995a:75–77, 81–82).

[1430] Baillie (1991a).

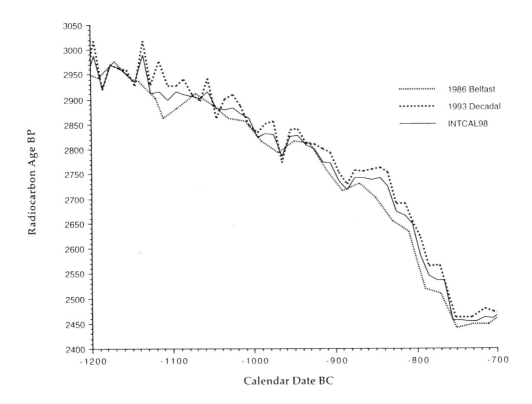

Fig. 60. Comparison of the 1993 decadal calibration curve data of Stuiver and Becker (1993) solely from German wood with the INTCAL98 dataset of Stuiver et al. (1998) and the Irish data of Pearson et al. (1986) for the period 1200–700BC. Errors on the calibration curve data are not shown.

climate regime. Cooler, wetter, conditions were good for tree growth in semi-arid central Anatolia, but bad for tree growth in the bogs of the north of Ireland or at the upper timber line in the White Mountains of California.[1431]

However, the association of the growth event beginning in relative ring 854 of the Anatolian chronology with 1628BC in the Irish chronology can be made even more secure. A period of about 15 years of unusually raised average growth in the mid-

---

[1431] Yamaguchi (1993:Table 1) notes this pattern, whereby the stratospheric aerosol from a major volcanic eruption can cause growing season frosts or cool growing seasons in areas at or near forest ecotones (i.e. the upper timber-line or subarctic tree-line), and thus frost damage in the wood, or narrow rings or low density 'light rings', whereas, in contrast, the same type of volcanic event and a cooler growing season in the case of semi-arid forests will promote wide late-season (latewood) growth. In the 1628/27BC case we see all the above: frost damage at the upper timber-line in western USA, narrow rings in northerly bog oak from Ireland and generally poor growth in northern European dendrochronologies, whereas in semi-arid Anatolia there is significantly increased (latewood) growth and very wide rings.

12th century BC in the Anatolian dendrochronology was noted briefly in Kuniholm (1990b).[1432] This begins clearly in relative ring 1329 (and arguably from ring 1324) and continues to relative ring 1343, some (470 to) 475 years after the relative ring 854 event. If one refers to the Irish dendrochronology, it is a remarkable coincidence that in 1159–1141BC, starting 469 years after the 1628BC event, there is a 20-year growth anomaly.[1433] Both anomalies are consistent with sustained cooler and wetter weather: good for tree growth in central Anatolia, bad for tree growth in the north of Ireland. A coincidence in timing is apparent, with the Anatolian trees merely being a little bit slower to be initially affected in the 1150s BC, but with both events falling in the same overall two-decade window. The 1628BC and 1159–1141BC tree-ring events are the only major tree-ring growth anomalies in the entire second millennium BC in the Irish dendrochronology.[1434] Therefore, the correlation, within the possible dating window established by the high-precision radiocarbon dating and wiggle-match, of the Anatolian and Irish dendrochronologies at both these decisive points provides a clear case for being able to apply the absolute dates from the Irish dendrochronology (and its European associates) to the Anatolian dendrochronology. Moreover, whereas the two-decade mid-12th century BC anomaly is obvious, but not a precise single event, the 1628–1627BC event is a clear and specific signal around the northern hemisphere, and so we may date the matching relative ring 854 event in the Anatolian dendrochronology precisely to 1628BC.[1435] This dating clearly has potential implications with regard to Thera (see below), but it has direct relevance to samples of wood from ancient buildings linked to the Aegean dendrochronology. Buildings such as the Waršama palace at Kültepe, and the Sarıkaya palace at Acemhöyük, where wood preserved out to the bark (cutting year) was recovered from wall footings and similar construction contexts, may now be dated exactly.[1436] Since documents preserved in these buildings provide links with the Assyrian King List, the dates offer the potential to contribute to the resolution of the long-running debate over the chronology of the Old Babylonian period (see discussion in Chapter VII below).

The second observation is that both in the 1503-year Anatolian chronology, and indeed in the total 6,500 years of Anatolian chronologies so far collected, the relative ring 854 event is unique in its scale. There are some other similar events, such as the

---

[1432] See also Baillie (1995a:86–87).

[1433] Baillie and Munro (1988); Baillie (1989; 1995a:77, Fig.5.3; 1996b:295).

[1434] Baillie and Munro (1988).

[1435] As in Kuniholm *et al.* (1996). Given the pattern of a 0–1 year lag time in trees picking up such events around the northern hemisphere, from observations from recent times, and also from compatible satellite observations of the timing of the global spread of volcanic eruption products (e.g. McCormick *et al.* 1993; 1995), a maximum error of ±1 year exists. Thus the relative ring 854 summer growth extension might conceivably have occurred in 1629BC, with Irish trees not being adversely affected until spring 1628BC, and maximum hemisphere cooling following in 1627BC when frost damage occurred in Bristlecone pines at the upper timber line in the White Mountains of California.

[1436] One final note of explanation and clarification is desirable. Kuniholm (1993) referred to a date for tree-rings from a bowl from Shaft Grave V at Mycenae. This was a mistake and should be expunged from the literature, and no longer referred to. Kuniholm was not able to measure properly the tree-rings in the bowl in question (in fact not able to measure them at all following accepted dendrochronological practice), and they should never have been included in the datelist (Peter Ian Kuniholm, pers. comm.).

one a little over 470 years later, and other much smaller but similar events matching historical eruptions such as Krakatau, but none are of the same order of magnitude as the relative ring 854 event: see Figure 61. Something very unusual and specific must be responsible for this 1628BC Aegean–Anatolian event.

What could cause such a sudden and short-lived cooling of the climate? The studies of Irish and American dendrochronologies have shown a clear link with major volcanic eruptions in the cases of distinct growth anomalies over the last several thousand years (see Chapter V.2 above). As we discussed in Chapter V.2, the correlation of dendrochronological and ice-core evidence further shows that the 1628/1627BC event in Irish, European, and American trees is very likely associated with a major volcanic eruption. Thus we can suggest that the Anatolian evidence is also recording the effects of a major volcanic eruption in 1628BC. The clear short-lived effect in the Anatolian trees (Figure 59) is entirely consonant with the c.1–3 year maximum effect of a major volcanic eruption. However, the 1159–1141BC event is somewhat problematic in this regard. Although the eruption of the Hekla III volcano in Iceland has been linked by some workers with the 1159BC tree-ring event in Ireland, others dispute this.[1437] The 1159BC event is not represented as frost damage – an extreme circumstance – in the dendrochronology of LaMarche and Hirschboeck (1984) from the White Mountains of California, nor did it show up clearly in some of the Greenland ice-core records. The length of the event (two decades), both in the Irish and Anatolian trees, is also too long for the short-lived effects of a volcanic eruption (0–3 years); similarly, the lack of a clear correlation for the start of the event between Ireland and Anatolia (up to a six year lag in Anatolia), mitigates against a clear, decisive, hemisphere-wide signal, such as a major, climatically-effective, volcanic eruption – which ought to be picked up everywhere within a 0–1 year dating window.[1438] If, nonetheless, a volcanic event was involved, then, because the eruption concerned (Hekla III?) is at a high northern latitude, the poleward direction of atmospheric circulation would have led to a much reduced impact in California versus the north of Ireland. The effect in Anatolia is also (consistently) relatively minor versus the dramatic relative ring 854 event. But it is more likely that some other, longer duration, climatic causal force is primarily responsible for the mid-12th century BC event. This situation may be contrasted with the clear case for a major volcanic eruption in 1628BC.

There remains one final observation of significance. Throughout the 6,500 years of Anatolian dendrochronologies constructed to date there have been a number of major volcanic eruptions. Most of these are detectable as small to very small positive growth year spikes in the Anatolian dendrochronology, but are statistically

---

[1437] See Buckland *et al.* (1997:588–591).

[1438] For example, the studies of McCormick *et al.* (1993; 1995) and Self *et al.* (1996) show how the aerosol from the mid-June 1991 low-latitude northern hemisphere Pinatubo eruption achieved peak mass about four months after the eruption, and had spread to cover most of the northern hemisphere and high southern hemisphere latitudes about seven months after the eruption. Climate change models had predicted that global average surface temperature cooling would begin in late 1991 with the largest effect (of c.0.5°C) in late 1992 (Hansen *et al.* 1992), and these models were proved basically correct (McCormick *et al.* 1995:402).

indistinguishable from normal tree-growth variation (e.g. Krakatau, or Tambora, in the recent past: see Figure 61). The reason they are relatively small to indistinguishable anomalies is because the Anatolian trees are growing in environments which are not especially marginal and so sensitive – in contrast to the trees at the upper timber line in California, or the bogs of the north of Ireland. Moreover, the relevant Anatolian environments are not critically affected by cooler weather – again, in complete contrast to the dendrochronologies of LaMarche and Hirschboeck, and Baillie. Instead, the main climate threat to the Anatolian trees is overly long, hot, and dry summers. Cooler and wetter weather is a boon. This positive effect will always be less dramatic and clear in a dendrochronology than the crisis of near-death – hence the cooler weather which promotes growth in Anatolia will be less dramatic in recorded effect in general, and may be contrasted with the clear and decisive evidence of low-growth and frost damage and thus near-death experiences which this same weather causes at the upper timber line in the White Mountains of California, or in bogs of the north of Ireland.

The extraordinary clarity and scale of growth exhibited across a number of trees of widely differing ages (19 to 244+ years old at the time of the event) and from different species (juniper, cedar, pine and fir) beginning in relative ring 854 of the Anatolian dendrochronology is thus remarkable, and requires a special explanation. The effect is similar to, but much more dramatic than, those caused by any other major volcanic eruption in 6,500 years of chronologies. Somehow it is a special, even unique, circumstance. The best explanation appears to be that the volcano responsible for the northern hemisphere-wide 1628BC surface cooling had an especially direct and dramatic effect on the climate of the Aegean region. There is of course a very suitable explanation and candidate available: an enormous volcanic eruption just 840km away, at the same latitude, and upwind (i.e. to the west) from where the relevant trees were growing, and already dated to more or less the right time. Further, the distribution of tephra fallout from the eruption of Thera is easterly towards Anatolia,[1439] and Heiken and McCoy (1984:8,451) noted evidence of southeasterly winds during the Plinian phase of the eruption. This is especially consistent with an eruption date in the spring–early summer period.[1440] The oxygen isotope profile in Hammer *et al.* (1987:Fig.3) places the major 'Thera' volcanic signal between the summer '1645BC' and summer '1644BC' $\delta^{18}O$ peaks (i.e. main winter snowfall), but, as Hammer *et al.* (1987:519) observe, the increased volcanic sulphuric acid levels begin during the preceding year, and in particular just as the $\delta^{18}O$ value changes to reflect warmer summer '1645BC' temperatures. Hence this too would support an eruption date during, or shortly before, the spring of this year – which is regarded here as in fact being either 1629BC or 1628BC. The 1628BC volcanic event is detected in spring wood onwards in Ireland, and the signal is present in spring onwards wood in Anatolia (of 1628BC, or possibly 1629BC). Thus a spring eruption is likely (or one in the preceding later winter after the previous growing season had finished), and this is consistent with the tree-ring data. The peak

---

[1439] Watkins *et al.* (1978); McCoy (1980); Sullivan (1990); Guichard *et al.* (1993); Eastwood *et al.* (1998). See Figure 21, p.72 above.
[1440] Doumas (1990:49); Sullivan (1988).

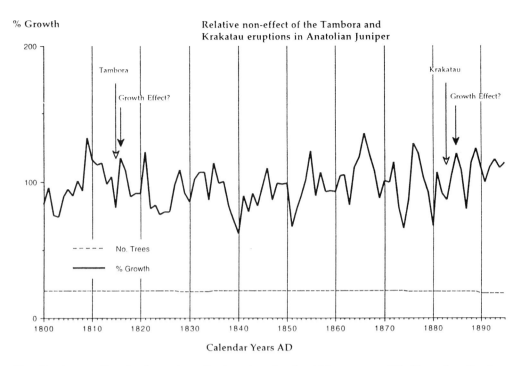

Fig. 61. Aegean Dendrochronology Project data for the 19th century AD. Note the effective non-impact of the Tambora and Krakatau eruptions. Small increases in growth do follow in each case, consistent with the model that cooler temperatures caused by volcanic aerosols promote tree growth in Anatolia, but the effect is very small and completely indistinguishable from normal growth variations. Data courtesy of Peter Ian Kunihom.

climate effect occurred into the following 1–2 years (e.g. ice-core main volcanic acid peak), and this correlates with the 1627BC frost damage in the bristlecone pines[1441] and the peak anomaly in the Anatolian trees over the period 1629/1628–1626/1625BC: Figures 57 and 59.[1442]

A reasonable circumstantial case therefore exists whereby the eruption of Thera could have been responsible for the absolutely dated 1628BC tree-ring events in the USA, Ireland, Europe, and Anatolia. The Thera eruption is established as potentially contemporary from the direct radiocarbon evidence from Akrotiri; the Thera eruption could have caused the climatic effects required (especially now the low petrologic estimates of its sulphur production are questionable); the Thera eruption seems to have occurred at the right time of the year to account for the tree-ring and ice-core evidence; and the volcano of Thera is in the right geographic location both to explain

---

[1441] LaMarche and Hirschboeck (1984).
[1442] Kuniholm *et al.* (1996:Fig.3).

the unique growth anomaly in the Anatolian trees and to be consistent with the nature
of the ice-core signal in Greenland (Chapter V.2 above). In the absence of any other
better (or as suitable) candidate, it is therefore a plausible working hypothesis that
the eruption of Thera caused the absolutely dated 1628/1627BC tree-ring events in
the USA, Ireland, Europe, and Anatolia.[1443] The discussion of the glass shards from
the c.1623BC layer of the GISP2 ice-core (Chapter V.3 above) only further adds to this
viewpoint, since these shards do not disprove a mid–later 17th century BC Thera
eruption date, and may in fact even prove to be potentially consistent with a Theran
eruption source within the respective measurement errors on the data.

Nothing in the Aegean dendrochronology suggests a potential major volcanic
event in between this 1628BC event and 1551BC when the replicated chronology
from the large group of trees from Porsuk ends (and nothing in the record of the
few Porsuk trees which continue a few years later – the last specimen has a ring of
1527BC – indicates a volcanic signal down to 1527BC). There are a few relatively
minor volcanic signals in the Greenland ice-cores from c.1622BC to c.1566BC (see
Table 13), but nothing in the tree-ring data from the Aegean, nor Ireland, nor the
USA, would indicate that these had either major hemisphere wide effects, or specific
local effects in the Aegean region. The minor volcanic events at c.1622BC (Dye 3
ice-core), c.1618BC (GRIP ice-core) or c.1602BC and c.1600BC (GISP2 ice-core),
mentioned in Chapter V.3, *could* be consistent with the calibrated radiocarbon age
range for the Thera eruption, and therefore are possible candidates if the sulphur
production of the Minoan eruption of Thera was low, however, the minor events at
c.1594BC and c.1577BC (GISP2 ice-core), 1569BC (Dye 3 ice-core) and 1566BC (GRIP
ice-core) are less ʼnan likely since they fall outside the most likely calibrated
radiocarbon age range for the eruption (see Chapter V.1). The two 1560s BC events
might possibly be argued to work with a 'compromise early' Aegean chronology,
but there is a lack of any supporting tree-ring evidence (including in the Aegean).

After the minor c.1566BC volcanic signal in the GRIP ice-core, there is in fact *no*
significant volcanic signal (small or large) in any of the major recent ice-cores until
the mid-15th century BC (see Table 13). There is similarly no tree-ring evidence for
any significant climate event. Thus it is very unlikely that a huge, VEI 6.9+, volcanic
eruption in the mid-latitudes of the northern hemisphere could have occurred and
not be evident in any of these records. Therefore, a Thera eruption date anywhere
from 1550 to 1479BC is most unlikely.

A potential caveat or objection to this hypothesis is that there is not at present a
good Aegean dendrochronological record for the later 16th century BC, and some
might argue that perhaps only proximate tree-ring data recorded the eruption
(especially if its sulphur production was relatively low, as has been argued by some
scholars). After the large group of Porsuk trees and their wood which lasts down to
1551BC, there are only a few trees providing data for the later 16th century BC. This
is not an appropriately large sample to smooth out individual tree-specific factors, or
local, micro-environmental, issues. Thus it might be argued that an Aegean volcanic

---

[1443] For additional details and data, see also Kuniholm *et al.* (1996).

eruption could have occurred in the later 16th century BC (as the low chronology would have Thera do so), but not yet be detected by Aegean dendrochronology. However, we already know that no significant tree-ring anomaly exists over the whole of the 16th century BC in the records from the USA and Ireland, and, more importantly, from ice-core records, that no significant/detectable volcanic eruption with a climatic impact (large to smaller) occurred in the northern hemisphere in the second half of the 16th century BC (previous paragraph, and see Chapter V.2 above). Nor, among the Aegean wood that *is* available for the later 16th century BC, is there any indication of a significant climate event consistent with a major volcanic eruption.[1444] Thera was a very large eruption; it cannot be 'hiding' in the later 16th century BC. Thera must instead belong with one of the known recorded eruptions.[1445]

We may therefore conclude that 1628BC is by far the most likely and plausible date for the Thera eruption given the unusual and specific evidence from the Anatolian dendrochronology. It is admitted that the Aegean tree-ring evidence by itself is nothing more than suggestive,[1446] but the package of evidence and argument presented in Chapter V Sections 1–3, together with the evidence of the Aegean dendrochronology, makes a compelling and specific case. In the future, it may even be possible to add to the picture. Work by Hall *et al.* (1990) showed that it is possible to detect a specific elemental signal linked to volcanic eruptions in tree-rings from the western USA, and it may thus prove possible with further work to prove beyond any doubt that the 1628BC tree-ring growth anomaly was associated with a volcanic eruption (and similarly to rule out the occurrence of a major local volcanic eruption in various other years).[1447] Whether a specific eruption source can ever be identified is perhaps asking too much.

[1444] Peter Ian Kuniholm, pers. comm.

[1445] The ice-core evidence reviewed in Chapter V.2, and in previous paragraphs in this Section, indicates that it is very unlikely that a major climatically-effective northern hemisphere volcanic eruption occurred in the 16th century BC *after* the early 1560s BC. This period may thus be discounted. But an eruption in the early 1560s BC or earlier in the 16th century BC was noted as possible from the ice-core evidence (and so the 'compromise early' chronology). It was merely noted that none of these possible volcanic signals in the ice-core data were consistent with a large eruption, and thus they are unlikely to represent Thera. The Aegean dendrochronology data may assist here. The Porsuk trees provide good replicated data into the 1550s BC (and a few trees continue on to a final ring in 1527BC). There is no likely clear and distinct major volcanic signal after the 1628BC episode discussed above in the late 17th century BC or the first half of the 16th century BC (to 1551BC, or in the few trees from Porsuk that continue afterwards down to a final ring of 1527BC). Nor is there any indication in the non-Porsuk wood from the later 16th century BC from Anatolia. It seems impossible if Thera did occur in this period that there would not be a clear signal in Anatolian wood. The only obvious and clear signal consistent with the effect of a major local volcanic eruption is the dramatic 1628BC growth spike.

[1446] Cf. Renfrew (1996).

[1447] Ongoing work by John Chiment, and others, of the Aegean Dendrochronology Project is investigating methods for identifying specifically volcanic signals in tree-rings. Preliminary indications are positive (John Chiment, pers. comm.; Peter Ian Kuniholm, pers. comm.). In particular, it seems possible that increased uptake of certain metals may be linked with volcanic aerosols. The hypothesis is that large volcanic aerosols may lead to increased soil acidity, and that this in turn creates increased mobility, and so tree up-take, of various metals. Up-take of toxic metals may, in their turn, also be predicted to lead to stress indicating glutathione and glutathione-based products in the wood. A particularly promising technique for the analysis of trace element compositions in wood appears to be laser ablation ICP-MS (see e.g. Garbe-Schönberg *et al.* 1997; Durand *et al.* 1999).

Chapter VI. Summary and Conclusions

'A brief summary will be sufficient to recall to the reader's mind the more salient points in this work. Many of the views which have been advanced are highly speculative, and some no doubt will prove erroneous; but I have in every case given the reasons which led me to one view rather than to another. ... False facts are highly injurious to the progress of science, for they often endure long; but false views, if supported by some evidence, do little harm, for every one takes a salutary pleasure in proving their falseness: and when this is done, one path towards error is closed and the road to truth is often at the same time opened.' (Darwin 1871 quoted from Darwin c.1948:909)

A large and very varied body of data and discussion has been presented in Chapters IV and V. It is time to draw this together to reach the likely conclusions available. It is inevitable that not everything is totally clearcut and decisive. In most circumstances neither nature nor culture have the neat and tidy divisions that archaeological chronologies pretend. The precise and accurate 'spot' dating of the specific event of the eruption of Thera therefore offers a fascinating problem, and an extraordinary chance, but we cannot expect it to be easy. It is a challenge involving both a test of archaeological dating and a test of science-dating, and, accordingly, it has become one of the standard examples in archaeological textbooks.[1448] In the process of investigation, we must guard against the tendency to 'suck in and smear': where the existence of one known event leads archaeologists, historians, and scientists to associate everything around-about with this event, whether or not it is appropriate.[1449] Similarly, the critical and sceptical observations of Buckland *et al.* (1997) should be noted: the existence of a possible correlation does not by itself establish a causal connection.

[1448] Renfrew and Bahn (1996:154–155); Greene (1997:103, 113–114).
[1449] See Baillie (1991b). A similar logical fault underlies the event-historical mode of traditional archaeology, where knowledge of the conquest of a site by a particular king in a given year leads to determined attempts to associate some specific destruction horizon at the site with this historical event. In fact, this may be inappropriate, since (as discussed in Chapter III) archaeological and historical evidence may reflect fundamentally different facets of historical reality.

The discussion in Chapter IV sought to review, critically examine, and analyse, the archaeological evidence for chronology both around, and specifically concerning, the eruption of Thera. The discussion in Chapter V did the same for the science-dating evidence. Each of these 'species' of data and scholarship were considered independently – however, *both* were found to point in the same direction (Aegean 'early' chronology) on the balance of probabilities. Neither the archaeological nor scientific data were privileged or prioritised. A case directly relevant to the Thera event was constructed, and short-comings, where found, were acknowledged. The aim was a rigorous study, considering, and integrating, both archaeology and science. The conclusions of this study are therefore broadly based and strong. They do *not* rely on one piece of evidence. They instead rest on different but consonant cases developed from *both* the archaeological *and* scientific datasets.

If one brings together the discussions in Chapters IV and V, we can identify first some problem issues, second a key archaeological area in need of further clarification and resolution, and finally, third, some likely conclusions.

1.a. Problem Issues: Archaeology

Although it has been argued that the corpus of archaeological evidence can plausibly be interpreted as consistent with the 'early' or 'high' Aegean chronology, it must be admitted that not everything is clearcut, nor are there no contradictions or problems. Much of the archaeological evidence available is undeniably open to, or capable of, *either* a 'high' or 'low' chronological interpretation (with neither necessarily correct from the evidence relevant to any individual case). The ten years of debate on this issue have been useful in deconstructing previous assumptions based on little solid data. Indeed, some evidence previously held central may now be dismissed. In certain cases, the evidence in fact clearly supports a chronology earlier than the conventional or 'low' chronology: for the LMIB to LMIIIA1 period in particular, an earlier chronology than the conventional or 'low' chronology is clearly required. This is important.

However, the evidence for the historical dating of the LMIA period in terms of Egypt and the Near East remains problematic. Since this period includes the eruption of Thera, the date for this event also remains problematic in terms of the archaeological chronology. Some things seem capable of definition, nonetheless. It seems clear that the LMIA period was contemporary (at least in part – and seemingly to at least the destruction of Akrotiri on Thera) with the later MBA of the Levant (and so the later Hyksos period/SIP in Egypt). The links between frescoes, art styles, and material culture are still few, but are compelling. It is further clear that LMIA was contemporary with more or less the initial LCIA period (onwards) on Cyprus, with a recent find at Maroni *Vournes* nicely confirming previous indications from Toumba tou Skourou. New evidence from Kommos in south central Crete now makes this conclusive: LC late handmade Red Slip in early LMIA, possible PWS? (the alternative is late WP=LCIA) in the middle of the three phases of LMIA at Kommos (LMIA Advanced), and Proto Base Ring, Monochrome, and initial BRI (contemporary with Thera early WSI bowl) in Final LMIA contexts. Since almost all scholars agree that LCIA began during the later MBA of the Levant (MBIIC or MBIII period), this confirms the link between the latter and LMIA. This is an important revision to past views, where at best early LMIA was seen to overlap with the late Hyksos/SIP. The later MBA Levantine trading world appears to have been in contact with, and included, the LMIA Aegean. The respective élites shared common practices and symbolism, with 'Aegean'-style wall-paintings, and common jewellery types, providing two of the more obvious manifestations (writing notation may possibly be another, or at least an area deserving greater study). This chronology and cultural synchronisation is in turn of wide relevance to the general history of new palace Crete. The major port of Akrotiri on Thera was apparently the key Aegean centre for this wider east Mediterranean trade system. The LMIA (Akrotiri) links appear especially to have been with the pre-Bichrome phase of later MBII (earlier MBIIC or MBIII) in the Levant.

The preceding synthesis can be broadly agreed upon because no absolute dates have yet been mentioned. Once they are, we meet the main problem: White Slip I pottery, and the general view of the date of its first appearance as no earlier than the start of the 18th Dynasty in Egypt. Since a WSI bowl was found in an LMIA volcanic destruction level context on Thera, this is held by several scholars to require the 'low' chronology. I spent considerable space on this issue in Chapter IV.4 and especially Chapter IV.5, and tried to explain, following Merrillees (1971), why this is in fact not a problem. I argued that Egypt (including Tell el-Dab^c a) received its Cypriot pottery from eastern/southeastern Cyprus, and that eastern/southeastern Cyprus remained largely 'MC' in style until the end of the LCIA period. With one or two rare exceptions, Egypt only received the new 'LC' styles of WSI and BRI once these styles had been adopted in eastern Cyprus in LCIB. This is early 18th Dynasty in Egyptian terms. Meanwhile, the 'LC' styles had developed in northwestern Cyprus rather earlier, in LCIA, and had been potentially available for export throughout this period. They were an already mature style when adopted by eastern Cyprus in LCIB. As it happens, eastern Cyprus seems to have dominated exports to Egypt in LCIA, and LCIA north-western Cypriot products are thus found only in the Levant, and, at present, more or less only at Tell el-^c Ajjul from current data. But some LMIA–LCIA exports/imports from the northwest of Cyprus to the Aegean, and the reverse, are evident. This is SIP in Egyptian terms (and so quite possibly compatible with the Aegean 'early' chronology).

However, I imagine some critics will not have been convinced. The evidence of quite different, regional/chronological, ceramic traditions over the MCIII–LCIA period on Cyprus, and of near exclusive trading contacts between one zone (eastern Cyprus) for Egypt including Tell el-Dab^c a and some of the Levant, and a contrary and quite different linkage (also) with another zone on Cyprus (northwest Cyprus) for Tell el-^c Ajjul and Thera (and presumably some other Levantine sites), appears not to have been appreciated nor accepted by much current scholarship outside Cyprus. Among Cypriot scholarship the position is, however, clear: Enkomi and east Cyprus was the pre-eminent, and largely discrete, polity of Cyprus in LCI, and, with some products of southeast Cyprus also, controlled almost all trade with Egypt and most of the Levant. To quote the recent statement of Pickles and Peltenburg (1998:87): 'the overwhelming eastern Cypriot character of pottery exports to sites like Tell el-Dab^c a point to its [Enkomi's] pre-eminence in Cyprus at this time'. In reverse, Levantine elements predominantly entered Cyprus at this time through eastern and southeastern Cyprus.[1450] Northwest Cyprus was different and outside this zone; its exports are not widely attested in the Levant in general on current data, but, for some special (but unknown) reason, they were imported into Tell el-ᶜAjjul.[1451] This region of Cyprus also seems to have cultivated some Aegean links (perhaps because the Levantine trade was largely controlled by Enkomi). A dichotomy, with LCI style northwestern products parallel with MCIII-style LCI eastern products, continuing over a significant chronological period, is quite possible, even plausible.

In the case of WSI, support for the 'early', or 'high', Aegean chronology case boils down to just one, problematic, site: Tell el-ᶜAjjul. If Petrie was correct to state that he found WSI in Palace I contexts at the site, then the 'early' chronology is required. Further, this would fit perfectly with the pre-Bichrome Ware links for LMIA/Late Cycladic I-style frescoes at Alalakh and Tel Kabri. In this case, only LCIB and mature to later WSI would correlate with the early 18th Dynasty. The fragment of a stone vase with the cartouche of Ahmose, first king of the 18th Dynasty, from a likely LCIB (onwards) context at Palaepaphos would co-ordinate nicely with such a view. Evidence from Saqqara, Memphis, and perhaps Abydos, would indicate that the *mature* LMIB and LHIIA periods in the Aegean were likewise correlative with the early 18th Dynasty.

However, it must be confessed that the Tell el-ᶜAjjul evidence is so far spectacularly singular. And the stratigraphic information is debatable and less than perfect. To date, no other site in the Levant or Egypt provides evidence of pre-LBI/18th Dynasty finds of WSI. Of course, few provide much evidence at all – Tell el-ᶜAjjul is unusual in every way – and none except Tell el-ᶜAjjul provides a link with initial LCIA northwest Cyprus where the early WSI style evolved. I have chosen to accept Petrie's basic record. This conclusion is not totally perverse. After originally accepting Albright's re-datings, Professor James R. Stewart (1974:62), probably the leading Cypriot archaeologist of the middle of the 20th century AD, reached the same view in light of the Stephania excavations, stating that: 'I now believe that Petrie's statement that White Slip I ware appeared in ᶜAjjul I is probably correct'. The evidence at the Theran end of the equation is also a little problematic. One WSI bowl found in the 19th century, which is now

[1450] Peltenburg (1996:34–35); Merrillees (1974a).

[1451] The material record of LCI Cyprus would indicate actual political divisions on the island (Knapp 1979; Peltenburg 1996:27–35). A territory controlled by forts can be proposed for Enkomi (see Peltenburg 1996:30–34; for the forts, see Fortin 1983; 1989). This implies rivalry, and presumably military rivalry, with other entities on the island: a northwestern grouping around the Toumba tou Skourou area, for example (cf. Peltenburg 1996:33). We may suspect that control, production, and distribution, of copper lay at the heart of these different polities. The Cypriot ceramics at Tell el-ᶜAjjul are notable, special, and require some explanation in this regard. No other site in the Levant or Egypt (including Tell el-Dabᶜa) has anywhere near as much MCIII–LCI material. The large quantity of WSI is particularly striking given its virtual absence at several other major sites in Palestine (e.g. Megiddo, Hazor, Lachish). Perhaps Tell el-ᶜAjjul acted as the main trade partner for copper exports from the northwest of Cyprus? Northwest Cyprus may, in addition to its Aegean links, have also had trade relations with sites in the north Levant and southern Anatolia (not yet recognised).

lost, is the sum of it. Although it seems likely that this bowl was found in an LMIA pre-eruption context on Thera near the modern excavation area at Akrotiri, we lack any actual account of its find context. Despite the extensive modern excavations from 1967 onwards on Thera, and the literally millions of finds, no other sherd of WSI (nor indeed equivalent Cypriot artefact) has ever been found. The Theran WSI bowl is thus unique, lost, and poorly documented.

The evidence of BRI is also problematic. It is argued by some that there is no indisputable evidence for pre-LBI/18th Dynasty finds of BRI, in agreement with the claims made about WSI. But Merrillees (1971) argues that this is because BRI really only appears in Egypt in the LCIB period after eastern Cyprus adopts the western/northwestern Cyprus LCI styles. In support of the Merrillees model and LCIA=SIP early BRI in west/northwest Cyprus, there is a recent BRI find from Memphis (although disputed by other scholars), and there are a few other instances where an early date is possible (just not demonstrated). But, since BRI appears to have been employed in the Levant for very different purposes to WS, a different import pattern is quite plausible. There is some early BR exported to the Aegean on present data (Kommos, Final LMIA, consistent with later LMIA equating with LCIA2 and in turn the MBIIC/MBIII period in the Levant and the SIP in Egypt). BRI was not reported from Tell el-ᶜAjjul Palace I, and there is no good evidence for when it appeared in the City strata at the site, so it may not have been exported to the site as early as WSI (but note again its different function/role). Nor, as noted, do the first appearances of this ware in the Levant and Egypt necessarily date its development on Cyprus. BRI was a long-lived type, and the majority of exports undeniably appear to equate with the later, LCIB, phase of its production (from eastern Cyprus, once eastern Cyprus had adopted the originally northwestern Cyprus LCI ceramic package in LCIB).

All in all, neither the 'early' Aegean chronology, nor the 'low' Aegean chronology, can claim proof solely on the basis of the archaeological evidence. Claims to the contrary depend on unproven assumptions, or deterministic views on other matters. The 'early' chronology is certainly not ruled out. Full consideration of the Aegean and Cypriot evidence and its contexts may even support it.

1.b. Problem Issues: Tell el-Dabᶜa

The chronology and evidence of this site is now central to the 'low' chronology case. It is the site where, for the first time, a few examples of WSI have been found in a stratified excavation context in Egypt. It has the finds of Theran pumice from an early 18th Dynasty workshop. It has impressive Aegean-style fresco fragments. And so on. I have spent considerable space in Chapter IV discussing this wonderful site and its finds, and explaining why none of them necessarily requires the 'low' Aegean chronology. I fully appreciate that the excavator of the site, Professor Manfred Bietak, will disagree with this assessment. I hope readers will, in contrast, consider the case from a neutral perspective.

The frescoes are fascinating, but chronologically rather irrelevant. Some at least seem quite possibly to exhibit LMIB elements, and so could support the 'early' chronology synthesis even with Bietak's re-dating of them all to the early 18th Dynasty. A case for some (with good LMIA stylistic links) being from destroyed Hyksos structures also remains possible. The pumice merely sets an irrelevant *terminus ante quem*. The WSI found to date at the site probably does all come from early 18th Dynasty contexts, although two finds might possibly be from earlier contexts, but could also be regarded as either LCIB in date (matching other LCIB imports in early 18th Dynasty contexts), or, if earlier WSI, from secondary contexts where the original import date and vessel use could very well be SIP. Moreover, in general, early LC west/northwest, and northcoast/Karpass, Cypriot products are simply not found/present at Tell el-Dabᶜa. Why? As argued repeatedly in Chapter IV, and summarised again earlier in this chapter, Tell el-Dabᶜa seems to have received all its later MC through LCI exports from eastern/southeastern Cyprus. This area remained largely in the MC tradition through LCIA, and developed Bichrome Ware at this time, whereas the west/northwest developed the LCI styles, including the earlier WSI of LCIA. Thus, while Tell el-ᶜAjjul and Thera received early LCIA WSI from northwest Cyprus in the later Levantine MBA period, Tell el-Dabᶜa received mainly the products of eastern/southeastern Cyprus (late WP to PWS). The Red on Black and Red Slip present already in stratum E/1, the dominance of WP PLS in the late MBA assemblages, and the appearance of WPV from stratum D/3, confirm that we are respectively already very close to, and then into, initial LCIA. I am prepared to envisage some 80–100 years separating the appearance of initial early WSI, in LCIA, as found at Thera, from the later mature WSI, in LCIB, as found from the beginning of the 18th Dynasty at Tell el-Dabᶜa (especially bowl 7949), and, overall, I consider plausible some 150+ years of total WSI production down to the earlier New Kingdom. Some other scholars will undoubtedly find this position difficult, although all standard current published estimates already offer a lifetime of 130 *or more* years to WSI production.

The absolute dating of the late MBA phases at Tell el-Dabᶜa is another problem. Bietak regards the final D/2 stratum as 30 years in duration, and allocates another 30 years to the preceding D/3 stratum. The time estimate comes from his view that the average span of each building phase at the site is 30 years (on the understanding that some strata lasted longer, others for shorter periods). Stratum D/2 sees the first appearance in the Tell el-Dabᶜa stratigraphy of Bichrome Ware and PWS. But Bichrome Ware appears in Tell el-ᶜAjjul (late) City 3 and clearly from City 2b, and, in the Palace sequence, Bichrome Ware is most common from Palace II, although, in some cases, it is reported from Palace I or the destruction debris between Palace I and II. PWS appears from the destruction debris between City 3 and 2b and in City 2b. The main City 2b/Palace II Bichrome Ware phase begins during the reign of Khyan, but is predominantly linked with Apophis. At Alalakh, Bichrome Ware appears in Level VI, after the destruction of Level VII by Hattusili I. A date of c.1600/1590BC is therefore often stated for the start of this main Bichrome phase in the Levant (based on standard Egyptian chronology, or the Middle to Low Babylonian and Hittite chronologies).[1452]

[1452] See Chapter VII for discussion. See, for standard position summarised above, Kempinski (1983:131–148, 216–224); Oren (1969:132–134; 1997b:271; n.d.).

To quote Oren (1997b:271): 'The appearance of Bichrome ware marks a clear demarcation line between the MBII and III, at about 1600 B.C.E.' It should further be noted that this c.1600BC datum is very much the minimum position, based on the main phase of Bichrome Ware exports. The first appearances of the ware are in fact a little earlier (see above). In view of this Bichrome Ware horizon from c.1600BC, one might therefore expect, in approximate terms, to correlate this date with the start of Tell el-Dabᶜa stratum D/2; Tell el-ᶜAjjul City 2b and Tell el-Dabᶜa stratum D/2 have many similarities.[1453] However, Bietak dates the start of stratum D/2 c.1560BC. It is tempting to suggest that stratum D/2 might well be a case for one of the longer '30-year average' phases, linking its beginning with the c.1600BC Bichrome Ware horizon.

The ceramic evidence from Tell el-Maskhuta in the Nile Delta might be held to support such a view.[1454] This site has a c.1700–1600BC assemblage,[1455] and should offer a good parallel sequence to the Hyksos levels at Tell el-Dabᶜa. However, as currently published, the 'quite late' dates of Bietak for his E/1 to D/2 strata create some problematic issues in the correlation of Maskhuta with Dabᶜa.[1456] The Maskhuta assemblage has flat bottomed cups as the dominant type; this type appears in Tell el-Dabᶜa stratum E/1, and is present in stratum D/3, but only becomes dominant in stratum D/2. Thus while the six phases of Maskhuta might overall be correlated with Tell el-Dabᶜa strata E/1 to D/2, it is D/2 which offers the best link for the key cup type. However, the remainder of the Maskhuta assemblage best compares to Tell el-Dabᶜa strata E/1 to D/3, and especially D/3, and, in general, Maskhuta lacks late MBIIC/MBIII types.[1457] Weinstein (1995:87–88) regards the assemblage as MBIIB. It might therefore seem that Tell el-Dabᶜa stratum D/2 should at least join/overlap. Moreover, Maskhuta has a few finds of LCI WPVI from Cyprus, from both early and late phases.[1458] Bietak reports WPVI only from Tell el-Dabᶜa stratum D/2. The implication of both the flat bottomed cups and the WPVI is that Tell el-Dabᶜa stratum D/2 needs to stretch upwards to at least c.1600BC to link with, or overlap with, the late MBIIB (mainly Tell el-Dabᶜa strata E/1 to D/3) assemblage at Maskhuta. This is consistent with the Bichrome Ware horizon from c.1600BC discussed above. Further, if a link or association is sustained between early LMIA/LHI/Late Cycladic I ceramic decoration and the development in eastern Cyprus in the LCIA period of Bichrome Ware (eastern Cyprus = mainly MCIII style but chronologically LCIA), as Artzy (n.d.) argues, then, in reverse, this nexus of evidence also provides support for the above, and, in turn, support also for the 'early' Aegean chronology.

Revision of some of the arbitrary assumptions for the dating of the later SIP phases at Tell el-Dabᶜa would then be a necessary consequence. It is important to remember that there is no basis to the dates cited in current literature for the later MBA strata.

[1453] Kempinski (1983:150–151); Oren (1997b; n.d.).

[1454] Redmount (1993; 1995).

[1455] Redmount (1995:67–68).

[1456] Redmount (1995:e.g. 81).

[1457] Redmount (1995:78).

[1458] Redmount (1993:4; 1995:71).

Bietak at present has a link with Sesostris III year 5 for early stratum K (so c.1868BC),[1459] and the end of stratum D/2 lies within the reign of Ahmose. Everything else is flexible within these limits. We are concerned with the Hyksos period. An indication of the upwards limit is provided by the observation that during the course of strata E/1 to D/3, characteristic Hyksos period scarab designs start to occur.[1460] Hence some part of stratum E/1 must be close to, or include, the start of the 15th Dynasty, and so a mid-17th century BC date is both required and feasible (start of the Hyksos 15th Dynasty c.1669BC, or c.1649/48BC, or c.1638/31/27BC according to the high, middle, and low Egyptian chronologies[1461]). Strata D/3 and D/2 in turn represent the timespan of the 15th Dynasty, with the latter appearing to be the rather longer phase. Overall, they may represent nearer 90 or 100 years, rather than the total of 60 years allowed by Bietak. Earlier stratum D/3 may thus include the date of 1628BC, and, on the 'early' chronology, both the eruption of Thera, and part of the mid LCIA period.

There is nothing in the material reported from Tell el-Dabᶜa which disproves such a slightly higher chronology. An initial arbitrary decision to allocate each of the nine SIP strata an equal 30 years has led to a mistaken belief in these dates, simply because they have been referred to many times. They were never facts. In 1979 Bietak wrote that 'satisfactory evidence for an absolute chronology has not yet emerged from the excavations at Tell el-Dabᶜa' (p.233), but he proceeds in that paper to reach several very low chronology positions, more than a little influenced by the work of Williams.[1462] Other possibilities are rejected (cf. pp.254–256). The particularly troublesome problem involved here is the very low date Bietak (1979:237) proposd for Tell el-Dabᶜa stratum F and the associated MBIIA–MBIIB transition: 1715/1680BC to 1690/1660BC. But it seems clear now that the 14th Dynasty kings Seshi and Nehsy (and the associated deputy treasurer Aamu) belong to stratum F,[1463] and that this stratum therefore probably dates to (or includes) the second half of the 18th century BC.[1464] This resolves the problem of the ultra-low chronology. The resolution, not surprisingly, comes out midway between Dever's (1985) ultra-high dating and Bietak's (1979; 1984) ultra-low dating. In sum, the whole set of 'dates' now conventionally attached to the Tell

---

[1459] Mentioned in Bietak and Hein (n.d.). Date from Kitchen (1996b). This is more or less the mainstream date in scholarship today (after Luft 1992b). Krauss (1998b:118–120) continues to support a lower option, whereby the Sothic date for Sesostris year 7 would be c.1830BC, and so Sesostris year 5 c.1832BC. This position has not, however, attracted general support. See further in Appendix 1.

[1460] Bietak (1991a:52–53); Weinstein (1995:87).

[1461] With, for the sake of argument, the fall of Avaris and the end of the 15th Dynasty equated with Ahmose year 11, and the overall span of the 15th Dynasty rounded up to 109 years (after Ryholt 1997:186–188). The high chronology date comes from either Hayes (1970) or Wente and Van Siclen (1976), the middle chronology from Ryholt (1997) and von Beckerath (1997), and the low chronology from Kitchen (1996a). See also Table 3 and Appendix 1.

[1462] See Bietak (1979:234–237); cf. Dever (1985:77). The PhD thesis of B. Williams, submitted in 1975, is now available via the internet: **http://www-oi.uchicago.edu/OI/DEPT/RA/BBW/BBWIntro.html** Williams notes in his introduction to this 1999 internet release that his Kerma chronology must now be significantly revised.

[1463] Ryholt (1997:46).

[1464] Cf. Ryholt (1997:200 Table 39).

el-Dabᶜa later SIP strata need to be reviewed and reworked.[1465] The strata are probably both of significantly differing temporal spans, and the later strata occupy rather more of the second half of the SIP than previously thought, with strata H through E/2 having to fit into the close of the 12th Dynasty (late 19th century BC) to earlier 17th Century BC period. This presents no serious difficulty.[1466]

The evidence from Tell el-Dabᶜa does not invalidate the c.1628BC date for the eruption of Thera, and the 'early' Aegean chronology. Current *interpretation* at the site is, however, not compatible with the 'early' Aegean chronology.

1.c. Problem Issues: Science-Based Dating

At present, the radiocarbon evidence on short-lived sample matter from the volcanic destruction level at Akrotiri on Thera is the only scientific evidence definitely and directly relevant to the date of the eruption of Thera. This evidence clearly supports a 17th century BC date range, but does not rule out a mid-16th century BC range. A date after c.1530/1525BC is a non-starter. Almost everyone accepts this; those supporting the 'low' chronology merely choose to disregard it, or claim to sneak in within the extreme lowest range possible for the Thera radiocarbon dates. The other scientific evidence may be argued to provide a compelling circumstantial case, but is not directly and unequivocally relevant. Ice-core and tree-ring evidence may be cited to show that it is very unlikely that any large volcanic eruption (including therefore Thera) occurred in the second half of the 16th century BC, or the early 15th century BC (the former covering the date range offered by the conventional or 'low' chronology), and that a suitable volcanic eruption did occur in the later 17th century BC. But irrefutable positive evidence is lacking to date. The claim that the volcanic glass in one later 17th century BC ice-core layer was not Theran has been shown to be unsupported when due attention is paid to the measurement errors and range of values for Theran glass, but this does not necessarily mean that it is Theran either.

Radiocarbon probability, a consonant set of circumstantial ice-core and tree-ring evidence, and an 'early' interpretation of the archaeological evidence (and acceptance of the Tell el-ᶜAjjul Palace I WSI), all lead to the 'early' Aegean chronology. The less likely, but possible, mid-16th century BC radiocarbon range for Thera, and acceptance of the raised LMIA–LMIIIA1 archaeological chronology and the compatible radiocarbon evidence from Chania and Myrtos-Pyrgos, could, alternatively, lead to the 'compromise early' chronology. This is because the LMIB radiocarbon evidence merely sets a date range of c.1525–1490BC for the close of the LMIB period. Thus, if the LMIB period was short (as previously thought by some scholars – *but* cf. next section), then the late LMIA period could still lie in the mid 16th century BC. Only if the LMIA period is considered to be longer is an 'early' or 'high' date for LMIA necessary. The 'compromise early' chronology could be made to work with Tell el-ᶜAjjul, WSI, and the rest of the

---

[1465] Cf. previously Manning (1995:120–122).

[1466] And is more than possible within the uncertainties and margins of error proposed by Weinstein (1995).

archaeological evidence. If one wished to avoid conflict, and seek to make everyone happy, then the 'compromise early' chronology would seem the obvious way forward. The problematic requirement, however, is that the eruption of Thera would have to be considered a low sulphur yield episode with minimal climatic effect, since there is no evidence for a large climatically effective volcanic eruption in the northern hemisphere in the mid to later 16th century BC. Moreover, any compromise is by definition unlikely to be correct, merely the least painful option for a majority. The science-dating evidence, direct or circumstantial, is simply not compatible with the low chronology, and most certainly it is not compatible with the extreme low chronologies which place the eruption of Thera outside the possible radiocarbon date range (i.e. those who date the eruption c.1520BC or later).

2. The limited scope for a 'post-eruption-LMIA phase' and the importance of recognising an earlier phase of what seem to be long overall LMIB/LHIIA periods

An obvious issue for the 'early' chronology (especially) is what lies between mature LMIA and the eruption of Thera, and the evidence for mature LMIB from the time of the earlier 18th Dynasty. In the last decade a so-called 'post-eruption-LMIA phase' has been proposed to account for some or even quite a portion of this time-period by some scholars. However, as I shall discuss below, this appears to cover at best a relatively short interval. I instead propose that the apparent 'gap' is most plausibly filled by the earlier part of the LMIB and LHIIA periods. In this regard, it is important to recall that the LMIB connections with earlier 18th Dynasty Egypt are with mature LMIB as known from the destruction deposits at the close of the period on Crete, hence the majority of the period on Crete was earlier. Further, whereas the LMIB period was originally considered to be relatively brief, it is now apparent that it was of significant duration. This is the major difference between the 'early' Aegean chronology and the 'low' Aegean chronology.

The suggested importance of a 'post-eruption-LMIA phase' (late final LMIA phase elsewhere) in Crete and the southern Aegean has become apparent. Like the problematic final MBA (MBIIC or MBIII) Bichrome Ware phase in Syria–Palestine, this putative period of time is thought to be critical to the overall chronological construction, but is tricky to tie down in clear stratigraphic terms. The basic questions are how long is this period, and can it carry us through to the evidence of LMIB/LHIIA links with Egypt? Since existing LMIB/LHIIA evidence comes from the early 18th Dynasty, it would be convenient if this post-eruption final LMIA phase was quite long. The trouble is that the evidence from the Aegean does not appear consistent with a very long 'post-eruption-LMIA phase' of final LMIA. Anything over 50 years seems simply impossible. This is of course a subjective judgement, but one shared by many of the ceramic specialists of the period; and the main argument against a significant phase is our failure to find or identify it despite intensive fieldwork. We must be talking about a relatively brief, transitional (in stylistic terms) period. The eruption of Thera is undoubtedly more than a little responsible for this 'hidden' phase. A number of sites in the southern and eastern Aegean may have been directly affected by the eruption, and there is a general malaise in the wider area following the eruption, as argued in detail by Driessen and Macdonald.[1467]

While too much may be made of inherently anachronistic judgements of style, it is difficult to avoid the fact that the LMIA ceramics present at Akrotiri at the time of the eruption include mature to late LMIA features, and that there are few LMIA deposits found on Crete which display significantly different, or later, stylistic features, or developments within the LMIA fashion canon. The Akrotiri assemblage at the time of the eruption (Marthari 1990 Group A) very much goes with mature to later LMIA as known from Crete.[1468] At Kommos, a site with a high-quality and recently analysed sequence, the ceramic material from the Akrotiri VDL links with the Advanced into Final LMIA phases, and at most some or all of the Final LMIA phase follows the eruption of Thera (Shaw *et al.* 1997; n.d.). A period of a few decades seems the likely maximum allowance for this Final, post-eruption, LMIA phase.

Another decade or so of time may easily be slotted in (there are no certain or fixed rules or data which provide a timescale[1469]), but no more. Overall, these decades represent the difference between completely later, final, LMIA, and the still somewhat archaic overall package at Akrotiri on Thera. Included here also is the interval during which clearing, repair, and re-occupation occurred between the final earthquake at Akrotiri – which provides our major VDL assemblages – and the actual volcanic eruption. This may involve 'a period of several years', since there was some incipient soil formation.[1470] Such an overall interval further allows for the missing final phase of LHI at Akrotiri, and also the supposed overlap of earliest LHIIA with latest LMIA.[1471]

However, a period of 50+ years would have left more trace, and would have been stratigraphically identified by now. The tephra falls found at Mochlos on Crete and Trianda on Rhodes, and the generally likely correlation of the eruption of Thera with an earthquake or related disruption on Crete,[1472] are all placed in the late LMIA period (even at its very end by some, cf. discussion in Chapter IV.1 above). Other indications all seem to combine to point to a relatively short interval between the eruption and the start of the LMIB period, such as: (i) arguments for evidence of what could be considered as proto-LMIB stylistic consciousness (or similar) already at Akrotiri in wall paintings,[1473] or (ii) the same via the famous later LMIA table of offerings found at Akrotiri on Thera with its Marine Style scene,[1474] or, (iii) in reverse, arguments that

---

[1467] Driessen and Macdonald (1997); see also Rehak and Younger (1998a:100, 149).

[1468] Betancourt (1985:133); Popham (1990:27); Niemeier (1979b; 1980); Marthari (1990:61–65); Warren and Hankey (1989:75).

[1469] Contra Popham (1990).

[1470] Limbrey (1990:esp.380).

[1471] See Warren and Hankey (1989:97–98). To date there is a lack of clear stratigraphic support if the contexts referred to are examined. One might, however, note again the bridge-spouted jar with a decoration consisting of double axes and dotted crosses from Akrotiri which must be very close to LHIIA in stylistic date (Marthari 1990:64 and fig.8; see Figure 15). This supports the early LHIIA/late LMIA overlap, *but* this is at the expense of much of the supposed post-eruption LMIA phase before this overlap begins (contra Warren 1990/1991:30 and fig.3 who tries to have both).

[1472] Advocated by Hood (1978c); see also Macdonald (1990).

[1473] Morgan (1984).

[1474] Marinatos (1968–1976, Vol. V:pls.C, 25 and 102); Doumas (1992:180, pls.142–144).

the LMIB Marine Style palatial pottery merely represents a new manifestation of the LMIA palatial art tradition in other media and cannot have been too far removed in temporal terms,[1475] or (iv) arguments for a relatively short interval between the eruption and the next LMIB phase because Middle Cycladic III–Late Cycladic I (pre-eruption) jugs were still in existence to be deposited at Myrtos-Pyrgos on Crete in an LMIB context,[1476] and because tephra and pumice from the eruption is found also in LMIB/LHIIA contexts, or (v) the evidence (despite some problems of details) from archaeomagnetic measurements which suggests a relatively short time interval between the eruption of Thera and the LMIB destructions on Crete.[1477]

We therefore appear to be discussing a period or phase which is not a major distinct entity, but rather something which must be accommodated within a final late LMIA phase, and a period of perhaps a few decades to at most 50 years, and not significantly longer. Warren and Hankey (1989:215) and Warren (1990/1991:35–36) allowed c.50 years (two 'generations') for this final, post-Theran-eruption, LMIA phase, and this seems a total maximum time interval, and one with which many in the field would be uneasy. The overall length of the LMIA period is a related issue. Its length has been quietly growing over the last generation of scholarship. It was originally about 50 years,[1478] or perhaps up to about three generations or c.70 years.[1479] But, with the recognition of SIP material at Akrotiri, the period was stretched out to a century or even 120 years in the 1980s.[1480] Even with a total period of 100–120 years duration, the implication of a supposed 50+ years post-Thera-eruption phase of final LMIA is that the end of Akrotiri must be placed about halfway through the overall LMIA period. This is exactly what Warren did in his 1990/1991 study:[1481] post-eruption LMIA became about half the total LMIA period! Such a chronology strikes many scholars of the period as implausible given the fact that the Akrotiri assemblage includes many vessels comparable with late or final LMIA assemblages elsewhere (and even a hint of LHIIA). It is true that the impressive nature and quantity of finds at Akrotiri have rather tended to define mature, or late, LMIA, and elsewhere in the absence of deposit-forming destruction episodes other later material may well exist, but allowing half the overall LMIA period for this post-eruption phase appears to be significantly overdoing it. One might indeed contrast the discussion of Warren and Hankey (1989:72–78) themselves, and especially their view on p.75, having discussed the Theran VDL later LMIA assemblage, that 'we cannot yet detect within or outside Crete a clear LMIA deposit *subsequent* to this stage. Moreover, some of the LMIA reed style stemmed cups or cup-rhyta are closely similar to those of LMIB'. Warren (1998) in his most recent publication on the subject has indeed retreated

---

[1475] Driessen and Macdonald (1997:62–63).

[1476] Cadogan (1984). Warren (1990/1991:36 and n.41) notes also 'the similarity of much of the destruction pottery of LMIB Gournia to that of LMIA Thera', *but* it is in fact quite plausible that the vases in question derive from an LMIA destruction horizon at Gournia, prior to the final LMIB destruction which is represented only in some parts of the site (Driessen and Macdonald 1997:22 n.2, 213–215).

[1477] Downey and Tarling (1984); Tarling and Downey (1990); cf. Evans and Mareschal (1988).

[1478] E.g. Cadogan (1978:210).

[1479] Hankey and Warren (1974:Table 3); Niemeier (1985:Fig.65).

[1480] Warren (1985:151); Warren and Hankey (1989:169 Table 3.1).

[1481] Warren (1990/1991:Fig.5).

markedly from his earlier positions; the eruption of Thera is now placed c.1520BC and the LMIA/LMIB transition c.1525–1490BC. Hence the previously long post-eruption phase is reduced to a possible range of –5 years to +30 years.

If we arbitrarily consider a maximum post-eruption-LMIA phase of c.30 years, what then fills the time period from here to mature LMIB and LHIIA by about the time of Amenhotep I/Tuthmosis I? For the 'early' chronology, the period at issue is the first half of the 16th century BC. Is this some insuperable problem for a longer LMI chronology? I do not believe so. Post-eruption LMIA may be limited to a couple of decades, however, I suggest that what really needs attention are the earlier LMIB and LHIIA periods. With mature LMB and later LHIIA being deposited in Egypt in the first few decades of the 18th Dynasty, it is a reasonable conclusion that earlier LMIB and LHIIA were contemporary with the last several decades of the SIP. There is at present no real control on this overlap (i.e. no data), hence it is potentially flexible enough to cover the gap between the end of the post-eruption final LMIA period, and the mature LMIB/late LHIIA period in the first few decades of the 18th Dynasty.

This is an important issue. Let us consider it in a little detail. If 1628BC is regarded as being the most likely date for the eruption of Thera, as argued in Chapters IV and V, then, at face value, it appears difficult to accommodate the 1628BC eruption date, and the pattern of Aegean correlation data, with the Egyptian chronology which does not begin the 18th Dynasty until c.1550 or c.1540BC, *unless* something can be found to stretch between mature LMIA at 1628BC, and mature LMIB by some point in the first one to four decades of the 18th Dynasty. The Egyptian chronology requires an interval of around a century between these points. But we have determined that a long post-Thera-eruption final phase of LMIA is not available as the primary answer. This post-eruption final LMIA phase probably gets us no further than c.1600BC, or at the very most c.1580BC. What about the missing 50–70 or so years? We must, as suggested above, consider the early LMIB/LHIIA periods. Mature LMIB and late LHIIA products were available for deposit in Egypt during the reigns of the first two (to three) kings of the 18th Dynasty (Saqqara and Memphis), and possibly even as early as the late Hyksos period (Abydos). This does imply that the preceding earlier LMIB and earlier LHIIA periods were contemporary with the later Hyksos period. As discussed below, it is now clear that the LMIB period overall was relatively long – perhaps as long as, or longer than, the LMIA period. Betancourt (1998b:293) states that 'it must surely be well over a century'. Hence it is quite feasible that the poorly known early LMIB and early LHIIA periods might resolve the tension above, and offer a (so far not attested) correlation in the time range from the early through mid 16th century BC. The LMIB period seems to end c.1525–1490BC; a century or so duration would therefore take us nicely to c.1600BC and the end of the post-eruption-LMIA phase.

Therefore, the major change involved, if one is seriously to consider the 'early' Aegean chronology, is the length of the LMIB period. I have quoted one opinion for a long phase, but this now requires some substantiation. The history of the supposedly short LMIB period began with the excavations of Evans at Knossos. Neither LMIB contexts nor material were well represented in his excavations at Knossos, and he accorded it a half century, from the beginning of the 15th century BC, parallel with the reign of Tuthmosis III, on the basis of correlations.[1482] This lack of a clear stratified sequence at the Palace of Knossos led also to the debates earlier this century over the stylistic phase's exact stratigraphic relationship vis à vis LMIA and LMII. Elsewhere, the LMIB period was recognised from a fairly homogeneous horizon of destructions marking the (often violent) close of the phase.[1483] Since there was relatively little evidence of stylistic variation in these close of LMIB assemblages, the art-historical approach led to the view that this was a short phase with just one or two generations of potters at work. Thus some scholars allotted as little as 25 years, or a 'generation'.[1484]

However, there is now a growing body of evidence indicating that the phase must have been rather longer, and that previous estimates relate only to the final mature part of the overall LMIB period. Judging the length of ceramic and architectural phases from relative criteria is, of course, difficult and subjective, but the indications of several building phases within LMIB, and the sheer quantity of LMIB ceramic material, would suggest that the period is quite long, and very possibly 'longer than LMIA'.[1485] Evidence from recent excavations at Palaikastro, for example, indicates that several building horizons and two separate fire destructions exist within LMIB.[1486] New work at Pseira likewise has revealed several building phases within the LMIB period.[1487] And, at Kommos, up to three building/stratigraphic phases within a long LMIB period exist in places (especially room 2 of House X: Shaw and Shaw 1993: 145–147), and, in general, two phases of LMIB are recognised in the ceramic-stratigraphic record (Jeremy B. Rutter, pers. comm.). Outside Crete, the evidence for a substantial LMIB period is also clear. At Ayia Irini on Keos, Period VIIa is an 'early' LMIB/LHIIA phase not well attested at sites excavated on Crete until the 1980s onwards. This in turn seems a little earlier than a 'comparatively early stage'[1488] of LMIB deposit found at Kastri on Kythera (deposits kappa and lambda).[1489] Both Kastri and Ayia Irini each then have major later LMIB phases, marked by the Marine Style and Alternating Style ceramics.[1490] An impression is given of a significant overall chronological span. Moreover, it is an impression which shows that the classic LMIB destruction deposit material from the sites on Crete is representative only of the final phase of the period.

It is the same classic LMIB, or later LHIIA, material from the final phases of these periods which correlates with the earlier 18th Dynasty. Earlier LMIB/LHIIA lies before

---

[1482] Evans (1921–1935, vol.IV:881).

[1483] E.g. Page (1970:1–8); Niemeier (1985:175–180); Warren (1990/1991); Manning (1994:247–251); Driessen and Macdonald (1997); Rehak and Younger (1998a:148–149).

[1484] E.g. Warren (1985:150); Popham (1990). Such views influenced, and were taken into account, by Manning (1988b:57).

[1485] Betancourt (1998b:293). This finding is significant also in terms of the politics and history of Crete and the Aegean in the New Palace period: on which, see e.g. Wiener (1990); Hägg and Marinatos (1984); Driessen and Macdonald (1997); Rehak and Younger (1998a).

[1486] See e.g. MacGillivray *et al.* (1991:123–132).

[1487] Betancourt *et al.* (1995).

[1488] Coldstream and Huxley (1972:126).

[1489] See Schofield (1984:181 with refs.).

[1490] Schofield (1984:181).

this. Material and contexts of this time are not well known on Crete (work in the 1990s is changing this situation). This is partly because the late LMIA disruptions evident in Crete, which were probably associated with the effects of the Theran eruption, appear to have had a profound effect in particular parts of Crete where a number of LMIA sites were not occupied in LMIB, and/or parts of sites were abandoned.[1491] However, this silence does not mean that a real temporal period did not occur – even a significant one – simply that there is no clear record of architecture and material culture discard. Earlier LMIB phases at some sites on Crete and at sites elsewhere in the Aegean clearly provide evidence of this chronological timespan. This earlier LMIB and earlier LHIIA period can comfortably fill the first half of the 16th century BC.

A great deal happened in the LMIB period; from the recovery after the late LMIA disruptions in Crete and especially the east Aegean, to the creation of new trade routes and partners following the obliteration of what seems to have been the major international port of the LMIA Aegean at Akrotiri on Thera, through several phases of building at several sites with material respectively from early through mature LMIB, to the well known late LMIB horizon. This mature, or late, LMIB phase seems in Egyptian terms to have stretched from Ahmose/Amenhotep I (/Tuthmosis I) through to about the beginning of the reign of Tuthmosis III. This is already some c.25 to 70 years; earlier LMIB may plausibly be regarded as at least as long in duration. The emergence of signs such as a 'special palatial tradition' in the ceramics of later LMIB[1492] indicate new forms of display and distinction by the élite of Crete. Indeed, the LMIB period is notable for such attempts by the élite on Crete to create a status 'propaganda'.[1493] At the same time, mainland centres start to imitate and emulate the LMIB ceramic styles, and vessels of their 'palatial' style are often nearly indistinguishable.[1494] This process will have taken time. It further signals not only the importance of LMIB Crete as the old regional core in the Aegean 'world system', but also the probable origins of its eventual collapse, since the Mycenaean mainland had the resources to overtake and out-compete the polities of Crete. The rise of rival mainland states may have increased competition within the polities/palaces of Crete, and led to the struggles which saw Knossos emerge in LMII–IIIA as the single, dominant, centre of most of central and west Crete.

3. Proposed Conclusions

i.   1628BC = the Thera eruption. 1628BC is (or remains) the most likely date for the eruption of Thera. It is potentially compatible with all the scientific *and* archaeological evidence. Definitive proof is still lacking, but a strong circumstantial case exists from several independent data sources. In reverse, the

---

[1491] See the review of the LMI period, and the site descriptions, in Driessen and Macdonald (1997).
[1492] Betancourt (1985:140–148).
[1493] Driessen and Macdonald (1997:35–83).
[1494] Mountjoy (1993:41–52); Niemeier (1985).

scientific evidence is explicitly *not* compatible with an eruption date anywhere between c.1525–1479BC, and there is no scientific evidence for any major volcanic eruption in the northern hemisphere across the whole period from c.1560–1479BC.

The main archaeological data which have been argued to oppose this view – the first appearance of WSI pottery, the Aegeanising frescoes at Tell el-Dabᶜa in Egypt, the finds of Theran pumice at Tell el-Dabᶜa (and elsewhere) – have each been shown not to provide good contrary evidence (and in fact to quite possibly offer compatible data). The one recent argument from science-dating evidence against this position – the paper of Zielinski and Germani (1998a) concerning the volcanic glass shards from the c.1623±36BC layer of the GISP2 ice-core from Greenland – has been shown to have based its views on selective comparanda and to have failed to consider the relevance of the stated measurement errors and the variability in the respective data (GISP2 and Thera), and between microprobe measurement suites. When a more realistic comparison is made, this c.1623±36BC volcanic glass *could* be compatible with Theran glass. Alternatively, the problematic dating of the GISP2 ice-core at this time, and its lack of correlation with the Dye 3 and GRIP ice-cores, render the negative case of Zielinski and Germani as likely irrelevant to a mid–later 17th century BC Thera eruption date.

The testing, and so confirmation, or negation, of this hypothesis is now a priority for Aegean and east Mediterranean prehistory. This may be anticipated via two routes. First, the identification of further volcanic glass in ice-cores, which may be comprehensively shown to originate, or not to originate, specifically from the Thera eruption, allied with continuing greater refinement of the accuracy and precision of the dating of the second millennium BC ice-core layers. The c.1636BC and c.1644BC layers of the GRIP and Dye 3 ice-cores are priority targets in this regard. Analysis is underway and results are expected during AD2000 (Claus Hammer, pers. comm.). However, eventually, an analysis must be made of all the ice-core layers covering the period c.1700–1450BC. Once all possibly relevant years have been assessed, and the volcanic glass potentially compatible with Theran glass within measurement errors is rigorously analysed to create a proper field of values, and rare earth and trace element analysis is conducted to refine provenance possibilities to a specific match, then we should know the date of the Thera eruption within the dating errors of the various ice-cores. If this date is consonant with the 1628BC tree-ring evidence, then we may have a precise date, if not, we may never have a date exact to the year. A decision between the later 17th century BC and the mid-16th century BC should, however, be possible. News is expected soon (above). This will provide a key test of the archaeological case developed in this book. A 17th century BC date is expected following my analysis. The only other viable possibility (same relative chronology but compressed) is a mid-16th century BC date ('compromise early' chronology). A date later than this (and the low or conventional relative chronology) should be impossible.

Second, dendrochronology may in time be able to offer further direct data, both through the identification of specifically volcanic signals in tree-ring series via elemental analysis, and, with luck, through the eventual discovery of a tree datable by dendrochronology[1495] which was demonstrably killed by the Thera eruption, and buried under the pumice on Thera, or elsewhere. Promising sounding samples have been discovered in the past.[1496] The bark would date the eruption within 0–1 years. It is also possible that tree-remains buried/killed elsewhere in the Aegean due to the associated seismic activity or tidal waves could offer relevant and precise dates.[1497]

ii. The mature–later LMIA ceramic period – as found in the VDL at Akrotiri – includes the date 1628BC. Whether there were just several years, or a few decades, between the abandonment of Akrotiri and the 'end' of the LMIA period is not clear at present. The missing last phase of LHI at Akrotiri, the slightly 'archaic' look of the assemblage from Akrotiri as a whole, and the apparent post-eruption LMIA horizon identified at Phylakopi on Melos, all suggest the possibility of a potentially significant interval with a 'post-eruption-LMIA phase' (of a few decades), but such a horizon has not yet been stratigraphically defined (see discussion above). New evidence from Kommos would, however, suggest its existence. A wide scholarly consensus agrees that an interval longer than a few decades is not possible. A date of c.1600BC, and at latest c.1580BC, is probably a reasonable and convenient approximation for the end of the overall LMIA phase.

iii. The LMIB period ends c.1525–1490BC. The LMIB period ended both by c.1525–1490BC in absolute terms (radiocarbon *and* archaeological evidence), or around the beginning of the reign of Tuthmosis III in relative terms (the pattern of finds and the earlier Keftiu representations are most easily explained if the LMIB phase at least overlaps with the start of Tuthmosis III's reign). The period probably began in the first half of the 16th century BC, plausibly c.1600/1580BC. The stylistically late LHIIA cup from a context dated to the very early 18th Dynasty, somewhere between the reigns of Ahmose and Amenhotep I (to Tuthmosis I), at Saqqara (Chapter IV.7 above) would certainly imply that LHIIA, and LMIB, began during the later Hyksos period (and the context of the LMIB sherd at Abydos can be interpreted most easily in a consonant fashion).

The LMIB evidence leads to one point of potential conflict between Aegean and Egyptian chronology (see also Appendix 1). The evidence from Saqqara, tied with the radiocarbon data and analysis in Housley *et al.* (1999) which was summarised in Chapter V.1, and the radiocarbon evidence from Jericho, creates some problems for the Egyptian 'low' chronology. Muhly (1998:212) appraised the situation in these terms: '...it seems to me that the new Aegean chronology is on a collision course with what passes for Egyptian chronology. One of them has to be wrong.' This is over-doing it, but there are some problems. The radiocarbon

---

[1495] Or high-precision radiocarbon wiggle-matching: see example of Sparks *et al.* (1995).

[1496] See Mamet (1874); Fouqué (1879:114, 120, 121, 129; 1999:114, 120, 121, 129) referring first to charcoal which he identifies as pine, second to 'decomposed organic material in which bits of straw and large numbers of pieces of wood are still recognizable', third to the 'trunk of an olive tree more than two metres long, with several branches', and fourth to 'the abundance of pieces of olive wood ... found in the ruins of Therasia and Akrotiri'; Olson and Broecker (1959:20, L-362); Luce (1969:63–64); Rackham (1978:758; 1990:388) referring to Mamet's report of the oak stump.

[1497] Cf. Yamaguchi *et al.* (1997).

evidence from Chania and Myrtos-Pyrgos, and also the other relevant data from Mochlos, Knossos, and Kommos (see Chapter V.1), provide a good case for an 'early' chronology, with the close of the LMIB period c.1525–1490BC. A date much lower is very unlikely. *If* the traditional arguments for linking at least some part of the timespan of the LMIB period with the reign of Tuthmosis III are considered valid (and this is a long-held view by many scholars),[1498] then the currently popular 'low' Egyptian chronology which places the accession of Tuthmosis III in 1479BC is barely compatible (even with the lowest feasible construction of the radiocarbon data). In contrast, the older, 'high', Egyptian chronologies which placed the accession of Tuthmosis III in 1504BC, or 1490BC, would be nicely compatible (and it may be noted that the 1504BC date best suits the available lunar evidence[1499]). I realise this runs contrary to the recent pronouncements of the dead-reckoners of the palimpsest of Egyptian chronological data who regard c.1479BC as absolute, but one may note that in his recent review of Egyptian absolute chronology Wiener (1998:315–317) regards the c.1490BC date, and the linked choice of 1290BC for the accession of Ramesses II, as still 'conceivable'.[1500] Ward (1992:59) likewise points out that the c.1279BC date for Ramesses II rests only on rhetoric and conjecture, and that 1290BC remains feasible. As already noted in Chapter V.1, I do not regard this (11–25 year shift) as an insuperable hurdle if one is critical and realistic about the available Egyptian evidence (see Appendix 1).

iv. The LMIIIA1 period began during the middle–later years of the reign of Tuthmosis III in relative terms, shown particularly by the Aegean design fashions recorded on the kilts in the paintings (or re-paintings) of Keftiu in the Menkheperraseneb and Rekhmire tombs. This now appears widely accepted,[1501] and is not a controversial view.

Thus, irrespective of the Thera question, the LMIB–LMIIIA1 evidence has been found to require a raised, or 'early', Aegean chronology for these periods. This is an important conclusion, and a major revision of the conventional views of the last generation of scholarship. It might be held in general also to favour the 'early' chronology for the LMIA period, but the two matters are in many ways discrete. In principle, the raised LMIB–LMIIIA1 chronology could go with either the 'early' or 'compromise early' dates for the LMIA period. The former is consistent with the range of science-dating evidence, the latter with the conventional interpretation of WSI, Tell el-Dabʿa, and the Egyptian low chronology. The 'low' chronology is the only definite casuality.

v. The LHIIIA2 period was underway by, or just before, the early 14th century BC at the latest, or by the early part of the reign of Amenhotep III. The general chronology of LHIIIA2 has been recently reviewed by Wiener (1998), and he offers dates for the period from 1390/70BC to 1320/00BC. These both raise and lengthen the

---

[1498] Re-stated most recently by Warren (1998:328): '...a number of finds link LMIB/LHIIA with Tuthmosis III'.

[1499] Casperson (1986).

[1500] Following Kitchen (1987:40–41).

[1501] Even to an extent by Warren (1996:288; 1998:328).

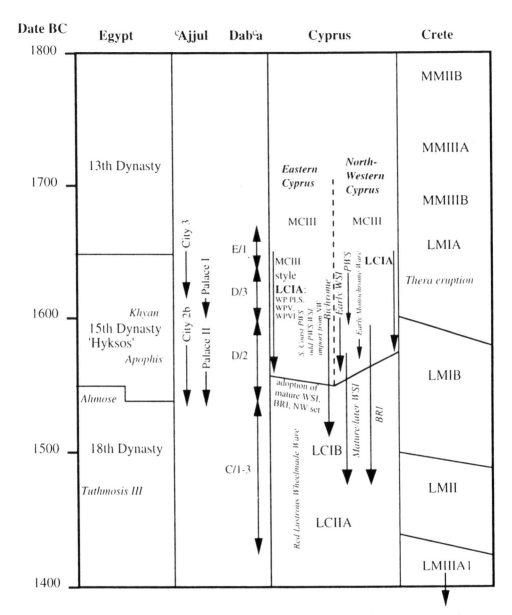

Fig. 62. Proposed 'early' Aegean chronology for the mid-second millennium BC and its east Mediterranean context. (Same as Fig. 36)

     period from the 1370/60BC to 1340/30BC dates in the conventional chronology of Warren and Hankey (1989:169 Table 3.1).

vi. The sum of these explorations and findings is support for a new chronology for the earlier Aegean LBA. The low, or conventional, chronology is shown to be incorrect

– that is too low and compressed – for the LMIB through LMIIIA1 periods. Moreover, the balance of probabilities favours an 'early' and long chronology for the LMIA through LMIB periods, although a 'compromise early' chronology is also possible. Final resolution between these two possibilities seems likely to come in the near future from the positive identification of Theran eruption volcanic glass in a Greenland ice-core. In general terms, the ideas and hypotheses behind the 'early' chronologies of Kemp and Merrillees (1980), Betancourt (1987), and Manning (1988b) have been found to be largely correct. However, it is also clear that these authors were a little over-enthusiastic (or polemical) in these initial works (mea culpa). This has already been noted and discussed.[1502] For the MMIII–LMIA periods, even critics had to concede that 'it is important to stress that the renewed investigations of the traditional synchronisms of the MMIII/LMIA material have shown the contexts – both the Egyptian/Near Eastern and Aegean – so dubious that a revised high chronology for the beginning of the LMIA is possible'.[1503] The early problems centered on LMIB. The arguments for a start date for the LMIB period before the reign of Tuthmosis III, and at least in the early 18th Dynasty (and probably the later SIP), have proved correct, with archaeological confirmation at Kom Rabiᶜa and Saqqara. But, in their first publications, Betancourt (1987) and Manning (1988b) were too sweeping in their choice of closing dates. Manning (1988b:57) noted that he was unclear on this border, and offered a 'blurred' boundary. Nonetheless, the attempt to end LMIB completely before the reign of Tuthmosis III was a mistake (and was the crux of the refusal of many scholars to accept or seriously to consider the early chronology when first proposed[1504]). As discussed in Manning (1995:217–229), it is clear that the LMIB period continued up to around, or into, at least the first years of Tuthmosis III. Nonetheless, new analysis (of textile patterns) confirms the views of Betancourt (1987) and Manning (1988b) that the LMIIIA1 period began before the end of the reign of Tuthmosis III. Thus the end of the LMIB period, the entire LMII period, and the beginning of the LMIIIA1 period, must all be accommodated within Tuthmosis III's long (54 year) reign.

For a proposed chronological scheme for the Aegean and east Mediterranean in the mid-second millennium BC, see Figure 62. Approximate dates for the LMI–IIIA1 periods are suggested as follows:

> LMIA c.1675±BC to c.1600/1580BC
> LMIB c.1600/1580BC to c.1500/1490BC
> LMII c.1500/1490BC to c.1440/1425BC
> LMIIIA1 c.1440/1425BC to c.1390/1370BC.

How this proposal stands the 'test of time' remains to be seen.[1505] I have no doubt that the judgement of Sir Charles Darwin (1886:422–423) will prove valid: 'any one whose disposition leads him to attach more weight to unexplained difficulties than to the explanation of a certain number of facts will certainly reject the theory'.

[1502] Manning (1991; 1995:217–229); Manning *et al.* (1994a:222–225).
[1503] Hallager (1988:12).
[1504] E.g. Dickinson (1994:18).
[1505] The analagous concept of the test of time for art is discussed in Savile (1982).

Chapter VII. Some implications, and the problem of dating Alalakh VII

As argued in an article of 1988, the eruption of Thera is potentially a pivotal event in Mediterranean history.[1506] If an absolute date is given, it may become the basis of the chronology and history of the Aegean and eastern Mediterranean for the couple of surrounding centuries. The general relative cultural sequences are now becoming increasingly clear in the immediate archaeological periods: the Aegean LMIA period corresponds with the late MBII world of greater Canaan (which includes SIP Delta Egypt) and the LCIA period of Cyprus; the Aegean LMIB period corresponds with the later SIP (second half of the 15th/Hyksos Dynasty) and then the early 18th Dynasty down to the first years of Tuthmosis III. This is a revision of previous syntheses, but only a fairly minor one. Moreover, this revision is *independent* of the arguments for the 1628BC Thera eruption date. An LMIA–SIP overlap had already been noted. I have merely argued that this is in fact the main characteristic of the LMIA period in terms of its east Mediterranean associations. The main social, economic, and cultural parameters are thus set, and the big picture in terms of trading, political, and socio-cultural systems may be described across the east Mediterranean to Aegean regions within this broad chronological framework.[1507] However, the potential of an absolute and specific date for the eruption of Thera, along with the development of a precise Aegean dendrochronology,[1508] raises the opportunity to try to begin to go beyond the recognition of broad cultural horizons. It may be possible to approach a chronology and archaeology of near historical scale, and so move beyond the previous limitations of chronology in the prehistoric Aegean towards a proto-historic time-frame in which individual agency, scale, and resolution are taken into consideration.[1509]

The outcome of the discussions in Chapters IV, V and VI is that the working hypothesis must now be a date of 1628BC for the LMIA eruption of Thera, and that there is evidence from the subsequent LMIB–LMIIIA1 periods in favour of a

---

[1506] Manning (1988b).
[1507] For such macro-scale analysis, see e.g. Sherratt and Sherratt (1998; 1991).
[1508] Kuniholm *et al.* (1996); Kuniholm (1996a).
[1509] For discussion, see Manning (1998c).

compatible 'early', and long, LBA chronology. The only possible, but I argue less likely, alternative for the Thera eruption is a date in the mid-16th century BC (which I have termed the 'compromise early' chronology). It is therefore time to begin to consider the impact of the early Aegean LBA chronology, and, at a total minimum, the 'compromise early' chronology. It does not relate merely to the Aegean, and should not be a debate only among Aegean archaeologists. Rather than simple rejection on the *a priori* grounds of convention, engagement is now required from those working in surrounding regions. As already discussed in detail in Chapter IV, two obvious extensions of the Aegean chronology are immediately available: first to Cyprus, and second to Syria–Palestine and Delta Egypt, and the site of Tell el-Dabᶜa in particular. Another relevant topic is, of course, Egyptian chronology, and, apart from a few comments expressed already, some discussion on this topic may be found in Appendix 1. However, many other long-standing debates in eastern Mediterranean archaeology and history are also affected, and are relevant. It is not possible here to review all of these. Indeed, it is impossible to envisage any one scholar today being able to write a study of the scale of Schaeffer's (1948) monumental *Stratigraphie comparée*. Thus I have instead chosen merely to review one major long-standing debate in second millennium BC west Asian chronology, which in turn links to several other issues (Babylonian chronology, Hittite chronology, Bichrome Ware, etc.), as an example, or case study, concerning some of the many issues and problems: the chronology of level VII of the site of Alalakh.

Other, and further, considerations of the effects, modifications, and relations of the 'early' Thera eruption date, and the early and long Aegean LBA chronology, must await discussion at another time. In general terms, one of the main objections to this new chronology has merely been the *apparent* 'violence' of the changes involved; major changes to convention are always difficult. The all-purpose argument that one cannot change anything as it must necessarily affect everything, and so 'convention', was immediately mounted against attempts to suggest an 'early' date for the eruption of Thera: 'a principal difficulty with introducing a radically different chronology is its "push-me-pull-you" effect'.[1510] This 'violence' is the sort of thing only a violent, unintelligible, barbarian would attempt against the established order, civilisation, and tradition of the Aegean and east Mediterranean.[1511] However, we must not be strait-jacketed by convention, by structures of our own making through the weight of tradition. Instead, we must examine the data and their analysis, and seek especially to consider as much independent data as possible. It is time to reconsider convention, to contemplate a paradigm-shift.

In fact, when one considers the issues – instead of just the labels and the numbers conventionally associated with them – the 'violence' required is more apparent than

---

[1510] Cadogan (1987).

[1511] Of course, an interesting feature of the original classical Greek 'barbarian' of the 5th century BC is that this is a relative classification entirely invented by the 'civilised' Greeks themselves, forming an oppositional definition by which the Greeks used another group, and anti-familiar, anti-'in'-group, anti-tradition, anti-convention, criteria to define their own 'civilisation' (Hall 1989; Hall 1997:45–47).

real. In the Aegean and its directly related areas, some important changes are necessary, but little else is involved which is revolutionary. Further, the argument that change is impossible collapses if the nature of the proposed change is actually examined. To say that one cannot make a big change and upset everything, since it is not possible for 'everything' to move because it would cause the world as we know it to end, is simply not true. At the upper end, what is necessary includes:

(i)   The shortening of the MM period. This is a period now widely accepted as lacking a solid, indeed any, absolute chronology towards its end, and is, overall, a period which has recently been significantly re-worked and re-understood in relative terms on Crete through the studies of MacGillivray and Momigliano.[1512]

(ii)   A shortening of the overall MC period. Again, the later MC period has long lacked coherence, or indeed a definable stratigraphic existence, and quite a bit of what is termed late MC-style pottery is in fact LCIA in date. The transition in northwest Cyprus may be placed in the earlier to mid-17th century BC.

(iii)   A reworking of the artificial chronology of Tell el-Dabᶜa by admitting a little 'natural' flexibility.[1513] And, in particular, to regard the D/3 and especially D/2 strata as being representative of longer time periods (and again it is all too evident that the 'chronology' of the late MBII period in Syria–Palestine is a controversial subject beset with rival or differing interpretations of ambiguous evidence[1514]).

(iv)   A *possible* case for a slightly 'higher' Egyptian chronology for the New Kingdom (by c.11 or 25 years). As noted in Chapter III, and again below in the study on Alalakh, this is independent of Old Babylonian chronology. The latter may be 'low', and the former 'high'. Although current consensus in Egyptian chronology is undoubtedly against a high chronology of the New Kingdom, the high chronology remains *feasible* (see Appendix 1). Moreover, while it is suggested that a slightly higher 18th Dynasty chronology would be more compatible with the radiocarbon evidence from Crete, and would better fit with the 'early' Aegean LB1 chronology, it is *not* necessary, *nor* a linked determinant. The combination of a few decades of a post-Thera-eruption final phase of LMIA, followed by earlier LMIB and LHIIA periods contemporary with the later Hyksos period, contains sufficient flexibility to co-ordinate with any of the low, middle, or high Egyptian chronologies.

In other words, the whole set of the MMIII, MCIII, and later Syro-Palestinian MBII periods are already problematic; Thera may help sort out a mess, and clarify thinking. They do not provide obstacles! Egyptian chronology is of course more difficult. Here many scholars believe we are dealing with near certain information. But the evidence is not so definite as sometimes claimed, and the necessary degree of flexibility (variously either c.11 or at most 25 years) remains (see Appendix 1). Further, nothing in pre- and proto-history can be expected to work perfectly given the types of data

---

[1512] MacGillivray (1986; 1998); Momigliano (1989; 1991).

[1513] See Chapter VI above. See also Weinstein (1995:85) for some pertinent observations.

[1514] Contrast Kempinski (1983; 1992b); Dever (1985; 1992); Bietak (1984; 1991).

available. If the eruption of Thera best offers a firm, precise, and independent absolute date, then other slightly flexible chronological constructs will have to fit in with Thera, and not the reverse.

The lower end is perhaps a little more difficult, because we think we know more about these periods, and that they are therefore more chronologically concrete. We do well, however, to remember the caution of French (1963:44):

> The very considerable quantity of Mycenaean pottery which has been discovered in the Mediterranean area and the studies of it which have been published in the last twenty-five years have produced the impression that Mycenaean pottery is 'well-known'. Indeed, such pottery is, on the whole, easily recognized but there is often great difficulty in dating it.

If one reflects for a minute, there is in fact still a reasonable degree of flexibility in our present state of knowledge. The start of the LHIIIB period in Egyptian terms remains highly problematic.[1515] LHIIIA2 ceramics characterise a 14th century BC, 'Amarna period', horizon in the eastern Mediterranean contemporary with the reigns of Amenhotep III through Akhenaten (and perhaps later).[1516] However, LHIIIB (early) ceramics were present at Amarna according to some specialists,[1517] although other experts dispute this.[1518] Needless to say, this fashion/style border is inherently fuzzy as most earlier LHIIIB motifs were also employed in LHIIIA2.[1519] And, notwithstanding, it is not clear whether this evidence (if accepted) belongs just to a last phase of use of Amarna during the reign of Tutankhamun,[1520] or to the main phase under Akhenaten. Some LHIIIB pottery was also found at Kamid el-Loz (Kumidi) in a context which is probably/possibly datable to Akhenaten. Thus there is a good half century of flexibility. In addition, there is dendrochronological evidence to consider. A sequence consisting of wood from the hull frame, and one small piece of cedar wood which was cargo/firewood/dunnage, on the spectacular Uluburun shipwreck[1521] can be matched with the Aegean Dendrochronology Project Bronze Age-Iron Age master chronology: see Figure 63.[1522] The cargo wood has a final preserved ring equivalent to relative ring 1177. On the basis of the absolute chronology proposed in Kuniholm *et*

[1515] See summary and references in Warren and Hankey (1989:149–154); and the discussion of Wiener (1998:311–315).

[1516] E.g. sites and finds summarised by Hennessy (1997:352–354); Wiener (1998).

[1517] Hankey (1981); Warren and Hankey (1989:149–151, figs.8–9); Hankey and Aston (1995:69); Hankey (1997).

[1518] E. French (pers. comm.); see also Wiener (1998:311–312).

[1519] On the chronology of LHIIIB, see recently Thomas (1992:esp.460–510).

[1520] And indeed, it is possible that one of the Amarna letters (EA16) from Assur-uballit I of Assyria was addressed to Ay (as king), successor of Tutankhamun (Moran 1992:39 n.1). How this would be at Amarna is not obvious. Amarna was by now the abandoned capital according to the conventional Egyptian history – unless the abandonment of the city did not really (or completely) occur until the reign of Haremhab, who clearly separated and distinguished himself from the group of rulers from Amenhotep III through Ay?

[1521] Bass (1987); Bass *et al.* (1989); Pulak (1997).

[1522] This figure revises the previously published match shown in Kuniholm (1996b:Fig.7). See next footnote for explanation.

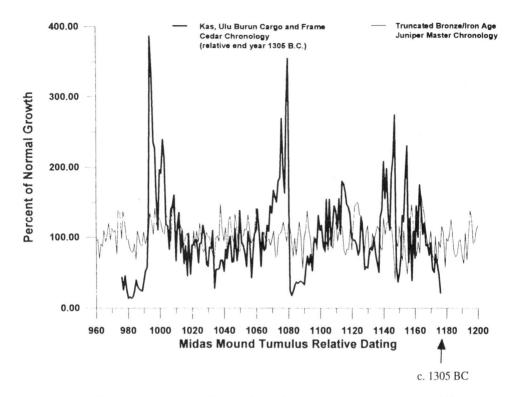

Fig. 63. Correlation of the Uluburun dendrochronological sequence, consisting of (for earlier part) one sample of cedar from shipframe and (for later part) one piece of cedar as cargo/ dunnage aboard the ship, with the Aegean Dendrochronology Project Master Chronology. Correlation determined by computer calculation and checked by eye. The dramatic variation up and down in the Uluburun curve is solely because this consists of just one or two samples. This is in contrast to the relatively smooth overall average pattern of the master curve. The Uluburun sequence ends at relative ring 1177 or c.1305BC. The cargo/dunnage sample was not preserved to bark, thus an unknown number of additional rings are missing. A date c.1300BC for the wreck is a likely approximation. Figure courtesy of Peter Ian Kuniholm.

al. (1996), this may be dated to 1305BC: see Figure 63.[1523] The wreck should, therefore, be dated no more than a few years later (c.1300BC).

The Aegean ceramic material from the Uluburun wreck is mainly LHIIIA2. A couple of the 14 fineware Mycenaean vessels are early LHIIIA2, and thus show that at least

---

[1523] Kuniholm (1997); Wiener (1998:314); Bass (1998:184 and n.7); Wiener in Bass (1998:190). The 1305BC date is a revision of the 1316BC date published in Kuniholm *et al.* (1996), following the recognition of traces of additional preserved rings on one part of the wood sample after drying. For the difficult nature of the samples from the wreck for dating analysis, see the picture in Kuniholm (1997:Fig.6) – see also **http://www.arts.cornell.edu/dendro/97news/97adplet.html**

some of this Aegean fineware had been around for a reasonable period by the time the ship sank.[1524] But one vase (a round-mouthed jug) is potentially early LHIIIB.[1525] It is therefore more than possible that the vessel sank in the (very) early LHIIIB period, with the rest of the, or all of the, small Aegean fine-ware component being somewhat old by this time (although a date of 'late LHIIIA2 to early LHIIIB' is the safest approximation). The Egyptian finds lack any Ramesside material, and are consistent with a date at the end of the 14th century BC, probably the reign of Haremhab.[1526] The Cypriot material is mainly – if not wholly – LCIIC in date,[1527] and should not date earlier than the late 14th century BC, and would be at home in the 13th century BC. Wiener (1998:313) reports the view of Oren that one of the Canaanite vessels from the wreck is 13th century BC; this emphasises that the latest material from the wreck must lie close to, or even just after, c.1300BC. The Aegean material is not part of sets of objects stored on the vessel for trade, in contrast to other groups of items on the wreck, and may therefore have been in use for a little while before the sinking. Hence a date for the LHIIIA2–LHIIIB transition might probably be placed somewhere in the fourth quarter of the 14th century BC (or a little earlier if LHIIIB material can indeed be securely linked with contexts datable to the reign of Akhenaten). Everyone seems happy to regard the LHIIIB period, with its several sub-phases, as a very long ceramic period, and the general outlines of the LHIIIB chronology are independently supported by radiocarbon dating.[1528]

From this base-line, LHIIIA2/LMIIIA2 can satisfactorily fill up the slack left between here and the LMIIIA1 period beginning late in the reign of Tuthmosis III and presumably running at least to the start of the 14th century BC. The LHIIIA2/ LMIIIA2 period is undoubtedly a little longer than the mere 30 years accorded it in the chronology of Warren and Hankey (1989:169 Table 3.1): see Wiener (1998). Much of the problem has been that a great deal of (misleading) effort has gone into defending an ambiguous (and increasingly unlikely) situation at Knossos in favour of an LMIIIA2 early 'destruction' *and* (solely LMIIIA2 early) Linear B archive, versus an LMIIIB archive.[1529] Further, whereas for many years on Crete, and on the mainland, clear LHIIIA2/LMIIIA2 stratigraphic sequences have been conspicuous by their absence, of late, and more or less as Warren and Hankey were writing/finishing their book, excavations of major sequences now suggest that this was not necessarily the short period previously thought.[1530] Thus there is every reason significantly to lengthen the

---

[1524] Pulak (1997:250).

[1525] Pulak (1997:250); Jeremy B. Rutter, pers. comm.; Bass *et al.* (1989:24 and n.119). I thank Dr. Cemal Pulak for kindly showing me the Uluburun finds stored at Bodrum.

[1526] Nicholson *et al.* (1997:151–152); Bass *et al.* (1989:17–29).

[1527] Based on a brief review of the material in the storerooms by this author; also the opinion of Professor Vassos Karageorghis, pers. comm.; the Cypriot material will be published by Nicolle Hirschfeld. For the LCIIC ceramic phase, see Russell (1986); South *et al.* (1989:1–21); and Kling (1989:6–55).

[1528] Manning and Weninger (1992); Christen and Litton (1995).

[1529] See e.g. Davis (1995:733); Rehak and Younger (1998:160).The point is that there was an LMIIIA2 early destruction at Knossos (Popham 1970b; 1997), however, this does not mean that all the final Linear B archive from the site also dates from this destruction.

[1530] See Warren and Hankey (1989:82–88, 99–101, 214 postscript to p.88).

LHIIIA2/LMIIIA2 period from the 'conventional' 30 years in Warren and Hankey (1989:169 Table 3.1). It can instead take us from the start of the 14th century BC through to the later 14th century BC.[1531]

We have seen that the later part of the reign of Tuthmosis III corresponds to the (early) LMIIIA1 period. There are then the reigns of Amenhotep II and Tuthmosis IV. A cartouche of Amenhotep II was inscribed on a monkey figurine found in an LHIIIA context at Tiryns,[1532] and we might interpolate an LHIIIA1 correlation as both possible and suitable.[1533] LHIIIA1 cannot be too much later. I have explained why the Sellopoulou scarab with the name of Amenhotep III could be regarded as (earlier) LHIIIA2, or at least late LHIIIA1 and possibly LHIIIA2 (and, on whether also as late LMIIIA1, or in fact early LMIIIA2, see Chapter IV.10 above). A plausible set of historical scenarios exists.

In conclusion, the general outlines of an 'early' chronology are both clear and likely. Inevitably, one or two problems, or contradictions, remain to be resolved or explained. But, we must expect a few problems given the nature of the data, and they are not insuperable; they are instead relatively minor issues of adjustment and interpretation. Further, the early chronology cannot simply be rejected just because one or two problematic areas may be identified. The much larger, and stronger, case in favour must be considered. And, in reverse, it must be remembered that the conventional, or low, chronology has just as many, and indeed rather more, 'problems', and is universally inconsistent with a wide range of independent scientific evidence. It seems that convention might have to change. The 'compromise early' chronology is perhaps the new *minimum* position.

Chronology of Alalakh VII

To conclude this work, I wish to explore briefly one example of the implications of the 1628BC date for the Thera eruption, and the early Aegean LBA chronology, in western Asia. The obvious case study is the famous (indeed infamous) long-running chronological controversy over the dating of Alalakh VII: see Figure 64.[1534] Many scholars regard Alalakh as a problem. Dates for this crucial site near the bend in the Orontes, where its heads for the Mediterranean, in the Turkish Province of Hatay (greater northwest Syria in ancient cultural terms),[1535] with Aegean, Cypriot, Hittite,

---

[1531] Other previous scholars have indeed accorded it as much as a century in the past: see Manning (1995:227 and refs.).

[1532] Cline (1991:34–38; 1994:132 no.6).

[1533] Warren (1998:325), despite taking the trouble to correct the text of Manning (1988b:36) which mistakenly ascribed an LHIIIA1 context, nonetheless proceeds to accept 'an early LHIIIA link with Amenophis II'!

[1534] For data and references to previous literature, see Heinz (1992; 1993); Eriksson (1992:187–193); Kempinski (1983:esp.80–90, 216–221; 1992b); Dever (1992:14); Niemeier (1991); Niemeier and Niemeier (1998:69–71, 82–85); McClellan (1989); Astour (1989:9–21, 56–63); Gates (1987; 1981); Collon (1977); Na'aman (1976); Muhly (1975); Woolley (1955:377–399).

[1535] Woolley (1953; 1955). The mound is named Tell Atchana. Alalakh is the ancient name for the MBA city.

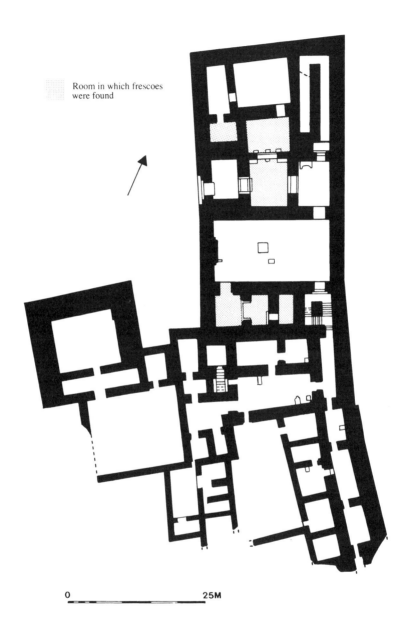

Room in which frescoes
were found

Fig. 64. Schematic plan of Alalakh VII, the Yarim Lim palace, after Woolley (1955:Fig.35).
Areas where LMIA-style frescoes found indicated (Rooms 4, 5, 11, 12 and 13: Woolley 1955:92,
94, 100, 102, 228–232). They were usually fallen from original locations on the floor above.

Syro-Palestinian, and, with the campaigns of Tuthmosis III, even Egyptian relations, have both varied dramatically over the past 50 years, and been of central importance to east Mediterranean and west Asian archaeology for the last 50 years.[1536] The dates given for the end of level VII at Alalakh differ by a good century in published literature from the last few decades.[1537] Can this uncertainty be resolved in any way? And how do both the 1628BC Thera date, and the Aegean dendrochronology,[1538] impinge on the problem?

The paradox over the last fifty years of debate is that we know a remarkable amount about Alalakh VII in historical terms, but, at the same time, since the site is at the crossroads (or margins of) the main Syrian–Palestinian, Anatolian, and Aegean worlds, this relative historical and prosopographical information floats vis à vis the general chronology of the ancient Near East. And, as always, it is often difficult to tie archaeology to history. Two archives of documents were found at the site,[1539] along with a large corpus of seal impressions.[1540] Among other things, these documents provide us with the names of, and an internal chronology for, the rulers of Alalakh VII and IV, and various of their contemporaries, during the later MBA and earlier LBA. Our attention here focuses on the dynasty of Alalakh VII: Figure 65. Alalakh is also mentioned in documents from other ancient archives in Anatolia and Syria from the MBA. However, at the same time, there are the archaeological finds, and, in particular, the ceramics from the various levels at Alalakh,[1541] and also the links provided by these to the relative ceramic chronology of Syria–Palestine. There has been an uneasy meeting, or collision, of all these ingredients over the last 50 years, not helped by Woolley's (1955) rather arbitrary and schematic publication of the ceramics simply by 'types' and by level, with little further detail on material or contexts. Recent studies of the material kept by Woolley have helped clarify some issues,[1542] but many problems remain due to the nature of the excavation and the recording. Some would say that rather than consider the problem of Alalakh, one must simply accept that the excavations and publication of Woolley on Alalakh are a problem, and so nothing can be satisfactorily resolved. But it is always informative to consider apparent problems and contradictions between different types and sources of evidence. Perspective is necessary, and I suggest that we can learn from this problem. First, let us explore the historical evidence and chronology.

Woolley studied and published Alalakh in terms of its architectural sequence (or stratigraphy). Alalakh level VII, with which we are primarily concerned, begins with the construction of the palace of king Yarim-Lim. Frescoes of general LMIA Aegean style were found in this palace,[1543] and so Alalakh VII appears to correlate with the

---

[1536] Since Smith (1940).

[1537] McClellan (1989:Fig.26).

[1538] Kuniholm *et al.* (1996).

[1539] Wiseman (1953).

[1540] Collon (1975).

[1541] McClellan (1989) – cf. Heinz (1993).

[1542] Gates (1981); Heinz (1992).

[1543] Woolley (1955:228–234, pls.26.b-29.c; 1953:76, pl.6.a); see with discussion of Niemeier and Niemeier (1998:69–71, 82–85 and refs.); previously Niemeier (1991).

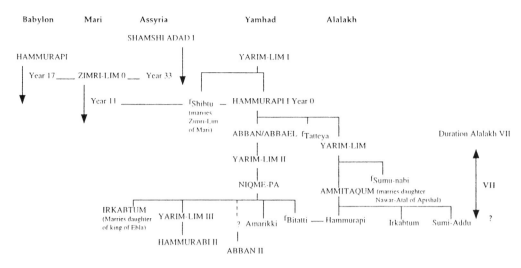

Fig. 65. The ruling house of Alalakh VII and the chronology of relationships with the ruling houses of other Near Eastern cities (after Collon 1977; Charpin and Durand 1985; Astour 1989). Kings shown in CAPITALS. Names of females preceded by a superscript 'f'. It is possible that Hammurapi of Alalakh became king shortly before the sack of Alalakh VII, but this is not attested.

LMIA period. The archive of Alalakh VII, in conjunction with sealing evidence, informs us that Yarim-Lim was the son of Hammurapi of the kingdom of Yamhad (capital at Aleppo or Halab/Haleb); the father is mentioned in the Mari archives and is attested as succeeding his father, Yarim-Lim I of Yamhad, during year 11 of Zimri-Lim of Mari. Zimri-Lim Year 0 = Hammurapi of Babylon year 17 = Samsi-Adad I of Assyria year 33.[1544] Thus Alalakh may be related to Babylonian and Assyrian chronology,[1545] constructed from preserved kinglists, chronicles, royal inscriptions, and dated administrative or religious documents.[1546]

[1544] Charpin and Durand (1985:306–308); see also Veenhof (1985:217–218). Whiting (1990:esp.210 n.205) argues against this view, and maintains the previous dates whereby Samsi-Adad I died in Hammurapi years 12 or 13, but the case for year 17 appears more compelling. The extreme possible range is after Hammurapi year 10 (last extant Babylonian evidence attesting Samsi-Adad I as alive) and before Hammurapi year 18 (accession of Zimri-Limi). The 4–5 years difference are irrelevant to the present discussion. The 33 year reign here is, it should be remembered, Samsi-Adad I's reign as king of Assyria (from the Assyrian King List) after his conquest of Assur and the ousting of the then encumbent Erisum. Samsi-Adad I was in fact a king and 'reigning' before this. Three years earlier he had conquered Ekallatum, and he was a minor ruler for some years before this. In total, he seems to have had a minimum reign (somewhere) of about 57+ years (see Birot 1985:224; Veenhof 1985:215; Whiting 1990:170 and passim). He probably lived to the age of 80+ years (Whiting 1990:171).
[1545] For recent reviews of the textual evidence from Alalakh and chronology, see e.g. Heinz (1992:190–197); and Gates (1987).
[1546] For a brief summary with further refs., see Gasche *et al.* (1998:47–48).

Observations of the planet Venus recorded during the reign of Ammisaduqa, penultimate ruler of the Babylonian Old (First) Dynasty, have been argued for many years to offer the basis of a chronology for the Dynasty of Hammurapi (Figure 66),[1547] and in wider terms, the Near East including Alalakh in the earlier second millennium BC. The problem is that such planetary observations are not unique, and, for Venus, repeat every c.60 years or so. Hence one must select a solution within the possible overall dating window established by other criteria. Given the broad chronology of the first half of the second millennium BC, most post-AD1930s scholarship has considered three possible solutions (180 year range), the so-called High, Middle, and Low chronologies, although an ultra-High, and an ultra-Low, chronology have been proposed by some (total of a 300 year range). The question of which of these options is correct has been the subject of decades of unresolved debate.[1548] The fundamental problem is that the astronomical data preserved are both incomplete and corrupt/unreliable,[1549] and so cannot really form the basis of a sound astronomical-chronological solution.[1550]

It would be hoped that dendrochronology might prove relevant in this regard. Documents (bullae) found in the destruction of the Sarıkaya palace at Acemhöyük[1551] include those with the seal of Samsi-Adad I.[1552] It is of course conceivable that these documents were 'old' and either kept or somehow placed in a later context, but, in general, it would be reasonable to conclude that it is most likely that such sealed documents come from the lifetime of the building concerned, and are preserved thanks to its burnt destruction. In this case, it is likely that some part of Samsi-Adad I's long reign post-dates the construction of the Sarıkaya palace.[1553] The 'reign' of Samsi-Adad I referred to in this context is his final 33 year reign as king of Assyria (and not his earlier 24+ years as a king). Meanwhile, analysis suggests that the Waršama palace of Kültepe IB[1554] was constructed either shortly before, or around, the beginning of the reign of Samsi-Adad I from Assur, with the first *limu* (eponym) evidence from Level IB belonging from some point in the reign of Samsi-Adad I of Assyria. Whiting (1990:212–213) in a brief analysis of the available data proposes that the preceding

---

[1547] For an early study with references to previous work, see Langdon and Fotheringham (1928).

[1548] See e.g. Smith (1940); Sidersky (1940–1941); Albright (1942); Rowton (1958; 1970:231–233); Tadmor (1970); Sachs (1970); Reiner and Pingree (1975); Huber (1982; 1987); Astour (1989:1–2); Heinz (1992:198–201).

[1549] Reiner and Pingree (1975:25).

[1550] See Neugebauer (1929); Gasche *et al.* (1998:9–10, 72–74); Gates (1987:76–77).

[1551] Possibly Burushattum/Purushattum in Assyrian texts, or Purushanda in Hittite texts: Bryce (1998:24).

[1552] And his officials and contemporaries, and even the slightly later king Aplakhanda of Carchemish (Özgüç 1980; Grayson 1987:61; Önhan 1989).

[1553] It has been stated in some publications (Kuniholm and Newton 1989:293; Kuniholm 1993:372; Manning 1995:112) that a year 10 of Samsi-Adad I is attested. Although this date was stated in a lecture (and accordingly incorporated by Kuniholm who heard it mentioned), it is in fact incorrect/nonexistent at this time. There are no published bullae so dated from the Sarıkaya palace (and, as Gasche *et al.* 1998:10 n.47 note, bullae are in fact rarely, if ever, dated). And, as Gasche *et al.* (1998:10 n.47) also point out, the complete sequence of eponyms for the reign of Samsi-Adad I has not yet been definitively established (cf. Whiting 1990:Fig.2 for a proposed chronology), and so a precise dating is not possible. Full publication of the documents from Acemhöyük is an urgent priority.

[1554] Ancient Kanes or Nesa, see Bryce (1998:22–24).

Fig. 66. Stela now in the Louvre, Paris, with a relief scene at the top showing Hammurapi of Babylon standing before the throne of the sun-god. Hammurapi's legal code is inscribed below on the stela under this relief scene. See Frankfort (1970:119–122, Fig.134–135); Kuhrt (1995:Fig.11). Drawing after previous refs.

Level II ends around the time Samsi-Adad I became king (his real year 1) and no later than his real year 14, whereas Level IB became active probably around Samsi-Adad real year 43 and no earlier than his real year 33. Samsi-Adad I became king of Assur/Assyria in his year 24 (start of 33 reign recorded in Assyrian King List), so we are approximately at his year 9 through 19 as king of Assyria. Kültepe Level IB was then quite long-lived, up to a century, and is thought to have continued in use until at least the 10th year of Samsuilana of Babylon.[1555] The Acemhöyük palace was destroyed first. Tree-ring evidence is available relating to the construction date of each of these MBA palaces.[1556] This information reveals that the Sarıkaya palace at Acemhöyük was built in or after 1752BC, and the Waršama palace in or after 1810BC.[1557]

We may thus compare these data with the relevant 'dates' from the High, Middle, and Low chronologies. Hammurapi's reign began according to the High, Middle, and Low scheme in 1848BC, 1792BC, or 1728BC. Samsi-Adad I had a 33 year long reign as king of Assyria according to the Assyrian Kinglist (raw figure: cf. Gasche *et al.* 1998:50 on lunar versus solar calendars). As noted above, his final year 33 (real year c.57+) equates with Hammurapi year 17. Thus the reign of Samsi-Adad I as king of Assyria lies in either 1864–1832BC, 1808–1776BC or 1744–1712BC.[1558] From the Acemhöyük evidence, we may conclude that, at a minimum, the end of Samsi-Adad I's reign (both total, and as king of Assyria) must have been after 1752BC (and probably by at least a few years). From the Kültepe evidence, Samsi-Adad I years 9 to 19 as king of Assyria post-date 1810BC (by an unknown amount). These two data offer similar, but not entirely consistent, information. The earliest Kültepe IB documents imply a further 14–24 years of Samsi-Adad I's reign. To be compatible with the 1752BC datum from Acemhöyük, it would be necessary to see these at best as dating from c.1776BC (Samsi-Adad I year 9 as king of Assyria), and there is a slightly uncomfortable gap of c.34 years from the cutting date of wood used in the construction date of the Waršama palace at 1810BC and this c.1776BC date with no (published) pre-Samsi-Adad I documentary evidence. Up to 33 years of this *could* be regarded as contemporary with the earlier years of Samsi-Adad I before his year 33 (total) or 9 (as king of Assyria) – with Kültepe II ending about the time of his accession, rather than later. And this seems about the neatest solution.

[1555] Özgüç (1968; 1986:xxi and n.3; 1988:23); Orlin (1970); Önhan (1989); Whiting (1990:212–213 and n.209). Much of the documentary evidence from Kültepe has not been published, and this is again an urgent priority.

[1556] Kuniholm *et al.* (1996); for tree-ring data and context, see Kuniholm (1993); Kuniholm *et al.* (1992); Kuniholm and Newton (1989).

[1557] It is worth emphasising that these dates are proposed as absolute. Gasche *et al.* (1998:10) refer to the 95% confidence error on the radiocarbon wiggle-match in Kuniholm *et al.* (1996). But the point of the paper of Kuniholm *et al.* (1996) was that *within* this dating window established by the radiocarbon evidence the two unusual dendrochronological anomalies in the second millennium BC permitted a precise fit against the absolutely dated Irish dendrochronology. Hence the final dates (some 13 years lower than the radiocarbon wiggle-match), and with, in effect, no error. See also Chapter V.4 above.

[1558] Note, most standard works employ the pre-Charpin and Durand (1985) correlation of Samsi-Adad I year 33 with Hammurapi year 12, and thus have dates 5 years higher, e.g. the 'standard' Middle chronology date of 1813–1781BC. The dates in the text should be preferred.

Reference to the dendrochronological dates significantly revises the possible absolute chronological range within which Samsi-Adad I must be placed. The High chronology is clearly ruled out by both the Kültepe and Acemhöyük dates. It may probably be deleted from further scholarly consideration. The Middle chronology could work with the Kültepe date, but is ruled out by the Acemhöyük date. To remain viable, it would require the Acemhöyük documents of Samsi-Adad I to be heirlooms of some three decades. This is always possible, but seems unlikely. Hence the Middle chronology can also probably be deleted from further consideration. The only chronology which works at face value is the Low chronology. Similarly, since the Acemhöyük palace ends before Kültepe IB, and thus by or around the last attested 'date' in the Kültepe IB archive (Samsuilana year 10: 1796BC, 1740BC or 1676BC), only the Low chronology plausibly allows a minimum of several decades of life to the Sarıkaya palace.

The Low chronology is therefore shown to be probably correct – or, rather, a chronology close to it – since it is more than likely that the Venus data are inherently problematic,[1559] or even 'wrong' (since Huber plausibly finds the relevant astronomy and statistics to support the High chronology, but absolutely dated dendrochronology renders this impossible).[1560] Hence the true chronology may be another one. For example, a chronology derived from the king lists in the sub–Low, Low, or low–Middle range, independent of the Venus tablet data.[1561] The constraint on any proposal is that it must lie within a couple of decades of the Low chronology to be viable.

It is at this point that a new study by Gasche *et al.* (1998) commands our attention. Based on a review of the archaeological, textual, and astronomical data, these authors propose a new chronology some two to four decades lower than the traditional Low chronology. In their preferred synthesis, the reign of Samsi-Adad I (as king of Assyria) is dated 1719–1688BC, some 25 years lower than the Low chronology.[1562] Their dead-reckoning maximum date from the textual evidence is 1737–1705BC.[1563] Without entering into a detailed analysis of the entire project of Gasche *et al.* (1998), we may note that their dates are possible, but problematic, in view of the dendrochronological data. The conventional approximate correlation of somewhere around years 9 to 19 of Samsi-Adad I's reign as king of Assyria with the start of, or at least an early stage of, Kültepe IB, which is dated shortly after 1810BC by dendrochronology, is rather difficult if Samsi-Adad I year 9 (real 33) is dated c.1710BC (or at a maximum 1728BC). The 82–100 year gap is too long to be represented by silence, and pre-Samsi-Adad I rulers ought to have been present in the documentary evidence. The plausible link of

---

[1559] See above; also Reiner and Pingree (1975); Gates (1981:37); Kudlek (1985); Oelsner (1988).

[1560] Huber (1982; 1987). Few have followed Huber's lead in recent Near Eastern scholarship. Dalley (1984) was one of the rare exceptions. I note also an article by Clayden (1992:143 n.2), which refers to Clayden's doctoral dissertation (which I have not seen) for support in arguing for the long chronology for the dynasty of Hammurapi.

[1561] See e.g. Weidner (1945–1951); Hachmann (1977); Na'aman (1984). But cf. Henige (1986); and Hallo (1978) on the general problems of this data. For the main specific uncertainties and possible variations, see Gasche *et al.* (1998:47–56 and refs.).

[1562] Gasche *et al.* (1998:56–68).

[1563] Gasche *et al.* (1998:62).

the end of the preceding Kültepe Level II with either the time of Samsi-Adad I's accession, or as late as his year 14, would, if correct, clearly make the Gasche *et al.* chronology impossible. The Acemhöyük dendrochronological data by itself could plausibly conform with a lower chronology – just with no documents dated to earlier rulers extant for years 1752BC to 1719BC (or 1737BC) – however, in combination with the Kültepe data, the Acemhöyük documents plausibly must belong to the mature to later part of Samsi-Adad's I reign. In this case, the gap from 1752BC again seems implausibly long given the pattern of documentary attestations. Thus at this stage the ultra-low chronology of Gasche *et al.* (1998) seems implausible, but, of course, not impossible. For the rest of this discussion I therefore refer both to the traditional 'Low' Venus tablet chronology (which I favour as it is within *about* the appropriate chronological range), and the new low chronology of Gasche *et al.* (1998). We will see later where some additional problems crop up, and why the extreme ultra-low dates are perhaps too low.

With these chronologies selected, we can offer dates for associated ancient Near Eastern rulers, and, with reference to our present discussion, Hammurapi of Yamhad in particular. He succeeded to the throne in c.1701BC on the Low chronology, or 1677/1669BC on the preferred chronology of Gasche *et al.* (1998).[1564] An elder son, Abban (or Abbael), succeeded him as king of Yamhad, and, in due course, gave Alalakh and some other territory to Yarim-Lim junior.[1565] The time interval is unknown. An 'average' generational count cannot always apply in every case. Abban is attested only once beyond the investiture treaties in the archives of Alalakh VII, so Astour (1989:10) argues that the handover was late in Abban's reign, but this is conjecture given the partial nature of the data sources, and we do not know how long Abban or the father lived. The latter in particular may not have had a long reign; he was born during the reign of his grandfather,[1566] which, assuming his father did have a typical lifespan, might well mean Abban was king only for a few years if he did not live to a great age. Further, the settlement with his brother sounds like something which would have been carried out at the beginning of a reign among adult siblings to ensure dynastic peace.

Thus although one cannot rule out a longer period, estimates for the one and a bit to almost two generations involved might range from c.20–50 years, with the odds favouring the shorter end of this range. Assuming Yarim-Lim got to work soon after, and built his palace, and so inaugurated Alalakh VII, we might state a *terminus post quem* for Alalakh VII of, variously, c.1681/1651BC to 1657/1619BC; the phase lasted through the reign of Yarim-Lim, his son Ammitaqum, and perhaps a part of the reign of his grandson Hammurapi (although, as he is attested as crown prince, only, in records from Alalakh VII, this is perhaps not necessary). There are also linkages to 3–

[1564] The different dates depend on whether one uses the end of reign/death date of 1688BC given by Gasche *et al.* (1998:91) for Samsi-Adad I = Zimri-Lim Year 0, or the 1696BC date given by Gasche *et al.* (1998:91) for the accession of Hammurapi, with Hammurapi year 17 = Zimri-Lim Year 0. There is an inconsistency (even allowing for the lunar calendar versus solar calendar issue).

[1565] I follow Collon (1977), and reject the family structure created by Na'aman (1976).

[1566] Villard (1986:394); Astour (1989:10).

4 generations of other families (just over 3 generations of rulers of Yamhad, and 3–4 generations of officials and merchants at Alalakh).[1567] Alalakh VII thus need not occupy a long time period, and Woolley (1955:385) thought it to be a relatively short phase, c.50 years. Some c.20–60 or so years might be allowed for the period. This is assuming that: Yarim-Lim was a young adult on gaining Alalakh and reigned for another c.10–30 years, that his son Ammitaqum then reigned for 10–30 years, and that 0 years are allowed for Hammurapi, or that he is given the last few years of the time span of one of the previous two reigns, since both are unlikely to have been long. Other published estimates tend to overlook the likelihood of one or other or both of the reigns being not particularly long.[1568] For example, the average reign length in the Assyrian King List data for kings 48 through 83 (from Belu-bani in the 17th century BC to Assur-dan I in the 12th century BC) is c.15.4 years.[1569] Therefore, the end of Alalakh VII might be placed within limits of c.1661/1591BC to 1637/1559BC. This is one evidential approach. Another is offered by the Hittites and their entry into Syria.

Textual evidence informs us that the Hittite king Hattusili I sacked Alalakh.[1570] Scholarship has thus tried to decide which destruction level at Alalakh may be associated with this statement. For the sake of argument I will do the same, but a serious caveat should be noted. There is no reason why this claimed sack should be archaeologically clear, and it need not correlate with one of the 'destructions' recognised by Woolley.[1571] It is *assumed* that the relevant destruction is that of Alalakh VII, since textual evidence ties Hattusili I, a certain Zukrasi, Ammitaqum of Alalakh, and Yarim-Lim III of Yamhad together within a generation at most.[1572] The record of Hattusili I's attack is in the second of six years of records, but where within his overall and presumably quite long reign (given known achievements, and succession by a grandson) these six years lie, we do not know for certain from the text itself – although Astour (1989:10) argues that the wording indicates that this was year 2 from the beginning of his reign, and an early date is consistent with what we know of the campaigns and events of his reign[1573]). Some guidance comes from the mention of a

---

[1567] Collon (1977:127–128).

[1568] E.g. Gates (1987:72) who allows 50–75 years; or Heinz (1992:206) who allows c.75 years. McClellan (1989:211) suggests an unquantified 'long' duration for Alalakh VII on the basis of his ceramic seriation analysis. But the textual evidence seems our best guide. Niemeier and Niemeier (1998:70) also support a long duration for Alalakh VII and cite others of the same view (p.70 n.17). Niemeier and Niemeier state that documents of Alalakh VII 'mention six kings of Yamhad' (p.70), but the first (Abban) and the last (Hammurapi II) at best overlap just with the very beginning and end of the period, and there are only three certain kings in between (Yarim-Lim II, Niqmepa, Yarim-Lim III). Hence there is no reason for a particularly long period.

[1569] Data set out by Gasche *et al.* (1998:62); note, this becomes c.15 years with their 'corrected' data on p.63.

[1570] From his annals: Kuhrt (1995:241); Bryce (1998:75–76); CTH 4.

[1571] See discussion in Chapter III above; see cautionary examples from the 1st millennium BC in the study of Forsberg (1995).

[1572] E.g. see summaries by Muhly (1975:78–81); and Astour (1989:11 and 84 ns.58–60); each with refs. to primary sources.

[1573] Bryce (1998:73–84, 88–89).

Zukrasi, described as commander of the regular troops (general of Yarim-Lim III of Yamhad), in a text (AT6.27) from what must be later/late Alalakh VII,[1574] who is also found in a Hittite text (KBo 7.14), where he is referred to as coming to the aid of Hassu at the request of Hammurapi II, son of Yarim-Lim III (the latter dead by this time[1575]). It is likely that the Hassu (Hassuwa) episode may be dated to the (second) Syrian campaign of Hattusili I dated from his *Annals* to his year 6.[1576] Because Zukrasi held exactly the same title in both mentions, and we know that Hammurapi II succeeded his father shortly before the sack of Alalakh VII and ruled into the beginning of Alalakh VI,[1577] we may conjecture that the events may not have been too far apart, and we might thus accept the view that the attack on Alalakh VII occurred before Hattusili I year 6 (and so probably in his year 2).[1578] Clearly this view is not certain, but it does appear to be the probable conclusion from a nexus of interrelated data.

Since Hattusili I's grandson and successor Mursili I is credited with being 'the man of Hatti' who in the time Samsuditana marched against Akkad according to a later insertion to the much later *Babylonian Chronicle*,[1579] and sacked the famous city of Babylon,[1580] and so probably also ended the reign of Samsuditana (although this additional 'fact' is not stated by any ancient record), the end of Alalakh VII may be dated from an alternative approach if we can calculate the time span involved. The end of the reign of Samsuditana is dated c.1531BC on the Low chronology, and c.1499BC by Gasche *et al.* (1998) on their preferred chronology. However, exact figures for the interval between Hattusili I's attack on Alalakh and Mursili I's raid on Babylon are not known. It seems likely, but by no means certain, that Alalakh VII was sacked early (even very early – year 2) in the reign of Hattusili I. He had a long reign – probably beginning relatively young as he was the grandson?/nephew of his predecessor – but no actual numbers exist for the length. An adult son was disinherited,

---

[1574] Will of Ammitaqum, last definite ruler of Alalakh VII, made in the time of of Yarim-Lim III of Yamhad (Wiseman 1953:33–34, pl.V.6).

[1575] Astour (1989:84 n.60).

[1576] On which, see Bryce (1998:82–83).

[1577] Astour (1989:11, 84 ns.61 and 62).

[1578] For the recognition of Zukrasi as the same individual in the different texts, see Landsberger (1954:52). For discussion of this famous correlation with further references, see Astour (1989:11); Muhly (1975:78); Bryce (1998:76).

[1579] Gasche *et al.* (1998:6–7) usefully highlight that there is no good contemporary evidence. The Hittite inscription of Telepinu is a century after the event and does not mention the name of the Babylonian king, and the Babylonian 'record' linking an attack on Akkad by the Hittites to the reign of Samsuditana is a later insertion on the tablet of the later 'Chronicle of Early Kings' in a small script (Grayson 1975:49). This insertion (Tablet B, reverse, sentence 11) reads: 'At the time of Samsu-ditana the Hittites marched against Akkad' (Grayson 1975:156). Just how reliable either of these records are, especially the latter, is not clear. Gasche *et al.* (1998:6) are thus correct to write: 'Babylon *seems* to have fallen to the Hittite king Mursili I' (my italics). Indeed, this is an understatement. The sentence added to the Chronicle of Early Kings neither actually states that the Hittites at this time captured, devastated, or otherwise succeeded in their march on Akkad. Nor is Mursili I mentioned in this, or the Hittite record. Much hypothesis has been built on very little evidence.

[1580] Edict of Telepinu: Kuhrt (1995:245–248 at p.245); see also Bryce (1998:102–103); CTH 19.

along with a son of a daughter.[1581] His eventual successor was a grandson who was then a minor/youth since Hattusili I asked his 'foremost servants' not to take him into the field for three years and to protect him.[1582] We can probably assume that Hattusili I was an adult when he himself became king, seemingly in the middle of a rebellion and crisis.[1583] He may already have had children. But, as noted above, since he was the grandson?/nephew of his predecessor, it seems unlikely he was more than in his 20s on accession. Hence about 20 (minimum) and up to about 30 (or more) years of reign are plausible, and necessary, to account for his recorded feats and the dynastic data known with regard to his own succession problems. Presumably Mursili I did not attack Babylon until at least his year 4, and quite possibly not for several more years (another 1–20? years – we have no actual evidence), and his early reign appears to have been concerned with re-establishing Hittite control within Anatolia.[1584] But it cannot have been too many years as his reign was evidently relatively short (few attested details except the Syrian campaign), and it seems that he died childless.[1585] The view that he was assassinated more or less immediately on his return from Babylon is based on no positive evidence,[1586] so a few additional years may have elapsed after the Syrian foray. Astour (1989) represents a minimalist view, and credits Mursili I with just a c.10 year reign; Bryce (1998:xiii) in contrast allows 30 years. The former seems more likely, but there is almost no actual evidence.

In consequence, it is difficult to see how to reduce the interval involved between the destruction of Alalakh VII by Hattusili I and the sack of Babylon by Mursili I below c.20–30 years,[1587] and it could easily be as much as almost two generations later (e.g. Hattusili I c.50 to 60 years old at his death after c.30–35 year reign, and Mursili I an adolescent on accession and launching his Syrian campaign at about age 20–35, some 5 to 20 years later). An interval of perhaps up to c.40–55 years maximum might be envisaged. Thus the sack of Alalakh VII would lie as early as c.1586BC on the Low chronology, or as late as 1519BC on the Gasche *et al.* (1998) preferred chronology. Here we start to hit problems or contradictions. Working from Hammurapi of Yamhad we got at the lowest to about 1591BC or 1559BC. A date in the later 16th century BC seems rather difficult. We need now also to consider the archaeological data, as this too sets parameters for acceptable solutions.

[1581] Bryce (1998:89–94).

[1582] Astour (1989:13 and n.79); CTH 6.

[1583] Bryce (1998:70–74).

[1584] Bryce (1998:101–102).

[1585] Astour (1989:13–14).

[1586] Bryce (1998:105 and n.14).

[1587] Unless it is argued that the sack of Alalakh in fact belongs with his later skirmishes with the kingdom of Aleppo (for which, see Bryce 1998:88–89). However, as discussed above, the textual data suggests it is likely that the attack on Alalakh was early in Hattusili I's reign (and perhaps during his year 2). Hence the potential minimum figure of 7 years employed by Gates (1987:74) may be ignored; likewise Kempinski's (1983:219–220) argument for a maximum interval of 15/20 years, which is based on other factors, and does not account for the Hittite data. The short c.20 year interval employed by Na'aman (1976:140) is due to his assumed Middle Babylonian chronology, and has no independent basis.

Despite the summary and arbitrary recording of Woolley (1955), the other main source of chronological data is the ceramic assemblage of Alalakh. As has been recognised since Kantor (1956:158–160) and Albright (1956), Alalakh level VII is later MBII in terms of the wider Syro-Palestinian archaeological sequence. On the basis of Woolley's excavation and publication (1955), and the re-analyses of Gates (1981) and Heinz (1992), Level VII is held specifically to lack Bichrome Ware and the other LCI imports characteristic of the close of MBA–early LBI period of the region.[1588] In contrast, Alalakh VIB appears to have crossed this threshold. I note that Eriksson (1992:187–193) makes a reasonable case for the very problematic nature of some of the Alalakh data. Woolley indeed seems to have mixed, confused, or been unable to resolve the stratigraphy in places, and scholarship has to accept the limitations of the data. Eriksson (1992:193) concludes that 'it seems one cannot place too much reliance on the stratigraphy of Alalakh for determining the finer points of chronology'. True. But the main patterns in the evidence do probably have some worth. And, it must also be borne in mind that Alalakh has been criticised or avoided so intensely because, as Woolley (1953:91) observed: '...at Atchana [Alalakh] we have a chronology not less well established than that of Cyprus and for our examples of the White Slip and Base-Ring pottery the Cyprus dating simply does not fit'.[1589] Alalakh instead supports an 'early' or 'high' chronology for the early LBA periods of both Cyprus and the Aegean.

It is therefore entirely reasonable to observe that Alalakh level VIB has recorded finds of mature LCIB wares, such as WSI, BRI, and also Bichrome Ware. Earlier LCI ought to be before this. The WSI in particular may be noted as including mature or classic parallel line style examples of the late phase of WSI,[1590] and indeed some altogether late looking WSI.[1591] These LCIB imports in level VIB follow the first signs of early or transitional LC types (Black on Red/Red on Black, and Monochrome) in the preceding Level VIA.[1592]. Indeed, these may not be the earliest LC products

---

[1588] A sentence in Woolley (1953:91) seems at first sight to provide an intriguing contradiction to this view. Woolley is discussing Cypriot WS and BR imports, and then writes 'two wish-bone handles turned up in Level VII, and in Level VI both wares become relatively common...'. However, it seems likely that the two wish-bone handles are the same as the two mentioned in Woolley (1955:364–365). Here he states that 'the ware did not seem to be Cypriote' (one was of a red fabric, the other grey). Woolley (1955:368) nonetheless further notes that these wish-bone handles were 'of the regular "Cypriote" form, but not in the normal Cypriote Monochrome ware'.

[1589] See also Woolley (1955:354–355).

[1590] Noted also by Popham (1972a:442).

[1591] Eliezer Oren (pers. comm.) has expressed the same opinion. I note that a supposed WSI(?) sherd was found in Alalakh level VIII: Woolley (1955:365); Gates (1981:18 and n.75); Heinz (1992:tafel 27 no.73) – Ashmolean Museum 1948.376. This could be from level VI? as suggested by Heinz. As a single stray find, it is to be discounted from any analysis.

[1592] See Woolley (1955:316, 355–357, 363–364, 368), and subsequently Gates (1981; 1987). I have noted Eriksson's (1992) cautions against the necessary reliability of the finds/stratigraphy at Alalakh, but to reject all the level VI imports (all the LCI finds, and the LHIIA finds) because of a few later intrusions and problems is perhaps going too far – moreover, her conclusion that only Alalakh V correlates with LCI and the early 18th Dynasty (p.192) leads to impossible contradictions unless an ultra-low Egyptian

at the site. Apart from the reference by Woolley (1953:91) to the 'two wish-bone handles ... in Level VII' (see footnote 1588 above), a 'WS' sherd from an 'effectually sealed' Level VIII context, and another 'WS'? sherd from under the Yarim-Lim palace, might, as Woolley suggests, represent 'early isolated imports from the source which later was to supply the normal White Slip wares'.[1593] LCIA might thus possibly span levels VII–VIA, and not just VIA. However, even if we discount these references (as most do), some considerable time interval may be involved across Level VIA to VIB. In addition, it is possible that some LHIIA sherds, and an LHIIA/LMIB sherd, were found in Alalakh VI.[1594] Eriksson and others argue against this, and point to stratigraphic problems,[1595] but it is important to observe that LHIIA finds would be entirely consistent with an LCIB date for this horizon. Indeed, this is a minimum position. Apart from the possible LC style handles in Level VII (above), Gates refers to the possibility of WSII as also present in the Alalakh VIB assemblage.[1596] If so, level VIB continued into LCIIA. Thus by the time of Alalakh VIB we are certainly well into the timespan of the earlier 18th Dynasty of Egypt and the Syro-Palestinian LBI period in general.[1597] What is rather absent at Alalakh is a clear late MBII (MBIIC or MBIII) horizon with PWS. This seems to lie in temporal terms between level VII and VI, or perhaps in the amorphous level VIA, but is not attested at the site.[1598]

To attempt to interpret this data, we need first to consider Bichrome Ware, especially since one of the major recent cases for the dating of Alalakh VII, the monograph and article by Gates,[1599] rests on the chronology of Bichrome Ware. Bichrome Ware has already been mentioned several times in the discussion above.[1600] Both in stylistic and compositional terms it appears linked to, and to develop out of, the Cypriot WP

18th Dynasty chronology is employed (Eriksson 1992 of course uses the ultra-low c.1530BC accession date for Ahmose after Helck 1987 – for a general survey of the Syro-Palestinian data contrary to the assumptions and views of Eriksson, see Kempinski 1983; 1992b).

[1593] Woolley (1955:365, and 367–368 n.3).

[1594] Gates (1981:Ill.7d, 26n.114); Woolley (1955:370 and pl.79 ATP/47/50).

[1595] Eriksson (1992:188); Åström (1989:68–71).

[1596] Gates (1987:64) referring to her Ph.D. thesis – which I have not seen.

[1597] Eriksson (1992:191) lists one of the problems with Level VIB as the finds of LHIII sherds. But, if there is WSII, and Level VIB did continue into (early) LCIIA, then the presence of LHIII sherds is not necessarily a serious problem. LM/LHIIIA1 began by late in the reign of Tuthmosis III (Chapter IV.9), and links with WSII. Thus the dramatic contradiction Eriksson imagines is in fact possibly non-existent.

[1598] Heinz (1992:204–206, 210) tries to link Alalakh levels VII–VI with Tell el-Dabʿa strata E/2 to D/2. Her general correlation of Alalakh level VII to Tell el-Dabʿa stratum E/1 is reasonable, but the subsequent linkages are quite problematic. She variously places Alalakh level VIA as contemporary with Tell el-Dabʿa stratum D/3, or D/2 (compare p.204 with p.206 and p.210), but Alalakh level VIA lacks the diagnostic late MBII (MBIIC/MBIII) types found in Tell el-Dabʿa stratum D/2. Her suggestion to date Alalakh level VIA c.1575–1540BC is thus odd and arbitrary. Following the conventional chronology, this is the time of Bichrome ware and the close of the MBA, but Alalakh level VIA provides no good evidence of belonging to this specific horizon. It instead seems to lie a little earlier (as Heinz suggested on p.204).

[1599] Gates (1981; 1987).

[1600] For the ware, see Epstein (1966).

tradition.[1601] It is a key pottery style, and has often been used to distinguish where to place an assemblage. It is therefore almost inevitable that its study has been marked by controversy.[1602] Study has shown that there are separate Cypriot and Palestinian Bichrome products.[1603] However, the problem concerns chronology. It has variously been argued that Cypriot Bichrome appeared first, in later MBII, that Bichrome generally started in, even marks, the late MBA phase, or alternatively that Bichrome does not pre-date the Palestinian LBI period, and so in effect delineates the LBA.[1604] On Cyprus, as noted in Chapter IV.4, some have argued for its appearance in MCIII, others in LCIA (and in effect probably the same temporal period is indicated, LCIA, but with the east of Cyprus continuing the later MC styles). It is fair to say that confusion reigns. Yet, paradoxically, Bichrome Ware assumes key importance in a number of chronological arguments in Syro-Palestinian archaeology. The study of Gates on the chronology of Alalakh is an example.[1605] Muhly (1985:25–26), with reference to her study, observes:

> The important point is that she has made the dating of Bichrome ware the crux of her chronological argument whereas anyone familiar with all the arguments that have gone on regarding the archaeological context of Bichrome ware in Cyprus and in Palestine would realise that a chronological system built upon Bichrome ware is a chronology built upon foundations of sand.

Further work has confirmed that Bichrome Ware does indeed appear in the final MBA phase in Palestine, and it is also found in the contemporary D/2 stratum at Tell el-Dabᶜa.[1606] Epstein (1966) in her classic study, while accepting Palace I occurrences at Tell el-ᶜAjjul, resisted a pre-LBI/pre-Ahmose date for Bichrome Ware, and so this Tell el-ᶜAjjul context, on the basis of the sequence at Megiddo. She insisted despite statements to the contrary that Bichrome Ware did not occur at Megiddo until the LBA level IX. Today we have to accept that this is incorrect. Bichrome Ware was found in Level X, and, in general, the appearance of Bichrome Ware very much defines the final MBII (MBIIC or MBIII) phase in Syria–Palestine.[1607] Kempinski (1983:131–148, 223) argued that the Bichrome Ware at Tell el-ᶜAjjul appeared in the final MBA phase, and more specifically around or a little before the time of the beginning of the reign of Apophis, penultimate ruler of the Hyksos dynasty. This allows us to estimate a date. Apophis has an attested year 33, and is assumed to have ruled for more than 40

[1601] Artzy (1973); Artzy *et al.* (1978); Knapp and Cherry (1994:56). For other analyses showing Cypriot origin, see also Artzy *et al.* (1973; 1981). An original Aegean late MBA or initial LBA source/inspiration/influence may further be argued (see Chapter IV.4; Artzy n.d.).

[1602] Muhly (1985:24–26).

[1603] Artzy *et al.* (1978); Wood (1982); Knapp and Cherry (1994:56–57).

[1604] For the last, see Wood (1982) with refs. to earlier literature. For a general review, see Bimson (1981:137–171).

[1605] Gates (1981; 1987).

[1606] Bietak (1991b:313; 1996a:63); Maguire (1992:117 Fig.2; 1995).

[1607] Gonen (1992:98–99) provides a useful brief sumary. See also Kempinski (1983); Oren (1997b:271). For the specific case of MBA level X (Area BB) finds at Megiddo, see Gonen (1987:86 and 96 Table; Gonen 1992:98–104); Kempinski (1989:61).

years (restoring 4[1] years in the Turin Canon).[1608] The length of reign of his successor and final Hyksos king, Khamudy, is more ambiguous (see Appendix 1). If the entry on the reverse of the Rhind Mathematical Papyrus, which refers to a year 11 of an unnamed king associated with bad omens and the encroachment of the Thebans, is an allusion to Khamudy,[1609] then his reign is 11+ years (since the actual siege of Avaris possibly took several further years). Otherwise, if this reference is instead associated with year 11 of Ahmose (or someone else), there is no direct evidence. Von Beckerath (1997:137) considers restoring c.9 years for Khamudy in the Turin Canon, and ends up awarding 11 years (p.189), but this is arbitrary, and dictated by a complete guess for the first king, 'Salitis'. Ryholt (1997:189, 201), in contrast, argues for just 1 year for Khamudy's reign. As argued in Appendix 1, I reject this minimalist approach, and suggest that 11+ years is the best available estimate. We might thus estimate c.50 to 55 years from the fall of Avaris to the beginning of the reign of Apophis. Therefore, at a minimum, on the low Egyptian chronology, with the accession of Ahmose c.1540BC, and the conquest of Avaris thus c.1534–1520BC (between Ahmose years 7–21), the beginning of the reign of Apophis is c.1589–1570BC. Bichrome Ware is around in Palestine a little before, or from about, this time. If the middle, or alternative current, Egyptian chronology is employed, and the accession of Ahmose is placed c.1552/1550BC,[1610] then these dates become 1601/1596BC to 1585/1580BC. The conventional date for the start of the Bichrome Ware phase in the Levant used by archaeologists is c.1600BC.[1611]

The assemblage of Alalakh VII should lie before these dates. A conflict with the ultra-low date – of as low as c.1519BC – for the destruction of Alalakh VII from the chronology of Gasche *et al.* (1998) is apparent, and it is very difficult if not impossible to see how to make these two different dating schemes compatible. The Egyptian chronology is regarded as sound (and the low Egyptian chronology is if anything a minimum base-line: see Appendix 1), so the Bichrome chronology cannot really go down more than a few years (according to judgement). Instead, a date range from the later 17th century BC, through to the first two to three decades of the 16th century BC (at most), seems required for the end of Alalakh level VII. It may fairly be pointed out that 'at Alalakh Bichrome Ware is found in Levels VI and V, but at most there are no more than twelve sherds', and that 'it may be better to evaluate the whole range of Cypriote wares and their general pattern of distribution, rather than relying heavily

---

[1608] On the Turin Canon, see Gardiner (1959); Redford (1986:1–18, 197–201); Kitchen (1995:540–550 no.288); von Beckerath (1964; 1997:19–23, 207–213); and especially now Ryholt (1997:9–33 and passim). Helck's (1992a) reconstruction is ignored, following the arguments of Ryholt (1997:21). The extant text is both fragmentary (incomplete) and late. It was written on the back of a Ramesside tax document, but presumably reflects earlier/extant kinglist records. It is usually regarded as the best (or only) useful source for the SIP. Manetho offers different reign lengths (for example: 61 years for Apophis versus the usual 4[1] from the Turin Canon), and a much longer overall SIP period. The Manetho-derived data for the SIP seem generally impractical.

[1609] As for example Bietak (1997:114 argues). See also el-Sabbahy (1993).

[1610] von Beckerath (1994a; 1997).

[1611] E.g. Oren (1997b:271).

on Bichrome Ware which, because of its scarcity, may provide a misleading sense of its date'.[1612]

However, general assessment of the Cypriot data leads to the same conclusion. Level VIB is contemporary with mature LCIB (even into LCIIA), and probably/possibly LHIIA/LMIB. This in turn means the Syro-Palestinian LBI period and the early 18th Dynasty down to about the reign of Tuthmosis III. It might be guessed that the preceding level VIA should therefore be contemporary in broad terms with at least part of the LCIA period, perhaps into early LCIB (since level VIB seems mature LCIB into perhaps even LCIIA). The finds from level VIA lack examples of the key diagnostic early LCIA types, such as PWS or Bichrome Ware, and in fact lack many Cypriot finds altogether. There is Cypriot Red on Black and Monochrome ware, typical respectively of MCIII–LCIA, and LCIA onwards, but nothing else. The rest of the local assemblage fits into a later MBA horizon, and the impression is that the specific close of MBA assemblage known from Palestine is not represented (for whatever reason: only small excavated areas of level VIA, no destruction deposits representing the – in effect missing – late VIA phase, a hiatus, etc.). This interval co-ordinates with final MBII (MBIIC or MBIII) period in Palestine, and the later Hyksos period. The extant level VIA Cypriot assemblage ranges from Red on Black (just two sherds) which links with Tell el-Dab'a stratum E/1,[1613] to initial Monochrome ware which links with late MBII (MBIIC or MBIII) into LBI (see Chapter IV.5). Missing at Alalakh is an entire lengthy period ranging from initial Bichrome Ware and PWS through earlier WSI. Whether this should be levels VII–VIA, or just VIA, or mainly VII, is totally unclear on existing evidence. This lack of good correlation criteria makes any ceramic-based chronology highly problematic. A mid-17th century BC (c.1650BC) beginning for level VII seems widely accepted.[1614] The LMIA-style frescoes from the construction of Yarim-Lim's palace thus co-ordinate perfectly with the early Aegean chronology. The debate is over the date for the close of the period. If the absence of Bichrome Ware from level VII is meaningful (from the dozen sherds found at the entire site!), then the close of level VII is appropriately dated no later than about the beginning of the reign of Apophis (and so before the appearance of Bichrome Ware), but it could easily have been a couple of decades earlier (e.g. c.1600BC[1615]).

If the nexus of textual data tying Hattusili I to the destruction of Alalakh VII is correct, then the only conclusion one can reach is either that the ultra-low chronology of Gasche *et al.* (1998) for the fall of Babylon is incorrect, or that the association of Mursili I's raid on Babylon with the end of the reign of Samsuditana is incorrect (the lack of contemporary evidence was noted above). If the latter conventional reconstruction is maintained, it may also be observed that the Low chronology – with its upper date of 1586BC for the end of Alalakh working back from Mursili I's raid on Babylon equalling the end of Samsuditana's reign – only just offers a suitable

---

[1612] McClellan (1989:192).

[1613] E.g. Maguire (1992:Fig.2).

[1614] E.g. Heinz (1992:204, 206, 210).

[1615] Compare the chronological scheme in Heinz (1992:204).

correlation range. Given that the Venus tablet chronological system is almost definitely to be regarded as inappropriate or non-existent (see above), this might be regarded as almost favouring a real Babylonian/Assyrian chronology in the 'raised Low' category, something about one to three decades earlier than the Venus-tablet Low chronology. This could fit the dendrochronological data from the Sarıkaya palace at Acemhöyük, the collection of textual data relevant to Alalakh VII, and the archaeological data relevant to Alalakh VII (especially if a high or middle Egyptian chronology were found to be appropriate).

We may now insert Thera. The frescoes from the Yarim-Lim palace at Alalakh are comparable to neopalatial Minoan and Late Cycladic I/LMIA Theran examples. If the 1628BC date for the eruption of Thera is accepted, then the Alalakh frescoes are likely to date from around this point. The Tel Kabri frescoes also come from a pre-Bichrome Ware late MBII context,[1616] and are likely to be closely contemporary. A mid to late 17th century BC to start of the 16th century BC date for Alalakh VII, as required by the 1628BC date for Thera, is exactly what we have already derived from the analysis and resolution of the textual and archaeological data relevant to Alalakh VII (start to end of period). The whole nexus of data ties together in a highly consistent and coherent manner with this chronological construction; a mid-16th century BC date for the Thera eruption would be possible – frescoes at Alalakh and Tel Kabri seen as earlier than those at Akrotiri – but is less satisfactory. A date for the Thera eruption 'between 1515 and 1460 B.C.', as argued by Bietak (1997:125), is almost impossible.[1617] In addition, some further refinements of the relative linkages between LMIA, MCIII–LCIA, and Syro-Palestinian later MBII, are now evident from the foregoing discussion. The neopalatial-style frescoes from Alalakh and Tel Kabri suggest a correlation with a pre-Bichrome Ware stage of late MBII. However, the find of the early WSI bowl on pre-eruption Thera indicates that, by the time of the eruption, and the destruction of Akrotiri, later/late LMIA had moved on into a correlation with the Bichrome Ware, earlier LCI, phase in general, and the Syro-Palestinian late MBII (MBIIC or MBIII) period. Thus we must place the earlier neopalatial, MMIIIB–LMIA, period as extending from the pre-Bichrome Ware phase, and so the late MCIII to early LCIA period,[1618] and the later Syro-Palestinian MBII period, through to the initial Bichrome Ware phase, and the general LCIA period, and the Syro-Palestinian final MBII (MBIIC or MBIII) period.

The most interesting conclusion from the foregoing discussion is therefore that the exploration of the chronology of Alalakh level VII leads to a date which is very much the conventional date. This is both irrespective of, and/or in agreement with, the

---

[1616] Kempinski (1992b:70–72); Niemeier and Niemeier (1998:73).

[1617] This conclusion applies also to the c.1520BC date for the Thera eruption advocated by Warren (1998:328) and, needless to say, to the c.1460BC date advocated by Eriksson (1992:219).

[1618] Note, as discussed in Chapter IV.4, although Bichrome Ware is regarded as an indicator of earliest LCIA (or MCIII = LCIA) by some scholars, it does not occur at some other important Cypriot sites until a more mature stage of LCIA or LCI (i.e. it appears with WSI and BRI): e.g. at Myrtou-Pigadhes, Kalopsidha, Enkomi, and Toumba tou Skourou (see review in Eriksson 1992:205–206, 212, 214). Thus the 'pre-Bichrome phase' may well include initial LCIA.

early 1628BC date for the Thera eruption. The early Thera date is shown not to lead to any radical upsets, and at most merely helps refine long-standing debate or ambiguity in West Asian chronology. And this is very much the point of this case study. The 'early' Thera–Aegean chronology applies only where directly relevant. The ripples outward are important, but they may well have little or no effect on distinct or independent cultures and chronologies (where approximately correct/valid). This de-coupling is crucial, and avoids the usual conclusion that if one thing changes then everything else necessarily must change with it (and the retort that this is impossible). Likewise, a 'high' or 'middle' Egyptian 18th Dynasty chronology can sit with a Low or raised-Low, Babylonian chronology.[1619] As Maguire (1992:esp.116–117) argues in a sensible study, considerable care and caution must be taken with synchronisms – especially ones based on few, or broadly dated, objects. Archaeologists in the Aegean and east Mediterranean tend to take too positive an approach, and to suffer from tunnel vision formed via tradition.[1620]

The most important outcome of the study of pre-historic Aegean chronology is that it permits the appropriate Aegean cultural periods/phases to be correlated with the Hittite, West Asian, and Egyptian chronologies and histories. This is the goal or raison d'être of the present enterprise. It is undoubtedly true that a real objectivity in history and historical analysis is impossible,[1621] but we can nevertheless achieve a useful 'historical objectivity' through the logic of comparison and the building of coherent frameworks.[1622] In the second millennium BC Aegean and east Mediterranean, I submit that the combination of relative and absolute chronology permits a better 'historical objectivity'. From this, appropriate interpretation may follow. The central conclusions of the present work are, therefore, the need to realign the LMIA period in the Aegean, and the LCIA period of Cyprus (comprising its distinct regional northwest and eastern/southeastern groupings), with the SIP period in Egypt, and the late MBII period in Syria–Palestine, and the recognition of an important east Mediterranean phase (what I have termed, loosely, a 'world system' in earlier chapters) at this time centred on greater Canaan and especially the major port cities such as Ugarit, Byblos, Ebla, Tell el-ʿAjjul, and the 14th–15th Dynasty kingdom, and the great city, of Avaris.

[1619] But not an ultra-low Babylonian chronology – however, the ultra-low of chronology of Gasche *et al.* (1998) has been shown to be unsatisfactory above. Alalakh continues to have its uses.

[1620] Here I wish to take the opportunity to correct a mistake in previous writing by this author where I have fallen victim to the very fault castigated in the text. Manning (1995:219 towards end) stated that a 'high' Aegean LBA chronology goes with a high Babylonian chronology. This was an error caused by the failure to extract my thinking there from the entire inter-locked mode of thought in relevant scholarship. I should have realised that each chronology at issue is entirely independent of the other (whilst the range of movement is constrained by various linkages between them in the Amarna period). As Astour (1989) argues, there is no reason why a 'low' Babylonian chronology cannot fit with a 'high' Egyptian chronology for the New Kingdom. And, indeed, as argued in the text, dendrochronological data lends strong support to a raised-low to low (or thereabouts) Babylonian chronology (revising views previously expressed by this author: Manning 1995:123, 111–113), whilst also lending support to an early chronology for the Aegean Late Bronze Age (Kuniholm *et al.* 1996; the present book).

[1621] Jenkins (1991); Bernstein (1983); Hall (1980); Collingwood (1994).

[1622] Bevir (1994).

The koine of LMIA Aegean-style frescoes around the Aegean and east Mediterranean at major sites is the epitome of this cultural horizon. The raised Aegean LMIB/LHIIA to LMIIIA1/LHIIIA1 chronology also has important implications for the interpretation of subsequent Aegean relations with the eastern Mediterranean. As noted previously, a good example is that the early Aegean-Hittite relations known from Hittite texts make much better sense with the 'early', or 'high', Aegean chronology.[1623] Moreover, such matters not only affect the material culture and archaeological linkages of the Aegean and east Mediterranean, but also the attempt to place the Aegean into its protocultural and protohistoric milieu, and the possibility of appropriate interpretation of the resonances of LBA epic (both Aegean and Near Eastern) found preserved in contemporary art and subsequent early Iron Age Greek literature.[1624]

[1623] Mee (1998:142).

[1624] For the suggestions of Aegean LBA wall paintings reflecting contemporary epic poetry/stories, see e.g. Morris (1989); Hiller (1990). For discussion of Near Eastern influences and elements in early Greek poetry, see West (1997). For the suggestions that the foundations, and expansionary activities, of early LBA Mycenaean Greece provide the basis to parts of the 8th century BC Homeric epic cycle tradition (formed in the earlier LBA, maintained during the palatial Mycenaean LBA, and then recreated in the early Iron Age), see e.g. Vermeule (1986; 1987) and Sherratt (1990). For the 8th century BC composition date of the Homeric epics (indeed, probably first half), see Janko (1998:1 and n.6 with further refs). Hood (1995) attempts to rebut these suggestions, and instead argues for a post-palatial LHIIIC origin. But he fails to engage with the overall argument put forward by Sherratt and Vermeule (e.g. accepting Sherratt's point about a stratigraphy of text at p.27 and n.24 but then not engaging with Sherratt's wider case). For a general review of archaeology and Homer, see Manning (1992c). For the recent work at Troy, and in particular the find of the large lower city, see the articles in *Studia Troica* vol.1 (1991) onwards.

Appendix 1: Egyptian Chronology

The chronology of the 18th Dynasty of Egypt has been referred to a number of times in this work, and is central to the entire controversy surrounding the date of the eruption of Thera, and the 'early' Aegean chronology.[1625] The standard modern chronological syntheses of Jurgen von Beckerath and Kenneth Kitchen have been cited in the main text.[1626] These place the accession of Ahmose respectively c.1552/1550BC or c.1540BC. Both regard the accessions of Tuthmosis III in 1479BC and Ramesses II in 1279BC as fixed points. Most recent scholarship by leading figures in Egyptology has reached very similar conclusions.[1627] In historical terms, these represent the middle and low chronologies of the New Kingdom (among 'respectable' scholarship). Helck proposed an ultra-low chronology (Ahmose from 1530BC),[1628] but this has been ruled out.[1629] However, it has also been noted in a couple of places in the main text that the evidence might be compatible with a higher Egyptian chronology. At the opening of the 20th century AD Breasted proposed such a higher chronology; he placed the start of the 18th Dynasty in 1580BC, and placed the accession of Tuthmosis III c.1501BC.[1630] Parker (1957) then supported a revision to such dates, placing the accessions of Tuthmosis III and Ramesses II at 1490BC and 1290BC respectively, based on analysis of the relevant lunar data. Hornung, Redford, and others supported the Parker dates in studies published in the 1960s.[1631] Redford (1966:124 Table 1) placed the accession of Ahmose in 1558BC according to such a chronology. Hayes meanwhile proposed a 'high' 1504BC accession date for Tuthmosis III, linked with a 1304BC accession date for Ramesses II. When incorporated in the *Cambridge Ancient History* by Hayes (1970), this became the best known Egyptian chronology outside the specialist field. The accession of Ahmose and the start of the 18th Dynasty were dated c.1570BC on this

---

[1625] For another recent review of Egyptian chronology by an Aegeanist, see Wiener (1998:315–317).

[1626] von Beckerath (1994a; 1997) – see with Krauss (1995); Kitchen (1987; 1991; 1996a).

[1627] See table in von Beckerath (1994a:124).

[1628] Helck (1987; 1992b).

[1629] von Beckerath (1992; 1994a) and Kitchen (1996a:6). Helck's ultra-low chronology struggles to work satisfactorily with the other Near Eastern, and Hittite, linkages.

[1630] Breasted (1962, vol.I:§38–§75). The dates for the 18th Dynasty are given in (§66).

[1631] Hornung (1964); Redford (1966; 1967).

chronology. The high chronology of Hayes was initially criticised by other scholars in the 1960s, but new studies in the 1970s offered strong support.[1632] An amalgamation high–low (i.e. long) chronology was also proposed in the mid-1970s by Wente and Van Siclen (1976). Scholarly opinion then changed in the late 1970s and 1980s. Today the 'high' chronology of Hayes is stated by many to be impossible, but, even those supporting the low chronology admit that the 'higher' Parker chronology remains a possibility.

The central questions which this Appendix seeks to review and investigate are: (i) exactly how secure is the conventional chronology of the 18th Dynasty, and (ii) whether, despite current scholarly opinion, a higher chronology is feasible?[1633] This may seem a great deal of concern over 11–25 years, but it is important.[1634]

BASIC APPROACHES: ASTROCHRONOLOGY, DEAD-RECKONING, AND PROBLEMS

With reference to the second millennium BC, what are the key facts of Egyptian chronology? First, a complete chronology from a fixed point does *not* exist! An agreed and known list of rulers in sequence with definite reign lengths from Greco-Roman times backwards to the middle of the second millennium BC is not available. There are certainly many lists, and many names, and they undoubtedly provide rulers for the whole of the period in question, but there are many problems, gaps, debated relationships, times when different parts of Egypt were ruled simultaneously by

---

[1632] See summary of Casperson (1986:140–141 with many references).

[1633] Kitchen (1996a:5) states that: 'The scepticism of Manning 1995, 16, n.5, concerning the 1279 date for Ramesses II (and 1479 for Tuthmosis III ...) was, frankly, unwarranted; he appeared not to have grasped the extent and relative value of our various source-materials'. The present Appendix therefore seeks to discuss and argue in some detail why the confidence of Kitchen in dead-reckoning, and in his exact chronology, is misplaced. Kitchen of course did not actually provide any arguments concerning my discussion in Manning (1995:16–17 n.5).

[1634] Giles (1997:81) would take the view that I, and also Kitchen, and von Beckerath, are guilty of making the mistake of trying to be overly precise. Giles argues 'that the whole chronology of this period is very difficult to establish, and is complicated further by the attempts of various modern scholars to force the scanty data remaining from the middle of the Second Millennium BC into a scheme of modern western year dates, the details of which they cannot determine among themselves'. Giles goes on to state that 'in Egypt, even the chronology of the Eighteenth Dynasty is not fixed', and he enumerates variable factors where 'alone more than half a century could be involved'. A response is difficult to such overwhelming pessimism and scepticism. I note that his views on the lack of a fixed chronology in Egypt, and his similar view that 'in Mesopotamia, the possibility of error over such a span of time, where dead reckoning is the principal tool, is manifest and unavoidable. The Babylonian King Lists and the Assyrian 'Limmu' lists are systems of dead reckoning, in which leading authorities in the field place a degree of faith which is frankly incomprehensible', support my general theme that there is sufficient flexibility to permit the Egyptian king-list/historical data to fit with the early Aegean chronology. There is a more informed, but similar, scepticism in the review of Cryer (1995). However, one must dispute Giles' sweeping dismissal of chronological studies. They are the basis and framework for the history he would like to write of the period. Further, it is through a more solid and precise chronology, and independent reference points such as the eruption of Thera, that scholarship concerned with the second millennium BC eastern Mediterranean region will be able to escape from completely relative and circular argumentation, and to evaluate competing hypotheses.

different dynasties, and so on. Some sets of reasonably well known blocks of rulers exist, for example: the Middle Kingdom of the 12th Dynasty, and the New Kingdom of the 18th and 19th Dynasties. In the case of the latter, attested data on some 18th Dynasty pharaohs come from several sources, and can moreover be correlated against inscriptions in tombs giving lengths of service of Viziers and various other court officials and soldiers. Thus the reigns of a few pharaohs are virtually absolute in terms of their length (e.g. Tuthmosis III at 53 years, 10 months, and 26 days[1635]). Likewise, the genealogical data on the high priests at Memphis secures the 22nd Dynasty in approximate terms. But these blocks of relative certainty float in time due to problems in the periods before and afterwards. In particular, at the end of the MBA and at the end of the LBA (not coincidental), central government collapses in Egypt, and complex and poorly understood periods with several contemporary dynasties ruling different areas occur: the so-called Second and Third Intermediate Periods.[1636]

In an attempt to circumvent these problems, Egyptologists have followed two approaches. The traditional one sought to establish fixed points of chronology, via retro-dating records of astronomical observations of either the star Sirius (Sothis) or the Moon, which can then tie down the various 'good' floating blocks of rulers.[1637] The other approach is to try through detailed prosopographical analysis and argument to reconstruct a best continuous sequence of kings, and regnal data, from the firm dates of the 6th and 7th centuries BC through to the 18th Dynasty, and so establish a chronology based on the 'dead-reckoning' of historical information.[1638] Unfortunately, few scholars outside Egyptology consider, or seem to wish to understand in any detail, the actual basis and mechanics of the Egyptian chronologies they employ; convenient dates are cited, but not the many pages of caveats and best guesses and discussions of problems. Some practiioners seem themselves to forget the assumptions, hypotheses, and caveats they employed in previous studies, or even elsewhere during the course of lengthy books, when finally stating their chronology.[1639]

The central astronomical bases to the second millennium BC chronology of Egypt concern the star Sirius (Sothis), the brightest star in the night sky. In Egypt, a key

---

[1635] Stated in the biography of Amenemheb (Breasted 1962, vol.II:§592). See e.g. Wente (1975:267–268); von Beckerath (1997:109).

[1636] For the former, see Ryholt (1997); Oren (1997a); von Beckerath (1964); Van Seters (1966); Redford (1970); for the latter, see Kitchen (1996b) – previously Kitchen (1986; 1973); Baer (1973); Wente (1967).

[1637] Leitz (1989); von Beckerath (1994a:8–16; 1997:41–51); Krauss (1985; 1998b). For the standard older study, see Meyer (1904).

[1638] Kitchen (1996a; 1996b).

[1639] For a critical, general, but brief, review of Egyptian chronology, see Ward (1992). For details on the chronological evidence, Egyptian calendars, time-keeping, and records, and the astronomical data and its interpretation, see, variously: Parker (1950); Hornung (1964); von Beckerath (1984; 1993; 1994a; 1997); Krauss (1985; 1994; 1995; 1998b); Redford (1986); Leitz (1989); Luft (1992a; 1992b); Spalinger (1992; 1994); and Kitchen (1987; 1996b). On Egyptian and general ancient Babylonian astronomy/astrology, see e.g. Neugebauer and Parker (1960–1969); Neugebauer (1975:347–566); Krauss (1997); Depuydt (1998). On the chronology of the 18th Dynasty, Redford (1967:esp.183–215) provides a useful compendium of scholarship to the late 1960s. The two extremes of mainstream scholarship in the 1970s are represented by Wente and Van Siclen (1976) and Krauss (1978), each with further references to the then current literature. For a current synthesis, see von Beckerath (1994a) with Krauss (1995).

event was the Nile flood which occurred every year; this event very much determined the Egyptian agricultural year. Because of Egypt's southerly latitude, Sirius is invisible for some of the year, but re-appears just before dawn at about the time of the Nile flood. This re-appearance, termed the heliacal rising, was New Year's Day in the Egyptian calendar (19 July in the second millennium BC). The agricultural calendar was linked to this astronomical observation, and, tied to observations of the moon for more refined detail, formed the basis of calendars and an absolute time keeping system in Egypt.[1640] A key problem was precision. The civil calendar ended up as a 365 day scheme, but the true sideral year is slightly over a quarter of a day longer. Thus every four years the civil calendar fell a day behind the sidereal (and so Sothis) calendar; over time, the civil calendar's New Year's Day fell on every day of the sidereal year (and largely nowhere near the Sirius-determined New Year's Day). A complete cycle, whereby there is a return to the civil calendar's New Year matching sideral time, is about 1460 years.[1641] This cycle is referred to as the Sothic Cycle.[1642]

By luck, the Roman writer Censorinus[1643] informs us that the heliacal rising of Sirius matched the New Year's Day of the Egyptian civil calendar on 20 July AD139.[1644] In confirmation, coins were minted at Alexandria in Egypt showing a phoenix/crane in a crown of rays with the legend AION.[1645] The previous such occasion would therefore be c.1321BC (and in fact probably some 4–7 years later). A manuscript with the work of Theon, writing in the fourth century AD, provides further consonant information (quite possibly not independent). It states that 1605 years had passed from Menophres to the end of the era of Augustus.[1646] By the era of Augustus the writer meant the introduction of the era of Diocletian on 29 August AD284.[1647] 1605 years before is also 1321BC. Thus we have an end/beginning of the Sothic cycle. And, by luck, there are a couple of records from ancient Egypt recording the day in terms of the civil calendar (and so also some specific Pharaoh's reign) on which the heliacal rising of Sirius occurred. An approximate date may therefore be calculated for these.

Who or what is Menophres? If this were a clear fact, then it would offer a good basis to later second millennium BC Egyptian chronology. Needless to say, this is a debated point. One school of thought holds that this is a Greek rendering of the throne name (*Men-pehty-re*) of Ramesses I.[1648] Ramesses I had a very short reign (less than

---

[1640] For the argument that the c.1460 year Sothic cycle can be explained through connecting the agricultural year with an annual astronomical phenomenon, see Neugebauer (1938). For general discussions of Egyptian and Near Eastern calendars, time, and measurement systems, see Hallo (1996:120–143); Spalinger (1996); Neugebauer (1969). The classic detailed work on Egyptian calendars remains Parker (1950).

[1641] Cf. Ingham (1969) for details and exact precision – the true figure is a couple of years less.

[1642] For a brief account, see Bickerman (1980:40–43).

[1643] Sallmann (1983).

[1644] Interpreting *De die natali* 21.10, and see 18.10 for details of calendars including Sothic cycle, see Meyer (1912:27–36).

[1645] Poole (1964:lxxxvi, 117 no.1004, pl.26 no.1004); Bickerman (1980:41); Astour (1989:79 n.13).

[1646] See Meyer (1912:36 and n.1, 37); Montet (1937); Rowton (1946:107–109); Long (1974:269–271); von Beckerath (1997:47; 1994a:13–14).

[1647] For this date, see Bickerman (1980:72 and n.59).

[1648] See Astour (1989:3 and refs.); Faulkner (1975:218); Montet (1937).

two full years), so this would provide a specific time fix. The so-called high Egyptian chronology placed the reign of Ramesses I at c.1320–1318BC based on a 1304BC accession of Ramesses II (one of three possibilities from lunar data: see below), and this would be entirely compatible. Some other scholars have suggested that Menophres could instead also be associated with the name of his successor, Sethos I (*Men-ma-re Sety mer-en ptah*), and/or his position as the practical founder of a new era.[1649] It is even possible that the reference could in effect be to these two kings combined, since their reigns began within a year (Sethos I initially as co-regent). King Merenptah, successor of Ramesses II, and whose name is also similar, is dismissed as definitely much too late – moreover, his reign cannot be seen as inaugerating any new era. The reign of Sethos I began c.1318BC on the high chronology. However, another school of thought argues that Menophres derives from the word for Memphis, and that the era of Menophres therefore refers to the renewal at Memphis under Haremhab.[1650] This interpretation is consonant with the low Egyptian chronology which places the accession of Haremhab c.1323BC[1651] or 1319BC.[1652] Such ambiguity is the hallmark of the chronology of the Egyptian New Kingdom: a tantalising precision, but inevitably a possible range of choices or interpretation over a c.25 year range. In this instance, the 'era of Memphis' argument appears to involve rather more special pleading than the simple link with Ramesses I. Despite his short reign, Ramesses I represented an historically important moment.[1653] Ramesses I appreciated that he was the founder of a new dynasty, and he specifically chose a throne name that echoed a re-founding of Egyptian kingship by imitating the throne name of Ahmose. So as Ahmose was *Neb-pehty-re*, lord of might is Re, so Ramesses I became *Men-pehty-re*, enduring of might is Re. Therefore, it makes sense both in terms of the similarity of the Greek name Menophres to this throne name, and in terms of the historical impression of this representing a new era. As second choice, the reign of Sethos I was also seen as the real beginning of a new era by later writers. Either of these supports a high/higher Egyptian chronology.

In principle, it might seem that careful analysis of the examples of extant Sothic data should form a secure chronological foundation for second millennium BC Egypt, and so it seemed for much of this century following the pioneering work of Meyer.[1654] The problems, however, are also plentiful.[1655] First, Censorinus is not a contemporary of the event he mentions, he is passing on data one hundred years old when he wrote, and we have no way to check the accuracy of transmission. Nor do we know if the

---

[1649] Rowton (1946:107–108) citing Sethe; Hayes (1970:190) who compares to Amenemhat I, founder of the 12th Dynasty; von Beckerath (1994a:13–14; 1997:47). For a brief survey of his reign, see Kitchen (1982:20–41).

[1650] Wente and Van Siclen (1976:233–234 and refs.); Rowton (1946:107–109).

[1651] Kitchen (1996a).

[1652] von Beckerath (1997).

[1653] Kitchen (1982:18–19).

[1654] Meyer (1904; 1912).

[1655] The attempt at a general critique by Long (1974) may be corrected on some points – e.g. Parker (1976) – but does highlight a number of problems and unproven assumptions.

rising was observed, or merely computed. Second, scholarship has to guess where the observation recorded in Censorinus was made; Sirius appeared earlier as one travelled south in Egypt: by about a day per degree of latitude further south. Hence, from the Mediterranean coast of Egypt at 31° latitude, to Elephantine at the First Cataract of the Nile at 24°, some 7 degrees of latitude, or seven days difference of observation of the Heliacal rising of Sirius, are possible. For example, the difference between the major northern capital of Memphis, and the Upper Egyptian capital of Thebes, is 5 days. This small variation in contemporary observation times, translates into a difference in calculated dates in the second millennium BC of a few decades. The usual assumption of observation at Memphis is reasonable, but may not necessarily be correct. It might have been Alexandria; although it may be noted that observation of the heliacal rising of Sirius at Memphis was the base point for the Egyptian sacred year throughout Egyptian history as far as we know (arguments for the observation point being moved to Thebes, or Elephantine in far south Egypt, during the New Kingdom are conjecture and lack any direct positive evidence).[1656] Third, the process of observation is difficult (Sirius must in fact be a couple of degrees above the horizon to be seen, and the Sun must also be a couple of degrees below the horizon) and may vary due to local conditions, and we do not know on which of the four years (the *tetraeteris*) in which the heliacal rising occurs on the same day the observation noted by Censorinus was made. Such observational issues and variability affect all other recorded data as well.

The end result is that we have a rocky start even at the beginning of our search for a precise Egyptian chronology from astronomy, since one may debate exactly what Censorinus provides by way of an initial linch pin for the Sothic chronology,[1657] and, in general, one may identify several problems in the application of Sothic dating.[1658] In addition, and almost inevitably, the ancient textual data incorporating the relevant astronomical observations are usually either not complete, or not without ambiguity. The disputed interpretation of the fundamental Papyrus Ebers, containing Sothic data from year 9 of Amenhotep I and long employed to establish the early chronology of the 18th Dynasty, is a good example.[1659] It is of concern that several other key records (e.g. the lunar data for Tuthmosis III and Ramesses II) usually require some form of 'emendation' or preferred reading, rendering an absolute resolution of the relevant debate[1660] impossible on strict evidential grounds.[1661] Thus, barring finds of new text/inscriptional evidence which offers more certain information, the astronomical

---

[1656] Von Beckerath (1994a) argues that observations of Sirius were not made just at one place, but were a local affair for religious and agricultural purposes (see also Ward 1992:61–62). Thus he argues that some records, e.g. the Ebers Papyrus, may record an observation made at Thebes, while other records, e.g. one from the reign of Tuthmosis III, may record an observation made at Elephantine. This argument is entirely possible (even likely), but positive proof is lacking.

[1657] See Ward (1992:58) and his caveats.

[1658] E.g. Ward (1992); Rose (1994); Depuydt (1995).

[1659] See Depuydt (1996b) with extensive bibliography of past work; see further below.

[1660] E.g. whether the reign of Tuthmosis III begins in 1504BC, 1490BC, or 1479BC, or Ramesses II in 1304BC, 1290BC, or 1279BC.

[1661] Manuelian (1987:3–19); Bryan (1991:14–20); Parker (1957); Wente and Van Siclen (1976:223–224).

approach can never hope to be totally precise. It probably provides key data (see below), but margins of error inherently exist.

The other approach to second millennium BC Egyptian chronology is to work out a sequence of rulers, from textual and inscriptional evidence, backwards from the last agreed fixed date (in terms of our modern calendar systems reaching through to the Roman and Greek periods). The relevant sources range from the contemporary or near contemporary, to those which are much later, even if based on ancient evidence or traditions. The contemporary or near contemporary sources include the Turin Canon, ancient kinglist inscriptions at several locations, pharaonic annals and daybooks, contemporary administrative documents, dated inscriptions, genealogies and prosopographical data on various individuals, families and offices, a few extant examples of royal correspondence, and a few specific links with the histories of surrounding cultures.[1662] The later evidence consists of texts of the first millennium BC or afterwards which preserve compendiums of ancient kinglist traditions and histories.[1663] The most notable example is the history of Egypt from the work of Manetho, known to us from excerpts preserved in several subsequent authors.[1664]

The last truly fixed date in Egyptian history is usually agreed to be 664BC and the end of the reign of Taharqa/accession of Psammetichus I,[1665] although (if one were strict) it is 525BC when Cambyses conquered Egypt,[1666] and the Persian kings were integrated into the Egyptian kinglists and dating schemes.[1667] Kitchen (1996a:1) confidently asserts that: 'from original, *contemporary* sources, we may construct a basic Egyptian chronology dependent on no other source'. I refer to this approach as 'dead-reckoning' (after Kitchen). Now, if there were in fact a real, completely continuous, set of chronological data available in the ancient texts and inscriptions (and a real truth to be found), then this approach could, when the right analysis is applied, provide an absolute chronology. However, this basic premise is not present. We do not know that we have complete and continuous (yet alone accurate) data. It is undoubtedly gratuitously unfair, but nonetheless appropriate, to cite Gardiner's (1961:63) reminder that:

> what is proudly advertised as Egyptian history is merely a collection of rags and tatters. It would be good if the quantitative defects of our documentation were offset by its qualitative excellence. Unhappily it is not ... .

[1662] For a review, see von Beckerath (1997:19–31, 59–71). For the some of the kinglists and the Turin Canon, see von Beckerath (1997:204–216). For an English translation of the Turin Canon, see Kitchen (1995:540–550 no.288). On kinglists, pharaonic annals, and daybooks, see the detailed study of Redford (1986). On the Turin Canon, see also footnote 1608 above. For an example of the assorted documentary administrative records potentially available from ancient Egypt, see the collection relevant to the Amarna period assembled and translated in Murnane (1995). For the standard set of major documentary sources for ancient Egypt, see Breasted (1962).

[1663] von Beckerath (1997:32–40).

[1664] For an English translation, see Waddell (1940). For the Greek text and its sources, see Jacoby (1958:no.609).

[1665] Kitchen (1996a:1–2; 1996b:161–163, 174); von Beckerath (1997).

[1666] Depuydt (1996a).

[1667] Barta (1992).

All the evidence available demonstrates only that our current corpus of data is incomplete, and in some cases ambiguous or conflicting (the preface to Kitchen 1996b:xiv–xlvi where he tries to account for and/or dismiss a whole variety of various counter-views – from the plausible to the absurd – provides eloquent testimony of this undeniable fact). Even in the last few years, new discoveries have been made which require modifications of existing chronologies and datasets,[1668] or scholarly and rigorous new interpretations have been proposed.[1669] Such new evidence or debate is not solely restricted to the 'murky' times, like the Third Intermediate Period, or the possible interregnum/power struggle in the period around or after the reign of Queen Tewosret.[1670] In the 18th Dynasty, there is the question of whether a Nefernefruaten is identical to Smenkhkare, or whether instead this individual (possibly a women since the throne name, Ankh-kheprure, has a female ending – i.e. Nefertiti?) was a ruler in her/his own right for some period following Akhenaten for a few (?) years.[1671] More minor, but still potentially significant, the lengths of the reigns of Haremhab and Tuthmosis I and II remain unknown,[1672] and debate continues over the question of a significant co-regency between Amenhotep III and Akhenaten.[1673] The negotiations between an Egyptian king's widow and the Hittite king Suppiluliuma I also hint at an interregnum of 6 months to a year or more.[1674] Another pertinent example of new data changing the known minimum chronology comes from the very recent evidence found to show that the Middle Kingdom pharaoh Sesostris III, to whom Kitchen and von

---

[1668] E.g. Dodson (1993); Allen (1988; 1994a; 1994b).

[1669] E.g. Ashton (1989); Leahy (1990); Dodson (1993); von Beckerath (1994c; 1995a); Dautzenberg (1995); Hagens (1996).

[1670] Recently, see Wiener (1998:316). The argument is that there may have been an interregnum during or after the reign of Queen Tewosret at the close of the 19th Dynasty. The Papyrus Harris indicates a period of civil turmoil. As Wiener discusses, scholarship in the past had considered a possible interregnum of between about 5 years to up to two decades at this time (see Bierbrier 1975:118 n.4 for further literature supporting an interregnum). However, Hornung (1964:97) dismissed the existence of any interregnum, and most recent scholarship has followed this lead (see discussion in Bierbrier 1975:15). The matter is inconclusive. An interregnum period of up to about five years may still be agreed as possible (Bierbrier 1975:15, 121 n.104). Hence there are a few available years at this time. Further, irrespective of the interregnum issue, another possible source of a couple of 'extra' years concerns whether the stated regnal years of Tewosret followed on from Siptah (and so both reigns may be considered as one – co-regents), or whether they were in fact separate. Recent scholarship favours the former option, but the latter could yet prove correct (noted by Bierbrier 1975:2).

[1671] Allen (1988; 1994b); Murnane (1995:10, 207). If this king is female, suggestions have been Princess Meritaten, daughter of Akhenaten and Nefertiti, or Nefertiti herself. Harris (1973; 1974; Allen 1988; 1994b) made the case for the mother, whereas Krauss (1978) argued for Meritaten. What happened to this individual is not clear. How long a chronological interval to allow is also totally unclear. A number of objects bearing the name of Nefernefruaten were used in the burial of Tutankhamun. Thus Harris (1992) wondered if this meant she/he did not receive a kingly burial and was interred under a different name. Alternatively, since there were several objects with the name of Akhenaten, one might see this merely as linking Tutankhamun with his two familial predecessors, or that he died unexpectedly, and existing royal objects were used as gifts in some cases.

[1672] Wente and Van Siclen (1976:225–227; 231–232); von Beckerath (1994a:110–112).

[1673] Murnane (1995:5); Johnson (1996); Allen (1994a); Hayes (1970:189).

[1674] Güterbock (1956:94 and 96); Bryce (1998:193–197); see further below.

Beckerath following the studies of Simpson accord a 19 year reign,[1675] not only celebrated a *Heb-sed*, a 'jubilee', and so reigned for 30+ years,[1676] *but* in fact probably has a year 39 attested, and thus reigned for 39+ years![1677] This conforms with the data in the Turin Canon, but is a potential 20 year variation to the accepted chronology of scholarship from the last three decades. In an effort to compromise the conflicting data, and Simpson's case that Amenemhat III seems to be pharaoh shortly after Sesostris III's year 19 from a body of circumstantial and prosopographical data, Wegner (1996) proposes a long (i.e. 20 year!) co-regency betwen Sesostris III and Amenemhat III. This, however, is not without problems. In addition, in the Middle Kingdom, whereas Kitchen allows for some dozen years of co-regencies with respect to the overall reign of Sesostris I,[1678] Obsomer (1995), in a comprehensive treatment of this pharaoh, makes a strong case that Sesostris I was not a co-regent at either end of his reign (a further variation of 12 and a bit years from the Kitchen chronology, since Obsomer also shows that Sesostris I reigned into a 46th year, whereas Kitchen allots him 45 years).[1679]

We simply do not know what else may be found, or what else may change. Nor are a number of current assumptions or hypotheses proven. We know there are unknown factors, and we know there are existing ambiguities or conflicts. But we have no control over the unknown. The most obvious instance (as noted above) is that only in some cases is the final year (total length of reign) of a king known for certain, often we merely have a highest attested year from available evidence: see Table 14. The New Kingdom chronology of Kitchen closely follows the highest attested year, except in a few instances (and there may be other as yet unknown instances). Subsequent years, not known or attested to us, must almost inevitably exist in at least some cases, especially in the less certain span of the Third Intermediate Period.[1680] The 'known' chronology is thus merely a *minimum* chronology.[1681] A mere one ruler back from the 664BC base line, Shebitku, older brother of Taharqa, we find a good case to illustrate this general point. Kitchen (1996a:2) states: 'We have no date for Shebitku beyond Year 3 at present, but he certainly reigned longer'.[1682]

[1675] Kitchen (1996a:9, 11; 1987:43); von Beckerath (1997:132–134); Simpson (1963; 1972; 1984).

[1676] Arnold (1992); Arnold and Oppenheim (1995:47–48, fig.5 and n.5); Yurco (1996:69–70). For celebration of the jubilee in the 12th Dynasty, see Simpson (1963:59–63); also Wente and Van Siclen (1976:219–221).

[1677] Wegner (1996).

[1678] Kitchen (1996a:11; 1987:49).

[1679] Although cf. Jansen-Winkeln (1997).

[1680] It is interesting to note, in situations where one can compare ancient lists tabulating overall reign lengths with modern finds of known highest attested year, that the figures in the lists tend to be typically slightly higher than the data for highest attested year. The Kassite dynasty of Babylon offers an example: Brinkman (1976:430).

[1681] This point is noted and accepted by practitioners (e.g. Bierbrier 1975:1–2). One possibly useful approach which might be investigated is the creation of a completeness measure of all the extant (contemporary documentary/inscriptional) data relevant to Egyptian chronology. An obvious analogy here comes from evolutionary biology, where work has gone into creating completeness measures of the extant fossil record (see Foote and Sepkoski 1999).

[1682] With Kitchen here disagreeing with Depudyt (1993) who took the literalist dead-reckoning position: see further in Kitchen (1996b:xxxix–xlii, 453, 553, 555–557).

King	Highest Attested Year of Reign	Years of Reign in Kitchen (1996a; 1987)	Difference
Ahmose	22	25	3
Amenhotep I	21	21	0
Tuthmosis I	9	12	3
Tuthmosis II	1	3 (13*)	2 (12*)
Tuthmosis III	54	54	0
Amenhotep II	26	26 (co-regent 2 years)	0 or 2
Tuthmosis IV	8	10	2
Amenhotep III	38	38	0
Akhenaten	17	16	≤1
Smenkhkare	3	2 (co-regent 1 year)	1 or 0
Tutankhamun	10	9	≤1
Ay	4	4	0
Haremhab	27 (28/29?)	28	0–1
Ramesses I	2	1	≤0–1
Sethos I	11	15	4
Ramesses II	67	66	≤1
Merenptah	10	10	0
Amenmesses	4	3	≤1
Sethos II	6	6	0
Siptah	7?	6	≤1
Tewosret	8	2 (co-regent 6 years)	6 or 0
Setnakht	3	2	≤1
Ramesses III	32	31	≤1
Ramesses IV	7	6	≤1
Ramesses V	4	4	0
Ramesses VI	8	7	≤1
Ramesses VII	8	7	≤1
Ramesses VIII	1	3	≤1
Ramesses IX	19	18	≤1
Ramesses X	3	9	6
Ramesses XI	28	29/30	1–2

* von Beckerath (1997; 1994a)

Table 14. Highest attested year of reign for 18–20th Dynasty pharaohs after von Beckerath (1994a:117; 1994:201–202) compared to conjectured or interpolated years of reign in Kitchen (1996a), and, for late 20th Dynasty, Kitchen (1987).

The number of years involved in such cases cannot usually be quantified. Thus there is a basic logical problem with dead-reckoning: it entirely fails to account for what we do not know, and this is rather a lot! Kitchen's own works as a whole only demonstrate this point very clearly. By his own admission he cannot find enough years in the records and attestations from the Third Intermediate Period through the 20th Dynasty to produce an acceptable date for Ramesses II via dead-reckoning, given his links with the independent Babylonian chronology.[1683] Kitchen has to make

---

[1683] Kitchen (1996a:4–5).

up some 11–17 years.[1684] But, if one can make up 11–17 years, then why not a few more? There can be no control over the unknown. The total period involved from the 664BC fixed point is a little over 600 years, and, with a few additional examples of unattested final years, another decade or two could easily 'appear'. The very ability of critics of Kitchen to offer radically different readings of his data for the Third Intermediate Period, and legitimately to claim that he has not demonstrated several of his assumptions, only confirms the lack of a truly solid, replicated, dataset.[1685]

Kitchen (1996a:3), however, argues that the approximate time period involved for a large part of the Third Intermediate Period can be independently controlled by the records of genealogies for several important priestly families, particularly during the timespan of the 22nd Dynasty,[1686] and the study of Bierbrier (1975) collates similar data for the late New Kingdom. But this is true only in approximate terms. The several genealogies linked to the names (and so reigns) of various kings do provide a coherent structure which precludes radical surgery to the chronology of the Third Intermediate Period. Kitchen (1996a:3) is thus correct to state that 'the biological implications of these data preclude any *appreciable* stretching or contraction of the 130 years *or so* covered by the 22nd Dynasty' (my italics). However, the available data in no way preclude an overall flexibility of c.11 or even c.25 years. The brief, but trenchant, critique of Bierbrier's attempt to extract precise chronology from genealogical data by Henige (1981) applies also to Kitchen's work. Henige demonstrates that Bierbrier's genealogical analysis can in no way be held to require, even usefully support, the low versus middle or high Egyptian New Kingdom chronologies. Henige (1981:184) concludes that: 'the counting of generations in undated or partly dated genealogies, especially over a long period of time, cannot help in establishing exact dates'. The fundamental problem is that, to quote Bryan (1991:23), 'the average lifespan for ancient Egypt is unknown, and individual variations are great in all populations'. There is nothing in these data (*in toto*) which precludes the necessary very small overall expansion to accommodate the middle or high Egyptian chronologies for the 18th Dynasty. There are a lack of specific numbers (and so no truly fixed chronology), and the 'biological implications' referred to are inherently flexible by a few years in almost every case. The records of Apis bulls also enter the fray. Here there are hard numbers, but not a continuous record, with effectively no data from the mid-11th through mid-9th centuries BC.[1687] The gaps provide plenty of potential (*minor*) flexibility.[1688]

[1684] Or 9–15 years in Kitchen (1987:39).

[1685] See James *et al.* (1998:32–34) with further refs.; Hagens (1996).

[1686] Full discussion in Kitchen (1996b:187–189).

[1687] Kitchen (1996b:489 Table 20).

[1688] In fairness, it should be noted that Bierbrier (1975:109–113) did not in fact claim certainty or proof in his case for the low Egyptian chronology (1279BC accession for Ramesses II). He concluded his chronological discussion merely stating that (p.113): '...the generational analysis of the period from the accession of Ramesses II to 664 B.C. *tends* to weaken the argument in favour of 1304 B.C. as the accession date of Ramesses II' (my italics). This is a less than decisive claim. It is subsequent writers who have claimed that Bierbrier's work offers a hard evidence platform for further discussion.

Egyptian and Israelite chronology?

The chronology of Kitchen further relies on several assumptions. The most infamous in recent literature concerns the issue of whether or not we can in fact precisely date Shoshenq I, and so Egyptian chronology, in the early first millennium BC via Israelite chronology and in turn Assyrian chronology.[1689] Kitchen believes that we can secure the Egyptian Third Intermediate Period chronology at c.925BC with the sack of Jerusalem recorded in the Bible: 'in the fifth year of Rehoboam's reign Shishak king of Egypt attacked Jerusalem'.[1690] The Egyptian king referred to as Shishak is conventionally equated with Sheshonq I. Kitchen argues that this is linguistically acceptable, in contrast to the other suggestions of Rohl, and others,[1691] but chooses to ignore the valid criticism of James *et al.* (1992:127) that there *are* other alternatives, and that there are problems with the Sheshonq I candidacy.[1692] Now, apart from the problem that James *et al.* (1991a:229–231) and Rohl (1995) plausibly question this *assumption*[1693] – and, rather than the radical alternatives of James *et al.* and Rohl, the real point is that there is another Shoshenq (II) in close proximity who might also be a candidate – there is the major problem of how the date of 926/925BC was derived in the first place. It comes from the work of Thiele,[1694] but, prior to a reference in the Assyrian annals under Shalmaneser III to King Ahab of Israel in 853BC,[1695] an independent check on Biblical data for the reign lengths of Israelite kings is lacking.[1696] This is serious; the Bible seems to record only total reign lengths, and does not mention co-regencies. We also have reason to believe that some numbers cited are stylised ones (long reign, short reign), and not real, specific, records. These data may therefore be no more reliable than the reign lengths given in Manetho for Egyptian rulers, many of which Kitchen is happy to dismiss. To take the example of the 25th Dynasty, and to quote Kitchen (1996b:554–555):

> The surviving Manethonian versions of the 25th Dynasty are (as they now stand) absolutely riddled with errors from end to end ... As these figures stand in the

---

[1689] Kitchen (1996a:3; 1996b:72–76); von Beckerath (1994a:30–34; 1997:68–70); compare Wente (1976); Wente and Van Siclen (1976:224); James *et al.* (1991a:229–231, 248–251; 1998:29–30); Rohl (1992; 1995:120–127); Cryer (1995:662).

[1690] 1 Kings 14.25–26; account confirmed in 2 Chronicles 12.2–10. Barnes (1991:57–71) finds the 'evidence is too imprecise to confirm or deny decisively any particular biblical chronology' (p.71), although he favours a chronology similar to the one proposed by Kitchen, and would place Rehoboam year 5 in 927BC (p.153). Lower chronologies have been proposed. The best known is the work of Albright (e.g. 1945; 1953), and a recent derivative is Hayes and Hooker (1988). The latter dates Rehoboam year 5 at 922–921BC.

[1691] Kitchen (1996b:xliv, 73 n.356).

[1692] Also James *et al.* (1991b:231; 1998:33–34).

[1693] See also Cryer (1995:662).

[1694] Thiele (1983:80) – although cf. pp.33–42 for some of the problems with the chronological tradition. For a critique of the work of Thiele (and also Albright), see Barnes (1991:esp.1–27).

[1695] Kuhrt (1995:488).

[1696] Cryer (1995:657); Tadmor (1985); Cogan (1985).

existing text, NOT ONE FIGURE IS CORRECT. They are WRONG. It is, therefore, preposterous to claim to base a sound, factually-grounded chronology of the 25th Dynasty upon these faulty data.

The current conventional chronology for the kings of Israel until 853BC was determined only by fitting the data to the correlations with Assyria.[1697] The Assyrian chronology is part of what might be termed the Assyro-Babylonian chronographic tradition.[1698] Babylonian chronology provides a fixed chronology to 747BC,[1699] and this then may be linked with the Assyrian annual eponym lists to provide an Assyrian chronology specific to the year back to the 10th century BC.[1700] But this precision in Assyrian data does not simply transfer to the Israelite chronology. The link with Egyptian chronology via Shishak and Rehoboam is not only open to some question, but is also not securely dated, since it is not known (versus assumed) when in the reign of Shoshonq I the campaign against Jerusalem occurred.[1701] It is true that monuments of Shoshonq I attest a Palestinian campaign,[1702] but this seems to have been primarily directed at the northern kingdom of Israel, and Jerusalem is not mentioned. An additional (to an already unknown amount) 20 years of uncertainty is thus introduced.

Further, one must raise the question of which Shoshonq is being referred to. Shoshonq I is well attested in Egypt, and celebrated a Palestinian campaign, but this does necessarily mean he is the Shishak referred to in the Bible. Our clue is that under the reign of Rehoboam's father, Solomon, the fugitive Jeroboam sheltered with king Shishak of Egypt, and heard of Solomon's death and the accession of Rehoboam in Egypt (Egyptian king at this subsequent time not stated).[1703] Kitchen uses this information as part of his case that the relevant campaign of Shoshonq I was thus late in his reign (years 20–21). And, no doubt, Shoshonq I does present the most plausible case. But, this does not mean that this hypothesis is correct. One might also consider that the Biblical account could easily mean Shosheng II, who may have been the active 'king' as co-regent with his father Osorkon I, and 'Army-Chief'. Since Shoshonq II pre-deceased his father, and is thought to have been in his 50s at death,[1704] one might even hypothesise a scenario where Jeroboam went into exile at the end of Shoshonq I's reign, and, after an exile of unknown duration (including death of Shoshonq I and accession of Osorkon I), and another five years of Rehoboam's reign, Army-Chief and co-regent (i.e. king) Shoshonq II marched on Jerusalem (to rival achievements of the great Shoshonq I and to out-do him since he did not claim Jerusalem's wealth). Therefore, Egyptian chronology

[1697] Thiele (1983); James *et al.* (1991a:266–267).
[1698] Cryer (1995:656).
[1699] Secured by an eclipse assumption (see Depuydt 1996c:99 and n.6) and the fact that the information seems correct, and the astronomy is consistent with known data (Depuydt 1996c:106–107).
[1700] Brinkman (1968; 1984; 1990); Depuydt (1996c); Cryer (1995:657).
[1701] Wente and Van Siclen (1976:224); Cryer (1995:662).
[1702] Kitchen (1996b:432–447).
[1703] 1 Kings 11.40, 12.2; 2 Chronicles 10.2.
[1704] Kitchen (1996b:117–120, 119 n.169 for age at death).

is by no means totally secure back to a supposed accession of Sheshonq I in 945BC. Things only get worse backwards through the Third Intermediate Period.

EGYPTIAN LINKS WITH BABYLONIAN, ASSYRIAN, AND HITTITE HISTORY AND CHRONOLOGY

In such fuzzy and uncertain circumstances, recourse is made to a few documented instances of relations with the Hittite and Babylonian–Assyrian worlds, and so, ultimately, to the independent Babylonian–Assyrian chronographic tradition.[1705] In particular, there are two sets of good linkages: the first during the reign of Ramesses II (involving the Babylonian king Kadasman-Enlil II and the Hittite king Hattusili III), and the second during the Amarna period (correspondence between the Babylonian kings Kadasman-Enlil I and possibly also Burna-Burias II and Amenhotep III of Egypt, and Burna-Burias II and both Akhenaten and Tutankhamun). These linkages are regularly cited in support of the conventional Egyptian chronology, the first to support the now conventional date of 1279BC for Ramesses II (against the high chronology date of 1304BC), and the second to support the conventional chronology of the Amarna period.

The key underlying assumption is that the Babylonian (Kassite), and via this, the core Assyrian, chronological data are totally secure. However, this is far from the case. In the major study of the Kassite period, Brinkman (1976) constructs a tentative absolute chronology (which is widely used). A careful reading of pages 6–34 reveals that Brinkman expresses a number of caveats, is forced to make several hypotheses, or inferences, and openly admits to areas of flexibility.[1706] The absolute dates come from Assyria and its kinglist tradition (tied to the Babylonian kings through 15 explicit synchronisms). Among the five extant versions of the Assyrian King List (three of which are relatively substantial) there are rival textual data for the reign lengths of some Assyrian kings (especially Puzur-Assur III, Assur-nadin-apli, Ninurta-apil-Ekur and Assur-dan I), and several scholars have not accepted Brinkman's decision to give Ninurta-apil-Ekur a 13 year reign (as attested in the Nassouhi kinglist[1707]), and have instead chosen to favour other later versions of the kinglist which give a reign of just three years. Thus their chronologies are 10 years lower.[1708] There are in addition some discrepancies between the Assyrian King List tradition and other textual data (e.g. eponym lists), for example during the reigns of Adad-nirari II and Tukulti-Ninurta II in the earlier first millennium BC,[1709] apart from a variety of other esoteric (and minor) problems.[1710] Hence a firm absolute

---

[1705] von Beckerath (1994a:23–29; 1997:59–68, 70–71).
[1706] See also Gasche *et al.* (1998:47–48); and the steadfastly pessimistic scepticism of Giles (1997:81–86).
[1707] See Brinkman (1973). For Assur-dan I choice among conflicting data is also significant: 36 or 45 years.
[1708] E.g. Wente and Van Siclen (1976:249); Boese and Wilhelm (1979).
[1709] Boese and Wilhelm (1979:19–20).
[1710] Poebel (1943:86–90). Yamada (1994) further makes a good case for the view that the Assyrian King List we have was not the outcome of a single composition (recension), but that there are several phases of composition (each of course later than the kings involved). This overall editorial history provides a number of occasions when errors may have been introduced.

chronological 'range' is available from this Assyrian–Babylonian data, but not a specific and precise absolute chronology.

With regard to the Amarna and Ramesses II periods, the most important caveats or problems concern the fact that the textual data from the Babylonian kinglist tradition for kings ?15 to ?21 in the Kassite sequence (Kara-indas to Nazi-Bugas) are problematic – there *could* even be other kings not attested: 'thus one can readily see that the arguments for the usually accepted sequence of rulers in this section of the dynasty are rather weak and, in many cases, circumstantial'.[1711] This period includes Kadasman-Enlil I (king ?18) and Burna-Burias II (king ?19), and so the Amarna period synchronism. Here 'the dates ... are subject to an even wider margin of variation because of the more than usually hypothetical nature of the reconstruction of that part of the dynasty'.[1712] At a basic level, Burna-Burias II, though amply attested, is not in the Babylonian kinglist A, and has to be inserted by modern scholarship. For the later Ramesses II period, problems of evidence continue. The crucial kinglist A[1713] is badly damaged for this period – and our text may be regarded as being derived from a source already damaged in antiquity[1714] – and only the beginnings of the royal names for kings 24 and 25 (Kadasman-Turgu and Kadasman-Enlil II) are preserved, and the regnal data are not legible for the latter (and can at best be hypothesised at 10 + x years[1715]). Brinkman (1976:28) concludes that 'although significant uncertainties remain in the reconstructions, it nonetheless seems advisable to propose a tentative absolute chronology'. However, this is hardly the same as stating that there is a firm absolute chronology!

Let us now consider the two episodes of linkages between Egypt and Babylonia: first the Ramesses II linkage, and then the Amarna period linkages.

In Ramesses II year 21 peace was made between Egypt and the Hittites under Hattusili III after a period of tension.[1716] This year 21 figure offers a potential reference point for several other diplomatic communications. A letter from Hattusili III to Kadasman-Enlil II of Babylon[1717] hopes that the new Babylonian ruler Kadasman-Enlil II will follow the pro-Hittite policies of his father (and not the anti-Hittite ones of the intervening regent/vizier Itti-Marduk-balatu). Much depends on when this letter was written (the text of this key letter is in fact damaged). On the one hand, some scholars have argued that it dates from before the peace at a time of implied Hittite–Egyptian hostilities (*but we know from this same document of earlier correspondence from Kadasman-Turgu, to Hattushili III offering support which better fits this time, and Hattusili III seems to refer to his problems with Ramesses II in the past tense:*

[1711] Brinkman (1976:14–16, 33 n.92).

[1712] Brinkman (1976:30 n.86).

[1713] See Brinkman (1976:424–439).

[1714] Brinkman (1976:426–427); Gasche *et al.* (1998:67 and n.278).

[1715] Brinkman (1976:23 n.60).

[1716] See Beckman (1996:90–95 no.15); Kitchen (1982:73–79, 250–251); Bryce (1998:291, 304–309). For the extant text of the treaty, and for commentary, see recently Edel (1997).

[1717] Beckman (1996:132–137 no.23); Oppenheim (1967:139–146); Bryce (1998:293); CTH 172; KBo 1.10 + KUB 3.72.

see below), on the other hand, there are scholars who date it after the year 21 peace.[1718] After the success of the Egyptian peace, Hattusili III might be interpreted as seeking to reach a similar diplomatic peace with the new ruler of Babylonia (especially as he was concerned about Assyria). We simply do not know for sure – we can only make best interpretations. The currently conventional 'before' position, adopted, for example, by Bryce (1998:292–293), is based largely on use of the (now) conventional dates for Babylonian chronology and Egyptian chronology, and not any actual evidence regarding this specific communication.[1719] Ironically, given the recent penchant for ever lower dates in second millennium BC chronological studies, the 'before' hypothesis works only if the ultra-low Assyrian chronology is discounted. This would place Kadasman-Enlil II's accession at c.1253BC,[1720] some six years after Ramesses year 21 and the Egyptian–Hittite treaty!

A date for this (and the associated) set of relationships comes from Babylonia, since Hittite chronology is entirely floating/flexible. The relevant Babylonian chronology is derived from correlations with the almost absolute Assyrian chronology.[1721] Although dates are given, it must be noted again (see above), and stressed, that Brinkman highlights a number of applicable or potential errors and possible variations. His best compromise/approximation date for the reign of Kadasman-Enlil II (on his general 'minimum' chronology interpretation[1722]) is 1263–1255BC ±5 years.[1723] Boese and Wilhelm (1979), meanwhile, place his reign ten years later. However, the only possible variation is not just downwards; as noted in Brinkman (1970:306), a maximum chronology date of 1283–1269 BC is also possible. Brinkman (1976:34) did in fact conclude by observing, with reference to his preferred minimum chronology, that 'in general, it may be said that, with the exception of possible revisions from the Assyrian side, most adjustments in dates for Babylonian events and reigns here set between 1374 and 1155 should be expected to be *upward*' (my italics – this is clearly assuming that his balance of probabilities arguments in Brinkman 1973 are correct). Gasche *et al.* (1998:66) employ a date of c. 1258–1250BC, selecting the lowest of the available options, and including their solar versus lunar calendar reduction.

On the one hand, those who wish to interpret the Hattusili III-Kadasman-Enlil II letter as before Ramesses II year 21 (years 16–20 are cited) see 1263BC + 16 as supporting the 1279BC accession choice for Ramesses II.[1724] But, in contrast, others might add 1283BC + 16–20 years to reach 1299–1303BC.[1725] On the other hand, those who instead see Ramesses II years 16–20 as linked with Kadasman-Turgu (Kadasman-

---

[1718] For critique of the 'before' position, see e.g. Rowton (1966:243–249); previously, Rowton (1960:16–18; 1959). For the opposite viewpoint, see e.g. Bierbrier (1975:109–110).

[1719] Cf. Bryce (1998:292 n.1 and caveat re-Brinkman 1983).

[1720] Boese and Wilhelm (1979); Wente and Van Siclen (1976:250).

[1721] See Brinkman (1970; 1976:28–29); Boese and Wilhelm (1979); Gasche *et al.* (1998:61–67).

[1722] See Brinkman (1970:305–307).

[1723] See Brinkman (1976:31; cf. pp.32–33 n.89) for further possible errors/variations.

[1724] E.g. Bierbrier (1975:109–111); von Beckerath (1992:25–26; 1994a:26–28).

[1725] E.g. Ward (1992:56).

Enlil II's father, with a regent in between as well?), and place the correspondence later, since the peace is hardly going to have ended diplomatic manoeuvrings, may link a later year, and so reach the 1304BC date for the accession of Ramesses II. This is not even considering some possible selection of higher dates from within Brinkman's ranges.

The only limits to potential flexibility are: (i) that Hattusili III became Hittite Great King by about (or a few years before) Ramesses II year 16,[1726] with an upper limit at about Ramesses II years 12/13;[1727] (ii) that correspondence[1728] probably shows that Hattusili III was also a contemporary (as Great King) of the Assyrian king Adad-nirari I (c.1305–1274BC in the older 'conventional' chronologies such as Brinkman 1977);[1729] (iii) that we also have to accommodate as contemporary with Hattusili III the dates of Kadasman-Turgu, c.1281–1264BC ±5 years (Brinkman low chronology);[1730] and (iv) that Hattusili III reigned for a long time (c.30 years): in Ramesses II's year 34 Hattusili III gave him a daughter in marriage, and a second such proposal was made perhaps in the years 40s of Ramesses II's reign, and it is generally concluded that Hattusili III probably lived at least into the later years 40s of Ramesses II's reign.[1731]

The letter attributed to Hattusili III, writing to Adad-nirari I, is clearly from relatively early in Hattusili III's reign. Based on what we know of Assyrian–Hittite activities and relations with Mitanni/Hanigalbat, Rowton (1959) made a good case for the letter also belonging to late in Adad-nirari's 32 year reign, but at least 6 years before its end. Hattusili III complains about the fact he has not been properly recognised as great king (did not receive the usual presents on becoming king), and makes it clear that there is now a new policy in Hatti in contrast to the previous reign of Urhi-Tesub.[1732] Thus, at a minimum (and very likely), we may conclude that a point within a few years after Hattusili III's accession, in the period from Ramesses II years 12/13 to 16 or so, must lie within the reign of Adad-nirari I (but probably before his year 27). Here the choice is stark. *If* the accession of Ramesses II is placed at 1279BC, then, to reach at least Ramesses II year 12/13 before the end of the reign of Adad-nirari I, only the ultra-low chronology is feasible (and even then only just!). This circular logic is in fact one of the reasons both 'low' sides in the Egyptian and Mesopotamina chronology debates choose the low dates. But the evidence in favour

---

[1726] Rowton (1960:16–18); Rowton (1966:244–245).

[1727] As employed by von Beckerath (1994a:107–108).

[1728] Beckman (1996:139–140 no.24B); Bryce (1998:282); KBo 1.14.

[1729] Other dates offered for this king in current literature include: c.1307–1275BC in Kuhrt (1995:351 Table 22); c.1305–1274BC in the Gasche *et al.* (1998:62) 'base chronology' from textual data; c.1300–1270BC in Gasche *et al.* (1998:63) correcting for lunar versus solar calendar; c.1295–1264BC in the ultra-short chronology of Boese and Wilhelm (1979); and c.1298/97–1265BC in von Beckerath (1994a:22, 25–26; 1997:67).

[1730] Or ten years later with Boese and Wilhelm (1979), or c.1301–1284BC (Brinkman maximum chronology), or c.1276–1259BC (Gasche *et al.* 1998:66).

[1731] Bryce (1998:310–315, 324 and n.96); Kitchen (1982:83–95).

[1732] Beckman (1996:140).

of the ultra-low Assyrian chronology is flimsy, and consists merely of choice and selection within the ambiguous issues. Employment of one of the slightly higher, conventional, Assyrian chronologies (even the pretty 'lowish' chronology of Gasche *et al.* 1998:63) renders 1279BC difficult.

And, as noted, there is reason not to equate Hattusili III's year of accession with the year of the death of Adad-nirari I. There may well have been a few to several years of overlap (but not much more). Indeed, the writer of the letter we have notes that there has been previous correspondence between the two correspondents (assumed to be Hattusili III and Adad-nirari I) on the subjects of the city of Turira and iron supply and crafting.[1733] Thus Rowton (1959) placed the correspondence no later than six years before Adad-nirari I's death. For example, our base line is that Hattusili III's accession has occurred by Ramesses II year 16, and so we might place this correspondence no later than about Ramesses II years 16–18 give or take a year or two. At a minimum, given that Adad-nirari I dies c.1275/1274BC, or 1270BC according to the conventional Assyrian chronology or the recent revision of Gasche *et al.* (1998), and allowing a couple of years for previous correspondence and so dating the present correspondence no later than six years before the death of Adad-nirari I following Rowton, we find that Ramesses II years 16–18 lie, at a rough minimum, by, or before, c.1281/1280BC or 1276BC. Ramesses II's accession would therefore be in the range c.1299–1291BC. This is significantly earlier than the supposed 1279BC accession date. In the past, a 1290BC ('lower–high', or 'middle', chronology) accession has been proposed for Ramesses II, based on the lunar data relevant to his year 52 which could place his accession at 1304BC, 1290BC, or 1279BC.[1734] But, this 1290BC date is now thought less likely, ditto a 1490BC accession option for Tuthmosis III.[1735] The least complicated, and so most likely, solutions for the astronomical data are either 1304BC or 1279BC. The dates above are likely approximate minima. Although Adad-nirari I was also a contemporary with Muwatalli II and Urhi-Tesub, and the Babylonian rulers Nazi-Maruttas and Kadasman-Turgu, and, it seems likely his seizure of Hanigalbat may be placed in the period just after the Egyptian–Hittite battle of Kadesh in Ramesses II year 5,[1736] there is no reason he could not have been corresponding with Hattusili III a little earlier than his last few years of life. Thus 1304BC is by no means impossible – unless a strong (i.e. positive) case can be made for the ultra-low Assyrian chronology of Boese and Wilhelm (1979).[1737]

In addition to the Assyrian link, we also know that Hattusili III corresponded with Kadasman-Turgu, as also did Adad-nirari I. We do not know when this occurred.

[1733] Beckman (1996:140).

[1734] E.g. Parker (1957); Hornung (1964).

[1735] See Casperson (1986; 1988); Wente and Van Siclen (1976:223–224).

[1736] As Kitchen (1982:63).

[1737] If the ultra-low Assyrian chronology is chosen here to avoid such problems for the Egyptian low chronology, then the correspondence between Hattusili III and Kadasman-Enlil II cannot be placed before the Egyptian–Hittite treaty of Ramesses year 21 (as Wente and Van Siclen 1976:250 also note), contrary to the currently popular synthesis. But this decision in turn supports an overall set of linkages among the texts and rulers most plausibly consistent with an earlier (and not the low) chronology (as Rowton 1966).

Bryce (1998:292) guesses that it was within a year or two of Kadasman-Turgu's death, but this view is solely because of the chronology adopted by Bryce. A reading of the letter from Hattusili III to Kadasman-Enlil II[1738] might lead to a different view. It seems apparent when Hattusili III reminds the new Babylonian king of the relationship between Hattusili III and his father, Kadasman-Turgu, that this correspondence was some long time ago:

> ...my brother [Kadasman-Enlil II] was a child in those days, and they did not read out the tablets in your presence. Now are none of those scribes still living? Are the tablets not filed? Let them read those tablets to you now.[1739]

> My brother was a youngster in those days and so I assume that no one ever read these tablets to him; now these old scribes are not alive any more, and none of the tablets are even kept in archives so that they could be read to you now.[1740]

Now Kadasman-Enlil II ruled for only c.10 years (10+x years). We may guess that he was perhaps relatively young on accession, as Hattusili III refers to the period between Kadasman-Turgu's death and the present letter as being 'in those days my brother was a child, and Itti-Marduk-balatu, that evil man, spoke as he pleased'.[1741] Indeed, the vicious tone taken against Itti-Marduk-balatu might imply Hattusili III knew Kadasman-Enlil II to be recently free of this influence, and also to have negative feelings about his former regent?/vizier (otherwise the critical references at several places in the letter would seem designed to undermine the express point of the letter: good relations between Hattusili III/the Hittites and Kadasman-Enlil II/the Babylonians). At the time of the letter Kadasman-Enlil II 'has become a grown man'.[1742] If one treats the information literally, one might hypothesise Kadasman-Enlil II to be a young child (i.e. 0–6? or so years of age) at the time of the Hattusili III-Kadasman-Turgu treaty, and yet still only a teenager at most on accession (hence role of Itti-Marduk-balatu), and so not a grown man until another c.1–5 or so years – with his 10th year as the limit.

Even if this is all some form of rhetorical pleasantry, the letter is carefully crafted, and this seems a fairly specific point: the new (just grown-up) king is not to blame for not knowing about the past relationship, and Hattusili III hopes to reactivate a friendly accord. In this case, the dealings with Kadasman-Turgu need not have been at the end of his reign at all. They may have occurred one to two decades earlier (Kadasman-Turgu reigned 17/18 years). Unless we place the Hattusili III letter late in the ten year reign of Kadasman-Enlil II, he must be assumed to have been an adult by about his year 5. Hence Hattusili III's treaty with his father when he was a child might easily be c.15 years earlier. The bold offer of Kadasman-Turgu to send, even lead, his troops alongside Hattusili III against Egypt perhaps best befits an impetuous new young

[1738] Beckman (1996:132–137 no.23); Oppenheim (1967:139–146); KBo 1.10 + KUB 3.72.
[1739] Beckman (1996:133–134).
[1740] Oppenheim (1967:140).
[1741] Beckman (1996:134).
[1742] Beckman (1996:137).

ruler.[1743] The whole tone of this section is written in the past tense. Hattusili III refers to when he and the king of Egypt became angry with one another in the time of Kadasman-Turgu, and links this to when his enemy fled to Egypt, and Ramesses II would not hand this enemy over. The enemy involved must almost certainly be the deposed Hittite king Urhi-Tesub.[1744] Since the treaty between Ramesses II and Hattusili III of Ramesses year 21 specifically makes detailed mention of the return of exiles or fugitives,[1745] it seems likely that the events relevant to the Hattusili III treaty with Kashman-Turgu were earlier, before this accord with Egypt.[1746] This past state of affairs is contrasted to the present, and Kadasman-Enlil II – 'now you are an adult', and the discussion about current dealings with Egypt.[1747] Hattusili III says it is now perfectly fine for Kadasman-Enlil II to correspond with Egypt. Clearly Hattusili III is thus no longer angry with Ramesses II, and it is no longer appropriate to expect friends to cease correspondence with Egypt (as Hattusili III says Kadasman-Turgu did when Hattusili III and Ramesses II became angry with one another). Indeed, the whole context of 'when the King of Egypt and I became angry with one another' is set in a past which is now no longer appropriate since such problems have been resolved. Hattusili III is just reminding Kadasman-Enlil II of the past alliance of himself and Kadasman-Turgu in difficult times.

In consequence, it seems likely that the treaty between Hattusili III and Kadasman-Turgu dates to soon after Hattusili III's accession, and the flight of Urhi-Tesub to Egypt. Since Urhi-Tesub had opened negotiations from exile with the king of Babylonia,[1748] Hattusili III would have wanted to tidy matters up rather rapidly, if possible. He clearly sought recognition from the main contemporary rulers, but was initially rebuffed by several (e.g Adad-nirari I[1749]). Unlike Ramesses II, and the Assyrians, Kadasman-Turgu appears to have happily accepted Hattusili III as the new king, and sided with him (both feared the Assyrians). Since we have seen that it is most likely that Hattusili III is writing to Kadasman-Enlil II after Ramesses II year 21 (by an unknown number of years), the earlier treaty with Kadasman-Turgu could be anywhere from one to two decades previously. Although proof is impossible, one might further reasonably hypothesise that the treaty between the new king Hattusili III was made with Kadasman-Turgu during the earlier (and not later) part of Kadasman-Turgu's reign. Hence scribes had died, records got lost, by the time of the

---

[1743] Beckman (1996:135).

[1744] Bryce (1998:289–291).

[1745] Beckman (1996:93–94).

[1746] Hattusili III still could not get Urhi-Tesub back, but his formal 'anger' with the king of Egypt seems unlikely after the year 21 treaty. A letter from Ramesses II which might date to the post-treaty period indicates he no longer has Urhi-Tesub (whether or not this is true: see Bryce 1998:310; CTH 156; KBo 1.15), while it is not entirely clear what to make of the sarcastic comment about Urhi-Tesub being in Egypt in the letter about marriage arrangements usually attributed to the Hittite queen Puduhepa, wife of Hattusili III, writing to Ramesses II (although the extant text preserves neither sender or receiver, and several other identifications have been proposed: Beckman 1996:125–129 no.22E; CTH 176; KUB 21.38).

[1747] Beckman (1996:135).

[1748] Bryce (1998:290).

[1749] Bryce (1998:305); CTH 216; KBo 8.14.

correspondence with his grown up son – perhaps up to a c.15–20 year period (perhaps as much as 10–15 years of treaty between the two, and up to 5 years of Kadasman-Enlil II's reign to this now grown up point?). When Hattusili III encourages Kadasman-Enlil II to attack the enemy,

> Do not keep sitting around, my brother, but go against an enemy land and defeat the enemy![1750]

> And so I say 'Go ahead now, and make a razzia into the land of the enemy (i.e. Assyria)'.[1751]

he is probably referring to Assyria, the main common enemy of the Hittites and Babylonians, especially after the successor of Adad-nirari I as king of Assyria, Salmaneser I, seems (claimed) to have gone further than his father, and conquered and destroyed the kingdom of Hanigalbat (Mitanni), and so brought Assyria right to the Hittite border.[1752]

If we therefore seek to correlate Hattusili III's first years (1–3 = potentially Ramesses II years 13–18) with some point in the first half of Kadasman-Turgu's reign, then the date of this correspondence would be: 1281–1272BC ±5,[1753] or 1301–1292BC,[1754] or c.1271–1262BC ±5,[1755] or 1276–1267BC.[1756] The minimum date for Ramesses II's accession would be placed somewhere in the range (from higher to lower): 1319–1305BC, 1299–1285BC ±5, 1294–1280BC, or 1289–1275BC ±5. If the interpretation of an early date for the initial Hattusili III-Kadasman-Turgu correspondence is correct, then a 1304BC or 1290BC accession date for Ramesses II would offer a possible fit with the Brinkman (1976) chronology, and, on all but the lowest construction of the ultra-low Boese and Wilhelm (1979) chronology, we are earlier than the 1279BC conventional low chronology accession date for Ramesses II. Such an argument is not, of course, necessarily correct, or even likely, but I am merely trying to demonstrate that the evidence we have does not require the conventional low chronology 1279BC accession date alone, and could be consistent with a higher 1290BC or 1304BC accession date. The current Assyrian, Babylonian, Egyptian, and Hittite historical data can plausibly fit with, or at least accommodate, a higher Egyptian chronology. Even honest adherents of the lower 1279BC date admit that 'the evidence from other Near Eastern countries cannot be regarded as decisive in determining the accession date of Ramesses II'.[1757]

Kitchen nonetheless claims that the genealogical data for the Third Intermediate Period and the late New Kingdom do enable him to rule out the 1304BC accession

[1750] Beckman (1996:137).
[1751] Oppenheim (1967:146).
[1752] Bryce (1998:303–304); cf. Wilhelm (1989:40).
[1753] Brinkman (1976, preferred minimum chronology).
[1754] Brinkman (1976, maximum chronology).
[1755] Boese and Wilhelm (1979).
[1756] Gasche *et al.* (1998:66).
[1757] Bierbrier (1975:111).

date.[1758] As noted above, this argument is simply nonsense. To quote Henige (1981:182): 'neither the genealogical data adduced by Bierbrier nor his interpretation of them can possibly warrant the conclusion that "the generation analysis of the period ... tends to weaken the argument in favour of 1304 BC as the accession date of Ramesses II"'. The data involved are relative, and not hard data consisting of continuous, definitively known, numerical series. Over the time periods at issue, a mere 25 years could easily be accommodated without breaching biological feasibility. Kitchen (1987:39) further masks the issue by pretending the 25 years must all be accommodated in the period of the Ramesside kings; in fact, bits of this quarter century could belong anywhere from 525BC back to the 13th century BC.

In conclusion, we must follow Ward (1992:56), and re-quote Brinkman (1970:307): 'It should also be clear that Babylonian chronology, in its present state of uncertainty, is not a reliable standard against which to measure other chronologies of the late second millennium'. Thus, although 1279BC as the accession date for Ramesses II has become a popular fixed point in recent scholarship,[1759] it is illusory. The necessary precision and accuracy is not present in the data to rule out the mere 11 years to 1290BC, nor the 25 years involved between 1279BC and 1304BC.

The other main set of international relationships with a bearing on Egyptian chronology occur during the Amarna period, when the only certain and direct Egyptian–Babylonian synchronisms are attested:[1760]

1. Kadasman-Enlil I – Amenhotep III.[1761]
2. Possibly Burna-Burias II – Amenhotep III.[1762]
3. Burna-Burias II – Akhenaten.[1763]
4. Burna-Burias II – probably Tutankhamun.[1764]

Although it is important to stress that the case is *not* certain (synchronisms 2 and 4 above), the general consensus nonetheless is that the reign of Burna-Burias II must therefore overlap with the end of Amenhotep III's reign, all of Akhenaten's reign, and the start of Tutankhamun's reign. Kitchen (1996a:5) regards this three-pharaoh overlap (or four/five?-pharaoh overlap adding the ephemeral Smenkhkare, and Nefernefruaten?, between Akhenaten and Tutankhamun) with Burna-Burias II as a

---

[1758] E.g. Kitchen (1987:39). For the data, see Kitchen (1996b) and Bierbrier (1975).

[1759] Contrast previously Rowton (1966:240–258) who constructed the same pattern of linkages around a 1304BC accession for Ramesses II (see also generally Rowton 1970).

[1760] Kühne (1973:49–75); Brinkman (1976:6 n.1, 108, 135); Giles (1997:76–101). For the links with Amenhotep III, see also the recent discussion of Kitchen (1998:253–256).

[1761] EA 1–3: Moran (1992:1–8).

[1762] EA 6: Moran (1992:12). The reading of the Egyptian king's name in sentence 1 is not certain. Kühne (1973:129 and n.642) suggests that Amenhotep III is possible, otherwise it must be Akhenaten.

[1763] EA 7–8, 11: Moran (1992:12–17, 21–23).

[1764] EA 9: Moran (1992:18–19); Kühne (1973:72–75, esp.72 n.363). Other letters from this period are not able to be so definitely assigned (EA4, 5, 6, 7, 10, 12, 13, 14). The Egyptian ruler's name is largely lost in EA5. It might be Amenhotep III (which would be appropriate as it is from Kadasman Enlil I). EA10 similarly involves the restoration of most of the Egyptian king's name. It is probably Akhenaten, and thus another letter from Burna-Burias II to Akhenaten.

fact. As noted above, Burna-Burias II is not in the Babylonian kinglist A, however, other textual evidence attests a highest regnal year of 27. Thus his reign is 27 + x years, but given other factors it is conventionally treated as 27 years (although, see above for problems with Babylonian kings ?18–?21, of which Burna-Burias II is king ?19). Akhenaten's reign lasted 16 or 17 years.[1765] The independent reign of Smenkhkare is usually accorded 1 or 2 years (but positive evidence for any particular figure is lacking), and a few years might be needed before this for Nefernefruaten.[1766] Thus it would be quite possible in the relative terms of his 27-year reign for Burna-Burias II to write to Amenhotep III at the beginning of his reign (and the close of the latter's), and still be alive to write to Tutankhamun, with some 7–8 or 4–5 years of leeway.

The real issue, however, is how do these data conform with Egyptian chronology? If we assume that the 1279BC accession date for Ramesses II is the *minimum* realistically possible chronology,[1767] then the death of Amenhotep III is reckoned as occurring about 1353BC,[1768] or 1351/1350BC.[1769] If Ramesses II's accession was in 1290BC, these dates would rise by c.11 years, or, if the accession was in 1304BC, then a c.25 year increase is neccessary. Minor flexibilities are, however, possible. Between Ramesses II and Amenhotep II, fairly firm data on the total reign lengths are known for only one ruler: Akhenaten at 16/17 years.[1770] Of the others, Ramesses I probably reigned for less than two full years, with the 16 months of Manetho preserved in Josephus agreeing with a highest attested year date of year 2. Although the highest attested year for Sethos I is 11, circumstantial evidence argues for not less than 14–15 years.[1771] The totals for Ay (4–5 years) and Tutankhamun (10 years) are solely based on highest attested years,[1772] and one or two additional years may well have existed. The length of Haremhab's reign has long been contentious,[1773] and, while the short reign view seems now unlikely, the case for 28/29 years is largely conjectural – the interpretation of a record of a year 58/59 is not certain. Finally, the situation with regard to Smenkhkare and Nefernefruaten is completely uncertain concerning whether or not these are two separate individuals, whether or not they had reigns independent of Akhenaten's, and how many years to allow for these.[1774]

Since Kadasman-Enlil I corresponded with Amenhotep III, and it seems probable that his successor, Burna-Burias II, did as well, the assumption must be that the latter's reign commenced in the later part of the reign of Amenhotep III. The text of EA6 makes it apparent that Burna-Burias had only recently become king of Babylonia,

---

[1765] For 16 years: Kitchen (1987:40–41; 1996a:5). For 17 years, or not more than 17 years, see von Beckerath (1994a:97–103; 1997:111–114); Murnane (1995:10, 207 no.93B).

[1766] Murnane (1995:10); Murnane allows 3 years at p.xiv.

[1767] The basis of Kitchen (1996a); von Beckerath (1994a; 1997); etc.

[1768] Kitchen (1996a).

[1769] von Beckerath (1997).

[1770] His reign was no longer than 17 years on the basis of an inscription on a jar originally dated to his 17th year which was erased and re-inscribed with the name of a successor (Murnane 1995:207 no.93B).

[1771] Bierbrier (1975) – cf. Wente and Van Siclen (1976:233).

[1772] von Beckerath (1997:114–115).

[1773] Wente and Van Siclen (1976:231–232); Kitchen (1996a:5); von Beckerath (1997:115–116).

[1774] It is also possible that there was a hiatus of some months to half a year or so between official Egyptian

when Burna-Burias II refers to how his father and Amenhotep III had been friends and how he too now wants to be friends with Amenhotep III. The reign of Burna-Burias II is dated variously: 1360–1333BC,[1775] 1359–1333BC ±5,[1776] or as early as c.1381–1355BC,[1777] or 1354–1328BC,[1778] or c.1349–1323BC ±5.[1779] Terminal dates for Amenhotep III on the middle or low Egyptian chronology, 1353BC or 1351/1350BC, permit the overlap with the accession of Burna-Burias II following the Brinkman (1976) preferred minimum chronology. They miss the ultra-low chronology of Boese and Wilhelm (1979), unless one starts to play around with the ±5 year error allowance (on both the Brinkman, and Boese and Wilhelm, preferred chronologies). The higher Egyptian chronology, for which there was some support in the nexus of data surrounding Ramesses II, could work with a 1290BC accession for Ramesses within the ±5 year error allowance of Brinkman (1976), while the 1304BC accession date would require either a higher Babylonian chronology with regard to Burna-Burias II, but one entirely within the limits of Brinkman's (1976) maximum chronology, or the Egyptian King in EA6 to in fact be Akhenaten (see footnote 1762 above). Nonetheless, it is fair to conclude that whereas the evidence surrounding Ramesses II perhaps favours an earlier Egyptian chronology, the Amarna evidence is more consistent with the middle or lower Egyptian chronology (although there is greater uncertainty over the Babylonian kinglist and chronology at this time: see above).

Meanwhile, in a detailed study of Hittite history and relations in western Asia, Astour finds strong evidence for a chronology consistent with the higher Egyptian chronology which starts the Egyptian 18th Dynasty c.1570BC – although one may note that there are another set of assumptions and slight preferential biases in operation (in particular a resolute rejection of a non-Memphite Sothic observation chronology for Egypt). Astour (1989:5–7) discusses the Hittite text which apparently refers to a solar eclipse in year 10 of the Hittite king Mursili II,[1780] and makes a good case that this is 1335BC (and not the eclipse of 1340BC) – Mursili II's accession is thus 1344BC. Mursili II's predecessor had a very short reign (1–2 years it is thought), and the king before that, Suppiluliuma I, therefore died c.1346/1345BC. The relevance of this to Egyptian chronology is that Suppiluliuma I had correspondence with the widow of an Egyptian pharaoh.[1781] Traditionally, this has been thought to be the widow of

---

kings on the death of Tutankhamun when his widow wrote to the Hittite king asking that he send her a son to marry: a son who would then become king of Egypt. The letter from the widow arrived during a campaigning season (summer?), and it is only the next spring when the messenger sent to Egypt in response returns (Güterbock 1956:94 and 96; Bryce 1998:193–197). It is not clear if Suppiluliuma I sends his son Zannanza immediately then, or only a little later again. See further below on this episode.

[1775] Kitchen (1998:253 and n.140). Kitchen's one year variation for accession date from the Brinkman (1976) dates results because he eliminates 'the common solecism of failing to credit their accession-year periods to Mesopotamian kings'.

[1776] Brinkman (1976, preferred minimum chronology).

[1777] Brinkman (1976, maximum chronology). Higher dates appeared in older literature. Burna-Burias II had a 1395BC accession following Rowton (1970).

[1778] Gasche *et al.* (1998:66).

[1779] Boese and Wilhelm (1979).

[1780] CTH 70; KUB 14.4.

[1781] Bryce (1998:193–197); Güterbock (1956:94–98, 107–108).

Tutankhamun, and, at a minimum, suggests Tutankhamun died no later than 1346/ 1345BC. Since Tutankhamun reigned for 9/10 years, his accession would have been no later than c.1356/1355BC. This runs quite contrary to both the overall short and low chronology of Kitchen, von Beckerath, Krauss, etc., where the reign of Tutankhamun is placed c.1336/35/33/32 to 1327/23BC,[1782] and the long 18th Dynasty chronology of Wente and Van Siclen (1976) which has Tutankhamun c.1334–1325BC.[1783] But, needless to say, the date of the eclipse is in fact debated,[1784] with other scholars proposing eclipses (full or partial) in 1312BC or 1308BC in order to accommodate the lower Egyptian chronology;[1785] whilst the identification of the widow's deceased husband has even been challenged, and either Akhenaten or Smenkhkare suggested.[1786] However, although Wilhelm and Boese (1987) seem correct to suggest that in EA41 Suppiluliuma I was writing to Smenkhkare,[1787] it remains most unlikely, all things considered, that the widow writing to the Hittite king was anyone other than the widow of Tutankhamun.[1788]

A further complication arises with EA16. It is not clear whom Assur-uballit I (king of Assyria) was addressing as king of Egypt, but the suggestion has been made that

---

[1782] Kitchen (1987:52; 1989:153; 1996a); von Beckerath (1997); Krauss (1985).

[1783] See Wente and Van Siclen (1976:249–250).

[1784] See e.g. Åström (1993); von Beckerath (1994a:15–16); Wilhelm and Boese (1987:105–107); Wente and Van Siclen (1976:249–250).

[1785] The 1312BC date seems unlikely as the eclipse (on June 24) is incompatible with the spring to beginning of summer date required by the text description (Wilhelm and Boese 1987:107; Astour 1989:7), but 1308BC is a reasonable alternative to 1335BC. 1308BC would provide the basis for a construction of Hittite chronology compatible with the low Egyptian chronology. If Miletus is the Millawanda of Hittite texts (see Niemeier and Niemeier 1997:200–202, 246–248; 1998), then this site might provide evidence in the future to assist in resolving this ambiguity. A major destruction episode occurs at Miletus towards the close of the LHIIIA2 ceramic period. The annals of Mursili II state: 'but when it was spring, because Uhhaziti joined the side of the king of the land of Ahhiyawa, and the land of Millawanda had gone over to the king of the land of Ahhiyawa ... I sent forth Gulla and Malaziti and troops and chariots; and they destroyed the land of Millawanda' (Bryce 1998:210). It is possible that the destruction level found by archaeology and this recorded sack are the same. The textual and ceramic evidence place both events in the second half of the 14th century BC. In this case it might be hoped that high-precision radiocarbon evidence relevant to the destruction episode will be able to help to resolve between the higher or lower options.

[1786] See Krauss (1978); Wilhelm and Boese (1987); Astour (1989:6–7).

[1787] Moran (1992:114). The father referred to in this letter (EA41), with whom Suppiluliuma I says he had various friendly contacts, will have been Amenhotep III (Smenkhkare and Tutankhamun were most plausibly sons of Amenhotep III). Thus contrary to the ultra-short chronology of Wilhelm and Boese (1987), Suppiluliuma I's accession must have occurred during the (late) reign of Amenhotep III. On the conventional low Egyptian chronology the end of Amenhotep III's reign is 1353BC or 1351/1350BC. Hence Suppiluliuma I was king before then (the Hittite chronology at this point in Bryce 1998:xiii needs similar revision). If one is not prepared to countenance a very long reign for Suppiluliuma (c.35 years or more), then this is an argument against the 1308BC eclipse scenario. If a very long reign is accepted (e.g. c.40 years: Astour 1989), then either the 1335BC or 1308BC eclipse scenarios are possible (see Astour 1989:7–9 for further discussion of, and problems with, the ultra-short Hittite chronology of Wilhelm and Boese 1987).

[1788] Kitchen (1989:156–157); Bryce (1998:193 and ns.98–99).

it was Ay.[1789] If this is the case, then, at a minimum, some part of their respective reigns must overlap. Moran regards this as being possible only on the ultra-low Assyrian chronology of Boese and Wilhelm (1979),[1790] but this is not necessarily correct, and depends on which of the conventional low Egyptian chronologies one follows. The reign of Ay commenced in 1327BC according to Kitchen (1996a) or 1323BC according to von Beckerath (1997).[1791] Assur-uballit I died after a 36 year reign in c.1328BC,[1792] or 1322BC,[1793] or 1318BC.[1794] Within stated errors, all current conventional chronologies could be made to accommodate this information. Further, this seems to be a non-correlation anyway. The letter refers to the recipient's father. Given Ay's total lack of a royal parent, it seems unlikely that a long-established foreign king would make this reference to Ay. Akhenaten seems instead the likely recipient.[1795]

It might be anticipated that the date of the Thera eruption and the LMIA period, and the dating of Alalakh VII and the fall of Babylon, would come into play in such matters, since it is necessary to link these with Hattusili I. Unfortunately, the chronology of the Hittite world in the 15th century BC is totally uncertain at present, which renders the situation problematic in the extreme. Astour (1989) makes a strong case for seven generations between Mursili I and Suppiluliuma I.[1796] The trouble is that we have neither an exact date for the death of Mursili I, nor do we know how long a generation is. If we were to assume a Low or raised Low Old Babylonian chronology (as required from the dendrochronological data: see Chapter VII), and hence place the death of Mursili I (shortly afterwards) in the range c.1550–1530BC, and allow 25 years per generation as being a fairly typical average for this period,[1797] then the accession of Suppiluliuma I is 'guesstimated' at c.1375–1355BC. This proves nothing, but is consistent with either the high, middle, or low Egyptian chronologies (and the general case for an Amenhotep III-Suppiluliuma I overlap, and long reign for Suppiluliuma I).

Where does this review of Egyptian–Babylonian–Assyrian–Hittite linkages leave us? The only conclusion from such tangled and debated data and interpretations is that the Egyptian New Kingdom chronology is floating; only by a small amount (and/or potential errors), yes, but floating nonetheless. It is ridiculous to pretend otherwise. The Ramesses II evidence in no way proves or necessitates the low Egyptian chronology (and a 1279BC accession date), and could plausibly be consistent with an earlier Egyptian chronology (c.1290BC or even 1304BC accession); the Suppiluliuma I-Egyptian linkage could go either way, while the Amarna period evidence better fits the middle or low Egyptian chronology, but could accommodate the higher Egyptian

---

[1789] Moran (1992:39 n.1).
[1790] Moran (1992:xxxix n.140).
[1791] Previously 1325BC in von Beckerath (1994a:118).
[1792] Brinkman (1977).
[1793] Gasche *et al.* (1998).
[1794] Boese and Wilhelm (1979).
[1795] Cf. Moran (1992:39 n.1) and the first and generally accepted reading.
[1796] Contra the nine generations in Wilhelm and Boese (1987).
[1797] But cf. Henige (1981).

chronology within the stated flexibility of the Babylonian chronology (and remember also that the main element favouring the middle or low Egyptian chronology here is the *possible* identification of Amenhotep III as the Egyptian king in EA6 – it may well be Akhenaten, and if so, the middle or higher Egyptian chronology is then more feasible). Thus there is no certain resolution, merely a possible range. The few other New Kingdom linkages one might adduce are less precise, or specific, and do not resolve this situation of potential ambiguity within an 11 to 25 year dating window. Such an 'error' factor is already ridiculously small for a time period from more than 3000 years ago! We should be realistic about what is possible given the less than perfect, and less than complete, data.

CHRONOLOGY OF THE 18TH DYNASTY OF EGYPT

The period of Egyptian chronology central to this book is the earlier 18th Dynasty, and in particular the dates for Ahmose and Tuthmosis III. The 1479BC accession of Tuthmosis III in the now conventional middle/low Egyptian chronology is linked with the 1279BC accession date for Ramesses II. Among recent work, only the chronology of Wente and Van Siclen (1976) broke with the (embarrassingly neat) 200 year interval between the accession years of these two key pharaohs. The lunar dates recorded during the reign of Tuthmosis III lead to possible accession dates of 1504BC, 1490BC, and 1479BC (other variations either earlier, or later, seem impossible today). Whereas Casperson (1988) found that analysis of the lunar observation data recorded in the reign of Ramesses II favoured 1279BC, because it offered perhaps the better match among the possibilities for the accession of Ramesses II,[1798] Casperson (1986) found that 1504BC seemed the best solution for Tuthmosis III.[1799] As noted previously, the data in question are not perfect, and emendation/assumption is required.[1800] Different scholars have argued for, and emended or not emended, or interpreted, the text data for the critical 'date'. Current views, whether through least emendation, or clever interpretation,[1801] favour solutions of either 1504BC or 1479BC.[1802] The 1490/1290BC dates proposed by Parker (1957) remain possible, but are currently considered less satisfactory, and require a key text emendation. Today, out of this conflicting/imperfect data and several possibilities, the low chronology 1479/1279BC date pair is favoured by the majority of scholarship. However, the evidence is by no means decisive (see above). As Kempinski (1992:72) was fully justified to observe: 'it seems that the Egyptian High chronology is still feasible', citing the studies of Leitz; and, for a slightly lower possibility, Luft (see above).

One route out of the current bind would be to extend somehow the length of the 18th Dynasty, such that one could have a 1279BC accession for Ramesses II, but a

---

[1798] See also Krauss (1989).
[1799] See also Leitz (1989:91–97; 1992); and cf. Luft (1989:231–233).
[1800] See review-discussion of Bryan (1991:14–19).
[1801] Esp. Lello (1978).
[1802] Wente (1975; see also Casperson 1986) argued for the former; Krauss (1985) for the latter.

1504BC accession for Tuthmosis III (or 1490BC and 1279BC, or 1504BC and 1290BC).
A 'long' chronology along these lines was proposed by Wente and Van Siclen (1976).
However, a 225 year interval between the accessions of Tuthmosis III and Ramesses
II is widely regarded as impossible in recent literature (and the authors of this
chronology have subsequently accepted this as likely, after a reconsideration of the
supposed jubilee references of Tuthmosis IV: see below).[1803] Wente and Van Siclen
(1976) achieved their elongation of the usual 18th Dynasty sequence by significantly
lengthening the reign of Tuthmosis IV, from the usual c.10 years to 33 years.[1804]
Tuthmosis IV was selected as one of the few 18th Dynasty kings where a certain
potential flexibility existed in the then available data. Van Siclen (1987:65 n.22) in fact
continues to state that 'the absolute length of the reign of Tuthmosis IV still remains
open to question'. Such a long reign for Tuthmosis IV was subsequently rejected in
detailed studies of Tuthmosis IV's reign by Bryan.[1805] She argues that he reigned for
10, and possibly 12, years. Bryan is undoubtedly likely to be correct, and her position
is widely accepted, but, it is instructive of the possible flexibilities still available in
the extant data to review several key details which *might* be argued to remain a little
ambiguous. I note the following issues as an exercise.[1806]

(i)   It is true that good evidence for year attestations goes only to Tuthmosis IV year
        8. Manetho gives 9 years and 8 months for the ruler probably to be considered
        as Tuthmosis IV (although, given Manetho's confused and garbled 18th Dynasty,
        this is hardly evidence – the reference could refer to Tuthmosis I, for example,
        who is missing in Manetho). Bryan (1991:6–9) argues at some length against
        two suggestions to the contrary which might provide evidence of a year 19 or
        20. The latter, a rock inscription at Tombos, is the most interesting, as several
        leading Egyptologists have thought it belonged to Tuthmosis IV. Bryan argues
        that this year 20 could be read as belonging to Tuthmosis III, and adduces various
        other points of detail, but, nonetheless, Tuthmosis IV cannot be absolutely
        excluded. Bryan's case is based on negative evidence, or possible alternatives,
        rather than clear positive evidence.

(ii)   Wente and Van Siclen (1976) placed great significance on attestations of *Heb-sed*
        (jubilee) festivals as indicating – at the first celebration – a year 30 for the ruling
        king.[1807] Since some inscriptions indicate the celebration of either a first *Heb-sed*
        for Tuthmosis IV (year 30) or even of a second (repeat) *Heb-sed* (year 33), Wente
        and Van Siclen therefore argued for a year 33 for Tuthmosis IV. Bryan (1991:20–
        23) argues against this. She does not dispute the inscriptions, rather the
        interpretation. She argues that there is no proof of the 30-year rule, especially in
        the New Kingdom. But this is less than convincing since Tuthmosis III and

---

[1803] Kitchen (1978) offered a rapid and detailed critique of the Wente and Van Siclen (1976) chronology.

[1804] Wente and Van Siclen (1976:229–230); Wente (1980b:252–254).

[1805] Bryan (1980:1–45; 1991:4–37); also Krauss (1978:169–172); Redford (1992:182–184).

[1806] From Wente and Van Siclen (1976); Wente (1980b); and Van Siclen (1987) versus Bryan (1991).

[1807] See esp. Wente and Van Siclen (1976:219–223). This is undoubtedly the usual position: see Van Siclen
(1987:60–61 and ns.16 and 27).

Amenhotep III both seem to have celebrated year 30 jubilees, following the 12th Dynasty model.[1808] Although Bryan is correct to argue that Wente and Van Siclen place undue faith in the link between a jubilee and 30 years of reign, she herself is arguing solely from silence, or instances of ambiguity, or poor evidence, or simple scepticism. She produces no evidence of direct relevance to Tuthmosis IV. One other counter argument is the possibility that the jubilees belong to Tuthmosis IV's father, Amenhotep II, and that Tuthmosis IV was merely a co-celebrant as co-regent. However, there is no evidence that there was a co-regency, and everything points against this scenario.[1809] The clear evidence of a first and second jubilee of specifically Tuthmosis IV from inscriptions on stone blocks from Karnak seemed to show, when Wente and Van Siclen 1976 was written, that this cannot have been the case (but see now Van Siclen's 1987 study: see below). Therefore, in summary, Bryan may be right to express scepticism, but she offers no proof, yet alone strong evidence for her view, and Wente and Van Siclen *may* be right, and Tuthmosis IV *may* have celebrated a first jubilee following the 30-year first jubilee rule, and *may* have celebrated or have been preparing to celebrate a second three years later (the formula 'first occasion and repetition of the jubilee').[1810] Finally, the appearance of Tuthmosis IV on one stela from Giza wearing the *shebiu* gold collar and gold armlets may be noted.[1811] I simply quote Bryan (1991:351): 'Raymond Johnson argues that the king would wear the *shebiu* collar only after a jubilee had taken place, since the gold denoted his new state of divinity and rejuvenation'. Bryan then of course procedes to try to explain this away, but the meaning may in fact be straightforward. The associated inscription, while only partially preserved, likewise suggests longevity and the sorts of phrases associated with a jubilee and renewal as the god Horemakhet states: 'I have given to you [millions of] years ... eternity [upon] the throne of Geb; all protection, life and stability behind him like Re...'.[1812]

New work by Van Siclen (1987) modifies the above debate. On the basis of an analysis of the Tuthmosis temple at Amada in lower Nubia, he finds evidence that the jubilee references of Tuthmosis IV seem to belong to relatively early in his reign, since he argues that they belong to the first of two phases of building at the site within the reign of Tuthmosis IV. He argues that if this analysis is correct, then the jubilee references cannot belong to a year 30 of Tuthmosis IV. To resolve the available data, Van Siclen then argues that the jubilee labels were attached to scenes originally carved for the forthcoming second jubilee of Amenhotep II, but, as he died before its celebration, they were then attributed to his son and successor Tuthmosis IV (who might have been expected in the future to celebrate a jubilee). Tuthmosis did not, however, actually celebrate a jubilee.

[1808] And recent evidence shows Sesostris III did properly celebrate a year 30 jubilee, contra Bryan (1991:22): see above this Appendix.
[1809] Bryan (1991:348–349).
[1810] Although see Van Siclen (1987): discussed below.
[1811] Bryan (1991:154, 350). On these collars, see Johnson (1998:86–87).
[1812] Bryan (1991:154).

Most Egyptologists will welcome this hypothesis, as it removes much of the 'evidence' in favour of a longer reign for Tuthmosis IV. However, the proposed building history is merely a best hypothesis, and in fact no trace remains *in situ* of the proposed second phase.[1813] Nor, because there are two Tuthmosis IV building phases, does the earlier one necessarily have to be placed early in his reign (and general stylistic comparisons to structures of Amenhotep II are plausible for either early or late in the reign of his son). There is just a presumption that as the temple was begun jointly by Tuthmosis III and Amenhotep II (as co-regents), that Tuthmosis IV will have immediately proceeded with its completion. But clearly, despite its beginning during the coregency of Amenhotep II with Tuthmosis III, the temple was not immediately finished in the next 20 odd years of Amenhotep II's sole rule. There are also jubilee references for Tuthmosis IV from Elephantine and Karnak. It might be questioned whether a re-attribution occurred at all three sites. The jubilee was an important event; given the celebrations of his father, this would have been well appreciated. Would a new king have wished to claim a jubilee that was not his? The suggestions that the labels were pious wishes seems unlikely as they specifically refer to a jubilee (and the hypothesis is without good parallels).[1814] Van Siclen (1987:60) notes that the absence of officials with real jubilee titles seems to argue against any actual celebration of a jubilee by Tuthmosis IV, but, at the same time, there is in fact rather limited prosopographical data available for his officials. It is of course conceivable that Tuthmosis IV was readying preparations for a jubilee which he did not live to celebrate; this could accommodate both a longer reign (to a later 20s year), and the lack of concrete evidence. Nothing is totally certain. All in all, Van Siclen (1987:61) simply admits that there is 'no physical proof' for his hypothesis.

(iii) There is rather limited prosopographical evidence concerning officials who are known to have served under Tuthmosis IV during their careers. Bryan (1991:23) thus cautions against the use of such evidence, stating that it 'should be weighed with scepticism'. Nonetheless, she identifies the career of a man named Horemhab as possibly relevant to the question of the length of Tuthmosis IV's reign.[1815] The weighing scene in Horemhab's tomb indicates that this individual served Amenhotep II, Tuthmosis IV, and Amenhotep III, and, when it comes to judgement of his life, four kings are indicated by their cartouches, with the addition of Tuthmosis III. Bryan argues that the inclusion of Tuthmosis III meant that this ruler also knew the deceased well enough to judge his truthfulness, and some scholars have even taken this to indicate that Horemhab must have served under Tuthmosis III. But since Horemhab does not state specifically that he was in the following (service) of Tuthmosis III, the latter view may be discounted. Bryan nevertheless assumes that he was at least 15–20 years old when Tuthmosis III died, but even this is not necessary. Apart from the possibility

---

[1813] Van Siclen (1987:55).

[1814] Van Siclen (1987:60 and ns.18 and 19).

[1815] Bryan (1991:23–24).

that Tuthmosis III appears as a necropolis deity,[1816] the evidence really requires only that Horemhab was born before the death of Tuthmosis III (and thus strictly he is one of his judges as king-god of his life – in this case his childhood). Bryan (1991:24) then asks whether the autobiography of Horemhab supports a short or long reign of Tuthmosis IV? Needless to say, one piece of data is no control, and can always be exceptional. If the long reign model of Wente and Van Siclen (1976) were correct, then, to have been born before Tuthmosis III died (conceivably even during his two year co-regency with Amenhotep II), and to have lived and then served through the reigns of Amenhotep II and Tuthmosis IV before dying in the service of Amenhotep III, Horemhab must have lived to be c.65+ years of age. Of course Bryan is therefore correct to suggest that a shorter reign for Tuthmosis IV would allow Horemhab to die younger, at an age more typical of the average age at death for the period. But there is also nothing extraordinary in a member of the Egyptian élite living to his later 60s – indeed, the general demographic pattern for the élite in the ancient world is that if individuals survived their juvenile–young adult years (which the majority did not, hence low average life expectancy), then they had a fair chance of living to old age (see e.g. Sallares 1991:116–117). Thus this evidence does not weigh against the long reign hypothesis.

We might also consider two other individuals, Heqareshu and Heqarneheh, father and son, and royal nurses/tutors of respectively Tuthmosis IV and Amenhotep III.[1817] Heqarneheh's tomb (TT64) was built (and presumably used) late in the reign of Tuthmosis IV – Amenhotep III is still only heir apparent in a scene in the tomb, and Tuthmosis is represented as the reigning king. Heqarneheh was tutor to the young prince Amenhotep III. Royal tutors were drawn usually from the ranks of the retired courtiers, and were not young men. Heqarneheh's father, Heqareshu, was the tutor of the young Tuthmosis IV, and is shown on a statue dedicated by Tuthmosis before he became king. Again, we may presume he was not a young man. He seems to have survived into the reign of Tuthmosis IV, whereupon he enjoyed a more honorific title. Although by no means impossible, it seems unlikely in the normal course of affairs that both father and son could be royal tutors (and die) within less than a decade as required by the short reign of Tuthmosis IV. A longer reign would be more convenient.

(iv) The Lateran obelisk was cut and inscribed for Tuthmosis III but was not erected during his reign. It was then subsequently set up under Tuthmosis IV who added an inscription stating that he was now erecting it for Tuthmosis III after it had 'spent thirty-five years lying on its side in the hands of the craftsmen on the southern side of Karnak'.[1818] Depending on when Tuthmosis IV erected this obelisk, the 35-year interval might indicate that Tuthmosis IV's father reigned up to 33/ 34 years, and not the 26 years usually assigned.[1819] There is no direct evidence on

---

[1816] Bryan (1991:37 n.161).
[1817] See Bryan (1991); Berman (1998:9); Bryan (1998:40–41).
[1818] Translation of Bryan (1991:24–25). For the text on the obelisk, see Breasted (1962, vol.II:§830–838).
[1819] Wente and Van Siclen (1976:227–228).

this point. It could theoretically date from the end of Tuthmosis IV's reign. But the evidence would suggest the contrary. The circumstances of the succession of Tuthmosis IV are somewhat murky.[1820] Even if previous views of his being a usurper are downplayed or dismissed, Bryan (1991:38–73), after a forensic examination of the available evidence, concludes that there may well have been a power struggle to be king at the death of Amenhotep II. In such circumstances, it would make best sense that the brand new ruler would look for visible opportunities to stress his legitimacy, and nothing would be as obvious as a specific linking of himself as son–father with, and as protector of, the great Tuthmosis III. A year 1–2 date for the setting up of the obelisk is thus quite plausible and likely. Such a view is in fact more or less required by the recent chronology of von Beckerath (1997), who gives Amenhotep II a 31 year reign (hence, given 2 year co-regency of Amenhotep II and Tuthmosis III, obelisk by Tuthmosis IV year 2/3). In conclusion, this evidence does not tell us anything about Tuthmosis IV's reign length, but does suggest that Amenhotep II had a long reign, and requires c.7 additional years compared to the chronology of Kitchen (1996a).

(v)   Wente and Van Siclen brought up the issue of providing time for two or three Great Queens to fit into the reign of Tuthmosis IV (and a couple of minor wives), as well as time for him to father several children.[1821] This argument was largely predicated on the idea that Tuthmosis IV was relatively young on accession (see (vi) below). However, although the 'young at accession' argument cannot be taken too far, the dynastic evidence (from family, to monuments, to tombs dated to his reign[1822]) is impressive for a reign of just 10 or fewer years. Bryan (1991:332) argues that Tuthmosis IV has been one of the lesser known Egyptian kings of the 18th Dynasty simply because he did not rule for a long time. This is an unnecessary assumption (and one that informs Bryan's whole analysis). Basically, Tuthmosis IV does not appear to have been particularly active in military or expansionary diplomatic terms,[1823] and did not do anything radical, such as change Egyptian religion, and no archive of his correspondence has been preserved. Therefore, he stands in poor comparison with Tuthmosis III, or Amenhotep III, or Akhenaten. But this circumstance hardly demonstrates that his reign was short. History is full of less dynamic or newsworthy rulers – not all of whom had short reigns. As Bryan (1991:354) notes, the royal administration prospered under Tuthmosis IV, and while 'the rank of "general" or "military officer" is practically unknown in the period ... that of "royal scribe" abounds ... The office of "scribe of recruits" was never so well-attested'. There is potentially plenty of evidence to belong to a longer reign.

[1820] Redford (1992:183); Wente and Van Siclen (1976:229); Van Siclen (1987:65 n.25).

[1821] Wente and Van Siclen (1976:229–230); Wente (1980b:252–254); cf. Bryan (1991:93–140).

[1822] See Bryan (1991:passim); Bryan (1998).

[1823] There is limited inscriptional evidence of at least one Asian campaign (Breasted 1962, vol.II:§816–822, also §837 from the Lateran Obelisk). He also clearly fought a campaign in Nubia (Breasted 1962, vol.II:§823–829, also §837 from the Lateran Obelisk).

(vi)   Wente and Van Siclen (1976:230) argue that Tuthmosis IV was young at his accession. Their arguments consist of the prominence of his mother, Tiaa, in the first six years of his reign, and the use of the term *inpw* to describe Tuthmosis IV at accession – which Wente and Van Siclen state was 'a term applied to young princes and kings who had not yet reached puberty'. Bryan (1991:42–43) argues strongly against this, explaining away the use of *inpw* as relevant only to the past (i.e. his childhood), and she follows a suggestion of James Weinstein that the specific inscription from Thebes at issue referred to the rebuilding of 'the house of his Majesty when he was very young'.[1824] There is also a statue of Tuthmosis IV as a prince (which shows a grown man), and before his accession he is described as able to race chariots. Bryan therefore concludes that Tuthmosis IV 'was of at least adolescent years at the death of Amenhotep II'. This debate bears only indirectly on the question of the length of Tuthmosis IV's reign (see (v) above), and neither argues for, or against, another several decades of life.

(vii)   The last piece of evidence which has been noted in this debate is the x-ray and other analysis of the mummy thought to belong to Tuthmosis IV.[1825] A programme of study of the royal mummies published in 1980 argued that the mummy of Tuthmosis IV is of a man who is thought to have died aged c.35 years of age (range 30–40),[1826] which, if he was *relatively* young on accession (c.≤15–20 years of age), would suggest a reign of c. 15–20±5 years, rather than the 10 years in Kitchen (1996a) and von Beckerath (1997). This is supported, apart from the prominence of the mother (because wives are not mentioned in his early years), because he seems potentially to have become heir only after the death/removal of another son of Amenhotep II. There are of course caveats over such x-ray datings.[1827] And it may be that the mummy identified as Tuthmosis IV is perhaps in fact not Tuthmosis IV at all! Wente and Harris (1992:11–13) suggest that, although Tuthmosis IV offers one of the better circumstantial cases for correct identification, it might make better sense if this mummy in fact belonged to Amenhotep III, and the mummy identified as Amenhotep II in fact belonged to Tuthmosis IV. If this revised assignment of mummies were correct, then it only strengthens the case for Tuthmosis IV's being relatively mature at death; the mummy for Amenhotep II/Tuthmosis IV(?) is estimated to have had an age at death of c.35–45 years.[1828] However, the appropriate conclusion must be that this x-ray evidence is less than conclusive. It could conceivably support either the short or long reign case (or neither if the identity of the mummy is not certain).

The outcome of this excursus on Tuthmosis IV is that the case is not completely closed with regard to the possibility of a longer reign (although I accept it is unlikely – I am more seeking to demonstrate the potential for a degree of minor flexibility in a specific

---

[1824] Bryan (1991:43).
[1825] Bryan (1991:9–13).
[1826] Krogman and Baer (1980:202 Table 6.3, 206–211 Table 6.4); Harris *et al.* (1980:333 Table 9.1).
[1827] E.g. Robins (1981); Bryan (1991:10–13); Wente and Harris (1992).
[1828] Krogman and Baer (1980:202, 210 Table 6.4).

case). I can only repeat the statement of Van Siclen (1987:65 n.22): 'the absolute length of the reign of Tuthmosis IV still remains open to question'.

We may briefly consider the data with regard to the other earlier 18th Dynasty kings. The length of Amenhotep III's reign is known fairly firmly to be 37/38 years, but the length of the reign of Amenhotep II is not specifically known.[1829] His highest attested year is 26. Our only further control is that 35 years represents the interval between some points in the reigns of Tuthmosis III and IV (Lateran obelisk inscription referred to above); if the points are the end and beginning of the reign, then Amenhotep's sole reign could be up to 35 years long.[1830] Given the other potential flexibilities already noted in the period between Ramesses II and Amenhotep III, it therefore remains possible that the 'fixed' interval of 200 years may not be completely unassailable.

The 54 year reign of Tuthmosis III is then certain, but there are grounds for debate over the lengths of the reigns of some of the earlier kings of the 18th Dynasty. Von Beckerath (1994a) specifically notes the paucity of dated documentary evidence for the 18th Dynasty kings prior to Tuthmosis III. The most uncertain is Tuthmosis II. As Bierbrier (1995) concludes, Tuthmosis II may have reigned for 15, 13, or as few as about 3 years. To this author, the weight of evidence favours the longer reign option.[1831] In particular, the view that Hatshepsut celebrated her jubilee in her year 16 as 30 years from the death of her father, Tuthmosis I, and thus 30 years after she became 'heiress', seems the most plausible construction of the evidence, and requires a longer reign for Tuthmosis II. No one is sure what to do with a now lost inscription which purportedly recorded a year 18 for Tuthmosis II.[1832] It may be correct that this was an inscription of Hatshepsut changed to Tuthmosis II by Tuthmosis III,[1833] but we do not know. This debate, however, only again emphasises that it is incorrect to claim that the chronology of the New Kingdom is known and secure from inscriptional and genealogical data. As Bierbrier (1995:18) concludes, concerning the chronology of the period of Hatshepsut: 'the problem of her age remains open, but it is open like so much in Egyptian history. The last and definitive word on the subject remains to be written'.

The length of Tuthmosis I's reign is also uncertain. He is securely attested only to year 4, but perhaps attested to years 8 and 9 on a debated stone block, and perhaps as far as years 12/13 from Manetho.[1834] The reigns of the first two rulers of the 18th Dynasty are widely agreed at c.21 years for Amenhotep I and c.25 years for Ahmose. Current opinion rules out a co-regency between the two. The total period from the

---

[1829] To the point that Kitchen (1987:41) proposes adding any extra years required if the reign of Sethos I is shortened to Amenhotep II.

[1830] From the usually credited 26 years: Kitchen (1996a); von Beckerath (1994a:118); or 31 years: von Beckerath (1997).

[1831] See also Wente and Van Siclen (1976:226–227); von Beckerath (1997:120–121); cf. Krauss (1992:86–90).

[1832] Wente and Van Siclen (1976:226); Breasted (1962, vol.II note a to §129).

[1833] As Kitchen (1996a:6 argues).

[1834] Krauss (1992:86–90); Kitchen (1996a:6); von Beckerath (1997:120, 125–126).

accession of Ahmose to the accession of Tuthmosis III thus ranges between about 74 to 55 years in recent scholarship. The longer option seems more likely. From the 1479BC accession date for Tuthmosis III, this suggests an accession date for Ahmose from c.1553BC (conventionally c.1550BC). The dates would be from c.1564BC, or from c.1578BC, if the higher 1490BC, or 1504BC, accession dates for Tuthmosis III were employed instead.

Until recently, the linch pin of the chronology of the early 18th Dynasty was an apparent reference to a heliacal rising of Sothis (Sirius) during the 9th year of Amenhotep I in the Papyrus Ebers. This has recently become contested as evidence,[1835] and debated as to interpretation, and place of observation.[1836] If one ignores recent arguments to discount this evidence entirely,[1837] then the Sothic information and some allied lunar data[1838] provides a date for Amenhotep year 9. Where was the observation made? The older conventional assumption was Memphis. In this case, the date is in the range of the c.1540s–1530s BC.[1839] However, some scholars argue for an observation point at Thebes – notably von Beckerath (1987 and since), who has also defended the utility of the papyrus data. In this case, the date is in the range of the 1520s–1510s BC (preferred date 1517BC).[1840] Von Beckerath is probably correct to argue for a general model of local observations of Sirius; in which case, Thebes must be the likely place of observation for this datum, given Theban find spot.[1841] Krauss made a case for an observation location at Elephantine, which would require a date another decade lower again (e.g. c.1506BC).[1842] There are of course many pages of advocacy for each of these three dates, and variations of a few years on each of them. The radically low Elephantine model of Krauss lacks any positive support from ancient evidence, and has not been widely accepted.[1843]

The choice between Memphis and Thebes is based on little solid evidence. Memphis was the traditional administrative capital, but the papyrus was found at Thebes, and some argue that Thebes was the effective capital of Egypt during the reigns of Ahmose and Amenhotep I. Circumstantial evidence through Egyptian history would favour Memphis as the location of such official observations, but one cannot be certain in the absence of explicit evidence. This choice is again between the high and the low Egyptian chronology. Memphis works with (and requires) the high chronology (but could accommodate the middle chronology); Thebes works with the low chronology (but could accommodate the middle chronology or lower high chronology of Parker).

[1835] von Beckerath (1992; 1994a:10–12, 112–113; 1997:45–46, 50); Helck (1983; 1992b); Luft (1986; 1992a:112–113); Barta (1988); Depuydt (1996b).

[1836] Ward (1992:59).

[1837] See esp. Helck (1983; 1988; 1992b).

[1838] ?: cf. esp. Luft (1992a:112 and refs.).

[1839] E.g Wente (1975). The traditional date in older literature is 1547BC from a Memphite observation.

[1840] For the Memphite or Theban options, see in addition variously Hornung (1964:20–21); Parker (1976:185–186); Kitchen (1987:42); Leitz (1992); von Beckerath (1994a:10–11, 112–113; 1997:45–46, 50).

[1841] See also Ward (1992:61–62) who supports local observations.

[1842] Krauss (1985; 1992; 1995).

[1843] E.g. see critique of Murnane (1983).

In one way it is very reassuring to see how all the various pieces of evidence available keep offering a compatible picture, but, at the same time, the basic c.11 to c.25 year possible range in dates remains. The current dismissal of the formerly traditional (high) Memphite date in recent literature stems from the belief in the 1479BC and 1279BC dates for the accessions of Tuthmosis III and Ramesses II; if these moved (see above), then the Memphite solution could again become relevant. However, since this now seems less likely, with a local observation model plausible, it is perhaps important to note that the Parker lower high chronology (with 1490BC and 1290BC dates) could be made to work with a Thebes observation point.

Working forward from the Middle Kingdom

We may also approach the problem of early 18th Dynasty dates from the other direction. The Middle Kingdom traditionally has its own fixed point via another Sothic datum from Sesostris III year 7 with associated lunar information from the reigns of Sesostris III and Amenemhat III.[1844] The place of observation is again debated. For the Middle Kingdom, the Elephantine hypothesis of Krauss (1985)[1845] seems very unlikely; Elephantine had no special association with the central government during the Middle Kingdom. Leitz (1989) presents a strong argument against Elephantine, although, as Ward (1992:60–62) summarises, both Leitz and Krauss undoubtedly apply inappropriate modern standards and viewpoints to ancient data which were never meant to be capable of supporting such specific and detailed analyses. Thebes is possible, but Memphis was the political centre of the Middle Kingdom, and the relevant texts were found in one of the pyramid towns (Illahun) of the Middle Kingdom pharaohs near Memphis. A stela from Memphis also provides at least consonant evidence of the observation of the heliacal rising (coming forth) of Sirius/Sothis during the 13th Dynasty.[1846] Most scholarship has thus favoured the Memphis region sighting, and the recent work of Luft adds additional strong support for this choice.[1847] The result is thus either the traditional Parker date of 1872BC, or the revised date of 1866BC calculated by Luft, for Sesostris III year 7.[1848] Since there is almost no significant difference, this matter (and a few minor associated debates) need not detain us further.

Indeed, if there has been a major critique, it has been of the astronomical data and calculations thereupon.[1849] Rose provided a critique of all the main attempts to calculate exact dates from the Illahun data, and concluded that: 'no one seems to have been able to establish an early second-millennium chronology for the Twelfth Dynasty by

---

[1844] Parker (1976:177–184); Luft (1992a; 1992b; 1994); Kitchen (1987:43); Ward (1992:59–60); von Beckerath (1997:44–45); Krauss (1998b).
[1845] Krauss (1998b). See also Franke (1988a).
[1846] Bourriau (1982:51–55, pl.3).
[1847] Luft (1989; 1992a; 1992b). Rose (1994:245–246) also offers several arguments in favour of the Memphis area and against Elephantine.
[1848] The preferred alternative low Elephantine date of Krauss is 1830BC (most recently Krauss 1998b).
[1849] Rose (1994; 1997); Long (1974).

calculating exact placements both for the Sothic date and for the El-Lahun lunar documents. In order to find a suitable anchorage for the Middle Kingdom, we shall apparently have to look elsewhere...'.[1850] Read (1995) takes up from this conclusion, and proposes again[1851] a change from regarding the recorded lunar data as being relevant not to morning risings (as argued by conventional scholarship) but to evening crescent observations, and so goes on (perversely only for the period 1800–1550BC, ignoring the rest of the conventionally relevant 19th century BC!) to offer a radically revised Egyptian chronology (quite impossible for other reasons – e.g. the 13th Dynasty most definitely existed! – contra Read[1852]). Parker (1970) previously rejected Read's case, and there is no reason to change this position. Nonetheless, the very lack of real certainty, of absolute precision, and the clear evidence of errors, of debate, and of flexibilities, are highlighted by the existence of such 'radical' literature.

If we ignore radical alternatives, and accept the likelihood of a date for Sesostris III year 7 c.1872/1866BC, the chronology of the Middle Kingdom then depends on some debates concerning the lengths of reigns and co-regencies.[1853] Formerly, based on the Turin Canon, Sesostris II was accorded 19 years, and Sesostris III 30+x years. Then Simpson and others attempted to shorten the reigns of Sesostris II and III, and so shorten the overall Middle Kingdom.[1854] Simpson's case was based on a set of evidence which indicated that Amenemhat III had become pharaoh by about Sesostris III year 19. Most scholarship readily accepted his case. There was no evidence that Sesostris reigned longer than about 19 years, and, if there was any discrepancy, it was argued that there were good grounds to suspect a co-regency between Sesostris III and his successor Amenemhat III. As noted earlier, recent evidence has created some problems. First, there is a reasonable case that Sesostris celebrated a *Heb-sed*, and so reached a 30th year as king, and, most recently, Wegner (1996) has found evidence for a Sesostris III year 39! How to explain these 20 additional years is not easy. Wegner makes a good case for there being a very long (20 years) co-regency between Sesostris III and Amenemhat III. If correct, then there is in effect no change to the post-Simpson conventional chronology of the 12th Dynasty around and following the Sesostris III year 7 Sothic datum. At this time, the arguments of Simpson, maintained by Wegner, appear convincing, and this seems the best solution (although one must note that some of the 'certainty' from extant records and lunar data appears misplaced[1855]).

The preceding reign of Sesostris II remains more problematic. The proposed six year reign in the shortened, or revised, chronology of Kitchen (1996a), and two years as co-regent, also appears rather short, given, if nothing else, the scale and nature of

---

[1850] Rose (1994:261).

[1851] See previously Read (1970).

[1852] See Ryholt (1997:69–93).

[1853] E.g. Kitchen (1987:43–44); von Beckerath (1997:132–135); Obsomer (1995); Wegner (1996). Note: Kitchen (1989:152) revises to 1856/55BC for a Memphis/Heliopolis observation for Sesostris III year 7, but the change is small.

[1854] Simpson (1972:50–54; 1984:900, 903–904, 906); Krauss (1984). See also Kitchen (1987:43 and refs.); von Beckerath (1995b; 1997).

[1855] Contra e.g. Luft (1992a:110 and n.15).

his pyramid at Illahun;[1856] further, Sesostris II is attested at least a year 8 (and, despite a generally 'compact' viewpoint of the 12th Dynasty, von Beckerath allows 10 years[1857]). A long co-regency with his predecessor Amenemhat II is one possible explanation. The internal chronology of the earlier 12th Dynasty is certainly fluid at present,[1858] and there is active debate over the existence and extent of several co-regencies. These debates, while relevant to the date of the start of the 12th Dynasty, do not concern our present discussion: the attempt to work forwards from the Sesostris III Sothic date to the 18th Dynasty.

The reigns after Sesostris III are more or less agreed. Amenemhat III reigned for a minimum of 45 years (and perhaps 1–2 more years), Amenemhat IV for 9 years, and Sobeknofru for 4 years. If one further assumes that the Wegner (1996) thesis is correct (and so the case of Simpson), the date of the end of the Middle Kingdom may be calculated by employing the 1872/1866BC Sesostris III year 7 date as c.1801BC,[1859] or c.1796BC,[1860] or c.1795BC,[1861] or c.1794/1793BC.[1862] Other variants exist: Parker's original date of 1786BC based on a (separate) 36 year reign for Sesostris III was proposed again by Kitchen (1989:153) on the basis of a revised Memphis Sothic date of 1856/55BC (but with shorter reign for Sesostris III); however, this Sothic dating appears to have attracted little support, and Kitchen (1996a:9) no longer mentions it. Let us thus work with the range 1801–1793BC.

The 13th Dynasty follows. It was based at Memphis. The first two kings of the 13th Dynasty were sons of the 12th Dynasty king Amenemhat IV, and the Dynasty represents continuity. However, it seems that at about the same time (even the very end of the 12th Dynasty), a new regional realm of Canaanite origin had developed in the Delta: the 14th Dynasty.[1863] Unfortunately, we have little solid data for the 13th Dynasty. Some recent literature has circumscribed its duration to less than 70 years,[1864] whereas the usual view is that it lasted for more than a century. It is certainly clear that it existed, and for some time – even more radical proposals to abolish or side-line the 13th Dynasty are incorrect.[1865] Ryholt (1997:72) argues for not less than 57 13th Dynasty 'kings'. One suggestion is that a strong vizierate (created under Sesostris III) took charge and ruled through largely puppet pharaohs (hence so many, and most with very short reigns). Others blame famine, plague, war and civil strife: the royal names and titles of some of the SIP kings are certainly suggestive of such problems.[1866]

[1856] Yurco (1996:69).
[1857] von Beckerath (1995b; 1997).
[1858] Delia (1997).
[1859] Kitchen (1987:49).
[1860] Luft (1992a; 1992b).
[1861] Kitchen (1996a).
[1862] von Beckerath (1995b; 1997). This employs the longest options available.
[1863] Ryholt (1997:75–76, 94–117).
[1864] Greenberg (1993).
[1865] E.g. von Beckerath (1964); Yurco (1996:86–87); Ryholt (1997:esp. 69–93).
[1866] Ryholt (1997:305–306). E.g. 'He who seizes through strength', 'the Might of Re which rescues Thebes', 'He who is beloved of his army', 'He who nourishes his city (i.e. Thebes), saving it from famine', etc.

The beginnings of what became the separate cultural realms of lower and upper Egypt in the times of the Hyksos and 16–17th Dynasty rulers may be seen here (whether or not one follows all the details of Ryholt's case); this division then existed until the wars of the late 17th Dynasty against the Hyksos, and their eventual conquest of lower Egypt under Ahmose.[1867] What we do not have through this period is chronological control. However, most of Egypt seems to have been ruled by the 13th Dynasty until at least the reign of Sobekhotep IV, perhaps some 49–56 years into the Dynasty,[1868] although Ryholt points out the lack of real evidence in favour of this impression.[1869] The big question in SIP studies is what happens thereafter. Here there have been many divergent views.

A major issue is when the Hyksos takeover of Memphis occurred in terms of the 13th Dynasty. Some have argued that this was during, or at the end of, the reign of the 13th Dynasty ruler Merneferre Ay or successor Merhetepre, some that it was during the reign of [Dudu]mose/mosre[1870] whose name is similar to the king 'Tutimaios' Manetho links with the Hyksos takeover,[1871] and others maintain that it was instead only at the end of the attested 13th Dynasty and possibly a hypothetical Dudumose II?[1872] Those who have advocated mid-13th Dynasty takeovers then have to discuss what happened elsewhere in Egypt. Since subsequent 13th Dynasty kings after Merneferre Ay[1873] in the Turin Canon list are attested only (if at all) from the monuments, inscriptions, and so on from upper Egypt,[1874] this has prompted some to argue that the 13th Dynasty perhaps moved to, and limped on at, Thebes.

Ryholt (1997:79) argues strongly against the idea of the 13th Dynasty re-locating. Ryholt argues that ancient Egyptian and Near Eastern kinglists grouped rulers by residence and not family – further, it is clear that the 13th Dynasty were not all one family. If the king had moved to Thebes, then this would have led to a new dynastic grouping in the kinglists. Moreover, Ryholt (1997:79–80) notes a meagre couple of stela which seem most plausibly to indicate late 13th Dynasty rule/presence at Memphis, and the fact that all known 13th Dynasty tombs are at Memphis. Thus the best interpretation at present appears to be to regard the entire 13th Dynasty as a Memphite dynasty. Its end comes with the conquest of Memphis by the 15th Dynasty.

When was this? The data available from the Turin Canon are less than useful. A

[1867] Bourriau (1997); O'Connor (1997).

[1868] Following Kitchen (1987:50).

[1869] Ryholt (1997:75–77).

[1870] King no.51 in Ryholt's (1997:73) Turin Canon reconstruction; no.37 in the Turin Canon list of the 13th Dynasty in von Beckerath (1997:138).

[1871] Although Bülow-Jacobsen in Ryholt (1997:327–329) removes this name from the text of Manetho entirely.

[1872] See von Beckerath (1964); Franke (1988b); Kitchen (1987:44–46; 1996a:7); Ryholt (1997).

[1873] No.33 in Ryholt's (1997:73) Turin Canon reconstruction; no.27 for Dynasty 13 in von Beckerath (1997:138).

[1874] O'Connor (1997:Fig.2.3). Bietak (1984:473) saw widespread 13th Dynasty rule as ending (or not attested) after the reigns Neferhotep I and Sebekhotep IV. This is three to five kings before Merneferre Ay in the Turin Canon list.

number of kings listed in the Turin Canon for this period have no preserved reign length, and several 13th Dynasty kings listed in the Turin Canon are known only from this record: there are at present no other attestations from archaeology or history. Despite its incomplete, fragmentary, nature, and the late date, the Turin Canon nonetheless seems the best source for the SIP; Manetho records rather different reign lengths, and altogether offers an SIP nearly twice as long, but his data appear mostly impractical. Different scholars have also included different kings (or not) in the late 13th Dynasty. The calculation on the basis of Kitchen (1996a:7) is that the entire 13th Dynasty represents at about a minimum c.150 years.[1875] However, Kitchen here, and elsewhere,[1876] includes in the late 13th Dynasty several kings whom Ryholt (1997), rather speculatively, assigns to the 16th Dynasty. Nonetheless, despite a different list (of 57 kings), Ryholt (1997:196) calculates an almost identical c.154 years for the 13th Dynasty. Given the attested data, this could well be an over-estimate (largely derived from the other perceived chronological constraints for the SIP). Yurco (1996:86–87) offers an alternative approach by calculating the period of the six 'ruling' viziers of this timespan. He achieves a figure of c.110–120 years (flexible). At Thebes, genealogies for some of the important families likewise span the late 13th through earlier 16th Dynasties,[1877] and such data may in the long run resolve some of the chronological problems. From the starting point of 1801–1793BC derived above, the c.150-year estimate suggests that the 13th Dynasty ended c.1651–1643BC (or later). Of course, complications abound. The 15th Dynasty need not have conquered Memphis almost immediately on coming to power at Avaris, nor, even when they did control Memphis, do we necessarily know that they replaced the ruling group there.[1878] A long and a shorter chronology are thus available: long with the entire the 13th Dynasty followed by the entire 15th Dynasty, short with some overlap of the early 15th and late 13th Dynasties.

To reach the 18th Dynasty and Ahmose, we need to consider the 15th Dynasty.[1879] An entry in the Turin Canon at the end of a list of this Dynasty states 'six [Hyk]sos kings ruling for 108 years' + x months and x days,[1880] and this figure is usually accepted. The Turin Canon preserves only the name of the last of the Hyksos, Khamudy, and a few reign lengths for which kings must be conjectured. The reign of 40 + x years is conventionally assigned to Apophis, as he is known to have ruled for more than 33 years on the basis of an attested year 33 on the Rhind Mathematical Papyrus. This entry may also fit as the penultimate one. The preceding entry of 10, or 20, or even 30 + years is probably Khyan. The two kings before him are assigned 8 and 3 years. Ryholt (1997:119–125) argues that the names of the first three kings are likely to be

---

[1875] Support for a figure close to this comes also from the usual emendation of Manetho's figure of 453 years to 153 years for the 13th Dynasty. Such numbers are of course dubious, and others are possible: cf. Barta (1979–1980).

[1876] Kitchen (1987:45, 51).

[1877] Ryholt (1997:306).

[1878] Ryholt (1997:323–327) argues against 'vassal' kings, but the evidence is not conclusive.

[1879] Ryholt (1997:118–150).

[1880] Ryholt (1997:118, 119 table 22); von Beckerath (1997:136, 212).

Samuquenu, 'Aper-'Anati, and Sakir-Har; the order of these three is mere guesswork.[1881] The Ianassi mentioned as a king's son of Khyan must be assumed either to have predeceased his father, or was perhaps violently usurped by Apophis.[1882] We may conclude that Manetho included Iannas as one of the Hyksos kings, and left out Khyan, by a simple copying mistake whereby he inverted the son for the father and king.[1883] The attested years for four of the six Hyksos kings therefore total between c.54–74, leaving 34–54 years to share between the first king and Khamudy.[1884]

It is usually thought that the end of Hyksos rule occurred in about the middle of the reign of Ahmosis. Some entries on the back of the Rhind Mathematical Papyrus seem relevant.[1885]

a. 11th regnal-year, 2nd month of Shemu: Heliopolis was entered.
b. 1st month of Akhet, 23rd day: He-of-the-South strikes against Sile.
c. 25th? or 26? day: It was heard that Sile had been entered.
d. 11th regnal-year, 1st month of Akhet, birth[day] of Seth: The majesty of this god gave a cry.
e. Birth[day] of Isis: The sky made rain.

In particular, there is reference to the 11th regnal year of an unnamed king dating events when 'He-of-the-South' entered and took various cities and territory which were formerly part of the 15th Dynasty territory. The context seems to be linked with the loss of cities/territory leading directly to the fall of Avaris.[1886] Who is the unnamed king to whom the year 11 belongs? It cannot be Apophis as the Papyrus itself is dated to his year 33, and these jottings are later. Ahmose and Khamudy seem the possible candidates. Cases can be made for either. It would seem inherently unlikely that a Hyksos document would refer to the year dates of the southern Theban kings, but it has been argued that perhaps these jottings were added by a former Hyksos subject now living in territory conquered by Ahmose (e.g. Memphis). Ryholt (1997:188), following Redford (1979), accepts this latter interpretation, and so dates the fall of Avaris to Ahmose year 11. But it is impossible to be certain. I find the balance of probabilities to favour Khamudy. First, it seems more likely that the 'He-of-the-South' (i.e. Ahmose) is distinguished from the writer's world (i.e. is the enemy), and is not the subject of the year dates given. Second, there is the reference to the god Seth. Seth seems to be the god of Avaris.[1887] Although Egyptian, Seth seems to have been adopted

---

[1881] Bietak (1996a:65) argues that Sakir-Har (rendered Seker-her by Bietak) was the first Hyksos king (thus representing the 'Salitis' in the list in Manetho).
[1882] Ryholt (1997:307–308).
[1883] See Ryholt (1997:120–121) for possible explanation.
[1884] It remains possible that additional Hyksos kings may be discovered, if finds of names found cannot be linked to the names of known rulers. Bietak (e.g. 1991a:52 and Fig.18) reports a possible case of a scarab of an unknown Hyksos ruler (Shenshek), although Bietak goes on to suggest that it might belong with Sheshi (the 14th Dynasty ruler), with the latter to be considered as a diminutive?
[1885] Ryholt (1997:187 with text and n.670 with further refs.).
[1886] See e.g. Bietak (1984:473 and ns.22–23).
[1887] Ryholt (1997:148–150).

by the Canaanite population of the Delta (and some argue that Seth became endowed with the qualities of an original Syrian weather god, and there is a close link to Canaanite Baal[1888]). The 14th Dynasty Canaanite king Nehesy is 'beloved of Seth, lord of Avaris'.[1889] This seems further grounds for suspecting that the writer of the jottings on the papyrus was Hyksos and perhaps at Avaris.

In consequence of this decision, I assign the 11th regnal year to Khamudy. Since Ahmose is close to surrounding Avaris from these notes, Khamudy may not have had many more years as king at Avaris. Nonetheless, later tradition suggests that the siege of Avaris perhaps took a few years. Let us assign his reign 11+ years. None of the arguments Ryholt advances in favour of a much shorter reign for Khamudy (Ryholt in fact argues for just 1 year) are strong, and they mostly rely on other assumptions.[1890] Many other scholars have been content to award c.11 years of reign to Khamudy.[1891] This would leave 23–43 years for the first king. Since Khyan was clearly an important historical figure and is well attested, it is likely his reign was relatively long,[1892] thus either the 20 + x years or 30 + x years options appear likely. Ryholt (1997:201) turns this into 40 years, but on no evidence (and partly the unnecessary Khamudy = 1 year assumption). Hence up to 23 or 33 years remain for the first king (Manetho has 19 years for Salitis/Saïtes as first Hyksos king). This seems reasonable.

There is no real chronological control from current data for the key fall of Avaris. Redford (1967:48) argues for a possible range between Ahmose years 7 to 17. The upper limit is Ahmose year 22,[1893] since Ahmose is by then employing spoils from his Syrian wars (undoubtedly several years after the capture of Avaris). Most other scholars have taken year 11 as the minimum number (for no good reason if one does not employ the Rhind Mathematical Papyrus as referring to Ahmose). However, the fall of Avaris may have been a little later in Ahmose's reign according to several recent studies, ranging from Ahmose years 11–18, or even years 18–22.[1894]

We concluded above that the c.150-year long 13th Dynasty ended c.1651–1643BC (or later). With 108/109 years for the 15th Dynasty, a date for the fall of Avaris, working forwards from the 12th Dynasty, becomes on the long chronology with the entire 13th Dynasty followed by the entire 15th Dynasty: 1543/42BC to 1535/34BC. It is possible that a few more years (up to 10?) might be either added to or removed from the 13th

---

[1888] Hoffmeier (1997:191 and 198 n.148).
[1889] Bietak (1996a:41).
[1890] Ryholt (1997:188, 189, 201).
[1891] E.g. von Beckerath (1997:189).
[1892] E.g. Ryholt (1997:120, 201).
[1893] Redford (1967:48–49); Eriksson (1992:163); Ryholt (1997:186). The relevant text is in Breasted (1962, vol.II:§26–28), with key reference in §27.
[1894] E.g. Bietak (1991a:48) calculates a date between Ahmose years 11–18; Bietak (1996a:81) favours 'after the fifteenth or even eighteenth year'; Weinstein (1995:85 and 89n.1 referring to el-Sabbahy 1993) also questions the exactitude of the year 11 date and leaves open a slightly later one; Franke (1988b:264) backs a year 18 or later conquest – although cf. Ryholt (1997:186–187 n.669); Bourriau (1997:159) places Ahmose's conquest of Avaris in his years 18–22. Recent investigations in the area of Ahmose's pyramid and cult complex at Abydos (Harvey 1994; 1995) will potentially be relevant to this question. Fragments of scenes showing battles with an Asiatic enemy have been identified.

Dynasty, and it is very possible that there was some early 15th Dynasty–late 13th Dynasty overlap which might remove a few years to a decade or two. If the above figures are employed as an approximation, then the accession of Ahmose occurred at some time during a range from c.1564–1541BC, or earlier if there was a significant early 15th Dynasty–late 13th Dynasty overlap. This date range nicely covers the range of the high/middle to low Egyptian New Kingdom chronologies.

One may also briefly consider when the 16th–17th Dynasties began in relation to the 13th and 15th Dynasties, and whether this has any bearing on the chronology of the SIP? Thebes seems to have acknowledged the 13th Dynasty until during the reign of Merneferre Ay,[1895] but it is not clear what happened afterwards. Some have argued that subsequent 13th Dynasty kings after Merneferre Ay in the Turin Canon list are attested only (if at all) from the monuments, inscriptions, and so on from upper Egypt,[1896] and, as noted above, this had led some to suggest that the 13th Dynasty perhaps moved to, and limped on at, Thebes. Others reject this scenario.[1897] It has sometimes been suggested that not all the names in the Turin Canon necessarily belong here. It is in fact possible that some of the unplaced kings assigned by von Beckerath (1964) to the 13th Dynasty instead belong to the 16th Dynasty,[1898] or less likely the 17th Dynasty,[1899] or that they may indeed belong outside this structure. Despite the confidence of Ryholt in the Turin Canon as our best source, it is difficult to be certain. There are a lot of 'kings' and relatively few years (unless overlapping Dynasties, or the inclusion of ancestors, are allowed for). Famine and plague go only so far.[1900]

Kitchen assumed that the 17th Dynasty either immediately followed the whole of the 13th Dynasty, or, alternatively, that it began during the 13th Dynasty, no earlier than Merneferre Ay, and perhaps after Dedumose II.[1901] He saw the start of the 17th Dynasty as effectively contemporary with the start of the 15th Dynasty in the Delta. Kitchen (1987:45, 51) estimated a minimum of 78 years for the 17th Dynasty.[1902] Kitchen

---

[1895] E.g. Bennett (1995b); O'Connor (1997:48). As noted previously, Bietak (1984:473) saw widespread 13th Dynasty rule as ending (or not attested) after the reigns Neferhotep I and Sebekhotep IV. This is three to five kings before Merneferre Ay in the Turin Canon list.
[1896] O'Connor (1997:Fig.2.3).
[1897] Ryholt (1997).
[1898] Ryholt (1997:151–158).
[1899] Bennett (1995a:27–28).
[1900] Cf. Ryholt (1997:196, 300–301).
[1901] Kitchen (1987; 1996a).
[1902] Bennett (1995a) likewise found >78 years, from an absolute minimum of >57 years, and probably 68 years: Bennett (1995a; 1995b). Bennett (1995b) attempts to establish a date for Nubkheperre Inyotef. However, his logic is flawed and overly concise given the quality of his data (Ryholt 1997:168–169 n.606 dismisses the work of Bennett). The typological analysis of coffins and canopic chests, Ward's scarab analysis, and Minemhat's jewellery box, are not as certain, accurate, or precise as he believes; nor are the actual placings of reigns free from debate (cf. his rejection of Turin Canon-Cairo Juridical stela linkage). Bennett believes he has established a low chronology which rules out a high accession date for Ahmose. But in fact it is only his 'date' ranges achieved from Minemhat's jewellery box and the hypothesis that the first three kings of the Abbott papyrus are chronologically close which create any conflict with a high accession date for Ahmose. Bennett's first dates from the coffin analysis, Ward's scarab analysis,

(1996a:7) was more generous, arguing for a total of 58 years plus about another 32/ 38 years, equals 90/96 years all up. Von Beckerath (1997) also allowed c.95 years. All is flexibility! and going up. The end result, with the 13th Dynasty at c.150 years, is that Kitchen (1996a) had the total minimum interval from the end of the 12th Dynasty to the accession of Ahmose at c.240–250 years. From the end of the 12th Dynasty (1801–1793BC), this brings us to 1561–1543BC, and, again, the conventional date range.

However, Ryholt (1997) makes a strong case for the view that the 16th Dynasty was not some irrelevant regional grouping.[1903] Instead, Ryholt proposes that the 16th Dynasty ruled at Thebes following the end of the 13th Dynasty (a case could be made for an overlap), until a proposed conquest of Thebes by the Hyksos 15th Dynasty – the latter proposal however lacks evidence and is speculative/questionable. On this model, the 17th Dynasty is the post-conquest new dynasty at Thebes. They are distinctly fighting a war of liberation. This model makes a mockery of Kitchen's previous chronological calculations. The 16th Dynasty cannot be inserted into the c.240–250 year period he had calculated. Ryholt (1997:167–171) proposes a much shortened 17th Dynasty, lasting only c.31 years (p.203)! Some of Kitchen's (1987:51) 17th Dynasty kings are placed instead in the 16th Dynasty by Ryholt (1997:158, 202).

Ryholt (1997:201) nonetheless conspires to calculate the 16th Dynasty at c.67 years, with the result that the combined 13th Dynasty, 16th Dynasty, and 17th Dynasty total is c.252 years. Oddly enough, this new SIP chronology offers a mid-16th century BC accession for Ahmose from the starting point of the end of the 12th Dynasty. Depite the careful research into sorting out the various SIP dynasties, Ryholt's (1997:184–204) chronology is in fact arbitrary in the sense that the numbers are calculated to fit the known interval and to accord with the c.108/109 years for the 15th Dynasty in the Turin Canon. Several key details, such as when the 16th Dynasty began in terms of the 13th Dynasty, and the 14th–15th Dynasties, and whether or not the Hyksos actually conquered Thebes, and when, are at best merely conjecture. It would be entirely possible to shorten slightly, or lengthen, the SIP constructed by Ryholt by the necessary 0–25 years, depending on a high, middle, or low chronology for the accession of Ahmose.

The outcome of an attempt to work forwards from the near-fixed date for Sesostris III through the SIP is thus an inability to offer a firm chronology for the start of the 18th Dynasty. There is an absence of firm and independent data. The recent, radical, and sometimes persuasive, re-working of the period by Ryholt (1997), demonstrates only that evidence has not been, and is not, clear and definite. Other scholars will reject Ryholt's arguments, but no certain alternative exists. The figure of 108 years for the 15th Dynasty from the Turin Canon is unfortunately not able to be tied to a specific

---

and the canopic chests, offer a good match for Nubkheperre Inyotef c.1626/1625–1616–1615BC with a 1701BC accession for Merhetepre, and a possible match with a 1690BC accession. If Bennett's analysis shows anything, it is the unlikely nature of the ultra-low Krauss chronology. However, the conclusion must be to advise caution.

[1903] Kitchen (1996a:7) had dismissed them as entirely parallel with the 13th, 15th, and 17th Dynasties, and so of zero relevance to chronology.

figure for the 13th Dynasty. Ambiguity means one can make plausible calculations in favour of any of the high, middle, or low Egyptian chronologies. Again it is reassuring that the available evidence does roughly mesh together, but an attempt to offer a firm sequence relies on making unproven assumptions, or taking the low New Kingdom chronology as a given. It is also worth remembering that the all important Sothic and lunar data from the Middle Kingdom are unsatisfactory,[1904] and that the entire Sesostris III year 7 date hangs on an assumption (since the pharaoh is not actually named in the key texts).

Discussion

The aim of this relatively lengthy and detailed discussion has been to highlight, on the one hand, that the conventional chronology of second millennium BC Egypt is sound in general terms, but, on the other hand, to show that it is not known with total precision and accuracy. As a result of painstaking detective work and wide erudition, it is 'best guesstimated' and 'argued' on the basis of incomplete and sometimes ambiguous or problematic data. There is sometimes poor control on this data, and it is not of a testable sort, nor capable of independent replication. There is a false mystique of fact. This situation may be contrasted with scientific measurement, where both accuracy and precision may be quantified and tested.

The low Egyptian chronology, and accession dates of 1479BC for Tuthmosis III and 1279BC for Ramesses II, may be currently regarded as virtual facts by some Egyptologists,[1905] but this is not so. The evidence available cannot sustain proof. The logic of dead-reckoning and reducing the data to the irreducible is a good means to the creation of an absolute minimum baseline. However, when it is clear that there are unknowns, and that we have few data specifically pertinent to total reign lengths (versus fortuitously preserved individual year dates), it is clear that such a *minimum* is just this. The real chronology is higher. It is inherently incorrect of Kitchen (1996a:6) to state that 'there is no possibility of intercalating any additional years' in the 18th Dynasty. The evidence is not this firm. Von Beckerath (1994a), one of the leading scholars of Egyptian chronology in the 20th century, specifically notes the paucity of documentary evidence relevant to the reign lengths of the first four 18th Dynasty kings prior to Tuthmosis III. Instead, it is clear from a review of the data that there is room for potential movement of up to about 11 or 25 years from the so-called low chronology. The biographical and genealogical data available for the New Kingdom and for the Third Intermediate Period provide good grounds to defend the approximate status quo in second millennium BC chronology. Egyptian chronology cannot be moved up or down by any *large* amount. But this data in no way precludes overall (versus any individual) movement upwards of some 11 or 25 years.[1906] Each

[1904] See esp. Rose (1994; 1997).
[1905] E.g. Krauss (1985:127) states there is no alternative.
[1906] See Henige (1981).

of the so-called low, middle, and high chronologies for New Kingdom Egypt are possible from present data. Claims to the contrary are not rigorously sound, but depend on assumptions, or non-explicit arguments. Archaeologists working elsewhere may choose to employ the conventional low Egyptian chronology (as one of the possible options) if they wish, but they cannot regard this as a proven fact upon which to base further argument.

To conclude, we can consider the relevance of the 'early' Aegean LBA chronology, and the c.1628BC Thera eruption date, in relation to Egyptian chronology. What is at issue? Bietak (1996a:76) alleges that the early Aegean chronology would require a dramatic shift of 130 years to Egyptian chronology. Kitchen (1996a:6) is clearly thinking along the same lines when he states that 'any idea of slipping in the odd extra century or so to link up (e.g.) with supposed dates for the Thera eruption can be resolutely and definitively dismissed'.[1907] But both are imagining non-existent conflicts. The true impact is in fact very little! Nothing is required beyond the existing flexibilities in the Egyptian chronology. The Thera eruption is during the SIP where, as we have seen, the data is less than solid. The seismic destruction at Thera (and earlier LMIA earthquakes on Crete) occurred during the late 13th Dynasty, and the eruption itself was early to mid Hyksos 15th Dynasty (depending on 18th Dynasty chronology), or earlier stratum D/3 at Tell el-Dab^{c}a.

The only real requirement is that not too long a gap exists between the mature LMIA eruption and the beginning of the 18th Dynasty. I admit that a higher Egyptian chronology would undoubtedly be more compatible, and the radiocarbon evidence relevant to the close of the LMIB period on Crete provides some grounds for supporting a high/higher (1504BC or 1490BC) accession date for Tuthmosis III *if* long-standing art-historical linkages are to be maintained (Chapter V.1). But the middle (or even low) Egyptian chronologies can easily be considered compatible: see Figure 62 above p. 339. The earlier LMIB period cannot explain everything, but it can account for several decades or more; WSI was a relatively long-lived style, and the LCIA period likewise may be considered to have lasted several generations. Moreover, as argued above, the state of Egyptian chronology (that is current conventional interpretation) cannot be held *a priori* to override a range of independent scientific evidence and compatible archaeological correlations. Nor, as I seek to stress, is there any actual conflict between the 1628BC Thera eruption date and the early Aegean LBA chronology, and the conventional (middle or low) Egyptian chronology. The conflict claimed in some recent literature (e.g. previous paragraph) in fact has nothing to do with Egyptian chronology, and is instead due to mistaken views on matters such as: the development and export appearances of the LCI ceramic styles of WSI, BRI, etc., without taking due regard of the regional processes at work on Cyprus; the relevance of mere *terminus ante quem* pumice from an eruption which may have easily occurred about a century earlier; and the belief that the existing relative chronological synthesis for the eastern Mediterranean is somehow more or less fixed, whereas, in reality, some

---

[1907] Kitchen is undoubtedly thinking of Baillie (1995a:149–158; 1996b:297).

things may be de-coupled and then be better associated elsewhere in a new, revised, framework (e.g. Figure 62 above p. 339).

The discussions in Chapters IV and VI suggest that the LMIA period is broadly synchronous with the later SIP (later 14th Dynasty until mid Hyksos 15th Dynasty), and the following LMIB/LHIIA period seems to have begun during the later Hyksos period and then run through the early 18th Dynasty to the beginning of the reign of Tuthmosis III. In accord, archaeological cross-dating also supports an upwards revision of the conventional Aegean–Egyptian chronology for the following periods through to LMIIIA1. Aegean-style frescoes broadly similar to those at Akrotiri buried by the Thera eruption have been found in pre-Bichrome Ware later MBII Syria–Palestine of likely later 17th century BC to early 16th century BC date. Early WSI could exist by the late 17th century BC. All in all, a potentially coherent chronological framework exists compatible with, and built around, the early Aegean LBA chronology and the 1628BC eruption of the volcano of Thera. An important potential new synchronisation of the Aegean and eastern Mediterranean in the mid-second millennium BC is at hand; final confirmation of which depends (most likely) on definitive finds of Thera Minoan eruption tephra in precisely dated contexts in Greenland ice-cores.

> Falls sich diese [finds of tephra] stratifiziert im Grönlandeis in Zukunft identifizieren lassen [see Chapter V.3] und damit die Datierung der Santorin-Eruption gegen Ende des 17. Jhs. v.Chr. bestätigt werden kann, wird es Aufgabe der Archäologen sein, die derzeit gültigen konventionellen mediterranen Basis-Chronologien völlig neu zu bearbeiten.[1908]

An absolute date for the Thera eruption thus offers a vital means to test and to refine Egyptian chronology – and is not some barbaric attempt wantonly to overthrow a century of scholarship. Kitchen (1991:205) in a presentation aimed at general archaeological readers stated that the potential error in dating in Egyptian chronology at c.1500BC was 10–20 years. We have seen that this is probably a reasonable minimum estimate for the true potential variability. And Kitchen had already ruled out the high or long 18th Dynasty chronology – still considered *possible* above. An absolute date for the Thera eruption, and other science-based dating programmes (particularly dendrochronology and high-precision radiocarbon dating), offer a means to resolve such debates and ambiguities of several decades in the existing chronology of Egypt, to move from an *almost* precisely dated chronology (with no truly independent checks, and no real quantification of what the 'almost' means) to a proper, independently verified, precise, and absolute chronology. Egyptology should actively embrace and pursue these possibilities.

[1908] Schoch (1997:61).

Appendix 2: Why the standard chronologies are approximately correct, and why radical re-datings are therefore incorrect

In the last decade a set of publications have argued for a radically lower chronology of the Bronze Age Mediterranean, centred on claims for a c.250 year 'reduction' in conventional dates. The initial and main proponents are Peter James *et al.*, who were then followed by David Rohl.[1909] The basic premise is that much of the so-called Dark Age between the end of the Late Bronze Age and the beginning of the 8th century Iron Age renaissance of Greece and its contemporaries, and especially the so-called Third Intermediate Period in Egypt, can be done away with or greatly compressed. This is the period of the 11th through 9th centuries BC on conventional chronological schemes.[1910]

This type of argument is not new. Periods lacking clear and obvious data – periods where considerable scholarly expertise is required in order to analyse and to interpret the data – have long attracted those who fancy rewriting history, eradicating 'dark ages', and generally 'beating the boffins'. The Third Intermediate Period of Egypt is a prime candidate in this respect, and forms the core of the work of James *et al.* and Rohl. Often there is also an underlying agenda: the most common is the attempt to create reality for the Old Testament. Velikovsky and his book *Ages in Chaos* (1953, and subsequent volumes, London: Sidgwick & Jackson) is seminal. Rohl essentially pursues the same approach, and, to their credit, this is the reason James *et al.* split from Rohl after original collaboration. The work of James *et al.* instead has scholarly pretensions. They have read very widely, and they seek to sustain academic debate. A number of the weaknesses they identify in conventional Mediterranean chronologies are entirely legitimate (and their critics sometimes should first remove the planks from their own eyes). But, of course, this does not necessarily mean that the whole conventional

---

[1909] See e.g. James *et al.* (1991a; 1991b; 1992; 1998); Rohl (1992; 1995). A slightly less radical version of the Third Intermediate Period compression supported by James *et al.* was proposed by Goldberg (1995). Others of like mind publish in the *Journal of the Ancient Chronology Forum* in particular; there are also a number of World Wide Web sites advocating such ideas.

[1910] For some responses to the books of James *et al.* and Rohl by area specialists, see Kitchen (1992; 1996b:xlii–xlvi); Kemp (1992); Postgate (1992); Snodgrass (1992); Sherratt and Sherratt (1992); papers in Leonard (1993). See in response in turn James *et al.* (1992; 1998) with further refs. For standard studies of Greece, Egypt, and the Levant, and of interconnections, through the so-called Dark Age or Third Intermediate Period, see Snodgrass (1971); Whitley (1991); Kuhrt (1995:385–646); Kitchen (1996b); Kopcke and Tokumaru (1992).

chronology is wrong, and should be radically altered. Their book (1991a) can fairly be described as a brave failure.

As in any good 'beat the boffins' debate, the entire argument structure and approach of James *et al.* is at odds with the conventional *mores* of the field. They would claim that this is just the point: they seek to alter the existing paradigm, not work within it. James *et al.* are very good at isolating – not infrequently out of appropriate context – selected issues and the mention by experts of any instances of problems, and then building an eclectic case around these without at any time dealing with the mainstream evidence. A classic recent example is their supposed rejection of the case of Manning and Weninger (1992) in support of the conventional later LBA chronology in the Aegean. Over three pages James *et al.* (1998:36–38) argue about all sorts of supposed problems with radiocarbon dating and the case presented by Manning and Weninger, but specifically fail to address the main data and analysis in that paper: namely the Archaeological Wiggle Matching of the entire large Kastanas radiocarbon date series so as to establish a relatively precise and robust chronology for the phases at the site, and so also the correlated southern Aegean archaeological periods. They instead just sneak in mention of 'statistical massage', without explaining how they can rebut the analysis (an analysis subsequently supported by other statistical specialists[1911]). Elsewhere, they concentrate on peripheral details, irrelevancies, or *non*-facts, and generally refuse actually to engage with the case of Manning and Weninger.[1912]

It is inherently difficult to refute James *et al.* on their own terms, as they do not accept the norms of a century or more of scholarship. Where something is, say, 90% likely, and fits with a web of other probable arguments, and is the generally accepted scholarly position, James *et al.* will invariably go with the 10% extreme possibility, and then link this with other unlikely options to build up an alternative case. It is clever, legalistic, debating; but this does not mean that it is at all likely to be correct.

The proof against the radically low chronologies comes from science, from data and

---

[1911] Christen and Litton (1995) achieve basically the same results as Manning and Weninger (1992), but employ a more sophisticated and holistic Bayesian approach to wiggle matching.

[1912] The page by James *et al.* (1998:37) on the 'old wood effect' is a good example. To begin, this issue has no bearing on the actual wiggle-match, only on the cultural application of this dating of the radiocarbon measurements as fitted to the radiocarbon calibration curve. Further, James *et al.* seem to fail to understand that wood from long-lived structural timbers typically are relevant to the date of the construction (and not the destruction) of a building (and so phase at a site). Manning and Weninger noted and discussed the relevance of the old wood effect to the cultural phases, and adopted a reasonable approximate correction. James *et al.* instead suggest that this correction could be much larger (citing extreme possibilities), and they wish to allow for it as modifying the lowest possible part of the overall calibrated date range for some dates. They ignore the narrow wiggle-match ranges for the seriated set as a whole. It is, of course, possible in some cases that older wood was dated, but it is unlikely in most random situations (ruling out known major structural timbers from large buildings). Typically 70% of the wood in a tree lies in the outer 30% of the rings; hence random charcoal (long-lived wood samples) is likely to come from the outer 30% of a tree, and the odds against true inner rings are high. Some trees grow to be very old, but many typical lower altitude (lowland or foothill) Mediterranean trees live rather shorter periods. Many types live around a century and few live over 300 years. Hence random charcoal in the Mediterranean is in fact likely to be around +50±50 (that is 0–100) years older than the date when the tree is cut down and used by humans. There will be exceptions, such as major structural beams from

methodologies independent of the history of Egypt and the Aegean. At present, this means a combination of Aegean and east Mediterranean dendrochronology with high-precision radiocarbon dating and American and northern European dendrochronology. The high-precision radiocarbon dating of a floating dendrochronological sequence from Gordion fixes in absolute time (based on the radiocarbon record in the absolutely dated German, Irish, and American tree-ring series), within a quantified possible range, a 1503 year dendrochronological sequence relevant to the chronology and history of the ancient Near East and Aegean (see Chapter V.4).[1913] This chronology both offers, and requires, links consistent with the conventional range of dates for both Mesopotamian chronology, and Egyptology. Radical change is no longer possible. As published, the chronological fit was defined within a 95% confidence range. Use of more recent calibration data (or use of the existing Belfast 1986 data) would only make the preferred fit a few decades *higher* (i.e. older).[1914] The required reductions in dates to suit the radical low chronologies of James *et al.* or Rohl are impossible, even at 3σ (99%) confidence.

Some readers may wonder about the reliability, accuracy, and precision of radiocarbon wiggle-matching.[1915] However, when employed on substantial fixed dendrochronological sequences, the results achieved by modern high-precision laboratories are consistently very close to known absolute dendrochronological dates. There is no possibility of a significant error here. Any error may be quantified, and, at the extreme, consists of the laboratory errors on the measurements on the samples dated, sample window mis-matching and ring-width variation in samples leading to minor radiocarbon level mis-matching, inter-laboratory offsets/variation, and the variation in relevant calibration curve datasets. The accuracy and precision are in fact so good that wiggle-matching may be employed in discussions attempting to resolve small regional differences in contemporary radiocarbon levels.[1916]

For Egyptology, the key date at present comes from the final preserved tree-ring on wood carried on the Uluburun ship. A date of c.1305BC has been proposed on the basis of a correlation of marker events in northern hemisphere dendrochronologies *within* the range established by the radiocarbon wiggle-match with German wood for the Aegean Dendrochronology Project Bronze-Iron Age chronology (see Chapter V.4). The actual radiocarbon wiggle-match date is 1318 +76/−22 years at c.95% confidence. Use of the new INTCAL98.14C radiocarbon curve, or the previous Belfast datasets on Irish oak, would make this match a little earlier (and the error range would become more symmetrical, but broadly similar in overall scale). There is thus less than a 5%

---

large structures, or wood from the various potentially very long-lived tree types (e.g. *pinus nigra*, or *cedrus libani*, or giant juniper), but these will not be the norm from non-monumental contexts.

[1913] Kuniholm *et al.* (1996).

[1914] See discussion in Chapter V.4. For examples of the small *upwards* shifts if Irish oak data from Belfast are employed (rather than the preferred German wood), see Manning (1998a:303–304).

[1915] For the technique and its evolution and examples, see e.g. Ferguson *et al.* (1966); Clark and Morgan (1983); Pearson (1986); Christen and Litton (1995); Kuniholm *et al.* (1996); Goslar and Madry (1998: 551). The OxCal computer programme of Ramsey (1995, and subsequent versions) provides the most commonly employed Bayesian implementation of wiggle-matching in use today. On good accuracy of wiggle-matching, see Goslar and Madry (1998).

[1916] van der Plicht *et al.* (1995).

chance of a date after c.1296BC on the *lowest* radiocarbon fit option. A date more than another few decades lower may be excluded as completely impossible. The final ring (bark) is not preserved on the relevant cedar sample (cargo/dunnage), so some unknown number of rings (years) are missing beyond c.1305BC. The nature of the sample (unworked – even root?) would indicate that the number involved should be relatively small. Hence a shipwreck date c.1300BC is proposed, with a likely error factor of a decade or so. The objects on board the ship also included a gold scarab of Nefertiti, wife of Akhenaten. This scarab was already old (that is it showed signs of wear) by the time of the shipwreck,[1917] but, at a total logical minimum, the scarab (and so Nefertiti) necessarily dates before c.1300BC to c.1290±BC. This confirms the approximate validity of the conventional 14th century BC Egyptian chronology, and so general LBA Egyptian chronology.[1918] It rules out any c.250 year reduction.

Apart from this one specific instance, James *et al.* and Rohl must also deliberately fail to notice that right across the Mediterranean and Europe modern high-precision calibrated radiocarbon dating on appropriate samples, and dendrochronology, offer a Bronze Age chronology *broadly* in line with (or sometimes slightly earlier than) the range of conventional chronologies in the Aegean and the Near East (and so Egypt) – and not one some 250 years later.[1919] This includes Egypt.[1920] In addition, in Europe, the radiocarbon dates on Bronze Age organic samples agree in general terms with the independent, and absolute, tree-ring chronologies available, and cannot be shifted downwards by 250 years. Any one instance may be debatable, or flexible, but the vast web of inter-connected data in question are not misplaced upwards by a whopping 250 years. It is difficult to describe the discussion on radiocarbon dating in James *et al.* (1998:36–38) as anything but perverse: it combines misinformation, with selective citation of extremes, and other statements out of context, and generally ignores much of the data. In particular, they seize on the 'old wood' issue, and then try to claim everything might be a couple of centuries later in date. Rather than spend several pages highlighting every error or misrepresentation in their discussion, I simply note that the 'old wood' issue does not apply for short-lived samples, such as seeds. These provide radiocarbon ages directly relevant to use context. Among recent examples, the sets of short-lived samples specifically relevant to the close of the LMIB and LMII

[1917] Bass *et al.* (1989:23).

[1918] Kuniholm *et al.* (1996); Wiener (1998:313–314).

[1919] For some examples of relevant literature, see Becker *et al.* (1985; 1989); Sperber (1987); Breunig (1987); Barfield (1991); Randsborg (1991); several papers in Randsborg (1996b); Weninger (1997); Kristiansen (1998:31–34, Fig.13); Vanzetti (1998); Korfmann and Kromer (1993); Manning (1995; 1997); Manning and Weninger (1992); Skeates and Whitehouse (1994).

[1920] From pre-dynastic times onwards: e.g. Görsdorf *et al.* (1998); Lange (1998); Hassan and Robinson (1987); Weninger (1990:223–226; 1997:96–101, 168–169, 182); appropriate samples in The David H. Koch Pyramids Radiocarbon Project, versus 'old wood' samples which are prevalent in ancient Egyptian contexts (see the preliminary report in *Archaeology* vol. 52(5), 1999:26–33). In Egypt, some samples have at various times been found to provide ages much older than expected (e.g. Haas *et al.* 1987; Geyh *et al.* 1989), whether through dating 'old wood', a reservoir effect in 'old' water, or the incorporation of carbonates into samples, etc. But analyses of more suitable samples lead, as in the studies above, to chronological conclusions broadly in line with the range of the conventional chronological schemes. The

periods on Crete,[1921] or the sets of short-lived samples from the late MBA destruction level at Jericho,[1922] each discussed in Chapter V.1, provide evidence in clear support/ requirement of the range of the conventional chronologies, and completely inconsistent with a radically lower one.[1923] Many more examples could be cited.

David H. Koch Pyramids Radiocarbon Project has re-investigated, and re-considered, the data and conclusions of the Haas *et al.* (1987) work, and now considers these anomalous early (by an average 374 years!) dates to result from the dating of inappropriate 'old wood' which did not reflect the archaeological contexts for which dates were sought (see *Archaeology* vol. 52(5), 1999:26–33).

[1921] Housley *et al.* (1999).

[1922] Bruins and van der Plicht (1995; 1996).

[1923] The radiocarbon data on short-lived samples analysed in Manning and Weninger (1992:Fig.12) for the later LBA Aegean also nicely matched the range of conventionally proposed dates. The new radiocarbon dates from Tell Abu al-Kharaz in Jordan offer another recent example of data on short-lived samples consonant with the range of the conventional chronologies, and *not* a chronology a couple of centuries later (Fischer 1999:17–19).

References

Note: An important set of recent publications is found in the *Aegaeum* series (Annales d'archéologie égéenne de l'Université de Liège et UT-PASP, Université de Liège: Service d'Histoire de l'art et archéologie de la Grèce antique, and Program in Aegean Scripts and Prehistory, The University of Texas at Austin). These volumes often have individual titles and editors/authors. However, unless a single/joint author book, they are listed below by *Aegaeum* volume as they can be found this way in any library, and a number of libraries shelve these volumes as a series/periodical.

Åberg, N. 1933. *Bronzezeitliche und früheisenzeitliche Chronologie. IV. Griechenland.* Stockholm: Kungl. Vitterhets Historie och Antikvitets Akademien.

Aczel, A.D. 1995. Improved radiocarbon age estimates using the bootstrap. *Radiocarbon* 37:845–849.

Adams, W.Y. 1988. Archaeological classification: theory versus practice. *Antiquity* 62:40–56.

Admiraal, S.M.L. 1982. Late Bronze Age tombs from Dromolaxia. *Report of the Department of Antiquities, Cyprus:* 39–59.

Aitchison, T., Ottaway, B. and Al-Ruzaiza, A.S. 1991. Summarizing a group of ^{14}C dates on the historical time scale: with a worked example from the Late Neolithic of Bavaria. *Antiquity* 65:108–116.

Aitken, M.J. 1961. *Physics and archaeology.* New York: Interscience.

Aitken, M.J. 1974. *Physics and archaeology.* Second edition. Oxford: Clarendon Press.

Aitken, M.J. 1988. The Minoan eruption of Thera, Santorini: a re-assessment of the radiocarbon dates. In R.E. Jones and H.W. Catling (eds.), *New aspects of archaeological science in Greece: proceedings of a meeting held at the British School of Athens, January 1987:* 19–24. Occasional Paper 3 of the Fitch Laboratory. London: British School at Athens.

Aitken, M.J. 1990. *Science-based dating in archaeology.* London: Longman.

Aitken, M.J. and Fleming, S.J. 1971. Preliminary application of thermoluminescent dating to the eruption of Thera. In S. Marinatos and D. Ninkovich (eds.), *Acta of the 1st International Scientific Congress on the Volcano of Thera:* 293–301. Athens: Archaeological Services of Greece.

Albright, W.F. 1938. The chronology of a south Palestinian city, Tell el-ᶜAjjul. *The American Journal of Semitic Languages and Literatures* 55:337–359.

Albright, W.F. 1942. A third revision of the early chronology of western Asia. *Bulletin of the American Schools of Oriental Research* 88:28–36.

Albright, W.F. 1945. The chronology of the divided monarchy of Israel. *Bulletin of the American Schools of Oriental Research* 100:16–22.

Albright, W.F. 1953. New light from Egypt on the chronology and history of Israel and Judah. *Bulletin of the American Schools of Oriental Research* 130:4–11.

Albright, W.F. 1956. Stratigraphic confirmation of the Low Mesopotamian chronology. *Bulletin of the American Schools of Oriental Research* 144:26–30.

Alexiou, S. 1964. Neue Wagendarstellungen aus Kreta. *Archäologischer Anzeiger:* 785–803.

Algaze, G. 1993.*The Uruk world system: the dynamics of expansion of early Mesopotamian civilization.* Chicago: Chicago University Press.

Allen, J.P. 1988. Two altered inscriptions of the late Amarna period. *Journal of the American Research Centre in Egypt* 25:117–126.

Allen, J.P. 1994a. Further evidence for the coregency of Amenhotep III and IV? *Göttinger Miszellen* 140:7–8.

Allen, J.P. 1994b. Nefertiti and Smenkh-ka-re. *Göttinger Miszellen* 141:7–17.

Alley, R.B., Meese, D.A., Shuman, C.A., Gow, A.J., Taylor, K.C., Grootes, P.M., White, J.W.C., Ram, M., Waddington, E.D., Mayewski, P.A. and Zielinski, G.A. 1993. Abrupt increase in Greenland snow accumulation at the end of the Younger Dryas event. *Nature* 362:527–529.

Alley, R.B., Shuman, C.A., Meese, D.A., Gow, A.J., Taylor, K.C., Cuffey, K.M., Fitzpatrick, J.J., Grootes, P.M., Zielinski, G.A., Ram, M., Spinelli, G. and Elder, B. 1997. Visual-stratigraphic dating of the GISP2 ice core: basis, reproducibility, and application. *Journal of Geophysical Research* 102, C12:26,367–26,381.

Amiran, R. 1970. *Ancient pottery of the Holy Land.* New Brunswick: Rutgers University Press.

Andreadaki-Vlasaki, M. and Papadopoulou, E. 1997. LMIIIA:1 pottery from Khamalevri, Rethymnon. In E. Hallager and B.P. Hallager (eds.), *Late Minoan III pottery: chronology and terminology. Acts of a meeting held at the Danish Institute at Athens August 12–14, 1994:* 111–151. Monographs of the Danish Institute at Athens 1. Athens: Danish Institute at Athens.

Andreou, E. 1974. M.E. Prokhous ek Thiras. *Athens Annals of Archaeology* 7:416–421.

Andres, R.J., Rose, W.I., Kyle, P.R., Desilva, S., Francis, P., Gardeweg, M. and Moreno Roa, H. 1991. Excessive sulfur dioxide emissions from Chilean volcanoes. *Journal of Volcanology and Geothermal Research* 46:323–329.

Appadurai, A. 1986. Introduction: commodities and the politics of value. In A. Appadurai (ed.), *The social life of things: commodities in cultural perspective.* Cambridge: Cambridge University Press.

Arnold, D. and Oppenheim, A. 1995. Reexcavating the Senwosret III pyramid complex at Dâshur. *KMT* 6(2):44–56.

Arnold, F. 1992. New evidence for the length of the reign of Senwosret III? *Göttinger Miszellen* 129:27–31.

Artzy, L.M. 1972. *The origin of the Palestinian Bichrome ware.* Ph.D. dissertation, Brandeis University. Ann Arbor: University Microfilms International.

Artzy, M. 1973. The Late Bronze Age 'Palestinian' Bichrome ware in its Cypriote context. In H.A. Hoffner Jr. (ed.), *Orient and Occident. Essays presented to Cyrus H. Gordon on the Occasion of his sixty-fifth birthday:* 9–16. Alter Orient und Altes Testament 22. Kevelaer and Neukirchener-Vluyn: Verlag Butzon & Bercker and Neukirchener Verlag.

Artzy, M. 1991. Conical cups and pumice, Aegean cult at Tel Nami, Israel. *Aegaeum* 7:203–206.

Artzy, M. 1995. Nami: a second millennium international maritime trading centre in the Mediterranean. In S. Gitin (ed.), *Recent excavations in Israel: a view to the west. Reports on Kabri, Nami, Miqne-Ekron, Dor, and Ashkelon:* 17–40. Archaeological Institute of America Colloquia and Conference Papers, No.1. Dubuque: Kendall/Hunt.

Artzy, M. n.d. The Aegean, Cyprus, Levant and the Bichrome Ware: eastern Mediterranean Middle Bronze Age koine? Manuscript.

Artzy, M., Asaro, F. and Perlman, I. 1973. The origin of the 'Palestinian' Bichrome Ware. *Journal of the American Oriental Society* 93:446–461.

Artzy, M., Perlman, I. and Asaro, F. 1978. Imported and local Bichrome ware in Megiddo. *Levant* 10:99–111.

Artzy, M., Perlman, I. and Asaro, F. 1981. Cypriote pottery imports at Ras Shamra. *Israel Exploration Journal* 31:37–47.

Aruz, J. 1995. Imagery and interconnections. *Ägypten und Levante* 5:33–48.

Ashton, D.A. 1989. Takeloth II – a king of the 'Theban' Twenty-Third Dynasty? *Journal of Egyptian Archaeology* 75:139–153.

Assmann, J. 1997. *Moses the Egyptian: the memory of Egypt in western monotheism.* Cambridge, Mass.: Harvard University Press.

Astour, M.C. 1989. *Hittite history and the absolute chronology of the Bronze Age.* Studies in Mediterranean Archaeology and Literature Pocket-book 73. Partille: Paul Åströms Förlag.

Åström, P. 1966. *Excavations at Kalopsidha and Ayios Iakovos in Cyprus*. Studies in Mediterranean Archaeology 2. Lund: Studies in Mediterranean Archaeology.

Åström, P. 1971. Three Tell el Yahudiyeh juglets in the Thera Museum. In S. Marinatos and D. Ninkovich (eds.), *Acta of the 1st International Scientific Congress on the Volcano of Thera*: 415–421. Athens: Archaeological Services of Greece.

Åström, P. 1972a. The Late Cypriote Bronze Age. Relative and absolute chronology, foreign relations, summary and historical conclusions. In L. Åström and P. Åström (eds.), *The Swedish Cyprus Expedition*, vol.IV, part 1D: 675–781. Lund: The Swedish Cyprus Expedition.

Åström, P. 1972b. The Middle Cypriote Bronze Age. In P. Åström, *The Swedish Cyprus Expedition*, vol.IV, part 1B. Lund: The Swedish Cyprus Expedition.

Åström, P. 1972c. Some aspects of the Late Cypriot I period. *Report of the Department of Antiquities, Cyprus*: 46–57.

Åström, P. 1972d. The Late Cypriote Bronze Age architecture and pottery. In P. Åström, *The Swedish Cyprus Expedition*, vol.IV, part 1C. Lund: The Swedish Cyprus Expedition.

Åström, P. 1978. Methodological viewpoints on Middle Minoan chronology. *Opuscula Atheniensia* 12:87–90.

Åström, P. 1979. A faience sceptre with the cartouche of Horemheb. In V. Karageorghis *et al.*, (eds.), *Studies presented in memory of Porphyrios Dikaios*: 46–48. Nicosia: Lions Club of Nicosia (Cosmopolitan).

Åström, P. 1984. The Middle Minoan chronology. In P. Åström, L.R. Palmer and L. Pomerance, *Studies in Aegean chronology*: 3–7. Studies in Mediterranean Archaeology Pocketbook 25. Gothenburg: Paul Åströms Förlag.

Åström, P. 1987. The chronology of the Middle Cypriote Bronze Age. In P. Åström (ed.), *High, middle or low? Acts of an International Colloquium on Absolute Chronology held at the University of Gothenburg 20th–22nd August 1987*, Part 1: 57–66. Studies in Mediterranean Archaeology and literature Pocket-book 56. Gothenburg: Paul Åströms Förlag.

Åström, P. (ed.). 1989. *High, middle or low? Acts of an International Colloquium on Absolute Chronology held at the University of Gothenburg 20th–22nd August 1987*, Part 3. Studies in Mediterranean Archaeology and literature Pocket-book 80. Gothenburg: Paul Åströms Förlag.

Åström, P. 1992. Implications of an ultra-low chronology. *Ägypten und Levante* 3:19–21.

Åström, P. 1993. The omen of the sun in the tenth year of the reign of Mursilis II. In P. Åström (ed.), *Horizons and styles: studies in early art and archaeology in honour of Professor Homer L. Thomas*: 11–17. Jonsered: Paul Åströms Förlag.

Åström, P. 1998. Ceramics: influences east and west. *Aegaeum* 18:257–263.

Avi-Yonah, M. 1975. *Encyclopedia of archaeological excavations in the Holy Land. Volume I*. London: Oxford University Press.

Baer, K. 1973. The Libyan and Nubian kings of Egypt: notes on the chronology of Dynasties XXII to XXVI. *Journal of Near Eastern Studies* 32:4–25.

Bailey, G.N. 1981. Concepts, time-scales and explanations in economic prehistory. In A. Sheridan and G.N. Bailey (eds.), *Economic archaeology: towards an integration of ecological and social approaches*: 97–117. British Archaeological Reports, International Series, 96. Oxford: British Archaeological Reports.

Bailey, G.N. 1983. Concepts of time in quaternary prehistory. *Annual Review of Anthropology* 12:165–192.

Bailey, G.N. 1987. Breaking the time barrier. *Archaeological Review from Cambridge* 6:5–20.

Baillie, M.G.L. 1982. *Tree-ring dating and archaeology*. Chicago: University of Chicago Press.

Baillie, M.G.L. 1989. Hekla 3: how big was it? *Endeavour* 13:78–81.

Baillie, M.G.L. 1990. Irish tree rings and an event in 1628BC. In D.A. Hardy and A.C. Renfrew (eds.), *Thera and the Aegean world III. Volume three: chronology*: 160–166. London: The Thera Foundation.

Baillie, M.G.L. 1991a. Marking in marker dates: towards an archaeology with historical precision. *World Archaeology* 23:233–243.

Baillie, M.G.L. 1991b. Suck-in and smear: two related chronological problems for the 1990s. *Journal of Theoretical Archaeology* 2:12–16.

Baillie, M.G.L. 1994. Dendrochronology raises questions about the nature of the AD 536 dust-veil event. *The Holocene* 4:212–217.

Baillie, M.G.L. 1995a. *A slice through time: dendrochronology and precision dating*. London: Batsford.

Baillie, M.G.L. 1995b. Dendrochronology and the chronology of the Irish Bronze Age. In J. Waddell and E. Shee-Twohig (eds.), *Ireland in the Bronze Age*: 30–37. Dublin: Stationery Office.

Baillie, M.G.L. 1996a. Extreme environmental events and the linking of the tree-ring and ice-core records. In J.S. Dean, D.M. Meko and T.W. Swetnam (eds.), *Tree rings, environment and humanity: proceedings of the International Conference, Tucson, Arizona, 17–21 May, 1994*: 703–711. Tucson: Radiocarbon.

Baillie, M.G.L. 1996b. The chronology of the Bronze Age 2354 BC to 431 BC. *Acta Archaeologica* 67:291–298.

Baillie, M.G.L. 1998. Bronze Age myths expose archaeological shortcomings? a reply to Buckland *et al.* 1997. *Antiquity* 72:425–427.

Baillie, M.G.L. and Munro, M.A.R. 1988. Irish tree rings, Santorini and volcanic dust veils. *Nature* 332:344–346.

Baines, J. 1996. Contextualizing Egyptian representations of society and ethnicity. In J.S. Cooper and G.M. Schwartz (eds.), *The study of the ancient Near East in the twenty-first century: the William Foxwell Albright centennial conference*: 339–384. Winona Lake: Eisenbrauns.

Baker, H.D. 1998. Empires on the Med: review of E.M. Meyers, *The Oxford encyclopedia of archaeology in the Near East. The Times Higher Education Supplement* May 1, no.1330:24.

Balmuth, M.S. and Tykot, R.H. (eds.). 1998. *Sardinian and Aegean chronology: towards the resolution of relative and absolute dating in the Mediterranean*. Studies in Sardinian Archaeology V. Oxford: Oxbow.

Barber, E.J.W. 1991. *Prehistoric textiles. The development of cloth in the Neolithic and Bronze Ages with special reference to the Aegean*. Princeton: Princeton University Press.

Barber, E.J.W. 1993. Late Bronze Age kilts and the reconstruction of Aegean textile connections. *American Journal of Archaeology* 97:350.

Barber, E.J.W. 1998. Aegean ornaments and designs in Egypt. *Aegaeum* 18:13–17.

Barber, R.N.L. 1987. *The Cyclades in the Bronze Age*. London: Duckworth.

Barber, R.N.L. 1992. The origins of the Mycenaean palace. In J.M. Sanders (ed.), *Pilolakon: Lakonian studies in honour of Hector Catling*: 11–23. London: The British School at Athens.

Barfield, L.H. 1991. Wessex with and without Mycenae: new evidence from Switzerland. *Antiquity* 65:102–107.

Barlow, J., Bolger, D. and Kling, B. (eds.). 1991. *Cypriot ceramics: reading the prehistoric record*. University Museum Monograph 74/University Museum Symposium Series vol.2. Philadelphia: The A.G. Leventis Foundation and the University Museum of Archaeology and Anthropology, University of Pennsylvania.

Barnes, W.H. 1991. *Studies in the chronology of the divided monarchy of Israel*. Cambridge: Harvard University Press.

Barratt, J.C. 1994. *Fragments from antiquity: an archaeology of social life in Britain, 2900–1200 BC*. Oxford: Blackwell.

Barta, W. 1979–1980. Die ägyptischen Sothisdaten und ihre Bezugsorte. *Jaarbericht Ex Oriente Lux* 26:26–34.

Barta, W. 1988. Das Kalendarium des Papyrus Ebers mit der Notiz eines Sothisaufgangs. *Göttinger Miszellen* 101:7–12.

Barta, W. 1992. Zur Datierungspraxis in Ägypten unter Kambyses und Darios I. *Zeitschrift für ägyptische Sprache und Altertumskunde* 119:82–90.

Barth, F. 1969. Introduction. In F. Barth (ed.), *Ethnic groups and boundaries: the social organization of culture difference*: 9–38. Bergen-Oslo: Universitetsforlaget, and London: George Allen & Unwin.

Barthes, R. 1971. Style and its image. In S. Chatman (ed. and in part trans.), *Literary style: a symposium*: 3–10. Oxford: Oxford University Press.

Bass, G.F. 1987. Oldest known shipwreck reveals Bronze Age splendors. *National Geographic Magazine* 172(6):692–733.

Bass, G.F. 1998. Sailing between the Aegean and the Orient in the second millennium BC. *Aegaeum* 18:183–191.

Bass, G.F., Pulak, C., Collon, D. and Weinstein, J. 1989. The Bronze Age shipwreck at Ulu Burun: 1986 campaign. *American Journal of Archaeology* 93:1–29.

Baurain, C. 1984. *Chypre et la Méditerranée Orientale au Bronze Récent: synthèse historique*. Études Chypriotes VI. Paris: École française d'Athenes.

Baxter, M.J. 1999. On the multivariate normality of data arising from lead isotope fields. *Journal of Archaeological Science* 26:117–124.

Bayliss, A., Ramsey, C.B. and McCormac, F.G. 1997. Dating Stonehenge. In B. Cunliffe and C. Renfrew (eds.), *Science and Stonehenge*: 39–59. Proceedings of the British Academy 92. Oxford: Oxford University Press.

Beck, P. and Zevulun, U. 1996. Back to square one. *Bulletin of the American Schools of Oriental Research* 304:64–75.

Becker, B., Billamboz, A., Egger, H., Gassmann, P., Orcel, A., Orcel, C. and Ruoff, U. 1985. *Dendrochronologie in der Ur- und Frühgeschichte. Die absolute Datierung von Pfahlbausiedlungen nördlich der Alpen im Jahrringkalendar Mitteleuropas.* Basel: Verlag Schweizerische Gesellschaft für Ur- und Frühgeschichte.

Becker, B., Krause, R. and Kromer, B. 1989. Zur absoluten Chronologie der Frühen Bronzezeit. *Germania* 67:421–442.

Beckerath, J. von. 1964. *Untersuchungen zur politischen Geschichte der Zweiten Zwischenzeit in Ägypten.* Glückstadt: J.J. Augustin.

Beckerath, J. von. 1984. *Handbuch der ägyptischen Königsnamen.* Munich: Deutscher Kunstverlag.

Beckerath, J. von. 1987. Das Kalendarium des Papyrus Ebers und das Sothisdatum vom 9. Jahr Amenophis I. *Studien zur altägyptischen Kultur* 14:27–33.

Beckerath, J. von. 1992. Das Kalendarium des Papyrus Ebers und die Chronologie des ägyptischen Neuen Reiches. Gegenwärtiger Stand der Frage. *Ägypten und Levante* 3:23–27.

Beckerath, J. von. 1993. Bemerkungen zum ägyptischen Kalender (I–II). *Zeitschrift für ägyptische Sprache und Altertumskunde* 120:7–22.

Beckerath, J. von. 1994a. *Chronologie des ägyptischen Neuen Reiches.* Hildesheimer ägyptologische Beiträge 39. Hildesheim: Gerstenberg Verlag.

Beckerath, J. von. 1994b. Zur Datierung Ramses' II. *Göttinger Miszellen* 142:55–56.

Beckerath, J. von. 1994c. Osorkon IV. = Herakles. *Göttinger Miszellen* 139:7–8.

Beckerath, J. von. 1995a. Beiträge zur Geschichte der Libyerzeit. *Göttinger Miszellen* 144:7–13.

Beckerath, J. von. 1995b. Nochmals zur Chronologie der XII. Dynastie. *Orientalia* 64:445–449.

Beckerath, J. von. 1997. *Chronologie des pharaonischen Ägypten. Die Zeitbestimmung der ägyptischen Geschichte von der Vorzeit bis 332 v. Chr.* Mainz am Rhein: Philipp von Zabern.

Beckman, G. 1996. *Hittite diplomatic texts.* Atlanta: Scholars Press.

Begét, J., Mason, O. and Anderson, P. 1992. Age, extent and climatic significance of the c.3400 BP Aniakchak tephra, western Alaska, USA. *The Holocene* 2:51–56.

Bennet, J. 1985. The structure of the Linear B administration at Knossos. *American Journal of Archaeology* 89:231–249.

Bennet, J. (D.J.L.) 1986. *Aspects of the administrative organization of LMII–IIIB Crete: a study based on archaeological and textual data.* Ph.D. dissertation, University of Cambridge.

Bennet, J. 1987a. The wild country east of Dikte: the problem of east Crete in the LMIII period. In J.T. Killen, J.L. Melena and J.-P. Olivier (eds.), *Studies in Mycenaean and Classical Greek presented to John Chadwick*: 77–88. Salamanca: Universidad de Salamanca. (= *Minos* 20–22).

Bennet, J. 1987b. Knossos and LMIII Crete: a post-palatial palace? In R. Hägg and N. Marinatos (eds.), *The Function of the Minoan palaces. Proceedings of the fourth international symposium at the Swedish Institute in Athens, 10–16 June, 1984*: 307–312. Skrifter Utgivna av Svenska Institutet i Athen, 4°, 35. Stockholm: Paul Åströms Förlag.

Bennet, J.D. 1988. 'Outside in the distance': problems in understanding the economic geography of Mycenaean palatial territories. In J.-P. Olivier and T.G. Palaima (eds.), *Texts, tablets and scribes. Studies in Mycenaean epigraphy and economy offered to Emmett L. Bennet Jr.*: 19–41. Suplementos a *Minos* 10. Salamanca: Universidad de Salamanca.

Bennet, J. and Galaty, M. 1997. Ancient Greece: recent developments in Aegean archaeology and regional studies. *Journal of Archaeological Research* 5:75–120.

Bennett, C. 1995a. The structure of the seventeenth Dynasty. *Göttinger Miszellen* 149:25–32.

Bennett, C. 1995b. The date of Nubkheperre Inyotef. *Göttinger Miszellen* 147:19–27.

Bennett, J. 1939. The Restoration Inscription of Tut'ankhamun. *Journal of Egyptian Archaeology* 25:8–17.

Bennett, K.D. 1994. Tephra geochemistry: a comment on Hunt and Hill. *The Holocene* 4:435–436.

Bennett, S.M. and Owens, G.A. 1999. The dating of the Linear A inscriptions from Thera. *Kadmos* 38:12–18.

Benson, J.L. 1961. The White Slip sequence at Bamboula, Kourion. *Palestine Exploration Quarterly* 93:61–69.

Benson, J.L. 1967. Review of V. Karageorghis, *Nouveaux documents pour l'étude du Bronze Récent à Chypre*. *American Journal of Archaeology* 71:316–317.

Benson, J.L. 1969. Bamboula at Kourion: the stratification of the settlement. *Report of the Department of Antiquities, Cyprus:* 1–28.

Benson, J.L. 1970. Bamboula at Kourion: the stratification of the settlement. *Report of the Department of Antiquities, Cyprus:* 25–74.

Benson, J.L. 1972. *Bamboula at Kourion: the necropolis and the finds*. Philadelphia: University of Pennsylvania Press.

Ben-Tor, A. and Ben-Ami, D. 1998. Hazor and the archaeology of the tenth century B.C.E. *Israel Exploration Journal* 48:1–37.

Ben-Tor, D. 1994. The historical implications of Middle Kingdom scarabs found in Palestine bearing private names and titles of officials. *Bulletin of the American Schools of Oriental Research* 294:7–22.

Bergoffen, C. 1989. *A comparative study of the regional distribution of Cypriote pottery in Canaan and Egypt in the Late Bronze Age*. Ph.D. dissertation, New York University.

Bergoffen, C.J. 1991. Overland trade in northern Sinai: the evidence of the Late Cypriot pottery. *Bulletin of the American Schools of Oriental Research* 284:59–76.

Bergoffen, C. n.d. The Proto White Slip and White Slip I pottery from Tell el Ajjul. Manuscript of paper presented to the White Slip Ware Conference held in Nicosia 29–30 October 1998. Paper to be published in the conference proceedings: V. Karageorghis (ed.), *White Slip Ware. Proceedings of an International Conference Organized by the Anastasios G. Leventis Foundation, Nicosia in Honour of Malcolm Wiener, Nicosia 29th–30th October 1998*. In Press.

Berman, L.M. 1998. Overview of Amenhotep III and his reign. In D. O'Connor and E.H. Cline (eds.), *Amenhotep III: perspectives on his reign:* 1–25. Ann Arbor: The University of Michigan Press.

Bernal, M. 1987. *Black Athena: the afroasiatic roots of classical civilization. Volume I: the fabrication of ancient Greece, 1785–1985*. London: Free Association Books.

Bernal, M. 1991. *Black Athena: the Afroasiatic roots of Classical civilization. Volume II: the archaeological and documentary evidence*. London: Free Association Books.

Bernard, A., Demaiffe, D., Mattielli, N. and Punongbayan, R.S. 1991. Anhydrite-bearing pumices from Mount Pinatubo: further evidence for the existence of sulphur-rich silicic magmas. *Nature* 354:139–140.

Bernini, L.E. 1995. Ceramics of the early neo-palatial period at Palaikastro. *Annual of the British School at Athens* 90:55–82.

Bernstein, R.J. 1983. *Beyond objectivism and relativism: science, hermeneutics, and praxis*. Oxford: Blackwell.

Betancourt, P.P. 1983. *The Cretan collection in the University Museum, University of Pennsylvania. Vol. I. Minoan objects excavated from Vasilike, Pseira, Sphoungaras, Priniatikos Pyrgos, and other sites*. University Museum Monograph 47. Philadelphia: The University Museum, University of Pennsylvania.

Betancourt, P.P. 1985. *The history of Minoan pottery*. Princeton, N.J.: Princeton University Press.

Betancourt, P.P. 1987. Dating the Aegean Late Bronze Age with radiocarbon. *Archaeometry* 29:45–49.

Betancourt, P.P. 1990a. High chronology or low chronology: the archaeological evidence. In D.A. Hardy and A.C. Renfrew (eds.), *Thera and the Aegean world III. Volume three: chronology:* 19–23. London: The Thera Foundation.

Betancourt, P.P. 1990b. *Kommos II: the Final Neolithic through Middle Minoan III pottery*. Princeton: Princeton University Press.

Betancourt, P.P. 1997. Relations between the Aegean and the Hyksos at the end of the Middle Bronze Age. In E.D. Oren (ed.), *The Hyksos: new historical and archaeological perspectives:* 429–432. Philadelphia: The University Museum, University of Pennsylvania.

Betancourt, P.P. 1998a. Middle Minoan objects in the Near East. *Aegaeum* 18:5–12.

Betancourt, P.P. 1998b. The chronology of the Aegean Late Bronze Age: unanswered questions. In M.S. Balmuth and R.H. Tykot (eds.), *Sardinian and Aegean chronology: towards the resolution of relative and absolute dating in the Mediterranean:* 291–296. Studies in Sardinian Archaeology V. Oxford: Oxbow.

Betancourt, P.P. and Davaras, C. 1986. Anaskaphiki Ereuna Pseiras: Periodou 1985 kai 1986. *Amaltheia* 17:183–200.

Betancourt, P.P. and Davaras, C. 1988. Excavations at Pseira, 1985 and 1986. *Hesperia* 57:207–225.

Betancourt, P.P., Davaras, K. and Banou, E.S. (eds.). 1995. *The Minoan buildings on the west side of Area A*. Pseira 1. University Museum Monograph 90. Philadelphia: University Museum, University of Pennsylvania.

Betancourt, P.P., Goldberg, P., Hope Simpson, R. and Vitaliano, C.J. 1990. Excavations at Pseira: the evidence for the Theran eruption. In D.A. Hardy and A.C. Renfrew (eds.), *Thera and the Aegean world III. Volume three: chronology:* 96–99. London: The Thera Foundation.

Betancourt, P.P. and Lawn, B. 1984. The Cyclades and radiocarbon chronology. In J.A. MacGillivray and R.N.L. Barber (eds.), *The prehistoric Cyclades:* 277–295. Edinburgh: Department of Classical Archaeology, University of Edinburgh.

Betancourt, P.P., Michael, H.N. and Weinstein, G.A. 1978. Calibration and the radiocarbon chronology of Late Minoan IB. *Archaeometry* 20:200–203.

Betancourt, P.P. and Weinstein, G.A. 1976. Carbon-14 and the beginning of the Late Bronze Age in the Aegean. *American Journal of Archaeology* 80:329–348.

Bevir, M. 1994. Objectivity in history. *History and Theory* 33:328–344.

Bichler, M., Egger, H., Preisinger, A., Ritter, D. and Stastny, P. 1997. NAA of the "Minoan pumice" at Thera and comparison to alluvial pumice deposits in the eastern Mediterranean region. *Journal of Radioanalytical and Nuclear Chemistry* 224:7–14.

Bickerman, E.J. 1980. *Chronology of the ancient world.* Revised edition. London: Thames and Hudson.

Bicknell, P. 1995. Santorini Project, 1993. *Mediterranean Archaeology* 8:137–138.

Bicknell, P. 1996/1997. The Monash University Santorini Project, 1996. *Mediterranean Archaeology* 9/10:233–235.

Biddle, M. and Ralph, E.K. 1980. Radiocarbon dates from Akrotiri: problems and a strategy. In C. Doumas (ed.), *Thera and the Aegean world II:* 247–252. London: Thera and the Aegean World.

Bienkowski, P. 1989. The division of Middle Bronze IIB–C in Palestine. *Levant* 21:169–179.

Bienkowski, P. 1990. Jericho was destroyed in the Middle Bronze Age, not the Late Bronze Age. *Biblical Archaeology Review* 16(5):45–49, 68–69.

Bierbrier, M.L. 1975. *The late New Kingdom in Egypt.* Warminster: Aris and Phillips.

Bierbrier, M.L. 1995. How old was Hatshepsut? *Göttinger Miszellen* 144:15–19.

Bietak, M. 1979. Avaris and Piramesse: archaeological exploration in the eastern Nile Delta. *Proceedings of the British Academy* 65:225–290.

Bietak, M. 1984. Problems of Middle Bronze Age chronology: new evidence from Egypt. *American Journal of Archaeology* 88:471–485.

Bietak, M. 1989a. The Middle Bronze Age of the Levant – a new approach to relative and absolute chronology. In P. Åström (ed.), *High, middle or low? Acts of an International Colloquium on Absolute Chronology held at the University of Gothenburg 20th–22nd August 1987,* Part 3: 78–120. Studies in Mediterranean Archaeology and literature Pocket-book 80. Gothenburg: Paul Åströms Förlag.

Bietak, M. 1989b. Archäologischer Befund und historische Interpretation am Beispiel der Tell el-Yahudiya-Ware. In S. Schoske (ed.), *Akten des vierten internationalen Ägyptologenkongresses, München, 1985,* Vol. 2: 7–34. Hamburg: Buske.

Bietak, M. 1991a. Egypt and Canaan during the Middle Bronze Age. *Bulletin of the American Schools of Oriental Research* 281:27–72.

Bietak, M. 1991b. *Tell el-Dabᶜa V.* Wien: Verlag der Österreichischen Akademie der Wissenschaften.

Bietak, M. 1992a. Die Chronologie Ägyptens und der Beginn der Mittleren Bronzezeit-Kultur. *Ägypten und Levante* 3:29–37.

Bietak, M. 1992b. Minoan wall-paintings unearthed at ancient Avaris. *Egyptian Archaeology* 2:26–28.

Bietak, M. 1994. Freskofragment, Stierspringer und Labyrinth; Stierspringer und Stierfänger; and Freskofragment, Stiersprungszene. In I. Hein (catalogue editor), *Pharaonen und fremde Dynastien im Dunkel:* 197–200. Vienna:Museen der Stadt Wien.

Bietak, M. 1995a. Connections between Egypt and the Minoan world: new results from Tell el-Dabᶜa / Avaris. In W.V. Davies and L. Schofield (eds.), *Egypt, the Aegean and the Levant: interconnections in the second millennium BC:* 19–28. London: British Museum Publications.

Bietak, M. (ed.). 1995b. *Trade, power and cultural exchange: Hyksos Egypt and the eastern Mediterranean world 1800–1500 B.C. An International Symposium Wednesday, November 3, 1993. Ägypten und Levante/Egypt and the Levant 5.* Wein: Verlag der Österreichischen Akademie der Wissenschaften.

Bietak, M. 1996a. *Avaris: the capital of the Hyksos. Recent excavations at Tell el-Dabᶜa.* London: British Museum Publications.

Bietak, M. 1996b. Le début de la XVIIIᵉ Dynastie et les Minoens à Avaris. *Bulletin de la Société Française d'Égyptologie* 135:5–29.

Bietak, M. 1997. Avaris, capital of the Hyksos kingdom: new results of excavations. In E.D. Oren (ed.), *The Hyksos: new historical and archaeological perspectives*: 87–139. Philadelphia: The University Museum, University of Pennsylvania.

Bietak, M. 1998. The Late Cypriot White Slip I-Ware as an obstacle of the high Aegean chronology. In M.S. Balmuth and R.H. Tykot (eds.), *Sardinian and Aegean chronology: towards the resolution of relative and absolute dating in the Mediterranean*: 321–322. Studies in Sardinian Archaeology V. Oxford: Oxbow.

Bietak, M., Dorner, J., Hein, I. and Jánosi, P. 1994. Neue Grabungsergebnisse aus Tell el-Dabᶜa und ᶜEzbet Helmi im östlichen Nildelta 1989–1991. *Ägypten und Levante* 4:9–80.

Bietak, M. and Hein, I. n.d. The context of White Slip wares in the stratigraphy of Tell el- Dabᶜa and some conclusions on Aegean chronology. Manuscript of paper presented to the White Slip Ware Conference held in Nicosia 29–30 October 1998. Paper to be published in the conference proceedings: V. Karageorghis (ed.), *White Slip Ware. Proceedings of an International Conference Organized by the Anastasios G. Leventis Foundation, Nicosia in Honour of Malcolm Wiener, Nicosia 29th–30th October 1998*. In Press.

Bietak, M. and Marinatos, N. 1995. The Minoan wall paintings from Avaris. *Ägypten und Levante* 5:49–62.

Bilde, P.G. 1993. Prehistoric pottery. In L. Wriedt Sørensen and D.W. Rupp (eds.), *The land of Paphian Aphrodite. Volume 2. The Canadian Palaipaphos Survey Project: artifact and ecofactual studies*: 1–36. Studies in Mediterranean Archaeology 104:2. Göteborg: Paul Åströms Förlag.

Bimson, J.J. 1981. *Redating the Exodus and conquest*. 2nd edition. Sheffield: JSOT Press.

Bimson, J.J. and Livingston, D. 1987. Redating the Exodus. *Biblical Archaeology Review* 13(5):40–53.

Bintliff, J.L. (ed.). 1991. *The Annales School and archaeology*. Leicester: Leicester University Press.

Birks, H.J.B. 1994. Did Icelandic volcanic eruptions influence the post-glacial vegetation history of the British Isles? *Trends in Ecology and Evolution* 9:312–314.

Birot, M. 1985. Les chroniques 'assyriennes' de Mari. *Mari: Annales de recherches interdisciplinaires* 4:219–242.

Bissing, W.F. von. 1936–1937. Das angebliche Weltreich der Hyksos. *Archiv für Orientforschung* 11:325–335.

Blackman, D.J. 1997–1998. Archaeology in Greece 1997–98. *Archaeological Reports* 44:1–128.

Blakolmer, F. 1997. Minoan wall-painting: the transformation of a craft into an art form. *Aegaeum* 16:95–105.

Blong, R.J. 1980. The possible effects of Santorini tephra fall on Minoan Crete. In C. Doumas (ed.), *Thera and the Aegean world II*: 217–226. London: Thera and the Aegean World.

Bluth, G.J.S., Schnetzler, C.C., Krueger, A.J. and Walter, L.S. 1993. The contribution of explosive volcanism to global atmospheric sulphur dioxide concentrations. *Nature* 366:327–329.

Bluth, G.J.S., Rose, W.I., Sprod, I.E., and Krueger, A.J. 1997. Stratospheric loading of sulfur from explosive volcanic eruptions. *Journal of Geology* 105:671–683.

Boardman, J. 1984. Signa tabulae priscae artis. *Journal of Hellenic Studies* 104:161–163.

Boese, J. and Wilhelm, G. 1979. Assur-dan I., Ninurta-apil-Ekur und die mittelassyrische Chronologie. *Wiener Zeitschrift für die Kunde des Morgenlandes* 71:19–38.

Bohman, J. 1997. Do practices explain anything? Turner's critique of the theory of social practices. *History and Theory* 36:93–107.

Bolton, K. 1976. Addendum to J.V. Luce's article: "Thera and the devastation of Minoan Crete: a new interpretation of the evidence". *American Journal of Archaeology* 80:17–18.

Bonani, G., Wölfli, W. and Doumas, C. 1989. AMS radiocarbon dating of Middle and Late Bronze Age settlements in Akrotiri prior to the Santorini (Thera) eruption. Paper presented to the Thera and the Aegean World III conference (but not published in the proceedings).

Bond, A. and Sparks, R.S.J. 1976. The Minoan eruption of Santorini, Greece. *Journal of the Geological Society of London* 132:1–16.

Boss, M. and Laffineur, R. 1997. Mycenaean metal inlay: a technique in context. *Aegaeum* 16:191–197.

Boulotis, C. 1992. Provlimata tis Aigaiakis zographikis kai oi toikhographies tou Akrotiriou. In C. Doumas (ed.), *Akrotiri Theras. Eikosi khronia (1967–1987)*: 81–94. Athens: Athenais Archaiologike Hetaireia.

Bourdieu, P. 1977. *Outline of a theory of practice*. Trans. R. Nice. Cambridge: Cambridge University Press.

Bourdieu, P. 1990. *The logic of practice*. Trans. R. Nice. Cambridge: Polity Press.

Bourke, S.J. 1993. The transition from the Middle to the Late Bronze Age in Syria: the evidence from Tell Nebi Mend. *Levant* 25:155–195.

Bourke, S.J. 1997. Pre-classical Pella in Jordan: a conspectus of ten years' work (1985–1995). *Palestine Exploration Quarterly* 129:94–115.

Bourriau, J. 1982. Three monuments from Memphis in the Fitzwilliam Museum. *Journal of Egyptian Archaeology* 68:51–59.

Bourriau, J. 1989. Aegean pottery from stratified contexts at Memphis, Kôm Rabî'a. Unpublished paper edited from a lecture presented to the Aegean Bronze Age Seminar, New York.

Bourriau, J. 1990. Memphis/Kom Rab'ia 1990. *Bulletin de Liaison du Groupe International d'étude de la Céramique Égyptienne* 15:7–8.

Bourriau, J. 1996. The dolphin vase from Lisht. In P. Der Manuelian (ed.), *Studies in honor of William Kelly Simpson. Volume I:* 101–116. Boston: Department of Ancient Egyptian, Nubian, and Near Eastern Art, Museum of Fine Arts.

Bourriau, J. 1997. Beyond Avaris. The Second Intermediate Period in Egypt outside the eastern delta. In E.D. Oren (ed.), *The Hyksos: new historical and archaeological perspectives:* 159–182. Philadelphia: The University Museum, University of Pennsylvania.

Bourriau, J. and Eriksson, K.O. 1997. A Late Minoan sherd from an early 18th Dynasty context at Kom Rabi'a, Memphis. In J. Phillips (ed.), *Ancient Egypt, the Aegean, and the Near East: studies in honour of Martha Rhoads Bell:* 95–120. San Antonio: Van Siclen Books.

Bouzek, J. 1994. Late Bronze Age Greece and the Balkans: a review of the present picture. *Annual of the British School at Athens* 89:217–234.

Bouzek, J. 1996. Greece and the Aegean area and its relationship with continental Europe. *Acta Archaeologica* 67:175–181.

Bowden, H. 1991. The chronology of Greek painted pottery: some observations. *Hephaistos* 10:49–59.

Bowman, S. 1990. *Radiocarbon dating.* London: British Museum.

Bowman, S. 1994. Using radiocarbon: an update. *Antiquity* 68:838–843.

Bowman, S. and Balaam, N. 1990. Using radiocarbon. *Antiquity* 64:315–318.

Bradley, R. 1991. Ritual, time and history. *World Archaeology* 23:209–219.

Bradley, R. 1998. *The significance of monuments: on the shaping of human experience in Neolithic and Bronze Age Europe.* London: Routledge.

Bradley, R.S. 1988. The explosive volcanic eruption signal in northern hemisphere continental temperature records. *Climatic Change* 12:221–243.

Braitseva, O.A., Melekestsev, I.V., Ponomareva, V.V. and Sulerzhitsky, L.D. 1995. Ages of calderas, large explosive craters and active volcanoes in the Kuril-Kamchatka region, Russia. *Bulletin of Volcanology* 57:383–402.

Braitseva, O.A., Ponomareva, V.V., Sulerzhitsky, L.D., Melekestsev, I.V. and Bailey, J. 1997. Holocene key-marker tephra layers in Kamchatka, Russia. *Quaternary Research* 47:125–139.

Braitseva, O.A., Sulerzhitsky, L.D., Litasova, S.N., Melekestsev, I.V. and Ponomareva, V.V. 1993. Radiocarbon dating and tephrachronology in Kamchatka. *Radiocarbon* 35:463–476.

Branigan, K. 1973. Radio-carbon and the absolute chronology of the Aegean Bronze Age. *Kretika Chronika* 25:352–374.

Braudel, F. 1993. *A history of civilizations.* Trans. R. Mayne. London: Penguin Books.

Braziunas, T.F., Fung, I.E., and Stuiver, M. 1995. The preindustrial atmospheric $^{14}CO_2$ latitudinal gradient as related to exchanges among atmospheric, oceanic, and terrestrial reservoirs. *Global Biogeochemical Cycles* 9:565–584.

Breasted, J.H. 1962 [1906–1907]. *Ancient records of Egypt: from the earliest times to the Persian conquest.* Volumes I–V. New York: Russell & Russell. This is a re-issue of the original edition of 1906–1907, in 5 volumes, from The University of Chicago Press.

Breunig, P. 1987. *^{14}C-Chronologie des vorderasiatischen, südost-und mitteleuropäischen Neolithikums.* Köln: In Kommission bei Böhlau.

Briffa, K.R. 1994. Mid and late Holocene climate change: evidence from tree-growth in northern Fennoscandia. In B.M. Funnell and R.L.F. Kay (eds.), *Palaeoclimate of the Last Glacial/Interglacial Cycle:* 61–65. London: NERC.

Briffa, K.R., Bartholin, T.S., Eckstein D., Jones, P.D., Karlén, W., Schweingruber, F.H. and Zetterberg, P. 1990. A 1,400-year tree-ring record of summer temperatures in Fennoscandia. *Nature* 346:434–439.

Briffa, K.R., Jones, P.D. and Schweingruber, F.H. 1988. Summer temperature patterns over Europe: a reconstruction from 1750 A.D. based on maximum latewood density indices of conifers. *Quaternary Research* 30:36–52.

Briffa, K.R., Jones, P.D. and Schweingruber, F.H. 1992. Tree-ring reconstructions of summer temperature patterns across western North America since 1600. *Journal of Climate* 5:735–754.

Briffa, K.R., Jones, P.D. and Schweingruber, F.H. 1994. Summer temperatures across northern North America: regional reconstructions from 1760 using tree-ring densities. *Journal of Geophysical Research* 99:25,835–25,844.

Briffa, K.R., Jones, P.D., Schweingruber, F.H. and Osborne, T.J. 1998. Influence of volcanic eruptions on Northern Hemisphere summer temperatures over the past 600 years. *Nature* 393:450–455.

Brinkman, J.A. 1968. *A political history of post-Kassite Babylonia, 1158–722 B.C.* Analecta Orientalia. Commentationes scientificae de rebus orientis antiqui 43. Rome: Pontificum Institutum Biblicum.

Brinkman, J.A. 1970. Notes on Mesopotamian history in the thirteenth century B.C. *Bibliotheca Orientalis* 27:301–314.

Brinkman, J.A. 1972. Foreign relations of Babylonia from 1600 to 625 B.C.: the documentary evidence. *American Journal of Archaeology* 76:271–281.

Brinkman, J.A. 1973. Comments on the Nassouhi Kinglist and the Assyrian Kinglist tradition. *Orientalia* 42:306–319.

Brinkman, J.A. 1976. *Materials and studies for Kassite History.* Chicago: Oriental Institute of the University of Chicago.

Brinkman, J.A. 1977. Mesopotamian chronology of the historical period. In A.L. Oppenheim, *Ancient Mesopotamia. Portrait of a dead civilisation:* 335–348. Revised edition, completed by E. Reiner. Chicago: University of Chicago Press.

Brinkman, J.A. 1983. Istanbul A.1988, Middle Babylonian chronology, and the statistics of the Nippur archives. *Zeitschrift für Assyriologie und Vorderasiatische Archäologie* 73:67–74.

Brinkman, J.A. 1984. *Prelude to empire: Babylonian society and politics, 747–626 B.C.* Philadelphia: Babylonian Fund, University Museum.

Brinkman, J.A. 1990. The Babylonian chronicle revisited. In T. Abusch, J. Hühnergard, and P. Steinkeller (eds.), *Lingering over words: studies in ancient Near Eastern literature in honor of William L. Moran:* 73–104. Harvard Semitic Studies 37. Atlanta: Scholars Press.

Broodbank, C. 1992. The spirit is willing. *Antiquity* 66:542–546.

Bruins, H.J. and Mook, W.G. 1989. The need for a calibrated radiocarbon chronology of Near Eastern archaeology. *Radiocarbon* 31:1,019–1,029.

Bruins, H.J. and Plicht, J. van der. 1995. Tell Es-Sultan (Jericho): radiocarbon results of short-lived cereal and multiyear charcoal samples from the end of the Middle Bronze Age. *Radiocarbon* 37:213–220.

Bruins, H.J. and Plicht, J. van der. 1996. The Exodus enigma. *Nature* 382:213–214.

Bruns, M., Levin, I., Münnich, K.O., Hubberten, H.-W. and Filippakis, S. 1980. Regional sources of volcanic carbon dioxide and their influence on the 14C content of present-day plant material. *Radiocarbon* 22:532–536.

Brunstein, F.C. 1996. Climatic significance of the Bristlecone Pine latewood frost-ring record at Almagre Mountain, Colorado, U.S.A. *Arctic and Alpine Research* 28:65–76.

Bryan, B.M. 1980. *The reign of Tuthmosis IV.* Ph.D. dissertation, Yale University. Ann Arbor: University Microfilms International.

Bryan, B.M. 1991. *The reign of Tuthmose IV.* Baltimore: Johns Hopkins University Press.

Bryan, B.M. 1998. Antecedents to Amenhotep III. In D. O'Connor and E.H. Cline (eds.), *Amenhotep III: perspectives on his reign:* 27–62. Ann Arbor: The University of Michigan Press.

Bryce, T.R. 1983. *The major historical texts of early Hittite history.* St. Lucia: University of Queensland.

Bryce, T.R. 1986. Madduwatta and Hittite policy in western Anatolia. *Historia* 35:1–12.

Bryce, T.R. 1989a. Ahhiyawans and Mycenaeans – an Anatolian viewpoint. *Oxford Journal of Archaeology* 8:297–310.

Bryce, T.R. 1989b. The nature of Mycenaean involvement in western Anatolia. *Historia* 38:1–21.

Bryce, T.R. 1998. *The kingdom of the Hittites.* Oxford: Clarendon Press.

Buchholz, H.-G. 1963. Steinerne Dreifußschalen des ägäischen Kulturkreises und ihre Beziehungen zum Osten. *Jahrbuch des Deutschen Archäologischen Instituts* 78:1–77.

Buchholz, H.-G. 1980. Some observations concerning Thera's contacts overseas during the Bronze Age. In C. Doumas (ed.), *Thera and the Aegean world II:* 227–240. London: Thera and the Aegean World.

Buchholz, H.-G. 1987. *Ägäische Bronzezeit.* Darmstadt: Wissenschaftliche Buchgesselschaft.

Buck, C.E., Cavanagh, W.G. and Litton, C.D. 1996. *Bayesian approach to interpreting archaeological data.* Chichester: J. Wiley and Son.

Buck, C.E., Kenworthy, J.B., Litton, C.D. and Smith, A.F.M. 1991. Combining archaeological and radiocarbon information: a Bayesian approach to calibration. *Antiquity* 65:808–821.

Buck, C.E., Litton, C.D. and Scott, E.M. 1994. Making the most of radiocarbon dating: some statistical considerations. *Antiquity* 68:252–263.

Buck, C.E., Litton, C.D. and Smith, A.F.M. 1992. Calibration of radiocarbon results pertaining to related archaeological events. *Journal of Archaeological Science* 19:497–512.

Buckland, P.C., Dugmore, A.J. and Edwards, K.J. 1997. Bronze Age myths? Volcanic activity and human response in the Mediterranean and North Atlantic regions. *Antiquity* 71:581–593.

Buckland, P.C., Dugmore, A.J. and Edwards, K.J. 1998. Comment. *Antiquity* 72:431–432.

Burnouf, É. 1879. *Mémoires sur l'antiquité.* Paris. [not seen by this author, cited from Merrillees (n.d.)]

Cadogan, G. 1972. Cypriot objects in the Bronze Age Aegean and their importance. In V. Karageorghis and A. Christodoulou (eds.), *Praktika tou Protou Diethnous Kyprologikou Synedriou:* 5–13. Nicosia: Hetaireia Kypriakon Spoudon.

Cadogan, G. 1976. Some faience, blue frit and glass from fifteenth century Knossos. *Temple University Aegean Symposium* 1:18–19.

Cadogan, G. 1978. Dating the Aegean Bronze Age without radiocarbon. *Archaeometry* 20:209–214.

Cadogan, G. 1979. Cyprus and Crete c.2000–1400 B.C. In V. Karageorghis (ed.), *Acts of the international archaeological symposium 'The relations between Cyprus and Crete ca.2000–500BC':* 63–68. Nicosia: Department of Antiquities.

Cadogan, G. 1983a. Early and Middle Minoan chronology. *American Journal of Archaeology* 87:507–518.

Cadogan, G. 1983b. Maroni I. *Report of the Department of Antiquities, Cyprus:* 153–162.

Cadogan, G. 1984. Cycladic jugs at Pyrgos. In J.A. MacGillivray and R.N.L. Barber (eds.), *The prehistoric Cyclades:* 162–164. Edinburgh: Department of Classical Archaeology, University of Edinburgh.

Cadogan, G. 1986. Maroni in Cyprus, between West and East. In V. Karageorghis (ed.), *Acts of the International Archaeological Symposium "Cyprus Between the Orient and the Occident" Nicosia, 8–14 September 1985:* 104–111. Nicosia: Department of Antiquities.

Cadogan, G. 1987. Unsteady date of a big bang. *Nature* 328:473.

Cadogan, G. 1988. Some Middle Minoan problems. In E.B. French and K.A. Wardle (eds.), *Problems in Greek prehistory. Papers presented at the Centenary Conference of the British School of Archaeology at Athens, Manchester, April 1986:* 95–99. Bristol: Bristol Classical Press.

Cadogan, G. 1989. Maroni and the monuments. In E.J. Peltenburg (ed.), *Early society in Cyprus:* 43–51. Edinburgh: Edinburgh University Press.

Cadogan, G. 1990. Thera's eruption into our understanding of the Minoans. In D.A. Hardy, C.G. Doumas, J.A. Sakellarakis and P.M. Warren (eds.), *Thera and the Aegean world III. Volume one: archaeology:* 93–97. London: The Thera Foundation.

Cadogan, G. 1991. *Palaces of Crete.* Reprint. London: Routledge.

Cadogan, G. 1996. Maroni: change in Late Bronze Age Cyprus. In P. Åström and E. Herscher (eds.), *Late Bronze Age settlement in Cyprus: function and relationship:* 15–22. Jonsered: Paul Åströms Förlag.

Cadogan, G. and Harrison, R.K. 1978. Evidence of tephra in soil samples from Pyrgos, Crete. In C. Doumas (ed.), *Thera and the Aegean world I:* 235–255. London: Thera and the Aegean World.

Cadogan, G., Harrison, R.K. and Strong, G.E. 1972. Volcanic glass shards in Late Minoan I Crete. *Antiquity* 46:310–313.

Cadogan, G., Herscher, E., Russell, P. and Manning, S. n.d. Maroni-Vournes: a long White Slip sequence and its chronology. Manuscript of paper presented to the White Slip Ware Conference held in Nicosia 29–30 October 1998. Paper to be published in the conference proceedings: V. Karageorghis (ed.), *White Slip Ware. Proceedings of an International Conference Organized by the Anastasios G. Leventis Foundation, Nicosia in Honour of Malcolm Wiener, Nicosia 29th–30th October 1998.* In Press.

Calderoni, G. and Turi, B. 1998. Major constraints on the use of radiocarbon dating for tephrachronology. *Quaternary International* 47/48:153–159.

Callinicos, A. 1989. *Against postmodernism: a Marxist critique.* Cambridge: Polity Press.

Cameron, M.A. 1967. Unpublished fresco fragments of a chariot composition from Knossos. *Archäologischer Anzeiger:* 330–344.

Cameron, M.A. 1978. Theoretical interrelations among Theran, Cretan and Mainland frescoes. In C.

Doumas (ed.), *Thera and the Aegean world I:* 579–592. London: Thera and the Aegean World.

Cardarelli, A. 1993. Le età dei metalli nell'Italia settentrionale. In A Guidi and M. Piperno (eds.), *Italia preistorica:* 366–419. Second edition. Rome: Editori Laterza.

Carroll, M.R. 1997. Volcanic sulphur in the balance. *Nature* 389:543–544.

Carpenter, J.R. 1981. Excavations at Phaneromeni, 1975–1978. In J.C. Biers and D. Soren (eds.), *Studies in Cypriote archaeology:* 59–78. Monograph 18. Los Angeles: Institute of Archaeology, University of California.

Carr, C. and Neitzel, J.E. (eds.). 1995. *Style, society, and person: archaeological and ethnological perspectives.* New York: Plenum Press.

Caseldine, C., Hutton, J., Huber, U., Chiverrell, R. and Woolley, N. 1998. Assessing the impact of volcanic activity on mid-Holocene climate in Ireland: the need for replicate data. *The Holocene* 8:105–111.

Casperson, L.W. 1986. The lunar dates of Tuthmosis III. *Journal of Near Eastern Studies* 45:139–150.

Casperson, L.W. 1988. The lunar date of Ramesses II. *Journal of Near Eastern Studies* 47:181–184.

Castleden, R. 1998. *Atlantis Destroyed.* London: Routledge.

Catling, H.W. 1962. Patterns of settlement in Bronze Age Cyprus. *Opuscula Atheniensia* 4:129–169.

Catling, H.W. 1979. The St. Andrews-Liverpool Museums Kouklia tomb excavation. *Report of the Department of Antiquities, Cyprus:* 270–275.

Catling, H.W. 1983. Archaeology in Greece, 1982–83. *Archaeological Reports* 29:3–62.

Catling, H.W. 1989. Some problems in Aegean prehistory, c.1450–1380 B.C. The Fourteenth J.L. Myres Memorial Lecture: a lecture delivered at New College, Oxford, on 5th May, 1987. Oxford: Leopard's Head Press.

Catling, H.W. 1991. A Late Cypriot import in Rhodes. *Annual of the British School at Athens* 86:1–7.

Chapin, A.P. 1997. A re-examination of the Floral Fresco from the Unexplored Mansion at Knossos. *Annual of the British School at Athens* 92:1–24.

Charpin, D. and Durand, J.-M. 1985. La prise du pouvoir par Zimri-Lim. *Mari: Annales de recherches interdisciplinaires* 4:293–343.

Charlson, R.J., Schwartz, S.E., Hales, J.M., Cess, R.D., Coakley, J.A. Jr., Hansen, J.E. and Hofmann, D.J. 1992. Climate forcing by anthropogenic aerosols. *Science* 255:423–430.

Chase-Dunn, C. and Hall, T. (eds.). 1991. *Core/periphery relations in precapitalist worlds.* Boulder: Westview Press.

Chase-Dunn, C. and Hall, T.D. 1995. Cross-world-system comparisons: similarities and differences. In S.K. Sanderson (ed.), *Civilizations and world systems: studying world-historical change:* 109–135. Walnut Creek: Altamira Press.

Cherry, J.F. 1983. Evolution, revolution, and the origins of complex society in Minoan Crete. In O. Krzyszkowska and L. Nixon (eds.), *Minoan society. Proceedings of the Cambridge colloquium 1981:* 33–45. Bristol: Bristol Classical Press.

Cherry, J.F. 1992. Beazley in the Bronze Age? Reflections on attribution studies in Aegean prehistory. *Aegaeum* 8:123–144.

Chester, D.K. 1988. Volcanoes and climate: recent volcanological perspectives. *Progress in Physical Geography* 12:1–35.

Childe, V.G. 1925. *The dawn of European civilization.* London: Kegan Paul.

Childe, V.G. 1928. *The most ancient East: the Oriental prelude to European prehistory.* London: Kegan Paul.

Childe, V.G. 1929. *The Danube in prehistory.* Oxford: Oxford University Press.

Christen, J.A. and Litton, C.D. 1995. A Bayesian approach to wiggle-matching. *Journal of Archaeological Science* 22:719–725.

Cita, M.B. and Rimoldi, B. 1997. Geological and geophysical evidence for a Holocene tsunami deposit in the eastern Mediterranean deep-sea record. *Journal of Geodynamics* 24:293–304.

Clark, R.M. 1975. A calibration curve for radiocarbon dates. *Antiquity* 49:251–266.

Clark, R.M. and Morgan, R.A. 1983. An alternative statistical approach to the calibration of floating tree-ring chronologies: two sequences from the Somerset levels. *Archaeometry* 25:3–15.

Clausen, H.B. and Hammer, C.U. 1988. The Laki and Tambora eruptions as revealed in Greenland ice cores from 11 locations. *Annals of Glaciology* 10:16–22.

Clausen, H.B., Hammer, C.U., Hvidberg, C.S., Dahl-Jensen, D., Steffensen, J.P., Kipfstuhl, J. and Legrand, M. 1997. A comparison of the volcanic records over the past 4000 years from the Greenland Ice Core Project and Dye 3 Greenland ice cores. *Journal of Geophysical Research* 102 C12:26,707–26,723.

Clayden, T. 1992. Kish in the Kassite period (c.1650–1150 B.C.). *Iraq* 54:141–155.

Clerc, G. 1990. Un fragment de vase au nom d'Ahmosis(?) à Palaepaphos-*Teratsoudhia*. In V. Karageorghis, Michaelides, D., *et al., Tombs at Palaepaphos. 1. Teratsoudhia. 2. Eliomylia:* 95–103. Nicosia: A.G. Leventis Foundation.

Cline, E.H. 1987. Amenhotep III and the Aegean: a reassessment of Egypto-Aegean relations in the 14th century BC. *Orientalia* 56:1–36.

Cline, E.H. 1990. An unpublished Amenhotep III faience plaque from Mycenae. *Journal of the American Oriental Society* 110:200–212.

Cline, E.H. 1990–1991. Contact and trade or colonization?: Egypt and the Aegean in the 14th–13th centuries B.C. *Minos* 25–26:7–36.

Cline, E.H. 1991. Monkey business in the Bronze Age Aegean: the Amenhotep II faience figurines at Mycenae and Tiryns. *Annual of the British School at Athens* 86:29–42.

Cline, E.H. 1994. *Sailing the wine-dark sea: international trade and the Late Bronze Age Aegean.* British Archaeological Reports International Series 591. Oxford: Tempus Reparatum.

Cline, E.H. 1995a. Tinker, tailor, soldier, sailor: Minoans and Mycenaeans abroad. *Aegaeum* 12:265–283.

Cline, E.H. 1995b. 'My brother, my son,' rulership and trade between the Late Bronze Age Aegean, Egypt and the Near East. *Aegaeum* 11:143–150.

Cline, E.H. 1996. Assuwa and the Achaeans: the 'Mycenaean' sword at Hattusas and its possible implications. *Annual of the British School at Athens* 91:137–151.

Cline, E.H. 1998a. Rich beyond the dreams of Avaris: Tell el-Dabʿa and the Aegean world – a guide for the perplexed. *Annual of the British School at Athens* 93:199–219.

Cline E.H. 1998b. Amenhotep III, the Aegean, and Anatolia. In D. O'Connor and E.H. Cline (eds.), *Amenhotep III: perspectives on his reign:* 236–250. Ann Arbor: The University of Michigan Press.

Cogan, M. 1985. The chronicler's use of chronology as illuminated by Neo-Assyrian royal inscriptions. In J.H. Tigay (ed.), *Empirical models for Biblical criticism:* 197–209. Philadelphia: University of Pennsylvania Press.

Coldstream, J.N. 1969. The Thera eruption: some thoughts on the survivors. *Bulletin of the Institute of Classical Studies* 16:150–152.

Coldstream, J.N. and Huxley, G.L. (eds.). 1972. *Kythera. Excavations and studies conducted by the University of Pennsylvania Museum and the British School at Athens.* London: Faber and Faber.

Cole, D.P. 1984. *Shechem I: the Middle Bronze IIB pottery.* Winona Lake: American Schools of Oriental Research.

Collingwood, R.G. 1994. *The idea of history.* Revised edition with Lectures 1926–1928. Paperback issue. Oxford: Oxford University Press.

Collon, D. 1975. *The seal impressions from Tell Atchana/Alalakh.* Alter Orient und Altes Testament 27. Kevelaer and Neukirchener-Vluyn: Verlag Butzon & Bercker and Neukirchener Verlag.

Collon, D. 1977. A new look at the chronology of Alalakh Level VII: a rejoinder. *Anatolian Studies* 27:127–131.

Collon, D. 1994. Bull-leaping in Syria. *Ägypten und Levante* 4:81–85.

Contu, E. 1992. L'inizio dell'età nuragica. In *La Sardegna nel Mediterraneo tra il Bronzo Medio il Bronzo Recente (XVI–XIII Sec. a.C.). Atti del III Convegno di studi 'Un millennio di relazioni fra la Sardegna e I Paesi del Mediterraneo', Selargius-Cagliari, 19–22 novembre 1987:* 13–40. Cagliari: Edizioni della Torre.

Cook, E.R. and Kairiukstis, L.A. (eds.). 1990. *Methods of dendrochronology: applications in the environmental sciences.* Dordrecht: Kluwer Academic Publishers.

Courtois, J.-C. 1981. *Alasia II: les tombes d'Enkomi, le mobilier funéraire (fouilles C.F.-A. Schaeffer 1947–1965).* Mission Archéologique d'Alasia 5. Paris: Mission Archéologique d'Alasia.

Courtois, J-C. 1986. A propos des apports Orientaux dans la civilisation du Bronze Récent à Chypre. In V. Karageorghis (ed.), *Acts of the International Archaeological Symposium "Cyprus between the Orient and the Occident" Nicosia, 8–14 September 1985:* 69–90. Nicosia: Department of Antiquities.

Courtois, L. 1970. Note preliminaire sur l'origine des differentes fabriques de la poterie du Chypriote Recent. *Report of the Department of Antiquities, Cyprus:* 81–85.

Courtois, L. and Velde, B. 1989. Petrographic studies of pottery (preliminary report). In A. South, P. Russell and P.S. Keswani, *Kalavasos-Ayios Dhimitrios II: ceramics, objects, tombs, specialist studies:* 73–77. Studies in Mediterranean Archaeology 71:3. Göteborg: Paul Åströms Förlag.

Crowley, J.L. 1989. *The Aegean and the east: an investigation into the transference of artistic motifs between the*

Aegean, Egypt, and the Near East in the Bronze Age. Studies in Mediterranean Archaeology and Literature Pocket-book 51. Jonsered: Paul Åströms Förlag.

Crowley, T.J., Criste, T.A. and Smith, N.R. 1993. Reassessment of Crête (Greenland) ice core acidity/ volcanism link to climate change. *Geophysical Research Letters* 20:209–212.

Crowley, T.J. and Kim, K.-Y. 1993. Towards development of a strategy for determining the origin of decadal-centennial scale climate variability. *Quaternary Science Reviews* 12:375–385.

Cryer, F.H. 1995. Chronology: issues and problems. In J.M. Sasson, J. Baines, G. Beckman and K.S. Rubinson (eds.), *Civilizations of the Ancient Near East*, volume II: 651–664. New York: Charles Scribner's Sons.

Cuffey, K.M., Clow, G.D., Alley, R.B., Stuiver, M., Waddington, E.D. and Saltus, R.W. 1995. Large Arctic temperature change at the Wisconsin-Holocene glacial transition. *Science* 270:455–458.

Cummer, W.W. and Schofield, E. 1984. *Keos III. Ayia Irini: House A.* Mainz am Rhein: Philipp von Zabern.

Dabney, M.K. and Wright, J.C. 1990. Mortuary customs, palatial society and state formation in the Aegean area: a comparative study. In R. Hägg and G.C. Nordquist (eds.), *Celebrations of death and divinity in the Bronze Age Argolid. Proceedings of the sixth international symposium at the Swedish Institute at Athens, 11–13 June, 1988:* 45–53. Skrifter Utgivna av Svenska Institutet i Athen, 4°, 40. Stockholm: Paul Åströms Förlag.

Dalley, S. 1984. *Mari and Karana: two Old Babylonian cities.* London: Longman.

Damon, P.E., Ferguson, C.W., Long, A. and Willick, E.I. 1974. Dendrochronologic calibration of the radiocarbon time scale. *American Antiquity* 39:350–366.

Damon, P.E. 1995a. A note concerning "location-dependent differences in the ^{14}C content of wood" by McCormac *et al. Radiocarbon* 37:829–830.

Damon, P.E. 1995b. Note concerning "intercomparison of high-precision ^{14}C measurements at the University of Arizona and the Queen's University of Belfast radiocarbon laboratories" by Kalin *et al.* (1995) and the regional effect. *Radiocarbon* 37:955–959.

Damon, P.E., Cheng, S. and Linick, T.W. 1989. Fine and hyperfine structure in the spectrum of secular variations of the atmospheric ^{14}C. *Radiocarbon* 31:704–718.

Daniel, G.E. 1943. *The three ages: an essay on archaeological method.* Cambridge: Cambridge University Press.

Dansgaard, W., Clausen, H.B., Gundestrup, N., Johnsen, S.J. and Rygner, C. 1985. Dating and climatic interpretation of two deep Greenland ice cores. In C.C. Langway Jr., H. Oeschger and W. Dansgaard (eds.), *Greenland ice core: geophysics, geochemistry, and the environment:* 71–76. American Geophysical Union, Geophysical Monograph 33. Washington: American Geophysical Union.

Dansgaard, W., Johnsen, S.J., Clausen, H.B., Dahl-Jensen, D., Gundestrup, N. and Hammer, C.U. 1984. North Atlantic climate oscillations revealed by deep Greenland ice cores. In J.E. Hansen and T. Takahashi (eds), *Climate processes and climate sensitivity:* 288–298. American Geophysical Union, Geophysical Monograph 29. Washington: American Geophysical Union.

Dansgaard, W., Johnsen, S.J., Clausen, H.B., Dahl-Jensen, D., Gundestrup, N.S., Hammer, C.U., Hvidberg, C.S., Steffensen, J.P., Sveinbjörnsdottir, S.E., Jouzel, J. and Bond, G. 1993. Evidence for general instability of past climate from a 250-kyr ice-core record. *Nature* 364:218–220.

Darwin, C. 1871. *The descent of man, and selection in relation to sex.* 2 vols. London: John Murray.

Darwin, C. 1886. *The origin of species by means of natural selection, or the preservation of favoured races in the struggle for life.* 6th edition with additions and corrections to 1872. London: John Murray.

Darwin, C. c.1948. *The origin of species by means of natural selection, or the preservation of favoured races in the struggle for life* and *The descent of man and selection in relation to sex.* New York: The Modern Library.

Dautzenberg, N. 1993. Bemerkungen zur Dynastie der Grossen Hyksos bei Manetho. *Göttinger Miszellen* 135:9–26.

Dautzenberg, N. 1995. Bemerkungen zu Schoschenq II., Takeloth II. und Pedubastis II. *Göttinger Miszellen* 144:21–29.

Davidson, D.A. 1978. Aegean soils during the second millennium BC with reference to Thera. In C. Doumas (ed.), *Thera and the Aegean world I:* 725–739. London: Thera and the Aegean World.

Davies, W.V. and Schofield, L. (eds.) 1995. *Egypt, the Aegean and the Levant: interconnections in the second millennium BC.* London: British Museum Publications.

Davis, E.N. 1990a. A storm in Egypt during the reign of Ahmose. In D.A. Hardy and A.C. Renfrew (eds.), *Thera and the Aegean world III. Volume three: chronology:* 232–235. London: The Thera Foundation.

Davis, E.N. 1990b. The Cycladic style of the Thera frescoes. In D.A. Hardy, C.G. Doumas, J.A. Sakellarakis and P.M. Warren (eds.), *Thera and the Aegean world III. Volume one: archaeology:* 214–228. London: The Thera Foundation.

Davis, J.L. 1977. Polychrome bird jugs: a note. *Athens Annals of Archaeology* 9:81–83.

Davis, J.L. 1995. An Aegean prehistory textbook for the 1990s? *American Journal of Archaeology* 99:732–735.

Davis, J.L. and Cherry, J.F. 1984. Phylakopi in Late Cycladic I: a pottery seriation study. In J.A. MacGillivray and R.L.N. Barber (eds.), *The prehistoric Cyclades: contributions to a workshop on Cycladic chronology:* 148–161. Edinburgh: Department of Classical Archaeology, University of Edinburgh.

Davis, J.L. and Cherry, J.F. 1990. Spatial and temporal uniformitarianism in Late Cycladic I: perspectives from Kea and Milos on the prehistory of Akrotiri. In D.A. Hardy, C.G. Doumas, J.A. Sakellarakis and P.M. Warren (eds.), *Thera and the Aegean world III. Volume one: archaeology:* 185–200. London: The Thera Foundation.

Davis, J.L. and Williams, D.F. 1981. Petrological examination of Late Middle Bronze Age pottery from Ayia Irini, Keos. *Hesperia* 50:291–300.

Day, S.P. and Mellars, P.A. 1994. 'Absolute' dating of Mesolithic human activity at Star Carr, Yorkshire: new palaeoecological studies and identification of the 9600 BP radiocarbon 'plateau'. *Proceedings of the Prehistoric Society* 60:417–422.

Dean, J.S. 1997. Dendrochronology. In R.E. Taylor and M.J. Aitken (eds.), *Chronometric dating in archaeology:* 31–64. New York: Plenum Press.

Decker, R.W. 1990. How often does a Minoan eruption occur? In D.A. Hardy, J. Keller, V.P. Galanopoulos, N.C. Flemming and T.H. Druitt (eds.), *Thera and the Aegean world III. Volume two: earth sciences:* 444–452. London: The Thera Foundation.

Delia, R.D. 1997. Review of C. Obsomer, *Sésostris Iᵉʳ: étude chronologique et historique de règne. Journal of the American Research Centre in Egypt* 34:267–268.

Demakopoulou, K. and Crouwel, J.H. 1993. More cats or lions from Thera? *Arkhaiologiki Ephemeris* 132:1–11.

Demakopoulou, K., Mangou, E., Jones, R.E., and Photos-Jones, E. 1995. Mycenaean black inlaid metalware in the National Archaeological Museum, Athens: a technical examination. *Annual of the British School at Athens* 90:137–153.

Depuydt, L. 1993. The date of Piye's Egyptian campaign and the chronology of the Twenty-Fifth Dynasty. *Journal of Egyptian Archaeology* 79:269–274.

Depuydt, L. 1995. On the consistency of the wandering year as backbone of Egyptian chronology. *Journal of the American Research Centre in Egypt* 32:43–58.

Depuydt, L. 1996a. Egyptian regnal dating under Cambyses and the date of the Persian conquest. In P. Der Manuelian (ed.), *Studies in honor of William Kelly Simpson. Volume I:* 179–190. Boston: Department of Ancient Egyptian, Nubian, and Near Eastern Art, Museum of Fine Arts.

Depuydt, L. 1996b. The function of the Ebers calendar concordance. *Orientalia* 65:61–88.

Depuydt, L. 1996c. More valuable than all gold: Ptolemy's Royal Canon and Babylonian chronology. *Journal of Cuneiform Studies* 47:97–117.

Depuydt, L. 1998. Ancient Egyptian star clocks and their theory. *Bibliotheca Orientalis* 55:6–44.

Dethlefsen, E. and Deetz, J. 1966. Death's heads, cherubs, and willow trees: experimental archaeology in colonial cemeteries. *American Antiquity* 31:502–511.

Dever, W.G. 1985. Relations between Syria–Palestine and Egypt in the 'Hyksos' period. In J.N. Tubb (ed.), *Palestine in the Bronze and Iron Ages: papers in honour of Olga Tufnell:* 69–87. London: Institute of Archaeology, University of London.

Dever, W.G. 1987. Palestine in the Middle Bronze Age: the zenith of the urban Canaanite era. *Biblical Archaeologist* 50:149–176.

Dever, W.G. 1990. 'Hyksos', Egyptian destructions, and the end of the Palestinian Middle Bronze Age. *Levant* 22:75–82.

Dever, W.G. 1991. Tell el-Dabᶜa and Levantine Middle Bronze Age chronology: a rejoinder to Manfred Bietak. *Bulletin of the American Schools of Oriental Research* 281:73–79.

Dever, W.G. 1992. The chronology of Syria–Palestine in the second millennium B.C.E.: a review of current issues. *Bulletin of the American Schools of Oriental Research* 288:1–25.

Dever, W.G. 1997. Settlement patterns and chronology of Palestine in the Middle Bronze Age. In E.D.

Oren (ed.), *The Hyksos: new historical and archaeological perspectives*: 285–301. Philadelphia: The University Museum, University of Pennsylvania.

Devine, J.D., Sigurdsson, H., Davis, A.N. and Self, S. 1984. Estimates of sulfur and chlorine yield to the atmosphere from volcanic eruptions and potential climatic effects. *Journal of Geophysical Research* 89:6,309–6,325.

Dickinson, O. 1994. *The Aegean Bronze Age.* Cambridge: Cambridge University Press.

Dickinson, O. 1997. Arts and artefacts in the Shaft Graves: some observations. *Aegaeum* 16:45–49.

Dietz, S. 1991. *The Argolid at the transition to the Mycenaean age. Studies in the chronology and cultural development in the Shaft Grave period.* Copenhagen: The National Museum of Denmark, Department of Near Eastern and Classical Antiquities.

Dikaios, P. 1969–1971. *Enkomi: excavations 1948–1958.* Mainz am Rhein: Philipp von Zabern.

Dimopoulou, N., Olivier, J.-P. and Réthémiotakis, G. 1993. Une statuette en argile MRIIIA de Poros/ Irakliou avec inscription en linéaire A. *Bulletin de Correspondance Hellénique* 117:501–521.

Dingwell, D.B. 1996. Volcanic dilemma: flow or blow? *Science* 273:1054–1055.

Dodson, A. 1993. A new king Shoshenq confirmed? *Göttinger Miszellen* 137:53–58.

Dominey-Howes, D.T.M. 1996. *The geomorphology and sedimentology of five tsunamis in the Aegean sea region, Greece.* Ph.D. dissertation, Coventry University.

Dorman, P.F. 1988. *The monuments of Senenmut: problems in historical methodology.* London: Keegan Paul International.

Doumas, C. 1974. The Minoan eruption of the Santorini volcano. *Antiquity* 48:110–115.

Doumas, C. (ed.). 1978a. *Thera and the Aegean world I.* London: Thera and the Aegean World.

Doumas, C. 1978b. The stratigraphy of Akrotiri. In C. Doumas (ed.), *Thera and the Aegean world I*: 777–782. London: Thera and the Aegean World.

Doumas, C. (ed.). 1980. *Thera and the Aegean world II.* London: Thera and the Aegean World.

Doumas, C. 1982. The Minoan thalassocracy and the Cyclades. *Archäologischer Anzeiger*: 5–14.

Doumas, C. 1983a. *Thera: Pompeii of the ancient Aegean.* London: Thames and Hudson.

Doumas, C. 1983b. Santorini et la fin du monde égéen. *La Recherche* 143:456–463.

Doumas, C. 1988. The prehistoric eruption of Thera and its effects. The evidence from Rhodes. In S. Dietz and I. Papachristodoulou (eds.), *Archaeology in the Dodecanese*: 34–38. Copenhagen: The National Museum of Denmark, Department of Near Eastern and Classical Antiquities.

Doumas, C. 1990. Archaeological observations at Akrotiri relating to the volcanic destruction. In D.A. Hardy and A.C. Renfrew (eds.), *Thera and the Aegean world III. Volume three: chronology*: 48–49. London: The Thera Foundation.

Doumas, C. 1991. High art from the time of Abraham. *Biblical Archaeology Review* 17:40–51.

Doumas, C. 1992. *The wall-paintings of Thera.* Athens: The Thera Foundation-Petros M. Nomikos.

Doumas, C. and Papazoglou, L. 1980. Santorini tephra from Rhodes. *Nature* 287:322–324.

Downey, W.S. and Tarling, D.H. 1984. Archaeomagnetic dating of Santorini volcanic eruptions and fired destruction levels of Late Minoan civilisation. *Nature* 309:519–523.

Doxey, D. 1987. Causes and effects of the fall of Knossos in 1375 B.C. *Oxford Journal of Archaeology* 6:301–324.

Drews, R. 1993. *The end of the Bronze Age: changes in warfare and the catastrophe ca. 1200 B.C.* Princeton: Princeton University Press.

Driessen, J. 1990. *An early destruction in the Mycenaean palace at Knossos: a new interpretation of the excavation field-notes of the south-east area of the West Wing.* Katholieke Universiteit Leuven Acta Archaeologica Lovaniensia Monographiae 2. Leuven: Katholieke Universiteit Leuven.

Driessen, J. and Farnoux, A. (eds.). 1997. *La Crète Mycénienne: actes de la table ronde internationale, 26–28 mars 1991.* Bulletin de Correspondance Hellénique Supplément 30. Athens: École française d'Athènes.

Driessen, J. and Macdonald, C. 1984. Some military aspects of the Aegean in the late fifteenth and early fourteenth centuries B.C. *Annual of the British School at Athens* 79:49–74.

Driessen, J. and Macdonald, C.F. 1997. *The troubled island: Minoan Crete before and after the Santorini eruption.* Aegaeum 17. Liège: Université de Liège, Histoire de l'art et archéologie de la Grèce antique.

Drower, M.S. 1973. Syria c.1550–1400 B.C. In I.E.S. Edwards, C.J. Gadd, N.G.L. Hammond and E. Sollberger (eds.), *The Cambridge Ancient History*, Vol.II, Part 1:417–525. Third edition. Cambridge: Cambridge University Press.

Druitt, T.H. and Francaviglia, V. 1990. An ancient caldera cliff line at Phira, and its significance for the topography and geology of pre-Minoan Santorini. In D.A. Hardy, J. Keller, V.P. Galanopoulos, N.C. Flemming and T.H. Druitt (eds.), *Thera and the Aegean world III. Volume two: earth sciences*: 362–369. London: The Thera Foundation.

Druitt, T.H. and Francaviglia, V. 1992. Caldera formation on Santorini and the physiography of the islands in the Late Bronze Age. *Bulletin of Volcanology* 54:484–493.

Duhoux, Y. 1998. Pre-Hellenic language(s) of Crete. *Journal of Indo-European Studies* 26:1–39.

Dumont, A. and Chaplain, J.C. 1888. *Les céramiques de la Grèce propre. Vol. I: histoire de la peinture des vases Grecs depuis les origines jusqu'au Vᵉ siècle avant Jésus-Christ.* Paris: Libraire de Firmin Didot et Cⁱᵉ.

Duncan, D.E. 1998. *The Calendar: the 5000-year struggle to align the clock and the heavens – and what happened to the missing ten days.* London: Fourth Estate.

Durand, S.R., Shelley, P.H., Antweiler, R.C. and Taylor, H.E. 1999. Trees, chemistry, and prehistory in the American Southwest. *Journal of Archaeological Science* 26:185–203.

Dutton, E.G. 1990. Comments on "major volcanic eruptions and climate: a critical evaluation". *Journal of Climate* 3:587–588.

Dutton, E.G. and Christy, J.R. 1992. Solar radiative forcing at selected locations and evidence for global lower troposphere cooling following the eruptions of El Chichón and Pinatubo. *Geophysical Research Letters* 19:2,313–2,316.

Dwyer, R.B. and Mitchell, F.J.G. 1997. Investigation of the environmental impact of remote volcanic activity on north Mayo, Ireland, during the mid-Holocene. *The Holocene* 7:113–118.

Dyson, S.L. 1993. From new to new age archaeology: archaeological theory and classical archaeology – a 1990s perspective. *American Journal of Archaeology* 97:195–206.

Eames, S.J. 1994. A re-examination of the definition, distribution, and relative chronology of Proto Base Ring ware. *Mediterranean Archaeology* 7:127–140.

Eastwood, W.J., Pearce, N.J.G., Westgate, J.A., Perkins, W.T. 1998. Recognition of Santorini (Minoan) tephra in lake sediments from Gölhisar Gölü, southwest Turkey by laser ablation ICP-MS. *Journal of Archaeological Science* 25:677–687.

Eastwood, W.J., Pearce, N.J.G., Westgate, J.A., Perkins, W.T., Lamb, H.F. and Roberts, N. 1999. Geochemistry of Santorini tephra in lake sediments from southwest Turkey. *Global and Planetary Change* 21:17–29.

Edel, E. 1997. *Der Vertag zwischen Rameses II. von Ägypten und Hattušili III. von Hatti.* Berlin: Mann.

Effinger, M. 1996. *Minoischer Schmuck.* British Archaeological Reports International Series 646. Oxford: Tempus Reparatum.

Ehrich, R.W. (ed.). 1993. *Chronologies in Old World archaeology.* Third edition. Chicago: University of Chicago Press.

el-Sabbahy, A.-F. 1993. The military entry on the verso of the Rhind Mathematical Papyrus. *Göttinger Miszellen* 133:97–100.

Epstein, C. 1966. *Palestinian bichrome ware.* Leiden: E.J. Brill.

Ericson, J.E. and Earle, T.K. (eds.). 1982. *Contexts for prehistoric exchange.* New York: Academic Press.

Eriksson, K. 1991. Red Lustrous Wheelmade Ware: a product of Late Bronze Age Cyprus. In J. Barlow, D. Bolger and B. Kling (eds.), *Cypriot ceramics: reading the prehistoric record*: 81–96. University Museum Monograph 74/University Museum Symposium Series vol.2. Philadelphia: The A.G. Leventis Foundation and the University Museum of Archaeology and Anthropology, University of Pennsylvania.

Eriksson, K.O. 1992. Late Cypriot I and Thera: relative chronology in the eastern Mediterranean. In P. Åström (ed.), *Acta Cypria: acts of an international congress on Cypriote archaeology held in Göteborg on 22–24 August 1991*, Part 3: 152–223. Studies in Mediterranean Archaeology and Literature Pocketbook 120. Jonsered: Paul Åströms Förlag.

Eriksson, K.O. 1993. *Red lustrous wheel-made ware.* Studies in Mediterranean Archaeology 103. Jonsered: Paul Åströms Förlag.

Eriksson, K.O. n.d. Cypriot Proto White Slip and White Slip I: chronological beacons on relations between Late Cypriot I Cyprus with contemporary societies of the eastern Mediterranean. Manuscript of paper presented to the White Slip Ware Conference held in Nicosia 29–30 October 1998. Paper to be published in the conference proceedings: V. Karageorghis (ed.), *White Slip Ware. Proceedings of an International Conference Organized by the Anastasios G. Leventis Foundation, Nicosia in Honour of Malcolm Wiener, Nicosia 29th–30th October 1998.* In Press.

Evans, A.J. 1900–1901. The palace of Knossos. Provisional report of the excavations for the year 1901. *Annual of the British School at Athens* 7:1–120.

Evans, A.J. 1903–1904. The palace of Knossos. *Annual of the British School at Athens* 10:1–62.

Evans, A.J. 1904–1905. The palace at Knossos and its dependencies. *Annual of the British School at Athens* 11:1–26.

Evans, A.J. 1905. The prehistoric tombs of Knossos. *Archaeologia* 59:391–562.

Evans, A.J. 1906. *Essai de classification des époques de la civilisation minoenne. Résumé d'un discours fait au congrès d'archéologie à Athènes.* London: B. Quaritch.

Evans, A.J. 1909. *Scripta Minoa. The written documents of Minoan Crete with special reference to the archives of Knossos. Volume I: the Hieroglyphic and Primitive Linear classes with an account of the discovery of the pre-Phoenician scripts, their place in Minoan story and their Mediterranean relations.* Oxford: Clarendon Press.

Evans, A.J. 1921–1935. *The palace of Minos at Knossos*, vols. I–IV. London: Macmillan.

Evans, M.E. and Mareschal, M. 1988. Secular variation and magnetic dating of fired structures in Greece. In R.M. Farquhar, R.G.V. Hancock, and L.A. Pavlish (eds.), *Proceedings of the 26th International Archaeometry Symposium held at University of Toronto, Toronto, Canada May 16th to May 20th, 1988:* 75–79. Toronto: Archaeometry Laboratory, Department of Physics, University of Toronto.

Evely, D. 1984. The other finds of stone, clay, ivory, faience, lead, etc. In M.R. Popham, *The Minoan Unexplored Mansion at Knossos:* 223–259. The British School of Archaeology at Athens, Supplementary Volume 17. London: Thames and Hudson.

Fagan, B.M., Beck, C., Michaels, G., Scarre, C. and Silberman, N.A. (eds.). 1996. *The Oxford companion to archaeology.* New York: Oxford University Press.

Fairman, H.W. and Grdseloff, B. 1947. Texts of Hatshepsut and Sethos I inside Speos Artemidos. *Journal of Egyptian Archaeology* 33:12–33.

Faulkner, R.O. 1975. Egypt: from the inception of the Nineteenth Dynasty to the death of Ramesses III. In I.E.S. Edwards, C.J. Gadd, N.G.L. Hammond and E. Sollberger (eds.), *The Cambridge Ancient History*, Vol.II, Part 2:217–251. Third edition. Cambridge: Cambridge University Press.

Faure, P. 1968. Toponymes créto-mycéniens dans une liste d'Aménophis III. *Kadmos* 7:138–149.

Faure, P. 1971. Remarques sur las présence et l'emploi de la Pierre Ponce en Crète du Néolithique à nos jours. In S. Marinatos and D. Ninkovich (eds.), *Acta of the 1st International Scientific Congress on the Volcano of Thera:* 422–427. Athens: Archaeological Services of Greece.

Federman, A.N. and Carey, S.N. 1980. Electron microprobe correlation of tephra layers from eastern Mediterranean abyssal sediments and the island of Santorini. *Quaternary Research* 13:160–171.

Ferguson, C.W. 1969. A 7104-year annual tree-ring chronology for bristlecone pine, pinus aristata, from the White Mountains, California. *Tree-Ring Bulletin* 29:2–29.

Ferguson, C.W., Huber, B. and Suess, H.E. 1966. Determination of the age of Swiss lake dwellings as an example of dendrochronologically-calibrated radiocarbon dating. *Zeitschrift für Naturforschung* 21A:1,173–1,177.

Fiacco, R.J. Jr., Palais, J.M., Germani, M.S., Zielinski, G.A. and Mayewski, P.A. 1993. Characteristics and possible source of a 1479 AD volcanic ash layer in a Greenland ice core. *Quaternary Research* 39:267–273.

Fiacco, R.J. Jr., Thordarson, T., Germani, M.S., Palais, J.M. and Whitlow, S. 1994. The 1783–84 Laki event in the GISP2 ice core: atmospheric loading and transport, and the climatic effects of aerosols produced by the Laki eruptions. *Quaternary Research* 42:231–240.

Figuier, L. 1872. *La terre et les mers.* 4th edition. Paris: Librairie Hachette.

Finkelberg, M. 1998. Bronze Age writing: contacts between East and West. *Aegaeum* 18:265–272.

Finkelstein, I. 1996a. The archaeology of the United Monarchy: an alternative view. *Levant* 28:177–187.

Finkelstein, I. 1996b. Toward a new periodization and nomenclature of the archaeology of the southern Levant. In J.S. Cooper and G.M. Schwartz (eds.), *The study of the ancient Near East in the twenty-first century: the William Foxwell Albright centennial conference:* 103–123. Winona Lake: Eisenbrauns.

Finkelstein, I. 1998a. Philistine chronology: high, middle or low? In S. Giten, A. Mazar and E. Stern (eds.), *Mediterranean peoples in transition: thirteenth to early tenth centuries BCE:* 140–147. Jerusalem: Israel Exploration Society.

Finkelstein, I. 1998b. Bible archaeology or archaeology of Palestine in the Iron Age? A rejoinder. *Levant* 30:167–174.

Finkelstein, I. 1999. Hazor and the north in the Iron Age: a low chronology perspective. *Bulletin of the American Schools of Oriental Research* 314:55–70.

Firth, C.M. and Gunn, B.G. 1926. *Excavations at Saqqara. Teti Pyramid cemeteries I–II.* Cairo: L'Institut français d'archéologie orientale.

Firth, R.J. 1992–1993. A statistical analysis of the Greekness of men's names on the Knossos Linear B tablets. *Minos* 27–28:83–97.

Fischer, P.M. 1999. Chocolate-on-White ware: typology, chronology, and provenance: the evidence from Tell Abu al-Kharaz, Jordan Valley. *Bulletin of the American Schools of Oriental Research* 313:1–29.

Fishman, B., Forbes, H. and Lawn, B. 1977. University of Pennsylvania radiocarbon dates XIX. *Radiocarbon* 19:188–228.

Fishman, B. and Lawn, B. 1978. University of Pennsylvania radiocarbon dates XX. *Radiocarbon* 20:210–233.

Fletcher, R. 1992. Time perspectivism, *Annales*, and the potential of archaeology. In A.B. Knapp (ed.), *Archaeology, Annales, and ethnohistory:* 35–49. Cambridge: Cambridge University Press.

Foote, M. and Sepkoski J.J. Jr. 1999. Absolute measures of the completeness of the fossil record. *Nature* 398:415–417.

Forsberg, S. 1995. *Near Eastern destruction datings as sources for Greek and Near Eastern Iron Age chronology. Archaeological and historical studies: the cases of Samaria (722 B.C.) and Tarsus (696 B.C.).* Boreas. Uppsala Studies in Ancient Mediterranean and Near Eastern Civilizations 19. Uppsala: Uppsala University.

Forsyth, P.Y. 1980. *Atlantis: the making of myth.* Montreal: McGill-Queen's University Press, and London: Croom Helm.

Forsyth, P.Y. 1996. The pre-eruption shape of Bronze Age Thera: a new model. *The Ancient History Bulletin* 10:1–10.

Forsyth, P.Y. 1998. *Thera in the Bronze Age.* New York: Peter Lang.

Fortin, M. 1983. Recherches sur l'architecture militaire de l'âge du bronze à Chypre. *Echos du Monde Classique/Classical Views* 27:206–219.

Fortin, M. 1989. La soi-disant forteresse d'Enkomi I (Chypre) à la fin du bronze moyen et au début du Bronze récent. *Aegaeum* 3:239–249.

Foster, K.P. and Ritner, R.K. 1996. Texts, storms, and the Thera eruption. *Journal of Near Eastern Studies* 55:1–14.

Fouqué, F. 1868. Premier rapport sur une mission scientifique à l'ile de Santorin. pp.1–30. Published by the Imprimerie Impériale, February 1868. Fouqué's report is dated by him as Paris, 1st June 1867.

Fouqué, F.A. 1879. *Santorin et ses éruptions.* Paris: G. Masson.

Fouqué, F.A. 1999. *Santorini and its eruptions.* Translated and annotated by A.R. McBirney. Baltimore: The Johns Hopkins University Press.

Francaviglia, V. 1990. Sea-borne pumice deposits of archaeological interest on Aegean and eastern Mediterranean beaches. In D.A. Hardy and A.C. Renfrew (eds.), *Thera and the Aegean world III. Volume three: chronology:* 127–134. London: The Thera Foundation.

Francis, E.D. 1990. *Image and idea in fifth-century Greece: art and literature after the Persian wars.* London: Routledge.

Francis, E.D. and Vickers, M. 1983. *Signa prisciae artis:* Eretria and Siphnos. *Journal of Hellenic Studies* 103:49–67.

Francis, E.D. and Vickers, M. 1985. Greek Geometric pottery at Hama and its implications for Near Eastern chronology. *Levant* 17:131–138.

Frank, A.G. and Gills, B.K. (eds.). 1993. *The world system: five hundred years or five thousand?* London: Routledge.

Franke, D. 1988a. Zur Chronologie des Mittleren Reiches (12.–18. Dynasty). Teil I: Die 12. Dynasty. *Orientalia* 57:113–138.

Franke, D. 1988b. Zur Chronologie des Mittleren Reiches. Teil II: Die sogenannte "Zweite Zwischenzeit" Altägyptens. *Orientalia* 57:245–274.

Frankel, D. 1974. *Middle Cypriot White Painted pottery: an analytical study of the decoration.* Studies in Mediterranean Archaeology 42. Göteborg: Paul Åströms Förlag.

Frankenstein, S. and Rowlands, M. 1978. The internal structure and regional context of Early Iron Age society in south-western Germany. *Bulletin of the Institute of Archaeology* 15:73–112.

References

Frankfort, H. 1970. *The art and architecture of the ancient orient*. Fourth edition. New Haven: Yale University Press.

French, E. 1963. Pottery groups from Mycenae: a summary. *Annual of the British School at Athens* 58:44–52.

French, E. 1993. Turkey and the east Aegean. In C. Zerner, F. Zerner and J. Winder (eds.), *Proceedings of the International Conference Wace and Blegen Pottery as evidence for trade in the Aegean Bronze Age 1939–1989 held at the American School of Classical Studies at Athens, December 2–3, 1989*: 155–158. Amsterdam: J.C. Gieben.

Frerichs, E.S. and Lesko, L.H. (eds.). 1997. *Exodus: the Egyptian evidence*. Winona Lake: Eisenbrauns.

Friedrich, W. L. 1994. *Feuer im Meer: Vulkanismus und die Naturgeschichte der Insel Santorin*. Heidelberg: Spektrum Akademischer Verlag.

Friedrich, W.L. 2000. *Fire in the sea: volcanism and the natural history of Santorini*. Cambridge: Cambridge University Press. In press.

Friedrich, W.L., Eriksen, U., Tauber, H., Heinemeier, J., Rud, N., Thomsen, M.S. and Burchardt, B. 1988. Existence of a water-filled caldera prior to the Minoan eruption of Santorini, Greece. *Naturwissenschaften* 75:567–569.

Friedrich, W.L., Friborg, R. and Tauber, H. 1980. Two radiocarbon dates of the Minoan eruption on Santorini (Greece). In C. Doumas (ed.), *Thera and the Aegean world II*: 241–243. London: Thera and the Aegean World.

Friedrich, W.L., Wagner, P. and Tauber, H. 1990. Radiocarbon dated plant remains from the Akrotiri excavation on Santorini, Greece. In D.A. Hardy and A.C. Renfrew (eds.), *Thera and the Aegean world III. Volume three: chronology*: 188–196. London: The Thera Foundation.

Frost, K.T. 1913. The *Critias* and Minoan Crete. *Journal of Hellenic Studies* 33:189–206.

Furtwaengler, A. and Loeschcke, G. 1886. *Mykenische Vasen*. Berlin: Verlag A. Asher & Co.

Furumark, A. 1941a. *The Mycenaean pottery: analysis and classification*. Stockholm: Kungl. Vitterhets Historie och Antikvitets Akademien. (Reprinted 1972 as Skrifter Utgivna av Svenska Institutet i Athen, 4°, 20.1.)

Furumark, A. 1941b. *The chronology of Mycenaean pottery*. Stockholm: Kungl. Vitterhets Historie och Antikvitets Akademien. (Reprinted 1972 as Skrifter Utgivna av Svenska Institutet i Athen, 4°, 20.2.)

Furumark, A. 1950. The settlement at Ialysos and Aegean history c. 1550–1450 BC. *Opuscula Archaeologica* 6:150–271.

Fuscaldo, P. 1998. A preliminary report on the pottery from the late Hyksos period settlement at ʿEzbet Helmi (Area H/III, strata D/3 and D/2). *Ägypten und Levante* 7:59–69.

Galanopoulos, A.G. and Bacon, E. 1969. *Atlantis: the truth behind the legend*. London: Nelson.

Gale, N.H. (ed.). 1991. *Bronze Age trade in the Mediterranean. Papers presented at the conference held at Rewley House, Oxford, in December 1989*. Studies in Mediterranean Archaeology 90. Jonsered: Paul Åströms Förlag.

Galloway, R.B., Liritzis, Y., Sampson, A. and Marketou, T. 1990. Radio-isotope analyses of Aegean tephras: contribution to the dating of Santorini volcano. In D.A. Hardy and A.C. Renfrew (eds.), *Thera and the Aegean world III. Volume three: chronology*: 135–145. London: The Thera Foundation.

Gamble, C. 1987. Archaeology, geography and time. *Progress in Human Geography* 11:227–246.

Garbe-Schönberg, C.-D., Reimann, C. and Pavlov, V.A. 1997. Laser ablation ICP-MS analyses of tree-ring profiles in pine and birch from N Norway and NW Russia – a reliable record of the pollution history of the area? *Environmental Geology* 32:9–16.

Gardiner, A.H. 1946. Davies's copy of the great Speos Artemidos inscription. *Journal of Egyptian Archaeology* 32:43–56.

Gardiner, A.H. 1959. *The Royal Canon of Turin*. Oxford: Printed for the Griffith Institute by Oxford University Press.

Gardiner, A.H. 1961. *Egypt of the pharaohs*. Oxford: Clarendon Press.

Gasche, H., Armstrong, J.A., Cole, S.W. and Gurzadyan, V.G. 1998. *Dating the fall of Babylon: a reappraisal of second-millennium chronology*. Ghent: University of Ghent and the Oriental Institute of the University of Chicago.

Gates, C. 1995. Defining boundaries of a state: the Mycenaeans and their Anatolian frontier. *Aegaeum* 12:289–298.

Gates, M.-H. Carre. 1981. Alalakh levels VI and V: a chronological reassessment. *Syro-Mesopotamian Studies* 4:11–50.

Gates, M.-H. 1987. Alalakh and chronology again. In P. Åström (ed.), *High, middle or low? Acts of an International Colloquium on Absolute Chronology held at the University of Gothenburg 20th–22nd August 1987*, Part 2: 60–86. Studies in Mediterranean Archaeology and literature Pocket-book 57. Gothenburg: Paul Åströms Förlag.

Gates, M.-H. 1988. Dialogues between ancient Near Eastern texts and the archaeological record: test cases from Bronze Age Syria. *Bulletin of the American Schools of Oriental Research* 270:63–91.

Gates, M.-H. 1996. Archaeology in Turkey. *American Journal of Archaeology* 100:277–335.

Geel, van B. and Mook, W.G. 1989. High-resolution ¹⁴C dating of organic deposits using natural atmospheric ¹⁴C variations. *Radiocarbon* 31:151–155.

Geel, van B., Plicht, van der J. and Renssen, H. 1999. Comment on "A large California flood and correlative global climatic events 400 years ago" (Schimmelmann *et al.*, 1998). *Quaternary Research* 51:108–110.

Gell, A. 1998. *Art and agency : an anthropological theory*. Oxford: Clarendon Press.

Gerlach, T.M., Westrich, H.R., Casadevall, T.J. and Finnegan, D.L. 1994. Vapor saturation and accumulation in magmas of the 1989–1990 eruption of Redoubt Volcano, Alaska. *Journal of Volcanology and Geothermal Research* 62:317–337.

Gerlach, T.M., Westrich, H.R. and Symonds, R.B. 1996. Preeruption vapor in magma of the climactic Mount Pinatubo eruption: source of the giant stratospheric sulphur dioxide cloud. In C.G. Newhall and R.S. Punongbayan (eds.), *Fire and mud: eruptions and lahars of Mount Pinatubo, Philippines*: 415–433. Seattle: University of Washington Press.

Geyh, M.A., Munro, P. and Germer, R. 1989. Zur absoluten Chronologie des Alten Reiches und der 1. Zwischenzeit nach konventionellen und kalibrierten ¹⁴C-Daten. *Studien zur altägyptischen Kultur* 16:65–81.

Giddens, A. 1984. *The constitution of society: outline of the theory of structuration*. Cambridge: Polity Press.

Giles, F.J. 1997. *The Amarna age: western Asia*. The Australian Centre for Egyptology Studies 5. Warminster: Aris and Phillips.

Gillis, C. 1995. Trade in the Late Bronze Age. In C. Gillis, C. Risberg and B. Sjöberg (eds.), *Trade and production in premonetary Greece: aspects of trade*: 61–86. Sudies in Mediterranean Archaeology and literature Pocket-book 134. Jonsered: Paul Åströms Förlag.

Gittlen, B.M. 1975. Cypriote White Slip pottery in its Palestinian stratigraphic context. In N. Robertson (ed.), *The archaeology of Cyprus: recent developments*: 111–120. Park Ridge, N.J.: Noyes Press.

Gittlen, B.M. 1977. *Studies in the Late Cypriote pottery found in Palestine*. Ph.D. dissertation, University of Pennsylvania. Ann Arbor: University Microfilms International.

Gittlen, B.M. 1981. The cultural and chronological implications of the Cypro-Palestinian trade during the Late Bronze Age. *Bulletin of the American Schools of Oriental Research* 241:49–59.

Gjerstad, E. 1926. *Studies on prehistoric Cyprus*. Uppsala: A. Börtzells Tryckeriaktiebolag.

Gjerstad, E., Lindros, J., Sjöqvist, E. and Westholm, A. 1934. Finds and results of the excavations in Cyprus 1927–1931. In E. Gjerstad, J. Lindros, E. Sjöqvist and A. Westholm, *The Swedish Cyprus Expedition* vol.I. Stockholm: The Swedish Cyprus Expedition.

Goedicke, H. 1986. The end of the Hyksos in Egypt. In L.H. Lesko (ed.), *Egyptological studies in honor of Richard A. Parker: presented on the occasion of his 78th birthday December 10, 1983*: 37–47. Hanover, N.H.: Brown University Press.

Goedicke, H. 1992. The chronology of the Thera/Santorin explosion. *Ägypten und Levante* 3:57–62.

Goldberg, J. 1995. Centuries of darkness and Egyptian chronology: another look. *Discussions in Egyptology* 33:11–32.

Gonen, R. 1987. Megiddo in the Late Bronze Age – another reassessment. *Levant* 19:83–100.

Gonen, R. 1992. *Burial patterns and cultural diversity in Late Bronze Age Canaan*. American Schools of Oriental Research Dissertation Series 7. Winona Lake: Eisenbrauns.

Gordon, C.H. 1966. *Evidence for the Minoan language*. Ventnor: Ventnor Publishers.

Görg, M. 1993. Zum Hyksoskönig Jannas. *Biblische Notizen* 70:5–8.

Görsdorf, J., Dreyer, G. and Hartung, U. 1998. ¹⁴C Dating Results of the Archaic Royal Necropolis Umm el-Qaab at Abydos. *Mitteilungen des Deutschen Archäologischen Instituts Abteilung Kairo* 54:169–175.

Gosden, C. 1994. *Social being and time*. Oxford: Blackwell.

Goslar, T. and Madry, W. 1998. Using the Bayesian method to study the precision of dating by wiggle-matching. *Radiocarbon* 40:551–560.

Grace, V.R. 1956. The Canaanite jar. In S.S. Weinberg (ed.), *The Aegean and the Near East: studies presented to Hetty Goldman on the occasion of her seventy-fifth birthday*: 80–109. Locust Valley: J.J. Augustin.

Gräslund, B. 1987. *The birth of prehistoric chronology*. Cambridge: Cambridge University Press.

Grattan, J. and Charman, D.J. 1994. Non-climatic factors and the environmental impact of volcanic volatiles: implications of the Laki fissure eruption of AD 1783. *The Holocene* 4:101–106.

Grattan, J.P. and Gilbertson, D.D. 1994. Acid-loading from Icelandic tephra falling on acidified ecosystems as a key to understanding archaeological and environmental stress in northern and western Britain. *Journal of Archaeological Science* 21:851–859.

Grayson, A.K. 1975. *Assyrian and Babylonian chronicles*. Locust Valley: J.J. Augustin.

Grayson, A.K. 1987. *Assyrian rulers of the third millennium and second millennium BC (to 1115 BC)*. Toronto: University of Toronto Press.

Graziadio, G. 1991. The process of social stratification at Mycenae in the Shaft Grave period: a comparative examination of the evidence. *American Journal of Archaeology* 95:403–440.

Graziadio, G. 1995. Egina, Rodi e Cipro: rapporti inter-insulari agli inizio del Tardo Bronzo? *Studi Micenei ed Egeo-Anatolici* 36:7–27.

Greenberg, G. 1993. Manetho rehabilitated – a new analysis of his Second Intermediate Period. *Discussions in Egyptology* 25:21–29.

Greene, K. 1997. *Archaeology: an introduction*. Third edition, fully revised, reprinted. London: Routledge.

Greene, M.T. 1992. *Natural knowledge in preclassical antiquity*. Baltimore: The Johns Hopkins University Press.

Guichard, F., Carey, S., Arthur, M.A., Sigurdsson, S. and Arnold, M. 1993. Tephra from the Minoan eruption of Santorini in sediments of the Black Sea. *Nature* 363:610–612.

Guidi, A. 1993. Le età dei metalli nell'Italia centrale e in Sardegna. In A. Guidi and M. Piperno (eds.), *Italia preistorica*: 420–470. Second edition. Rome: Editori Laterza.

Guidi, A. and Whitehouse, R. 1996. A radiocarbon chronology for the Bronze Age: the Italian situation. *Acta Archaeologica* 67:271–282.

Gulliksen, S. and Scott, M. 1995. Report of the TIRI workshop, Saturday 13 August 1994. *Radiocarbon* 37:820–821.

Gurney, O.R. 1982. Review of S. Heinhold-Krahmer, I. Hoffman, A. Kammenhuber, and G. Mauer, *Probleme der Textdatierung in der Hethitologie (Beiträge zu umstrittenen Datierungskriterien für Texte des 15. bis 13. Jahrhunderts v. Chr. Orientalistische Literaturzeitung* 77:560–563.

Gurney, O.R. 1990. *The Hittites*. Revised edition. London: Penguin.

Güterbock, H.G. 1956. The deeds of Suppiluliuma as told by his son, Mursili II. *Journal of Cuneiform Studies* 10:41–68, 75–98, 107–130.

Güterbock, H.G. 1967. Lexicographical notes III. *Revue hittite et asianique* 25:141–150.

Güterbock, H.G. 1983. The Hittites and the Aegean world. Part 1: the Ahhiyawa problem reconsidered. *American Journal of Archaeology* 87:133–138.

Güterbock, H.G. 1984. Hittites and Akhaeans: a new look. *Proceedings of the American Philosophical Society* 128:114–122.

Haas, H., Devine, J., Wenke, R., Lehner, M., Wölfli, W. and Bonani, G. 1987. Radiocarbon chronology and the historical calendar in Egypt. In O. Aurenche, J. Evin and F. Hours (eds.), *Chronologies du Proche Orient/Chronologies in the Near East. Relative chronologies and absolute chronology 16.000–4.000 BP. C.N.R.S. International Symposium Lyon (France) 24–28 November 1986*: 585–606. British Archaeological Reports International Series 379. Oxford: British Archaeological Reports.

Habachi, L. 1972. *The second stela of Kamose and his struggle against the Hyksos ruler and his capital*. Glückstadt: J.J. Augustin.

Hachmann, R. 1977. Assyrische Abstandsdaten und absolute Chronologie. *Zeitschrift des Deutschen Palästina Vereins* 93:97–130.

Hadjisavvas, S. 1977. The archaeological survey of Paphos: a preliminary report. *Report of the Department of Antiquities, Cyprus*: 222–231.

Hagens, G. 1996. A critical review of dead-reckoning from the 21st Dynasty. *Journal of the American Research Centre in Egypt* 33:153–163.

Hägg, R. and Marinatos, N. (eds.). 1984. *The Minoan Thalassocracy: myth and reality. Proceedings of the third international symposium at the Swedish Institute in Athens, 31 May–5 June, 1982*. Skrifter Utgivna av Svenska Institut i Athen, 4°, 32. Stockholm: Paul Åströms Förlag.

Haider, P.W. 1990. Ägäer in ägyptischen Diensten zwischen ca.1550 und 1200 v. Chr. *Laverna* 1:18–49.

Haider, P.W. 1996. Menschenhandel zwischen dem ägyptischen Hof und der minoisch-mykenischen Welt? *Ägypten und Levante* 6:137–156.

Hall, E. 1989. *Inventing the barbarian: Greek self-definition through tragedy.* Oxford: Clarendon Press.

Hall, G.S., Yamaguchi, D.K. and Rettberg, T.M. 1990. Multielemental analyses of tree rings by inductively coupled plasma mass spectrometry. *Journal of Radioanalytical and Nuclear Chemistry* 146:255–265.

Hall, H.R. 1901–1902. Keftiu and the peoples of the sea. *Annual of the British School at Athens* 8:157–189.

Hall, J.M. 1997. *Ethnic identity in Greek antiquity.* Cambridge: Cambridge University Press.

Hall, J.R. 1980. The time and the history of times. *History and Theory* 19:113–131.

Hall, V.A., Pilcher, J.R. and McCormac, F.G. 1994. Icelandic volcanic ash and the mid-Holocene Scots pine (*Pinus sylvestris*) decline in the north of Ireland: no correlation. *The Holocene* 4:79–83.

Hallager, B. 1993. Mycenaean pottery in Crete. In C. Zerner, F. Zerner and J. Winder (eds.), *Proceedings of the International Conference Wace and Blegen Pottery as evidence for trade in the Aegean Bronze Age 1939–1989 held at the American School of Classical Studies at Athens, December 2–3, 1989*: 263–269. Amsterdam: J.C. Gieben.

Hallager, B.P. 1997. Terminology – the Late Minoan goblet, kylix and footed cup. In E. Hallager and B.P. Hallager (eds.), *Late Minoan III pottery: chronology and terminology. Acts of a meeting held at the Danish Institute at Athens August 12–14, 1994*: 15–47. Monographs of the Danish Institute at Athens 1. Athens: Danish Institute at Athens.

Hallager, B.P. and Hallager, E. 1995. The Knossian bull: political propaganda in Neo-Palatial Crete? *Aegaeum* 12:547–556.

Hallager, E. 1978. The history of the palace at Knossos in the Late Minoan period. *Studi Micenei ed Egeo-Anatolici* 19:17–33.

Hallager, E. 1988. Final palatial Crete. An essay in Minoan chronology. In A. Damsgaard-Madsen, E. Christiansen and E. Hallager (eds.), *Studies in ancient history and numismatics presented to Rudi Thomsen*: 11–21. Aarhus: Aarhus University Press.

Hallo, W.W. 1978. Assyrian historiography revisited. *Eretz-Israel* 14:1–7.

Hallo, W.W. 1996. *Origins: the ancient Near Eastern background of some modern western institutions.* Leiden: E.J. Brill.

Halstead, P. 1989. The economy has a normal surplus: economic stability and social change among early farming communities of Thessaly, Greece. In P. Halstead and J. O'Shea (eds.), *Bad year economics. Cultural responses to risk and uncertainty*: 68–80. Cambridge: Cambridge University Press.

Halstead, P. 1994. The north–south divide: regional paths to complexity in prehistoric Greece. In C. Mathers and S. Stoddart (eds.), *Development and decline in the Mediterranean Bronze Age*: 195–219. Sheffield: John Collis Publications.

Hammer, C.U. 1977. Past volcanism revealed by Greenland ice sheet impurities. *Nature* 270:482–486.

Hammer, C.U. 1980. Acidity of polar ice cores in relation to absolute dating, past volcanism, and radio-echoes. *Journal of Glaciology* 25:359–372.

Hammer, C.U. 1984. Traces of Icelandic eruptions in the Greenland ice sheet. *Jökull* 34:51–65.

Hammer, C.U. n.d. What can Greenland ice core data tell about the Thera eruption in the 2nd millennium BC? Paper to be published from a symposium of the Austrian Academy of Sciences held in 1998.

Hammer, C.U., Clausen, H.B. and Dansgaard, W. 1980. Greenland ice sheet evidence of post-glacial volcanism and its climatic impact. *Nature* 288:230–235.

Hammer, C.U., Clausen, H.B., Friedrich, W.L. and Tauber, H. 1987. The Minoan eruption of Santorini in Greece dated to 1645 BC? *Nature* 328:517–519.

Handler, P. 1989. The effect of volcanic aerosols on global climate. *Journal of Volcanology and Geothermal Research* 37:233–249.

Hankey, V. 1973. The Aegean deposit at El Amarna. In V. Karageorghis (ed.), *Acts of the International Archaeological Symposium 'The Mycenaeans in the Eastern Mediterranean'*: 128–136. Nicosia: Department of Antiquities.

Hankey, V. 1981. The Aegean interest in El Amarna. *Journal of Mediterranean Anthropology and Archaeology* 1:38–49.

Hankey, V. 1987. The chronology of the Aegean Late Bronze Age. In P. Åström (ed.), *High, middle or low? Acts of an International Colloquium on Absolute Chronology held at the University of Gothenburg 20th–*

22nd August 1987, Part 2: 39–59. Studies in Mediterranean Archaeology and literature Pocket-book 57. Gothenburg: Paul Åströms Förlag.

Hankey, V. 1991/1992. From chronos to chronology: Egyptian evidence for dating the Aegean Bronze Age. *Journal of the Ancient Chronology Forum* 5: 99–105.

Hankey, V. 1993. A Theban 'battle axe', Queen Aahotep and the Minoans. *Minerva* 4(3):13–14.

Hankey, V. 1997. Aegean pottery at El-Amarna: shapes and decorative motifs. In J. Phillips (ed.), *Ancient Egypt, the Aegean, and the Near East: studies in honour of Martha Rhoads Bell*: 193–218. San Antonio: Van Siclen Books.

Hankey, V. and Aston, D. 1995. Mycenaean pottery at Saqqara: finds from excavations by the Egyptian Exploration Society of London and the Rijksmuseum Van Oudheden, Leiden, 1975–1990. In J.B. Carter and S.P. Morris (eds.), *The ages of Homer: a tribute to Emily Townsend Vermeule*: 67–91. Austin: University of Texas Press.

Hankey, V. and Leonard, A. Jr. 1998. Aegean LBI–II pottery in the east: 'who is the potter, pray, and who the pot?'. *Aegaeum* 18:29–37.

Hankey, V. and Tufnell, O. 1973. The tomb of Maket and its Mycenaean import. *Annual of the British School at Athens* 68:103–111.

Hankey, V. and Warren, P. 1974. The absolute chronology of the Aegean Late Bronze Age. *Bulletin of the Institute of Classical Studies* 21:142–152.

Hannestad, L. 1996. Absolute chronology: Greece and the Near East c.1000–500 BC. *Acta Archaeologica* 67:39–49.

Hansen, J.E., Lacis, A., Ruedy, R. and Sato, M. 1992. Potential climate impact of Mount Pinatubo eruption. *Geophysical Research Letters* 19:215–218.

Hardy, D.A., Doumas, C.G., Sakellarakis, J.A., and Warren, P.M. (eds.). 1990a. *Thera and the Aegean world III. Volume one: archaeology*. London: The Thera Foundation.

Hardy, D.A., Keller, J., Galanopoulos, V.P., Flemming, N.C. and Druitt, T.H. (eds.). 1990b. *Thera and the Aegean world III. Volume two: earth sciences*. London: The Thera Foundation.

Hardy, D.A. and Renfrew, A.C. (eds.). 1990. *Thera and the Aegean world III. Volume three: chronology*. London: The Thera Foundation.

Hari, R. 1980. Review of R. Krauss, *Das Ende der Amarnazeit: Beiträge zur Geschichte und Chronologie des Neuen Reiches. Bibliotheca Orientalia* 37:319–321.

Harris, J.E., Storey, A.T. and Ponitz, P.V. 1980. Dental diseases in the royal mummies. In J.E. Harris and E.F. Wente (eds.), *An X-Ray atlas of the royal mummies*: 328–346. Chicago: The University of Chicago Press.

Harris, J.R. 1973. Nefernefruaten. *Göttinger Miszellen* 4:15–17.

Harris, J.R. 1974. Nefernefruaton regnans. *Acta Orientalia* 36:11–21.

Harris, J.R. 1992. Akhenaten and Nefernefruaten in the Tomb of Tut'ankhamun. In C.N. Reeves (ed.), *After Tut'ankhamun: research and excavations in the Royal Necropolis at Thebes*: 55–72. London: Kegan Paul International.

Harvey, S.P. 1994. Monuments of Ahmose at Abydos. *Egyptian Archaeology* 4:3–5.

Harvey, S.P. 1995. The monuments of Ahmose: new perspectives on the earliest Eighteenth Dynasty at Abydos. In C. Eyre (ed.), *Seventh International Congress of Egyptologists Cambridge, 3–9 September 1995. Abstracts of papers*: 81–82. Oxford: Oxbow books for International Association of Egyptologists.

Haskell, H.W. 1989. LMIII Knossos: evidence beyond the palace. *Studi Micenei ed Egeo-Anatolici* 27:81–110.

Hassan, F.A. 1986. The restoration of time: radiocarbon dating 1965–1985/6. *Quarterly Review of Archaeology* 7(2):5–6.

Hassan, F.A. and Robinson, S.W. 1987. High-precision radiocarbon chronometry of ancient Egypt, and comparisons with Nubia, Palestine and Mesopotamia. *Antiquity* 61:119–135.

Hayes, J.H. and Hooker, P.K. 1988. *A new chronology for the kings of Israel and Judah and its implications for Biblical history and literature*. Atlanta: John Knox Press.

Hayes, W.C. 1970. Chronology I. Egypt – to the end of the twentieth dynasty. In I.E.S. Edwards, C.J. Gadd and N.G.L. Hammond (eds.), *The Cambridge Ancient History*, vol.I, Part 1:173–193. Third edition. Cambridge: Cambridge University Press.

Hayes, W.C. 1973. Egypt: internal affairs from Tuthmosis I to the death of Amenophis III. In I.E.S. Edwards, C.J. Gadd, N.G.L. Hammond and E. Sollberger (eds.), *The Cambridge Ancient History*, Vol.II, Part 1:313–416. Third edition. Cambridge: Cambridge University Press.

Hayes, W.C. 1990. *The Scepter of Egypt: a background for the study of the Egyptian antiquities in the Metropolitan*

Museum of Art. Period II: the Hyksos period and the New Kingdom (1675–1080 B.C.). Fourth Printing (revised). New York: The Metropolitan Museum of Art.

Hedges, R.E.M., Housley, R.A., Bronk, C.R. and van Klinken, G.J. 1990. Radiocarbon dates from the Oxford AMS system: *Archaeometry* datelist 11. *Archaeometry* 32:211–237.

Heidegger, M. 1962. *Being and time.* Trans. J. MacQuarrie and E. Robinson. Oxford: Blackwell.

Heiken, G. and McCoy, F.W. 1984. Caldera development during the Minoan eruption, Thira, Cyclades, Greece. *Journal of Geophysical Research* 89 B10:8,441–8,462.

Heiken, G., McCoy, F. and Sheridan, M. 1990. Palaeotopographic and palaeogeologic reconstruction of Minoan Thera. In D.A. Hardy, J. Keller, V.P. Galanopoulos, N.C. Flemming and T.H. Druitt (eds.), *Thera and the Aegean world III. Volume two: earth sciences:* 370–376. London: The Thera Foundation.

Hein, I. 1994a. Erste Beobachtungen zur Keramik aus ᶜEzbet Helmi. *Ägypten und Levante* 4:39–43.

Hein, I. (catalogue editor) 1994b. *Pharaonen und fremde Dynastien im Dunkel.* Vienna: Museen der Stadt Wien.

Hein, I. 1998. ᶜEzbet Helmi – Tell el-Dabᶜa: chronological aspects of pottery. In C.J. Eyre (ed.), *Proceedings of the Seventh International Congress of Egyptologists, Cambridge, 3–9 September 1995:* 547–554. Orientalia Lovaniensia Analecta 82. Leuven: Uitgeverij Peeters.

Heinhold-Krahmer, S., Hoffman, I., Kammenhuber, A. and Mauer, G. 1979. *Probleme der Textdatierung in der Hethitologie (Beiträge zu umstrittenen Datierungskriterien für Texte des 15. bis 13. Jahrhunderts v. Chr.* Texte der Hethiter 9. Heidelberg: Carl Winter.

Heinz, M. 1992. *Tell Atchana/Alalakh: Die Schichten VII–XVII.* Alter Orient und Altes Testament 41. Kevelaer and Neukirchener-Vluyn: Verlag Butzon & Bercker and Neukirchener Verlag.

Heinz, M. 1993. Anmerkung zu T. McClellan, "The Chronology and Ceramic Assemblages of Alalakh". *Akkadica* 83:1–28.

Helck, W. 1975. *Historisch-Biographische Texte der 2. Zwischenzeit und Neue Texte der 18. Dynastie.* Wiesbaden: Harrassowitz.

Helck, W. 1979. *Die Beziehungen Ägyptens und Vorderasiens zur Ägäis bis ins 7. Jahrhundert v. Chr.* Erträge der Forschung 120. Darmstadt: Wissenschaftliche Buchgesellschaft.

Helck, W. 1983. Haremhab und das Sothisdatum des Pap. Ebers. *Göttinger Miszellen* 67:47–49.

Helck, W. 1987. "Was kann die Ägyptologie wirklich zum Problem der absoluten Chronologie in der Bronzezeit beitragen?" Chronologische Annäherungswerte in der 18. Dynastie. In P. Åström (ed.), *High, middle or low? Acts of an International Colloquium on Absolute Chronology held at the University of Gothenburg 20th–22nd August 1987,* Part 1: 18–26. Studies in Mediterranean Archaeology and literature Pocket-book 56. Gothenburg: Paul Åströms Förlag.

Helck, W. 1988. Erneut das angebliche Sothis-Datum des Pap. Ebers und die Chronologie der 18. Dynastie. *Studien zur altägyptischen Kultur* 15:149–164.

Helck, W. 1992a. Anmerkungen zum Turiner Königspapyrus. *Studien zur altägyptischen Kulture* 19:151–216.

Helck, W. 1992b. Zur Chronologiediskussion über das Neue Reich. *Ägypten und Levante* 3:63–68.

Helck, W. 1993. Das Hyksosproblem. *Orientalia* 62:60–66.

Helck, W. 1995. *Die Beziehungen Ägyptens und Vorderasiens zur Ägäis bis ins 7. Jahrhundert v. Chr.* 2nd ed., (ed.) R. Drenkhahn. Erträge der Forschung 120. Darmstadt: Wissenschaftliche Buchgesellschaft.

Hellbing, L. 1979. *Alashia problems.* Studies in Mediterranean Archaeology 57. Göteborg: Paul Åströms Förlag

Helms, M.W. 1988. *Ulysses' sail: an ethnographic odyssey of power, knowledge, and geographical distance.* Princeton: Princeton University Press.

Helms, M.W. 1992. Long-distance contacts, élite aspirations, and the age of discovery in cosmological context. In E.M. Schortman and P.A. Urban (eds.), *Resources, power, and interregional interaction:* 157–174. New York: Plenum Press.

Helms, M.W. 1993. *Craft and the kingly ideal: art, trade, and power.* Austin: University of Texas Press.

Henige, D. 1981. Generation-counting and late New Kingdom chronology. *Journal of Egyptian Archaeology* 67:182–184.

Henige, D. 1986. Comparative chronology and the ancient Near East: a case for symbiosis. *Bulletin of the American Schools of Oriental Research* 261:57–68.

Hennessy, J.B. 1963. *Stephania: a Middle and Late Bronze Age cemetery in Cyprus.* London: Quaritch.

Hennessy, J.B. 1997. Some observations on the archaeology of the Amarna age in Cyprus and the Levant. In F.J. Giles, *The Amarna age: western Asia:* 349–379. The Australian Centre for Egyptology Studies 5. Warminster: Aris and Phillips.

Herscher, E. 1976. South coast ceramic styles at the end of the Middle Cypriot. *Report of the Department of Antiquities, Cyprus:* 11–19.

Herscher, E. 1981. Southern Cyprus, the disappearing Early Bronze Age and the evidence from Phaneromeni. In J.C. Biers and D. Soren (eds.), *Studies in Cypriote archaeology:* 79–85. Monograph 18. Los Angeles: Institute of Archaeology, University of California.

Herscher, E. 1984. The pottery of Maroni and regionalism in Late Bronze Age Cyprus. In V. Karageorghis and J.D. Muhly (eds.), *Cyprus at the close of the Late Bronze Age:* 23–28. Nicosia: A.G. Leventis Foundation.

Herscher, E. 1991. Beyond regionalism: toward an islandwide Early and Middle Cypriot sequence. In J. Barlow, D. Bolger and B. Kling (eds.), *Cypriot ceramics: reading the prehistoric record:* 45–50. University Museum Monograph 74/University Museum Symposium Series vol.2. Philadelphia: The A.G. Leventis Foundation and the University Museum of Archaeology and Anthropology, University of Pennsylvania.

Herscher, E. and Fox, S.C. 1993. A Middle Bronze Age tomb from western Cyprus. *Report of the Department of Antiquities, Cyprus:* 69–80.

Heurtley, W.A. 1939. A Palestinian vase-painter of the sixteenth century B.C. *Quarterly of the Department of Antiquities of Palestine* 8:21–37.

Higgins, R. 1997. *Minoan and Mycenaean art.* New revised edition. London: Thames and Hudson.

Hiller, S. 1975. Die Explosion des Vulkans von Thera. *Gymnasium* 82:32–74.

Hiller, S. 1978. Minoan Qe-Ra-Si-Ja. The religious impact of the Thera volcano on Minoan Crete. In C. Doumas (ed.), *Thera and the Aegean world I:* 675–679. London: Thera and the Aegean World.

Hiller, S. 1984. Pax Minoica versus Minoan Thalassocracy. Military aspects of Minoan culture. In R. Hägg and N. Marinatos (eds.), *The Minoan thalassocracy: myth and reality. Proceedings of the third international symposium at the Swedish Institute in Athens, 31 May–5 June, 1982:* 27–30. Skrifter Utgivna av Svenska Institutet i Athen, 4°, 32. Stockholm: Paul Åströms Förlag.

Hiller, S. 1990. The Miniature Frieze in the West House – evidence for Minoan poetry? In D.A. Hardy, C.G. Doumas, J.A. Sakellarakis and P.M. Warren (eds.), *Thera and the Aegean world III. Volume one: archaeology:* 229–236. London: The Thera Foundation.

Hiller, S. 1995. Der SM II-Palaststil. Ausdruck politischer Ideologie? *Aegaeum* 12:561–573.

Hiller, S. 1996. Zur Rezeption Ägyptischer Motive in der Minoischen Freskenkunst. *Ägypten und Levante* 6:83–105.

Hobbs, P.V. (ed.). 1993. *Aerosol–cloud–climate interactions.* San Diego: Academic Press.

Höckmann, O. 1974. Die Katastrophe von Thera: Archäologische Gesichtspunkte. *Jahrbuch des Römisch-Germanischen Zentralmuseums, Mainz* 21:46–92.

Hodder, I. 1991. *Reading the past: current approaches to interpretation in archaeology.* Second edition. Cambridge: Cambridge University Press.

Hodder, I. 1992. *Theory and practice in archaeology.* London: Routledge.

Hodder, I. 1995. Material culture in time. In I. Hodder, M. Shanks, A. Alexandri, V. Buchli, J. Carmen, J. Last and G. Lucas (eds.), *Interpreting archaeology: finding meaning in the past:* 164–168. London: Routledge.

Hodder, I. (ed.). 1996. *On the surface.* London: British Institute of Archaeology at Ankara/Cambridge: McDonald Institute.

Hodder, I. 1997. 'Always momentary, fluid and flexible': towards a reflexive excavation methodology. *Antiquity* 71:691–700.

Hodder, I. 1999. *The archaeological process: an introduction.* Oxford: Blackwell Publishers.

Hoffmeier, J.K. 1989. Reconsidering Egypt's part in the termination of the Middle Bronze Age in Palestine. *Levant* 21:181–193.

Hoffmeier, J.K. 1990. Some thoughts on William G. Dever's '"Hyksos", Egyptian destructions, and the end of the Palestinian Middle Bronze Age'. *Levant* 22:83–89.

Hoffmeier, J.K. 1991. James Weinstein's 'Egypt and the Middle Bronze IIC/Late Bronze IA transition': a rejoinder. *Levant* 23:117–124.

Hoffmeier, J.K. 1997. *Israel in Egypt: the evidence for the authenticity of the Exodus tradition.* New York: Oxford University Press.

Hogg, A.G., Higham, T., Robertson, S., Beukens, R., Kankainen, T., McCormac, F.G., van der Plicht, J. and Stuiver, M. 1995. Radiocarbon age assessment of a new, near background IAEA ^{14}C quality assurance material. *Radiocarbon* 37:797–803.

Holladay, J.S. Jr. 1997. The eastern Nile Delta during the Hyksos and pre-Hyksos periods: toward a systemic/socioeconomic understanding. In E.D. Oren (ed.), *The Hyksos: new historical and archaeological perspectives:* 183–252. Philadelphia: The University Museum, University of Pennsylvania.

Holmes, Y. 1975. The foreign trade of Cyprus during the Late Bronze Age. In N. Robertson (ed.), *The archaeology of Cyprus: recent developments:* 90–110. Park Ridge, N.J.: Noyes Press.

Hood, S. 1964. To the editor. *Nestor* 2:342–343.

Hood, S. 1970. The International Scientific Congress on the Volcano of Thera. *Kadmos* 9:98–106.

Hood, S. 1978a. Discrepancies in 14C dating as illustrated from the Egyptian New and Middle Kingdoms and from the Aegean Bronze Age and Neolithic. *Archaeometry* 20:197–199.

Hood, S. 1978b. *The arts in prehistoric Greece.* London: Penguin.

Hood, S. 1978c. Traces of the eruption outside Thera. In C. Doumas (ed.), *Thera and the Aegean world I:* 681–690. London: Thera and the Aegean World.

Hood, S. 1995. The Bronze Age context of Homer. In J.B. Carter and S.P. Morris (eds.), *The ages of Homer: a tribute to Emily Townsend Vermeule:* 25–32. Austin: University of Texas Press.

Hood, S. 1996. Back to basics with Middle Minoan IIIB. In D. Evely, I.S. Lemos and S. Sherratt (eds.), *Minotaur and Centaur: studies in the archaeology of Crete and Euboea presented to Mervyn Popham:* 10–16. British Archaeological Reports International Series 638. Oxford: Tempus Reparatum.

Hornung, E. 1964. *Untersuchungen zur Chronologie und Geschichte des Neuen Reiches.* Wiesbaden: Harrassowitz.

Housley, R.A., Hedges, R.E.M., Law, I.A. and Bronk, C.R. 1990. Radiocarbon dating by AMS of the destruction of Akrotiri. In D.A. Hardy and A.C. Renfrew (eds.), *Thera and the Aegean world III. Volume three: chronology:* 207–215. London: The Thera Foundation.

Housley, R.A., Manning, S.W., Cadogan, G., Jones, R.E. and Hedges, R.E.M. 1999. Radiocarbon, calibration, and the chronology of the Late Minoan IB phase. *Journal of Archaeological Science* 26:159–171.

Houwink ten Cate, P.H.J. 1970. *The records of the early Hittite empire (c.1450–1380 BC).* Uitgaven van het Nederlands Historisch-Archaeologisch Instituut et Istanbul 26. Ankara: Nederlands Historisch-Archaeologisch Instituut in het Nabije Oosten.

Hubberten, H-W., Bruns, M., Calamiotou, M., Apostolakis, C., Filippakis, S. and Grimanis, A. 1990. Radiocarbon dates from the Akrotiri excavations. In D.A. Hardy and A.C. Renfrew (eds.), *Thera and the Aegean world III. Volume three: chronology:* 179–187. London: The Thera Foundation.

Huber, P.J. with the collaboration of A. Sachs, M. Stol, R.M. Whiting, E. Leichty, C.B.F. Walker and G. van Driel. 1982. *Astronomical dating of Babylon I and Ur III.* Occasional Papers on the Near East 1.4. Malibu: Undena Publications.

Huber, P.J. 1987. Astronomical evidence for the Long and against the Middle and Short chronologies. In P. Åström (ed.), *High, middle or low? Acts of an International Colloquium on Absolute Chronology held at the University of Gothenburg 20th–22nd August 1987,* Part 1: 5–17. Studies in Mediterranean Archaeology and literature Pocket-book 56. Gothenburg: Paul Åströms Förlag.

Hughes, M.K. 1988. Ice layer dating of the eruption of Santorini. *Nature* 335:211–212.

Hunt, J.B. 1993. Volcanology, volcanic eruptions, aerosols and climate: a post-Pinatubo assessment. *Quaternary Newsletter* 69:17–22.

Hunt, J.B. and Hill, P.G. 1993. Tephra geochemistry: a discussion of some persistent analytical problems. *The Holocene* 3:271–278.

Hunt, J.B. and Hill, P.G. 1994. Geochemical data in tephrachronology: a reply to Bennett. *The Holocene* 4:436–438.

Imai, A., Listanco, E.L. and Fujii, T. 1993. Petrologic and sulphur isotopic significance of highly oxidized and sulphur-rich magma of Mt. Pinatubo, Philippines. *Geology* 21:699–702.

Immerwahr, S.A. 1990. *Aegean painting in the Bronze Age.* University Park, Pennsylvania State University: Pennsylvania State University Press.

Ingham, M.F. 1969. The length of the Sothic cycle. *Journal of Egyptian Archaeology* 55:36–40.

International Study Group 1982. An inter-laboratory comparison of radiocarbon measurements in tree rings. *Nature* 298:619–623.

Jacobsson, I. 1994. *Aegyptiaca from Late Bronze Age Cyprus.* Studies in Mediterranean Archaeology 112. Jonsered: Paul Åströms Förlag.

Jacoby, F. 1958. *Die Fragmente der Griechischen Historiker.* Part III.C. Leiden: E.J. Brill.

James, P. 1995. *The sunken kingdom: the Atlantis mystery solved.* London: Pimlico.

James, P., Thorpe, I.J., Kokkinos, N., Morkot, R. and Frankish, J. 1991a. *Centuries of darkness*. London: Jonathan Cape.

James, P., Thorpe, I.J., Kokkinos, N., Morkot, R. and Frankish, J. 1991b. Centuries of darkness: context, methodology and implications. *Cambridge Archaeological Journal* 1:228–235.

James, P., Thorpe, I.J., Kokkinos, N., Morkot, R. and Frankish, J. 1992. Centuries of darkness: a reply to critics. *Cambridge Archaeological Journal* 2:127–130.

James, P., Kokkinos, N. and Thorpe, I.J. 1998. Mediterranean chronology in crisis. In M.S. Balmuth and R.H. Tykot (eds.), *Sardinian and Aegean chronology: towards the resolution of relative and absolute dating in the Mediterranean*: 29–43. Studies in Sardinian Archaeology V. Oxford: Oxbow.

Janko, R. 1998. The Homeric poems as oral dictated texts. *Classical Quarterly* 48:135–167.

Jánosi, P. 1995. Die Stratigraphische Position und Verteilung der minoischen Wandfragmente in den Grabungsplätzen H/I und H/IV von Tell el-Dabᶜa. *Ägypten und Levante* 5:63–71.

Jansen-Winkeln, K. 1997. Zu den Koregenzen der 12. Dynastie. *Studien zur altägyptischen Kultur* 24:115–135.

Jenkins, K. 1991. *Re-thinking history*. London: Routledge.

Jirikowic, J.L. and Kalin, R.M. 1993. A possible ENSO indicator in the spatial variation of tree-ring radiocarbon. *Geophysical Research Letters* 20:439–442.

Johnsen, S.J., Clausen, H.B., Dansgaard, W., Fuhrer, K., Gundestrup, N., Hammer, C.U., Iversen, P., Jouzel, J., Stauffer, B. and Steffensen, J.P. 1992. Irregular glacial interstadials recorded in a new Greenland ice core. *Nature* 359:311–313.

Johnson, G.A. 1982. Organisational structure and scalar stress. In C. Renfrew, M.J. Rowlands and B.A. Segraves (eds.), *Theory and explanation in archaeology: the Southampton conference*: 389–421. New York: Academic Press.

Johnson, J. 1980. *Maroni de Chypre*. Studies in Mediterranean Archaeology 59. Gothenburg: Paul Åströms Förlag.

Johnson, J.W. 1962. Chronological writing: its concepts and development. *History and Theory* 2:124–145.

Johnson, P. 1982. The Middle Cypriote pottery found in Palestine. *Opuscula Atheniensia* 14:49–72.

Johnson, W.R. 1996. Amenhotep III and Amarna: some new considerations. *Journal of Egyptian Archaeology* 82:65–82.

Johnson, W.R. 1998. Monuments and monumental art under Amenhotep III: evolution and meaning. In D. O'Connor and E.H. Cline (eds.), *Amenhotep III: perspectives on his reign*: 63–94. Ann Arbor: The University of Michigan Press.

Johnstone, B. 1997. Who killed the Minoans? *New Scientist* 154 (no.2087):36–39.

Johnstone, W. 1971. A Late Bronze Age tholos tomb at Enkomi. In C.F.-A. Schaeffer (ed.), *Alasia I*: 51–122. Mission Archéologique d'Alasia IV. Paris: Mission Archéologique d'Alasia/Klincksieck.

Jones, P.D., Briffa, K.R. and Schweingruber, F.H. 1995. Tree-ring evidence of the widespread effects of explosive volcanic eruptions. *Geophysical Research Letters* 22:1,333–1,336.

Jones, R.E. 1986. *Greek and Cypriot pottery: a review of scientific studies*. Fitch Laboratory Occasional Paper 1. Athens: The British School at Athens.

Jones, S. 1997. *The archaeology of ethnicity: constructing identities in the past and present*. London: Routledge.

Jong, A.F.M. de, Mook, W.G. and Becker, B. 1979. Confirmation of the Suess wiggles: 3200–700 BC. *Nature* 280:48–49.

Kaiser, B. 1976. *Untersuchungen zum minoischen Relief*. Bonn: Dr. Rudolf Habelt.

Kalela-Brundin, M. 1999. Climatic information from tree-rings of *Pinus sylvestris* L. and a reconstruction of summer temperatures back to AD1500 in Femundsmarka, eastern Norway, using partial least squares regression (PLS) analysis. *The Holocene* 9:59–77.

Kalin, R.M., McCormac, F.G., Damon, P.E., Eastoe, C.J. and Long, A. 1995. Intercomparison of high-precision ^{14}C measurements at the University of Arizona and the Queen's University of Belfast radiocarbon laboratories. *Radiocarbon* 37:33–38.

Kanta, A. 1980. *The Late Minoan III period in Crete: a survey of sites, pottery and their distribution*. Studies in Mediterranean Archaeology 58. Göteborg: Paul Åströms Förlag.

Kantor, H.J. 1947. The Aegean and the Orient in the second millennium B.C. *American Journal of Archaeology* 51:1–103. [reprinted in 1997 by the Archaeological Institute of America]

Kantor, H.J. 1956. Syro-Palestinian ivories. *Journal of Near Eastern Studies* 15:153–174.

Kantor, H.J. 1965. The relative chronology of Egypt and its foreign correlations before the Late Bronze Age. In R.W. Ehrich (ed.), *Chronologies in Old World archaeology*: 1–46. Chicago: University of Chicago Press.

Kaplan, M.F. 1980. *The origin and distribution of Tell el Yahudiyeh ware*. Studies in Mediterranean Archaeology 62. Göteborg: Paul Åströms Förlag.

Karageorghis, V. 1965. *Nouveaux documents pour l'étude du Bronze Récent à Chypre*. Études Chypriotes 3. Paris: Boccard.

Karageorghis, V. 1990. *The end of the Late Bronze Age in Cyprus*. Nicosia: Pierides Foundation.

Karageorghis, V. 1995. Relations between Cyprus and Egypt – Second Intermediate Period and XIIIth Dynasty. *Ägypten und Levante* 5:73–79.

Karageorghis, V., Michaelides, D., *et al.* 1990. *Tombs at Palaepaphos. 1. Teratsoudhia. 2. Eliomylia*. Nicosia: A.G. Leventis Foundation.

Karlsson, H. 1997. *Being and post-processual archaeological thinking: reflections upon post-processual archaeologies and anthropocentrism*. Göteborg: Göteborg University, Department of Archaeology.

Kastens, K.A. and Cita, M.B. 1981. Tsunami-induced sediment transport in the abyssal Mediterranean Sea. *Geological Society of America Bulletin* 92:845–857.

Keller, J., Rehren, T. and Stadlbauer, E. 1990. Explosive volcanism in the Hellenic Arc: a summary and review. In D.A. Hardy, J. Keller, V.P. Galanopoulos, N.C. Flemming and T.H. Druitt (eds.), *Thera and the Aegean world III. Volume two: earth sciences*: 13–26. London: The Thera Foundation.

Kelly, P.M. and Sear, C.B. 1984. Climatic impact of explosive volcanic eruptions. *Nature* 311:740–743.

Kemp, B.J. 1980. Egyptian radiocarbon dating: a reply to James Mellaart. *Antiquity* 54:25–28.

Kemp, B.J. 1983. Old Kingdom, Middle Kingdom and Second Intermediate Period c.2686–1552 BC. In B.G. Trigger, B.J. Kemp, D. O'Connor and A.B. Lloyd, *Ancient Egypt: a social history*. Cambridge: Cambridge University Press.

Kemp, B.J. 1992. Explaining ancient crises. *Cambridge Archaeological Journal* 1:239–244.

Kemp, B.J. and Merrillees, R.S. 1980. *Minoan pottery in second millennium Egypt*. Mainz am Rhein: Philipp von Zabern.

Kempinski, A. 1974. Tell el-ʿAjjul – Beth-Aglayim or Sharuhen? *Israel Exploration Journal* 24:145–152.

Kempinski, A. 1983. *Syrien und Palästina (Kanaan) in der letzten Phase der Mittelbronze IIB Zeit (1650–1570 v. Chr.)*. Weisbaden: Harrassowitz.

Kempinski, A. 1989. *Megiddo: a city-state and royal centre in north Israel*. Munich: C.H. Beck Verlag.

Kempinski, A. 1992a. The Middle Bronze Age. In A. Ben-Tor (ed.), *The archaeology of ancient Israel*: 159–210. Trans. R. Greenberg. New Haven and London: Yale University Press and The Open University of Israel.

Kempinski, A. 1992b. The Middle Bronze Age in northern Israel, local and external synchronisms. *Ägypten und Levante* 3:69–73.

Kempinski, A. 1997. The Hyksos: a view from northern Canaan and Syria. In E.D. Oren (ed.), *The Hyksos: new historical and archaeological perspectives*: 327–334. Philadelphia: The University Museum, University of Pennsylvania.

Kenyon, K.M. 1960. *Excavations at Jericho. Volume One: the tombs excavated in 1952–4*. London: British School of Archaeology in Jerusalem.

Kenyon, K.M. 1965. *Excavations at Jericho. Volume Two: the tombs excavated in 1955–8*. London: British School of Archaeology in Jerusalem.

Kenyon, K. 1973. Palestine in the time of the Eighteenth Dynasty. In I.E.S. Edwards, C.J. Gadd, N.G.L. Hammond and E. Sollberger (eds.), *The Cambridge Ancient History*, Vol.II, Part 1:526–556. Third edition. Cambridge: Cambridge University Press.

Keswani, P.F.S. 1989a. *Mortuary ritual and social hierarchy in Bronze Age Cyprus*. Ph.D. dissertation, University of Michigan. Ann Arbor: University Microfilms International.

Keswani, P.S. 1989b. Dimensions of social hierarchy in Late Bronze Age Cyprus: an analysis of the mortuary data from Enkomi. *Journal of Mediterranean Archaeology* 2:49–86.

Keswani, P.S. 1996. Hierarchies, heterarchies, and urbanization processes: the view from Bronze Age Cyprus. *Journal of Mediterranean Archaeology* 9:211–250.

Killen, J. 1977. The Knossos texts and the geography of Mycenaean Crete. In J. Bintliff (ed.), *Mycenaean Geography. Proceedings of the Cambridge Colloquium, September 1976*: 40–47. Cambridge: British Association for Mycenaean Studies.

Kitchen, K.A. 1973. *The Third Intermediate Period in Egypt (1100–650 B.C.)*. Warminster: Aris & Phillips.

Kitchen, K.A. 1978. Review of E.F. Wente and J.H. Johnson (eds.), *Studies in honor of George R. Hughes, January 12, 1977. Serapis* 4:65–80.

Kitchen, K.A. 1982. *Pharaoh triumphant: the life and times of Ramesses II.* Warminster: Aris & Phillips.

Kitchen, K.A. 1986. *The Third Intermediate Period in Egypt (1100–650 B.C.).* Second Edition. Warminster: Aris & Phillips.

Kitchen, K.A. 1987. The basics of Egyptian chronology in relation to the Bronze Age. In P. Åström (ed.), *High, middle or low? Acts of an International Colloquium on Absolute Chronology held at the University of Gothenburg 20th–22nd August 1987,* Part 1: 37–55. Studies in Mediterranean Archaeology and literature Pocket-book 56. Gothenburg: Paul Åströms Förlag.

Kitchen, K.A. 1989. Supplementary notes on 'the basics of Egyptian chronology'. In P. Åström (ed.), *High, middle or low? Acts of an International Colloquium on Absolute Chronology held at the University of Gothenburg 20th–22nd August 1987,* Part 3: 152–159. Studies in Mediterranean Archaeology and literature Pocket-book 80. Gothenburg: Paul Åströms Förlag.

Kitchen, K.A. 1991. The chronology of ancient Egypt. *World Archaeology* 23:201–208.

Kitchen, K.A. 1992. Egyptian chronology: problem or solution? *Cambridge Archaeological Journal* 1:235–239.

Kitchen, K.A. 1995. *Ramesside inscriptions translated and annotated. Translations. Volume II: Ramesses II, royal inscriptions.* Oxford: Blackwell.

Kitchen, K.A. 1996a. The historical chronology of ancient Egypt, a current assessment. *Acta Archaeologica* 67:1–13.

Kitchen, K.A. 1996b. *The Third Intermediate Period in Egypt (1100–650 BC).* Second revised edition with supplement. Warminster: Aris & Phillips.

Kitchen, K.A. 1998. Amenhotep III and Mesopotamia. In D. O'Connor and E.H. Cline (eds.), *Amenhotep III: perspectives on his reign:* 250–261. Ann Arbor: The University of Michigan Press.

Kleinmann, B. 1974. Die Katastrophe von Thera: Geologie eines Vulkans. *Jahrbuch des Römisch-Germanischen Zentralmuseums, Mainz* 21:12–45.

Kling, B.B. 1989. *Mycenaean IIIC:1b and related pottery in Cyprus.* Studies in Mediterranean Archaeology 87. Göteborg: Paul Åströms Förlag.

Klinken, G.J. van, Bowles, A.D. and Hedges, R.E.M. 1994. Radiocarbon dating of collagenase peptides isolated from contaminated fossil bone collagen by reversed-phase chromatography. *Geochimica et Cosmochimica Acta* 58:2,543–2,551.

Klinken, G.J. van and Hedges, R.E.M. 1992. Experiments on ^{14}C dating of contaminated bone using peptides resulting from enzymatic cleavage of collagen. *Radiocarbon* 34:292–295.

Knapp, A.B. 1979. *A re-examination of the interpretation of Cypriote material culture in the MCIII–LCI period in the light of textual data.* Ph.D. dissertation, University of California, Berkeley. Ann Arbor: University Microfilms International.

Knapp, A.B. 1985. *Alashiya, Caphtor/Keftiu,* and eastern Mediterranean trade: recent studies in Cypriote archaeology and history. *Journal of Field Archaeology* 12:231–250.

Knapp, A.B. 1986a. Production, exchange and socio-political complexity on Bronze Age Cyprus. *Oxford Journal of Archaeology* 5:35–60.

Knapp, A.B. 1986b. *Copper production and divine protection: archaeology, ideology and social complexity on Bronze Age Cyprus.* Studies in Mediterranean Archaeology Pocket-book 42. Göteborg: Paul Åströms Förlag.

Knapp, A.B. (ed.). 1992. *Archaeology, Annales, and ethnohistory.* Cambridge: Cambridge University Press.

Knapp, A.B. 1994. Emergence, development and decline on Bronze Age Cyprus. In C. Mathers and S. Stoddart (eds.), *Development and decline in the Mediterranean Bronze Age:* 271–304. Sheffield: J.R. Collis Publications.

Knapp, A.B. (ed.). 1996. *Sources for the history of Cyprus. Volume II: Near Eastern and Aegean texts from the third to the first millennia BC.* Altamont: Greece and Cyprus Research Centre.

Knapp, A.B. 1997. *The archaeology of Late Bronze Age Cypriot society: the study of settlement, survey and landscape.* Glasgow: Department of Archaeology, University of Glasgow.

Knapp, A.B. 1998. Mediterranean Bronze Age trade: distance, power and place. *Aegaeum* 18:193–207.

Knapp, A.B. and Cherry, J.F. 1994. *Provenience studies and Bronze Age Cyprus: production, exchange and politico-economic change.* Monographs in World Archaeology no.21. Madison: Prehistory Press.

Knapp, A.B. and Marchant, A. 1982. Cyprus, Cypro-Minoan and Hurrians. *Report of the Department of Antiquities, Cyprus:* 15–30.

Kohler, E.L. and Ralph, E.K. 1961. C-14 dates for sites in the Mediterranean area. *American Journal of Archaeology* 65:357–367.

Kopcke, G. and Tokumaru, I. (eds.). 1992. *Greece between east and west: 10th–8th centuries BC*: Mainz am Rhein: Philipp von Zabern.

Kopytoff, I. 1986. The cultural biography of things: commoditization as process. In A. Appadurai (ed.), *The social life of things: commodities in cultural perspective:* 64–91. Cambridge: Cambridge University Press.

Korfmann, M. 1997. Troia – Ausgrabungen 1996. *Studia Troica* 7:1–71.

Korfmann, M. and Kromer, B. 1993. Demircihüyük, Besik-Tepe, Troia – Eine Zwischenbilanz zur Chronologie dreier Orte in Westanatolien. *Studia Troica* 3:135–171.

Krauss, R. 1978. *Das Ende der Amarnazeit: Beiträge zur Geschichte und Chronologie des Neuen Reiches.* Hildesheimer Ägyptologische Beiträge 7. Hildesheim: Gerstenberg Verlag.

Krauss, R. 1984. Korrekturen und Ergänzungen zur Chronologie des MR und NR – ein Zwischenbericht. *Göttinger Miszellen* 70:37–43.

Krauss, R. 1985. *Sothis -und Monddaten. Studien zur astronomischen und technischen Chronologie altägyptens.* Hildesheimer Ägyptologische Beiträge 20. Hildesheim: Gerstenberg Verlag.

Krauss, R. 1989. Note on modern computational errors in astronomical dating. In P. Åström (ed.), *High, middle or low? Acts of an International Colloquium on Absolute Chronology held at the University of Gothenburg 20th–22nd August 1987*, Part 3: 160–162. Studies in Mediterranean Archaeology and literature Pocket-book 57. Gothenburg: Paul Åströms Förlag.

Krauss, R. 1992. Das Kalendarium des Papyrus Ebers und seine chronologische Verwertbarkeit. *Ägypten und Levante* 3:75–96.

Krauss, R. 1993. Zur Problematik der Nubienpolitik Kamoses sowie der Hyksosherrschaft in Oberägypten. *Orientalia* 62:17–29.

Krauss, R. 1994. Zur Chronologie des Mittleren Reiches. *Orientalistische Literaturzeitung* 89:5–18.

Krauss, R. 1995. Zur Chronologie des Neuen Reiches. *Orientalistische Literaturzeitung* 90:237–251.

Krauss, R. 1997. *Astronomische Konzepte und Jenseitsvorstellungen in den Pyramidentexten.* Wiesbaden: Harrassowitz.

Krauss, R. 1998a. An examination of Khyan's place in W.A. Ward's seriation of Hyksos royal scarabs. *Ägypten und Levante* 7:39–42.

Krauss, R. 1998b. Altägyptische Sirius- und Monddaten aus dem 19. Und 18. Jahrhundert vor Christi Geburt (Berliner Illahun-Archiv). *Ägypten und Levante* 8:113–123.

Kress, V. 1997. Magma mixing as a source for Pinatubo sulphur. *Nature* 389:591–593.

Kristiansen, K. 1985. The place of chronological studies in archaeology: a view from the Old World. *Oxford Journal of Archaeology* 4:251–266.

Kristiansen, K. 1998. *Europe before history.* Cambridge: Cambridge University Press.

Krogman, W.M. and Baer, M.J. 1980. Age at death of pharaohs of the New Kingdom, determined from X-Ray films. In J.E. Harris and E.F. Wente (eds.), *An X-Ray atlas of the royal mummies:* 188–233. Chicago: The University of Chicago Press.

Kromer, B., Ambers, J., Baillie, M.G.L., Damon, P.E., Hesshaimer, V., Hofmann, J., Jöris, O., Levin, I., Manning, S.W., McCormac, F.G., Plicht, J. van der, Spurk, M., Stuiver, M. and Weninger, B. 1996. Summary of the workshop "Aspects of high-precision radiocarbon calibration". *Radiocarbon* 38:607–610.

Krueger, A.J., Walter, L.S., Bhartia, P.K., Schnetzler, C.C., Krotkov, N.A., Sprod, I. and Bluth, G.J.S. 1995. Volcanic sulfur dioxide measurements from the total ozone mapping spectrometer instruments. *Journal of Geophysical Research* 100:14,057–14,076.

Kudlek, M. 1985. Review of P.J. Huber *et al.*, *Astronomical dating of Babylon I and Ur III. Archiv für Orientforschung* 32:114–115.

Kühne, C. 1973. *Die Chronologie der internationalen Korrespondenz von El-Amarna.* Alter Orient und Altes Testament 17. Kevelaer and Neukirchener-Vluyn: Verlag Butzon & Bercker and Neukirchener Verlag.

Kuhrt, A. 1995. *The ancient Near East c.3000–330 BC.* London: Routledge.

Kuniholm, P.I. 1977. *Dendrochronology at Gordion and the Anatolian Plateau.* Ph.D. dissertation, University of Pennsylvania. Ann Arbor: University Microfilms International.

Kuniholm, P.I. 1990a. Overview and assessment of the evidence for the date of the Eruption of Thera. In D.A. Hardy and A.C. Renfrew (eds.), *Thera and the Aegean world III. Volume three: chronology:* 13–18. London: The Thera Foundation.

Kuniholm, P.I. 1990b. Archaeological evidence and non-evidence for climate change. *Philosophical Transactions of the Royal Society of London*, Series A, 330:645–655.

Kuniholm, P.I. 1993. A date-list for Bronze Age and Iron Age monuments based on combined dendrochronological and radiocarbon evidence. In M.J. Mellink, E. Porada and T. Özgüç (eds.), *Aspects of art and iconography: Anatolia and its neighbours. Studies in honor of Nimet Özgüç*: 371–373. Ankara: Türk Tarih Kurumu.

Kuniholm, P.I. 1996a. The prehistoric Aegean: dendrochronological progress as of 1995. *Acta Archaeologica* 67:327–335.

Kuniholm, P.I. 1996b. Aegean Dendrochronology Project 1995–1996 results. *XII. Arkeometri Sonuçlari Toplantisi*: 163–175. Ankara: Kültür Bakanligi, Anitlar ve Müzeler Genel Müdürlügü.

Kuniholm, P.I. 1996c. Aegean Dendrochronology Project December 1996 progress report. (available also at **http://www.arts.cornell.edu/dendro/**)

Kuniholm, P.I. 1997. Aegean Dendrochronology Project December 1997 progress report. (available also at **http://www.arts.cornell.edu/dendro/**)

Kuniholm, P.I. 1998a. Aegean Dendrochronology Project December 1998 progress report. (available also at **http://www.arts.cornell.edu/dendro/**)

Kuniholm, P.I. 1998b. Aegean Dendrochronology Project 1996–1997 results. *XIII. Arkeometri Sonuçlari Toplantisi*: 49–63. Ankara: Kültür Bakanligi, Anitlar ve Müzeler Genel Müdürlügü.

Kuniholm, P.I., Kromer, B., Manning, S.W., Newton, M., Latini, C.E. and Bruce, M.J. 1996. Anatolian tree-rings and the absolute chronology of the east Mediterranean 2220–718BC. *Nature* 381:780–783.

Kuniholm, P.I. and Newton, M.W. 1989. A 677 year tree-ring chronology for the Middle Bronze Age. In K. Emre, B. Hrouda, M. Mellink and N. Özgüç (eds.), *Anatolia and the ancient Near East: studies in honor of Tahsin Özgüç*: 279–294. Ankara: Türk Tarih Kurumu.

Kuniholm, P.I. and Striker, C.L. 1982. Dendrochronological investigations in the Aegean and neighboring regions, 1977–1982. *Journal of Field Archaeology* 10:411–420.

Kuniholm, P.I. and Striker, C.L. 1987. Dendrochronological investigations in the Aegean and neighboring regions, 1983–1986. *Journal of Field Archaeology* 14:385–398.

Kuniholm, P.I., Tarter, S.L., Newton, M.W. and Griggs, C.B. 1992. Preliminary report on dendro-chronological investigations at Porsuk/Ulukisla, Turkey 1987–1989. *Syria* 69:379–389.

Lacovara, P. 1990. *Deir el-Ballas. Preliminary report on the Deir el-Ballas expedition, 1980–1986*. American Research Centre in Egypt Reports 12. Winona Lake: Eisenbraun.

Lacovara, P. 1997. Egypt and Nubia during the Second Intermediate Period. In E.D. Oren (ed.), *The Hyksos: new historical and archaeological perspectives*: 69–83. Philadelphia: The University Museum, University of Pennsylvania.

Laffineur, R. 1990–1991. Material and craftmanship in the Mycenae Shaft Graves: imports vs local production. *Minos* 24–25:245–295.

Laffineur, R. 1998. From west to east: the Aegean and Egypt in the early Late Bronze Age. *Aegaeum* 18:53–67.

LaMarche, V.C. Jr. 1970. Frost-damage rings in subalpine conifers and their application to tree-ring dating problems. *The University of British Columbia, Faculty of Forestry, Bulletin* 7:99–100.

LaMarche, V.C. Jr. 1974. Paleoclimatic inferences from long tree-ring records. *Science* 183:1,043–1,048.

LaMarche, V.C. Jr. and Hirschboeck, K.K. 1984. Frost rings in trees as records of major volcanic eruptions. *Nature* 307:121–126.

Lamb, H.H. 1988. *Weather, climate & human affairs: a book of essays and other papers*. London: Routledge.

Landsberger, B. 1954. Assyrische Königsliste und 'dunkles Zeitalter'. *Journal of Cuneiform Studies* 8:31–73.

Langdon, S. and Fotheringham, J.K. 1928. *The Venus tablets of Ammizaduga: a solution of Babylonian chronology by means of the Venus observations of the First Dynasty*. Oxford and London: Oxford University Press and Humphrey Milford.

Lange, M. 1998. Wadi Shaw 82/52: ¹⁴C dates from a peridynastic site in northwest Sudan, supporting the Egyptian historical chronology. *Radiocarbon* 40:687–692.

Last, J. 1995. The nature of history. In I. Hodder, M. Shanks, A. Alexandri, V. Buchli, J. Carmen, J. Last and G. Lucas (eds.), *Interpreting archaeology: finding meaning in the past*: 141–157. London: Routledge.

Leahy, A. 1990. Appendix: the Twenty-Third Dynasty. In A.M. Leahy (ed.), *Libya and Egypt c.1300–750 BC*: 177–200. London: SOAS Centre of Near and Middle Eastern Studies, and the Society for Libyan Studies.

Leitz, C. 1989. *Studien zur ägyptischen Astronomie.* Ägyptologische Abhandlungen 49. Wiesbaden: Harrassowitz.

Leitz, C. 1992. Bemerkungen zur astronomischen Chronologie. *Ägypten und Levante* 3:97–102.

Lello, G. 1978. Tuthmose III's first lunar date. *Journal of Near Eastern Studies* 37:327–330.

Lemeche, N.P. 1991. *The Canaanites and their land. The tradition of the Canaanites.* Sheffield: Sheffield Academic Press.

Lemeche, N.P. 1996. Where should we look for Canaan? *Ugarit-Forschungen* 28:767–772.

Lemeche, N.P. 1998. Greater Canaan: the implications of a correct reading of EA151:49–67. *Bulletin of the American Schools of Oriental Research* 310:19–24.

Leonard, A. Jr. 1988. Some problems inherent in Mycenaean/Syro-Palestinian synchronisms. In E.B. French and K.A. Wardle (eds.), *Problems in Greek prehistory. Papers presented at the centenary conference of the British School of Archaeology at Athens, Manchester April 1986:* 319–330. Bristol: Bristol Classical Press.

Leonard, A. Jr. (ed.). 1993. *A Review of Peter James et al. Centuries of Darkness: A Challenge to the Conventional Chronology of Old World Archaeology. A workshop held at the 93rd Annual Meeting of the AIA, Chicago, Illinois 1991.* Colloquenda Mediterranea A/2.1. Bradford: Loid Publishing.

Leonard, A. Jr. 1994. *An index to the Late Bronze Age Aegean pottery from Syria–Palestine.* Studies in Mediterranean Archaeology 114. Jonsered: Paul Åströms Förlag.

Leonard, A. Jr. 1996. "Canaanite jars" and the Late Bronze Age Aegeo-Levantine wine trade. In P.E. McGovern, S.J. Fleming and S.H. Katz (eds.), *The origins and ancient history of wine:* 233–254. New York: Gordon and Breach.

Leonard, A. Jr., Hughes, M., Middleton, A. and Schofield, L. 1993. The making of Aegean stirrup jars: technique, tradition, and trade. *Annual of the British School at Athens* 88:105–123.

Levi, S.T., Vanzetti, A., Cioni, R., Fratini, F. and Pecchioni, E. n.d. Pyroclastic temper in Apulian Bronze Age pottery: the far reaching impact of a Vesuvian eruption. Manuscript to appear in the acts of the 'Colloquium on the cultural response to the volcanic landscape' (Medford, MA, 16 to 17 November 1996), eds. M. Balmuth, D. Chester and P. Johnston. Forthcoming.

Levin, I., Bösinger, R., Bonani, G., Francey, R.J., Kromer, B., Münnich, K.O., Suter, M., Trivett, N.B.A. and Wölfli, W. 1992. Radiocarbon in atmospheric carbon dioxide and methane: global distribution and trends. In R.E. Taylor, A. Long and R.S. Kra (eds.), *Radiocarbon after four decades: an interdisciplinary perspective:* 503–518. New York: Springer-Verlag.

Libby, W.F. 1955. *Radiocarbon dating.* Second edition. Chicago: University of Chicago Press.

Lightfoot, C.S. 1998. Hittite vases with Minoan links excite archaeologists. *Minerva* 9(1):3–4.

Lilliu, G. 1982. *La civiltà nuragica.* Sassari: Carlo Delfino.

Lilyquist, C. 1993. Granulation and glass: chronological and stylistic investigations at selected sites, ca.2500–1400 B.C.E. *Bulletin of the American Schools of Oriental Research* 290–291:29–94.

Lilyquist, C. 1994. Objects attributable to Kamid el-Loz and comments on the date of some objects in the 'Schatzhaus'. In W. Adler, *Kamid el-Loz 11. Das 'Schatzhaus' im Palastbereich. Die Befunde des Königsgrabes:* 207–220. Bonn: Dr. Rudolf Habelt.

Lilyquist, C. 1996. Stone vessels at Kamid el-Loz: Egyptian, Egyptianizing, or non-Egyptian? A question at sites from the Sudan to Iraq to the Greek mainland. In R. Hachmann, *Kamid el-Loz 16. Schatzhausstudien:* 133–173. Bonn: Dr. Rudolf Habelt.

Lilyquist, C. 1997. Egyptian stone vases? Comments on Peter Warren's paper. *Aegaeum* 16:225–228.

Limbrey, S. 1990. Soil studies at Akrotiri. In D.A. Hardy, J. Keller, V.P. Galanopoulos, N.C. Flemming and T.H. Druitt (eds.), *Thera and the Aegean world III. Volume two: earth sciences:* 377–382. London: The Thera Foundation.

Liritzis, Y. 1985. Archaeomagnetism, Santorini volcanic eruptions and fired destruction levels on Crete. *Nature* 313:75–76.

Liritzis, I., Michael, C. and Galloway, R.B. 1996. A significant Aegean volcanic eruption during the second millennium B.C. revealed by thermoluminescence dating. *Geoarchaeology* 11:361–371.

Liritzis, Y. and Thomas, R. 1980. Palaeointensity and thermoluminescence measurements on Cretan kilns from 1300 to 2000 BC. *Nature* 283:54–55.

Liverani, M. 1990. *Prestige and interest: international relations in the Near East ca.1600–1000 B.C.* Padua: Sargon.

Lloyd, A.B. 1975. Once more Hammamat inscription 191. *Journal of Egyptian Archaeology* 61:54–66.

Lohman, H. 1998. Die Santorin-Katastrophe – ein archäologischer Mythos. In E. Olshausen and H. Sonnabend (eds.), *Naturkatastrophen in der antiken Welt:* 337–363. Stuttgarter Kolloquium zur historischen geographie des Altertums 6, 1996. Stuttgart: Franz Steiner Verlag.

Lolos, Y.G. 1987. *The Late Helladic I pottery of the southern Peloponnesos and its local characteristics.* Studies in Mediterranean Archaeology and Literature Pocket-book 50. Gothenburg: Paul Åströms Förlag.

Lolos, Y.G. 1990. On the Late Helladic I of Akrotiri, Thera. In D.A. Hardy and A.C. Renfrew (eds.), *Thera and the Aegean world III. Volume three: chronology:* 51–56. London: The Thera Foundation.

Long. R.D. 1974. A re-examination of the Sothic chronology of Egypt. *Orientalia* 43:261–274.

Lorius, C., Jouzel, J. and Raynaud, D. 1992. The ice core record: past archive of the climate and signpost to the future. *Philosophical Transactions of the Royal Society of London,* Series B, 338:227–234.

Loud, G. 1948. *Megiddo II: seasons of 1935–39.* Chicago: The University of Chicago Press.

Lough, J.M. and Fritts, H.C. 1987. An assessment of the possible effects of volcanic eruptions on North American climate using tree-ring data, 1602–1900 A.D. *Climatic Change* 10:219–239.

Lowe, D.J. and Higham, T.F.G. 1998. Hit-or-myth? Linking a 1259 AD acid spike with an Okataina eruption. *Antiquity* 72:427–431.

Luce, J.V. 1969. *The end of Atlantis: new light on an old legend.* London: Thames and Hudson.

Luce, J.V. 1973. More thoughts about Thera. *Greece & Rome* 19:37–46.

Luce, J.V. 1976. Thera and the devastation of Minoan Crete: a new interpretation of the evidence. *American Journal of Archaeology* 80:9–16.

Luckman, B.H., Briffa, K.R., Jones, P.D. and Schweingruber, F.H. 1997. Tree-ring based reconstruction of summer temperatures at the Columbia Icefield, Alberta, Canada, AD 1073–1983. *The Holocene* 7:375–389.

Luft, U. 1986. Noch einmal zum Ebers-Kalender. *Göttinger Miszellen* 92:69–77.

Luft, U. 1989. Illahunstudien, IV: Zur chronologischen Verwertbarkeit des Sothisdatums. *Studien zur altägyptischen Kultur* 16:217–233.

Luft, U. 1992a. Remarks of a philologist on Egyptian chronology. *Ägypten und Levante* 3:109–114.

Luft, U. 1992b. *Die chronologische Fixierung des ägyptischen Mittleren Reiches nach dem Tempelarchiv von Illahun.* Wein: Österreichische Akademie der Wissenschaften.

Luft, U. 1994. "Weil … nicht sein kann, was nicht sein darf": Replik einer Kritik. *Göttinger Miszellen* 141:109–111.

Luhr, J.F. 1991. Mount Pinatubo: volcanic shade causes cooling. *Nature* 354:104–105.

Luhr, J.F., Carmichael, I.S.E. and Varekamp, J.C. 1984. The 1982 eruptions of El Chichón Volcano, Chiapas, Mexico: mineralogy and petrology of the anhydrite-bearing pumices. *Journal of Volcanology and Geothermal Research* 23:69–108.

Luhr, J.F. and Melson, W.G. 1996. Mineral and glass compositions in June 15, 1991, pumices: evidence for dynamic disequilibrium in the dacite of Mount Pinatubo. In C.G. Newhall and R.S. Punongbayan (eds.), *Fire and mud: eruptions and lahars of Mount Pinatubo, Philippines:* 733–750. Seattle: University of Washington Press.

Macdonald, C. 1990. Destruction and construction in the palace at Knossos: LMIA–B. In D.A. Hardy and A.C. Renfrew (eds.), *Thera and the Aegean world III. Volume three: chronology:* 82–88. London: The Thera Foundation.

Macdonald, C.F. 1996. Notes on some Late Minoan IA contexts from the Palace of Minos and its immediate vicinity. In D. Evely, I.S. Lemos and S. Sherratt (eds.), *Minotaur and Centaur: studies in the archaeology of Crete and Euboea presented to Mervyn Popham:* 17–26. British Archaeological Reports International Series 638. Oxford: Tempus Reparatum.

MacGillivray, J.A. 1986. *Pottery of the Old Palace at Knossos and its implications.* Ph.D. dissertation, University of Edinburgh.

MacGillivray, J.A. 1995. A Minoan cup at Tell el-Dabᶜa. *Ägypten und Levante* 5:81–84.

MacGillivray, J.A. 1997a. Late Minoan II and III pottery and chronology at Palaikastro: an introduction. In E. Hallager and B.P. Hallager (eds.), *Late Minoan III pottery: chronology and terminology. Acts of a meeting held at the Danish Institute at Athens August 12–14, 1994:* 193–202. Monographs of the Danish Institute at Athens 1. Athens: Danish Institute at Athens.

MacGillivray, J.A. 1997b. The re-occupation of eastern Crete in the Late Minoan II–IIIA:1/2 periods. In J. Driessen and A. Farnoux (eds.), *La Crète Mycénienne: actes de la table ronde internationale, 26–28 mars 1991:* 275–279. Bulletin de Correspondance Hellénique Supplément 30. Athens: École française d'Athènes.

MacGillivray, J.A. 1998. *Knossos: pottery groups of the old palace period.* British School at Athens Studies 5. London: The British School at Athens.

MacGillivray, J.A., Sackett, L.H., Driessen, J., Farnoux, A. and Smyth, D. 1991. Excavations at Palaikastro, 1990. *Annual of the British School at Athens* 86:121–147.

MacGillivray, J.A., Sackett, L.H., Driessen, J.M. and Hemingway, S. 1992. Excavations at Palaikastro, 1991. *Annual of the British School at Athens* 87:121–152.

MacGillivray, J.A., Sackett, L.H. and Driessen, J.M. 1998. Excavations at Palaikastro, 1994 and 1996. *Annual of the British School at Athens* 93:221–268.

Mader, H.M., Phillips, J.C., Sparks, R.S.J. and Sturtevant, B. 1996. Dynamics of explosive degassing of magma: observations of fragmenting two-phase flows. *Journal of Geophysical Research* 94:15,703–15,721.

Maguire, L.C. 1986. *The Middle Cypriot pottery from Tell el-Dabᶜa, Egypt.* MA dissertation, Department of Archaeology, University of Edinburgh.

Maguire, L.C. 1990. *The circulation of Cypriot pottery in the Middle Bronze Age.* Ph.D. dissertation, University of Edinburgh. [A revised version edited by R.S. Merrillees will be published in the publication series of the Verlag der Österreichischen Akademie der Wissenschaften.]

Maguire, L.C. 1991. The classification of Middle Bronze Age painted pottery: wares, styles ... workshops? In J. Barlow, D. Bolger and B. Kling (eds.), *Cypriot ceramics: reading the prehistoric record:* 59–66. University Museum Monograph 74/University Museum Symposium Series vol.2. Philadelphia: The A.G. Leventis Foundation and the University Museum of Archaeology and Anthropology, University of Pennsylvania.

Maguire, L.C. 1992. A cautious approach to the Middle Bronze Age chronology of Cyprus. *Ägypten und Levante* 3:115–120.

Maguire, L.C. 1995. Tell el-Dabᶜa: the Cypriot connection. In W.V. Davies and L. Schofield (eds.), *Egypt, the Aegean and the Levant: interconnections in the second millennium BC:* 54–65. London: British Museum Publications.

Maier, F.G. and Karageorghis, V. 1984. *Paphos: history and archaeology.* Nicosia: A.G. Leventis Foundation.

Malamat, A. 1997. The Exodus: Egyptian analogies. In E.S. Frerichs and L.H. Lesko (eds.), *Exodus: the Egyptian evidence:* 15–26. Winona Lake: Eisenbrauns.

Maliszewski, D. 1997. Notes on the Bronze Age settlement patterns of western Cyprus c.2500–c.1050 BC. *Report of the Department of Antiquities, Cyprus:* 65–84.

Mamet, H. 1874. *De insula Thera.* Thesis, Facultati Litterarum Parisiensi. Insulis: E. Thorin.

Manning, S.W. 1987. The volcano of Thera and the destruction of Minoan Crete. *Kretika Chronika* KZ':59–85.

Manning, S.W. 1988a. Dating of the Santorini eruption. *Nature* 332: 401.

Manning, S.W. 1988b. The Bronze Age eruption of Thera: absolute dating, Aegean chronology and Mediterranean cultural interrelations. *Journal of Mediterranean Archaeology* 1(1): 17–82.

Manning, S.W. 1990a. The eruption of Thera: date and implications. In D.A. Hardy and A.C. Renfrew (eds.), *Thera and the Aegean world III. Volume three: chronology:* 29–40. London: The Thera Foundation.

Manning, S.W. 1990b. The Thera eruption: the Third Congress and the problem of the date. *Archaeometry* 32: 91–100.

Manning, S.W. 1991. Response to J.D. Muhly on problems of chronology in the Aegean Late Bronze Age. *Journal of Mediterranean Archaeology* 4:249–262.

Manning, S.W. 1992a. Thera, sulphur, and climatic anomalies. *Oxford Journal of Archaeology* 11: 245–253.

Manning, S.W. 1992b. Santorini, ice-cores and tree-rings: resolution of the 1645 or 1628BC debate? *Nestor* 19:2,511–2,512.

Manning, S.W. 1992c. Archaeology and the world of Homer: introduction to a past and present discipline. In C. Emlyn-Jones, L. Hardwick and J. Purkis (eds.), *Homer: readings and images:* 117–142. London: Duckworth.

Manning, S.W. 1994. The emergence of divergence: development and decline on Bronze Age Crete and the Cyclades. In C. Mathers and S. Stoddart (eds.), *Development and decline in the Mediterranean Bronze Age:* 221–270. Sheffield Archaeological Monographs 8. Sheffield: J.R. Collis Publications.

Manning, S.W. 1995. *The absolute chronology of the Aegean Early Bronze Age: archaeology, history and radiocarbon.* Monographs in Mediterranean Archaeology 1. Sheffield: Sheffield Academic Press.

Manning, S.W. 1997. Troy, radiocarbon, and the chronology of the northeast Aegean in the Early Bronze Age. In C.G. Doumas and V. La Rosa (eds.), *I Poliochni kai i proimi epochi tou Chalkou sto Boreio Aigaio/*

Poliochni e l'antica età del bronzo nell'Egeo settentrionale: 498–520. Athens: Scuola archeologica italiana di Atene.

Manning, S.W. 1998a. Aegean and Sardinian chronology: radiocarbon, calibration, and Thera. In M.S. Balmuth and R.H. Tykot (eds.), *Sardinian and Aegean chronology: towards the resolution of relative and absolute dating in the Mediterranean*: 297–307. Studies in Sardinian Archaeology V. Oxford: Oxbow.

Manning, S.W. 1998b. Correction. New GISP2 ice-core evidence supports 17th century BC date for the Santorini (Minoan) eruption: response to Zielinksi and Germani (1998). *Journal of Archaeological Science* 25:1,039–1,042.

Manning, S.W. 1998c. From process to people: longue durée to history. *Aegaeum* 18:311–327.

Manning, S.W. 1998d. Changing pasts and socio-political cognition in Late Bronze Age Cyprus. *World Archaeology* 30:39–58.

Manning, S.W., De Mita, F.A. Jr., Monks, S.J. and Nakou, G. 1994a. The Fatal Shore, the Long Years, and the Geographical Unconscious. Considerations of Iconography, Chronology and Trade in Response to Negbi's 'The "Libyan Landscape" from Thera: A Review of Aegean Enterprises Overseas in the Late Minoan IA Period' (*JMA* 7.1). *Journal of Mediterranean Archaeology* 7:219–235.

Manning, S.W., Collon, D., Conwell, D.H., Jansen, H.-G., Sewell, D., Steel, L. and Swinton, A. 1994b. Tsaroukkas, Mycenaeans and Trade Project: preliminary report on the 1993 season. *Report of the Department of Antiquities, Cyprus, 1994*: 83–106.

Manning, S.W., Bolger, D., Ponting, M.J., Steel, L. and Swinton, A. 1994c. Maroni Valley Archaeological Survey Project: preliminary report on 1992–1993 seasons. *Report of the Department of Antiquities, Cyprus, 1994*: 345–367.

Manning, S.W. and De Mita, F.A. Jr. 1997. Cyprus, the Aegean and Maroni-*Tsaroukkas*. In D. Christou *et al.* (eds.), *Proceedings of the International Archaeological Conference Cyprus and the Aegean in Antiquity from the prehistoric period to the 7th century A.D. Nicosia 8–10 December 1995*: 101–142. Nicosia: Department of Antiquities.

Manning, S.W. and Monks, S.J. with contributions by Steel, L., Ribeiro, E.C. and Weinstein, J.M. 1998. Late Cypriot tombs at Maroni *Tsaroukkas*, Cyprus. *Annual of the British School at Athens* 93:297–351.

Manning, S.W. and Weninger, B. 1992. A light in the dark: archaeological wiggle matching and the absolute chronology of the close of the Aegean Late Bronze Age. *Antiquity* 66:636–663.

Manuelian, P. der. 1987. *Studies in the reign of Amenophis II*. Hildesheim: Gerstenberg Verlag.

Marazzi, M. and Re, L. 1986. Importazioni egeo-micenee dall'isola di Vivara (Procidea). In M. Marazzi, S. Tusa and L. Vagnetti (eds.), *Traffici Micenei nel Mediterraneo: problemi storici e documentazione archeologica*: 155–174. Taranto: Istituto per la Storia e l'Archeologia della Magna Grecia.

Marchetti, N., Nigro, L. and Sarieᶜ, I. 1998. Preliminary report on the first season of excavations of the Italian–Palestinian expedition at Tell es-Sultan/Jericho, April–May 1997. *Palestine Exploration Quarterly* 130:121–144.

Marinatos, N. 1994. The 'export' significance of Minoan bull hunting and bull leaping scenes. *Ägypten und Levante* 4:89–93.

Marinatos, N. 1998. The Tell el-Dabᶜa paintings: a study in pictorial tradition. *Ägypten und Levante* 8:83–99.

Marinatos, S. 1939. The volcanic destruction of Minoan Crete. *Antiquity* 13:425–439.

Marinatos, S. 1968–1976. *Excavations at Thera I–VII*. Athens: Arkhaiologike Hetaireia.

Marinatos, S. and Hirmer, M. 1960. *Crete and Mycenae*. Trans. J. Boardman. London: Thames and Hudson.

Marinatos, S. and Ninkovitch, D. (eds.). 1971. *Acta of the 1st International Scientific Congress on the Volcano of Thera*. Athens: Archaeological Services of Greece. [Note a supplementary volume of 'indices', including individual photographs of the participants at the conference, was published in 1973 by the Ministry of Culture and Science, Athens.]

Marketou, T. 1988. New evidence on the topography and site history of prehistoric Ialysos. In S. Dietz and I. Papachristodoulou (eds.), *Archaeology in the Dodecanese*: 27–33. Copenhagen: Department of Near Eastern and Classical Antiquities, The National Museum of Denmark.

Marketou, T. 1990. Santorini tephra from Rhodes and Kos: some chronological remarks based on the stratigraphy. In D.A. Hardy and A.C. Renfrew (eds.), *Thera and the Aegean world III. Volume three: chronology*: 100–113. London: The Thera Foundation.

Marketou, T. 1996. Excavations at Trianda (Ialysos) on Rhodes: new evidence for the Late Bronze Age I period. *Bulletin of the Institute of Classical Studies* 41:133–134.

Marthari, M. 1980. Akrotiri, keramiki ME paradosis sto stroma tis ifaisteiakis katastrofis. *Arkhaiologiki Ephemeris:* 182–211.

Marthari, M. 1984. The destruction of the town at Akrotiri, Thera, at the beginning of LCI: definition and chronology. In J.A. MacGillivray and R.N.L. Barber (eds.), *The prehistoric Cyclades:* 119–133. Edinburgh: Department of Classical Archaeology, University of Edinburgh.

Marthari, M. 1987. The local pottery wares with painted decoration from the volcanic destruction level of Akrotiri, Thera: a preliminary report. *Archäologischer Anzeiger:* 359–379.

Marthari, M. 1990. The chronology of the last phases of occupation at Akrotiri in the light of the evidence from the West House pottery groups. In D.A. Hardy and A.C. Renfrew (eds.), *Thera and the Aegean world III. Volume three: chronology:* 57–70. London: The Thera Foundation.

Mass, C. and Portman, D. 1989. Major volcanic eruptions and climate: a critical review. *Journal of Climate* 2:566–593.

Mass, C. and Portman, D.A. 1990. Reply. *Journal of Climate* 3:589–590.

Masson, O. 1961–1962. Remarques sur les rapports entre la Crète et Chypre à la fin de l'Age du Bronze. *Kretika Chronika* 15–16:156–161.

Matthäus, H. 1980. *Die Bronzegefäße der kretisch-mykenischen Kultur.* Prähistorische Bronzefunde II.1. München: C.H. Beck'sche Verlagsbuchhandlung.

Matthäus, H. 1985. *Metallgefäße und Gefäßuntersätze der Bronzezeit, der geometrischen und archaischen Periode auf Cypern.* Prähistorische Bronzefunde II.8. München: C.H. Beck'sche Verlagsbuchhandlung.

Matthäus, H. 1995. Representations of Keftiu in Egyptian tombs and the absolute chronology of the Aegean Late Bronze Age. *Bulletin of the Institute of Classical Studies* 40:177–194.

Matthews, S.W. 1976. What's happening to our climate? *National Geographic Magazine* 150(5):576–615.

Matthiae, P. 1997. Ebla and Syria in the Middle Bronze Age. In E.D. Oren (ed.), *The Hyksos: new historical and archaeological perspectives:* 379–414. Philadelphia: The University Museum, University of Pennsylvania.

Mattingly, H.B. 1996. *The Athenian empire restored: epigraphic and historical studies.* Ann Arbor: The University of Michigan Press.

Maxwell-Hyslop, K.R. 1971. *Western Asiatic jewellery c.3000–612 B.C.* London: Methuen & Co.

Mazar, A. 1997. Iron Age chronology: a reply to I. Finkelstein. *Levant* 29:157–167.

McArthur, J.K. 1981. The textual evidence for location of place-names in the Knossos tablets. *Minos* 17:147–210.

McClellan, T.L. 1989. The chronology and ceramic assemblages of Alalakh. In A. Leonard Jr. and B.B. Williams (eds.), *Essays in ancient civilization presented to Helene J. Kantor:* 181–212. Studies in Ancient Oriental Civilization 47. Chicago: Oriental Institute of the University of Chicago.

McCormac, F.G., Baillie, M.G.L., Pilcher, J.R. and Kalin, R.M. 1995. Location-dependent differences in the ^{14}C content of wood. *Radiocarbon* 37:395–407.

McCormac, F.G., Hogg, A.G., Higham, T.G.F., Lynch-Stieglitz, J., Broecker, W.S., Baillie, M.G.L., Palmer, J., Xiong, L., Pilcher, J.R., Brown, D. and Hoper, S.T. 1998. Temporal variation in the interhemispheric ^{14}C offset. *Geophysical Research Letters* 25:1,321–1,324.

McCormick, M.P., Thomason, L.W. and Trepte, C.R. 1995. Atmospheric effects of the Mt. Pinatubo eruption. *Nature* 373:399–404.

McCormick, M.P., Wang, P.-H., Poole, L.R. 1993. Stratospheric aerosols and clouds. In P.V. Hobbs (ed.), *Aerosol–cloud–climate interactions:* 205–222. San Diego: Academic Press.

McCoy, F.W. 1980. The upper Thera (Minoan) ash in deep-sea sediments: distribution and comparison with other ash layers. In C. Doumas (ed.), *Thera and the Aegean world II:* 57–78. London: Thera and the Aegean World.

McCoy, F.W. and Heiken, G. n.d. Tsunami generated by the Late Bronze Age eruption of Thera (Santorini), Greece. In F.W. McCoy and G. Heiken (eds.), *Volcanic hazards and disasters in human antiquity.* Special Paper of the Geological Society of America. In Press.

McGovern, P.E. 1985. *Late Bronze Palestinian pendants: innovation in a cosmopolitan age.* Sheffield: JSOT for the American Schools of Oriental Research.

McGovern, P.E., Bourriau, J., Harbottle, G. and Allen, S. 1994. The archaeological origin and significance of the dolphin vase determined by Neutron Activation Analysis. *Bulletin of the American Schools of Oriental Research* 296:31–41.

McGovern, P.E. and Harbottle, G. 1997. "Hyksos" trade connections between Tell el Dabᶜa (Avaris) and the Levant: a neutron activation study of the Canaanite jar. In E.D. Oren (ed.), *The Hyksos: new historical and archaeological perspectives:* 141–157. Philadelphia: The University Museum, University of Pennsylvania.

Mee, C.B. 1988. A Mycenaean thalassocracy in the eastern Aegean? In E.B. French and K.A. Wardle (eds.), *Problems in Greek prehistory. Papers presented at the Centenary Conference of the British School of Archaeology at Athens, Manchester, April 1986:* 301–306. Bristol: Bristol Classical Press.

Mee, C.B. 1998. Anatolia and the Aegean in the Late Bronze Age. *Aegaeum* 18:137–148.

Meese, D.A., Gow, A.J., Alley, R.B., Zielinski, G.A., Grootes, P.M., Ram, M., Taylor, K.C., Mayewski, P.A. and Bolzan, J.F. 1997. The Greenland Ice Sheet Project 2 depth-age scale: methods and results. *Journal of Geophysical Research* 102, C12:26,411–26,423.

Meillassoux, C. 1972. From reproduction to production. *Economy and Society* 1:92–105.

Melekestsev, I.V. and Miller, T.P. 1997. The origin of the 1645 B.C. acidic peak in the Greenland ice sheet is the caldera-generating Aniyakchak eruption, Alaska, U.S.A. [in Russian] *Vulkanologiya i Seysmologiya* 1997 volume, part 2:32–35 (not seen by author).

Mellaart, J. 1979. Egyptian and Near Eastern chronology: a dilemma? *Antiquity* 53:6–18.

Mellaart, J. 1980. James Mellaart replies to his critics. *Antiquity* 54:225–227.

Mellink, M.J. 1995. New perspectives and initiatives in the Hyksos period. *Ägypten und Levante* 5:85–89.

Melnik, O.E. 1999. Fragmenting magma. *Nature* 397:394–395.

Merrillees, R.S. 1965. Reflections on the Late Bronze Age in Cyprus. *Opuscula Atheniensia* 6:139–148.

Merrillees, R.S. 1968. *The Cypriote Bronze Age pottery found in Egypt.* Studies in Mediterranean Archaeology 18. Göteborg: Paul Åströms Förlag.

Merrillees, R.S. 1971. The early history of Late Cypriot I. *Levant* 3:56–79.

Merrillees, R.S. 1972a. Aegean Bronze Age relations with Egypt. *American Journal of Archaeology* 76:281–294.

Merrillees, R.S. 1972b. Alasia. In *Praktika tou Protou Dieuthnos Kyprologikou Synedriou,* vol.A: 111–119. Nicosia: Hetaireia Kypriakon Spoydon.

Merrillees, R.S. 1974a. *Trade and transcendence in the Bronze Age Levant.* Studies in Mediterranean Archaeology 39. Paul Åströms Förlag.

Merrillees, R.S. 1974b, Tell el-ʿAjjul fine and imported wares. In J.R. Stewart, *Tell el ʿAjjul: the Middle Bronze Age remains:* 86–111. Edited by H.E. Kassis. Studies in Mediterranean Archaeology 38. Göteborg: Paul Åströms Förlag.

Merrillees, R.S. 1975. The Cypriote Bronze Age pottery found in Egypt: a reply. *Report of the Department of Antiquities, Cyprus:* 81–90.

Merrillees, R.S. 1977. The absolute chronology of the Bronze Age in Cyprus. *Report of the Department of Antiquities, Cyprus:* 33–50.

Merrillees, R.S. 1978. El-Lisht and Tell el-Yahudiya ware in the archaeological museum of the American University of Beirut. *Levant* 10:75–98.

Merrillees, R.S. 1980. An essay in provenance: the Late Minoan IB pottery from Egypt. *Berytus* 28:1–45.

Merrillees, R.S. 1982. Review of J. Strange, *Caphtor/Keftiu: a new investigation. Report of the Department of Antiquities, Cyprus:* 244–253.

Merrillees, R.S. 1986. A 16th century B.C. tomb group from central Cyprus with links both east and west. In V. Karageorghis (ed.). *Acts of the international archaeological symposium "Cyprus between the Orient and the Occident", Nicosia, 8–14 September 1985:* 114–148. Nicosia: Department of Antiquities.

Merrillees, R.S. 1987. *Alashia revisited.* Cahiers de la Revue Biblique 22. Paris: J. Gabalda et Cᵉ, Éditeurs.

Merrillees, R.S. 1992. The absolute chronology of the Bronze Age in Cyprus: a revision. *Bulletin of the American Schools of Oriental Research* 288:47–52.

Merrillees, R.S. 1994. Review of G. Hult, *Nitovikla reconsidered. Opuscula Atheniensia* 20:256–258.

Merrillees, R.S. 1998. Egypt and the Aegean. *Aegaeum* 18:149–158.

Merrillees, R.S. n.d. Some Cypriote White Slip pottery from the Aegean. Manuscript of paper presented to the White Slip Ware Conference held in Nicosia 29–30 October 1998. Paper to be published in the conference proceedings: V. Karageorghis (ed.), *White Slip Ware. Proceedings of an International Conference Organized by the Anastasios G. Leventis Foundation, Nicosia in Honour of Malcolm Wiener, Nicosia 29th–30th October 1998.* In Press.

Meulengracht, A., McGovern, P. and Lawn, B. 1981. University of Pennsylvania radiocarbon dates XXI. *Radiocarbon* 23:227–240.

Meyer, E. 1904. *Aegyptische Chronologie.* Berlin: Abhandlungen der Konigl. Preuss. Akademie der Wissenschaften vom Jahre 1904.

Meyer, E. 1912. *Chronologie Égyptienne.* Trans. A. Moret. Annales du Musé Guimet 24.2. Paris: Ernest Leroux. (Translation of Meyer 1904)

Meyers, E.M. (ed.). 1997. *The Oxford encyclopedia of archaeology in the Near East.* New York: Oxford University Press.

Michael, H.N. 1976. Radiocarbon dates from Akrotiri on Thera. *Temple University Aegean Symposium* 1:7–9.

Michael, H.N. 1978. Radiocarbon dates from the site of Akrotiri, Thera, 1967–1977. In C. Doumas (ed.), *Thera and the Aegean world I:* 791–795. London: Thera and the Aegean World.

Michael, H.N. and Betancourt, P.P. 1988. The Thera eruption: II. Further arguments for an early date. *Archaeometry* 30:169–175.

Michaelidis, P. 1995. Ägyptische Sphinx aus Malia. *Praehistorische Zeitschrift* 70:90–95.

Milojčić, V. 1967. Die absolute Chronologie der Jungsteinzeit in Südosteuropa und die Ergebnisse der Radiocarbon -(C14-) Methode. *Jahrbuch des Römisch-Germanischen Zentralmuseums, Mainz* 14:9–37.

Momigliano, N. 1989. *MMIA pottery from Evans' excavations at Knossos.* Ph.D. dissertation, University College London.

Momigliano, N. 1991. MMIA pottery from Evans' excavations at Knossos: a reassessment. *Annual of the British School at Athens* 86:149–271.

Mommsen, H., Beier, T., Diehl, U. and Podzuweit, C. 1992. Provenance determination of Mycenaean sherds found in Tell el Amarna by neutron activation analysis. *Journal of Archaeological Science* 19:295–302.

Money, J. 1973. The destruction of Acrotiri. *Antiquity* 47:50–53.

Montet, P. 1937. L'ère de Menophrès. *Academie des Inscriptions & Belles-Lettres. Comptes Rendus des Scéances de l'anné 1937:* 418–426.

Moran, W. 1992. *The Amarna letters.* Baltimore: The Johns Hopkins University Press.

Morgan, L. 1984. Morphology, syntax and the issue of chronology. In J.A. MacGillivray and R.N.L. Barber (eds.), *The prehistoric Cyclades:* 165–177. Edinburgh: Department of Classical Archaeology, University of Edinburgh.

Morgan, L. 1988. *The miniature wall paintings of Thera: a study in Aegean culture and iconography.* Cambridge: Cambridge University Press.

Morgan, L. 1990. Island iconography: Thera, Kea, Milos. In D.A. Hardy, C.G. Doumas, J.A. Sakellarakis and P.M. Warren (eds.), *Thera and the Aegean world III. Volume one: archaeology:* 252–266. London: The Thera Foundation.

Morgan, L. 1995. Minoan painting and Egypt: the case of Tell el-Dabᶜa. In W.V. Davies and L. Schofield (eds.), *Egypt, the Aegean and the Levant: interconnections in the second millennium BC:* 29–53. London: British Museum Publications.

Morgan, L. 1998. Power of the beast: human–animal symbolism in Egyptian and Aegean art. *Ägypten und Levante* 7:17–31.

Morissette, A. 1995. Ironic. From 'Jagged Little Pill'. MCA Music.

Morris, C. 1993. Hands up for the individual! The role of attribution studies in Aegean prehistory. *Cambridge Archaeological Journal* 3:41–66.

Morris, I. 1987. *Burial and ancient society: the rise of the Greek city-state.* Cambridge University Press.

Morris, S.P. 1989. A tale of two cities: the miniature frescoes from Thera and the origins of Greek poetry. *American Journal of Archaeology* 93:511–535.

Morris, S.P. 1998. Bearing Greek gifts: Euboean pottery on Sardinia. In M.S. Balmuth and R.H. Tykot (eds.), *Sardinian and Aegean chronology: towards the resolution of relative and absolute dating in the Mediterranean:* 361–362. Studies in Sardinian Archaeology V. Oxford: Oxbow.

Mountjoy, P.A. 1986. *Mycenaean decorated pottery: a guide to identification.* Studies in Mediterranean Archaeology 73. Göteborg. Paul Åströms Förlag.

Mountjoy, P.A. 1993. *Mycenaean pottery: an introduction.* Oxford: Oxbow.

Mountjoy, P.-A., Jones, R.E. and Cherry, J.F. 1978. Provenance studies of the LMIB/LHIIA marine style. *Annual of the British School at Athens* 73:143–171.

Muhly, J.D. 1972. The land of Alashiya: references to Alashiya in the texts of the second millennium B.C.

and the history of Cyprus in the Late Bronze Age. In *Praktika tou Protou Dieuthnos Kyprologikou Synedriou,* vol.A: 201–219. Nicosia: Hetaireia Kypriakon Spoydon.

Muhly, J.D. 1975. Near Eastern chronology and the date of the Late Cypriot I period. In N. Robertson (ed.), *The archaeology of Cyprus: recent developments:* 76–89. Park Ridge, N.J.: Noyes Press.

Muhly, J.D. 1982. The nature of trade in the LBA eastern Mediterranean: the organization of the metals trade and the role of Cyprus. In J.D. Muhly, R. Maddin and V. Karageorghis (eds.), *Acta of the international archaeological symposium: Early Metallurgy in Cyprus, 4000–500 BC:* 251–266. Larnaca: Pierides Foundation.

Muhly, J.D. 1985. The Late Bronze Age in Cyprus: a 25 year retrospect. In V. Karageorghis (ed.), *Archaeology in Cyprus 1960–1985:* 20–46. Nicosia: Department of Antiquities.

Muhly, J.D. 1991. Egypt, the Aegean and Late Bronze Age chronology in the eastern Mediterranean: a review article. *Journal of Mediterranean Archaeology* 4:235–247.

Muhly, J.D. 1998. On re-reading Helene Kantor. *Aegaeum* 18:211–214.

Mullins, R.A. 1999. The excavation at Tel Rehov: the chronology of Iron Age II. *American Schools of Oriental Research Newsletter* 49(1):7–9.

Munn-Rankin, M. 1980. Mesopotamian chronology: a reply to James Mellaart. *Antiquity* 54:128–129.

Murnane, W.J. 1971. Once again the dates of Tuthmose III and Amenhotep II. *Journal of the Near Eastern Society of Columbia University* 3:1–7.

Murnane, W.J. 1977. *Ancient Egyptian coregencies.* Studies in Ancient Oriental Civilization 40. Chicago: Oriental Institute.

Murnane, W.J. 1983. Review of R. Krauss, *Das Ende der Amarnazeit: Beiträge zur Geschichte und chronologie des Neuen Reiches. Orientalia* 52:264–284.

Murnane, W.J. 1995. *Texts from the Amarna period in Egypt.* Atlanta: Scholars Press.

Myres, J.L. 1893–1895. Some pre-historic pottery from Kamarais, in Crete. *Proceedings of the Society of Antiquaries of London* 15:351–356.

Na'aman, N. 1976. A new look at the chronology of Alalakh VII. *Anatolian Studies* 26:129–143.

Na'aman, N. 1984. Statements of time-spans by Babylonian and Assyrian kings and Mesopotamian chronology. *Iraq* 46:115–123.

Na'aman, N. 1994a. The Hurrians and the end of the Middle Bronze Age in Palestine. *Levant* 26:175–187.

Na'aman, N. 1994b. The Canaanites and their land: a rejoinder. *Ugarit-Forschungen* 26:397–418.

Na'aman, N. 1999. Four notes on the size of Late Bronze Age Canaan. *Bulletin of the American Schools of Oriental Research* 313:31–37.

Needler, W. 1962. A dagger of Ahmose I. *Archaeology* 15:172–175.

Neer, R. 1997. Beazley and the language of connoisseurship. *Hephaistos* 15:7–30.

Negbi, O. 1970. *The hoards of goldwork from Tell el-ʿAjjul.* Studies in Mediterranean Archaeology 25. Göteborg: Paul Åströms Förlag.

Negbi, O. 1978. Cypriote imitations of Tell-el-Yahudiyeh ware from Toumba tou Skourou. *American Journal of Archaeology* 82:137–151.

Negbi, O. 1986. The climax of urban development in Bronze Age Cyprus. *Report of the Department of Antiquities, Cyprus:* 97–121.

Negbi, O. 1989. Bronze Age pottery. In Z. Herzog, G. Rapp Jr. and O. Negbi (eds.), *Excavations at Tel Michal, Israel:* 43–63. Minneapolis and Tel Aviv: University of Minnesota Press and the Sonia and Marco Nadler Institute of Archaeology, Tel Aviv University.

Negbi, O. 1994. The 'Libyan landscape' from Thera: a review of Aegean enterprises overseas in the Late Minoan IA period. *Journal of Mediterranean Archaeology* 7:73–112.

Nelson, D.E., Vogel, J.S. and Southon, J.R. 1990. Another suite of confusing radiocarbon dates for the destruction of Akrotiri. In D.A. Hardy and A.C. Renfrew (eds.), *Thera and the Aegean world III. Volume three: chronology:* 197–206. London: The Thera Foundation.

Neugebauer, O. 1929. Zur Frage der astronomischen Fixierung der babylonischen Chronologie. *Orientalistische Literaturzeitung* 32:913–921.

Neugebauer, O. 1938. Die Bedeutungslosigkeit der 'Sothisperiode' für die älteste ägyptische Chronologie. *Acta Orientalia* 17:169–195.

Neugebauer, O. 1969. *The exact sciences in antiquity.* Second edition. New York: Dover Publications.

Neugebauer, O. 1975. *A history of ancient mathematical astronomy.* Berlin: Springer-Verlag.

Neugebauer, O. and Parker, R.A. 1960–1969. *Egyptian astronomical texts.* 3 vols, 1960, 1964, 1969. Providence: Brown University Press.

Neve, P. 1993. *Hattusa: Stadt der Götter und Tempel: Neue Ausgrabungen in der Hauptstadt der Hethiter.* Mainz am Rhein: Philipp von Zabern.

Newhall, C.G. and Punongbayan, R.S. (eds.). 1996. *Fire and mud: eruptions and lahars of Mount Pinatbo, Philippines.* Quezon City: Philippine Institute of Volcanology and Seismology, and Seattle: University of Washington Press.

Newhall, C.G. and Self, S. 1982. The volcanic explosivity index (VEI): an estimate of explosive magnitude for historical volcanism. *Journal of Geophysical Research* 81:1,231–1,238.

Newton, C.T. 1878. Dr. Schliemann's exploration of Mycenae. *Edinburgh Review* 147:220–256 (reprinted in Newton, C.T. 1880. *Essays on Art and archeology.* London: Macmillan)

Nicholson, P.T., Jackson, C.M. and Trott, K.M. 1997. The Ulu Burun glass ingots, cylindrical vessels and Egyptian glass. *Journal of Egyptian Archaeology* 83:143–153.

Nicolaou, I and Nicolaou, K. 1989. *Kazaphani. A Middle/Late Cypriot tomb at Kazaphani-Ayios Andronikos: T.2A, B.* Nicosia: Department of Antiquities, Cyprus.

Niemeier, B. and Niemeier, W.-D. 1997. Milet 1994–1995. Projekt «Minoisch-mykenisches bis protogeometrisches Milet»: Zielsetzung und Grabungen auf dem Stadionhügel und am Athena-tempel. *Archäologischer Anzeiger:* 189–248.

Niemeier, W.-D. 1979a. Towards a new definition of Late Minoan II. *American Journal of Archaeology* 83:212–214.

Niemeier, W.-D. 1979b. The master of the Gournia octopus stirrup jar and a Late Minoan I pottery workshop at Gournia exporting to Thera. *Temple University Aegean Symposium* 4:18–26.

Niemeier, W.-D. 1980. Die Katastrophe von Thera und die spätminoische Chronologie. *Jahrbuch des Deutschen Archäologischen Instituts* 95:1–76.

Niemeier, W.-D. 1983. The character of the Knossian palace society in the second half of the fifteenth century B.C.: Mycenaean or Minoan? In O. Krzyszkowska and L. Nixon (eds.), *Minoan society. Proceedings of the Cambridge Colloquium 1981:* 217–236. Bristol: Bristol Classical Press.

Niemeier, W.-D. 1985. *Die Palaststilkeramik von Knossos: Stil, Chronologie und Historischer Kontext.* Archäologische Forschungen 13. Berlin: Mann.

Niemeier, W.-D. 1986. Creta, Egeo e Mediterraneo agli inizi del bronzo tardo. In M. Marazzi, S. Tusa and L. Vagnetti (eds.), *Traffici Micenei nel Mediterraneo: problemi storici e documentazione archeologica:* 245–270. Taranto: Istituto per la Storia e l'Archeologia della Magna Grecia.

Niemeier, W.-D. 1990. New archaeological evidence for a 17th century date of the 'Minoan eruption' from Israel (tel Kabri, western Galilee). In D.A. Hardy and A.C. Renfrew (eds.), *Thera and the Aegean world III. Volume three: chronology:* 120–126. London: The Thera Foundation.

Niemeier, W.-D. 1991. Minoan artisans travelling overseas: the Alalakh frescoes and the painted plaster floor at Tel Kabri (western Galilee). *Aegaeum* 7:189–201.

Niemeier, W.-D. 1994. Knossos in the New Palace period (MMIII–LMIB) In D. Evely, H. Hughes-Brock and N. Momigliano (eds.), *Knossos: a labyrinth of history. Papers presented in honour of Sinclair Hood:* 71–88. Oxford: The British School at Athens.

Niemeier, W.-D. 1995a. Tel Kabri: Aegean fresco paintings in a Canaanite palace. In S. Gitin (ed.), *Recent excavations in Israel: a view to the west. Reports on Kabri, Nami, Miqne-Ekron, Dor, and Ashkelon:* 1–15. Archaeological Institute of America Colloquia and Conference Papers, No.1. Dubuque: Kendall/Hunt.

Niemeier, W.-D. 1995b. Minoans and Hyksos: Aegean frescoes in the Levant. *Bulletin of the Institute of Classical Studies* 40:258–260.

Niemeier, W.-D. 1998. The Mycenaeans in western Anatolia and the problem of the origins of the Sea Peoples. In S. Gitin, A. Mazar and E. Stern (eds.), *Mediterranean peoples in transition: thirteenth to early tenth centuries BCE:* 17–65. Jerusalem: Israel Exploration Society.

Niemeier, W.-D. and Niemeier, B. 1998. Minoan frescoes in the eastern Mediterranean. *Aegaeum* 18:69–98.

Ninkovich, D. and Heezen, B.C. 1965. Santorini tephra. *Submarine Geology and Geophysics (Colston Papers)* 17:413–453.

Obsomer, C. 1995. *Sésostris Iᵉʳ: étude chronologique et historique de règne.* Brussels: Connaissance de l'Égypte ancienne.

O'Connor, D. 1997. The Hyksos period in Egypt. In E.D. Oren (ed.), *The Hyksos: new historical and archaeological perspectives:* 45–67. Philadelphia: The University Museum, University of Pennsylvania.

O'Connor, D. and Cline, E.H. (eds.). 1998. *Amenhotep III: perspectives on his reign.* Ann Arbor: The University of Michigan Press.

Oelsner, J. 1988. Review of P.J. Huber *et al., Astronomical dating of Babylon I and Ur III. Orientalistische Literaturzeitung* 83:554–558.

Oeschger, H. and Siegenthaler, U. 1988. How has the atmospheric concentration of CO_2 changed? In F.S. Rowland and I.S.A. Isaksen (eds.), *The changing atmosphere:* 5–23. New York: John Wiley & Sons.

Olivier, J.-P. (ed.). 1992. *Mykenaïka: actes du IXe Colloque international sur les textes mycéniens et égéens organisé par le Centre de l'Antiquité Grecque et Romaine de la Fondation Hellénique de Recherches Scientifiques et l'École française d'Athènes.* Bulletin de Correspondance Hellénique Supplément 25. Athens: École française d'Athènes.

Olson, E.A. and Broecker, W.A. 1959. Lamont natural radiocarbon measurements V. *Radiocarbon* 1:1–28.

Önhan, T. 1989. Cylinder seal inscriptions of Samsi-Adad I and his officials from Acemhöyük. In K. Emre, B. Hrouda, M. Mellink and N. Özgüç (eds.), *Anatolia and the ancient Near East. Studies in honor of Tahsin Özgüç:* 481–483. Ankara: Türk Tarih Kurumu.

Oppenheim, A.L. 1967. *Letters from Mesopotamia* Chicago: University of Chicago Press.

Oren, E.D. 1969. Cypriote imports in the Palestinian Late Bronze I context. *Opuscula Atheniensia* 9:127–150.

Oren, E.D. (ed.). 1997a. *The Hyksos: new historical and archaeological perspectives.* Philadelphia: The University Museum, University of Pennsylvania.

Oren, E.D. 1997b. The "Kingdom of Sharuhen" and the Hyksos Kingdom. In E.D. Oren (ed.), *The Hyksos: new historical and archaeological perspectives:* 253–283. Philadelphia: The University Museum, University of Pennsylvania.

Oren, E.D. n.d. Early White Slip pottery in Canaan: spatial and chronological perspectives. Manuscript of paper presented to the White Slip Ware Conference held in Nicosia 29–30 October 1998. Paper to be published in the conference proceedings: V. Karageorghis (ed.), *White Slip Ware. Proceedings of an International Conference Organized by the Anastasios G. Leventis Foundation, Nicosia in Honour of Malcolm Wiener, Nicosia 29th–30th October 1998.* In Press.

Oren, E., Olivier, J.-P., Goren, Y., Betancourt, P.P., Myer, G.H. and Yellin, J. 1996. A Minoan graffito from Tel Haror (Negev, Israel). *Cretan Studies* 5:91–118.

Orlin, L.L. 1970. *Assyrian colonies in Cappadocia.* Studies in Ancient History 1. The Hague: Mouton.

Otten, H. 1969. *Sprachliche Stellung und Datierung des Madduwatta-Textes.* Studien zu den Bogazköy-Texten 11.Weisbaden: Harrassowitz.

Özgüç, N. 1968. *Kanis Karumu Ib Kati Mühürleri ve Mühür Baskilari/Seals and seal impressions of level Ib from Karum Kanish.* Ankara: Türk Tarih Kurumu.

Özgüç, N. 1980. Seal impressions from the palaces at Acemhöyük. In E. Porada (ed.), *Ancient art in seals:* 61–100. Princeton: Princeton University Press.

Özgüç, N. 1988. Anatolian cylinder seals and impressions from Kültepe and Acemhöyük in the second millennium BC. In H.I.H. Prince T. Mikasa (ed.), *Essays on Anatolian studies in the second millennium B.C.:* 22–34. Wiesbaden: Harrassowitz.

Özgüç, T. 1986. *Kültepe-Kanis. II. New researches at the trading centre of the ancient Near East.* Ankara: Türk Tarih Kurumu.

Padgett, M. 1990. White Slip. In E.D.T. Vermeule and F.Z. Wolsky, *Toumba tou Skourou. A Bronze Age potter's quarter on Morphou Bay in Cyprus. The Harvard University–Museum of Fine Arts, Boston Cyprus Expedition:* 371–376. Cambridge, Mass.: Harvard University Press.

Page, D.L. 1970. *The Santorini volcano and the desolation of Minoan Crete.* London: Society for the Promotion of Hellenic Studies.

Page, D.L. 1978. On the relation between the Thera eruption and the destruction of eastern Crete, c.1450 B.C. In C. Doumas (ed.), *Thera and the Aegean world I:* 691–698. London: Thera and the Aegean World.

Palaima, T.G. 1989. Cypro-Minoan scripts: problems of historical context. In Y. Duhoux, T.G. Palaima and J. Bennet (eds.), *Problems in decipherment:* 121–187. Louvain-la-Neuve: Peeters.

Palais, J.M., Germani, M.S. and Zielinski, G.A. 1992. Inter-hemispheric transport of volcanic ash from a 1259 AD volcanic eruption to the Greenland and Antarctic ice sheets. *Geophysical Research Letters* 19:801–804.

Palais, J.M., Kirchner, S. and Delmas, R.J. 1990. Identification of some global volcanic horizons by major element analysis of fine ash in Antarctic ice. *Annals of Glaciology* 14:216–240.

Palais, J.M., Kyle, P.R., Mosley-Thompson, E. and Thomas, E. 1987. Correlation of a 3,200 year old tephra in ice cores from Vostok and South Pole Stations, Antarctica. *Geophysical Research Letters* 14:804–807.

Pallister, J.S., Hoblitt, R.P., Meeker, G.P., Knight, R.J. and Siems, D.F. 1996. Magma mixing at Mount Pinatubo: petrographic and chemical evidence from the 1991 deposits. In C.G. Newhall and R.S. Punongbayan (eds.), *Fire and mud: eruptions and lahars of Mount Pinatubo, Philippines*: 687–731. Seattle: University of Washington Press.

Palmer, L.R. 1964. To the editor. *Nestor* 2:323–325.

Palmer, L.R. 1981. The Khyan Lid deposit at Knossos. *Kadmos* 20:108–128.

Palmer, L.R. 1984. The Linear B palace at Knossos. In P. Åström, L.R. Palmer and L. Pomerance, *Studies in Aegean chronology*: 26–119. Studies in Mediterranean Archaeology and Literature, Pocket-book 25. Gothenburg: Paul Åströms Förlag.

Pålsson Hallager, B. 1988. Mycenaean pottery in LMIIIA1 deposits at Khania, western Crete. In E.B. French and K.A. Wardle (eds.), *Problems in Greek prehistory. Papers presented at the Centenary Conference of the British School of Archaeology at Athens, Manchester, April 1986*: 173–183. Bristol: Bristol Classical Press.

Panagiotaki, M. 1998. Dating the Temple Repositories vases. *Annual of the British School at Athens* 93:185–198.

Pang, K.D. and Chou, H-h. 1985. Three very large volcanic eruptions in antiquity and their effects on the climate of the ancient world. *EOS. Transactions, American Geophysical Union* 66:816.

Pang, K.D., Srivastava, S.K. and Chou, H.-h. 1988. Climatic impacts of past volcanic eruptions: inferences from ice-core, tree ring and historical data. *EOS. Transactions, American Geophysical Union* 69:1,062.

Pang, K.D., Keston, R., Srivastava, S.K. and Chou, H-h. 1989. Climatic and hydrologic extremes in early Chinese history: possible causes and dates. *EOS. Transactions, American Geophysical Union* 70:1,095.

Papadopoulos, J.K. 1996. Euboians in Macedonia? A closer look. *Oxford Journal of Archaeology* 15:151–181.

Papadopoulos, J.K. 1997. Phantom Euboians. *Journal of Mediterranean Archaeology* 10:191–219.

Papadopoulos, J.K. 1998. From Macedonia to Sardinia: problems of Iron Age Aegean chronology, and assumptions of Greek maritime primacy. In M.S. Balmuth and R.H. Tykot (eds.), *Sardinian and Aegean chronology: towards the resolution of relative and absolute dating in the Mediterranean*: 363–369. Studies in Sardinian Archaeology V. Oxford: Oxbow.

Papale, P. 1999. Strain-induced magma fragmentation in explosive eruptions. *Nature* 397:425–428.

Parker, D.E. 1985. Frost rings in trees and volcanic eruptions. *Nature* 313:160–161.

Parker, R.A. 1950. *The calendars of ancient Egypt*. Chicago: University of Chicago Press.

Parker, R.A. 1957. The lunar dates of Tuthmosis III and Ramesses II. *Journal of Near Eastern Studies* 16:39–43.

Parker, R.A. 1970. The beginning of the lunar month in ancient Egypt. *Journal of Near Eastern Studies* 29:217–220.

Parker, R.A. 1976. The sothic dating of the Twelfth and Eighteenth Dynasties. In J.H. Johnson and E.F. Wente (eds.), *Studies in honour of George R. Hughes, January 12, 1977*: 177–189. Studies in Ancient Oriental Civilization 39. Chicago: Oriental Institute.

Parr, P.J. 1973. The origin of the Canaanite jar. In D.E. Strong (ed.), *Archaeological theory and practice*: 173–181. London: Seminar Press.

Pearson, G.W. 1986. Precise calendrical dating of known growth-period samples using a 'curve fitting' technique. *Radiocarbon* 28:292–299.

Pearson, G.W. 1987. How to cope with calibration. *Antiquity* 61:98–103.

Pearson, G.W., Pilcher, J.R. and Baillie, M.G.L. 1983. High precision ^{14}C measurements of Irish oaks to show the natural ^{14}C variations from 200BC to 4000BC. *Radiocarbon* 25:179–186.

Pearson, G.W., Pilcher, J.R., Baillie, M.G.L., Corbet, D.M. and Qua, F. 1986. High precision C-14 measurements of Irish oaks to show the natural C-14 variations from AD 1840–5210 BC. *Radiocarbon* 28:911–934.

Pearson, G.W., Pilcher, J.R., Baillie, M.G.L., and Hillam, J. 1977. Absolute radiocarbon dating using a low altitude European tree-ring calibration. *Nature* 270:25–28.

Pearson, G.W. and Qua, F. 1993. High-precision ^{14}C measurement of Irish oaks to show the natural ^{14}C variations from AD 1840–5000 BC: a correction. *Radiocarbon* 35:105–123.

Pearson, G.W. and Stuiver, M. 1986. High-precision calibration of the radiocarbon time scale, 500–2500 BC. *Radiocarbon* 28:839–862.

Pearson, G.W. and Stuiver, M. 1993. High-precision bidecadal calibration of the radiocarbon time scale, 500–2500 BC. *Radiocarbon* 35:25–33.

Peltenburg, E. 1996. From isolation to state formation in Cyprus, c.3500–1500 B.C. In V. Karageorghis and D. Michaelides (eds.), *The development of the Cypriot economy from the prehistoric period to the present day:* 17–43. Nicosia: University of Cyprus and the Bank of Cyprus.

Petrie, W.M.F. 1890. The Egyptian bases of Greek history. *Journal of Hellenic Studies* 11:271–277.

Petrie, W.M.F. 1891a. *Illahun, Kahun and Gurob, 1889–90.* London: David Nutt.

Petrie, W.M.F. 1891b. Notes on the antiquities of Mykenae. *Journal of Hellenic Studies* 12:199–205.

Petrie, W.M.F. 1894. *Tell el Amarna.* London: Methuen.

Petrie, W.M.F. 1931–1934. *Ancient Gaza, I–IV.* London: British School of Archaeology in Egypt and Bernard Quaritch.

Petrie, W.M.F., Mackay, E.J.H., and Murray, M.A. 1952. *City of shepherd kings* and *Ancient Gaza V.* London: British School of Egyptian Archaeology and Bernard Quaritch.

Philip, G. 1995. Tell el-Dabᶜa metalwork: patterns and purpose. In W.V. Davies and L. Schofield (eds.), *Egypt, the Aegean and the Levant: interconnections in the second millennium BC:* 66–83. London: British Museum Publications.

Philip, G.M. and Watson, D.F. 1989. Some geometric aspects of the ternary diagram. *Journal of Geological Education* 37:27–29.

Phillips, J.S. 1991. *The impact and implications of the Egyptian and 'Egyptianizing' material found in Bronze Age Crete ca.3000 – ca.1100 B.C.* Ph.D. dissertation, University of Toronto. Ann Arbor: University Microfilms International.

Pichler, H. and Schiering, W. 1980. Der spätbronzezeitliche Ausbruch des Thera-Vulkans und seine Auswirkungen auf Kreta. *Archäologischer Anzeiger:* 1–33.

Pickles, S. and Peltenburg, E. 1998. Metallurgy, society and the Bronze/Iron transition in the east Mediterranean and the Near East. *Report of the Department of Antiquities, Cyprus:* 67–100.

Piggott, S. 1966. *Approach to archaeology.* Harmondsworth: Penguin Books.

Pilcher, J.R., Baillie, M.G.L., Schmidt, B. and Becker, B. 1984. A 7272-year tree-ring chronology for western Europe. *Nature* 312:150–152.

Pilcher, J.R., Hall, V.A. and McCormac, F.G. 1995. Dates of Holocene Icelandic volcanic eruptions from tephra layers in Irish peats. *The Holocene* 5:103–110.

Pilides, D. 1992. Monochrome Ware: its regional variation. In P. Åström (ed.), *Acta Cypria: acts of an international congress on Cypriote archaeology held in Göteborg on 22–24 August 1991,* Part 2: 289–305. Studies in Mediterranean Archaeology and Literature Pocket-book 120. Jonsered: Paul Åströms Förlag.

Pinto, J.P., Turco, R.P. and Toon, O.B. 1989. Self-limiting physical and chemical effects in volcanic clouds. *Journal of Geophysical Research* 94:11,165–11,174.

Platon, N. 1984. De nouveau le problème de la destruction des centres néopalatiaux minoens. In *Aux origines de l'Hellénisme. La Crète et la Grèce. Hommage à Henri van Effenterre présenté par le Centre G. Glotz:* 101–109. Paris: Publications de la Sorbonne.

Plicht, van der J. 1993. The Groningen radiocarbon calibration program. *Radiocarbon* 35:231–237.

Plicht, van der J. and McCormac, F.G. 1995. A note on calibration curves. *Radiocarbon* 37:963–964.

Plicht, van der J., Jansma, E. and Kars, H. 1995. The "Amsterdam Castle": a case study of wiggle-matching and the proper calibration curve. *Radiocarbon* 37:965–968.

Poebel, A. 1943. The Assyrian king list from Khorsabad – concluded. *Journal of Near Eastern Studies* 2:56–90.

Pomerance, L. 1970. *The final collapse of Santorini (Thera): 1400 B.C. or 1200 B.C.?* Studies in Mediterranean Archaeology 26. Göteborg: Paul Åströms Förlag.

Pomerance, L. 1971. The final collapse of Santorini (Thera). 1400B.C. or 1200 B.C.? In S. Marinatos and D. Ninkovich (eds.), *Acta of the 1st International Scientific Congress on the Volcano of Thera:* 384–394. Athens: Archaeological Services of Greece.

Pomerance, L. 1975. Comments on the Vitaliano geological report. *American Journal of Archaeology* 79:83–84.

Pomerance, L. 1976. The peripatetic Santorini tephra. *American Journal of Archaeology* 80:305.

Pomerance, L. 1979. Thera and the Aegean World: the interdisciplinary meeting held at Thera, 18–25 August 1978. *Kadmos* 18:178–180.

Pomerance, L. 1984. A note on the carved stone ewers from the Khyan lid deposit. In P. Åström, L.R. Palmer and L. Pomerance, *Studies in Aegean chronology:* 15–26. Studies in Mediterranean Archaeology and Literature, Pocket-book 25. Gothenburg: Paul Åströms Förlag.

Ponomareva, V., Pevzner, M.M. and Melekestsev, I.V. 1998. Large debris avalanches and associated eruptions in the Holocene eruptive history of Shiveluch Volcano, Kamchatka, Russia. *Bulletin of Volcanology* 59:490–505.

Poole, R.S. 1964 [reprint 1892 original]. *Catalogue of the coins of Alexandria and the nomes.* Bologna: Arnaldo Forni.

Popham, M.R. 1962. The Proto White Slip pottery of Cyprus. *Opuscula Atheniensia* 4:277–297.

Popham, M.R. 1963. Two Cypriot sherds from Crete. *Annual of the British School at Athens* 58:89–93.

Popham, M.R. 1966. White Slip ware. In P. Åström, *Excavations at Kalopsidha and Ayios Iakovos in Cyprus:* 94–97. Studies in Mediterranean Archaeology 2. Lund: Studies in Mediterranean Archaeology.

Popham, M.R. 1967. Late Minoan pottery, a summary. *Annual of the British School at Athens* 62:337–351.

Popham, M.R. 1970a. Late Minoan chronology. *American Journal of Archaeology* 74:226–228.

Popham, M.R. 1970b. *The destruction of the palace at Knossos: pottery of the Late Minoan IIIA period.* Studies in Mediterranean Archaeology 12. Göteborg: Paul Åströms Förlag.

Popham, M.R. 1972a. White Slip ware. In P. Åström, *The Swedish Cyprus Expedition,* vol.IV, part 1C: 431–471. Lund: The Swedish Cyprus Expedition.

Popham, M.R. 1972b. A note on the relative chronology of White Slip ware. In L. Åström and P. Åström, *The Swedish Cyprus Expedition,* vol.IV, part 1D: 699–705.

Popham, M.R. 1973. Sellopoulou Tomb 4. Some aspects of the finds. In *Pepragmena tou G' Diethnous Kretologikou Synedriou,* Vol A':268–273. Athens.

Popham, M.R. 1975. Late Minoan II Crete: a note. *American Journal of Archaeology* 79:372–374.

Popham, M.R. 1977. Notes from Knossos, part 1. *Annual of the British School at Athens* 72:185–195.

Popham, M.R. 1979. Thera and the Aegean world. *Antiquity* 53:57–59.

Popham, M.R. 1980. Cretan sites occupied between c.1450 and 1400 BC. *Annual of the British School at Athens* 75:163–167.

Popham, M.R. 1984. *The Minoan Unexplored Mansion at Knossos.* London: The British School at Athens.

Popham, M.R. 1988. The historical implications of the Linear B archive at Knossos dating to either c.1400 B.C. or 1200 B.C. *Cretan Studies* 1:217–227.

Popham, M.R. 1990. Pottery styles and chronology. In D.A. Hardy and A.C. Renfrew (eds.), *Thera and the Aegean world III. Volume three: chronology:* 27–28. London: The Thera Foundation.

Popham, M.R. 1997. The final destruction of the palace at Knossos: seals, sealings and pottery: a reconsideration. In J. Driessen and A. Farnoux (eds.), *La Créte Mycénienne: actes de la table ronde internationale, 26–28 mars 1991:* 375–385. Bulletin de Correspondance Hellénique Supplément 30. Athens: École française d'Athènes.

Popham, M.R., Catling, E.A. and Catling, H.W. 1974. Sellopoulou tombs 3 and 4, two Late Minoan graves near Knossos. *Annual of the British School at Athens* 69:195–257.

Popper, K.R. 1972. *The logic of scientific discovery.* 6th revised impression. London: Hutchinson.

Porter, B. and Moss, R.L.B. 1994. *Topographical bibliography of ancient Egyptian hieroglyphic texts, reliefs and paintings. II. Theban Temples.* Second edition, revised and augmented. Oxford: Griffith Institute, Ashmolean Museum.

Porter, S.C. 1986. Pattern and forcing of northern hemisphere glacier variations during the last millennium. *Quaternary Research* 26:27–48.

Portugali, Y. and Knapp, A.B. 1985. Cyprus and the Aegean: a spatial analysis of interaction in the 17th–14th centuries B.C. In A.B. Knapp and T. Stech (eds.), *Prehistoric production and exchange: the Aegean and eastern Mediterranean:* 44–78. Monograph 25. Los Angeles: Institute of Archaeology, University of California.

Postgate, N. 1992. The chronology of Assyria – an insurmountable obstacle. *Cambridge Archaeological Journal* 1:244–246.

Prag, A.J.N.W. 1989. Reconstructing King Midas: a first report. *Anatolian Studies* 39:159–165.

Prag, J. and Neave, R. 1997. *Making faces: using forensic and archaeological evidence.* College Station: Texas A&M University Press.

Pulak, C. 1997. The Uluburun shipwreck. In S. Swiny, R.L. Hohlfelder and H. Wylde Swiny (eds.), *Res maritimae: Cyprus and the eastern Mediterranean from prehistory to late antiquity:* 233–262. Atlanta: Scholars Press.

Pyle, D.M. 1989. Ice-core acidity peaks, retarded tree growth and putative eruptions. *Archaeometry* 31:88–91.

Pyle, D.M. 1990a. New estimates for the volume of the Minoan eruption. In D.A. Hardy, J. Keller, V.P. Galanopoulos, N.C. Flemming and T.H. Druitt (eds.), *Thera and the Aegean world III. Volume two: earth sciences:* 113–121. London: The Thera Foundation.

Pyle, D.M. 1990b. The application of tree-ring and ice-core studies to the dating of the Minoan eruption. In D.A. Hardy and A.C. Renfrew (eds.), *Thera and the Aegean world III. Volume three: chronology:* 167–173. London: The Thera Foundation.

Pyle, D.M. 1992. On the 'climatic effectiveness' of volcanic eruptions. *Quaternary Research* 37:125–129.

Pyle, D.M. 1997. The global impact of the Minoan eruption of Santorini, Greece. *Environmental Geology* 30:59–61.

Pyle, D.M. 1998. How did the summer go? *Nature* 393:415–417.

Pyle, D.M., Beattie, P.D. and Bluth, G.J.S. 1996. Sulphur emissions to the stratosphere from explosive volcanic eruptions. *Bulletin of Volcanology* 57:663–671.

Quack, J.F. 1996. Kft3w und i3sy. *Ägypten und Levante* 6:75–81.

Rackham, O. 1978. The flora and vegetation of Thera and Crete before and after the great eruption. In C. Doumas (ed.), *Thera and the Aegean world I:* 755–764. London: Thera and the Aegean World.

Rackham, O. 1990. Observations on the historical ecology of Santorini. In D.A. Hardy, J. Keller, V.P. Galanopoulos, N.C. Flemming and T.H. Druitt (eds.), *Thera and the Aegean world III. Volume two: earth sciences:* 384–391. London: The Thera Foundation.

Rainey, A.F. 1993. Sharhân/Sharuhen – the problem of identification. *Eretz-Israel* 24:178–187.

Rainey, A.F. 1996. Who is a Canaanite? A review of the textual evidence. *Bulletin of the American Schools of Oriental Research* 304:1–15.

Ramage, E. (ed.). 1978. *Atlantis: fact or fiction?* Bloomington: Indiana University Press.

Rampino, M.R. and Self, S. 1982. Historic eruptions of Tambora (1815), Krakatau (1883), and Agung (1963), their stratospheric aerosols, and climatic impact. *Quaternary Research* 18:127–143.

Rampino, M.R. and Self, S. 1993. Climate-volcanism feedback and the Toba eruption of ~74,000 years ago. *Quaternary Research* 40:269–280.

Rampino, M.R., Self, S. and Fairbridge, R.W. 1988. Volcanic winters. *Annual Review of Earth and Planetary Sciences* 16:73–99.

Ramsey, C.B. 1995. Radiocarbon calibration and analysis of stratigraphy: the OxCal program. *Radiocarbon* 37:425–430.

Randsborg, K. 1991. Historical implications: chronological studies in European archaeology 2000–500 B.C. *Acta Archaeologica* 62:89–108.

Randsborg, K. 1996a. The Nordic Bronze Age: chronological dimensions. *Acta Archaeologica* 67: 61–72.

Randsborg, K. (ed.). 1996b. *Absolute chronology: archaeological Europe 2500–500 B.C. Acta Archaeologica* 67 and Acta Archaeologica Supplementa 1. København: Munksgaard.

Rapp, G. Jr., Cooke, S.R.B. and Henrickson, E. 1973. Pumice from Thera (Santorini) identified from a Greek mainland archaeological excavation. *Science* 179:471–473.

Read, J.G. 1970. Early Eighteenth Dynasty chronology. *Journal of Near Eastern Studies* 29:1–11.

Read, J.G. 1995. Placement of El-Lahun lunar dates and resulting chronology. *Discussions in Egyptology* 33:87–113.

Redford, D.B. 1966. On the chronology of the Egyptian Eighteenth Dynasty. *Journal of Near Eastern Studies* 25:113–124.

Redford, D.B. 1967. *History and chronology of the Eighteenth Dynasty of Egypt: seven studies.* Toronto: University of Toronto Press.

Redford, D.B. 1970. The Hyksos invasion in history and tradition. *Orientalia* 39:1–51.

Redford, D.B. 1979. A gate inscription from Karnak and Egyptian involvement in western Asia during the early 18th Dynasty. *Journal of the American Oriental Society* 99:270–287.

Redford, D.B. 1986. *Pharaonic king-lists, annals and day-books. A contribution to the study of the Egyptian sense of history.* Mississauga: Benben Publications.

Redford, D.B. 1992. *Egypt, Canaan, and Israel in ancient times.* Princeton: Princeton University Press.

Redford, D.B. 1997. Textual sources for the Hyksos period. In E.D. Oren (ed.), *The Hyksos: new historical and archaeological perspectives:* 1–44. Philadelphia: The University Museum, University of Pennsylvania.

Redmount, C.A. 1993. Tell el-Maskhuta. Hyksos pottery. *Bulletin de Liaison du Groupe International d'étude de la céramique Égyptienne* 17:2–17.

Redmount, C.A. 1995. Pots and peoples in the Egyptian Delta: Tell el-Maskhuta and the Hyksos. *Journal of Mediterranean Archaeology* 8:61–89.

Rehak, P. 1996. Aegean breechcloths, kilts, and the Keftiu paintings. *American Journal of Archaeology* 100:35–51.

Rehak, P. 1997. Interconnections between the Aegean and the Orient in the second millennium B.C. *American Journal of Archaeology* 101:399–402.

Rehak, P. 1998. Aegean natives in the Theban tomb paintings: the Keftiu revisited. *Aegaeum* 18:39–51.

Rehak, P. and Younger, J.G. 1998a. Review of Aegean prehistory VII: Neopalatial, Final Palatial, and Postpalatial Crete. *American Journal of Archaeology* 102:91–173.

Rehak, P. and Younger, J.G. 1998b. International styles in ivory carving in the Bronze Age. *Aegaeum* 18:229–256.

Reiner, E. and Pingree, D. 1975. *Babylonian planetary omens: part one. The Venus tablet of Ammisaduqa.* Bibliotheca Mesopotamica 2.1 Malibu: Undena Publications.

Renaudin, L. 1922. Vases préhelléniques de Thera, à l'École française d'Athènes. *Bulletin Correspondance Hellénique* 66:113–159.

Renfrew, C. 1970. The tree-ring calibration of radiocarbon: an archaeological evaluation. *Proceedings of the Prehistoric Society* 36:280–311.

Renfrew, C. 1971. Obsidian and pumice: the use of recent igneous rocks in Aegean prehistory. In S. Marinatos and D. Ninkovich (eds.), *Acta of the 1st International Scientific Congress on the Volcano of Thera:* 430–436. Athens: Archaeological Services of Greece.

Renfrew, C. 1972. *The emergence of civilization. The Cyclades and the Aegean in the third millennium B.C.* London: Methuen.

Renfrew, C. 1973. *Before civilisation. The radiocarbon revolution and prehistoric Europe.* London: Jonathan Cape.

Renfrew, C. 1978. Phylakopi and the Late Bronze I period in the Cyclades. In C. Doumas (ed.), *Thera and the Aegean world I:* 403–421. London: Thera and the Aegean World.

Renfrew, C. 1979. The eruption of Thera and Minoan Crete. In P.D. Sheets and D.K. Grayson (eds.), *Volcanic activity and human ecology:* 565–585. New York: Academic Press.

Renfrew, C. 1996. Kings, tree rings and the Old World. *Nature* 381:733–734.

Renfrew, C. 1998. Word of Minos: the Minoan contribution to Mycenaean Greek and the linguistic geography of the Bronze Age Aegean. *Cambridge Archaeological Journal* 8:239–264.

Renfrew, C. and Bahn, P. 1996. *Archaeology: theories, methods and practice.* Second edition. London: Thames and Hudson.

Reza, Y. 1998. *The unexpected man.* Trans. C. Hampton. London: Faber and Faber.

Rice, M. 1998. *The power of the bull.* London: Routledge.

Riefstahl, E. 1972. An enigmatic faience figure. *Miscellanea Wilbouriana* 1:137–142.

Robins, G. 1981. The value of the estimated ages of the royal mummies at death as historical evidence. *Göttinger Miszellen* 45:63–68.

Robock, A. and Mao, J. 1995. The volcanic signal in surface-temperature observations. *Journal of Climate* 8:1,086–1,103.

Rodziewicz, M. 1988. Pottery studies in the Alexandrian region and the conference organised by the 'Ecole française d'Athènes'. *Bulletin de liaison du groupe international d'étude de la céramique égyptienne* 13:44–46.

Rohl, D.M. 1992. Some chronological conundrums of the 21st Dynasty. *Ägypten und Levante* 3:133–141.

Rohl, D.M. 1995. *A test of time. Volume one: the Bible – from myth to history.* London: Century.

Rose, L.E. 1994. The astronomical evidence for dating the end of the Middle Kingdom of ancient Egypt to the early second millennium: a reassessment. *Journal of Near Eastern Studies* 53:237–261.

Rose, L.E. 1997. Review of U. Luft, *Die chronologische Fixierung des ägyptischen Mittleren Reiches nach dem Tempelarchiv von Illahun. Journal of Near Eastern Studies* 56:119–121.

Ross, J.M. 1977. Is there any truth in Atlantis? *The Durham University Journal* 69:189–199.

Rowton, M.B. 1946. Mesopotamian chronology and the 'Era of Menophres'. *Iraq* 8:94–110.

Rowton, M.B. 1958. The date of Hammurabi. *Journal of Near Eastern Studies* 17:97–111.

Rowton, M.B. 1959. The background of the treaty between Ramesses II and Hattusilis III. *Journal of Cuneiform Studies* 13:1–11.

Rowton, M.B. 1960. Comparative chronology at the time of Dynasty XIX. *Journal of Near Eastern Studies* 19:15–22.

Rowton, M.B. 1966. The material from western Asia and the chronology of the Nineteenth Dynasty. *Journal of Near Eastern Studies* 25:240–258.

Rowton, M.B. 1970. Chronology. II. Ancient western Asia. In I.E.S. Edwards, C.J. Gadd and N.G.L. Hammond (eds.), *The Cambridge Ancient History*, vol.I, part 1:193–239. Third edition. Cambridge: Cambridge University Press.

Rozanski, K., Stichler, W., Gonfiantini, R., Scott, E.M., Beukens, R.P., Kromer, B. and van der Plicht, J. 1992. The IAEA ¹⁴C intercomparison exercise 1990. *Radiocarbon* 34:506–519.

Russell, P.J. 1986. *The pottery from the Late Cypriot IIC settlement at Kalavassos-Ayios Dhimitrios, Cyprus: the 1979–1984 excavation seasons.* Ph.D. dissertation, University of Pennsylvania. Ann Arbor: University Microfilms International.

Rutter, J.B. 1993. Review of Aegean prehistory II: the prepalatial Bronze Age of the southern and central Greek mainland. *American Journal of Archaeology* 97:745–797.

Rutter, J.B. 1999. Cretan external relations during Late Minoan IIIA2–B (ca. 1370–1200 BC): a view from the Mesara. In W. Phelps, Y. Lolos and Y. Vichos (eds.), *The Point Iria Wreck: interconnections in the Mediterranean ca. 1200 BC. Proceedings of the international conference, island of Spetses, 19 September 1998:* 139–186. Athens: Hellenic Institute of Marine Archaeology.

Ryholt, K.S.B. 1997. *The political situation in Egypt during the Second Intermediate Period c.1800–1550 B.C.* Carsten Niebuhr Institute Publications volume 20. Copenhagen: The Carsten Niebuhr Institute of Near Eastern Studies, University of Copenhagen, and Museum Tusculanum Press.

Sachs, A. 1970. Absolute dating from Mesopotamian records. In T.E. Allibone (ed.), *The impact of the natural sciences on archaeology: a joint symposium of the Royal Society and the British Academy:* 19–22. Philosophical Transactions of the Royal Society of London, Series A, 269. London: Oxford University Press for The British Academy.

Sadler, J.P. and Grattan, J.P. 1999. Volcanoes as agents of past environmental change. *Global and Planetary Change* 21:181–196.

Saidah, R. (ed. H. Seeden) 1993–1994. Beirut in the Bronze Age: the Kharji Tombs. *Berytus* 41:137–210.

Sakellarakis, E. and Sakellarakis, Y. 1984. The Keftiu and the Minoan thalassocracy. In R. Hägg and N. Marinatos (eds.), *The Minoan thalassocracy: myth and reality. Proceedings of the third international symposium at the Swedish Institute in Athens, 31 May–5 June, 1982:* 197–203. Skrifter Utgivna av Svenska Institut i Athen, 4°, 32. Stockholm: Paul Åströms Förlag.

Sallares, R. 1991. *The ecology of the ancient Greek world.* London: Duckworth.

Sallmann, N. (ed.). 1983. *Censorini de die natali liber ad Q. Caerellium.* Leipzig: Teubner.

Saltz, D.L. 1977. The chronology of the Middle Cypriote period. *Report of the Department of Antiquities, Cyprus:* 51–70.

Sanderson, S.K. (ed.). 1995. *Civilizations and world systems: studying world-historical change.* Walnut Creek: Altamira Press.

Sarpaki, A. 1990. 'Small fields or big fields?' That is the question. In D.A. Hardy, J. Keller, V.P. Galanopoulos, N.C. Flemming and T.H. Druitt (eds.), *Thera and the Aegean world III. Volume two: earth sciences:* 422–431. London: The Thera Foundation.

Savile, A. 1982. *The test of time: an essay in philosophical aesthetics.* Oxford: Clarendon Press.

Schaeffer, C.F.-A. 1948. *Stratigraphie comparé et chronologie de l'Asie Occidentale (IIIe et IIe millénaires).* Oxford: The Griffith Institute, Ashmolean Museum.

Schaeffer, C.F.-A. 1949. *Ugaritica II.* Mission de Ras Shamra Tome V. Paris: Paul Geuthner.

Schiffer, M.B. 1986. Radiocarbon dating and the 'old wood' problem: the case of the Hohokam chronology. *Journal of Archaeological Science* 13:13–30.

Schiffer, M.B. 1987. *Formation processes of the archaeological record.* Albuquerque: University of New Mexico Press.

Schilpp, P.A. (ed.). 1974. *The philosophy of Karl Popper.* La Salle: Open Court Publishing.

Schimmelmann, A., Zhao, M., Harvey, C.C. and Lange, C.B. 1998. A large California flood and correlative global climatic events 400 years ago. *Quaternary Research* 49:51–61.

Schimmelmann, A., Zhao, M., Harvey, C.C. and Lange, C.B. 1999. Reply to Van Geel *et al.*'s comment on "A large California flood and correlative global climatic events 400 years ago". *Quaternary Research* 51:111–112.

Schneider, J. 1977. Was there a pre-capitalist world system? *Peasant Studies Newsletter* 6(1):20–29.

Schnetzler, C.C., Bluth, G.J.S., Krueger, A.J. and Walter, L.S. 1997. A proposed volcanic sulfur dioxide index (VSI). *Journal of Geophysical Research* 102 B9:20,087–20,091.

Schoch, M. 1997. Die naturwissenschaftlichen Datierungen des spätbronzezeitlichen Vulkanausbruchs von Santorin. Eine kritische Diskussion. *Thetis* 4:51–62.

Schoep, I. 1999. Tablets and territories? Reconstructing Late Minoan IB political geography through undeciphered documents. *American Journal of Archaeology* 103:201–221.

Schofield, E. 1984. Destruction deposits of the earlier Late Bronze Age from Ayia Irini, Kea. In J.A. MacGillivray and R.L.N. Barber (eds.), *The prehistoric Cyclades: contributions to a workshop on Cycladic chronology:* 179–183. Edinburgh: Department of Classical Archaeology, University of Edinburgh.

Schofield, E. 1985. Ayia Irini, Keos, in Late Cycladic II. *Bulletin of the Institute of Classical Studies* 32: 155.

Scholes, K. 1956. The Cyclades in the later Bronze Age: a synopsis. *Annual of the British School at Athens* 51:9–40.

Schoo, J. 1937–1938. Vulkanische und seismische Aktivität des ägäischen Meeresbeckens im Spiegel der griechischen Mythologie. *Mnemosyne* Series 3, vol.4:257–294.

Schortman, E.M. and Urban, P.A. (eds.). 1992. *Resources, power, and interregional interaction.* New York: Plenum Press.

Schweingruber, F. 1988. *Tree rings: basics and applications of dendrochronology.* Dordrecht: Reidel.

Scott, E.M., Harkness, D.D. and Cook, G.T. 1997. Analytical protocol and quality assurance for ¹⁴C analyses: proposal for a further intercomparison. *Radiocarbon* 39:347–350.

Scott, E.M., Harkness, D.D. and Cook, G.T. 1998. Interlaboratory comparisons: lessons learned. *Radiocarbon* 40:331–340.

Scott, E.M., Long, A. and Kra, R. (eds.). 1990. *Proceedings of the international workshop on intercomparison of radiocarbon laboratories. Radiocarbon* 32(3):253–397.

Scott, W.E., Hoblitt, R.P., Torres, R.C., Self, S., Martinez, M.M.L. and Nillos, T. Jr. 1996. Pyroclastic flows of the June 15, 1991, climactic eruption of Mount Pinatubo. In C.G. Newhall and R.S. Punongbayan (eds.), *Fire and mud: eruptions and lahars of Mount Pinatubo, Philippines:* 545–570. Seattle: University of Washington Press.

Scranton, R.L. 1976. Of myth and Santorin. In J.H. Johnson and E.F. Wente (eds.), *Studies in honour of George R. Hughes, January 12, 1977:* 191–199. Studies in Ancient Oriental Civilization 39. Chicago: Oriental Institute.

Scuderi, L.A. 1990. Tree-ring evidence for climatically effective volcanic eruptions. *Quaternary Research* 34:67–85.

Scuderi, L.A. 1992. Climatically effective volcanism. *Quaternary Research* 37:130–135.

Sear, C.B., Kelly, P.M., Jones, P.D. and Goodness, C.M. 1987. Global surface-temperature responses to major volcanic eruptions. *Nature* 330:365–367.

Searle, J.R. 1995. *The construction of social reality.* London: Penguin.

Seger, J.D. 1965. *The pottery of Palestine at the close of the Middle Bronze Age: being a study of the MBIIC ceramic remains from biblical Shechem and their Palestinian correspondences.* Ph.D. dissertation, Harvard University. Harvard, Cambridge, Mass: Library Office Microfilms.

Seger, J.D. 1974. The Middle Bronze IIC date of the East Gate at Shechem. *Levant* 6:117–130.

Seger, J.D. 1975. The MBII fortifications at Shechem and Gezer: a Hyksos retrospective. *Eretz-Israel* 12:34–45.

Self, S. and King, A.J. 1996. Petrology and sulphur and chlorine emissions of the 1963 eruption of Gunung Agung, Bali, Indonesia. *Bulletin of Volcanology* 58:263–285.

Self, S., Zhao, J.-X., Holasek, R.E., Torres, R.C. and King, A.J. 1996. The atmospheric impact of the 1991 Mount Pinatubo eruption. In C.G. Newhall and R.S. Punongbayan (eds.), *Fire and mud: eruptions and lahars of Mount Pinatubo, Philippines:* 1,089–1,115. Seattle: University of Washington.

Seol, D.-I. and Yamazaki, K. 1998. QBO and Pinatubo signals in the mass flux at 100 hPa and stratospheric circulation. *Geophysical Research Letters* 25:1,641–1,644.

Shanks, M. 1992. *Experiencing the past: on the character of archaeology.* London: Routledge.

Shanks, M. 1996. *Classical archaeology of Greece: experiences of the discipline.* London: Routledge.

Shaw, J.W. 1986. Excavations at Kommos (Crete) during 1984–1985. *Hesperia* 55:219–269.

Shaw, J.W., van de Moortel, A., Day, P.M. and Kilikoglou, V. 1997. A LMIA pottery kiln at Kommos, Crete. *Aegaeum* 16:323–331.

Shaw, J.W., Van de Moortel, A., Day, P.M. and Kilikoglou, V. n.d. *A LMIA ceramic kiln in south-central Crete: function and pottery production.* Hesperia Supplement, in press.

Shaw, J.W. and Shaw, M.C. 1993. Excavations at Kommos (Crete) during 1986–1992. *Hesperia* 62:129–190.

Shaw, M. 1995. Bull leaping frescoes at Knossos and their influence on the Tell el-Dab'a murals. *Ägypten und Levante* 5:91–120.

Shaw, M. 1996. The bull-leaping fresco from below the Ramp House at Mycenae: a study in iconography and artistic transmission. *Annual of the British School at Athens* 91:167–190.

Shea,W.H. 1979. The conquest of Sharuhen and Megiddo reconsidered. *Israel Exploration Journal* 29:1–5.

Shelmerdine, C.W. 1992. Historical and economic considerations in interpreting Mycenaean texts. In J.-P. Olivier (ed.), *Mykenaïka: acts du IXe Colloque international sur les textes mycénians et égéens organisé par le Centre d'Antiquité Grecque et Romaine de la Fondation Hellénique de Recherches Scientifiques et l'École française d'Athènes*: 567–589. Bulletin de Correspondance Hellénique Supplément 25. Athens: École française d'Athènes.

Sherratt, A. 1993. What would a Bronze-Age world system look like? Relations between temperate Europe and the Mediterranean in later prehistory. *Journal of European Archaeology* 1.2:1–57.

Sherratt, A. and Sherratt, S. 1991. From luxuries to commodities: the nature of Mediterranean Bronze Age trading systems. In N.H. Gale (ed.), *Bronze Age trade in the Mediterranean. Papers presented at the conference held at Rewley House, Oxford, in December 1989*: 351–386. Studies in Mediterranean Archaeology 90. Jonsered: Paul Åströms Förlag.

Sherratt, A. and Sherratt, S. 1992. Urnfield reflections. *Cambridge Archaeological Journal* 1:247–251.

Sherratt, A. and Sherratt, S. 1998. Small worlds: interaction and identity in the ancient Mediterranean. *Aegaeum* 18:329–343.

Sherratt, S. (E.S.) 1990. Reading the texts: archaeology and the Homeric question. *Antiquity* 64:807–824.

Sherratt, S. 1994. Comment on Ora Negbi, 'The "Libyan Landscape" from Thera: a review of Aegean enterprises overseas in the Late Minoan IA period'. *Journal of Mediterranean Archaeology* 7:237–240.

Shott, M.J. 1998. Status and role of formation theory in contemporary archaeological practice. *Journal of Archaeological Research* 6:299–329.

Sidersky, D. 1940–1941. Nouvelle étude sur la chronologie de la dynastie hammurapienne. *Revue d'Assyriologie et d'Archéologie Orientale* 37:45–54.

Sigurdsson, H. 1982. Volcanic pollution and climate: the 1783 Laki eruption. *EOS. Transactions, American Geophysical Union* 63:601–602.

Sigurdsson, H., Carey, S. and Devine, J.D. 1990. Assessment of mass, dynamics and environmental effects of the Minoan eruption of Santorini volcano. In D.A. Hardy, J. Keller, V.P. Galanopoulos, N.C. Flemming and T.H. Druitt (eds.), *Thera and the Aegean world III. Volume two: earth sciences*: 100–112. London: The Thera Foundation.

Sigurdsson, H., Devine, J.D. and Davis, A.N. 1985. The petrologic estimation of volcanic degassing. *Jökull* 35:1–8.

Silva, S.L. de and Zielinksi, G.A. 1998. Global influence of the AD 1600 eruption of Huaynaputina, Peru. *Nature* 393:455–458.

Silverman, 1978. *The Gournia collection in the University Museum: a study in east Cretan pottery.* Ph.D. dissertation, University of Pennsylvania. Ann Arbor: University Microfilms International.

Simkin, T. 1994. Distant effects of volcanism–how big and how often? *Science* 264:913–914.

Simkin, T. and Fiske, R.J. (eds.). 1983. *Krakatau 1883: the volcanic eruption and its effects.* Washington, DC: Smithsonian Institution Press.

Simkin, T. and Siebert, L. 1994. *Volcanoes of the world.* Tucson: Geoscience Press.

Simpson, W.K. 1963. Studies in the Twelfth Egyptian Dynasty: I–II. *Journal of the American Research Centre in Egypt* 2:53–63.

Simpson, W.K. 1972. A tomb chapel relief of the reign of Amunemhet III and some observations on the length of the reign of Sesostris III. *Chronique d'Égypte* 47:45–54.

Simpson, W.K. 1984. Sesostris II, Sesostris III. In W. Helck and W. Westendorf (eds.), *Lexikon der Ägyptologie* V/6:899–906. Wiesbaden: Harrassowitz.

Sjöqvist, E. 1940. *Problems of the Late Cypriote Bronze Age.* Stockholm: The Swedish Cyprus Expedition.

Skeates, R. 1994. A radiocarbon date-list for prehistoric Italy (c.46,400BP–2450BP/400 cal. BC). In R. Skeates and R. Whitehouse (eds.), *Radiocarbon dating and Italian prehistory*: 147–288. Volume 3 Accordia

Specialist Studies on Italy, Volume 8 Archaeological Monographs of the British School at Rome. London: The British School at Rome, Accordia Research Centre, University of London.

Skeates, R. and Whitehouse, R. (eds.). 1994. *Radiocarbon dating and Italian prehistory.* Volume 3 Accordia Specialist Studies on Italy, Volume 8 Archaeological Monographs of the British School at Rome. London: The British School at Rome, Accordia Research Centre, University of London.

Smith, H.S. and Smith, A. 1976. A reconsideration of the Kamose text. *Zeitschrift für ägyptische Sprache und Altertumskunde* 103:48–76.

Smith, S. 1940. *Alalakh and chronology.* London: Lusac and company.

Smith, W.S. 1965. *Interconnections in the ancient Near East: a study of the relationship between the arts of Egypt, the Aegean and western Asia.* New Haven: Yale University Press.

Snodgrass, A.M. 1971. *The Dark Age of Greece: an archaeological survey of the 11th to the 8th centuries BC.* Edinburgh: Edinburgh University Press.

Snodgrass, A.M. 1983. Archaeology. In M. Crawford (ed.), *Sources for ancient history:* 137–184. Cambridge: Cambridge University Press.

Snodgrass, A.M. 1985. The new archaeology and the classical archaeologist. *American Journal of Archaeology* 89:31–37.

Snodgrass, A.M. 1987. *An archaeology of Greece: the present state and future scope of a discipline.* Berkeley: University of California Press.

Snodgrass, A. 1992. The Aegean angle. *Cambridge Archaeological Journal* 1:246–247.

Soles, J.S. 1997. A community of craft specialists at Mochlos. *Aegaeum* 16:425–431.

Soles, J.S. and Davaras, C. 1990. Theran ash in Minoan Crete: new excavations on Mochlos. In D.A. Hardy and A.C. Renfrew (eds.), *Thera and the Aegean world III. Volume three: chronology:* 89–95. London: The Thera Foundation.

Soles J.S. and Davaras, C. 1996. Excavations at Mochlos, 1992–1993. *Hesperia* 65:175–230.

Soles, J.S., Taylor, S.R. and Vitaliano, C.J. 1995. Tephra samples from Mochlos and their chronological implications for Neopalatial Crete. *Archaeometry* 37:385–393.

South, A.K., Russell, P.J. and Keswani, P.S. 1989. *Vasilikos Valley Project 3: Kalavassos-Ayios Dhimitrios II: ceramics, objects, tombs, special studies.* Studies in Mediterranean Archaeology 71:3. Göteborg: Paul Åströms Förlag.

South, S. 1977. *Method and theory in historical archaeology.* New York: Academic Press.

Spalinger, A.J. 1992. Night into day. *Zeitschrift für ägyptische Sprache und Altertumskunde* 119:144–156.

Spalinger, A.J. (ed.). 1994. *Revolutions in time: studies in ancient Egyptian calendrics.* San Antonio: Van Siclen Books.

Sparks, R.J., Melhuish, W.H., McKee, J.W.A., Ogden, J., Palmer, J.G. and Molloy, B.P.J. 1995. ^{14}C calibration in the southern hemisphere and the date of the last Taupo eruption: evidence from tree-ring sequences. *Radiocarbon* 37:155–163.

Sparks, R.S.J. 1976. Comment on "The volcanic eruption of Thera and its effects on the Mycenaean and Minoan civilizations" by I.G. Nixon. *Journal of Archaeological Science* 13:289–290.

Sparks, R.S.J. 1985. Archaeomagnetism, Santorini volcanic eruptions and fired destruction levels on Crete. *Nature* 313:74–75.

Sperber, L. *Untersuchungen zur Chronologie der Urnenfelderkultur im nördlichen Alpenvorland von der Schweiz bis Oberösterreich.* Bonn: Dr. Rudolf Habelt.

Sperling, J.W. 1973. *Thera and Therasia.* Athens: Athens Centre of Ekistics.

Stanley, D.J. and Sheng, H. 1986. Volcanic shards from Santorini (upper Minoan ash) in the Nile Delta, Egypt. *Nature* 320:733–735.

Steel, L. 1998. The social impact of Mycenaean imported pottery in Cyprus. *Annual of the British School at Athens* 93:285–296.

Stern, E. (ed.). 1993. *The new encyclopedia of archaeological excavations in the Holy Land.* Jerusalem: The Israel Exploration Society and Carta.

Stewart, J.R. 1974. *Tell el ʿAjjul: the Middle Bronze Age remains.* Edited by H.E. Kassis. Studies in Mediterranean Archaeology 38. Göteborg: Paul Åströms Förlag.

Stokes, M.A. and Smiley, T.L. 1968. *An introduction to tree-ring dating.* Chicago: University of Chicago Press.

Stokes, S. and Lowe, D.J. 1988. Discriminant function analysis of late Quaternary tephras from five volcanoes in New Zealand using glass shard major element chemistry. *Quaternary Research* 30:270–283.

Stokes, S., Lowe, D.J. and Froggatt, P.C. 1992. Discriminant function analysis and correlation of Late

Quaternary rhyolitic tephra deposits from Taupo and Okataina volcanoes, New Zealand, using glass shard major element composition. *Quaternary International* 13/14:103–117.

Stos-Gale, Z.A. and Gale, N.H. 1990. The role of Thera in the Bronze Age trade in metals. In D.A. Hardy, C.G. Doumas, J.A. Sakellarakis and P.M. Warren (eds.), *Thera and the Aegean world III. Volume one: archaeology*: 72–91. London: The Thera Foundation.

Stothers, R.B. and Rampino, M.R. 1983. Historic volcanism, European dry fogs, and Greenland acid precipitation, 1500 BC to AD 1500. *Science* 222:411–413.

Stothers, R.B., Wolff, J.A., Self, S. and Rampino, M.R. 1986. Basaltic fissure eruptions, plume heights, and atmospheric aerosols. *Geophysical Research Letters* 13:725–728.

Strange, J. 1980. *Caphtor/Keftiu: a new investigation*. Acta Theologica Danica 14. Leiden: E.J. Brill.

Stuiver, M. 1982. A high-precision calibration of the AD radiocarbon time scale. *Radiocarbon* 24:1–26.

Stuiver, M. and Becker, B. 1986. High-precision decadal calibration of the radiocarbon time scale, AD 1950–2500 BC. *Radiocarbon* 28:863–910.

Stuiver, M. and Becker, B. 1993. High-precision decadal calibration of the radiocarbon time scale, AD 1950–6000 BC. *Radiocarbon* 35:35–65.

Stuiver, M. and Braziunas, T.F. 1998. Anthropogenic and solar components of hemispheric ^{14}C. *Geophysical Research Letters* 25:329–332.

Stuiver, M., Braziunas, T.F., Grootes, P.M. and Zielinski, G.A. 1997. Is there evidence for solar forcing of climate in the GISP2 oxygen isotope record? *Quaternary Research* 48:259–266.

Stuiver, M. and Pearson, G.W. 1986. High-precision calibration of the radiocarbon time scale, AD 1950–500 BC. *Radiocarbon* 28:805–838.

Stuiver, M. and Pearson, G.W. 1992. Calibration of the radiocarbon time scale, 2500–5000 BC. In R.E. Taylor, A. Long and R.S. Kra (eds.), *Radiocarbon after four decades: an interdisciplinary perspective*: 19–33. New York: Springer-Verlag.

Stuiver, M. and Pearson, G.W. 1993. High-precision bidecadal calibration of the radiocarbon time scale, AD 1950–500 BC and 2500–6000 BC. *Radiocarbon* 35:1–23.

Stuiver, M. and Reimer, P.J. 1986. A computer program for radiocarbon age calibration. *Radiocarbon* 28:1,022–1,030.

Stuiver, M. and Reimer, P. J. 1993. Extended ^{14}C database and revised CALIB radiocarbon calibration program. *Radiocarbon* 35:215–230.

Stuiver, M., Reimer, P.J., Bard, E., Beck, J.W., Burr, G.S., Hughen, K.A., Kromer, B., McCormac, G., Plicht, J. van der, and Spurk, M. 1998. INTCAL98 radiocarbon age calibration, 24,000–0 cal BP. *Radiocarbon* 40:1,041–1,083.

Sullivan, D.G. 1988. The discovery of Santorini Minoan tephra in western Turkey. *Nature* 333:552–554.

Sullivan, D.G. 1990. Minoan tephra in lake sediments in western Turkey: dating the eruption and assessing the atmospheric dispersal of the ash. In D.A. Hardy and A.C. Renfrew (eds.), *Thera and the Aegean world III. Volume three: chronology*: 114–119. London: The Thera Foundation.

Sullivan, D.G. 1993. Effects of the Santorini eruption on Bronze Age settlement in Aegean Turkey. *American Journal of Archaeology* 97:330.

Swiny, S. 1979. *Southern Cyprus, c.2000–1500 B.C.* Ph.D. dissertation, University of London.

Swiny, S. 1981. Bronze Age settlement patterns in southwest Cyprus. *Levant* 13:51–87.

Swiny, S. 1997. So near and yet so far: Cyprus and Crete in the Early Bronze Age. In D. Christou *et al.* (eds.), *Proceedings of the international archaeological conference Cyprus and the Aegean in antiquity from the prehistoric period to the 7th century A.D. Nicosia 8–10 December 1995*: 47–55. Nicosia: Department of Antiquities.

Tabazadeh, A. and Turco, R.P. 1993. Stratospheric chlorine injection by volcanic eruptions: HCl scavenging and implications for ozone. *Science* 260:1,082–1,086.

Tadmor, H. 1970. Chronology of the ancient Near East in the second millennium BCE. In B. Mazar (ed.), *The world history of the Jewish people. II. Patriachs*: 63–101. London: W.H. Allen.

Tadmor, H. 1985. Nineveh, Calah and Israel: on Assyriology and the origins of Biblical archaeology. In *Biblical archaeology today: proceedings of the International Congress on Biblical archaeology, Jerusalem, April 1984*: 260–268. Jerusalem: Israel Exploration Society.

Tarling, D.H. and Downey, W.S. 1989. Archaeomagnetic study of the Late Minoan Kiln 2, Stratigraphical Museum Extension, Knossos. *Annual of the British School at Athens* 84:345–352.

Tarling, D.H. and Downey, W.S. 1990. Archaeomagnetic results from Late Minoan destruction levels on

Crete and the 'Minoan' tephra on Thera. In D.A. Hardy and A.C. Renfrew (eds.), *Thera and the Aegean world III. Volume three: chronology:* 146–158. London: The Thera Foundation.

Taylor, R.E. 1987. *Radiocarbon dating: an archaeological perspective.* Orlando: Academic Press.

Taylor, R.E. 1997. Radiocarbon dating. In R.E. Taylor and M.J. Aitken (eds.), *Chronometric dating in archaeology:* 65–96. New York: Plenum Press.

Taylor, R.E. and Aitken, M.J. (eds.). 1997. *Chronometric dating in archaeology.* New York: Plenum Press.

Taylor, R.E., Long, A. and Kra, R.S. (eds.). 1992. *Radiocarbon after four decades: an interdisciplinary perspective.* New York: Springer-Verlag.

Televantou, C. 1984. Kosmimata apo tin proïstoriki Thira. *Arkhaiologiki Ephemeris:* 14–54.

Thiele, E.R. 1983. *The mysterious numbers of the Hebrew kings.* New revised edition. Grand Rapids: Academie Books, Zondervan Publishing House.

Thomas, J. 1996. *Time, culture and identity: an interpretative archaeology.* London: Routledge.

Thomas, P.M. 1992. *LHIIIB:1 pottery from Tsoungiza and Zygouries.* Ph.D. dissertation, The University of North Carolina at Chapel Hill. Ann Arbor: University Microfilms International.

Thordarson, T., Self, S., Oskarsson, N. and Hulsebosch, T. 1996. Sulfur, chlorine, and fluorine degassing and atmospheric loading by the 1783–1784 AD Laki (Skaftar Fires) eruption in Iceland. *Journal of Volcanology and Geothermal Research* 58:205–225.

Tiradritti, F. (ed.). 1999. *Egyptian treasures from the Egyptian Museum in Cairo.* New York: Harry N. Abrams.

Tomlinson, R.A. 1996. Archaeology in Greece 1995–96. *Archaeological Reports* 42:1–47.

Trepte, C.R. and Hitchman, M.H. 1992. Tropical stratospheric circulation deduced from satellite aerosol data. *Nature* 355:626–628.

Trigger, B.G. 1989. *A history of archaeological thought.* Cambridge: Cambridge University Press.

Trigger, B.G. 1998. *Sociocultural evolution: calculation and contingency.* Oxford: Blackwell.

Tsountas, C. and Manatt, J.I. 1897. *The Mycenaean age.* London: Macmillan.

Tufnell, O. 1962. The Courtyard Cemetery at Tell el-ʿAjjul, Palestine. *Bulletin of the Institute of Archaeology, University of London* 3:1–37.

Tufnell, O. 1984. *Studies on scarab seals. II. Scarab seals and their contribution to history in the early second millennium BC.* Warminster: Aris & Phillips.

Tufnell, O., Inge, C.H. and Harding, L. 1940. *Lachish II (Tell ed Duweir): the Fosse Temple.* London: Oxford University Press for the Trustees of the late Sir Henry Wellcome.

Tufnell, O. *et al.* 1958. *Lachish IV (Tell ed-Duweir): the Late Bronze Age.* London: Oxford University Press for the Trustees of the late Sir Henry Wellcome.

Turner, S. 1994. *The social theory of practices: tradition, tacit knowledge, and pre-suppositions.* Chicago: University of Chicago Press.

Tykot, R.H. 1994. Radiocarbon dating and absolute chronology in Sardinia and Corsica. In R. Skeates and R. Whitehouse (eds.), *Radiocarbon dating and Italian prehistory:* 115–145. Volume 3 Accordia Specialist Studies on Italy, Volume 8 Archaeological Monographs of the British School at Rome. London: The British School at Rome, Accordia Research Centre, University of London.

Tyldesley, J. 1996. *Hatchepsut: the female pharaoh.* London: Viking.

Ugas, G. 1992. Considerazioni sullo sviluppo dell'architettura e della società nuragica. In R.H. Tykot and T.K. Andrews (eds.), *Sardinia in the Mediterranean: a footprint in the sea. Studies in Sardinian archaeology presented to Miriam S. Balmuth:* 221–234. Monographs in Mediterranean Archaeology 3. Sheffield: Sheffield Academic Press.

Vagnetti, L. 1993. Mycenaean pottery in Italy: fifty years of study. In C. Zerner, F. Zerner and J. Winder (eds.), *Proceedings of the International Conference Wace and Blegen Pottery as evidence for trade in the Aegean Bronze Age 1939–1989 held at the American School of Classical Studies at Athens, December 2–3, 1989:* 143–154. Amsterdam: J.C. Gieben.

Vallianou, D. 1996. New evidence of earthquake destructions in Late Minoan Crete. In S. Stiros and R.E. Jones (eds.), *Archaeoseismology:* 153–167. Fitch Laboratory Occasional Paper 7. Athens: Institute of Geology and Mineral Exploration and the British School at Athens.

Van de Moortel, A.M.P.A. 1997. *The transition from the protopalatial to the neopalatial society in south-central Crete: a ceramic perspective.* Ph.D. dissertation, Bryn Mawr College.

Vandenabeele, F. 1985. La chronologie des documents en Linéaire A. *Bulletin de Correspondance Hellénique* 109:3–20.

Vandersleyen, C. 1967. Une tempête sous le règne d'Amosis. *Revue d'Egyptologie* 19:123–159.

Vandersleyen, C. 1968. Deux nouveaux fragments de la stèle d'Amosis relatant une tempête. *Revue d'Egyptologie* 20:127–134.

Vandersleyen, C. 1971. *Les guerres d'Amosis, fondateur de la XVIIIe dynastie.* Monographes Reine Elisabeth 1. Brussels: Fondation égyptologique reine Elisabeth.

Vandersleyen, C. 1995. *L'Égypte et la vallée du Nil. Tome II. De la fin de l'Ancien Empire à la fin du Nouvel Empire.* Paris: Presses Universitaires de France.

van Effenterre, H. 1974. *La seconde fin du monde. Mycènes et la mort d'une civilisation.* Toulouse: Editions des Hespirides.

Van Schoonwinkel, J. 1990. Datation de l'éruption minoenne de Théra (Santorin). Bibliographie thématique. *PACT* 25:117–124.

Van Seters, J. 1966. *The Hyksos: a new investigation.* New Haven: Yale University Press.

Van Siclen III, C.C. 1987. The building history of the Tuthmosid Temple at Amada and the jubilees of Tuthmosis IV. *Varia Aegyptiaca* 3:53–66.

Vanzetti, A. 1998. La data dell'eruzione delle pomici di Avellino nel quadro della cronologia comparata dell'età del bronzo, tra Egeo e Europa centrale. In P.G. Guzzo and R. Peroni (eds.), *Archeologia e Vulcanologia in Campania. Atti del Convegno Pompei, 21 dicembre 1996*: 167–210. Naples: Arte Tipografica.

Vaughan, S. 1991. Material and technical classification of Base Ring ware: a new fabric typology. In J. Barlow, D. Bolger and B. Kling (eds.), *Cypriot ceramics: reading the prehistoric record:* 119–130. University Museum Monograph 74/University Museum Symposium Series vol.2. Philadelphia: The A.G. Leventis Foundation and the University Museum of Archaeology and Anthropology, University of Pennsylvania.

Veenhof, K.R. 1985. Limu of the later Old Assyrian period and Mari chronology. *Mari: Annales de recherches interdisciplinaires* 4:191–218.

Vercoutter, J. 1947. Les Haou-nebut. *Bulletin de l'Institut Français d'Archéologie Orientale* 46:125–158.

Vercoutter, J. 1956. *L'Égypte et le monde égéen préhellénique.* Bibliothèque d'Étude 22. Cairo: Institut français d'Archéologie Orientale.

Vermeule, E.D.T. 1964. *Greece in the Bronze Age.* Chicago: University of Chicago Press.

Vermeule, E.D.T. 1974. *Toumba tou Skourou: the mound of darkness. A Bronze Age town on Morphou Bay in Cyprus.* Boston: The Harvard University Cyprus Archaeological Expedition and the Museum of Fine Arts.

Vermeule, E.D.T. 1986. 'Priam's castle blazing': a thousand years of Trojan memories. In M.J. Mellink (ed.), *Troy and the Trojan War:* 77–92. Bryn Mawr: Department of Classical and Near Eastern Archaeology.

Vermeule, E.D.T. 1987. Baby Aigisthos and the Bronze Age. *Proceedings of the Cambridge Philological Society* 33:122–152.

Vermeule, E.D.T. and Karageorghis, V. 1982. *Mycenaean pictorial vase painting.* Cambridge, Mass.: Harvard University Press.

Vermeule, E.D.T. and Wolsky, F.Z. 1978. New Aegean relations with Cyprus: the Minoan and Mycenaean pottery from Toumba tou Skourou, Morphou. *Proceedings of the American Philosophical Society* 122:294–317.

Vermeule, E.D.T. and Wolsky, F.Z. 1990. *Toumba tou Skourou. A Bronze Age potter's quarter on Morphou Bay in Cyprus. The Harvard University–Museum of Fine Arts, Boston Cyprus Expedition.* Cambridge, Mass.: Harvard University Press.

Vickers, M. 1985. Early Greek coinage: a reassessment. *Numismatic Chronicle* 145:1–44.

Vickers, M. 1987. Dates, methods and icons. In C. Bérard (ed.), *Actes du Colloque International 'Images et société en Grèce ancienne: l'iconographie comme méthode d'analyse', 1984:* 19–25. Lausanne: Institut d'archéologie et d'histoire ancienne, Université de Lausanne.

Villard, P. 1986. Un roi de Mari à Ugarit. *Ugarit-Forschungen* 18:387–412.

Vitaliano, C.J., Taylor, S.R., Norman, M.D., McCulloch, M.T. and Nicholls, I.A. 1990. Ash layers of the Thera volcanic series: stratigraphy, petrology and geochemistry. In D.A. Hardy, J. Keller, V.P. Galanopoulos, N.C. Flemming and T.H. Druitt (eds.), *Thera and the Aegean world III. Volume two: earth sciences:* 53–78. London: The Thera Foundation.

Vitaliano, D.B. 1973. *Legends of the Earth: their geological origins.* Bloomington: Indiana University Press.

Vitaliano, D.B. and Vitaliano, C.J. 1974. Volcanic tephra on Crete. *American Journal of Archaeology* 78:19–24.

Vitaliano, D.B. and Vitaliano, C.J. 1978. Tephrachronological evidence for the time of the Bronze Age eruption of Thera. In C. Doumas (ed.), *Thera and the Aegean world I*: 217–219. London: Thera and the Aegean World.

Vladár, J. and Bartonèk, A. 1977. Zu den Beziehungen des Ägäischen, Balkanischen und Karpathischen Raumes in der mittleren Bronzezeit und die Kulturelle Ausstrahlung der Ägäischen Schriften in den Nachbarländer. *Slovenska Archeologia* 25:371–431.

Vogel, J.S., Cornell, W., Nelson, D.E. and Southon, J.R. 1990. Vesuvius/Avellino, one possible source of seventeenth century BC climatic disturbances. *Nature* 344:534–537.

Vogel, R.B., Egger, H and Schweingruber, F.H. 1996. Interpretation extremer Jahrringwerte in der Schweiz anhand von klima-historischen Aufzeichnungen zwischen 1525 und 1800 A.D. *Vierteljahrsschrift der Naturforschenden Gesellschaft in Zürich* 141/2:65–76.

Voutsaki, S. 1995. Value and exchange in premonetary societies: anthropological debates and Aegean archaeology. In C. Gillis, C. Risberg and B. Sjöberg (eds.), *Trade and production in premonetary Greece: aspects of trade*: 7–17. Studies in Mediterranean Archaeology and literature Pocket-book 134. Jonsered: Paul Åströms Förlag.

Wace, A.J.B. and Blegen, C.W. 1916–1918. The pre-Mycenaean pottery of the mainland. *Annual of the British School at Athens* 22:175–189.

Wace, A.J.B. and Blegen, C.W. 1939. Pottery as evidence for trade and colonisation in the Aegean Bronze Age. *Klio* 32:131–147.

Wachsmann, S. 1987. *Aegeans in the Theban tombs.* Orientalia Lovaniensia Analecta 20. Leuven: Peeters.

Wachsmann, S. 1998. *Seagoing ships & seamanship in the Bronze Age Levant.* College Station and London: Texas A&M University Press and Chatham Publishing.

Waddell, W.G. 1940. *Manetho.* The Loeb Classical Library. London and Cambridge, Mass.: William Heinemann Ltd. and Harvard University Press.

Walberg, G. 1976. *Kamares: a study of the character of palatial Middle Minoan pottery.* Uppsala: University of Uppsala.

Walberg, G. 1983. *Provincial Middle Minoan pottery.* Mainz am Rhein: Philipp von Zabern.

Walberg, G. 1984. The Tôd Treasure and Middle Minoan absolute chronology. *Opuscula Atheniensia* 15:173–177.

Walberg, G. 1986. *Tradition and innovation: essays in Minoan art.* Mainz am Rhein: Philipp von Zabern.

Walberg, G. 1987. Middle Minoan chronology: relative and absolute. In P. Åström (ed.), *High, middle or low? Acts of an International Colloquium on Absolute Chronology held at the University of Gothenburg 20th–22nd August 1987*, Part 1: 67–73. Studies in Mediterranean Archaeology and literature Pocket-book 56. Gothenburg: Paul Åströms Förlag.

Walberg, G. 1992. The finds at Tell el-Dabᶜa and Middle Minoan chronology. *Ägypten und Levante* 3:157–159.

Walberg, G. 1998. The date and origin of the Kamares cup from Tell el- Dabᶜa. *Ägypten und Levante* 8:107–108.

Wallerstein, I. 1974. *The modern world-system, vol. 1. Capitalist agriculture and the origins of the European world-economy in the sixteenth century.* New York: Academic Press.

Ward, G.K. and Wilson, S.R. 1978. Procedures for comparing and combining radiocarbon age determinations: a critique. *Archaeometry* 20:19–31.

Ward, W.A. 1987. Scarab typology and archaeological context. *American Journal of Archaeology* 91:507–532.

Ward, W.A. 1992. The present status of Egyptian chronology. *Bulletin of the American Schools of Oriental Research* 288:53–66.

Ward, W.A. 1993–1994. Egyptian objects from the Beirut tombs. *Berytus* 41:211–222.

Ward, W.A. and Joukowsky, M. (eds.). 1992. *The crisis years: the 12th century B.C. from beyond the Danube to the Tigris.* Dubuque: Kendall/Hunt.

Warner, R. 1990. The 'prehistoric' Irish annals: fable or history? *Archaeology Ireland* 4(1):30–33.

Warren, P.M. 1969. *Minoan stone vases.* Cambridge: Cambridge University Press.

Warren, P.M. 1973. Review of J.N. Coldstream and G.L. Huxley, *Kythera. Excavations and studies conducted by the University of Pennsylvania Museum and the British School at Athens. Gnomon* 45:173–178.

Warren, P. M. 1976a. Radiocarbon dating and calibration and the absolute chronology of Late Neolithic and Early Minoan Crete. *Studi Micenei ed Egeo-Anatolici* 17:205–219.

Warren, P.M. 1976b. Did papyrus grow in the Aegean? *Athens Annals of Archaeology* 9:89–95.

Warren, P.M. 1979. The stone vessels from the Bronze Age settlement at Akrotiri, Thera. *Arkhaiologike Ephemeris*: 82–113.

Warren, P.M. 1980. Problems of chronology in Crete and the Aegean in the third and earlier second millennium BC. *American Journal of Archaeology* 84:487–499.

Warren, P.M. 1984. Absolute dating of the Bronze Age eruption of Thera (Santorini). *Nature* 308:492–493.

Warren, P.M. 1985. Minoan pottery from Egyptian sites. *Classical Review* 35:147–151.

Warren, P.M. 1987. Absolute dating of the Aegean Late Bronze Age. *Archaeometry* 29:205–211.

Warren, P.M. 1988. The Thera eruption: continuing discussion of the dating. III. Further arguments against an early date. *Archaeometry* 30:176–179, 181–182.

Warren, P.M. 1990. Summary of evidence for the absolute chronology of the early part of the Aegean Late Bronze Age derived from historical Egyptian sources. In D.A. Hardy and A.C. Renfrew (eds.), *Thera and the Aegean world III. Volume three: chronology:* 24–26. London: The Thera Foundation.

Warren, P.M. 1990/1991. The Minoan civilisation of Crete and the volcano of Thera. *Journal of the Ancient Chronology Forum* 4:29–39.

Warren, P.M. 1991a. A new Minoan deposit from Knossos, c.1600 BC, and its wider relations. *Annual of the British School at Athens* 86:319–340.

Warren, P.M. 1991b. A merchant class in Bronze Age Crete? The evidence of Egyptian stone vessels from the city of Knossos. In N.H. Gale (ed.), *Bronze Age trade in the Mediterranean. Papers presented at the conference held at Rewley House, Oxford, in December 1989:* 295–301. Studies in Mediterranean Archaeology 90. Jonsered: Paul Åströms Förlag.

Warren, P.M. 1995. Minoan Crete and Pharaonic Egypt. In W.V. Davies and L. Schofield (eds.), *Egypt, the Aegean and the Levant: interconnections in the second millennium BC:* 1–18. London: British Museum Publications.

Warren, P.M. 1996. The Aegean and the limits of radiocarbon dating. *Acta Archaeologica* 67:283–290.

Warren, P.M. 1997. The lapidary art – Minoan adaptations of Egyptian stone vessels. *Aegaeum* 16:209–223.

Warren, P.M. 1998. Aegean Late Bronze 1–2 absolute chronology – some new contributions. In M.S. Balmuth and R.H. Tykot (eds.), *Sardinian and Aegean chronology: towards the resolution of relative and absolute dating in the Mediterranean:* 323–331. Studies in Sardinian Archaeology V. Oxford: Oxbow.

Warren, P.M. and Hankey, V. 1989. *Aegean Bronze Age chronology*. Bristol: Bristol Classical Press.

Warren, P.M. and Puchelt, H. 1990. Stratified pumice from Bronze Age Knossos. In D.A. Hardy and A.C. Renfrew (eds.), *Thera and the Aegean world III. Volume three: chronology:* 71–81. London: The Thera Foundation.

Waterbolk, H.T. 1971. Working with radiocarbon dates. *Proceedings of the Prehistoric Society* 37:15–33.

Watkins, N.D., Sparks, R.S.J., Sigurdsson, H., Huang, T.C., Federman, A., Carey, S. and Ninkovich, D. 1978. Volume and extent of the Minoan tephra from Santorini volcano: new evidence from deep sea sediment cores. *Nature* 271:122–126.

Watrous, L.V. 1981. The relationship of Late Minoan II to Late Minoan III A1. *American Journal of Archaeology* 85:75–77.

Watrous, L.V. 1992. *Kommos III: the Late Bronze Age pottery*. Princeton: Princeton University Press.

Watson, G.S. and Nguyen, H. 1985. A confidence region in a ternary diagram from point counts. *Mathematical Geology* 17:209–213.

Watson, R.T., Rodhe, H., Oeschger, H. and Siegenthaler, U. 1990. Greenhouse gases and aerosols. In J.T. Houghton, G.J. Jenkins and J.J. Ephraums (eds.), *Climate change: the IPCC scientific assessment:* 1–40. Cambridge: Cambridge University Press.

Webster, G.S. 1988. Duos Nuraghes: preliminary results of the first three seasons of excavation. *Journal of Field Archaeology* 15:465–472.

Webster, G.S. 1996. *A prehistory of Sardinia 2300–500BC*. Sheffield: Sheffield Academic Press.

Wegner, J.W. 1996. The nature and chronology of the Senwosret III-Amenemhat III regnal succession: some considerations based on new evidence from the mortuary temple of Senwosret III at Abydos. *Journal of Near Eastern Studies* 55:249–279.

Wegner, J.W. 1998. Excavations at the town of *Enduring-are-the-Places of Khakaure-Maa-Kheru-in-Abydos*: a preliminary report on the 1994 and 1997 seasons. *Journal of the American Research Centre in Egypt* 35:1–44.

Weidner, E.F. 1945–1951. Bemerkungen zur Königsliste aus Chorsabad. *Archiv für Orientforschung* 15:85–102.

Weinstein, G.A. and Betancourt, P.P. 1978. Problems of interpretation of the Akrotiri radiocarbon dates. In C. Doumas (ed.), *Thera and the Aegean world I:* 805–814. London: Thera and the Aegean World.

Weinstein, G.A. and Michael, H.N. 1978. Radiocarbon dates from Akrotiri, Thera. *Archaeometry* 20:203–209.

Weinstein, J.M. 1980. Palestinian radiocarbon dating: a reply to James Mellaart. *Antiquity* 54:21–24.

Weinstein, J.M. 1981. The Egyptian empire in Palestine: a reassessment. *Bulletin of the American Schools of Oriental Research* 241:1–28.

Weinstein, J.M. 1982. Review of B.J. Kemp and R.S. Merrillees, *Minoan pottery in second millennium Egypt. Journal of the American Research Centre in Egypt* 19:157–159.

Weinstein, J.M. 1983. Tomb SA17 at Aniba and its 'Aegean' vase. In P.P. Betancourt (ed.), *Minoan objects excavated from Vasilike, Pseira, Sphoungaras, Priniatikos Pyrgos, and other sites:* 83–86. Philadelphia: University Museum, University of Pennsylvania.

Weinstein, J.M. 1991. Egypt and the Middle Bronze IIC/Late Bronze IA transition in Palestine. *Levant* 23:105–115.

Weinstein, J.M. 1992. The chronology of Palestine in the early second millennium B.C.E. *Bulletin of the American Schools of Oriental Research* 288:27–46.

Weinstein, J.M. 1995. Reflections on the chronology of Tell el-Dabᶜa. In W.V. Davies and L. Schofield (eds.), *Egypt, the Aegean and the Levant: interconnections in the second millennium BC:* 84–90. London: British Museum Publications.

Weinstein, J.M. 1996. A wolf in sheep's clothing: how the high chronology became the middle chronology. *Bulletin of the American Schools of Oriental Research* 304:55–63.

Weinstein, J. 1997. Exodus and archaeological reality. In E.S. Frerichs and L.H. Lesko (eds.), *Exodus: the Egyptian evidence:* 87–103. Winona Lake: Eisenbrauns.

Wells, R.A. 1989. On chronology in Egyptology. *Göttinger Miszellen* 108:87–95.

Weninger, B. 1990. Theoretical radiocarbon discrepancies. In D.A. Hardy and A.C. Renfrew (eds.), *Thera and the Aegean world III. Volume three: chronology:* 216–231. London: The Thera Foundation.

Weninger, B. 1995. Stratified ¹⁴C dates and ceramic chronologies: case studies for the Early Bronze Age at Troy (Turkey) and Ezero (Bulgaria). *Radiocarbon* 37:443–456.

Weninger, B. 1997. *Studien zur dendrochronologischen Kalibration von archäologischen ¹⁴C-Daten.* Bonn: Dr. Rudolf Habelt.

Wente, E.F. 1967. On the chronology of the Twenty-first Dynasty. *Journal of Near Eastern Studies* 26:155–176.

Wente, E.F. 1975. Tuthmosis III's accession and the beginning of the New Kingdom. *Journal of Near Eastern Studies* 34:265–272.

Wente, E.F. 1976. Review of K.A. Kitchen, *The Third Intermediate Period in Egypt (1100–650 B.C.). Journal of Near Eastern Studies* 35:275–278.

Wente, E.F. 1980a. Genealogy of the Royal family. In J.E. Harris and E.F. Wente (eds.), *An X-Ray atlas of the royal mummies:* 123–162. Chicago: The University of Chicago Press.

Wente, E.F. 1980b. Age at death of pharaohs of the New Kingdom, determined from historical sources. In J.E. Harris and E.F. Wente (eds.), *An X-Ray atlas of the royal mummies:* 234–285. Chicago: The University of Chicago Press.

Wente, E.F. and Harris, J.E. 1992. Royal mummies of the Eighteenth Dynasty: a biologic and Egyptological approach. In C.N. Reeves (ed.), *After Tut'ankhamun: research and excavations in the Royal Necropolis at Thebes:* 2–20. London: Keegan Paul International.

Wente, E.F. and Van Siclen, C.C. 1976. A chronology of the New Kingdom. In J.H. Johnson and E.F. Wente (eds.), *Studies in honour of George R. Hughes, January 12, 1977:* 217–261. Studies in Ancient Oriental Civilization 39. Chicago: Oriental Institute.

West, D.R.F. 1982. *Ternary equilibrium diagrams.* Second edition. London: Chapman and Hall.

West, M.L. 1997. *The east face of Helicon: West Asiatic elements in Greek poetry and myth.* Oxford: Clarendon Press.

Westgate, J.A., Shane, P.A.R., Pearce, N.J.G., Perkins, W.T., Korisettar, R., Chesner, C.A., Williams, M.A.J. and Acharyya, S.K. 1998. All Toba tephra occurrences across peninsular India belong to the 75,000 yr B.P. eruption. *Quaternary Research* 50:107–112.

Whiting, R.M. 1990. Tell Leilan/Šubat-Enlil: Chronological problems and perspectives. In S. Eichler, M. Wäfler, and D. Warburton (eds.), *Tall al-Hamidiya 2. Recent excavations in the upper Khabur region. Symposion, Berne, December 9–11, 1986:* 167–218. Orbis biblicus et orientalis. Series Archaeologica 6. Freiberg, Göttingen: Universitätsverlag Freiburg, Vandenhoeck & Ruprecht.

Whitley, D.S. (ed.). 1998. *Reader in archaeological theory: post-processual and cognitive approaches.* London: Routledge.

Whitley, J. 1991. *Style and society in Dark Age Greece.* Cambridge: Cambridge University Press.

Whitrow, G.J. 1989. *Time in history: views of time from prehistory to the present day.* Paperback edition. Oxford: Oxford University Press.

Wiener, M.H. 1984. Crete and the Cyclades in LMI: the tale of the conical cups. In R. Hägg and N. Marinatos (eds.), *The Minoan Thalassocracy: myth and reality. Proceedings of the third international symposium at the Swedish Institute in Athens, 31 May–5 June, 1982:* 17–25. Skrifter Utgivna av Svenska Institut i Athen, 4°, 32. Stockholm: Paul Åströms Förlag.

Wiener, M.H. 1987. Trade and rule in palatial Crete. In R. Hägg and N. Marinatos (eds.), *The function of the Minoan palaces. Proceedings of the fourth international symposium at the Swedish Institute in Athens, 10–16 June, 1984:* 261–266. Skrifter Utgivna av Svenska Institutet i Athen, 4°, 35. Stockholm: Paul Åströms Förlag.

Wiener, M.H. 1990. The isles of Crete? The Minoan Thalassocracy revisited. In D.A. Hardy, C.G. Doumas, J.A. Sakellarakis and P.M. Warren (eds.), *Thera and the Aegean world III. Volume one: archaeology:* 128–161. London: The Thera Foundation.

Wiener, M.H. 1991. The nature and control of Minoan foreign trade. In N.H. Gale (ed.), *Bronze Age trade in the Mediterranean. Papers presented at the conference held at Rewley House, Oxford, in December 1989:* 325–350. Studies in Mediterranean Archaeology 90. Jonsered: Paul Åströms Förlag.

Wiener, M.H. 1998. The absolute chronology of Late Helladic IIIA2. In M.S. Balmuth and R.H. Tykot (eds.), *Sardinian and Aegean chronology: towards the resolution of relative and absolute dating in the Mediterranean:* 309–319. Studies in Sardinian Archaeology V. Oxford: Oxbow.

Wiener, M.H. n.d. The White Slip I of Dab[c]a and Thera: critical challenge for the Aegean long chronology. Manuscript of paper presented to the White Slip Ware Conference held in Nicosia 29–30 October 1998. Paper to be published in the conference proceedings: V. Karageorghis (ed.), *White Slip Ware. Proceedings of an International Conference Organized by the Anastasios G. Leventis Foundation, Nicosia in Honour of Malcolm Wiener, Nicosia 29th–30th October 1998.* In Press.

Wiener, M.H. and Allen, J.P. 1998. Separate lives: the Ahmose tempest Stela and the Theran eruption. *Journal of Near Eastern Studies* 57:1–28.

Wijngaarden, G.-J. van. 1999a. An archaeological approach to the concept of value: Mycenaean pottery at Ugarit (Syria). *Archaeological Dialogues* 6:2–23.

Wijngaarden, G.-J. van. 1999b. The value of an archaeological approach: a reply. *Archaeological Dialogues* 6:35–39.

Wilhelm, G. 1989. *The Hurrians.* Trans. J. Barnes. Warminster: Aris & Phillips.

Wilhelm, G and Boese, J. 1987. Absolute Chronologie und die hethitische Geschichte des 15. und 14. Jahrhunderts v. Chr. In P. Åström (ed.), *High, middle or low? Acts of an International Colloquium on Absolute Chronology held at the University of Gothenburg 20th–22nd August 1987,* Part 1: 74–117. Studies in Mediterranean Archaeology and literature Pocket-book 56. Gothenburg: Paul Åströms Förlag.

Williams, J.L. and Oren, E.D. n.d. The composition of White Slip pottery from Cyprus and the east Mediterranean – the petrographic characterisation of pillow lava pastes and their archaeological significance. Manuscript kindly shown to this author.

Wilson, A.L. 1976. The presence in Crete of volcanic ash from Thera. *American Journal of Archaeology* 80:419–420.

Wilson, A.L. 1977. The place-names in the Linear B tablets from Knossos. Some preliminary considerations. *Minos* 16:67–125.

Wiseman, D.J. 1953. *The Alalakh tablets.* London: The British Institute of Archaeology at Ankara.

Wölfli, W. 1992. Möglichkeiten und grenzen der Beschleunigermassenspekrometrie in der Archäologie. In *10 Jahre Beschleunigermassenspektrometrie in der Schweiz. Symposium Institut für Mittelenergiephysik der ETHZ Zürich, Schweiz:* 30–44. PSI-Proceedings 92–04. Zürich: Eidgenössische Technische Hochschule.

Wood, B. 1982. The stratigraphic relationship of local and imported Bichrome ware at Megiddo. *Levant* 14:73–79.

Wood, B.G. 1990. Dating Jericho's destruction: Bienkowski is wrong on all counts. *Biblical Archaeology Review* 16(5):45–49, 68–69.

Woolley, L. 1953. *A forgotten kingdom: being a record of the results obtained from excavation of two mounds, Atchana and Al Mina, in the Turkish Hatay.* London: Penguin Books.

Woolley, L. 1955. *Alalakh: an account of the excavations at Tell Atchana in the Hatay, 1937–1949*. Oxford: Oxford University Press for the Society of Antiquaries.

Xenaki-Sakellariou, A. and Chatziliou, C. 1989. *'Peinture en métal' à l'époque mycénienne*. Athens: Ekdotike Athenon.

Yadin, Y., Aharoni, Y., Amiran, R., Dothan, T., Dunayevsky, I., and Perrot, J. 1960. *Hazor II: an account of the second season of excavations, 1956*. Jerusalem: Magnes Press.

Yamada, S. 1994. The editorial history of the Assyrian King List. *Zeitschrift für Assyriologie* 84:11–37.

Yamaguchi, D.K. 1993. On tree-ring records of volcanic events in Kamchatka and elsewhere. *Quaternary Research* 40:262–263.

Yamaguchi, D.K., Atwater, B.F., Bunker, D.E., Benson, B.E. and Reid, M.S. 1997. Tree-ring dating the 1700 Cascadia earthquake. *Nature* 389:922–923.

Young, R.S. 1981. *The Gordion excavations. Final reports volume I: three great early tumuli*. Philadelphia: University Museum, University of Pennsylvania.

Younger, J.G. 1995. Bronze Age representations of Aegean bull-games, III. *Aegaeum* 12:507–545.

Yurco, F.J. 1996. Black Athena: an Egyptological review. In M.R. Lefkowitz and G.M. Rogers (eds.), *Black Athena revisited*: 62–100. Chapel Hill: The University of North Carolina Press.

Yurco, F.J. 1997. Merenptah's Canaanite campaign and Israel's origins. In E.S. Frerichs and L.H. Lesko (eds.), *Exodus: the Egyptian evidence*: 27–55. Winona Lake: Eisenbrauns.

Zaccagnini, C. 1983. Patterns of mobility among Near Eastern craftsmen. *Journal of Near Eastern Studies* 42:245–264.

Zangger, E. 1992. *The flood from Heaven: deciphering the Atlantis legend*. London: Sidgwick & Jackson.

Zangger, E. 1993. Plato's Atlantis account – a distorted recollection of the Trojan war. *Oxford Journal of Archaeology* 12:77–87.

Zeuner, F.E. 1946. *Dating the past: an introduction to geochronology*. London: Methuen.

Zeuner, F.E. 1958. *Dating the past: an introduction to geochronology*. Fourth edition, revised and enlarged. London: Methuen.

Zielinski, G.A. 1995. Stratospheric loading and optical depth estimates of explosive volcanism over the last 2100 years derived from the GISP2 ice core. *Journal of Geophysical Research* 100:20,937–20,955.

Zielinski, G.A. and Germani, M.S. 1998a. New ice-core evidence challenges the 1620s BC age for the Santorini (Minoan) eruption. *Journal of Archaeological Science* 25:279–289.

Zielinski, G.A. and Germani, M.S. 1998b. Reply to: Correction. New GISP2 ice-core evidence supports 17th century BC date for the Santorini (Minoan) eruption. *Journal of Archaeological Science* 25:1,043–1,045.

Zielinski, G.A., Germani, M.S., Larsen, G., Baillie, M.G.L., Whitlow, S., Twickler, M.S. and Taylor, K. 1995. Evidence of the Eldgjá (Iceland) eruption in the GISP2 Greenland ice core: relationship to eruption processes and climatic conditions in the tenth century. *The Holocene* 5:129–140.

Zielinski, G.A., Mayewski, P.A., Meeker, L.D., Grönvold, K., Germani, M.S., Whitlow, S., Twickler, M.S. and Taylor, K. 1997. Volcanic aerosol records and tephrachronology of the Summit, Greenland, ice-cores. *Journal of Geophysical Research* 102, C12:26,625–26,640.

Zielinski, G.A., Mayewski, P.A., Meeker, L.D., Whitlow, S., and Twickler, M.S. 1996. A 110,000-yr record of explosive volcanism from the GISP2 (Greenland) ice core. *Quaternary Research* 45:109–118.

Zielinski, G.A., Mayewski, P.A., Meeker, L.D., Whitlow, S., Twickler, M.S., Morrison, M., Meese, D.A., Gow, A.J. and Alley, R.B. 1994a. Record of volcanism since 7000 B.C. from the GISP2 Greenland ice core and implications for the volcano-climate system. *Science* 264:948–952.

Zielinski, G.A., Fiacco, R.J., Whitlow, S., Twickler, M.S., Germani, M.S., Eno, K. and Yasui, M. 1994b. Climatic impact of the AD 1783 eruption of Asama (Japan) was minimal: evidence from the GISP2 ice core. *Geophysical Research Letters* 21:2,365–2,368.

Zielinski, G.A., Mayewski, P.A., Meeker, L.D., Whitlow, S., Twickler, M.S., Morrison, M., Meese, D.A., Gow, A.J. and Alley, R.B. 1995. The GISP ice core record of volcanism since 7000 B.C. *Science* 267:257–258.

Plates

Plate 1. View of the Thera volcanic caldera looking south from Phira town. This overall caldera represents the outcome and evolution of a long series of volcanic eruptions.

Plate 2. View of the massive Minoan eruption deposits in the Megalochori Quarry on Thera.

Plate 3. View of part of the site of the Bronze Age settlement at Akrotiri buried by the eruption.

Plate 4. View of part of the site of the Bronze Age settlement at Akrotiri buried by the eruption.

Plate 5. View of a stream bed filled by the Minoan eruption deposits in the Phira Quarry on Thera.

Plate 6. The Minoan land surface preserved directly beneath the pumice from the Minoan eruption (the straight dark line under the grey-white Minoan eruption pumice).

Plate 7. Diver (Kate Mackay) recording one of the 45+ LBA-type stone anchors found on the seabed off the site of Maroni Tsaroukkas, southern Cyprus.

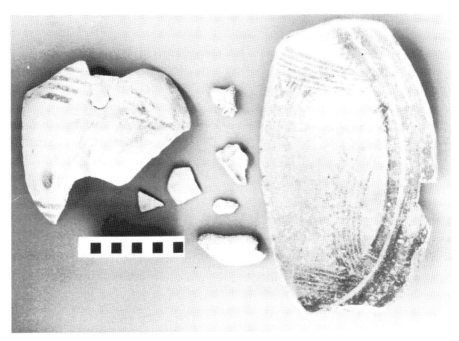

Plate 8. White Painted pottery from an LCI deposit on the seabed off the site of Maroni Tsaroukkas, southern Cyprus.

Plate 9. Proto White Slip sherd from an LCI deposit on the seabed off the site of Maroni Tsaroukkas, southern Cyprus.

Plates

Plate 10. Part of a Canaanite Jar from an LCI deposit on the seabed off the site of Maroni Tsaroukkas, southern Cyprus.

Plate 11. LMIA sherd from an early LCIA context at Maroni Vournes in southern Cyprus (P80 from trench M11 layer 12 #8814). Photograph courtesy of Gerald Cadogan.

Plate 12. *A view of the Midas Mound tumulus at Gordion in Winter. Photograph courtesy of Peter Ian Kuniholm.*

Plate 13. *View of parts of the wooden structure inside the Midas Mound tumulus. Sections through some of the giant juniper logs preserved out to bark can be seen on the left. Photograph courtesy of Peter Ian Kuniholm.*

Plate 14. Two examples of sections of logs taken as samples from the Midas Mound tumulus at Gordion. Photograph courtesy of Peter Ian Kuniholm.

Plate 15. Peter Ian Kuniholm collecting one of the wood samples at Porsuk, Turkey. Photograph courtesy of Peter Ian Kuniholm.

Index

Abban (Abael), son of Hammurapi of Yamhad 355

Åberg, N. 9

Abbreviations xvi–xviii

absolute dating, definition of 231–232

Abydos (Egypt) 204, 324, 333

academic controversies, nature of xxxi

Acemhöyük (Turkey): *Sarıkaya palace* 314, 351, 353, 354; *tree-ring data* 308, 355

Acknowledgements xxxii–xxxiii

Admiraal, S.M.L. 179

Aegean / Cypriot sequence, suggested: 188–192, Fig.36, Fig.62; *early LMIB / LHIIA = LCIA/B transition to early LCIB* 191; *early-mature LMIA = LCIA* 190; *late MMIII / MMIII–LMIA transition = late MC* 188–190; *LCIB = mature LMIB / LHIIA-end LMIB / LHIIA; mature LMIA = LCIA* 190; *mature-late LMIA synchronisms* 190–191; *see also* 'high' chronology for Aegean LBA

Aegean Dendrochronology Project 34, 307–319

Aegean-East Mediterranean Radiocarbon Calibration Project 241, 311

'Ahhiyawa' 225–227, 229

Ahhotep: *axe and other items of Aegean influence* 111; *inlaid dagger blade* 140–141, 144

Ahmose: 41–42, 61–62, 81, 84, 89, 90–93, 95–97, 103, 105, 142, 144, 146, 166–167, 183, 187, 195–201, 203, 206, 258–260, 328, 335, 337; *see* Tempest Stele of Ahmose; *see also* Egyptian chronology

Aitken, M.J. 23

Akhenaten (Amenhotep IV) 2, 344, 346; *see also* Egyptian chronology

Akkad 357

Akrotiri (Thera Greece): 4, 7, 9, 10, 15–17, 19, 26, 30, 55, 70–71, 77, 80, 100–101, 109, 113–115, 323, 329, 331–332, 335, 337; *frescoes* 138–139, 142, 144, 148, 150–151, 156, 164, 171, 174, 178, 181, 187–188, 190, 203,

263; *Levantine imports at* 26, 30; 113–115, 131; *LH imports at* 19; *radiocarbon dates* 232–247; *seeds from* 233; *relationship of Alalakh frescoes to* 364; *Tell el-Yahudiyeh juglets at* 113; *WSI bowl at* 34–35, 118, 150–158; *no WSII bowl at* 152

Alalakh (Turkey) 31, 80, 88, 97, 101, 135–136, 148, 176, 188, 190, 206, 347–364; *Bichrome Ware at* 326, 360–363; *Cypriot imports at* 359; *frescoes* 324, 354; *phase VII chronology* 347–358; *WSI at* 359–360

Alasiya 211–225

Albright, W.F. 182

Alexiou, S. 216

Alley, R.B. *et al.* 301

Almagre Mountain (Colorado USA) *tree-ring data* 279

Amarna Letters 228; *see also* Tell el-Amarna, Egypt

Amman Airport (Jordan) 59

Amenemhat IV 84; *see also* Egyptian chronology

Amenhotep I 92, 97, 258, 333, 335, 337; *see also* Egyptian chronology

Amenhotep II 93, 95, 214, 223–224, 227, 347; *see also* Egyptian chronology

Amenhotep III: 207, 218, 220–225, 227–229; *and Aegean chronology* 220–229; *and the Hittites* 224–229; *diplomatic and political links* 222–229, 344, 347; *see also* Egyptian chronology

Ammisaduqa 351

Ammitaqum of Alalakh 356

Aniakchak II (Alaska USA) volcanic eruption 282, 284, 300

Aniba 218

Antalya (Turkey) 149–150

Apophis 86–87, 90, 91, 99, 143, 183, 185, 326, 361, 362; *see also* Egyptian chronology

archaeomagnetic data 17–18

Ariano Irpino (Italy) 283

Arnold, D. 218

Arnuwanda I 225, 227

Arpera *Mosphilos* (Cyprus) 130, 132

Artapanos 196

Artzy, M. 139

Arzawans 227

Asama (Japan) volcanic eruption 278

Asmunikal, daughter of Tudhalya I 227

Assur-dan 356

Assyrian / Babylonian chronology 66, 380–393

Assyrian King List 314

Astour, M.C. 227, 355–356, 358

Åström 120, 122–124, 139, 154, 157, 168, 180, 190

Athens (ancient) xxxi

Atlantis xxvii, 10, 202

Attarisiya of Ahhiya (Ahhiyawa) 225–226

Avachinsky (Kamchatka) volcanic eruption 282–283, 285

Avellino (Italy) volcanic eruption 282–283, 285, 300

Avaris / Tell el-Dabʿa *see* Tell el-Dabʿa / Avaris (Egypt)

Ayia Irini (Keos) 80, 158, 205, 334

Ayia Triadha (Crete) 116, 142, 207

Babylonian Chronicle 357

Baillie, M.G.L. and Munro, M.A.R. 23–24

Baillie, M.G.L. xxviii, 36, 38, 301, 304, 316

Balos (Thera, Greece) 151

Barber, E. 31, 214

Barthes, R. 144

Baurain, C. 78

Beazley, Sir John x

Beckerath, J. von 66–67, 187, 362

Bergoffen, C. 154, 156–157, 159, 183

Belfast Radiocarbon Laboratory: 240, 242, 311; *1986 bi-decadal radiocarbon calibration curve* 240–241, Fig.45

Belu-bani 356

Bernini, L.E. 73–75

Betancourt, P.P. xxx, 27–28, 30, 34, 101, 108, 202, 215, 333, 340

Bichler, M. *et al.* 149–150

Bichrome Ware 61, 98; *at Alalakh* 360–363; *dating evidence* 122–123

Bietak, M. and Hein, I. 159, 161, 163

Bietak, M. and Marinatos, N. 99–101, 104

Bietak, M. 32, 33–36, 40–42, 49, 78, 80–107, 114, 120–121, 124, 130, 135–136, 145, 150, 158, 160, 164, 166–168, 170, 186–188, 258–259, 325–328, 364; *change of dates* 35, 82–83, 90

Bimson, J. 61

Bluth, G.J.S. *et al.* 287

Bodin, J. 46–47

Boss, M. and Laffineur, R. 142

Bourke, S. 60

Bournouf, É. 152, 153

Bourriau, J. and Eriksson, K. 42, 145, 203, 204, 207

Bourriau, J. 110

BRI (Base Ring I) Ware: *archaeological dating, review of* 325; *at Kommos* 325; *at Memphis* 167

Briffa, K.R. *et al.* 277, 278, 279

Bruins, H.J. and van der Plicht, J. 225, 256

Brunstein, F.C. 278, 279

Bryce, T.R. 358

Buckland, P.C. *et al.* 24, 36, 264, 278–279, 321

Byblos (Lebanon) 365

Cadogan, G. 23, 71, 174

Cambyses 260

Cameron, M. 215–216, 217

Catling, H. 168

ceramic terminology: *Aegean / Cretan ceramic style phases* x–xvi; *Cypriot ceramic types* xvi

Chania (Crete) 208, 247–248, 250, 254; *LMIB destruction radiocarbon dates* 247–250, 329, 337

Cherry, J.F. 75

Childe, V.G. 1

Chios (Greece) 149–150

chronological systems / terms: *absolute dating, definition* 231–232; *Aegean system/terms* vii–x; *astrochronology* 368–377; *Babylonian / Assyrian / Hittite chronology* 380–393; *Biblical chronology* 378–380; *Cretan system/ terms* vii–x; *'cross-dating' and trade* 55–60; *dead-reckoning* 368–377; *differences between historical and archaeological timescales* 53–54; *Egyptian chronology* 2, 65–68; 367–414; *history of Aegean prehistoric chronology* 2–5, 12–13, 19–20; *history of archaeological chronology* 1–2; *outline chronology / event sequence* 188–192, 335–340, Fig. 36, Fig.62; *problems / errors in archaeological dating* 52–65; *proto-historical framework, possibility of* 341; *traditional tripartite system* vii–viii

Clausen, H.B. *et al.* 38, 273, 280, 288, 302

climatic anomalies: *history of debate* 263–266; *later 17th century BC, northern hemisphere* 263–307; *circumstantial links between 17th century BC disruption and Thera eruption* 272–285; *multiple eruption scenario, critique of* 286–287; *possible hemisphere-scale effects of Thera eruption* 268–269

Cline, E.H. 33, 83, 116–118, 220, 222–224, 229

Coldstream, N. 13

Collingwood, R.G. 47

Copenhagen Radiocarbon Laboratory Thera short-lived radiocarbon data 238–239, Tables 7–8, 243–246, Fig.46–47

Cusae (Egypt) 206

Cypriot-east Mediterranean links, significance of 129

Darwin, C. xxviii, 321, 340

Davis, J.L. and Cherry, J.F. 18

Davis, E.N. 192

Davis, J.L. 34, 75

Deir el-Bahri (Egypt) 213

Deir el-Ballas (Egypt) 90, 92, 110, 196

Dendera (Egypt) 195

dendrochronology / tree rings: *accuracy / precision of dating* 52; *Acemhöyük data* 308; *Aegean / Anatolian data and 1628BC climate-event* 307–319; *Aegean Dendrochronological Project* 34, 307–319; *Almagre Mountain, Colorado, tree-ring data* 279; *and dating of volcanic activity* 22–24, 30; *and major 17th century BC climatic anomaly* 263–266, Fig. 50, 280–282; *and past temperature reconstruction* 266–267; *Irish bog oak data* 316; *late 16th century BC caveat in Aegean / Anatolian dendrochronological sequence* 318–319; *Kültepe, Turkey, tree ring data* 308; *old wood problem* 50; *locational evidence for volcanic activity from* 284–285; *negative evidence for 16th century BC date for Thera eruption* 274–280; *Porsuk, Turkey, tree-ring data* 308, 318; *sensitivity as index of volcanic activity* 276–279; *Uluburun dendrochrono-logical dates* 344–346, Fig.63; *White Mountains, California, tree ring data* 276, 279, 312, 315, 316; *see also relative ring 854 growth anomaly*

Dever, W.G. 63, 87–88, 186, 328

Dhiarizos River (Cyprus) 171

Dickinson, O.T.P.K. 142

Dietz, S. 19

Dikaios, P. 171

Djahi (Syria) 258

Doumas, C. 9, 18, 143, 144

Doumas, C. and Papazoglou, L. 18

Downey, W.S. and Tarling, D.H. 17–18

Driessen, J. and Macdonald, C. 5, 213, 331

Dromolaxia *Trypes* (Cyprus) 179

Dumont, A. and Chaplain, J.C. 152, 153, 156

Duos Nuraghes (Sardinia) 262

Dye 3 ice core 318, 336

Ebla (Syria) 365

Edwards, I.E.S. 222

Ebers papyrus 258, 260

Egyptian chronology: 2, 65–68, 367–414; *18th Dynasty chronology* 393–402; *astrochronology in* 368–377; *Babylonian / Assyrian / Hittite chronology, links with* 380–393; *Biblical chronology, links with* 378–380; *dead-reckoning in* 368–377; *working forward from the Middle Kingdom* 402–411

El Chichón (Mexico) volcanic eruption 270, 278, 287

Eldgjá (Iceland) volcanic eruption 285, 302

El-Lisht 25; *jug* 78–79

Enkomi (Cyprus) 125–126, 145, 154, 172, 176, 179, 190, 323, 324

Episkopi *Phaneromeni* (Cyprus) 173

Epstein, C. 182, 184, 187, 361

Eriksson, K.O. 40, 129, 132, 145, 169, 173, 205, 359, 360

Evans, Sir Arthur 10, 25, 77, 79, 103, 127, 136, 148, 333

Exodus 10, 202

'Ezbet Helmi (Tell el-Dab'a) 127, 157, 160, 162, 164, 165, 166, 168, 182, 184, 185

Federman, A.N. and Carey, S.N. 295, 296

Fennoscandia 281

'flying gallop' motif 141–142

figural wall-painting: *New Palace appearance of* 80; *see also frescoes*

Foster, K.P. and Ritner, R.K. 192–197, 200–201

Fouqué, F. 9, 12, 151, 152

French, E. 160, 340

frescoes: *as part of unified east Mediterranean trading network* 135–136; *and jewellery* 138–139; *at Miletus* 135; *at Yarim-Lim place, Alalakh* 364; *bull-leaping in* 101–104; *Chariot fresco, Knossos* 216–219, 220, 221, 222, 224; *Nilotic motifs see Nilotic motifs*; *Procession fresco, Knossos* 211, 214–215; *relative dating of Tell el-Dab'a and Aegean frescoes* 147–149; *stylistic date of Egyptian elements in Tell el-Dab'a frescoes* 106–107; *stylistic date*

of *Tell el-Dabᶜa frescoes in Aegean terms* 100–105; *stylistic relationship to Keftiu kilts* 214–217; *Toreador fresco, Knossos* 103
Friedrich, W.L. *et al.* 238–239
Furtwaengler, A. and Loeschke, G. 151–153
Furumark, A. 13, 19–20, 24, 140–141, 143, 209
Fuscaldo, P. 127

Gasche, H. *et al.* 66, 354, 355, 357–358, 363
Gates, C. 359–361
Genesis 41, 202
Gerlach, T.M. *et al.* 270
Gezer (Israel) 121
Giles, F. xxviii
GISP2 ice-core: 283–284, 288–307, 336; *comparison of volcanic glass with Mochlos samples* 297–299, Fig.56; *dating accuracy* 301–305; *negative evidence for non-Theran sources of volcanic glass* 300–301; *Zielinski and Germani hypothesis on source of volcanic glass* 288–300, 318
Gittlen, B.M. 63, 119, 129, 161, 166
Goedicke, H. 197
Gonen, R. 61
Gorceix, H. 9, 150
Gordion (Turkey) Midas Mound tumulus 307–308
Gournia (Crete) 117
GRIP ice core 318, 336
Groningen Radiocarbon Laboratory 242

Hagens, G. 66
Hall, V.A. *et al.* 37
Hall, G.S. *et al.* 319
Hallager, B.P. and Hallager, E. 104
Hallager, E. 108
Hammer, C.U. 21, 23, 264, 285, 307, 316
Hammurapi: 350, 351, 353; *of Yamhad* 355, 358
Hammurapi II 357
Hankey, V. and Leonard, A. 78, 110
Hankey, V. 40
Haremhab 346
Hatshepsut: 213; *Speos Artemidos, inscription* 200
Hattusa / Bogazköy (Turkey) 136
Hattusili I 103, 326, 356–358, 363
Hattusili III 227
Hazor (Israel) 184
Heidelberg Radiocarbon laboratory 236, 240, 311
Heiken, G. and McCoy, F.W. 316
Hein, I. 88–89, 94
Heinz, M. 359
Hekla III (Iceland) volcanic eruption: 285, *dating of* 37, 315

Helck, W. 258
Herculaneum (Italy) 12
Hesiod, *Theogony* 202
'high' chronology for Aegean LBA: *historical implications of* 341–347; *implications for Near East* 364–366; *outline of* 338–340, Fig.62
'high' chronology for Egyptian New Kingdom, proposed 343
Hood, S. 13, 16
Housley, R.A. *et al.* 238, 337
Housley, R.A. 247
Huayanaputina (Peru) volcanic eruption 267, 284
Huber, P.J. 354
Hughes, M. 24

Ibani 167
ice cores: *accuracy / precision of dating* 52, 266; *and dating of volcanic activity* 21, 23–24, 30–31, 33, 37–39, 264–266; *and major 17th century climatic anomaly* 263, 266, 282–284; *and positive 17th century BC link with Thera eruption* 280; *GISP2 core* 288–307; *locational evidence of volcanic activity from* 284–285; *see also* GISP2 ice-core
Immerwahr, S. 80, 100, 216
inlaid daggers: *Aegean examples* 141–142; *Ahhotep dagger* 140–141
INTCAL98 radiocarbon calibration dataset/curve: 39, 234, 241–242, 244, 246–247, 262, 311, 312, Fig.44
Irish bog oak tree ring data 316
Italy, Aegean imports in 260–262

James, P. *et al.*, critique of 415–418
Jánosi, P. 90, 94–95
Jericho (Palestine West Bank): *and Egyptian historical chronologies* 258–260; *and MBA Syro-Palestinian chronology* 256–259; *radiocarbon dates* 255–260, Table 11; *synchronisms with Tell el-Dabᶜa* 259
jewellery 54–55; 138–39
Johnson, J.W. 46
Joseph, famine in *Genesis* 41, 202
Julian-Gregorian calendar 231

Kahun (Egypt) 2
Kalopsidha (Cyprus) 123–125
Kamares (Potamos), Thera 9
Kamares Ware 2
Kamid el-Loz (Kumidi Lebanon) 344
Kamose 62, 86, 91, 96, 98, 120, 137, 191, 195–197; *stela of* 86, 91, 98–99, 110, 206; *see also* Egyptian chronology
Kantor, H. 141, 359
Karageorghis, V. 155–157, 176
Karnak / Thebes (Egypt) 192, 196, 198, 218
Kastri (Kythera Greece) 205, 334

Kato Zakro (Crete) 116–117, 178, 190
Katsambas (Crete) 218
Keftiu 31, 109, 202, 209, 211, 213–214, 217–218, 219–220, 223, 225; *in Theban tombs and chronology* 31, 209–220, Fig.38–41, 338; *kilts worn by* see kilts; *metal objects carried by* 217
Kemp, B.J. and Merrillees, R.S. 204, 340
Kemp, B.J. 26–28
Kempinski, A. 62, 361
Kenyon, K. 256
Keos (Greece) 70
Kerma (Egypt) 110–111; *and Aegean (?) sherd* 110–111
Khamudy 86–87, 91, 259, 362
Khyan 25, 79, 86–87, 183–184, 187–188, 219, 326; *lid* 79, 115, 136; see also Egyptian chronology; see also royal gift exchange
kilts: *and chronology* 211–217, 218; *stylistic links with LMII–LMIIIA1 ceramics and frescoes* 214–217; *textiles as prestige goods* 214, 218–220
Kisnapili 225
Kitchen, K.A. 66–67, 258
Knossos (Crete): 10, 71, 78–79, 97, 100, 116–117, 136, 142, 174, 176, 208–209, 333, 335, 346; *Amenhotep III scarab at Sellopoulou Tomb 4* 220–223; *as LMII/LMIIIA1 'super-site'* 219–220; *Chariot fresco* 216–219, 220–222, 224; *late WSI at* 176; *Procession fresco* 211, 214–215; *Toreador fresco* 103; *Unexplored Mansion, LMII radiocarbon dates* 252–255, 338
Kommos (Crete): 70–71, 79, 117–118, 181, 188, 190, 208, 218, 250–251, 254, 322, 331, 334, 337; *early BR imports* 325; *LMII radiocarbon date* 252–255, 338; *MMIII/early LMIA radiocarbon dates* 250–252, Table 9
Kom Rabiᶜa / Memphis (Egypt) 203, 205, 222, 340
Korfmann, M. 78
Kos (Greece) 149
Kourion *Bamboula* (Cyprus) 157, 162
Krakatau (Indonesia) volcanic eruption 271–272, 284, 306, 315–316
Krauss, R. 258
Kress, V. 271
Kuhrt, A. 258
Kuniholm, P.I. *et al.* 344
Kuniholm, P.I. 307, 308, 310–313
Kültepe (Turkey): *tree ring data* 308; *Waršama palace* 314, 351, 353, 354, 355
Kurustama treaty 227

Lachish (Israel): 184, *Fosse temple at* 207
Laffineur, R. 101

Laki (Iceland) volcanic eruption 278, 285
LaMarche, V.C. and Hirschboeck, K.K. 21–22, 276–279, 315– 316
LCI: *dating through archaeological linkages* 107–192; *debate regarding start of period* 122–126; *imports at MBA Tell el-Dabʿa* 120; *imports in Syria-Palestine and Egypt* 124; *start date during later MBA (Palestine) and SIP (Egypt)* 119–121; *uncommonness of early types in MM-LMIA Crete* 127–128; *uncommonness of early types in Syria-Palestine and Egypt* 127, 129
LCI (LCIA/LCIB) Cypriot regionalism: 120; 123–124; *and interregional contacts* 125–127, 134–135, 178–180, 326; *and PWS* 171–172; *and WSI* 150–192
LCIB: *correlation of earliest phase with LMIB-LMII (not LMIA)* 145
Leonard, A. 60
LHI–II imports in southern Italy 261–262
LHIIA: *LMIB/LHIIA imports in Egypt* 202–204, 206–208; *LMIB/LHIIA period, earlier phase* 330–335; *relationship with LMIB* 205; *see also* LMIB
LHIIIA2 chronology 358
LHIIIB, start date 344–347
Lilliu, G. 261
Lilyquist, C. 204
LMIA: *ceramic style* 13, 19–20, 24; *dating through archaeological linkages* 107–192, 322–323; *equated with LCIA* 117–119; *import pattern in LMIA Aegean and relevance to chronology* 113–119; *imports in early LCI Cyprus* 126–127; *synchronism with Hyksos period* 144; *synchronism with LCIA, late MBA (Palestine) and SIP (Egypt)* 121–122, 132; *see also* 'post-eruption LMIA phase'
LMIB: *chronology* 202–208; *end date* 337–338; *first appearance of 18th Dynasty, Syro-Palestinian LB types, and LCIB types* 117–119; *LMIB/ LHIIA imports in Egypt* 202–204, 206–208; *LMIB/LHIIA period, earlier phase* 330–335; *relationship with LHIIA* 205; *see also* LHIIA
LMII: *chronology* 208–209
LMII/LMIIIA1: *chronology* 254
LMIIIA1: *chronology* 338; *pottery decoration* 215, Figs.42–43
Linkages between the Late Minoan IA period, the Late Cypriot IA period, and Egypt and the Levant 107–148
Liritzis, Y. *et al.* 283
Lolos, Y.G. 19
Lough, G.M. and Fritts, H.C. 284

Macdonald, C. 145
MacGillivray, J.A. 77–78, 160, 343
Madduwatta, indictment of 225–226
Maguire, L.C. 125–126, 159, 161, 166–167, 170, 190, 365
Malia (Crete) 117, 209
Maliszewski, D. 171
Malkata (Egypt) Amenotep III temple at 229
Mamet, C. 9, 150
Manetho 196
Manning, S.W. 17, 24, 28, 34, 38, 187, 218, 299, 340
Mari (Syria) 80
Marinatos, S. xxvii, 9, 10, 12–13, 15
Maroni valley (Cyprus) 64, 123, 172, 178; Maroni *Kapsaloudhia* 131; Maroni *Tsaroukkas* 176; Maroni *Vournes* 126, 135, 145, 165, 188, 190, 322
Matthäus, H. 40, 217
Matthiae, P. 61
Mattingly, H.B. xxxi
MBA Syro-Palestinian imports: *in late MC-LCI Cyprus* 122; *in LMIA Akrotiri* 122
MBII: *links to Aegean and Cypriot evidence* 119–129; *importance of MBIIC/MBIII phase* 186; *Jericho and MBIIB-C chronology* 256–259
MB/LB transition: *debates and problems of interregional correlation* 60–65, 119–129
McCormac, F.G. 240
McCoy, F.W. and Heiken, G. 146
McGovern, P.E. *et al.* 78
MC period, proposed shortening of 343
MCIII–LCIA: *regional development pattern in Cyprus* 35, 49, 63–65
Medinet el-Gurob (Egypt) 206–207
Mee, C. 226–227
Meese, D.A. *et al.* 301
Megiddo (Israel) 61, 184, 187, 206–207, 361
Mellink, M. 136
Melos (Greece) 70
Memphis (Egypt): 110, 120, 324, 333; *BRI vessel* 167, 206, 254, 325; *LMIB rim sherd at* 203–204, Fig.37.a
Menkheparaseneb 212, 214–215, 219, 338; *see also* Egyptian chronology
Merrillees, R.S. 26–28, 35, 64, 124–125, 139, 152–153, 157, 161, 164, 178, 180–181, 206, 323, 325
Miletus (Turkey): 97; *frescoes at* 135; *PWS at* 174
Minoan exports, general pattern 109–113
Mitanni 227
MM period, proposed shortening of 343
MMII archaeological chronology 76–78

MMIII archaeological chronology 77–79
Mochlos (Crete): 73–74, 208, 250, 254, 294, 297, 299, 331; *LMII radiocarbon dates* 252–255, 338
Momigliano, N. 343
Money, J. 17
Morgan, L. 104, 106
Morphou Bay (Cyprus) 172–173
Morris, I. 59
Mount Pinatubo (Phillippines) volcanic eruption 22, 31, 268, 270, 287
Mount St Helens (Washington USA) *Yn tephra eruption* 282; 283–285, 300
Muhly, J.D. 40, 124, 361
Mursili I 357, 358, 363
Mycenae (Greece) 115–116, 142, 190, 224
Myres, J.L. 2
Myrtos-Pyrgos (Crete): 4, 247–248, 250, 254, *LMIB destruction radiocarbon dates* 247–250, 329, 337
Myrtou *Pigadhes* (Cyprus) 123

Negbi, O. 62–63, 129–130, 132, 182
Newhall, C.G. and Self, S. Volcanic Explosivity Index 282
'New Kingdom' ceramic types, first appearance in 17th Dynasty 120
Niemeier, W.-D. 29–31, 80
Nilotic motifs in New Palace art 140–143
Nissyros (Greece): *volcanic eruption* 282–283, 285; *thermoluminescence dates* 149–150
Novarupta (Katmai) Aleutian islands volcanic eruption 277, 285

O'Connor, D. 84
Oren, E. 88, 137–138, 183, 326, 346
Oxford Radiocarbon Laboratory 236–237, 246–247, 250
OxCal radiocarbon calibration programme 243, 262

Padgett, M. 154, 157, 173–174, 178
Page, D. 13, 17
Palaikastro (Crete) 73–75
Palaima, T. 128
Palaepaphos *Teratsoudhia* (Cyprus) 154, 157, 174, 176–177
Palma Campania (Italy) 283
Palmer, L.R. 79
Paphos (Cyprus) 172
Parker, D.E. 264
Pearson, G.W. and Qua, F. 240
Pelée (Martinique) volcanic eruption 277
Peltenberg, E. 125–126
Pendaya *Mandres* (Cyprus) 155–157, 172–173
Pennsylvania Radiocarbon Laboratory ('first phase') Thera dates 236

Petrie, Sir Flinders 2, 182, 324
petrologic analysis of volcanic sulphur emissions: *critique of* 269–272, 305–306
Phillips, J.S. 222
Phylakopi (Melos): 18, 71, 80, 139, 163, 174–176, 337; *late WSI at* 176–178
Pickles, S. and Peltenburg, E. 323
Pilcher, J.R. *et al.* 37
Politiko (Cyprus) 173
Pomerance, L. 14
Pompeii (Italy) 12
Popper, K.R. 100
Popham, M. R. 64, 71, 108, 152, 156–157, 171, 174, 176, 209, 222
Poros (Crete) 18, 116
Porsuk (Turkey) tree-ring data 308, 318
'post-eruption LMIA phase', possibility of, and length of 330–335, 337
pre-Bichrome Ware (late MBII [earlier MBIIC/MBIII]) 98
prestige economy, inter-élite communication, fashion and artistic fusion, late MBA-SIP-LMIA/LHI 136–144, 365–366; *metals trade, possible importance of* 128; *stylistic components of* 139
Pretoria Radiocarbon Laboratory 242
Pseira (Crete) 73, 334
pumice: *at Tell el-Dab'a* 145–150, 336; *craft-use* 146–148, 149–150; *chronological relationship to Tell el-Dab'a frescoes* 147–150; *'rose' pumice* 297; *scientific examination of* 149
PWS (Proto White Slip) Ware: *at Tell el-Dab'a* 167–168; *and early WSI in Aegean* 174–176
PWS / WSI transition 173–174
Pyle, D. 263–264, 270, 273, 280, 282, 305–306

Qatna (Syria) 135

radiocarbon: *Aegean-East Mediterranean Radiocarbon Calibration Project* 241, 311; *calibration curves* 240–242; Sardinian dates 262–263, Table 12; *Jericho dates* 255–260, Table 11; *non-Theran Aegean radiocarbon data* 247–255, Fig.48–49, Tables 9–10; *principles* 232–233; *problems* 50–52, 233–236; *suggestions for a radiocarbon-based resolution of Thera eruption date debate* 247; *Thera dates* 232–247; *variations and errors* 242
Ramesses II 66–67, 338; *see also* Egyptian chronology
Rampino, M.R. *et al.* 272
Ramsey, C.B. 243
Reck, H. 14

Redford, D.B. 192, 194–196, 198
Rehak, P. 101, 104, 214–215
Rekhmire: 213, 216; *tomb of* 212, 214, 218–220, 338; *see also* Egyptian chronology
Relative date of the Thera eruption in the Aegean and beyond 69–76
relative ring 854 growth anomaly in Anatolian tree-ring sequence: 308–318, Fig.57; *absolute dating of* 310–312, Fig.58; *comparison with effects of known volcanic events* 314–315; *correspondence with Akrotiri radiocarbon dates* 317; *correspondence with Irish and California tree-ring data* 312–314; *environmental factors in Anatolian tree growth* 315–317; *links with Near Eastern historical chronologies* 314; *see also* dendrochronology / tree rings
Renaudin, L. 10
Renfrew, C. 18, 30
Rhind Mathematical Papyrus 196, 361
Rhodes (Greece) 18
royal gift exchange: *Hyksos period (Khyan)* 136–138; *lack of in 18th Dynasty* 136
Ryholt, K.S.B. 259, 362

Salitis 86, 362
Samsi-Adad I 350–351
Samsuditana 357, 363
Samsuilana of Babylon 353
Santa Maria (Guatemala) volcanic eruption 277
Saqqara (Egypt): 180, 324, 333, 337, 340, 353–355; *contents of Tomb NE 1* 204; *Teti Pyramid at* 204–205, 209
Sardinia: *Aegean imports in* 260–262; *radiocarbon dates* 262–263, Table 12
scarabs: *Amenhotep III scarab at Knossos* 220–223, 347; *and MBA-SIP élite trading* 137
Schaeffer, C.F.-A. 342
Schiffer, M.B. 50
Scholes, K. 13
science-based dating: *history of dating of Thera eruption by* 4–5, 20–40; *problems of* 329–330; *see also* radiocarbon, dendrochronology / tree rings, ice cores
scripts: *relationship between Minoan, Cypriot and Eastern Mediterranean systems* 127–128
Seattle Radiocarbon Laboratory: 240, 242, 311; *1993 decadal radiocarbon calibration curve* 240, 243–245, Fig.45
'second phase' Thera radiocarbon dates 236
Self, S. and King, A.J. 272
Sellopoulou (Crete): 218, 220, 222–223, 347; *see also Knossos, Crete*

Senmut: 212; *tomb of* 213, 217; *see also* Egyptian chronology
Sharuhen 166, 183, 258
Sidmant tomb 137, 207
Shaw, M. 104
Sigurdsson, H. *et al.* 270, 273, 275, 277–278, 305–306
Simon Fraser versus Oxford radiocarbon controversy 237–240
Soles, J.S. *et al.* 73–74
Soles, J.S. 252, 254
Soufrière (St. Vincent) volcanic eruption 278
Stephania (Cyprus) 158, 161
Stewart, J.R. 324
Stuiver, M. and Becker, B. 245, 308
Stuiver, M. *et al.* 242, 311
stylistic exchanges: 139; *source of* 143
Suez Canal xxvii, 9
sulphur emissions: *and climate disruptions* 264, 268–269, 276–279; *and 17th century climatic anomaly* 281; *estimation of volcanic emissions by petrologic analysis* 269–272, 305–306; *recorded in ice cores* 263
Suppiluliuma I 225
Swiny, S. 127

Tambora (Indonesia) volcanic eruption 281, 284, 316
Tanaja, equation with Greek mainland 223–224
Tarhunaradu, King of Arzawa 228
TAW III Conference 29–30, 236
Tell el-Dab'a / Avaris (Egypt) 32–34, 49, 62–63, 77, 107–112, 114, 119–120, 124–125, 127, 130, 132, 134–137, 138, 142, 145, 147–149, 159, 160–161, 164–167, 170–171, 174, 178, 180–182, 184–185, 188, 190–191, 196, 199, 201, 203, 205, 258–259, 323, 325–329, 338, 342, 361, 363; *Cypriot imports at* 159–160, 325–327; *discontinuity of MC/LCIA and LCIB finds at* 164–166; *'Ezbet Helmi area of site see* 'Ezbet Helmi (Tell el-Dab'a); *frescoes* 80–107, 335; *historical dating* 326–329; *LMIA material at* 107–113; *pumice at* 32–33, 35, 145–150, 336; *'missing' stratum* 166, 168; *problem issues* 325–329; *PWS at* 167–168 *WSI at* 34–35, 49, 93, 158–170; *WSI finds and regional contacts* 180–181
Tell el-Amarna (Egypt) 2; *see also* Amarna Letters
Tell el-'Ajjul (Gaza) 36, 55, 61–64, 127, 129, 134–135, 156–158, 162, 164–166, 169, 323–325, 327, 361, 365; *gold jewellery and links with frescoes* 138–139; *relative chronology* 176, 181–182 184–187, 190–191; *WSI at* 181–187, 324–326, 329

Tell el-Maskhuta (Egypt): 190–191, 327; *Cypriot imports at* 327

Tell el-Yahudiyeh Ware 62–63, 122, 129–135, 138, 178, 190–191; *at Toumba tou Skourou (Cyprus)* 130–131; *biconical (late) types* 134–135; *Cypriot influence on Tell el-Dabʿa finds and chronological implications* 130; *distribution map and discussion* 133–134; *juglets at Thera* 113, 132, 135; *phases represented in Cyprus and Egypt* 132–134; *relative Cypriot date* 129–130; *relative date in Thera* 132; *significance for LMIA/MBA/SIP correlation* 132

Tell es-Sultan see *Jericho*

Tell Taʿannek (Palestine West Bank) 206–207, 218

Tel Kabri (Israel): 29–30, 80, 97, 101, 135–136, 148, 188, 190, 259; *frescoes* 324, 364

Tel Nami (Israel) 146

Tempest Stele of Ahmose: 41–42, 192–202; *alternative interpretations of text* 193–195; *and similar texts* 196–197; *critique of Foster and Ritner hypothesis* 199–201; *location, date and context* 195–196; *non-literal interpretation* 201; *no Thera link* 201–202; *political-cultural context* 197–199; *relevance of human agency* 201

tephra: 331; *distinctive Theran tephra* 11, Fig.13; *relative dating of Thera by tephra / pumice finds* 16–18

Thebes (Egypt) 12, 97, 120, 196, 254

Thera: *pre-eruption shape* 15, Fig.14

Thera eruption: 267, 271–272, 280, 282, 284, 286–287, 292, 294–295, 330; *possibility of less dramatic volcanic acid signal* 305–306; *possible hemisphere-scale effects* 268–269

Thera eruption date debate: *1628 BC date, summary of argument for* 335–337; *alternative candidates for 17th century volcanic eruption* 282–286; *circumstantial climatic links between 17th century BC disruption and* 272–285; *current state of debate* 40–45; *eruption/abandonment of Akrotiri LMIA (not LMIB)* 13, 15–19; *Gölcük glass data and* 296; *history of* 9–45; *history of science-dating of* 4–5, 20–40; *local effects* 267–268; *negative climatic evidence for 16th century BC date* 274–280; *positive climatic evidence for 17th century BC date* 280–287; *relevance to wider history* xxvii–xxviii, xxix–xxx, 1, 7, 11–12, 41–42, 43–44, 75–76; *suggestions for a radiocarbon-based resolution* 247;

'rose pumice' and 297; *traditional dating of* 13, 19–20

time: *role in archaeology* xxviii–xxix, 46–48

Tiryns (Greece) 347

Tiyi, Queen 222

Total Ozone Mapping Spectrometer (TOMS) Satellite 270

Toumba tou Skourou (Cyprus) 123, 125–126, 129–131, 135, 154, 157–158, 162, 163, 170, 172–173, 176, 178–179, 181, 190–191, 322; *Egyptian razor* 145

tree rings see dendrochronology / tree rings

Trianda (Rhodes) 72, 97, 118, 331

Trondheim, 12th International Radiocarbon Conference 240

tsunamis from Thera 72, 146

Tudhaliya I 225, 227

Tudhaliya II 227, 228, 229

Turin Canon 187, 361

Tutankhamun: *Restoration Stela of* 198, 200; 344; *see also* Egyptian chronology

Tuthmosis I 42, 92, 146, 203, 333, 337; see also Egyptian chronology

Tuthmosis III 13, 19, 24, 26, 30–31, 37, 42, 61, 67, 90, 92–93, 96–97, 122, 145, 188, 202–204, 206–207, 209, 211–214, 218–220, 223–225, 227, 254, 258, 334, 335, 337–338, 340–341, 346–347, 349, 363; *see also* Egyptian chronology

Tuthmosis IV 223–224, 227, 347; *see also* Egyptian chronology

Tykot, R.H. 260, 262

Tylissos (Crete) 116

Ugarit (Syria) 365

Uluburun shipwreck (south Turkish coast) 344–345

Useramun, tomb of 217

Vandersleyen, C. 195

Vasilikos Valley (Cyprus) 172

Venus, observations and relation to chronology of Hammurapi 351, 354

Vercoutter, J. 212–213

Vermeule, E.D.T. and Wolsky, F.Z. 125–126, 130

Vesuvius (Italy) volcanic eruption 300, 302

Vitaliano, D.B. and Vitaliano, C.J. 16

Vivara (Italy) 283

Vogel, J.S. *et al.* 283

volcanic glass: *Gölcük glass data* 296; *in GISP2 ice-core* 283–284, 288–307; *sourcing techniques* 267, 288; *see also* GISP2 ice-core

Wace, A.J.B. and Blegen, C.W. 206

Wachsmann, S. 212, 214

Ward, W.A. 474

Warren. P.M. and Hankey, V. 119, 144, 204, 206–207, 220–222, 254, 332, 346–347

Warren, P.M. 17, 22–23, 26, 28, 40, 77, 108, 144–145, 147–148, 264, 275, 278, 332, 338

Watkins, N.D. *et al.* 268

Watrous, L.V. 218

Webster, G.S. 261–262

Weinstein, G.A. 27

Weinstein, J.M. 26–28

Westgate, J.A. *et al.* 292

White Mountains (California USA) tree ring data 276, 279, 313, 315–316

Whiting, R.M. 351

Wiener, M.H. and Allen, J.P. 192–196, 199, 201

Wiener, M.H. 40, 150, 338, 346

Wijngaarden, G.-J. van 59

Williams, B. 328

Woolley, L. 349, 356, 359–360

WP / PWS transition 173

WSI (White Slip I) Ware: *and the start of the LCI and LMIA periods* 150–192; *and feasting* 170; *at Alalakh* 360–363; *at Tell el-ʿAjjul* 181–187, 324–325; *at Tell el-Dabʿa* 158–170; *bowl from Thera* 150–158; *island-wide homogeneity LCIB* 172; *late WSI in Aegean* 176–178; *more typical of LCIB than LCIA* 123–124; *non-stratified nature of Tell el-Dabʿa finds* 160–161; *outline of chronological debate* 150; *relative dating of Thera and Tell el-Dabʿa finds* 161–164; *relative chronology/ sequence* 170–188, 323–325; *significance of absence from Tell el-Dabʿa stratum D/2:* 166–167

Yamhad 356

Yarim-Lim I, palace at Alalakh, 349–350, 360, 363

Yarim-Lim III of Yamhad 356–357

Yiali (Greece) 149

Younger, J. 104

Zakros see *Kato Zakro (Crete)*

Zielinski, G.A. and Germani, M.S. 37–39, 284, 288–290, 292, 294–297, 299–301, 304, 306, 336

Zielinski, G.A. *et al.* 305

Zimri-Lim of Mari 350

Zukrasi 356–357

Zürich Radiocarbon Laboratory 235

A TEST OF TIME REVISITED

Acknowledgements

I thank Felix Höflmayer, Bernd Kromer, David Aston, Christopher Bronk Ramsey, Mike Dee, Jeffrey Leon and Catherine Kearns for their very helpful comments and assistance. I thank Malcolm Wiener for his forensic interest, and criticisms of past work, which in turn encourage progressively better and more robust studies.

Note

- Figures in the Revisit Essay are labeled as Figure RE1 to RE32.
- Tables in the Revisit Essay are labeled as Table RE1 to RE12.
- References cited in the Revisit Essay are listed at the end of the Revisit Essay.
- Figures RE33 to RE44 follow in the Postscript, along with Tables RE13 to RE17.

Contents

A schematic map of the Aegean and East Mediterranean showing the locations of the main sites discussed in the Revisit Essay

A schematic and approximate representation of the Aegean archaeological and calendar-^{14}C time periods discussed in the Revisit Essay

Revisit Essay: The Thera/Santorini Debate 13+ years on

1. Introduction   1

2. Approaches and viewpoints: relativity and objectivity in the Thera/ Santorini debate   13

3. *A Test of Time Revisited*: The State of the Debate and Key Evidence as of AD 2012 to earlier 2013   19
   - *a.* Note concerning WWW document on developments AD 1999 to AD 2006   19
   - *b.* Note concerning discussion to AD 2004, and then to AD 2012   19
   - *c.* State of the Debate (AD 2012 to earlier 2013)   20
     Introductory remarks (and Egyptian and Mesopotamian chronology)
     - (I) What we can put aside at present with regard to the Thera date debate   26
       - (i) Ice-cores   26
       - (ii) Speleothems *and* Postscript (and change in characterisation)   27
       - (iii) Tree-ring growth anomalies (except Porsuk) and suggested linkages to major volcanic eruptions   27
       - (iv) Aegean tree-ring growth anomaly   29
       - (v) Thera pumice (qua pumice – and not airfall tephra)   31
       - (vi) Tell el-Dab'a   32
       - (vii) Archaeomagnetism   33
     - (II) The archaeological connections between the Aegean, east Mediterranean and Egypt   34
       - (i) Khyan Lid (and dating of Khyan)   35
       - (ii) Egyptian stone vessels   37
       - (iii) Vessel with the name of Ahmose from Palaepaphos *Teratsoudhia*, Cyprus   38
       - (iv) White Slip (WS) I   39
       - (v) Rhyta   42
     - (III) The radiocarbon (^{14}C) evidence   42
       - (i) The ^{14}C evidence for the date of the end of the Akrotiri VDL, and for the Aegean phases before, contemporary with, and after the Thera eruption   43

(a) Akrotiri VDL ^{14}C dates in isolation   60
(b) Aegean Sequence analysis   66
(c) Thera olive branch   74
(d) Robustness?   79
(e) Conclusions   79
(ii) Claims of problems as undermining radiocarbon dating in
      the Aegean and especially as regards Thera put forward
      by Wiener (2012)   80
      (a) Regional ^{14}C offsets   80
      (b) Calcareous growth context for plant samples   81
      (c) Analysis and calibration   81
(iii) Radiocarbon conclusions   94
(IV) Approximate Chronology to use AD 2013 versus Manning
      (1999: 340 and Fig. 62)?   95

4. Response to, and critique of, Bietak (2004)   99

5. Corrections/mistakes in Manning (1999)
    (a) Corrections/Mistakes – which were errors/mistakes in 1999 – and discussion 108
        (i)   Supposed 12th century BC dendrochronological anomaly   109
        (ii) Uluburun and dendrochronology   109
        (iii) The dating of the Anatolian juniper dendrochronology   110
        (iv) Is the Gordion/Anatolian dendrochronology sound?   111
        (v)   Has Anatolian dendrochronology always been appropriately
              undertaken and reported?   112
    (b) Other Corrigenda and Addenda to A Test of Time   113

6. Revisit Essay Appendix 1: Details on Egyptian New Kingdom
    chronology results following Aston (2012) and re-running the
    Bronk Ramsey et al. (2010) radiocarbon model   116

7. Revisit Essay Appendix 2: Radiocarbon date listing regarding
    Figures RE1–4 and Manning et al. (2006a)   134

8. Revisit Essay Appendix 3: Testing ^{14}C Sequence analysis in the
    period 1700–1500 BC against known age data   143

9. References (for the Revisit Essay)   149

10. Postscript   169
    (i)   Comparisons and Differences Between the IntCal09 and IntCal13
           Calibration Datasets with regard to the Thera VDL Date Range   169
    (ii)   IntCal13 and the Thera Olive Branch   175
    (iii) IntCal13 and the ^{14}C Chronology of New Kingdom Egypt 181
    (iv)   IntCal13, Tree-rings, and Mesopotamian Chronology   189
    (v)   IntCal13 and the date of the Uluburun Ship   189
    (vi)   IntCal13 and dating Late Minoan IB-II   191
    (vii) Final words on the anti-radiocarbon case: comments on Wiener
           and Earle (2014)   195
    (vii) Additional References in the Postscript not in the Revisit Essay   198

Index   200

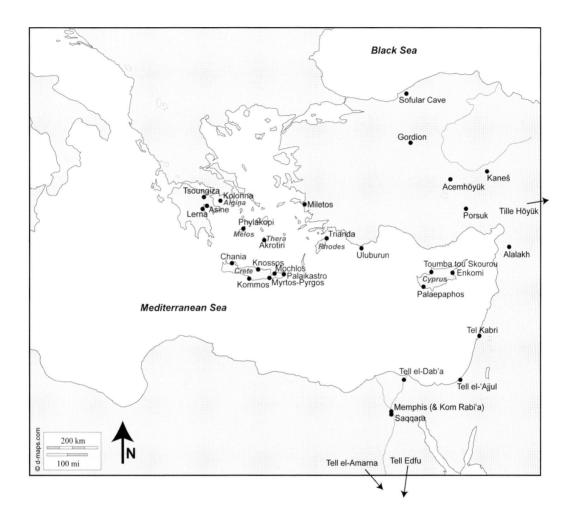

Schematic map of the Aegean and East Mediterranean showing the locations of the main sites discussed in the Revisit Essay. Base map from d-maps.com.

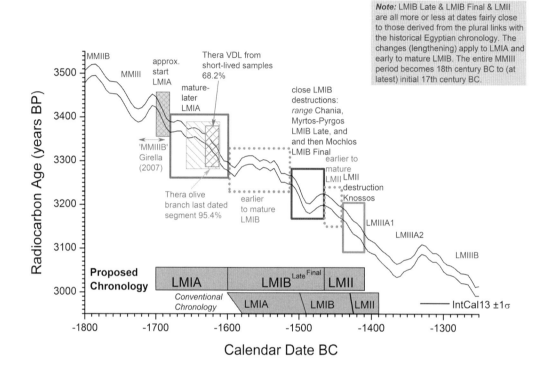

Schematic and approximate representation of the calendar time periods of the Aegean Late Minoan IA to Late Minoan II phases set against the IntCal13 radiocarbon calibration curve on the basis of the discussions in the Revisit Essay and the Postscript, and contrasted with the previous conventional (or 'low') chronology (e.g. Cadogan 1978; Warren 1984; Warren and Hankey 1989; Wiener 2006a).
Note: x axis of boxes = calendar years; y axis of boxes is not to scale.

REVISIT ESSAY

The Thera/Santorini Debate 13+ years on

1. Introduction

The test envisaged in the title *A Test of Time: The Volcano of Thera and the chronology and history of the Aegean and east Mediterranean in the mid second millennium BC* (Manning 1999) was of two forms. First, the obvious: what was the correct and precise (as possible) dating of the enormous mid-second millennium BC eruption of the Thera (Santorini) volcano in the southern Aegean, and, in turn, what was the correct dating scheme (chronology) and historical synthesis for the associated archaeological phases in the Aegean and east Mediterranean in the mid-second millennium BC? There was a conventional set of assumptions and interpretations which, by the AD 1970s, placed the eruption more or less at about 1500 BC. However, starting with results from Michael (1976 – see also Betancourt and Weinstein 1976), radiocarbon (^{14}C) dating started to suggest a date for the eruption, and thence the beginning of the Late Bronze Age (LBA) in the Aegean, some 100 or so years earlier than previously thought (17th century BC versus about 1500 BC for the eruption and c.1700 BC versus c.1600 BC for the start of the LBA).[1] This began the belated impact of the so-called second radiocarbon revolution (dendrochronologically calibrated radiocarbon dates: see Renfrew 1973) on the world of the second millennium BC Aegean and east Mediterranean. In the period from the later AD 1980s to AD 1990s, a debate formed between those who defended the conventional position, and those who argued instead that the radiocarbon-based dating was perhaps correct and that the archaeological evidence and other indications could be reinterpreted to yield a new 'high' chronology and history for the period (especially Betancourt 1987; Manning 1988a). Manning (1999) sought to review the ups and downs of this debate, and the various data and arguments deployed, and to address this debate (favouring, on analysis, a 'high' Aegean chronology – given the evidence then to hand).

---

[1] For one recent short summary of the whole Thera date topic as of 2010, see Manning (2010); on the Thera/Santorini volcano generally (including date of the Minoan eruption) see Friedrich (2009), and on the Minoan eruption and impacts see Sewell (2001) – available at http://santorini-eruption.org.uk/; on Akrotiri, see Doumas (2010). For a review of the history of the Thera date topic to AD 1999, see Manning (1999: 7–40).

Second, the other aspect of 'a test of time' was the long process of resolving this debate: the 'high' v. 'low' chronology controversy in Aegean prehistory and associated fields was already over two decades old in AD 1999, and is now well into its 4th decade, and yet remains to be settled. The debate has become something of an agonistic struggle between opposing viewpoints and interpretations, that has even been characterized by one leading 'low' chronology figure as 'Science versus Archaeology' (Bietak 2003). Resolution of the debate is, however, fundamental to establishing an accurate and precise timeframe for the archaeology and proto-history of the second millennium BC in the Aegean and east Mediterranean regions – and so the ability to move then to more refined, higher-resolution, nuanced and human scale and agent-centered analyses, interpretations and syntheses of the rich interrelated cultural legacies of these civilizations (and from thence to successful wider Eurasian syntheses). All scholars involved realize this, and hence the vigour and passion of the debate. Establishing the correct timescale will directly shape the writing of the history of this era. Already we may note that some leading scholars working on syntheses of European prehistory have observed that the "traditional low chronology" of the Aegean for the mid second millennium BC "as employed by Kilian-Dirlmeier (1993: Abb.2) and Warren and Hankey (1989), is problematic from a central and north European perspective, in terms of both chronology and cultural relations" (Kristiansen and Larsson 2005: 118) – these scholars instead employ the 'high' Aegean chronology.

In the period from mid-AD 1999 to the end of AD 2012, an enormous amount of literature has appeared concerned with the topics and scholarship discussed in the original publication of this book, *A Test of Time* (Manning 1999) – reprinted as first published (unrevised) in this second edition.[2] The question of the correct dates for the Minoan eruption of the Thera/Santorini volcano (hereafter I use Thera as in Manning 1999), and for the associated archaeological phases in the Aegean and across the east Mediterranean region, remain hotly contested and of wide interest. It is fair to say that the divide between the 'high' chronology, and the previously conventional and now 'low' chronology, is one of the main scholarly controversies in the fields of Aegean and east Mediterranean prehistory. For example, Manfred Bietak (2000a: 11), having observed that the east Mediterranean in the 3rd and 2nd millennia BC is the region that shaped the Ancient World (as relevant to the subsequent Near Eastern, Mediterranean and European civilisations), then remarks that:

---

[2] The most important and comprehensive volume with new work and synthesis unfortunately appeared after this essay was finished: Höflmayer (2012b). I thank Felix Höflmayer (pers. comm. January 2013) for the following assessment. This book provides a thorough summary of the archaeological and scientific arguments, with rich documentation on all the archaeological evidence (and thus is much more complete and comprehensive than earlier partial studies such as e.g. Höflmayer 2007; 2009). Höflmayer regards his 2012 *Radiocarbon* paper (Höflmayer 2012a) as an update, certainly in viewpoint and general assessment. This Höflmayer (2012a) paper is cited a number of times in this Revisit Essay. Höflmayer (2012b) is valuable, however, for some specific arguments and for its forensic discussions concerning early LBA Aegean pottery in Egypt, and Egyptian material in the Aegean; in both cases it provides some new critical comments (while still being more conservative in viewpoint and assessment than the subsequently written Höflmayer 2012a paper). The Höflmayer (2012b) volume should thus be consulted with regard to discussions in Section 3.c, and especially Section 3.c.II, of this Revisit Essay.

Our knowledge of this period proves to be, upon close examination, based on such uneven and controversial research that the basis of its history has to be reestablished and reexamined.

The most unbearable aspect of the status quo in research is chronological differences of up to 150 years from one region to another resulting in uncertainty over which situation in one region corresponds to which conditions in another region. ...

An example for such a disarrangement was the attempt to give the eruption of the Santorini volcano a high date, which was moved, based on natural scientific research, from the previous c.1500 BC to 1628 BC

Bietak (2001a: 11–12) then continues to cite – and use the Santorini/Thera case as the main example of such an 'unbearable aspect' or 'disarrangement', as he sees it.

And so, whereas there was apparent certainty in the general range of Aegean and east Mediterranean chronology up to the mid AD 1970s, there is now doubt or ambiguity, and textbooks end up offering both the 'high' and the 'low' chronologies (e.g. Shelmerdine 2008: 5 Table 1.2). As Bietak (2000a: 11) notes, this is problematic, since it means we are unclear in the period around the Thera eruption (c.1700–1500 BC) about which archaeological phases in the Aegean or Cyprus (and regions) are linked with which rulers in Egypt, and with which archaeological phases in Egypt and the Levant. We cannot write history without chronology. This controversy, ambiguity, and uncertainty – apparently pitting radiocarbon versus archaeology – is indeed doubly ironic, even problematic, in the 21st century AD when, outside the (often rather introspective) Aegean-east Mediterranean fields, areas as relevant as ancient Egypt itself, or at the opposite end of Europe from V. Gordon Childe's (1928) 'most ancient East' (southern Britain and Ireland), or as far away as southeast Asia, have each witnessed concerted, successful, recent efforts to create large-scale, highly precise, and accurate chronologies *integrating* radiocarbon and archaeology (see especially Bronk Ramsey *et al.* 2010; Whittle *et al.* 2011; Higham and Higham 2009). As reviewed and propounded by Bayliss (2009), a new (third) radiocarbon revolution, integrating archaeological sequences with radiocarbon dating via Bayesian chronological modelling (Bronk Ramsey 2009a), is revolutionizing archaeological chronology around the world. Therefore, despite the arcane and conservative scholarly traditions in Classical and Aegean archaeology, its long literary inferiority complex and art history tendencies, and the sometimes problematic mix of protohistory and archaeology which has often served to keep Aegean and Classical archaeology separate from the rest of European and Near Eastern prehistory (e.g. Whitley 2001: 12–15; Manning 2008a: 36–40), we should, nonetheless, expect that a refined high-resolution archaeological chronology integrating archaeology and radiocarbon via Bayesian chronological modelling (the third radiocarbon revolution) should also be possible for the Aegean and east Mediterranean in the second millennium BC. Some starts have been made (e.g. Manning *et al.* 2006a; Wild *et al.* 2010), but much more remains to be done. Creating a highly-resolved timeframe is fundamental to sophisticated and refined archaeological analysis and interpretation (Bayliss and Whittle 2007; Whittle *et al.* 2008; Whittle *et al.* 2011: 1–4; Bayliss 2009: 141–142).

Apart from this sort of general logic (the correct synchronisation of the civilisations of the Aegean and east Mediteranean in the 2nd millennium BC), and a simple desire to have the correct date for textbooks and museum labels, there are also (at least) three main reasons for investigating the Thera date debate,[3] and for trying to reach a resolution:

First: the Thera volcanic eruption was one of the largest volcanic eruptions of the last several thousand years (Sigurdsson *et al.* 2006),[4] and proximate to the civilizations of Minoan Crete, the early Mycenaean world (and the rest of the Aegean), and the Ancient Near East, and has been tentatively (or speculatively) associated with the stories of Atlantis, even the Exodus (Luce 1969; Bruins and van der Plicht 1996; Friedrich 2009: 188–201; Sivertsen 2009), enhanced loss of visibility of the planet Venus as recorded in Old Babylonian texts from the reign of Ammisaduqa (de Jong and Foertmeyer 2010),[5] or some Egyptian texts discussing major storms and unusual circumstances either from the start of the reign of Ahmose or from the reign of Hatshepsut/Tuthmosis III (e.g. Foster and Ritner 1996; Foster *et al.* 2009: 176–179; Goedicke 1992; 2004; MacGillivray 2009: 159–161),[6] and possibly a few other ancient text sources including some Chinese

---

[3] A separate question to the calendar date is when (the season) within the relevant year the eruption occurred? Sewell (2001; Manning and Sewell 2002) from a study of wind patterns through the year versus tephra distribution from the Thera eruption argues that (spring-) summer is the most likely time, and, as MacGillivray (2009: 158–159) summarises, the archaeology at Akrotiri appears to offer a consistent impression (also e.g. Doumas 1990: 49). The very recent and more sophisticated study of Johnston *et al.* (2012) modelling tephra distribution versus wind patterns for the Thera eruption also argues for a spring to summer timing. Postscript: the detailed new study of insect pests by Panagiotakopulu *et al.* (2013) also points to an early summer date (shortly after harvest).

[4] Recent work by Johnston *et al.* in fact indicates that this is a minimum estimate and that the real erupted volume is another c.20–40% larger: see http://www.academia.edu/2391529/Revised_Estimates_for_the_Volume_of_the_Minoan_Eruption. This would make Thera arguably the largest Holocene volcanic eruption in terms of erupted Dense Rock Equivalent. A publication is in preparation: Emma Johnston, pers. comm, 2013.

[5] The link (visual extinction) is with the well-known 1628–1626 BC climate event indicated from tree-ring evidence widely spread around the northern hemisphere (e.g. Salzer and Hughes 2007: 64–66; Grudd *et al.* 2000; Baillie and Munro 1988). Whether or not the cause of this event might be the massive Thera/Santorini volcanic eruption (as suggested by de Jong and Foertmeyer 2010: 153–155) is a separate issue. Some major climate impact clearly seems to have occurred in these years (and a large volcanic eruption – whichever – is one possible cause among others). It is a nice coincidence that one plausible solution for the dating of the Old Babylonian period from the Venus tablet data of Ammisaduqa – the low-Middle chronology – which fits with the available dendrochronology and the other evidence indicating most likely a Middle to low-Middle chronology date (see Section 3.c below) – offers a possible linkage of substantially reduced visibility of the planet Venus (suggested to be consistent with the effects of a major aerosol from a large volcanic eruption) with these very years known for a notable widespread climate event (as noted by de Jong and Foertmeyer 2010; see also de Jong 2012: 403; 2013a).

[6] Manning (1999: 192–202) argued against any literal linkage between the so-called Tempest Stele of Ahmose and the Thera eruption (see also Wiener and Allen 1998). In a recent discussion, Schneider (2010b) reviews this text and notes that it is interesting and perhaps more literal than Manning (1999) argued (see esp. p.409), but nonetheless Schneider holds that it likely does not refer/link to a volcanic eruption, i.e. Thera (esp. p.408). However, in recent (AD 2012) lectures, Robert Ritner and Nadine Moeller have put the case again, perhaps, for more directly linking the destructive and violent storm and effects described in the stele with the Thera eruption (see now forthcoming article in *Journal of*

and other material,[7] and more prosaically, but famously (since an article of 1939 by Marinatos), with the supposed destruction of Minoan civilization (more recently, see Driessen and Macdonald 1997). Thus it seems an interesting and challenging quest to get an accurate and precise date for the Thera eruption as this would have wide potential interest and relevance. More recent studies have claimed to identify the effects of a Thera tsunami on Crete (Bruins *et al.* 2008; 2009), and, in detail, work has intriguingly hinted at the possible arrival and influence of Theran refugees on Crete (presumably some of those who abandoned the island immediately before the eruption) at the end of Late Minoan IA, and as a factor in new buildings and practices in early Late Minoan IB (Soles 2009: 113–116). In all cases, establishing a date and refining a concrete absolute timeframe, and ending current century-scale uncertainties, would allow for more historical-level analysis in Aegean archaeology at the scale (human lives, and experiences) at which challenges, opportunities and changes were experienced by individuals and their communities, and choices made. As Whittle *et al.* (2011: 4) write: "Without time there is no history, and without history our view of human agency, identity, choice and values must remain substantially incomplete".

Second: if the Thera volcanic eruption can be precisely dated, it would in turn provide a specific calendar point applicable to a wide horizon of archaeological contexts/horizons and palaeoenvironmental contexts across the entire east Mediterranean region from the Aegean to Egypt, based both on finds of air-fall Thera tephra in archaeological and palaeoenvironmental contexts (see e.g. Narcisi and Vezzoli 1999: 42–43 regarding the Z2 tephra; Eastwood *et al.* 1999; Bichler *et al.* 2003), and the wide material culture links with the large assemblage of artefacts buried by the eruption in the early Late Bronze Age time-capsule at Akrotiri on Thera (see e.g. Doumas 1983; Forsyth 1997; Palyvou 2005), ranging from imports and exports of ceramic and stone objects to wall paintings and the items depicted (e.g. Warren 1979: 88–90, 106–107 and n.2; Buchholz 1980; Cadogan 1990: 95; Doumas 1998; Manning 1999: 136–144; Niemeier and Niemeier 2000; Sørensen 2009: 269, Merrillees 2009; Earle 2012: 14 with summary listing from Cline 1994).[8] There is thus the potential, with a much more high-resolution timeframe,

---

Near Eastern Studies). If the start of the New Kingdom is raised somewhat into the 2nd quarter of the 16th century BC as Aston (2012) proposes, then it may be more possible to try even to consider how a 'high' (late 17th century BC) or a compromise early chronology (early to mid 16th century BC) date for the Thera eruption might indeed perhaps have an association with this text. In reverse, the 'low' chronology dates around c.1530/1525 BC and later would not work.

[7] For some of the other claims (in e.g. Greek, Chinese and Irish texts), see literature cited by Manning (1999: 202 and n.952). Review of the chronology of the Chinese records, however, appeared quickly to undermine the claims for a link with Thera around 1600 BC (e.g. by Pang *et al.* 1989): see Pankenier (1998). The usefulness of the dating available from these early Chinese astronomical records has also been criticized (see Keenan 2002b; 2007 – against Pankenier 2007). The comments of Keenan (2007: 147) regarding ^{14}C require some modification. The more dramatic claims in Keenan (2004) have been shown not to be correct with further data and work (Manning and Kromer 2011b – see with footnote 15 below).

[8] The major recent Middle Cycladic discoveries at Akrotiri are, as Doumas (2010: 754–755) writes "revolutionizing our knowledge about this period not only in the Cycladic islands but also in the entire Aegean". The extraordinary bichrome painted ceramic vessels (e.g. Nikolakopoulou 2010), and their imagery (griffin, felines chasing in 'flying gallop' pose, birds), in particular raise again the issue of whether there are connections with the art of the Levant at this period (for some previous

to write a new fine grain history of the entire mid-second millennium BC Aegean and east Mediterranean world at the level of individual lives.

Third: if the 'high' chronology is correct, it requires a significant re-thinking (of the conventional 'low' chronology view) of a web of archaeological, historical and cultural associations (a re-thinking of the 'orthodox' history of the Aegean and east Mediterranean in the mid-second millennium BC). In particular, it necessitates a new emphasis on the period c.1700–1550 BC, and so the world of the Hyksos in Egypt, and the associated Levantine maritime world (e.g. Oren 1997a; Bietak 1995). We would need to rewrite history to give much greater importance to this Canaanite world in the formation of the initial Late Bronze Age societies of Cyprus, the east Aegean, new palace Crete, the Cyclades, and early Mycenaean Greece (among other things).[9] Although rich pre-Classical east-west cultural interactions in the eastern Mediterranean region have been (belatedly) recognized and highlighted both in literature, archaeology and art (e.g. West 1997; Morris 1992; 1997; Kopcke and Tokumaru 1992; Cline 1994; Davies and Schofield 1995; Niemeier and Niemeier 2000; Brysbaert 2007), a new focus on the Hyksos-Levantine world, and the period (18th–16th centuries BC) when it was a major maritime trading centre of gravity in the eastern Mediterranean region,[10] and so (thus) wider cultural influence and force, has the potential to reshape a number of existing interpretations and syntheses. Specifically, it would re-raise debates that have been partly quashed by the 'low' chronology cultural synthesis, such as the wider relevance of both the Semitic aspects of Linear A on Crete, and several other Levantine-Aegean connections in mythology/tradition, archaeology, and art, reaching back at least to the mid-second millennium BC (Gordon 1962; 1993; Astour 1967; Bernal 1987; 1991; and see literature cited at the end of the previous paragraph). This may lead to a different and exciting new writing of history for the mid-second millennium BC – and the un-invention of the now orthodox tradition. It calls for a plea *opposite* that of MacGillivray (2009: 170), who, after proposing a conventional date of 1500 BC for the Thera eruption (see previously e.g. Warren 1984 defending this orthodox approximate date), then ends his essay by stating that this 1500 BC date is "close to those proposed

---

thoughts see, for example, the discussion in Manning 1999: 139), and the direction of transfer, and so on, and take this exchange/transference clearly into the pre-New Kingdom period before the Late Bronze Age. This is an area for new and exciting work.

[9] Balter (2006: 508) quotes Jeremy B. Rutter's lovely pithy statement: "The Hyksos have gotten lousy press." In the Aegean, apart from re-considering Levantine-Hyksos interaction and influence on Crete, the role of Thera and Aigina as gateway ports not only for Cretan (current general view: see discussion of Maran 2011), but also for Levantine influences and technologies (MBA to early LBA) into the emerging Mycenaean world offers rich potential for another potentially important reassessment.

[10] The Kamose inscription refers to hundreds of ships of the Retenu ('Syrians') in the harbor of Avaris (Redford 1997: 14), and whether or not there is any exaggeration, the large scale of the maritime trading world of the Hyksos, and the associated coast-port cities of the Levant (e.g. Oren 1997b), is very clear (Manning 1999: 136–144). Tell el-Dab'a was one of the largest cities (and ports) of Egypt and likely the entire Levant in the later Middle Bronze Age. The considerable aspirations of the Hyksos ruler Khyan may be guessed at based on royal, king-to-king, gifts he seems to have sent to both Knossos on Crete and Hattusa in Anatolia, as highlighted by Mellink (1995), as well as the wide distribution of other finds with his name (Moeller and Marouard 2011: 106 and n.59 with refs.).

by prominent Aegean archaeologists like Sinclair Hood before the calibrated ^{14}C dates introduced uncertainty" and that "I trust that closer scrutiny and re-calibration of those samples with dates averaging at approximately 3350 BP will remove that uncertainty and allow us to return to our task of writing this chapter of early European, Egyptian and Southwest Asian history with the confidence that scholars displayed before the ^{14}C dispute". Instead, if the 'high' chronology synthesis is correct, we can and should re-think such (pre-radiocarbon) orthodoxy entirely, and consider a new history (and stop trying to ignore both the second and third radiocarbon revolutions). This is an intellectual and ethical imperative. As a principal conduit to, and then narrator of, the past – via the archaeological 'time machine' (Schnapp 2002: 139) – it is incumbent on archaeologists to try to be fair arbiters: critical of tradition and of context (original, intervening and modern).

Thus much more than a simple date in a table in a book, or on a label in a museum, is at stake. The Thera debate is at the heart of the correct synchronisation of the civilisations in the eastern Mediterranean in the second millennium BC, and so, in turn, it is fundamental to the correct proto to early history of the millennium that forms the background to the Classical World and the general beginnings of what can loosely be called Western Civilisation. The 'high' chronology, if correct, means a different history and cultural context for the mid-second millennium BC – something appreciated very early in the debate by Martin Bernal, who spotted the relevance of the 'high' 17th century BC date for the eruption of Thera for his wide challenge to the historiography of the Classical world (1987). The vigour and relentlessness of the defense of the orthodox or standard position (now the 'low' chronology) against the 'high' chronology challenge is notable, but to be expected, and serves only to highlight the importance of the topic to a number of inter-locking syntheses and modes of thought regarding the analysis of the history of the second millennium BC Aegean and east Mediterranean worlds. Even when an archaeological expert but – on this topic – non-committed scholar like Colin Renfrew is quoted as saying (of two independent studies in 2006 reporting findings in strong support of the 'high' Aegean chronology) that the studies "convincingly solve the problem of the dating of the Thera eruption" (Balter 2006: 508), and so one might think the 'high' chronology had at least reached the position of a reasonable or likely viewpoint on the part of the man on the Clapham omnibus (the ordinary sensible person),[11] the resolute total rejection of such change, and the defense of the 'low' chronology, has nonetheless continued. These defenses start from the premise that the 'low' chronology is correct (by tradition), and take the line of demanding, in legalistic fashion, that the 'low' chronology should stand until every possible hypothetical or real objection is dealt with – regardless of what seems to be most likely if one makes a fresh review, or applies common sense.

The field is now divided into four approximate groupings with regard to this controversy:

(i)   A group persuaded that critique of the pre-radiocarbon archaeological orthodoxy is justified, and who accept that a large body of radiocarbon data

---

[11] For the term in legal history and use, see the summary of McCaughran (2011: 614–615).

(from several laboratories and techniques) and other consonant findings, and a plausible re-reading of the archaeological evidence, seem to indicate the need for a new, revised, 'high' chronology for the Thera eruption in the late 17th century BC, and so a start for the Aegean and Cypriot Late Bronze Age periods no later than the mid 17th century BC. This group treats the radiocarbon and other scientific evidence as at least as important as the material culture and art-historical data and interpretations, while seeking a way to find solutions plausible to both types of data and argument. This was the main position adopted in Manning (1999; see further Manning 2007), and initially in Manning (1988a). Even taking this position, it is apparent that the later the Thera eruption is placed in the 17th century BC, the more potentially palatable this date could be to many archaeologists, and to the general pattern of the archaeological evidence. Thus, if the eruption were placed c.1650 BC or 1645 BC, then this is much more difficult to accept than 1628BC; and, if the eruption date ended up somewhere in the range 1630–1600 BC, then this could be even more palatable and can be more easily or plausibly accommodated in terms of the archaeological evidence. The most recent review and re-consideration of the Thera radiocarbon evidence suggests that it might be plausible to consider a most likely date in the last three decades of the 17th century BC (Manning and Kromer 2012; Höflmayer 2012a; and see below). Meanwhile, very recent work in fact indicates that perhaps the Egyptian historical chronology for the early 18th Dynasty might be able to go back another couple of decades (Aston 2012), in line with radiocarbon findings from Egyptian samples (Bronk Ramsey *et al.* 2010; and see below). This would further help substantially to reduce the apparent offset between the Aegean 'high' chronology and Egyptian dates (also Höflmayer 2012a), and would assist to make a late 17th century BC date for the Thera Volcanic Destruction Level (VDL) and subsequent eruption rather easier to accommodate within the wider pattern of evidence.

(ii)   A group determined to resist change, and wanting to retain more or less the pre-radiocarbon 'low' or traditional chronology with the eruption of Thera around (variously) 1530–1480 BC, and who therefore actively focus on trying to find any and all means to try to criticize or question or malign the science and especially the radiocarbon-based work employed by the scholarship in (i), and instead to recommend versions of the traditional pre-radiocarbon archaeological linkages and connections. This group regards the material culture and art-historical evidence and their standard interpretations of this as inherently correct and seeks to find every way to downplay or dismiss outright apparently contradictory indications from archaeological science methods such as radiocarbon dating. Some of the critique produced by this group is of course valid, and has prompted further, better, and more robust work and analyses by scholars supporting the 'high' position in recent years. I discuss some of this scholarship below and the responses to its criticisms. Scholars in this group tend to ignore the critiques of the security or precision or accuracy of the chronological conclusions which can be appropriately drawn from the cited archaeological and art historical data, and the fact that on critical study these really in no way rule out a higher (or even the 'high') chronology (Höflmayer 2012a – and see the 'high' chronology archaeological discussions and syntheses of e.g. Manning 2007; 1999; 1988a; Betancourt 1990; 1987; Kemp and Merrillees 1980).

(iii)   A new, if small, group which accepts that, while always less than perfect, the weight and strength of the radiocarbon data are considerable and cannot simply be ignored, and, while important, that much of the key archaeological evidence relevant to the Aegean or Cypriot late Middle Bronze Age or initial Late Bronze Age is either capable of some wider or more flexible interpretation, or is ambiguous, or is less than secure, or depends on *ex silencio* arguments. Thus some form of compromise is required between the 'high' and 'conventional' chronologies, and between 'science' and 'conventional archaeology'. This was more or less the case and logic for the possible "shortened 'compromise' early chronology" in Manning (1999); this position notes that the radiocarbon evidence all but excludes a Thera eruption date after about 1530 BC, but could be made to work with a date in the earlier to mid 16th century BC if there are strong reasons not to prefer the most likely radiocarbon date range in the later/late 17th century BC. After a further decade with little serious take-up, Höflmayer (2012a) has now argued for just such a compromise logic and position, and this position is of course attractive (trying to make everything 'sort of' work together). The question then is when exactly to place such a compromise date for the Thera eruption: does it put the eruption in the earlier to mid 16th century BC, or in fact in the late 17th century BC (as suggested to be possible, even most likely, by Manning and Kromer 2012; and see below).

(iv)   A group of indeterminate proportions (but sizable) who regard this topic as controversial but unsolved (Höflmayer 2012b falls into this category, with its conclusion p.244 col.2 "... konnte das chronologische Problem der ägäischen Chronologie nicht lösen": Höflmayer, pers. comm. January 2013). They acknowledge that the challenge to the traditional chronology and its historical and cultural assumptions since the AD 1980s has some validity, and they accept that radiocarbon dating works in most areas of archaeology around the world and seems consistently since the mid AD 1970s to indicate one course (upwards) for this Thera dating debate. However, they do not know how much trust they really have in this science technique that they do not entirely understand when applied to their own field, and worry about all the claims of problems and errors made repeatedly by the scholarship in (ii), and do not know whether to believe some of these claims or not. They therefore see this topic as a 'debate', set it as a nice exam or essay question for students, and are content enough to leave it as happily unsettled.

The aims of this essay revisiting the Thera debate and Manning (1999) some 13 years later are:

1.   To review the state of the debate, in terms of new evidence and claims. Is the (i) group position above – the position reviewed and advanced in Manning

(1999) – still the most likely one given the range of evidence and what we know by the end of AD 2012? And to answer the question: what is the most likely date of the Thera eruption? The relevance of a raising of the Egyptian historical chronology, and the start of the Egyptian New Kingdom, by some c.15/25 to 26/36 years (Aston 2012) versus older standard dates of c.1550 BC or 1540 BC (von Beckerath 1997; Kitchen 2000 – as in Manning 1999: 68 Table 3) is also considered. This greatly reduces the difference or offset between radiocarbon and the conventional scenario (which is already rather smaller than many believe: Höflmayer 2012a). This raising of the start of the Egyptian New Kingdom would make it much more feasible to try to compromise or accommodate both the radiocarbon and the (more conventionally interpreted) archaeological synthesis – and so seems potentially very attractive. Thus we need to consider whether this seems the best answer, or whether instead it offers a better set of circumstances to synthesise the 'high' Aegean chronology with the rest of the east Mediterranean archaeological and historical record?

2.   To highlight both the problems or lack of scientific basis to a number of claims from scholarship in the (ii) group above, and the problems with the traditional chronological synthesis, and to outline why some (upwards) changes are necessary for Aegean (and linked) chronology in the period around the time of the Thera volcanic eruption.

3.   To seek to persuade those members of the (iv) group of the relevance and importance of resolving the topic, and to provide a case for why they should consider joining groups (i or iii) if this can be shown to be the most likely position on current evidence.

4.   To acknowledge, note, and either correct, or accept, some errors and flaws in the original Manning (1999) study, and in some work it (mistakenly) relied on.

As noted already above, perhaps the most noticeable feature in scholarship concerned with the Thera eruption date, and Aegean and east Mediterranean Bronze Age chronology over the past dozen years, has been the determined and prolific campaign by a relatively small group of scholars to try to reject the Aegean 'high' chronology as supported in Manning (1999), both by claiming that the archaeological evidence supports the conventional or 'low' chronology and contradicts the 'high' chronology, and by trying to claim, via reference to all and any possible reasons that can be thought of (whether plausible or not), that the large body of Aegean radiocarbon data indicating support for the Aegean 'high' chronology must be wrong. There is no point citing and discussing every such paper; there is also an element of "[T]he lady doth protest too much, methinks" in the endless rhetoric. I just list a number of examples from three of the main scholars engaged in this effort from the past decade post-Manning (1999): Wiener 2001; 2003; 2006a; 2006b; 2007; 2009a; 2009b; 2010; 2012; Warren 2006; 2009; 2010; Bietak 2003; 2004; Bietak and Höflmayer 2007 (and see Postscript (vii) below).[12]

---

[12] There are of course a number of other papers just by these scholars also, apart from similar papers

I do not propose to offer multiple critiques of each of these rejectionist papers – this would end up as an extremely repetitious discussion – nor do I wish to fail to recognize that some valid and useful criticisms and observations have been made, which, by addressing these, serve to strengthen the 'high' or 'higher' or radiocarbon-based position (and so there is a debt of gratitude for the forensic attention of critical scholars). Just from the last decade, a reading of some of the work written or co-written by this author shows the benefit of answering the questions and critiques raised and made by rejectionist scholars, and illustrates how much stronger, better-based, and robust the resultant studies have become as a result, see e.g., Manning and Bronk Ramsey (2003); Manning *et al.* (2006a; 2009a); Manning (2007); Manning and Kromer (2011a; 2011b; 2012).

Instead, with one exception, I review below some of the main categories of evidence or topics, and in the course of these discussions I offer commentary and critique of the main 'low' chronology defense papers and arguments as relevant. The exception is a response to, and critique of, the long negative review of Manning (1999) by Manfred Bietak (2004): see Section 4 below (see also Postscript (iii) for some comments on a subsequent paper by Bietak). For various previous responses and comments by this author to earlier literature, see also especially Manning (2007); Manning and Kromer (2011a); Manning *et al.* (2009a). Some of the debate is about differences in approach and mentalité (see previously Manning 2007: 101–103), some about misunderstandings, and some about different types of, and sometimes non-compatible, data and their interpretation. Section 2 of this revisit essay discusses approaches and mentalité. The new evidence published in the years since AD 1999 has more or less uniformly supported or been consistent with the 'high' chronology position, and in contradiction with the 'low' chronology. Most important were the new radiocarbon dates and analyses relevant to Thera published in Friedrich *et al.* (2006) and Manning *et al.* (2006a). The aim of this revisit essay in Section 3 is to list and review the most important post-AD 1999 evidence and arguments, and to assess the current best dating for the Thera eruption and the initial Late Bronze Age phases in the Aegean. Within the space of a relatively modest update and assessment of the Manning (1999) book some 13 years after its initial publication, it is not possible to cite and discuss everything; indeed, not even more than a small fraction of the possible literature – this would otherwise require an entirely new major book-length treatment. This essay is therefore not a page by page detailed update, revision, and correction, nor can it focus on all and every point of detail covered in the original book. Instead, it focuses on the main issue – the date – and the main arguments raised by critics.

In closing this introduction, I wish to note that I do not have some ideological or other background reason which means that I 'believe' in the 'high' Aegean chronology and Thera date (regardless of the evidence). I became interested in the topic of the date of the Thera eruption as an undergraduate student simply because it seemed, on reading about the topic, that there was a potential problem: the radiocarbon dating evidence seemed at odds with the (then, and still) traditional interpretation of the archaeological evidence. Leading archaeologists were publishing papers suggesting

---

written by various other writers, such as, to give one instance, Fantuzzi (2007; 2009).

that the radiocarbon had to be wrong, for whatever reason, since they stated that the Aegean chronology derived from Egypt was fairly strong. But to my mind a critical examination of the archaeological evidence revealed much that was assumption and mere orthodox interpretation, and rather little that was solid for the key period around the time of the Thera eruption. Undoubtedly this was because I was new to the field, and had not been trained to 'know' the correct (orthodox) position. Meanwhile, the radiocarbon evidence was pretty coarse at that time, in terms both of measured data from the Aegean and the radiocarbon calibration curves. It seemed that probably nothing could be done, but then the first high-precision radiocarbon calibration curve to include the second millennium BC was published (Pearson *et al.* 1983), and, with this clearer picture (and then the subsequent set of high-precision radiocarbon calibration curves published in AD 1986 in *Radiocarbon* vol. 28 (2B)), it really did seem reasonable to ask what gave us the best chronology for the Aegean Bronze Age: the existing archaeological interpretation, or radiocarbon? And could the two different datasets and approaches (radiocarbon and archaeology) offer a coherent picture – rather than being forced to choose one scheme over the other? I did not see why one source of evidence and scholarship (archaeology) was necessarily better (or worse) than another (archaeological science). Others were of course wondering and thinking along similar lines at this time, with the dramatic paper of Betancourt (1987) and the subsequent debate papers in *Archaeometry* (vol. 29(2): 205–213; vol. 30(1): 165–182) offering the best known examples.

Since my first written work on the topic (would-be articles all politely rejected by various journals from AD 1984–1987[13]), to my first published articles on the Thera date topic in AD 1988 (Manning 1988a; 1988b), and subsequently, I have tried to offer what seems to me to be the best and most plausible synthesis of the evidence available as a whole at the time of writing. I have changed views on many issues as new or better evidence or arguments have become available, or mistakes or errors have been revealed in previous data or arguments. For example, what seemed like a potentially convincing linkage of radiocarbon, ice-core and tree-ring data in the late AD 1980s (e.g. Hughes 1988) broke apart with both new data and much critical scrutiny in the following years and especially by the early AD 2000s, and I have clearly stated such changes in subsequent publications (e.g. Manning 2007: 103–104). The suggested most likely date for the Thera eruption at 1628 BC in Manning (1999) is thus to be revised now. Something happened then that affected trees widely in the northern hemisphere, but, at this time, we do not know the cause. The ice-core evidence of a major volcanic eruption is also now more problematic, with debates around both the date (1640s BC, or maybe 20 years later: see Muscheler 2009), and the question of whether or not this volcanic eruption is Thera (no say some, yes or perhaps say others – see below). The radiocarbon evidence is substantially improved since Manning (1999), and now seems

---

[13] Several of these rejections came with very kind inclusions of recent offprints from (anonymous – sic) scholars concerned that somehow I was unaware that archaeology had rejected all and any such thinking. In those pre-internet and pre-PDF days, and as a student in Australia where the library only received the journals months after publication in Europe or North America, these inclusions were very gratefully received (even though they did not have the desired effect). I particularly thank an 'anonymous' reviewer who several times generously sent such offprints from Bristol.

to best support a date somewhere around the last three decades of the 17th century BC, and this date range (and thus a date possibly a decade or more later than 1628 BC) seems the best dating to use as of AD 2013 (Manning and Kromer 2012; Höflmayer 2012a; and see below: also see Postscript). If the weight of evidence at any stage has seemed to contradict or question the 'high' chronology, I have happily published saying this.

The radiocarbon evidence provides an example. The radiocarbon dating of the volcanic destruction level (VDL) on Thera in isolation usually provides a somewhat ambiguous outcome, with a majority of probability favouring a 17th century BC date range, and a lesser probability falling in the mid-16th century BC. Around the time of the *Thera and the Aegean World III Congress* in AD 1989, the odds seemed to be about 70:30 in favour of the 17th century BC, and so the 17th century BC seemed the more likely candidate just from radiocarbon (e.g. Manning 1990a), but, with a revised radiocarbon calibration curve of AD 1993, the balance of probabilities seemed less clear and I noted this (e.g. Manning 1999: 32–33 and p.245 Fig. 47), just as I noted that the subsequent further improved and revised radiocarbon calibration curve of AD 1998 returned the odds clearly in favour of the 17th century BC (Manning 1999: 243–246). I have tried to note such problems and to address or solve them. For example, I (Manning 1990b: 36–37) noted some troubling issues evident by the end of the *Thera and the Aegean World III Congress*, including 'a slight bimodal tendency' in the (then available) radiocarbon data relevant to the Thera volcanic destruction level, and in a paper published 22 years later (Manning and Kromer 2012), we returned to this subjectively observed slight bi-modal tendency issue and wondered if we can use this observation to offer a latest plausible date for the eruption. Similarly attempts (new data, new methods) to resolve the 17th/16th century BC dating ambiguity can be seen in papers across two decades (e.g. Manning 1992; Housley *et al.* 1999; Manning *et al.* 2006a). I have also worked to try to better refine and understand the radiocarbon record of the Aegean and east Mediterranean (Kromer *et al.* 2001; Manning *et al.* 2001; 2003; 2010; 2013; Manning and Kromer 2011a; 2011b; 2012).

2. Approaches and viewpoints: relativity and objectivity in the Thera/Santorini debate

The Thera date debate is a set of classic conflicts and contrasts between both approaches to evidence, and very different types of evidence, with scholars entering with diverse (often contradictory) training and pre-conceived worldviews. Needless to say, if a scholar arrives with a firm pre-determined position, then that scholar tends to dismiss or downgrade contrary evidence, and ends up claiming that somehow what s/he regards as the best evidence supports their pre-determined view. Similarly, many Aegean and east Mediterranean archaeologists and art-historians not only are *not* scientists, but inherently they are more than a little skeptical if not suspicious of 'scientific' data. This author has once been labeled or associated with 'natural scientists' (Negbi 1994: 81) – as if this is a pejorative term! Under the excuse of not understanding a scientific technique they then ignore it, or, armed with partial knowledge at best, they feel qualified to criticize and to cast doubt on work by others recognized as experts in their 'scientific' field (without really providing the rigorous and appropriate evidence and argument), while yet others then cite such unproven assertions as if they carry weight, while in all cases of course rejecting or ignoring any and all critiques of archaeological scholarship and its interpretations. And vice versa. Needless to say, real progress comes from the integration of both archaeology and archaeological science (Pollard and Bray 2007). In the case of radiocarbon dating, this has become much more possible with the advent and development of Bayesian chronological modelling approaches, which explicitly integrate archaeological and radiocarbon information (e.g. Bayliss 2009; Bronk Ramsey 2009a). The Manning *et al.* (2006a) investigation represented the first such major Bayesian chronological modelling study for the second millennium BC Aegean, and as directly relevant to the Thera date debate.

The archaeological chronology of the Aegean-east Mediterranean has been built up by assessing evidence (material culture or stylistic) of linkages between cultures. To get dates, scholars concentrate on instances and patterns of linkages between the various Aegean and east Mediterranean cultures and Egypt, where an historical chronology can be applied against archaeological contexts or objects in instances that can be linked with one of the Egyptian kings. Each step of such an analysis has possible issues (e.g. Höflmayer 2012b: 40–42), for example: was the object or style transferred immediately or buried only after much use, was the object or style from the start, middle or end of its period of currency in its source culture, is the Egyptian context precisely dated to just one king and even then where within his/her reign – or is there some flexibility over the exact association, and so on. Where there are lots of linkages all within a relatively short period and the Egyptian chronology is secure, it is difficult to see how one should not link culture period *x* with Egyptian context and thence king *y*, and so get an approximate date for *x*. This sort of situation exists for the mid-14th century BC and Late Helladic (LH) IIIA2 and a tie to the Amarna period in Egypt and hence to a generally very well dated horizon in the ancient Near East in terms of the historical chronologies and diplomatic texts which tightly link Egypt, Assyria and Babylonia at this time (see in Hornung *et al.* 2006; Moran 1992). When radiocarbon dating is applied to the period – for example the dating of Amarna itself, or of a ship (Uluburun) from this period – it finds dates closely compatible with those determined by archaeology from the standard Egyptian historical chronology and wider ancient Near Eastern chronology (Bronk Ramsey *et al.* 2010; Manning *et al.* 2009b; 2013). And so everything works happily.

However, when the archaeological chronology is built on just one or very few material culture or stylistic linkages, or less than clear-cut claimed linkages, or rhetoric more than any clear linkages, then the archaeologically-based dates are much less certain, and perhaps even completely wrong. To a scientist, the suggestion of uncertainty leads to the obvious question: how uncertain? But this is a key difference between the conventional Aegean archaeological (and art historical) versus scientific worlds. There is no way to quantify how uncertain a supposed stylistic association is, nor to apply an error factor to the suggested date or date range. This is in contrast to scientific dating methods which produce quantified data and a stated measurement or analytical error at a level of probability (which can be tested in terms of accuracy and precision). Thus even if a radiocarbon date gives a reasonably wide calendar age range, this is quantified information, whereas a supposed association between (for example) some (loosely dated) Egyptian imitations of the (assumed to be only source) Aegean rhyton form known from several possible Aegean cultural phases and areas is entirely unquantifiable and vague information and comes without any ability to assess its accuracy or precision. And yet some scholars inherently trust the latter versus the former. Conventional archaeologists of this variety are good at noting or suggesting possible (sometimes vaguely at best) and even esoteric additional errors or complications in radiocarbon dating, and then try to propose the legalistic logic that, even if 95% or 99% of the evidence indicates *x*, if just 5% or 1% could suggest *y*, then we must not accept *x*, and, in fact, that maybe we should in fact favour *y* because of …*n* other arguments drawing in other assertions. A notable feature of this debate is that these same ultra-critics of the radiocarbon data and analyses will uncritically and in un-quantified ways employ poorly constrained and poorly replicated material culture and stylistic associations (without requiring the same 'perfect' criteria just demanded of the science data) – and of course as part of the above *n* arguments against radiocarbon.

A few (just three) stone bowls which are stated to be Egyptian (although some other experts have questioned this) offer a good example (e.g. Warren 2006). Each of the main critics of radiocarbon dating (Bietak, Warren, Wiener) cite one or more of these rare items as strong evidence against the 'high' chronology and for the 'low' chronology – but this case moves from weak to not established (see also further below). The claim is that two of the bowls compare to known 18th Dynasty types and thus the contexts in the Aegean with such items must date after c.1550/1540 BC (standard dates for the start of the 18th Dynasty in Egypt prior to Aston 2012 – see e.g. Krauss and Warburton 2006; Schneider 2010a; Kitchen 2000; von Beckerath 1997). But what is not stated is that whereas we have a reasonable body of 18th Dynasty (and especially Tuthmosid era) assemblages including stone bowls to offer comparanda, we have very few *early* 18th Dynasty and even less Second Intermediate Period (SIP) assemblages. Thus, since stone bowl types appear conservative, it seems entirely inappropriate to rule out the likelihood of SIP comparanda if only we had more data. To quote Höflmayer (2012a: 444), who in his AD 2012a study (see pp. 440–441, 444) rethinks his own earlier arguments (e.g. Höflmayer 2009) along the lines above regarding these bowls:

> Given the unsatisfactory state of research in the field of Egyptian stone vessels of the Second Intermediate Period and the early New Kingdom, it does not seem impossible that the 2 Egyptian stone vessels from the Mycenaean shaft-graves could have been produced 1 or 2 generations earlier than previously suggested (i.e. in the late Second Intermediate Period). A new critical re-evaluation of the development of Egyptian stone vessels from the Second Intermediate Period to the New Kingdom might be desirable in order to check a possible earlier dating of these crucial synchronisms.

In other words, there is or could be reasonable (or more) doubt in the low chronology assessment of these few data. They cannot be relied upon given our current knowledge, and can hardly be held to form a sound basis on which to reject a large body of (comparatively) high-quality and coherent radiocarbon data and their detailed and robust analysis (e.g. Manning *et al.* 2006a; 2009a; Manning and Kromer 2011a; 2012; Weninger *et al.* 2010).

In periods where we have a vague and uncertain archaeological chronology such as LMIA – i.e. in contrast with the Late Helladic IIIA to B period where we have many dozens to hundreds of material culture linkages and exchanges (depending on criteria applied) (e.g. Warren and Hankey 1989: 146–158) – then, if a good body of radiocarbon data is produced which offers a different date range to existing assumptions and best guesses based on very few or ambiguous archaeological data, one might suspect that it is in fact possible that the radiocarbon dates give us the best guidance. This assertion in essence summarises the entire Thera dating controversy. In contrast to the Amarna period and its plural and relatively precise Aegean archaeological associations (e.g. Hankey 1997; 1981; 1973; Warren and Hankey 1989: 149–151), or to the Middle Kingdom and its plural associations (even if a bit less precise or numerous: e.g. MacGillivray 1998: 103–105; Warren and Hankey 1989: 131–135), the period around the time of the Thera eruption is in something of an archaeologically-dated 'gap' in the Aegean sequence. This time period is approximately the 17th through 16th centuries BC. There is no body of clear imports and exports to/from the Aegean to provide a chronology for the Late Minoan (LM) IA period, nor for the preceding Middle Minoan (MM) III period,[14] nor for the earlier part of the succeeding LMIB period, in terms of Egypt (or Mesopotamia). This was the case when Cadogan offered his succinct and clear assessment in 1978, when Manning re-stated the same in 1999, and it remains the case in AD 2012 (as evident in the reassessment of the archaeological data in Höflmayer 2012a: 440–444; see also 2012b).

Thus, when radiocarbon offers a date range for the Thera eruption and the Late Minoan IA cultural period, it is effectively filling a void. It is not contrary to any large set of sound archaeological associations. It merely offers evidence versus what was a best guess based on almost no concrete or unambiguous data. Since, in those cases where we have a good set of archaeological data regarding cross-links with Egypt we find that archaeology and radiocarbon yield compatible and very similar date ranges (such as for the Amarna period: see above and discussed further in Section 3.c.III), and since a large sophisticated study of radiocarbon dates on Egyptian materials finds that radiocarbon offers dates for the Egyptian kings which are entirely compatible with the range of the standard Egyptian historical chronology (Bronk Ramsey *et al.* 2010), it seems to be the reasonable corollary that where a good body of radiocarbon data (including a recent high-quality sub-set) are available, as they are, then these should offer us the best chronology for the Thera eruption and the Late Minoan IA period. And, should a decent body of archaeological evidence ever exist relevant to this period, we should hypothesize that it will likely offer a similar date assessment. The fact that radiocarbon dates from the site of Tell el-Dab'a contradict the 'low' chronology assessment (see Kutschera *et al.* 2012), and instead could be compatible with the Aegean 'high' (and radiocarbon-based) chronology and its proposed revised interpretation of Aegean-east Mediterranean cultural linkages for the late Middle Bronze Age to initial Late Bronze Age, only serves to support this assessment in the view of this author (see also Manning and Kromer 2011a).

This is not a unique situation. Among other examples, one might note the revision of the dating of the Iron Age destruction at Gordion. A long-held archaeological

---

[14] On the question of the definition of MMIII (and on the difference between a ceramic 'style' and a ceramic 'period'), see Girella (2007).

assessment, based in fact on very little solid evidence, came under (more serious) question when radiocarbon dates suggested a different date range. After some debate and argument, and attempts to dismiss or downplay the radiocarbon data, the archaeological and historical side of the topic was re-thought, and further radiocarbon data confirmed the initial radiocarbon position, and now a new chronology combining archaeology and science evidence has been presented and seems to have become the standard position for most scholars (see Rose and Darbyshire 2011).[15]

We should, moreover, remember that the weaknesses of, or the question of perhaps needing to re-think, the archaeologically-based chronology for the start of the Late Bronze Age in the Aegean and the associated chronology of Cyprus is not solely because of science-based evidence. Indeed, the orthodox archaeological chronologies were already being critiqued and questioned before radiocarbon came into play, with the work of Merrillees (e.g. 1968; 1971; 1972; 1975; 1977; Kemp and Merrillees 1980) notable here, in particular (I note also Muhly 1975). Hallager (1988: 12) likewise noted the absence of strong archaeological evidence (almost none) for the chronology of the Middle Minoan III–Late Minoan IA periods, and thus concluded "…it is important to stress that the renewed investigations of the traditional synchronisms of the MMIII/LMIA material have shown the contexts – both the Egyptian/Near Eastern and Aegean – so dubious that a revised high chronology for the beginning of the LMIA is possible".

Is change possible? One of the usual responses, or concerns, expressed about changes in archaeological chronologies is that a change in one period affects several other surrounding periods, and then the links of all these periods with other sequences elsewhere, and so on (what Cadogan 1987 referred to as the 'push-me-pull-you' effect). The implication is that one cannot change anything without changing everything. This is a non-issue for the Thera case. The change that is at issue is the dating of the Aegean and Cypriot archaeological phases and their correlation with which particular rulers in Egypt and with which particular associated archaeological phases in the Levant. No one is proposing to change dramatically the dating of Egyptian kings, nor to radically re-date of the whole ancient Near East (and in fact radiocarbon dating provides key data to disprove attempts to promote significantly different chronologies: e.g. Manning *et al.* 2001; 2009; 2010; 2013; Manning and Kromer 2011b). The study of Bronk Ramsey *et al.* (2010) has clearly shown that appropriate and sophisticated radiocarbon dating finds a chronology in Egypt which is compatible with the range of standard historical chronology. Egypt stays more or less where it is. Where there are good sets of material culture linkages between the Aegean and Egypt the traditional archaeological chronology remains valid (e.g. 14th century BC), and radiocarbon dating where available merely confirms this existing picture. It is only in the periods where there is not a well-based archaeological chronology (thus a lack of plural connections

---

[15] I note that while Keenan (2004) confidently pronounced that the radiocarbon dating of Iron Age Gordion by DeVries *et al.* (2003) was incorrect, a more extensive follow-up study clearly supports the DeVries *et al.* (2003) position, and not the claims of Keenan (see Manning and Kromer 2011b). I note that there were a few unfortunate typos and a missing line of text in the published version of the Manning and Kromer (2011b) paper. For the corrections, and for discussion of these, please see: https://www.academia.edu/1110679/Manning_S.W._and_Kromer_B._2011._Radiocarbon_Dating_Iron_Age_Gordion_and_the_Early_Phrygian_Destruction_in_Particular

from relatively precise contexts) that radiocarbon can offer alternative and better guidance and where, if radiocarbon indicates a different chronology, we may have to re-think. In the Aegean in the second millennium BC, this seems to apply to the period from about 1700 BC to 1500 BC. What does this mean? It means a longer Late Minoan IB period (Manning 2009), and a long Late Minoan IA period (Manning and Bronk Ramsey 2009), and a shorter overall Middle Minoan period (ending by around the earlier 17th century BC): see e.g. Manning *et al.* (2006a: Fig. 3) or Manning and Bronk Ramsey (2009: Fig. 10). It means revising which (of these) Aegean periods (and the linked Cypriot periods) equate with which periods of time in Egypt (and not radically changing any chronology in Egypt). While perhaps seemingly dramatic 20+ years ago, when the LMIB period was argued to be short (no more than a generation), this is not the case today. LMIB is recognised as a much longer period (see already views to this effect cited in Manning 1999: 334), with several phases at least at several sites (see especially Rutter 2011),[16] and the former short temporal estimate really only applies at best to what is now known to be the final part(s) of the (now) long overall period.

Of course, if one somehow *knows* that the pre-radiocarbon interpretation is more or less correct, then one rejects such thinking, and tries to question the radiocarbon evidence and its worth. Similarly, if one somehow *knows* the chronology of one's own site and interprets everything around it on this basis, then one also rejects any such possibilities, even when radiocarbon data from one's own site seem to contradict this (whereas it works very well elsewhere including in Egypt). Hence we have the current Thera dating controversy, as different approaches are applied, and not all the evidence and interpretations are weighted fairly and appropriately by all scholars (see e.g. Bietak 2003; Bietak and Höflmayer 2007). This contradiction of preconceived archaeology versus radiocarbon dating is now highlighted and made very concrete at the excavations of Manfred Bietak at the site of Tell el-Dab'a (Kutschera *et al.* 2012). The detailed radiocarbon dating of his own site does not support either his chronological interpretation, or his reading of the site stratigraphy and associations.

---

[16] The papers in Brogan and Hallager (2011) offer a rich review of the ceramics and phasing of the LMIB period as currently understood. Several sites show multiple LMIB phases, but not all do, and there is less than universal agreement on intra-LMIB phasing. A number of scholars recognize at least a new (or extra) LMIB Final sub-phase after the more standard LMIB Late phase known from various destruction horizons on Crete. The study of Rutter (2011) is a wonderful first attempt at a grander synthesis. Rutter (2011: 326) in his review of the Crete-wide evidence concludes that "The evidence from Kommos and Mochlos, as perhaps also that from Chania, strongly suggests that LMIB was longer-lived than the 50–60 years … conventionally assigned to it according to the traditional Aegean absolute chronology… or even than the expanded span of 70 to 90 years … more recently accorded to the phase by adherents of this low chronology. The duration of roughly a century accorded to the period by Manning … with the Aegean 'high chronology' seems more appropriate".

3. A Test of Time Revisited: *The State of the Debate and Key Evidence as of AD 2012 to earlier 2013*

(a) Note concerning WWW document on developments AD 1999 to AD 2006.

In various webpages and finally in a 'fixed' pdf,[17] I have provided discussion and references to post-publication developments relevant to Manning (1999) and the general Thera dating topic up to AD 2006. The interested reader can still read this material in its fixed AD 2006 form at the address listed in footnote 17 below. I do not propose here to simply repeat the information presented and discussed there – for those readers interested, please see the pdf. The one exception is the list of corrections/addenda below in Section 5, which repeats the list in the pdf document.

(b) Note concerning discussions up to AD 2004 and then to AD 2012

An essay on the topic of the 'high' versus 'low' chronology by Manning (2007) provides relatively detailed discussion and assessment current through AD 2004 (although the paper was not published until AD 2007) of approaches, issues of interpretation, and reviews of the salient data and key points of dispute. A version of this essay can also be found online.[18] Again, I see no reason merely to repeat this discussion here, and refer interested readers to this paper.

This author has published or co-published a number of studies relevant to the Thera date topic since AD 1999 and up to the present time of writing (AD 2012). Obviously sometimes more recent studies improve or update older ones. The relevant papers are:

Manning and Kromer (2012)	Manning *et al.* (2006b)
Lindblom and Manning (2011)	Manning (2005)
Manning and Kromer (2011a)	Bronk Ramsey *et al.* (2004)
Manning (2010)	Galimberti *et al.* (2004)
Manning *et al.* (2010)	Manning and Bronk Ramsey (2003)
Manning (2009)	Manning *et al.* (2003)
Manning and Bronk Ramsey (2009)	Manning and Sewell (2002)
Manning *et al.* (2009a)	Manning *et al.* (2002a)
Pearson and Manning (2009)	Manning *et al.* (2002b)
Pearson *et al.* (2009)	Kromer *et al.* (2001)
Manning (2007)	Manning (2001)
Manning *et al.* (2006a)	Manning *et al.* (2001)

---

[17] The fixed AD 2006 document can be found at the following location: http://cornell.academia.edu/SturtWManning/Books/326586/Manning_S.W._1999._A_Test_of_Time_the_volcano_of_Thera_and_the_chronology_and_history_of_the_Aegean_and_east_Mediterranean_in_the_mid-second_millennium_BC._Oxford_Oxbow_Books.

[18] The paper can be found at the following location: https://www.academia.edu/1822410/Manning_S.W._2007._Clarifying_the_high_v._low_Aegean_Cypriot_chronology_for_the_mid_second_millennium_BC_assessing_the_evidence_interpretive_frameworks_and_current_state_of_the_debate.

(c) State of the Debate (AD 2012 to earlier 2013)

INTRODUCTORY REMARKS (AND EGYPTIAN AND MESOPOTAMIAN CHRONOLOGY)

Away from Aegean and east Mediterranean prehistory, there has been considerable debate in the last generation of scholarship about the relationship of time with archaeology. This was already well advanced when Manning (1999) was published (see e.g. Murray 1999; McGlade 1999 and literature cited). Such post-modern concerns have not, however, troubled the worlds of Aegean and east Mediterranean prehistory and early history. Nor, yet, has wider Aegean and east Mediterranean archaeology grappled with the recent return elsewhere in archaeology to a focus on high-resolution chronological investigations aimed at creating rigorous timeframes which allow life-time, even agent-centred, assessment of the archaeological record (e.g. Bayliss and Whittle 2007; Whittle *et al.* 2008; Whittle *et al.* 2011: 1–4; Bayliss 2009: 141–142). The conceptions of time for the inhabitants of the ancient world (see Feeney 2007; for the basis of calendars in the Ancient Near East, see e.g. Steel 2010), and the difference of relative and relational time versus modern absolute (calendar) time, are likewise not the concern of those working on the chronology of the second millennium BC – much though the ancient views of, and descriptions of, temporal information are relevant to the so-called historical chronology of Egypt and the Ancient Near East and to the success of the synchronisms from there onwards that form bases to the now standard western calendar time and history (Momigliano 1977).

Instead, the last dozen years have seen relentless attention and debate trying to prove or disprove certain specific calendar dates simply in modern numerical terms, and associated absolute chronological schemes, and only thence the relevant cultural/historical reconstructions, with particularly frenetic activity focusing on two topics: (i) the chronology of Iron Age Israel, and (ii) the dating of the Thera (Santorini) eruption. The first is not the topic of Manning (1999), nor this essay; the second is. But it may nonetheless be noted in passing that intensive radiocarbon dating of numerous short-lived samples in studies addressing the early Iron Age of Israel have provided fairly consistent calendar dates and that the differences of interpretation are increasingly small (to the point of being almost beyond the resolution or precision possible from the dating method in some cases) (see e.g. Mazar and Bronk Ramsey 2008, 2010; Lee *et al.* 2013; Finkelstein and Piasetzky 2010a, 2010b, 2011).

With regard to the Thera debate, we can divide the debate into (a) the evidence which can be put aside as either not necessarily relevant, or not conclusive, as of AD 2013, (b) the evidence from archaeological connections between the Aegean and the east Mediterranean and Egypt, and (c) the directly relevant radiocarbon dating evidence. However, before discussing these topics, we may note that one basic starting point for our discussion is now much better fixed: the chronological placement of the historical Egyptian chronology. I reviewed this topic in Manning (1999: 367–413 and see also Manning 2007: 127–130) and employed a standard Egyptian historical chronology in the main text (favouring von Beckerath 1997), but noted a few possible areas of uncertainty. A publication in AD 2010 reporting the radiocarbon findings and analyses from a large and impressive research project involving several laboratory teams has now demonstrated that radiocarbon offers data and chronological resolution consistent with, and in support of, the standard Egyptian historical chronology (Bronk Ramsey *et al.* 2010). In particular, this work is even capable of indicating that the 'higher' historical chronology (e.g. starting the 18th Dynasty about c.1550 BC, or even in the preceding 20 years) is more likely than the somewhat lower historical chronology reconstructions of e.g. Krauss and Warburton (2006) and especially Krauss and Warburton (2009). Thus it is no longer possible to somehow claim that radiocarbon gives substantially different results in Egypt versus elsewhere (like the Aegean). Instead, we see that sophisticated radiocarbon dating (including the recognition of a small growing season-related offset in Egypt – linked to the pre-modern hydrological cycle operating along the Nile: see Dee *et al.* 2010) yields dates very consistent with (and even allowing resolution of) the standard Egyptian historical chronology (see also various papers in Shortland and Bronk Ramsey 2013). In turn, this suggests that sophisticated and careful radiocarbon dating in the Aegean should also yield calendar dates which are both valid and compatible with Egyptian historical chronology (see also Manning and Kromer 2011a). This is a key change in base-line knowledge, and viewpoint, compared to previously where it was assumed or asserted (by several scholars at least) that radiocarbon and Egyptian chronology were (or could be) somehow incompatible and thus one could also question radiocarbon-based chronology generally (to pick just a few examples: Hood 1978; Bietak 2003; Bietak and Höflmayer 2007; Wiener 2007). No more. Since Bronk Ramsey *et al.* (2010), we instead know that sophisticated radiocarbon analysis is entirely consistent with (and can even refine) standard Egyptian historical chronology; we can therefore assume that radiocarbon also offers the appropriate chronology elsewhere in the Mediterranean. Thus what in the AD 1970s seemed to be "problems with the LMIA and LMIB [^{14}C] dates from Thera and Crete" (Weinstein and Betancourt 1978: 809), turn out instead to have been missed (until Betancourt 1987) early indications of problems with an assumed archaeological chronology for this period in the Aegean (late Middle Minoan to mid LMIB), which was based on almost no direct, specific, or unambiguous evidence (see scholarship cited by Manning 1999: 108; see Section 3.c.II below).

And there is more. The reconsideration of Egyptian chronology by Schneider (2010a) assessed errors of about 15 years for the New Kingdom. He started the New Kingdom at c.1548 BC, placed the accession of Hatshepsut/Tuthmosis III at 1476 BC, and accepted that another 3 years could be added to match the astronomical possibilities (e.g. 1479 BC for Tuthmosis III). And so it seemed that more or less the status quo continued. But an exciting, important and refreshing new paper by Aston (2012) raises strong arguments for a slightly earlier start and longer duration for the New Kingdom chronology – from a combined (re-)consideration of New Kingdom wine dockets, the apparent links between Horemheb and Mursilis II of Hatti, and the possible dates – given possible ranges – from the lunar data for the reigns of Tuthmosis III, Ramesses II, Tauseret and Ramesses III (I thank David Aston for kindly sending me a copy of the paper, and for discussion). Aston favours a date of 1493 BC for the accession of Thuthmosis III (Aston's 'high' chronology), but will also consider an 'ultra-high' date of 1504 BC (so +14 to +25 years versus Krauss and Warburton 2006 and +25 and +36 years versus Krauss and Warburton 2009). This new chronology is very compatible with the radiocarbon study of Bronk Ramsey *et al.* (2010). Thus Aston's analyses support this ^{14}C-based study (or the reverse), offering mutually compatible data and arguments leading to a similar conclusion. Oddly enough, it is also very much in keeping with the 'wonderings' of

Manning (1999: 367–413) over a possible 11–25 year raise and extension to the standard 1479 BC date for Tuthmosis III and so on, or the higher astronomical assessment of Huber (2011: 191–195). The study of Aston (2012) changes a few of the reign lengths versus those employed by Bronk Ramsey *et al.* (2010), in particular, it finds evidence for a much longer reign of Tuthmosis IV: either 27+ years or even 38 years versus 10 years (9 years 8 months in Schneider 2010a: 402). There is also the often vexed question of co-regencies, starting with Amenhotep I from somewhere in the last years of Ahmose (for example, as Aston 2012 speculates, did Amenhotep I in fact reign for c.30 years with 9 as co-regent and therefore for 21 as sole ruler – the usual number employed for his reign length – offering one explanation of references to a *Heb sed*? – since as Aston notes a first *Heb sed* festival should only occur in a year 30 following standard practice). If we follow Schneider (2010a: 402) for Ahmose to Tuthmosis II, and Aston (2012 'high' or 'ultra-high') for Tuthmosis III to Ramesses II, then the changes versus the Bronk Ramsey *et al.* (2010) study (OxCal runfile in their Table S6) are: (i) longer independent reigns for Tuthmosis I of 13 years versus 12, for Tuthmosis III/Hatshepsut of 54 years in total versus 52 years, for Amenhotep II of c.31 years (sole reign) versus 27 years (or 25 years and 10 months in Schneider 2010a: 402), for Tuthmosis IV of 38 years (ultra-high) or 27 years (high) versus 10 years, for Amenhotep IV=Akhenaten of 17 years versus 14 years, for the combined period of independent reigns by Smenkhare/Neferneferuaten and Ankhetkheperure of 3 or 4 total years (after 1 year of co-regency with Akhenaten) versus the 2 years allowed for Neferneferuaten, etc., in Bronk Ramsey *et al.* (2010), for Ramesses I of 2 years versus 1 year, for Ramesses II of 67 years in total versus 66 years (Schneider 2010: 402 has 66 years and 2 months); and (ii) shorter independent reigns for Horemhab of 15 years versus 28 years and Sety I of 9 years (he died before the wine harvest of his year 9 – whereas Schneider 2010a: 402 uses 10 years as halfway between the year 9 figure and what Aston 2012 discredits as a record of a year 11) versus 15 years. Overall, in net round terms, these changes mean a longer duration for the period from the accession of Ahmose to the death of Ramesses II, by around 12 or 23 years. A re-run of the Bronk Ramsey *et al.* (2010) model (using the OxCal runfile from Table S6 of their modified SOM of 17 May 2011 and excluding data now regarded as not from New Kingdom contexts/material – OxA-18520 – and associating OxA-18960 with Siamun as noted in Table S1 addendum – added April 2011, and accordingly adding intervals for Osochor, Siamun and Psusennes II), but adjusting some of the New Kingsom reign lengths as noted above, leads to accession date estimates for the 18th Dynasty to early 19th Dynasty rulers as set out in Table RE1 (right) and compared with those of Bronk Ramsey *et al.* (2010) (left). For further details, some possible variations, and some discussion of such re-runs, see the Revisit Essay Appendix 1 below. We may observe that using the Aston (2012) 'high' or 'ultra-high' reign lengths pushes up the start of the 18th Dynasty a little versus the Bronk Ramsey *et al.* (2010) study – but not by very much – and finds dates for the accession of Tuthmosis III nicely compatible with the 1493 BC or 1504 BC dates in the Aston (2012) chronology, and (predictably) forces some (modest) changes due to the changes of reign lengths for Tuthmosis IV, Horemheb, etc., but in fact leaves the accession of Ramesses II almost stable and at a placement compatible with the 1290 BC accession date in either the 'high' or 'ultra-high' chronology of Aston (2012) or the chronology of Schneider (2010a).

The revised Egyptian chronology following Aston (2012) would get us to as early as c.1575–1565 BC for the beginning of the New Kingdom! The Bronk Ramsey *et al.* (2010) re-run using the Aston ultra-high chronology places the beginning of the New Kingdom very similarly ca 1578–1569 BC (68.2% probability, or 1582–1563 BC at 95.4% probability: see Table RE1). And so we start to have a situation where there is only a modest, even rather small, offset between the late 17th century BC Thera date from ^{14}C and the conventional interpretation of archaeological links with the Egyptian historical chronology. When we then consider and allow that, for example, the Egyptian (or Levantine-Egyptian) stone vessels claimed to set 18th Dynasty *terminus post quem* ranges for their Aegean contexts could in fact include at least the later SIP (see below), that the White Slip I finds at Tell el-Dab'a only set *terminus ante quem* ranges for the production of the ware on Cyprus (and *not* a *terminus post quem*: see below), and so on, then it would be fairly easy to accommodate a late 17th century BC date for the Akrotiri VDL and Thera eruption (the date which seems most likely from the ^{14}C evidence: see below) within the framework of the available archaeological linkages (see also Höflmayer 2012a).[19]

Recent work also suggests that one other important and long-running chronological debate seems to be drawing to a possible conclusion and resolution. This is the topic of the dating of the Mesopotamian chronologies in the second millennium BC (for a brief summary of the topic, see Hunger 2009; for a detailed review, see Pruzsinszky 2009). At the time Manning (1999) was written, there was significant debate covering High, Middle, Low and Ultra-Low chronologies. Serious scholarship placed the same historical event – e.g. the accession of Hummurabi – up to 152 years apart (contrast the High chronology of Huber *et al.* 1982 versus the Ultra-Low chronology of Gasche *et al.* 1998) – an uncertainty which made it problematic to try to synchronise much of ancient western Asian early history and related east Mediterranean prehistory. At the

---

[19] The raised start for the New Kingdom in Aston (2012), or as modelled in Table RE1, could also be argued to make an earlier to mid-16th century BC Thera date more plausible, if one tries to favour the possible but less likely calendar range available from the Akrotiri ^{14}C evidence. It might be argued that the archaeology and historical chronology could better, or more easily, fit the possible early to mid-16th century BC range, and allow a potentially satisfactory solution, whereas to now scholars of the 'low' grouping have been restricted (by the old lower Egyptian chronology) to an earliest possible date for the Thera eruption (c.1530–1520 BC) – squeezed into the very last very unlikely end of the possible calibrated calendar ^{14}C probability range. This has always seemed a major problem (because it is very unlikely), unless one ignores the radiocarbon evidence (which seems unreasonable). This early-mid 16th century BC scenario is possible (and is similar to the possible alternative compromise early chronology discussed in Manning 1999), and seems the only feasible alternative to the 'high' chronology which could try to incorporate most evidence (contra the 'low' chronology). I favour the position in the text (late 17th century BC date for the Thera eruption) for two reasons: first, as this is much more likely given the available radiocarbon data and their analysis (see Section 3.c.III below); and second, I consider the evidence (archaeology, pumice, etc.) as suggesting that the Akrotiri VDL and the eruption were likely prior to, or no later than the very beginning of, the New Kingdom (or 18th Dynasty) (see Section 3.c below). This then points at the latest to an early 16th century BC date given likely revisions to Egyptian chronology (Aston 2012; Table RE1 above) – and not a mid-16th century BC date – hence, since if there is an ambiguity available in the ^{14}C data it is more for the mid-16th century BC, this leaves the ^{14}C data clearly in favour of the late 17th century BC option given the likely available choices. The archaeological indications for a long overall LMIB period on Crete also seem compatible (see below).

	Accession Dates BC										
	Modelled Highest Posterior Density (hpd) Ranges from Bronk Ramsey *et al.* (2010: Tables 1, S8)				Modelled hpd Ranges from revised model using Aston (2012) 'high' chronology				Modelled hpd Ranges from revised model using Aston (2012) 'ultra-high' chronology			
	68.2%		95.4%		68.2%		95.4%		68.2%		95.4%	
King/Queen	from	to	from	to	from	to	from	to	from	to	from	to
Ahmose	1566	1552	1570	1544	1574	1565	1579	1559	1578	1569	1582	1563
Amenhotep I	1541	1527	1545	1519	1549	1540	1554	1534	1553	1544	1557	1539
Tuthmosis I	1520	1507	1524	1498	1528	1519	1533	1514	1532	1524	1536	1518
Tuthmosis II	1507	1495	1511	1487	1515	1506	1519	1502	1519	1511	1522	1506
Tuthmosis III	1494	1483	1498	1474	1502	1493	1506	1489	1507	1499	1510	1493
Amenhotep II	1441	1431	1445	1423	1448	1440	1452	1436	1453	1446	1457	1440
Tuthmosis IV	1414	1403	1418	1396	1417	1409	1422	1405	1423	1415	1426	1410
Amenhotep III	1404	1393	1408	1386	1390	1382	1395	1379	1386	1378	1389	1372
Amenhotep IV = Akhenaten	1365	1355	1370	1348	1353	1344	1357	1341	1348	1341	1352	1335
Smenkhare/ Neferneferuaten* & Ankhetkheperure	1351	1340	1356	1333	1336	1328	1341	1324	1332	1324	1336	1318
Tutankhamun	1349	1338	1353	1331	1333	1325	1338	1322	1330	1322	1334	1316
Ay	1339	1329	1344	1322	1324	1316	1330	1313	1321	1313	1326	1307
Horemheb	1336	1325	1341	1318	1321	1312	1326	1309	1318	1309	1322	1303
Ramesses I	1308	1297	1313	1290	1306	1297	1312	1293	1303	1294	1308	1288
Sety I	1307	1296	1312	1288	1304	1295	1310	1291	1301	1292	1306	1286
Ramesses II	1292	1281	1297	1273	1296	1286	1302	1282	1293	1283	1298	1276

Table RE1. Modelled accession dates (first regnal year) for kings and queens of the New Kingdom from Ahmose to Ramesses II (18th Dynasty and early 19th Dynasty) from the Egyptian historical chronology, comparing the dates in Bronk Ramsey et al. *(2010: Tables 1 and S8) versus those found from re-runs of the Bronk Ramsey* et al. *(2010) model (using the OxCal runfile from the modified SOM of 17 May 2011 – excluding samples no longer considered to be of NK origin – OxA-18520 – and associating OxA-18960 with Siamun: see Table S1 addendum – added April 2011 and accordingly adding intervals for Osochor, Siamun and Psusennes II) but adjusting some of the reign lengths of rulers between Ahmose to Rameses II following the Aston (2012) paper 'high' and 'ultra high' chronologies (see text). The reign of Tuthmosis I is also adjusted +1 year following Schneider (2010a: 402). *Bronk Ramsey* et al. *(2010: Tables 1 and S8) only use Neferneferuaten but the relevant Boundary is Neferneferuaten, etc. – I combine the independent (non-coregency) overall reign periods for Smenkhare and Ankhetkheperure with her reign (total c.3 years following Aston 2012) in the re-run model. I thank Mike Dee and Christopher Bronk Ramsey for advice with this model re-run. Typical values shown – each run of such an analysis can offer small variations (usually of 0–1 or 0–2 years). The OxCal Convergence values for each of the accession Boundaries reported above in Table RE1 are greater than or equals 95. Note that the model includes an allowance for small errors on the stated reign lengths (Bronk Ramsey 2010: 1555). For further details, variations, and discussion, see the Revisit Essay Appendix 1 below.*

time Manning (1999) was written, using the placement of the Gordion dendrochronology published in Kuniholm *et al.* (1996), it seemed that the tree-ring evidence offered grounds in support of the Low chronology (on the basis of the dating of timbers used in the construction of palaces at Kaneš near Kültepe and Acemhöyük which were linked by finds of sealings with the reign of Šamši-Adad I: see Manning 1999: 351–355).

But, since AD 1999, several things have changed, and changed significantly. Subsequent programmes of dendro-^{14}C wiggle-match dating on elements of the Gordion dendrochronology employing many more samples and ^{14}C dates (52 dates in AD 2001 versus the original 18 dates in AD 1996, through to 128 dates in AD 2010 versus the original 18 dates in AD 1996) revealed that the chronological placement for the Gordion dendrochronology proposed in AD 1996 was definitely incorrect. And one of the assumptions of the Kuniholm *et al.* (1996) paper regarding the 12th century BC section of the dendrochronology was not really valid (see Section 5.a.i below). A revised and much more robust placement of the Gordion dendrochronology since AD 2001 puts it about 22–23 years earlier within a possible error range at 95% probability of less than a decade (Manning *et al.* 2001; 2003; 2010; Kromer 2001; Manning and Kromer 2011b). This in turn means that the dendro data relevant to Šamši-Adad I are much more compatible with a Middle or low-Middle chronology (e.g. Manning *et al.* 2001: 2534), and it is possible that a solar eclipse linked with the year after the birth of Šamši-Adad I might offer specific guidance (Michel 2002). These new data, and reanalysis and critique of the other evidence, started to suggest that the much maligned or criticised Middle chronology (or a low-Middle chronology) might be in fact turn out to be plausible and even likely (see also Banjević 2005; Pruzsinszky 2006; Muhly 2009: 7–9; de Jong 2013b).

Meanwhile, Barjamovic *et al.* (2012) have published a long reconstruction of the Old Assyrian eponym list from Kaneš (near Kültepe), and, linking this list with the near absolute dendrodates from the bark of beams from the construction of the Waršama Palace at Kaneš (Manning *et al.* 2001; Newton and Kuniholm 2004; Manning *et al.* 2010), they have argued for the placement of their eponym list and thence the reign dates for Šamši-Adad I, within margins of about 10 years – with the death of Šamši-Adad I at 1776 ± 10 BC. In turn, with the death of Šamši-Adad I synchronised with the 18th year of Hammurabi (Charpin and Ziegler 2003 – note Manning 1999 used spelling of Hammurapi), this places the accession of Hammurabi c.1793 ± 10 BC, and the fall of Babylon c.1596 ± 10 BC. These dates correlate remarkably with the standard Middle chronology (which has long placed the accession of Hammurabi c.1792 BC), suggesting we are very near a workable and sensible solution to this long-running dating dilemma. Such data, compatible with the range of the Middle chronology, at the same time fundamentally undermine or contradict the Low and especially the Ultra-Low chronological schemes and their assumptions and hypotheses (Roaf 2012; de Jong 2013b). Recent additional work within this 'Middle chronology window' on the astronomical data might further suggest that the so-called low-Middle chronology, some 8 years later than the standard Middle chronology, is perhaps the comprehensive best solution (de Jong and Foertmeyer 2010; de Jong 2012; 2013a).[20]

---

[20] This recent work in support of a Middle Chronology (and especially it might seem a low-Middle Chronology some 8 years later than the Middle Chronology) necessarily means the rejection of the

While the resolution of the Old Babylonian chronology does not directly impinge on the Thera date date, it is a corollary issue, and a Middle or low-Middle solution – as now seems plausible and likely – creates a wider western Asian historical-archaeological synthesis in good accord with the Aegean 'high' chronology (and offers a revised and somewhat better scenario than in Manning 1999: 347–364). For example, with the Middle chronology, and the attested historical linkages, the LMIA-style wall paintings known from Alalakh Level VII (Niemeier and Niemeier 2000) are therefore dated to the 17th century BC (see the summary of the textual and archaeological data by Bergoffen 2005: 55–57 *but* with Middle chronology or low-Middle chronology dates applied as now likely contra her discussion and preference; or revising Manning 1999: 347–364 to the Middle chronology or low-Middle chronology dates). This, together with recent analysis indicating a likely 17th century BC date for similar paintings at Tel Kabri (Cline *et al.* 2011), creates a context where we may suggest that the 'high' Aegean chronology date in the 17th century BC for the similar LMIA-style wall paintings on Thera becomes both plausible (rather than too early), and indeed likely, as part of a wider eastern Mediterranean synthesis where similar art forms were used in similar ways by communicating elites in the same general time horizon.

(I) What we can put aside at present with regard to the Thera date debate

There is little to be gained in a lengthy discussion of data or arguments which are not necessarily relevant, or are indecisive, regarding the dating of the Thera eruption as of AD 2012. I thus give only a summary listing (often merely up-dating Manning 2007):

(i)   *Ice-cores.* Although Vinther *et al.* (2008) provide some reasonable arguments why the evidence pertaining to the large Greenland ice-core volcanic signal in the 17th century BC might nonetheless be Thera, there is at present no satisfactory case for the recognition of a definite (versus possible) Thera identification for any volcanic signal in any ice-core, and previous suggestions to the contrary can be treated as unproven at best (and the exact dating of the relevant ice-cores is also under something of a question mark).[21] This assessment is agreed

radical recent alternatives like the so-called New (or Ultra-Low) Chronology: see discussion by Roaf 2012. It also suggests that arguments based on statistical analyses of attested versus predicted month lengths in the Venus Tablet data (and versus other ancient records) are ultimately not robust – since these can produce findings (e.g. the High Chronology: Huber 1982; or the low chronology of Mebert 2010) outside the plausible range of other constraints (de Jong 2013a, 2013b) – and a number of scholars have noted previously that such results cannot be decisive as it is impossible to demonstrate the reliability of the available data (Pruzsinszky 2009: 72–73).

[21] Hammer *et al.* (2003) first claimed to identify volcanic glass particles as from Thera. Keenan (2003), Pearce *et al.* (2004; 2007) and Denton and Pearce (2008) argued that this appeared flawed/incorrect, and Pearce *et al.* argued instead for an association with the eruption of Aniakchak. Vinther *et al.* (2008) explain why, nonetheless, they felt a Thera association remained possible. The dating of at least some of the ice-core records meanwhile came under some question, with Southon (2002; 2004) demonstrating significant problems in the dating of especially the GISP2 ice-core in the mid second millennium BC. Finally, Muscheler (2009) argued from a comparison of isotope records that perhaps the key GICC05 ice-core timescale (including the relevant Dye 3, GRIP and NGRIP ice-cores) has a dating error of up to 20 years in the time window of the Thera eruption – which could have the effect

by those arguing both for, and against, the 'high' or 'early' chronology (e.g. Manning 2007: 104; Wiener 2010: 368–369). Of course, at some point in the future, it is possible, even likely, that volcanic glass particles most plausibly associated with Thera will be (securely) recognized in a well-dated ice-core and this could offer important dating evidence. But not yet.

(ii) *Speleothems*. A couple of papers have noted signals in speleothems which they have suggested might be associated with Thera eruption impacts (e.g. Frisia *et al.* 2008 and Siklósy *et al.* 2009). However, there is no definite association, merely at best a circumstantial case, and thus I leave these claims aside for the present (it is clearly a source of information to be followed in research going forward).

Postscript (and change in characterisation): After the above text was written, a new paper makes a strong case for an association between the Thera eruption and subsequent changes in trace elements (sulphur, bromine and molybdenum) in the high-resolution speleothem record from Sofular Cave in northern Turkey (Badertscher *et al.* 2014; Fleitmann *et al.* 2012; Dominik Fleitmann, pers. comm., 2013). It is argued that bromine may be the most sensitive indicator, offering a clear short-lived peak at 1621 ± 25 BC, with molybdenum following at 1617 ± 25 BC and sulphur later at 1589 ± 25 BC. While the authors note that the speleothem dating resolution is not sufficient to resolve small differences (e.g. resolving between the Thera olive branch or Akrotiri VDL seeds dating, versus ice-core claims, and so on), this work is important, and offers another strong set of independent data in general support of the 'high' dating of the Thera eruption in the mid-late 17th century BC (and *not* in the range of the 'low' chronology dating in mid-later 16th century BC or early 15th century BC).

(iii) *Tree-ring growth anomalies (except Porsuk) and suggested linkages to major volcanic eruptions*. The study of Salzer and Hughes (2007), reviewing the Bristlecone pine data from the western USA and several other long tree-ring records, represents the best, most comprehensive, review at present of this topic. They note in all 7 possible tree-ring growth anomalies which might link with volcanism within the plausible timeframe of the Thera eruption: 1652 BC, 1649 BC, 1626 BC, 1597 BC, 1544 BC, and 1524 BC and a suppressed growth episode in two northern chronologies 1619–1617 BC (pp.65–66). They note the good volcano case especially for 1628–1626 BC, but in no case is there any evidence to link these growth anomalies definitely to Thera (and while one might anticipate that a Thera signal is likely in such tree-ring records sensitive to major northern hemisphere volcanism since the eruption likely had a 1+ calendar year climate impact and so should be represented in at least one relevant growing season for sensitive trees in the northern hemisphere, it is also possible that Thera

---

of bringing the date of the ice-core signal for the major volcanic eruption (whether Thera, Aniakchak, or another volcano) down to during the 1620s BC. The end result, at present, is a somewhat uncertain exact date, and no clear association with Thera. Hence we should exclude the ice-core evidence from our arguments for now.

is not represented in any given record for local or other reasons). The events in the 1640s BC, 1620s BC and 1610s BC show up fairly widely across several tree-ring datasets from different parts of the northern hemisphere, whereas those in 1544 BC (only one chronology) or 1524 BC (only two chronologies) are less impressive and lack apparent possible correlations to volcanic signals in ice-core records. One of the more widely represented later/late 17th century BC records may well represent Thera, and one might suspect one of the more prominent records (since the scale of the Thera eruption has been assessed as even larger than formerly thought: Sigurdsson *et al.* 2006 – and see in addition footnote 4 above), but we have no direct evidence at present.

Is it in fact likely that dendrochronology can contribute in a specific way to the Thera debate? While dendrochronology has the potential to offer annual-scale chronological resolution even thousands of years ago where there are suitable tree-ring chronologies,[22] the challenge is to tie a given annual tree-ring to the event we wish to date: in this case the eruption of Thera. Thus, if a group of trees of a species which produces clear annual rings, and of at least 'mature' age (ideally around 100+ years of life = rings), were to be demonstrably killed by the Thera eruption (buried by pumice or tephra fall, etc.) with the growth increment of this last 'death' year preserved (the bark), then – if the growth patterns of these trees could be cross-dated against a long dendrochronology – it would be entirely possible to claim a dendro-date for the eruption. However, this seems highly unlikely at present. Despite past reports of an oak stump in the 19th century AD, and a pine sample used for one early radiocarbon date (see references cited by Manning 1999: 337 n.1496), the wood samples found on Thera from volcanic destruction level contexts in recent decades have been either non-dendro-friendly species (like olive – with its lack of clear, visible, annual growth increments) and/or small and/or with very few tree-rings. Preservation of non-burnt wood at the archaeological site of Akrotiri on Thera is poor. And in this case we need living trees which were killed by the eruption, and more than one such tree since a replicated pattern would be necessary to create a strong case demonstrating a specific dramatic death/destruction event consistent with the impact of the eruption. The odds on finding such a set of samples seem low and would require a special context (on Thera or in the eastern Aegean or southwestern Turkey) where preservation conditions have been favourable.

If samples with clear tree-ring patterns apparently tied to the eruption's destruction horizon could be found (again with bark for this year of death = eruption), but not be capable of dendro cross-dating (whether because they are not of a species suitable to match available tree-ring sequences, or the sequences are too short, or because they are idiosyncratic), then ^{14}C-dendro wiggle-matching (e.g. Bronk Ramsey *et al.* 2001; Galimberti *et al.* 2004; Bayliss

---

[22] To give just one recent and dramatic (and very nicely illustrated) example, Tegel *et al.* (2012) report the precise dendro-dating of oak timbers from Neolithic wells in eastern Germany between 5469 and 5098 BC against the long, absolutely placed, sub-fossil oak chronology of central Europe.

and Tyers 2004; Tyers 2008) could plausibly hope to provide an eruption date within about a decade or so of error margin – and this would be an important step – but, as above, finding such a set of samples remains the challenge.

If non-dendro-friendly wood is found and tied to an eruption context, then, even in the absence of detectable annual rings, one can still consider the analysis of an ordered sequence of ^{14}C dates from the inner (older) to outer (more recent) wood to the bark against the known pattern of ^{14}C levels in the atmosphere and so get an approximate date range for date of death = eruption (on such Sequence analyses, see Revisit Essay Appendix 3). We can apply this logic to the olive wood sample from Thera reported by Friedrich *et al.* (2006) *even if* it is argued that growth increments (tree-rings) cannot in fact be detected in this sample by X-ray tomography, as argued by Wiener (2009b: 204–206; 2010: 373 and citations – and since see the study of Cherubini *et al.* 2013), contra the original claims that annual growth increments could be identified at least approximately (Friedrich *et al.* 2006; 2009; see also Friedrich and Heinemeier 2009). Hence the olive branch remains as evidence to consider. See Section 3.c.III.i.c below.

Apart from the olive branch, there are no other direct dendrochronological data at present. Other tree-ring derived data and arguments at best rely on attempts to build less clear-cut or indirect linkages: e.g. finding unusual wood chemistry or growth anomalies and hypothesizing that these could be the result of a volcanic eruption. The link for any specific eruption to signal case will always be open to debate. If a long tree-ring sequence exists and it can be shown that most large volcanic events over several centuries or more (to millennia) seem to correlate with the tree-ring based indicator (e.g. Salzer and Hughes 2007; Briffa *et al.* 1998), then the volcano linkage can be argued to be strong: but even then the specific linkage for any one signal to a specific eruption is only a hypothesis.

The attempt to date Thera by dendrochronology is thus a difficult challenge and really needs a set of samples from a clear Thera destruction context. Anything else will only ever be a hypothesis. Although building long Aegean-region dendrochronologies offers huge potential to clarify Aegean and east Mediterranean archaeological chronology, such as the presently near-absolutely placed Gordion juniper time series (Manning *et al.* 2001; 2010 – hopefully to be absolutely placed through dendrochronology alone at some point in the future), such tree-ring series by themselves will do nothing to resolve the Thera date debate.

(iv) *Aegean tree-ring growth anomaly.* A dramatic short-term growth spike has been recognized in a large set of trees (conifers: juniper, cedar, pine) of several species recovered from the archaeological site of Porsuk in Turkey, with the start of the growth spike currently dated around 1651/1650 BC with only very small margins of error (Manning *et al.* 2001; 2003; 2010; Pearson *et al.* 2009). This c.1651/1650 BC date is a revision (by about 22–23 years) of the date of 1628 BC in Kuniholm *et al.* (1996) (and as used in Manning 1999). The revision is because the hypothesis (as used in Kuniholm *et al.* 1996) that the Porsuk growth anomaly could be synchronized with the more widely recognized

1628 BC tree-ring growth anomaly just about within the possible range of the radiocarbon wiggle-match dating of the Aegean tree-ring chronology – which seemed possible in AD 1996 although it was a mistake (see Section 5 below) – was definitely no longer possible in AD 2001 after an extensive further programme of high-precision ^{14}C dating as reported in Kromer *et al.* (2001) and Manning *et al.* (2001). In AD 1996 the wiggle-match comprised just 18 ^{14}C dates (some not really high-precision), whereas the much more closely defined analysis published in AD 2001 employed 52 high-precision ^{14}C dates and also identified an issue with the dates in the period leading to and around the major solar minimum in the mid-8th century BC relevant to the dating of the overall dendrochronology (Kromer *et al.* 2001; Manning *et al.* 2001). Manning *et al.* (2003) added an additional 6 dates and further confirmed the placement in Manning *et al.* (2001); and Manning *et al.* (2010) then re-did the analysis but now with 128 high-precision ^{14}C data and covering much more of the overall dendrochronology – again finding a best fit within about 1 year of the Manning *et al.* (2001) analysis. These new and much more extensive data placed the start of the Porsuk growth anomaly c.1651/1650 BC with a leeway of only a handful of years up or down. (Note: see p. 189 below.)

A volcanic eruption might be responsible for this marked growth anomaly, and it has been suggested that Thera could be a candidate. However, there is no proof, just a circumstantial case (and some potentially compatible chemistry: Pearson *et al.* 2009) that this anomaly was caused by a volcanic impact, and, of course, there is no evidence other than proximity that, even if a volcano was involved, it is Thera. This growth anomaly might almost be linkable with tree-ring growth anomalies in 1649–1648 BC reported by Salzer and Hughes (2007), and might perhaps also link with the major Greenland ice-core volcanic signal in the 1640s BC (Vinther *et al.* 2008). But then, if so, this might be the result of the Aniakchak eruption if Pearce *et al.* (2004) and Denton and Pearce (2008) are correct to argue that analysis of the volcanic glass particles from this ice-core layer rules out Thera and instead indicates Aniakchak, leaving Thera as separate and at another (unknown) point in time (and meanwhile the chronology of the Dye 3, GRIP and NGRIP cores in this interval might need revision and the volcanic acidity layer could become c.15–20 years later – Muscheler 2009 – further removing its relevance to the Porsuk tree growth anomaly). It is also not certain that the growth anomaly and chemical changes observed in the Anatolian trees are uniquely the result of a volcanic eruption. Other scenarios are possible, though there is as yet no positive evidence in their favour: in particular, one might consider the recovery of tree stands after the effects of a (likely major – since trees from several species were affected) forest fire (although none of the Porsuk samples examined show any indication of fire scars as one might expect in such a case), or some other such traumatic episode. In all cases, there is no evidence securely linking this growth anomaly with Thera. One may also observe – see Section 3.c.III below – that the radiocarbon dating case for the date of the Thera eruption as of AD 2012 tends to place c.1651/1650BC outside the most likely date range for the eruption; this too suggests that the c.1651/1650 BC growth anomaly perhaps represents something else (and, if a volcanic event, then perhaps an eruption *other than* Thera).

(v)   *Thera pumice (qua pumice – and **not** airfall tephra).* This material when identified as Theran and when found at an archaeological site at best sets an unknown *terminus ante quem* for the Thera eruption. It was used for centuries to millennia after the eruption by humans and was a very useful craft resource (Manning 1999: 146 and n.712; Wiener 2010: 374 and n.68). Archaeological representation reflects such subsequent use, and perhaps even post-eruption trade in the resource from the Aegean. Hence, considering the Levant-Egypt, it perhaps shows up especially in the 18th Dynasty period (Wiener 2010: 374), when Late Minoan IB-III Cretans and Late Helladic IIA to III Greeks were trading actively into the east Mediterranean. We have very few samples analysed from pre-Tuthmosid and pre-18th Dynasty contexts, thus what was happening in these periods is largely unknown. Sterba *et al.* (2009) appropriately conclude that this means the pumice data are not conclusive. On the basis of the current stratigraphic analysis, the finds at Tell el Dab'a in Stratum C merely illustrate use 50–75+ years *later* than the Thera eruption even for adherents of the 'low' Aegean chronology (see (vi) below next sub-section) – i.e. an irrelevant *terminus ante quem* – while finds at Tell el-'Ajjul in contrast indicate use apparently likely some c.50–100+ years earlier (Fischer 2009) and could be compatible either with a late 17th century BC Thera eruption date or one in the 16th century BC. They also highlight how long the *ante* in the *terminus ante quem* set by the finds of pumice (like at Tell el Dab'a) can be. If the radiocarbon dates for the Tell el-Dab'a strata were used (see Kutschera *et al.* 2012), then the Thera pumice could be more or less contemporary to a little later. But, all in all, the pumice is inconclusive (an unquantified *terminus ante quem*) and is not appropriate evidence as highlighted in the recent review of Höflmayer (2012a: 441–442), who concludes (p.442):

> For these reasons, the only conclusion that can be drawn from the occurrence of Theran pumice in Egypt and the Levant is that the Minoan Thera eruption must have happened *earlier* than the early New Kingdom. We are not able to quantify the years between eruption and disposal. The conclusion therefore has to be that pumice is not a reliable indicator for dating the Thera eruption.

In contrast to the water-borne (or human transported) pumice, if a substantial and secure *in situ* airfall Thera tephra deposit could be precisely dated in terms of secure dates above and below its stratigraphic context, whether on land or more likely in a sediment sequence from a lake, then this could provide a very promising route to a chronological resolution. Lakes in Turkey would seem the obvious targets for such a study. The evidence available so far is very limited and inconclusive (e.g. Sullivan 1990; Eastwood *et al.* 2002: 433),[23] and also lacks a rigorous programme of analysis aimed at this problem.

---

[23] Just two radiocarbon dates are published by Eastwood *et al.* (2002: 433 – from Eastwood *et al.* 1999: 19). One at 3300±70 BP could support a 'high' or a 'low' chronology given the large measurement error. The other at 3225±45 BP is still not decisive given the large error, but clearly more favours the 'low' chronology date range. A proper dating programme would be desirable to see if this evidence could be better defined and, if replicated (etc.), perhaps decisive.

(vi)   *Tell el-Dab'a*. Significant concern has to be expressed about aspects of the current chronology of this important site. Warburton (2009b) offers trenchant critique of the data published and the stratigraphic interpretations offered (and of the 'methods' being used generally to create and report the archaeological record of the site). The lack of published sections, and the unclear methods for creating strata which end up neatly comprised of certain sets of ceramic groups when often the material is residual and not primary, all seem at odds with reality – even in the few cases from the site where pictures and descriptions are available, it seems that there is in fact a much more complicated stratigraphic story. This general situation, and the extraordinary complete mis-match – by around 120 years on average (Kutschera *et al.* 2012: Fig. 5)[24] – of the detailed (substantial) radiocarbon chronology for the site employing short-lived sample material versus the excavator-constructed (supposed historical) archaeological chronology for the site (Kutschera *et al.* 2012), all lead this author to be highly skeptical of the Tell el-Dab'a stratigraphy and chronology at present (also Manning and Kromer 2011a). Something is wrong. I applaud Walter Kutschera and Manfred Bietak for finally publishing the Tell el-Dab'a radiocarbon data in full. I note that another (and similar) potential major problem for the Bietak chronology of Tell el-Dab'a is emerging, if new evidence suggesting the need for a much earlier date for Khyan is correct (Moeller and Marouard 2011): see Section 3.c.II.i below.

      At present Bietak would have Theran pumice first appearing at Tell el-Dab'a in the reign of Tuthmosis III and would place the (earlier) Minoan style wall-paintings around the beginning of his reign also, and some later ones into the reign of Amenhotep II (e.g. Bietak and Höflmayer 2007: 15 Fig. 2; Bietak *et al.* 2007: 16 Fig. 5). If the paintings are LMIB to LMII in style in Aegean terms, then this could be fine (Manning 2009: 222–223) – it is more challenging if they are regarded as LMIA in style (I note that in one of three beautifully illustrated

---

[24] It is worth highlighting that the situation is in reality more complicated and perhaps subtle. The Tell el-Dab'a sequence employed in the Kutschera *et al.* (2012) paper integrates material from several different areas of excavations from the large overall site. But, and contrary the impression given in figures published many times by Bietak (and as in Kutschera *et al.* 2012: Fig. 3), there is not in reality a secure master stratigraphy across all the site areas at Tell el-Dab'a. Rather, these various areas are synchronized on the basis of the ceramics found, the architecture and its forms, first appearances of various traits, and so on. Thus a fundamental problem is whether the supposed overall site sequence used by Kutschera *et al.* (2012) is in fact correct and appropriate? It may be that analysis of the data and sub-sequences from the separate areas of the site would in fact allow a somewhat different picture, with varying 'offsets' versus the expected data – and not with all areas offering the fairly consistent c.120 years offset seen in the Kutschera *et al.* (2012) paper. Nonetheless, as evident from the non-modelled calibrated age ranges reported in Kutschera *et al.* (2012: Table 1A), the key problems for the Bietak chronology are that (i) the supposed Tuthmosid palace area data (Phases C2, C2–3) are pre-New Kingdom (whereas numerous radiocarbon dates on samples linked to Hatshepsut and Tuthmosis III from other contexts have produced dates and analysis compatible with the expected age range in the 15th century BC: e.g. Bronk Ramsey *et al.* 2010), and (ii) the other Tell el-Dab'a data generally do all indicate varying older dates, of at least 50+ years to 100+ years, versus the Bietak chronology. Thus there is a problem at the site. I thank Felix Höflmayer for comments and previously Ezra Marcus for discussions.

recent discussions in *Ägypten und Levante* 20, Morgan 2010: 265 places the earlier Tuthmose III context paintings as LMIB in Aegean terms based on the conventional Aegean-Egyptian cultural correlations = chronology). But the pumice (Bietak and Höflmayer 2007: 15 Fig. 2 place it between c.1470–1440 BC; Bietak *et al.* 2007: 16 Fig. 5 as after 1450 BC) is around 50+ or 75+ years after the date of the Thera eruption even as proposed by the Aegean 'low' chronology (e.g. c.1525 BC in Wiener 2010: 387) – this either proves the irrelevance of finds of pumice in workshops to the debate (see (v) above previous sub-section), or suggests that the Tuthmosis III dating is questionable. It should be noted that the evidence for the dating of some of the palatial platforms is less than secure (and some could yet turn out to be Hyksos, as Bietak first suggested, before changing his mind: see Manning 1999: 83 with refs.), and there need be no relation (a hiatus in between) with some of the scrappier 18th Dynasty structures. For the SIP/New Kingdom divide one must also note that there is precious little evidence for the supposed 'datum line' of 1530 BC = Ahmose conquest of Avaris.[25] Much depends on whether the appearance of Upper Egyptian Marl A pottery at Tell el-Dab'a (and flint implements of Theban origin) equates with the 18th Dynasty in terms of the Egyptian historical chronology. Bietak *et al.* (2007: 39 n.71) state these are nearly absent throughout the SIP at Avaris, but they are dated 17th Dynasty in Upper Egypt, and one has to ask whether they only appeared at Tell el-Dab'a because of the Ahmose conquest (the Bietak hypothesis) or whether they did not appear there through trade and interaction in the time of the (later) 17th Dynasty.

(vii) *Archaeomagnetism.* Downey (2011a: 163 and Fig. 14) suggests that comparison of some archaeomagnetic inclination data on Thera tephra against the available secular variation (SV) curves of Evans (2006) and Tema and Kondopoulou (2011) leads to dates for the Thera eruption perhaps c.1540 BC or c.1500 BC. However, this is a completely non-independent and irrelevant statement. Why? Because the calendar 'dates' for the curve of Evans (2006) for Greece with which Downey compares his data come from the conventional archaeological chronology! To quote Evans (2006: Table 1, notes): "Cretan chronology follows Arthur Evans's classic scheme, as tabulated in Huxley (2000)". Thus this is entirely circular – the conventional chronology offers the conventional chronology dates – and irrelevant for the discussion here. The paper of Tema and Kondopoulou (2011) uses the same Cretan data (and 'dates') – see their Fig. 1 – so see above, but also highlights some other key issues. They note that archaeomagnetic data from the region for the period 2200–1600 BC are relatively sparse (p.605), and inclination data – as used by Downey (2011a: Fig. 14) – are notably sparse for the period c.1750–1550 BC in Tema and Kondopoulou (2011: Fig. 4b). They

---

[25] I note that in the caption to Figure 3 in Kutschera *et al.* (2012) it is merely stated that the "abandonment of Avaris was *supposedly* caused by the conquest of Ahmose (~1530 BC)" [my italics] – a somewhat less than certain statement of what was formerly a 'datum line' at the site c.1530 BC (e.g. Bietak and Höflmayer 2007: Fig. 2). This c.1530 BC date would of course be some 14+ to 25+ years earlier following the chronology of Aston (2012).

go on to identify the period around 1600BC as a time of one of the apparent archaeomagnetic jerks (AMJ) evident in the data they analyse, and other records (pp. 609–611). Thus the simplistic dating strategy proposed in Downey (2011a: Fig. 14) is likely inappropriate. More particularly, the comparison of the Balkan region data versus the CALS7K.2 dataset – a largely independent record based on archaeomagnetic, volcanic and lake sediment data (Korte *et al.* 2005)[26] – in Tema and Kondopoulou (2011a: Fig. 6) shows a marked divergence in inclination – which Downey (2011a: Fig. 14) is trying to use to date – and intensity at exactly the 'Thera' period. Thus we may conclude that there is no independent or useful basis to the dates in Downey (2011a) as regards the Thera date question.[27] However, the issue of the apparent relative difference in archaeomagnetic age between the fired LMIB destructions in central versus east Crete (Downey and Tarling 1984; Tarling and Downey 1990; Downey 2011b), and the relationship of these to a better definition of a long and complicated LMIB period, remains a topic which deserves more investigation.

(II) The archaeological connections between the Aegean, east Mediterranean and Egypt

Very little new or decisive archaeological evidence has entered the debate in the last 13 years, and in most cases no evidence can be argued to be decisive unless one or more prior assumptions or guesses are made, and then accorded special status. Clear linkages for LMIA with Egypt remain absent. In contrast (mature to late) LMIB or late LHIIA objects occur in contexts in Egypt at a minimum taking us into the first decades of the 15th century BC (Tuthmosis I to Hatshepsut: e.g. Warren 2006: 310–313 nos.4 and 5 from Saqqara), or, into the 18th Dynasty and sometimes, even as an heirloom (cf. Saqqara finds and context as dated by Warren, last reference), into the reign of Tuthmosis III (Warren 2006: 313–316 nos. 6 and 7) (see also Höflmayer 2009: 191–193). Subsequent LHIIB material appears to be buried in Egypt by later in the reign of Tuthmosis III (e.g. c.1440 BC) (Warren 2006: 316–317 nos. 8 and 9; Höflmayer 2009: 189–190). Therefore, a close of the LMIB period around or shortly into the reign of Tuthmosis III is plausible (with the Egyptian finds of course providing *terminus ante quem* dates for the relevant material or phases in the Aegean). No such control exists for the LMIA period. The main items noted in recent discussions by those arguing against the 'high' chronology, and in favour of the 'low' Aegean chronology, may be briefly noted and critiqued (see also e.g. Manning 2007: 115–124). It is also worth noting that a number of other items and arguments have been dropped or abandoned even by the advocates of the 'low'

---

[26] But note that for Greece the data from archaeological sites for the second millennium BC will – as noted above – follow the conventional chronology given the sources cited on p.9 in Korte *et al.* (2005). However, the Greek data are 'swamped' out by those from other areas (and other, largely ¹⁴C-based, chronologies).

[27] Of course, this discussion highlights another reason to try to resolve the Thera data debate and Aegean chronology in the mid second millennium BC, so that Aegean and related archaeomagnetic data may be appropriately placed in calendar time.

chronology if one compares recent discussions versus discussions of a couple of decades ago (e.g. Hankey and Warren 1974; Warren and Hankey 1989; Eriksson 1992). Recent critical reassessment by Höflmayer has shown that in several cases items formerly cited in scholarship do not in fact have entirely secure contexts or associations, and thus are of little specific chronological value: Höflmayer (2011a).

(i) *Khyan Lid (and dating of Khyan).* As noted several times in the past, the dating of the find context of this item at Knossos has been argued to not be well-defined (Phillips 2008 vol.II: 97–98 and refs; Manning 1999: 79 and refs.). Phillips (2008 vol.II: 97–98) summarises the situation, and how the relevant fill seems at best to set a *terminus* date for its deposit in LMIII, much later than the MMIIIA date assigned by Evans. She also notes, against its attribution to the MMIIIA burnt stratum (as Evans stated), that "the lid itself shows no marks of burning. Considering its material, which would have been affected by any fire, *the described context itself may be questioned*" [my italics]; on p.93 while discussing another Egyptian item Phillips suggests that "[a]s with the Khyan lid … Evans apparently erred in reading his notes". Phillips (2008 vol.II: 98) suggests the lid was likely "imported onto Crete long after Khyan's reign, and probably not before the New Kingdom". Nonetheless, there has been a recent effort to try to rehabilitate this item as almost useful evidence for the 'low' chronology (Wiener 2010: 374–375; see also Warren 2010: 390–391). Höflmayer recently adds to this case in favour of – despite the problems – perhaps accepting the approximate MMIII date of Evans,[28] noting both that Mackenzie accepted the date for the relevant charcoal layer (see Mackenzie's entry in his daybook from 3 April 1901: Phillips 2008 vol.II: 97 – but cf. her note 540), and – following Macdonald (2002: 44–45; 2003; 2005: 133–135) – pointing out that the latest material associated with the stone cist found nearby, and also associated with the charcoal layer, is MMIIIB, and that the Khyan lid therefore likely comes from (and so ante dates) what seems to be the MMIIIB destruction of this entire area. Macdonald (2005: 134) concludes that if the Khyan lid is

> related to the destruction of the lustral basin, as seems most likely, then a Middle Minoan IIIA date is inadmissible for this event – whereas a Middle Minoan IIIB date or later … would harmonise with the evidence.

However, the lid may of course have arrived on Crete earlier, perhaps indeed in Evan's MMIIIA period. Thus, whereas previously it has seemed that the lack of a good find context rendered the lid entirely irrelevant for precise chronology, it may be that it should be considered anew despite some remaining uncertainties. But, ironically, as I discuss in the next paragraph, this rethinking occurs just as recent finds in Egypt undermine the conventional date placement of Khyan, and instead indicate that his reign was substantially earlier than previously thought! Hence *even if* we were to accept a possible MMIIIA (or MMIII) date for the Knossos context of the Khyan lid (it can hardly ever be considered definite

[28] Höflmayer (2012b: 172–175, with review of literature) – Höflmayer pers. comm. January 2013.

given what is unclear), this link for MMIIIA may turn out to be with a point no later than the earlier 17th century BC, and perhaps even before this. In which case, this find, even if MMIIIA, does not undermine the 'high' chronology, and in fact may end up being regarded as potential evidence in its favour.

With regard to Khyan, the real excitement is the important new study of Moeller and Marouard (2011) which appears to undermine all existing convention concerning the dating and placement of Khyan (also spelt as 'Khayan' as in Moeller and Marouard 2011). Moeller and Marouard (2011) report on finds of sealings with the cartouche of Khyan at Tell Edfu in a context which requires an earlier date for Khyan than previously thought (and not immediately before Apophis), and perhaps even for an overlap (or near association) of his reign with the late 13th Dynasty (since his sealings are associated with those of Sobekhotep IV – dated e.g. 1709–1701 BC by Krauss and Warburton 2006, or 1738–1731 BC by Kitchen 2000). All of this could push Khyan back at least into the earlier 17th century BC (or even to the late 18th Century BC), and so, ironically, might make it possible – despite the caveats (still) over the find context of the inscribed lid at Knossos – to envisage contact between this ruler and Knossos in late MM or early LMIA on the 'high' chronology. It would also entirely undermine (and *reverse*) the arguments cited above by Wiener or Warren based on placing Khyan in the region of c.1610–1580 BC (see and contrast with Wiener 2010: 375; or 2006b: 327).

Another, even more intriguing, scenario is also highlighted. The Hyksos palace at Tell el-Dab'a linked by the excavators to Khyan is dated to late Stratum E/1 and Stratum D/3 (Bietak and Forstner-Müller 2009: 93; Bietak 2010). According to the Bietak chronology for the site, this means about 1600 BC to about 1560 BC (see e.g. Kutschera *et al.* 2012: Fig. 3; Bietak and Höflmayer 2007: Fig. 2). But the suggested earlier dating of Khyan by Moeller and Marouard (2011) would mean that the dating of this palace would have to be substantially earlier. If Khyan were in fact placed as contemporary with, or shortly after, the late 13th Dynasty as the Tell Edfu finds suggest, then the dating for the Tell el-Dab'a Khyan palace would have to be c.100 years earlier in date than Bietak proposes. Such an earlier date range is exactly where the radiocarbon evidence (modelled or unmodelled) from Tell el-Dab'a places Stratum E1 and Stratum D/3 (Kutschera *et al.* 2012: Figs. 4, 6a, 7)! Thus the finds at Tell Edfu may demonstrate the need for a significant revision of the Tell el-Dab'a site chronology, and point to a timeframe that is likely more or less compatible with the radiocarbon data from the site (and so a solution to the conflict left unresolved by Kutschera *et al.* 2012, esp. pp. 420–421). This would, in turn, offer strong support for the Aegean 'high' chronology – and largely remove the basis for the Aegean 'low' chronology. Other evidence may offer further support for this view. A link between Khyan and the Old Babylonian period has been raised by recent finds of cuneiform artefacts at Tell el-Dab'a (Bietak and Forstner-Müller 2009: 115–118; Schneider 2010a: 401). In particular, the find context for a letter fragment assigned to one of the last two kings of the Old Babylonian period is said to be the same Hyksos palace linked by the excavators to Khyan of late Stratum E/1 and Stratum D/3. This find points towards an approximate correlation of Khyan with the later Old Babylonian period. Since the Middle or low-Middle chronologies for Mesopotomia seem the most likely on current data (see Section 3.c above), this suggests also an earlier date for Khyan than currently assumed. The general range in time indicated by the Tell Edfu finds would work nicely.

(ii) *Egyptian stone vessels.* Warren (2006: 305–310; see also Warren 2010: 393–394 – noting especially corrections p.393 n.64; see also Höflmayer 2012b: 175–181 – Höflmayer pers. comm. January 2013) has drawn attention to three stone vessels found in the Aegean which he argues are Egyptian and of 18th Dynasty date in two cases and from LHI or LMIA contexts before or around the time of the Thera eruption. Hence he argues they are evidence for the eruption likely falling in the early 18th Dynasty (also Wiener 2010: 378–381). The first is National Museum 829 from Shaft Grave V at Mycenae which is dated to the late Second Intermediate Period (SIP) by Warren (2006: 308) but merely as SIP by Phillips (2008 vol.II: 281) – a position also maintained by Christine Lilyquist (see Wiener 2010: 380 and n.117). The second is National Museum 592 from Shaft Grave IV at Mycenae which Warren dates as 18th Dynasty (2006: 308) but for which Wiener (2010: 380) reports Lilyquist and Dorothea Arnold as not ruling out a 17th Dynasty date, and Lilyquist as in fact noting that it differs from known Egyptian examples and so the whole argument is perhaps rather weak. The third example is from Akrotiri on Thera (Akr* 1800), which, contrary to his initial assessments, Warren (2006: 310) now regards as Egyptian (but cf. e.g. Phillips 2008 vol.II: 277 n.1420) and dates as 18th Dynasty while admitting it is a singleton and that he cannot really cite good parallels (Wiener 2010 chooses not to mention this vessel). All in all reviewing these three items I cannot regard them (singly or as a group) as decisive evidence in such poorly established circumstances – and the actual solid information for the chronology of these types in Egypt is, on critical review, both scarce and less concrete than often thought, since it is largely derived from interpretations of fragmentary material without close dating control (Höflmayer 2012a: 440–441). There is, moreover, a fundamental 'hole' in the logic of these claims: namely we know something about 18th Dynasty material, and can more easily find comparanda; whereas, we do not know the SIP material as well, and thus we may tend to exclude its relevance inappropriately. The Egyptian origin of the vessels is also less than certain. Lilyquist suggested that some of these sorts of vessels were in fact Levantine products (1996; 1997; see further discussion of the Lilyquist position by Wiener 2010: 278–280; Höflmayer 2009: 194). Bevan (2003: 66) concludes: "There are indeed a number of imported vessels from the Aegean that fall into a putative, Egypto-Levantine category and that may just as well have been products of a centre such as Tell el-Ajjul, as from Egypt itself".[29] Bevan says that it is impossible to resolve this issue at present (Sparks

---

[29] Bevan (2007: 130) makes the observation that preference for white-coloured stones for the stone vessels found in the Shaft Graves at Mycenae corresponds to a similar preference at Akrotiri – and

2003: 40 also notes the issue, but says that it does not apply so far to any vessels with Egyptian inscriptions, hence e.g. the Khyan lid at Knossos, and in contrast to the non-inscribed items from Thera and Mycenae which might fall into the 'Egypto-Levantine' category). Thus at present we can say that three stone vessels of possible Egyptian, or Levantine-Egyptian origin, and whose date is less than closely defined in each case, and for two of which several experts include the SIP as a likely dating, are found in Aegean contexts from before or around the time of the Thera eruption. If SIP, there is no problem at all for the 'high' chronology. If it can ever be demonstrated that these vessels are specifically (and only) 18th Dynasty in type/date, then they would present a very strong argument for either a 'compromise' early chronology or the Aegean 'low' chronology – but this is very much *not* the case at present. As Höflmayer (2012a: 444) concludes, after also noting that earlier pre-Tuthmosid or pre-18th Dynasty dates for the stone vessels cannot at present be excluded given our lack of knowledge (pp. 440–441, 443):

> Given the unsatisfactory state of research in the field of Egyptian stone vessels of the Second Intermediate Period and the early New Kingdom, it does not seem impossible that the 2 Egyptian stone vessels from the Mycenaean shaft-graves could have been produced 1 or 2 generations earlier than previously suggested (i.e. in the late Second Intermediate Period). A new critical re-evaluation of the development of Egyptian stone vessels from the Second Intermediate Period to the New Kingdom might be desirable in order to check a possible earlier dating of these crucial synchronisms.

I agree – and it is therefore entirely premature and inappropriate to claim that this evidence offers any solid information against the 'high' Aegean chronology.

Meanwhile, on a positive note, we might note one other Egyptian stone vessel, following Höflmayer (2009: 189–190; Höflmayer 2011b). This is an imitation of a Base Ring I vessel found in Mycenae chamber tomb 102, a context dated LHIIA. Since the earliest secure BR imitations date to Tuthmosid period (and end with Amarna), this find seems nicely compatible with the (standard) scenario that the LMIB/LHIIA periods end *after* the start of the reign of Tuthmosis III.

(iii) *Vessel with the name of Ahmose from Palaepaphos* Teratsoudhia, *Cyprus.* Wiener (2010: 377) highlights this item and claims that it supports the 'low' chronology as otherwise the Egyptian vessel is an heirloom (something that is hardly uncommon – e.g. Pomerance 1980; Bevan 2003: 68). There seems to be a failure to

---

that this is in contrast to the range of material and colours found on Crete. Bevan suggests that this "reinforces the general impression of strong Cycladic links in the Shaft Graves". Warren (e.g. 2009: 181 n.5) observes this point, and then argues that perhaps the vessels went from Crete to Thera and then Mycenae. But, there is perhaps no reason to involve Crete! Perhaps these whitish vessels went direct from source of manufacture to Thera (major international Aegean port – and thence to Mycenae). If so, perhaps this was from the Levant, home of some other east-Mediterranean connections evident at Akrotiri (noting especially jewellery and inlaid daggers/swords, which specifically link Akrotiri and Mycenae: e.g. Manning 1999: 137–138, 141–142), and not Egypt? Perhaps these vessels are not Egyptian but Levantine in manufacture (as has been suggested for some such vessels: see scholars cited in the text)? If so, the supposed strict chronological value of these items as argued by Warren is undermined.

examine the find context carefully as published. This find cannot be "associated directly with any of the other contents" (Eriksson 2007: 176; Karageorghis and Michaelides *et al.* 1990: 31–32) – as stated with references to the primary publication in Manning (1999: 177–178 and ns. 856–860). Other finds from the tomb include Late Cypriot (LC) IA to IB material (i.e. into the 18th Dynasty) and, based especially on those items from the proximate area, a LCIB date for this Ahmose vessel is entirely possible and plausible. But in strict terms the associated elements of the tomb complex (see Karageorghis and Michaelides *et al.* 1990: 24 stage 2), chambers N and O, have material to LCIIIA (Karageorghis and Michaelides *et al.* 1990: 61–66), and so the vessel is of no chronological relevance (and it certainly provides no evidence for the 'low' chronology).

(iv) *White Slip (WS) I.* This has become one of the most misrepresented or misunderstood arguments in Manning (1999). A fairly thorough statement of my position and responses to some of the earlier incorrect or misrepresenting discussions is to be found in Manning (2007: 117–122). The dramatic claims that Manning created or supports some 'intra-island barrier' thesis, etc., on Cyprus as claimed by Eriksson (2007; also 2009: 49 n.2) are simply not true. Apparent (but never claimed to be exclusive) regional patterns were discussed, taking up the previous observations of Merrillees (1971 – for recent discussion of the regionalism topic and complexities, see Frankel 2009) , and it was argued that various sites/regions on Cyprus developed links with various sites/regions on the mainland (and preferentially versus other sites/areas on Cyprus). Recent work on Cyprus supports exactly such rich regional patterns and distinctions in LCI (both internal and external), see for example Crewe (2007: 155; 2009: 96–97; 2013 with further refs.). As one instance, Crewe (2009: 97) notes from her study of Galinoporni Tomb 1 (1956) that:

> Evidence for stronger material connections with the surrounding Mediterranean than with populations in other regions of Cyprus at this time [LCI] is also attested at Enkomi and *Toumba tou Skourou* (Crewe 2007, 155) and it would seem likely that individual links were being forged between Cypriot and mainland groups, rather than mediated through a hierarchical system on Cyprus.

It is further stated by critics that WSI appears in Egypt and Canaan entirely or almost entirely after 1500 BC (Wiener 2010: 275–376). Thus, since a WSI bowl was found in a pre-eruption context on Thera, the argument is that the eruption occurred around or after this date. When exactly? Wiener (2010: 375–377) starts by saying that WSI appears entirely or almost entirely Tuthmosid and after 1500 BC, then allows for a small number of sherds from Tell el-'Ajjul which are arguably earlier, and then cites Oren for a date of nowhere earlier than 1550–1470 BC (at the earliest). Returning to the subject at the top of column 2 of p.377, Wiener (2010) states that at the new (and so far very limited) excavations of Peter Fischer at Tell el-'Ajjul WSI first appears in his Stratum H5 (yes: see Fischer 2009), but Wiener claims Stratum H5 is 18th Dynasty and perhaps Tuthmosid, whereas the radiocarbon dates indicate that H5 is 16th century BC, and that its finds could be compatible with the Aegean 'high' chronology (while they could also be compatible with a Thera eruption date in the mid-16th century BC:

see Fischer 2009: Fig. 4). Eriksson (2007: 13 Table 1B) in fact allows the (initial) Thera-relevant Rope Lattice Group of WSI to start c.1560 BC. Thus even within the 'low' chronology camp there is more than 50-years of flexibility for the start of WSI! Of course, if the radiocarbon dates for the relevant Tell el-Dab'a strata were used (Kutschera *et al.* 2012), then these dates would place WSI at this site into a timeframe entirely compatible with the 'high' Aegean-Cypriot chronology.

I recapitulate my arguments in brief. I regard the WSI bowl reported from Thera[30] to be an early style of WSI decoration (see Manning 2007: 118–119; Manning *et al.* 2006b: 483–486 and n.3; Manning *et al.* 2002b: 98–106, 160–162; Manning 1999: 153–192); Eriksson (2007) in agreement also places this 'Rope Lattice' group at the very beginning of WSI. Wiener (2010: 377 and n.94) states that at Trianda on Rhodes WSI only appears after the Thera eruption – *but* since the Trianda WSI finds reported to date are of the mature to later WSI styles, and so more likely Late Cypriot (LC) IB in date, this observation really only serves to highlight that later LMIA finds (such as the Thera find) correlate with an earlier phase of WSI (and LCIA1/2 to 2 on Cyprus). I in turn place this early WSI bowl from Thera around the LCIA1/2 border to early LCIA2 in Cypriot terms (as does Eriksson 2007:13 Table 1B – but see Merrillees 2009: 248 for a summary of some other opinions). Some sherds in a similar style were found in what seems likely to be a MBIII context at Tell el-'Ajjul (Bergoffen 2001). I regard the stratified (versus the majority residual material: a point noted also by Höflmayer 2012a: 442–443) WSI from Tell el-Dab'a as of the later LCIB styles of WSI (and thus irrelevant: Manning 1999: 159–164). On Cyprus some areas and sites seem to have adopted WSI (and associated wares) earlier than others (as substantive elements of their site assemblages); some of the east of island seems to have been relatively slow to take up a new fashion and yet this is where most of the Cypriot material found at Tell el-Dab'a (and Egypt generally) seems to have come from. The Thera WSI bowl had a brown fabric and this could be consistent with a northwest Cyprus origin and is somewhat against a SE or SW origin[31] (see Manning 2007: 119; Manning *et al.* 2006b: 484–485). Maguire (2012: 91) further observes that in terms of the brush-stroke behavior the Thera WSI bowl belongs in the group of WSI bowls known from Toumba tou Skourou.[32] The absolute chronology of LCI is of course debated, but a coherent

---

[30] A single example, now lost (Merrillees 2001). I am accepting this evidence (as in Manning 1999), and am not trying to dismiss its use simply on the basis of its being a singleton and not extant for over 90 years (contrast arguments by some against the relevance of the olive branch because it is a single find – despite the olive branch, and a second such find, being a recent and well documented find in comparison to the WSI bowl).

[31] And this is in contrast to e.g. the white fabric WSI from Phylakopi – on such white fabric WSI, see Manning *et al.* (2006b: 482–483).

[32] The study of Maguire (2012) further enriches our knowledge. She argues that whereas the stylistic origins of Proto White Slip (PWS) and WSI are in the north, northwest and centre (NNWC) of the Cyprus (the traditional view), the painting practices (in particular painting the vessel when upside down) derive from the White Painted wares of the east and the Karpass (Maguire 2012: 76–77, 102). How to imagine this cross-island interaction at the end of the Middle Bronze Age/start of the Late

set of analyses by Merrillees (e.g. 2002) places the start of the period about 1650 BC, and, adjusting this now in light of subsequent analysis and evidence to a likely Middle and especially low-Middle Mesopotamian chronology (contra Merrillees 2002: 5; or Manning 1999; 2001 – for this change see the discussion in Section 3.c above), then this, or Manning (2001: 78–80), plausibly becomes a date range of around 1700–1650 BC. Thus the early WSI on Thera might be OK as mid-later 17th century BC before a (subsequent) Thera eruption in the late 17th century BC down to c.1600BC following Merrillees' analyses of the Cypriot-Egyptian linkages – whereas this is not the case if one of the lower Cypriot chronological schemes is selected instead. As Merrillees (2009: 251) observes, the closer the Thera eruption is placed to the end of the 17th century BC, then the easier it is to accommodate all the archaeological evidence. So: if it can be independently established that LCI only began c.1600BC or c.1550 BC, etc., then, yes, the Theran WSI bowl would be a major obstacle to the 'high' Aegean chronology, *but* if a Merrillees-style LC chronology is possible, then so is the Aegean 'high' chronology. Especially if the Thera eruption date is late 17th century BC (as Manning and Kromer 2012 suggest is most likely), and as is discussed and supported below, then a potentially satisfactory scenario can exist accommodating (very well) both the radiocarbon *and* archaeological evidence.

Bronze Age is not addressed – the period has of course long been identified as a period of change and reorientation on the island as Maguire notes (e.g. 2012: 104). I am less than convinced in all respects for the following reasons. This distinction is based on a tiny sample from the east/Karpass: just 14 pots (and we should consider the non-WP Karpass and eastern wares when defining painter/site/region practices). Nor is it very consistent. The WPIII-IV PLS, IV-VI CLS and WPV 'eastern Mesaoria' styles group fail to show any evidence of being painted upside down (Maguire 2012: 61) as the east/Karpass is meant to prefer – and indeed the WPV vessel discussed from Nitovikla in the Karpass (Nitovikla Tb2 no.47 in Maguire 2012: 61–64) was painted both upright and upside down (Maguire 2012: 64 col.1). The shapes are not compared rigorously – vessels with painted rounded bases are often done upside down for common sense reasons in all areas when Maguire's text is read (e.g. Dhenia Kafkalla Tb 2 no.1 in Maguire 2012: 43–46 or likely Dhenia Kafkalla Tb 3 no.9 in Maguire 2012: 47 despite being in the 'upright' NNWC area). Likewise, tankard shapes are painted on their sides or both upright or upside down as suitable (such as WSI Maroni Tb 28 in Maguire 2012: 93). A PWS bowl (Maguire 2012: Fig. 62) is painted partly on either its side or upside down (Maguire 2012: 87 col.2) but then also in an upright position (Maguire 2012: 88 col.1). Handedness (right versus left) was not recognized by Maguire (2012: 30) although around 10% or a little more of the population of painters should be left handed unless atypical of normal human populations (for example strongly or moderately left handed at c.10% in the study of Perelle and Ehrman 1994 and up to c.20% in the earlier study of Perelle and Ehrman 1983). Thus although sets of practices may successfully link products to workshops or areas, it seems premature to hypothesize movements of people from the Karpass to the northwest (Maguire 2012: 104 col.2) on the basis of the existing evidence which may plausibly have other and even practical explanations. We may also as much be witnessing a shift in vessel shapes/types and decorative syntax which favoured some elements of the overall available set of painting practices, as substantive movements of painters/people across the island. In general terms, ceramic production in the Middle Bronze Age to Late Cypriot I period on Cyprus is recognized as complicated (macro and micro patterns), with highly localized production and yet quite a range of movement of pots (and associated influences) across/around the island.

(v)   *Rhyta.* Some Egyptian vessels are argued to be imitations of Aegean LMIA to
      LMIB conical rhyta (Koehl 2000; 2006: 238–239, 342–345; Bietak 2004: col. 210;
      Warren 2009: 182–184). The argument is that some examples of imitations of
      Koehl's type III of LMIA style come from late SIP or early 18th Dynasty contexts
      in Egypt through to Tuthmosid (Tell el-Dab'a Phases C/3–2) contexts (note the
      down-dating from early 18th Dynasty to Tuthmosid between Koehl 2000 and
      e.g. Bietak 2004: col. 210), and that other LMIB style imitations are known
      from other mid-18th Dynasty contexts or thereabouts – including depictions in
      Theban tombs dated to the reign of Tuthmosis III. The earliest tomb depiction
      of a LMIB style Type III rhyton comes from the Tomb of Useramun (uncle
      of Rekhmire) from the *earlier* part of Tuthmosis' reign. Thus since LMIB style
      rhyta are being depicted by the earlier part of the reign of Tuthmosis III,
      the LMIA style rhyta from Tuthmosid Tell el-Dab'a are 'old' style (heirloom
      representations) and merely set an irrelevantly later *terminus ante quem* for the
      Aegean period of original inspiration. This leaves a fairly general influence of
      LMIA from late SIP to the early 18th Dynasty in Egypt – thus a *terminus ante
      quem* of this period for LMIA in the Aegean. Especially as the start date of
      the 18th Dynasty seems to be moving earlier, into the 2nd quarter of the 16th
      century BC (Aston 2012), this *terminus ante quem* seems perfectly consonant with
      the 'high' chronology and a Thera eruption date late in the 17th century BC,
      and in no way provides strong evidence in reverse. LMIB style influences follow
      by the reign of Tuthmosis III, consistent with other indications of exchanges
      and influences of LMIB/LHIIA date from his reign (Warren and Hankey 1989:
      138–144). These observations parallel those made of the vessels carried by
      the Keftiu in wall paintings from the reigns of Hatshepsut and Tuthmosis
      III (Matthäus 1995). The earlier paintings (tombs of Senmut and Useramun
      linked to Hatshepsut) include items of LMIA/LHIA and LMIB date, whereas
      the paintings from later in the reign of Tuthmosis III include items of LHIIB/
      LMII to perhaps LHIIIA/LMIIIA date. These linkages can be consistent with
      the observations noted at the start of this section. Again, this evidence does
      not require the 'low' chronology, nor run against the 'high' chronology (and
      especially if 18th Dynasty chronology from Ahmose to Tuthmosis III is raised
      a little, as Aston 2012 proposes).[33]

(III) The radiocarbon (^{14}C) evidence

At present, arguably the only direct evidence strictly relevant to the dating of the
Thera eruption comes from radiocarbon: first, from dating short-lived plant matter
from the volcanic destruction level on Thera harvested and stored (very) shortly
prior to the eruption, second from dating elements of one or more olive trees buried
by (and likely killed by) the Thera eruption, and third from dating a sequence of

---

[33] Höflmayer (2012b: 147–149) discusses the rhyta topic, reaching a more or less similar assessment:
i.e., general parallel between early to mid 18th Dynasty rhyta and LM IA to LMIB rhyta, but no clear
synchronism (Höflmayer, pers. comm. January 2013).

archaeologically recovered organic samples from the Aegean providing dates relevant to the LMIA to LMII phases before, contemporary with, and after the Thera eruption. Much new evidence has become available since I wrote Manning (1999: 232–263), although the general picture remains the same. This new material has been extensively published, see especially Manning *et al.* (2006a; 2009a); Manning and Kromer (2011a; 2012); Friedrich *et al.* (2006; 2009); Friedrich and Heinemeier (2009); Friedrich (2009: 109–121); Heinemeier *et al.* (2009); Bronk Ramsey *et al.* (2004); Galimberti *et al.* (2004); Manning and Bronk Ramsey (2003; 2009); Manning *et al.* (2002a); Manning (2009); Maniatis (2010). Probably because these data clearly and consistently contradict the Aegean 'low' chronology,[34] there has been an intense effort to try to claim that there is something wrong with radiocarbon when applied to this topic, and that scholarship should ignore the radiocarbon evidence. What I would like to do in this section is first, in (i), to outline and assess the main data we have, comment on some of the supposed problems which have been raised concerning the use of radiocarbon in this case, and to summarise the current best assessment of the radiocarbon evidence for the date of the Thera eruption. Then, in (ii) at the end, I discuss some specific criticisms and issues Wiener (2012) has raised with regard to the radiocarbon evidence. Note: for a succinct outline and review of modern radiocarbon dating in general, readers should consult Bronk Ramsey (2008).

(i) *The ^{14}C evidence for the date of the end of the Akrotiri VDL, and for the Aegean phases before, contemporary with, and after the Thera eruption*
Several sets of data on short-lived sample material (so samples with no or little in-built age factor – contrast with tree-ring samples unless known to be outermost tree-rings) exist relevant to the final volcanic destruction level (VDL) on Thera from the site of Akrotiri, and these should offer ages shortly before the Thera eruption (the data are shown in Figures RE1–4 and listed in Revisit Essay Appendix 2 below). These samples – stored crop produce (primarily *Lathyrus* sp. and *Hordeum* sp.)[35] – should all reflect a very similar if not identical calendar time period, whether of one to a few years (the twig forming K-4255 is the exception comprising c.10 years in total – Friedrich *et al.* 1990: 195, 192–193). Sarpaki (2001: 38 n.20) suggests that cereals and legumes can be stored for periods of 1–2 years (Sarpaki 1992: 229 says storage "perhaps up to two years"), and the arrangements found so far at Akrotiri reflect household (normal use), and *not* large-scale (e.g. granary), nor specialist longer-term (e.g. sealed pits – as discussed in Currid and Navon 1989), nor communal storage. The fact the samples we have were preserved at Akrotiri as they were found reflects an unusual circumstance, which Sarpaki (2001: 28–30) argues was heat from the hot tephra and associated gases, etc., of the (main) Thera eruption

---

[34] The (lovely) recent book of Neer (2012) on Greek art and archaeology reaches this observation: he states that the "seemingly solid radiocarbon dates put the eruption in the last third or so of the 17th century BCE" (p.37) – but then of course there and on p.20 he notes the contradiction with the previous (and one continuing) view based on connections/correlations with Egypt and the Near East. Taking a refreshing approach to the excitement of ongoing scholarly discussion, Neer offers the opinion that "The fact that there is wide disagreement about something so fundamental as dates may seem alarming. On the bright side, the situation is also exciting: we still have a lot to learn" (p.20).

[35] For discussion and inferences about the crops found stored at Akrotiri, see Sarpaki (1990; 1992; 2001).

enveloping the site (of around 300°C).[36] This means that the preserved stored material we have from the site should all come from the 0–2 years prior to the eruption. This view is further supported by observations on the nature and state of preservation of insect pest remains among the stored crops at Akrotiri (Panagiotakopulu and Buckland 1991), which suggests that there was an active insect population and use of the jars by humans until sudden extinction and charring by the eruption. Thus, if anything, the sum of the indications suggests that the eruption was in fact in the c.0–1 year subsequent period to the time when most of the stored crop elements were likely growing, and that there was hence very much *no* substantial interval of time involved. We can therefore treat the date of the stored crop elements and the date of the Thera eruption as effectively the same age in calendar and radiocarbon terms (within 0–1 or 0–2 calendar years), especially when considered against a radiocarbon calibration curve (IntCal09: Reimer *et al.* 2009) known (modelled) at 5 calendar years resolution for this period. The very similar weighted averages (and date distributions) for both the *Lathyrus* sp. and *Hordeum* sp. samples (Manning and Kromer 2012: Fig. 10; see also Figure RE5 below) are entirely consistent with this view that we are dealing with material all from the same very short (e.g. 0–1 or 0–2 years) calendar window and all of approximately the same radiocarbon age in average terms. Therefore, despite Wiener (2012: 429) claiming that "it is not clear whether some of the seeds were collected before the preliminary eruption that caused the population to flee, or between that point and the final phase…", it would seem that we are in fact dealing with material all from a very short, approximately 0–1 or 0–2 years, calendar window which may be considered as one set which all reflects approximately the same radiocarbon age.

From the geological side we get similar information. The estimate of the time from the abandonment of the Akrotiri settlement (and earthquakes) – so end of the VDL – to the beginning of the eruption sequence, is short and represents "probably not longer than a year" (Cioni *et al.* 2000: 721, 724 – with the longest estimate as a few years: Limbrey 1990: esp. 380), and the time from the precursor eruption (not sufficient to char seed material) to the start of the main eruption was only "a few months, certainly no more than a year" (McCoy 2009: 80). Therefore, all the available information indicates that it is appropriate to consider the Akrotiri VDL radiocarbon data as effectively dating the same event, and thus they can be treated as offering estimates of approximately the same ^{14}C age range, and so combined together with a weighted average offering the best estimate of the correct ^{14}C age, and tested (for this hypothesis) via a Chi-square test (Ward and Wilson 1978, Case I situation).

The notable feature of the Akrotiri VDL data sets available today is how

---

[36] High temperatures of around 300 degrees Celius are likely on the basis of the observed charring (compare Braadbaart and van Bergen 2005), and as indicated by geological analysis (McClelland and Druitt 1989).

consistent the trends (averages) are, and, especially for the more recently measured data, or data from carefully selected appropriate samples and standard pretreatment regimes. We see measurements yielding consistent dates with similar spreads of ages around very similar average values (noted regarding the smaller set of, and less high-precision, evidence available to AD 1999, at Manning 1999: 239 n.1134 – although in the AD 1980s-1990s this picture was less clear than it is today), as discussed regarding post-AD 1999 data, and all the data, in Manning and Kromer (2011a; 2012); Manning (2007: 104–114); Manning *et al.* (2006a; 2009a). Despite data from several laboratories (and differing pretreatment regimes) and from different technologies and from over a considerable period of time (and technical improvements in measurement precision), very similar ^{14}C ages have been repeatedly produced (with precision and accuracy improving in the more recent data): see Figures RE1–6.[37]

Figure RE1 shows the 43 data available, comprising 12 dates run in the AD 1970s-1980s from the University of Pennsylvania laboratory on what are stated to be definite short-lived samples from the Akrotiri VDL (although not all these data received either NaOH pretreatment or carbon-13 normalisation – and thus they are less 'sound' than the data in the 28 date set which all did), along with the 28 dates employed in Manning *et al.* (2006a), and 3 data from the ETH laboratory (Kutschera and Stadler 2000: table 2, comprising ETH-3315, 3323 and 3324) (as Manning and Kromer 2011a: Fig. 1 no.3); the central 37 data in this set offer a fairly tight, coherent set with a weighted average of 3346 ± 7 ^{14}C years BP. Only 6 of 43 dates (14%) are outliers (for the data, see Revisit Essay Appendix 2 below). Figure RE2 shows just the 28 date set employed by Manning *et al.* (2006a) on the basis that they were the datasets available with current normal pretreatment procedures (acid-base-acid) and with correction for isotopic (δ^{13}C) fractionation. On reflection, the 3 Heidelberg data – run in the AD 1980s and not high precision – should not have been included.[38] This

---

[37] It is worth noting that the Thera samples are are all from carbonised plant material, and these samples do not therefore have any of the added complications potentially linked to state of preservation, source of dietary intake and hence source of the carbon in the bone collagen, etc., that can surround radiocarbon dates on bone samples, or other problematic materials which include reservoir ages (like marine shell). For a recent discussion of suitable samples for radiocarbon dating and some of the selection and pretreatment issues, see Bayliss *et al.* (2011: 38–42, 43–44). Human bones, in particular, can be problematic and variable depending on the choices and selections in diet by the humans in question. Where diet can lead to the incorporation (directly or via the food chain) of a ^{14}C reservoir age (from a marine reservoir or a freshwater reservoir – e.g. geothermally derived river or spring water sources) via fish or other marine/riverine food resources, this can lead to anomalous ^{14}C ages versus contemporary terrestrial atmospheric levels (e.g. Cook *et al.* 2001; 2002; Bayliss *et al.* 2004; Ascough *et al.* 2007; Bonsall *et al.* 2012). Such human bone offsets can sometimes be recognized and contrasted with unaffected ^{14}C dates either on plant remains, or, as in the case of a study of the Klin Yar site, to ^{14}C dates on pasture grazing ungulates (Higham *et al.* 2010). It is tempting to speculate that some such issues may yet be determined to lie behind the anomalous ^{14}C dates reported from human bones from Nineveh in Taylor *et al.* (2010).

[38] Their inclusion or exclusion makes no real practical difference as the spread of ages in this 3 date Heidelberg set, as very recent, middling and very old, balances out near the mean of the other samples,

set of 3 data has far too large a spread of values. This leaves 25 data for best consideration. These data offer a fairly symmetrical distribution around the set mean with a weighted average age of 3346 ± 8 BP. The central 20 data (all those whose mid-point values are within 1 Standard Deviation, SD, of the set mean, unweighted) form an especially tight (total range of 90 ^{14}C years across mid-point values), coherent, set with a weighted mean age of 3345 ± 8 BP. Figure RE3 shows the central 20 date set from the 25 date set in Figure RE2 in more detail. Figure RE4 shows and compares the weighted averages for each of the four constituent data sets comprising the 25 date set in Figure RE2, two from the AD 1980s (Copenhagen and Oxford Series I) and two from the AD 2000s (Oxford and VERA).

While precision increases substantially from the older to more recent period, the data remain very stable, despite different laboratories, equipment, and varying exact pretreatment regimes, with just 20 ^{14}C years covering the mid-points of the 4 weighted averages. The data on the two main plant species which provide sample material, *Lathyrus* sp. and *Hordeum* sp., yield almost identical weighted averages also, as shown (weighted average 3346 ± 13 BP for *Lathyrus* sp. and 3345 ± 10 BP for *Hordeum* sp.) – indicating there is no difference by (or because of) plant type. Figure RE5 shows the total (summed) ^{14}C dating probability from all 13 of the ^{14}C dates measured in the AD 2000s

and, since they are data with large measurement errors their value is down-weighted in terms of the weighted average calculated for the overall set. The large errors mean that they can be part of a 28 date weighted average which passes a Chi-square test (and without biasing the weighted average) as in Manning *et al.* (2006a). But, on reflection, it seems more appropriate – as in the text here – to exclude these obviously poor quality data and just use the other 25 dates. There is almost no difference in weighted average (in rounded whole years). The 28–date set yields a weighted average of 3345 ± 8 BP with T = 31.5 < 39.9 for df27 at the 5% level; the 25–date set yields a weighted average of 3346 ± 8 BP with T = 19.7 < 36.4 for df24 at the 5% level (Ward and Wilson 1978 as implemented in Bronk Ramsey 1995 and since). The 25–date set has a noticeably tighter spread, however: see Figure RE2.

I take this opportunity to note a minor error in the Manning *et al.* 2006a SOM with regard to these 3 Heidelberg dates (Hd-7092–6795, Hd-6058–5519, Hd-6059–7967). In the original SOM of 2006 Table S1 on p.40 the three Hd data are shown with grey shading apparently indicating they were not employed in the analysis – whereas they were included in the set of dates (28 dates in all) employed to calculate the weighted average value for the Akrotiri VDL in the model runs in Manning *et al.* (2006a) as evident or stated in Figure S2F (bottom) and Figure S2G, and Table S2 page 46 of the Manning *et al.* 2006a SOM, and as evident from adding up the number of ^{14}C dates on short-lived samples from the Akrotiri VDL in Table S1 required to get to the total of 28 dates referred to in Manning *et al.* 2006a. I thank Malcolm Wiener for highlighting this error to me. As just noted, the inclusion or exclusion of these 3 Heidelberg dates in the Manning *et al.* 2006a analysis makes almost no difference. The Manning *et al.* 2006a analysis used the weighted average value of the Akrotiri short-lived sample VDL set and there is just a 1 ^{14}C year difference between the weighted average value for the 25 date set (without the Hd dates) versus the weighted average value for the 28 date set with the Hd dates (see previous paragraph this footnote). The change of 1 ^{14}C year makes no substantive difference. But, as discussed in the text and the previous paragraph in this footnote, probably not using the 3 Heidelberg dates makes better sense given their wide spread – hence see the analyses in this Revisit Essay using only the 25–date set. A corrected version of the Manning *et al.* 2006a SOM Table S1 is provided below in Revisit Essay Appendix 2.

from the Oxford and VERA laboratories (data from Manning *et al.* 2006a – data indicated in Figures RE1–RE3). This shows a fairly normal (symmetrical) spread from the 13 data out of an assumed real and much larger population of data (if one could date many more similar samples from the Akrotiri VDL). There is every reason to consider the data as representative of a normal probability distribution and to use the weighted average of the set as the best estimate of the appropriate ^{14}C value for the set – consistent with the comfortable pass of the Chi-square test. In detail, the weighted mean is a little to the low side of the overall range of the data (only 45.2% of the range is below the average and 54.8% above) and there is a slightly longer tail of values to the high side. The weighted mean already reflects to an extent this slight bias to the lower end of the probability distribution – but not quite as far as the median value which is at 3339 BP – but this is very minor. A subjective case for perhaps considering the slight clumping in the data in the set in an area just to the low side of the weighted mean, in the period covered by the bins c.3307.5 BP to 3337.5 BP in Figure RE5, is discussed below in this Section (see also Manning and Kromer 2012). Figure RE6 shows the calibrated calendar probability distributions for each of the four date sets in Figure RE4, and the most likely calibrated age ranges from these at 68.2% and 95.4% probability. In each case, a period in the 17th century BC is clearly the most likely date range. Figure RE7 shows the calibrated calendar probability distributions and most likely calibrated age ranges from these at 68.2% and 95.4% probability for (top) the weighted averages of the 25 date set (from Figure RE2) and (bottom) for the 13 date set of samples run in the AD 2000s by Oxford and VERA (from Manning *et al.* 2006a). The two are almost identical. In each case, a period in the later 17th century BC is clearly the most likely date range. As Figures RE1–7 demonstrate, we have data showing consistent, repeated, findings on short-lived samples from the Akrotiri VDL with (coherent) weighted average ages centered between 3346 to 3344 ^{14}C years BP.

Nonetheless, Wiener (2012 – and in previous studies) makes contrary claims. Let us review (some of) these. Wiener (2012: 425) asserts that "no information was provided [by Manning *et al.* 2006a] with respect to whether any measurements were rejected as failing the chi-squared test". This is simply not true. The Manning *et al.* (2006a) paper in the caption to their Figure 2 makes it clear all 28 of the Akrotiri VDL data passed a Chi-squared (χ^2) test – i.e. no data of the 28 stated as used were excluded – and the Manning *et al.* (2006a) SOM p.6 clearly states that if one instead uses just the AD 2000s measured data (n=13) then they too all passed the Chi-square test. Wiener (2012: 425) states that "measurements of seeds from the same location in the final destruction horizon produced ages with central dates as much as 250 yr apart (with seeds of the same species providing central dates 215 yr apart)". These are of course the very most extreme cases in the whole set – ignoring the strong central trend (for which see Figures RE1 to Figure RE4 above, and see Manning and Kromer 2011a: Fig. 1; 2012: Fig. 9). The implication of Wiener is that somehow these data indicate dramatic variability and thus could not yield a satisfactory

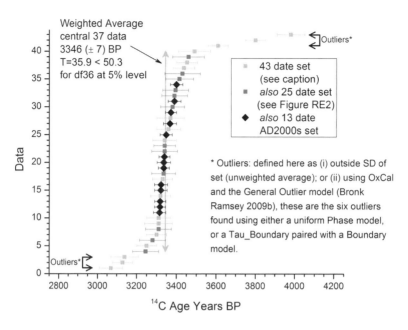

Figure RE1. The 43 date set of ¹⁴C ages reported for short-lived samples from the Akrotiri or Thera Volcanic Destruction Level (VDL) from Manning and Kromer (2011a: Fig. 1 no.3). Data shown with 1 Standard Deviation (1SD or 1σ) errors. This includes all radiocarbon dates published (with details) for definite short-lived sample matter from the VDL at Akrotiri or on Thera (thus adding 12 of the Penn data listed in Manning 1988b: table 4, comprising P-1697, 1885, 1888, 1889, 1892, 1894, 1895, 2559, 2560, 2561, 2565 and 2791; and three ETH data from Kutschera and Stadler 2000: table 2, comprising ETH-3315, 3323 and 3324). Six outliers (three too old and three too recent) are indicated – these data (mid-point values) are outside the SD of the mean of the 43-date set, leaving 37 dates. Removing the outliers excludes, visually, the very obviously outlying data, and, especially, two much too old values where some contamination or other issue seems apparent (compare Weninger 1990: 218–219). For the data, see Revisit Essay Appendix 2 below. Note: despite being included in Manning and Kromer (2011a: Fig. 1 no.3), the reported find context of P-1894 ("under paved floor": Fishman et al. 1977: 193) might in fact indicate that it is not very latest final VDL (see also Revisit Essay Appendix 2).

weighted average – but this also entirely ignores the relevant measurement errors on the 'central dates'. In the 28–date set employed in Manning *et al.* (2006a), the 4 most recent ages and the 4 oldest ages all have measurement errors greater than or equals 65 ¹⁴C years (range 65–90 ¹⁴C years), thus their 2SD ranges are ± 130 to 180 ¹⁴C years. Hence, in fact, even the extreme most recent and oldest ages all can overlap and so combine within 95% confidence limits (the Ward and Wilson 1978 test), as consistent with representing the same real age. But, as data with much larger measurement errors than others in the set, their contribution to the weighted mean is also down-weighted. To take the 215 ¹⁴C year difference example Wiener cites (two *Lathyrus* sp. samples, OxA-1549 and OxA-1555), both samples have measurement errors of 65 ¹⁴C

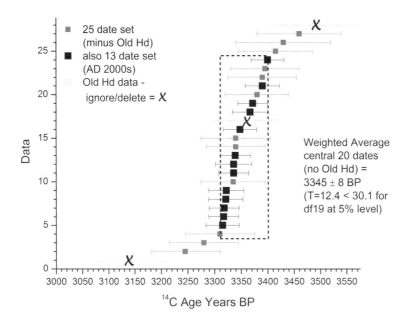

Figure RE2. The 28 date set of ¹⁴C dates on short-lived samples from the Akrotiri VDL employed in Manning et al. (2006a). Data shown with 1SD errors. Although these 28 data can combine and pass a Chi-square test at the 5% level, the 3 data from Heidelberg measured before AD 1990 are clearly much less good quality since there is a major spread of ages among these 3 data. Hence they should probably be excluded. These data are indicated in the figure and the X marks their exclusion here. This leaves 25 dates. The dates which are also in the set of 13 dates measured in the AD 2000s and reported in Manning et al. (2006a) are also denoted (within the 25 date set). Five of the remaining dates have mid-point values outside the SD of the (unweighted) mean of the 25-date set, leaving 20 data with a very tight age range – mid-points covering just 90 ¹⁴C years in total for the central 20 data and with 18 of the 20 data overlapping within their 1SD ranges – and a fairly symmetrical distribution about the weighted average value of 3345 BP (the same weighted average as for the original 28 date set – indicating all the data are more or less symmetrically distributed around the mean). For the data, see Revisit Essay Appendix 2 below.

years, and thus comfortably overlap at 2SD, and so could be compatible with being estimates of the same age. *And, note:* these are the oldest and most recent of the 14 data on *Lathyrus* sp. – the other 12 data fall in between with a tight spread around the set weighted average value of 3346 ¹⁴C years BP – and in fact these examples are the oldest and most recent ages in the entire 25 date set of Oxford, VERA and Copenhagen data (see Figure RE2)! Thus this is not some typical difference; it is the extremes of the entire set.[39] The majority of the data form a much tighter range. In the 28-date set, if one discounts the 3

---

[39] The larger difference Wiener notes does not exist when the Heidelberg data are discounted, as proposed in the text above, and see Figure RE2. See also the note concerning the 3 Heidelberg dates at the end of footnote 38 above.

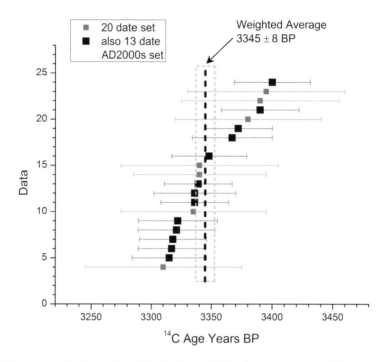

Figure RE3. The central 20 date set identified in Figure RE2 shown in more detail. Data shown with 1SD errors. Those data in the AD 2000s-measured 13 date set are also indicated. All but 2 data overlap with the 1SD range of the weighted average and all data comfortably overlap within their 2SD ranges (and hence the good Chi-square test value of 12.4 < 30.1 for df19 at the 5% level). The data are fairly symmetrically distributed about the mean. 12 values are lower than the mean and 8 above. There is (accordingly) a slightly tighter range to the low side (range mean to lowest value mid-point = 35 ¹⁴C years) than to the high side (range mean to highest value mid-point = 55 ¹⁴C years).

oldest and 3 most recent data (see Manning and Kromer 2011a: Fig. 1 no.1), then 78.6% of the data (n = 22) fall in a range of 'central dates' of just 105 ¹⁴C years, and all of these data comfortably include the weighted mean within their 2SD measurement errors making this a very consistent set. If one looks at the central 20 data identified in Figure RE3, then a 90 ¹⁴C year range covers the spread of mid-point values. If one only considers the more recent technology data since AD 2000, then there are 13 data (data indicated in Figures RE2 and RE3 – for data, see Manning *et al.* 2006a; Manning and Kromer 2011a: Fig. 1 no.2), which all include the weighted mean within their 2SD measurement errors and which comprise a total range of mid-point values of just 85 ¹⁴C years. These data are tight, coherent, and the outcome of repeated work; they are robust.

What about volcanic CO_2 and similar? This topic has become the last great hope of the 'low' chronology. Somehow (and any and all possible scenarios from the plausible to the very unlikely are raised) volcanic CO_2, which is ¹⁴C

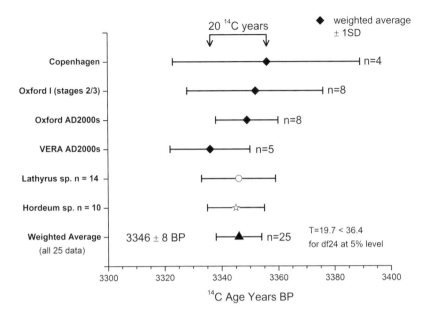

Figure RE4. Weighted average values ± 1SD for four different sets of measurements (25 data in total) on definite short-lived samples (or including one 10-year twig in the Copenhagen set) from the Akrotiri VDL as calculated by OxCal 4.1.7 (Ramsey 2009a) implementing Ward and Wilson (1978) (note: one can get 0-1 year differences from rounding versus doing by hand as reported in Manning 1999 for example p.239 n. 1134). Copenhagen date set available AD 1989 from Friedrich et al. (1990) weighted average 3356 ± 33 BP, Oxford Series I data just on the Stages 2/3 samples available AD 1989 (the final pre-eruption occupation and destruction phases) from Housley et al. (1990) weighted average 3352 ± 24 BP, Oxford data run in the AD 2000s from Bronk Ramsey et al. (2004) and Manning et al. (2006a) – note different accelerator compared to the earlier Oxford data – weighted average 3349 ± 11 BP, VERA data run in the AD 2000s from Manning et al. (2006a) weighted average 3336 ± 14 BP. Each set comfortably passes a Chi-square test for representing the same age (see Figure RE5). There is only a 20 ^{14}C year spread between the central weighted average values across the four sets. The data on the two main plant species offering samples, Lathyrus *sp. and* Hordeum *sp., are almost identical as shown (weighted average 3346 ± 13 BP for* Lathyrus *sp. and 3345 ± 10 BP for* Hordeum *sp.). The weighted average of the 25 data in each of the above four sets is shown at the bottom: 3346 ± 8 BP.*

depleted, or something else similar, is argued to affect the Thera samples, and so lead to too old ages (e.g. Wiener 2007: 34–37; 2009a: 282–283, 321–323, 329–330; 2009b: 200–206; 2010: 371–372). Several responses to many of these points have already been published (e.g. Manning *et al.* 2009a: 300–304; Friedrich 2009: 120–121; Friedrich *et al.* 2009; Heinemeier *et al.* 2009). There are some very simple and common sense arguments to show why this issue does not appear a substantive problem, despite however many hypothetical problems from various citations are proposed.

First: as Manning *et al.* (2006a) demonstrated, the analysis of a sequence of ^{14}C date sets from the Aegean for the period before, contemporary with, and

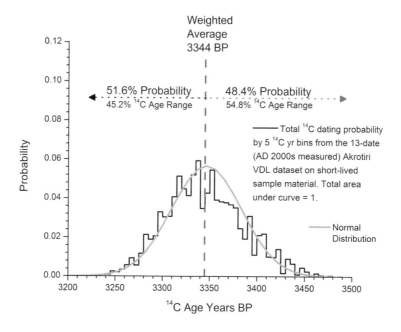

Figure RE5. Approximate total ^{14}C dating probability, normalised (summed probability to 4SD for each date) by 5 ^{14}C year bins for the 13 date set of AD 2000s measured data (see data indicated in Figures RE1–RE3) in black, and compared to the shape of a normal probability distribution curve (0.25 SD resolution) in grey. The ^{14}C probability is relatively symmetrical around the weighted average, with a slight concentration of probability to the lower side of the mean – bins centered c.3307.5 to 3337.5 BP). The range to the low side of the weighted average is also less (45.2% of the total range) than to the older side (54.8% of the total range).

after the Thera eruption using only Aegean samples which did *not* come from Thera (and so are immune from the hypothetical volcanic CO_2) still yielded a date range for the Thera VDL (1659–1624 BC at 68.2% probability and c.1668–1585 BC at 95.4% probability) which is consistent with (very similar to) those achieved with the Thera data included (see also Manning *et al.* 2009a: 303 Table 1). The non-Thera range is slightly wider, since there were fewer dates and constraints in the dating model, but the calendar ranges found for the Akrotiri VDL, and for the LMIA and LMIB date sets, were consonant with the 'high' chronology and not compatible with the 'low' chronology. The similarity in ranges, with or without the Thera data, implies that the Thera data do not suffer (on average at least) from any substantive volcanic CO_2 effect.

Second: sets of recent radiocarbon dates from sites well away from Thera, from Kolonna on Aigina (Wild *et al.* 2010), Lerna in the Argolid of mainland Greece (Lindblom and Manning 2011), and Palaikastro in east Crete (Bruins *et al.* 2008; 2009) all yield results which are compatible with the 'high' chronology date for LMIA and *not* with the 'low' chronology date (see also Höflmayer 2012a:

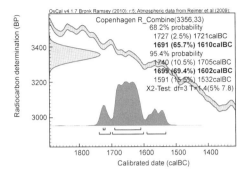
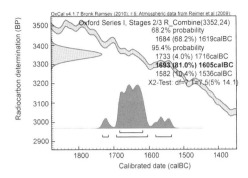
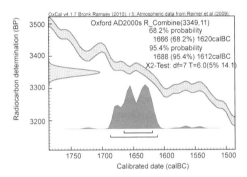
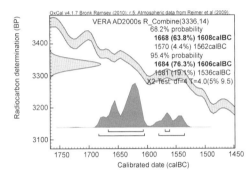

Figure RE6. Calibrated calendar age probability distributions and age ranges at 68.2% and 95.4% probability for the four weighted averages in Figure RE4. As labeled: top left = Copenhagen date set available AD 1989 from Friedrich et al. *(1990), top right = Oxford Series I data just on the Stages 2/3 samples available AD 1989 from Housley* et al. *(1990) (note: just the final pre-eruption occupation and destruction phases – Housley* et al. *1990: 209), bottom left = Oxford data run in the AD 2000s from Bronk Ramsey* et al. *(2004) and Manning* et al. *(2006a), and bottom right = VERA data run in the AD 2000s from Manning* et al. *(2006a). Each set comfortably passes a Chi-square test for representing the same age. Where there are multiple possible age ranges the more likely one is in bold. Data from IntCal09 (Reimer* et al. *2009) and OxCal 4.1.7 (Bronk Ramsey 2009a) with curve resolution set at 5.*

438–440 regarding Kolonna and Palaikastro). As did data from Miletos and Trianda reported in Manning *et al.* (2006a); and see also the 'high' chronology compatible ^{14}C data in Voutsaki *et al.* 2009a, 2009b from Middle Helladic Lerna and Asine. The fact that these contemporary or near contemporary archaeological contexts yield ^{14}C ages for later LMIA (or equivalent Aegean periods) similar to the ^{14}C ages measured on short-lived samples from the later LMIA period at Akrotiri is strong evidence that no substantive volcanic CO_2 (or similar) effect applies to the Akrotiri VDL dataset in Figure RE2. Nor are the current findings from Thera, from the Aegean, or from the above recent studies, somehow all just a result of one particular implementation of Bayesian probability analysis – similar results are found applying a deliberately more conservative and robust approach (Weninger *et al.* 2010).

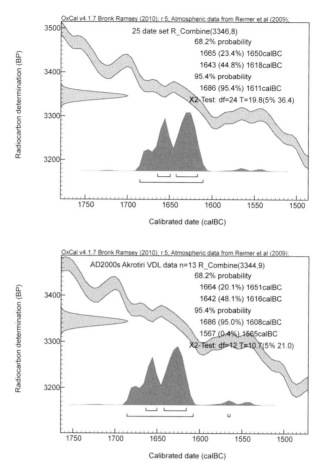

Figure RE7. Calibrated calendar age probability distributions and most likely age ranges at 68.2% and 95.4% probability for the (top) 25 date set in Figure RE2 and (bottom) the 13 date set of data on short-lived samples from the Akrotiri VDL measured in the AD 2000s by the Oxford and VERA laboratories from Manning *et al. (2006a). Each set comfortably passes a Chi-square test for representing the same age. Data from IntCal09 (Reimer* et al. *2009) and OxCal 4.1.7 (Bronk Ramsey 2009a) with curve resolution set at 5.*

Third: the sequence of radiocarbon dates from the olive branch sample from Thera (Friedrich *et al.* 2006) shows that radiocarbon ages were *declining* over time to the last dated sample (Figure RE18 below; Manning *et al.* 2009a: Fig. 1). Whereas, if there was a real and substantive volcanic CO_2 effect relevant to the last years or decades before the eruption, then a spike upwards to older ^{14}C ages, or generally an upwards trajectory (or at least one that is not downwards) towards too old ^{14}C ages, would be expected. The sequence of measured ^{14}C ages on the olive branch sample furthermore offers a very close match to the average mid-latitude northern hemisphere radiocarbon record. These patterns indicate that it is highly unlikely that this sample, and thus one may assume much of Thera away from the active volcanic vents/fumaroles, was effected to any substantive, let alone significant, way by old (depleted) volcanic CO_2 (Manning *et al.* 2009a: 300 and Fig. 1; Heinemeier *et al.* 2009: 288, 292; Höflmayer 2012a: 437–438): see also Section 3.c.III.i.d below. The radiocarbon age (3331 ± 10 ^{14}C years BP) for the last dated sample of the olive branch is very similar to the weighted average for the Akrotiri VDL, and especially for the low-date 'clump' of ages noted by Manning and Kromer (2012) (respectively 3345± 8 BP, and 3328 ± 9 BP or 3326 ± 11 BP). Thus, since the history of the radiocarbon record across the olive branch contradicts a substantive volcanic CO_2 effect, the similarity of the last dated segment with the Akrotiri VDL data on short-lived samples indicates that they too likely reflect radiocarbon ages that have not (typically) been affected to any material degree by volcanic CO_2. The other circumstances surrounding the location of the olive tree – several kilometers from the active volcanic area, high up a caldera wall in a location where there would have been good vertical and horizontal mixing of the atmosphere (and not the sort of location where volcanic CO_2, which is heavier than air, would, or could, accumulate) – also indicate that it is unlikely to have been affected by volcanic CO_2 (Friedrich and Heinemeier 2009; Friedrich 2009: 120–121).

Fourth: the overwhelming majority of the Akrotiri VDL data form a tight, coherent grouping, as evident in Figure RE1 above. Within the 28 date set used in Manning *et al.* (2006a), or the preferred 25–date set above (see Figure RE2), or the more recent 13 date subset published in that paper, there are no instances of substantially older ^{14}C ages of the sort that would typically identify samples affected by volcanic CO_2. Evidence from volcanic contexts where plants have been studied usually indicate significantly varying and localized (over time and by distance from source) but marked effects (that is hundreds to many hundreds to greater than 1000 ^{14}C years of effect where present) (Manning *et al.* 2009a: 301, 304 and Fig. 3 and citations) and see Figure RE8. The study of Pasquier-Cardin *et al.* (1999) of plant samples from degassing and non-degassing areas at Furnas volcano, Azores, provides a good and relevant example: see Figure RE8. Plants from areas with significant degassing exhibit marked (very clear) ^{14}C aging, and variable such marked effects. All the sites with these clear effects were in fields with degassing or close to fumaroles or bubbling water sources (Pasquier-Cardin *et al.* 1999: Table 1). Site HT had very low soil degassing but was *inside* the active caldera, and within a few hundred meters of marked fumaroles (Pasquier-Cardin *et al.* 1999: 198, Fig. 1, Table 1). This site exhibited some (2 of 5) samples with zero ^{14}C aging, but also two with minor to larger ^{14}C aging (22 and 72 ^{14}C years), but also one sample with large ^{14}C aging (369 ^{14}C years). Such clear variability is *not* evident in the 25–date or 13–date Akrotiri VDL dataset (see Figure RE2).[40] The control site *outside* the

---

[40] If the Akrotiri data had variation on the scale of even site HT (so 20% of the data +369 ^{14}C years, 20% +72 ^{14}C years, 20% +22 ^{14}C years and 40% plus 0 ^{14}C years), then we would not expect the data to pass a Chi-square test. For example, to take the 13 date set of ^{14}C measurements on short-lived samples from the Akrotiri VDL made in the AD2000s (Manning *et al.* 2006a), if we adjust these data

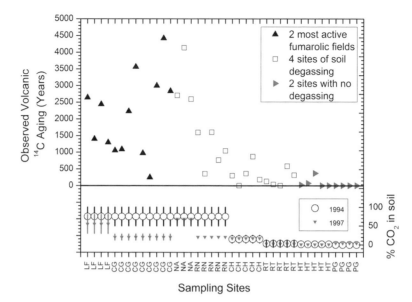

Figure RE8. Top: the observed apparent ^{14}C *aging of plant material from sites around the Furnas volcano, Azores, caused by volcanic* CO_2 *reported by Pasquier-Cardin* et al. *(1999). Samples collected in AD 1996 and AD 1997. Bottom: the percent* CO_2 *measured in the soil (in AD 1994 and then in AD 1997). Sites LF on the northern edge of Furnas Lake and CG in the eastern part of Furnas village had the most active fumarolic fields. Sites NA, RN, CH and RT from Furnas village had soil degassing of various levels and are all in the active caldera area. Site HT had low soil degassing but was inside the active caldera area and relatively close (few hundred meters to <1km) from marked fumaroles. Site PG was outside the active caldera and had very low soil degassing.*

younger caldera area and at least 1km away from the fumaroles marked in Pasquier-Cardin *et al.* (1999: Fig. 1) – site PG – showed zero (0) ^{14}C aging. The elevated site where the olive tree dated by Friedrich *et al.* (2006) grew was at least 3.5km from the active area of the volcano in the second millennium BC and it grew on a "thick, deeply weathered volcanic tuff" which attests to a lack of volcanic activity in this area (and so no likely significant degassing) (Friedrich 2009: 120); Akrotiri and its likely fields were this distance, and further, from the active volcanic area, and outside the caldera. Based on the Pasquier-Cardin *et al.* (1999) data from an active volcanic area, the likely volcanic ^{14}C aging effect

pro rata even on the least possible basis (so largest adjustment to the oldest data, etc.) – that is deduct 369 ^{14}C years from the 2 oldest ^{14}C data in the set, deduct 72 ^{14}C years from the next two oldest data, deduct 22 ^{14}C years from the next two latest data, and deduct 0 from the rest of the data – then the set dramatically fails a Chi-square test: T = 145.6 > 21.0 for df12 at the 5% level (following Ward and Wilson 1978). The same least possible exercise with the 25 date set from the Akrotiri VDL leads to a similar result and a dramatically failed Chi-squared test: T = 119.7 > 36.4 at df 24 at the 5% level. The contrast is clear with the actual ^{14}C data in either the 13 date set or the 25 date set, which both pass a Chi-square test (see Figure RE7). Hence we may reasonably conclude that there is no such volcanic CO_2 effect, even at the more minor site HT level from the study of Pasquier-Cardin *et al.* (1999), in the 25 or 13 date Akrotiri VDL datasets.

we may expect for the olive tree sample from Thera, and for the majority of the agricultural plant material found stored at Akrotiri on Thera, is zero.

Other evidence from areas with volcanic lakes or fossil CO_2 vents also indicates a clear – that is large – effect when present, such as in the results reported on two trees growing in the Ansanto Valley in Italy (Capano *et al.* 2012: Table 2, Fig. 2). Further, the effect (dilution) "appears to be variable for a range of years and different trees, probably due to their distance from the emitting source, the wind direction, and the intensity of the diluted CO_2 fumes" (Capano *et al.* 2012: 708). The study of Marzaioli *et al.* (2005) likewise demonstrated that a tree growing *very close (20m)* to a fossil emission source in Italy exhibited a clear (i.e. large) dilution offset versus the non-affected atmospheric record (Marzaioli *et al.* 2005: Table 1) – and even then – they note that this tree-ring record of a fossil diluted CO_2 effect reveals a non-constant enrichment of CO_2 (p.261). Soter (2011) in his review of the topic also notes the issue of spatial and temporal variability, commenting on p.66 that:

> The expected result is that while old CO_2 levels sufficient to produce measurable ^{14}C age increments would be found within large areas, *plants grown even in the same cultivated field may show a substantial range of apparent ages*. [my italics]

All these sorts of reports (and the other literature cited by e.g. Soter 2011), are not consistent with the Thera data sets, where evidence for a steadily declining ^{14}C level across time from the olive branch is the opposite of what should be expected if there was a volcanic/fossil CO_2 effect (both in terms of trend direction, and lack of variation/spikes) (see Figure RE18 below), and where there is a very consistent set of ages on different plants from different fields reported from the Akrotiri VDL (whereas some marked variability, or at least an inconsistent patterning, would be expected if a substantive volcanic/fossil CO_2 effect applied). To quote the conclusion of Soter (2011: 66):

> In such [tectonically active] areas … if short-lived samples from the same stratigraphic horizon yield a *wide range of ^{14}C ages*, the lower values may be the least altered by old CO_2. [my italics]

But the ^{14}C data on short-lived samples from the Akrotiri VDL, or on the olive branch, do *not* yield a "wide range of ^{14}C ages" – indeed the exact reverse, as discussed above (and see Figures RE1 to RE10 and Figures RE16 to RE18). Hence there seems little reason to believe any substantive volcanic (or similar) CO_2 effect applies in this case – and, as noted above ('second' argument), the ^{14}C dates from later LMIA Thera are similar to the ^{14}C ages available from a variety of other Aegean archaeological contexts of later LMIA or equivalent date where no volcanic CO_2 issue applies, which confirms this conclusion.

Overall, we may conclude that there is no obvious evidence for a volcanic/fossil CO_2 effect on the Akrotiri data, as noted in AD 1990 (Weninger 1990: 218–219) or AD 2009 (Manning *et al.* 2009a: 300–304). Among data from Akrotiri run some time ago (AD 1970s), two ages are far too old (two oldest data top right in Figure RE1, and two oldest data on right in Manning and Kromer 2011a: Fig. 1 no.3) – and in the past it has been speculated that these (alone) might reflect a volcanic CO_2 effect (Weninger 1990: 218–219). Otherwise, the 28 date set (or 25 date set if one removes the old Heidelberg data as admittedly an inconsistent three-date set), or the AD 2000s run 13 date set, are consistent sets as indicated by the fact that each passes a Chi-square test (as also Heinemeier *et al.* 2009: 288 regarding the initial 28 date set). They do not contain data with substantial and varying volcanic/fossil CO_2 input.

Wiener (2012: 429) raises the question whether a Ward and Wilson (1978) Type I situation applies to the data set on short-lived sample material from the Akrotiri VDL – all the data reflect radiocarbon estimates of the same real age – but it is reasonable or likely that all or nearly all these samples do in fact reflect a very short calendar interval (a year, to a few years, to around a decade at most) and thus can reasonably all be combined as an average in terms of a radiocarbon record resolved on decadal samples and modelled to 5-year increments (see text above). The samples from different plant species, and especially barley (*Hordeum* sp.) and vetch (*Lathyrus* sp.) for which we have several samples and dates for each, likely grew in different fields (Sarpaki 1990), and the harvested parts of each form at different heights off the ground. Yet they yield very similar radiocarbon results (Manning and Kromer 2012: 459–461 and Fig. 10). This too runs against the relevance of the volcanic CO_2 hypothesis, since such effects are typically localized and variable over space and through time. Alternatively, as discussed below, treating the Akrotiri VDL data instead as a distribution biased to the recent side – to accommodate fully the Wiener critique and so an 'even if' argument – yields an almost identical outcome in terms of a tight dating range from the set requiring a 'high' chronology age in the late 17th century BC (also Höflmayer 2012a: 436–437).

Fifth: as discussed in Manning and Kromer (2012), despite the Akrotiri VDL data yielding a satisfactory weighted average and every indication that the weighted average of the set of Akrotiri VDL ^{14}C ages indicates the appropriate ^{14}C age for the set (see text above), if one nonetheless observes that there is something of a low-date 'clump' in the Akrotiri datasets (whether 28 date set, or 13 date set – for the latter, see Figure RE5 above, and discussion in text and caption), and speculates that this might be (despite *no* actual positive evidence) because of some minor volcanic CO_2 or similar effect on some of the data (as suggested by the discussion of Soter 2011),[41] then one still ends

---

[41] The very weak positive evidence that does exist is the shape of the distribution of the ^{14}C dates (ages) within the sets. These distributions are biased a (very) little to the more recent side, and there is a slight low-date 'clump' of ages both with a substantial grouping of the data and also effectively defining the lowest end of the overall data spread (see Manning and Kromer 2012: Figs. 9 and 10) – and see Figure RE5 above. It is only a small issue and subjective (since the overall datasets also pass the Chi-square test with all the data being consistent with being the same event and the distribution observed may therefore just be within the expected random variation within any smaller set drawn from the assumed normal larger real population): the median of the 28 date set is 3340 BP versus the average (unweighted) of 3350 BP; and the median of the 13 date set is 3336 BP versus the (unweighted) average of 3345 BP (or median of total ^{14}C probability at 3339 BP versus weighted average value of 3344 BP for the 13 date set: as in Figure RE5). It might also be suggested that there is also something

up with a weighted average age for the Akrotiri VDL (from the low-date 'clumps') consistent with the last dated segment of the olive branch and with a most likely late 17th century BC date (when considered in isolation), or very clearly a most likely date in the late 17th century BC if considered as part of the Aegean sequence of data from before, contemporary with, and after the Akrotiri VDL. Use of the Tau_Boundary paired with a Boundary model – modelling an expected exponential distribution of the data biased to the recent end – also allows for the low-date 'clump' issue, and achieves the same late 17th century BC date range (see Section 3.c.III.1.b below; Höflmayer 2012a: 436–437). Thus, *even if* some small volcanic CO_2 effect might be present for some of the samples, the late 17th century BC dating remains the more appropriate conclusion.

Sixth: for many years a fall-back argument was that radiocarbon did not work in Egypt and thus perhaps somehow it did not work in other Old World areas – like the Aegean and east Mediterranean – south and east of the Renfrew's famous chronological fault line (1973: 116 Fig. 21). Keenan's (2002a) hypothesis of up-welling/de-gassing causing generally too old radiocarbon ages in the east Mediterranean is a similar line of argument. And scholars pointed to apparent inconsistencies, such as in Hood's article of AD 1978 entitled "Discrepancies in ^{14}C dating as illustrated from the Egyptian New and Middle Kingdoms and from the Aegean Bronze Age and Neolithic" (Hood 1978). In many cases the existing radiocarbon data from Egypt did in fact offer (or could be plausibly argued to offer) a reasonable, if rather approximate, picture (e.g. Manning 2006), but many were not convinced. However, this all changed with the large-scale sophisticated project on the radiocarbon dating and analysis of Egyptian samples reported by Bronk Ramsey *et al.* (2010). Radiocarbon was demonstrated to yield a good, precise, chronology fully consistent with the range of the historical Egyptian chronology – indeed it could offer grounds to favour which historical chronology was more likely accurate. New radiocarbon analyses of samples from the historically narrowly dated site of Tell el-Amarna in Egypt closely repeat this finding (Manning *et al.* 2013), and other recent studies have also shown a good correspondence between a radiocarbon based dating of Egyptian contexts and the Egyptian historical chronology (e.g. Franzmeier *et al.* 2011; Hassler and Höflmayer 2008). Thus, if radiocarbon could achieve an accurate and precise chronology in Egypt (disproving, again, the claim of Keenan 2002a for too old ^{14}C ages by several centuries for the region), there is now every reason to expect that it can do the same elsewhere in the east

---

of a more obvious if relatively minor tail off in ages to the higher side (see Figure RE3 and caption for example), and this could possibly reflect some varying very minor volcanic CO_2 (or other effect) on some of these dates. Choosing, subjectively, the low-date 'clump' might rule out any possible minor volcanic CO_2 effect (following the logic of Soter 2011), and offers the latest plausible date estimate for the Akrotiri VDL. But at the same time it should be stressed that this is a subjective view, and is a choosing of the latest possible ^{14}C age range for the VDL, and that the Soter hypotheses are, as he states, without actual positive evidence/support and have not as yet been observed/demonstrated in the field (Soter 2011: 66).

Mediterranean and Aegean. The close fit of detailed ^{14}C time-series from Aegean-region tree-ring series from both western Anatolia (Miletos) and central Anatolia (Gordion) during the mid second millennium BC further confirms that there seems to be no large-scale or region-wide aberrations in Aegean ^{14}C levels – but instead a fairly good agreement with the mid-latitude Northern Hemisphere record as represented by the IntCal dataset (Manning *et al.* 2010). Fine resolution and relatively very minor issues like possible small growing season offsets (as resolved for samples growing in Egypt: Dee *et al.* 2010) could be determined from such a large-scale and comprehensive project, and are being investigated for elsewhere in the Aegean and east Mediterranean (e.g. Manning *et al.* 2010; Manning and Kromer 2012). All evidence to date indicates that any offset relevant to the southern Aegean region is small to (effectively) non-existent, and would not change the chronological conclusions to be drawn from the available data.

In light of the good correspondence between radiocarbon analyses and Egyptian historical chronology elsewhere, the fact that the radiocarbon dating of the site of Tell el-Dab'a in Egypt consistently finds dates around a century or so older than those estimated by the excavator, based on his interpretation of stratigraphy and material culture and stylistic associations (Kutschera *et al.* 2012), must now lead to serious questions about this particular site and its supposed archaeological chronology for the contexts selected and for the site in general (Warburton 2009b), and *not* to questions about radiocarbon dating in general for the region. Moreover, the fact that the radiocarbon chronology for Tell el-Dab'a in fact offers a chronology more or less consonant with the Aegean 'high' chronology, and past suggestions for a revision of the dating of the site, might be argued to be yet more circumstantial evidence against some claim of an anomaly in Aegean or Thera radiocarbon dating in the LMIA period because of, e.g., volcanic CO_2, or something else, and instead for the likely approximate validity of the Akrotiri VDL radiocarbon data along with the other Aegean radiocarbon date sets.

Beyond the basic situation just summarized, if we consider the calendar date range indicated for the Akrotiri VDL and the Thera eruption from the radiocarbon data, we may further observe the following points:

(a) Akrotiri VDL ^{14}C dates in Isolation. In isolation, the Akrotiri VDL ^{14}C dates on short-lived samples indicate most likely a later to late 17th century BC date, whether treated as a weighted average (see discussion above for why this seems a reasonable approximation) – see above and Figures RE6 and RE7 – or instead as a phase (grouping) of data not necessarily all of identical (or very near identical) age and distributed with most coming from close to the final use of the relevant VDL contexts (a Tau_Boundary with Boundary model in OxCal: see Bronk Ramsey 2009a) (and as discussed also by Höflmayer 2012a: 437 and Fig. 2). Figure RE7 shows the calibrated calendar age probability and ranges for the weighted average of the data in the 25-date and 13-date sets discussed above (and see Figures RE1–5). Figure RE9 shows the calendar age

probability for a *terminus post quem* (TPQ) Boundary 'End' for, and/or a date for, the eruption from the same data modelled as a Phase with a Tau_Boundary to start and a Boundary ('End') to end (so there is an exponential distribution towards the end date – a point in late LMIA as exhibited by the Akrotiri VDL – which includes, or is very shortly before, e.g. by no more than c.0–2 years or so – see above, the eruption date). Figure RE9A uses all 28 data from Manning *et al.* (2006a), Figure RE9B uses the 25–date set (as in Figure RE2) excluding the 3 Heidelberg data, and Figure RE9C uses just the 13 dates run in the AD 2000s from Manning *et al.* (2006a). One of the 28 dates – Hd-6059–7967 with Posterior v. Prior of 15 v. 5 – is found to be a (clear) outlier applying the General outlier model of Bronk Ramsey (2009b). And as discussed above, there are good grounds for excluding the three Heidelberg dates altogether and instead using just the 25–date set in Figure RE2. The analysis of the 25–date set has no outliers and good Amodel and Aoverall values of 119.1 and 113.9 both well above the 60% threshold value in OxCal. The 13–date set also has no outliers and good Amodel and Aoverall values of 122.2 and 118.9. The findings from all three models are almost identical: see Figures RE9A-RE9C – as is the finding using a similar model reported by Höflmayer (2012a: 437 and Fig. 2). In Figure RE9B at 68.2% probability we see a date for mature to late LMIA and a date or short TPQ for the eruption of 1635–1609 BC (1661–1602 BC at 95.4% probability), and in Figure RE9C at 68.2 probability the date range is 1633–1607 BC (1663–1595 BC at 95.4% probability).

The Tau_Boundary model – a feature of OxCal 4 (Bronk Ramsey 2009a) which was not available when Manning *et al.* (2006a) was written – is arguably the most appropriate analytical approach for the Akrotiri data. Why? Well, notwithstanding the discussion above, as Wiener (2012: 429) writes with regard to the Manning *et al.* (2006a) analysis and the Akrotiri VDL dataset:

> For example, the Ward and Wilson Case I analysis has been applied to seeds from the Volcanic Destruction Level at Thera (Manning *et al.* 2006a, b). Here, however, it is not clear whether some of the seeds were collected before the preliminary eruption that caused the populace to flee, or between that point and the final phase, during which some returned to try to rescue items of value, nor whether all the seeds measured came from the same location with regard to its distance from preexisting point, fault, or field of gas emissions capable of producing distorting reservoir effects.

Thus, to allow for the possible reality of such concerns, and as Höflmayer (2012a: 437) also outlines, we could argue that the short-lived material from the Akrotiri VDL may not all represent exactly the same point in time, and so should rather be treated as a Phase in OxCal, since it is an unordered grouping of events, *but* with the data tending to represent the very latest time interval within this Phase (i.e. latest increment within the overall period of time represented by the short-lived sample materials recovered from the Aktoriri VDL). The following Boundary thus gives a date for the end of the VDL and a short *terminus post quem* for the closely subsequent eruption. The time period from the abandonment of the Akrotiri settlement (and earthquakes) – so end

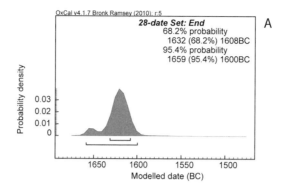

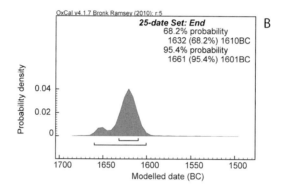

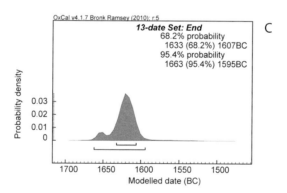

Figure RE9. The modelled End of the Akrotiri VDL phase = 'End' based on short-lived samples from the Akrotiri VDL grouped as a Phase with a Tau_Boundary as the start of the Phase and a Boundary at the end – to model exponentially distributed events tending towards the end of the Phase – using OxCal 4.1.7 (Bronk Ramsey 2009a) and IntCal09 with curve resolution set at 5. (A) employs the 28-date set in Manning et al. (2006a), (B) employs the 25-date subset of this set excluding the 3 Heidelberg dates as discussed above and as shown in Figure RE2, and (C) employs just the 13-date sub-set of measurements run in the AD 2000s as reported by Manning et al. (2006a). Note: it is possible to get slight variations in outputs from modelling runs in OxCal, typically within 0-2 years at most.

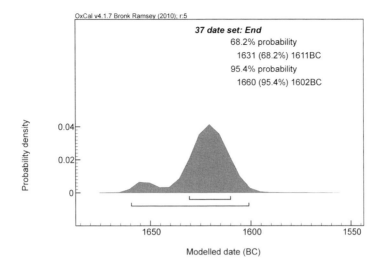

Figure RE10. The modelled End of the Akrotiri VDL phase = 'End' based on 37 short-lived samples from the Akrotiri VDL (Figure RE1 dataset minus 6 outliers indicated there) grouped as a Phase with a Tau_Boundary as the start of the Phase and a Boundary at the end – to model exponentially distributed events tending towards the end of the Phase – using OxCal 4.1.7 (Bronk Ramsey 2009a) and IntCal09 (Reimer et al. 2009) with curve resolution set at 5. Note: it is possible to get slight variations in outputs from modelling runs in OxCal, typically within 0-2 years at most. The model has satisfactory Amodel and Aoverall values of 89.2 > 60 and 73.5 > 60 and only 1 very minor (6 > 5) outlier (P-1888) applying the General model of Bronk Ramsey (2009b).

of the VDL – to the beginning of the eruption sequence, while short, represents at least a short period of time but "probably not longer than a year" (Cioni *et al.* 2000: 721, 724), or maybe at most as long as a few years (Limbrey 1990: esp. 380). In general terms, therefore, the Tau_Boundary paired with a Boundary dating of the Boundary after the VDL data represents both the end of the VDL, and, within no more than 1 to a few years, the date of the subsequent eruption, since the geological and archaeological evidence indicates only a short-lived timespan between the precursor eruption and the very violent main eruption ("a few months, certainly no more than a year": McCoy 2009: 80) (see also: Sparks and Wilson 1990; Cioni *et al.* 2000: 720–721; Friedrich 2009: 83–90; McCoy 2009). As discussed above, the fact we have charred seeds from the Akrotiri buildings also indicates material both charred by the main eruption and likely not in their storage vessels for more than 0–2 years – hence again from a very short (few years at most) range of time before the end of the VDL and the shortly subsequent eruption. The date of the final Boundary on such a model, grouping all the Akrotiri VDL short-lived samples as a Phase using a Tau_Boundary paired with a Boundary to define the final Boundary of what is assumed to be more or less an exponential distribution of the data ramped towards the end of the Phase, is as shown in Figure RE9. This model, which best accommodates the concerns highlighted by Wiener (2012: 249), and could be held to be more appropriate than treating all samples as being of (more or less) the same age (even if this is likely true for most of the samples in question), yields a clear date solution for the end of the late LMIA VDL at Akrotiri (and so a date generally for the late LMIA period in the Aegean) in the late 17th century BC.

How robust are the data and this finding? We can consider two experiments. First we can try a Tau_Boundary paired with a Boundary model on the larger set of 43 published radiocarbon dates on short-lived samples from the Thera VDL collected in Manning and Kromer (2011a: Fig. 1 no.3; see Figure RE1 above) – this includes older technology data on definite short-lived sample material from the University of Pennsylvania laboratory (now long closed) and three data on short-lived samples from the ETH Laboratory included in the list of data in Kutschera and Stadler (2000: Table 2). Six of these data are outliers from the General outlier model of Bronk Ramsey (2009b);[42] the Tau_boundary paired with a Boundary model from the remaining 37 data (86% of the initial set) yields the probability distribution for the late LMIA VDL at Akrotiri shown in Figure RE10. The second and alternative possibilities are to consider what if the samples do not distribute towards the very end of the VDL Phase. We can consider a middle alternative and an extreme alternative scenario. The middle alternative – the default assumption in OxCal – is to assume that the group of dates (events) represented are a random sample from a uniform distribution, i.e., that we have a random scatter of events between a start Boundary and an end Boundary. Thus the samples can distribute themselves as they like within a uniform Phase rather than with the assumption of an exponential distribution towards the end of the Phase (as in Figure RE9). If we follow this strategy and take the 25 date set (see Figure RE2) and treat all the dates as a Phase with a Boundary at the start and a Boundary at the end, then the End Boundary represents a date estimate for the end of the Akrotiri VDL and a close TPQ estimate for the shortly subsequent Thera eruption. This is shown in Figure RE11A. The distribution is very similar to the ones with the Tau_Boundary paired with Boundary model (Figure RE9) – highlighting that we have a tight, consistent, set of data which – as a set or Phase – describe a (very) short calendar interval. The extreme alternative scenario is to reverse the assumptions shown in Figure RE9. Thus we suppose that the samples dated were perhaps all in their storage jars for the maximum likely storage period and even perhaps a little longer – abandoned by their owners – before being charred by the eruption. Thus perhaps the samples in fact are distributed towards the older (and not most recent) end of the range available in the VDL ^{14}C dataset. We can model this with a Boundary paired with a Tau_Boundary model – the opposite of

---

[42] The dates found to be outliers are (far too old end of the set) P-2560 (Posterior v. Prior of 98 > 5), P-2561 (97 > 5), ETH-3315 (86 > 5), and (from the far too recent end of the set) Hd-6059–7967 (31 > 5), P-1888 (91 > 5), and P-1697 (97 > 5).

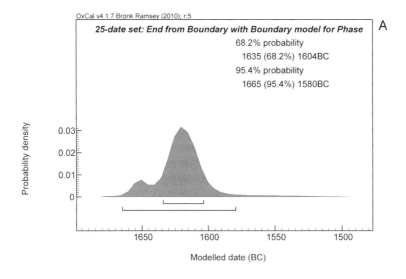

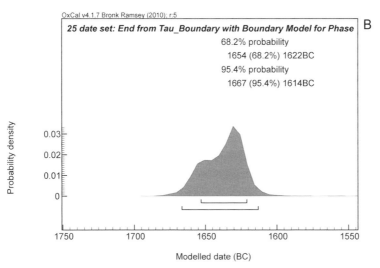

Figure RE11. Alternative End Boundaries for the 25 date set of ^{14}C ages on short-lived samples from the Akrotiri VDL (see Figure RE2). A at the top shows the End Boundary if the 25 date set is treated as a Phase with start and end Boundaries and thus an assumption of a uniform distribution of dates within the Phase. B at the bottom shows the opposite of the models in Figures RE9 and RE10. It assumes a Phase with the dates exponentially distributed towards the start (old end) of the Phase using a Boundary paired with a Tau_Boundary model. Data from OxCal 4.1.7 (Bronk Ramsey 2009a) and IntCal09 (Reimer et al. 2009) with curve resolution set at 5. Note: it is possible to get slight variations in outputs from modelling runs in OxCal, typically within 0-2 years at most.

	Date Range for the End Boundary of the Akrotiri late LMIA VDL and TPQ for the Thera volcanic eruption assuming ¹⁴C dates exponentially distributed towards the end of the VDL Phase (see text)	
	68.2% Probability	*95.4% Probability*
37 (from 43) date set	1631–1611 BC	1660–1602 BC
28 date set	1632–1608 BC	1659–1600 BC
25 date set	1632–1610 BC	1661–1601 BC
13 date set	1633–1607 BC	1663–1595 BC

Table RE2. Calibrated calendar date ranges at 68.2% and 95.4% probability for the Boundary describing a date for late in, or at the close of, the late LMIA VDL at Akrotiri on Thera and thus a (short) terminus post quem (TPQ) date range for the subsequent eruption of the Akrotiri/Thera volcano. Starting data sets comprising 43 ¹⁴C dates (using 37 dates: see Figure RE1), 28 ¹⁴C dates (see Figure RE2), 25 ¹⁴C dates (see Figure RE2), or 13 ¹⁴C dates: see text. For the probability distributions, see Figures RE9 and RE10; data from a Tau_Boundary paired with a Boundary model for the Phase of Akrotiri VDL radiocarbon dates on short-lived samples using OxCal 4.1.7 (Ramsey 2009a; 2009b) and IntCal09 (Reimer et al. 2009) with curve resolution set at 5.

the examples in Figures RE9 and RE10. If we consider this scenario for the 25 date set, we get the alternative probability distribution shown in Figure RE11B. The notable observation is that the age range (1654–1622 BC at 68.2% probability) is only slightly older than for the opposite Tau_Boundary paired with Boundary model in Figure RE9B (1632–1610 BC). Thus again we see that the Akrotiri VDL dataset on short-lived samples is a tight one describing a single short period/event and cannot be manipulated to describe a substantially different period by making different assumptions.

If we assume that the distribution towards the end of the VDL Phase – the Tau_Boundary paired with Boundary model – is in fact the more plausible and likely one from the archaeology (as also Höflmayer 2012a: 437 and Fig. 2) – then we get a date range for the End Boundary, the close of the Akrotiri VDL Phase and a short TPQ for the Thera eruption, from the various date sets discussed and illustrated above as summarized in Table RE2. The date ranges are all almost identical. Thus this late 17th century BC date range (1633/32/31 to 1611/10/08/07 BC at 68.2% probability) for the end of the late LMIA VDL at Akrotiri, and close TPQ for the shortly subsequent volcanic eruption, is a robust date – and a date entirely compatible with the date estimated from the last extant growth increment of the olive branch argued to have been killed by the eruption (see (c) below this Section). This finding provides strong support for the view that this branch was *not* long dead at the time of the eruption, and instead was living and part of a tree killed and buried by the eruption as argued by Friedrich *et al.* (2006; 2009; Friedrich and Heinemeier 2009).

(b) Aegean Sequence analysis. When placed in the available Aegean stratigraphic-archaeological sequence of radiocarbon data from before, around the time

of, and after the Thera eruption, as published in Manning *et al.* (2006a), or with some subsequent data added (e.g. Manning and Bronk Ramsey 2009; Manning and Kromer 2012: Fig. 13), or with additional considerations (such as calibration dataset to be employed or possible small-scale regional growing-season related ^{14}C offsets: Manning *et al.* 2010; Manning and Kromer 2011a; 2012), the Akrotiri VDL is also dated most likely and robustly in the later/late 17th century BC (Manning *et al.* 2006a; 2009a; Manning and Bronk Ramsey 2009; Manning and Kromer 2011a; 2012): see Figures RE12 to RE14 for three examples. The sequence of data helps eliminates the otherwise possible 16th century BC ambiguity – since some of the subsequent LMIB data occupies the 16th century BC time range. Figure RE12 shows the sequence of data as published in Manning *et al.* (2006a) but using just the 25–date Akrotiri VDL set (see above) and adding some other data (from Akrotiri from Maniatis 2010 – except two too old data, i.e. residual charcoal or charcoal from inner tree-rings, DEM-1455, DEM-1646, with OxCal Agreement Index values <10 – and from Mochlos LMIB Final from Soles 2004) using weighted averages for the sets of short-lived data from the same 'destruction' contexts but with the Chania data treated as a Phase with a Tau_Boundary paired with a Boundary since these data (i) range somewhat in ^{14}C time and (ii) do not all come from the same find contexts even if all are from LMIB 'destruction' contexts at the site, and so might be best modelled as within a Phase but distributed towards the end of the Phase (as in Manning and Kromer 2012: Fig. 13). The LMIB period archaeological phasing follows Rutter (2011). To allow for and test for any apparent southern Aegean region growing season or similar ^{14}C offset – believed to be small to effectively negligible based on current data (Manning *et al.* 2010; Manning and Kromer 2012) – a ΔR factor of 0 ± 10 ^{14}C years is also added. Figure RE13 considers the same sequence but with the Akrotiri VDL, the Chania LMIB Phase, the Myrtos-Pyrgos LMIB Late Phase, the Mochlos LMIB Final Phase, and the Knossos LMII Destruction Phase all considered as Phases with the constituent dates distributed towards the end of the Phases employing a Tau_Boundary paired with a Boundary model (and not weighted averages). Figure RE14 is the same as Figure RE13 except that it adds consideration of, and a test for, a ΔR factor of 0 ± 10 ^{14}C. Figure RE15 shows in more detail the main Tau_Boundary start and End Boundaries for the period from the Akrotiri VDL to the LMII destruction at Knossos from Figure RE13. The dates for five of the main findings (End Boundaries) from the models shown in Figures RE13 to RE14 are listed in Table RE3B.

In each case, the models show a clear late 17th century BC date range for the end of the Akrotiri VDL, and so the closely subsequent Thera eruption. All the models indicate a lengthy period of around or more than a century from the Thera eruption (late 17th century BC) to the LMIB destructions in the early to mid 15th century BC (see further in Manning 2014; see Postscript (vi)). This is an important change compared to the previous conventional chronologies with short LMIB periods, but appears consistent with the archaeological evidence which now indicates a long overall LMIB period (see discussion in Section 2

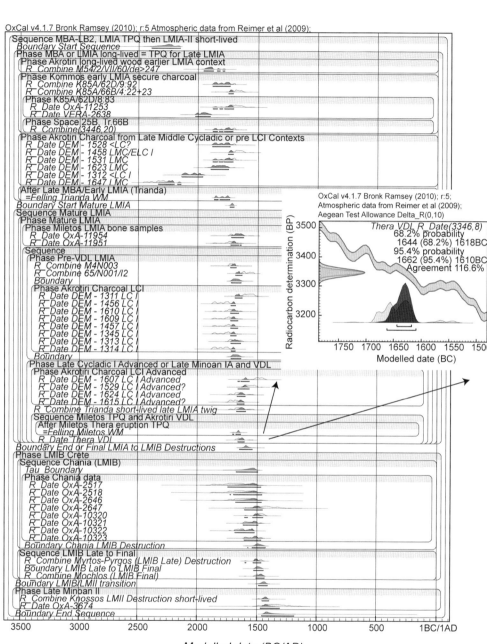

above), and especially as summarized by Rutter (2011). The dates for the LMIB destructions and for the LMII destruction at Knossos are more or less compatible with the conventional chronology, and with the (non-disputed) evidence of linkages of late LMIB products and influences into the reign of Tuthmosis III (see also Manning 2009). What is changed is the date for LMIA – where we have very poor, scarce, or absent secure archaeological correlations – and the length of the LMIB period. The well-known LMIB correlations with Egypt – and certainly those from the reign of Tuthmosis III – are it seems mainly from the later even late part of the long LMIB period. We lack recognition so far of earlier LMIB material in the east Mediterranean.

It is very possible that some of this 'gap' in apparent material and trade relates to the impacts of the enormous Thera volcanic eruption. As Knappett *et al.* (2011) have discussed and modelled, the catastrophic destruction of Thera and the major Aegean and international port there, likely would have had serious systemic knock-on effects *over time* for the rest of the Aegean and especially Crete. These problems and the elimination of previous modes and routes of trade, not only may have played a general role in creating conditions for economic (and political) change (Minoan palatial collapse or reorientation later in LMIB), but may have led to various individuals and groups on Crete actively looking for, and trying to develop, new and alternative trade connections. This could potentially account for the *later* LMIB connections seen (somewhat all of a sudden) in Egypt, even potentially a scenario where the

---

Figure RE12 (opposite). Analysis of the sequence of data as published in Manning et al. *(2006a) but using just the 25-date Akrotiri VDL set (see text above) and adding some additional data (from Akrotiri from Maniatis 2010 – except two too old data, i.e. residual charcoal or charcoal from inner tree-rings, DEM-1455, DEM-1646, with OxCal Agreement Index values <10 – and from Mochlos LMIB Final from Soles 2004). The model employs weighted averages for the sets of short-lived data from the same 'destruction' contexts, except for the Chania data which are treated as a Phase with a Tau_Boundary paired with a Boundary since these data (i) range somewhat in ¹⁴C time and (ii) do not all come from the same find contexts even if they are all from LMIB 'destruction' contexts at the site, and so might be best modelled as within a Phase but distributed towards the end of the Phase (as in Manning and Kromer 2012: Fig. 13). The LMIB period archaeological phasing follows Rutter (2011). To allow for and test for any apparent southern Aegean region growing season or similar ¹⁴C offset – believed to be small to effectively negligible based on current data (Manning* et al. *2010; Manning and Kromer 2012) – a ΔR factor of 0 ± 10 ¹⁴C years is also added. This returns a ΔR distribution with a μ±σ value of -3.3 ± 6.9 which is small to negligible. Results for some key events are listed in Table RE3A below. Data from OxCal 4.1.7 (Bronk Ramsey 2009a) and IntCal09 (Reimer* et al. *2009) with curve resolution set at 5. Amodel 80.2 > 60 and Aoverall 72 > 60. The horizontal lines under each probability distribution indicate the 95.4% modelled ranges. Note: it is possible to get slight variations in outputs from modelling runs in OxCal, typically within 0-2 years at most. The Inset shows in detail the probability modelled for the weighted average of the 25-date set of short-lived samples from the Akrotiri VDL.*

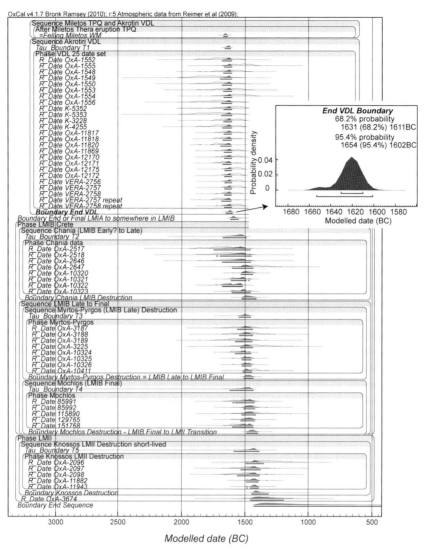

Figure RE13. Analysis of the same sequence and data as in Figure RE12 but with the Akrotiri VDL, the Chania LMIB Phase, the Myrtos-Pyrgos LMIB Late Phase, the Mochlos LMIB Final Phase and the Knossos LMII Destruction Phase all considered as Phases with the constituent dates distributed towards the end of the Phases employing a Tau_Boundary paired with a Boundary model (and so not using weighted averages). Only the results for the sequence that differ from those shown in Figure RE12, i.e. from the first Tau_Boundary (start of the Akrotiri VDL Phase), are shown in order to keep the number of elements in the plot down to a reasonable number (and so legible). The dates for the End Boundary for these five Phases are listed in Table RE3B below. Data from OxCal 4.1.7 (Bronk Ramsey 2009a) and IntCal09 (Reimer et al. 2009) with curve resolution set at 5. The horizontal lines under each probability distribution indicate the 95.4% modelled ranges. Amodel = 76.5 > 60 and Aoverall = 76.4 > 60. Note: it is possible to get slight variations in outputs from modelling runs in OxCal, typically within 0-2 years at most. The Inset shows in detail the probability modelled for the weighted average of the 25-date set of short-lived samples from the Akrotiri VDL.

	Akrotiri VDL	*End* Chania LMIB	Myrtos-Pyrgos LMIB Late Destruction	Mochlos LMIB Final Destruction	Knossos LMII Destruction
Figure RE12 68.2%	1644–1618 BC	1512–1463 BC	1521–1495 BC	1484–1449 BC	1439–1414 BC
Figure RE12 95.4%	1662–1610 BC	1577–1419 BC	1599–1465 BC	1508–1437 BC	1456–1399 BC
Figure RE12 μ ± σ	1634 ± 15 BC	1489 ± 28 BC	1510 ± 22 BC	1471 ± 18 BC	1427 ± 14 BC
No ΔR 68.2%	1639–1618 BC	1509–1461 BC	1518–1495 BC	1482–1449 BC	1437–1413 BC
No ΔR 95.4%	1656–1612 BC	1525–1434 BC	1529–1468 BC	1502–1438 BC	1451–1400 BC
No ΔR μ ± σ	1631 ± 12 BC	1484 ± 24 BC	1505 ± 16 BC	1468 ± 16 BC	1425 ± 13 BC

Table RE3A. Top: the calibrated calendar age ranges modelled for the weighted averages for the end of site phase destructions at the Akrotiri VDL, LMIB Late Myrtos-Pyrgos, LMIB Final Mochlos and LMII Knossos and the end of phase (Tau_Boundary paired with a Boundary) Boundary for LMIB Chania from the model in Figure RE12. The Figure RE12 model includes an extra ΔR factor of 0 ± 10 ¹⁴C years to allow for possible small regional ¹⁴C differences (versus the IntCal09 calibration curve record). This leads to a couple of much wider ranges, notably for the Myrtos-Pyrgos set at 95.4% probability and the end of the Chania Phase at 95.4% probability: compare with the data outputs without the ΔR factor of 0 ± 10 ¹⁴C years listed in the lower half of Table RE3A. Bottom: as top but from the model in Figure RE12 run without the ΔR factor of 0 ± 10 ¹⁴C.

	End Akrotiri VDL	*End* Chania LMIB	*End* Myrtos-Pyrgos LMIB Late	*End* Mochlos LMIB Final	*End* Knossos LMII
Figure RE13 68.2%	1631–1611BC	1509–1452 BC	1496–1456 BC	1466–1424 BC	1431–1386 BC
Figure RE13 95.4%	1654–1602 BC	1526–1413 BC	1510–1435 BC	1489–1402 BC	1447–1316 BC
Figure 13 μ ± σ	1623 ± 11 BC	1477 ± 30 BC	1473 ± 19 BC	1444 ± 21 BC	1396 ± 37 BC
Figure RE14 68.2%	1637–1611 BC	1513–1454 BC	1501–1457 BC	1469–1425 BC	1435–1385 BC
Figure RE14 95.4%	1657–1604 BC	1573–1409 BC	1516–1436 BC	1494–1404 BC	1453–1311 BC
Figure 14 μ ± σ	1627 ± 14 BC	1482 ± 33 BC	1477 ± 21 BC	1447 ± 22 BC	1398 ± 40 BC

Table RE3B. The calibrated calendar age ranges modelled for the End Boundaries in Figures RE13 and RE14 for the Akrotiri VDL Phase, Chania LMIB Phase, Myrtos-Pyrgos LMIB Late Phase, the Mochlos LMIB Final Phase and the Knossis LMII Phase. These ranges are terminus ante quem ranges, for the relevant Phase of data (e.g the Myrtos-Pyrgos LMIB Late destruction, and so on). Note that the recent end of the LMII distribution, seen especially in the 95.4% probability range, is poorly constrained (see Figures RE12–RE14) as the model stops with the LMII data.

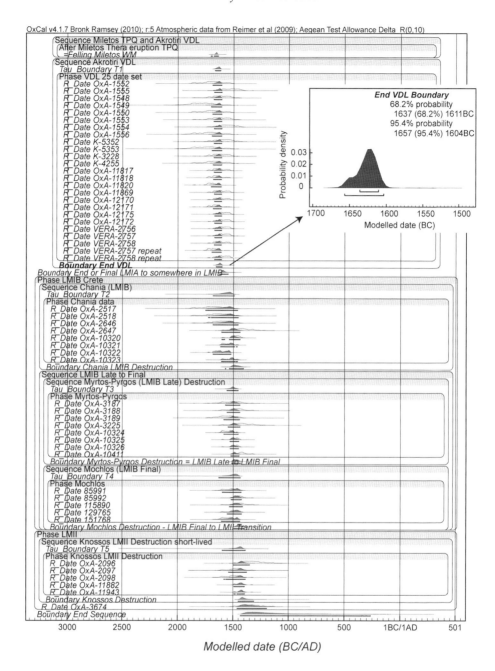

Figure RE14. As Figure RE13 but with an allowance for, and test for, any apparent southern Aegean region growing season or similar ¹⁴C offset – believed to be small to effectively negligible based on current data (Manning et al. 2010; Manning and Kromer 2012) – by incorporating a ΔR factor of 0 ± 10 ¹⁴C years. This returns a ΔR distribution with a µ±σ value of -4.2 ± 6.9 which is small to negligible (as found in the model in Figure RE12). Amodel = 99.8 > 60 and Aoverall = 89.2 > 60.

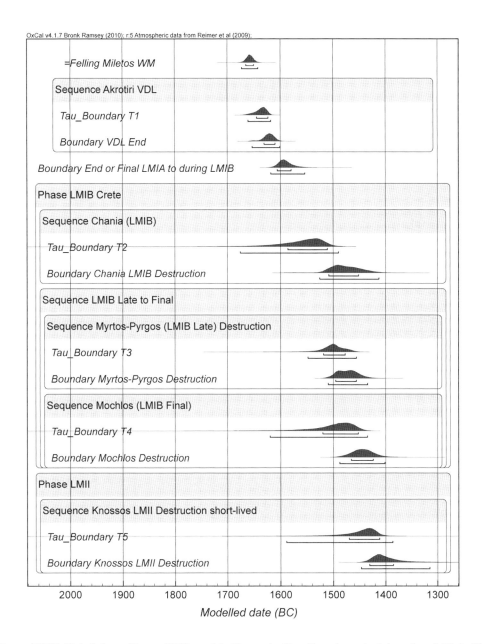

Figure RE15. Detail from Figure RE13 model. The main Tau_Boundary start (numbered T1 to T5) and End Boundaries for the period from the Akrotiri VDL through to the LMII destruction at Knossos are shown from Figure RE13. The upper and lower horizontal lines under each probability distribution indicate, respectively, the modelled 68.2% and 95.4% probability ranges (as also listed in Table RE3B).

Minoans (Keftiu)[43] were seeking alliances (and even help) during the reign of Tuthmosis III. We can note that this is the time when LMI style Keftiu start to appear in wall paintings in some Theban tombs in upper Egypt in such an ambassadorial/embassy/tribute guise from the earlier part of the reign of Tuthmosis III, and Aegean products and influences appear visibly in Egypt (as summarized by e.g. Warren and Hankey 1989: 138–144; Höflmayer 2009: 189–194; for other basic information and references on the Keftiu scenes, see Manning 1999: 209–213 – and more recently Panagiotopoulos 2001), and before the subsequent LMII-IIIA style Keftiu follow by late in the long reign of Tuthmosis III (Manning 1999: 213–220 and references).

(c) Thera olive branch. Friedrich *et al.* (2006) reported an olive tree branch found in the Plinian pumice fall on Thera and argued that this tree (and branch) was killed by the eruption. Since olive wood is not suitable for normal dendrochronological methods (it lacks visible regular annual growth rings), this team employed X-ray tomography to try to resolve what they argued were annual growth increments in the wood and they used this information to undertake a ^{14}C dendro wiggle-match on the sample to estimate the date of the last extant growth ring, which they argued was the year of the tree's death, and so the year of the Thera eruption (see also Friedrich *et al.* 2009; Friedrich and Heinemeier 2009; Friedrich 2009: 109–117). Recognising the lack of control on their estimated 'ring' counting, Friedrich *et al.* (2006) considered error estimates on the ring count up to 50% and yet found similar dates – hence they claimed they had a robust date.

Since the analysis of Friedrich *et al.* (2006) found a late 17th century BC eruption date (1627–1600 BC at 95.4% probability, sometimes stated as 1613 ± 13 BC), consistent with the 'high' chronology, this evidence has come under attack by the 'low' chronology grouping (e.g. Wiener 2009a: 282–283, 321–323, 329–330; 2009b: 204–206; 2010: 373 and citations). The most obvious line of criticism has been the supposed 'ring' count (72) on the olive sample as used in the ^{14}C wiggle-match – since recognizing such annual growth increments in olive wood is problematic at best (as noted by Wiener 2010: 373 – and subsequently see the more detailed study of Cherubini *et al.* 2013, which discusses and highlights the same problem). However, this is in fact not a major issue, since we do not need any ring count to achieve a reasonably precise dating of the olive branch. A Sequence analysis simply using the direction of growth (and no tree-rings) on the olive branch sample allows a fairly precise dating while entirely circumventing any arguments over whether or not Friedrich *et al.* were correct about being able to recognize annual growth increments in olive using X-ray tomography (on such relative sequence analyses, see Revisit Essay Appendix 3 below; see also the Postscript (ii) below). Such an analysis (see Figure RE16) places the centre of the last dated wood segment at 1637–1610

---

[43] This usual assumption – the equivalence of Keftiu with Crete – is, however, questioned by Vandersleyen (2003), who argues that there is no good evidence to make the link – but against, see Quack (2007: 334–337).

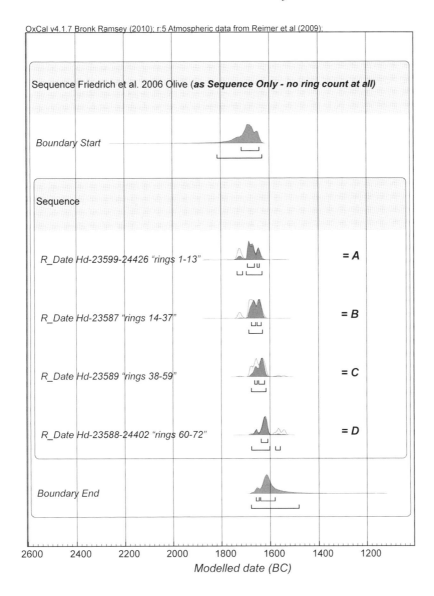

Figure RE16. Sequence analysis of the ¹⁴C data reported from the olive branch from Thera/Santorini (Friedrich et al. 2006) with no ring count input, and instead just using the sequence of oldest innermost segment to most recent outermost segment as required by tree growth (regardless of whether tree-growth increments, such as rings, can or cannot be observed). The individual calibrated probability distributions are shown by the light grey histograms; the modelled calibrated probability distributions are indicated by the dark grey histograms. The upper and lower lines under each probability distribution indicate (respectively) the most likely 68.2% and 95.4% modelled age ranges. For a detail of the placement of the last (outermost) dated segment, see Figure RE17. Data from OxCal 4.1.7. (Bronk Ramsey 2009a) and IntCal09 (Reimer et al. 2009) with curve resolution set at 5. Amodel 124.8 > 60, Aoverall 124.2 > 60.

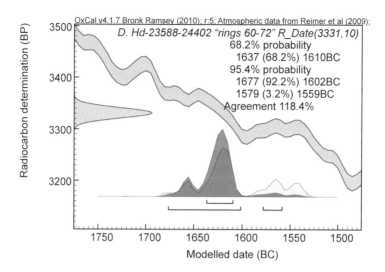

Figure RE17. Detail of the calendar dating probability distribution and most likely 68.2% and 95.4% probability age ranges for the outermost segment of the olive branch from the Sequence analysis shown in Figure RE16.

BC at 68.2% probability: see Figure RE17. But in this case we do not know how many years lie between this point and the exterior of the sample (if we dismiss the claimed ring count), and there is also a lack of clarity over whether or not bark was present or whether there may be missing years between the last preserved wood on the sample and the original bark. Thus the date calculated in Figure RE17 is a *terminus post quem* for the Thera eruption – and the length of the 'post' is not known, though we may guess it is not too long (nonetheless, this evidence usefully helps change one aspect of the Thera debate: it helps rule out a mid-17th century BC date and instead points towards a date for the Thera eruption especially in the late 17th century BC, or potentially a little later).

Some estimate of the scale of the time interval from the middle of the last dated segment of the olive branch (Figure RE17) to the last wood extant in the sample (argued to be the likely time of death) can be made by comparing the calculated calendar intervals between the mid-points of the four dated segments of the olive sample (A, B, C, D) versus the scale of these intervals in terms of the overall physical sample length (based on visual examination of the images in the Frontispiece to Warburton 2009a). I estimate that the percentage distance between the centre of segment A to the centre of segment B is c.27% of the overall sample length, from B to C c.36% and from C to D c.25%. Interestingly, these values are relatively similar to the percentages based on the approximate ring counts reported from X-ray tomography – which make the centre of A to centre of B distance 26% of the total (72 rings) sample, B to C 32% of the total and C to D 24% of the total. The calendar intervals calculated by OxCal from the modelling shown in Figure RE16 between the mid-points of segments A-B, B-C and C-D are -2 to 23 years, -2 to 19 years and -2 to 18 years at 68.2% probability (μ±σ of 18±18, 14±14, 15±18 years). If we use the μ±σ values, about 88% of the sample represents about 47±27 years or 20 to 74 calendar years. The distance from the centre of the last dated segment (D) to the recent edge of the sample (stated to be "the last ring … formed in the year of the eruption": Warburton 2009a: Frontispiece) is about 7% of the total sample length. Thus this distance on an approximate average basis would likely equate to between c.2 and 7 years (using the μ±σ ranges above and rounding to the nearest whole integer). This range of course includes the estimate of 6 years from the X-ray tomography. In very round terms, we could say that less than about 10 years is indicated.

We can easily and approximately quantify the resultant outer growth increment date: if we allow for ten extra years from the mid-point of the last dated section to original bark, then the date for the last increment is approximately 1627–1600 BC at 68.2% probability (1667–1592 BC at 92.2% probability and 1569–1549 BC at 3.2% probability looking at the 95.4% probability range), or, if we allow even double this, and so x10 to almost x3 from our above estimate (of 2–7 years), and so allow 20 years, then the date is 1617–1590 BC at 68.2% probability and so on. We thus find that even without the ring count employed by Friedrich *et al.* (2006), the likely date of the last extant growth increment is very similar to the dates proposed by Friedrich *et al.* (2006), and very likely to be in the last three decades of the 17th century BC. This late 17th century BC date range is therefore fairly robust.

At this point, the only real counter argument is to argue that this tree, or this branch anyway, was not in fact killed by the eruption, but was perhaps already dead at the time of the eruption (for just this argument, see e.g. Wiener 2009b: 204–206; 2010: 373 and citations – see against Friedrich *et al.* 2009; Friedrich and Heinemeier 2009; Friedrich 2009: 117–120). This is of course special pleading – but at the same time it is true that dead branches can be found on olive trees, and Wiener (2009b: 205) finds two experts (O. Rackham and H. Blitzer) to support this assertion. It is more or less impossible to disprove this possibility – much though Friedrich *et al.* (2009; Friedrich and Heinemeier 2009) provide grounds for thinking the branch and tree were both alive at the time of the eruption. But it is an extraordinary coincidence that the ^{14}C wiggle match of the olive branch gives a date for the last growth increment that is almost exactly compatible with the analysis of the large set of short-lived samples from the Akrotiri VDL. The ^{14}C wiggle match tells us that this branch stopped growing/ died likely somewhere in the last 3 decades of the 17th century BC. The Wiener argument is that this dead branch was then borne by the olive tree for another 50–100 years before the 'low' chronology date of the Thera eruption. The dead branch scenario (Wiener 2009b: 205) while possible in isolation, becomes very implausible when the large set of short-lived samples from the Akrotiri VDL indicate a date range around the very same time as, or just before, the date for the last growth increment of the olive branch. This coincidence seems to have only one obvious and plausible explanation: the olive branch (and tree) was in fact alive until killed and buried by the Thera volcanic eruption.

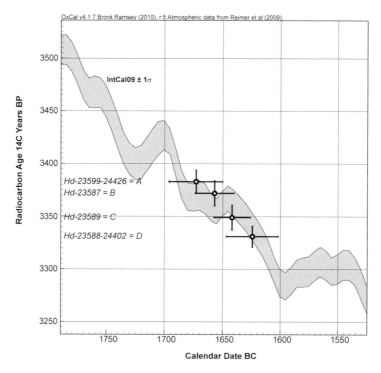

Figure RE18. Comparison of the pattern and placement of the ^{14}C dates on the dated segments from the Thera/Santorini olive branch (Friedrich et al. 2006) in Figure RE16 against the mid-latitude Northern Hemisphere atmospheric ^{14}C record of IntCal09 (Reimer et al. 2009). The olive branch data are shown as the $\mu \pm \sigma$ ranges (of the modelled ranges in Figure RE16) on the calendar (x) axis, and as the published ^{14}C ages from Friedrich et al. (2006) $\pm 1\sigma$ on the ^{14}C (y) axis. The olive branch data match the shape and trend of the IntCal09 curve closely, and do not exhibit any indications of too old ^{14}C values – as would be anticipated if there had been any substantial volcanic CO_2 effect relevant to these samples.

It has also been argued that this olive branch is a single (if large) sample and – for some unspecified/unknown reasons – it needs further replication before we can be sure. Of course, such a standard requiring strict replication of any unique find before it can be employed would rule out a great deal of archaeological data (and the entire 'low' chronology case for the MMIII to LMII period, starting of course with the single and now lost WSI bowl from Thera). In contrast, it is one of the strengths of the 'high' chronology case: multiple samples run at multiple laboratories yielding approximately the same outcomes. Nonetheless, replication is the foundation of science, and other olive/tree samples from Thera would (of course) be desirable. A second olive branch has in fact been mentioned and shown in preliminary statements (e.g. Friedrich and Heinemeier 2009: 59–61; Friedrich 2009: 118–119 box 7.7), and a multi-laboratory radiocarbon dating project is being carried out (at the time I write) to compare age findings on some samples of the first olive branch (J. Heinemeier, pers. comm 2011; B. Kromer, pers. comm. 2012). Full publication of the second branch and these new data is awaited, but the indications are that the dating reported from the original olive branch is probably reasonably sound (as above) – a contiguous pattern and period of ^{14}C ages best placed as leading down towards the marked dip in the ^{14}C calibration curve shortly after 1600 BC (e.g. c.1685–1595 BC with IntCal09 covering 3394–3321 ^{14}C years BP at 1σ, see Figure RE18 – and e.g. 1690–1590 BC with IntCal13, see Figure RE40 below, covering 3414–3264 ^{14}C years BP at 1σ).

   A further line of would-be criticism is to speculate whether volcanic CO_2 could be relevant to the olive branch sample (e.g. Wiener 2009b: 205 also pp. 201–203): see Section 3.c.III.i.a above. In this case, as noted above, the data from the olive branch indicate the exact opposite (Manning *et al.* 2009a: 300). The four sequential ^{14}C dates from the olive branch sample – an older to most recent sequence regardless of whether or not any 'ring' count is possible (as discussed above) – show a pattern over time (c.20–74 years at 1SD based solely on the ^{14}C data and the sequence – see above) of *declining* ^{14}C ages: see Figure RE18 (and see Manning *et al.* 2009a: Fig. 1). If there was any significant volcanic CO_2 input within the period of growth of the olive branch then one would expect to see evidence of a spike or trend towards too old ^{14}C ages. Instead, there is none, and the samples offer a close match to the mid-latitude northern hemisphere pattern. It is difficult to see how this sample yields such a pattern and such a close match to the mid-latitude northern Hemisphere ^{14}C record if a substantive volcanic CO_2 effect was operating, whether for short periods, or over several years, to decades.

(d) Robustness? Even when allowances are made for a range of likely appropriate or plausible or possible to implausible and extreme regional differences or offsets in radiocarbon calibration datasets, or for other plausible to possible inter- or intra-annual variability factors, the dating of the Thera VDL radiocarbon datasets remains robustly in favour of a later/late 17th century BC date range in almost all circumstances, and especially when the overall Aegean sequence (from before, during, and following the Thera eruption) is considered (Manning and Bronk Ramsey 2003; Manning *et al.* 2006a; 2009a; 2010; Manning and Kromer 2011a; 2012) – and as discussed above. See also the Postscript (i) and (ii) regarding the relevance of IntCal13.

(e) Conclusions. Let us now summarise this review of the basic radiocarbon evidence and case. In general, whether from the assessment of the ^{14}C ages available on short-lived radiocarbon samples from the Akrotiri VDL as a weighted average (which appears approximately appropriate) (see Figures RE6 and RE7), or (perhaps better) as data distributed within a Phase but tending towards the end of the Phase using the Bayesian chronological modelling software OxCal and the Tau_Boundary paired with a Boundary model (see Figures RE9 and RE10), or via an *even if* argument in Kromer and Manning (2012) using the lowest plausible/possible data grouping from within the Akrotiri VDL ^{14}C date set, we find that a date range in the later or late 17th century BC is either required or clearly most likely. This is especially the

case if the archaeological sequence of available Aegean data is considered from before, contemporary with, and after the Akrotiri VDL (Manning *et al.* 2006a; 2009a; Manning and Bronk Ramsey 2009; Manning 2009; Manning and Kromer 2011a; 2012): Figures RE12–RE15. Such a Sequence analysis employing Bayesian chronological modelling methods also offers the most appropriate and robust analytical approach (see also Revisit Essay Appendix 3 below; and see Postscript (vi)). As noted in Manning *et al.* (2006a; 2009a: 303 Table 1), a consistent finding in favour of the 'high' chronology is made even if one does not include any of the ^{14}C data from Thera. Finally, radiocarbon data published since the Manning *et al.* (2006a) study offer further, independent, support, yielding date ranges compatible with the Akrotiri VDL data and generally in line with the 'high' chronology scenario (and *not* the 'low' chronology): (i) the sequence analysis of radiocarbon data from Kolonna on Aigina (Wild *et al.* 2010; Höflmayer 2012a: 438 and Fig. 4), (ii) samples from Palaikastro on Crete (Bruins *et al.* 2009; Manning and Kromer 2011a: Fig. 2; Höflmayer 2012a: 438–439 and Fig. 5), and (iii) samples from the Lerna Shaft Graves from Greece (Lindblom and Manning 2011).

(ii)   *Claims of problems as undermining radiocarbon dating in the Aegean and especially as regards Thera put forward by Wiener (2012)*
Wiener (e.g. 2003; 2007; 2009a; 2009b; 2010; 2012) has been the leading voice trying to dismiss or downplay the ^{14}C evidence as relevant to the Thera debate, and to Aegean chronology in this period. He has sought to assert that there are all sorts of problems with radiocarbon dating. Often unrelated issues are cited, and always in the context of a constant argument that there are unexplained variations, or marked differences, which affect the Thera, and other Aegean, ^{14}C date sets especially. The preceding discussions, Section 3.c.III.i, have already covered and rejected a number of these sorts of supposed criticisms: in particular, the consistency of the Akrotiri VDL ^{14}C date set has been highlighted, and the case against the relevance of substantive volcanic CO_2 (or similar) has been summarised. I go through some of the other 'problems' raised in Wiener (2012) and offer responses.

(a) Regional ^{14}C offsets. Wiener (2012: 424) highlights this topic as a possible problem. The existing research on this topic however finds typically only very small offsets for the Aegean and east Mediterranean region (Manning *et al.* 2010; Manning and Kromer 2012). Egypt and its almost entirely opposite (winter) growing season in pre-modern times (before the Nile dams) is very different and the likely extreme case. Yet even there the observed growing season offset is just 19 ± 5 ^{14}C years (Dee *et al.* 2010). This is relevant at high-precision, and allows better correlation of large ^{14}C data sets and analyses thereof with both the radiocarbon calibration curve and Egyptian historical chronology (Bronk Ramsey *et al.* 2010; Manning *et al.* 2013). However, typically, it is still only a very small issue and Dee *et al.* (2010: 689) state that the "impact of this uplift is almost imperceptible". Recent studies have considered allowances for both the observed scale of regional offsets, and for use even of an east Mediterranean region ^{14}C

calibration curve, and do not find that so doing substantially affects analyses and findings with regard to the Thera date (Manning *et al.* 2010; Manning and Kromer 2011a; Manning and Kromer 2012). The dating models shown in Figures RE12 and RE14 above allow for, and test for, a likely more than adequate 0 ± 10 ^{14}C years possible offset, and find (i) no evidence for a substantial offset in the data sets, and (ii) date ranges still clearly requiring the Aegean 'high' chronology. The small regional offset observed in the 9th-8th centuries BC associated with the major solar minimum is not a typical situation, and no such episode occurred in the period c.1700–1500 BC. While apparently real, continued work and many more data have also reduced the scale of this offset (Manning *et al.* 2010: 1594) versus our original report (Kromer *et al.* 2001; Manning *et al.* 2001) – the figure in Wiener (2012: Fig. 1) shows the original situation only.

(b) Calcareous growth context for plant samples. Wiener (2012: 426) argues that plant samples growing in limestone areas may be affected by old carbon and so yield too old ^{14}C ages. This was a potential concern raised in the past (e.g. Damon *et al.* 1978: 469). Wiener wonders about the data from Chania, Crete. However, the study of Tauber (1983), which investigated this issue for highly calcareous soils, found no significant effect in a comparison of same age wood samples and concluded: "Hence, a significant assimilation of soil CO_2 or soil carbonate during photosynthesis could *not* be detected" (p. 420 – my italics). Earlier work by Olsson *et al.* (1972: 268–269) testing for the influence of dissolved carbonates also shows no significant variation. The general similarity of ^{14}C dates on Bristlecone Pine samples from the dolomite (limestone) area around Schluman Grove in the White Mountains versus ^{14}C dates on same age material from trees from a variety of other geologies provides further consonant evidence (e.g. Taylor *et al.* 2010: Fig. 5; Fuller *et al.* 2012; Linick *et al.* 1986: Fig. 1). More work could be done to check on this issue, but it seems unlikely to be a major or general factor. *Note*: effects on bone samples via diet from the incorporation of carbon material from marine or riverine reservoir sources – or the direct dating of riverine food sources like fish and mollusks – are an entirely different issue (see footnote 37 above) – and even then are not always clear-cut (Hart and Lovis 2007).

(c) Analysis and calibration. Wiener (2012: 428–430) argues there are two problems worth noting in this regard. His first point is the claim that stated results are based on "the duration of intersection between the ^{14}C age range obtained and the relevant calibration curve measurements" – and that if there is a 2 decade intersection versus a 1 decade intersection then 'ceteris paribus' there should be 66.7% probability for the 2 decade period. But, Wiener claims, this is not the case, and cites his Figure 3 as an illustration. This argument seems at best confused. To begin, for the example that Wiener uses of 3305 BP in his Figure 3, the result is exactly what he says it is not: a clear higher probability for the large 16th century BC period of intersection (59.5%) and a much lower one for the short 17th century BC intersection (8.7%) from the most likely 68.2% range of the total probability (OxCal 4.1.7 using IntCal09: Bronk Ramsey 2009a; Reimer *et al.* 2009). Two other misconceptions seem to

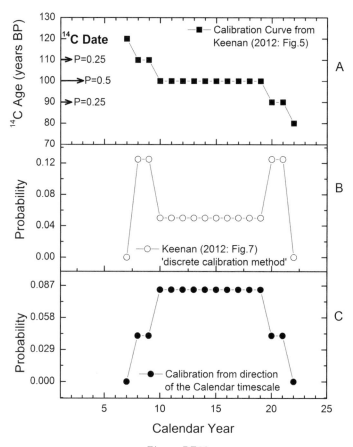

Figure RE19.

Panel A: *simple radiocarbon calibration curve with annual values of exactly 120, 110, 100, 90 and 80 ^{14}C years BP (no errors) after Keenan (2012: Fig. 5). Only the annual values (the square symbols) are used (as in Keenan 2012) – I add the linking grey lines merely to make it look more like a calibration curve but do not use any intervening values. On left, a representation of the [14]C 'date' for transformation into calendar year dating probability: with probability ½ (or 0.5) for 100 ^{14}C years BP and ¼ (0.25) for each of 110 and 90 ^{14}C years BP (as Keenan 2012: Table 1).*

Panel B: *the supposed calibration of the ^{14}C date in Panel A (after Keenan 2012: Table 1) into a calendar dating probability distribution via his 'discrete calibration method' – after Keenan (2012: Fig. 7). Only the specified annual values are employed – I add the linking grey lines (unlike Keenan 2012: Fig. 7) merely to make the plot look more like a typical calibrated calendar probability distribution. Because, inappropriately, the viewpoint of the ^{14}C timescale is used, the probability of most likely age, 100 ^{14}C years BP, is divided among the possible calendar dates and each (counter-intuitively) ends up less likely than dates before or after.*

Panel C: *the calibration of the ^{14}C date in Panel A (after Keenan 2012: Table 1) but – contrast with Panel B and Keenan (2012) – from the viewpoint of the calendar timescale and following the standard approaches in the field (see text). Only the specified annual values are employed – I add the linking grey lines (unlike Keenan 2012: Fig. 5) just to make the plot look more like a typical calibrated calendar probability distribution. By starting from the calendar timescale, each calendar year (and its probability of a ^{14}C age – here specific with no error following Keenan 2012) that intersects with the most likely ^{14}C age of the sample to be calibrated, ends up with an equally likely probability of being the most likely calendar date. The shape of the calibrated calendar probability distribution is not the same as the symmetrical shape of the ^{14}C probability (a normal probability distribution in real examples) of the ^{14}C date to be calibrated (unless the ^{14}C curve is a line at 45°), but the properties of the ^{14}C distribution are appropriately transformed and represented on the calendar timescale when the calibration process is performed from the perspective of the calendar timescale.*

apply in addition. One is that the calibration 'curve' is illustrated as a band seemingly all of equal weight. In fact it is a probability profile (the central 68.2%) based around modelled probability distributions (normal distributions) spaced every 5 calendar years (in the period under discussion). Thus Wiener's red line in his Figure 3 intersects with a range of probabilities from the high (centre of a normal probability distribution) to the edges of the 68.2% (1SD) ranges of various of the probability distributions making up the calibration curve. Hence it is not a case of comparing a 1 versus 2 decade contact.

The other issue is the direction of analysis. As discussed in several papers written in the period when the initial generation of calibration software became available, calibration of radiocarbon dates should be viewed from the calendar timescale and not the radiocarbon timescale (e.g. Dehling and van der Plicht 1993; Michczynska *et al.* 1990; Stuiver and Reimer 1989; Weninger 1986). Each calendar year has its own solution, whereas from the perspective of the ^{14}C timescale there can be a variable number of solutions. Only the former viewpoint achieves an outcome appropriate to the calendar timescale for archaeology, history, and so on. As noted by Weninger *et al.* (2011: 4–6), initially this was simply the implementation of practical or reasonable observations in order for early calibration software to work, subsequently it was given a more robust foundation in terms of an application of Bayesian theory. This calendric v. ^{14}C viewpoint issue, and inappropriately *not* using the calendric perspective, is the key flaw in the paper of Keenan (2012), which (mistakenly) claims to identify an error in the now standard approach to radiocarbon calibration (with Bronk Ramsey 2009a now the best known, and used, statement).[44] Keenan (2012) does not cite the earlier published work on how the now standard calibration methods were discussed and developed. Analysis from the calendar timescale avoids the unreasonable outcomes Keenan (2012) finds via what he describes as his 'discrete calibration method'. Figure RE19 provides an example of the problem from Keenan (2012), and the more reasonable solution when analysis is viewed instead from the calendar timescale.[45] Keenan (2012: Fig. 5) proposes a simple calibration curve with annual values of exactly 120, 110, 100, 90 and 80 ^{14}C years BP (no errors) (see Figure RE19 panel A) and considers the calibration into calendar year dating probability of a (simplified) ^{14}C date with probability of ½ for exactly 100 ^{14}C years BP and ¼ for exactly 110 ^{14}C years BP and ¼ for exactly 90 ^{14}C years BP (Keenan 2012: Table 1) (also Figure RE19 panel A). Keenan (2012: Fig. 7) shows the problem if analysis is not viewed from the calendar timescale as the years equating with the most likely range of the date end up less likely because of the plateau in the calibration curve (see Figure RE19 panel B after Keenan 2012: Fig. 7). In contrast, following standard practice

---

[44] See also Weninger *et al.* (2011) who, despite some discussion and question-raising regarding Bayesian approaches, nonetheless find in effect the same outcomes. In particular, they too note the importance of viewing calibration from the calendar timescale.

[45] The specific plateau problem case discussed by Keenan (2012), and a sensible solution of this, has of course been considered previously – for one example, see Weninger (1986: Fig. 11; Weninger *et al.* 2011: Fig. 4).

in the radiocarbon and archaeological fields stemming out of discussions in papers such as those of Dehling and van der Plicht (1993), Michczynska *et al.* (1990); Stuiver and Reimer (1989), Weninger (1986), calibration from viewpoint of the calendar timescale – the relevant one for humans and the study of archaeology, history, climate – instead leads to the appropriate outcome shown in Figure RE19 panel C.

In reality, the calibration dataset, and the ^{14}C age we wish to transform into calendar years, are all probability distributions. Each calendar year (or other increment) is unique in a linear sequence (contrast the radiocarbon timescale – hence calibration). There is a best estimate of the radiocarbon age (a normal probability distribution) for each calendar increment (5 years in IntCal09 in the period we are discussing and this can be modelled down to e.g. 1 year as an option in OxCal). Calibration – of a single measured ^{14}C age in simplified terms – is then the intersection of all these calendar placed probabilities for a radiocarbon age versus the normal probability distribution of the measured radiocarbon age we wish to try to place into calendar time. Figure RE20 shows this process schematically in terms of the ^{14}C calibration curve for the ^{14}C ages of 3305 BP, 3326 BP and 3345 BP. Note: I am ignoring the measurement errors on the incoming ^{14}C dates of interest (i.e. the ^{14}C dates to be calibrated into calendar age ranges) here – as in Wiener (2012: Fig. 3) – to keep Figure RE20 relatively simple. 3305 BP is selected as this is the ^{14}C date illustrated in Wiener (2012: Fig. 3); 3326 BP is shown for comparison as this is the weighted average ^{14}C age for the 'low date clump' from the 13 dates on short-lived samples from the Akrotiri VDL run in the AD2000s in Manning *et al.* (2006a) after Manning and Kromer (2012: 462) and represents what seems to be about the lowest (most recent) ^{14}C age possible/plausible as an estimate of the correct ^{14}C age of the Akrotiri VDL (see discussion of Manning and Kromer 2012); and 3345 BP is shown as this is the weighted average ^{14}C value of the 28 date set of ^{14}C data on short-lived samples from the Akrotiri VDL as employed in Manning *et al.* (2006a) or the preferred 25 date (sub-set) used above (from Figure RE2). We see that 3305 BP intersects at several places, with most intersections with the most likely 1SD ranges in the earlier to mid 16th century BC. In contrast, 3326 BP intersects in the area around 1615 BC and does not intersect with any of the 1SD ranges in the 16th century BC – hence 3326 BP most likely dates in the late 17th century BC. 3345 BP intersects in the 17th century BC around 1625 BC and does not intersect even with any of the 2SD ranges in the 16th century BC – hence it is very unlikely to date in the 16th century BC.

Figure RE21 illustrates the situation for the same ^{14}C ages of 3305 BP, 3326 BP and 3345 BP when viewed from the opposite direction (starting with the calendar time scale – the time scale of real interest to us). The probabilities for a given ^{14}C age for each of the 5-year calendar increments of IntCal09 are shown for the period from 1630 BC to 1530 BC. These are the probabilities that any ^{14}C age to be calibrated encounters if it dates in this calendar age range, and it is the intersection (combination) of all these probabilities that yields the probability, by calendar increment, that a ^{14}C age of interest (a single date or a combined

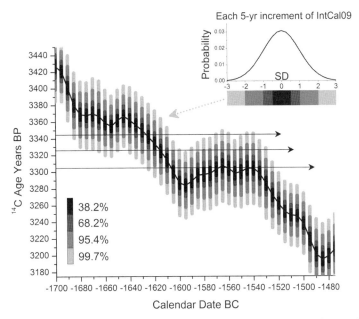

Figure RE20. The radiocarbon calibration curve (IntCal09: Reimer et al. 2009) comprises probabilities for a given ¹⁴C value spaced by 5 calendar year increments in the period shown (1700 BC to 1475 BC), and as relevant to dating the Thera eruption. Each of the 5 year points of the IntCal curve is a normal probability distribution estimate of the ¹⁴C age for that calendar date. Although often shown as, e.g., a 1 standard deviation (SD) band (as in Wiener 2012: Fig. 3 – not in fact noted to be a 1SD band there), we instead must envisage a probability band around the quoted value – as above. I simplify in the figure here and show the quoted value – the black line – the 0.5 SD range (most likely 38.2% probability), the 1 SD range (next 15% either side = altogether the most likely 68.2%), the 2 SD range (next 13.6 either side = altogether the most likely 95.4% range) and then the 3 SD range (next 2.15% either side = altogether the most likely 99.7% range) for each 5 year interval of IntCal09 in the period from 1700-1475 BC (compare Wiener 2012: Fig.3). The intersections of the ¹⁴C ages of 3345 BP, 3326 BP and 3305 BP (see text) are indicated against the constituent ¹⁴C date probabilities for each 5 calendar year increment of IntCal09.

age from several dates) belongs to the particular calendar increment.[46] Again we can see why we get quite different results for 3305 BP versus 3326 BP and especially versus 3345 BP.

---

[46] To keep the figure relatively simple and to parallel Wiener (2012: Fig. 3), the incoming ¹⁴C ages of interest (to be calibrated into a calendar age range) are shown just as single year ¹⁴C ages without a measurement error. In reality, the ¹⁴C age to be calibrated is itself a normal probability distribution (defined by the statement of the date and its standard deviation). Thus instead of a line coming down in Figure RE21, one should imagine an intersecting normal probability distribution. It is then the intersections of all the probability values, the normal probability distribution of the measured ¹⁴C age of interest of unknown calendar age intersecting – combining – with each and all of the normal probability distributions for what ¹⁴C age belongs to the given calendar ages of IntCal09, which yields the probability distribution for this date on the calendar time scale (the calibrated calendar age probability distribution). See for example Figures RE6 and RE7 above. For the calendar probability distributions for the (no errors) examples illustrated in Figures RE20 and RE21, see Figure RE22.

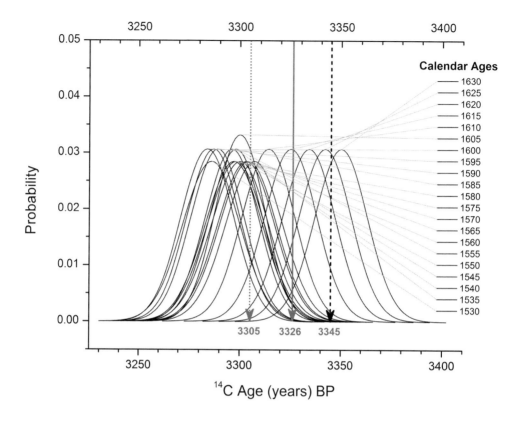

Figure RE21. Schematic illustration of the probabilities for a given ¹⁴C age for each of the 5 calendar intervals from 1530 BC to 1630 BC (shown to 4SD) from the standard mid-latitude Northern Hemisphere dataset of IntCal09 (Reimer et al. 2009). The differing heights in some cases reflect the slightly different standard deviations given for some calendar years for the IntCal09 ¹⁴C value. Due to the irregular shape of the radiocarbon calibration curve (history of past natural atmospheric ¹⁴C levels) – see Figure RE20 – the probabilities for given ¹⁴C ages are sometimes spaced out (e.g. 1630 to 1610 BC and ¹⁴C ages c.3360-3310 BP) and at other times bunched (e.g. 1605 to 1530 BC and ¹⁴C ages c.3305-3275 BP). A range of calendar ages at varying probabilities intersect with a ¹⁴C age of 3305 BP, especially in a range around 1570 BC, 1565 BC, and 1545 BC, 1540 BC but broadly c.1610 to 1535 BC – thus a ¹⁴C age of 3305 BP considered in isolation could belong to a wide range of likely calendar dates with most probability in the earlier to mid 16th century BC. This is the ¹⁴C age illustrated in Wiener (2012: Fig. 3). In contrast, a much smaller group of calendar placed probabilities for a ¹⁴C age intersect with 3326 BP. It scores an almost direct hit at 1615 BC and generally intersects at higher probability from 1620 to 1610 BC. There are only a few and lower probability intersections with any other calendar dates. Thus, considered in isolation, a ¹⁴C age of 3326 BP date would likely belong to a much narrower range of likely calendar dates in the late 17th century BC with only a small amount of probability for any other date. The ¹⁴C age of 3345 BP offers calendar date intercepts especially around 1630–1615 BC (and, if the probabilities for 1635–1665 BC were also shown in the figure, then there would be some older calendar intercepts in this range in addition), whereas by about 1605 BC (or later) it no longer offers any substantial intercept. A calendar date in the mid-later 17th century BC date is clearly most likely for the ¹⁴C age.

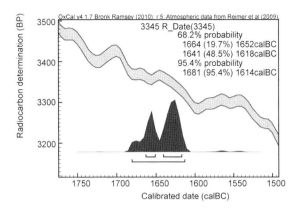

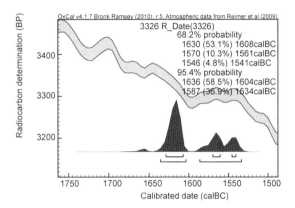

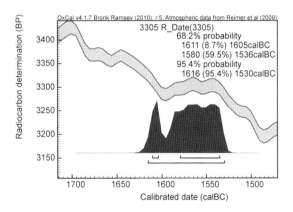

Figure RE22. Calendar age probability distributions and most likely age ranges at 68.2% and 95.4% probability for the ¹⁴C *ages, without errors, which are illustrated and discussed in Figures RE20 and RE21. Data from IntCal09 (Reimer* et al. *2009) and OxCal 4.1.7 (Bronk Ramsey 2009a) with curve resolution set at 5.*

Figure RE22 illustrates the calendar dating probabilities for the three ^{14}C ages illustrated and discussed in Figures RE20 and RE21. Again, as in Figures RE20 and RE21, this is with no error attached to the ^{14}C age being converted into the appropriate calendar age range. For the actual situation, with error (and so a normal probability distribution on the ^{14}C age scale to intersect with the time-series of normal probability distributions on the calendar timescale), for the weighted average ^{14}C ages relevant to the Akrotiri VDL, see Figure RE7 above and discussion there.

Wiener (2012) does not specifically explain why he uses the value of 3305 BP in his Fig. 3, but his mentions of the essentially flat period of the ^{14}C calibration curve and the "beginning of the Late Bronze Age in the Aegean, when measurements may intersect the calibration curve at various places between ~1615 and 1525 BC" on his p.427, and discussion of the Thera case pp.429–430, give the impression that somehow he regards this age as relevant to the Thera case, and so a 16th century BC date. Let us therefore briefly consider this, and return to the question of what is the most appropriate ^{14}C age for the Akrotiri VDL (see discussion above in Section 3.c.III.i). Figure RE23 shows (as in Figure RE5) the total ^{14}C dating probability (approximately, calculated to 4SD or to 99.994% for each date) by 5 ^{14}C year bins from the most recent high-quality set of data for short-lived samples from the Akrotiri VDL – the 13–date set from Manning *et al.* (2006a) (see Figures RE2–RE4 and RE7 lower above). The vertical lines then compare some ^{14}C ages against this probability distribution: (i) the weighted average value from the 13 dates at 3344 BP, (ii) the lowest of the weighted average values for the subjectively defined latest possible/plausible dating low-date 'clump' in Manning and Kromer (2012) at 3326 BP, and (iii) the arbitrary value of 3305 BP shown in Wiener (2012: Fig. 3). We may observe that the only value that is more or less in the centre of the probability distribution – with the distribution fairly symmetrically distributed around it as one would expect – is the weighted average value of (i) 3344 BP. The probability distribution from this random sample of 13 dates, out of the hypothetical total population of such possible date estimates, is consistent with being in the form of a normal probability distribution – and this is visibly the case (see Figures RE2, RE3, RE5, RE23) – and it comfortably passes a Chi-square test (Figure RE7 lower). The low-date 'clump' value (ii) at 3326 BP leaves 61.5% of the total probability to the older side, but does describe the latest region of available higher probability, and so can be used to offer an *even if* and latest possible/plausible date scenario as in Manning and Kromer (2012). However, the (iii) 3305 BP value is well into the less likely probability range, with 83.2% of the probability distribution older than this age, and this value clearly does *not* describe the probability distribution available from the dates on short-lived samples from the Akrotiri VDL. There is instead every reason to consider a central ^{14}C age value around 3344 to 3346 BP as the most appropriate for the population of short-lived material found in the Akrotiri VDL (Figures RE2–RE4, RE7), and see discussion above.

The second problem Wiener (2012: 428–429) identifies is that "All calibration

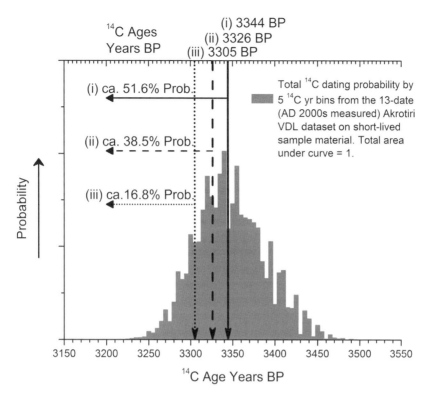

Figure RE23. A comparison of the total ¹⁴C dating probability from the 13 date set of measurements run in the AD2000s from short-lived samples from the Akrotiri VDL (Manning et al. 2006a) (see Figure RE5 above) by 5 ¹⁴C year bins against (i) the weighted average value of this set, 3344 BP, (ii) the low-date 'clump' weighted average value of 3326 BP from Manning and Kromer (2012), and (iii) the ¹⁴C age of 3305 BP highlighted in Wiener (2012: Fig. 3).

programmes narrow stated error ranges in direct response to the number of measurements included … without great regard to the consistency or inconsistency (even when substantial) of the measurements themselves, provided the measurements meet the chi-squared test". This statement is inaccurate at best. The particular narrowing Wiener is focused on is the use of a weighted average as the best estimate of the real age of a set of data from the same event where each date is regarded as a random sample from a population of estimates for the correct age and the pooled mean of a set of such estimates will give the best estimate of the real age. This has nothing to do with calibration or Bayesian modelling, but is just applying normal probability theory. The Chi-square test is the classic test that the data are consistent with the above hypothesis – hence the use of the approach outlined in Ward and Wilson (1978) with respect to ¹⁴C data from the same event (their Case I). I have noted already Wiener's claim that the data from the Akrotiri VDL may not conform to the criterion of belonging to the same event, and we have

90   *A Test of Time Revisited*

seen that in fact they do seem to in approximate terms and as relevant to the level of precision available for ^{14}C analysis and calibration (Section 3.c.III). In particular, contrary Wiener's claim, we have seen that the large central group of Akrotiri VDL data (the 25 date set, or the 13 date set: see Figures RE2 to RE7) comprise tight, coherent, sets of data centered fairly closely on their weighted means. I have also discussed an alternative analytical approach which allows for Wiener's objection, and we have seen that it, nonetheless, yields a calendar date range in the late 17th century BC for the Akrotiri VDL data (see Figures RE9 and 10 above and discussion).

Wiener's principal objection to the weighted average value regarding the Thera case is that the standard deviation on this when combining the set of consistent measurements for the Akrotiri VDL is small enough that it renders a 17th century BC calibrated age the clear most likely result. This is entirely incompatible with the 'low' chronology dating scheme. Wiener thus wonders why a much larger error value, ± 35 ^{14}C years, might not be used instead. This value is larger than any of the individual stated measurement errors for any of the dates in the 13 date set from the AD 2000s, and is almost 4x larger than the SD on the weighted average value following standard methods (i.e. Ward and Wilson 1978 for ^{14}C dates). Indeed, what an error term of ± 35 ^{14}C years on the weighted average of, e.g., the AD 2000s 13-date set from the Akrotiri VDL (Manning *et al.* 2006a) means is that on average each of the constituent dates would have a measurement error of ± 125 ^{14}C years BP – or c.3.7x to 4.5x their published measurement errors (of 28 to 34 ^{14}C years BP)! This is despite known age tests for the two laboratories involved during the period of the Manning *et al.* (2006a) project, OxA = Oxford and VERA = Vienna, demonstrating that their data are accurate and precise at a level much closer to their stated measurement errors (as detailed at the time in Manning *et al.* 2006a: Fig. 1 nos. 20–25, and SOM pp.4–5). Known age data since from Oxford continues to show very high levels of accuracy (e.g. Bronk Ramsey *et al.* 2010: Fig. S1), and good inter-laboratory agreement with Vienna data on shared identical samples (Bronk Ramsey *et al.* 2010: Table S3). Of course, if one arbitrarily for no sound reason makes the error term large enough (and so the probability curve flatter and wider), then some probability starts to fall in the 16th century BC and the calibration eventually would become more ambiguous: see Figure RE24. However, regardless of applying arbitrary, larger and larger (and unrealistic or inappropriate), error terms, we see in Figure RE24 that the 17th century BC remains the most likely date range. Even if the error on the weighted average is more than doubled to 25 ^{14}C years (so 2.77x the actual value), there is no calibrated calendar age probability within the most likely 68.2% range after 1600 BC. Wiener (2012: 430) is correct that by arbitrarily making the error ± 35 ^{14}C years (instead of the calculated ± 9) that the calibrated age ranges start to include the 16th century BC. But even then 71% of the total probability lies before 1599 BC, and, of the most likely 68.2% of probability, 59% lies 1688–1607 BC and only 9% lies between 1571–1560 BC and 1548–1540 BC. Hence, *even then*, the 16th century BC is the unlikely result.

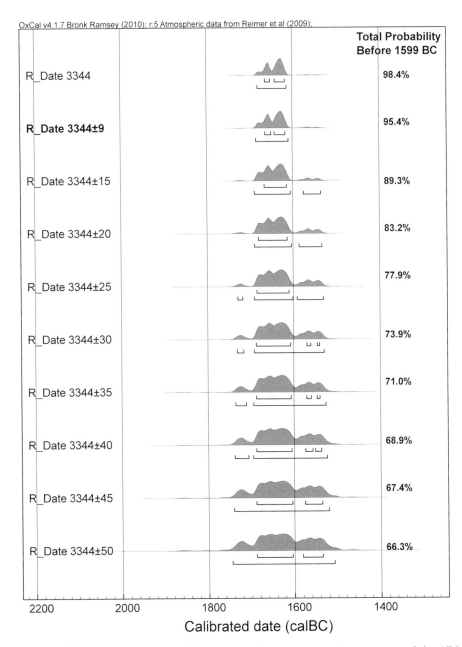

Figure RE24. Calibrated calendar probability distributions for the weighted average of the AD2000s measured 13-date set of ^{14}C measurements on short-lived samples from the Akrotiri VDL from Manning et al. (2006a) given a range of errors from 0 to 50. The actual weighted average value of the set is 3344 ± 9 BP (shown). The upper and lower lines under each probability distribution indicate, respectively, the most likely 68.2% and 95.4% ranges. The percentage of the total probability older (before) 1599 BC is stated to the right of each probability distribution. Data from OxCal 4.1.7 (Bronk Ramsey 2009a) and IntCal09 (Reimer et al. 2009) with the calibration curve resolution set at 5.

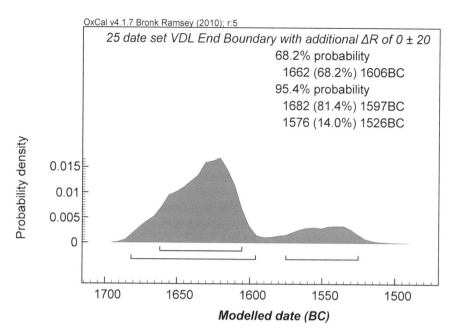

Figure RE25. Revised version of Figure RE9B when re-run adding an additional allowance for an uncertainty of 20 ¹⁴C years to cover a hypothetical local CO_2 reservoir offset of some form – for which there is at present no evidence and indeed evidence to the contrary (see Section 3.c.III.1 above). This is the 25 date set of measurements on short-lived samples from the Akrotiri VDL (Figure RE2) modelled as a Phase with a Tau_Boundary paired with a Boundary, so that the data are assumed to be distributed exponentially towards the end of the Phase. Data from OxCal 4.1.7 (Bronk Ramsey 2009a) and IntCal09 (Reimer et al. 2009) with curve resolution set at 5.

Another way of considering the robustness of the 17th century BC finding is to take the Tau_Boundary paired with a Boundary model for the dates on short-lived samples from the Akrotiri VDL – argued to perhaps be the most appropriate analytical model in discussions above in Section 3.c.III.i and in Höflmayer (2012a: 436 and Fig. 2) – and allow for a possible or hypothetical local CO_2 reservoir offset at varying levels (despite the lack of evidence for such an offset – see discussions above Section 3.c.III). Heinemeier *et al.* (2009: 288–289 and Fig. 8) consider such a test on the wiggle-match of the Thera/Santorini olive branch sample and find that its later 17th century BC dating is robust unless there is a large offset – for which there is no evidence. Let us consider the 25 date set in Figure RE2 modelled as a Phase with an exponential distribution towards the end of the Phase (as in Figures RE9 and RE10) using the Tau_Boundary paired with a Boundary model from Bronk Ramsey (2009a) and also consider what effect allowing for some hypothetical (or test) variation in the local CO_2 reservoir (for whatever reason – but we assume likely volcanic CO_2 input) makes using the Delta-R (ΔR) function in OxCal. I consider adding a possible variation of 0 ± 20 ¹⁴C years – as this is approximately the extreme

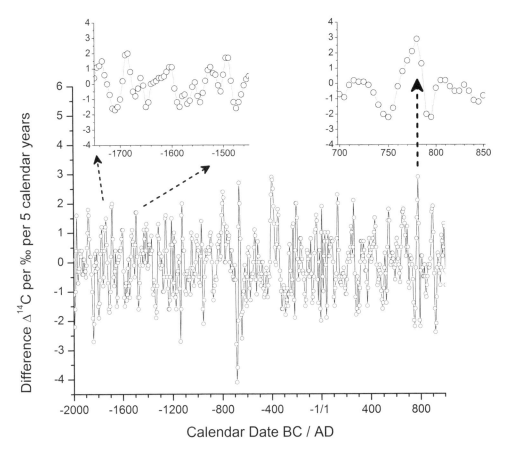

Figure RE26. Change in Δ¹⁴C per 5 calendar years (data resolution of modelled record) from IntCal09 record (Reimer et al. *2009) for the period 2000 BC to AD 1000 (lower plot) and – details – for 1750 BC to 1450 BC (top left) and AD 700–AD 850 (top right). The period 1750–1450 BC shows no very large changes that might denote an unusual or special factor applying at this time – no change per 5 calendar years is greater than or less than 2‰. Indeed, the later 17th century BC, especially, is quite calm. We can contrast the period 1750–1450 BC with the period around AD 775 when there is a dramatic sudden change in 5 years of almost 3‰ and there has been recent discussion of a possible major solar flare or even a gamma ray burst (Miyake* et al. *2012; Merlott and Thomas 2012; Hambaryan and Neuhäuser 2013), or other periods when there were dramatic/significant variations such as around 685-665 BC or 400 BC.*

variation known in the wider region from the alternative growing season context of Nile Egypt (Dee *et al.* 2010) (very much not the case on Thera), and much larger than any offset observed for the rest of the Aegean and east Mediterranean region in data reported so far (Manning *et al.* 2010; Manning and Kromer 2012): see Figure RE25. As illustrated in Figure RE25, even such a larger additional uncertainty factor does not change the clear dating in the later 17th century BC for the end of Akrotiri VDL estimate. The most likely 68.2% range is 1662–1606 BC and even the 95.4% range only has 14% probability in the range 1576–1526 BC versus 81.4% probability for the range 1682–1597 BC. These ranges are wider than those in Figure RE9B because of the substantially increased uncertainty allowed for in this robustness test, but the pattern is the same. In fact, even if an additional uncertainty, ΔR, of up to 35 ^{14}C years is allowed for, and so, at 2SD, an allowance for a local offset of up to 70 ^{14}C years – a very large offset and one for which there is no positive evidence and quite a strong case against: Section 3.c.III – this in fact still leaves a 17th century BC date as clearly most likely for the End of the Akrotiri VDL (most likely 68.2% ranges 1663–1606 BC with 45.1% of the total probability versus 1564–1527 BC with just 23.1 % of the total probability).

A final general issue is whether there is some unusual variation in the radiocarbon record (the record of natural variations in atmospheric ^{14}C) during the period potentially relevant to the dating of the Thera eruption. Figure RE26 shows the variation by 5 calendar year increments (the modelled resolution for this period) of the Δ^{14}C record from IntCal09 (Reimer *et al.* 2009) for the period 2000 BC to AD 1000. The variation in the period around the time of the Thera eruption, so broadly defined as within 1750 BC to 1450 BC, is not remarkable, and is in fact relatively modest compared to some other periods. The period 1750–1450 BC shows no very large changes that might denote some unusual or special factor which might apply. There is no change greater than ± 2‰ in this period, and the later 17th century BC is especially calm. We can contrast the Thera period with the timespan around AD 775, when there is a dramatic change in 5 years of almost 3‰, and there has been recent discussion of a possible major solar flare or even a gamma ray burst (Miyake *et al.* 2012; Merlott and Thomas 2012; Hambaryan and Neuhäuser 2013). Some other periods of substantial rapid change, such as around 685–665 BC, or 400 BC, also stand out as of potential interest – but again in clear contrast to the Thera period. Thus no special factor seems to apply regarding the Thera eruption period.

(iii) *Radiocarbon Conclusions*
To draw together the main conclusions from the above discussions:

- The radiocarbon dating of the Akrotiri VDL appears to provide an appropriate ^{14}C age estimate for this event – and there is no evidence that any substantial ^{14}C offset or other special circumstance seems to apply.
- Analyses of the radiocarbon dates, whether on the short-lived samples from Akrotiri or from the olive branch found buried by the Thera eruption pumice, and whether in isolation or as part of a wider sequence of Aegean ^{14}C data, all place the end of the Akrotiri VDL and the Minoan eruption of the Thera volcano in the later or late 17th century BC at a high level of probability.
- These findings are robust within any reasonable known tolerances, or plausible variations or errors (with regard to Sequence analyses, see also Revisit Essay Appendix 3 below).

More widely, we may also conclude that:

- a sequence of Aegean radiocarbon date sets offers a coherent ^{14}C-based timeframe for the LMIA through LMII periods (Manning *et al.* 2006a and subsequent versions including Figures RE12–RE14 above) – this places the LMIA period in the 17th century BC, requires a long overall LMIB period covering most of the 16th century BC and into the earlier 15th century BC (see also Manning 2009; 2014; and Postscript (vi) – note in addition the recent paper of Höflmayer *et al.* 2013), followed by the LMII period running to late in the 15th century BC;

- radiocarbon dating has recently provided a detailed and highly-resolved chronology for Egypt compatible with the historical chronology (and even helping refine it) (Bronk Ramsey *et al.* 2010; see also Appendix 1 to this Revisit Essay), removing a long-standing perception that ^{14}C and Egypt were incompatible, and hence, *a priori*, we should expect the same finding in the Aegean and so should use the Aegean ^{14}C-based chronology as the likely best measure of time for this region; and

- various possible sources of variation and error at high-resolution, such as regional growing-season-related offsets, deserve more attention in the Mediterranean, but initial data for non-Nile Valley contexts in the Aegean and east Mediterranean do not indicate more than small factors (e.g. Manning *et al.* 2010; Manning and Kromer 2012), which are unlikely to substantially affect dating case studies in the southern Aegean on appropriate and carefully selected samples.[47]

(IV) Approximate Chronology to use AD 2013 versus Manning (1999: 340 and Fig. 62)?

The dates proposed in Manning (1999: 340) have stood the test of time fairly well. Subsequent analyses with many more radiocarbon data, and with more sophisticated approaches, have supported fairly similar dates (see above). Other new evidence and reports have also supported the general 'high' chronology position, ranging from the recent indications of a need to completely reassess the date (and so associations) of Khyan (Moeller and Marouard 2011 and see Section 3.c.II.i above), to the plausibility of returning to a longer New Kingdom Egyptian chronology that would start earlier (Aston 2012 and discussions in Section 3.c above and Revisit Essay Appendix 1 below), to the analysis of the Sofular Cave speleothem which suggests changes in its chemistry which are very plausibly associated with a major (arguably the largest Holocene: see footnote 4) regionally relevant volcanic eruption (i.e. Thera) starting in the later/late 17th century BC (Badertscher *et al.* 2014 and see Section 3.c.I.ii above). Any final summary table of dates is necessarily an approximation and selection from a range of evidence,

---

[47] The need to select appropriate samples which come from secure contexts and which will be able to offer ^{14}C ages contemporary with the date of the archaeological event, object or element for which a date is sought, is critical to accurate high-resolution dating in archaeology (e.g. Bayliss *et al.* 2011; Dee *et al.* 2012). The necessity to focus on the careful selection and screening of samples against likely problems (for the case of Egypt, see Dee *et al.* 2012) has become more and more important as the precision of both radiocarbon dating itself, and especially of the associated chronological modelling methods (e.g. Bayliss 2009), has increased.

which both varies somewhat, and all the constituent data do not necessarily date the same thing. In this case, considering just the radiocarbon-based information, the main 'balance' is between using dates from the weighted average values for some destruction horizons at various sites, and using modelled dates for a subsequent Boundary marking the end of such a Phase (so compare for example the values in Table RE3A versus Table RE3B). The latter will be slightly to somewhat later than the former (see also the date ranges listed in e.g. Manning *et al.* 2006a; 2009a: Table 1; etc.) depending on the data, their spread, and the surrounding constraints. In round terms, I suggest the dates below as an AD 2013 approximate chronology for the LMIA to LMII periods.

These dates allow a reasonable correspondence with the Egyptian historical chronology (and especially to a higher New Kingdom chronology such as Aston 2012) for the periods where there is good evidence of material and stylistic connections between the Aegean and Egypt. The new findings from Tell Edfu which seem to indicate a significant re-dating (earlier) for Khyan (Moeller and Marouard 2011 and see discussion in Section 3.c.II.i above) are compatible, and may well provide key, even decisive, archaeological evidence in support of the overall 'high' chronological-archaeological synthesis for the 17th-16th centuries BC. Moving into the New Kingdom, the proposed chronology allows the later part of the LMIB period to overlap with the earlier part of the reign of Tuthmosis III, consistent with Aegean material links of LMIB and LHIIA date especially, and the end of LMIB and the change to LMII can fall in the later part of his reign again consistent with ceramic finds, the clothing designs worn by Keftiu in representations from later in the reign of Tuthmosis, and the changing typology of the metal vessels represented in the Keftiu paintings (Matthäus 1995; Manning 1999: 209–220). At present we lack evidence of secure or precise or non-ambiguous archaeological synchronisms for earlier LMIB and LMIA with Egypt – as discussed in Section 3.c.II above. Radiocarbon provides our best evidence. The 17th century BC date for the LMIA period and the wall paintings at Thera also seems potentially compatible with stylistically similar artworks of around this date (and not the mid or later 16th century BC) known from Alalakh Level VII (Niemeier and Niemeier 2000) – to

	Manning (1999: 340)		AD 2013		Other Source
	Start BC	End BC	Start BC	End BC	
LMIA	1675±	1600/1580	1700–1675	1610–1580	1
LMIB	1600/1580	1500/1490	1610–1580	1500–1450	2
LMII	1500/1490	1440/1425	1470–1450	1440–1410	2

Table RE4. Approximate Summary Aegean Chronology in Manning (1999: 340) versus AD 2013. This reflects mainly the balance between the dates in Figures RE12 and RE13 and in Tables RE3A and 3B – dates for the short-lived samples from various end of phase destruction sets directly (Table RE3A) versus the end of Phase Boundaries, and so terminus ante quem *ranges for the Phase from Table RE3B. The other main sources apart from this Revisit Essay above are: 1. Manning and Bronk Ramsey (2009), 2. Manning (2009; 2014). The date range given for the end of LMIB covers the range from the LMIB Late destruction at Myrtos-Pyrgos through to the LMIB Final destruction at Mochlos. The time period covering the later LMIB Late and LMIB Final phases seems to cover several decades in the first half of the 15th century BC (note: this can be consistent with the new date and discussion in Höflmayer et al. 2013 – if the dates for the reign of Tuthmosis III are raised slightly as in Aston 2012 there is an even nicer correlation of* ¹⁴C *and historical chronology).*

be dated in the 17th century BC following the Middle or low-Middle Chronology for Mesopotamia, which, importantly, now seems the most plausible solution (see Section 3.c above) – and Tel Kabri (Cline *et al.* 2011).[48]

To conclude, I suggest we are at (or almost at) a tipping point for study of the Aegean and east Mediterranean in the second millennium BC. Forty years ago it was entirely reasonable to regard radiocarbon as not useful to Late Bronze Age Aegean chronology (Hankey and Warren 1974: 142–143); it offered neither accuracy nor, especially, precision. But the situation has changed and changed radically in the decades since, and especially from the AD 1990s with the widespread application of both Accelerator Mass Spectrometry (AMS) dating technology and Bayesian chronological modelling. We may observe that what seemed like an obviously wrong or aberrant intrusion to the archaeological timescale from radiocarbon starting in the mid AD 1970s has not gone away, but has instead become a sustained, replicated, robust and relatively refined alternative timescale (see this Revisit Essay; and e.g. Manning *et al.* 2006a; Manning and Bronk Ramsey 2009; Manning 2009; Wild *et al.* 2010; etc.). Indeed, radiocarbon now appears to offer a better timescale for the Aegean not only for the third millennium BC (e.g. Manning 1995; 2008b; Renfrew *et al.* 2012), but also for the second millennium BC, and to provide a coherent and valid basis for best comparisons with the chronology of Egypt since the ground-changing study of Bronk Ramsey *et al.* (2010) (and, in time, will do so also for the Levant, Anatolia, Cyprus, etc.). If we compare the present status of Aegean chronology versus the standard position of a little over four decades ago, it is evident how far we have come and how our evidence has changed. Stubbings (1970: 240) wrote of the Aegean Bronze Age that: "'Absolute' chronology can be achieved only in patches … For most of the Bronze Age our dates are based … on cross-contacts with Egypt". Today we still have plenty of work to do, but increasingly radiocarbon best provides a framework for the whole of the Aegean Bronze Age, with cross-contacts usefully informative only in those patches where they form sets of coherent linkages (and on critical analysis many instances of cross-cultural contacts have been removed

---

[48] It is relevant to note that the 'high' Aegean chronology for the start of the LBA also works in terms of looking to the west and north. For example, in contrast with the 'low' chronology, the 'high' chronology is either entirely consistent with (or arguably even supported by) material linkages for the LHI period with Italy and Sardinia and the radiocarbon dates from there (as argued some time ago: Manning 1998 – and work since in the central Mediterranean continues to indicate a somewhat raised, versus traditional, EBA-MBA chronological framework consistent with the Aegean 'high' chronology: e.g. Alberti 2011 for Sicily). Looking even further, the remarkable similarities of amber items (and association with gold, and of social practices) between the Shaft Grave world of Mycenae (MHIII and LHI) and the Wessex Culture (Wessex 1 to 2 or Period 3 and into 4 of the southern Britain sequence) of the later Early Bronze Age of southern Britain (Maran 2013: 148–149 and references) make most plausible sense if they were at least relatively contemporary. The Wessex contexts are radiocarbon dated from the first quarter of the second millennium BC into the 17th century BC for a transitional Wessex 2 grave (Needham *et al.* 2010), while the Mycenae contexts would be dated from the 18th to 17th centuries BC on the Aegean 'high' chronology. And, generally, it has been observed that the traditional 'low' Aegean chronology is "problematic from a central and north European perspective, in terms of both chronology and cultural relations" (Kristiansen and Larsson 2005: 118), whereas the 'high' Aegean chronology seems to work well.

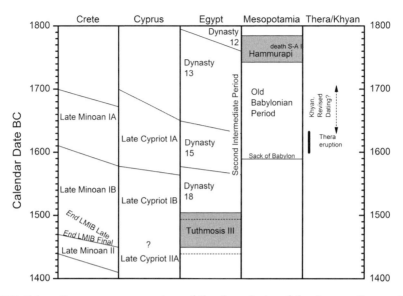

Figure RE27. Schematic summary comparison of the chronologies of the Aegean, Cyprus, Egypt and Mesopotamia in the period around the time of the Thera eruption and as reviewed and discussed in this Revisit Essay. The date range of the Thera eruption is regarded as lying somewhere from the late 1630s BC and by/before 1600 BC (see text above). The Late Minoan IA to II period dates follow the discussion in this text above. The dates for the Late Cypriot IA to IIA periods follow the text above and Merrillees (1992; 2002) and Manning (2001) all modified to a Middle or low-Middle Mesopotamian chronology and to the Aston (2012) or the RE Table 1 Egyptian chronology above (and see Revisit Essay Appendix 1). The transition of Late Cypriot IB to IIA is not especially clear, but is assumed to occur later/late in the reign of Tuthmosis III or thereabouts. The Egyptian dates follow the Egyptian chronology of Table RE1 above (and see Revisit Essay Appendix 1) and/or the chronology of Aston (2012) for the New Kingdom, with the range of Middle Kingdom to Second Intermediate Period dates shown covering von Beckerath (1997); Kitchen (2000) and Krauss and Warburton (2006). The accession of Tuthmosis III is either 1504 BC or 1493 BC. The Mesopotamian dates follow the low-Middle chronology (see Section 3.c above). The revised early approximate placement of Khyan (contemporary with the later to late 13th Dynasty) following the findings reported by Moeller and Marouard (2011; and see Section 3.c.II.i above) is also indicated.

as *not* chronologically useful or relevant data: Höflmayer 2011a; 2012a; 2012b). This ^{14}C disruption, and now new ^{14}C-based chronological framework for some periods, like the 17th-16th centuries BC, means that the field cannot go on with the conventional synthesis and merely note that radiocarbon is divergent (and hope that this 'problem' will go away if ignored for long enough). Instead, taking the radiocarbon-based timescale as our best guide (and actively working to improve this ^{14}C-based timescale in terms of resolution and robustness and with further ^{14}C dating programmes for, e.g., the late 3rd millennium BC, the MBA, and the late LBA to early Iron Age), we need now to analyse, synthesise, and write new critical histories for the Aegean and east Mediterranean in the mid second millennium BC.

A schematic approximate summary of the Aegean 'high' chronology as discussed in the Revisit Essay in terms of some of the main elements of the chronologies of Cyprus, Egypt and Mesopotamia is shown in Figure RE27.

4. Response to, and critique of, Bietak (2004)

Bietak (2004) is a 12 page review and (supposed) critique of Manning (1999), and has been repeatedly referenced by those who – for whatever reason – are against the 'high' Thera or Aegean chronology for the mid second millennium BC (some dwelling on, or putting copies on the internet highlighting, passages where Bietak makes claims that Manning failed to present rigorous scholarship, etc., etc.). I respond following the column numbers of Bietak (2004). While some issues are, undoubtedly, differences in opinion, interpretation, or approach – and I accept that everyone is entitled to their own opinions and these may vary – some of the (supposed serious) claims and arguments made by Bietak in this paper are simply incorrect or reflect poor scholarship on Bietak's part, and I respond regarding these points. I also note a couple of wider issues (which are then discussed in detail in Section 5 below).

(i) Cols. 199–202. Bietak starts by in fact citing a book by someone called "Manning, W."; it should be Manning, Sturt W. or Manning, S.W. (Bietak 2004: Col. 201 states that Manning 1999 has "…a very useful and bulky bibliography, albeit containing a few mistakes (which is uncommon these days)." The mistakes – apparently uncommon these days – are unfortunately not listed (which would of course be a useful corrective). Bietak 2004 has a mistake in his one, and only, opening citation of the book that he is reviewing – this is perhaps even more uncommon?)

Bietak's introduction makes some general observations and notes that Manning (1999) is a "courageous attempt", but already from Col. 200 Bietak complains about the "strong bias" of the author (i.e. Manning) and wishes to give the impression that somehow it is bias, and not the strength of data and argument/analysis, that leads to the views in Manning (1999). See Section 2 above. It is an interesting approach, Bietak complaining of prior bias, and pretending to want objective scholarship; this from an author who, in Bietak (2000b: 187 n.3, towards end), was then happy to dismiss the arguments of Manning (1999) *even without having read them* but merely claiming to have seen them on the internet:

> The new publication by S.W. Manning, *A Test of Time* (Oxford, 2000), which I consulted only on the internet, offers no convincing evidence…

And, in this case, we may further note that the year is incorrect (both for the book and the website which, I assume, he did actually visit: they are each originally dated 1999), and so the appearance of scholarly rigour on Bietak's part slips at least slightly (or further).[49]

(ii) Col. 201 bottom begins the criticisms with some argumentation, versus mere assertion. Here Bietak claims that Manning mistakenly dates some items from Tell el-'Ajjul to the Middle Bronze Age (MBA) when they are really he argues – and as he seeks to demonstrate – from later find contexts. Bietak (or Christa Mlinar who is thanked in Bietak 2004: 201 n.3) has failed to read the text of Manning (1999) carefully or fully! In the text discussion of these items on p.137 and n.658 and pp.138–139 and n.668, Manning (1999) explains the dating (the items are also briefly mentioned on

---

[49] For a discussion and response to the specific claim Bietak is trying to dismiss with this comment, see Manning *et al.* (2002b: 148–152).

p.55 and illustrated pp.56–58 – note that p.55 line 6 specifically says "see discussion in Chapter IV" – where the pp.137–139 discussion is located, and the Index p.493 has the entry under Tell el-'Ajjul (Gaza) "gold jewellery and links with frescoes 138–139" – again directing the reader to the discussion with cited scholarship regarding the likely later MB original manufacture date of these items). Yes, these items have usually been dated Late Bronze I and were found in such later find contexts, *but* I followed the (then recent) scholarship I cite at Manning (1999: 137 n.658 and 139 n.668) which suggests that these jewellery items are (nonetheless) in fact later MBII in origin (as in when they were produced, which is what is relevant when I compare their design/form with other artwork). And hence I date them later MBII when considering contemporary linkages for the style embodied in these items. Thus, and somewhat typical of the supposed overwhelming critique of the Bietak (2004) review, this first much trumpeted supposed criticism by Bietak (20 lines of text and ending in an exclamation mark) is in fact (i) incorrect, and (ii) betrays a failure to correctly read and follow the Manning (1999) text and arguments in detail. I note that I made the above points previously (Manning 2007: 123–124). Bietak in Col. 208 then has the temerity to claim against Manning (1999) that:

> These are just some of the numerous and quite deplorable mistakes which show an utmost lack of care in dealing with archaeological sources.

When in fact it is Bietak – as in the example just reviewed – who has failed to 'deal' carefully, fully and correctly – i.e. read properly – the archaeological sources.

(iii) Col. 202. Bietak complains about my terminology in Manning (1999) and in particular the term 'Compromise Early Chronology' for the possibility of a date for the Thera eruption around the mid 16th century BC. I offer an explanation here. When Manning (1999) was written Bietak placed the eruption c.1515–1460 BC (Bietak 1996; 1997), and the earliest date suggested by the current 'low' chronology scholarship was 1520 BC (Warren 1998). These dates envisaged the eruption as during the 18th Dynasty at a minimum and (for much of the Bietak range above) likely the Tuthmosid period. This 18th Dynasty link was, and is, regarded as the absolute requirement for the 'low' chronology position. The 'early' chronology from the start has argued that the eruption occurred likely *before* the 18th Dynasty. The possibility of a date in the mid 16th century BC, unless merely treated as the very latest possible (and hence highly unlikely) date allowed within the extremes of the 95.4% radiocarbon range, means a date from a couple of decades before, to the very start of, the 18th Dynasty. While – as Bietak complains – this is not so far in temporal terms from the 'low' range and further from the 'high' date in the later 17th century BC, such a pre-18th Dynasty to start 18th Dynasty date nonetheless requires the re-evaluation (i.e. rejection) of a number of supposed facts or absolutes and interpretations repeatedly stated by the 'low' chronology scholarship. Thus the logic and requirements of the mid-16th century BC date are more similar to the 'high' chronology – i.e. a significant rethink of 'convention' – and *not* the 'low' chronology. This mid 16th century BC range was not the most likely from the radiocarbon – but possible – and the archaeology could be interpreted to work; hence my choice (in Manning 1999) to refer to this position as the 'Compromise Early Chronology'. Of course another name could be chosen – but it is most definitely not the 'low' chronology, since the archaeological synthesis has to be significantly changed to one inherently more similar to the 'high' chronology arguments from Kemp and Merrillees (1980); Betancourt (1987); Manning (1988a); and much scholarship onwards.

If the date for the start of the Egyptian New Kingdom were to be raised by a couple of decades (which, very conveniently, Aston 2012 proposes), then this would be a way of trying to keep some or more of the 'low' chronology archaeological synthesis while also having a position potentially compatible with the radiocarbon evidence – both in the Aegean and from Egypt. Recently Höflmayer (2012a) has argued for just such a re-think of the 'low' chronology position. If this were to be the case, then, with a little reassessment of the less than clear or known information – like the chronology of Egyptian stone vessel forms from the later Second Intermediate Period through the early 18th Dynasty, and the original import date of the White Slip I sherds found in secondary if not tertiary contexts at Tell el-Dab'a, and so on – we could envisage a chronological synthesis where even a late 17th century BC date for the Thera eruption[50] could work against the archaeological-historical data (as suggested by Höflmayer 2012a). It may end up that the supposed dramatic, large, impossible-to-bridge, etc., gap (of 100–150 years) between the radiocarbon date for the Thera eruption and the VDL at Akrotiri, and the archaeological synthesis linking the Aegean and east Mediterranean and Egyptian cultures – one of the main reasons that Bietak (e.g. 2003; 2004, etc.; Wiener e.g. 2009) believes that the 'high' chronology must *a priori* be wrong – does not really exist, or is at least very much smaller, and so almost manageable (Höflmayer 2012a).

(iv) Bottom of Col. 202 and Col. 203 Bietak returns again to the argument that I change 'register' – and let claims go from supposed uncertainty to certainty – and he magisterially states that "Such changes in register should not be used in an objective scholarly publication. This should set alarms bells ringing". Pots and kettles come to mind.[51] I can only suggest that any 'objective' reader read some of the bibliography of Bietak on the topic of east Mediterranean chronology and ask themselves who argues entire positions based on subjective readings of the evidence, arbitrary assumptions regarding stratigraphy, time, and selected synchronisms (which then over time become 'factoids': e.g. Bietak 1979 to Bietak 2000b), and *a priori* rejections of whole bodies of 'objective' evidence (Bietak 2003). Read Warburton (2009b). Ask who took over 6 years to finally publish radiocarbon data from his own site which both undermine his

---

[50] It is worth highlighting that – in 2012 – the available radiocarbon evidence and analytical options favour a date in the last 3 decades of the 17th century BC (see this Revisit Essay; see subsequently the Postscript (i), which expands this to the last four decades, perhaps favouring c.1630–1610 BC). There have been changes in the likely date over the period 1999 to present. When Manning (1999) was written 1628 BC seemed to be a strong candidate – but the (then) associated arguments to select this date from the wider mid-later 17th century BC radiocarbon range may now be discounted. Similarly, arguments made about an ice-core acidity layer dated c.1645/1644 BC may now be either discounted with regard to Thera, or perhaps even be re-dated 20 years later (Muscheler 2009 – and perhaps then be potentially relevant again) (see Section 1 and 3.c.I above; Manning 2007; 2010). We are left at present with best dating evidence for the date of the Thera eruption somewhere in the last 3 decades of the 17th century BC (see now Postscript (i)).

[51] Since linguistic difficulties are raised by Bietak (2004: Col. 208), I provide a reference for this English idiom: http://en.wikipedia.org/wiki/The_pot_calling_the_kettle_black

archaeological chronology, and the entire interpretative scheme for his own site (see Warburton 2009b; Manning and Kromer 2011a; Kutschera *et al.* 2012)?

The specific subject for this supposed general attack on Manning (1999) is the Kom Rabi'a Aegean sherd. Manning (1999)'s sin was to follow the scholarly publication of the sherd by Bourriau and Eriksson (1997) – the latest and only scholarly account available when Manning (1999) was written. The Manning text recounted the history of the sherd's identification and – hardly unreasonably – went with the published statement of Bourriau and Eriksson (1997). Bietak cites Manning (1999: 28 and 42) – whereas the major discussion of the sherd is actually on pp.203–204 (not cited by Bietak – and again, as in (ii) above – an instance where Bietak does not seem to have read my text fully or accurately), and this is where I offer *my* case for why, when I wrote Manning (1999), I thought the sherd was most likely to be LMIB in date (versus just citing Bourriau and Eriksson 1997 and some earlier mentions in the literature as on pp. 28 and 42).[52] Bietak then goes on to argue that the Kom Rabi'a find context is not in fact secure and might be later. With the benefit of studies available *since* 1999, this is possible and even likely (see Höflmayer 2009: 191). I (in writing a book published in 1999) used and relied on the available published information; if later critique of this and new work (e.g. the Aston study cited by Bietak 2004 as forthcoming = Aston 2007) subsequently demonstrate that this previous published assessment is not sound or not secure, then of course this evidence becomes less valuable – such is normal scholarly progress achieved. But this does not mean I did anything wrong in citing the published evidence as it was when I wrote Manning (1999). Bietak (2004) uses anachronistic hindsight when it suits him – but neither fairly, nor always appropriately. If we are only ever to use archaeological evidence once all its associated context and site have been fully published, then we would also never be able to do research or make progress. To pick just one random major site: so much is not published fully or properly or at all from Tell el-Dab'a – or what is available suggests likely serious problems with stratigraphy or interpretation (Warburton 2009b) – that no evidence at all should be considered from this site. Reasonable? I am sure Bietak will say 'no' – but it would be entirely in keeping with the line of his argument in Bietak (2004).

(v) Cols. 203–204. Bietak (2004) criticizes Manning for basically just recounting what Niemeier (1990) had published (about finds at Tel Kabri) in what is an introductory review section of the Manning (1999) book (pp.29–30). As noted above, Bietak fails to cite any of my subsequent more detailed discussions in the book – he just sticks to the brief review introduction to the history of the topic (Manning 1999: 7–45). Bietak spends 70 lines rejecting the Niemeier case and the likelihood, or even possibility, of the Tel Kabri evidence supporting the 'high' chronology. Rather than critique each of his non-arguments here (and see the subsequent publication of Kempinski 2002), I refer readers to the work of an entirely new Israeli-American team working now at Tel Kabri. Cline *et al.* (2011) report on finds at Tel Kabri of many new fragments belonging to an

---

[52] Despite Bietak (2004: Cols. 202–203) stressing that Manning (1999) is incorrect for arguing that the sherd is most likely LMIB in date, one can note that Aston (2007: 212) and Höflmayer (2009: 191) also support a LMIB date. The latter ends his discussion: "a LMIB-date … seems clear" (see also Höflmayer 2012b: 125–128).

Aegean-style fresco and painted floor and they state that their new work very much replicates and supports the previous studies of Niemeier and Kempinski. In particular, the fresco/floor finds are stated to be Middle Bronze II and probably 17th century B.C.E. in origin (i.e. painting and use) (Cline *et al.* 2011: 254–257) – i.e. exactly the scenario discussed in Manning (1999) from Niemeier. Cline *et al.* (2011: 257) explicitly conclude that their findings at Tell Kabri leave "open a chronological scheme that will fit the "high" chronology for the Theran eruption". Thus this is exactly the opposite of the claims of Bietak (2004: Col.204) that "the Kabri paintings cannot be used to support a date just before 1600 BC". Instead, the Tel Kabri data are at least compatible with the 'high' Aegean chronology, and could reasonably be argued to offer some support.

(vi) Col. 205. Bietak accepts in his view that the Alalakh VII paintings may be LMIA in style/association, but then says that the dating could be much later than the 17th century BC following the ultra-Low or even Low Mesopotamian chronology. Work since Manning (1999) has provided a pretty robust and detailed radiocarbon wiggle-match for the dendrochronology covering the MBA in central Anatolia (Manning *et al.* 2001; 2003; 2010; Kromer *et al.* 2001), and this work (revising Kuniholm *et al.* 1996 and the situation when Manning 1999 was written) provides strong grounds for the Middle chronology or a chronology close to the Middle chronology – especially the low-Middle chronology (see Section 3.c above). Work from the textual/historical side further provides strong support for the Middle chronology (or one very close to it) and thus altogether offers a very strong solution paired with the radiocarbon-wiggle-matched dendrochronology in support of generally a Middle chronology solution (Barjamovic *et al.* 2012) and perhaps particularly a low-Middle chronology about 8 years later (de Jong 2013a). In turn, a 17th century BC date for the (plausibly or likely) LMIA-style Alalakh paintings is likely, and this either is compatible with, or even offers some support for, the 'high' Aegean chronological synthesis.

(vii) Col. 205 bottom. Bietak expresses mystification that I suggested that his method of dating Tell el-Dab'a via arbitrary intervals and in terms of prior views on Syro-Palestinian chronology might prove open to at least 'a little flexibility'. I am hardly alone in expressing concern about the stratigraphy and chronology construction at Tell el-Dab'a (Warburton 2009b); and the paper by Kutschera *et al.* (2012) highlighting an unexplainable offset of on average a little over a century between a large set of modern radiocarbon dates from Tell el-Dab'a versus the Bietak chronology for the site only begs the question even more. Since a large set of radiocarbon dates from a number of other defined Egyptian contexts offers very good agreement with the Egyptian historical chronology (Bronk Ramsey *et al.* 2010), one has to ask what is wrong at Tell el-Dab'a? If it is not the radiocarbon – which works very well elsewhere in Egypt – then perhaps it is the dates assigned or stated for the contexts and stratigraphy declared at Tell el-Dab'a? Oddly enough, the radiocarbon dates from Tell el-Dab'a offer a chronology which would allow the strata of the site to align nicely with the 'high' Aegean chronology synthesis – an alignment suggested from the archaeology alone for many years (e.g. Manning *et al.* 2002b: 148–154).

(viii) Col. 206 middle. Bietak writes that at Tell el-Dab'a "White Slip I (WSI) Ware did not make its first appearance before the 18th Dynasty". Bietak returns to this topic again in Cols. 211–213. This (and some other such 'first appearances') is held to be a key datum, and one that requires a date for the Thera eruption after the start of the Egyptian New Kingdom since a WSI bowl was found on Thera under the pumice. Apart from saying please read Manning (1999: 153–192) and the short review statement above in Section 3.c.II.iv (and references there), I quote the recent statement of Höflmayer (2012a) after his review of the WSI issue (pp.442–443) where he offers exactly the opposite conclusion to the one so firmly stated by Bietak:

> There are important limitations that have to be considered regarding the chronological value of this argument. Although White Slip I pottery does not occur in Tell el-Dab'a earlier than Str. C/3 (reign of Thutmose III), it has to be remembered that no complete vessels were found and that the published fragments only come from secondary or tertiary contexts, i.e. no material was found *in situ*. The first appearance of White Slip I ware in Egypt and the Levant is based on sherds, so far only from residual material. In fact, only a few fragments of White Slip I come from Str. C at Tell el- Dab'a: Bietak and Hein (2001) mention only 6 sherds of clear White Slip I attribution found in Str. C (without differentiating between C/2 and C/3) and Maguire (2009) mentions only a few fragments coming from Str. C (although for 2 fragments even a date in Str. D/2, dated to the late Hyksos period, has not been ruled out: DAB 378 and 383).
>
> One should thus regard the first appearance of White Slip I ware in the early 18th Dynasty in the eastern Mediterranean only as a *terminus ante quem* for the start of the White Slip sequence on Cyprus, which should then start earlier than ~1540 BCE based on the Egyptian historical chronology. (Höflmayer 2012a: 442)

To emphasise the key points: the WSI from Tell el-Dab'a comes from secondary or even tertiary contexts; it is not in situ. Its 'first' appearances in the excavated Tell el-Dab'a record thus only set a *terminus ante quem* – by an unknown amount – for when the ware was being made in Cyprus. This means, to again quote Höflmayer:

> Cypriot White Slip pottery therefore provides no convincing argument against an eruption date of ~1600 BCE or shortly before. (Höflmayer 2012a: 443)

I think this White Slip I argument against the 'high' Aegean-Cypriot chronology by Bietak (see Bietak 1998 onwards; and those who followed like Wiener 2001) can be now dropped as lacking both merit or rigour.

(ix) Col. 206 bottom to Col. 208. Bietak says (criticizing Manning 1999) that "It is also most unwise without the expertise and inside knowledge of a complex research project to try to reinterpret the results". The other way to read this situation is to note how unsatisfactory and incomplete and contradictory is much of the published record of the large and complex excavations at Tell el-Dab'a (Warburton 2009b). This is now even more apparent with the publication of the radiocarbon data from the site (Kutschera *et al.* 2012), which indicate the potential for some serious misunderstandings of the stratigraphy/archaeology, or misinterpretations of this record (Manning and Kromer 2011a). Manning (1999) tried to assess what was then published. I (of course) made some mistakes or misunderstandings (for just one example: I did not appreciate then that the grain silo stratum I mentioned from Bietak 1997 – Manning 1999: 92 – in fact indicated two new strata, D/1. 1–2, and that the stratigraphic summary I published in Manning 1999: Fig. 23 after Bietak 1996 therefore already needed significant revision) – but one might also blame the sources of information if so much is unclear, inadequate, or contradictory. Bietak's series of publications in the AD 1990s confused or confounded a number of readers. The article of Cline (1998) is the obvious example of this to cite. Only retrospectively – and after Manning (1999) was written – did Bietak (e.g. 2000b) offer a clearer statement declaring that, for example, all the wall painting fragments came from what he considered a Tuthmosid context (as Bietak 2004: Cols. 207–208 – citing literature written by himself and colleagues in his footnote 17 which only appeared *after* Manning 1999 was published).[53] Bietak chastises Manning (1999) for, e.g., thinking there might possibly be two phases of wall paintings. I fully accept that Bietak now says there are not. But, writing in 1996–1999 – when Manning (1999) was written – this was not so clear, especially when, for example, none other than Bietak himself in an article with Marinatos (Bietak and Marinatos 1995: 49) wrote: "the Minoan wall paintings date to *two periods…*" [my italics]. It is hardly odd that some took this at face value, or failed fully to appreciate a sharp change of interpretation in the following years – sometimes even after they had written/published the relevant text (and so could hardly be able to take subsequent literature into account).

(x) Cols. 208 bottom to top of Col. 209. Bietak seems to accept as possible that the Tell el-Dab'a wall paintings might in fact be LMIB (and more likely later LMIB and into LMII to LMIIIA) in date in Aegean stylistic terms as argued by Manning (1999: 100–107) – and *not* LMIA as Bietak has usually argued to this point (and sometimes afterwards also). For further discussion on this topic and the LMIB (at earliest) to LMII/IIIA dating of the Tell el-Dab'a wall paintings, see Manning (2009: 222–223); Shaw (2009); Younger (2009). If this material is all Tuthmosid, as Bietak now firmly states, then the Aegean stylistic date of LMIB to LMII/IIIA certainly does not contradict the Aegean 'high' chronology (and its dates for LMIB and LMII: see Manning 2009), and might even tend to support it.

(xi) Cols. 210–213. Regarding rhyta, Egyptian stone vessels, and WSI, see discussions above in this Revisit Essay. Bietak also criticizes Manning (1999: 120) for referring to the Base Ring (BR) I sherd from Memphis that had been published as from a SIP context. Ignoring Manning's point about regionalism, Bietak states that BRI does not appear at Ezbet Helmi until the Tuthmosid period (Col. 211). However, the Tell el-Dab'a evidence itself makes it apparent that this is not really clear (or correct). DAB 388 is stated by Maguire (2009: 173) to be from Stratum D/2–B – and thus not a definite Tuthmosid context at all. DAB 387 is given a Tuthmosid Stratum C context (Maguire 2009: 172), but is just a sherd (residual?) and from the description and drawing could be BRII. As in the case of the WSI, all the evidence in fact makes clear is that a *terminus ante quem* for BRI lies *before* the Tell el-Dab'a contexts. Since one of the two BR items in the study of Maguire (2009) could have derived from a late Hyksos (Stratum D/2) context (and even then as secondary material), this in fact yields a possible *minimum* date for BR entirely contradictory to the position of Bietak.

(xii) Col. 212 bottom to Col. 213 top. Bietak refers to the jug with incised figural decoration from Toumba tou Skourou Tomb 5 and claims it somehow disproves the

---

[53] Bietak (2011: 21–26) provides a succinct summary of his current interpretation of the history of the site from the Hyksos abandonment through the Tuthmosid period.

'high' chronology, because, if he applies his 'low' Tell el-Dab'a date against the 'high' Aegean-Cypriot chronology, he says there is a mis-match. Of course: he is mixing apples and oranges. Manning (2007: 123) reviewed this case in some detail. It can be compatible with the 'high' chronology (early/earlier 17th century BC jug deposited in late Middle Cypriot III tomb in earlier 17th century BC). It very certainly does *not* go "right against Manning's chronology" as Bietak asserts.

   Note: in their recent magisterial synthesis of Tell el-Yahudiya Ware, Aston and Bietak (2012: 193) argue that this vessel is of the Levantine-Egyptian J.1 group (and not a local Cypriot imitation as Negbi 1978 proposed) and of "Late Thirteenth Dynasty/Second Intermediate Period date". They argue that if Late Cypriot IA then it is an heirloom (whereas I would argue that this need not be the case). The dating proposed (late 13th Dynasty/Second Intermediate Period) in fact seems to offer a good and plausible synchronism either with late Middle Cypriot or Late Cypriot IA, and very clearly could be compatible with the 'high' chronology synthesis.

(xiii) Cols. 214–215. Pumice. See Section 3.c.I.v above.

(xiv) Col. 215. Bietak begins discussion of the scientific dating evidence and this part of the Manning (1999) book. He takes issue with my not regarding historical chronology and astrochronology for Egypt as 'absolute', and states that "It is a great illusion to believe that sciences are more reliable, at least for now, in obtaining absolute dates". Bietak is confidently (then at least) of the view that (Col. 218) "It is well known that ^{14}C is about 50–100 years higher than the historical dates of the New Kingdom" – no basis for this view is provided – one assumes it was already the first ^{14}C dates at Tell el-Dab'a (which started to be mentioned at meetings and conferences around this time – for example in Vienna in 2004 and 2005, and Walter Kutschera presented them at the radiocarbon conference in Oxford in 2006, but for some reason – excavator perhaps did not like the results? – these were not formally and properly published for more than half a dozen years…: see now the excellent report of Kutschera *et al.* 2012). As it turned out, the "at least for now" was short-lived. The publication of Bronk Ramsey *et al.* (2010) does exactly what Bietak most feared: this large-scale and sophisticated radiocarbon study provides a precise chronology for second millennium BC Egypt which is not only of similar resolution to the historical chronology, but can even offer resolution between some of the rival historical chronologies and suggest which date range is more likely. Since such a sophisticated analysis of a sequence of radiocarbon sets provides a good chronology for Egypt and one compatible with the standard historical chronology (if a slightly higher standard range – harking back to e.g. Wente and van Siclen 1976; Hayes 1970; or as recently proposed by Aston 2012 for the earlier 18th Dynasty: see also Appendix 1 to this Revisit Essay), there seems an *a priori* likelihood that similar high-quality radiocarbon sequence analyses using substantial data sets from loci elsewhere in the second millennium BC east Mediterranean will also yield correct and appropriate age ranges – such as the Aegean sequence published by Manning *et al.* (2006a). It must also, as Warburton (2009b) argues, raise serious questions about the stratigraphic analyses, archaeological interpretations, and/or the linkages drawn between contexts and historical dates for a site – such as Tell el-Dab'a – when a large series of radiocarbon dates and similar sophisticated analysis finds an offset of over a century between the claimed archaeological dating and the refined radiocarbon chronology (Kutschera *et al.* 2012). There seems no plausible reason why radiocarbon dating should work very well elsewhere in Egypt over the course of the second millennium BC, and just not work, solely, at Tell el-Dab'a. As Warburton (2009b: 144) concludes:

> In this volume, Wiener notes that the ^{14}C dates dates from Tell el-Dab'a differ radically from the dates of the various layers proposed by the excavators, and remarks that "the cause of the anomaly remains unknown". Yet, in fact, the situation is exactly the opposite. The excavators at Tell el-Dab'a insist that all of the dates for all of the levels at Tell el-Dab'a are off by a century and more. It is no longer possible to speak of an anomaly: the anomaly is the archaeological dating.

(xv) Cols. 215–218. Radiocarbon evidence for the dating of the Thera eruption and the Aegean from the MMIII to LMII period. The data and their analysis have changed considerably since Manning (1999) was published. Much new data and sophisticated analyses of these data have been published (in particular Manning *et al.* 2002a; Manning and Bronk Ramsey 2003; Galimberti *et al.* 2004; Bronk Ramsey *et al.* 2004; Friedrich *et al.* 2006; Manning *et al.* 2006a; 2009a; Manning and Bronk Ramsey 2009; Manning 2009; Heinemeier *et al.* 2009; Wild *et al.* 2010; Lindblom and Manning 2011), along with a number of papers considering the dating issues and demonstrating how robust this evidence is in general, and how a date range in the later 17th century BC for the late LMIA VDL at Akrotiri and the closely subsequent eruption of Thera is the most likely finding across a range of scenarios (Manning and Bronk Ramsey 2003: 124–129; 2009; Manning 2005; 2007; 2009; Manning *et al.* 2006a; 2009a; Friedrich *et al.* 2009; Manning and Kromer 2011a; 2012; Höflmayer 2012a). For a current assessment, see above Section 3.c.III. The particularist comments of Bietak trying to undermine the Manning (1999) radiocarbon discussion and questioning why the extreme (low) parts of probability ranges could not also be possible,[54] and the evidence as it was in 1999, are for most purposes no longer relevant and nothing is to be gained by going over these discussions now when we instead have much more and high-quality evidence and much more sophisticated and appropriate analyses of this large body of evidence. Thus see the discussions earlier in Section 3.c.III.

(xvi) Col. 218 lower. Bietak observes that Manning (1999) favoured the 1628 BC dendro and ice-core package dating within the wider range indicated by the radiocarbon. But then Bietak notes that the date for the ice-core acidity layer became more precise in publications, and was incompatible with 1628 BC at around 1645/1644 BC give or take it was stated ±7 and then ±4 years, and Bietak sees a problem. Yes, Bietak is correct. As discussed earlier in this Revisit Essay, this area is one where there has been a major change since Manning (1999) was written – in my (more critical) assessment of some of the data, in the data available, and general associated information. What seemed a fairly convincing coincidence of radiocarbon, tree-ring, and ice-core dating in the mid-AD 1980s to late AD 1990s around a hypothetical Thera eruption date of 1628 BC, has

---

[54] The answer of course is yes it is possible – but by definition these extremes of the overall ranges are very unlikely (see further discussion in Section 3.c.III.iii above) – hence the arguments made in Manning (1999) and against which Bietak complains.

fallen apart since, both because of new and better data, and because critical assessment has highlighted that there were flaws in the argument that pushed this coincidence of different observations together in the first place (see e.g. Manning 2007: 103–104). On the ice-core evidence and why it is not presently useful, see Section 3.c.I.i above; on the non-Porsuk tree-ring evidence, which might indicate a major volcanic eruption, but, as of yet, in no case is actually linked in any positive way to Thera, see Section 3.c.I.iii above. On the Porsuk tree-ring growth anomaly and why it no longer has a date compatible with c.1628 BC and is instead to be dated c.1651/1650 BC (see Postscript (iv)), and why, although it might show a volcanic association, there is no evidence to link this with Thera, see Section 3.c.I.iv above. This means that the radiocarbon data – now a much larger more high-quality dataset compared to 1999 – directly relevant to the VDL on Thera and to Aegean archaeological sites before, contemporary with, and after the late LMIA at Thera, are currently our only and best definite scientific dating source for the Thera debate (and perhaps also forthcoming work on the Sofular speleothem: see Section 3.c.I.ii above).

(xvii) Cols. 218 bottom, 221–222. Dating of the Gordion dendrochronology and related matters. Bietak questions whether the dating of this dendrochronology was changed (between Kuniholm *et al.* 1996 and Manning *et al.* 2001) to match the ice-core dates, and how the chronology has been so easily 'reconstructed', and so implies that it is all some flexible exercise and thus of no value, and he questions the dating of the Uluburun ship, and raises some concerns about dendrochronologically matching (i.e. crossdating) different tree species. This set of questions and topics raises some important issues, and painful reminders of uncomfortable lessons for this author since AD 1999. I have already briefly explained the redating of the Gordion tree-ring chronology based on many more additional ^{14}C dates and the much more highly resolved ^{14}C dendro wiggle match analyses (of 52 dates in AD 2001 versus just 18 in AD 1996, and then with 128 dates in AD 2010) (Manning *et al.* 2001; 2010): see Section 3.c.I.iv. It had nothing to do with ice-core dates (Manning *et al.* 2001 merely noted that – then – the redating of the Aegean dendrochronology offered a date for the ring 854 growth anomaly that might be compatible with the 1645/1644 BC major volcanic acidity layer – subsequently it has become even less clear whether this acidity layer has anything to do with Thera: see Section 3.c.I.i above). With regard to the Aegean dendrochronological issues (some specific, some general), I go through these in some detail in Section 5 below – please see there. None of these matters impact on the question of the Thera date, now that the ring 854 growth anomaly in the Aegean dendrochronology is dated c.1651/1650 BC (see Postscript (iv)) and is discounted as regards Thera. But they do raise important issues about what should and should not be relied on in Aegean and east Mediterranean dendrochronology.

5. *Corrections/mistakes in Manning (1999)*

(a) Corrections/Mistakes – which were errors/mistakes in 1999 – and discussion

There are a few things in the original Manning (1999) text which I would correct, delete or change, not because of new findings, debate, and general progress in research, but because they were mistakes or errors in 1999, whether by my error, or my lack of knowledge at the time. Some of the more important of these relate to the Aegean Dendrochronology Project work up to that time.

(i) Supposed 12th century BC dendrochronological anomaly in the Aegean Dendrochronology Project data and relevance (pp. 313–315). The paper of Kuniholm *et al.* (1996) claimed that there was a significant tree ring growth anomaly starting in relative ring 1324 in the Anatolian dendrochronology (which became ring 1329 in Manning 1999: 314). However, there is in fact no such significant 12th century BC anomaly in the available Anatolian dendrochronology (whether significant in the statistical sense, or as in just fairly convincing) – as evident from an examination of the graph and data in Kuniholm *et al.* (2005). It was a mistake to believe the non-demonstrated assertions that such a significant 12th century BC anomaly existed, whereas, in fact, there was no strong evidence and thus nothing to be tied with the relative ring 854 growth anomaly to help place the dendrochronology (as was incorrectly argued by Kuniholm *et al.* 1996: 781–782).

The best placement of the floating Anatolian dendrochronology on the basis of a large-scale radiocarbon wiggle-match analysis has been most recently considered in Manning *et al.* (2010 – see previously Manning *et al.* 2003; 2001; Kromer *et al.* 2001), and I regard this dating as the best estimate available as of AD 2013. This dating means that the ring 854 growth anomaly in the Anatolian dendrochronology lies around 1651/1650 BC (see Postscript (iv)), give or take a relatively small (sub 10 years) error on any calculation (Manning *et al.* 2010). Therefore, the ring 854 growth anomaly is distinct from the 1628/1627 BC growth anomalies noted in several other northern hemisphere tree-ring series. It is also distinct from the likely date range of the Thera eruption from [14]C. For a more general statement about the reliability of Anatolian dendrochronology, see below.

(ii) Uluburun and dendrochronology (p.345 and Fig. 63). The supposed dating of the Uluburun ship by dendrochronology reported/repeated in Manning (1999) from Kuniholm *et al.* (1996) was a mistake (and is withdrawn). Again the supposed dendrochronology was in fact not (at all) sound, as tentatively indicated already in Manning *et al.* (2001: 2535 n.38), and subsequently firmly stated in Manning *et al.* (2009b). This 'dendrodate' should never have been put into the literature.

A best effort near-absolute dating of the last voyage of the Uluburun ship, through a combination of radiocarbon dating and dendro-^{14}C-wiggle-matching, has since been published (Manning *et al.* 2009b). This dating and discussion should be employed. Criticisms of the supposed dendro dating of the Uluburun wood in AD 1996 and AD 1999 by e.g. Peter James (see James 2012: 146 and references) – are correct. The near-absolute dating in the subsequent study of Manning *et al.* (2009b) yields a likely date range for the last voyage of the Uluburun ship c.1320 ± 15 BC, compatible otherwise with the arguments and discussions of Manning (1999: 344–346, 417–418).[55] See Postscript (v) for update.

---

[55] James (2012: 147) tries to use rhetoric to negate or undervalue the study on the Uluburun ship date in Manning *et al.* (2009b) – but in so doing sacrifices correct representation of the data and what is

For more general statements about the dating and reliability of Anatolian dendrochronology, see below.

(iii)   The dating of the Anatolian juniper dendrochronology reported in 2001 (Manning *et al.* 2001; Kromer *et al.* 2001) and tested further in 2003 (Manning *et al.* 2003) was based solely on the detailed radiocarbon dating of dendrochronologically sequenced samples of juniper from the Gordion dendrochronology and their wiggle-matching to the (then current) radiocarbon calibration curve. This produced a date for the dendrochronology some 22 years earlier than the date mistakenly proposed in AD 1996 (note the radiocarbon analysis in the AD 1996 paper – on many fewer samples, n=18 – in fact preferred a date within 9 years of the placement in AD 2001, and we should have used this – but see the mea culpa in (i) above). This 22-year dating change was made solely because the date proposed in the 1996 paper was no longer possible within the dating range available from the analysis of the substantial body of radiocarbon wiggle-match data (n=52 ^{14}C dates in the AD 2001 papers), and the new date offered came solely from the dendro-sequenced wiggle-matching analysis. With over twice as many radiocarbon dates compared to AD 2001, this work was again repeated and further tested a decade later, and found almost the same date for the Gordion dendrochronology (within about 0–1 years – so change from AD 1996 of 22–23 years): Manning *et al.* (2010). Information on the Gordion dendrochronology is published in Kuniholm *et al.* (2011); the

---

being done in order to achieve his desired ends. The first main argument by James is that because it is not possible to dendrochronologically crossdate the cedar wood from the Uluburun ship (which is stated by Manning *et al.* 2009b and supports previous claims by James that dendro cross-dating is not possible), then somehow there also cannot be clear tree-ring sequences (ring following ring) in the samples which can at least be separated out into sequential sets of tree-rings for ^{14}C wiggle-match dating (on which see e.g. Galimberti *et al.* 2004; Bayliss and Tyers 2004). This is incorrect: there are sequential ring sequences in the cedar samples as one would expect for the species (the tree-ring sequences available are shown in Manning *et al.* 2009b: Fig. 6 and those used for the ^{14}C wiggle-matches are shown in Manning *et al.* 2009b: Figs. 8, 10, 12, 14 and 16) – and if one looks closely at Manning *et al.* (2009b: Fig. 6) tree-rings are visible in KAS-7 especially on the right side of the sample as shown. Thus over the short tree-ring sequences available from the samples, one can divide up sets of sequential tree rings, radiocarbon date these, and match these tree-ring defined patterns against the radiocarbon calibration curve (see Manning *et al.* 2009b). Despite James' criticizing of the language used – he claims it is buzzwords and such – this is straightforward science and the analyses provide good matches and relatively precise dates and overall the analysis offers a fairly precise date for the last voyage of the Uluburun ship. The second misleading tactic of James (and a fairly standard one for those who wish to avoid radiocarbon evidence when inconvenient to their arguments) is to cite the extreme lowest possible date of a range, without stating the range, nor the very low probability of this last extreme age, and then pretend that somehow this is the date and argue from here. Thus whereas Manning *et al.* (2009b: Fig. 17) find a fairly clearly defined most likely date range of 1333–1307 BC at 68.2% probability and an overall 1343–1274 BC range at 95.4% probability – with still the area around c.1320 BC the most likely (the mode) – James just cites the extreme lowest end of the 95.4% range, 1274 BC, on p.147 and argues from there (the probability of a date of c.1274 BC or later is of course less than 3%). This type of minimalist, selective, special pleading logic always allows one to avoid the obvious (in this case simply look at Manning *et al.* 2009b: Fig. 17).

security of the dendrochronology relevant to the specific samples employed for the radiocarbon wiggle-match work is discussed and illustrated, and all the radiocarbon data are made available, in Manning *et al.* (2010).

Unfortunately, Manning (1999) was written before the 2001 re-analysis of the ^{14}C data on the Gordion dendrochronology, and so used the Kuniholm *et al.* (1996) paper and its mistaken assumptions (see (i) and (ii) above). Thus all references to the Anatolian dendrochronology dates in Manning (1999) should be adjusted backwards (older) by around 22–23 years as subsequently shown (see above). This means, for example, that the Gordion dendrochronology supports a Middle to low-Middle Babylonian chronology range, and *not* (as in the Kuniholm 1996 paper) the Low Babylonian chronology (this revision of Low to Middle or low-Middle was stated in Manning *et al.* 2001; the much more robust analysis of Manning *et al.* 2010 found the same result within about 0–1 years). For a detailed case for a likely Middle (or near-Middle, i.e. low-Middle) Babylonian chronology, which is consistent with the textual and dendrochronological data at Kültepe Kaneš, see now Barjamovic *et al.* (2012) and the discussion and references to other recent scholarly work in Section 3.c above.

(iv) Is the Gordion/Anatolian dendrochronology sound? This is a more general question, raised by Keenan (2002a: 232–233) and also in a WWW paper on Keenan's website (http://informath.org/ATSU04a.pdf), and repeated from there in summary form by e.g. Liphschitz (2007: 164–165)[56] who concludes (p.165) that "[t]he Anatolian master chronology has proved to be untrustworthy". Keenan (2002a: 233) for his part ends stating: "[i]n conclusion, Anatolian dendrochronology should be regarded as suspect and in need of independent scrutiny". For the question of the wiggle-match dating discussed in (i) and (ii) and Bietak's (2004) complaints that it moved, and, indeed generally, the fundamental issue is the Gordion juniper dendrochronology. This is the dendrochronology that was radiocarbon wiggle-match dated and which forms the major core of the Bronze-Iron Age Anatolian dendrochronology. So, how do we know that this chronology is sound, and why can we reject claims that it is suspect? The two key reasons are:

(a) The Gordion area dendrochronology (of archaeologically recovered *juniperus* spp. – there is also a separate *Pinus nigra* chronology) has been twice built from the beginning, independently (different investigators and in different laboratories), and by use of entirely different techniques (skeleton plotting versus curve-matching), and yet the same dendrochronology has been the result. This two strand history is summarized by Kuniholm *et al.* (2011: 80–82). The initial study by Jeffrey S. Dean at the Laboratory of Tree-Ring Research, University of Arizona, working on samples obtained by Bryant Bannister, is by someone widely regarded as one of the leading

---

[56] But note that Liphschitz's (2007:164) citation of Keenan (2004) is incorrect regarding dendrochronology (Keenan 2004 is a short paper about the radiocarbon dating of the Gordion Iron Age destruction – criticisms shown to be entirely incorrect: see Manning and Kromer 2011b). I assume Liphschitz in fact means the WWW document of Keenan cited above in the text.

dendroarchaeological specialists of North America over the past generation. The chronology built by Kuniholm (1977) has itself been re-built and tested by Maryanne Newton and others over time. Thus, as a replicated study, we can regard the dendrochronology as sound. Therefore, despite whatever faults may have been exhibited in dendrochronological work published by Kuniholm (see discussion below and as claimed by Keenan and Liphschitz; see also James 2012), the Gordion dendrochronology has, as noted, been independently replicated/verified, and may thus be considered to be valid notwithstanding. Keenan in his WWW document cited above dwells on the fact that Kuniholm used *t* scores, and he (correctly) argues for potential problems with using these without due care.[57] Thus it is important to note that Dean built his Gordion dendrochronology via skeleton plotting, using no *t* scores or similar statistical approaches, nor relying just on ring-width measurements, but instead via direct study of the wood (on skeleton plotting, see the classic brief introduction in Stokes and Smiley 1968; and for an earlier summary, see Brown 1937). The Gordion dendrochronology, or the ^{14}C dated elements therefrom, also offer good long crossdates and appropriate good *t* scores and correlation coefficients if using curve-fitting approaches, and passes the standard crossdate quality control test employed in dendrochronology via the COFECHA software (e.g. Kuniholm *et al.* 2011: Table 5.6; Manning *et al.* 2010: Tables 2 and 3).

(b) The large time-series of dendro-sequenced high-precision radiocarbon data obtained from the Gordion dendrochronology (n=128) offer a very close fit to the shape of the northern hemisphere radiocarbon calibration curve over almost 1000 years (Manning *et al.* 2010). The one minor exception in the 9th-8th centuries BC appears consistent with a major solar-driven climate change episode affecting growing seasons in this period (Kromer *et al.* 2001), and subsequent work, while not inconsistent with this hypothesis, has in fact only reduced the apparent offset making the overall similarity (Anatolia v. Northern Hemisphere record) closer (Manning *et al.* 2010; Manning and Kromer 2011b: Fig. 6.4). This long, detailed, correlation over most of a millennium inherently confirms that the underlying dendrochronology must be correct within very small margins, otherwise this situation would not occur. It also demonstrates no significant offset for the regional atmospheric radiocarbon levels versus the mid-latitude Northern Hemisphere record of IntCal (e.g. IntCal09: Reimer *et al.* 2009).

(v) But has Anatolian dendrochronology always been appropriately undertaken

---

[57] It is of course correct that the modified student t-test scores as employed in dendrochronology (Baillie and Pilcher 1973) must be used with caution and the appreciation that they offer only an exploratory statistic or guide (Wigley *et al.* 1987), and as part of an overall analysis of the samples in question. To quote a recent sensible policy: "t-values below 3.5 are mostly disregarded, as they do not indicate a match; t-values between 3.5 and 6 indicate a possible match; and t-values higher than 6 are a clear indication of correct dating position" (Sass-Klaassen *et al.* 2008: 101). Miles (1997) offers similar observations (p.40) and goes on to stress the likely problems trying to date short sequences, whereas usually longer sequences offer less ambiguous information.

and reported? I refer to work published by Kuniholm and before 2006 (when Manning became Director of the Cornell Tree Ring Laboratory and had access to the relevant tree-ring data). This is a different question. I make a few remarks commenting on the two criticisms/issues raised by Liphschitz (2007: 164):

(a) Uluburun shipwreck (see above). This supposed dendrochronological dating was a mistake and should not have been stated/published. If all the co-authors of the Kuniholm *et al.* (1996) paper had had full knowledge of/access to the relevant data, then it would not have been included as a dendro date in the paper. There are several problems. The samples from the shipwreck do not crossdate, and are short sequences only, and the supposed dating was based on just two samples (which is clearly too few given problematic material). There is further no reason to expect or to assume that cedar (from e.g. Lebanon) should crossdate with juniper from central Anatolia. The current best estimate of the wrecking date for the Uluburun ship, based on a combination of radiocarbon wiggle-match dating some of the wood elements, and radiocarbon dating short-lived material on board the ship, is published in Manning *et al.* (2009b): c.1320±15 BC. (Note: see now Postscript (v) with small revision.) This date should be used instead of the supposed and withdrawn dendro date. Sections of Manning (1999) referring to the Uluburun ship and its date should therefore be accordingly revised as noted above.

(b) Gateway at Tille Höyük. The dendrochronological analysis and supposed dating of Kuniholm *et al.* (1993) has already been withdrawn, and a revised statement published: see Griggs and Manning (2009). There were several errors in the work reported by Kuniholm *et al.* (1993); most obviously, it was inappropriate ever to expect oak from the Tille Höyük area to crossdate with juniper from near Gordion, and dendro sequences that were too short were supposedly crossdated to build the site dendrochronology. Subsequent work has in fact indicated that the original chronology was put together in the wrong order (see Griggs and Manning 2009).

(b) Other Corrigenda and Addenda to A Test of Time

I list below the typos and corrections/errors I am aware of to the AD 1999 text (citing the original 1999 pagination as kept in this printing also) as were known to me by the end of AD 1999: Table RE5. I have *not* sought to identify further typos. This AD 1999 list is taken from the pdf (via WWW) companion to: Sturt W. Manning, *A test of time: the volcano of Thera and the chronology and history of the Aegean and east Mediterranean in the mid second millennium BC* which was put online originally in 1999 (at the University of Reading), and maintained through to 2006 (first at the University of Toronto, and subsequently at Cornell University) and is now (as an historical record of the final 2006 document) available at: http://cornell.academia.edu/SturtWManning/Books/326586/Manning_S.W._1999._A_Test_of_Time_the_volcano_of_Thera_and_the_chronology_and_history_of_the_Aegean_and_east_Mediterranean_in_the_mid-second_millennium_BC._Oxford_Oxbow_Books.

p.vii Fig. 4	On the map of Cyprus Palaepaphos not Paleapaphos, and Toumba tou Skourou not Tomba ...
p.xviii	The spelling should be Alasiya and not Alasia.
p.44 item (iii)	Data are plural. Should read 'Significant new data have started to emerge ... these data ...'.
p.71 and footnote 297	Add to references re-Knossos find of Theran pumice the description in Warren, P.M. 1999. Aspects of Minoan chronology. In P.P. Betancourt, V. Karageorghis, R. Laffineur and W.-D. Niemeier (eds.), *Meletemata: studies in Aegean archaeology presented to Malcolm H. Wiener as he enters his 65th year. Vol.III:* 893–903. Aegaeum 20. Université de Liège: Service d'Histoire de l'art et archéologie de la Grèce antique, and Austin: Program in Aegean Scripts and Prehistory, The University of Texas at Austin.
p.72, Fig. 21	Tephra depths fail to appear on figure. Should be, from inside contour line outwards, 30cm, 20cm, 10cm, 5cm and 1cm. See figure below.
pp.113–114 and footnote 510	There are now two additional late MB type Canaanite jars from LMIA Akrotiri on Thera. See p.134 and Figs. 1–2 in Doumas, C. 1998. Aegeans in the Levant: myth and reality. In S. Getin, A. Mazar and E. Stern (eds.), *Mediterranean peoples in transition: thirteenth to early tenth centuries BCE:* 129–137. Jerusalem: Israel Exploration Society.
p.128 footnote 602	Tel Haror sherd with Minoan graffito. This has now been shown to be Cretan, as noted very briefly at p.109 footnote 493. See Day *et al.* paper in P.P. Betancourt, V. Karageorghis, R. Laffineur and W.-D. Niemeier (eds.), *Meletemata: studies in Aegean archaeology presented to Malcolm H. Wiener as he enters his 65th year. Vol.I:* 191–196. Aegaeum 20. Université de Liège: Service d'Histoire de l'art et archéologie de la Grèce antique, and Austin: Program in Aegean Scripts and Prehistory, The University of Texas at Austin.
p.163 lines 26–27	The 'be' should be an 'is'. Thus '...but nothing is certain'.
p.225, p.226 Table 6, pp.227–229, p.228 footnote 1108	There is some confusion/error in my text about who is Tudhaliya I and II, and whether they are the same person (as several scholars assume), or in fact different persons. Likewise, there is a problem over whether one or two Tudhaliyas reigned between Arnuwanda I and Suppiluliuma I. This issue of exactly how many early New Kingdom rulers there were, and how many Tudhaliyas, has been a long-running debate/confusion in Hittite studies (Bryce 1998:132–133 and footnote 7). Let me correct/explain the errors in the text. I thank Eric H. Cline for drawing this confusion to my attention. **1. How many Tudhaliyas at the very start of the Hittite New Kingdom before Arnuwanda I? One or two? Most scholars assume one.** re-footnote 1108 on p. 228. The Tudhaliya II referred to by Cline (1996) *is* the same person as the Tudhaliya I of Astour (1989) – referred to as Tudhaliya I/II in Bryce (1998:133). Cline, Astour and Bryce are all talking about the same person. There are not two kings who claim victory over Assuwa, just the one who lived c.1450–1420BC (Astour 1989 dates). This affects my discussion in footnote 1108. There is just the one king and one Assuwa victory. This correction in fact favours the high chronology historical synthesis (as the early 14th century BC Tudhaliya II option discussed in my footnote is incorrect). Elsewhere in my text, references to Tudhaliya I refer to Tudhaliya I (Astour) or Tuhaliya I/II (Bryce). Gurney (1990:181) has a different chronology again. He has the early New Kingdom rulers before Arnuwanda I as Tudhaliya I(?), Hattusilis II(?), and Tudhaliya II. **2. How many Tudhaliyas after Arnuwanda I and before Suppiluliuma I? One or two? Bryce and Gurney say one (called Tudhaliya III). Astour (1989) has two, called Tudhaliya II and Tudhaliya III.** At p.225 footnote 1093 and in Table 6 on p.226, I followed Astour (1989) and have two Tudhaliyas in this interval: Tudhaliya II and Tudhaliya III. The caption to Table 6 thus should be corrected to read: 'Table 6. List of Hittite Kings after Bryce (1998), except for early New Kingdom which follows Astour (1989)'. In footnote 1093 I sought some support from the evidence that Suppiluliuma's father was a Tudhaliya (see also Bryce 1998:161 and footnote 85 with further refs.), but this is by no means a necessary corollary. Again, some confusion results. On page 229, for example, where I have Tudhaliya II, this would be Tudhaliya III for Bryce or Gurney, and yet we all mean the same person. Thus, in general, my Tudhaliya II = Bryce's/Gurney's Tudhaliya III.

p.259 n.1191	The mention here of forthcoming radiocarbon data from Tel Kabri relevant to the late MB palace destruction and the Aegean-style fresco fragments overlooked two dates from the Zurich laboratory already published by G. Bonani, 1994. The C[14] data. In A. Kempinski and W.-D. Niemeier (eds.), *Excavations at Kabri: preliminary report of 1992–1993 seasons (nos.7–8): 8*. Tel Aviv: Tel Aviv Expedition, Tel Aviv University. The two data in question come from Area D locus 723 – a fill layer under threshold 698 – and relate to late in the MBA. It is not stated what the samples consist of. We may guess charcoal given the delta 13C figures quoted and no specific information to the contrary. The dates are: Lab no. 8817, 3260±60BP, and Lab no. 8819, 3480±70BP. The calibrated ages with INTCAL98.[14]C employing the OxCal calibration programme (round ranges 'on') at 1 standard deviation are 1620–1450BC and 1890–1690BC respectively. Clearly the dates are not very similar and likely reflect charcoal of quite differing real ages. The combined calibrated calendar age range is 1690–1600, 1570–1530BC, but with a poor agreement statistic (since the data appear to reflect significantly different real ages). The note to these data states "The date of 1638± B.C. fits well the destruction date of the palace at the end of the Middle Bronze Age". This is clearly misleading. Neither date by itself in fact supports this age, only a likely inappropriate average/combining. However, given just two data, and limited to insufficient information about sample material, context, and so on, it is difficult to say much further. Hopefully further, and better quality, data will be forthcoming.
p.268 footnote 1244 line 1	sulphur and not suphur.
p.274 Fig. 51	London is the un-named dot left of Paris.
p.485 plate 9	PWS sherd should best be oriented as shown on the cover of the 1999 printing of Manning (1999) (rim at top).
p.72 Figure 21	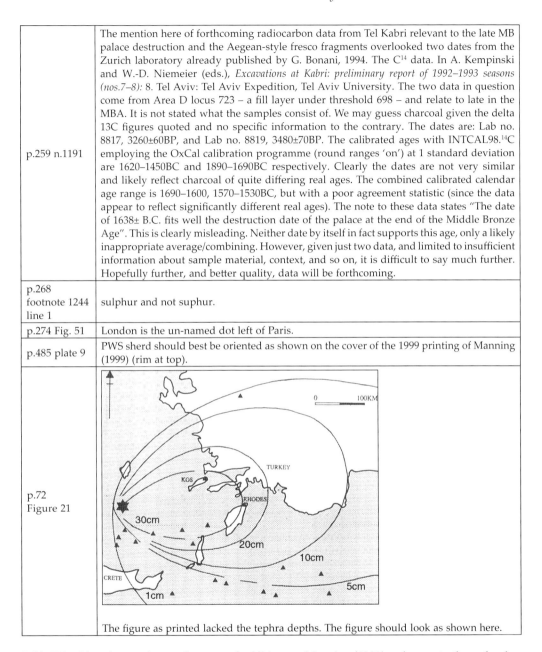 The figure as printed lacked the tephra depths. The figure should look as shown here.

Table RE5. *List of corrections and typos and additions to Manning (1999) as known to the author by the end of AD 1999.*

6. Revisit Essay Appendix 1: Details on Egyptian New Kingdom chronology results following Aston (2012) and re-running the Bronk Ramsey et al. (2010) radiocarbon model

This Appendix provides some more details on the re-running of the Bronk Ramsey *et al.* (2010) New Kingdom ^{14}C chronology model reported in brief in Table RE1.

The basic OxCal runfile of Bronk Ramsey *et al.* (2010 – from the modified SOM of 17 May 2011) was employed (but excluding samples no longer considered to be of NK origin – OxA-18520 – and associating OxA-18960 with Siamun, see Table S1 addendum – added April 2011 in the Bronk Ramsey *et al.* 2010 SOM, and accordingly adding intervals for Osochor, Siamun and Psusennes II: see Table RE10 below) (I thank Mike Dee and Christopher Bronk Ramsey for their assistance and advice). The total number of ^{14}C data employed is 128. The Bronk Ramsey *et al.* (2010) runfile includes the 19 ± 5 ^{14}C years seasonal offset (ΔR) for pre-modern (pre-Nile dams) Egypt and its growing season as discussed in that paper, and as quantified in Dee *et al.* (2010). The changes then made were to adjust some of the reign lengths of rulers between Ahmose to Rameses II following the Aston (2012) paper 'high' and 'ultra high' chronologies. I note that these are the contiguous (one after another, no overlaps) reign lengths – thus co-regencies where present have been discounted. The whole year intervals employed are listed in Table RE6 – separate 'high' and 'ultra-high' models were then run. For completeness, the full OxCal runfile for one example of the revised models used in these re-runs – the 'ultra-high' chronology in Table RE9A – is listed below in full in Table RE12. For comparison, the reign lengths in the Schneider (2010a) paper are also shown in Table RE6 – and these are used for the rulers from Ahmose to Tuthmosis II. The main difference between the Schneider (2010a) and Aston (2012) schemes is that Aston allots a much longer reign to Tuthmosis IV based on a detailed reassessment of the evidence. The differences in reign lengths for the two models ('high' and 'ultra-high') versus those employed in the Bronk Ramsey *et al.* (2010) paper are listed in the right column of Table RE6.

The results of the re-running of the Bronk Ramsey New Kingdom (NK) model for the 'high' and 'ultra-high' chronologies adjusting just as noted above are listed in summary form in Table RE1, and in full in Table RE7 below. Note, with regard to these and the other OxCal model runs reported below, different runs of these models can see small variations, typically within the range of 0–1 or 0–2 calendar years (where the convergence is greater than or equal to 95). Typical values from several runs are listed in Tables RE1, RE7, RE9 and RE11.

In the models reported in Tables RE1 and RE7, I have not adjusted the reign lengths of rulers after Ramesses II to reflect recent scholarship. I have simply used the Bronk Ramsey *et al.* (2010) model. For reference, I list the reign lengths used in the Bronk Ramsey *et al.* (2010) model versus those in Schneider (2010a) in Table RE8 for the rulers from Merneptah to Psusennes II. There are only very small differences even in the largest case (Ramesses X), and overall only a very small net difference in length of time (of at most 7 years and perhaps only 5 or less years if the question mark cases added the possible extra year and if Ramesses VIII perhaps got beyond 1 year and 6

Rulers	Schneider (2010a) Reign Length Whole Years	Aston (2012) 'High' Reign Length Whole Years	Aston (2012) 'Ultra High' Reign Length Whole Years	Difference versus Bronk Ramsey *et al.* (2010) Years
Ahmose	25			0
Amenophis I	21			0
Tuthmosis I	13			0
Tuthmosis II	13			+1
Tuthmosis III	54	54	54	+2
Amenophis II	26	31	31	+4
Tuthmosis IV	10	27	38	+17 / +28
Amenophis III	39	38	38	0
Akhenaten	17	17	17	+3
Smenkhare/ Neferneferuaten & Ankhetkheperure	4	3	3	+1 / +2
Tutankhamun	9	9	9	0
Ay	3	4	4	0
Horemheb	14	15	15	-13
Ramesses I	1	2	2	+1
Sety I	10	9	9	-6
Ramesses II	66	67	67	+1

Table RE6. Comparison of the approximate rounded whole year independent reign lengths of the rulers of Egypt from Ahmose to Ramesses II from Schneider (2010a: 402) versus Aston (2012) 'high' and 'ultra-high' chronologies (i.e. deducting co-regencies – e.g. Amenhotep II with Tuthmosis III in the Aston 'ultra-high' chronology, Smenkhare/Neferneferuaten with Akhenaten in the Aston 'high' and 'ultra-high' chronologies). The main difference is the much longer reign of Tuthmosis IV. The analyses reported in Tables RE1 and RE7 use the reign lengths from the Aston (2012) 'high' and 'ultra-high' chronologies above for the rulers listed above from Tuthmosis III to Ramesses II and from Schneider (2010a) for Ahmose to Tuthmosis II (and otherwise employ the Bronk Ramsey et al. 2010 information in their OxCal runfile in their Table S6). The right column shows the net differences between the reign lengths used for the 'high' and 'ultra' high models (the only difference is 27 or 38 years for Tuthmosis IV) reported in Tables RE1 and RE7) versus the Bronk Ramsey et al. (2010) OxCal runfile.

months). This should therefore have little impact on the overall model. However, to check, Table RE9A reports both the 'high' and 'ultra-high' models re-run again for Ahmose to Ramesses II, but this time using the Schneider (2010a) minimum reign lengths (and order) for the rulers from Merneptah to Psusennes II (by minimum I mean that if Schneider writes, e.g., "28 (or 29?) y." as for Ramesses XI, then I use 28 years). The outcomes, comparing Table RE9A versus Tables RE1 and RE7, are only very small differences to the dates for the 18th Dynasty and to Ramesses II – the period of interest in this study. As one further variation, Table RE9B reports the accession date ranges in Table RE9A *but* with the entire Bronk Ramsey *et al.* (2010) New Kingdom model re-run employing only the Schneider (2010a) reign lengths (thus primarily the much shorter reign of Tuthmosis IV). Again, we see relatively little change for the dates in the earlier New Kingdom – where the model has most data and there are the main 'tie points' to the shape of the radiocarbon calibration curve (see Figures RE28 and RE29, Tables RE7 and RE12). We may thus regard the results in Tables RE1, RE7 and RE9 as all very similar and relatively robust. Note, as discussed in Bronk Ramsey *et al.* (2010: 1555), the model allows for small errors (assumed typically to be of around 1–2 years) in reign length estimates using a Student's t distribution ($v = 5$). Thus the model findings are fairly robust against anything other than larger changes in reign lengths (and/or overall sequence length). Even then, the modest differences between the Bronk Ramsey (2010) model findings and those from the re-runs as reported in Tables RE1, RE7 and RE9 – even when some quite significant changes have been made to the reign lengths of Tuthmosis IV and Horemheb, especially – demonstrates the general stability of the findings.

The New Kingdom models reported in Bronk Ramsey *et al.* (2010) or here in Tables RE1, RE7 and RE9 employed all of the 128 ^{14}C data in the initial model (Bronk Ramsey *et al.* 2010: Table S6 and as modified – see text descriptions above and Table RE10). Outliers were identified (see Bronk Ramsey *et al.* 2010: Fig. 2B, Table S1) but left in the model runs. The Bayesian chronological analysis downweights such outlying data, but nothing has been excluded. For the New Kingdom Bronk Ramsey *et al.* (2010: Fig. 2 Caption) observe that there is a scatter of outliers "but these show no systematic pattern and have no single explanation". For interest and as a test, Table RE11 and Figure RE28 report a re-run of the model in Table RE9A for the 'ultra-high' chronology with all the outliers with outlier probability greater than or equal to 95 (compare Bronk Ramsey *et al.* 2010: Table S1 far right column) excluded (n = 21).[58] The aesthetics of the fit of the plotted data versus the radiocarbon calibration curve when such outliers are excluded improves noticeably – compare Figure RE28 with outliers excluded versus Figure RE29 with no outliers excluded – but the calculated accession date Boundaries are all more or less identical within 0–1 years (compare Table RE11 to Table RE9A 'ultra-high').

Interestingly, regardless of whether the original Bronk Ramsey *et al.* (2010) reign lengths, or the Aston 'high' or 'ultra-high' reign lengths are used, and/or the Schneider reign lengths for the post Ramesses II rulers, or for all the rulers, or the extreme outliers are excluded (so any of the results in Tables RE1, RE7, RE9 and RE11), a fairly similar date range is found for the accession of Ahmose and the start of the New Kingdom: at 68.2% probability within a range of c.1579–1552 BC and at 95.4% probability within a range of 1584 to 1544 BC. As in the original Bronk Ramsey *et al.* (2010) study, this finding suggests that the ^{14}C data support one of the higher historical chronologies for New Kingdom Egypt – such as the Aston (2012) 'high' or 'ultra-high' proposals, or at least a chronology no later than e.g. Schneider (2010a) – and that they do not support

---

[58] The 21 dates excluded are: OxA-19788, OxA-19715, OxA-19008, SacA-11168, OxA-19151, SacA-11155, OxA-18508, OxA-19556, VERA-4788A, SacA-11135, OxA-19004, OxA-19263, VERA-4686, VERA-4686B, OxA-20482, OxA-18501, OxA-18958, OxA-19006, OxA-20213, OxA-18051, OxA-20201.

the various lower chronologies which place the accession of Ahmose c.1540 BC or later (e.g. Krauss and Warburton 2006; 2009).

The main sets of ^{14}C data, and the main tie points to the shape of the radiocarbon calibration curve (the history of past natural variations in atmospheric ^{14}C content), lie in the period of the early 18th Dynasty to the Amarna period (see Figures RE28 and RE29, Tables RE7 and RE12). These placements (including the date for the accession of Ahmose) remain fairly stable across all the models as noted. Thus changes between the model outcomes are reflected more in changes in the date ranges for accessions in the later New Kingdom. For example, the dates calculated for the accession of Shoshenq I at the end of the model vary (quoting the 68.2% probability ranges) from: 981–969 BC (Table RE9B) to 979–964 BC or 976–950 BC (Table RE9A), to 976–949 BC (Table RE11), to 971–946 BC or 959–945 BC (Table RE7). If – and it is an 'if' – the standard view is taken that the reign of Shoshenq I can be tied to the reign lengths of the kings of Israel and Judah and to two synchronisms with Assyrian chronology, then the accession of Shoshenq I is placed about 946 or 945 BC (Jansen-Winkeln 2006: 232–233 and literature cited – cf. Manning 1999: 378–380). And the usual alternative is a few years later such as c.943 BC (Krauss and Warburton 2006: 474 – who note skepticism regarding the biblically-derived dates) or even later, e.g. c.930 BC (Krauss and Warburton 2009: 127). The only ^{14}C models for the New Kingdom which are more or less compatible within their most likely 68.2% probability are those using either the long 'ultra-high' Aston (2012) chronology for the earlier New Kingdom, or, in Table RE7, the Aston (2012) 'high' chronology. Even at 95.4% probability, the model employing the overall Schneider (2010a) chronology of reign lengths for all rulers from Ahmose to Psusennes II (Table RE11) places the accession of Shoshenq I 988–963 BC – rather too early for the standard historical estimates for this ruler and the start of the 22nd Dynasty. This circumstance seems to provide an argument in favour of a relatively long historical chronology for the New Kingdom being appropriate (given that the placement of the period from the early 18th Dynasty to the Amarna period is fairly fixed and robust from the ^{14}C evidence): thus something like the Aston (2012) 'high' or especially 'ultra-high' schemes.

Accession Dates BC

King/Queen	^{14}C dates re specific ruler	Bronk Ramsey et al. (2010: Table 1, Table S8) 68.2% from	to	95.4% from	to	Aston (2012) 'high' 68.2% from	to	95.4% from	to	Aston (2012) 'ultra-high' 68.2% from	to	95.4% from	to
17th Dynasty (Start)		1596	1582	1601	1573	1604	1595	1609	1589	1608	1599	1612	1593
Ahmose	0	1566	1552	1570	1544	1574	1565	1579	1559	1578	1569	1582	1563
Amenhotep I	0	1541	1527	1545	1519	1549	1540	1554	1534	1553	1544	1557	1539
Tuthmosis I	1	1520	1507	1524	1498	1528	1519	1533	1514	1532	1524	1536	1518
Tuthmosis II		1507	1495	1511	1487	1515	1506	1519	1502	1519	1511	1522	1506
Tuthmosis III	24	1494	1483	1498	1474	1502	1493	1506	1489	1507	1499	1510	1493
Hatshepsut	25	1488	1477	1492	1468	1496	1487	1500	1484	1501	1493	1503	1487
Hatshepsut End		1473	1462	1477	1454	1481	1473	1485	1469	1486	1478	1489	1473
Amenhotep II	1	1441	1431	1445	1423	1448	1440	1452	1436	1453	1446	1457	1440
Tuthmosis IV	1	1414	1403	1418	1396	1417	1409	1422	1405	1423	1415	1426	1410
Amenhotep III	2	1404	1393	1408	1386	1390	1382	1395	1379	1386	1378	1389	1372
Amenhotep IV = Akhenaten	17	1365	1355	1370	1348	1353	1344	1357	1341	1348	1341	1352	1335
Smenkhare/Neferneferuaten* & Ankhetkheperure	0	1351	1340	1356	1333	1336	1328	1341	1324	1332	1324	1336	1318
Tutankhamun	7	1349	1338	1353	1331	1333	1325	1338	1322	1330	1322	1334	1316
Ay	0	1339	1329	1344	1322	1324	1316	1330	1313	1321	1313	1326	1307
Horemheb	0	1336	1325	1341	1318	1321	1312	1326	1309	1318	1309	1322	1303
Ramesses I	0	1308	1297	1313	1290	1306	1297	1312	1293	1303	1294	1308	1288
Seti I	0	1307	1296	1312	1288	1304	1295	1310	1291	1301	1292	1306	1286
Ramesses II	2	1292	1281	1297	1273	1296	1286	1302	1282	1293	1283	1298	1276
Merneptah	1	1226	1215	1231	1207	1229	1219	1236	1215	1226	1216	1232	1209
Amenmesse + Seti II**	0	1216	1201	1221	1194	1219	1205	1226	1201	1216	1203	1222	1196
Siptah	0	1207	1189	1212	1187	1211	1199	1218	1195	1207	1197	1214	1190
Tewosre	1	1201	1189	1206	1181	1205	1193	1213	1189	1202	1191	1209	1183

Ruler													
Sethnakhte	0	1198	1187	1204	1179	1203	1191	1211	1187	1200	1188	1207	1181
Ramesses III	0	1196	1185	1202	1176	1201	1188	1209	1184	1198	1186	1205	1179
Ramesses IV	3	1165	1154	1171	1145	1170	1157	1179	1153	1167	1155	1175	1147
Ramesses V	0	1159	1148	1165	1139	1164	1151	1173	1147	1161	1149	1169	1141
Ramesses VI	0	1155	1144	1161	1135	1160	1146	1170	1143	1157	1145	1166	1137
Ramesses VII	0	1148	1137	1153	1127	1153	1139	1163	1135	1149	1138	1159	1130
Ramesses VIII	0	1141	1130	1146	1120	1145	1132	1157	1128	1142	1130	1153	1123
Ramesses IX	0	1137	1127	1143	1117	1148	1128	1154	1125	1139	1127	1150	1120
Ramesses X	2	1119	1109	1125	1099	1131	1110	1137	1107	1121	1109	1133	1102
Ramesses XI	0	1110	1100	1116	1090	1123	1101	1128	1097	1112	1100	1124	1093
Smendes	1	1080	1069	1085	1060	1093	1071	1099	1067	1082	1069	1095	1063
Amenemnesu	9	1054	1044	1059	1033	1068	1045	1073	1041	1056	1043	1069	1037
Psusennes I	1	1050	1039	1055	1029	1065	1041	1069	1037	1052	1039	1066	1033
Amenemope	1	1004	993	1010	983	1019	994	1024	990	1006	993	1020	987
Osochor***	0	995	984	1002	975	1010	985	1015	981	998	984	1011	978
Siamun	1	NS	NS	NS	NS	1004	979	1009	975	992	978	1005	971
Psusennes II	0	NS	NS	NS	NS	985	960	991	956	973	959	986	952
Shoshenq I	0	NS	NS	NS	NS	971	946	977	941	959	945	973	938

*Table RE7. Extended version of Table RE1 reporting all the accession Boundaries calculated by the re-run models ('high' and 'ultra-high') from Ahmose to Shoshenq I. Otherwise see caption to Table RE1 and see text above in this Appendix. NS = Not Stated (these rulers were not in the Bronk Ramsey et al. (2010) OxCal runfile – added subsequently (see text, for details of the additional code: see Table RE10 below). Notes: *Bronk Ramsey et al. (2010: Table 1 and Table S8) only use Neferneferuaten but the relevant Boundary is 'Neferneferuaten, etc.' – I combine the independent (non-coregency) overall reign periods for Smenkhare and Ankhetkheperure with her reign (total c.4 years) in the re-run model. ** Bronk Ramsey et al. (2010) have the reign order as Amenmesse and then Seti II, whereas the standard view in more recent scholarship of this complicated topic (see Schneider 2010a: 394–396) is that Seti II was the ruler and Amenmesse the rival and their reigns are either concurrent or perhaps Amenmesse continues in a separate reign after Seti II before the reign of Sethnakhte (following Schneider 2010a: 395–396) – however, as the Bronk Ramsey et al. (2010) model has no ^{14}C data for either of these two reigns this little detail in fact makes no difference to the model outcomes. Here I conflate the two reigns into one stated period in the table. ***Bronk Ramsey et al. (2010) use the name Osorkon the Elder. All convergence values greater than or equal to 95. The total number of ^{14}C dates in the model is 128; 100 dates are specifically associated with a named ruler – 28 other dates have other associations (e.g. 17/18th Dynasty Boundary) or slightly less specific associations such as early 18th Dynasty before Hatshepsut, or 20th Dynasty between Sethnakhte and Smendes, etc. (see Bronk Ramsey et al. 2010: Table S6 or Table RE12 below).*

A Test of Time Revisited

Rulers (Merneptah to Shoshenq)	Bronk Ramsey *et al.* (2010) reign length in years	Schneider (2010a) reign length in years	Difference
Merneptah	10	10	0
Seti II	6	6	0
Amenmesse	3	2	-1
Siptah and Tewosre	8	8	0
Sethnakhte	2	3	+1
Ramesses III	31	31	0
Ramesses IV	6	8	+2
Ramesses V	4	4	0
Ramesses VI	7	8	+1
Ramesses VII	7	7 or 8?	0 or +1
Ramesses VIII	3	1 +?	-2 / -?
Ramesses IX	18	18	0
Ramesses X	9	3	-6
Ramesses XI	30	28 or 29?	-2 / -1
Smendes	26	26	0
Amenemnesu	4	4	0
Psusennes I	46	46	0
Amenemope	9	9	0
Osochor	6	6	0
Siamun	19	19	0
Psusennes II	14	14	0

Table RE8. Comparison of the reign lengths of the rulers of Egypt from Merneptah to Psusennes II used by Bronk Ramsey et al. *(2010) versus Schneider (2010a) – chosen as an example of recent scholarship. There are very small to negligible differences and the net difference in length of time is at most c.7 years and perhaps only 5 or even 4 years (if Ramesses VIII were to make it over 1 year 6 months). The use of the Bronk Ramsey* et al. *(2010) intervals for this period versus those of Schneider (2010a) should therefore have a net minimal impact on the model outcomes. Other recent assessments can be cited to offer reign lengths that are about the same as or closer to each of the Bronk Ramsey* et al. *(2010) figures where there is a difference (for example from Krauss and Warburton 2009: 126–128; or Kitchen 2000; or von Beckerath 1997), with the exception of Ramesses X where most recent scholarship has allotted a shorter reign of 3 or 4 years as the solution to what is a complicated situation for the history and succession from Ramesses IX to XI (see Schneider 2010a: 396–397). One point of detail to note: Bronk Ramsey* et al. *(2010) have the reign order as Amenmesse and then Seti II, whereas the standard view in more recent scholarship of this complicated topic (see Schneider 2010a: 394–396) is that Seti II was the ruler and Amenmesse the rival and their reigns are either concurrent or perhaps Amenmesse continues in a separate reign after Seti II before the reign of Sethnakht (following Schneider 2010a: 395–396) – however, as the Bronk Ramsey* et al. *(2010) model has no* ¹⁴*C data for either of these two reigns, this little detail in fact makes no difference to the model outcomes.*

	Accession Dates BC							
	Modelled hpd Ranges from revised model using Aston (2012) 'high' chronology and Schneider (2010) reign lengths for Tuthmosis II and for Merneptah to Psusennes II				Modelled hpd Ranges from revised model using Aston (2012) 'ultra-high' chronology and Schneider (2010) reign lengths for Tuthmosis II and for Merneptah to Psusennes II			
	68.2%		95.4%		68.2%		95.4%	
King/Queen	from	to	from	to	from	to	from	to
Ahmose	1575	1566	1580	1560	1579	1570	1583	1563
Amenhotep I	1550	1541	1555	1536	1554	1545	1558	1539
Tuthmosis I	1529	1520	1533	1515	1533	1524	1536	1518
Tuthmosis II	1516	1507	1520	1502	1520	1512	1523	1505
Tuthmosis III	1503	1494	1507	1490	1507	1499	1510	1493
Amenhotep II	1449	1441	1453	1437	1455	1447	1458	1440
Tuthmosis IV	1419	1410	1422	1407	1424	1416	1428	1409
Amenhotep III	1392	1384	1396	1380	1387	1379	1391	1372
Amenhotep IV = Akhenaten	1354	1346	1358	1342	1350	1341	1354	1334
Smenkhare/ Neferneferuaten & Ankhetkheperure	1337	1330	1341	1326	1334	1325	1338	1318
Tutankhamun	1335	1327	1339	1323	1331	1323	1335	1315
Ay	1326	1318	1330	1314	1323	1314	1327	1307
Horemheb	1323	1315	1327	1310	1320	1310	1324	1302
Ramesses I	1309	1300	1313	1295	1306	1295	1310	1287
Seti I	1307	1298	1311	1292	1304	1293	1308	1285
Ramesses II	1299	1289	1303	1283	1296	1284	1300	1276
Shoshenq I	979	964	983	949	976	950	980	944

Table RE9A. Accession date ranges from further re-runs of the 'high' and 'ultra-high' models (Table RE7) for the rulers from Ahmose to Ramesses II and then the end of the model Boundary for the accession of Shoshenq I, but this time using the Schneider (2010a) minimum reign lengths (and order) for the rulers from Merneptah to Psusennes II – see Table RE8 (by minimum I mean that if Schneider writes, e.g., "28 (or 29?) y." as for Ramesses XI, then I use 28 years), as well as his reign length for Tuthmosis II (as in Tables RE1 and RE7). Otherwise: as Tables RE1 and RE7.

King/Queen	Accession Dates BC			
	Modelled hpd Ranges from revised model using only the Schneider (2010a) reign lengths for Ahmose to Psusennes II			
	68.2%		95.4%	
	from	to	from	to
Ahmose	1566	1554	1571	1548
Amenhotep I	1541	1530	1546	1523
Tuthmosis I	1520	1509	1524	1502
Tuthmosis II	1507	1496	1511	1490
Tuthmosis III	1493	1484	1498	1477
Amenhotep II	1439	1430	1442	1424
Tuthmosis IV	1412	1404	1416	1398
Amenhotep III	1402	1393	1406	1388
Amenhotep IV = Akhenaten	1363	1354	1367	1349
Smenkhare/ Neferneferuaten & Ankhetkheperure	1345	1337	1345	1328
Tutankhamun	1341	1333	1345	1328
Ay	1332	1324	1336	1319
Horemheb	1329	1321	1334	1316
Ramesses I	1316	1307	1320	1302
Seti I	1314	1306	1319	1301
Ramesses II	1304	1296	1309	1291
Shoshenq I	981	969	988	963

Table RE9B. Accession date ranges from a further re-run of the Bronk Ramsey et al. *(2010) model for the rulers from Ahmose to Ramesses II and then the end of the model Boundary for the accession of Shoshenq I, but this time using the Schneider (2010a) minimum reign lengths (and order) for all the rulers from Ahmose to Psusennes II – otherwise as Table RE9A.*

A.
```
......
Boundary("Amenemope");
Phase("Amp")
{
R_Date("18960", 2805, 29)
{Outlier(0.05);};
R_Date("19794", 2904, 27)
{Outlier(0.05);};
Interval("Amp Int",9 + T(5));
};
Boundary("Osorkon the Elder");
};
};
```

B.
```
......
Boundary("Amenemope");
 Phase("Amp")
 {
 R_Date("19794", 2904, 27)
 {
  Outlier(0.05);
 };
 Interval("Amp Int",9 + T(5));
 };
 Boundary("Osorkon the Elder");
 Phase("Ors")
 {
 Interval("Ors Int", 6 + T(5));
 };
 Boundary("Siamun");
```

```
Phase("Sia")
{
R_Date("18960", 2805, 29)
{
 Outlier(0.05);
};
Interval("Sia Int", 19 + T(5));
};
Boundary("Psusennes II");
Phase("Psu II")
{
Interval("Psu II Int", 14 + T(5));
};
Boundary("Shoshenq I");
};
};
```

Table RE10. A: The last part of the Oxcal runfile for the New Kingdom (NK) model as documented in Bronk Ramsey et al. (2010: Table S6). B: the modified OxCal code for the last part of the OxCal runfile employed for the models reported in Tables RE1 and RE7. Note: Osorkon the Elder = Osochor.

King/Queen	Accession Dates BC			
	Modelled hpd Ranges from revised model using Aston (2012) 'ultra-high' chronology and Schneider (2010a) reign lengths for Tuthmosis II and for Merneptah to Psusennes II *and* excluding outliers (n = 21) with greater than or equals 95% probability from the model runs reported in Table RE9 (remaining data: n = 107)			
	68.2%		95.4%	
	from	to	from	to
Ahmose	1579	1570	1583	1563
Amenhotep I	1554	1545	1558	1539
Tuthmosis I	1533	1524	1536	1518
Tuthmosis II	1520	1512	1523	1505
Tuthmosis III	1507	1499	1510	1493
Amenhotep II	1455	1446	1458	1440
Tuthmosis IV	1424	1416	1428	1409
Amenhotep III	1387	1379	1391	1372
Amenhotep IV = Akhenaten	1350	1341	1354	1334
Smenkhare/ Neferneferuaten & Ankhetkheperure	1334	1325	1338	1317
Tutankhamun	1331	1322	1335	1315
Ay	1323	1313	1327	1306
Horemheb	1320	1309	1324	1301
Ramesses I	1305	1294	1310	1286
Seti I	1304	1292	1308	1284
Ramesses II	1295	1283	1300	1275
Merneptah	1229	1216	1233	1208
Seti II + Amenmesse	1219	1200	1224	1191
Siptah + Tewosre	1212	1191	1216	1182
Sethnakhte	1205	1189	1209	1180
Ramesses III	1202	1186	1206	1177
Ramesses IV	1172	1155	1176	1145
Ramesses V	1164	1147	1168	1137
Ramesses VI	1161	1142	1165	1133
Ramesses VII	1153	1133	1157	1125
Ramesses VIII	1147	1125	1151	1117
Ramesses IX	1146	1123	1149	1116
Ramesses X	1128	1105	1132	1098
Ramesses XI	1126	1101	1129	1095
Smendes	1098	1073	1102	1067
Amenemnesu	1072	1046	1076	1041
Psusennes I	1069	1042	1072	1037
Amenemope	1023	996	1027	990
Osochor	1014	987	1018	981
Siamun	1008	981	1012	975
Psusennes II	990	963	994	956
Shoshenq I	976	949	980	942

Table RE11. A re-run of the 'ultra-high' model in Table RE9 but after excluding the 21 14C dates with outlier probability greater than or equal to 95 (so remaining n = 107). The data are shown plotted against the radiocarbon calibration curve in Figure RE28. The outcomes are all within 0–1 year of those in Table RE9 'ultra-high'.

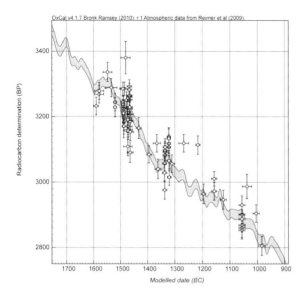

Figure RE28. Calendar placement (μ ± σ) of the 107 ¹⁴C data (1σ) in the re-run New Kingdom model excluding the largest outliers (data with outlier probability greater than or equal to 95) following the 'ultra-high' model in Table RE9 – the re-run data from this model excluding the largest outliers are listed in Table RE11 (note: many of the data points overlie each other and so they are not all visible). All data are within the field of view. Compare to Bronk Ramsey et al. (2010: Fig. 2B). The IntCal09 radiocarbon calibration curve (Reimer et al. 2009) is shown as a 1σ band. Compare this view and fit with the one including all 128 data in Figure RE29. Note that the ¹⁴C data nicely and specifically pick up the radiocarbon calibration curve shape in the later 16th century BC, the wiggle in the early 15th century BC, and the wiggle in the late 14th century BC – these are the main tie points and where the model has significant data.

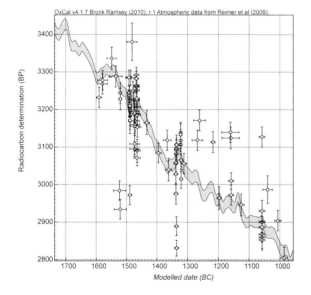

Figure RE29. Calendar placement (μ ± σ) of all the 128 ¹⁴C data (1σ) in the re-run New Kingdom model (except for 6 extreme outlier data not within the view shown) following the 'ultra-high' model in Table RE9 (note: many of the data points overlie each other and so they are not all visible). Compare to Bronk Ramsey et al. (2010: Fig. 2B). The IntCal09 radiocarbon calibration curve (Reimer et al. 2009) is shown as a 1σ band. Compare this all data view and fit with the one excluding the largest outliers in Figure RE28 (data in Table RE11). Note that the ¹⁴C data pick up the radiocarbon calibration curve shape in the later 16th century BC, the wiggle in the early 15th century BC, and the wiggle in the late 14th century BC – these are the main tie points and where the model has significant data.

```
Options()
{
Resolution=1;
kIterations=100;
};
Plot()
{
Outlier_
Model("General",T(5),U(0,4),"t");
 Delta_R("Seasonal Effect", 19,
5);
 Sequence("Extra Dates 1
17th/18th Dynasty Boundary")
{
 Boundary("=Start 17th
Dynasty");
 Phase("17th/18th Boundary")
{
 R_Date("20018", 3268, 27)
{
 Outlier(0.05);
};
 R_Date("20015", 3278, 26)
{
 Outlier(0.05);
};
};
 Boundary("=Amenhotep I");
};
 Sequence("Extra Dates 2 Early
18th Dynasty")
{
 Boundary("=Ahmose");
 Phase("Early 18th")
{
 R_Date("18417", 3336, 30)
{
 Outlier(0.05);
};
 R_Date("19715", 2934, 26)
{
 Outlier(0.05);
};
 R_Date("19716", 3288, 28)
{

 Outlier(0.05);
};
 R_Date("19788", 2984, 26)
{
 Outlier(0.05);
};
};
 Boundary("=Queen
Hatshepsut");
};
 Sequence("Extra Dates 3
Hatshepsut or Thutmose III")
{
 Boundary("=Thutmose III");
 Phase("Hst or Thut III")
{
 R_Date("SacA 11134", 3225, 20)
{
 Outlier(0.05);
};
 R_Date("SacA 11135", 3095, 20)
{
 Outlier(0.05);
};
 R_Date("SacA 11137", 3170, 25)
{
 Outlier(0.05);
};
 R_Combine("Hst or Thut III
Combine 1", 8)
{
  R_Date("19452", 3227, 30);
  R_Date("SacA-11139", 3225,
25);
 Outlier(0.05);
};
 R_Date("SacA 11140", 3250, 25)
{
 Outlier(0.05);
};
 R_Date("SacA 11144", 3380, 50)
{
 Outlier(0.05);
};
 R_Date("SacA 11145", 3195, 20)

{
 Outlier(0.05);
};
 R_Date("SacA 11163", 3285, 20)
{
 Outlier(0.05);
};
 R_Date("SacA 11164", 3160, 20)
{
 Outlier(0.05);
};
 R_Date("SacA 11165", 3195, 30)
{
 Outlier(0.05);
};
 R_Date("SacA 11166", 3155, 25)
{
 Outlier(0.05);
};
 R_Date("SacA 11172", 3190, 25)
{
 Outlier(0.05);
};
 R_Date("18508", 3482, 29)
{
 Outlier(0.05);
};
 R_Date("18513", 3108, 28)
{
 Outlier(0.05);
};
 R_Combine("Hst or Thut III
Combine 2", 8)
{
  R_Date("19556", 2589, 26);
  R_Date("VERA-4788A", 2649,
35);
 Outlier(0.05);
};
};
 Boundary("=Amenhotep II");
};
 Sequence("Extra Dates 4 Late
18th Dynasty")
{
```

```
Boundary("=Tutankhamun");
Phase("Late 18th")
{
R_Date("18509", 3056, 27)
{
 Outlier(0.05);
};
};
Boundary("=Rameses I");
};
Sequence("Extra Dates 5 20th
Dynasty")
{
Boundary("=Sethnakht");
Phase("20th")
{
R_Date("18958", 3124, 29)
{
 Outlier(0.05);
};
R_Date("19006", 3139, 27)
{
 Outlier(0.05);
};
};
Boundary("=Smendes");
};
Sequence("New Kingdom
Model")
{
Boundary("Start 17th
Dynasty");
Phase("17th Dynasty")
{
R_Date("18554", 3232, 27)
{
 Outlier(0.05);
};
Interval("17th Int", 30 + T(5));
};
Boundary("Ahmose");
Phase("Ahm")
{
Interval("Ahm Int", 25 + T(5));
};

Boundary("Amenhotep I");
Phase("Ahp I")
{
Interval("Ahp I Int", 21 + T(5));
};
Boundary("Thutmose I");
Phase("Thut I")
{
R_Date("18506", 3244, 27)
{
 Outlier(0.05);
};
R_Date("18411", 3228, 29)
{
 Outlier(0.05);
};
Interval("Thut I Int", 13 + T(5));
};
Boundary("Thutmose II");
Phase("Thut II")
{
Interval("Thut II Int", 13 + T(5));
};
Boundary("Thutmose III");
Phase("Thut III")
{
Interval("Thut III Int I", 6 +
T(5));
};
Boundary("Queen
Hatshepsut");
Phase("Hst")
{
R_Combine("Hst Combine 1",
8)
{
 R_Date("16833", 3179, 31);
 R_Date("VERA-4070", 3249,
32);
 Outlier(0.05);
};
R_Combine("Hst Combine 2",
8)
{
 R_Date("16834", 3191, 31);

 R_Date("VERA-4071", 3203,
29);
 Outlier(0.05);
};
R_Combine("Hst Combine 3",
8)
{
 R_Date("16835", 3245, 31);
 R_Date("VERA-4072", 3204,
30);
 Outlier(0.05);
};
R_Combine("Hst Combine 4",
8)
{
 R_Date("16836", 3191, 31);
 R_Date("VERA-4073", 3240,
31);
 Outlier(0.05);
};
R_Combine("Hst Combine 5",
8)
{
 R_Date("16837", 3193, 32);
 R_Date("VERA-4074", 3173,
30);
 Outlier(0.05);
};
R_Date("19008", 2972, 26)
{
 Outlier(0.05);
};
R_Combine("Hst Combine 6",
8)
{
 R_Date("19448", 3245, 30);
 R_Date("SacA-11129", 3165,
30);
 Outlier(0.05);
};
R_Combine("Hst Combine 7",
8)
{
 R_Date("19449", 3275, 31);
 R_Date("SacA-11130", 3200,
```

25);
 Outlier(0.05);
};
R_Combine("Hst Combine 8",
8)
{
 R_Date("19450", 3291, 31);
 R_Date("19451", 3237, 30);
 R_Date("SacA-11131", 3230,
20);
 Outlier(0.05);
};
R_Date("SacA 11132", 3170, 35)
{
 Outlier(0.05);
};
R_Date("19154", 3209, 28)
{
 Outlier(0.05);
};
R_Date("SacA 11170", 3285, 20)
{
 Outlier(0.05);
};
R_Date("19546", 3237, 26)
{
 Outlier(0.05);
};
R_Date("19252", 3210, 31)
{
 Outlier(0.05);
};
R_Date("19547", 3171, 25)
{
 Outlier(0.05);
};
R_Date("SacA 11168", 3760, 60)
{
 Outlier(0.05);
};
Interval("Hst Int", 15 + T(5));
};
Boundary("Hatshepsut End");
Phase("Thut III")
{

R_Date("19147", 3261, 32)
{
 Outlier(0.05);
};
R_Date("19148", 3186, 28)
{
 Outlier(0.05);
};
R_Date("19453", 3264, 29)
{
 Outlier(0.05);
};
R_Date("SacA 11148", 3090, 30)
{
 Outlier(0.05);
};
R_Date("19480", 3251, 26)
{
 Outlier(0.05);
};
R_Date("SacA 11150", 3185, 30)
{
 Outlier(0.05);
};
R_Combine("Thut III Combine
1", 8)
{
 R_Date("19481", 3233, 25);
 R_Date("SacA-11152", 3180,
25);
 Outlier(0.05);
};
R_Date("19150", 3153, 27)
{
 Outlier(0.05);
};
R_Date("SacA 11153", 3260, 30)
{
 Outlier(0.05);
};
R_Combine("Thut III Combine
2", 8)
{
 R_Date("19482", 3277, 26);
 R_Date("SacA-11154", 3305,

25);
 Outlier(0.05);
};
R_Combine("Thut III Combine
3", 8)
{
 R_Date("19151", 3107, 27);
 R_Date("SacA-11155", 3040,
25);
 Outlier(0.05);
};
R_Combine("Thut III Combine
4", 8)
{
 R_Date("19581", 3258, 26);
 R_Date("SacA-11156", 3200,
25);
 Outlier(0.05);
};
R_Combine("Thut III Combine
5", 8)
{
 R_Date("19483", 3226, 26);
 R_Date("SacA-11158", 3285,
20);
 Outlier(0.05);
};
R_Combine("Thut III Combine
6", 8)
{
 R_Date("19484", 3257, 26);
 R_Date("SacA-11159", 3305,
25);
 Outlier(0.05);
};
R_Combine("Thut III Combine
7", 8)
{
 R_Date("19485", 3262, 25);
 R_Date("SacA-11160", 3200,
20);
 Outlier(0.05);
};
R_Combine("Thut III Combine
8", 8)

```
{
 R_Date("19152", 3249, 28);
 R_Date("SacA-11161", 3205,
30);
 Outlier(0.05);
};
Interval("Thut III Int II", 33 +
T(5));
};
Boundary("Amenhotep II");
Phase("Ahp II")
{
R_Date("18507", 3165, 32)
{
 Outlier(0.05);
};
Interval("Ahp II Int", 31 + T(5));
};
Boundary("Thutmose IV");
Phase("Thut IV")
{
R_Date("19549", 3084, 26)
{
 Outlier(0.05);
};
Interval("Thut IV Int", 38 +
T(5));
};
Boundary("Amenhotep III");
Phase("Ahp III")
{
R_Date("18510", 3040, 30)
{
 Outlier(0.05);
};
R_Date("19548", 3118, 27)
{
 Outlier(0.05);
};
Interval("Ahp III Int", 38 + T(5));
};
Boundary("Amenhotep IV");
Phase("Ahp IV")
{
R_Date("18057", 3082, 29)
```

```
{
 Outlier(0.05);
};
R_Date("18407", 3096, 28)
{
 Outlier(0.05);
};
R_Combine("Ahp IV Combine
1", 8)
{
 R_Date("18512", 3051, 27);
 R_Date("18412", 3064, 28);
 Outlier(0.05);
};
R_Date("18953", 3092, 27)
{
 Outlier(0.05);
};
R_Date("18954", 2976, 28)
{
 Outlier(0.05);
};
R_Combine("Ahp IV Combine
2", 8)
{
 R_Date("19004", 2862, 26);
 R_Date("19263", 2798, 27);
 Outlier(0.05);
};
R_Combine("Ahp IV Combine
3", 8)
{
 R_Date("VERA-4686", 2847,
36);
 R_Date("VERA-4686B", 2918,
30);
 Outlier(0.05);
};
R_Combine("Ahp IV Combine
4", 8)
{
 R_Date("18955", 3115, 30);
 R_Date("VERA-4687", 3094,
37);
 R_Date("VERA-4687B", 3070,
```

```
37);
 Outlier(0.05);
};
R_Date("18956", 3028, 27)
{
 Outlier(0.05);
};
R_Date("20482", 2787, 31)
{
 Outlier(0.05);
};
R_Combine("Ahp IV Combine
5", 8)
{
 R_Date("VERA-4685", 3096,
34);
 R_Date("VERA-4685B", 3116,
35);
 Outlier(0.05);
};
Interval("Akh Int", 17 + T(5));
};
Boundary("Neferneferuaten,
ETC");
Phase("Nef")
{
Interval("Nef Int", 3 + T(5));
};
Boundary("Tutankhamun");
Phase("Tut")
{
R_Date("17868", 3065, 31)
{
 Outlier(0.05);
};
R_Date("18950", 3138, 28)
{
 Outlier(0.05);
};
R_Date("18951", 3137, 29)
{
 Outlier(0.05);
};
R_Date("18952", 3117, 29)
{
```

```
Outlier(0.05);
};
R_Date("19003", 3106, 26)
{
 Outlier(0.05);
};
R_Date("19132", 3133, 29)
{
 Outlier(0.05);
};
R_Date("19550", 3015, 25)
{
 Outlier(0.05);
};
Interval("Tut Int", 9 + T(5));
};
Boundary("Ay");
Phase("Ay Phase")
{
Interval("Ay Int", 4 + T(5));
};
Boundary("Horemheb");
Phase("Hhb")
{
Interval("Hhb Int", 15 + T(5));
};
Boundary("Rameses I");
Phase("Ram I")
{
Interval("Ram I Int", 2 + T(5));
};
Boundary("Sety I");
Phase("Set I")
{
Interval("Sety I Int", 9 + T(5));
};
Boundary("Rameses II");
Phase("Ram II")
{
R_Date("18501", 3171, 28)
{
 Outlier(0.05);
};
R_Date("18505", 3118, 27)
{
```

```
Outlier(0.05);
};
Interval("Ram II Int", 67 + T(5));
};
Boundary("Merneptah");
Phase("Mpt")
{
R_Date("19131", 3113, 28)
{
 Outlier(0.05);
};
Interval("Mpt Int",10 + T(5));
};
Boundary("Sety II");
Phase("Set II")
{
Interval("Sety II Int", 6 + T(5));
};
Boundary("Amenmessu");
Phase("Amu")
{
Interval("Amu Int", 2 + T(5));
};
Boundary("Saptah");
Phase("Sap")
{
Interval("Sap Int", 6 + T(5));
};
Boundary("Queen Tausret");
Phase("Tau")
{
R_Date("19143", 2964, 30)
{
 Outlier(0.05);
};
Interval("Tau Int",2 + T(5));
};
Boundary("Sethnakht");
Phase("Seth")
{
Interval("Seth Int", 3 + T(5));
};
Boundary("Rameses III");
Phase("Ram III")
{
```

```
Interval("Ram III Int", 31 +
T(5));
};
Boundary("Rameses IV");
Phase("Ram IV")
{
R_Combine("Ram IV Combine
1", 8)
{
 R_Date("19554", 3020, 26);
 R_Date("VERA-4790A", 2995,
31);
 Outlier(0.05);
};
R_Date("20189", 2972, 27)
{
 Outlier(0.05);
};
Interval("Ram IV Int", 8 + T(5));
};
Boundary("Rameses V");
Phase("Ram V")
{
Interval("Ram V Int", 4 + T(5));
};
Boundary("Rameses VI");
Phase("Ram VI")
{
Interval("Ram VI Int", 8 + T(5));
};
Boundary("Rameses VII");
Phase("Ram VII")
{
Interval("Ram VII Int", 7 +
T(5));
};
Boundary("Rameses VIII");
Phase("Ram VIII")
{
Interval("Ram VIII Int", 1 +
T(5));
};
Boundary("Rameses IX");
Phase("Ram IX")
{
```

R_Date("20213", 2771, 28)
{
 Outlier(0.05);
};
R_Date("20214", 2946, 29)
{
 Outlier(0.05);
};
Interval("Ram IX Int", 18 +
T(5));
};
Boundary("Rameses X");
Phase("Ram X")
{
Interval("Ram X Int", 3 + T(5));
};
Boundary("Rameses XI");
Phase("Ram XI")
{
Interval("Ram XI Int", 28 +
T(5));
};
Boundary("Smendes");
Phase("Sme")
{
R_Date("18051", 2768, 27)
{
 Outlier(0.05);
};
Interval("Sme Int", 26 + T(5));
};
Boundary("Amenemnisu");
Phase("Ame")
{
R_Date("20060", 2901, 27)
{
 Outlier(0.05);
};
R_Combine("Ame Combine

1", 8)
{
 R_Date("20061", 2856, 27);
 R_Date("20062", 2880, 27);
 Outlier(0.05);
};
R_Date("20063", 2900, 28)
{
 Outlier(0.05);
};
R_Date("20064", 2930, 28)
{
 Outlier(0.05);
};
R_Date("20065", 2853, 27)
{
 Outlier(0.05);
};
R_Date("20066", 2860, 30)
{
 Outlier(0.05);
};
R_Date("20067", 2887, 28)
{
 Outlier(0.05);
};
R_Date("20201", 3127, 27)
{
 Outlier(0.05);
};
Interval("Ame Int", 4 + T(5));
};
Boundary("Psusennes I");
Phase("Psu")
{
R_Date("18959", 2987, 37)
{
 Outlier(0.05);
};

Interval("Psu Int", 46 + T(5));
};
Boundary("Amenemope");
Phase("Amp")
{
R_Date("19794", 2904, 27)
{
 Outlier(0.05);
};
Interval("Amp Int",9 + T(5));
};
Boundary("Osorkon the Elder");
Phase("Ors")
{
Interval("Ors Int", 6 + T(5));
};
Boundary("Siamun");
Phase("Sia")
{
R_Date("18960", 2805, 29)
{
 Outlier(0.05);
};
Interval("Sia Int", 19 + T(5));
};
Boundary("Psusennes II");
Phase("Psu II")
{
Interval("Psu II Int", 14 + T(5));
};
Boundary("Shoshenq I");
};
};

Table RE12. The OxCal runfile – the New Kingdom Model – for the 'ultra-high' model reported in Table RE9A (Aston 2012 'ultra-high' reign lengths for Tuthmosis III to Ramesses II, and Schneider 2010a reign lengths for Ahmose to Tuthmosis II and for Merneptah to Psusennes II). This is the OxCal runfile of Bronk Ramsey et al. (2010 – from the modified SOM of 17 May 2011), but excluding samples no longer considered to be of NK origin (OxA-18520), and associating OxA-18960 with Siamun (see Table S1 addendum – added April 2011 in the Bronk Ramsey et al. 2010 SOM), and accordingly adding intervals for Osochor, Siamun and Psusennes II: see Table RE10 above. I thank Mike Dee and Christopher Bronk Ramsey for their assistance and advice.

7. *Revisit Essay Appendix 2: Radiocarbon date listing regarding Figures RE 1–4 and Manning* et al. *(2006a)*

This Appendix lists:

   (i)   a corrected (see footnote 38 above) version of Manning *et al.* (2006a) SOM Table S1. The correction applies especially to the 3 Heidelberg dates (Hd-7092–6795, Hd-6058–5519, Hd-6059–7967). This listing includes the set of 28 dates (including the 3 Heidelberg dates) on short-lived samples from the Akrotiri VDL shown in Figures RE1 and 2, and as used in Manning *et al.* (2006a). The sub-set of 13 AD 2000s measured data are indicated within this listing.

  (ii)   a listing of the other 15 ^{14}C dates on (what is stated to be) definite short-lived (or shorter-lived) sample material from the Akrotiri VDL or equivalent and not on under-sized samples from work published in the AD1970s-1980s *not* employed in Manning *et al.* (2006a), *but* included in the 43–date set of ^{14}C data shown in Figure RE1 above and as used in Manning and Kromer (2011a: Figure 1).

I note that Höflmayer (2012b: 247–250) also conveniently lists many of the relevant Aegean ^{14}C data, including all those in the Manning *et al.* (2006a) study (and in Manning and Bronk Ramsey 2009; and Manning 2009).

(i) Corrected and edited version of Manning et al. (2006a) SOM Table S1.

The Table below lists all the samples and radiocarbon dates obtained for, or used in, the Manning *et al.* (2006a) study but with some minor edits/corrections as noted below. Source Laboratories: Oxford Radiocarbon Accelerator Unit – OxA (OxA samples with nos. 1548 to 3225 come from Housley *et al.* 1990; 1999), Vienna Environmental Research Accelerator – VERA, Heidelberg Radiocarbon Laboratory – Hd (samples Hd-7092–6795, Hd-6058–5519, Hd-6059–7967 come from Hubberten *et al.* 1990), Copenhagen Radiocarbon Laboratory – K (K samples come from Friedrich *et al.* 1990). For discussion of samples used/not used in the Manning *et al.* (2006a) study in the principle Models 1 and 2 analyses (those not used are shaded grey), see the Manning *et al.* (2006a) paper and SOM, and see notes in right hand column of the Table below and see Manning *et al.* (2006a) SOM Table S2 and notes. The samples employed in Models 1 and 2 are the non-shaded entries. Dark grey shaded entries were excluded altogether from the analysis in Manning *et al.* (2006a) for the reasons indicated. The light grey shaded entries are single data for samples or contexts, or are irrelevant early *terminus post quem* data for Late Minoan IB or Late Minoan II samples. These samples were not included in the Models 1 and 2 analyses in Manning *et al.* (2006a), but are included in the Model 1 run "with extras" shown in Manning *et al.* (2006a) SOM Fig. S4 and Table S3. The 13 dates on short-lived samples from the Akrotiri VDL measured in the AD2000s and reported in Manning *et al.* (2006a) are in bold in the Table below starting with OxA-11817. The other (15) dates in the 28–date set on short-lived samples from the Akrotiri VDL employed by Manning *et al.* (2006a) then follow down to Hd-6059–7967. These data form the 28–date and 13–date sets referred to in the text above and shown in Figures RE 1–2.

Site	Submitter's reference	Material*	Species	OxA	VERA	Hd	K	¹⁴C BP	±1σ	δ¹³C	Phase	Context
Miletos, Turkey	AT 99.915	bone	sheep/goat	11951				3423	23	-19.5	LMIA	Secure
Miletos, Turkey	AT 99.729	bone	sheep/goat	11952				3243	22	-20.1	Intrusive into LMIA†	Bad
Miletos, Turkey	AT 99.779	bone	sheep/goat	11953				3279	26	-20	Intrusive into LMIA†	Bad
Miletos, Turkey	AT 99.811	bone	sheep/goat	11954				3377	24	-19.4	LMIA	Secure
Akrotiri, Thera	M54/2/VII/60/SE>247	charcoal	Olea europaea	11250				3550	45	-23.4	LMIA(early)	Secure
						22037		3552	19	-25.04		
Kommos, Crete	Space 25B Tr.66B	charcoal	Cupressaceae sp.? ◆	3429				3350	70	-27.8	LMIA(early)	Secure
Kommos, Crete	Space 25B Tr.66B	charcoal	Cupressaceae sp.? ◆	11833				3485	33	-25.3	LMIA(early)	Secure
Kommos, Crete	Space 25B Tr.66B	charcoal	Cupressaceae sp.? ◆	11944				3435	25	-24.4	LMIA(early)	Secure
Kommos, Crete	TP-KE-30	charcoal		10618				3270	45	-22.6	LMIA(early)‡	poor/bad‡
Kommos, Crete	TP-KE-30	charcoal		10619				3295	45	-22.8	LMIA(early)‡	poor/bad‡
Kommos, Crete	K85A/62D/9:92	charcoal	Quercus sp.	11251				3505	40	-23.6	LMIA(early)	Secure
					2636§			3445	25	-23.4		
Kommos, Crete	K85A/66B/4:22+23	charred twig		11252				3375	45	-23.6	LMIA(early)	Secure
					2637§			3390	20	-21.0		
Kommos, Crete	K85A/62D/8:83	charcoal	Quercus sp.	11253				3397	38	-23.2	LMIA(early)	Secure
					2638§			3600	19	-20.5		
Kommos, Crete	38/TP-KC-22	charcoal		10731				3450	45	-24.1	LMIA(early)	secure – but single
Trianda, Rhodes	Trianda 1	charcoal		10623				3245	45	-23.5	?LMIA(early)	? phased – disturbed context‖
Trianda, Rhodes	Trianda 9	charcoal	?Olea sp.	10642				3333	39	-25.2	LMIA(early)	phased – single
Trianda, Rhodes	34/AE1024/A rings 2 1–30 (bark)	charcoal	Quercus sp.	10728				3455	45	-25.3	Late MB/ LMIA(early)	Secure
Trianda, Rhodes	34/AE1024/B rings 11–20	charcoal	Quercus sp.	10729				3410	45	-25.9	Late MB/ LMIA(early)	Secure

Site	Submitter's reference	Material*	Species	OxA	VERA	Hd	K	14C BP	±1σ	δ13C	Phase	Context
Trianda, Rhodes	36/AE1024/C rings 1 (pith) – 10	charcoal	Quercus sp.	10730				3490	45	-25.5	Late MB/ LMIA(early)	Secure
Trianda, Rhodes	34/AE1024/A rings 2 1–30 (bark)	charcoal	Quercus sp.	11945				3473	24	-24.9	Late MB/ LMIA(early)	Secure
					2740			3481	32	-25.5		
Trianda, Rhodes	34/AE1024/B rings 11–20	charcoal	Quercus sp.	11946				3474	24	-26.1	Late MB/ Late MB/ LMIA(early)	Secure
					2741			3485	28	-26.4		
Trianda, Rhodes	36/AE1024/C rings 1 (pith) -10	charcoal	Quercus sp.	11948				3526	25	-25.2	Late MB/ LMIA(early)	Secure
					2742			3476	28	-24.7		
Trianda, Rhodes	Trianda 4	charcoal		10640				3338	40	-25.4	LMIA	phased – single
Akrotiri, Thera	F/65/N001/I2 ring 3 (bark)	charcoal	Tamarix sp.	10312				3293	27	-24	LMIA(late)	Secure
					2748			3319	28	-24.6		
Akrotiri, Thera	G/65/N001/I2 ring 2	charcoal	Tamarix sp.	10313				3353	27	-24.1	LMIA(late)	Secure
					2749			3335	33	-25		
Akrotiri, Thera	H/65/N001/I2 ring 1 (pith)	charcoal	Tamarix sp.	10314				3330	27	-24.5	LMIA(late)	Secure
					2750			3325	28	-25.7		
Akrotiri, Thera	A/M4N003 rings 6–8 (bark)	charcoal	Olea europaea	10315				3446	39	-24	LMIA(late)	Secure
					2743			3413	28	-24.3		
Akrotiri, Thera	B/M4N003 rings 3–5	charcoal	Olea europaea	10316				3342	38	-24.4	LMIA(late)	Secure
					2744			3427	31	-20.4		
Akrotiri, Thera	C/M4N003 rings 7–8 (bark)	charcoal	Olea europaea	10317				3440	35	-24.1	LMIA(late)	Secure
					2745			3386	28	-22.9		
Akrotiri, Thera	D/M4N003 rings 5–6	charcoal	Olea europaea	10318				3355	40	-24.2	LMIA(late)	Secure
					2746			3471	28	-18.1		
Akrotiri, Thera	E/M4N003 rings 3–4	charcoal	Olea europaea	10319				3424	38	-24.4	LMIA(late)	Secure
					2747			3386	30	-26.4		

Site	Submitter's reference	Material*	Species	OxA	VERA	Hd	K	^{14}C BP	±1σ	δ^{13}C	Phase	Context
Kommos, Crete	TP-KE-31	charcoal		10620				3269	38	-22.4	LMIA(late)	phased – single
Kommos, Crete	40/TP-KC-20	charcoal		10761				3440	38	-24.3	LMIA(late)	Phased – TPQ
Kommos, Crete	39/TP-KC-21	charcoal		10769				3555	60	-24.7	LMIA(late)	Phased – TPQ
Miletos, Turkey	1:C-TU-MIL-1/ RY1000–1010	charcoal	Quercus sp.	12301				3439	30	-25.4	LMIA(late)	Secure
Miletos, Turkey	1:C-TU-MIL-1/ RY1000–1010	charcoal	Quercus sp.	12302				3386	31	-26	LMIA(late)	Secure
Miletos, Turkey	2:C-TU-MIL-1/ RY1010–1020	charcoal	Quercus sp.	12303				3467	31	-25.5	LMIA(late)	Secure
Miletos, Turkey	3:C-TU-MIL-1/ RY1020–1030	charcoal	Quercus sp.	12304				3404	31	-25.5	LMIA(late)	Secure
Miletos, Turkey	3:C-TU-MIL-1/ RY1020–1030	charcoal	Quercus sp.	12305				3459	31	-25.7	LMIA(late)	Secure
Miletos, Turkey	4:C-TU-MIL-1/ RY1030–1040	charcoal	Quercus sp.	12306				3416	31	-25.7	LMIA(late)	Secure
Miletos, Turkey	4:C-TU-MIL-1/ RY1030–1040	charcoal	Quercus sp.	12307				3425	31	-25.6	LMIA(late)	Secure
Miletos, Turkey	5:C-TU-MIL-1/ RY1040–1050	charcoal	Quercus sp.	12308				3361	31	-26	LMIA(late)	Secure
Miletos, Turkey	5:C-TU-MIL-1/ RY1040–1050	charcoal	Quercus sp.	12309				3397	31	-26	LMIA(late)	Secure
Miletos, Turkey	6:C-TU-MIL-1/ RY1050–1060	charcoal	Quercus sp.	12310				3345	32	-26.3	LMIA(late)	Secure
Miletos, Turkey	6:C-TU-MIL-1/ RY1050–1060	charcoal	Quercus sp.	12311				3397	32	-26.3	LMIA(late)	Secure
Miletos, Turkey	7:C-TU-MIL-1/ RY1060–1070	charcoal	Quercus sp.	12312				3388	30	-26.3	LMIA(late)	Secure
Miletos, Turkey	7:C-TU-MIL-1/ RY1060–1070	charcoal	Quercus sp.	12313				3352	31	-26.1	LMIA(late)	Secure
Miletos, Turkey	2:C-TU-MIL-1/ RY1010–1020	charcoal	Quercus sp.	12407				3385	34	-25.8	LMIA(late)	Secure

Site	Submitter's reference	Material*	Species	OxA	VERA	Hd	K	¹⁴C BP	±1σ	δ¹³C	Phase	Context
Trianda, Rhodes	Trianda 8	charcoal		10641				3498	39	-24.4	LMIA(late)	phased – single, TPQ
Trianda, Rhodes	Trianda 13	charred twig	Quercus sp.	10643				3367	39	-26.3	LMIA(late)	Secure
Trianda, Rhodes	Trianda 13	charred twig	Quercus sp.	11884				3344	32	-26	LMIA(late)	Secure
Tsoungiza, Nemea	Tsoungiza 4	charcoal		11312				3215	38	-24.2	LHI(late) (LMIA(late))%	phased*
Tsoungiza, Nemea	Tsoungiza 5	charcoal		11313				3261	39	-24.1	LHI(late) (LMIA(late))%	phased*
Tsoungiza, Nemea	Tsoungiza 6	charcoal	Allium sp.	11314				3202	38	-22.7	LHI(late) (LMIA(late))%	phased*
Akrotiri, Thera	M2/76 N003	charred seed	? Lathyrus sp.	11817				3348	31	-22.9	LMIA(VDL)	Secure
Akrotiri, Thera	M7/68A N004	charred seed	Hordeum sp.	11818				3367	33	-25.8	LMIA(VDL)	Secure
Akrotiri, Thera	M10/23A N012	charred seed	Hordeum sp.	11820				3400	31	-25.2	LMIA(VDL)	Secure
Akrotiri, Thera	M31/43 N047	charred seed	Hordeum sp.	11869				3336	34	-22.8	LMIA(VDL)	Secure
Akrotiri, Thera	M2/76 N003	charred seed	? Lathyrus sp.	12170				3336	28	-22.9	LMIA(VDL)	Secure
					2757			3315	31	-24.1		
					repeat¶			3390	32	-21.5		
Akrotiri, Thera	M7/68A N004	charred seed	Hordeum sp.	12171	2758			3372	28	-25.7	LMIA(VDL)	Secure
					repeat			3339	28	-26.5		
								3322	32	-24.7		
Akrotiri, Thera	M31/43 N047	charred seed	Hordeum sp.	12172	2756			3321	32	-23.1	LMIA(VDL)	Secure
								3317	28	-21.6		
Akrotiri, Thera	M10/23A N012	charred seed	Hordeum sp.	12175				3318	28	-24.7	LMIA(VDL)	Secure
Akrotiri, Thera	1	charred seed	Lathyrus sp.	1548				3335	60	-23	LMIA(VDL)	Secure
Akrotiri, Thera	1	charred seed	Lathyrus sp.	1549				3460	80	-23	LMIA(VDL)	Secure
Akrotiri, Thera	2	charred seed	Lathyrus sp.	1550				3395	65	-23	LMIA(VDL)	Secure
Akrotiri, Thera	4	charred seed	Lathyrus sp.	1552				3390	65	-23	LMIA(VDL)	Secure
Akrotiri, Thera	8	charred seed	Lathyrus sp.	1553				3340	65	-23	LMIA(VDL)	Secure
Akrotiri, Thera	8	charred seed	Lathyrus sp.	1554				3280	65	-23	LMIA(VDL)	Secure
Akrotiri, Thera	9	charred seed	Lathyrus sp.	1555				3245	65	-23	LMIA(VDL)	Secure
Akrotiri, Thera	11	charred seed	Hordeum sp.	1556				3415	70	-23	LMIA(VDL)	Secure
Akrotiri, Thera	041079-1, 220976	pulses					5352	3310	65	-22.5	LMIA(VDL)	Secure
Akrotiri, Thera	011079-1, 021069	pulses					5353	3430	90	-20.5	LMIA(VDL)	Secure

Site	Submitter's reference	Material*	Species	OxA	VERA	Hd	K	^{14}C BP	±1σ	δ^{13}C	Phase	Context
Akrotiri, Thera	20579–3	pulses					3228	3340	55	-20.6	LMIA(VDL)	Secure
Akrotiri, Thera	250780	charred twig	*Tamarix* sp.				4255	3380	60	-23.8	LMIA(VDL)	Secure
Akrotiri, Thera	West House	peas	peas			7092–6795		3360	60		LMIA(VDL)	Secure – *see correction below*
Akrotiri, Thera		grains				6058–5519		3490	80		LMIA(VDL)	Secure – *see correction below*
Akrotiri, Thera		grains				6059–7967		3140	70		LMIA(VDL)	Secure – *see correction below*
Tsoungiza, Nemea	Tsoungiza 2	charred seed	*Vitis vinifera*	11309				3308	39	-23.4	LHI-II (LMIA/LMIB)	phased*
Tsoungiza, Nemea	Tsoungiza 3	charcoal	? *Quercus* sp.	11310				3503	38	-24.5	LHI-II (LMIA/LMIB)	phased*
Tsoungiza, Nemea	Tsoungiza 3	charcoal	? *Quercus* sp.	11311				3487	38	-22.7	LHI-II (LMIA/LMIB)	phased*
Chania, Crete	15/TR10,Rm E	charred seed	*Pisum sativum*	2517				3380	80	-25.6	LMIB	Secure
Chania, Crete	13/TR17,1984,Rm C	charred seed	*Vicia faba*	2518				3340	80	-24.9	LMIB	Secure
Chania, Crete	14/TR17,1984,Rm C	charred seed	*Hordeum* sp.	2646				3315	70	-23.9	LMIB	Secure
Chania, Crete	16/TR24,1989,L6,BA1	charred seed		2647				3315	70	-23.9	LMIB	Secure
Chania, Crete	13/TR17,1984,Rm C	charred seed	*Vicia faba*	10320				3208	26	-22.8	LMIB	Secure
Chania, Crete	14/TR17,1984,Rm C	charred seed	*Hordeum* sp.	10321				3268	27	-22.1	LMIB	Secure
Chania, Crete	15/TR10,Rm E	charred seed	*Pisum sativum*	10322				3338	26	-23.9	LMIB	Secure
Chania, Crete	16/TR24,1989,L6,BA1	charred seed		10323				3253	25	-23.3	LMIB	Secure
Kommos, Crete	TP-KE-29	charcoal		10617				3190	40	-24.2	LMIB	phased – single
Myrtos-Pyrgos, Crete	17/K5,2,1	charred seed	*Hordeum* sp.	3187				3230	70	-22.2	LMIB	Secure
Myrtos-Pyrgos, Crete	18/K5,2,4	charred seed	*Hordeum* sp.	3188				3200	70	-26.5	LMIB	Secure
Myrtos-Pyrgos, Crete	19/K5/K6,2,1	charred seed	*Vicia ervilia*	3189				3270	70	-26	LMIB	Secure
Myrtos-Pyrgos, Crete	20/K5/L6,2,2	charred seed	*Vicia ervilia*	3225				3160	80	-23.6	LMIB	Secure

Site	Submitter's reference	Material*	Species	OxA	VERA	Hd	K	¹⁴C BP	±1σ	δ¹³C	Phase	Context
Myrtos-Pyrgos, Crete	17/K5,2,1	charred seed	*Hordeum* sp.	10324				3270	26	-22.4	LMIB	Secure
Myrtos-Pyrgos, Crete	19/K5/K6,2,1	charred seed	*Vicia ervilia*	10325				3228	26	-23.4	LMIB	Secure
Myrtos-Pyrgos, Crete	20/K5/L6,2,2	charred seed	*Vicia ervilia*	10326				3227	25	-22.4	LMIB	Secure
Myrtos-Pyrgos, Crete	18/K5,2,4	charred seed	*Hordeum* sp.	10411				3150	40	-26.5	LMIB	Secure
Miletos, Turkey	AT 99.787	bone	sheep/goat	11955				3233	23	-17.8	LMIB/II	phased (non-specific date, so not used – excluded) – single
Knossos, Crete	MUMK	charred seed	*Hordeum* sp.	2096				3070	70	-23.3	LMII	Secure
Knossos, Crete	MUMK	charred seed	*Hordeum* sp.	2097				3190	65	-23.6	LMII	Secure
Knossos, Crete	MUMK	charred seed	*Hordeum* sp.	2098				3220	65	-22.9	LMII	Secure
Knossos, Crete	MUMK	charred seed	*Hordeum* sp.	11882				3156	33	-22.7	LMII	Secure
Knossos, Crete	MUMK	charred seed	*Hordeum* sp.	11943				3148	23	-23	LMII	Secure
Kommos, Crete	TP-KE-28	charcoal		10793				3382	37	-23.7	LMII	Phased, TPQ
Kommos, Crete	43/TP-KC-17	charcoal		10732				3095	45	-22.2	LMII	Phased, TPQ
Kommos, Crete	42/TP-KC-18	charcoal		10762				7440	50	-23.4	LMII	phased – aberrant Neolithic age sample, excluded
Kommos, Crete	41/TP-KC-19	charcoal		10770				3040	190	-26.9	LMII	Phased, TPQ
Known Age test												
Çatacık, Turkey	AD1640-1649	tree rings	*Pinus nigra*			19597		246	13	-23.64	AD1640-49	Absolute
					2751			227	31	-22.1		
					2752			271	37	-21.5		
					2753			252	31	-22.1		
					2754			259	31	-22.4		
					2755			243	28	-23.7		

Notes on the Table:

* In terms of the Oxford Laboratory varying sample pretreatment strategies (RR, ZR or AF) depending on sample nature as summarized in Manning *et al.* (2006a) SOM, all the bone samples (OxA-11951, 11952, 11953, 11954, 11955) were AF pretreated, samples OxA-3429, 10793 and 11833 (from Kommos), OxA-11869 (from Akrotiri) and OxA-2096, 2097, 2098, 11882, 11943 (from Knossos) were RR pretreated, and all other Oxford samples were ZR pretreated.

† Two bone samples from Miletos were received and originally dated on the basis of being from Late Minoan IA contexts. Subsequently, the excavator of the site, W.-D. Niemeier, informed us that these two samples derive from what was later recognized as an intrusive (probably Mycenaean) pit cut into the LMIA stratum. These two dates may therefore be dismissed as irrelevant to LMIA and were excluded from analysis in Manning *et al.* (2006a) (see Bronk Ramsey *et al.* 2004: 339).

‡ These two samples were taken from Building T in the space under Gallery P5 hearth. While this context is regarded as LMIA early, the Kommos excavation team's archaeological analysis of the context has concluded that it was also "possibly contaminated by LMIIIA2 fill" (Jeremy B. Rutter, pers. comm.). Hence these two radiocarbon samples and dates must be regarded as suspect as they could relate to post-LMIA disturbance/material. They were thus not employed in the Manning *et al.* (2006a) analysis.

§ These VERA samples are the weighted averages of two measurements for VERA-2636 and 2637, and of three measurements for VERA-2638.

|| See Bronk Ramsey *et al.* (2004).

¶ This sample received only HCl pretreatment. For other variations in VERA sample pretreatment, see discussion in section 2 of the Manning *et al.* (2006a) SOM.

% Three of the samples from the southern Greek mainland site of Tsoungiza are an unexplained problem as they do not agree with the other data: OxA-11312 at 3215±38BP, 11313 at 3261±39BP, 11314 at 3202±38BP, and especially OxA-11312 and 11314. These two samples, regarded as Late Helladic I (approximately contemporary with LMIA), offer ages rather too late to conform with the other secure samples of this age range and indeed are mainly too late even for the (lower) conventional archaeological chronology. Calibrated age ranges are, respectively, 1513–1441 BC and 1499–1434 BC at 1σ. OxA-11312 and 11313 come from contexts also previously dated using other charcoal fragments by the Arizona radiocarbon lab with respective ages of 3322 ± 54 BP (AA-10816) and 3317 ± 55 BP (AA-10818). These ages are both rather older than the OxA measurements, in the first case by quite a large margin. This might suggest either (i) some problem (or contexts not in fact clear), or (ii) that the material from these contexts is mixed in age and some might be intrusive. We note in contrast, that the three samples regarded as subsequent, and of Late Helladic I-II context, seem fine. OxA-11309 on grape seeds, and so a short-lived sample, yields a calibrated range of 1625–1526 BC at 1σ, while OxA-11310 and 11311 on long-lived wood fragments yield rather older ages but these are acceptable given the sample material and clear possibility of also being residual (and so they offer largely irrelevant *terminus post quem* data for their phase: see Bronk Ramsey *et al.* 2004). The quality controls on the overall OxA dataset presented here, and generally for the laboratory, suggest there was nothing unusual which affected the measurements of OxA-11312 to 11314. We can note that the samples were not freshly acquired, but had been in storage for a number of years and so some form of contamination cannot be ruled out. However, a more economical explanation would seem to be unrecognized intrusive or mixed material at the site. None of the Tsoungiza data are employed in the analyses in the Manning *et al.* (2006a) paper.

Corrections to Manning *et al.* (2006a) SOM Table S1:

1. Three samples marked with the ♦ notation. Following Manning and Bronk Ramsey (2009), I note a correction to previous publications where this sample (3 radiocarbon dates: OxA-3429, OxA-11833, OxA-11944) was by mistake labelled as *Chamaecyparis* sp. – false cypress. This is a species not found on pre-modern Crete – whereas we assume it should instead be labelled *Cupressus* sp. (for the Cretan Cypress, see: Rackham and Moody 1997: 60), and I use a generic description of *Cupressaceae* sp. Bronk Ramsey *et al.* (2004: 339) listed OxA-11944 mistakenly as *Olea europaea*.

2. The 3 Heidelberg dates (Hd-7092–6795, Hd-6058–5519, Hd-6059–7967) were incorrectly shaded grey in the original Manning *et al.* (2006a) SOM. These data were included in the 28–date set of short-lived samples from the Akrotiri VDL (see Manning *et al.* 2006a SOM: Figures S2F and S2G and Table S2) – and as listed for 28 dates on short-lived sample material by Höflmayer (2012b: 249 – starting K-3228 to bottom of page). The weighted average for the Akrotiri VDL as employed in the Manning *et al.* (2006a) paper with these data is 3345 ± 8 BP (T = 31.5 < 39.9 for df27 at the 5% level); the weighted average without these data is almost the same at 3346 ± 8 BP (T = 19.7 < 36.4 for df24 at the 5% level) (Ward and Wilson 1978 as implemented in Bronk Ramsey 1995 and since). There is a one (1) ^{14}C year difference only. The inclusion/exclusion of these 3 dates is thus not a substantive issue for this analysis using a weighted average value for the Akrotiri short-lived samples VDL set (for an alternative analytical approach employing Tau_Boundary, Boundary modelling, see e.g. Figure RE9 above). I thank Malcolm Wiener for drawing this issue to my attention.

(ii) Listing of the other 15 ^{14}C dates on (what is stated to be) definite short-lived (or shorter-lived) sample material from the Akrotiri VDL or equivalent and not on under-sized samples from work published in the AD1970s–1980s not employed in Manning et al. (2006a), but included in the 43–date set of ^{14}C data shown in Figure RE1 above and as used in Manning and Kromer (2011a: Figure 1).

Lab ID	Context	Material	^{14}C Date BP	SD (1σ)	Reference
P-1697	Under pumice in jug	Carbonized beans	3070	60	Fishman *et al.* (1977: 193)
P-1888	Akrotiri VDL, Structure D	charcoal, shrubs	3130	50	Fishman *et al.* (1977: 192)
P-1885	Akrotiri VDL, Structure D room 1 jar 3	charred seed	3250	50	Fishman *et al.* (1977: 193)
P-1889	Akrotiri VDL, Structure D	charcoal, shrubs	3300	50	Fishman *et al.* (1977: 192)
P-1894*	Akrotiri VDL, Structure Delta, Room 3	charcoal, shrubs	3310	70	Fishman *et al.* (1977: 193)
P-2565	Akrotiri VDL, π5, Δ2	grain	3310	60	Fishman and Lawn (1978: 216)
P-1895	Akrotiri VDL, Structure Beta	charcoal, shrubs	3320	50	Fishman *et al.* (1977: 193)
P-1892	Akrotiri VDL, Bronos Bridge, Area 6	charcoal, shrubs	3330	50	Fishman *et al.* (1977: 193)
P-2791	Akrotiri VDL, Δ1, π2,	seeds & charred material	3340	60	Meulengracht *et al.* 1981: 229
P-2559	Akrotiri VDL, π1, Δ2	grain	3370	70	Fishman and Lawn (1978: 215)
ETH-3323	Akrotiri VDL	seed	3437	54	Kutschera and Stadler (2000: 74)
ETH-3324	Akrotiri VDL	seed	3453	52	Kutschera and Stadler (2000: 74)
ETH-3315	Akrotiri VDL	seed	3610	51	Kutschera and Stadler (2000: 74)
P-2561	Akrotiri VDL, π3, Δ1	grain	3800	50	Fishman and Lawn (1978: 216)
P-2560	Akrotiri VDL, π2, Δ1	grain	3980	70	Fishman and Lawn (1978: 215)

*Although P-1894 was employed in Manning and Kromer (2011a) and is listed here and plotted in Figure RE1, it is questionable whether this sample is in fact strictly from a VDL context as the publication states that it was from "under paved floor" (also e.g. Betancourt and Weinstein 1976: 344) – thus it might not be final VDL but could instead be pre-final VDL Late Cycladic I.

Note: the sample material listed above is as stated in the publication. For some the University of Pennsylvania (P) dates we can compare with the samples from the same loci (of the West House at Akrotiri) reported in Housley *et al.* (1990: 211). Although they note that the sample material sometimes differed even if from the same provenance, we may assume that the P samples were probably similar and thus likely (from Housley *et al.* 1990: Table 3) comprised the following for four of the P dates:

(Area) Δ1, (Pot) π2 = *Lathyrus* sp. = P-2560, P-2791
(Area) Δ1, (Pot) π3 = *Lathyrus* sp. = P-2561
(Area) Δ2, (Pot) π1 = *Lathyrus* sp. = P-2559

All of these associations should be considered with a question mark in view of the note to Table 4 in Housley *et al.* (1990).

8. Revisit Essay Appendix 3: Testing ^{14}C Sequence analysis in the period 1700–1500 BC against known age data

The logic and visual reasonableness of dendrochronological-^{14}C-wiggle-matching – that is fitting a sequence of ^{14}C data at known tree-ring spacings from a dendrochronological sample of unknown date (so a floating but fixed sequence) against a similarly constructed but absolutely placed 'master' radiocarbon calibration curve in order to achieve a close dating of the floating but fixed sequence – seems widely understood and accepted, with a variety of applications over nearly 50 years available in the literature (e.g. Ferguson *et al.* 1966; Weninger 1986; Pearson 1986; Christen and Litton 1995; Bronk Ramsey *et al.* 2001; Galimberti *et al.* 2004; Bayliss and Tyers 2004; Tyers 2008). Whether the fitting is achieved by *ad hoc* methods or a holistic Bayesian approach, very similar results emerge, and the method appears relatively robust (Bronk Ramsey *et al.* 2001; Galimberti *et al.* 2004). A detailed example illustrating this observation of similar results, comparing a least squares placement versus a Bayesian modelled placement, is offered, for example, by Manning *et al.* (2001: Figs. 2 and 3).

To give just one relevant instance of the much increased dating resolution available from such dendro-^{14}C-wiggle-match dating, Figure RE30 shows the dendro-^{14}C-wiggle-match placement of the dendrochronologically spaced ^{14}C data on an oak sample from Miletos found under a layer of Theran tephra (for the Miletos sample and data, see Bronk Ramsey *et al.* 2004: 327, 340; Galimberti *et al.* 2004: 921; Manning *et al.* 2006a). The waney edge (ring immediately below bark) of this sample thus provides a *terminus post quem* for the Thera eruption. The sample provided a sequence of 72 rings in total ending in what was believed to be the waney edge. It was dissected into seven 11-year samples, rings 1000–1010, 1010–1020, 1020–1030 … 1060–1070, and two ^{14}C dates were then obtained on each 11-year sample. These pairs of ^{14}C ages were then combined and wiggle-matched on the basis of fitting the mid-points of each 11-year sample (which are each 10-years apart) against the IntCal09 radiocarbon calibration curve (Reimer *et al.* 2009) modelled at 1 calendar year resolution employing OxCal (Bronk

Ramsey 2009a). Figure RE30A shows the Dendro Sequenced analysis, contrasting the individual non-modelled calibrated age probability distributions in light grey versus the much reduced modelled calibrated age probability distributions in black. Figure RE30C shows the modelled age ranges at 68.2% probability fitted against the IntCal09 radiocarbon calibration curve (shown as a 1SD band) – we see a close fit of the data to the shape of the ^{14}C calibration curve (indicating at most that a very small to no substantive regional/local offset applies: Manning *et al.* 2010: 1586, Figs. 11, 12). Figure RE30B shows the modelled calibrated age range for the final ring (to waney edge) of the sample – providing a *terminus post quem* for the Thera eruption (this *terminus post quem* was incorporated in the dating model in Manning *et al.* 2006a).

In contrast, there is less willingness in some circles to accept that Bayesian chronological modelling using just relative sequences of samples from, e.g., stratigraphic criteria (often referred to as Sequence analysis), can necessarily offer both greater precision and also reasonable accuracy for archaeology. Despite the explanations and equations in Bronk Ramsey (2009a), and the previous literature cited there (especially Buck *et al.* 1991; 1996; Buck and Millard 2004 – and see also the OxCal manual and the large body of work cited there: http://c14.arch.ox.ac.uk/oxcalhelp/hlp_contents.html) , and detailed examples in the literature (e.g. Needham *et al.* 1997; Manning *et al.* 2006a; Bayliss and Whittle 2007; Whittle *et al.* 2008; 2011), and checks by other teams (e.g. Weninger *et al.* 2010), skepticism is sometimes expressed, whether at the general to theoretical level relevant to some specific conditions (e.g. Weninger *et al.* 2011), or from the viewpoint of the archaeologist (e.g. Wiener 2003: 397–398 and footnote 168; 2006b: 331-332; 2012: 430).

In light of such expressions of concern, two reasonable questions from the archaeological perspective are: (i) can we check that Sequence analyses using Bayesian chronological modelling work (i.e. give a correct age), and (ii) how much more precise are the ranges calculated by such Bayesian chronological modelling approaches versus simple calibration?

In this Appendix I therefore offer a brief consideration of the period 1700–1500 BC – since this is the focus period for this book – to indicate the level of accuracy, and the scale of increased precision, available from Sequence analysis. To consider accuracy, I employed ^{14}C data of known calendar age (from dendrochronology) taken from IntCal09 (Reimer *et al.* 2009). I considered four different scenarios for the period 1700–1500 BC, moving from relatively few data and a coarse model to more data, and then to data with increased precision, and so ending with a relatively fine-grained model (which in the real world would come from e.g. combining 3 or 4 dates on identical samples – like short-lived seeds – from a context into a weighted average or from analyzing groups of data as Phases and thus being able to define Boundaries for one or more associated Phases with good precision). In each case, the sequence of data had no information about spacing, just the relative order. A Boundary was employed at the start and end of each Sequence to avoid the problem of an inappropriate prior (see discussion and references of Bronk Ramsey 2009a: 342–345).

Test 1 used just 5 ^{14}C dates each separated by 50 calendar years (^{14}C ages from IntCal09 for 1700 BC, 1650 BC, 1600 BC, 1550 BC and 1500 BC) and each assigned a measurement error of 30 ^{14}C years, which is about typical for many modern AMS measurements. Test 2 employed 9 data spaced every 25 years 1700–1500 BC from IntCal09, again with all

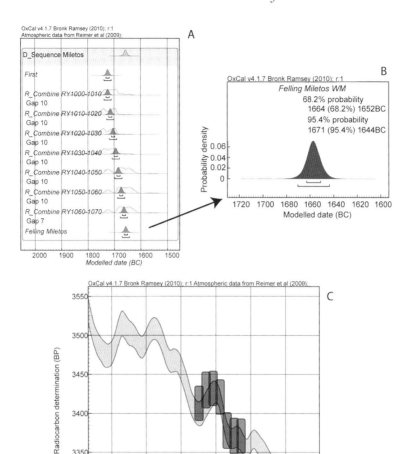

Figure RE30. Dendro-^{14}C-wiggle-match of ^{14}C data (pairs of ^{14}C dates, combined) on 7 dendrochronologically spaced samples (each of 11 tree-rings = years) from a tree-ring (charcoal, oak) sequence/sample from Miletos, western Turkey against the IntCal09 radiocarbon calibration curve. The waney edge (ring below bark) was 7 tree-rings (years) after the mid-point of the final dated 11-year sample. Figure RE30A shows the Dendro Sequenced analysis, contrasting the individual non-modelled calibrated age probability distributions in light grey versus the much reduced modelled calibrated age probability distributions in black. Figure RE30C shows the modelled age ranges at 68.2% probability fitted against the IntCal09 radiocarbon calibration curve (shown as a 1SD band) – we see a close fit of the data to the shape of the ^{14}C calibration curve. Figure RE30B shows the modelled calibrated age range for the final ring (to waney edge) of the sample. This provides a terminus post quem *for the Thera eruption since the sample was found covered (i.e. below) a layer of Theran tephra (this* terminus post quem *was incorporated in the dating model in Manning et al. 2006a). Data from IntCal09 (Reimer et al. 2009) and OxCal 4.1.7 (Bronk Ramsey 2009a) with curve resolution set at 1.*

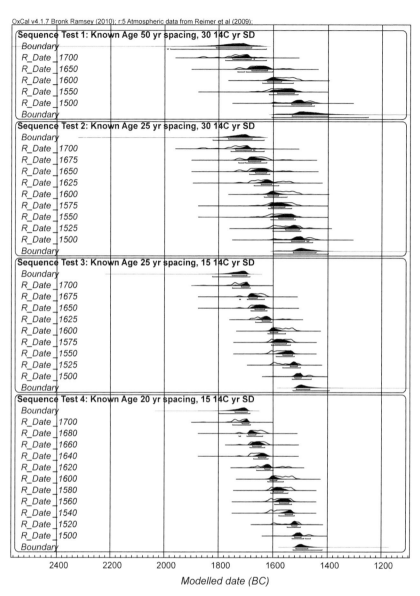

Figure RE31. Four Sequence analyses of ^{14}C data in a relative order (oldest to most recent) with no other constraints/information relevant to the years 1700-1500 BC. The ^{14}C data BP are taken from IntCal09 (Reimer et al. 2009) for the years indicated. The measurement errors are (arbitrarily) assigned as 30 ^{14}C years (Tests 1 and 2) or 15 ^{14}C years (Test 3 and 4). The data were taken at the spacings listed from IntCal09 but the analysis is not informed of this information, just that a set of n samples comes from a relative sequence. The hollow probability plots show the non-modelled calibrated age probability distributions; the solid (smaller) probability plots show the modelled calibrated age probability distributions. The two lines under each plot show (upper line) the 68.2% probability modelled range and (lower line) the 95.4% probability modelled range. Data from OxCal 4.1.7 (Bronk Ramsey 2009a) and IntCal09 (Reimer et al. 2009) with curve resolution set at 5. For details of the analysis, see Figure RE32.

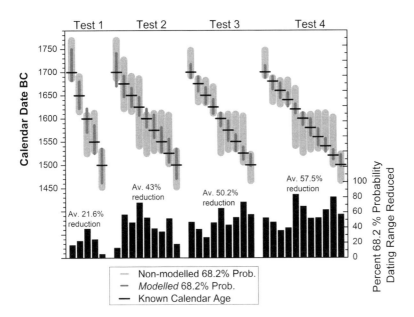

Figure RE32. Comparison of the test Sequence analysis models in Figure RE31. Top: the grey bars indicate the non-modelled 68.2% probability calibrated age ranges for each date. The narrower and smaller darker grey bars indicate the modelled 68.2% probability age ranges for each date. The black line intersecting each plot is the known real calendar age of the sample. Bottom: the percentage reduction in the 68.2% probability range moving from the non-modelled to modelled calibrated ranges for each date in the four test sequences.

data with measurement errors of 30 ^{14}C years. Test 3 employed the same data as test 2 except that the measurement error was halved to 15 ^{14}C years in each case. Test 4 employed 11 data spaced every 20 years from 1700–1500 BC from IntCal09 and with measurement errors at 15 ^{14}C years. The four different analyses are shown in Figure RE31. The hollow probability plots show the non-modelled calibrated age probability distributions for each date. The solid (smaller) probability plots show the modelled calibrated age probabilities. The two lines under each plot show (upper line) the 68.2% probability modelled range and (lower line) the 95.4% probability modelled range. Looking from Test 1 down to Test 4, we can see that as the density of data increase, and as the measurement resolution improves, the modelled calibrated ranges get smaller (more precise) and offer progressively greater resolution compared to the individual non-modelled calibrated probability ranges.

Figure RE32 compares the non-modelled versus modelled ranges at 68.2% probability for each date in Figure RE31, and plots these ranges against the known age of each sample. The percentage improvement (reduction = greater precision) in calibrated ranges from the non-modelled to the modelled data is also shown at the bottom (both for each individual date, and as an average for the whole of each sequence of data). Looking at Figure RE31 and especially Figure RE32, we can see that:

(i)   in each case the modelled calibrated calendar range is smaller (more precise) than the non-modelled calibrated calendar age range, and that, moving from Test 1 to Test 4, there is a substantial improvement in precision as the density of data increases and as the basic measurement precision increases (moving on average from a 21.6% reduction in Test 1 to a 57.5% reduction in Test 4).

(ii)   in each case the known calendar age is included within the modelled 68.2% calendar range; this indicates the approximate accuracy of the method – as well as the potential for increased precision.

(iii) where there are only relatively few and widely spaced data, e.g. Test 1, Sequence analysis can in general only make modest improvements to our dating resolution; in contrast, as soon as the density of data increases and reaches more the levels shown in Tests 2–4, then, whether with standard single-date AMS precision, or better, it is possible to get substantially increased precision (for example more than halving the likely calibrated ranges at 68.2% probability, on average, in Tests 3 and 4 and resolving some individual dated elements up to 6x more precisely – 1620 BC date in Test 4!).

While they are merely four indicative examples, the results in Figures RE31 and RE32 illustrate the potential and power of Sequence analysis to better resolve chronology when applied to data of known relative order (but no known spacings). As evident from Figures RE31 and RE32, the key to substantially improving chronological resolution is relatively dense data (and where possible reducing the relevant measurement errors via the combining of data or having sets of data which allow for well-defined constraints within a Sequence). While there are of course many complications – and especially the need to ensure the use of appropriate samples from secure contexts with appropriate laboratory pretreatment (see footnote 47 above) – the examples in Figure RE31 and RE32 illustrate that Sequence analyses of ^{14}C data are capable of producing precise and accurate information, and for the period 1700–1500 BC.

9. References

Alberti, G. 2011. Radiocarbon Evidence from the Middle Bronze Age Settlement at Portella (Aeolian Islands, Italy): Chronological and Archaeological Implications. *Radiocarbon* 53 (1): 1–12.

Ascough, P.L., Cook, G.T., Church, M.J., Dugmore, A.J., McGovern, T.H., Dunbar, E., Einarsson, Á. Friðriksson, A. and Gestsdóttir, H. 2007. Reservoirs and radiocarbon: ^{14}C dating problems in Mývatnssveit, northern Iceland. *Radiocarbon* 49(2): 947–961.

Aston, D.A. 2007. Kom Rabi'a, Ezbet Helmi, and Saqqara NK 3507. A Study in Cross-Dating. In Bietak, M. and Czerny, E. (eds.), *The Synchronisation of Civilisations in the Eastern Mediterranean in the Second Millennium B.C. III. Proceedings of the SCIEM 2000 – 2nd EuroConference*: 207–248. Vienna 28th of May – 1st of June 2003. Wien: Verlag der Österreichischen Akademie der Wissenschaften.

Aston, D. 2012. Radiocarbon, Wine Jars and New Kingdom Chronology. *Ägypten und Levante* 22: 289–315.

Aston, D.A. and Bietak, M. 2012. *The Classification and Chronology of Tell el-Yahudiya Ware*. Tell el-Dab'a VIII. Wien: Verlag der Österreichischen Akademie der Wissenschaften.

Astour, M.C. 1967. *Hellenosemitica; an ethnic and cultural study in West Semitic impact on Mycenaen Greece*. Leiden: Brill.

Badertscher, S., Borsato, A., Frisia, S., Cheng, H., Edwards, R.L., Tüysüz, O. and Fleitmann, D. 2014. Speleothems as sensitive recorders of volcanic eruptions – the Bronze Age Minoan eruption recorded in a stalagmite from Turkey. *Earth and Planetary Science Letters* 392: 58–66.

Baillie, M.G.L. and Munro, M.A.R. 1988. Irish tree rings, Santorini and volcanic dust veils. *Nature* 332: 344–346.

Baillie, M.G.L. and Pilcher, J.R. 1973. A simple cross-dating program for tree-ring research. *Tree-Ring Bulletin* 33: 7–14.

Balter, M. 2006. New Carbon Dates Support Revised History of Ancient Mediterranean. *Science* 312: 508–509.

Banjević, B. 2005. Ancient Eclipses and the Fall of Babylon. *Akkadica* 126: 169–193.

Barjamovic, G., Hertel, T. and Larsen, M.T. 2012. *Ups and Downs at Kanesh – Observations on Chronology, History and Society in the Old Assyrian period*. Leiden: Nederlands Instituut voor het Nabije Oosten.

Bayliss, A. 2009. Rolling out revolution: using radiocarbon dating in archaeology. *Radiocarbon* 51(1): 123–147.

Bayliss, A., Shepherd Popescu, E., Beavan-Athfield, N., Bronk Ramsey, C., Cook, G.T., Locker, A. 2004. The potential significance of dietary offsets for the interpretation of radiocarbon dates: an archaeologically significant example from medieval Norwich. *Journal of Archaeological Science* 31: 563–575.

Bayliss, A. and Tyers, I. 2004. Interpreting radiocarbon dates using evidence from tree-rings. *Radiocarbon* 46(2): 957–964.

Bayliss, A., van der Plicht, J., Bronk Ramsey, C., McCormac, G., Healy, F., Whittle, A. 2011. Towards generational time-scales: the quantitative interpretation of archaeological chronologies. In A. Whittle, F. Healy and A. Bayliss (eds.), *Gathering Time: Dating the Early Neolithic Enclosures of Southern Britain and Ireland*: 17–59. Oxford: Oxbow Books.

Bayliss, A. and Whittle, A. (eds.). 2007. *Histories of the dead: building chronologies for five southern British long barrows. Cambridge Archaeological Journal* 17(1), Supplement.

Beckerath, J. von. 1997. *Chronologie des pharaonischen Ägypten. Die Zeitbestimmung der ägyptischen Geschichte von der Vorzeit bis 332 v. Chr.* Mainz: Philipp von Zabern.

Bergoffen, C. 2001. The Proto White Slip and White Slip I Pottery from Tell el-Ajjul. In V. Karageorghis (ed.), *The White Slip Ware of Late Bronze Age Cyprus. Proceedings of an International Conference Organized by the Anastasios G. Leventis Foundation, Nicosia in Honour of Malcolm Wiener*: 145–156. Wien: Verlag der Österreichischen Akademie der Wissenschaften.

Bergoffen, C.J. 2005. *The Cypriot Bronze Age Pottery from Sir Leonard Woolley's Excavations at Alalakh (Tell Atchana)*. Wien: Verlag der Österreichischen Akademie der Wissenschaften.

Bernal, M. 1987. *Black Athena: The Afroasiatic Roots of Classical Civilization, Vol. I: The Fabrication of Ancient Greece, 1785–1985*. London: Free Association Books.

Bernal, M. 1991. *Black Athena: the Afroasiatic roots of Classical civilization. Volume II: the archaeological and documentary evidence*. London: Free Association Books.

Betancourt, P.P. 1987. Dating the Aegean Late Bronze Age with radiocarbon. *Archaeometry* 29: 45–49.

Betancourt, P.P. 1990. High chronology or low chronology: the archaeological evidence. In D.A. Hardy and A.C. Renfrew (eds.), *Thera and the Aegean world III. Volume three: chronology*: 19–23. London: The Thera Foundation.

Betancourt, P.P. and Weinstein, G.A. 1976. Carbon-14 and the beginning of the Late Bronze Age in the Aegean. *American Journal of Archaeology* 80: 329–348.

Bevan, A. 2003. Reconstructing the role of Egyptian culture in the value regimes of the Bronze Age Aegean: stone vessels and their social contexts. In R. Matthews and C. Roemer (eds.), *Ancient Perspectives on Egypt*: 57–73. London: University College London Press.

Bevan, A. 2007. *Stone Vessels and Values in the Bronze Age Mediterranean*. Cambridge: Cambridge University Press.

Bichler, M., Exler, M., Peltz, C. and Saminger, S. 2003. Thera Ashes. In Bietak, M. (ed.), *The synchronisation of civilisations in the eastern Mediterranean in the second millennium BC (II). Proceedings of the SCIEM2000 EuroConference Haindorf, May 2001*: 11–21. Wien: Verlag der Österreichischen Akademie der Wissenschaften.

Bietak, M. 1979. Avaris and Piramesse: archaeological exploration in the eastern Nile Delta. *Proceedings of the British Academy* 65: 225–290.

Bietak, M. (ed.). 1995. *Trade, power and cultural exchange: Hyksos Egypt and the eastern Mediterranean world 1800–1500 B.C. An International Symposium Wednesday, November 3, 1993. Ägypten und Levante/ Egypt and the Levant* 5. Wien: Verlag der Österreichischen Akademie der Wissenschaften.

Bietak, M. 1996. *Avaris: the capital of the Hyksos. Recent excavations at Tell el-Dab'a*. London: British Museum Publications.

Bietak, M. 1997. Avaris, capital of the Hyksos kingdom: new results of excavations. In E.D. Oren (ed.), *The Hyksos: new historical and archaeological perspectives*: 87–139. Philadelphia: The University Museum, University of Pennsylvania.

Bietak, M. 1998. The Late Cypriot White Slip I-Ware as an obstacle of the high Aegean chronology. In M.S. Balmuth and R.H. Tykot (eds.), *Sardinian and Aegean chronology: towards the resolution of relative and absolute dating in the Mediterranean*: 321–322. Studies in Sardinian Archaeology V. Oxford: Oxbow Books.

Bietak, M. 2000a. Introduction to the Research Programme. In M. Bietak (ed.), *The Synchronisation of Civilisations in the Eastern Mediterranean in the Second Millennium B.C. Proceedings of an International Symposium at Schloß Haindorf, 15th-17th of November 1996 and at the Austrian Academy, Vienna, 11th-12th of May 1998*: 11–12. Wien: Verlag der Österreichischen Akademie der Wissenschaften.

Bietak, M. 2000b. 'Rich beyond the Dreams of Avaris: Tell el-Dab'a and the Aegean world – A Guide for the Perplexed': a response to Eric H. Cline. *Annual of the British School at Athens* 95: 185–205.

Bietak, M. 2003. Science versus archaeology: problems and consequences of high Aegean chronology. In M. Bietak (ed.), *The Synchronisation of Civilisations in the Eastern Mediterranean in the Second Millennium B.C. II. Proceedings of the SCIEM 2000 – EuroConference Haindorf, 2nd of May – 7th of May 2001*: 23–33. Contributions to the Chronology of the Eastern Mediterranean II. Wien: Verlag der Österreichischen Akademie der Wissenschaften.

Bietak, M. 2004. Review of Manning, W. [sic] — *A Test of Time*. *Bibliotheca Orientalis* 61 (1–2): 199–222.

Bietak, M. 2010. Le hyksôs Khayan, son palais, et une letter cunéiforme. *Comptes rendus des séances de l'Académie des inscriptions et belles-lettres* (Fascicule II, April-June): 973–990.

Bietak, M. 2011. The Aftermath of the Hyksos in Avaris. In R. Sela-Sheffy and G. Toury (eds.), *Culture Contacts and The Making of Cultures. Papers in Homage to Itamar Even-Zohar*: 19–65. Tel Aviv: Unit of Culture Research, Tel Aviv University.

Bietak, M. and Forstner-Müller, I. with Radner, F and van Koppen, F. 2009. Der Hyksospalast bei Tell el-Dab'a. Zweite und Dritte Grabungskampagne (Frühling 2008 und Frühling 2009). *Ägypten und Levante* 19: 91–119.

Bietak, M. and Höflmayer, F. 2007. Introduction: high and low chronology. In M. Bietak and E. Czerny (eds), *The Synchronisation of Civilizations in the Eastern Mediterranean in the Second Millennium B.C. – III*: 13–23. Wien: Verlag der Österreichischen Akademie der Wissenschaften.

Bietak, M. and Marinatos, N. 1995. The Minoan wall paintings from Avaris. *Ägypten und Levante* 5: 49–62.

Bietak, M., Marinaros, N., and Palyvou, C. 2007. *Taureador scenes in Tell el-Dab'a (Avaris) and Knossos*. Wien: Verlag der Österreichischen Akademie der Wissenschaften.

Bonsall, C., , A., Soficaru, A., McSweeney, K., Higham, T., Mirițoiu, N., Pickard, C. and Cook, G. 2012. Interrelationship of age and diet in Romania's oldest human burial. *Naturwissenschaften* 99: 321–325.

Bourriau, J. and Eriksson, K.O. 1997. A Late Minoan sherd from an early 18th Dynasty context at Kom Rabi'a, Memphis. In J. Phillips (ed.), *Ancient Egypt, the Aegean, and the Near East: studies in honour of Martha Rhoads Bell*: 95–120. San Antonio: Van Siclen Books.

Braadbaart, F. and van Bergen, P.F. 2005. Digital imaging analysis of size and shape of wheat and pea upon heating under anoxic conditions as a function of temperature. *Vegetation History and Archaeobotany* 14: 67–75.

Briffa, K.R., Jones, P.D., Schweingruber, F.H. and Osborne, T.J. 1998. Influence of volcanic eruptions on Northern Hemisphere summer temperatures over the past 600 years. *Nature* 393: 450–455.

Brogan, T.M. and Hallager, E. (eds). 2011. *LM IB pottery: relative chronology and regional differences. Acts of a workshop held at the Danish Institute at Athens in collaboration with the INSTAP Study Center for East Crete, 27–29 June 2007*. Monographs of the Danish Institute at Athens Volume 11. Athens: The Danish Institute at Athens.

Bronk Ramsey, C. 1995. Radiocarbon calibration and analysis of stratigraphy: The OxCal program. *Radiocarbon* 37(2): 425–430.

Bronk Ramsey, C. 2008. Radiocarbon dating: revolutions in understanding. *Archaeometry* 50: 249–275.

Bronk Ramsey, C. 2009a. Bayesian Analysis of Radiocarbon Dates. *Radiocarbon* 51(2): 337–360.

Bronk Ramsey, C. 2009b. Dealing with Outliers and Offsets in Radiocarbon Dating. *Radiocarbon* 51(3): 1023–1045.

Bronk Ramsey, C., Dee, M.W., Rowland, J.M., Higham, T.F.G., Harris, S.A., Brock, F.A., Quiles, A., Wild, E., Marcus, E.S. and Shortland, A.J. 2010. Radiocarbon-based chronology for Dynastic Egypt. *Science* 328: 1554–1557.

Bronk Ramsey, C., Manning, S.W. and Galimberti, M. 2004. Dating the volcanic eruption at Thera. *Radiocarbon* 46(1): 325–344.

Bronk Ramsey, C., van der Plicht, J., Weninger, B. 2001. 'Wiggle matching' radiocarbon dates. *Radiocarbon* 43(2A): 381–389.

Brown, F.M. 1937. Dendrochronology. *Antiquity* 11: 409–426.

Bruins, H.J., MacGillivray, J.A., Synolakis, C.E., Benjamini, C., Keller, J., Kisch, H.J., Klügel, A. and van der Plicht, J. 2008. Geoarchaeological tsunami deposits at Palaikastro (Crete) and the Late Minoan IA eruption of Santorini. *Journal of Archaeological Science* 35: 191–212.

Bruins, H.J. and van der Plicht, J. 1996. The Exodus enigma. *Nature* 382: 213–214.

Bruins, H.J., van der Plicht, J., and MacGillivray, J.A. 2009. The Minoan Santorini eruption and tsunami deposits in Palaikastro (Crete): dating by geology, archaeology, ^{14}C and Egyptian chronology. *Radiocarbon* 51(2): 397–411.

Brysbaert, A. 2007. Cross-craft and cross-cultural interactions during the Aegean and Eastern Mediterranean Late Bronze Age. In S. Antoniadou and A. Pace (eds.), *Mediterranean Crossroads*: 325–359. Oxford: Pierides Foundation.

Buchholz, H.-G. 1980. Some observations concerning Thera's contacts overseas during the Bronze Age. In C. Doumas (ed.), *Thera and the Aegean world II*: 227–240. London: Thera and the Aegean World.

Buck, C.E., Cavanagh, W.G. and Litton, C.D. 1996. *Bayesian Approach to Interpreting Archaeological Data*. Chichester: J. Wiley and Son.

Buck, C.E., Kenworthy, J.B., Litton, C.D., Smith, A.F.M. 1991. Combining archaeological and radiocarbon information: a Bayesian approach to calibration. *Antiquity* 65: 808–821.

Buck, C.E., Millard, A.R. (eds.). 2004. *Tools for Constructing Chronologies: Crossing Disciplinary Boundaries*. London: Springer.

Cadogan, G. 1978. Dating the Aegean Bronze Age without radiocarbon. *Archaeometry* 20: 209–214.

Cadogan, G. 1987. Unsteady date of a big bang. *Nature* 328: 473.

Cadogan, G. 1990. Thera's eruption into our understanding of the Minoans. In D.A. Hardy, C.G. Doumas, J.A. Sakellarakis and P.M. Warren (eds.), *Thera and the Aegean World III. Volume One: Archaeology:* 93–97. London: The Thera Foundation.

Capano, M., Marzaioli, F., Passariello, I., Pignatelli, O., Martinelli, N., Gigli, S., Gennarelli, I., De Cesare, N and Terrasi, F. 2012. Preliminary Radiocarbon Analyses of Contemporaneous and Archaeological Wood from the Ansanto Valley (Southern Italy). *Radiocarbon* 54 (3–4): 70 1–714.

Charpin, D. and Ziegler, N. 2003. *Florilegium marianum: V, Mari et le proche-orient à l'époque amorrite: essai d'historie politique.* Memoires de N.A.B.U. 6. Antony: SEPOA, Société pour l'étude du Proche-orient ancient.

Cherubini, P., Humbel, T., Beeckman, H., Gärtner, H., Mannes, D., Pearson, C., Schoch, W., Tognetti, R. and Lev-Yadun, S. 2013. Olive Tree-Ring Problematic Dating: A Comparative Analysis on Santorini (Greece). *PLoS ONE* 8(1): e54730. doi:10.1371/journal.pone.0054730

Childe, V.G. 1928. *The most ancient East: the Oriental prelude to European prehistory.* London: Kegan Paul, Trench, Trübner & Co.

Christen, J.A. and Litton, C.D. 1995. A Bayesian approach to wiggle-matching. *Journal of Archaeological Science* 22: 719–725.

Cioni, R., Gurioli, L., Sbrana, A. and Vougioukalakis, G. 2000. Precursors to the Plinian Eruptions of Thera (Late Bronze Age) and Vesuvius (AD 79): Data from Archaeological Areas. *Physics and Chemistry of the Earth, Part A: Solid Earth and Geodesy* 25: 719–724.

Cline, E.H. 1994. *Sailing the wine-dark sea: international trade and the Late Bronze Age Aegean.* BAR International Series 591. Oxford: Tempus Reparatum.

Cline, E.H. 1998. Rich beyond the dreams of Avaris: Tell el-Dab'a and the Aegean world – a guide for the perplexed. *Annual of the British School at Athens* 93: 199–219.

Cline, E.H., Yasur-Landau, A. and Goshen, N. 2011. New Fragments of Aegean-Style Painted Plaster from Tel Kabri, Israel. *American Journal of Archaeology* 115: 245–261.

Cook, G.T., Bonsall, C., Hedges, R.E.M., McSweeney, K., Boronean, V., Pettitt, P.B. 2001. A freshwater diet-derived ^{14}C reservoir effect at the Stone Age sites in the Iron Gates Gorge. *Radiocarbon* 43(2A): 453–460.

Cook, G.T., Bonsall, C., Hedges, R.E.M., McSweeney, K., Boroneant, V., Bartosiewicz, L., Pettitt, P.B. 2002. Problems of dating human bones from the Iron Gates. *Antiquity* 76: 77–85.

Crewe, L. 2007. *Early Enkomi: Regionalism, Trade and Society at the Beginning of the Late Bronze Age on Cyprus.* BAR International Series 1706. Oxford: Archaeopress.

Crewe, L. 2009. Tomb 1 (1956) at Galinoporni and the Middle-Late Cypriot transition in the Karpass Peninsula. *Report of the Department of Antiquities, Cyprus:* 89–115.

Crewe, L. 2013. Regional connections during the Middle–Late Cypriot transition: new evidence from Kissonerga-*Skalia. Pasiphae* 7: 47–55.

Currid, J.D. and Navon, A. 1989. Iron Age Pits and the Lahav (Tell Halif) Grain Storage Project. *Bulletin of the American Schools of Oriental Research* 273: 67–78.

Damon, P.E., Lerman, J.C. and Long, A. 1978. Temporal functions of ^{14}C: Causal factors and implications. *Annual Review of Earth and Planetary Science* 6: 457–494.

Davies, W.V. and Schofield, L. (eds.) 1995. *Egypt, the Aegean and the Levant: interconnections in the second millennium BC.* London: British Museum Publications.

Dee, M.W., Brock, F., Harris, S.A., Bronk Ramsey, C., Shortland, A.J., Higham, T.F.G., Rowland, J.M. 2010. Investigating the likelihood of a reservoir offset in the radiocarbon record for ancient Egypt. *Journal of Archaeological Science* 37(4): 687–693.

Dee, M.W., Rowland, J.M., Higham, T.F.G., Shortland, A.J., Brock, F., Harris, S.A. and Bronk Ramsey,

C. 2012. Synchronising radiocarbon dating and the Egyptian historical chronology by improved sample selection. *Antiquity* 86: 868–883.

Dehling, H. and van der Plicht, J. 1993. Statistical Problems in Calibrating Radiocarbon Dates. *Radiocarbon* 35(1): 239–244.

de Jong, T. 2012. Babylonian observations of Venus: arcus visionis, atmospheric extinction and observational practice. *Journal for the History of Astronomy* 43: 391–409.

de Jong, T. 2013a. Astronomical Fine-Tuning of the Chronology of the Hammurabi Age. *Jaarbericht van het Vooraziatisch-Egyptisch Genootschap "Ex Oriente Lux"* 44: 147–167.

de Jong, T. 2013b. Review of Mebert, Joachim, *Die Venustafeln des Ammī-saduqa und ihre Bedeutung für die astronomische Datierung der altbabylonischen Zeit*. *Journal American Oriental Society* 133: 366–370.

de Jong, T. and Foertmeyer, V. 2010. A new look at the Venus observations of Ammisaduqa: Traces of the Santorini eruption in the atmosphere of Babylon? *Jaarbericht van het Vooraziatisch-Egyptisch Genootschap "Ex Oriente Lux"* 42: 143–59.

Denton, J.S. and Pearce, N.J.G. 2008. Comment on "A synchronized dating of three Greenland ice cores throughout the Holocene" by B. M. Vinther *et al.*: No Minoan tephra in the 1642 B.C. layer of the GRIP ice core. *Journal of Geophysical Research* 113: D04303, doi:10.1029/2007JD008970.

DeVries, K., P.I. Kuniholm, G.K. Sams and M.M. Voigt. 2003. New Dates for Iron Age Gordion. *Antiquity* 77 (no. 296), Project Gallery: http://antiquity.ac.uk/ProjGall/devries/devries.html

Doumas, C. 1983. *Thera: Pompeii of the ancient Aegean*. London: Thames and Hudson.

Doumas, C. 1990. Archaeological observations at Akrotiri relating to the volcanic destruction. In D.A. Hardy and A.C. Renfrew (eds.), *Thera and the Aegean world III. Volume three: chronology*: 48–49. London: The Thera Foundation.

Doumas, C.G. 1998. Aegeans in the Levant: Myth and Reality. In S. Gitin, A. Mazar and E. Stern (eds.), *Mediterranean Peoples in Transition: Thirteenth to Early Tenth Centuries BCE. In Honor of Professor Trude Dothan*: 129–137. Jerusalem: Israel Exploration Society.

Doumas, C. 2010. Akrotiri. In E.H. Cline (ed.), *The Oxford Handbook of The Bronze Age Aegean (c.3000–1000 BC)*: 752–761. New York: Oxford University Press.

Downey, W.S. 2011a. Palaeomagnetic Results from Minoan Ash Deposits in (RV VEMA) Cores V10–50 and V10–58, South Aegean Sea. *Mediterranean Archaeology and Archaeometry* 11: 151–168.

Downey, W.S. 2011b. Archaeomagnetic Directional Determinations on Various Archaeological Ma-terials from the Late Minoan Destruction Site at Malia, Crete. *Mediterranean Archaeology and Archaeometry* 11: 21–31.

Downey, W.S. and Tarling, D.H. 1984. Archaeomagnetic Dating of Santorini Volcanic Eruptions and Fired Destruction Levels of Late Minoan Civilization. *Nature* 309: 519–523.

Driessen, J. and Macdonald, C.F. 1997. *The troubled island: Minoan Crete before and after the Santorini eruption*. Aegaeum 17. Liège: Université de Liège, Histoire de l'art et archéologie de la Grèce antique.

Earle, J.W. 2012. A Cycladic Perspective on Mycenaean Long-Distance Exchanges. *Journal of Mediterranean Archaeology* 25: 3–25.

Eastwood, W.J., Pearce, N.J.G., Westgate, J.A., Perkins, W.T., Lamb, H.F. and Roberts, N. 1999. Geochemistry of Thera tephra in lake sediments from southwest Turkey. *Global and Planetary Change* 21: 17–29.

Eastwood, W.J., Tibby, J., Roberts, N., Birks, H.J.B. and Lamb, H.F. 2002. The environmental impact of the Minoan eruption of Thera (Thera): statistical analysis of palaeoecological data from Gölhisar, southwest Turkey. *The Holocene* 12: 431–444.

Eriksson, K.O. 1992. Late Cypriot I and Thera: relative chronology in the eastern Mediterranean. In P. Åström (ed.), *Acta Cypria: acts of an international congress on Cypriote archaeology held in Göteborg on 22–24 August 1991,* Part 3: 152–223. Studies in Mediterranean Archaeology and Literature Pocket-book 120. Jonsered: Paul Åströms Förlag.

Eriksson, K.O. 2007. *The creative Independence of Late Bronze Age Cyprus: An Account of the Archaeological Importance of White Slip Ware*. Wien: Verlag der Österreichischen Akademie der Wissenschaften.

Eriksson, K.O. 2009. Regionalism and Island-wide Analysis: Some Observations Regarding White Painted V and VI Wares from Middle Cypriot III/Late Cypriot I Tombs from the Northwest Region of Cyprus. In I. Hein (ed.), *The Formation of Cyprus in the 2nd Millennium B.C.: Studies in Regionalism during the Middle and Late Bronze Ages. Proceedings of a workshop held at the 4th Cyprological Congress, May 2nd 2008, Lefkosia, Cyprus*: 49–63. Wien: Verlag der Österreichischen Akademie der Wissenschaften.

Evans, M.E. 2006. Archaeomagnetic investigations in Greece and their bearing on geomagnetic secular variation. *Phyics of the Earth and Planetary Interior* 159: 90–95.

Fantuzzi, T. 2007. The debate on Aegean high and low chronologies: an overview through Egypt. *Rivista di Archaeologia* 31: 53–65.

Fantuzzi, T. 2009. The Absolute Chronology of the Egyptian S.I.P. – N.K. Transition and Its Implications for Late Minoan Crete. *Creta Antiqua* 10(2): 477–500.

Feeney, D. 2007. *Caesar's Calendar: Ancient Time and the Beginnings of History.* Berkeley: University of California Press.

Ferguson, C.W., Huber, B. and Suess, H.E. 1966. Determination of the age of Swiss lake dwellings as an example of dendrochronologically-calibrated radiocarbon dating. *Zeitschrift für Naturforschung* 21A: 1173–1177.

Finkelstein, I. and Piasetzky, E. 2010a. The Iron I/IIA Transition in the Levant: A Reply to Mazar and Bronk Ramsey and a New Perspective. *Radiocarbon* 52(4): 1667–1680.

Finkelstein, I. and Piasetzky, E. 2010b. Radiocarbon Dating the Iron Age in the Levant: A Bayesian Model for Six Ceramic Phases and Six Transitions. *Antiquity* 84: 374–385.

Finkelstein, I. and Piasetzky, E. 2011. The Iron Age Chronology Debate: Is the Gap Narrowing? *Near Eastern Archaeology* 74(1): 50–54.

Fischer, P. M. 2009. The chronology of Tell el-'Ajjul, Gaza. In D.A. Warburton (ed.), *Time's Up! Dating the Minoan eruption of Santorini. Acts of the Minoan Eruption Chronology Workshop, Sandbjerg November 2007 initiated by Jan Heinemeier & Walter L. Friedrich*: 253–265. Monographs of the Danish Institute at Athens Volume 10. Athens: The Danish Institute at Athens.

Fishman, B., Forbes, H and Lawn, B. 1977. University of Pennsylvania Radiocarbon Dates XIX. *Radiocarbon* 19(2): 188–228.

Fishman, B. and Lawn, B. 1978. University of Pennsylvania Radiocarbon Dates XX. *Radiocarbon* 20(2): 210–233.

Fleitmann, D., Borsato, A., Frisia, S., Badertscher, S., Cheng, H., Edwards, R.L. and Tüysüz, O. 2012. Speleothems as sensitive recorders of volcanic eruptions – the Bronze Age Minoan eruption recorded in a stalagmite from Turkey. EGU General Assembly 2012, held 22–27 April, 2012 in Vienna, Austria., p.9293. http://meetingorganizer.copernicus.org/EGU2012/EGU2012-9293.pdf

Forsyth, P.Y. 1997. *Thera in the Bronze Age.* New York: Peter Lang.

Foster, K.P. and Ritner, R.K. 1996. Texts, storms, and the Thera eruption. *Journal of Near Eastern Studies* 55: 1–14.

Foster, K.P., Sterba, J.H., Steinhauser, G. and Bichler, M. 2009. The Thera eruption and Egypt: pumice, texts, and chronology. In D.A. Warburton (ed.), *Time's Up! Dating the Minoan eruption of Santorini. Acts of the Minoan Eruption Chronology Workshop, Sandbjerg November 2007 initiated by Jan Heinemeier & Walter L. Friedrich*: 171–180. Monographs of the Danish Institute at Athens Volume 10. Athens: The Danish Institute at Athens.

Frankel, D. 2009. What do we mean by 'regionalism'? In I. Hein (ed.), *The Formation of Cyprus in the 2nd Millennium B.C. Studies in Regionalism during the Middle and Late Bronze Age*: 15–25. Wien: Verlag der Österreichischen Akademie der Wissenschaften.

Franzmeier, H., Höflmayer, F., Kutschera, W., Wild, E.M. 2011. Radiocarbon Evidence for new Kingdom Tombs: Sedment 254 and 246. *Ägypten und Levante* 21: 15–29.

Friedrich, W.L. 2009. *Santorini: Volcano, Natural History, Mythology.* Trans. A.R. McBirney. Aarhus: Aarhus University Press.

Friedrich, W.L. and Heinemeier, J. 2009. The Minoan eruption of Thera radiocarbon dated to 1613 ± 13 BC – geological and stratigraphic considerations. In D.A. Warburton (ed.), *Time's Up! Dating the Minoan eruption of Santorini. Acts of the Minoan Eruption Chronology Workshop, Sandbjerg November 2007 initiated by Jan Heinemeier & Walter L. Friedrich*: 57–63. Monographs of the Danish Institute at Athens Volume 10. Athens: The Danish Institute at Athens.

Friedrich, W., Kromer, B., Friedrich, M., Heinemeier, J., Pfeiffer, T. and Talamo, S. 2006. Santorini Eruption Radiocarbon Dated to 1627–1600 BC. *Science* 312: 548.

Friedrich, W., Kromer, B., Friedrich, M., Heinemeier, J., Pfeiffer, T. and Talamo, S. 2009. Santorini Eruption Radiocarbon Dated to 1627–1600 BC: Further Discussion. In S.W. Manning and M.J. Bruce, (eds.), *Tree-Rings, Kings and Old World Archaeology and Environment: Papers Presented in Honor of Peter Ian Kuniholm*: 293–298 and 327. Oxford: Oxbow Books.

Friedrich, W.L., Wagner, P. and Tauber, H. 1990. Radiocarbon dated plant remains from the Akrotiri excavation on Santorini, Greece. In D.A. Hardy and A.C. Renfrew (eds.), *Thera and the Aegean world III. Volume three: chronology*: 188–196. London: The Thera Foundation.

Frisia, S., Badertscher, S., Borsato, A., Susini, J., Göktürk, O.M., Cheng, H., Edwards, R.L., Kramers, J., Tüysüz, O. and Fleitmann, D. 2008. The use of stalagmite geochemistry to detect past volcanic eruptions and their environmental impacts. *PAGES News* 16(3): 25–26.

Fuller, B.T., Fahmi, S., Southon, J.R. and Taylor, R.E. 2012. PP33A-2112: Annual bristlecone pine and german oak ^{14}C data sets confirm 2625 BP ^{14}C wiggle: major two decade reduction in ^{14}C production? American Geophysical Union Fall Meeting, San Francisco, 3–7 December 2012. http://fallmeeting.agu.org/2012/eposters/eposter/pp33a-2112/

Galimberti M., Bronk Ramsey C. and Manning S.W. 2004. Wiggle-match dating of tree ring sequences. *Radiocarbon* 46(2): 917–924.

Girella, L. 2007. Toward a Definition of the Middle Minoan III Ceramic Sequence in South-Central Crete: Returning to the Traditional MMIIIA and MMIIIB Division? In Felten, F., Gauss, W. and Smetana, R. (eds.), *Middle Helladic Pottery and Synchronisms. Proceedings of the International Workshop held at Salzburg October 31st – November 2nd, 2004*: 233–255. Wien: Verlag der Österreichischen Akademie der Wissenschaften.

Goedicke, H. 1992. The chronology of the Thera/Santorin explosion. *Ägypten und Levante* 3: 57–62.

Goedicke, H. 2004. *The Speos Artemidos inscription of Hatshepsut and related discussions*. Oakville: HALGO.

Gordon, C.H. 1962. *Before the Bible; the common background of Greek and Hebrew civilisations*. New York: Harper & Row.

Gordon, C.H. 1993. Review of M. Bernal, *Black Athena: The Afroasiatic Roots of Classical Civilization, Vol. I: The Fabrication of Ancient Greece, 1785–1985. Journal of the American Oriental Society* 113: 489–490.

Griggs, C.B. and Manning, S.W. 2009. A reappraisal of the dendrochronology and dating of Tille Höyük (1993). *Radiocarbon* 51(2): 711–720.

Grudd, H., Briffa, K.R., Gunnarson, B.E. and Linderholm, H.W. 2000. Swedish tree rings provide new evidence in support of a major, widespread environmental disruption in 1628 BC. *Geophysical Research Letters* 27: 2957–2960.

Hallager, E. 1988. Final palatial Crete. An essay in Minoan chronology. In A. Damsgaard-Madsen, E. Christiansen and E. Hallager (eds.), *Studies in ancient history and numismatics presented to Rudi Thomsen*: 11–21. Aarhus: Aarhus University Press.

Hambaryan, V.V. and Neuhäuser, R. 2013. A Galactic short gamma-ray burst as cause for the ^{14}C peak in AD 774/5. *Monthly Notices of the Royal Astronomical Society* 430: 32–36.

Hammer, C.U., Kurat, G., Hoppe, P., Grum, W. and Clausen, H.B. 2003. Thera Eruption Date 1645 BC Confirmed By New Ice Core Data? In Bietak, M. (ed.), *The synchronisation of civilisations in the eastern Mediterranean in the second millennium BC (II). Proceedings of the SCIEM2000 EuroConference Haindorf, May 2001*: 87–94. Wien: Verlag der Österreichischen Akademie der Wissenschaften.

Hankey, V. 1973. The Aegean deposit at El Amarna. In V. Karageorghis (ed.), *Acts of the International Archaeological Symposium 'The Mycenaeans in the Eastern Mediterranean'*: 128–136. Nicosia: Department of Antiquities.

Hankey, V. 1981. The Aegean interest in El Amarna. *Journal of Mediterranean Anthropology and Archaeology* 1: 38–49.

Hankey, V. 1997. Aegean pottery at El-Amarna: shapes and decorative motifs. In J. Phillips (ed.), *Ancient Egypt, the Aegean, and the Near East: studies in honour of Martha Rhoads Bell*: 193–218. San Antonio: Van Siclen Books.

Hankey, V. and Warren, P. 1974. The absolute chronology of the Aegean Late Bronze Age. *Bulletin of the Institute of Classical Studies* 21: 142–152.

Hassler, A. and Höflmayer, F. 2008. Mostagedda 1874 and Gurob 23: Notes on some Recent Radiocarbon Dates and their Importance for Egyptian Archaeology and Chronology. *Ägypten und Levante* 18: 145–155.

Hart, J.P. and Lovis, W.A. 2007. The Freshwater Reservoir and Radiocarbon Dates on Cooking Residues: Old Apparent Ages or a Single Outlier? Comments on Fischer and Heinemeier (2003). *Radiocarbon* 49 (3): 1403–1410.

Hayes, W.C. 1970. Chronology I. Egypt – to the end of the twentieth dynasty. In I.E.S. Edwards, C.J. Gadd and N.G.L. Hammond (eds.), *The Cambridge Ancient History,* vol.I, part 1: 173–193. Third edition. Cambridge: Cambridge University Press.

Heinemeier, J., Friedrich, W.L., Kromer, B. and Bronk Ramsey, C. 2009. The Minoan eruption of Santorini radiocarbon dated by an olive tree buried by the eruption. In D.A. Warburton (ed.), *Time's Up! Dating the Minoan eruption of Santorini. Acts of the Minoan Eruption Chronology Workshop, Sandbjerg November 2007 initiated by Jan Heinemeier & Walter L. Friedrich*: 285–293. Monographs of the Danish Institute at Athens Volume 10. Athens: The Danish Institute at Athens.

Higham, C. and Higham, T. 2009. A new chronological framework for prehistoric Southeast Asia, based on a Bayesian model from Ban Non Wat. *Antiquity* 83: 125–144.

Higham, T.F.G., Warren, R., Belinski, A, Harke, H. and Wood, R. 2010. Radiocarbon dating, stable isotope analysis, and diet-derived offsets in ^{14}C ages from the Klin Yar site, Russian north Caucasus. *Radiocarbon* 52(2–3): 653–670.

Höflmayer, F. 2009. Aegean-Egyptian synchronisms and radiocarbon chronology. In D.A. Warburton (ed.), *Time's Up! Dating the Minoan eruption of Santorini. Acts of the Minoan Eruption Chronology Workshop, Sandbjerg November 2007 initiated by Jan Heinemeier & Walter L. Friedrich*: 187–195. Monographs of the Danish Institute at Athens Volume 10. Athens: The Danish Institute at Athens.

Höflmayer, F. 2011a. Egyptian Pots, Aegean Chronology and Radiocarbon Dating: Recent Research on Egypt and the Aegean Early Late Bronze Age. In M. Horn, J. Kramer, D. Soliman, N. Staring, C. van den Hoven and L. Weiss (eds.), *Current Research in Egyptology 2010. Proceedings of the Eleventh Annual Symposium which took place at Leiden University, the Netherlands January 2010*: 62–70. Oxford: Oxbow Books.

Höflmayer, F. 2011b. Egyptian Imitations of Cypriote Base Ring Ware in the Eastern Mediterranean. In K. Duistermaat and I. Regulski (eds.), *Intercultural Contacts in the Ancient Mediterranean. Proceedings of the international conference at the Netherlands-Flemish Institute in Cairo, 25th to 29th October 2008*: 347–361. OLA 202. Leuven: Peeters.

Höflmayer, F. 2012a. The Date of the Minoan Santorini Eruption: Quantifying the "Offset". *Radiocarbon* 54(3–4): 435–448.

Höflmayer, F. 2012b. *Die Synchronisierung der minoischen Alt- und Neupalastzeit mit der ägyptischen Chronologie.* Contributions to the Chronology of the Eastern Mediterranean 32. Wien: Verlag der Österreichischen Akademie der Wissenschaften.

Höflmayer, F., Hassler, A., Kutschera, W. and Wild, E.M. 2013. Radiocarbon Data for Aegean Pottery in Egypt: New Evidence from Saqqara (Lepsius) Tomb 16 and its Importance for LMIB/LHIIA. In A.J. Shortland and C. Bronk Ramsey (eds.), *Radiocarbon and the Chronologies of Ancient Egypt*: 110–120. Oxford: Oxbow Books.

Hood, S. 1978. Discrepancies in ^{14}C dating as illustrated from the Egyptian New and Middle Kingdoms and from the Aegean Bronze Age and Neolithic. *Archaeometry* 20: 197–199.

Hornung, E., Krauss, R. and Warburton, D.A. (eds.). 2006. *Ancient Egyptian Chronology*. Leiden: Brill.

Housley, R.A., Hedges, R.E.M., Law, I.A. and Bronk, C.R. 1990. Radiocarbon dating by AMS of the destruction of Akrotiri. In D.A. Hardy and A.C. Renfrew (eds.), *Thera and the Aegean world III. Volume three: chronology:* 207–215. London: The Thera Foundation.

Housley, R.A., Manning, S.W., Cadogan, G., Jones, R.E. and Hedges, R.E.M. 1999. Radiocarbon, calibration, and the chronology of the Late Minoan IB phase. *Journal of Archaeological Science* 26: 159–171.

Huber, P.J. 2011. The astronomical basis of Egyptian chronology of the second millennium BC. *Journal of Egyptian History* 4: 172–227

Huber, P.J. with the collaboration of A. Sachs, M. Stol, R.M. Whiting, E. Leichty, C.B.F. Walker and G. van Driel. 1982. *Astronomical dating of Babylon I and Ur III*. Occasional Papers on the Near East 1.4. Malibu: Undena Publications.

Hubberten, H-W., Bruns, M., Calamiotou, M., Apostolakis, C., Filippakis, S. and Grimanis, A. 1990. Radiocarbon dates from the Akrotiri excavations. In D.A. Hardy and A.C. Renfrew (eds.), *Thera and the Aegean world III. Volume three: chronology*: 179–187. London: The Thera Foundation.

Hughes, M.K. 1988. Ice layer dating of the eruption of Santorini. *Nature* 335: 211–212.

Hunger, H. 2009. How uncertain is Mesopotamian chronology? In D.A. Warburton (ed.), *Time's Up! Dating the Minoan eruption of Santorini. Acts of the Minoan Eruption Chronology Workshop, Sandbjerg November 2007 initiated by Jan Heinemeier & Walter L. Friedrich*: 145–152. Monographs of the Danish Institute at Athens Volume 10. Athens: The Danish Institute at Athens.

Huxley, D. (ed.), 2000. *Cretan Quests: British explorers, excavators and historians*. London: British School at Athens.

James, P. 2012. Review Article: Tree-Rings, Kings and Old World Archaeology and Environment. *Palestine Exploration Quarterly* 144: 144–150.

Jansen-Winkeln, K. 2006. Dynasty 21. In E. Hornung, R. Krauss and D.A. Warburton (eds.), *Ancient Egyptian Chronology*: 218–233. Leiden: Brill.

Johnston, E.N., Philips, J.C., Bonnadona, C. and Watson, I.M. 2012. Reconstructing the tephra dispersal pattern from the Bronze Age eruption of Santorini using an advection-diffusion model. *Bulletin of Volcanology* 74: 1485–1507.

Karageorghis, V., Michaelides, D., *et al.* 1990. *Tombs at Palaepaphos. 1. Teratsoudhia. 2. Eliomylia*. Nicosia: A.G. Leventis Foundation.

Keenan, D.J. 2002a. Why early-historical radiocarbon dates downwind from the Mediterranean are too early. *Radiocarbon* 44(1): 225–337.

Keenan, D.J. 2002b. Astro-historiographic chronologies of early China are unfounded. *East Asian History* 23: 61–68.

Keenan, D.J. 2003. Volcanic ash retrieved from the GRIP ice core is not from Thera. *Geochemistry, Geophysics, Geosystems* 4(11) 1097, doi:10.1029/2003GC000608.

Keenan, D.J. 2004. Radiocarbon dates from Iron Age Gordion are confounded. *Ancient West & East* 3: 100–103.

Keenan, D.J. 2007. Defence of planetary conjunctions for early Chinese chronology is unmerited. *Journal of Astronomical History and Heritage* 10: 142–147.

Keenan, D.J. 2012. Calibration of a radiocarbon age. *Nonlinear Processes in Geophysics* 19: 345–350.

Kemp, B.J. and Merrillees, R.S. 1980. *Minoan pottery in second millennium Egypt*. Mainz am Rhein: Philipp von Zabern.

Kempinski, A. 2002. *Tel Kabri: the 1986–1993 Excavations Seasons*. Tel Aviv: Emery and Claire Yass Publications in Archaeology, Institute of Archaeology, Tel Aviv University.

Kilian-Dirlmeier, I. 1993. *Die Schwerter in Griechenland (ausserhalb Peloponnes), Bulgarien und Albanien*. Prähistorische Bronzefunde. Abteilung IV, 12. Stuttgart: F. Steiner.

Kitchen, K.A. 2000. Regnal and Genealogical data of Ancient Egypt (Absolute Chronology I). The Historical Chronology of Ancient Egypt, A Current Assessment. In M. Bietak (ed.), *The Synchronisation of Civilisations in the Eastern Mediterranean in the Second Millennium B.C. Proceedings of an International Symposium at Schloß Haindorf, 15th–17th of November 1996 and at the Austrian Academy, Vienna, 11th–12th of May 1998*: 39–52. Wien: Verlag der Österreichischen Akademie der Wissenschaften.

Knappett, C., Rivers, R. and Evans, T. 2011. The Thera eruption and Minoan palatial collapse: new interpretations gained from modeling the maritime network. *Antiquity* 85: 1008–1023.

Koehl, R.B. 2000. Minoan rhyta in Egypt. In A. Karetsou (ed.), Κρητη–Αιγυπτοσ (Catalogue for an exhibition in the Heraklion Museum, 2000): 94–100. Athens: Ipourgeio Politismou.

Koehl, R.B. 2006. *Aegean Bronze Age Rhyta*. Philadelphia: INSTAP Academic Press.

Kopcke, G. and Tokumaru, I. (eds.). 1992. *Greece between East and West: 10th–8th Centuries BC. Papers of the Meeting at the Institute of Fine Arts, New York University, March 15–16th, 1990*. Mainz am Rhein: Philipp von Zabern.

Korte, M., Genevey, A., Constable, C.G., Frank, U. and Schepp, E. 2005. Continuous geomagnetic field models for the past 7 millennia: 2. CALS7K. *Geochemistry, Geophysics, Geosystems* 6(2): Q02H16, doi:10.1029/2004GC000801.

Krauss, R. and Warburton, D.A. 2006. Conclusions. In E. Hornung, R. Krauss and D.A. Warburton (eds.), *Ancient Egyptian Chronology*: 473–498. Leiden: Brill.

Krauss, R. and Warburton, D.A. 2009. The basis for the Egyptian dates. In D.A. Warburton (ed.), *Time's Up! Dating the Minoan eruption of Santorini. Acts of the Minoan Eruption Chronology Workshop, Sandbjerg November 2007 initiated by Jan Heinemeier & Walter L. Friedrich*: 125–144. Monographs of the Danish Institute at Athens Volume 10. Athens: The Danish Institute at Athens.

Kristiansen, K. and Larsson, T.B. 2005. *The Rise of Bronze Age Society: Travels, Transmissions and Transformations*. Cambridge: Cambridge University Press.

Kromer, B., Manning, S.W., Kuniholm, P.I., Newton, M.W., Spurk, M. and Levin, I. 2001. Regional $^{14}CO_2$ offsets in the troposphere: magnitude, mechanisms, and consequences. *Science* 294: 2529–2532.

Kuniholm, P.I. 1977. *Dendrochronology at Gordion and the Anatolian Plateau*. Ph.D. dissertation, University of Pennsylvania. Ann Arbor: University Microfilms International.

Kuniholm, P.I., Kromer, B., Manning, S.W., Newton, M., Latini, C.E. and Bruce, M.J. 1996. Anatolian tree-rings and the absolute chronology of the east Mediterranean 2220–718BC. *Nature* 381: 780–783.

Kuniholm, P.I., Newton, M.W., Griggs, C.B. and Sullivan, P.J. 2005. *Dendrochronological Dating in Anatolia: the Second Millennium B.C.* In Ü. Yalçın (ed.), *Anatolian Metal 3*: 41–47. Veröffentlichungen aus dem Deutschen Bergbau-Museum 124, Anschnitt Beiheft 18, Bochum: Deutsches Bergbau-Museum.

Kuniholm, P.I., Newton, M.W. and Liebhart, R.F. 2011. Dendrochronology at Gordion. In C.B. Rose and G. Darbyshire (eds.), *The New Chronology of Iron Age Gordion*: 79–122. Gordion Special Studies VI. Philadelphia: University of Pennsylvania Museum of Archaeology and Anthropology.

Kuniholm, P.I., Tarter, S.L., Griggs, C.B. 1993. Dendrochronological report. In G.D. Summers, *Tille Höyük 4: The Late Bronze Age and the Iron Age Transition*: 179–190. Ankara: The British Institute of Archaeology at Ankara.

Kutschera, W., Bietak, M., Wild, E.M., Bronk Ramsey, C., Dee, M., Golser, R., Kopetzky, K., Stadler, P., Steier, P., Thanheiser, U and Weninger, F. 2012.The chronology of Tell el-Daba: a crucial meeting point of ^{14}C dating, archaeology, and Egyptology in the 2nd millennium BC. *Radiocarbon* 54(3–4): 407–422.

Kutschera, W. and Stadler, P. 2000. ^{14}C Dating for absolute chronology of eastern Mediterranean cultures in the second millennium BC with accelerator mass spectrometry. In M. Bietak (ed.), *The Synchronisation of Civilisations in the Eastern Mediterranean in the Second Millennium B.C. Proceedings of an International Symposium at Schloß Haindorf, 15th–17th of November 1996 and at the Austrian Academy, Vienna, 11th–12th of May 1998*: 68–81. Wien: Verlag der Österreichischen Akademie der Wissenschaften.

Lee, S., Bronk Ramsey, C. and Mazar, A. 2013. Iron Age Chronology in Israel: Results from Modeling with a Trapezoidal Bayesian Framework. *Radiocarbon* 55(2–3): 731-740.

Lilyquist, C. 1996. Stone vessels at Kamid el-Loz: Egyptian, Egyptianizing, or non-Egyptian? A question at sites from the Sudan to Iraq to the Greek mainland. In R. Hachmann, *Kamid el-Loz 16. Schatzhausstudien*: 133–173. Bonn: Dr. Rudolf Habelt.

Lilyquist, C. 1997. Egyptian stone vases? Comments on Peter Warren's paper. *Aegaeum* 16: 225–228.

Limbrey, S. 1990. Soil studies at Akrotiri. In D.A. Hardy, J. Keller, V.P. Galanopoulos, N.C. Flemming and T.H. Druitt (eds.), *Thera and the Aegean world III. Volume two: earth sciences*: 377–382. London: The Thera Foundation.

Lindblom, M. and Manning, S.W. 2011. The Chronology of the Lerna Shaft Graves. In W. Gauß, M. Lindblom, R.A.K. Smith, J.C. Wright (eds.), *Our Cups Are Full: Pottery and Society in the Aegean Bronze Age. Papers presented to Jeremy B. Rutter on the occasion of his 65th birthday*: 140–153. BAR International Series 2227. Oxford: Archaeopress.

Linick, T.W., Long, A., Damon, P.E. and Ferguson, C.W. 1986. High-precision radiocarbon dating of Bristlecone Pine from 6554 to 5350 BC. *Radiocarbon* 28(2B): 943–953.

Liphschitz, N. 2007. *Timber in Ancient Israel: Dendroarchaeology and Dendrochronology.* Monograph 26. Emery and Claire Yass Publications in Archaeology. Tel Aviv: Institute of Archaeology, Tel Aviv University.

Luce, J.V. 1969. *The end of Atlantis: new light on an old legend.* London: Thames and Hudson.

Macdonald, C.F. 2002. The Neopalatial Palaces of Knossos. In J. Driessen, I. Schoep and R. Laffineur (eds.), *Monuments of Minos: Rethinking the Minoan Palaces. Proceedings of the International Workshop "Crete of the hundred Palaces" held at the Université Catholique de Louvain, Louvaine-la-Neuve, 14–15 December 2001*: 35–54. Aegeaum 23. Liège and Austin: Histoire de l'art et archeologie de la Grèce antique, Université de Liège and Program in Aegean Scripts and Prehistory, University of Texas at Austin.

Macdonald, C.F. 2003. The Palaces of Minos at Knossos. *Athena Review* 3(3): 36–43.

Macdonald, C.F. 2005. *Knossos.* London: The Folio Society.

MacGillivray, J.A. 1998. *Knossos: Pottery Groups of the Old Palace Period.* London: The British School at Athens.

MacGillivray, J.A. 2009. Thera, Hatshepsut, and the Keftiu: crisis and response. In D.A. Warburton (ed.), *Time's Up! Dating the Minoan eruption of Santorini. Acts of the Minoan Eruption Chronology Workshop, Sandbjerg November 2007 initiated by Jan Heinemeier & Walter L. Friedrich*: 154–170. Monographs of the Danish Institute at Athens Volume 10. Athens: The Danish Institute at Athens.

Maguire, L.C. 2009. *The Cypriot Pottery and its Circulation in the Levant.* Tell el-Dab'a XXI. Wien: Verlag der Österreichischen Akademie der Wissenschaften.

Maguire, L.C. 2012. *Painting Practices in White Painted and White Slip Wares.* Wien: Verlag der Österreichischen Akademie der Wissenschaften.

Maniatis, Y. 2010. New Radiocarbon Dates From Akrotiri, Thera. *Pasiphae* 4: 41–52.

Manning, S.W. 1988a. The Bronze Age eruption of Thera: absolute dating, Aegean chronology and Mediterranean cultural interrelations. *Journal of Mediterranean Archaeology* 1(1): 17–82.

Manning, S.W. 1988b. Dating of the Thera eruption. *Nature* 332: 401.

Manning, S.W. 1990a. The Thera eruption: the Third Congress and the problem of the date. *Archaeometry* 32: 91–100.

Manning, S.W. 1990b. The eruption of Thera: date and implications. In D.A. Hardy and A.C. Renfrew (eds.), *Thera and the Aegean world III, volume three: chronology*: 29–40. London: The Thera Foundation.

Manning, S.W. 1992. Thera, sulphur, and climatic anomalies. *Oxford Journal of Archaeology* 11: 245–253.

Manning, S.W. 1995. *The Absolute Chronology of the Aegean Early Bronze Age: archaeology, history and radiocarbon.* Monographs in Mediterranean Archaeology 1. Sheffield: Sheffield Academic Press.

Manning, S.W. 1998. Aegean and Sardinian chronology: radiocarbon, calibration, and Thera. In M.S. Balmuth and R.H. Tykot (eds.), *Sardinian and Aegean chronology: towards the resolution of relative and absolute dating in the Mediterranean*: 297–307. Studies in Sardinian Archaeology V. Oxford: Oxbow Books.

Manning, S.W. 1999. *A Test of Time: the volcano of Thera and the chronology and history of the Aegean and east Mediterranean in the mid-second millennium BC.* Oxford: Oxbow Books.

Manning, S.W. 2001. The chronology and foreign connections of the Late Cypriot I period: times they are a-changin. In P. Åström (ed.), *The chronology of Base-Ring ware and Bichrome wheel-made ware*: 69–94. Stockholm: The Royal Academy of Letters, History and Antiquities.

Manning, S. 2005. Simulation and the Thera eruption: outlining what we do and do not know from Radiocarbon. In A. Dakouri-Hild and S. Sherratt (eds.), *Autochthon: Papers presented to O.T.P.K. Dickinson on the occasion of his retirement*: 97–114. BAR International Series 1432. Oxford: Archaeopress.

Manning, S.W. 2006. Radiocarbon dating and Egyptian chronology. In E. Hornung, R. Krauss and D.A. Warburton (eds.), *Ancient Egyptian Chronology*: 327–355. Leiden: Brill.

Manning, S.W. 2007. Clarifying the "high" v. "low" Aegean/Cypriot chronology for the mid second millennium BC: assessing the evidence, interpretive frameworks, and current state of the debate. In Bietak, M. and Czerny, E. (eds.), *The Synchronisation of Civilisations in the Eastern Mediterranean in* the Second Millennium B.C. III. Proceedings of the SCIEM 2000 – 2nd EuroConference: 101–137. Vienna 28th of May – 1st of June 2003. Wien: Verlag der Österreichischen Akademie der Wissenschaften.

Manning, S.W. 2008a. An Edited Past: Aegean Prehistory and Its Texts. In M.A. Cheetham, E. Legge and C.M. Soussloff (eds.), *Editing the Image: Strategies in the Production and Reception of the Visual*: 33–65. Toronto: University of Toronto Press.

Manning, S.W. 2008b. Some initial wobbly steps towards a Late Neolithic to Early Bronze III radiocarbon chronology for the Cyclades. In N.J. Brodie, J. Doole, G. Gavalas and C. Renfrew (eds.), Ὁρίζων: *A colloquium on the prehistory of the Cyclades*: 55–59. Cambridge: McDonald Institute for Archaeological Research.

Manning, S.W. 2009. Beyond the Santorini eruption: some notes on dating the Late Minoan IB period on Crete, and implications for Cretan-Egyptian relations in the 15th century BC (and especially LMII). In D.A. Warburton (ed.), *Time's Up! Dating the Minoan eruption of Santorini. Acts of the Minoan Eruption Chronology Workshop, Sandbjerg November 2007 initiated by Jan Heinemeier & Walter L. Friedrich*: 207–226. Monographs of the Danish Institute at Athens Volume 10. Athens: The Danish Institute at Athens.

Manning, S.W. 2010. Eruption of Thera. In E.H. Cline (ed.), *The Oxford Handbook of The Bronze Age Aegean (c.3000–1000 BC)*: 457–474. New York: Oxford University Press.

Manning, S.W. 2014. Two notes: Dating the LMIB Destruction at Myrtos-Pyrgos, Crete, and the spatial setting of Maroni Vournes, Cyprus. In C.F. Macdonald, E. Hatzaki and S. Andreou (eds.), *The Great Islands. Studies of Crete and Cyprus presented to Gerald Cadogan*. Athens: Kapon Editions. In press.

Manning, S.W. and Bronk Ramsey, C. 2003. A Late Minoan I–II absolute chronology for the Aegean – combining archaeology with radiocarbon. In M. Bietak (ed.), *The synchronisation of civilisations in the eastern Mediterranean in the second millennium BC (II). Proceedings of the SCIEM2000 EuroConference Haindorf, May 2001*: 111–133. Wien: Verlag der Österreichischen Akademie der Wissenschaften.

Manning, S.W. and Bronk Ramsey, C. 2009. The dating of the earlier Late Minoan IA period: a brief note. In D.A. Warburton (ed.), *Time's Up! Dating the Minoan eruption of Santorini. Acts of the Minoan Eruption Chronology Workshop, Sandbjerg November 2007 initiated by Jan Heinemeier & Walter L. Friedrich*: 227–245. Monographs of the Danish Institute at Athens Volume 10. Athens: The Danish Institute at Athens.

Manning, S.W., Bronk Ramsey, C., Doumas, C., Marketou, T., Cadogan, G. and Pearson, C.L. 2002a. New evidence for an early date for the Aegean Late Bronze Age and Thera eruption. *Antiquity* 76: 733–744.

Manning, S.W., Bronk Ramsey, C., Kutschera, W., Higham, T., Kromer, B., Steier, P. and Wild, E. 2006a. Chronology for the Aegean Late Bronze Age. *Science* 312: 565–569.

Manning, S.W., Bronk Ramsey, C., Kutschera, W., Higham, T., Kromer, B., Steier, P. and Wild, E.M. 2009a. Dating the Santorini/Thera Eruption by Radiocarbon: Further Discussion (AD 2006–2007). In S.W. Manning and M.J. Bruce (eds.), *Tree-Rings, Kings and Old World Archaeology and Environment: Papers Presented in Honor of Peter Ian Kuniholm*: 299–316 and 327–328. Oxford: Oxbow Books.

Manning, S.W., Crewe, L. and Sewell, D.A. 2006b. Further light on early LCI connections at Maroni. In E. Czerny, I. Hein, H. Hunger, D. Melman and A. Schwab (eds.), *Timelines. Studies in honour of Manfred Bietak, Volume II*: 471–488. OLA 149. Leuven: Peeters.

Manning, S.W. and Kromer, B. 2011a. Radiocarbon Dating Archaeological Samples in the Eastern Mediterranean 1730–1480 BC: Further Exploring the Atmospheric Radiocarbon Calibration Record and the Archaeological Implications. *Archaeometry* 53: 413–439.

Manning, S.W. and Kromer, B. 2011b. Radiocarbon Dating Iron Age Gordion and the Early Phrygian Destruction in Particular. In C.B. Rose and G. Darbyshire (eds.), *The New Chronology of Iron Age Gordion*: 123–153. Gordion Special Studies VI. Philadelphia: University of Pennsylvania Museum of Archaeology and Anthropology. [I note that there were a few unfortunate typos and a missing line of text in the published version of the Manning and Kromer (2011b) paper. For the corrections, and for discussion of these, please see: https://www.academia.edu/1110679/Manning_S.W._and_Kromer_B._2011._Radiocarbon_Dating_Iron_Age_Gordion_and_the_Early_Phrygian_Destruction_in_Particular.

Manning, S.W. and Kromer, B. 2012. Considerations of the scale of radiocarbon offsets in the east Mediterranean, and considering a case for the latest (most recent) likely date for the Santorini eruption. *Radiocarbon* 54(3–4): 449–474.

Manning, S.W., Kromer, B., Bronk Ramsey, C., Pearson, C.L., Talamo, S., Trano, N. and Watkins, J.D. 2010. [14]C Record and Wiggle-Match Placement for the Anatolian (Gordion Area) Juniper Tree-Ring Chronology ~1729 to 751 Cal BC, and typical Aegean/Anatolian (growing season related) regional ^{14}C offset assessment. *Radiocarbon* 52(4): 1571–1597.

Manning, S.W., Kromer, B., Dee, M., Friedrich, M., Higham, T. and Bronk Ramsey, C. 2013. Radiocarbon calibration in the mid to later 14th century BC and radiocarbon dating Tell el-Amarna, Egypt. In A.J. Shortland and C. Bronk Ramsey (eds.), *Radiocarbon and the Chronologies of Ancient Egypt*: 121–145. Oxford: Oxbow Books.

Manning, S.W., Kromer, B., Kuniholm, P.I. and Newton, M.W. 2001. Anatolian tree-rings and a new chronology for the east Mediterranean Bronze-Iron Ages. *Science* 294: 2532–2535.

Manning, S.W., Kromer B., Kuniholm P.I. and Newton M.W. 2003. Confirmation of near-absolute dating of east Mediterranean Bronze-Iron Dendrochronology. *Antiquity* 77 (295): http://antiquity.ac.uk/ProjGall/Manning/manning.html.

Manning, S.W., Pulak, C., Kromer, B., Talamo, S., Bronk Ramsey, C. and Dee, M. 2009b. Absolute Age of the Uluburun Shipwreck: A Key Late Bronze Age Time-Capsule for the East Mediterranean. In S.W. Manning and M.J. Bruce (eds.), *Tree-Rings, Kings and Old World Archaeology and Environment: Papers Presented in Honor of Peter Ian Kuniholm*: 163–187. Oxford: Oxbow Books.

Manning, S.W. and Sewell, D.A. 2002. Volcanoes and history: a significant relationship? The case of Thera. In R. Torrence and J. Grattan, (eds) *Natural disasters and cultural change*: 264–291. London: Routledge.

Manning, S.W., Sewell, D.A. and Herscher, E. 2002b. Late Cypriot I A Maritime Trade in Action: Underwater Survey at Maroni Tsaroukkas and the Contemporary East Mediterranean Trading System. *The Annual of the British School at Athens* 97: 97–162.

Maran, J. 2011. Lost in Translation: the Emergence of Mycenean Culture as a Phenomenon of Glocalization. In T.C. Wilkinson, S. Sherratt and J. Bennet (eds.), *Interweaving Worlds: Systemic Interactions in Eurasia, 7th to 1st Millennia BC. Papers from a conference in memory of Professor Andrew Sherratt – What Would a Bronze Age World System Look Like? World systems approaches to Europe and western Asia 4th to 1st millennia BC*: 282–294. Oxford: Oxbow Books.

Maran, J. 2013. Bright as the sun: the appropriation of amber objects in Mycenaean Greece. In H.P. Hahn and H. Weiss (eds.), *Mobility, Meaning and the Transformations of Things*: 147–169. Oxford: Oxbow Books.

Marinatos, S. 1939. The volcanic destruction of Minoan Crete. *Antiquity* 13: 425–439.

Marzaioli, F., Lubritto, C., Battipaglia, G., Passariello, I., Rubino, M., Rogalla, D., Strumia, S., Miglietta, F., D'Onofrio, A., Cotrufo, M.F. and Terrasi, F. 2005. Reconstruction of past CO_2 concentration at a natural CO_2 vent site using radiocarbon dating of tree rings. *Radiocarbon* 47(2): 257–263.

Matthäus, H. 1995. Representations of Keftiu in Egyptian tombs and the absolute chronology of the Aegean Late Bronze Age. *Bulletin of the Institute of Classical Studies* 40: 177–194.

Mazar, A. and Bronk Ramsey, C. 2008. [14]C Dates and the Iron Age Chronology of Israel: A Response. *Radiocarbon* 50(2): 159–180.

Mazar, A., and Bronk Ramsey, C. 2010. A Response to Finkelstein and Piasetzky's Criticism and "New Perspective". *Radiocarbon* 52(4): 1681–1688.

McCaughran, J. 2011. Implied Terms: The Journey of the Man on the Clapham Omnibus. *The Cambridge Law Journal* 70: 607–622.

McClelland, E. and Druitt, T.H. 1989. Palaeomagentic estimates of emplacement temperatures of pyroclastic deposits on Santorini, Greece. *Bulletin of Volcanology* 51: 16–27.

McCoy, F.W. 2009. The eruption within the debate about the date. In D.A. Warburton (ed.), *Time's Up! Dating the Minoan eruption of Santorini. Acts of the Minoan Eruption Chronology Workshop, Sandbjerg November 2007 initiated by Jan Heinemeier & Walter L. Friedrich*: 73–90. Monographs of the Danish Institute at Athens Volume 10. Athens: The Danish Institute at Athens.

McGlade, J. 1999. The times of history: archaeology, narrative and non-linear causality. In T. Murray (ed.), *Time and Archaeology*: 139–163. Routledge: London and New York.

Mebert, J. 2010. *Die Venustafeln des Ammī-ṣaduqa und ihre Bedeutung für die astronomische Datierung der altbabylonischen Zeit.* Archiv fur Orientforschung, Beiheft 31. Wien: Institut für Orientalistik der Universität Wien.

Mellink, M.J. 1995. New perspectives and initiatives in the Hyksos period. *Ägypten und Levante* 5: 85–89.

Merlott, A.L. and Thomas, B.C. 2012. Causes of an AD 774–775 ¹⁴C increase. *Nature* 491: E 1–2

Merrillees, R.S. 1968. *The Cypriote Bronze Age pottery found in Egypt.* Studies in Mediterranean Archaeology 18. Göteborg: Paul Åströms Förlag.

Merrillees, R.S. 1971. The early history of Late Cypriot I. *Levant* 3: 56–79.

Merrillees, R.S. 1972. Aegean Bronze Age relations with Egypt. *American Journal of Archaeology* 76: 281–294.

Merrillees, R.S. 1975. The Cypriote Bronze Age pottery found in Egypt: a reply. *Report of the Department of Antiquities, Cyprus*: 81–90.

Merrillees, R.S. 1977. The absolute chronology of the Bronze Age in Cyprus. *Report of the Department of Antiquities, Cyprus*: 33–50.

Merrillees, R.S. 1992. The absolute chronology of the Bronze Age in Cyprus: a revision. *Bulletin of the American Schools of Oriental Research* 288: 47–52.

Merrillees, R.S. 2001. Some Cypriote White Slip pottery from the Aegean. In V. Karageorghis (ed.), *The White Slip Ware of Late Bronze Age Cyprus. Proceedings of an International Conference Organized by the Anastasios G. Leventis Foundation, Nicosia in Honour of Malcolm Wiener*: 89–100. Wien: Verlag der Österreichischen Akademie der Wissenschaften.

Merrillees, R.S. 2002. The relative and absolute chronology of the Cypriote White Painted Pendent Line Style. *Bulletin of the American Schools of Oriental Research* 326: 1–9.

Merrillees, R.S. 2009. Chronological conundrums: Cypriot and Levantine imports from Thera. In D.A. Warburton (ed.), *Time's Up! Dating the Minoan eruption of Santorini. Acts of the Minoan Eruption Chronology Workshop, Sandbjerg November 2007 initiated by Jan Heinemeier & Walter L. Friedrich*: 247–251. Monographs of the Danish Institute at Athens Volume 10. Athens: The Danish Institute at Athens.

Meulengracht, A., McGovern, P. and Lawn, B. 1981. University of Pennsylvania Radiocarbon Dates XXI. *Radiocarbon* 23(2): 227–240.

Michael, H.N. 1976. Radiocarbon dates from Akrotiri on Thera. *Temple University Aegean Symposium* 1: 7–9.

Michczynska, D.J., Pazdur, M.F. and Walanus, A. 1990. Bayesian approach to probabilistic calibration of radiocarbon ages. In W.G. Mook and H.T. Waterbolk (eds.), *¹⁴C and Archaeology: Proceedings of the Second International Symposium, Groningen 1987*: 69–79. PACT (Journal of the European Study Group on Physical, Chemical and Mathematical Techniques Applied to Archaeology) 29. Strasbourg: Council of Europe/Rixensart.

Michel, C. 2002. Nouvelles données pour la chronologie du IIᵉ millénaire. *NABU: Nouvelles Assyriologiques Brèves et Utilitaires* 20(1): 17–18.

Miles, D. 1997. The Interpretation, Presentation and Use of Tree-Ring Dates. *Vernacular Architecture* 28: 40–56.

Miyake, F., Nagaya, K., Masuda, K. and Nakamura, T. 2012. A signature of cosmic-ray increase in AD 774–775 from tree rings in Japan. *Nature* 486: 240–242.

Moeller, N. and Marouard, G. (with a contribution by Ayers, N.) 2011. Discussion of late Middle Kingdom and early Second Intermediate Period history and chronology in relation to the Khayan Sealings from Tell Edfu. *Ägypten und Levante* 21: 87–121.

Momigliano, A. 1977. Time in ancient historiography. In A. Momigliano, *Essays in ancient and modern historiography*: 179–204. Oxford: Blackwell.

Moran, W. 1992. *The Amarna letters.* Baltimore: The Johns Hopkins University Press.

Morgan, L. 2010. A Pride of Leopards: A Unique Aspect of the Hunt Frieze from Tell el-Dab'a. *Ägypten und Levante* 20: 263–301.

Morris, S.P. 1992. *Daidalos and the origins of Greek art*. Princeton: Princeton University Press.

Morris, S.P. 1997. Homer and the Near East. In I. Morris and B. Powell (eds.), *A New Companion to Homer*: 600–623. Leiden: Brill.

Muhly, J.D. 1975. Near Eastern chronology and the date of the Late Cypriot I period. In N. Robertson (ed.), *The archaeology of Cyprus: recent developments*: 76–89. Park Ridge, N.J.: Noyes Press.

Muhly, J. 2009. Perspective: Archaeology, History, and Chronology from Penn to the Present and Beyond. In S.W. Manning and M.J. Bruce (eds.), *Tree-Rings, Kings, and Old World Archaeology and Environment*: 3–11. Oxford: Oxbow Books.

Murray, T. 1999. A return to the 'Pompeii premise'. In T. Murray (ed.), *Time and Archaeology*: 8–27. Routledge: London and New York.

Muscheler, R. 2009. ^{14}C and ^{10}Be around 1650 cal BC. In D.A. Warburton (ed.), *Time's Up! Dating the Minoan eruption of Santorini. Acts of the Minoan Eruption Chronology Workshop, Sandbjerg November 2007 Initiated by Jan Heinemeier & Walter L. Friedrich*: 275–284. Monographs of the Danish Institute at Athens Volume 10. Athens: The Danish Institute at Athens.

Narcisi, B., Vezzoli, L., 1999. Quaternary stratigraphy of distal tephra layers in the Mediterranean-an overview. *Global and Planetary Change* 21: 31–50.

Needham, S., Bronk Ramsey, C., Coombs, D., Cartwright, C., and Pettitt, P.B. 1997. An independent chronology for British Bronze Age metalwork: the results of the Oxford Radiocarbon Accelerator Programme. *Archaeological Journal* 154: 55–107.

Needham, S., Parker Pearson, M., Tyler, A., Richards, M. and Jay, M. 2010. A first 'Wessex 1' date from Wessex. *Antiquity* 84 (2010): 363–373.

Neer, R.T. 2012. *Art & Archaeology of the Greek World c.2500–c.150 BCE*. London: Thames & Hudson.

Negbi, O. 1978. Cypriote Imitations of Tell el-Yahudiyeh Ware from Toumba tou Skourou. *American Journal of Archaeology* 82: 137–149.

Negbi, O. 1994. The 'Libyan Landscape' from Thera: A Review of Aegean Enterprises Overseas in the Late Minoan IA Period. *Journal of Mediterranean Archaeology* 7: 73–112.

Newton, M.W. and Kuniholm, P.I. 2004. A Dendrochronological Framework for the Assyrian Colony Period in Asia Minor. *TUBA-AR (Türkiye Bilimler Akademisi Arkeoloji Dergisi)* 7: 165–176.

Niemeier, W.-D. 1990. New archaeological evidence for a 17th century date of the 'Minoan eruption' from Israel (tel Kabri, western Galilee). In D.A. Hardy and A.C. Renfrew (eds.), *Thera and the Aegean world III. Volume three: chronology*: 120–126. London: The Thera Foundation.

Niemeier, B. and Niemeier, W.-D. 2000. Aegean Frescoes in Syria-Palestine: Alalakh and Tel Kabri. In S. Sherratt (ed.), *The Wall Paintings of Thera. Proceedings of the First International Symposium, Petros M. Nomikos Conference Centre, Thera, Hellas, 30 August – 4 September 1997*: 763–802. Athens: Petros M. Nomikos and the Thera Foundation.

Nikolakopoulou, I. 2010. Middle Cycladic iconography: a social context for 'A new chapter in Aegean art'. In O. Krzyszkowska (ed.), *Cretan Offerings: Studies in Honour of Peter Warren*: 213–222. London: The British School at Athens.

Olsson, I.U., Klasson, M. and Abd-el-Mageed, A. 1972. Uppsala Natural Radiocarbon Measurements XI. *Radiocarbon* 14(1): 247–271.

Oren, E.D. (ed.). 1997a. *The Hyksos: new historical and archaeological perspectives*. Philadelphia: The University Museum, University of Pennsylvania.

Oren, E.D. 1997b. The "Kingdom of Sharuhen" and the Hyksos Kingdom. In E.D. Oren (ed.), *The Hyksos: new historical and archaeological perspectives*: 253–283. Philadelphia: The University Museum, University of Pennsylvania.

Palyvou, C. 2005. *Akrotiri Thera: An Architecture of Affluence 3,500 Years Old*. Philadelphia: INSTAP Academic Press.

Panagiotakopulu, E. and Buckland, P.C. 1991. Insect pests of stored products from Late Bronze Age Santorini, Greece. *Journal of Stored Products Research* 27: 179–184.

Panagiotakopulu, E., Higham, T., Sarpaki, A., Buckland, P. and Doumas, C. 2013. Ancient pests: the season of the Santorini Minoan volcanic eruption and a date from insect chitin. *Naturwissenschaften* 100: 683-689.

Panagiotopoulos, D. 2001. Keftiu in context: Theban Tomb-Paintings as a historical source. *Oxford Journal of Archaeology* 20: 263–283.

Pang, K.D., Keston, R., Srivastava, S.K. and Chou, H-h. 1989. Climatic and hydrologic extremes in early Chinese history: possible causes and dates. *EOS. Transactions, American Geophysical Union* 70: 1095.

Pankenier, D.W. 1998. Heaven-Sent: Understanding Cosmic Disaster in Chinese Myth and History. In B.J. Peiser, T. Palmer and M.E. Bailey (eds.), *Natural catastrophes during Bronze Age civilisations: archaeological, geological, astronomical, and cultural perspectives*: 187–197. BAR International Series 728. Oxford: Archaeopress.

Pankenier, D.W. 2007. Caveat lector: Comments on Douglas J. Keenan, 'Astro-historiographic Chronologies of Early China are Unfounded'. *Journal of Astronomical History and Heritage* 10: 137–141.

Pasquier-Cardin, A., Allard, P., Ferreira, T., Hatte, C., Coutinho, R., Fontugne, M. and Jaudon, M. 1999. Magma-derived CO_2 emissions recorded in ^{14}C and ^{13}C content of plants growing in Furnas caldera, Azores. *Journal of Volcanology and Geothermal Research* 92: 195–207.

Pearce, N., Westgate, J., Preece, S., Eastwood, W. and Perkins, W. 2004. Identification of Aniakchak (Alaska) Tephra in Greenland Ice Core Challenges the 1645 BC Date for Minoan Eruption of Santorini. *Geochemistry, Geophysics, Geosystems* 5(3) Q03005, doi:10.1029/2003GC000672.

Pearce, N.J.G., Westgate, J.A., Preece, S.J., Eastwood, W.J., Perkins, W.T. and Hart, J.S. 2007. Reinterpretation of Greenland Ice-core Data Recognises the Presence of the Late Holocene Aniakchak Tephra (Alaska), not the Minoan Tephra (Santorini), at 1645 BC. In M. Bietak (ed.), *The synchronisation of civilisations in the eastern Mediterranean in the second millennium BC (II). Proceedings of the SCIEM2000 EuroConference Haindorf, May 2001*: 139–147. Wien: Verlag der Österreichischen Akademie der Wissenschaften.

Pearson, C.L., Dale, D.S., Brewer, P.W., Kuniholm, P.I., Lipton, J. and Manning, S.W. 2009. Dendrochemical analysis of a tree-ring growth anomaly associated with the Late Bronze Age eruption of Thera. *Journal of Archaeological Science* 36: 1206–1214.

Pearson, C.L. and Manning, S.W. 2009. Could Absolutely Dated Tree-ring Chemistry Provide a Means to Dating the Major Volcanic Eruptions of the Holocene? In S.W. Manning and M.J. Bruce (eds.), *Tree-Rings, Kings and Old World Archaeology and Environment: Papers Presented in Honor of Peter Ian Kuniholm*: 97–109. Oxford: Oxbow Books.

Pearson, G.W. 1986. Precise calendrical dating of known growth-period samples using a 'curve fitting' technique. *Radiocarbon* 28: 292–299.

Pearson, G.W., Pilcher, J.R. and Baillie, M.G.L. 1983. High-precision ^{14}C measurement of Irish oaks to show the natural ^{14}C variations from 200 BC to 4000 BC. *Radiocarbon* 25(2): 179–186.

Perelle, I. B. and Ehrman, L. 1983. The development of laterality. *Behavioral Science* 28: 284–297.

Perelle, I.B. and Ehrman, L. 1994. An international study of human handedness: the data. *Behavior Genetics* 24: 217–227.

Phillips, J. 2008. *Aegyptiaca on the Island of Crete in Their Chronological Context: A Critical Review.* Wien: Verlag der Österreichischen Akademie der Wissenschaften.

Pollard, A.M. and Bray, P. 2007. A Bicycle Made for Two? The Integration of Scientific Techniques into Archaeological Interpretation. *Annual Review of Anthropology* 36: 245–259.

Pomerance, L. 1980. The Possible Role of the Tomb Robbers and Viziers of the 18th Dynasty in Confusing Minoan Chronology. *Acts of the Fourth International Cretological Congress, Iraklion, 29 August-3 September, 1976. Vol. 1*: 447–453. Athens.

Pruzsinszky, R. 2006. Šamši-Adads I. "neue" Regierungsdaten und assyrische Distanzangaben. In E. Czerny, I. Hein, H. Hunger, D. Melman and A. Schwab (eds.), *Timelines: Studies in Honor of Manfred Bietak, Volume III*: 73–79. OLA 149. Leuven: Peeters.

Pruzsinszky, R. 2009: *Mesopotamian Chronology of the 2nd Millennium B.C. An Introduction to the Textual Evidence and Related Chronological Issues.* Wien: Verlag der Österreichischen Akademie der Wissenschaften.

Quack, J.F. 2007. Das Problem der H3w-nb.wt. In R. Rollinger, A. Luther and J. Wiesehöfer (eds.), *Getrennte Wege? Kommunikation, Raum und Wahrnehmung in der Alten Welt*: 331-362. Frankfurt am Mein: Verlag Antike.

Rackham, O. and Moody, J. 1997. *The Making of the Cretan Landscape*. Manchester: Manchester University Press.

Redford, D. 1997. Textual Sources for the Hyksos Period. In E.D. Oren, (ed), *The Hyksos: New Historical and Archaeological Perspectives*: 1–44. Philadelphia: The University Museum, University of Pennsylvania.

Reimer, P.J., Baillie, M.G.L., Bard, E., Bayliss, A., Beck, J.W., Blackwell, P.G., Bronk Ramsey, C., Buck, C.E., Burr, G.S., Edwards, R.L., Friedrich, M., Grootes, P.M., Guilderson, T.P., Hajdas, I., Heaton, T.J., Hogg, A.G., Hughen, K.A., Kaiser, K.F., Kromer, B., McCormac, F.G., Manning, S.W., Reimer, R.W., Richards, D.A., Southon, J.R., Talamo, S., Turney, C.S.M., van der Plicht, J., Weyhenmeyer, C.E. 2009. IntCal09 and Marine09 Radiocarbon Age Calibration Curves, 0–50,000 Years cal BP. *Radiocarbon* 59(4): 1111–1150.

Renfrew, C. 1973. *Before Civilization: The radiocarbon revolution and prehistoric Europe*. London: Jonathan Cape.

Renfrew, C., Boyd, M. and Bronk Ramsey, C. 2012. The oldest maritime sanctuary? Dating the sanctuary at Keros and the Cycladic Early Bronze Age. *Antiquity* 86: 144–160.

Roaf, M. 2012. The Fall of Babylon in 1499 NC or 1595 MC. *Akkadica* 133: 147–174.

Rose, C.B. and Darbyshire, G. (eds.). 2011. *The New Chronology of Iron Age Gordion*. Gordion Special Studies VI. Philadelphia: University of Pennsylvania Museum of Archaeology and Anthropology.

Rutter, J.B. 2011. Late Minoan IB at Kommos: a sequence of at least three distinct stages. In T.M. Brogan and E. Hallager (eds.), *LM IB pottery: relative chronology and regional differences. Acts of a workshop held at the Danish Institute at Athens in collaboration with the INSTAP Study Center for East Crete, 27–29 June 2007*: 307–343. Monographs of the Danish Institute at Athens Volume 11. Athens: The Danish Institute at Athens.

Salzer, M.W. and Hughes, M.K. 2007. Bristlecone pine tree rings and volcanic eruptions over the last 5000 yr. *Quaternary Research* 67: 57–68.

Sarpaki, A. 1990. 'Small fields or big fields?' That is the question. In D.A. Hardy, J. Keller, V.P. Galanopoulos, N.C. Flemming and T.H. Druitt (eds.), *Thera and the Aegean world III. Volume two: earth sciences*: 422–431. London: The Thera Foundation.

Sarpaki, A. 1992. A Palaeoethnobotanical Study of the West House, Akrotiri, Thera. *Annual of the British School at Athens* 87: 219–230.

Sarpaki, A. 2001. Processed cereals and pulses from the Late Bronze Age site of Akrotiri, Thera: preparations prior to consumption, a preliminary approach to their study. *Annual of the British School at Athens* 96: 27–41.

Sass-Klaassen, U., Vernimmen, T. and Baittinger, C. 2008. Dendrochronological dating and provenancing of timber used as foundation piles under historic buildings in The Netherlands. *International Biodeterioration & Biodegradation* 61: 96–105.

Schnapp. A. 2002. Between antiquarians and archaeologists – continuities and raptures. *Antiquity* 76: 134–140.

Schneider, T. 2010a. Contributions to the Chronology of the New Kingdom and the Third Intermediate Period. *Ägypten und Levante* 20: 373–403.

Schneider, T. 2010b. A Theophany of Seth-Baal in the Tempest Stele. *Ägypten und Levante* 20: 405–409.

Sewell, D.A. 2001. *Earth, air, fire and water. An elemental analysis of the Minoan eruption of the Santorini volcano in the Late Bronze Age*. Ph.D. dissertation, University of Reading. Available at: http://santorini-eruption.org.uk/.

Shaw, M.C. 2009. A Bull-Leaping Fresco from the NileDelta and a Search for Patrons and Artists. *American Journal of Archaeology* 113: 471–477.

Shelmerdine, C.W. (ed). 2008. *The Cambridge companion to the Aegean Bronze Age*. Cambridge: Cambridge University Press.

Shortland, A.J. and Bronk Ramsey, C. (eds.). 2013. *Radiocarbon and the Chronologies of Ancient Egypt*. Oxford: Oxbow Books.

Sigurdsson, H., Carey, S., Alexandri, M., Vougioukalakis, G., Croff, K., Roman, C., Sakellariou, D., Anagnostou, C., Rousakis, G., Ioakim, C., Gogou, A., Ballas, D., Misaridis, T., Nomikou, P., 2006.

Marine investigations of Greece's Santorini volcanic field. *EOS, Transactions American Geophysical Union* 87 (24): 337–342.

Siklósy, Z., Demény, A., Vennemann, T.W., Pilet, S., Kramers, J., Leél-Őssy, S., Bondár, M., Chuan-Chou Shen, C.-C. and Hegner, E. 2009. Bronze Age volcanic event recorded in stalagmites by combined isotope and trace element studies. *Rapid Communications in Mass Spectrometry* 23: 801–808.

Sivertsen, B.J. 2009. *The Parting of the Sea: How Volcanoes, Earthquakes, and Plagues Shaped the Story of Exodus.* Princeton: Princeton University Press.

Sørensen, A.H. 2009. An update on the chronological value of Minoica in the Levant and Cyprus. In D.A. Warburton (ed.), *Time's Up! Dating the Minoan eruption of Santorini. Acts of the Minoan Eruption Chronology Workshop, Sandbjerg November 2007 initiated by Jan Heinemeier & Walter L. Friedrich*: 267–273. Monographs of the Danish Institute at Athens Volume 10. Athens: The Danish Institute at Athens.

Soles, J.S. 2004. Radiocarbon results. In J.S. Soles, *et al., Mochlos IC. Period III. Neopalatial settlement on the coast: the Artisan's Quarter and the Farmhouse at Chalinomouri. The Small Finds*: 145–149. Philadelphia: INSTAP Academic Press.

Soles, J.S. 2009. The impact of the Minoan eruption of Santorini on Mochlos. In D.A. Warburton (ed.), *Time's Up! Dating the Minoan eruption of Santorini. Acts of the Minoan Eruption Chronology Workshop, Sandbjerg November 2007 initiated by Jan Heinemeier & Walter L. Friedrich*: 107–116. Monographs of the Danish Institute at Athens Volume 10. Athens: The Danish Institute at Athens.

Soter, S. 2011. Radiocarbon Anomalies from Old CO_2 in the Soil and Canopy Air. *Radiocarbon* 53(1): 55–69.

Southon, J.R. 2002. A first step to resolving the GISP2 and GRIP ice-core chronologies, 0–14,500 yr BP. *Quaternary Research* 57: 32–37.

Southon, J. 2004. A Radiocarbon Perspective on Greenland Ice-Core Chronologies: can we use ice cores for ^{14}C calibration? *Radiocarbon* 46(3): 1239–1259.

Sparks, R. 2003. Egyptian Stone Vessels and the Politics of Exchange (2617–1070 BC). In R. Matthews and C. Roemer (eds.), *Ancient Perspectives on Egypt*: 39–56. London: University College London Press.

Sparks, R.S.J. and Wilson, C.J.N. 1990. The Minoan Deposits: a Review of their Characteristics and Interpretation. In D.A. Hardy, J. Keller, V.P. Galanopoulos, N.C. Flemming and T.H. Druitt (eds.), *Thera and the Aegean World III. Vol. 2: Earth Sciences. Proceedings of the Third International Congress, Santorini, Greece, 3–9 September 1989*: 89–99. London: The Thera Foundation.

Steel, J.M. (ed.). 2010. *Calendars and Years: Astronomy and Time in the Ancient Near East.* Oxford: Oxbow Books.

Sterba, J.H., Foster, K.P., Steinhauser, G. and Bichler, M. 2009. New light on old pumice: the origins of Mediterranean volcanic material from ancient Egypt. *Journal of Archaeological Science* 36: 1738–1744.

Stokes, M.A. and Smiley, T.L. 1968. *An Introduction to Tree-Ring Dating.* Chicago: University of Chicago Press.

Stubbings, F.H. 1970. The Aegean Bronze Age. In I.E.S. Edwards, C.J. Gadd and N.G.L. Hammond (eds.), *The Cambridge Ancient History*, vol. I, part 1: 239–247. Third edition. Cambridge: Cambridge University Press.

Stuiver, M. and Reimer, P.J. 1989. Histograms obtained from computerized radiocarbon age calibration. *Radiocarbon* 31(3): 817–823.

Sullivan, D.G. 1990. Minoan tephra in lake sediments in western Turkey: dating the eruption and assessing the atmospheric dispersal of the ash. In D.A. Hardy and A.C. Renfrew (eds.), *Thera and the Aegean world III. Volume three: chronology*: 114–119. London: The Thera Foundation.

Tarling, D.H. and Downey, W.S. 1990. Archaeomagnetic results from Late Minoan destruction levels on Crete and the 'Minoan' tephra on Thera. In D.A. Hardy and A.C. Renfrew (eds.), *Thera and the Aegean world III. Volume three: chronology*: 146–158. London: The Thera Foundation.

Tauber, H. 1983. Possible Depletion in ^{14}C in trees growing in calcareous soils. *Radiocarbon* 25(2): 417–420.

Taylor, R.E., Beaumont, W.C., Southon, J., Stronach, D. and Pickworth, D. 2010. Alternative Explanations for Anomalous ^{14}C Ages on Human Skeletons Associated with the 612 BCE Destruction of Nineveh. *Radiocarbon* 52(2): 372–382.

Tegel, W., Elburg, R., Hakelberg, D., Stäuble, H. and Büntgen, U. 2012. Early Neolithic Water Wells

Reveal the World's Oldest Wood Architecture. *PLoS ONE* 7(12): e51374.doi:10.1371/journal. pone.0051374.

Tema, E. and Kondopoulou, D. 2011. Secular variation of the Earth's magnetic field in the Balkan region during the last eight millennia based on archaeomagnetic data. *Geophysical Journal International* 186: 603–614.

Tyers, C. 2008. Bayesian Interpretation of Tree-Ring Dates in Practice. *Vernacular Architecture* 39: 91–106.

Vandersleyen, C. 2003. Keftiu: a cautionary note. *Oxford Journal of Archaeology* 22: 209–212.

Vinther B.M., Clausen, H.B., Johnsen, S.J., Rasmussen, S.O., Andersen, K.K., Buchardt, S.L., Dahl-Jensen, D., Seierstad, I.K., Siggaard-Andersen, M.-L., Steffensen, J.P., Svensson, A., Olsen, J. and Heinemeier, J. 2008. Reply to comment by J. S. Denton and N. J. G. Pearce on "A synchronized dating of three Greenland ice cores throughout the Holocene". *Journal of Geophysical Research* 113: D12306, doi:10.1029/2007JD009083.

Voutsaki, S., Dietz, S. and Nijboer, A. 2009a. Radiocarbon Analysis and the History of the east Cemetery, Asine. *Opuscula. Annual of the Swedish Institutes at Athens and Rome* 2: 31-52.

Voutsaki, S., Nijboer, A.J. and Zerner, C. 2009b. Middle Helladic Lerna: Relative and Absolute Chronologies. In S.W. Manning and M.J. Bruce (eds.), *Tree-Rings, Kings and Old World Archaeology and Environment: Papers Presented in Honor of Peter Ian Kuniholm*: 151–161. Oxford: Oxbow Books.

Warburton, D.A. (ed.). 2009a. *Time's Up! Dating the Minoan eruption of Santorini. Acts of the Minoan Eruption Chronology Workshop, Sandbjerg November 2007 initiated by Jan Heinemeier & Walter L. Friedrich*. Monographs of the Danish Institute at Athens Volume 10. Athens: The Danish Institute at Athens.

Warburton, D. A., 2009b, Chronology, stratigraphy, typology & Tell el-Dab'a. Postscript. In D.A. Warburton (ed.), *Time's Up! Dating the Minoan eruption of Santorini. Acts of the Minoan Eruption Chronology Workshop, Sandbjerg November 2007 initiated by Jan Heinemeier & Walter L. Friedrich*: 139–144. Monographs of the Danish Institute at Athens Volume 10. Athens: The Danish Institute at Athens.

Ward, G.K. and Wilson, S.R. 1978. Procedures for comparing and combining radiocarbon age determinations: a critique. *Archaeometry* 20: 19–31.

Warren, P.M. 1979. The stone vessels from the Bronze Age settlement at Akrotiri, Thera. *Arkhaiologike Ephemeris*: 82–113.

Warren, P. 1984. Absolute dating of the Bronze Age eruption of Thera (Santorini). *Nature* 308: 492–493.

Warren, P. 1998. Aegean Late Bronze 1–2 absolute chronology – some new contributions. In M.S. Balmuth and R.H. Tykot (eds.), *Sardinian and Aegean chronology: towards the resolution of relative and absolute dating in the Mediterranean*: 323–331. Studies in Sardinian Archaeology V. Oxford: Oxbow.

Warren, P. 2006. The Date of the Thera Eruption in Relation to Aegean-Egyptian Interconnections and the Egyptian Historical Chronology. In E. Czerny, I. Hein, H. Hunger, D. Melman and A. Schwab (eds.), *Timelines: Studies in Honor of Manfred Bietak, Volume II*: 305–321. OLA 149. Leuven: Peeters.

Warren, P. 2009. The date of the Late Bronze Age eruption of Santorini. In D.A. Warburton (ed.), *Time's Up! Dating the Minoan eruption of Santorini. Acts of the Minoan Eruption Chronology Workshop, Sandbjerg November 2007 initiated by Jan Heinemeier & Walter L. Friedrich*: 181–186. Monographs of the Danish Institute at Athens Volume 10. Athens: The Danish Institute at Athens.

Warren, P.M. 2010. The Absolute Chronology of the Aegean circa 2000 B.C.–1400 B.C. A Summary. In W. Müller (ed.), *Die Bedeutung der minoischen und mykenischen Glyptik. VI. Internationales Siegel-Symposium aus Anlass des 50 jährigen Bestehens des CMS Marburg, 9.-12. Oktober 2008*: 383–394. CMS Beiheft 8. Mainz: Philipp von Zabern.

Warren, P. and Hankey, V. 1989. *Aegean Bronze Age chronology*. Bristol: Bristol Classical Press.

Weinstein, G.A. and Betancourt, P.P. 1978. Problems of interpretation of the Akrotiri Radiocarbon dates. In C. Doumas (ed.), *Thera and the Aegean World I*: 805–814. London: Thera and the Aegean World.

Weninger, B. 1986. High-precision calibration of archaeological radiocarbon dates. In *Acta Interdisciplinaria Archaeologica* 4: 11–53. (= Papers of the symposium held at the Institute of Archaeology of the Slovak Academy of Sciences, Nové Vozokany, October 28–31, 1985, Nitra: Archeologický ústav Slovenskej akadémie vied.)

Weninger, B. 1990. Theoretical radiocarbon discrepancies. In D.A. Hardy and A.C. Renfrew (eds.), *Thera and the Aegean world III. Volume three: chronology*: 216–231. London: The Thera Foundation.

Weninger, B., Edinborough, K., Clare, L. and Jöris, O. 2011. Concepts of probability in radiocarbon analysis. *Documenta Praehistorica* 38: 1–20.

Weninger, F., Steier, P., Kutschera, W. and Wild, E.M. 2010. Robust Bayesian Analysis, an Attempt to Improve Bayesian Sequencing. *Radiocarbon* 52(3): 962–983.

Wente, E.F. and van Siclen, C.C. 1976. A chronology of the New Kingdom. In J.H. Johnson and E.F. Wente (eds.), *Studies in honour of George R. Hughes, January 12, 1977*: 217–261. Studies in Ancient Oriental Civilization 39. Chicago: Oriental Institute.

West, M.L. 1997. *The East Face of Helicon: West Asiatic Elements in Greek Poetry and Myth.* Oxford: Oxford University Press.

Whitley, J. 2001. *The Archaeology of Ancient Greece.* Cambridge: Cambridge University Press.

Whittle, A., Bayliss, A. and Healey, F. 2008. The timing and tempo of change: examples from the fourth millennium cal BC in southern England. *Cambridge Archaeological Journal* 18: 65–70.

Whittle, A., Healy, F. and Bayliss, A. (eds.). 2011. *Gathering Time: Dating the Early Neolithic Enclosures of Southern Britain and Ireland.* Oxford: Oxbow Books.

Wiener, M.H. 2001. The White Slip I of Tell el-Dab'a and Thera: critical challenge for the Aegean Long Chrobology. In V. Karageorghis (ed.), *The White Slip Ware of Late Bronze Age Cyprus. Proceedings of an International Conference Organized by the Anastasios G. Leventis Foundation, Nicosia in Honour of Malcolm Wiener*: 195–202. Wien: Verlag der Österreichischen Akademie der Wissenschaften.

Wiener, M.H. 2003. Time out: the current impasse in Bronze Age archaeological dating. In K.P. Foster and R. Laffineur (eds.), *Metron: measuring the Aegean Bronze Age*: 363–399. Aegaeum 24. Liège: Université de Liège, Service d'histoire de l'art et d'archéologie de la Grèce antique and University of Texas, Program in Aegean Scripts and Prehistory.

Wiener M.H. 2006a. Chronology going forward (with a query about 1525/4 B.C.). In E. Czerny, I. Hein, H. Hunger, D. Melman and A. Schwab (eds.), *Timelines: Studies in Honor of Manfred Bietak, Volume III*: 317–328. OLA 149. Leuven: Peeters.

Wiener, M.H. 2006b. Egypt & Time. *Ägypten und Levante* 16: 325–339.

Wiener, M.H. 2007. Times Change: The Current State of the Debate in Old World Chronology. In M. Bietak and E. Czerny (eds.), *The Synchronisation of Civilisations in the Eastern Mediterranean in the Second Millennium B.C. – III*: 25–47. Wien: Verlag der Österreichischen Akademie der Wissenschaften.

Wiener, M.H. 2009a. Cold fusion: the uneasy alliance of history and science. In S.W. Manning and M.J. Bruce (eds.), *Tree-Rings, Kings and Old World Archaeology and Environment: Papers Presented in Honor of Peter Ian Kuniholm*: 277–292, 317–327, 329–330. Oxford: Oxbow Books.

Wiener M.H. 2009b. The state of the debate about the date of the Theran eruption. In D.A. Warburton (ed.), *Time's Up! Dating the Minoan Eruption of Santorini. Acts of the Minoan Eruption Chronology Workshop, Sandbjerg November 2007 initiated by Jan Heinemeier & Walter L. Friedrich*: 197–206. Monographs of the Danish Institute at Athens Volume 10. Athens: The Danish Institute at Athens.

Wiener, M.H. 2010. A point in time. In O. Krzyszkowska (ed.), *Cretan Offerings: Studies in Honour of Peter Warren*: 367–394. London: The British School at Athens.

Wiener, M.H. 2012. Problems in the Measurement, Calibration, Analysis, and Communication of Radiocarbon Dates (with Special Reference to the Prehistory of the Aegean World). *Radiocarbon* 54 (3–4): 423–434.

Wiener, M.H. and Allen, J.P. 1998. Separate lives: the Ahmose tempest Stela and the Theran eruption. *Journal of Near Eastern Studies* 57: 1–28.

Wigley, T.M.L., Jones, P.D. and Briffa, K.R. 1987. Cross-dating methods in Dendrochronology. *Journal of Archaeological Science* 14: 51–64.

Wild, E.M., Gauß, W., Forstenpointner, G., Lindblom, M., Smetana, R., Steier, P., Thanheiser, U., Weninger, F. 2010. ^{14}C dating of the Early to Late Bronze Age stratigraphic sequence of Aegina Kolonna, Greece. *Nuclear Instruments and Methods in Physics Research B* 268 (7–8): 1013–1021.

Younger, J.G. 2009. The Bull-Leaping Scenes from Tell el-Dab'a. *American Journal of Archaeology* 113: 479–480.

10. Postscript

After the Revisit Essay was written and this second edition went into production, a new revised international radiocarbon (^{14}C) calibration curve has been published for use for the northern hemisphere: IntCal13 (Reimer *et al.* 2013). IntCal13 makes only small changes in the time period relevant to the Santorini/Thera topic when compared to the previous IntCal09 (as used in the Revisit Essay). Some additional tree-ring data are included (evident for example in the mid 14th through 13th centuries BC – see also discussion regarding part of this period concerning IntCal09 in Manning *et al.* 2013), and some small changes were implemented in the modelling. In this postscript I review in brief the significance and impact of the IntCal13 calibration to the Thera date topic, and to some of the discussions in the Revisit Essay above.

(i) Comparisons and Differences Between the IntCal09 and IntCal13 Calibration Datasets with regard to the Thera VDL Date Range

Figure RE33 compares the previous IntCal09 calibration curve (Reimer *et al.* 2009) versus the new IntCal13 calibration curve (Reimer *et al.* 2013) for the Thera-relevant period of 1800–1100 BC. In several sections there is almost no change; however, a relatively small but substantial change – to slightly older ^{14}C values for the calibration curve – is evident for the period from the mid-14th through 13th centuries BC, and some very small changes – mainly to slightly more recent ^{14}C ages – can be observed in the period from the later 17th through 16th centuries BC. The latter are of course directly relevant to the Thera dating topic. The small 17th–16th century BC changes have the effect of slightly *reducing* the Thera dating ambiguity in the mid-16th century BC, and of *increasing* the (already strong) likelihood of a 17th century BC date for the eruption. Figure RE34 shows the comparison for the period 1700–1450BC in greater detail – highlighting that the point (in terms of ^{14}C age) of 16th century BC ambiguity (1σ calibration curve ranges) is lower/later with IntCal13, thus reducing the probability of a 16th century BC date for the plausible/possible weighted average ^{14}C age estimates for the Thera Volcanic Destruction Level (VDL) from short-lived samples (see Revisit Essay above; Manning and Kromer 2012; 2011a).

Figure RE35A shows a comparison of the calibrated calendar age probabilities and ranges for (a) the two weighted average ages for sets of data on short-lived samples from the Akrotiri VDL discussed and shown in Figure RE7 but employing IntCal13 versus IntCal09, and (b) the comparison for the 'even if' lowest plausible ^{14}C date range for the Akrotiri VDL subjectively selecting the low date clump of data from the overall set of short-lived samples as discussed in Manning and Kromer (2012). When comparing the IntCal13 probability ranges versus those from IntCal09, we see a noticeable small shift to older calendar ages in the 17th–16th century BC period. Thus for the 3344 ± 9 ^{14}C years BP average there is now *no* 16th century BC range even within the 95.4% probability range (and there is none for the 3346 ± 8 ^{14}C years BP value from either calibration dataset), and, even for the lowest plausible weighted average value of 3326 ± 11 ^{14}C years BP from a subjective choice to use the clump of lower ages in the overall Akrotiri VDL set (see Manning and Kromer 2012), there is now a much clearer

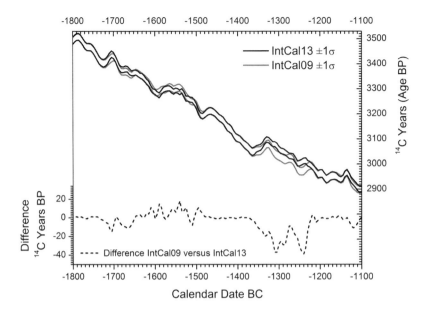

Figure RE33. Top: comparison of the IntCal13 ¹⁴C calibration curve (Reimer et al. 2013) (1σ range) versus the previous IntCal09 ¹⁴C calibration curve 1800–1100 BC (Reimer et al. 2009) (1σ range). Where IntCal09 is not visible it is hidden by (so effectively identical to) IntCal13. Bottom: Difference in ¹⁴C years of IntCal09 versus IntCal13.

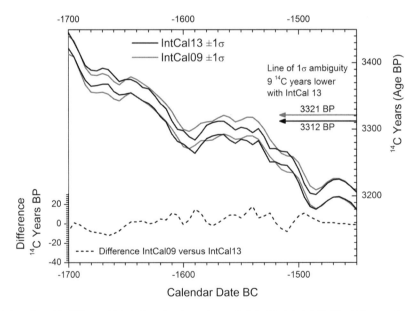

Figure RE34. Detail of Figure RE33 showing just the period 1700–1450 BC. The ¹⁴C age where the 16th century BC ambiguity (17th century BC or 16th century BC) starts at 1σ is also indicated – it is 9 ¹⁴C years later/lower with IntCal13.

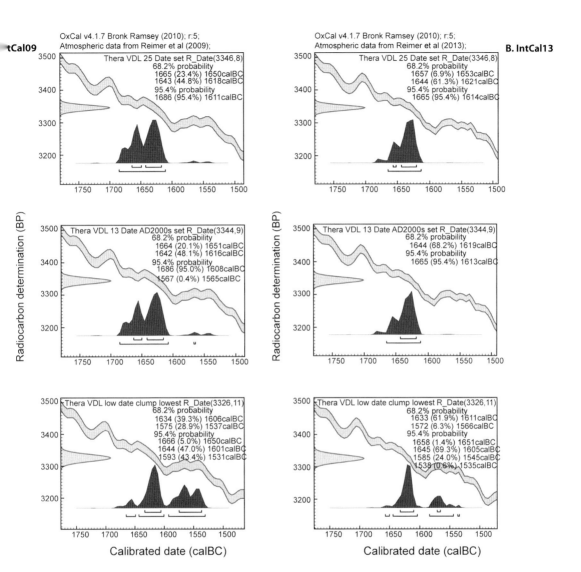

Figure RE35A. A comparison of the calibrated calendar probability distributions and most likely 68.2% and 95.4% probability calendar age ranges for (top) the weighted average value from the most appropriate 25-date set of short-lived samples from the Akrotiri VDL (see Figure RE7 above), (middle) the weighted average value for the 13-date AD2000s-run set of short-lived samples from the Akrotiri VDL (see Figure RE7 above), and (bottom) the lowest of the possible/plausible weighted averages for the subjective low-date clump of ages in the overall Akrotiri VDL date set of short-lived samples (see Manning and Kromer 2012). On the left are the probabilities and ranges employing the IntCal09 (Reimer et al. 2009) calibration dataset; on the right are the values employing the new IntCal13 (Reimer et al. 2013) calibration dataset. Data from OxCal 4.1.7 with curve resolution set at 5 (Bronk Ramsey 2009a).

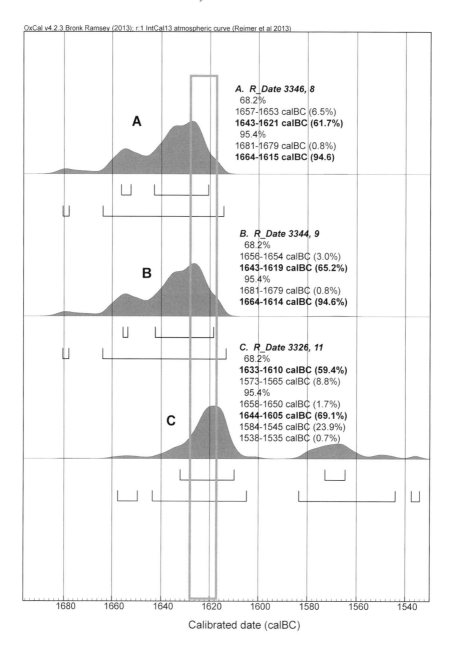

*Figure RE35B. The three weighted average ages for the Thera VDL shown in Figure RE35A, but re-run employing IntCal13 (Reimer et al. 2013) with the calibrated curve resolution now set at 1. A = 3346 ± 8 ^{14}C years BP, B = 3344 ± 9 ^{14}C years BP and C = 3326 ± 11 ^{14}C years BP. Data from OxCal 4.2.3 (Bronk Ramsey 2009a). The grey box indicates the common mode region c.1628–1617BC. The main calibrated calendar age ranges, where there are several, are in **bold**.*

preference for a 17th century BC date range: 61.9% probability with IntCal13 versus 39.3% probability with IntCal09 within the most likely 68.2% probability range, and, when looking at the 95.4% probability ranges, there is just a 24.6% probability for a date after 1600BC with IntCal13 versus a 43.4% with IntCal09. If re-run again with the calibration curve modelled at 1-year resolution, the modes (single most likely year) of the three IntCal13 calibrated probability distributions shown in Figure RE35A all lie between c.1628 to 1617 BC: see Figure RE35B. The overall common 68.2% region (or main 68.2% region for Figure RE35B no. C) lies 1643–1605 BC. In other words, the new IntCal13 calibration curve makes the Thera dating case advocated in the Revisit Essay above even a little more likely.

Figure RE36A shows the analyses in Figures RE9 (above) re-run employing the IntCal13 ^{14}C calibration curve – these consider the date of the Thera VDL by modelling the dates on short-lived samples using a Tau_Boundary paired with a Boundary in OxCal (see discussion of Figure RE9 above). There is very little difference comparing Figure RE36A with Figure RE9, but the probability of a 17th century BC date is slightly increased, and the possibility of a 16th century BC ambiguity is further slightly reduced. In the Revisit Essay, Section 3.III.ii.c, a further robustness model was considered: re-running the Tau_Boundary paired with a Boundary model for the Phase of 25 ^{14}C dates on short-lived material from the Akrotiri VDL (so Figures RE9B and RE36A no. B) but adding, arbitrarily and rather expansively, a ΔR allowance of 0 ± 20 ^{14}C years (Figure RE25). Let us thus consider this Figure RE25 case employing IntCal13: see Figure RE36B. If we compare Figure RE36B with Figure RE25 we see very little difference. Even adding such a large extra error still leaves the entire most likely 68.2% probability in the mid-late 17th century BC: 1654–1610 BC. Looking at the overall 95.4% probability range, 84.9% of the total probability range falls between 1681-1597 BC, and there is only a small unlikely 16th century range of 1575–1530 BC with a probability of just 10.5%. The change to IntCal13 has slightly narrowed the likely 17th century BC range, and slightly reduced (from 14% to 10.5%) the low probability and unlikely mid-16th century BC range within the overall 95.4% range.

Therefore, it is clear that use of the new IntCal13 ^{14}C calibration curve only adds additional support for the likelihood that the 'high' Aegean Late Bronze Age chronology is both the correct, and appropriate, timescale for the mid-second millennium BC Aegean (and the basis for the synchronization of the Aegean civilizations with the rest of the east Mediterranean and ancient Near East at this time) – reinforcing the arguments reviewed above in the Revisit Essay. Whereas with IntCal09 it seemed, if simplifying and rounding, that the most likely date for the Thera VDL and eruption was somewhere around the last three decades of the 17th century BC, it is perhaps more accurate with IntCal13 to revise this statement to the last four decades of the 17th century BC if one considers the most likely 68.2% ranges in Figures RE35A, RE35B and RE36A. A betting person would suggest a narrower most likely range, between c.1630 and 1610 BC.

Finally, we can consider re-runs of (some of) the Aegean late MBA through LMII sequences (adaptations and up-dates of the Manning *et al.* 2006a analysis) employing IntCal13. Figure RE37 shows a re-run of the original Manning *et al.* (2006a) Model 1 sequence, and Figure RE38 shows a re-run of the modified sequence as in Figure RE12 above. The date ranges for various elements of each figure are listed in Table RE13

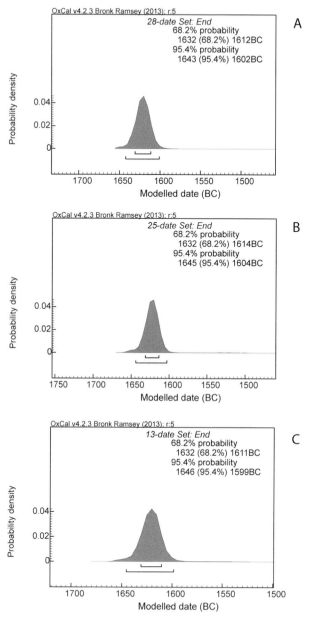

Figure RE36A. Re-run of Figure RE9 employing IntCal13 (Reimer et al. 2013). The modelled End of the Akrotiri VDL phase = 'End' based on short-lived samples from the Akrotiri VDL grouped as a Phase with a Tau_Boundary as the start of the Phase and a Boundary at the end – to model exponentially distributed events tending towards the end of the Phase – using OxCal 4.2.3 (Bronk Ramsey 2009a) and IntCal13 with curve resolution set at 5. (A) Employs the 28-date set in Manning et al. (2006a); (B) Employs the 25-date subset of this set excluding the 3 Heidelberg dates as shown in Figure RE2; and (C) Employs just the 13-date sub-set of measurements run in the AD 2000s as reported by Manning et al. (2006a). Note: it is possible to get slight variations in outputs from such modelling runs in OxCal, typically within 0–2 years at most.

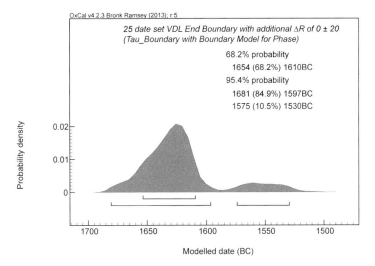

OxCal v4.2.3 Bronk Ramsey (2013): r:5

25 date set VDL End Boundary with additional ΔR of 0 ± 20 (Tau_Boundary with Boundary Model for Phase)

68.2% probability
1654 (68.2%) 1610BC
95.4% probability
1681 (84.9%) 1597BC
1575 (10.5%) 1530BC

Figure RE36B. Re-run of Figure RE25 employing IntCal13 (Reimer et al. 2013). This is thus a revised version of Figure RE36A, no. B, when re-run adding an additional allowance for an uncertainty of 20 ^{14}C years to cover a hypothetical local CO_2 reservoir offset of some form – for which there is at present no evidence and indeed evidence to the contrary (see Revisit Essay Section 3.c.III.1 above, and the text discussion of Figure RE25). This plot is of the 25 date set of measurements on short-lived samples from the Akrotiri VDL (Figure RE2) modelled as a Phase with a Tau_Boundary paired with a Boundary, so that the data are assumed to be distributed exponentially towards the end of the Phase. Data from OxCal 4.2.3 (Bronk Ramsey 2009a) with curve resolution set at 5.

(compare to Tables RE3A and RE3B above). Again we see that use of IntCal13 only introduces small changes in some cases, and, if anything, provides a slightly clearer case in favour of the 'high' Aegean LBA chronology. The Akrotiri VDL (and Thera eruption) lie in the later 17th century BC, the Late and Final LMIB destructions lie in a period from the late 16th century BC through to the earlier to mid 15th century BC – leaving the earlier through late LMIB period prior to the LMIB Late destructions in the time-span from the close of the 17th century BC to the late 16th century BC as part of a long LMIB overall period – and the LMII destruction at Knossos is placed in the later-late 15th century BC.

(ii) IntCal13 and the Thera Olive Branch

Examination of the results of calibrating the ^{14}C dates on the olive branch sample (Friedrich *et al.* 2006) with IntCal13 instead of IntCal09 (e.g. re-running the data shown in Figures RE16 and RE17) yields findings similar to those discussed above for the Thera VDL dates. If we abstain from using any claimed ring-counts at all for the olive sample – see Revisit Essay Section 3.c.III.i.c above – and merely use the sequence from inner to outer parts of the growth history of the branch sample, then the date for the final dated segment employing IntCal13 is as shown in Figure RE39. This is very similar to (and in fact very slightly older than) the IntCal09 results shown in Figure

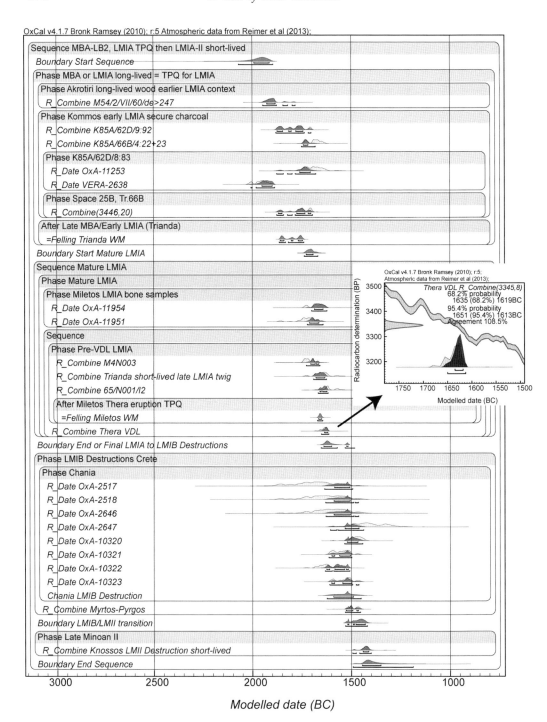

OxCal v4.1.7 Bronk Ramsey (2010); r:5 Atmospheric data from Reimer et al (2013);

Figure RE37. A re-run of the Model 1 sequence analysis in Manning et al. *(2006a) but employing the IntCal13 ¹⁴C calibration dataset (Reimer* et al. *2013) and OxCal 4.1.7 (Bronk Ramsey 2009a).*

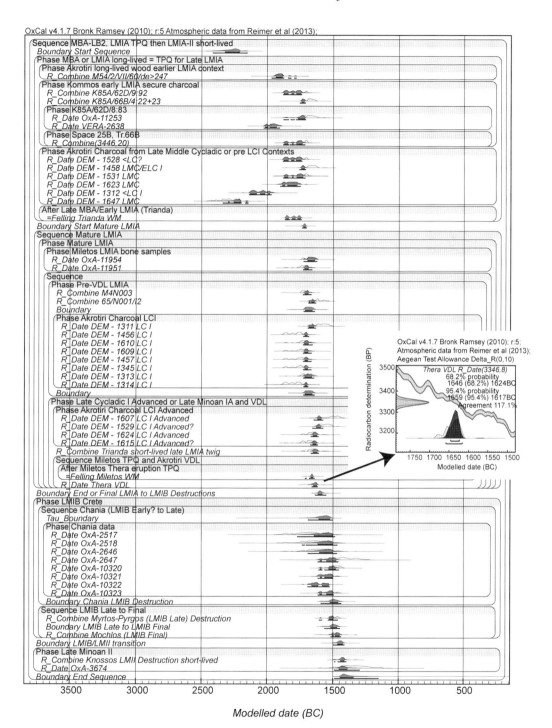

Figure RE38. A re-run of the Aegean sequence analysis in Figure RE12 but employing IntCal13 (Reimer et al. 2013) and OxCal 4.1.7 (Bronk Ramsey 2009a).

A Test of Time Revisited

	Akrotiri VDL	End Chania LMIB	Myrtos-Pyrgos LMIB Late Destruction	Mochlos LMIB Final Destruction	Knossos LMII Destruction
Manning *et al.* 2006a Model 1 (IntCal04) 68.2%	1656–1651 BC (11.3%) 1639–1616 BC (56.9%)	Not Stated	1517–1491 BC (58.1%) 1475–1467 BC (10.1%)	Not in Model	1439–1414 BC
Manning *et al.* 2006a Model 1 (IntCal04) 95.4%	1660–1612 BC	Not Stated	1522–1456 BC	Not in Model	1457–1399 BC
Figure RE37 68.2%	1635–1619 BC	1589–1490 BC	1526–1494 BC (60.4%) 1473–1466 BC (7.8%)	Not in Model	1443–1415 BC
Figure RE37 95.4%	1651–1613 BC	1622–1452 BC	1531–1455 BC	Not in Model	1494–1477 BC (6.5%) 1460–140 BC (88.9%)
Figure RE37 μ ± σ	1630 ± 9 BC	1534 ± 44 BC	1498 ± 21 BC	Not in Model	1434 ± 20 BC
Figure RE38 68.2%	1646–1624 BC	1522–1462 BC	1527–1499	1504–1496 BC (10.1%) 1482–1452 BC (58.1%)	1441–1416 BC
Figure RE38 95.4%	1659–1617 BC	1589–1568 BC (4.7%) 1560–1440 BC (90.7%)	1602–1583 BC (10.2%) 1536–1465 BC (85.2%)	1516–1440	1487–1483 BC (0.6%) 1461–1400 BC (94.8%)
Figure RE38 μ ± σ	1636 ± 11 BC	1500 ± 34 BC	1520 ± 29 BC	1476 ± 21 BC	1431 ± 17 BC
Figure RE38 No ΔR 68.2%	1639–1621 BC	1510–1458 BC	1520–1495 BC	1481–1448 BC	1437–1413 BC
Figure RE38 No ΔR 95.4%	1651–1615 BC	1537–1428 BC	1531–1464 BC	1502–1439 BC	1451–1400 BC
Figure RE38 No ΔR μ ± σ	1631 ± 8 BC	1487 ± 27 BC	1506 ± 19 BC	1468 ± 16 BC	1424 ± 14 BC

Table RE13. The calibrated calendar age ranges modelled for the end of site phase destructions at the Akrotiri VDL, LMIB Late Myrtos-Pyrgos, LMIB Final Mochlos and LMII Knossos and the end of phase (Tau_Boundary paired with a Boundary) Boundary for LMIB Chania from the models shown in Figures RE37 and RE38 employing IntCal13 – compare with Figures RE12–14 and Table 3A and Table 3B above (using IntCal09). The Figure RE38 model (like the Figure RE12 model) includes an extra ΔR factor of 0 ± 10 ¹⁴C years to allow for possible small regional ¹⁴C differences (versus the IntCal13 calibration curve record). The calibrated calendar age ranges with no ΔR factor are shown below.

RE17 above. The fit at 95.4% probability with the IntCal13 calibration curve of the 4 dates treated just as an ordered Sequence in OxCal and ignoring the supposed ring counts is shown in Figure RE40. Since the ^{14}C date for the outermost dated section of the wood provides a mid-point age (of the dated segment) at least some (unknown) period before the outermost preserved wood of the sample, the actual *terminus post quem* is after the last dated segment. As discussed in the Revisit Essay above, we might try to estimate such an interval based on the measurements (scale) of the segments versus the approximate calendar period indicated by the ^{14}C dates, or via other approaches. These sorts of estimates seem to indicate that the appropriate number is likely in single digits and not much more. If we were to allow up to 10 years, or even up to 20 years (which seems over generous: see discussion above in Revisit Essay Section 3.c.III.i.c), this still only takes the *terminus post quem* down to 1646–1599 BC or 1636–1589 BC, and clearly this date range supports the 'high' Aegean LBA chronology and a date for the Thera eruption in the late 17th century BC, or, at the very latest, in the very early 16th century BC. In no way are these data compatible with the 'low' or conventional chronology and dates after 1530 BC.

In addition to the Cherubini *et al.* (2013) paper which was noted in Revisit Essay Section 3.c.III.i.c above, another paper by Cherubini *et al.* (2014) argues, again, that no viable ring-counting/recognition is possible for olive sections and so the Thera/Santorini olive branch. These authors thus claim that the dating of the olive branch reported by Friedrich *et al.* (2006) should be treated with caution. The problems with recognizing

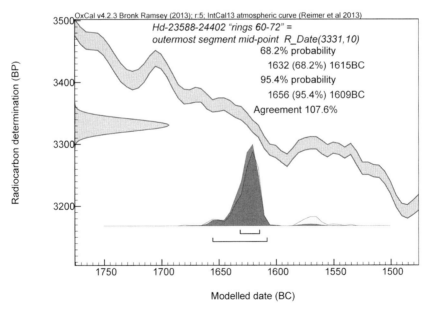

Figure RE39. Re-run of Figure RE17 employing IntCal13 and OxCal 4.2.3 (Bronk Ramsey 2009a). Plot shows the calendar dating probability distribution and most likely 68.2% and 95.4% probability age ranges for the mid-point of the outermost segment of the olive branch from the Sequence analysis shown in Figure RE16 – but here using IntCal13. No "rings" employed – just the ordered sequence from the innermost to outermost segments of the sample.

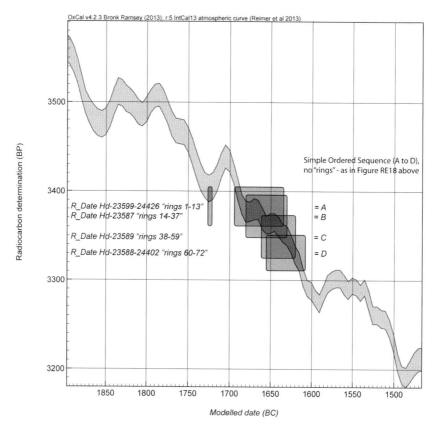

Figure RE40. Re-run of the data shown in Figure RE16 using IntCal13 (Reimer et al. 2013) and OxCal 4.2.3 (Bronk Ramsey 2009a). The figure shows the placements of the 95.4% probability fits of the mid-points of each of the dated segments of the Friedrich et al. (2006) olive branch against the IntCal13 ¹⁴C calibration curve (which is shown as a 1σ band). No "rings" are used, only the ordered sequence running from the innermost to the outermost segments of the olive branch (labeled as A, B, C, D in Figures RE16–18 above).

annual growth rings in olive are well-known, and this finding is entirely reasonable – however, the second claim is completely incorrect. I note (again – see Revisit Essay Section 3.c.III.i.c above) that it is important to appreciate that *even if* no ring-count sequence (of any robust sort) is possible for the Thera olive branch sample, then a simple Sequence analysis of the ¹⁴C dates on the sample, assuming no other information than the sequence of inner (older) to outer (more recent) sections of the olive sample nonetheless finds – see Figures RE16, RE17, RE18 and RE39 and RE40 – a likely later 17th century BC date for the outermost segment of the Thera olive branch. The 95.4% range ends (latest date) for the last dated segment at 1609 BC (see Figures RE39 and RE40). This is exactly contrary the claims of Cherubini *et al.* (2014). The Cherubini *et al.* (2014) paper otherwise exhibits poor or selective scholarship: it fails to take account of key literature relevant to the Thera dating topic subsequent to 2010 (such as any of the several important papers in *Radiocarbon* 54(3–4)), and is unaware that there is much less certainty over some of the archaeological evidence than they suggest or indicate via selective citation (instead, see e.g. the review and critique of Höflmayer 2012a, or, for the need to reconsider the date of Khyan from archaeological evidence and so the chronology of Tell e-Dab'a, see Moeller and Marouard 2011 – and of course see the Revisit Essay above). The Cherubini *et al.* (2014) paper ends in a simple nonsense claim when the authors state "Accordingly, caution should be taken with the dating by Friedrich *et al.* (2006) and their proposal cannot be used to discount a date range for the eruption of 1525–1490 BC proposed by numerous other radiocarbon studies". There are *no* numerous radiocarbon-based studies arguing for a date 1525–1490 BC. Indeed, in the debates over the Thera date question among knowledgeable scholars, it is generally accepted that the radiocarbon evidence offers effectively no dating probability after about 1525 BC (see Revisit Essay above; previously see e.g. Manning and Kromer 2011a; 2012).

(iii) IntCal13 and the ^{14}C Chronology of New Kingdom Egypt

The use of the new IntCal13 ^{14}C calibration curve (versus IntCal09) leads to minor changes in the date placements of the Egyptian dating models based on the study of Bronk Ramsey *et al.* (2010) as considered in the Revisit Essay. Table RE14 compares the results reported from the original Bronk Ramsey *et al.* (2010) model (as in their revised SOM – corrected 17 May 2011) from a re-run (adding three rulers at end: Siamun, Psusennes II and Shoshenq I) using all data and employing IntCal13 (compare to Tables RE1 and RE7). Only small differences are evident, and especially in the case of the 18th Dynasty rulers: all changes are less than 10 years. But it is noticeable that all changes are to slightly older date ranges – thus the findings of the Bronk Ramsey *et al.* (2010) paper in favour of the higher range of the historical chronologies of New Kingdom Egypt are only further reinforced when the new and improved IntCal13 ^{14}C calibration dataset is employed.[1]

Table RE15 provides the results from a re-run of the Bronk Ramsey *et al.* (2010) New Kingdom model but modifying the reign length data following the Aston (2012) 'high' historical chronology (the one Aston prefers) – so as reported in Tables RE1 and RE7 – and now employing IntCal13. A comparison of the age ranges reported in Table RE15 versus those for the Aston (2010) 'high' model in Tables RE1 and RE7 indicates only small changes, but, again, any movement in the dates of the 18th Dynasty rulers is towards slightly older dates – accentuating the findings of Bronk Ramsey *et al.* (2010) in favour of a higher historical chronology and the case and arguments presented above in the Revisit Essay using IntCal09.

---

[1] Since writing the Revisit Essay, the book of Shortland and Bronk Ramsey (2013) is now published, and should be consulted. This book includes additional details and discussion and some up-dates on the sample selection, pretreatment, accuracy and modelling work summarised in the Bronk Ramsey *et al.* (2010) study. All the analyses in Shortland and Bronk Ramsey (2013) however employ IntCal09 – so see this Postscript for reconsideration in light of IntCal13 – and they also do not include consideration of the revised and lengthened Egyptian historical chronology of Aston (2012) – so see the Revisit Essay above, and this Postscript.

King/Queen	Accession Dates BC							
	Modelled Highest Posterior Density (hpd) Ranges from Bronk Ramsey *et al.* (2010: Tables 1, S8) – IntCal09 as Tables RE1 and RE7				Modelled Highest Posterior Density (hpd) Ranges from Bronk Ramsey *et al.* (2010: Tables 1, S8) – *IntCal13*			
	68.2%		95.4%		68.2%		95.4%	
	from	to	from	to	from	to	from	to
Ahmose	1566	1552	1570	1544	1568	1556	1575	1548
Amenhotep I	1541	1527	1545	1519	1543	1531	1550	1523
Tuthmosis I	1520	1507	1524	1498	1522	1510	1529	1503
Tuthmosis II	1507	1495	1511	1487	1509	1498	1517	1491
Tuthmosis III	1494	1483	1498	1474	1496	1486	1504	1479
Amenhotep II	1441	1431	1445	1423	1444	1434	1452	1427
Tuthmosis IV	1414	1403	1418	1396	1417	1406	1425	1400
Amenhotep III	1404	1393	1408	1386	1407	1396	1415	1390
Amenhotep IV = Akhenaten	1365	1355	1370	1348	1369	1358	1377	1352
Smenkhare/ Neferneferuaten* & Ankhetkheperure	1351	1340	1356	1333	1355	1344	1364	1338
Tutankhamun	1349	1338	1353	1331	1353	1341	1362	1336
Ay	1339	1329	1344	1322	1344	1332	1353	1327
Horemheb	1336	1325	1341	1318	1340	1328	1350	1323
Ramesses I	1308	1297	1313	1290	1312	1300	1322	1294
Sety I	1307	1296	1312	1288	1311	1298	1321	1293
Ramesses II	1292	1281	1297	1273	1297	1283	1307	1278
Merneptah	1226	1215	1231	1207	1231	1217	1241	1212
Amenmesse + Seti II**	1216	1201	1221	1194	1221	1204	1232	1198
Siptah	1207	1189	1212	1187	1212	1198	1223	1192
Tewosre	1201	1189	1206	1181	1207	1191	1217	1186
Sethnakhte	1198	1187	1204	1179	1204	1189	1215	1184
Ramesses III	1196	1185	1202	1176	1202	1187	1213	1181
Ramesses IV	1165	1154	1171	1145	1171	1156	1183	1150
Ramesses V	1159	1148	1165	1139	1165	1149	1177	1144
Ramesses VI	1155	1144	1161	1135	1160	1145	1173	1140
Ramesses VII	1148	1137	1153	1127	1160	1137	1166	1133
Ramesses VIII	1141	1130	1146	1120	1153	1130	1160	1125
Ramesses IX	1137	1127	1143	1117	1150	1127	1157	1122
Ramesses X	1119	1109	1125	1099	1133	1109	1139	1104

Ramesses XI	1110	1100	1116	1090	1125	1099	1131	1095
Smendes	1080	1069	1085	1060	1095	1069	1101	1065
Amenemnesu	1054	1044	1059	1033	1070	1043	1075	1039
Psusennes I	1050	1039	1055	1029	1066	1039	1071	1035
Amenemope	1004	993	1010	983	1020	993	1025	989
Osochor***	995	984	1002	975	1011	984	1017	980
Siamun	NS	NS	NS	NS	1005	978	1011	973
Psusennes II	NS	NS	NS	NS	986	958	992	954
Shoshenq I	NS	NS	NS	NS	972	944	979	940

Table RE14. Comparison of the published Bronk Ramsey et al. (2010: Tables 1, S8) results, which used the IntCal09 ¹⁴C calibration dataset (Reimer et al. 2009) – on left with grey shading – versus a re-run of their (revised) model adding the three kings at the end (Siamun, Psusennes II and Shoshenq I – as in Tables RE1 and 7 above) employing the IntCal13 ¹⁴C calibration dataset (Reimer et al. 2013) – on right in table. Notes (as to Table RE7 above): *Bronk Ramsey et al. (2010: Table 1 and Table S8) only use Neferneferuaten but the relevant Boundary is 'Neferneferuaten, etc.' – I combine the independent (non-coregency) overall reign periods for Smenkhare and Ankhetkheperure with her reign (total c.4 years) in the re-run model. **Bronk Ramsey et al. (2010) have the reign order as Amenmesse and then Seti II, whereas the standard view in more recent scholarship of this complicated topic (see Schneider 2010a: 394–396) is that Seti II was the ruler and Amenmesse the rival and their reigns are either concurrent or perhaps Amenmesse continues in a separate reign after Seti II before the reign of Sethnakhte (following Schneider 2010a: 395–396) – however, as the Bronk Ramsey et al. (2010) model has no ¹⁴C data for either of these two reigns this little detail in fact makes no difference to the model outcomes. Here I conflate the two reigns into one stated period in the table. ***Bronk Ramsey et al. (2010) use the name Osorkon the Elder. Note: runs of such a model achieve slightly varying results each time, usually with variations of 0 to a couple of years; typical results from several runs shown.

With the accession date for Ahmose placed in Table RE15 from 1581-1571 BC at 68.2% probability (and 1585–1563 BC at 95.4% probability), and so a requirement for a high historical chronology for the early New Kingdom, the issue of the relationship of Egyptian history to the Thera question is very different when contrasted with scholarship that instead placed the accession of Ahmose c.1540 BC or so. With the high Egyptian dates, the accession of Ahmose could be within a few decades of the Thera eruption. The supposed great (and problematic) chronological 'gap' between the eruption horizon and the early 18th Dynasty (contrast e.g. Bietak 2003; Bietak and Höflmayer 2007; Eriksson 2007) is much reduced, and accordingly many of the claimed problems with the Aegean 'high' chronology largely evaporate (as also observed by Höflmayer 2012a, and see above in the Revisit Essay). Whether it is possible directly to link the accession of Ahmose with the Thera eruption (see discussion in the Revisit Essay Section 1 and footnote 6 above) based around the Ahmose Tempest Stele perhaps remains difficult if the eruption is late 17th century BC. It seems implausible to move the Egyptian dates much higher given the historical data constraints and the ¹⁴C data

	Accession Dates BC			
	Modelled hpd Ranges from re-runs of model in Tables RE1 and RE7 above using Aston (2012) 'high' chronology reign lengths *and* excluding outliers with greater than or equals 95% probability from initial model runs			
	68.2%		95.4%	
King/Queen	from	to	from	to
Ahmose	1581	1571	1585	1563
Amenhotep I	1556	1546	1559	1539
Tuthmosis I	1535	1526	1538	1518
Tuthmosis II	1522	1513	1525	1505
Tuthmosis III	1510	1500	1512	1492
Amenhotep II	1456	1447	1459	1440
Tuthmosis IV	1425	1416	1428	1409
Amenhotep III	1399	1389	1402	1382
Amenhotep IV = Akhenaten	1361	1351	1364	1345
Smenkhare/Neferneferuaten & Ankhetkheperure	1345	1334	1348	1328
Tutankhamun	1342	1331	1345	1325
Ay	1333	1323	1337	1316
Horemheb	1330	1318	1334	1312
Ramesses I	1315	1304	1319	1297
Seti I	1314	1301	1318	1294
Ramesses II	1305	1293	1309	1285
Merneptah	1239	1226	1243	1218
Seti II + Amenmesse	1229	1213	1233	1205
Siptah + Tewosre	1220	1200	1225	1192
Sethnakhte	1213	1198	1217	1190
Ramesses III	1211	1196	1215	1188
Ramesses IV	1180	1165	1185	1157
Ramesses V	1175	1159	1179	1150
Ramesses VI	1171	1153	1175	1146
Ramesses VII	1165	1145	1169	1139
Ramesses VIII	1158	1138	1162	1132
Ramesses IX	1156	1134	1159	1129
Ramesses X	1138	1116	1142	1110
Ramesses XI	1129	1106	1133	1101
Smendes	1100	1076	1103	1071
Amenemnesu	1074	1049	1078	1044
Psusennes I	1070	1045	1074	1040

Amenemope	1025	1000	1028	994
Osochor	1016	991	1020	985
Siamun	1010	985	1014	979
Psusennes II	991	966	995	960
Shoshenq I	978	952	982	946

Table RE15. Re-run of the 'high' models in Tables RE1 and RE7 after excluding dates in initial runs with outlier probabilities greater than or equals 95 employing IntCal13 (Reimer et al. 2013): 20 dates in all. Data from OxCal 4.1.7 (Bronk Ramsey 2009a). Each run of such a model produces slightly varying results – typical results from several runs listed. All individual convergence values are 95 or greater.

and calibration curve, and most evidence relevant to the Thera date indicates a likely placement a little earlier than potentially compatible (i.e. late 17th century BC versus early 16th century BC). Instead, the Thera eruption might perhaps more likely be placed in the reign of the Hyksos ruler Apophis (if Thera eruption is 1620s BC or later) or his predecessor (if a slightly earlier date for the Thera eruption).

These circumstances, and in addition the recent findings indicating that the important Hyksos (15th Dynasty) king Khyan, who had widespread links including to the Aegean (Knossos), is much earlier than previously thought and likely more or less contemporary with the late 13th Dynasty (Moeller and Marouard 2011), leaves the main 'Hyksos' period, and the associated east Mediterranean maritime trading world, from Khyan down to the Thera eruption, as lying in the period from the late 18th century BC to late 17th century BC. This century-scale era saw an important fusion of the Levantine, Egyptian and east Mediterranean worlds and cultures, and important transfers in technologies (e.g. metal-working, warfare) and material culture which were linked, or associated, with the Levantine-Hyksos world. East met west and north met south in a dynamic period in art, trade and societal change (e.g. Manning 1999: 136–144 and refs.). This was the time of the Shaft Graves and polity formation processes of Mycenaean Greece, the time of the MMIIIB-LMIA 'New Palaces' of Crete and the acme of the Minoan world and influence (its 'thalassocracy' if one prefers the term), and the time that large settlements, the first monumental structures, and initial urban processes develop on Cyprus (Knapp 2013: 350–351, 353, 360–363). The historical context for these key structural and structuring changes across the east Mediterranean region to the Aegean was the Levantine-led east Mediterranean trading world of the late Middle Bronze Age, with the Hyksos capital and its great harbour (with the hundreds of trading ships described by Kamose: see Redford 1997: 13–15) one of the focal points.

To date the Hyksos period has not received the attention it deserves, partly because of the dearth of written source material from the Hyksos themselves, and only a very limited and biased (negative) picture from the available Egyptian records (situation summarized by Schneider 2010: 157). Despite uncertainties over the site's dating/stratigraphy, the many finds at Tell el-Dab'a illustrate the extraordinary fusion of Levantine and Egyptian traditions and culture that marks the period from the later Middle Kingdom to the end of the Second Intermediate Period (nicely summarised by

Schneider 2010: 157–159). From early on (Bietak Stratum G) this includes evidence of contacts with the Aegean world (MacGillivray 1995; Walberg 1991). With the evidence to hand pointing fairly clearly to a 'high' Aegean LBA chronology, to a high Egyptian historical chronology for the earlier New Kingdom, and to a significant re-thinking of both the Hyksos (15th Dynasty) period and the dating and stratigraphic associations at the site of Tell el-Dab'a, we are now in a position to start to resolve the "disconcerting uncertainty as to precisely how the acme on Crete and contemporary Aegean societies fit with the wider pattern" (Broodbank 2013: 372).

To conclude this Egyptian-related discussion, I briefly mention the long article of Bietak (2013) which only appeared after the Revisit Essay was in production. This is another long and in places rather confused attempt by Bietak to defend positions undermined by ^{14}C evidence – and, of course, the problem that extensive ^{14}C dates and analysis indicates a different chronology for his own site, Tell el-Dab'a, and highlight problems with Bietak's assessment of the stratigraphy and supposed historical-archaeological associations. It of course includes further claims that the 'high' Aegean chronology is impossible. A few comments follow:

1. Bietak (2013: 76–77) generally accepts the importance of the Bronk Ramsey *et al.* (2010) study and agrees that it "seems to rule right out the low chronology of Hornung *et al.* (2006)". He notes that some minor revisions to reign lengths are necessary – something discussed in the Revisit Essay and this Postscript.

2. Bietak (2013: 77) suggests the 120 years offset between the ^{14}C chronology (Kutschera *et al.* 2012) and his chronology at Tell el-Dab'a might somehow be reduced to 80 years – still a major offset – and then re-asserts the view that the ^{14}C dates are too high (i.e. wrong) for some unstated reason. He refuses to consider that there are clearly reasons now critically to reassess his stratigraphic analyses and associations and instead re-summarises his published assessments (pp. 78–79). Bietak re-states the linkage of Strata late E/1 and early D/3 with Khyan (Khayan spelling in Bietak 2013). Oddly Bietak does not mention or cite the finds at Tell Edfu, despite Moeller and Marouard (2011) publishing in the journal (*Ägypten und Levante*) edited by Bietak. As noted in the Revisit Essay and this Postscript, these finds appear entirely contradictory to the Bietak placement of Strata late E1 and early D/3 around and after c.1600 BC (he dates Khyan's accession c.1602–1595 BC: pp.100–101 n.4 and his reign c.1600–1580 BC: p.86), and instead indicate that the correct age is around a century earlier linked to the late Middle Kingdom (mid 13th Dynasty)-early Second Intermediate Period (potentially very compatible with the ^{14}C dating results from Tell el-Dab'a). This of course would also significantly change/reverse the logic of Bietak (2013: 80–84) and the *stratigraphie comparée* model proposed there, and very especially Bietak's view drawn from the possible Khyan-Old Babylonian linkage (p.84) – if in reality this context is about a century earlier. To quote from the conclusions of Moeller and Marouard (2011: 109):

> "The sealings of Khayan were found in a secure archaeological context that has been identified as the last phase of activity and subsequent abandonment of an important

administrative complex, which can be securely dated by the ceramic evidence to the late Middle Kingdom (mid 13th Dynasty) – early Second Intermediate Period.

The presence of Khayan in the same context together with the other sealings of the late Middle Kingdom tradition, especially Sobekhotep IV, and those of the Palestinian series combined with the ceramic evidence and the ^{14}C date is very strong evidence for a chronological overlap of the late 13th and early 15th Dynasties. This discovery has certainly consequences for the overall length of the Second Intermediate Period".

3. Bietak (2013: 84) tries to dismiss the relevance of dendrochronology at Acemhöyük by saying all the wood could be re-used. Of course this claim can be made. But it seems implausible that it could apply consistently to a number of samples, and in the case of two structures at the site, and also to wood from another site (Kültepe).

4. Bietak (2013: 84–86) then starts his re-statement over several pages that the Aegean 'high' chronology and the late 17th century BC dating of the Thera eruption are impossible. First up is the Khyan lid from Knossos (see Revisit Essay Section 3.c.II.i). Bietak dates Khyan c.1600–1580 BC (p.86) and the Knossos context following Colin Macdonald as MMIII, most likely MMIIIB. Thus Bietak states the subsequent LMIA period must be later and so the ^{14}C dates for Thera are wrong. But, again, see the curiously non-cited (by Bietak) finds and analysis of Moeller and Marouard (2011) – which mean that Khyan must be significantly earlier, and so this whole argument from Bietak collapses. Correctly dated, Khyan may well offer a useful date for MMIIIB to initial LMIA about a century earlier. And this in turn undermines the rest of the Bietak argument from here and on much of his page 86.

5. Bietak (2013: 88) returns again to the WSI bowl from Thera. See the discussion above in the Revisit Essay Section 3.c.II.iv. Bietak mixes some correct information with incorrect assertions. For example, he states that "As regards WS I, there is strong scientific evidence that this ware was produced at the foothills of the Troodos mountains around Sanidha and Kalavasos in the south of the island". The first part of the sentence about the link to the geology of the foothill regions around the Troodos Mountains of Cyprus is correct (e.g. Eriksson 2007: 16–17, 22, 48–49 and refs.), but the second part betrays a lack of careful scholarship, as no WSI has been reported from Sanidha – it produced WSII! Instead the evidence indicates several sources on Cyprus using clay and minerals from the foothills region (available directly to north, centre-east, south and west Cyprus) (Hatcher 2007). The Sanidha site, however, has no relevance to the WSI bowl from Thera, and does not support Bietak's attempt to argue against my suggestion of perhaps a likely northwest Cypriot origin for the early WSI bowl found at Thera (a plausible hypothesis given a combination of circumstances: including early, LMIA, links between the Aegean and this area of Cyprus, the colour of the Thera WSI bowl's fabric, and the similarity of examples known from this area to the now lost WSI bowl from Thera – but another source area on Cyprus is not ruled out). Of course, it is correct that the chronology of WSI is less than clear, coming as it does from typological study

of material mainly from tomb groups, but the evidence adduced by Bietak (or Eriksson 2007) does not rule out the approximate scenario proposed by this author, and indeed the available data appears relatively consistent with my scenario (and of a Late Cypriot IA1/2 to Late Cypriot IA2 date for the Thera bowl, WSI 'RL' in Eriksson 2007, and for a correlation with LMIA) – especially with Khyan shown to date earlier as noted again in the previous paragraph, and with the dating of the Tell el-Dab'a strata now clearly (from science and archaeology evidence) in need of revision.

6.   Bietak (2013: 89) mentions again the supposed 100-years gap he sees, and then on pages 89–90 he argues on the basis of his dates for the Tell el-Dab'a strata for Middle Cypriot necessarily dating down "into the second half, possibly to the end of the 17th century and even beyond". This of course is meant to disprove a late 17th century BC Thera eruption date and the Aegean 'high' LBA chronology. Bietak is now simply entirely ignoring that ^{14}C clearly undermines his supposed chronology of Tell el-Dab'a (Kutschera *et al.* 2012), and (ever more conspicuously) is ignoring the archaeological evidence indicating that the dating of Khyan needs serious reconsideration (Moeller and Marouard 2011), as noted above, and that this evidence entirely undermines Bietak's Tell el-Dab'a chronology and seems to indicate a timescale roughly comparable to the one indicated by the ^{14}C evidence from the site. Once the Second Intermediate Period and Tell el-Dab'a chronologies are re-worked in light of the Moeller and Marouard (2011) finds and the ^{14}C evidence (and hopefully additional data and ^{14}C analysis of other SIP contexts), it seems likely that the Cyprus finds of Tell el-Yahudiya jugs and related material will in fact be consonant with the 'high' Aegean LBA chronology and the corresponding 'high' chronology for the start of the Late Cypriot I period.

7.   Bietak (2013: 94–100) ends with a discursive critique of ^{14}C dating and argues from rather random examples (some on inappropriate, long-lived, materials or where context associations are not especially strong or dubious, or where inappropriate fixed sequence wiggle-matching is employed) that there seem to be problems and offsets especially in the period from just before to a little after the Thera eruption. In response, I suggest reading the Revisit Essay and Postscript above. Bietak ends this discussion raising the argument that while ^{14}C seems about OK for Middle and Upper Egypt, he wonders if somehow more coastal areas in the east Mediterranean are affected by the sea and its activity (p.99): upwelling and an "estuary effect when seawater reaches inland". How this is meant to affect terrestrial plant matter is left unstated by Bietak – nor is any substantive sea up-welling attested in this period in the east Mediterranean. 'Riverine activity' and volcanic activity are then mentioned more in hope than with any possible relevance to Lower Egypt or many other areas of the east Mediterranean. The striking fact ignored by Bietak is that good quality ^{14}C dates from secure contexts and their analysis now offer a consistent chronological synthesis from the Aegean to Egypt. There is no general wide problem that needs solving: just in particular the need to re-think the chronology of Tell el-Dab'a as shown to be clearly necessary by recent archaeological evidence (Moeller and Marouard 2011).

(iv) IntCal13, Tree-rings, and Mesopotamian Chronology

Use of the IntCal13 calibration dataset (Reimer *et al.* 2013) makes some very small changes to the fit and placement of the dendro-sequenced ^{14}C dates on the Gordion juniper tree-ring chronology (as in Manning *et al.* 2010). The best fit, following the approach in the Manning *et al.* (2010) paper, moves the Gordion chronology just a couple of years older: about +2 years using all the 50 data relative rings 776.5 to 1145.5, and about +3 years if the 5 main outliers are then discounted. This thus has very little impact on existing discussions.

Of more relevance, however, is the security of the various dendrochronological linkages if one tries to extend the near-absolute Gordion chronology placement to other tree-ring sequences. The Gordion chronology itself is sound, as summarized above in the Revisit Essay Section 5(iv). With regard to the Middle Bronze Age palaces in Anatolia with associations via Šamši-Adad I to Mesopotamian historical chronology, the Kültepe and Acemhöyük juniper chronologies also each seem solid and cross-date, as does a juniper chronology from Karahöyük-Konya (KBK). The area of some possible potential concern at the time of writing is Porsuk, which has been employed as the bridge and link from the Gordion juniper chronology to the MBA juniper group (see e.g. Kuniholm and Newton 2004: Table 1). A re-investigation of this topic is ongoing at the time of writing (so if this is of interest to you, please look for a publication likely in the next couple of years). I note that if there is movement in the near-absolute calendar dates for the MBA juniper chronologies (or at least Porsuk) then it seems on current indications that this is to slightly *older* dates. Thus any change (if required) is only going to make a Low or ultra-Low Mesopotamian chronology even more impossible. The maximum scale of any possible movement would not seem sufficient, however, to bring the High chronology into play – thus the most likely scenario would remain the Middle or similar chronology as stated (and see references given) in the Revisit Essay above, Section 3.c.

(v) IntCal13 and the date of the Uluburun Ship

The Uluburun ship and its dating have been mentioned in the Revisit Essay Section 5. I briefly consider the impact of using IntCal13 (Reimer *et al.* 2013) for the analyses published in Manning *et al.* (2009b), especially since the later 14th through 13th centuries BC is one period where there are visible small changes when one compares IntCal13 to IntCal09/IntCal04 (see Figure RE33 above). Figures RE41 and RE42 show the dates for the Last Voyage (LV) of the Uluburun ship re-running Model A and Model B from Manning *et al.* (2009b) but employing IntCal13 (so compare Figure RE41 with Manning *et al.* 2009b: Figs. 11 and 13, and Figure RE42 with Manning *et al.* 2009b: Figs. 15 and 17). The results reported in Manning *et al.* (2009b) using IntCal04 are compared with those using IntCal13 in Table RE16.

The revised date ranges are only slightly different. There is very little change to the start (older end) of the modelled ranges, and the most likely 68.2% ranges remain as starting in the 1330s BC. However, as predicted in the 'Note added in Proof' to Manning *et al.* (2009b: 187), subsequent calibration data (revising the IntCal04/IntCal09 datasets) have had the effect of extending a little the modelled Last Voyage range in the recent

	Manning et al. (2009b) using IntCal04		Re-run results employing IntCal13	
	68.2% Dates BC	*95.4% Dates BC*	*68.2% Dates BC*	*95.4% Dates BC*
Model A (res 1)	1333–1319	1381–1364 (10%) 1341–1312 (85.4%)	1338–1329 (24.2%) 1325–1308 (44%)	1347–1299
Model A (res 5)	Not Stated	Not Stated	1338–1309	1352–1297
Model B (res 5)	1332–1311	1340–1289	1331–1291	1343–1263

Table RE16. Modelled calendar age ranges for the Last Voyage (LV) of the Uluburun ship, comparing the results from Models A and B in Manning et al. (2009b) employing the IntCal04 calibration dataset (Reimer et al. 2004) versus results from re-runs of the same models employing the IntCal13 calibration dataset (Reimer et al. 2013) and OxCal 4.2.3 (Bronk Ramsey 2009a). Curve resolution either 1 or 5, as indicated.

(i.e. later) direction, thus adding some 11 or 20 years to the 68.2% ranges and 13 and 26 years to the 95.4% ranges looking at Table RE16. If we examine the 68.2% ranges in Figures RE41 and RE42, approximate and similar dates in round terms of either 1325 ± 15 BC or 1310 ± 20 BC suggest themselves for the wrecking date. The figure of 1320 ± 15 BC in Manning *et al.* (2009b: 184) is thus still a reasonable estimate. However, if we wish now to cover all the 68.2% ranges (both models re-run), and so reflect the later extension to the dating range from IntCal13, we might propose a revised and safer approximate round-terms date of 1315 ± 25 BC for the Last Voyage of the Uluburun ship. The *terminus post quem* for the ship's construction and first voyage – the 'Ship Fitted Out Boundary' from Model B in Manning *et al.* (2009b), employing IntCal13, is 1362–1332 BC (68.2% probability) and 1370–1315 BC (95.4% probability). Thus the Uluburun ship was built and first used in the mid-14th century BC (Amarna period), and wrecked on its last voyage a few decades later, likely in the post-Amarna reigns of one of the rulers from Horemheb to early in the reign of Rameses II (adopting a higher Egyptian chronology following Aston 2012 and Bronk Ramsey *et al.* 2010 – as revised in the Revisit Essay and this Postscript).

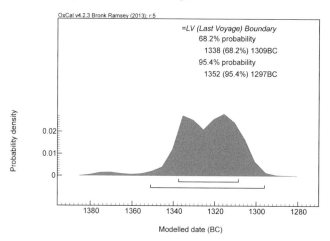

Figure RE41. The modelled calendar age estimate for the Last Voyage (LV) of the Uluburun ship from a re-run of Model A in Manning et al. (2009b: 174 and Fig. 10) employing IntCal13. Curve resolution set at 5. Time constant of 10 years employed (as in Manning et al. 2009: Fig. 10).

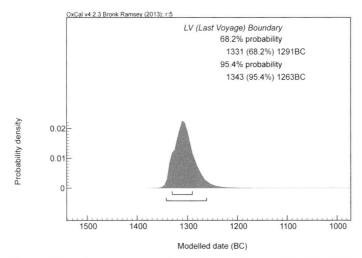

Figure RE42. The modelled calendar age estimate for the Last Voyage (LV) of the Uluburun ship from a re-run of Model B in Manning et al. *(2009b: 174–176 and Fig. 12) employing IntCal13. Curve resolution set at 5.*

(vi) IntCal13 and dating Late Minoan IB–II

The new IntCal13 calibration dataset has only a minor impact on the dating of the LMIB to LMII periods when comparing with analyses employing the IntCal04 or IntCal09 datasets (e.g. Manning *et al.* 2006a; Manning 2009), since there are only small changes to the calibration curve in the 16th–15th centuries BC. Nonetheless, the new calibration dataset offers the opportunity to reassess the best dating of these periods via radiocarbon (including Figures RE12–15 and Table 3A and 3B above), and to consider a slightly revised modelling versus previous work (see also Manning 2014).

The good quality and most useful data for the LMIB period comprise three datasets on short-lived samples from LMIB destructions at their respective sites (i.e. the end of the LMIB period at each site) (see Manning 2009). The destruction at Myrtos-Pyrgos is a specific event and the dates all come from seeds from a single room (room 9 of the 'Country House'). We can assume the seeds had been stored at most a couple of years and likely only a year. There were four samples, each dated twice. We can take a weighted average of each pair of dates as the best estimate for each sample, and regard a weighted average of the dates on the four samples as the best description of the date of this destruction event. The Myrtos-Pyrgos archaeological context is placed as LMIB Late by Rutter (2011). The Mochlos dates are on samples from different loci, and rather than use an average value, they might best be treated as a group of events likely distributed towards the end of a Phase, thus the Tau_Boundary paired with a Boundary model in OxCal seems appropriate (Bronk Ramsey 2009a). The archaeological context is placed as LMIB Final in Rutter (2011). There is thus a known archaeological sequence of data, with the Mochlos LMIB Final destruction *after* the Myrtos Pyrgos LMIB Late destruction. This can be modelled as a Sequence in OxCal, with Myrtos Pyrgos > Mochlos. The final set of data comes from Chania. There are four samples, each dated twice. We can take the average of the pairs as the best estimate for each. The data come from different loci at the site, and, again, rather than use an average, the Tau_Boundary paired with a Boundary model appears appropriate (and allows most of the data to lie close/at the end of the Phase, but not all). This LMIB context is not phased by Rutter. It could be a little earlier than, about the same age as, or just after the Myrtos-Pyrgos or Mochlos sets; our only secure knowledge is that it is a LMIB destruction set. This situation can be modelled in OxCal by creating a Phase (LMIB Destructions), with the Chania Sequence separate from the Myrtos-Pyrgos to Mochlos Sequence, with no relation between the two – the data are allowed to place the Chania Sequence relative to the other Sequence and vice versa.

We have useful constraints for the overall LMIB period. A *terminus post quem* is available from the LMIA period. Here our best data are (i) a dendro-^{14}C-wiggle-match on an oak sample from Miletos stratified below (so older than) Thera eruption tephra, and (ii) the short-lived data from Thera from the Volcanic Destruction Level (VDL) at Akrotiri (Manning *et al.* 2006a; Manning and Bronk Ramsey 2009). For the last we can here just consider the 13 date set run in the AD2000s as our best evidence, and we can consider the Akrotiri VDL data as exponentially distributed towards the end of the final phase, and so, using a Tau_Boundary paired with a Boundary model, regard the final Boundary as dating the Thera eruption (as Figure RE9C and RE36C). There is also a sequence: the VDL destruction lies *after* the Miletos oak's waney edge (outermost ring before bark). The period of time between the post VDL set Boundary (the Thera eruption) and the LMIB destruction date sets is, in archaeological terms, the time of any post-VDL-LMIA final period through the entirety of the early and mid LMIB period *before* the close of phase LMIB destructions at Chania, Myrtos-Pyrgos and Mochlos. We can model this time period with a Boundary in the overall Sequence between the LMIA Sequence (Miletos to Akrotiri VDL) and the subsequent LMIB destruction Phase.

We also have a *terminus ante quem* for the LMIB period in the form of a set of data from the LMII destruction at Knossos (Manning *et al.* 2006a; Manning 2009). These data come from a single context and a weighted average can best describe the date of this event. This event is the end of LMII at its locus. We may therefore assume there is an earlier period of LMII (start through mature LMII) *before* the LMII destruction at Knossos dated by our samples. We can model this time period with a Boundary after the LMIB destructions and before the LMII destruction date set.

A Bayesian chronological model running the overall sequence of data just described and reviewed against IntCal13 (modelled at 1 year resolution), using OxCal (Bronk Ramsey 2009a), is shown in Figure RE43. The General Outlier model of Bronk Ramsey (2009b) is employed. There are no outliers and the model has a very high overall agreement index value (Amodel = 188.9 > 60). Details of the key Boundaries and events in the model are shown in Figure RE44, and the date ranges for these elements are set out in Table RE17. The model in Figures RE43 and RE44 with the IntCal13 radiocarbon calibration curve yields a coherent chronology (late LMIA through LMII); the date ranges for the LMIB–II periods/phases require the 'high' Aegean chronology. The date ranges are similar to those proposed in Table RE4 above. The LMIB period, overall, is shown to represent a considerable timespan (likely over a century) – this is a key finding and aspect of the Aegean 'high' chronology synthesis (see p.18 and n.16 above). Even the

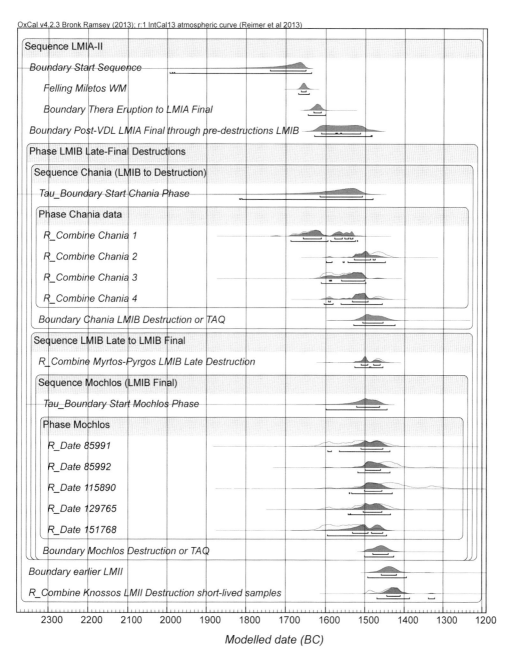

Figure RE43. *Sequence analysis of selected LMIA-II data and archaeological relationships in a chronological dating model as discussed in the text. Not all LMIA elements are shown (e.g. only waney edge = felling date for Miletos oak, and end Boundary = Thera eruption for the Akrotiri VDL set are shown). The model is run employing OxCal 4.2.3 (Bronk Ramsey 2009a) and IntCal13 (Reimer et al. 2013) with curve resolution set at 1. Amodel 188.9 > 60 and Aoverall 182.3 > 60. The horizontal lines under each probability distribution indicate the 68.2% and 95.4% modelled ranges respectively. Note: it is possible to get slight variations in outputs from modelling runs in OxCal, typically within 0-2 years at most.*

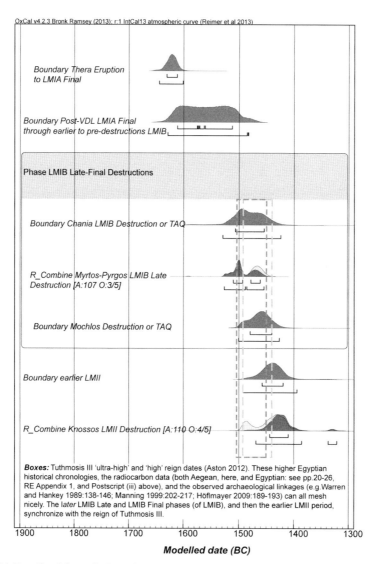

OxCal v4.2.3 Bronk Ramsey (2013); r:1 IntCal13 atmospheric curve (Reimer et al 2013)

Figure RE44. Details of the main Boundaries and events in the model shown in Figure RE43. The 68.2% and 95.4% ranges are indicated under each histogram – these are listed in Table RE17. The Ultra-High and High historical chronology dates for Tuthmosis III from Aston (2012) are also indicated.

last part of the LMIB period, the time from the LMIB Late destruction at Myrtos-Pyrgos to the LMIB Final end Boundary at Mochlos, represents some decades (0–39 calendar years at 68.2% probability, or 0-70 calendar years at 95.4% probability in the model in Figure RE43). In contrast to the substantial expansion of the LMIB timeframe, the period from the Mochlos LMIB Final end Boundary to the LMII Destruction at Knossos (so the LMII period) is relatively concise: 9–51 calendar years at 68.2% probability and 0–96 calendar years at 95.4% probability.

Event/Period of Time	68.2% Probability Calendar Date Range BC	95.4% Probability Calendar Date Range BC
Felling Date Miletos Oak	1662–1650	1669–1642
Thera VDL	1631–1612	1645–1602
Post-VDL LMIA Final through earlier LMIB (pre-LMIB destructions)	1612–1513*	1629–1484*
Chania LMIB Destruction	1507–1455	1530–1425
Myrtos-Pyrgos LMIB Late Destruction	1511–1494 (44.0%) 1479–1462 (24.2%)	1527–1489 (60.4%) 1486–1455 (35.0%)
Mochlos LMIB Final Destruction	1480–1441	1501–1427
Earlier LMII (pre-LMII destruction at Knossos)	1458–1420	1493–1395
LMII Destruction Knossos	1444–1411	1469–1386 (92.0%) 1338–1322 (3.4%)

*Table RE17. Calibrated calendar date ranges for the probability distributions shown in Figure RE44. *Note: whole range – very minor sub-divisions are not listed.*

(vii) Final words on the anti-radiocarbon case: comments on Wiener and Earle (2014)

As this book was in final proof, a paper entitled "Radiocarbon dating of the Theran eruption" appeared by Wiener and Earle (2014) – I thank Erio Valzolgher for bringing this paper to my attention. This paper largely re-states most of the arguments made previously by Wiener trying to undermine, question, or reject the radiocarbon-based dating of the Thera volcanic destruction level (VDL) (see previously e.g. Wiener 2003; 2006a; 2007; 2009a; 2009b; 2010; 2012). Wiener and Earle (2014: 60–62) generally present another version of Wiener's previous 'all-possible-problems-with-^{14}C' arguments – while not demonstrating that any of these issues are actually relevant to the Thera case, and ignoring much evidence to the contrary. Nearly all of these points have been discussed, critiqued, rejected, or dismissed as significant, both in previous work (e.g. Manning *et al.* 2006a; 2009a; Manning and Kromer 2011a; 2012), or especially in this Revisit Essay (see Section 3.III, pp. 42–94, and elsewhere in the Appendices and above in the Postscript). I make just a few additional comments:

(a) Wiener and Earle (2014: 60) state: "The traditional chronology is based on Egyptian and Near Eastern textual/historical and astronomical records and numerous archaeological interconnections now buttressed by analyses of pumice from the Theran eruption found in connection with Egyptian New Kingdom material". *Response*: there are no 'numerous' (and especially good, clear-cut) archaeological interconnections for MMIII-LMIA (see Section 3.c.II, pp. 34–42 above; see Höflmayer 2012a) – and the pumice *terminus ante quem* is unclear and irrelevant at best (see Section 3.c.I.v – p. 31 above, and (h) below).

(b) Wiener and Earle (2014: 60) state that there are some "unresolved disparities in [^{14}C] measurements of trees of known dendrochronological date" and suggest that this means the radiocarbon calibration curve should be less precise, and that this invalidates a precise dating of the Thera VDL. The reference to the period 850–750 BC and the comparison of Turkish trees versus German trees at this time and a small observed offset in ^{14}C ages is irrelevant to Thera – this relates to a period of a major solar minimum (see also p.81 above). The issue noted by Kromer *et al.* (2010) and Manning *et al.* (2013) regarding the 14th–13th centuries BC has been addressed in IntCal13 (see Postscript (i) above) – but again it does not apply to the Thera period (see Figures RE33–34 above). The mention of claimed disparities regarding ^{14}C dates on Gordion wood at ca. 1580 BC, 1570 BC, and 1560 BC or on German wood at 1550 BC suggest a wider problem when there is not one. For example, of the 128 ^{14}C dates on Gordion wood published in Manning *et al.* (2010: Table 4) on the exact same tree-ring years – 11 pairs of data – only 1 pair is not consistent with the hypothesis of indicating the same ^{14}C age at the 95% confidence level, and, comparing those pairings where the dates are on tree-ring sets within ±1 year of each other (38 instances including the previous 11), there are only 5 instances of differences over 60 ^{14}C years (worst two cases 94 and 71 ^{14}C years). The pairs or near-pairs in the 17–16th centuries BC (10 instances) are all consistent with representing the same ^{14}C age at the 95% confidence level (and in turn match the IntCal ^{14}C record well: see e.g. Manning *et al.* 2010: Fig. 6). As illustrated in Manning and Kromer (2011a: Figs. 3–8), the radiocarbon calibration data from the Heidelberg laboratory for the 17th–16th centuries BC offer a pretty clearly defined, and consistent, record with only a few noisy data in a large dataset. Wiener and Earle (2014: 60), by mentioning German samples at 1550 BC, appear to be pointing to the single largest difference between near contemporary (not identical) tree-rings out of a large set (48 ^{14}C years) – this one case does narrowly fail the Ward and Wilson (1978) test at the 95% confidence level (adding just an additional 2 ^{14}C years to each date's quoted error would see them pass – so this one pair is a little overly precisely stated) – but none of the other pairs or near contemporary pairs in Kromer *et al.* (2010: Fig. 2) fail this test.

(c) On issues of intra-annual and similar variations regarding ^{14}C (Wiener and Earle 2014: 60–61), see discussions in Section 3.c.II, and, in particular, note that even allowing for large possible errors (for whatever reason) the most likely late 17th century BC date range for the radiocarbon dating of the Thera VDL remains a robust finding: see Figures RE24, RE25, RE36B above. As another example, Wiener and Earle (2014: 60) suggest that the weighted average age of the 28 date set of Akrotiri VDL data (as employed in Manning *et al.* 2006a) would indicate a different calendar age range if (arbitrarily) it is given a ±20 ^{14}C year error (versus the calculated error of 7.5 ^{14}C years in Manning *et al.* 2006a: Fig.2 caption). But the IntCal13 (Reimer *et al.* 2013) calibrated calendar age range for 3345±20 ^{14}C years BP at 68.2% probability is entirely in the 17th century BC at 1681–1614 BC, and the 95.4% probability range is also strongly in favour of the 17th century BC (1690–1604 BC with 81.5% of the total probability versus 1587–1535 BC with just 13.9% of the total probability) (using OxCal with curve resolution set at 5). Meanwhile, there is no positive evidence for substantive upwelling affecting Aegean or east Mediterranean radiocarbon ages in the mid second millennium BC (the Keenan 2002a hypothesis – cited by Wiener and Earle 2014: 61) and instead much evidence against (Manning *et al.* 2002c). In particular, we can observe that large scale studies of Egyptian samples show no such effect (Bronk Ramsey *et al.* 2010; Dee *et al.* 2009; 2013) – this is important as supposed discrepancies in Egyptian dating was one of the reasons for the Keenan (2002a) suggestion – and that wood from Miletos on the west coast of Turkey, and likely from a tree which grew in the general area of the site, offers a 7 decade sequence of ^{14}C ages in the late 18th through mid-17th centuries BC with close comparison to the northern hemisphere ^{14}C curve and again showing no such offset, as does the large set of ^{14}C dates on wood from Gordion in central Turkey for the 18th–15th centuries BC (e.g. Manning *et al.* 2010: Fig. 11).

(d) On the issue of volcanic CO_2 (Wiener and Earle 2014: 61), and why it appears not to be a substantive issue with regard to the available Thera dating evidence, see pp. 50–58 above. In particular, we may note that a sequence analysis of Aegean ^{14}C data *without* any data from Thera, and thus only using data not plausibly affected by any hypothetical volcanic CO_2 effect on/around Thera, nonetheless yields results similar to those with the Thera data included, and points to the 'high' chronology and not the 'low' chronology (Manning *et al.* 2006a). Radiocarbon dates from other Aegean sites published since 2006 yield a similar story: results compatible with the Thera VDL dataset, and all pointing towards the 'high' chronology (see studies cited pp. 52–53 above; Höflmayer 2012a: 436–440). Some of the other literature cited by Wiener and Earle (2014: 61) is not really relevant. For example, an article cited by Fischer and Heinemeier (2003) on riverine (fish, mollusk) derived reservoir ages is not relevant to the Thera case (nor even entirely clear-cut in its own case: Hart and Lovis 2007). The article they cite by Turfa (2006) does not say that ^{14}C dates from clearly dated (*sic*) Italian archaeological sites are "often 70–250 years too early" (Wiener and Earle 2014: 61) – and indeed Turfa states "some scholars will still disagree, but most will be satisfied (or relieved) that, in general, the traditional systems seem to be supported by many recent [i.e. ^{14}C] developments". And, while degassing and releases of CO_2 are well known (and especially in Italy) – as discussed in a number of the papers cited by Wiener and Earle – it is not demonstrated in most cases that these issues are relevant to the dating of terrestrial archaeological samples, and especially not to those from a variety of sites/areas in the Aegean. Indeed, it is important to observe the strikingly consistent ^{14}C picture from terrestrial samples from archaeological sites of the earlier to mid second millennium BC from data from mainland Greece, Aigina, Thera, Rhodes, western Anatolia (Miletos), and Crete (see e.g. Manning *et al.* 2006a; Friedrich *et al.* 2006; Wild *et al.* 2010; Lindblom and Manning 2011; Voutsaki *et al.* 2009a; 2009b; Bruins *et al.* 2008; 2009; Maniatis 2010). This consistent pattern is in contrast to the marked and varying – in time and space – anomalies which one would expect *if* substantive degassing, etc., applied in one or some areas.

(e) Wiener and Earle (2014: 61) raise again whether a Ward and Wilson (1978) Case I analysis is appropriate for the Thera VDL data. The reasons why it is likely approximately valid have been discussed above (pp. 43–50), *and* an alternative and more appropriate analytical strategy has also been discussed and shown to yield a closely defined date for the end of the Akrotiri VDL and so Thera eruption in the late 17th century BC (see above pp. 58–59, 61–64, 173).

(f) On ^{14}C calibration and probability and claims that the Thera VDL set is not coherent (Wiener and Earle 2014: 61–62), see the discussions and responses, and the evidence to the contrary, as presented above (pp. 45–50, 80–94). On the issue of how most appropriately and robustly to estimate the calibration curve from the data available, see Niu *et al.* (2013); for discussion on the data included in the IntCal13 Calibration dataset, see the paper of Reimer, Bard *et al.* (2013).

(g) Wiener and Earle (2014: 62) again try to dismiss the relevance of the ^{14}C dates on the Thera olive branch. For a response and critique, and case why – regardless of whether or not any growth rings can be identified – a likely 17th century BC date applies to the most recent dated segment, see above pp. 74–79, 175–181. Wiener and Earle (2014: 62) argue that the descending ^{14}C ages on the sequence of dates from inner to outer wood of the olive branch could be compatible with all segments all consistently having e.g. an 1% reservoir of ^{14}C-deficient carbon (e.g. volcanic source CO_2). But this is unrealistic. The evidence of volcanic CO_2 effects – including the several studies cited by Wiener and Earle (2014: 61) and as reviewed above pp. 51–58 – shows typically highly varying effects both over time and in area affected. A consistent minor effect over several or many decades in one place is implausible. Thus the fact that the sequence of ^{14}C dates on the olive branch, inner to outer segments, shows no older age anomaly within the sequence, and offers a close match to the northern hemisphere standard ^{14}C record (IntCal), combine to imply that there was no relevant volcanic CO_2 effect with regard to the olive branch.

(h) Wiener and Earle (2014: 62) end with the pumice argument, which we can discount as already noted (and see p. 31 above; Manning and Kromer 2011a: 433; and especially see Höflmayer 2012a: 441–442). They close with discussion of the chronology of Tell el-'Ajjul. They misrepresent the data from the site. Fischer (2009: 262) argues that the pattern of Theran pumice finds at the site points to the Thera eruption as occurring *before* Phase 5 (or perhaps in initial Phase 5 = 5B). As Fischer (2009: 262–265) discusses, the Tell el-'Ajjul ^{14}C data are not clearcut, but can be compatible with the 'high' Aegean chronology and a date for the Thera eruption late in the 17th century BC. The Tell el-'Ajjul evidence does not require the 'low' chronology, and, as Höflmayer (2012a: 441–442) argues, it offers a very different date of first appearance (as currently known from a very small excavated area) versus the Tell el-Dab'a pumice horizon (as dated by Bietak – but see in contrast pp. 32–33 above) – merely highlighting that the appearance of pumice offers a *terminus ante quem* with the length of the *ante* unknown. All that the available evidence (of course most is 18th Dynasty and not SIP) seems to show is that the Thera eruption likely occurred before the 18th Dynasty, which, given the revised Egyptian historical chronology (see pp. 21–24, 116–133, 181–188) suggests a minimum date either in the first decades (only) of the 16th century BC or in the later 17th century BC (the 'high' Aegean chronology position). Indeed, the ^{14}C dates from from Tell el-'Ajjul Phase H5 set an OxCal Boundary for the transition from Phase 6 to Phase 5 – so likely a *terminus ante quem* date for the Thera eruption following the analysis of Fischer (2009: Fig. 4) – from the late 17th century BC through the 16th century BC – a position which can correlate well with both the raised historical chronology for Egypt (see pp. 21–24, 116–133, 181–188) – since Phase 5 is linked with the early 18th Dynasty – and the 'high' Aegean chronology and a late 17th century BC date for the Thera eruption. There is no problem, and this evidence in fact might be regarded as more supporting the 'high' Aegean chronology.

(viii) Additional References in the Postscript not in the Revisit Essay

Bietak, M. 2013. Antagonisms in historical and radiocarbon chronology. In A.J. Shortland and C. Bronk Ramsey (eds.), *Radiocarbon and the Chronologies of Ancient Egypt*: 76–109. Oxford: Oxbow Books.
Broodbank, C. 2013. *The Making of the Middle Sea: A History of the Mediterranean from the Beginning to the Emergence of the Classical World*. London: Thames & Hudson.

Cherubini, P., Humbel, T., Beeckman, H., Gärtner, H., Mannes, D., Pearson, C., Schoch, W., Tognetti, R. and Lev-Yadun, S. 2014. The olive-branch dating of the Santorini eruption. *Antiquity* 88: 267–273.

Dee, M.W., Bronk Ramsey, C., Shortland, A.S., Higham, T.F.G., Rowland, J.M. 2009. Reanalysis of the chronological discrepancies obtained by the Old and Middle Kingdom Monuments Project. *Radiocarbon* 51(3): 1061–1070.

Dee, M., Wengrow, D., Shortland, A., Stevenson, A., Brock, F., Girdland Flink, L. and Bronk Ramsey, C. 2013. An absolute chronology for early Egypt using radiocarbon dating and Bayesian statistical modeling. *Proceedings of the Royal Society* A 469: 20130395.

Fischer, A. and Heinemeier, J. 2003. Freshwater reservoir effect in ^{14}C dates of food residue on pottery. *Radiocarbon* 45 (3): 449-466.

Hatcher, H. 2007. *A Provenance Study on White Slip Wares from Late Bronze Age Cyprus and the Levant.* PhD thesis, Department of Archaeology School of Human and Environmental Sciences, University of Reading.

Knapp, A.B. 2013. *The Archaeology of Cyprus: From Earliest Prehistory through the Bronze Age.* Cambridge: Cambridge University Press.

Kromer, B., Manning, S.W., Friedrich, M., Talamo, S., and Trano, N. 2010. ^{14}C calibration in the 2nd and 1st millennia BC – Eastern Mediterranean Radiocarbon Comparison Project (EMRCP). *Radiocarbon* 52(3): 875–886.

MacGillivray, J.A. 1995. A Minoan cup at Tell el-Dab'a. *Ägypten und Levante* 5: 81-84.

Manning, S.W., Barbetti, M., Kromer, B., Kuniholm, P.I., Levin, I., Newton, M.W. and Reimer, P.J. 2002c. No systematic early bias to Mediterranean ^{14}C ages: radiocarbon measurements from tree-ring and air samples provide tight limits to age offsets. *Radiocarbon* 44(3): 739–754.

Niu, M., Heaton, T.J., Blackwell, P.G., Buck, C.E. 2013. The Bayesian approach to radiocarbon calibration curve estimation: the IntCal13, Marine13, and SHCal13 methodologies. *Radiocarbon* 55(4): 1905–1922.

Reimer P.J., Baillie M.G.L., Bard E., Bayliss A., Beck J.W., Bertrand C.J.H., Blackwell P.G., Buck C.E., Burr G.S., Cutler K.B., Damon P.E., Edwards R.L., Fairbanks R.G., Friedrich M., Guilderson T.P., Hogg A.G., Hughen K.A., Kromer B., McCormac G., Manning S., Bronk Ramsey C., Reimer R.W., Remmele S., Southon J.R., Stuiver M., Talamo S., Taylor F.W., van der Plicht J., Weyhenmeyer C.E. 2004. IntCal04 terrestrial radiocarbon age calibration, 0–26 cal kyr BP. *Radiocarbon* 46(3): 1029–1058.

Reimer, P.J., Bard, E., Bayliss, A., Beck, J.W., Blackwell, P.G., Bronk Ramsey, C., Buck, C.E., Cheng, H., Edwards, R.L., Friedrich, M., Grootes, P.M., Guilderson, T.P., Haflidason, H., Hajdas, I., Hatté, C., Heaton, T.J., Hoffmann, D.L., Hogg, A.G., Hughen, K.A., Kaiser, K.F., Kromer, B., Manning, S.W., Niu, M., Reimer, R.W., Richards, D.A., Scott, E.M., Southon, J.R., Staff, R.A., Turney, C.S.M. and van der Plicht, J. van der. 2013. IntCal13 and Marine13 Radiocarbon Age Calibration Curves 0–50,000 Years Cal BP. *Radiocarbon* 55(4): 1869–1887.

Reimer, P.J., Bard, E., Bayliss, A., Beck, J.W., Blackwell, P.G., Bronk Ramsey, C., Brown, D.M., Buck, C.E., Edwards, R.L., Friedrich, M., Grootes, P.M., Guilderson, T.P., Haflidason, H., Hajdas, I., Hatté, C., Heaton, T.J., Hogg, A.G., Hughen, K.A., Kaiser, K.F., Kromer, B., Manning, S.W., Reimer, R.W., Richards, D.A., Scott, E.M., Southon, J.R., Turney, C.S.M. and van der Plicht, J. 2013. Selection and Treatment of Data for Radiocarbon Calibration: An Update to the International Calibration (IntCal) Criteria. *Radiocarbon* 55(4): 1923–1945.

Schneider, T. 2010. Foreigners in Egypt: archaeological evidence and cultural context. In W. Wendrich (ed.), *Egyptian Archaeology*: 143–163. Malden: Wiley-Blackwell.

Turfa, J.M. 2006. Review of Gilda Bartoloni, Filippo Delpino, *Oriente e Occidente: metodi e discipline a confronto. Riflessioni sulla cronologia dell'età del ferro in Italia, Atti dell'Incontro di studi, Roma, 30-31 ottobre 2003. Mediterranea, 1 (2004). Bryn Mawr Classical Review* 2006.08.10. Available from: http://bmcr.brynmawr.edu/2006/2006-08-10.html

Walberg, G. 1991. A gold pendant from Tell el-Dab'a. *Ägypten und Levante* 2: 111–112.

Wiener, M.H. and Earle, J.W. 2014. Radiocarbon dating of the Theran eruption. In RH Tykot (ed.), *Proceedings of the 38th International Symposium on Archaeometry – May 10th–14th 2010, Tampa, Florida. Open Journal of Archaeometry* 2: 5265 (pp. 60–64).

Index

Acemhöyük, Turkey 25, 187, 189
Aegean Dendrochronology, and issues 108–113, 189
Aegean-east Mediterranean connections 5–6
Ahmose 4, 22, 33, 38–39, 42, 116–119, 183
Akrotiri, Middle Cycladic 5 n.8
Alalakh, Turkey 26, 96, 103
Amarna, Tell el-, Egypt 14, 16, 59
Amenhotep II 32
Aniakchak, Alaska, USA 26 n.21, 30
Ankhetkheperure 22
Ansanto Valley, Italy 57
Archaeological chronology, methods, issues 14–15, 17
Archaeology and time 3, 20
Archaeomagnetism 33–34
Asine, Greece 53
Aston, D., revised Egyptian historical dates 8, 10, 15, 21–24, 106, 116–120, 123, 126, 181, 184, 190
Azores and volcanic CO_2 55–57

Bernal, M. 6–7
Betancourt, P.P. 12
Bevan, A. 37
Bietak, M. 2–3, 11, 99–108, 186–188
Broodbank, C. 186

Chania, Crete 67, 81, 191–195
Cherubini, P. 74, 179–181
Chronology, key to archaeology and history 3
Classical archaeology 3
Cline, E.H. 103, 105, 114
Crewe, L. 39
Cypriot chronology 38–41, 104–106
Cyprus, regionalism, MC–LCI 39

Dean, J.S. 111–112
Dee, M.W. 80
Dendrochemistry and volcanic eruption? 30
Dendrochronology 108–113, 189
Dendrochronology and t test 112 and n.57

Egyptian chronology 20–23, 116–133, 181–185
Egyptian stone vessels 15, 37–39
Eriksson, K. 39–40
Gordion, Anatolian juniper dendrochronology 30, 60, 109–113, 108, 189
Gordion, Iron Age chronology 16–17

Hallager, E. 17
Hammurabi 23–25
Hatshepsut 4, 21–22, 32 n.24, 42
Heb sed 22
Höflmayer, F. 2 n.2, 9, 15, 31, 35, 38, 104
Hood, S. 7, 59
Horemheb 22
High chronology, rejectionist positions 8–9, 10
High chronology synthesis 2013 98 Figure RE27
Hyksos, reassessing history and role 6 and n.9

Ice-cores, volcanic eruptions and Thera 12, 26–27, 107–108
IntCal13, changes v. IntCal09 re Revisit Essay 169–185, 191–192
Israel, Iron Age chronology debate 20
Italy, Aegean and radiocarbon 97 n.48

James, P. 109–110 n.55

Kamose 6 n.10
Kaneš, Turkey 25, 111, 187, 189
Keenan, D.J. 5 n.7, 17 n.15, 59, 82–83, 111–112, 196
Keftiu 74, 96
Khyan (Khayan) and Khyan Lid 6 n.10, 35–37, 95–96, 186–187
Knossos, Crete 35, 69, 191–192
Kolonna, Aigina, Greece 52–53, 80
Kommos, Crete 18 n.16, 141
Kom Rabi'a, Egypt, Aegean (LMIB) sherd 102 and n.52, 105
Kom Rabi'a, Egypt, Base Ring I 105

Kuniholm, P.I., issues with dendrochronology 109–113

Kutschera, W. 32, 106

Late Minoan IB 18 and n.16, 67–74, 191–195
Late Minoan II 67–74, 191–195
Lerna, Greece 52, 80
Lilyquist, C. 37
Liphschitz, N. 111 and n.56

MacGillivray, J.A. 6–7
Maguire, L.C. 40 n.32
Man on Clapham omnibus 7
Merrillees, R.S. 17, 39, 41
Mesopotamian chronology 23–26, 103, 111, 189
Miletos (Miletus), Turkey 53, 60, 141, 143, 192
Mochlos, Crete, Greece 67, 191–195
Moeller, N. and Marouard, G. 35–37, 186–187
Myrtos-Pyrgos, Crete, Greece 67, 191–195

Neferneferuaten 22
Neer, R.T. 43 n.34
Nineveh, Iraq 45 n.37

Olive branch, Thera, and dating 29, 54–55, 66, 74–79, 175, 178–179, 197–198
Osochor 22

Palaepaphos, Cyprus 38–39, 114
Palaikastro, Crete, Greece 52–53, 80
Pasquier-Cardin, A. 55–57
Phillips, J. 35
Phylakopi, Melos 40 n.31
Porsuk, Turkey 29–31, 108, 189
Psusennes II 22

Radiocarbon (^{14}C), Aegean sequence analysis 66–74, 173–175
Radiocarbon and Egyptian chronology 21–23, 59–60, 116–133, 181–186
Radiocarbon, appropriate samples 95 n.47
Radiocarbon, Bayesian chronological modelling 3, 14, 53, 79–80, 83, 97, 118, 143–148
Radiocarbon, calcareous soil 81
Radiocarbon, calibration 81–94
Radiocarbon, marine/riverine reservoirs 45 n.37
Radiocarbon, regional (growing season) offsets 21, 60, 67, 80–81, 93, 95, 112, 116

Radiocarbon, solar flare/gamma ray burst 93–94
Radiocarbon, wiggle-matching 25, 28–30, 74, 77, 92, 103, 108–113, 143, 145, 189, 197
Ramesses I 22
Ramesses II 22
Renfrew, C. 7
Rhyta, Aegean-style 15, 42
Rutter, J.B. 18 and n.16

Šamši-Adad I 25, 189
Schneider, T. 4 n.6, 21–22, 116–118
Sety I 22
Shoshenq I, dating 119
Siamun 22
Smenkhare 22
Sobekhotep IV 36
Sofular Cave, speleothem 27, 95, 108
Soter, S. 57–58
Speleothems 27
Stubbings, F.H. 97

Tauber, H. 81
Tel Kabri, Israel 26, 97, 102–103, 115
Tell el-Amarna, see Amarna
Tell el-'Ajjul, Gaza 39–40, 99–100, 198
Tell el-'Ajjul, Gaza, jewellery and date 99–100
Tell el-Dab'a, Egypt 16, 18, 32–33, 60, 99–107, 186, 188
Tell el-Dab'a, Egypt, cuneiform finds 36–37
Tell el-Dab'a, Egypt, wall paintings 32–33, 105
Tell el-Yahudiya Ware 106, 188
Tell Edfu, Egypt 36, 96, 186
Tempest Stele of Ahmose 4 n.6
Thera date, scholarly groupings/perspectives 7–9
Thera date and new history c.1700–1500BC 6–7, 95–98, 185
Thera date and pumice 31, 32, 33, 114
Thera debate, reasons to resolve 4–7
Thera, Heidelberg ^{14}C dates 45–46 n.38
Thera, possible text allusions 4–5 and n.7
Thera, olive branch: see olive branch
Thera, ^{14}C dates, dating, quality and robustness 44–50, 60–67, 134–143, 169–175
Thera, seeds, preservation and time 43–44
Thera, time from abandonment to eruption 43–44, 62–63
Thera, tsunami 5

Thera volcanic eruption, aerosol and Babylonia 4 n.5
Thera volcanic eruption, season 4 n.3
Thera volcanic eruption, size 4 n.4
Thera volcanic eruption, knock effects 69
Tille Höyük, Turkey 113
Toumba tou Skourou, Cyprus 105–106
Tree-rings, volcanoes, and Thera 27–31, 108
Trianda, Rhodes, Greece 40, 53
Tsoungiza, Greece 141
Tuthmosis I 22
Tuthmosis III 4, 21–22, 32 n.24, 34, 42, 69, 74, 96
Tuthmosis IV 22

Uluburun ship and dating 109, 189–190

Venus tablets, Ammisaduqa 4 and n.5, 26 n.20
Volcanic CO_2, ^{14}C dating, and Thera date 50–58, 79, 92

Warburton, D.A. 32, 106–107
Wessex Culture 97 n.48
White Slip I and chronology 39–41, 103–104
Whittle, A. 5
Wiener, M.H. 47–49, 58, 61, 74, 77, 80–83, 88–90, 142, 195–198